THE

WRITER'S
HANDBOOK
1998

THE WRITER'S COMPANION

The essential guide to being published

Barry Turner

The Writer's Companion is a route map through the media jungle, an indispensable guide for established writers and newcomers alike who seek to make the best commercial use of their talents.

Drawing on the cumulative experiences of its sister volume, *The Writer's Handbook,* which is now in its eleventh year, *The Writer's Companion* is packed with a wealth of practical advice taking in:

- book publishing
- freelance journalism
- film and television
- radio drama
- theatre and poetry

Everyday concerns, financial and legal, from how to avoid contractual pitfalls to minimising the risk of libel are given full coverage and there is up-to-date advice on raising funds for creative projects on stage and screen.

Published by Macmillan

THE
WRITER'S
HANDBOOK
1998

EDITOR
BARRY TURNER

MACMILLAN

First published 1988
This edition published 1997 by
MACMILLAN
an imprint of Macmillan Publishers Ltd,
25 Eccleston Place, London SW1W 9NF
and Basingstoke
Associated companies throughout the world

10 9 8 7 6 5 4 3 2 1

A CIP catalogue record for this book is available from the British Library

ISBN 0–333–67538X

Typeset by Heronwood Press
Printed and bound in Great Britain
by Mackays of Chatham plc, Kent

If you would like an entry in *The Writer's Handbook 1998*,
please write or send a fax to:
The Writer's Handbook,
34 Ufton Road,
London N1 5BX.
Fax 0171 241 0118

Contents

Preface

I am steering clear of all money matters this year. Traditionally, *The Writer's Handbook* tries to give guidance on what writers can expect by way of book advances and freelance fees for press and broadcasting. This made sense when there was a consensus amongst publishers and editors on who should get what. But with the burgeoning of small presses, (*The Writer's Handbook* lists 150 of the best but the full number in business, if often marginally, is closer to 5000) broadcasting outlets and niche journals and papers appealing to every conceivable interest, there are no longer any rules that have general application. Thanks to the communications revolution it is easier to be published than ever before but it is also easier for newcomers to the writing business to be duped. Every post brings examples of publishing casualties; freelance journalists whose work has been accepted without any reference to the likely payment for services rendered, authors who have been conned into accepting low royalties and the surrender of all subsidiary rights, contributors to radio and television programmes whose fees are so derisory as to warrant a handout in postage stamps.

This is not to say that everyone in publishing and broadcasting is dishonest. Even if some of the big names do try it on, given half a chance, those listed in *The Writer's Handbook* can generally be relied on for a measure of fair treatment. But out towards the fringe where the multitude gathers, there are traps for the unwary and more chances of losing money (or doing work for nothing which comes to the same thing) than at a night out at the casino. Why is it that despite all the warnings, there are so many willing victims? The casino parallel does not carry through. It cannot be the gambling instinct that leads writers into bad company. Rather, I deduce, it is a readiness, born perhaps of a thousand rejection slips, to do anything for the chance of seeing themselves in print.

While the communications revolution has created more opportunities to be published it has also stimulated a mighty increase in the number of writers wanting to be published. At the same time the media leaders, ever interested in maximising profits, are relying on tried and trusted formulas that

"The age of the book is almost gone.'
George Steiner

'The first principle is never to write about anything you know and the second is never to read modern fiction.'
Peter Ackroyd on his essential principles of aesthetics

'It is a sad feature of modern life that only women for the most part have time to write novels, and they seldom have much to write about.'
Auberon Waugh

'It is one of the advantages of our century that childhood and adolescence now possess a language all their own, and can be freely explored; not only as a narrative device but as an emotional and psychological realm.'
Rachel Cusk - Whitbread Awards judge 1995

tend to exclude those newcomers who cannot show an immediate and brilliant talent. When I started in journalism in the early sixties, it was so easy to mount the first step on the ladder. A first job in television came when I made the short walk from the London School of Economics where I was a postgraduate student to what was then Rediffusion studios on the Kingsway corner of Aldwych. I asked for an audition and they gave me one. Nowadays, they would call the police. Similarly, when I moved over to newspapers, a letter and a bunch of cuttings were enough to get me a three-month tryout on *The Observer*. Today, no national editor would have the patience to read an application from an untried unless of course the name was the same as that of a famous media elder.

No wonder there are writers who do it for free in the hope of making a reputation that will carry them on to greater glory and no wonder there are authors who respond to the vanity publishers, knowing full well that others have been let down but believing, or trying to believe, that it will not happen to them. I have lost count of the number of correspondents who want to know if putting up large sums of money to cover the costs of book production is normal practice. I say, yet again, no, it is not normal practice and any writer who puts his trust in vanity publishing is at best naive and at worst a sucker. Those who want to know more about how easy it is to get caught, should refer to Graham King's article, *What Price Vanity?*, on page 170

But so much for the bad news. Like all revolutions, the upheaval in communications will eventually settle, allowing for a period of readjustment and taking stock. By the time we get to our twelfth edition a semblance of financial order may have reappeared in the writers' market. Meanwhile, the best advice I can give is never to trust to luck and always to remember to check the small print.

As another year passes, another debt of gratitude is owing to Jill Fenner, who distributes and collates the questionnaires that are the chief source of *The Writer's Handbook* intelligence, Jayne Jenkinson who makes us ready for the printer and Dominic Taylor, our Macmillan editor who tries to tell us where we are going wrong before it is too late. If he has missed anything it is my fault not his.

Barry Turner

UK Publishers

AA Publishing
The Automobile Association, Fanum House, Basingstoke, Hampshire RG21 4EA
☎01256 201234   Fax 01256 22575

Managing Director *John Howard*
Editorial Director *Michael Buttler*

Publishes maps, atlases and guidebooks, motoring and leisure. About 100 titles a year.

Authors' Rating Benefiting from a clearly defined market, the AA has advanced strongly in the publication of maps and tour guides. Travel writers who know how to churn out the facts are among the beneficiaries.

Abacus
See **Little, Brown & Co (UK)**

ABC – All Books For Children (a division of The All Children's Co. Ltd)
33 Museum Street, London WC1A 1LD
☎0171 436 6300   Fax 0171 240 6923

Managing Director *Sue Tarsky*

Publishes children's titles only, including the successful *Angelina Ballerina* and *Ned* books and toys. About 40 titles a year. *Specialises* in co-editions worldwide. **SoftbABCks** paperback imprint launched 1991 and **FactbABCks** non-fiction imprint launched 1995. Unsolicited material welcome but no novels. All material should be addressed to *Carol MacKenzie*, the Editorial Department; s.a.e. essential for return.
Royalties paid twice-yearly.

ABC–Clio Ltd
Old Clarendon Ironworks, 35a Great Clarendon Street, Oxford OX2 6AT
☎01865 311350   Fax 01865 311358

Managing Director *Tony Sloggett*
Editorial Director *Dr Robert G. Neville*

Formerly Clio Press Ltd. *Publishes* academic and general reference works, social sciences and humanities. Markets, outside North America, the CD-ROM publications of the American parent company. Art Bibliographies *S. Pape*. SERIES *World Bibliographical; International Organisations; World Photographers; Clio Montessori.*
Royalties paid twice-yearly.

Abington Publishing
See **Woodhead Publishing Ltd**

Absolute Classics
See **Oberon Books**

Absolute Press
Scarborough House, 29 James Street West, Bath BA1 2BT
☎01225 316013   Fax 01225 445836

Managing/Editorial Director *Jon Croft*

FOUNDED 1979. *Publishes* food and wine-related subjects as well as travel guides and the *Streetwise Maps* series of city maps. About 10 titles a year. *Outlines*, launched in summer 1997, is a new series of monographs on gay and lesbian creative artists. No unsolicited mss. Synopses and ideas for books welcome.
Royalties paid twice-yearly.

Abson Books London
5 Sidney Square, London E1 2EY
☎0171 790 4737   Fax 0171 790 7346

Chairman *M. J. Ellison*

FOUNDED 1971 in Bristol. *Publishes* language glossaries, literary quizzes and puzzles. No unsolicited mss; synopses and ideas for books welcome.
Royalties paid twice-yearly.

Academic Press
See **Harcourt Brace and Company Ltd**

Academy Group Ltd
42 Leinster Gardens, London W2 3AN
☎0171 402 2141   Fax 0171 723 9540

Chairman *John Jarvis*
Managing Director *John Stoddart*
Managing Editor *Maggie Toy*
Approx. Annual Turnover £2 million

FOUNDED 1969. Part of John Wylie & Sons, Inc. group. *Publishes* architecture, art and design. Welcomes unsolicited mss, synopses and ideas.
Royalties paid annually.

Acair Ltd
Unit 7, 7 James Street, Stornoway, Isle of Lewis, Scotland HS1 2QN
☎01851 703020   Fax 01851 703294

Specialising in matters pertaining to the Gaid-healtachd, Acair publishes books on Scottish history, culture and the Gaelic language. 75% of their children's books are targeted at primary

school usage and are published exclusively in Gaelic.
Royalties paid twice-yearly.

Ace Books
1268 London Road, London SW16 4ER
☎0181 679 8000   Fax 0181 679 6069
Approx. Annual Turnover £500,000
Publishing arm of Age Concern England. *Publishes* related non-fiction only. No fiction. About 18 titles a year. Unsolicited mss, synopses and ideas welcome.

Acropolis Books
See **Anness Publishing Ltd**

Actinic Press
See **Cressrelles Publishing Co. Ltd**

Addison Wesley Longman Ltd
Edinburgh Gate, Harlow, Essex CM20 2JE
☎01279 623623   Fax 01279 431059
Contracts & Copyrights Department
  Brenda Gvozdanovic
FOUNDED 1724 by Thomas Longman. Restructured in 1994 to focus solely on educational publishing. A subsidiary of Pearson plc. *Publishes* a range of curriculum subjects, including English language teaching for students at primary and secondary school level, college and university. All unsolicited mss should be addressed to the Manager, Contracts and Copyrights Department.
  Royalties twice-yearly. *Overseas associates* worldwide.

Authors' Rating With well over 800 titles a year rolling off its educational presses, Addison Wesley Longman ranks as one of the top six for title output. Uncertainties in the domestic education market have been offset by a strong export performance, particularly in the area of English Language Teaching. You never read about them in the literary pages but some of our top authors are into ELT. Louis Alexander, who is with Longman, has even appeared in the *Guinness Book of Records* as a world bestseller.

Adelphi
See **David Campbell Publishers Ltd**

Adlard Coles Ltd
See **A & C Black (Publishers) Ltd**

Adlib
See **Scholastic Ltd**

African Books Collective
The Jam Factory, 27 Park End Street, Oxford OX1 1HU
☎01865 726686   Fax 01865 793298
FOUNDED 1990. Collectively owned by its 17 founder member publishers. Exclusive distribution in N. America, UK, Europe and Commonwealth countries outside Africa for 50 African member publishers. Aims to promote and disseminate African-published material outside Africa. No unsolicited mss.

Airlife Publishing Ltd
101 Longden Road, Shrewsbury, Shropshire SY3 9EB
☎01743 235651   Fax 01743 232944
Chairman/Managing Director
  A. D. R. Simpson
Editorial Head *Peter Coles*
Approx. Annual Turnover £3 million
IMPRINTS
  Airlife Specialist aviation titles for pilots, historians and enthusiasts. Also naval and military history. About 60 titles a year. TITLES *Battles with the Luftwaffe; Airwar Bosnia; Suez: The Forgotten Invasion; Tupolev – The Man and His Aircraft.*
  Swan Hill Press Country pursuits, horse riding, mountaineering, fishing, natural history and decorative art. About 35 titles a year. TITLES *An Illustrated Guide to English Jugs; The World of Weather; Roe Deer; Lives of Salmon.*
  Waterline Books Practical sailing books for yachtsmen, nautical history and narrative. About 10 titles a year. TITLES *In Darwin's Wake; The DIY Yachtsman; Yachtsman's GPS Handbook; Classic One-Designs.* Unsolicited mss, synopses and ideas for books welcome.
  Royalties paid annually, twice-yearly by arrangement.

Ian Allan Ltd
Coombelands House, Coombelands Lane, Addlesdown, Surrey KT15 1HY
☎01932 855909   Fax 01932 854750
Chairman *David Allan*
General Manager *Tony Saunders*
Publishes atlases and maps, aviation, hobbies, guidebooks, defence and militaria, nautical, reference, transport, travel and topography. About 100 titles a year. Send sample chapter and synopsis (with s.a.e.). Manages distribution and sales for third party publishers.
  IMPRINT **Dial House** sporting titles.

J. A. Allen & Co. Ltd

1 Lower Grosvenor Place, Buckingham Palace Road, London SW1W 0EL
☎0171 834 0090   Fax 0171 976 5836

Executive Director *Caroline Burt*
Marketing Manager *Hugh Davie*
Editor *Jane Lake*
Approx. Annual Turnover £750,000

FOUNDED 1926 as part of J. A. Allen & Co. (The Horseman's Bookshop) Ltd, and became a separate independent company in 1960. *Publishes* equine and equestrian non-fiction. About 20 titles a year. Mostly commissioned, but willing to consider unsolicited mss of technical/instructional material related to all aspects of horses and horsemanship.
    Royalties paid twice-yearly.

Allen Lane

See **Penguin Books Ltd**

Allison & Busby

114 New Cavendish Street, London W1M 7FD
☎0171 636 2942   Fax 0171 323 2023

Publisher *Peter Day*
Editor *Vanessa Unwin*

FOUNDED 1967. *Publishes* literary fiction and non-fiction, including 20th-century classics, writers' guides and crime. About 36 titles a year. Send synopses with two sample chapters. No replies without s.a.e..

Authors' Rating After living dangerously for three years, Peter Day has sold his company to the Spanish newspaper group, Editorial Prensa Iberia. This will bring joy to the many who have a soft spot for Allison & Busby which has published bravely if not always financially wisely.

Amber Lane Press Ltd

Cheorl House, Church Street, Charlbury, Oxfordshire OX7 3PR
☎01608 810024   Fax 01608 810024

Chairman *Brian Clark*
Managing Director/Editorial Head
    Judith Scott

FOUNDED 1979 to publish modern play texts. *Publishes* plays and books on the theatre. About 4 titles a year. TITLES *Steaming; The Business of Murder; The Dresser* (play texts); *Playwrights' Progress – Patterns of Postwar British Drama* Colin Chambers & Mike Prior; *The Sound of One Hand Clapping: A Guide to Writing for the Theatre* Sheila Yeger. 'Expressly *not* interested in poetry.' No unsolicited mss. Synopses and ideas welcome.
    Royalties paid twice-yearly.

AMCD (Publishers) Ltd

PO Box 182, Altrincham, Cheshire WA15 9UA
☎0161 434 5105   Fax 0161 434 5105

Managing Director *John Stewart Adams*
Approx. Annual Turnover £1 million

FOUNDED 1988. *Publishes* financial directories, books on China, local history, business books. Took over the **Jensen Business Books** imprint in 1993 and is well placed in electronic reference after developing its own software. In conjunction with JHC (Technology) Ltd, AMCD offers publishers access to the electronic book market with their reference, dictionary and directory Pop-Up© software packages which can handle most languages. About 5 titles a year. TITLES *Financing China's Electricity; Around Haunted Croydon; Buying and Selling a Shop; Depression Challenges.* Ideas for business books and books on China or the Far East welcome in synopsis form (no mss). No poetry, fiction or historical romance. Final mss must be on disk.
    Royalties paid twice yearly.

Amsco

See **Omnibus Press**

Andersen Press Ltd

20 Vauxhall Bridge Road, London SW1V 2SA
☎0171 973 9720   Fax 0171 233 6263

Managing Director/Publisher *Klaus Flugge*
Editorial Director *Janice Thomson*
Editor, Fiction *Audrey Adams*

FOUNDED 1976 by Klaus Flugge and named after Hans Christian Andersen. *Publishes* children's high-quality picture books and hardback fiction. Seventy per cent of their books are sold as co-productions abroad. TITLES *Elmer* David McKee; *Greyfriars Bobby* Ruth Brown; *I Want My Potty* Tony Ross; *Badger's Parting Gifts* Susan Varley; *Teddy, Where Are You?* Ralph Steadman; *Jack's Fantastic Voyage* Michael Foreman; *Suddenly!* Colin McNaughton; *Cry of the Wolf* Melvin Burgess. Unsolicited mss welcome for picture books; synopsis in the first instance for books for young readers up to age 12.
    Royalties paid twice-yearly.

Anness Publishing Ltd

Hermes House, 88–89 Blackfriars Road, London SE1 8HA
☎0171 401 2077   Fax 0171 633 9499

Chairman/Managing Director *Paul Anness*
Publisher/Partner *Joanna Lorenz*

FOUNDED 1989. Successful, small entrepreneurial publisher of highly illustrated co-edition titles.

Publishes illustrated general non-fiction: cookery, crafts, interior design, gardening, photography, decorating, lifestyle and children's. About 400 titles a year. Unsolicited summaries and proposals welcome, no manuscripts.

IMPRINTS **Lorenz Books; Acropolis Books; Anness Publishing; Hermes House**.

Antique Collectors' Club

5 Church Street, Woodbridge, Suffolk
IP12 1DS
☎01394 385501   Fax 01394 384434
Managing Director *Diana Steel*
Sales Director *Brian Cotton*

FOUNDED 1966. Has a five-figure membership spread over the United Kingdom and the world. The Club's magazine *Antique Collecting* is sold on a subscription basis (currently £19.50 *p.a.*) and is published 10 times a year. It is sent free to members who may also buy the Club's books at special pre-publication prices. *Publishes* specialist books on antiques and collecting. The price guide series was introduced in 1968 with the first edition of *The Price Guide to Antique Furniture*. Subject areas include furniture, silver/jewellery, metalwork, glass, textiles, art reference, ceramics, horology. Also books on architecture and gardening. RECENT TITLES *Opera Houses of Europe* Andras Kaldor; *Farm Animal Portraits* Elspeth Moncrieff; *Understanding Antique Silver Plate* Stephen Helliwell; *Lucy Kemp Welch* Laura Wortley. Unsolicited synopses and ideas for books welcome. No mss.

Royalties paid quarterly as a rule, but can vary.

Anvil Press Poetry Ltd

Neptune House, 70 Royal Hill, London
SE10 8RT
☎0181 469 3033   Fax 0181 469 3363
Editorial Director *Peter Jay*

FOUNDED 1968 to promote English-language and foreign poetry, both classic and contemporary, in translation. English list includes Peter Levi, Dick Davis and Carol Ann Duffy. Translated books include Bei Dao, Celan, Dante, Lalić. Preliminary enquiry required for translations. Unsolicited book-length collections of poems are welcome from writers whose work has appeared in poetry magazines.

Authors' Rating Celebrating 30 years of independent publishing, Peter Jay has achieved wonders in opening up English poetry to new work. Immune to the dictates of short-lived fashions, Anvil has had great success in building the reputation of younger poets.

Apollos

See **Inter-Varsity Press**

Apple

See **Quarto Publishing** under **UK Packagers**

Appletree Press Ltd

19–21 Alfred Street, Belfast BT2 8DL
☎01232 243074   Fax 01232 246756
Managing Director *John Murphy*
Creative Manager *Nicola Lavery*

FOUNDED 1974. *Publishes* cookery and other small-format gift books, plus general non-fiction of Irish and Scottish interest. TITLES *Little Cookbook* series (about 40 titles); *Ireland: The Complete Guide; Northern Ireland: The Background to the Conflict*. No unsolicited mss; send initial letter or synopsis. Appletree's London office is at Aquarius House, 80–82 Chiswick High Road, London W4 1SY (☎0181 987 9439), but all editorial approaches should be sent to Belfast.

Royalties paid twice-yearly in the first year, annually thereafter. For the *Little Cookbook* Series, a standard fee is paid.

Arc Publications

Nanholme Mill, Shaw Wood Road, Todmorden, Lancashire OL14 6DA
☎01706 812338   Fax 01706 818948
Publishers *Rosemary Jones, Angela Jarman, Tony Ward*
General Editor *Tony Ward*
Associate Editors *Michael Hulse* (International), *David Morley* (UK)

FOUNDED in 1969 to specialise in the publication of contemporary poetry from new and established writers both in the UK and abroad. Runs the annual **Northern Short Story Competition** and *publishes* an anthology of winning entries. AUTHORS include John Kinsella (Australia), Glyn Maxwell, Tariq Latif, C. K. Stead (New Zealand), Donald Atkinson, Tomas Saluman (Slovenia), Jacqueline Brown. 8 titles a year. Authors submitting material should ensure that it is compatible with the current list and should enclose s.a.e. if they wish mss to be returned.

Aris & Phillips Ltd

Teddington House, Warminster, Wiltshire
BA12 8PQ
☎01985 213409   Fax 01985 212910
Managing/Editorial Director *Adrian Phillips*
Editor, Hispanic Classics *Lucinda Phillips*

FOUNDED 1972 to publish books on Egyptology. A family firm which has remained independent. *Publishes* academic, classical, oriental and hispanic. About 20 titles a year. With such a highly specialised list, unsolicited mss and synopses are not particularly welcome, but synopses will be considered.

Royalties paid twice-yearly.

Arkana
See **Penguin Books Ltd**

Arms & Armour Press
See **Cassell**

Arnefold
See **George Mann Books**

Edward Arnold
See **Hodder Headline plc**

Arrow
See **Random House UK Ltd**

Artech House
Portland House, Stag Place, London
SW1E 5XA
☎0171 973 8077   Fax 0171 630 0166

Managing Director (USA) *William M. Bazzy*
Commissioning Editor *Dr Julie Lancashire*

FOUNDED 1969. European office of Artech House Inc., Boston. *Publishes* electronic engineering, especially telecommunications, computer communications, computing, optoelectronics, signal processing and solid-state materials and devices (books, software and videos). 50–60 titles a year. Unsolicited mss and synopses considered.

Royalties paid twice-yearly.

Ashgate Publishing Co. Ltd
Gower House, Croft Road, Aldershot,
Hampshire GU11 3HR
☎01252 331551   Fax 01252 344405

Chairman *Nigel Farrow*

FOUNDED 1967. *Publishes* in social sciences, business, arts and humanities under the **Gower** imprint for professional books and **Ashgate** imprint for academic books.

Julia Scott Business and management; *Sarah Markham* Social sciences; *John Irvin* Political science, international relations and legal studies; *Alec McAulay* History; *John Smedley* Variorum collected studies; *Rachel Lynch* Music and literary studies; *Pamela Edwardes* Art history; *John Hindley* Aviation studies; *Jo Gooderham* Social work.

Ashmolean Museum Publications
Ashmolean Museum, Beaumont Street,
Oxford OX1 2PH
☎01865 278009   Fax 01865 278018

Publisher/Editorial Head *Ian Charlton*
Approx. Annual Turnover £200,000

The Ashmolean Museum, which is wholly owned by Oxford University, was founded in 1683. The first publication appeared in 1890 but publishing did not really start in earnest until the 1960s. *Publishes* European and Oriental fine and applied arts, European archaeology and ancient history, Egyptology and numismatics, for both adult and children's markets. About 8 titles a year. No fiction, American/African art, ethnography, modern art or post-medieval history.

IMPRINTS
Ashmolean Museum Publications and **Griffith Institute** (Egyptology imprint). Recent TITLES *Coinage of the Crusades and the Latin East; Miniatures; Eighteenth-Century French Porcelain; Contemporary Chinese Paintings; Oxford Food; Demotic Grammar; Stone Vessels, etc., From the Tomb of Tut'ankhamun.* No unsolicited mss.

Royalties paid annually.

Associated University Presses (AUP)
See **Golden Cockerel Press Ltd**

The Athlone Press
1 Park Drive, London NW11 7SG
☎0181 458 0888   Fax 0181 201 8115

Managing Director *Doris Southam*
Editorial Head *Brian Southam*

FOUNDED 1949 as the publishing house of the University of London. Now wholly independent, but preserves links with the University via an academic advisory board. *Publishes* archaeology, architecture, art, economics, film studies, history, history-of-ideas, history-of-science, law, eating disorders, psychiatry, literary criticism, psychic, medical, Japan, philosophy, politics, religion, science, sociology, women's/feminist issues. Anticipated developments in the near future: more emphasis on cultural studies, history of ideas, women's/feminist studies and environmental issues, including medicine. About 35 titles a year. Unsolicited mss, synopses and ideas for academic books welcome.

Royalties paid annually. *Overseas associates* The Athlone Press, 165 First Avenue, Atlantic Highlands, NJ 07716, USA.

Atlantic Europe Publishing Co. Ltd

Greys Court Farm, Greys Court,
Nr Henley on Thames, Oxon RG9 4PG
☎01491 628188   Fax 01491 628189

Directors *Dr B. J. Knapp, D. L. R. McCrae*

Closely associated, since 1990, with Earthscape Editions packaging operation. *Publishes* full-colour, highly illustrated children's non-fiction in hardback for international co-editions. Not interested in any other material. Main focus is on National Curriculum titles, especially in the fields of mathematics, science, technology, social history and geography. About 25 titles a year. Unsolicited synopses and ideas for books welcome but s.a.e. essential for return of submissions.

Royalties or fees paid depending on circumstance.

Attic Books

The Folly, Rhosgoch, Painscastle, Builth Wells, Powys LD2 3JY
☎01497 851205

Managing Director/Editorial Head
Jack Bowyer

FOUNDED 1984 by its architect owners. *Publishes* books on building crafts, architecture and engineering. Mostly technical books for the industry, dealing mainly with restoration and conservation.

Royalties paid annually.

AUP (Associated University Presses)

See **Golden Cockerel Press Ltd**

Aurum Press Ltd

25 Bedford Avenue, London
WC1B 3AT
☎0171 637 3225   Fax 0171 580 2469

Chairman *André Deutsch*
Managing Director *Bill McCreadie*
Editorial Director *Piers Burnett*

FOUNDED 1977. Formerly owned by Andrew Lloyd Webber's Really Useful Group, now owned jointly by Piers Burnett, Bill McCreadie and Sheila Murphy, all of whom worked together in the '70s for André Deutsch. Committed to producing high-quality, illustrated/non-illustrated adult non-fiction in the areas of general human interest, art and craft, lifestyle, sport and travel. About 40 titles a year.

Royalties paid twice-yearly.

Autumn Publishing Ltd

North Barn, Appledram Barns, Birdham Road, Near Chichester, West Sussex PO20 7EQ
☎01243 531660   Fax 01243 774433

Managing Director *Campbell Goldsmid*
Editorial Director *Ingrid Goldsmid*

FOUNDED 1976. Publisher of highly illustrated non-fiction: mainly children's, including activity books. About 20 titles a year. Unsolicited synopses and ideas for books welcome if they come within relevant subject areas.

Payment varies according to contract; generally a flat fee.

B & W Publishing Ltd

233 Cowgate, Edinburgh EH1 1NQ
☎0131 220 5551   Fax 0131 220 5552

Joint Managing Directors *Campbell Brown, Steven Wiggins*

FOUNDED 1990. *Publishes* fiction, memoirs, sport and guidebooks. 15 titles in 1996 with around 70 titles in print. Unsolicited mss, synopses and ideas for books welcome. No children's books.

Royalties paid twice-yearly.

Baillière Tindall

See **Harcourt Brace and Company Ltd**

Bantam/Bantam Press

See **Transworld Publishers Ltd**

Barefoot Books Ltd

PO Box 95, Kingswood, Bristol BS15 5BH
☎0117 9328885   Fax 0117 9328881

Rights & Management: 18 Highbury Terrace, London N5 1UP
☎0171 704 6492   Fax 0171 359 5798

Managing Director *Nancy Traversy*
Publisher *Tessa Strickland* (at Bristol office)
Approx. Annual Turnover £1 million

FOUNDED in 1993. *Publishes* high-quality children's picture books, particularly new and traditional stories from a wide range of cultures. 27 titles in 1997. TITLES *How Do Animals Say Hello?* Stella Blackstone; *The Emperor Who Hates Yellow* Jim Edmiston; *Storm Boy* Paul Owen Lewis. No unsolicited mss.

Royalties paid twice-yearly.

Barny Books

The Cottage, Hough on the Hill, Near Grantham, Lincolnshire NG32 2BB
☎01400 250246

Managing Director/Editorial Head
Molly Burkett

Business Manager *Tom Cann*
Approx. Annual Turnover £10,000

FOUNDED with the aim of encouraging new writers and illustrators. *Publishes* mainly children's books. TITLES *Once Upon a Wartime* series, Molly Burkett; *Dear James – Letters From a Serving Wren* Susan Slater; *Old Dykes I Have Known: History of Drainage of the Fens* Peter Charnley; *Tom Goes to the Seaside* Divya Malde; *Orston – History of a Nottinghamshire Village* Paul Barnes. Too small a concern to have the staff/resources to deal with unsolicited mss. Writers with strong ideas should approach Molly Burkett by letter in the first instance. Also runs a readership and advisory service for new writers (£10 fee for short stories or illustrations; £20 fee for full-length stories).
   Royalties division of profits 50/50.

Authors' Rating While Molly Burkett has been chasing about the world promoting her small but select list, she has also found time to organise the company to put it on to a more business-like footing. One of the friendliest of publishers, Molly has to be in the running for 'double-take title of the year' for her *Old Dykes I Have Known* which turns out to be a history of Fen drainage.

Baron Birch
See **The Barracuda Collection/Quotes Ltd**

The Barracuda Collection/ Quotes Ltd
The Book Barn, Church Way, Whittlebury, Northamptonshire NN12 8XS
☎01327 858301   Fax 01327 858302
Publisher *Clive Birch*

Barracuda was formed in 1974, Quotes in 1985. *Publishes* local and natural history, country and sporting life, military, transport, church, family and institutional histories. About 30 titles a year.

IMPRINTS
The Barracuda Collection TITLES *The Book of Sleaford; Fowlness – the Mystery Isle.* **Quotes in Camera** TITLES *Tyne & Wear Buses; Yorkshire Collieries.* **Sporting & Leisure Press** TITLE *Dons in the League.* **Baron Birch** TITLES *White Funnels, Middlesex Mills.* Synopses and ideas for books welcome with sample mss page, extent of words and pictures.
   Royalties paid annually.

Barrie & Jenkins
See **Random House UK Ltd**

Bartholomew
See **HarperCollins Publishers Ltd**

B. T. Batsford Ltd
583 Fulham Road, London SW6 5BY
☎0171 471 1100   Fax 0171 471 1101
Chairman *Gerard Mizrahi*
Chief Executive *Jules Perel*
Approx. Annual Turnover £5 million

FOUNDED in 1843 as a bookseller, and began publishing in 1874. An independent publisher until 1996 when it was bought by Labyrinth Publishing UK Ltd. A world leader in books on chess, arts and craft. *Publishes* non-fiction: archaeology, school reference, cinema, crafts and hobbies, equestrian, fashion and costume, graphic design, horticulture, botany and gardening. Acquired Faber chess list in 1994. About 130 titles a year.

DIVISIONS
Arts & Crafts; Archaeology & Ancient History; Chess; Horticulture; Country Sports; Graphic Design.
   Royalties paid twice in first year, annually thereafter.

Authors' Rating Explaining the sale of the long-established archaeology and Roman history lists to Routledge, Jules Perel backed the future of Batsford as a 'speciality, illustrated non-fiction publisher'. Radical management changes followed with the promotion of a new generation of commissioning editors.

Bay View Books Ltd
The Red House, 25–26 Bridgeland Street, Bideford, Devon EX39 2PZ
☎01237 479225/421285   Fax 01237 421286
Managing Directors *Charles Herridge, Bridgid Herridge*

FOUNDED 1986. *Publishes* transport books only, including series: all-colour classic car restoration guides; A–Zs of cars, motorcycles and racing cars. About 15 titles a year.
   Payment varies according to contract.

BBC Consumer Publishing
80 Wood Lane, London W12 0TT
☎0181 576 2623   Fax 0181 576 2858
Publishing Director *Christopher Weller*
Editorial Director *Sheila Ableman*
Approx. Annual Turnover £30 million

BBC Consumer Publishing is a division of BBC Worldwide Ltd. *Publishes* TV tie-in titles, including books which, though linked with

BBC television or radio, may not simply be the 'book of the series'. Books with no television or radio link are of no interest. About 80 titles a year. TITLES *Delia Smith's Winter Collection; Shooting Stars; Rhodes' Around Britain.* Unsolicited mss (which come in at the rate of about 15 weekly) are rarely read. However, strong ideas well expressed will always be considered, and promising letters will stand a chance of further scrutiny.

IMPRINTS
Network Books A new range of non-fiction tie-ins to TV programmes broadcast on channels other than BBC1 or BBC2. Includes cookery, gardening, crafts, plus some children's fiction. **BBC Penguin** A co-publishing deal which gives BBC Books a mass-market paperback outlet,
Royalties paid twice-yearly.

Authors' Rating It looks easy but publishing the book of the television series is no guarantee of a bestseller. On the other hand, it can help to get a television or radio proposal off the ground if there is an obvious book tie-in.

BBC Penguin
See **BBC Consumer Publishing**

Bedford Square Press
See **NCVO Publications**

Belair
See **Folens Ltd**

Bellew Publishing Co. Ltd
Nightingale Centre, 8 Balham Hill, London SW12 9EA
☎0181 673 5611   Fax 0181 675 3542
Chairman *Ian McCorquodale*
Managing Director *Ib Bellew*
Approx. Annual Turnover £600,000

FOUNDED 1983. Publisher and packager. *Publishes* craft, art and design, fiction, illustrated non-fiction, general interest, religion and politics. About 15 titles a year. TITLES *We Believe* Alfred Gilbey; *Chronicle* Alan Wall; *The Awakening of Willie Ryland* Tom Hart; *On Depiction: Critical Essays on Art* Avigdor Arikha. No unsolicited mss. Synopses with specimen chapters welcome.
Royalties paid annually.

Berg Publishers Ltd
150 Cowley Road, Oxford OX4 1JJ
☎01865 245104   Fax 01865 791165
Managing Director *Peter Cowell*

Editorial Director *Kathryn Earle*
Approx. Annual Turnover £600,000

Also **Oswald Wolff Books** imprint. *Publishes* scholarly books in the fields of history, social sciences and humanities. About 45 titles a year. No unsolicited mss. Synopses and ideas for books welcome.
Royalties paid annually.

Berkswell Publishing Co. Ltd
PO Box 420, Warminster, Wiltshire BA12 9XB
☎01985 840189   Fax 01985 840189
Managing Director *John Stidolph*
Approx. Annual Turnover £250,000

FOUNDED 1974. *Publishes* illustrated books, royalty, heritage, country sports, biography and books about Wessex. No fiction. About 4 titles a year. Unsolicited mss, synopses and ideas for books welcome.
Royalties paid according to contract.

Berlitz Publishing Co. Ltd
Berlitz House, Peterley Road, Oxford OX4 2TX
☎01865 747033   Fax 01865 779700
Chairman *H. Yokoi*
Managing Director *R. Kirkpatrick*
Approx. Annual Turnover £6 million

FOUNDED 1970. Part of Berlitz International, which also comprises language instruction and translation divisions. *Publishes* travel and language-learning products only: travel guides, phrasebooks and language courses. DIVISION **Berlitz Publishing** TITLES *Pocket Guides; Discover Guides; Berlitz Complete Guide to Cruising and Cruise Ships; Business Phrase Books; Berlitz Live.* No unsolicited mss.

BFI Publishing
British Film Institute, 21 Stephen Street, London W1P 2LN
☎0171 255 1444   Fax 0171 436 7950
Head of Sales *John Atkinson*
Approx. Annual Turnover £500,000

FOUNDED 1982. Part of the **British Film Institute**. *Publishes* academic and general film/television-related books. About 30 titles a year. TITLES *Film Classics* (series); *Modern Classics* series; *Derek Jarman* Michael O'Pray; *Fetishism & Curiosity* Laura Mulvey; *BFI Film & Television Handbook* Eddie Dyja. Unsolicited synopses and ideas preferred to complete mss.
Royalties paid annually.

Bible Society

Stonehill Green, Westlea, Swindon, Wiltshire
SN5 7DG
☎01793 418100   Fax 01793 418118
Executive Director *Neil Crosbie*
Approx. Annual Turnover £4 million

The Bible Society was founded in 1804 and was
granted a royal charter in 1948. It is now part of
a worldwide fellowship of Bible Societies, working in over 180 countries. A mission agency with
the specific task of enabling the Church to use
the Bible in her mission. *Publishes* Bibles, Bible-
related resources, group study, religious education and video materials. TITLES *The Good News
Bible, Contemporary English Version; Emmaus: The
Way of Faith; Learn New Testament Greek*. 22 titles
in 1996. Unsolicited synopses and ideas welcome. No Christian biography, fiction, poetry,
general religious or commentaries.
Royalties paid twice-yearly.

Clive Bingley Books
See **Library Association Publishing Ltd**

A. & C. Black (Publishers) Ltd

35 Bedford Row, London WC1R 4JH
☎0171 242 0946   Fax 0171 831 8478
Chairman *Charles Black*
Deputy Chairman *David Gadsby*
Managing Directors *Charles Black, Jill
    Coleman*
Approx. Annual Turnover £6.5 million

Publishes children's and educational books,
including music, for 3–15-year-olds, arts and
crafts, ceramics, fishing, ornithology, nautical,
reference, sport, theatre and travel. About 125
titles a year. Acquisitions brought the Herbert
Press' art, design and general books, Adlard
Coles' sailing list and Christopher Helm's natural history and ornithology lists into A. & C.
Black's stable.

IMPRINTS **Adlard Coles**; **Christopher Helm**;
The Herbert Press (see entry). TITLES *New
Mermaid* drama series; *Who's Who*; *Writers' &
Artists' Yearbook*; *Know the Game* sports series;
Blue Guides travel series. Initial enquiry appre-
ciated before submission of mss.
Royalties payment varies according to contract.

Black Ace Books

PO Box 6557, Forfar DD8 2YS
☎01307 465096   Fax 01307 465494
Managing Director *Hunter Steele, Boo Wood*
FOUNDED 1991. *Publishes* new fiction, Scottish
and general; some non-fiction including bi-
ography, history, philosophy and psychology.
26 titles in print. IMPRINTS **Black Ace Books**,
Black Ace Paperbacks TITLES *The Hawthorn
Hedge* Mercedes Clarasó; *The Song of the Forest*
Colin Mackay; *Empty Footsteps* Lorn
Macintyre; *The Bowels of Christ* Graham Lironi.
Completed books only. No unsolicited mss.
No submissions from outside UK. 'Send only:
1-page covering letter, 1-page synopsis, 1 full
page of text and large s.a.e.. If possible, include
1-page recommendation from suitable referee
such as published author, book reviewer or
university teacher of literature. No poetry,
children's, cookery, DIY, religion.'
Royalties paid twice-yearly.

Black Dagger Crime
See **Chivers Press Ltd**

Black Lace
See **Virgin Publishing Ltd**

Black Spring Press Ltd

63 Harlescott Road, Nunhead, London
SE15 3DA
☎0171 639 2492   Fax 0171 639 2508
Directors *Simon Pettifar, Maja Prausnitz*
FOUNDED 1986. *Publishes* fiction, literary criti-
cism, biography, theatre and cinema studies.
About 5 titles a year. TITLES *And the Ass Saw
the Angel* Nick Cave; *Death of a Lady's Man*
Leonard Cohen; *My Original Sin* Marie-
Victoire Rouillier; *The Terrible News* collection
of Russian short stories by Zamyatin, Babel,
Kharms, *et al*; *The Mortdecai Trilogy* Kyril
Bonfiglioli. No unsolicited mss.
Royalties paid twice-yearly.

Black Swan
See **Transworld Publishers Ltd**

Blackie
See **Penguin Books Ltd**

Blackstaff Press Ltd

3 Galway Park, Dundonald, Belfast BT16 0AN
☎01232 487161   Fax 01232 489552
Director/Editorial Head *Anne Tannahill*
FOUNDED 1971. *Publishes* mainly, but not
exclusively, Irish interest books, fiction, poetry,
history, politics, illustrated and fine editions,
natural history and folklore. About 25 titles a
year. Unsolicited mss considered, but preliminary submission of synopsis plus short sample
of writing preferred. Return postage *must* be
enclosed.
Royalties paid twice-yearly.

Authors' Rating Past winner of the *Sunday Times* Small Publisher of the Year Award, this Belfast publisher is noted for a strong backlist, 'wonderfully well-presented catalogues and promotional material'.

Blackwell Publishers Ltd
108 Cowley Road, Oxford OX4 1JF
☎01865 791100   Fax 01865 791347
Chairman *Nigel Blackwell*
Managing Director *René Olivieri*
FOUNDED 1922. Rapid growth since the 1970s included the establishment of a wholly owned distribution company, Marston Book Services, a joint venture with **Polity Press** (see entry). The focus is on international research journals and undergraduate textbooks in social sciences, business and humanities; computer-aided instruction on p.c. applications. About 300 titles a year and over 150 journals.

DIVISIONS
Books *Philip Carpenter, Stephan Chambers* **Journals** *Sue Corbett, Claire Andrews*. Unsolicited synopses with specimen chapter and table of contents welcome.
    Royalties paid annually. *Overseas associates* Blackwell Publishers Inc., Cambridge, Massachusetts; InfoSource Inc., Orlando, Florida.

Authors' Rating Investing heavily in computer-based training for the further and higher education markets, Blackwell is putting its faith in a booming US market which now accounts for more than half of the company's turnover.

Blackwell Science Ltd
Osney Mead, Oxford OX2 0EL
☎01865 206206   Fax 01865 721205
Chairman *Nigel Blackwell*
Managing Director *Robert Campbell*
Editorial Director *Peter Saugman*
Approx. Annual Turnover (Group) £95 million
FOUNDED 1939. Rapid growth since the 1970s culminated with expansion into Europe in the late 1980s with the acquisition of Medizinische Zeitschriften Verlagsgesellschaft (MZV), Vienna; Ueberreuter Wissenschaft Verlag (now Blackwell Wissenschafts-Verlag), Berlin; Arnette, Paris; more recently, Grosse Verlag, Germany; and the academic publishing of Paul Parey. Also 75% owner of Danish general publisher Munksgaard. *Publishes* medical, professional and science. About 300 titles a year, plus 220 journals. TITLES *Diseases of the Liver and Biliary System* Sherlock; *Essential Immunology* Roitt; *Textbook of Dermatology* Rook. Unsolicited mss and synopses welcome.
    Royalties paid annually. *Overseas subsidiaries* in USA, Australia, Paris, Berlin and Vienna; editorial offices in London and Edinburgh.

Authors' Rating Blackwell Science's main business is in scientific journals, mostly produced in partnership with learned societies, and medical publishing. Much of the growth is in mainland Europe where Blackwell Science has offshoots in Berlin, Paris and Vienna. Munksgaard, Blackwell's Danish subsidiary, hit the jackpot with Peter Høeg's *Miss Smilla's Feeling for Snow* but while this was a highly profitable bestseller, it does not mark a departure from core publishing.

Blake Publishing
3 Bramber Court, 2 Bramber Road, London W14 9PB
☎0171 381 0666   Fax 0171 381 6868
Chairman *David Blake*
Managing Director *John Blake*
Approx. Annual Turnover £1 million
FOUNDED 1991 and rapidly expanding. *Publishes* mass-market non-fiction. No cookery, children's, specialist or non-commercial. 22 titles in 1996. No unsolicited mss; synopses and ideas welcome. Please enclose s.a.e..
    Royalties paid twice-yearly.

Authors' Rating As a former editor of *The People*, John Blake knows a thing or two when it comes to eye-catching titles. *The Duchess of York Uncensored* is typical of a list that is 'unashamedly mass-market'. Strong on big money serial rights.

Blandford Press
See **Cassell**

Bloodaxe Books Ltd
PO Box 1SN, Newcastle upon Tyne NE99 1SN
☎0191 232 5988   Fax 0191 222 0020
Chairman *Simon Thirsk*
Managing/Editorial Director *Neil Astley*
Publishes poetry, literature and criticism, and related titles by British, Irish, European, Commonwealth and American writers. 95 per cent of their list is poetry. About 50 titles a year. TITLES include two major anthologies, *The New Poetry* Hulse, Kennedy and Morley (eds); *Sixty Women Poets* Linda France (ed); *The Gaze of the Gorgon* Tony Harrison – winner of the **Whitbread Award** for poetry in 1992; *No*

Truth With the Furies R. S. Thomas (Nobel Prize nominee); *Selected Poems* Jenny Joseph. Unsolicited poetry mss welcome; send a sample of no more than 10 poems. Authors of other material should write in the first instance.

Royalties paid annually.

Authors' Rating Assisted by regional Arts Council funding, Bloodaxe is one of the liveliest and most innovative of poetry publishers with a list that takes in some of the best of the younger poets.

Bloomsbury Publishing Plc

38 Soho Square, London W1V 5DF
☎0171 494 2111   Fax 0171 434 0151
Chairman/Managing Director *Nigel Newton*
Publishing Directors *Liz Calder, David Reynolds, Kathy Rooney, Alan Wherry Mathew Hamilton, Sarah Odedina*

FOUNDED 1986 by Nigel Newton, David Reynolds, Alan Wherry and Liz Calder. In the following years Bloomsbury titles appeared regularly in *The Sunday Times* bestseller lists, and many of its authors have gone on to win prestigious literary prizes. In 1991 Nadine Gordimer won the **Nobel Prize for Literature**, Michael Ondaatje's *The English Patient* won the 1992 **Booker Prize,** and Tobias Wolff's *In Pharaoh's Army* won the Esquire/Volvo/Waterstone's Non-Fiction Award in 1994.

Publishes literary fiction and non-fiction, including general reference books. TITLES *The Best of Friends* Joanna Trollope; *Debatable Land* Candia McWilliam; *The Piano* Jane Campion; *Crossing the River* Caryl Phillips; *The Robber Bride* Margaret Atwood; *Thomas Hardy: The Definitive Biography* Martin Seymour-Smith; *The Unlikely Spy* Paul Henderson; *Bloomsbury Thesaurus; Guide to Human Thought; Guide to Women's Literature; Bloomsbury Classics.* Unsolicited mss and synopses welcome; no poetry.

Royalties paid twice-yearly.

Authors' Rating While other middle-range publishers were suffering from a depressed book market, Bloomsbury continued to do well thanks largely to a shelf-load of strong sellers and high-quality design. The latest growth areas are in children's books and home reference.

Boatswain Press

See **Kenneth Mason Publications Ltd**

Bobcat

See **Omnibus Press**

Bodley Head

See **Random House UK Ltd**

The Book Guild Ltd

Temple House, 25 High Street, Lewes, East Sussex BN7 2LU
☎01273 472534   Fax 01273 476472
Chairman *George M. Nissen CBE*
Managing Director *Carol Biss*

FOUNDED 1982. *Publishes* fiction, academic, general non-fiction, naval and military, autobiography, art. Expanding children's list. Approx. 85 titles a year.

DIVISIONS/TITLES
Children's *Underneath the Underground* Anthea Turner and Wendy Turner; *Travel Joy* Roberta Edwards. **Fiction** *A Reasonable Man* Vaughan James; *Breakfast at Tesco's* Pam Moses. **Biography** *Man of Courage: The Life and Career of Tommy Farr* Bob Lonkhurst; *Grand Hotelier* Ronald F. Jones OBE. **General** *A Natural History of the Cuckmere Valley* Patrick Coulcher; *Out of My Head* Viv Martin. **Military** *Soldier in the Circus* Edward Lyme; *Silently into the Midst of Things* Athol Sutherland Brown.

IMPRINTS **Temple House Books** Fiction: *Drug Squad* Brian Windmill. Non-fiction: *Colditz, Last Stop* Jack Pringle; *The Fitzroy* Sally Fiber. All forthcoming paperbacks are now Book Guild titles. Unsolicited mss. Ideas and synopses welcome.

Royalties paid twice-yearly.

Authors' Rating Regularly advertises for authors who may be asked to cover their own production costs. But in promoting its services, The Book Guild is more up-front with its clients than the typical vanity publisher who promises the earth and delivers next to nothing.

Boulevard Books & The Babel Guides

8 Aldbourne Road, London W12 0LN
☎0181 743 5278   Fax 0181 743 5278
Managing Director *Ray Keenoy*

Specialises in contemporary world fiction by young writers in English translation. Existing or forthcoming series of fiction from Brazil, Italy, Latin America, Low Countries, Greece, and elsewhere. The Babel Guides series of popular guides to fiction in translation started in 1995.

DIVISONS
Latin American *Ray Keenoy* TITLES *Tattoo* Ednodio Quintero; *Hotel Atlantico* J. G. Noll.

Italian *Fiorenza Conte* TITLES *The Toy Catalogue* Sandra Petrignani; *Run!* Valeria Viganò. **Brazil** *Dr David Treece* TITLES *From the Heart of Brazil* (anthology). **Low Countries** *Prof. Theo Hermans.* **Greece** *Marina Coriolano-Likourezos.* **Babel Guides to Fiction in Translation** *Ray Keenoy* series editor TITLES *Babel Guide to Italian Fiction in Translation; Babel Guide to the Fiction of Portugal, Brazil & Africa in Translation; Babel Guide to French Fiction in English Translation.*

Suggestions and proposals for translations of contemporary fiction welcome. Also seeking contributors to forthcoming Babel Guides (all literatures).

Royalties paid twice-yearly.

Bowker–Saur Ltd

Maypole House, Maypole Road, East Grinstead, West Sussex RH19 1HU
☎01342 330100   Fax 01342 330191
Managing Director *Charles Halpin*
Publishers *Geraldine Turpie, Yolanda Dolling*

Owned by Reed Elsevier, Bowker-Saur is part of Reed Business Information in the UK. *Publishes* library reference, library science, bibliography, biography, African studies, politics and world affairs, business and professional directories. Unsolicited mss will not be read. Approach with ideas only.

Royalties paid annually.

Boxtree

See **Macmillan Publishers Ltd**

Marion Boyars Publishers Ltd

24 Lacy Road, London SW15 1NL
☎0181 788 9522   Fax 0181 789 8122
Managing Director/Editorial Director
  Marion Boyars
Editor, Non-fiction *Ken Hollings*

FOUNDED 1975, formerly Calder and Boyars. *Publishes* biography and autobiography, economics, fiction, literature and criticism, medical, music, philosophy, poetry, politics and world affairs, psychology, sociology and anthropology, theatre and drama, film and cinema, women's studies. About 30 titles a year. AUTHORS include Georges Bataille, Ingmar Bergman, Heinrich Böll, Hortense Calisker, Jean Cocteau, Clive Collins, Warwick Collins, Julian Green, Ivan Illich, Pauline Kael, Ken Kesey, Kenzaburo Oe, Michael Ondaatje, Hubert Selby, Igor Stravinsky, Frederic Tuten, Eudora Welty, Judith Williamson. Unsolicited mss not welcome for fiction; submissions from agents preferred. Unsolicited synopses and ideas welcome for non-fiction.

Royalties paid annually. *Overseas associates* Marion Boyars Publishers Inc., 237 East 39th Street, New York, NY 10016, USA.

Authors' Rating Marion Boyars caters exclusively for the intellectual top end of the book market which does not deter writers of more modest pretensions showering her with submissions. Either they lack self awareness or they are not studying the list.

Boydell & Brewer Ltd

PO Box 9, Woodbridge, Suffolk IP12 3DF
☎01394 411320

Publishes non-fiction only, principally medieval studies. All books commissioned. No unsolicited material.

BPS Books

St Andrews House, 48 Princess Road East, Leicester LE1 7DR
☎0116 2549568   Fax 0116 2470787
Publications Manager *Joyce Collins*
Editor *Susan Pacitti*

Book publishing division of The British Psychological Society. *Publishes* a wide range of academic and applied psychology, including specialist monographs, textbooks for teachers, managers, doctors, nurses, social workers, and schools material; plus general psychology and some electronic publishing. 10–15 titles a year. Proposals considered.

Bracken Books

See **Random House UK Ltd**

Brampton Publications

See **SB Publications**

Brassey's (UK) Ltd

33 John Street, London WC1N 2AT
☎0171 753 7777   Fax 0171 753 7794
Chairman *Lord Holme of Cheltenham*
Managing Director *Jenny Shaw MA*
Approx. Annual Turnover £2.65 million

Began life as *Brassey's Naval Annual* in 1886 to become the most important publisher of serious defence-related material in the world. Owned by Robert Stephen Holdings. *Publishes* books and journals on defence, international relations, military history, maritime and aeronautical subjects and defence terminology. Launched its new imprint **Brassey's Sports** in 1996 with the International Olympic

Committee's Official Handbook *The IOC Olympic Companion 1996*.

IMPRINTS **Brassey's (UK)**; **Brassey's Inc**; **Brassey's Sports**; **Conway Maritime Press** Naval history and ship modelling; **Putnam Aeronautical Books** Technical and reference.

Royalties paid annually.

Nicholas Brealey Publishing Ltd

36 John Street, London WC1N 2AT
☎0171 430 0224   Fax 0171 404 8311
Managing Director *Nicholas Brealey*

FOUNDED 1992 with a backlist of major titles from The Industrial Society. Independent non-fiction publisher focusing on high-profile, practical books for business that inspire, enable, inform and entertain. *Publishes* 'readable reference' on management, employment, law, training and human resources. TITLES *Coaching for Performance; Managing Without Management; Reengineering the Corporation; NLP at Work; Megatrends Asia; The Fifth Discipline Fieldbook; China Wakes; Transforming the Bottom Line; The Future of Capitalism*. No fiction, poetry or leisure titles. No unsolicited mss; synopses and ideas welcome.

Royalties paid twice-yearly.

Authors' Rating A recent entry into the booming management book market, Nicholas Brealey looks to be succeeding in breaking away from the usual computer-speak business manuals to publish information and literate texts. Lead titles have a distinct trans-Atlantic feel.

The Breedon Books Publishing Co. Ltd

44 Friar Gate, Derby DE1 1DA
☎01332 384235   Fax 01332 292755
Chairman/Managing Director *A. C. Rippon*
Approx. Annual Turnover £1 million

FOUNDED 1983. *Publishes* autobiography, biography, heritage and sport. 32 titles in 1996. Unsolicited mss, synopses and ideas welcome if accompanied by s.a.e.. No poetry or fiction.

Royalties paid annually.

Breese Books Ltd

164 Kensington Park Road, London W11 2ER
☎0171 727 9426   Fax 0171 229 3395
Chairman/Managing Director *Martin Ranicar-Breese*

FOUNDED 1975 to produce specialist conjuring books and then went on to establish a more general list. Breese Books has now closed its general publishing division and is concentrating on two specific areas: conjuring/sleight of hand/illusions and Sherlock Holmes pastiches. There is little point in submitting material on any subjects other than the above.

Authors' Rating Having cut back on his publishing programme, Martin Breese is offering a **Critical Eye Service** to advise authors on how to make their work saleable. There are no guarantees of publication and there is a charge but for some, straight practical advice may be useful.

Brimax Books

See **Reed Books**

Bristol Classical Press

See **Gerald Duckworth & Co. Ltd**

British Academic Press

See **I. B. Tauris & Co. Ltd**

The British Academy

20–21 Cornwall Terrace, London NW1 4QP
☎0171 487 5966   Fax 0171 224 3807
Publications Officer *J. M. H. Rivington*
Publications Assistant *J. English*

FOUNDED 1901. The primary body for promoting scholarship in the humanities, the Academy publishes many series stemming from its own long-standing research projects, or series of lectures and conference proceedings. Main subjects include history, philosophy and archaeology. About 10–15 titles a year. SERIES *Auctores Britannici Medii Aevi; Early English Church Music; Fontes Historiae Africanae; Records of Social and Economic History*. Proposals for these series are welcome and are forwarded to the relevant project committees. The British Academy is a registered charity and does not publish for profit.

Royalties paid only when titles have covered their costs.

The British Library

Marketing & Publishing Office, 41 Russell Square, London WC1B 3DG
☎0171 412 7704   Fax 0171 412 7768
Managing Director *Jane Carr*
Publishing Manager *David Way*
Approx. Annual Turnover £750,000

FOUNDED 1979 as the publishing arm of The British Library's London Collections to publish works based on the historic collections and

related subjects. *Publishes* bibliographical reference, manuscript studies, illustrated books based on the Library's collections, and book arts. TITLES *The Image of the World: 20 Centuries of World Maps; Women Bookbinders 1880 – 1920; Five Hundred Years of Printing; The Lindisfarne Gospels; The Gutenberg Bible*. About 30 titles a year. Unsolicited mss, synopses and ideas welcome if related to the history of the book, book arts or bibliography. No fiction or general non-fiction.
Royalties paid annually.

British Museum Press
46 Bloomsbury Street, London WC1B 3QQ
☎0171 323 1234   Fax 0171 436 7315
Managing Director *Patrick Wright*
Head of Publishing *Emma Way*
The book publishing division of The British Museum Company Ltd. FOUNDED 1973 as British Museum Publications Ltd; relaunched 1991 as British Museum Press. *Publishes* ancient history, archaeology, ethnography, art history, exhibition catalogues, guides, children's books, and all official publications of the British Museum. Around 50 titles a year. TITLES *The Discovery of the Past; Making Faces; Money: a History; Pottery in the Making; Early Celtic Designs*. Synopses and ideas for books welcome.
Royalties paid twice-yearly.

The Brockhampton Press
See **Hodder Headline plc**

John Brown Publishing Ltd
The Boathouse, Crabtree Lane, Fulham, London SW6 6LU
☎0171 470 2400   Fax 0171 381 3930
Chairman/Managing Director *John Brown*
FOUNDED 1986. *Publishes* adult comic annuals; *Viz* magazine; strange phenomena. 15 titles in 1996.
DIVISION **Fortean Times Books** *Mike Dash* TITLES *Book of Weird Sex; Book of Strange Dreams; Fortean Studies Vol II*. Does not welcome unsolicited mss.
Royalties paid twice-yearly.

Brown, Son & Ferguson, Ltd
4–10 Darnley Street, Glasgow G41 2SD
☎0141 429 1234   Fax 0141 420 1694
Chairman/Joint Managing Director
  T. Nigel Brown
FOUNDED 1850. *Specialises* in nautical textbooks, both technical and non-technical. Also Boy Scout/Girl Guide books, and Scottish

one-act/three-act plays. Unsolicited mss, synopses and ideas for books welcome.
Royalties paid annually.

Brown Watson Ltd
The Old Mill, 76 Fleckney Road, Kibworth Beauchamp, Leicestershire LE8 0HG
☎0116 2796333   Fax 0116 2796303
Managing Director *Michael B. McDonald*
FOUNDED 1980. *Publishes* children's books only. About 150 titles a year. Most books are commissioned. Unsolicited mss and synopses are not welcome.
Authors' Rating Children's books for the cheaper end of the market. Authors must work fast to make money.

Bucknell University Press
See **Golden Cockerel Press Ltd**

Burns & Oates
See **Search Press**

Business Books
See **Random House UK Ltd**

Business Education Publishers Ltd
Leighton House, 10 Grange Crescent, Sunderland, Tyne & Wear SR2 7BN
☎0191 567 4963   Fax 0191 514 3277
Managing Director *P. M. Callaghan*
Approx. Annual Turnover £400,000
FOUNDED 1981. *Publishes* business education, economics and law for BTEC and GNVQ reading. Currently expanding into further and higher education, computing, community health services, travel and tourism, occasional papers for institutions and local government administration. Unsolicited mss and synopses welcome.
Royalties paid annually.

Butterworth-Heinemann International
See **Reed Educational & Professional Publishing**

Cadogan Books plc
3rd Floor, 27–29 Berwick Street, London W1V 3RF
☎0171 287 6555   Fax 0171 734 1733
Managing Director *Bill Colegrave*
Publisher, Cadogan Guides & Chess *Rachel Fielding*
Approx. Annual Turnover £1.2 million
Now merged with **David Campbell Publishers Ltd**. *Publishes* the *Cadogan Travel Guide*

series, and chess and bridge titles. About 55 titles a year. No unsolicited mss; send introductory letter with synopsis only. Synopses and ideas welcome.

Royalties paid twice-yearly.

Calder Publications Ltd

179 Kings Cross Road, London WC1X 9BZ
☎0171 833 1300

Chairman/Managing Director/Editorial Head *John Calder*

Formerly John Calder (Publishers) Ltd. A publishing company which has grown around the tastes and contacts of John Calder, the iconoclast of the literary establishment. The list has a reputation for controversial and opinion-forming publications; Samuel Beckett is perhaps the most prestigious name. The list includes all of Beckett's prose and poetry. *Publishes* autobiography, biography, drama, literary fiction, literary criticism, music, opera, poetry, politics, sociology. AUTHORS Roy Calne, Marguerite Duras, Erich Fried, Trevor Hoyle, P. J. Kavanagh, Robert Pinget, Julian Semyonov, Claude Simon, Howard Barker (plays), ENO opera guides. *No new material accepted.*

Royalties paid annually.

Authors' Rating Operating in Paris and London and points between, John Calder is said to be 'overflowing with geniuses and eccentric talents'. But according to the publisher, times are hard and there is never enough money to pay all the bills. He is much revered in France as a free and far-ranging intellectual.

California University Press

See **University Presses of California, Columbia & Princeton Ltd**

Cambridge University Press

The Edinburgh Building, Shaftesbury Road, Cambridge CB2 2RU
☎01223 312393   Fax 01223 315052

Chief Executive *A. K. Wilson*
Managing Director, Publishing *R. J. Mynott*

The oldest press in the world. Over the last few years CUP has been diversifying into reference, electronic, legal and medical publishing and has expanded its activities in Europe, the Far East, Latin America, Australia and the USA. Recent developments include editorial offices at Stanford University, California, Cape Town, South Africa and Barcelona; new offices in Bologna and Mexico; the acquisition of

Grotius Publications (International Law); major National Curriculum and ELT course publications; Cambridge Encyclopedia programme; the Cambridge International Dictionary of English; low-price editions for the developing world; new Cambridge Guides and Illustrated Histories; the paperback imprint **Canto**.

Publishes academic/educational books for international English-language markets, at all levels from primary school to postgraduate. Also bibles and over 100 academic journals. Over 20,000 authors in 100 different countries, and about 1500 new titles a year.

PUBLISHING GROUPS
Bibles *C. J. Wright* **ELT** *C. J. F. Hayes* **Education** *A. C. Gilfillan* **Humanities** *A. M. C. Brown* **Social Sciences** *M. Y. Holdsworth* **Journals** *C. Guettler* **Science, Technology, Medicine** *S. Mitton.* Synopses and ideas for educational, ELT and academic books are welcomed (and preferable to the submission of unsolicited mss). No fiction or poetry.

Royalties paid twice-yearly.

Authors' Rating Not so many monographs from the obscure corners of academia but CUP has adapted to changing times and shrinking literary budgets by expanding into reference, English Language Teaching and foreign language publishing.

Camden Large Print

See **Chivers Press Ltd**

David Campbell Publishers Ltd

79 Berwick Street, London W1V 3PF
☎0171 287 0035   Fax 0171 287 0038

Chairman *Alewyn Birch*
Managing Director *David Campbell*
Approx. Annual Turnover £3.5 million

FOUNDED 1990 with the acquisition of **Everyman's Library** (established 1906) bought from **J. M. Dent**. Now merged with **Cadogan Books plc**. *Publishes* classics of world literature, pocket poetry anthologies, music companion guides and travel guides. AUTHORS include Bulgakov, Bellow, Borges, Forster, Grass, Mann, Nabokov, Orwell, Rushdie, Updike and Waugh. No unsolicited mss; ideas or synopsis welcome. IMPRINT **Adelphi** Illustrated books.

Royalties paid annually.

Campbell Books

See **Macmillan Publishers Ltd**

Canongate Books Ltd

14 High Street, Edinburgh EH1 1TE
☎0131 557 5111 Fax 0131 557 5211
Joint Managing Directors *Jamie Byng, Hugh Andrew*
Approx. Annual Turnover £1.25 million

FOUNDED 1973. Independent again, following a management buyout in September 1994. *Publishes* general fiction and non-fiction, children's fiction (age 8+), and Scottish interest. Also have an audio list (see entry under **Audio Books**).

IMPRINTS **Canongate Classics** Adult paperback series; **Kelpie** Children's paperback fiction series; **Payback Press** Afro-American, Black orientated fiction and non-fiction; music, history, politics, biography and poetry; **Rebel Inc.** promotion of new writing – fiction, poetry and non-fiction – as well as underground and neglected classics. About 60 titles a year. Synopses preferred to complete mss.

Royalties paid twice-yearly.

Authors' Rating Having increased turnover by 50 per cent in 18 months, with more than a little help from sales of the music reference book, *The Great Rock Discography*, Canongate is pushing out into choppier waters with such as Payback Press for black writers. The enthusiasm for bright and original ideas remains undiminished.

Canterbury Press Norwich

See **Hymns Ancient & Modern Ltd**

Canto

See **Cambridge University Press**

Capall Bann Publishing

Freshfields, Chieveley, Berkshire RG20 8TF
☎01635 46455 Fax 01635 46455
Chairman *Julia Day*
Editorial Head *Jon Day*

FOUNDED 1993 with three titles and now have over 100 in print. Family-owned and run company which *publishes* British traditions, folklore, computing, boating, animals, environmental, Celtic lore, mind, body and spirit. 42 titles in 1996. TITLES *Sacred Lore of Horses; Practical Meditation; Runic Astrology; Wildlife Gardening; Talking to the Earth; Bruce Roberts' Boatbuilding.* No unsolicited mss; synopses and ideas for books welcome. No fiction or poetry.

Royalties paid quarterly.

Jonathan Cape Ltd

See **Random House UK Ltd**

Carcanet Press Ltd

Conavon Court, 12–16 Blackfriars Street, Manchester M3 5BQ
☎0161 834 8730 Fax 0161 832 0084
Chairman *Kate Gavron*
Managing Director/Editorial Director *Michael Schmidt*

Since 1969 Carcanet has grown from an undergraduate hobby into a substantial venture. Robert Gavron bought the company in 1983 and it has established strong Anglo-European and Anglo-Commonwealth links. *Publishes* poetry, academic, literary biography, fiction in translation and translations. About 40 titles a year, including the *P. N. Review* (six issues yearly). AUTHORS John Ashbery, Edwin Morgan, Elizabeth Jennings, Iain Crichton Smith, Natalia Ginzburg, Eavan Boland, Stuart Hood, Leonardo Sciascia, Christine Brooke-Rose, Pier Paolo Pasolini, C. H. Sisson, Donald Davie.

Royalties paid annually.

Authors' Rating One of the four leading poetry publishers, Carcanet combines quality with profit. William Boyd says of Carcanet that it is 'everything an independent publisher should be'.

Cardiff Academic Press

St Fagans Road, Fairwater, Cardiff CF5 3AE
☎01222 560333 Fax 01222 554909
Marketing Manager *Mary de Lange*

Academic publishers.

Carlton Books Ltd

20 St Anne's Court, Wardour Street, London W1V 3AW
☎0171 734 7338 Fax 0171 434 1196
Managing Director *Jonathan Goodman*
Approx. Annual Turnover £11 million

FOUNDED 1992. Owned by Carlton Communications, Carlton books are aimed at the mass market for subjects such as computer games, sport, health, puzzles, popular science and rock'n'roll. *Publishes* illustrated leisure and entertainment. Prime UK customers include the Book Club and W H Smith. A second arm of the company, established late 1992, was set up to create a promotional books business. No unsolicited mss; synopses and ideas welcome.

Royalties paid twice-yearly.

Authors' Rating Linked to the largest programme producer in the ITV network, Carlton Books has built a reputation on co-editions for the international market. Now it is moving into television tie-ins. Noted for speed of taking a book from first idea to publication.

Frank Cass & Co Ltd

Newbury House, 890–900 Eastern Avenue, Newbury Park, Ilford, Essex IG2 7HH
☎0181 599 8866   Fax 0181 599 0984
Managing Director *Frank Cass*
Managing Editor *Robert Easton*

Publishes books and journals in the fields of politics, international relations, military and security studies, history, Middle East and African studies, economics, development studies and law. TITLES *Masters of War: Classical Strategy* Michael Handel; *Roots of Realism* ed. Benjamin Franklin; *Islamic Endowments in Jerusalem* Itzhak Reiter; *Kenyan Running* John Bale and Joe Sang; *Counterrevolution in China* Thomas A. Marks; *Capturing the Political Imagination* Diane Stone.

DIVISIONS
Woburn Press Educational list TITLES *The First Teenagers: The Lifestyle of Young Wage-Earners in Interwar Britain* David Fowler; *Teaching Science* eds. Jenny Frost *et al.* **Vallentine Mitchell/Jewish Chronicle Publications** Books of Jewish interest TITLES *Will We Have Jewish Grandchildren? Jewish Continuity and How to Achieve It* Chief Rabbi Dr Jonathan Sacks; *New Women's Writing From Israel* Risa Domb; *Library of Holocaust Testimonies* series: *An End to Childhood* Miriam Akavia; *Jewish Year Book; Jewish Travel Guide.* Unsolicited mss considered but synopsis with covering letter preferred.

Royalties paid annually.

Cassell

Wellington House, 125 Strand, London WC2R 0BB
☎0171 420 5555   Fax 0171 240 7261
Chairman/Managing Director
Philip Sturrock
Approx. Annual Turnover £25 million
FOUNDED 1848 by John Cassell. Bought by Collier Macmillan in 1974, then by CBS Publishing Europe in 1982. Finally returned to independence in 1986 as Cassell plc and a string of acquisitions followed: Tycooly's book publishing division; Link House Books (now Blandford Publishing Ltd); Mansell; then Mowbray and Ward Lock, publisher of Mrs Beeton, (in print continuously since 1861); Victor Gollancz Ltd in 1992 and Pinter Publishers Ltd in February 1995. *Publishes* business, education and academic, general non-fiction, primary and secondary school books, poetry, religion. About 800 titles a year.

IMPRINTS
Cassell General Books *Alison Goff* TITLES *Poems on the Underground; Cordon Bleu Complete Cookery Techniques; Cacti: The Illustrated Dictionary; Shaker.* PAPERBACK IMPRINTS **Indigo** *Mike Petty;* **Vista** *Humphrey Price.*
Cassell Academic Books *Janet Joyce, Naomi Roth* TITLES *Cassell Guide to Literature in French; Supervisory Management; Reflective Teaching in Primary Schools.*
Mansell *Janet Joyce* TITLES *Index of English Literary Manuscripts; Facts About the Prime Ministers.*
Arms & Armour Press *Roderick Dymott* TITLES *First World War Sourcebook; Napoleonic Weapons & Warfare; Great Battles of the Royal Navy.*
Blandford Press *Roderick Dymott* TITLES *Celebration of Maritime Art; Spiders of the World; Celtic Art Sourcebook; Make Your Own Electric Guitar.*
Ward Lock *Alison Goff* TITLES *Mrs Beeton's Book of Cookery and Household Management; Home & Garden Style; Ward Lock Gardening Encyclopedia.*
Victor Gollancz *Jane Blackstock* TITLES *Lost Gardens of Heligan; High Fidelity* Nick Hornby; *Hogfather* Terry Pratchett.
Geoffrey Chapman *Gill Paterson* TITLES *New Jerome Biblical Commentary; The Catechism of the Catholic Church; Storykeepers.*
Mowbray *Gill Paterson* TITLES *Why God* Bishop of Bath & Wells, Mervyn Stockwood.
Leicester University Press *Janet Joyce* TITLES *Museums and Popular Culture; Language of Displayed Art; Medieval Fortifications.*
Pinter *Janet Joyce* TITLES *States and Markets; European Union, Work for All?.*

Authors' Rating Cassell has grown by taking over and revitalising famous names down on their luck such as Ward Lock and Victor Gollancz and by title output which increased from 550 to 800 titles last year. The weakness in the mid-list of general books where sales have not kept up with the rest of the company has been offset by strong growth in the new paperback lists, Vista and Indigo.

Castle Publications

See **Nottingham University Press**

Kyle Cathie Ltd

20 Vauxhall Bridge Road, London SW1V 2SA
☎0171 973 9710   Fax 0171 821 9258
Publisher/Managing Director *Kyle Cathie*
Sales Director *Emma Bittleston*

FOUNDED 1990 to publish and promote 'books

we have personal enthusiasm for'. *Publishes* non-fiction: history, natural history, health, biography, food and drink, craft, gardening and reference. TITLES *50 Great Curries of India* Camellia Panjabi; *Jekka's Complete Herb Book*; Jekka McVicar; *Dictionary of Idioms* Linda and Roger Flavell. About 25 titles a year. No unsolicited mss. 'Synopses and ideas are considered in the fields in which we publish.'

Royalties paid twice-yearly.

Catholic Truth Society

192 Vauxhall Bridge Road, London SW1V 1PD
☎0171 834 4392   Fax 0171 630 1124
Chairman *Rt. Rev. Mgr. Peter Smith*
General Secretary *Fergal Martin*
Approx. Annual Turnover £500,000

FOUNDED originally in 1869 and re-founded in 1884. *Publishes* religious books – Roman Catholic and ecumenical; a variety of doctorial, moral, biographical, devotional and liturgical publications, including a large body of Vatican documents and sources. Unsolicited mss, synopses and ideas welcome if appropriate to their list.

Royalties paid annually.

Causeway Press Ltd

PO Box 13, 129 New Court Way, Ormskirk, Lancashire L39 5HP
☎01695 576048   Fax 01695 570714
Chairman/Managing Director *M. Haralambos*
Approx. Annual Turnover £2 million

FOUNDED in 1982. *Publishes* educational textbooks only. 16 titles in 1996. TITLES *Causeway Maths Series; Discovering History Series; Economics/Business Studies; Sociology in Focus; Politics; Causeway GNVQ; Design and Technology.* Unsolicited mss, synopses and ideas welcome.

Royalties paid annually.

CBA Publishing

Bowes Morrell House, 111 Walmgate, York YO1 2UA
☎01904 671417   Fax 01904 671384
Managing Editor *Christine Pietrowski*
Approx. Annual Turnover £25,000

Publishing arm of the **Council for British Archaeology**. *Publishes* academic archaeology reports, practical handbooks, yearbook, *British Archaeology* (monthly magazine), monographs, archaeology and education. TITLES *Recording Timber-framed Buildings: An Illustrated Glossary; Excavations at Caldicot; A Multi-period Sale* Production Site at Droitwich; Church Archaeology: Research Directions for the Future; Teaching Archaeology: A UK Directory of Resources.

Royalties not paid.

CBD Research Ltd

Chancery House, 15 Wickham Road, Beckenham, Kent BR3 5JS
☎0181 650 7745   Fax 0181 650 0768
Chairman *G. P. Henderson*
Managing Director *S. P. A. Henderson*
Approx. Annual Turnover £300,000

FOUNDED 1961. *Publishes* directories and other reference guides to sources of information. Increased output over the last few years. About 6 titles a year. No fiction.

IMPRINT **Chancery House Press** Non-fiction of an esoteric/specialist nature for 'serious researchers and the dedicated hobbyist'. Unsolicited mss, synopses and ideas welcome.

Royalties paid quarterly.

Centaur Press

Fontwell, Arundel, West Sussex BN18 0TA
☎01243 543302
Managing Director *Jon Wynne-Tyson*

FOUNDED 1954. A one-man outfit publishing some 20 titles a year at its peak. Then became increasingly preoccupied with humane education and reduced output to around 5 titles a year. After a semi-dormant period in the 1980s, Centaur went on to launch *The Kinship Library*, a series on the philosophy, politics and application of humane education, with special focus on the subject of animal rights and its relevance to the human condition.

IMPRINT **Linden Press** TITLES *Victims of Science; The Universal Kinship; Publishing Your Own Book.*

Authors' Rating With Centaur 40-plus and himself 70-plus, and with turnover too modest to tempt conglomerate predators, Jon Wynne-Tyson wants to sell out to a compatible firm or entrepreneur wanting a starter list. Submissions not encouraged until new owner found.

Century

See **Random House UK Ltd**

Chadwyck-Healey Ltd

The Quorum, Barnwell Road, Cambridge CB5 8SW
☎01223 215512   Fax 01223 215513
Chairman *Sir Charles Chadwyck-Healey*
Managing Director *Steven Hall*

Editorial Head *Michael Healy*
FOUNDED 1973. *Publishes* literary full-text and humanities reference databases on microform, CD-ROM and the World Wide Web. No monographs. About 50 titles a year. TITLES *Literature Online; The English Poetry Full-Text Database; Periodical Contents Index.* No unsolicited mss. Synopses and ideas welcome for reference works only.
Royalties paid annually.

Authors' Rating Another success story for niche publishing, Chadwyck-Healey has won two Export Achievement awards for its high price CD-ROM reference list aimed at the world library market. The latest venture is to put 200,000 literary works on the Internet to be delivered on-line on subscription. This may not attract domestic users but will not seem at all steep for most university campuses.

Chambers/Chambers Harrap Publishers Ltd
See **Larousse plc**

Chameleon
See **André Deutsch Ltd**

Chancery House Press
See **CBD Research Ltd**

Chansitor Publications Ltd
See **Hymns Ancient & Modern Ltd**

Chapman
4 Broughton Place, Edinburgh EH1 3RX
☎0131 557 2207   Fax 0131 556 9565
Managing Editor *Joy Hendry*

A venture devoted to publishing works by the best of the Scottish writers, both up-and-coming and established, published in *Chapman* magazine, Scotland's leading literary quarterly. Has expanded publishing activities considerably over the last two years and is now publishing a wider range of works though the broad policy stands. *Publishes* poetry, drama, short stories, books of contemporary importance in 20th-century Scotland. About 4 titles a year. TITLES *Carlucco & the Queen of Hearts; The Blasphemer* George Rosie; *Gold of Kildonan; Songs of the Grey Coast; Whins;* George Gunn; *The Collected Shorter Poems* Tom Scott; *Alien Crop* Janet Paisley; *Good Girls Don't Cry* Margaret Fulton Cook. No unsolicited mss; synopses and ideas for books welcome.
Royalties paid annually.

Geoffrey Chapman
See **Cassell**

Paul Chapman Publishing Ltd
144 Liverpool Road, London N1 1LA
☎0171 609 5315   Fax 0171 700 1057
Managing Director *Paul R. Chapman*
Editorial Director *Marianne Lagrange*
Publishes business, management, accountancy and finance, education, geography, environment, planning and economics, for the academic and professional markets.
Royalties paid twice-yearly.

Chapmans Publishers
See **The Orion Publishing Group Ltd**

Chatham Publishing
See **Gerald Duckworth & Co Ltd**

Chatto & Windus Ltd
See **Random House UK Ltd**

Cherrytree Press Children's Books
See **Chivers Press Ltd**

Child's Play (International) Ltd
Ashworth Road, Bridgemead, Swindon, Wiltshire SN5 7YD
☎01793 616286   Fax 01793 512795
Chairman *Michael Twinn*
FOUNDED 1972. This Swindon-based publisher has pioneered learning-through-play since the early days of its inception. *Publishes* children's books: picture books, fiction, science, art, activity books and dictionaries. TITLES *Tooth Fairy; Oxfam Discovery Flap Range; Big Hungry Bear; There Was an Old Lady; Ten in a Bed; Wally Whale; Puzzle Island.* Unsolicited mss welcome. Send s.a.e. for return or response. Expect to wait 2 months for a reply.
Royalties payment varies according to contract.

Chivers Press Ltd
Windsor Bridge Road, Bath BA2 3AX
☎01225 335336   Fax 01225 310771
Managing Director *Julian R. Batson*
Part of the Gieves Group. *Publishes* reprints for libraries mainly, in large-print editions, including biography and autobiography, children's, crime, fiction and spoken word cassettes. No unsolicited material.

IMPRINTS
Chivers Large Print; Gunsmoke Westerns;

Galaxy Children's Large Print; Camden Large Print; Paragon Softcover Large Print; Cherrytree Press Children's Books; Windsor Large Print; Black Dagger Crime. Chivers Audio Books (see entry under **Audio Books**.

Royalties paid twice-yearly.

Christian Focus Publications

Geanies House, Fearn, Tain, Ross-shire
IV20 1TW
☎01862 87541   Fax 01862 87699
Chairman *R. W. M. Mackenzie*
Managing Director *William Mackenzie*
Editorial Head *Malcolm Maclean*
Approx. Annual Turnover £600,000

FOUNDED 1979 to produce children's books for the co-edition market. Now a major producer of Christian books. *Publishes* Christianity, adult and children's books, including some fiction for children but not adults. About 70 titles a year. Unsolicited mss, synopses and ideas welcome from Christian writers. Publishes for all English-speaking markets, as well as the UK. Books produced for Australia, USA, Canada, South Africa. IMPRINTS **Christian Focus** General books; **Mentor** Specialist books; **Christian Heritage** Classic reprints.

Royalties paid twice-yearly.

Churchill Livingstone

Robert Stevenson House, 1–3 Baxter's Place, Leith Walk, Edinburgh EH1 3AF
☎0131 556 2424   Fax 0131 558 1278
Managing Director *Andrew Stevenson*
Vice-President, Professional and Reference Publishing *Jennifer Mitchell*
Director, Nursing and Allied Health, Medical Education *Peter Shepherd*

Originally an amalgamation of E. & S. Livingstone and J. & A. Churchill in the early 1970s. Now part of Pearson Professional. *Publishes* books, journals, CD-ROMs and loose-leaf material in medicine, nursing and allied health matters, plus complementary therapies. About 150 titles a year. No unsolicited mss. Synopses and ideas welcome.

Royalties paid annually. *Overseas associates* worldwide.

Cicerone Press

2 Police Square, Milnthorpe, Cumbria
LA7 7PY
☎015395 62069   Fax 015395 63417
Managing Director *Dorothy Unsworth*

Editorial Director *Walt Unsworth*

FOUNDED 1969. Guidebook publisher for outdoor enthusiasts. About 30 titles a year. No fiction or poetry. TITLES *A Trekker's Handbook*; various *Country Walking* guides; *LD Footpath Guides*. No unsolicited mss; synopses and ideas considered.

Royalties paid twice-yearly.

Clarendon Press

See **Oxford University Press**

Claridge Press

33 Canonbury Park South, London N1 2JW
☎0171 226 7791   Fax 0171 354 0383
Chairman/Managing Director/Editorial Head *Roger Scruton*
Managing Editor *Merrie Cave*

FOUNDED 1987. Developed from the quarterly *Salisbury Review* (see entry under **Magazines**). *Publishes* current affairs – political, philosophical and sociological – from a right-wing viewpoint. SERIES *Thinkers of our Time*. TITLES *Falsification of the Good; Understanding Youth; Some Turn to Mecca to Pray: Islamic Values in the Modern World; KGB Lawsuits*. Unsolicited mss welcome within given subject areas.

Royalties paid according to contract.

Clarion

See **Elliot Right Way Books**

T. & T. Clark

59 George Street, Edinburgh EH2 2LQ
☎0131 225 4703   Fax 0131 220 4260
Managing Director/Editorial Head *Geoffrey Green*

FOUNDED 1821. *Publishes* religion, theology, law and philosophy, for academic and professional markets. About 35 titles a year, including journals. TITLES include *Church Dogmatics* Karl Barth; *A Textbook of Christian Ethics* ed. Robin Gill; *Scottish Law Directory; The Law of Contracts and Related Obligations in Scotland* David M. Walker. Unsolicited mss, synopses and ideas for books welcome.

Royalties paid annually.

James Clarke & Co.

PO Box 60, Cambridge CB1 2NT
☎01223 350865   Fax 01223 366951
Managing Director *Adrian Brink*

Parent company of **The Lutterworth Press**. *Publishes* scholarly and academic works, mainly theological, directory and reference titles. TITLES *The Encyclopedia of the Early Church; The*

Libraries' Directory. Approach in writing with ideas in the first instance.

Richard Cohen Books Ltd

The Basement Offices, 7 Manchester Square, London W1M 5RE
☎0171 935 2099   Fax 0171 935 2199

Chairman/Managing Director
  Richard Cohen
Approx. Annual Turnover £1 million

FOUNDED in 1994. *Publishes* fiction, biography, current affairs, travel, history, politics, the arts, and sport. First titles published in 1995 with plans to expand from 20 books a year to 30. No erotica, DIY, children's, reference, science fiction, fantasy, or historical romance.

DIVISIONS **RCB General Books** *Richard Cohen* TITLES *Memoirs* Al Alvarez; *Mrs Rochester* Emma Tennant; *Running Free* Robin Knox-Johnston; *Alastair Cooke* Nick Clarke. No unsolicited mss.
Royalties paid twice-yearly.

Authors' Rating Having by his own admission 'bought ahead too ambitiously', Richard Cohen has had to struggle to keep his fledgling list alive. But there is much sympathy and support for a gifted publisher who gets on well with authors.

Peter Collin Publishing Ltd

1 Cambridge Road, Teddington, Middlesex TW11 8DT
☎0181 943 3386   Fax 0181 943 1673

Chairman *P. H. Collin*

FOUNDED 1985. *Publishes* dictionaries only, including specialised dictionaries in English for students and specialised bilingual dictionaries for translators (French, German, Swedish, Spanish, Greek, Chinese, Hungarian). About 5 titles a year. Synopses and ideas welcome. No unsolicited mss; copy must be supplied on disk.
Royalties paid twice-yearly.

Collins

See **HarperCollins Publishers Ltd**

Collins & Brown

London House, Great Eastern Wharf, Parkgate Road, London SW11 4NQ
☎0171 924 2575   Fax 0171 924 7725

Chairman *Cameron Brown*
Managing Director *Mark Collins*
Approx. Annual Turnover £8.25 million

FOUNDED 1989. Independent publisher. *Publishes* illustrated non-fiction: crafts, gardening, practical photography, illustrated letters and

history. No fiction, children's, poetry or local interest. About 30 adult and 60 children's titles a year. No unsolicited mss; outlines with s.a.e. only.
Royalties paid twice-yearly.

Colonsay Books

See **House of Lochar**

Columbia University Press

See **University Presses of California, Columbia & Princeton Ltd**

Condé Nast Books

See **Random House UK Ltd**

Condor

See **Souvenir Press Ltd**

Conran Octopus

See **Reed Books**

Constable & Co. Ltd

3 The Lanchesters, 162 Fulham Palace Road, London W6 9ER
☎0181 741 3663   Fax 0181 748 7562

Chairman/Managing Director
  Benjamin Glazebrook
Editorial Director *Carol O'Brien*
Approx. Annual Turnover £3 million

FOUNDED in 1890 by Archibald Constable, a grandson of Walter Scott's publisher. Controlling interest was bought by Benjamin Glazebrook in 1967 and the remaining 48% was purchased by Hutchinson, now owned by **Random House**, in 1968. A small but select publisher whose list includes Muriel Spark and Francis King. *Publishes* archaeology, architecture and design, biography and autobiography, cookery, fiction, guidebooks, history and antiquarian, natural history, psychology, sociology and anthropology, travel and topography, wines and spirits. About 80 titles a year. TITLES *Reality and Dreams* Muriel Spark; *Life in an Irish Country House* Mark Bence-Jones; *The Younger Pitt* John Ehrman. Unsolicited mss, synopses and ideas for books welcome.
Royalties paid twice-yearly.

Authors' Rating Keeping its distance from the conglomerates, even with Random holding a minority stake, Constable is highly regarded by authors who recognise a straight deal when they see it. The recession hit hard in the early '90s but Constable is now back into profit.

Consultants Bureau

See **Plenum Publishing Ltd**

Consumers' Association
See **Which? Books/Consumers' Association**

Context Limited
See entry under **Stop Press**

Conway Maritime Press
See **Brassey's (UK) Ltd**

Thomas Cook Publishing
PO Box 227, Peterborough PE3 6PU
☎01733 503571   Fax 01733 503596
Head of Publishing *Jennifer Rigby*
Approx. Annual Turnover £1.7 million

Part of the Thomas Cook Group Ltd, publishing commenced in 1873 with the first issue of Cook's Continental Timetable. *Publishes* guidebooks, maps and timetables. 20 titles in 1996. No unsolicited mss; synopses and ideas welcome as long as they are travel-related.
Royalties paid annually.

Leo Cooper/
Pen & Sword Books Ltd
190 Shaftesbury Avenue, London WC2H 8JL
☎0171 836 3141   Fax 0171 240 9247
Chairman *Sir Nicholas Hewitt*
Editorial Consultant *Leo Cooper*

FOUNDED 1990 following the acquisition of the Leo Cooper imprint from Octopus Publishing. *Publishes* military history, naval and aviation history, autobiography and biography. About 40 titles a year. Unsolicited synopses and ideas welcome; no unsolicited mss.
Royalties paid twice-yearly. *Associated company* **Wharncliffe Publishing Ltd**.

Authors' Rating One of the last of the gentleman publishers, Leo Cooper has, by virtue of good writing, brought a specialist area of publishing to a wider public.

Corgi
See **Transworld Publishers Ltd**

Cornwall Books
See **Golden Cockerel Press Ltd**

Coronet Books
See **Hodder Headline plc**

Countryside Books
2 Highfield Avenue, Newbury, Berkshire
RG14 5DS
☎01635 43816   Fax 01635 551004
Publisher *Nicholas Battle*
FOUNDED 1976. *Publishes* mainly paperbacks on regional subjects, generally by county. Local history, genealogy, walking and photographic, some transport. Over 250 titles available. Unsolicited mss and synopses welcome but, regretfully, no fiction, poetry, natural history or personal memories.
Royalties paid twice-yearly.

Crabtree Publishing
73 Lime Walk, Headington, Oxford
OX3 7AD
☎01865 67575   Fax 01865 750079
President *Peter Crabtree*
Editorial Director *Bobbie Kalman*

FOUNDED 1980. *Publishes* ecological and educational books in series. About 30 titles a year. SERIES *Animals and Their Ecosystems; Lands, Peoples and Culture; The Arctic World; Endangered Animals; Historic Communities; Primary Ecology.* New series: *Extraordinary Animals; Animal Trackers; Crabapples; Great African Americans* and the *Wonders of our World.*
Royalties paid twice-yearly.

Cressrelles Publishing Co. Ltd
10 Station Road Industrial Estate, Colwall, Malvern, Worcestershire WR13 6RN
☎01684 540154
Managing Director *Leslie Smith*

Publishes a range of general books, drama and chiropody titles. IMPRINTS **Actinic Press** Specialises in chiropody; **J. Garnet Miller Ltd** Plays and theatre texts; **Kenyon-Deane** Plays and drama textbooks.

Croom Helm
See **Routledge**

Crossway
See **Inter-Varsity Press**

The Crowood Press Ltd
The Stable Block, Crowood Lane, Ramsbury, Marlborough, Wiltshire SN8 2HR
☎01672 520320   Fax 01672 520280
Chairman *John Dennis*
Managing Director *Ken Hathaway*

Publishes sport and leisure titles, including animal and land husbandry, climbing and walking, maritime, country sports, equestrian, fishing and shooting; also chess and bridge, crafts, dogs, gardening, natural history and motoring. About 70 titles a year. Preliminary letter preferred in all cases.
Royalties paid annually.

James Currey Publishers

73 Botley Road, Oxford OX2 0BS
☎01865 244111   Fax 01865 246454
Chairman/Managing Director *James Currey*
FOUNDED 1985. A small specialist publisher. *Publishes* academic books on Africa, the Caribbean and Third World: history, anthropology, economics, sociology, politics and literary criticism. Approach in writing with synopsis if material is 'relevant to our needs'.
Royalties paid annually.

Curzon Press Ltd

15 The Quadrant, Richmond, Surrey
TW9 1BP
☎0181 948 4660   Fax 0181 332 6735
Managing Director *Malcolm G. Campbell*
Specialised scholarly publishing house. *Publishes* academic/scholarly books on history and archaeology, languages and linguistics, philosophy, religion and theology, sociology and anthropology, cultural studies and reference, all in the context of Africa and Asia. IMPRINT **Japan Library**.

Cygnus Arts

See **Golden Cockerel Press Ltd**

Dalesman Publishing Co. Ltd

Stable Courtyard, Broughton Hall, Skipton,
West Yorkshire BD23 3AE
☎01756 701381   Fax 01756 701326
Editor *Terry Fletcher*
Publishers of *Dalesman, Cumbria* and *Pennine* magazines and regional books covering Yorkshire and the Lake District. Subjects include crafts and hobbies, geography and geology, guidebooks, history and antiquarian, humour, travel and topography. Unsolicited mss considered on all subjects. About 20 titles a year.
Royalties paid annually.

Terence Dalton Ltd

Water Street, Lavenham, Sudbury, Suffolk
CO10 9RN
☎01787 247572   Fax 01787 248267
Director/Editorial Head *Elisabeth Whitehair*
FOUNDED 1967. Part of Lavenham Holdings plc, a family company. *Publishes* non-fiction: aviation and maritime history, river series and East Anglian interest. TITLES *Imperial Airways and the First British Airline* Capt. Archie Jackson. No unsolicited mss; send synopsis with two or three sample chapters. Ideas welcome.
Royalties paid annually.

The C. W. Daniel Co. Ltd

1 Church Path, Saffron Walden, Essex
CB10 1JP
☎01799 521909   Fax 01799 513462
Managing Director *Ian Miller*
Approx. Annual Turnover £1 million
FOUNDED in 1902 by a man who knew Tolstoy, the company was taken over by its present directors in 1973. Output has increased following the acquisition in 1980 of health and healing titles from the Health Science Press, and the purchase of Neville Spearman Publishers' metaphysical list in 1985. *Publishes* New Age: alternative healing and metaphysical. About 15 titles a year. No fiction, diet or cookery. Unsolicited synopses and ideas welcome; no unsolicited mss.
Royalties paid annually.

Darf Publishers Ltd

277 West End Lane, London NW6 1QS
☎0171 431 7009   Fax 0171 431 7655
Chairman/Managing Director *M. B. Fergiani*
Editorial Head *A. Bentaleb*
Approx. Annual Turnover £500,000
FOUNDED 1982 to publish books and reprints on the Middle East, history, theology and travel. *Publishes* geography, history, language, literature, oriental, politics, theology and travel. About 10 titles a year. TITLES *Moslems in Spain; Travels of Ibn Battuta; The Barbary Corsairs; Elementary Arabic; Travels in Syria and the Holy Land* Burckhardt.
Royalties paid annually. *Overseas associates* Dar Al-Fergiani, Cairo and Tripoli.

Darton, Longman & Todd Ltd

1 Spencer Court, 140–142 Wandsworth High Street, London SW18 4JJ
☎0181 875 0155   Fax 0181 875 0133
Editorial Director *Morag Reeve*
Approx. Annual Turnover £1 million
FOUNDED by Michael Longman, who broke away from Longman Green in 1959 when they decided to cut their religious list. In July 1990 DLT became a common ownership company, owned and run by staff members. The company is a leading ecumenical, predominantly Christian, publisher, with a strong emphasis on spirituality and the ministry and mission of the Church. About 50 titles a year. TITLES include *Jerusalem Bible; New Jerusalem Bible; God of Surprises; Audacity to Believe*. Sample material for books on theological or spiritual subjects considered.
Royalties paid twice-yearly.

David & Charles Publishers

Brunel House, Forde Road, Newton Abbot,
Devon TQ12 4PU
☎01626 61121   Fax 01626 334998

Publishing Director *Piers Spence*
Managing Director *Neil Page*

FOUNDED 1960 as a specialist company.
Bought back from **Reader's Digest** in 1997
by a management team. *Publishes* crafts and
hobbies, art techniques, gardening, equestrian
and countryside, natural history and field
guides. No fiction, poetry, memoirs or children's. About 50 titles a year. TITLES *Jo Verso's
Cross Stitch for Beginners; Hillier Gardener's Guide
to Trees and Shrubs; The Encyclopedia of Fungi;
The Artist's Guide to Mixing Colours; The
Countryman's Year*. Unsolicited mss will be
considered if return postage is included, synopses and ideas welcome.
Royalties paid twice-yearly.

Authors' Rating The management buyout of
David & Charles was one of the good news
stories of 1997. It is early days but first signs are
of a reinvigorated company set on building its
list of illustrated books.

Christopher Davies Publishers Ltd

PO Box 403, Swansea, West Glamorgan
SA1 4YF
☎01792 648825   Fax 01792 648825

Managing Director/Editorial Head
    Christopher T. Davies
Approx. Annual Turnover £100,000

FOUNDED 1949 to promote and expand Welsh-
language publications. By the 1970s the company was publishing over 50 titles a year but a
subsequent drop in Welsh sales led to the establishment of a small English list which has continued. *Publishes* biography, cookery, history, sport
and literature of Welsh interest. About 4 titles a
year. TITLES *English/Welsh Dictionaries; Famous
Cricketers of Glamorgan; Historic Gower; Who's
Who in Welsh History*. No unsolicited mss.
Synopses and ideas for books welcome.
Royalties paid twice-yearly.

Authors' Rating A favourite for Celtic readers and writers.

Giles de la Mare Publishers Ltd

3 Queen Square, London WC1N 3AU
☎0171 465 0045   Fax 0171 465 0034

Chairman/Managing Director *Giles de la
    Mare*
Approx. Annual Turnover £60,000

FOUNDED 1995 and commenced publishing in
April 1996. *Publishes* mainly non-fiction, espe-
cially art and architecture, biography, history,
music. TITLES *William Nicholson, Painter* ed.
Andrew Nicholson; *Inherit the Truth 1939–1945*
Anita Lasker-Wallfisch; *Short Stories 1895–1926*
Walter de la Mare; *Sir John Soane, Architect*
Dorothy Stroud. Unsolicited mss, synopses and
ideas welcome after initial telephone call.
Royalties paid twice-yearly.

Debrett's Peerage Ltd

73–77 Britannia Road, PO Box 357, London
SW6 2JY
☎0171 736 6524   Fax 0171 731 7768

Chairman *Ian McCorquodale*
Managing Director *Simone Kesseler*
General Manager *Jonathan Parker*

FOUNDED 1769. The company's main activity
(in conjunction with **Macmillan**) is the quin-
quennial *Debrett's Peerage and Baronetage* (published in 1995) and annual *Debrett's People of
Today* (also available on CD-ROM). Debrett's
general books are published under licence
through **Headline**.
Royalties paid twice-yearly.

Dedalus Ltd

Langford Lodge, St Judith's Lane, Sawtry,
Cambridgeshire PE17 5XE
☎01487 832382   Fax 01487 832382

Chairman *Juri Gabriel*
Managing Director *George Barrington*
Approx. Annual Turnover £175,000

FOUNDED 1983. *Publishes* contemporary
European fiction and classics and original literary fiction in the fields of magic realism, surrealism, the grotesque and bizarre. 14 titles in
1996. TITLES *The Decadent Cookbook; The
Arabian Nightmare* Robert Irwin; *Pfitz* Andrew
Crumey; *Memoirs of a Gnostic Dwarf* David
Madsen; *Music in a Foreign Language* Andrew
Crumey (winner of the **Saltire Best First
Book Award** in 1994). Welcomes submissions
for original fiction and books suitable for its list
but 'most people sending work in have no idea
of what kind of books Dedalus publishes and
merely waste their efforts'. Particularly interested in intellectually clever and unusual fiction. A letter about the author should always
accompany any submission. No replies without
s.a.e..

DIVISIONS/IMPRINTS **Original Fiction in
Paperback; Contemporary European
Fiction 1992–1997; Dedalus European
Classics; Surrealism; Empire of the Senses;
Literary Concept Books.**

Royalties paid annually. *Overseas associates* Hippocrene Books, Inc., New York; Ariadne Press, California.

Authors' Rating A small publisher triumphing against powerful competition by the simple expedient of putting quality first.

University of Delaware
See **Golden Cockerel Press Ltd**

J. M. Dent
See **The Orion Publishing Group Ltd**

André Deutsch Ltd
106 Great Russell Street, London WC1B 3LJ
☎0171 580 2746   Fax 0171 631 3253
Managing Director *T. J. Forrester*
Editorial Manager *Louise Dixon*

FOUNDED in 1950 by André Deutsch, who sold the company between 1984 and 1987 and ended his long association with it in 1991. By then a major fiction list had been established, with writers such as V. S. Naipaul, Philip Roth and Norman Mailer. In 1995 the company was acquired by audio and video publisher and distributor VCI Plc, of which it is now a wholly owned but separately managed subsidiary whose editorial policy remains enduringly successful with the recent addition of high profile books such as the Spice Girls' *Girl Power* and Ian Greer's *One Man's Word*. Since the VCI acquisition, five defined imprints have developed, two for children: **André Deutsch Classics**, a range of hardback classic books at paperback prices, and **Madcap**, offering innovative, fun and accessible titles. For adults there is **Chameleon**, the commercial label covering film, TV tie-ins, music, comedy and sport, and the **André Deutsch** imprint which covers hardback fiction, biography, politics and current affairs, photography and music. In 1996, the VCI Group also acquired the publishing interests of Manchester United Football Club and created the **Manchester United Books** imprint. AUTHORS include Gore Vidal, Penelope Lively and Tom Sharpe.

Authors' Rating Born again Deutsch has changed personality from a cottage-run, quality fiction list to a mass-market publisher linked to television and video. The new owners want to keep what they can from the old Deutsch list but how long the Spice Girls can rub shoulders with Penelope Lively remains to be seen.

Dial House
See **Ian Allan Ltd**

Disney
See **Ladybird Books Ltd**

Dolphin Book Co. Ltd
Tredwr, Llangrannog, Llandysul SA44 6BA
☎01239 654404   Fax 01239 654002
Managing Director *Martin L. Gili*
Approx. Annual Turnover £5000

FOUNDED 1957. A small publishing house specialising in Catalan, Spanish and South American books for the academic market. TITLES *Proceedings of the First Conference on Contemporary Catalan Studies in Scotland* ed. Chris Dixon; *Elegies de Bierville/Bierville Elegies* Carles Riba, Catalan text with English translation by J. L. Gili; *The Discerning Eye Studies* presented to Robert Pring-Mill; *The Late Poetry of Pablo Neruda* Christopher Perriam; *Hispanic Linguistic Studies in Honour of F. W. Hodcroft; Salvatge cor/Savage Heart* Carles Riba; Catalan text with English translations by J. L. Gili. Unsolicited mss not welcome. Approach by letter.

Royalties paid annually.

John Donald Publishers Ltd
138 St Stephen Street, Edinburgh EH3 5AA
☎0131 225 1146   Fax 0131 220 0567
Publishing & Production *Donald Morrison*
Commissioning Editor *Russell Walker*

Publishes academic and scholarly, agriculture, archaeology, architecture, economics, textbooks, guidebooks, local, military and social history, religious, sociology and anthropology. About 30 titles a year.

Royalties paid annually.

Donhead Publishing Ltd
Lower Coombe, Donhead St Mary, Shaftesbury, Dorset SP7 9LYU
☎01747 828422   Fax 01747 828522
Contact *Jill Pearce*

FOUNDED 1990 to specialise in publishing how-to books for building practitioners; particularly interested in architectural conservation material. *Publishes* building and architecture only. 6 titles a year. TITLES *Encyclopaedia of Architectural Terms; A Good Housekeeping Guide to Churches and their Contents; Cleaning Historic Buildings; Brickwork; Practical Stone Masonry; Conservation of Timber Buildings; Surveying Historic Buildings; English Heritage Directory of Building Limes; Journal of Architectural Conservation* (3 issues yearly). Unsolicited mss, synopses and ideas welcome.

Dorling Kindersley Ltd

9 Henrietta Street, London WC2E 8PS
☎0171 836 5411   Fax 0171 836 7570

Chairman *Peter Kindersley*
Deputy Chairman *Christopher Davis*
FOUNDED 1974. Packager and publisher of illustrated non-fiction: cookery, crafts, gardening, health, travel guides, atlases, natural history and children's information and fiction. Launched a US imprint in 1991 and an Australian imprint in 1997. About 175–200 titles a year.

DIVISIONS **Adult; Children's; Multimedia; Vision** (video). TITLES *Eyewitness Guides*; *BMA Complete Family Health Encyclopedia*; *RHS A–Z Encyclopedia of Garden Plants*; *Children's Illustrated Encyclopedia*; *The Way Things Work*. Unsolicited synopses/ideas for books welcome.

Authors' Rating Leading the way in the publishing of CD-ROM titles, DK has hit a few squalls in a notoriously turbulent market. Over production and falling prices in the US caused trouble last year and, lately, the strength of the pound has affected export sales. But the company has a firm base of popular titles with international appeal, and innovation, it is said, brings its own rewards. Writers who sign up with DK must be ready to work as part of an editorial and design team. Loners had best look elsewhere.

Doubleday

See **Transworld Publishers Ltd**

Ashley Drake Publishing Ltd

18 Park Grove, Cardiff CF1 3BN
☎01223 383648

Managing Director *Ashley Drake*
Approx. Annual Turnover £70,000

FOUNDED 1995. *Publishes* academic and Welsh-language books. 14 titles in 1996. No unsolicited mss; synopses and ideas for the Welsh Academic Press imprint welcome. No non-academic, scientific or computing books.

IMPRINTS
Welsh Academic Press English language academic, scholarly humanities and social sciences. TITLES *The Path to Freedom*; *Who's Who in Scottish History*; *The Basques*; *Ivor Novello A Biography*.

Gwasg Addysgol Cymru Welsh-language titles. TITLES *Dyddiadur Anne Frank* (*Diary of Anne Frank*).

Y Ddraig Fach Welsh-language titles for children. TITLES *Llew Frenin*(*Lion King*); *Pocahontas*.

Royalties paid annually.

Drake Educational Associates

St Fagans Road, Fairwater, Cardiff CF5 3AE
☎01222 560333   Fax 01222 554909

Contact *R. G. Drake*
Educational publishers.

Dryden Press

See **Harcourt Brace and Company Limited**

Gerald Duckworth & Co. Ltd

The Old Piano Factory, 48 Hoxton Square,
London N1 6PB
☎0171 729 5986   Fax 0171 729 0015

Managing Director *Robin Baird-Smith*
Editorial Director *Deborah Blake*
FOUNDED 1898. A joint ownership company. Some of the company's early credits include authors like Hilaire Belloc, August Strindberg, Henry James and John Galsworthy. *Publishes* academic material in the main, with some trade books, including fiction. About 80 titles a year.
IMPRINTS **Bristol Classical Press** Classical texts and modern languages; **Chatham Publishing** Maritime history. No unsolicited mss; synopses and sample chapters only. Enclose s.a.e. or return postage for response/return.

Royalties paid twice-yearly at first, annually thereafter.

Martin Dunitz Ltd

The Livery House, 7–9 Pratt Street, London
NW1 0AE
☎0171 482 2202   Fax 0171 267 0159

Chairman/Managing Director *Martin Dunitz*
FOUNDED 1978. Dunitz sold the successful *Positive Health Guides* series to former Macdonald in the '80s and now concentrates solely on specialist medical and dental titles aimed at an international market, with co-editions for the USA and Europe. The company won the Queen's Award for Export Achievement (1991). 50–60 titles a year. Unsolicited synopses and ideas welcome but no mss. Publisher of *Journal of Dermatological Treatment*; *International Journal of Psychiatry in Clinical Practice; Journal of Cytokines and Molecular Therapy*.

Royalties paid twice-yearly.

Dunrod Press

8 Brown's Road, Newtownabbey, Co.
Antrim BT36 8RG
☎01232 832362   Fax 01232 848780

Managing Director/Editorial Head
  Ken Lindsay
FOUNDED 1979. *Publishes* politics and world

affairs. About 3 titles a year. Preliminary letter essential. Synopses and ideas for books welcome.
Royalties paid annually.

Dutton
See **Penguin Books Ltd**

Eagle
See **Inter Publishing Ltd**

Earthscan Publications Ltd
See **Kogan Page Ltd**

Ebury Press
See **Random House UK Ltd**

Economist Books
See **Profile Books**

Edinburgh University Press
22 George Square, Edinburgh EH8 9LF
☎0131 650 4218   Fax 0131 662 0053
Chairman *David Martin*
Editorial Director *Jackie Jones*

Publishes academic and scholarly books (and journals): gender studies, history, Islamic studies, legal theory, linguistics, literary criticism, media and cultural studies; philosophy, politics, Scottish studies, social sciences, theology and religious studies. About 100 titles a year.

IMPRINTS
Polygon Editorial Director *Marion Sinclair* Creative writing and Scottish studies. *Publishes* fiction and poetry. SERIES *Determinations* (Scottish cultural polemics); *Living Memory* (oral history).

Keele University Press Commissioning Editor *Nicola Carr* American studies, international relations, landscape history, politics.

No unsolicited mss for EUP titles; mss welcome for Polygon but must be accompanied by s.a.e. for reply/return; letter/synopsis preferred in the first instance.
Royalties paid annually.

Element Books
The Old School House, The Courtyard, Bell Street, Shaftesbury, Dorset SP7 8BP
☎01747 851448   Fax 01747 855721
Chairman/Publisher *Michael Mann*
Editorial/Managing Director *Julia McCutchen*
Approx. Annual Turnover £10 million
FOUNDED 1978. An independent general publishing house whose policy is 'to make available knowledge and information to aid humanity in

a time of major transition'. *Publishes* general non-fiction in hardback and paperback, including full-colour, illustrated and gift books. TITLES *The Complete Illustrated Guide to Feng Shui; Bloodline of the Holy Grail; Emotional Excellence.* SERIES *Elements Of; Little Books; The Natural Way; Self Help; Health Essentials; Element Guides; Colour Health Reference Series; Earth Quest.* Unsolicited mss, synopses and ideas welcome. No fiction or poetry. 'We are always interested to hear from authors who have an original contribution to make based on quality and integrity.'
Royalties paid twice-yearly.

Authors' Rating Way-out authors are attracted to Element with its leaning towards books with a world message. Editorial advice is said to be helpful but there have been worries over late payments and poor royalties on US sales.

Elliot Right Way Books
Kingswood Buildings, Lower Kingswood, Tadworth, Surrey KT20 6TD
☎01737 832202   Fax 01737 830311
Managing Directors *Clive Elliot, Malcolm G. Elliot*

FOUNDED 1946 by Andrew G. Elliot. *Publishes* how-to titles and instruction books on a multifarious list of subjects including cookery, DIY, family financial and legal matters, family health, fishing, looking after pets and horses, motoring, popular education, puzzles, jokes and quizzes. All the early books were entitled *The Right Way to . . .* but this format became too restrictive. No fiction.

IMPRINTS
Right Way Instructional paperbacks in B format; **Clarion** Promotional/bargain series of 'how-to' books. Unsolicited mss, synopses and ideas for books welcome.
Royalties paid annually.

Ellipsis London Ltd
55 Charlotte Road, London EC2A 3QT
☎0171 739 3157   Fax 0171 739 3175
Contact *Tom Neville*

FOUNDED 1992. Formerly a subsidiary of Zurich-based Artemis Verlags AG but now an independent publishing house. *Publishes* architecture; contemporary art on CD-ROM. About 15 titles a year. No unsolicited mss, synopses or ideas.
Royalties paid annually.

Aidan Ellis Publishing

Whinfield, Herbert Road, Salcombe, South
Devon TQ8 8HN
☎01548 842755   Fax 01548 844356
Partners/Editorial Heads *Aidan Ellis,
Lucinda Ellis*
Approx. Annual Turnover £150,000
FOUNDED in 1971. *Publishes* gardening, fiction
and general trade books. About 8 titles a year.

DIVISIONS
Non-Fiction TITLES *The Royal Gardens in
Windsor Great Park* Charles Lyte/Tim Sandall;
Gardening Down a Rabbit Hole Josephine
Saxton; *Equestrian Statues* Maurice H. Grant;
Autobiography III Marguerite Yourcenar.
Fiction AUTHORS include José Miguel Roig,
Jonathan Maslow, Alan Bloom and Dana Fuller
Ross. Unsolicited non-fiction synopses (with
s.a.e.) welcome. No fiction, please.
   Royalties paid twice-yearly. *Overseas associates*
worldwide.

Elm Publications

Seaton House, Kings Ripton, Huntingdon,
Cambridgeshire PE17 2NJ
☎01487 773254   Fax 01487 773359
Managing Director *Sheila Ritchie*
FOUNDED 1977. *Publishes* textbooks, teaching
aids, educational resources, educational software and languages, in the fields of business
and management for adult learners. Books and
teaching/training resources are generally commissioned to meet specific business, management and other syllabuses. About 30 titles a
year. Ideas are welcome for new textbooks –
first approach in writing with outline or by a
brief telephone call.
   Royalties paid annually.

Elsevier Science Ltd

The Boulevard, Langford Lane, Kidlington,
Oxford OX5 1GB
☎01865 843000   Fax 01865 843010
Managing Director *Frans Visscher*
Parent company **Elsevier**, Amsterdam. Now
incorporates Pergamon Press. *Publishes* academic and professional reference books, scientific, technical and medical books, journals,
CD-ROMs and magazines.

DIVISIONS
Elsevier Advanced Technology and
Elsevier Trends Journals *David Bousfield;*
Elsevier and Pergamon *Barbara Barrett,
Michael Mabe, Chris Lloyd, Jim Gilgunn-Jones,*

Gerry Dorey. Unsolicited mss, synopses and
ideas for books welcome.
   Royalties paid annually.

Authors' Rating An offshoot of the largest
Dutch publisher. Refreshingly open with
authors in the tradition of northern European
publishers – early news on print runs and royalties paid promptly.

Emissary Publishing

PO Box 33, Bicester, Oxfordshire OX6 7PP
☎01869 323447   Fax 01869 324096
Editorial Director *Val Miller*
FOUNDED 1992. *Publishes* mainly humorous
paperback books; no poetry or children's. Runs
a biennial Humorous Novel Competition in
memory of the late Peter Pook and publishes
the winning novel (s.a.e. for details). No unsolicited mss or synopses.
   Royalties paid twice-yearly.

Enitharmon Press

36 St George's Avenue, London N7 0HD
☎0171 607 7194   Fax 0171 607 8694
Director *Stephen Stuart-Smith*
FOUNDED 1968 by Alan Clodd. An independent company with an enterprising editorial
policy, Enitharmon has established itself as one
of Britain's leading poetry presses. Patron of
'the new and the neglected', Enitharmon
prides itself on the success of its collaborations
between writers and artists. *Publishes* poetry,
literary criticism, fiction, art and photography.
About 20 titles a year. TITLES include *A Box of
Silver Birch* Phoebe Hesketh; *In a Valley of This
Restless Mind* Hilary Davies; *Our Lady of Europe*
Jeremy Hooker; *Swimming Through the Grand
Hotel* Judith Kazantzis; *Selected Poems* Anthony
Thwaite. Limited edition series: *The Man
Within* Victor Pasmore. No unsolicited mss.
   Royalties paid according to contract.
Distribution in Europe by Password (Books)
Ltd, Manchester; in the USA by Dufour
Editions Inc., Chester Springs, PA 19425.

Epworth Press

c/o Methodist Publishing House, 20 Ivatt Way,
Peterborough, Cambridgeshire PE3 7PG
☎01733 332202   Fax 01733 331201
Chairman *Dr John A. Newton*
Editor *Gerald M. Burt*
Formerly based in Manchester, Epworth now
operates from Peterborough. *Publishes* Christian
books only: philosophy, theology, biblical
studies, pastoralia and social concern. No fiction,

poetry or children's. A series based on the text of the *Revised English Bible*, entitled *Epworth Commentaries*, has proved very successful and two new series *Exploring Methodism* and *Thinking Things Through* have just been launched. About 10 titles a year. TITLES *Clinging to Faith* Peter Bishop; *The Bible* C. S. Rodd; *Acts of the Apostles* James Dunn. Unsolicited mss considered but write to enquire in the first instance. Authors wishing to have their mss returned must send sufficient postage.

Royalties paid annually.

Eros Plus
See **Titan Books**

Euromonitor
60–61 Britton Street, London EC1M 5NA
☎0171 251 8024   Fax 0171 608 3149
Chairman *R. N. Senior*
Managing Director *T. J. Fenwick*
Approx. Annual Turnover £6 million

FOUNDED 1972. International business information publisher specialising in library and professional reference books, market reports, electronic databases, journals and CD-ROMs. *Publishes* business reference, market analysis and information directories only. About 80–85 titles a year.

DIVISIONS
Market Direction & Reports *S. Holmes*;
Reference Books & Directories *S. Hunter*.
TITLES *Credit & Charge Cards: The International Market*; *Europe in the Year 2000*; *European Marketing Handbook*; *European Directory of Trade and Business Associations*; *World Retail Directory and Sourcebook*.

Royalties payment is generally by flat fee.

Europa Publications Ltd
18 Bedford Square, London WC1B 3JN
☎0171 580 8236   Fax 0171 636 1664
Chairman *C. H. Martin*
Managing Director *P. A. McGinley*
Approx. Annual Turnover £5 million

Owned by Staples Printers Ltd. FOUNDED 1926 with the publication of the first edition of *The Europa Year Book*. *Publishes* annual reference books on political, economic and commercial matters. About 3 titles a year. No fiction, biography or poetry. Enquiries in writing only.

Royalties paid annually.

Evangelical Press of Wales
See **Gwasg Bryntirion Press**

Evans Brothers Ltd
2A Portman Mansions, Chiltern Street,
London W1M 1LE
☎0171 935 7160   Fax 0171 487 5034
Managing Director *Stephen Pawley*
International Publishing Director *Brian Jones*
Managing Editor *Su Swallow*
Approx. Annual Turnover £3 million

FOUNDED 1908 by Robert and Edward Evans. Originally published educational journals, books for primary schools and teacher education. After rapid expansion into popular fiction and drama, both were sacrificed to a major programme of educational books for schools in East and West Africa. A new UK programme was launched in 1986 followed by the acquisition of **Hamish Hamilton**'s non-fiction list for children in 1990. *Publishes* UK children's and educational books, and educational books for Africa, the Caribbean and Far East. About 70 titles a year. Unsolicited mss, synopses and ideas for books welcome.

Royalties paid annually. *Overseas associates* in Kenya, Cameroon, Sierra Leone; Evans Bros (Nigeria Publishers) Ltd.

Everyman
See **The Orion Publishing Group Ltd**

Everyman's Library
See **David Campbell Publishers Ltd**

University of Exeter Press
Reed Hall, Streatham Drive, Exeter, Devon
EX4 4QR
☎01392 263066   Fax 01392 263064
Publisher *Simon Baker*

FOUNDED 1956. *Publishes* academic books: archaeology, classical studies, mining, history, maritime studies, English literature (especially medieval), linguistics, European studies, modern languages and literature, American studies, film history, cultural studies, Arabic studies and books on Exeter and the South West. About 40 titles a year. Unsolicited mss welcomed in the subject areas mentioned above.

Royalties paid annually.

Exley Publications Ltd
16 Chalk Hill, Watford, Hertfordshire
WD1 4BN
☎01923 248328   Fax 01923 818733
Managing/Editorial Director *Helen Exley*

FOUNDED 1976. Independent family company. *Publishes* gift books, quotation anthologies, social stationery and humour. All in series only – no individual titles. Has a substantial children's non-fiction list. About 65 titles a year.

DIVISIONS
Gift Series TITLES *To a Very Special Friend, Daughter, Mother, ...; The Fanatics Guide to Golf, Cats, Dads, etc; The Crazy World of Aerobics, Golf, Learning to Drive; Golf, Book Lovers, Dog, Friendship Quotations; So-Much-More-Than-A-Card Collection.* No unsolicited mss. 'Joke and gag writers are very badly needed. Also writers who can create personal "messages", rather like not-too-sugary greetings cards.'

Faber & Faber Ltd
3 Queen Square, London WC1N 3AU
☎0171 465 0045   Fax 0171 465 0034
Chairman/Managing Director
   Matthew Evans
Approx. Annual Turnover £8.8 million

Geoffrey Faber and Richard de la Mare founded the company in the 1920s, with T. S. Eliot as an early recruit to the board. The original list was based on contemporary poetry and plays (the distinguished backlist includes Eliot, Auden and MacNeice). *Publishes* poetry and drama, art, children's, fiction, film, music, politics, biography, specialist cookery and wine. Unsolicited mss will be considered; synopses and ideas for books welcome. Return postage required.

DIVISIONS
Children's *Suzy Jenvey* AUTHORS Gene Kemp, Russell Stannard, Susan Price; **Cookery and Wine** *Belinda Matthews* TITLES *Kettle Broth to Gooseberry Fool*; *Pastability*; *Burgundy*; **Fiction** *Julian Loose* AUTHORS P. D. James, Peter Carey, William Golding, Milan Kundera, Mario Vargas Llosa, Garrison Keillor, Caryl Phillips, Paul Auster; **Plays** *Peggy Butcher*, **Film** *Walter Donohue.* AUTHORS Samuel Beckett, Alan Bennett, David Hare, Harold Pinter, Tom Stoppard, John Boorman, Woody Allen, Martin Scorsese, Quentin Tarantino; **Poetry** *Christopher Reid* AUTHORS Seamus Heaney, Ted Hughes, Douglas Dunn, Tom Paulin, Simon Armitage; **Non-fiction** *Julian Loose* AUTHORS John Carey, Adam Phillips, Darian Leader.
   Royalties paid twice-yearly. *Overseas office* Boston.

Authors' Rating With the grandson of the founder named as managing director in waiting, the younger generation are set to move in on Faber. They could not hope for a better start with one of the strongest backlists of any publisher and a healthy income from subsidiary rights. Faber has long been the leading poetry publisher and is now pre-eminent on books about the cinema.

FactbABCks
See **ABC – All Books For Children**

Fairleigh Dickinson University Press
See **Golden Cockerel Press**

Falmer Press
27 Palmeira Mansions, Church Road, Hove, East Sussex BN3 2FA
☎01273 775154   Fax 01273 205612
Managing/Editorial Director *Malcolm Clarkson*
Acquisitions Editor *Anna Clarkson*
Editorial Secretary *Emma Jackson*

Part of **Taylor & Francis**. *Publishes* educational books/materials for all levels. Largely commissioned. Unsolicited mss considered.
   Royalties paid annually.

Farming Press Books & Videos
Wharfedale Road, Ipswich, Suffolk IP1 4LG
☎01473 241122   Fax 01473 240501
Manager *Roger Smith*

Owned by United News & Media plc. *Publishes* specialist books/videos on farming, plus a range of humorous and countryside titles. About 35 books and videos a year. No unsolicited mss; synopses and ideas welcome provided material is suitable for their list.
   Royalties paid twice-yearly.

Fernhurst Books
Duke's Path, High Street, Arundel, West Sussex BN18 9AJ
☎01903 882277   Fax 01903 882715
Chairman/Managing Director *Tim Davison*

FOUNDED 1979. For people who love watersports. *Publishes* practical, highly illustrated handbooks on sailing and watersports. No unsolicited mss; synopses and ideas welcome.
   Royalties paid twice-yearly.

Findhorn Press
The Park, Findhorn, Moray IV36 0TZ
☎01309 690582   Fax 01309 690036
Partners *Karin Bogliolo, Thierry Bogliolo*
Approx. Annual Turnover £200,000

FOUNDED 1971. *Publishes* mind, body, spirit, new age and healing. 14 titles in 1996. Unsolicited mss, synopses and ideas welcome if they come within their subject areas.
   Royalties paid twice-yearly.

First & Best in Education Ltd

32 Nene Valley Business Park, Oundle,
Peterborough PE8 4HJ
☎01832 274716   Fax 01832 275281
Publisher *Tony Attwood*
Senior Editor *Kirsty Meadows*

Publishers of over 700 educational books of all
types for all ages of children and for parents and
teachers. All books are published as being suitable for photocopying and/or as electronic
books. Currently launching 10 new titles a
month and 'keenly looking for new authors all
the time'. TITLES *The Perfect Assembly; Children,
Their Discipline and Behaviour; Jean de Florette
livret de travail*. IMPRINT **Multi-Sensory
Learning** (see entry). Also publishers of *Schools
Internet*. In the first instance send s.a.e. for
details of requirements and current projects to
Nikki Robinson, Editorial Dept. at the above
address.
   Royalties paid twice-yearly.

Fitzjames Press
See **Motor Racing Publications**

Fitzroy Dearborn Publishers

11 Rathbone Place, London W1P 1DE
☎0171 636 6627   Fax 0171 636 6982
Managing Director *Daniel Kirkpatrick*
Commissioning Editor *Lesley Henderson*

Publishes reference books: business, history, art,
literature, science and social sciences. About 30
titles a year. TITLES *Encyclopedia of Literary
Translation* ed. Olive Classe; *Dictionary of Women
Artists* ed. Delia Gaze; *Reader's Guide to American
History* ed. Peter J. Parish. IMPRINT **Glenlake
Business Books**. Unsolicited mss, synopses and
ideas welcome for reference books.
   Royalties twice yearly. *US associate* Fizroy
Dearborn Publishers, 70 East Walton Street,
Chicago, IL 60611.

Flamingo
See **HarperCollins Publishers Ltd**

Flicks Books

29 Bradford Road, Trowbridge, Wiltshire
BA14 9AN
☎01225 767728   Fax 01225 760418
Publishing Director *Matthew Stevens*

FOUNDED 1986. Devoted solely to publishing
books on the cinema and related media. 10
titles in 1996. TITLES *Queen of the 'B's: Ida
Lupino Behind the Camera* ed Annette Kuhn; *By
Angels Driven: The Films of Derek Jarman* ed

Chris Lippard. Unsolicited mss, synopses and
ideas within the subject area are welcome.
   Royalties paid annually and twice yearly.

Flint River Press Ltd
See **Philip Wilson Publishers Ltd**

Floris Books

15 Harrison Gardens, Edinburgh EH11 1SH
☎0131 337 2372   Fax 0131 346 7516
Managing Director *Christian Maclean*
Editor *Christopher Moore*
Approx. Annual Turnover £350,000

FOUNDED 1977. *Publishes* books related to the
Steiner movement, including arts & crafts,
children's, the Christian Community, history,
religious, science, social questions and Celtic
studies. No unsolicited mss. Synopses and ideas
for books welcome.
   Royalties paid annually.

Fodor's
See **Random House UK Ltd**

Folens Limited

Albert House, Apex Business Centre,
Boscombe Road, Dunstable, Bedfordshire
LU5 4RL
☎01582 472788   Fax 01582 472575
Chairman *Dirk Folens*
Managing Director *Malcolm Watson*

FOUNDED 1987. Leading educational publisher. About 150 titles a year. IMPRINTS
Folens; **Belair**. Unsolicited mss, synopses and
ideas for educational books welcome.
   Royalties paid annually.

Fontana
See **HarperCollins Publishers Ltd**

Fortean Times Books
See **John Brown Publishing Ltd**

G. T. Foulis & Co Ltd
See **Haynes Publishing**

W. Foulsham & Co.

The Publishing House, Bennetts Close,
Cippenham, Berkshire SL1 5AP
☎01753 526769   Fax 01753 535003
Chairman *R. S. Belasco*
Managing Director *B. A. R. Belasco*
Approx. Annual Turnover £2.2 million

FOUNDED 1816 and now one of the few
remaining independent family companies to
survive takeover. *Publishes* non-fiction on most

subjects including astrology, gardening, cookery, DIY, business, hobbies, sport, health and marriage. No fiction. IMPRINT **Quantum** Mind, Body and Spirit titles. Unsolicited mss, synopses and ideas welcome. Around 60 titles a year.

Royalties paid twice-yearly.

Fount
See **HarperCollins Publishers Ltd**

Fountain Press Ltd
2 Gladstone Road, Kingston-upon-Thames, Surrey KT1 3HD
☎0181 541 4050   Fax 0181 547 3022
Managing Director *H. M. Ricketts*
Approx. Annual Turnover £700,000

FOUNDED 1923 when it was part of the Rowntree Trust Group. Owned by the British Electric Traction Group until 1982 when it was bought out by the present managing director. *Publishes* mainly photography, natural history and travel. About 25 titles a year. TITLES *Photography Yearbook; Wildlife Photographer of the Year; Antique and Collectable Cameras; Camera Manual* (series). Unsolicited mss and synopses are welcome.

Royalties paid twice-yearly.

Authors' Rating Highly regarded for production values, Fountain has the reputation for involving authors in every stage of the publishing process.

Fourmat Publishing
See **Tolley Publishing Co. Ltd**

Fourth Estate Ltd
6 Salem Road, London W2 4BU
☎0171 727 8993   Fax 0171 792 3176
Chairman/Managing Director *Victoria Barnsley*
Publishing Director *Christopher Potter*
Approx. Annual Turnover £3.5 million

FOUNDED 1984. Independent publisher with strong reputation for literary fiction and up-to-the-minute non-fiction. *Publishes* fiction, popular science, current affairs, biography, humour, self-help, travel, reference. About 75 titles a year.

DIVISIONS

Literary Fiction/Non-fiction TITLES *Hanging Up* Delia Ephron; *Wonder Boys* Michael Chabon; *The Stone Diaries* Carol Shields; *The Shipping News* E. Annie Proulx; *Revolution in the Head* Ian MacDonald; *Out of Control* Kevin Kelly; *Longitude* Dava Sobel. **General Fiction/Non-**

Fiction TITLES *Real Good Food* Nigel Slater; *Mrs Merton's Friendship Book; Che Guevara's Motorcycle Diaries; Bestseller* Celia Brayfield. No unsolicited mss; synopses welcome.

IMPRINT **Guardian Books** in association with *The Guardian.*

Royalties paid twice-yearly.

Authors' Rating Half-owned by *The Guardian* and named Publisher of the Year in the *Publishing News* 1997 Book Awards, Fourth Estate has ambitions to quadruple turnover in the next three years. Its track record of initiative and inspiration (*Longitude*, the biography of an obscure 18th-century scientist, was the unlikeliest bestseller of 1997) suggests that the objective of rapid growth is entirely realistic. Authors praise the attention to detail and friendly editorial.

Free Association Books Ltd
57 Warren Street, London W1P 5PA
☎0171 388 3182   Fax 0171 388 3187
Managing Director *T. E. Brown*
Publishing Director *Gill Davies*

Publishes psychoanalysis and psychotherapy, cultural studies, sexuality and gender, women's studies, applied social sciences. TITLES *The Politics of Attachment; Betrayal of Trust; An Introduction to Object Relations; The Many Faces of Eros; Complementary and Alternative Medicine.* Always write a letter in the first instance accompanied by a book outline.

Royalties paid twice-yearly. *Overseas associates* New York University Press, USA; Astam, Australia.

W. H. Freeman
Macmillan Press, Houndsmill, Basingstoke, Hampshire RG21 6XS
☎01256 29242   Fax 01256 330688
President *Robert Beiwen* (New York)
Sales Director *Elizabeth Warner*

Part of W. H. Freeman & Co., USA. *Publishes* academic, agriculture, animal care and breeding, archaeology, artificial intelligence, biochemistry, biology and zoology, chemistry, computer science, economics, educational and textbooks, engineering, geography and geology, mathematics and statistics, medical, natural history, neuroscience, palaeontology, physics, politics and world affairs, psychology, sociology and anthropology, and veterinary. Freeman's editorial office is in New York (Basingstoke is a sales and marketing office only) but unsolicited mss can go through Basingstoke. Those which are obviously unsuitable will be sifted out; the rest will be forwarded to New York.

Royalties paid annually.

Samuel French Ltd

52 Fitzroy Street, London W1P 6JR
☎0171 387 9373   Fax 0171 387 2161
Chairman *Charles R. Van Nostrand*
Managing Director *John Bedding*

FOUNDED 1830 with the object of acquiring acting rights and publishing plays. *Publishes* plays only. About 50 titles a year. Unsolicited mss considered only after initial submission of synopsis and specimen scene. Such material should be addressed to the Performing Rights Department.

Royalties paid twice-yearly for books; performing royalties paid monthly, subject to a minimum amount.

Authors' Rating Thrives on the amateur dramatic societies who are forever in need of play texts. Editorial advisers give serious attention to new material but a high proportion of the list is staged before it goes into print. Non-established writers are advised to try one-act plays, much in demand by the amateur dramatic societies but rarely turned out by well-known playwrights.

David Fulton (Publishers) Ltd

Ormond House, 26/27 Boswell Street,
London WC1N 3JD
☎0171 405 5606   Fax 0171 831 4840
Chairman/Managing Director *David Fulton*
Editorial Director *John Owens*
Approx. Annual Turnover £750,000

FOUNDED 1987. *Publishes* non-fiction: books for teachers and teacher training at B.Ed and PGCE levels for primary, secondary and special education; geography for undergraduate and professional. In 1995, David Fulton set up a Fulton Fellowship (see under **Bursaries, Fellowships and Grants**). About 50 titles a year. No unsolicited mss; synopses and ideas for books welcome.

Royalties paid twice-yearly.

Authors' Rating Now in his tenth year of business, David Fulton has shown how niche publishing can succeed even in a difficult market. Known chiefly for books on learning difficulties, David Fulton gets most of his ideas and authors by going to education conferences.

Funfax

See **Henderson Publishing Ltd**

Gaia Books Ltd

66 Charlotte Street, London W1P 1LR
☎0171 323 4010   Fax 0171 323 0435
Also at: 20 High Street, Stroud,
Gloucestershire GL5 1AS
☎01453 752985   Fax 01453 752987
Managing Director *Joss Pearson*

FOUNDED 1983. *Publishes* ecology, health, natural living and mind, body & spirit, mainly in practical self-help illustrated reference form for Britain and the international market. About 12 titles a year. TITLES *Sacred Journeys; The Young Gaia Atlas of Earthcare; The Feng Shui Handbook; Reflexology – A Step by Step Guide*. Most projects are conceived in-house but outlines and mss with s.a.e. considered. 'From submission of an idea to project go ahead may take up to a year. Authors become involved with the Gaia team in the editorial, design and promotion work needed to create and market a book.'

Gairm Publications

29 Waterloo Street, Glasgow G2 6BZ
☎0141 221 1971   Fax 0141 221 1971
Chairman *Prof. Derick S. Thomson*

FOUNDED 1952 to publish the quarterly Gaelic periodical *Gairm* and soon moved into publishing other Gaelic material. Acquired an old Glasgow Gaelic publishing firm, Alexander MacLaren & Son, in 1970. *Publishes* a wide range of Gaelic and Gaelic-related books: dictionaries, grammars, handbooks, children's, fiction, poetry, biography, music and song. Catalogue available.

Galaxy Children's Large Print

See **Chivers Press Ltd**

J. Garnet Miller Ltd

See **Cressrelles Publishing Co. Ltd**

Garnet Publishing Ltd

8 Southern Court, South Street, Reading,
Berkshire RG1 4QS
☎0118 9597847   Fax 0118 9597356
Managing Director *Ken Banerji*

FOUNDED 1992 and purchased Ithaca Press in the same year. *Publishes* art, architecture, photography, archive photography, cookery, travel classics, travel, comparative religion, Islamic culture and history, foreign fiction in translation. Core subjects are Middle Eastern but list is rapidly expanding to be more general. Published about 30 titles 1997.

IMPRINTS
Ithaca Press *Adel Kamal* Specialises in post-

graduate academic works on the Middle East, political science and international relations. About 20 titles in 1997. TITLES *Palestine and the Law*; *The Israeli Labour Party*; *Abbas Hilmi II: Memoirs of the Last Khedive of Egypt*; *Islamist and Leftist Forces in Jordan*; *Oman and the Southern Shore of the Persian Gulf.* **Garnet Publishing** Anna Watson TITLES *Arab Women Writers* series (winner of the 1995 WiP New Venture Award); *Traditional Spanish Cooking*; *Architecture of Oman*; *Architecture of the UAE*; *Jerusalem: Caught in Time* series; *International Women Writers* series. Unsolicited mss not welcome – write with outline and ideas first. Not interested in sport or general fiction.

Royalties paid twice-yearly. *Sister companies*: All Prints, Beirut; Garnet France, Paris.

The Gay Men's Press
(GMP Publishers Ltd)
PO Box 247, Swaffham, Norfolk PE37 8PA
☎01366 328101   Fax 01366 328102
Directors *David Fernbach, Aubrey Walter*

Publishes primarily books by gay authors about gay-related issues: art, photography, biography and autobiography, literary fiction and popular (historical romance to crime and science fiction), health and leisure. No poetry. Works should generally be submitted by the author on disk.

DIVISIONS
Art & Photography *Aubrey Walter*; **General Books** (including **Fiction**) *David Fernbach*. TITLES *Dares to Speak* Joseph Geraci; *For a Lost Soldier* Rudi van Dantzig; *Serbian Diaries* Boris Davidovich; *Jack Fritscher's American Men*; *Unholy Ghosts* Richard Zimler; *Young Men at War* Noel Currer-Briggs. Send synopsis with sample chapters rather than complete mss.
Royalties negotiable.

Geddes & Grosset Ltd
David Dale House, New Lanark ML11 9DJ
☎01555 665000   Fax 01555 665694
Managing Director *P. Michael Miller*
Approx. Annual Turnover £3.2 million
FOUNDED 1989. Publisher and packager of children's and reference books. Unsolicited mss, synopses and ideas welcome. No adult fiction.

Authors' Rating Now almost ten years old, Geddes & Grosset really came to eminence with Tarantula, a children's imprint launched three years ago which sells almost exclusively through supermarket chains.

Stanley Gibbons Publications
5 Parkside, Christchurch Road, Ringwood, Hampshire BH24 3SH
☎01425 472363   Fax 01425 470247
Chairman *P. I. Fraser*
Managing Director *A. J. Pandit*
Editorial Head *D. Aggersberg*
Approx. Annual Turnover £3 million

Long-established force in the philatelic world with over a hundred years in the business. *Publishes* philatelic reference catalogues and handbooks. Approx. 15 titles a year. Reference works relating to other areas of collecting may be considered. TITLES *Stanley Gibbons British Commonwealth Stamp Catalogue; Collect British Stamps; How to Arrange and Write Up a Stamp Collection; Stamps of the World; Collect Aircraft on Stamps.* Foreign catalogues include Japan and Korea, Portugal and Spain, Germany, Middle East. Monthly publication *Gibbons Stamp Monthly* (see entry under **Magazines**). Unsolicited mss, synopses and ideas welcome.
Royalties by negotiation.

Robert Gibson & Sons
Glasgow Limited
17 Fitzroy Place, Glasgow G3 7SF
☎0141 248 5674   Fax 0141 221 8219
Chairman/Managing Director
R. G. C. Gibson

FOUNDED 1850 and went public in 1886. *Publishes* educational books only, and has been agent for the Scottish Certificate of Education Examination Board since 1902. About 40 titles a year. Unsolicited mss preferred to synopses/ideas.
Royalties paid annually.

Ginn & Co
See **Reed Educational & Professional Publishing**

Mary Glasgow Publications
See **Stanley Thornes (Publishers) Ltd**

Glenlake Business Books
See **Fitzroy Dearborn Publishers**

Godsfield Press Ltd
Laurel House, Station Approach, Alresford, Hampshire SO24 9JH
☎01962 735633   Fax 01962 735320
Approx. Annual Turnover £0.5 million
Publishes mind/body/spirit titles in colour for adults and children.

Golden Cockerel Press Ltd
16 Barter Street, London WC1A 2AH
☎0171 405 7979   Fax 0171 404 3598
Directors *Tamar Lindesay, Andrew Lindesay*
FOUNDED 1980 to distribute titles for US-based
Associated University Presses Inc., New Jersey.
Publishes academic titles mostly: art, film, history,
literary criticism, music, philosophy, sociology
and special interest. About 120 titles a year.
IMPRINTS **AUP: Bucknell University
Press; University of Delaware; Fairleigh
Dickinson University Press; Lehigh
University Press; Susquehanna University
Press; Cygnus Arts** Non-academic books on
the arts; **Cornwall Books** Trade hardbacks.
Unsolicited mss, synopses and ideas for appro-
priate books welcome.

Authors' Rating Very much attuned to
American interests with trans-Atlantic spelling
and punctuation predominating. Some writers
may find the process wearisome but those who
persevere win through to a wider market.

Victor Gollancz
See **Cassell**

Gomer Press
Wind Street, Llandysul, Dyfed SA44 4BQ
☎01559 362371   Fax 01559 363758
Chairman/Managing Director *J. H. Lewis*
FOUNDED 1892. *Publishes* adult fiction and
non-fiction, children's fiction and educational
material in English and Welsh. About 100 titles
a year (65 Welsh; 35 English).
IMPRINTS **Gomer Press** *Dr D. Elis-Gruffydd*;
Pont Books *Mairwen Prys Jones*. No unsolicited
mss, synopses or ideas.
Royalties paid twice-yearly.

Gower
See **Ashgate Publishing Co. Ltd**

GPC Books
See **University of Wales Press**

Grafton
See **HarperCollins Publishers Ltd**

Graham & Trotman
See **Kluwer Law International**

Graham & Whiteside Ltd
Tuition House, 5–6 Francis Grove, London
SW19 4DT
☎0181 947 1011   Fax 0181 947 1163
Managing Director *Alastair M. W. Graham*

FOUNDED 1995. *Publishes* annual directories for
the business and professional market with titles
dating back to 1975 originally published by
Graham & Trotman. TITLES 22 annual dir-
ectories, including: *Major Companies of Europe;
Major Companies of the Arab World; Major
Companies of the Far East and Australasia.*
Proposals for new projects welcome.
Royalties paid annually.

Graham-Cameron Publishing
The Studio, 23 Holt Road, Sheringham,
Norfolk NR26 8NB
☎01263 821333   Fax 01263 821334
Editorial Director *Mike Graham-Cameron*
Art Director *Helen Graham-Cameron*
FOUNDED 1984 as a packaging operation.
Publishes illustrated factual books for children,
institutions and business; also biography, edu-
cation and social history. TITLES *Up From the
Country; In All Directions; The Holywell Story;
Let's Look at Dairying.* Please do not send unso-
licited mss.
Royalties paid annually. *Subsidiary company*:
Graham-Cameron Illustration (agency).

Granta Books
2–3 Hanover Yard, Noel Road, London
N1 8BE
☎0171 704 9776   Fax 0171 354 3469
Publisher *Frances Coady*
FOUNDED 1979. *Publishes* literary fiction and
general non-fiction. About 35 titles a year. No
unsolicited mss; synopses and sample chapters
welcome.
Royalties paid twice-yearly.

Authors' Rating Backed by American media
mogul Rae Hederman, publisher of the *New
York Review of Books*, Granta has relaunched
with 'a mix of new and established writers'
while putting out the welcome sign for 'good
writing and challenging ideas'.

W. Green (Scotland)
See **Sweet & Maxwell Ltd**

Green Books
Foxhole, Dartington, Totnes, Devon
TQ9 6EB
☎01803 863843   Fax 01803 863843
Chairman *Satish Kumar*
Managing Editor *John Elford*
Approx. Annual Turnover £120,000
FOUNDED in 1987 with the support of a number
of Green organisations. Closely associated with

Resurgence magazine. *Publishes* high-quality books on a wide range of Green issues, particularly ideas, philosophy and the practical application of Green values. No fiction or books for children. TITLES *Forest Gardening* Robert A. de J. Hart; *Eco-Renovation* Edward Harland; *The Growth Illusion* Richard Douthwaite; *The Living Tree* John Lane; *Tongues in Trees* Kim Taplin. No unsolicited mss. Synopses and ideas welcome.
Royalties paid twice-yearly.

Green Print
See **The Merlin Press Ltd**

Greenhill Books/
Lionel Leventhal Ltd
Park House, 1 Russell Gardens, London
NW11 9NN
☎0181 458 6314   Fax 0181 905 5245
Managing Director *Lionel Leventhal*
FOUNDED 1984 by Lionel Leventhal (ex-**Arms & Armour Press**). *Publishes* aviation, military and naval books, and its Napoleonic Library series. Synopses and ideas for books welcome. No unsolicited mss.
Royalties paid twice-yearly.

Gresham Books
See **Woodhead Publishing Ltd**

Gresham Books Ltd
PO Box 61, Henley on Thames, Oxfordshire
RG9 3LQ
☎01734 403789   Fax 01734 403789
Managing Director *Mary V. Green*
Approx. Annual Turnover £175,000
Bought by Mary Green from Martins Publishing Group in 1980. A small specialist publishing house. *Publishes* hymn and service books for schools and churches, also craft-bound choir and orchestral folders and Records of Achievement. TITLES include music and melody editions of *Hymns for Church and School*; *The School Hymnal*; *Praise and Thanksgiving*. No unsolicited material but ideas welcome.

Griffith Institute
See **Ashmolean Museum Publications Ltd**

Grisewood & Dempsey
See **Larousse plc**

Grove's Dictionary of Music
See **Macmillan Publishers Ltd**

Grub Street
The Basement, 10 Chivalry Road, London
SW11 1HT
☎0171 924 3966   Fax 0171 738 1009
Managing Director *John Davies*
FOUNDED 1982. *Publishes* cookery, health and aviation history books. About 20 titles a year. TITLES *Complete Asian Cookbook*; *Everyday Diabetic Cookbook*; *Above the Trenches*; *Aces High*. Unsolicited mss and synopses welcome in the above categories.
Royalties paid twice-yearly.

Grune & Stratton
See **Harcourt Brace and Company Limited**

Guardian Books
See **Fourth Estate Ltd**

Guild of Master Craftsman
Publications Ltd
166 High Street, Lewes, East Sussex
BN7 1XU
☎01273 477374   Fax 01273 487962
Chairman *A.E. Phillips*
Approx. Annual Turnover £2 million
FOUNDED 1979. Part of G.M.C. Services Ltd. *Publishes* woodworking and craft books and magazines. 30 titles in 1997. Unsolicited mss, synopses and ideas for books welcome. No fiction.
Royalties paid twice-yearly.

Guinness Publishing Ltd
338 Euston Road, London NW1 3BA
☎0171 891 4567   Fax 0171 891 4501
Chairman *Ian Chapman, CBE*
Managing Director *Christopher Irwin*
Joint Publishing Directors *Ian Castello-Cortes, Michael Feldman*
FOUNDED 1954 to publish *The Guinness Book of Records*, now the highest-selling copyright book in the world, published in 35 languages. In the late 1960s the company set about expanding its list with a wider range of print and electronic titles. About 12 titles a year. Ideas and synopses for books welcome if they come within their fields of sport, human achievement (with the emphasis on facts and feats), popular music and family reference.

Authors' Rating Said by *The Bookseller* to be 'a strong contender for the title of most profitable adult trade publisher', all activity is centred on the founding title. The emphasis now is on using the Guinness name to broaden the publishing base.

Gunsmoke Westerns
See **Chivers Press Ltd**

Gwasg Addysgol Cymru
See **Ashley Drake Publishing Ltd**

Gwasg Bryntirion Press (formerly Evangelical Press of Wales)
Bryntirion House, Bridgend, Mid-Glamorgan CF31 4DX
☎01656 655886   Fax 01656 656095
Chairman *Reverend S. Jones*
Chief Executive *G. Wyn Davies*
Approx. Annual Turnover £85,000
Owned by the Evangelical Movement of Wales. *Publishes* Christian books in English and Welsh. 6 titles in 1996. TITLES *Encounters with God; Fire in the Thatch; Following the Shepherd; Pursued by God; Taught to Serve; Sally Jones – Rhodd Duw I Charles.* No unsolicited mss; synopses and ideas welcome.
Royalties paid annually.

Gwasg Carreg Gwalch
12 Iard Yr Orsaf, Llanrwst, Conwy LL26 0EH
☎01492 642031   Fax 01492 641502
Managing Editor *Myrddin Ap Dafydd*
FOUNDED in 1990. *Publishes* Welsh language; English books of Welsh interest – history, folklore, guides and walks. 40 titles in 1996. Unsolicited mss, synopses and ideas welcome.
Royalties paid.

Gwasg Prifysgol Cymru
See **University of Wales Press**

Peter Haddock Ltd
Pinfold Lane Industrial Estate, Bridlington, East Yorkshire YO16 5BT
☎01262 678121   Fax 01262 400043
Managing Director *Peter Haddock*
Contact *Pat Hornby*
FOUNDED 1952. *Publishes* children's picture story and activity books. About 200 series a year. Ideas for picture books welcome.
Royalties payments vary according to each contract.

Authors' Rating Cheap end of the market. Writers need to work fast to make a living.

Peter Halban Publishers
42 South Molton Street, London W1Y 1HB
☎0171 491 1582   Fax 0171 629 5381
Directors *Peter Halban, Martine Halban*
FOUNDED 1986. Independent publisher. *Publishes* biography, autobiography and memoirs, history, philosophy, theology, politics, literature and criticism, Judaica and world affairs. 4–5 titles a year. No unsolicited material. Approach by letter in first instance.
Royalties paid twice-yearly for first two years, thereafter annually in December.

Robert Hale Ltd
Clerkenwell House, 45–47 Clerkenwell Green, London EC1R 0HT
☎0171 251 2661   Fax 0171 490 4958
Chairman/Managing Director *John Hale*
FOUNDED 1936. Family-owned company. *Publishes* adult fiction (but not interested in category crime, romance or science fiction) and non-fiction. No specialist material (education, law, medical or scientific). Acquired **NAG Press Ltd** in 1993 with its list of horological, gemmological, jewellery and metalwork titles. Over 200 titles a year. TITLES *The Black Country* Harold Parsons; *Buying and Selling Pictures Successfully* Alan G. Thompson; *Tom Cruise, A Biography* Robert Sellers; *Writing a Musical* Richard Andrews; *The Auld Inns of Scotland* Dane Love; *The Purple Plain* H. E. Bates; *Flowering Thorn* Mary Williams. Unsolicited mss, synopses and ideas for books welcome.
Royalties paid twice-yearly.

Authors' Rating Takes good care of authors but can be tough on advances. Favours the popular end of the fiction market.

Halsgrove
Halsgrove House, Lower Moor Way, Tiverton, Devon EX16 6SS
☎01884 243242   Fax 01884 243325
Joint Managing Directors *Simon Butler, Steven Pugsley*
Approx. Annual Turnover £1.5 million
FOUNDED in 1990 from defunct Maxwell-owned publishing group. Grown into the region's largest publishing and distribution group, specialising in books, video and audio tapes. *Publishes* local history, cookery, biography. 50 titles in 1996. No fiction or poetry. Unsolicited mss, synopses and ideas for books of regional interest welcome.
Royalties paid annually.

The Hambledon Press

102 Gloucester Avenue, London NW1 8HX
☎0171 586 0817   Fax 0171 586 9970

Chairman/Managing Director/Editorial Head *Martin Sheppard*

FOUNDED 1980. *Publishes* English and European history from post-classical to modern. Currently expanding its list to include history titles with a wider appeal. 25–30 titles a year. TITLES *Jane Austen and Food* Maggie Lane; *Victorian Girls: Lord Lyttelton's Daughters* Sheila Fletcher; *Riddles in Stone* Richard Hayman. No unsolicited mss; send preliminary letter. Synopses and ideas welcome.

Royalties paid annually. *Overseas associates* **The Hambledon Press (USA)**, Ohio.

Hamilton & Co (Publishers)

115 Stamford Road, London E6 1LP
☎0181 548 1814

Managing Editor *James Dalton*

FOUNDED 1997. *Publishes* fiction and non-fiction: memoirs, autobiography, biography, war, poetry, religion. Planning to publish 15–20 titles in their first year. Unsolicited synopses and ideas for books (with s.a.e.) welcome. Authors who wish to have their mss returned must send sufficient postage.

Hamish Hamilton Ltd/Hamish Hamilton Children's

See **Penguin Books Ltd**

Hamlyn/Octopus

See **Reed Books**

Harcourt Brace and Company Limited

24–28 Oval Road, London NW1 7DX
☎0171 267 4466Fax 0171 482 2293/485 4752

Managing Director *Peter H. Lengemann*

Owned by US parent company. *Publishes* scientific, technical and medical books, college textbooks, educational & occupational test. No unsolicited mss. IMPRINTS **Academic Press**; **Baillière Tindall**; **Dryden Press**; **Grune & Stratton**; **Holt Rinehart and Winston**; **T. & A. D. Poyser**; **W. B. Saunders & Co. Ltd.**; **Saunders Scientific Publications**,.

Harlequin Mills & Boon Ltd

Eton House, 18–24 Paradise Road, Richmond, Surrey TW9 1SR
☎0181 948 0444   Fax 0181 288 2899

Managing Director *R. Guzner*

Editorial Director *Karin Stoecker*

FOUNDED 1908. Owned by the Canadian-based Torstar Group. *Publishes* romantic fiction and historical romance. Over 600 titles a year.

IMPRINTS

Mills & Boon Presents (50–55,000 words) contemporary romances with international settings, focusing intensely on hero and heroine, with happy endings assured. **Mills & Boon Enchanted**; **Mills & Boon Medical Romance**; *Elizabeth Johnson* (50–55,000 words) Modern medical practice provides a unique background to love stories. **Mills & Boon Historical Romance** *Elizabeth Johnson* (75–80,000 words) Historical romances; **Mira** *Linda Fildew* (minimum 100,000 words) Individual women's fiction.

Silhouette Desire, **Special Edition**, **Sensation** and **Intrigue** imprints are handled by US-based **Silhouette Books** (see **US Publishers**). Please send query letter in the first instance. Tip sheets and guidelines for the Harlequin Mills & Boon series available from Harlequin Mills & Boon Editorial Dept. (please send s.a.e.).

Royalties paid twice-yearly.

Authors' Rating There has been a shift in the romance market towards harder, sexier themes but rumours of the death of the old-fashioned love story have proved premature. The distinctive HMB titles continue to roll off the presses in great numbers. But there are hints of diversification, into children's educational products, for example.

Harley Books

Martins, Great Horkesley, Colchester, Essex CO6 4AH
☎01206 271216   Fax 01206 271182

Managing Director *Basil Harley*

FOUNDED 1983. Natural history publishers specialising in entomological and botanical books. Mostly definitive, high-quality illustrated reference works. TITLES *The Moths and Butterflies of Great Britain and Ireland; Spiders of Great Britain and Ireland; Dragonflies of Europe; The Flora of Hampshire.*

Royalties paid twice-yearly in the first year, annually thereafter.

HarperCollins Publishers Ltd

77–85 Fulham Palace Road, London W6 8JB
☎0181 741 7070   Fax 0181 307 4440

Also at: Freepost PO Box, Glasgow G4 0NB
☎0141 772 3200   Fax 0141 306 3119

Chief Executive *Anthea Disney*

Executive Chairman/Publisher *Eddie Bell*
Group Managing Director *Les Higgins*
Approx. Annual Turnover £200 million

Publisher of high-profile authors like Jeffrey Archer, James Herbert, Fay Weldon and Len Deighton. Owned by News Corporation. Since 1991 there has been a period of consolidated focus on key management issues within the HarperCollins empire. This has led to various imprints being phased out in favour of others, among them Grafton and Fontana, which have been merged under the HarperCollins paperback imprint. Title output has been reduced by about 20%.

DIVISIONS

Trade *Adrian Bourne*, Divisional Managing Director, *Malcolm Edwards*, Deputy Managing Director, *Stuart Profitt*, Publisher; **Fiction** *Malcolm Edwards, Nick Sayers*; **Non-Fiction** *Michael Fishwick*. IMPRINTS **Collins Crime**; **Flamingo** (literary fiction, both hardback and paperback); **HarperCollins Paperbacks**; **Tolkien**; **HarperCollins Science Fiction and Fantasy**; **Fontana Press**; **HarperCollins**. Over 650 titles a year, hardback and paperback. No longer accepts unsolicited submissions.

Thorsons *Eileen Campbell*, Divisional Managing Director. Health, nutrition, business, parenting, popular psychology, positive thinking, self-help, divination, therapy, recovery, feminism, women's issues, mythology, religion, yoga, tarot, personal development, sexual politics, biography, history, popular culture. About 250 titles a year.

Children's *To be appointed* IMPRINTS **Picture Lions**; **HarperCollins Audio** (see entry under **Audio Books**); **Jets**; **Collins Tracks**; **Collins Non-Fiction** Quality picture books and book and tape sets for under 7s; all categories of fiction for the 6–14 age group; dictionaries and general reference for pre-school and primary. About 250 titles a year. No longer accepts unsolicited mss.

Reference *Robin Wood*, Divisional Managing Director IMPRINTS **HarperCollins**; **Collins New Naturalist Library**; **Collins Gems**; **Collins Willow** (sport); **Janes** (military) Encyclopedias, guides and handbooks, phrase books and manuals on popular reference, art instruction, cookery and wine, crafts, DIY, gardening, military, natural history, pet care, Scottish, sports and pastimes. About 120 titles a year.

Educational *Kate Harris*, Divisional Managing Director. Textbook publishing for schools and FE colleges (5–18-year-olds): all subjects for primary education; strong in English, history, geography, science and technology for secondary education; sociology, business studies and economics in FE. (Former Holmes McDougall, Unwin Hyman, Mary Glasgow Primary Publications, and part of Harcourt, Brace & Co. educational imprints have been incorporated under Collins Educational.) About 90 titles a year.

Dictionaries *Robin Wood* IMPRINTS **Collins**; **Collins Cobuild**; **Collins Gem** Includes the *Collins English Dictionary* range with dictionaries and thesauruses, *Collins Bilingual Dictionary* range (French, German, Spanish, Italian, etc.), and the *Cobuild* series of English dictionary, grammars and EFL books. About 50 titles a year.

HarperCollege *Kate Harris* IMPRINT **HarperCollins College** Selected US academic titles, mostly imported from College Division, Basic Books, Harper Business and Harper Perennial. Most of the titles stocked are university-level texts, previously published under the Harper & Row and Scott Foresman imprints. A programme to publish UK editions of some of these commenced in 1994. Strength areas are economics, psychology, allied health and business. About 550 titles stocked in the UK.

HarperCollins World *Robin Wood*. IMPRINTS **HarperCollins US**; **Australia**; **New Zealand**; **Canada**; **India** General trade titles imported into the UK market.

Religious *Eileen Campbell*, Divisional Managing Director. A broad-based religious publisher across all denominations. IMPRINTS **HarperCollins**; **Fount**; **Marshall Pickering** Extensive range covering both popular and academic spirituality, music and reference. Marshall Pickering, bibles, missals, prayer books, and hymn books. About 150 titles a year.

HarperCollins Cartographic *Jeremy Westwood* The cartographic division, with Bartholomew and Times Books now joined as one division. IMPRINTS **Bartholomew**; **Collins**; **Harper-Collins Audiobooks** (see entry under **Audio Books**); **Invincible Press**; **Longman Nicholson**; **Nicholson/Ordnance Survey**; **Sun Crosswords**; **Times Atlases**; **Times Books**; **Times Crosswords** Maps, atlases and guides (Bartholomew; Collins; Collins Longman; Times Atlases); leisure maps; educational titles (Collins Longman); London titles (Nicholson); waterway guides (Nicholson/Ordnance Survey); sports titles for *The Sun* and *News of the World* (Invincible Press); reference and non-fiction (Times Books). About 30 titles a year.

HarperCollins Interactive *Steve Paul* Supports the company's electronic publishing activities on CD-ROM, floppy disk and on-line. *Specialises* in special interest, children's, reference and interactive fiction.

Broadcasting Consultancy *Cresta Norris* Newly formed to exploit TV and film rights across the country.

Authors' Rating There are those who say that Rupert Murdoch does not count HarperCollins as among his core activities while others claim that the media giant has a soft spot for book publishing. But even if HarperCollins does fall short as the creative power-house for the rest of News Corp. entertainment, it is unlikely to be sold while buyers are so downbeat. As new chief executive, Anthea Disney is said to be forging closer links with other sectors of the Murdoch empire. An early sign of this is the sale of the contents of HarperCollins' reference, children's and audiobook titles to LineOne, the News International on-line service on the Internet. But the most welcome news is of the shift of emphasis away from poaching authors at ridiculous sums towards building lists on new talent.

Harrap

See **Larousse plc**

Harvard University Press

Fitzroy House, 11 Chenies Street, London WC1E 7ET
☎0171 306 0603   Fax 0171 306 0604
Director *William Sisler*
General Manager *Ann Sexsmith*

Part of **Harvard University Press**, USA. *Publishes* academic and scholarly works in history, politics, philosophy, economics, literary criticism, psychology, sociology, anthropology, women's studies, biological sciences, astronomy, history of science, art, music, film, reference. All mss go to the American office: 79 Garden Street, Cambridge, MA 02138.

The Harvill Press Ltd

84 Thornhill Road, London N1 1RD
☎0171 609 1119   Fax 0171 609 2019
Chairman *Christopher MacLehose*
Managing Director *John Mitchinson*
Editorial Director *Guido Waldman*
  Managing Editor *Donna Poppy*

FOUNDED in 1946, the list was bought by Collins in 1959, of which it remained an imprint until returning to its original independent status in early 1995. *Publishes* literature in translation (especially Russian, Italian and French), literature, quality thrillers, illustrated books and Africana, plus an occasional literature anthology. 50–60 titles in 1996. AUTHORS Mikhail Bulgakov, Raymond Carver, Richard Ford, Alan Garner, Peter Høeg, Robert Hughes, Giuseppe T. di Lampedusa, Peter Matthiessen, Cees Nooteboom, Boris Pasternak, Georges Perec, Aleksandr Solzhenitsyn, Marguerite Yourcenar. Mss usually submitted by foreign publishers and agents. Synopses and ideas welcome. No educational or technical books.
Royalties paid twice-yearly.

Authors' Rating The buyout from HarperCollins is beginning to look like a gamble that will pay off handsomely. What Harvill does best, fiction in translation, does not seem to fit comfortably in a conglomerate but can thrive with an independent publisher. The two-way traffic means that Harvill's English language writers tend to do well in Europe. Relations with authors are said to be close and friendly.

Haynes Publishing

Sparkford, Near Yeovil, Somerset BA22 7JJ
☎01963 440635   Fax 01963 440825
Chairman *John H. Haynes*
Approx. Annual Turnover £20 million

FOUNDED in 1960 by John H. Haynes. A family-run business. The mainstay of its programme has been the *Owners' Workshop Manual*, first published in the mid 1960s and still running off the presses today. Indeed the company maintains a strong bias towards motoring and transport titles. *Publishes* DIY workshop manuals for cars and motorbikes, railway, aviation, military, maritime, model-making and general leisure.

IMPRINTS
G. T. Foulis & Co. Cars and motoring-related books; **J. H. Haynes & Co. Ltd** *Scott Mauck* Workshop manuals; **Oxford Illustrated Press** Photography, sports and games, gardening, travel and guidebooks; **Haynes** Home and leisure titles; **Oxford Publishing Co.** Railway titles; **Patrick Stephens Ltd** *Darryl Reach* Motoring, rail, aviation, military, maritime, model-making. Unsolicited mss welcome if they come within the subject areas covered.
Royalties paid annually. *Overseas associates* Haynes Publications Inc., California, USA.

Hazar Publishing Ltd

147 Chiswick High Road, London W4 2DT
☎0181 742 8578   Fax 0181 994 1407
**Managing Director/Editorial Head
   (Children's)** *Gregory Hill*
Editorial Head (Adult) *Marie Clayton*
Approx. Annual Turnover £700,000

FOUNDED 1993, Hazar is a new independent publisher of high-quality illustrated books. *Publishes* children's fiction and adult non-fiction: design and architecture. Planning to expand the children's list. About 15 titles a year.
   Royalties paid twice-yearly.

Hazleton Publishing

3 Richmond Hill, Richmond, Surrey
TW10 6RE
☎0181 948 5151   Fax 0181 948 4111
Chairman/Managing Director *R. F. Poulter*
Publisher of the leading Grand Prix annual *Autocourse*, now in its 47th edition. *Publishes* high-quality motor sport titles including annuals. TITLES *Motocourse; Rallycourse; British Motorsport Year; Autocourse PG Cart World Series.* About 13 titles a year. No unsolicited mss; synopses and ideas welcome. Interested in all motor sport titles.
   Royalties payment varies.

Headline

See **Hodder Headline plc**

Headstart

See **Hodder Headline plc**

Headway

See **Hodder Headline plc**

Health Education Authority

Publishing Department, Hamilton House,
Mabledon Place, London WC1H 9TX
☎0171 413 1846   Fax 0171 413 0339
General Manager (Publishing) *Simon Boyd*
Approx. Annual Turnover £600,000

Publishes public information leaflets, training manuals, professional guides and open learning material for the Health Education Authority. Over 300 titles in print. TITLES cover nutrition, physical activity, cancer, sexual health, oral health, immunisation, alcohol, smoking, primary health care, accidents, mental health and drugs. No unsolicited mss; synopses and ideas welcome.

William Heinemann

See **Random House UK Ltd**

Heinemann Educational/ Heinemann English Language Teaching

See **Reed Educational & Professional Publishing**

Heinemann Young Books

See **Reed Books**

Helicon Publishing

42 Hythe Bridge Street, Oxford OX1 2EP
☎01865 204204   Fax 01865 204205
Managing Director *David Attwooll*
Publishing Director *Michael Upshall*
Editorial Director *Anne-Lucie Norton*
Associate Editorial Director *Hilary McGlynn*

FOUNDED 1992 from the management buy-out of former Random Century's reference division. Led by David Attwooll, the buy-out (for an undisclosed sum) included the Hutchinson Encyclopedia titles and databases, along with other reference titles. The Helicon list, which is now distributed by Penguin, is increasing the range of reference titles, particularly in history, science and current affairs and is maintaining its lead in electronic publishing. TITLES *The Hutchinson Encyclopedia; J. M. Robert's History of Europe.* Electronic titles: *The Hutchinson Multimedia Encyclopedia; The Penguin Hutchinson Reference Library.*

Christopher Helm Publishers Ltd

See **A. & C. Black (Publishers) Ltd**

Henderson Publishing Limited

Marsh House, Tide Mill Way, Woodbridge,
Suffolk IP12 1BY
☎01394 380622   Fax 01394 380618
Managing Director *Barrie Henderson*
Managing Editor *Lucy Bater*
Approx. Annual Turnover £7 million

FOUNDED 1990. Bought by **Dorling Kindersley** in 1995 and now a wholly-owned subsidiary of Dorling Kindersley Holdings plc. *Publishes* children's books for the international mass markets; non-fiction information, novelty, puzzle and some fiction books. All ideas are generated in-house to specific formats across the range of imprints. Freelance writers are commissioned to write to an agreed brief with strict guidelines. Texts are then edited in-house to suit a particular Henderson style. Unsolicited synopses and ideas for books welcome. No mss. New authors welcome (send c.v. and introductory letter to Lucy Bater).
   IMPRINTS include **Funfax; Microfax; FX**

Pax; **Mad Jack Activity Packs**; **Magic Jewellery**.

Ian Henry Publications Ltd

20 Park Drive, Romford, Essex RM1 4LH
☎01708 749119   Fax 01708 749119

Managing Director *Ian Wilkes*

FOUNDED 1976. *Publishes* local history, transport history and Sherlockian pastiches. 8–10 titles a year. TITLES *Essex Miscellany; Portrait of Great Wakering; 'After You, Holmes …'; Legends of Leigh*. No unsolicited mss. Synopses and ideas for books welcome.
Royalties paid twice-yearly.

The Herbert Press Ltd

35 Bedford Row, London WC1R 4JH
☎0171 242 0946   Fax 0171 404 7706

Chairman *Charles Black*
Managing Director *Jill Coleman*

Subsidiary of **A. & C. Black (Publishers) Ltd.**
Publishes archaeology, architecture and design, botanical art, crafts and hobbies, exhibition catalogues, fashion and costume, fine art and art history, photography. About 8 titles a year.
Royalties paid twice-yearly.

Hermes House

See **Anness Publishing Ltd**

Nick Hern Books

14 Larden Road, London W3 7ST
☎0181 740 9539   Fax 0181 746 2006

Chairman/Managing Director *Nick Hern*
Approx. Annual Turnover £300,000

FOUNDED 1988. Fully independent since 1992. *Publishes* books on theatre: from how-to and biography to plays. About 30 titles a year. No unsolicited playscripts. Synopses, ideas and proposals for other theatre material welcome. Not interested in material unrelated to the theatre.

High Risk Books

See **Serpent's Tail**

Hippo

See **Scholastic Ltd**

HMSO

See **The Stationery Office Publishing**

Hobsons Publishing

Bateman Street, Cambridge CB2 1LZ
☎01223 354551   Fax 01223 323154

Chairman/Managing Director *Martin Morgan*

Approx. Annual Turnover £17.7 million

FOUNDED 1973. A division of Harmsworth Publishing Ltd, part of the Daily Mail & General Trust. *Publishes* course and career guides, under exclusive licence and royalty agreements for CRAC (Careers Research and Advisory Bureau); computer software; directories and specialist titles for employers, government departments and professional associations. TITLES *Graduate Employment and Training; The Student HelpBook Series; Degree Course Guides; The Which Degree Series; Which University* (CD-ROM); *The POSTGRAD Series: The Directory of Graduate Studies; The Directory of Further Education; CRAC GNVQ Assignment Series; CRAC Core Skills Series*. Also publisher of *Johansens Hotel Guides*.

Hodder & Stoughton

See **Hodder Headline plc**

Hodder Headline plc

338 Euston Road, London NW1 3BH
☎0171 873 6000   Fax 0171 873 6024

Group Chief Executive *Tim Hely Hutchinson*
Deputy Chief Executive *Mark Opzoomer*
Approx. Annual Turnover £92 million

Formed in June 1993 through the merger of **Headline Book Publishing** and **Hodder & Stoughton**. Headline was formed in 1986 and had grown dramatically, whereas Hodder & Stoughton was 125 years old with a diverse range of publishing.

DIVISIONS
Headline Book Publishing Managing Director *Amanda Ridout*. **Non-fiction** *Heather Holden-Brown*; **Fiction** *Jane Morpeth*. *Publishes* commercial fiction (hardback and paperback) and popular non-fiction including biography, cinema, design and film, food and wine, countryside, TV tie-ins and sports yearbooks. IMPRINTS **Headline**; **Headline Feature**; **Headline Review**; **Headline Delta Liaison** (erotic fiction). AUTHORS Raymond Blanc, Harry Bowling, Martina Cole, Josephine Cox, John Francome, Dean Koontz, Richard Laymon, Lyn Macdonald, James Patterson and Ellis Peters.

Hodder & Stoughton General Managing Director *Martin Nield*, Deputy Managing Director *Sue Fletcher*. **Non-fiction** *Roland Philipps*; **Horror** *Nick Austin*; **Sceptre** *Carole Welch*; **Fiction** *Carolyn Mays, Carolyn Caughey*; **Audio** (See entry under **Audio Books**).

Publishes commercial and literary fiction; biography, autobiography, history, self-help, humour, travel and other general interest non-fiction; audio. IMPRINTS **Hodder & Stoughton; Coronet; New English Library; Sceptre**. AUTHORS Melvyn Bragg, John le Carré, James Clavell, Elizabeth George, Stephen King, Stephen Leather, Gavin Lyall, Ed McBain, Malcolm Gluck and Mary Stewart, Terry Waite.

Hodder & Stoughton Educational Managing Director *Brian Steven*. **Humanities, Science & Mathematics** *Liz Wright*; **Language, Business and Psychology** *Tim Gregson-Williams*; **Teach Yourself; Headway** *Lucy Purkis*. Textbooks for the primary, secondary, tertiary and further education sectors and for self-improvement. IMPRINTS **Hodder & Stoughton Educational**.

Hodder Children's Books Managing Director *Mary Tapissier*. IMPRINTS **Hodder & Stoughton; Knight; Picture Knight; Hodder Dargaud; Headstart; Test Your Child**. AUTHORS Goscinny & Uderzo (*Asterix*), Rolf Harris, Mick Inkpen, Christopher Pike.

Hodder & Stoughton Religious Managing Director *Charles Nettleton*. **Bibles & Liturgical** *Emma Sealey*; **Christian paperbacks** *Judith Longman*. Bibles, commentaries, liturgical works (both printed and software), and a wide range of Christian paperbacks. IMPRINTS **New International Version of the Bible; Hodder Christian paperbacks**.

Edward Arnold Managing Director *Richard Stileman*. **Humanities** *Chris Wheeler*; **Medical, Science and Engineering** *Nicki Dennis*; **Health Sciences** *Georgina Bentliff*. Academic and professional books and journals.

The Brockhampton Press Managing Director *John Maxwell*. Promotional books. *Royalties* paid twice-yearly.

Authors' Rating Like all the big publishers, Hodder Headline has had a few wobbles in the last two years but seems now to be back on expansionist course with an impressive number of titles in the *Guardian* fast seller list. Strong marketing has led to the appearance of more Hodder Headline books on the supermarket shelves. New writing is encouraged and talent nurtured.

Holmes McDougall
See **HarperCollins Publishers Ltd**

Holt Rinehart & Winston
See **Harcourt Brace and Company Limited**

Honeyglen Publishing Ltd
56 Durrels House, Warwick Gardens, London W14 8QB
☎0171 602 2876   Fax 0171 602 2876
Directors *N. S. Poderegin, J. Poderegin*

FOUNDED 1983. A small publishing house whose output is 'extremely limited'. *Publishes* history, philosophy of history, biography and selective fiction. No children's or science fiction. TITLES *The Soul of India; A Child of the Century* Amaury de Riencourt; *With Duncan Grant in South Turkey* Paul Roche; *Vladimir, The Russian Viking* Vladimir Volkoff; *The Dawning* Milka Bajic-Poderegin; *Quicksand* Louise Hide. Unsolicited mss welcome. No synopses or ideas.

House of Lochar
Isle of Colonsay, Argyll PA61 7YR
☎01951 200232   Fax 01951 200232
Chairman *Kevin Byrne*
Managing Director *Georgina Hobhouse*
Approx. Annual Turnover £80,000

FOUNDED 1995 on the basis of some 24 titles formerly published by Thomas and Lochar of Nairn. *Publishes* Scottish fiction and non-fiction – history, topography, transport. IMPRINTS **House of Lochar** *Kevin Byrne* TITLES *Country Houses of Scotland; The Light in the Glen; The Rise and Fall of the Puffer Trade*. **Colonsay Books** *Georgina Hobhouse* TITLES *Summer in the Hebrides; Place Names of Colonsay and Oronsay; Antiquities of Colonsay*. No poetry or books unrelated to Scotland or Celtic theme. Unsolicited mss, synopses and ideas welcome if relevant to subjects covered.
Royalties paid annually.

How To Books Ltd
3 Newtec Place, Magdalen Road, Oxford OX4 1RE
☎01865 247711   Fax 01865 248780
Managing Director *Miles Lewis*

There are now over 200 titles in the How To Books series, many in revised and updated new editions. TITLES take the form of 'how to achieve a specific goal or benefit' in the areas of employment, business, education, family reference, international opportunities and self-development: *How to Become an Au Pair; How to Survive Divorce; How to Master Languages*. Well-structured proposals from qualified and experienced professionals welcome.
Royalties paid annually.

The University of Hull Press/ The Lampada Press

Cottingham Road, Hull, East Yorkshire
HU6 7RX
☎01482 465322   Fax 01482 466858
Assistant Registrar *Miss J. M. Smith*

The University of Hull Press *publishes* books of academic merit and those that command a wide general market. TITLES *An Historical Atlas of East Yorkshire* eds. Susan Neave and Stephen Ellis; *Superior Force: The Conspiracy Behind the Escape of Goeben and Breslau* Geoffrey Miller; *The Desperate Faction? The Jacobites of North-East England 1688–1745* Leo Gooch; *Aspects of Political Censorship 1914–1918* Tania Rose. The Lampada Press *publishes* well-researched popular works, mainly of local interest. Welcomes unsolicited mss, synopses and ideas for books.

Royalties paid annually. *Overseas representatives*: Paul & Company Publishers Consortium Inc., USA; St Clair Press, Australia.

Human Horizons
See **Souvenir Press Ltd**

Human Science Press
See **Plenum Publishing Ltd**

Hunt & Thorpe

Laurel House, Station Approach, Alresford, Hampshire SO24 9JH
☎01962 735633   Fax 01962 735320
Approx. Annual Turnover £1.5 million

Publishes children's and religious titles only. About 25 titles a year. Unsolicited material welcome.

C. Hurst & Co.

38 King Street, London WC2E 8JZ
☎0171 240 2666   Fax 0171 240 2667
Chairman/Managing Director
  Christopher Hurst
Editorial Heads *Christopher Hurst,*
  Michael Dwyer

FOUNDED 1967. An independent company, cultivating a concern for literacy, detail and the visual aspects of the product. *Publishes* contemporary history, politics and social science. About 20 titles a year. TITLES *The Origins of Japanese Trade Supremacy; The Rwanda Crisis – History of a Genocide; Listening People, Speaking Earth: Contemporary Paganism; Yugoslavia's Bloody Collapse; Following Ho Chi Minh – Memoirs of a North Vietnamese Colonel.* No unsolicited mss. Synopses and ideas welcome.

Royalties paid twice in first year, annually thereafter.

Hutchinson Books Ltd
See **Random House UK Ltd**

Hymns Ancient & Modern Ltd

St Mary's Works, St Mary's Plain, Norwich, Norfolk NR3 3BH
☎01603 616563   Fax 01603 624483
Chairman *Very Rev. Dr Henry Chadwick KBE*
Chief Executive *G. A. Knights*
Publisher, The Canterbury Press Norwich
  Christine Smith
Publisher, RMEP *Mary Mears*
Approx. Annual Turnover £3.2 million

Publishes hymn books for churches, schools and other institutions. All types of religious books, both general and educational.

IMPRINTS
The Canterbury Press Norwich General religious books TITLES *The Desert; Stars and Angels; Every Gate; Pilgrim Guides.* **Chansitor Publications Ltd** TITLES *The Sign; Home Words* – two monthly, nationwide parish magazine inserts. **Religious and Moral Education Press (RMEP)** Religious books for schools, primary, middle secondary, assembly material, etc. **G. J. Palmer & Sons Ltd** TITLES *Church Times* (see entry under **Magazines**). Ideas welcome; no mss.

Royalties paid annually.

Icon Books Ltd

Grange Road, Duxford, Cambridge CB2 4QF
☎01763 208008   Fax 01763 208080
Managing Director *Peter Pugh*
Editorial Head *Richard Appignanesi*
Publishing Director *Jeremy Cox*

FOUNDED 1992. *Publishes* 'Beginners' – cartoon introductions to the key figures and issues in the history of science, psychology, philosophy, religion and the arts. 50 titles in 1996. TITLES *Barthes for Beginners; Thatcher for Beginners; Foucault for Beginners; Sociology for Beginners.* No unsolicited mss; synopses and ideas for information non-fiction welcome.

Royalties paid twice yearly. *Overseas associates* Totem Books, USA.

Idol
See **Virgin Publishing Ltd**

Impact Books Ltd

Axe and Bottle Court, 70 Newcomen Street, London SE1 1YT
☎0171 403 3541   Fax 0171 407 6437
Managing Director *Jean-Luc Barbanneau*
Approx. Annual Turnover £150,000

FOUNDED 1985 by Jean-Luc Barbanneau, also Managing Director of Websters International Publishers. *Publishes* travel, practical guides, reference, illustrated books. About 20 titles a year. TITLES *By Bicycle in Ireland* (new edition) M. Ryle; *Chasing the Lizard's Tail* J. Finke; *French Glossary of Banking Terms*. Unsolicited mss not welcome – send detailed synopses and sample chapters first.
Royalties paid twice-yearly.

Indigo

See **Cassell**

Institute of Personnel and Development

IPD House, Camp Road, London SW19 4UX
☎0181 263 3387

Part of IPD Enterprises Limited. *Publishes* management and training. 30 titles in 1996. Unsolicited mss, synopses and ideas welcome.
Royalties paid annually.

Inter Publishing Ltd

St Nicholas House, The Mount, Guildford, Surrey GU2 4NH
☎01483 306309   Fax 01483 579196
Managing Director *David Wavre*
Approx. Annual Turnover £500,000

FOUNDED 1990. *Publishes* religious plus some gift and art books. About 24 titles a year. IMPRINT **Eagle**. Unsolicited mss, synopses and ideas for books welcome.
Royalties paid quarterly.

Inter-Varsity Press

38 De Montfort Street, Leicester LE1 7GP
☎0116 2551754   Fax 0116 2542044
Chairman *Ralph Evershed*
Chief Executive *Frank Entwistle*

FOUNDED mid-30s as the publishing arm of Universities and Colleges Christian Fellowship, it has expanded to wider Christian markets worldwide. *Publishes* Christian belief and lifestyle, reference and bible commentaries. About 50 titles a year. No secular material or anything which fails to empathise with orthodox Protestant Christianity.

IMPRINTS **IVP**; **Apollos**; **Crossway** TITLES *The Bible Speaks Today; Sociology through the Eyes of Faith* Campolo & Fraser. No unsolicited mss; synopses and ideas welcome.
Royalties paid twice-yearly.

Intrigue

See **Harlequin Mills & Boon Ltd**

Invincible Press

See **HarperCollins Publishers Ltd**

Isis Publishing Limited

7 Centremead, Osney Mead, Oxford OX2 0ES
☎01865 250333   Fax 01865 790358
Managing Director *John Durrant*

Publishes large-print books – fiction and non-fiction; audio books (see entry under **Audio Books**). TITLES *The Colour of Magic* Terry Pratchett; *The Book of Guys* Garrison Keillor; *The Rise and Fall of the House of Windsor*. No unsolicited mss as Isis undertake no original publishing.
Royalties paid twice-yearly.

Ithaca Press

See **Garnet Publishing Ltd**

IVP

See **Inter-Varsity Press**

JAI Press Ltd

38 Tavistock Street, London WC2E 7PB
☎0171 379 8834   Fax 0171 379 8835
Chairman *Herbert M. Johnson*
Managing Director *Piers R. Allen*

FOUNDED 1976. Subsidiary of JAI Press, Inc., USA. *Publishes* research-level scholarly publications in business, economics, social sciences, computer sciences, chemistry and life sciences, spanning the complete range of social and economic sciences, natural, pure and applied physical sciences. *Specialises* in the publication of research serials and monograph series, as well as journals. About 170 titles a year. TITLES *Advances in Biosensors; Research in Organizational Behavior; Research in Accounting in Emerging Economies; Studies in Qualitative Methodology*. No undergraduate texts. Unsolicited mss discouraged. Synopses and ideas welcome.
Royalties paid annually. *Overseas associates* JAI Press, Inc./Ablex Publishing Corp., Greenwich, Connecticut, USA.

Arthur James Ltd

70 Cross Oak Road, Berkhamsted,
Hertfordshire HP4 3HZ
☎01442 877511   Fax 01442 873019
Editorial Office: Deershot Lodge, Park Lane,
Ropley, Nr Alresford, Hampshire SO24 0BE
Managing Director *Ian Carlile*
Editorial Director *Mr J. Hunt*
Approx. Annual Turnover £165,000

FOUNDED 1944 by a Fleet Street journalist, A. J.
Russell. *Publishes* day books, devotional classics,
psychological, healing, religious, social work and
New Testament translations. AUTHORS include
Karen Armstrong, William Barclay, Jacques
Duquesne, Laurence Freeman, Monica Furlong,
Rosemary Harthill, Sara Maitland, Chuck
Spezzano, Angela Tilby, Robert Van de Weyer,
Marina Warner, John Woolley. No unsolicited
mss.
  Royalties paid annually. *Overseas associates*
Buchanan, Australia; Omega, New Zealand.

Jane's Information Group

163 Brighton Road, Coulsdon, Surrey
CR5 2NH
☎0181 700 3700   Fax 0181 763 1006
Managing Director *Alfred Rolington*
Approx. Annual Turnover £18 million

FOUNDED 1898 by Fred T. Jane with the publication of *All The World's Fighting Ships*. Now
part of The Thomson Corporation. In recent
years management, has been focusing on growth
opportunities in its core business and in enhan-
cing the performance of initiatives like Jane's
yearbooks on CD-ROM. *Publishes* reviews and
yearbooks on defence, aerospace and transport
topics, with details of equipment and systems;
plus directories and strategic studies. Also *Jane's
Defence Weekly* (see entry under **Magazines**).
  Publishing Division *Robert Hutchinson*
TITLES *Jane's Defence Weekly; Jane's International
Defense Review; Jane's Intelligence Review; Jane's
Defence Upgrades; Jane's Navy International;
Defence, Aerospace Yearbooks; Jane's Airport Review;
Foreign Report; Jane's Sentinel* (regional security
assessment); *Transportation Yearbooks*; CD-ROM
and electronic development and publication.
Unsolicited mss, synopses and ideas for books
welcome.
  Royalties paid twice-yearly. *Overseas associates*
Jane's Information Group Inc., USA.

Janus Publishing Company Ltd

Edinburgh House, 19 Nassau Street, London
W1N 7RE
☎0171 580 7664   Fax 0171 636 5756

Managing Director *Ronald Ross Stanton*
Publishes fiction, human interest, memoirs/biog-
raphy, mind, body and spirit, religion and theol-
ogy, social questions, popular science, history,
spiritualism and the paranormal, poetry, children
and young adults. About 70 titles. TITLES *Not
Just Another Club – The Story of Manchester United*
Stan Liversedge; *Spinozan Power* Tom Rubens;
In Pursuit of Physical Mediumship Robin Foy; *The
Unknown Coleridge* Raymonde Hainton; *Kaptan
June & the Turtles* June Haimoff. Unsolicited mss
welcome.
  Royalties paid twice-yearly. Agents in the
USA, Australia, South Africa and Asia.

Authors' Rating Authors may be asked to
cover their own productions costs.

Japan Library

See **Curzon Press Ltd**

Jarrold Publishing

Whitefriars, Norwich, Norfolk NR3 1TR
☎01603 763300   Fax 01603 662748
Managing Director *Antony Jarrold*
Part of Jarrold & Sons Ltd, long-established
printing/publishing company. *Publishes* UK
travel, leisure and calendars. Material tends to be
of a high pictorial content. About 30 titles a
year. Unsolicited mss, synopses and ideas welcome but before submitting anything, approach
in writing to Donald Greig, Managing Editor.
  Royalties paid twice-yearly.

Jensen Business Books

See **AMCD (Publishers) Ltd**

Jets

See **HarperCollins Publishers Ltd**

Jewish Chronicle Publications

See **Frank Cass & Co Ltd**

Michael Joseph Ltd

See **Penguin Books Ltd**

Kahn & Averill

9 Harrington Road, London SW7 3ES
☎0181 743 3278   Fax 0181 743 3278
Managing Director *Mr M. Kahn*
FOUNDED 1967 to publish children's titles but
now specialises in music titles. A small independent publishing house. *Publishes* music and
general non-fiction. No unsolicited mss; synopses and ideas for books considered.
  Royalties paid twice-yearly.

Karnak House
300 Westbourne Park Road, London W11 1EH
☎0171 221 6490   Fax 0171 221 6490
Chairman *Dimela Yekwai*
Managing Director *Amon Saba Saakana*
FOUNDED 1979. *Specialises* in African and Caribbean studies. *Publishes* anthropology, education, Egyptology, history, language and linguistics, literary criticism, music, parapsychology, prehistory. No poetry, humour or sport. About 12 titles a year. No unsolicited mss; send introduction or synopsis with one sample chapter. Synopses and ideas welcome.

Royalties paid twice–yearly. *Overseas subsidiaries* The Antef Institute, and Karnak House, Illinois, USA.

Keele University Press
See **Edinburgh University Press**

Kelpie
See **Canongate Books Ltd**

Kenilworth Press Ltd
Addington, Buckingham, Buckinghamshire MK18 2JR
☎01296 715101   Fax 01296 715148
Chairman/Managing Director *David Blunt*
Approx. Annual Turnover £500,000
FOUNDED 1989 with the acquisition of Threshhold Books. The UK's principal instructional equestrian publisher, producing the official books of the British Horse Society, the famous *Threshold Picture Guides*, and a range of authoritative titles sold around the world. About 10 titles a year.

IMPRINTS **Kenilworth Press** TITLES *British Horse Society Manuals*; *Endurance Riding: From First Steps to 100 Miles*; *A Modern Horse Herbal*; *Learn to Ride Using Sports Psychology*; *Threshold Picture Guides 1–39*. Unsolicited mss, synopses and ideas welcome but only for titles concerned with the care or riding of horses or ponies.

Royalties paid twice–yearly.

Kenyon-Deane
See **Cressrelles Publishing Co. Ltd**

Laurence King
71 Great Russell Street, London WC1B 3BN
☎0171 831 6351   Fax 0171 831 8356
Chairman *Robin Hyman*
Managing Director *Laurence King*
FOUNDED 1991. Publishing imprint of UK packager **Calmann & King Ltd** (see entry under **UK Packagers**). *Publishes* full-colour illustrated books on art history, the decorative arts, carpets and textiles, graphic design, architecture and interior design. Unsolicited material welcome.

Royalties paid twice–yearly.

Kingfisher
See **Larousse plc**

Jessica Kingsley Publishers Ltd
116 Pentonville Road, London N1 9JB
☎0171 833 2307   Fax 0171 837 2917
Managing Director *Jessica Kingsley*
Senior Editor *Charles Catton*
FOUNDED 1987. Independent publisher of books for professionals and academics on social and behavioural sciences, including arts therapies, child psychology, psychotherapy (especially forensic psychotherapy), social work, regional studies and higher education policy. Approx. 75 titles a year. 'We welcome suggestions for books and proposals from prospective authors, especially in the areas of social issues and working with children. Proposals should consist of an outline of the book, a contents list, assessment of the market, and author's c.v.. Complete manuscript should not be sent.'

Royalties paid twice yearly.

Kingsway Publications
Lottbridge Drove, Eastbourne, East Sussex BN23 6NT
☎01323 410930   Fax 01323 411970
Chairman *Peter Fenwick*
Joint Managing Directors *John Paculabo, Brian Davies*
Editorial Contact *Mrs J. Oldroyd*
Approx. Annual Turnover £1.5 million
Part of Kingsway Communications Ltd, a charitable trust with Christian objectives. *Publishes* Christian books: Bibles, Christian testimonies, renewal issues, devotional. No poetry please. About 40 titles a year.

IMPRINT
Kingsway TITLES *The Life Application Bible*; *The Father Heart of God* Floyd McClung; *Growing in the Prophetic* Mike Bickle; *Questions of Life* Nicky Gumble. Unsolicited mss welcome, but partial submissions/synopses preferred. Return postage appreciated; all submissions should be addressed to the Editorial Department.

Royalties paid annually.

Kluwer Academic Publishers

PO Box 55, Lancaster LA1 1PE
☎01524 34996   Fax 01524 32144

Managing Director Mr J. Smith
Approx. Annual Turnover £1.5 million

A member of the Dutch Kluwer Group, publisher of approximately 200 scholarly journals and 500 titles a year across an extensive range of scientific disciplines. Kluwer Academic (UK) specialises in medical, scientific and technical publishing at the postgraduate level. *Publishes* research monographs, postgraduate textbooks, colour atlases and texts for family physicians. Particular areas of medical specialisation include cardiology, nephrology, radiology, oncology, pathology, neurosciences and immunology. Mss are not considered in the UK; all material must be addressed to Wolters Kluwer Academic Publishers, PO Box 17, 3300 AA Dordrecht, The Netherlands.

Kluwer Law International

Sterling House, 66 Wilton Road, London SW1V 1DE
☎0171 821 1123   Fax 0171 630 5229

Director of Operations Marcel Nieuwenhuis

FOUNDED 1995. Parent company: Wolters Kluwer Group. Kluwer Law International consists of three components: the law list of Graham & Trotman, Kluwer Law and Taxation and Martinus Nyhoff. *Publishes* international law. Plans to publish 200 titles a year. Unsolicited synopses and ideas for books on law at an international level welcome.

Royalties paid annually. North American sales and marketing: Kluwer Law International, 675 Massachusetts Avenue, Cambridge, MA 02139.

Knight

See **Hodder Headline plc**

Charles Knight Publishing

See **Tolley Publishing Co Ltd**

Kogan Page Ltd

120 Pentonville Road, London N1 9JN
☎0171 278 0433   Fax 0171 837 3768/6348

Managing Director Philip Kogan
Approx. Annual Turnover £8 million

FOUNDED 1967 by Philip Kogan to publish *The Industrial Training Yearbook*. Member of the Euro Business Publishing Network. In 1992 acquired Earthscan Publications and launched a new management research series. *Publishes* business and management reference books and monographs, education and careers, marketing, personal finance, personnel, small business, training and industrial relations, transport, plus journals. Further expansion is planned, particularly in the professional and human resource areas, yearbooks and directories, and international business reference. About 240 titles a year.

DIVISIONS

Kogan Page *Pauline Goodwin, Philip Mudd, Peter Chadwick.* TITLES *Training and Enterprise Directory; British Vocational Qualifications.* SERIES *Working for Yourself; Careers; Better Management Skills.*

Earthscan Publications *Jonathan Sinclair Wilson* Has close associations with the International Institute for Environment and Development and with the Worldwide Fund for Nature. *Publishes* Third World issues and their global implications, and general environmental titles, both popular and academic. About 30 titles a year. TITLES *European Environmental Technology Directory.* Unsolicited mss, synopses and ideas for books welcome.

Royalties paid twice-yearly.

Authors' Rating The biggest and the best independent publisher of business books thrives on strong marketing particularly in airports and other gathering places for hungry executives.

Ladybird Books Ltd

Beeches Road, Loughborough, Leicestershire LE11 2NQ
☎01509 268021   Fax 01509 234672

Chair *Michael Lynton*
Managing Director L. F. A. *James*
Publishing Director M. H. *Gabb*
     International Director D. *King*
Approx. Annual Turnover £19 million

FOUNDED in the 1860s. Introduced just before the First World War, the Ladybird name and format was fully established as a result of the development of a children's list during the Second World War. In the early 1960s the commercial print side of the operation was abandoned in favour of publishing Ladybird titles only and in 1971 the company was bought by the Pearson Longman Group. From 1st January 1995, Ladybird has been integrated into the Penguin Group. *Publishes* children's consumer books for the mass market internationally. About 200 titles a year.

IMPRINTS

Ladybird; Key Words Reading Scheme; Picture Ladybird; Ladybird Discovery

Storybooks; Disney. TITLES *Dan and Pip's Ship; You'll Lose that Bear!; My Storytelling Sticker Activity Book; The Rainforest Animals Sticker Book; Peter Rabbit; Johnny Town Mouse; 101 Dalmatians Live Action; Toy Story*; plus the Ladybird audio cassette/book series (see entry under **Audio Books**). Non-fiction mss and ideas welcome; no unsolicited fiction; no poetry.

The Lampada Press
See **The University of Hull Press**

Langley Publishing Ltd
32 Sheen Park, Richmond, Surrey TW9 1UW
☎0181 286 3594   Fax 0181 948 0937
Chairman *Tim Little*

FOUNDED 1995. *Publishes* management training, personal development and skills for business. About 6–8 titles a year. IMPRINT **Straightforward Guides** TITLES *Answering the Tough Interview Questions; Power CVs and Interview Letters – That Really Work; Redundancy – Threat or Opportunity*. Unsolicited mss welcome, 'but our style is important – phone for the Authors' Information Pack first'. Synopses and ideas welcome.

Royalties paid quarterly.

Larousse plc
Elsley House, 24–30 Great Titchfield Street, London W1P 7AD
☎0171 631 0878   Fax 0171 323 4694
Chairman *John Clement*

FOUNDED 1994 when owners, Groupe de la Cité (also publishers of the Larousse dictionaries in France), merged their UK operations of **Grisewood & Dempsey** and **Chambers Harrap Publishers Ltd**. Larousse publishes under the **Kingfisher, Chambers, Harrap** and **Larousse** imprints.

IMPRINTS
Chambers *Maurice Shepherd, Min Lee* Editorial offices: 7 Hopetoun Crescent, Edinburgh EH7 4AY. ☎0131 556 5929 Fax: 0131 556 5313. *Publishes* dictionaries, reference, and local interest. The imprint was founded in the early 1800s to publish self-education books, but soon diversified into dictionaries and other reference works. Acquired by Groupe de la Cité in 1989. The acquisition of **Harrap Publishing Group**'s core business strengthened its position in the dictionary market, adding bilingual titles, covering almost all the major European languages, to its English-language dictionaries. Send synopsis with accompanying letter rather than completed mss.

Kingfisher *Ann-Janine Murtagh* Fiction, *Ann Davies* Non-fiction (Based at London address above.) Founded in 1973 by **Grisewood & Dempsey Ltd**. *Publishes* children's fiction and non-fiction in hardback and paperback: story books, rhymes and picture books, fiction and poetry anthologies, young non-fiction, activity books, general series and reference.

Royalties paid bi-annually where applicable.

Lawrence & Wishart Ltd
99A Wallis Road, London E9 5LN
☎0181 533 2506   Fax 0181 533 7369
Managing Director *Sally Davison*
Editors *Sally Davison, Bertie Vitry*

FOUNDED 1936. An independent publisher with a substantial backlist. *Publishes* current affairs, cultural politics, economics, history, politics and education. 15–20 titles a year. TITLES *Reclaiming Truth: A Contribution to a Critique of Cultural Relativism; The Acceptable Face of Feminism, A History of the Women's Institute; The Body Language: The Meaning of Modern Sport*. Synopses preferred to complete mss. Ideas welcome.

Royalties paid annually, unless by arrangement.

Authors' Rating One of the few genuine left-wing publishers. Authors should expect to surrender profit to principles.

Legend
See **Random House UK Ltd**

Lehigh University Press
See **Golden Cockerel Press Ltd**

Leicester University Press
See **Cassell**

Lennard Associates Ltd
Windmill Cottage, Mackerye End, Harpenden, Hertfordshire AL5 5DR
☎01582 715866   Fax 01582 715121
Chairman/Managing Director *Adrian Stephenson*

FOUNDED 1979. Publisher of sporting yearbooks, personality books, and television associated titles. TITLES *The Cricketers' Who's Who; Official PFA Footballers' Factfile; Wooden Spoon Society Rugby World; British Boxing Yearbook*. No unsolicited mss.

IMPRINTS **Lennard Publishing; Queen Anne Press**. Acquired the latter and most of its assets in 1992.

Payment both fees and royalties by arrangement.

Charles Letts
See **New Holland (Publishers) Ltd**

Levinson Children's Books
Greenland Place, 115–123 Bayham Street, London NW1 0AG
☎0171 424 0488   Fax 0171 424 0499
Managing Director *Joanna Levinson*
Senior Editor *Kate Burns*

FOUNDED in 1994 by Joanna Levinson to publish children's books. *Specialises* in novelty and picture books for the under-sevens. Unsolicited mss, synopses and ideas welcome.
Royalties paid twice yearly.

Liaison
See **Hodder Headline plc**

John Libbey & Co. Ltd
13 Smiths Yard, Summerley Street, London SW18 4HR
☎0181 947 2777   Fax 0181 947 2664
Chairman/Managing Director *John Libbey*

FOUNDED 1979. *Publishes* medical books only. TITLES *Progress in Obesity Research; Current Problems in Epilepsy.* About 20 titles a year. Synopses and ideas welcome for both specialist areas. *Overseas subsidiaries* John Libbey Eurotext Ltd, France; John Libbey-Cic, Italy; John Libbey & Co. Pty. Ltd, Australia.

Librapharm Ltd
Gemini House, 162 Craven Road, Newbury, Berkshire RG14 5NR
☎01635 522651   Fax 01635 522651
Chairman *Dr R. B. Smith*
Managing Director *Dr P. L. Clarke*
Approx. Annual Turnover £500,000

FOUNDED 1995 as a partial buyout from Kluwer Academic Publishers (UK) academic list. *Publishes* medical and scientific books and periodicals. 8 titles a year. IMPRINT **Petroc Press**. TITLES *Fry's Common Diseases; Neighbour: The Inner Consultation; Current Medical Research and Opinion* (journal). Unsolicited mss, synopses and ideas for medical books welcome.
Royalties paid twice-yearly.

Library Association Publishing
7 Ridgmount Street, London WC1E 7AE
☎0171 636 7543   Fax 0171 636 3627
Chairman *Michael Carmel*
Managing Director *Janet Liebster*

Publishing arm of **The Library Association**. *Publishes* library and information science,
monographs, reference, IT books and bibliography. About 30 titles a year.
IMPRINTS **Library Association Publishing**; **Clive Bingley Books** Over 200 titles in print, including *Walford's Guide to Reference Material* and *AACR2*. Unsolicited mss, synopses and ideas welcome provided material falls firmly within the company's specialist subject areas.
Royalties paid annually.

Frances Lincoln Ltd
4 Torriano Mews, Torriano Avenue, London, NW5 2RZ
☎0171 284 4009   Fax 0171 267 5249
Managing Director *Frances Lincoln*

FOUNDED 1977. *Publishes* highly illustrated non-fiction: gardening, interiors, health, crafts, cookery; children's picture and information books, art and religion books; and stationery. About 45 titles a year.

DIVISIONS
Adult Non-fiction *Erica Hunningher* TITLES *The Gardener's Book of Colour* Andrew Lawson; *Paint: Decorating with Water-based Paints* John Sutcliffe; *Easy Exercises for Pregnancy* Janet Balaskas; **Children's General Fiction and Non-fiction** *Janetta Otter-Barry* TITLES *The Wanderings of Odysseus* Rosemary Sutcliffe, illus. Alan Lee; *Amazing Grace, Grace & Family* Mary Hoffman, illus. Caroline Binch; **Children's Art and Religion** *Kate Cave* TITLES *My Sticker Art Gallery* Carole Armstrong; *Stories from the Old Testament* illustrated with paintings from art galleries around the world. Synopses and ideas for books considered.
Royalties paid twice-yearly.

Linden Press
See **Centaur Press**

Lion Publishing
Peter's Way, Sandy Lane West, Oxford OX4 5HG
☎01865 747550   Fax 01865 747568
Managing Director *Paul Clifford*
Approx. Annual Turnover £7 million

FOUNDED 1971. A Christian book publisher, strong on illustrated books for a popular international readership, with rights sold in over 100 languages worldwide. *Publishes* a diverse list with Christian viewpoint the common denominator. All ages, from board books for children to multi-contributor adult reference, educational, paperbacks and colour co-editions and gift books. Also developing a strong multimedia list.

DIVISIONS **Adult** *Lois Rock*; **Children's** *Su Box*; **Giftlines** *Meryl Doney*; **Multimedia** *Tim Hubbard*. Unsolicited mss welcome provided they have a positive Christian viewpoint intended for a wide general and international readership. Synopses, proposals and ideas also welcome.

Royalties paid twice-yearly.

Little, Brown & Co. (UK)

Brettenham House, Lancaster Place, London WC2E 7EN
☎0171 911 8000   Fax 0171 911 8100
Chief Executive/Publisher *Philippa Harrison*
Approx. Annual Turnover £33 million
FOUNDED 1988. Part of Time-Warner Inc. Began by importing its US parent company's titles and in 1990 launched its own illustrated non-fiction list. Two years later the company took over former Macdonald & Co. *Publishes* hardback and paperback fiction, literary fiction, crime, science fiction and fantasy; and general non-fiction, including illustrated: architecture and design, fine art, photography, biography and autobiography, cinema, gardening, history, humour, travel, crafts and hobbies, reference, cookery, wines and spirits, DIY, guidebooks, natural history and nautical.

IMPRINTS
Abacus *Richard Beswick* Literary fiction and non-fiction paperbacks; **Orbit** *Tim Holman* Science fiction and fantasy; **Little Brown/Warner** *Alan Samson, Barbara Boote, Hilary Hale* Mass-market fiction and non-fiction; **X Libris** *Helen Pisano* Women's erotica; **Illustrated** *Julia Charles* Hardbacks; **Virago** (see entry). Approach in writing in the first instance. No unsolicited mss.

Royalties paid twice-yearly.

Authors' Rating At the smaller end of the major publishers, Little, Brown combines editorial inspiration with strong marketing, living proof that quality can thrive in a highly competitive market.

Liverpool University Press

Senate House, Abercromby Square, Liverpool L69 3BX
☎0151 794 2233   Fax 0151 794 2235
Managing Director/Editorial Head
   Robin Bloxsidge
The principal activity of LUP, since its foundation in 1899, has been in the humanities and social sciences. *Publishes* academic and scholarly hardback and paperback books in the fields of archaeology, education, geography, ancient and modern history, science fiction criticism, modern French literature, English literature, Hispanic languages and literature, town planning and veterinary medicine. 30–40 titles a year. TITLES *Charles Reilly and the Liverpool School of Architecture; Sigmar Polke: Back to Postmodernity; Donatist Martyr Stories; 'The Angle Between Two Walls'; The Fiction of J. G. Ballard; The Plays of Lord Byron; The Erotics of Passage; Liverpool Accents: Seven Poets and a City*. Unsolicited mss, synopses and ideas for books welcome.

Royalties paid annually.

Livewire Books for Teenagers
See **The Women's Press**

Living Books

Allen House, Station Road, Egham, Surrey TW20 9NT
☎01784 431000   Fax 01784 431382
Chairman (Europe) *Jo Wood*
Managing Director (Europe) *Pilar Cloud*
FOUNDED 1994. Subsidiary of the US leading producer of children's multimedia storybooks on CD-ROM. Part of Broderbund Software Ltd. 4 titles in 1996. TITLES *Dr Seuss' ABC; Harry and the Haunted House; Little Monster at School; The Tortoise and the Hare*.

IMPRINT **Living Books/TAG Developments** TITLES *Just Grandma and Me, Teacher's Guide; Sheila Rae, The Brave Teacher's Guide*. No unsolicited mss.

Lord of Barton Publications

The Chippings, Wark, Northumberland NE48 3LB
☎01434 230000   Fax 01434 230000
Chairman *Arnold Baker, Kt.S., Baron of Barton*
Managing Director *Baroness Baker of Barton*
Approx. Annual Turnover £250,000
FOUNDED 1995 due to the receipt of a large legacy. A small family publisher with 'ambitious plans for expansion in 1998'. *Publishes* cookery, antique clocks, fishing, history and fiction. 6 titles in 1996. TITLES *A Fisherman's Tale; Food for Thought; In Search of Tranquility; A Clock Fit for a Duke*. No political, religious, violent, travel or children's books. Unsolicited mss, synopses and ideas welcome.

Royalties paid twice yearly.

Lorenz Books
See **Anness Publishing Ltd**

Peter Lowe (Eurobook Ltd)

PO Box 52, Wallingford, Oxfordshire
OX10 0XU
☎01865 749033   Fax 01865 749044

Managing Director *Peter Lowe*

FOUNDED 1968. *Publishes* children's natural
history, popular science and illustrated adult
non-fiction. No unsolicited mss; synopses and
ideas (with s.a.e.) welcome. No adult fiction.

Lund Humphries Publishers Ltd

Park House, 1 Russell Gardens, London
NW11 9NN
☎0181 458 6314   Fax 0181 905 5245

Chairman *Lionel Leventhal*
Editorial Director *Lucy Myers*

Publisher of fine art books. First title appeared
in 1895. *Publishes* art, architecture, photography, design and graphics. Publishers of exhibition catalogues in association with museums
and galleries, and of the annual *Calendar of Art
Exhibitions*. About 20 titles a year. There are
plans to expand the graphic arts and design list
in the years to come. Unsolicited mss welcome
but initial introductory letter preferred.
Synopses and ideas for books considered.
  Royalties paid twice-yearly.

The Lutterworth Press

PO Box 60, Cambridge CB1 2NT
☎01223 350865   Fax 01223 366951

Managing Director *Adrian Brink*

The Lutterworth Press dates back to the 18th
century when it was founded by the Religious
Tract Society. In the 19th century it was best
known for its children's books, both religious
and secular, including *The Boys' Own Paper*.
Since 1984 it has been an imprint of **James
Clarke & Co**. *Publishes* religious books for
children and adults, children's fiction and non-
fiction, adult non-fiction. TITLES *Cruden's
Concordance to the Bible* (new format); *Christopher:
The Holy Giant*; *Armies of Pestilence*. Approach in
writing with ideas in the first instance.
  Royalties paid annually.

Authors' Rating The list is expanding but it
still has its anchor in evangelical publishing.
Imaginative children's list.

Lynx

See **Society for Promoting Christian
Knowledge**

M & N Publishing Company Ltd

1–3 Lion Chambers, John William Street,
Huddersfield, West Yorkshire HD1 1ES
☎01535 559377(M&N Books)/559101(Falcon)
Fax 01484 559293

Managing Director *R. S. Byram*

Publishes general fiction and non-fiction.
Unsolicited synopses and ideas welcome. Initial
contact by phone or in writing; do not submit
mss in the first instance.
  IMPRINTS **M & N Books** *Jennifer Todd*
Literary fiction and general non-fiction paperbacks; **Blot Books** *Jennifer Todd* Books for
children in interesting formats; **Falcon Books**
H. L. Byram Fiction, biography and autobiography, general non-fiction paperbacks.

Authors' Rating Liable to ask authors to contribute towards costs of publication.

Macdonald & Co.

See **Little, Brown & Co. (UK)**

Macdonald Young Books

See **Wayland Publishers Ltd**

McGraw-Hill Book Co. Europe

McGraw-Hill House, Shoppenhangers Road,
Maidenhead, Berkshire SL6 2QL
☎01628 23432   Fax 01628 770958

Group Vice President, Europe *Kevin O'Brian*

FOUNDED 1899. Owned by US parent company. Began publishing in Maidenhead in 1965.
Publishes business and economics, engineering,
computer science, business computing and
training for the academic, student, trade and
professional markets. Around 100 titles a year.
Unsolicited mss, synopses and ideas welcome.
  Royalties paid twice-yearly.

Authors' Rating Number 5 in the list of publishers by title output, McGraw-Hill is heavily
into electronic publishing.

Macmillan Publishers Ltd

25 Eccleston Place, London SW1W 9NF
☎0171 881 8000   Fax 0171 881 8001

Chairman *Nicholas Byam Shaw*
Deputy Chairman, Pan Macmillan
  Christopher Paterson
**Managing Director, UK Book Publishing
  Division** *Adrian Soar*
Approx. Annual Turnover £90 million
(Book Publishing Group)

FOUNDED 1843. Macmillan is one of the largest
publishing house in Britain, publishing approximately 1400 titles a year. In 1995, Verlags-

gruppe Georg von Holtzbrinck, a major German publisher, acquired a majority stake in the Macmillan Group. In 1996 Macmillan bought Boxtree, the successful media tie-in publisher. Unsolicited proposals, synopses and mss are welcome in all divisions of the company (with the exception of Macmillan Children's Books). Authors who wish to send material to Macmillan General Books should note that there is a central submissions procedure in operation. For these divisions, send a synopsis and the first 3–4 chapters with a covering letter and return postage to the Submissions Editor, 25 Eccleston Place, London SW1W 9NF.

DIVISIONS

Macmillan Press Ltd Brunel Road, Houndsmill, Basingstoke, Hampshire RG21 6XS ☎01256 329242 Fax 01256 479476 Managing Director *Dominic Knight*. **Academic** *T. M. Familoe*; **Higher Education** *S. Kennedy*; **Further Education** *J. Winckler*, **Business and Economics** *S. Rutt*. *Publishes* textbooks and monographs in academic, professional and vocational subjects; medical and scientific journals; directories. Publications in both hard copy and electronic format.

Macmillan Education Basingstoke (address as for Macmillan Press). Managing Director *Chris Harrison*, Publishing Director *Alison Hubert*. *Publishes* regional ELT titles and a wide list for the international education market.

Macmillan General Books (Eccleston Place address). Managing Director *Ian S. Chapman*, Editor-in-Chief *Clare Alexander*. Publishes under **Macmillan**, **Pan**, **Papermac**, **Sidgwick & Jackson**

Macmillan (FOUNDED 1865) Executive Editorial Director (fiction) *Suzanne Baboneau*. *Publishes* novels, detective fiction, sci-fi, fantasy and horror. Publishing Director (non-fiction) *Georgina Morley,* Editorial Director (non-fiction) *Catherine Hurley*. *Publishes* autobiography, biography, business and industry, crafts and hobbies, economics, gift books, health and beauty, history, humour, natural history, travel, philosophy, politics and world affairs, psychology, theatre and drama, gardening and cookery, encyclopedias.

Pan (FOUNDED 1947) Publisher *Peter Lavery*. *Publishes* fiction: novels, detective fiction, sci-fi, fantasy and horror. Non-fiction: sports and games, theatre and drama, travel, gardening and cookery.

Papermac (FOUNDED 1965) Publisher *Jon Riley*, Senior Editor *Tanya Stobbs*. Serious non-fiction: history, biography, science, political economy, cultural criticism and art history.

Picador (FOUNDED 1972) Publisher *Jon Riley*, Editorial Director *Ursula Doyle*. *Publishes* literary international fiction and non-fiction.

Sidgwick & Jackson (FOUNDED 1908) Publishing Director *Georgina Morley*. *Publishes* military and war, music, pop and rock. Mss, synopses and ideas welcome.

Macmillan Children's Books (Eccleston Place address). Publisher *Kate Wilson*; **Fiction** *Marion Lloyd*; **Non-fiction** *Susie Gibbs*; **Picture Books** *Alison Green*. IMPRINTS **Macmillan, Pan, Campbell Books**. *Publishes* novels, board books, picture books, non-fiction (illustrated and non-illustrated), poetry and novelty books in paperback and hardback. No unsolicited material.

Macmillan Reference Ltd (Eccleston Place address). Managing Director *Ian Jacobs*. **Science** *Gina Fullerlove*; **Grove's Dictionaries of Music** *Margot Levy*; **Directories** *Neil Smith*. *Publishes* works of reference in academic, professional and vocational subjects; dictionaries; *The New Grove Dictionary of Music and Musicians*, ed. Stanley Sadie; and *The Dictionary of Art*, ed. Jane Turner.

Boxtree (Eccleston Place address). Managing Director *Adrian Sington*, Editorial Director *Susanna Wadeson*. *Publishes* books linked to and about television; also video and music. About 150 titles a year. TITLES *Mr Bean, Dilbert, Coronation Street, Lost World – Jurassic Park, Friends, James Bond*, also Robert Carrier and Anton Mosimann.

Royalties paid annually or twice-yearly depending on contract.

Authors' Rating The strength of Macmillan is in its big investment projects like *Grove's Dictionary of Music* and *The Dictionary of Art*. The general divisions present a less happy picture with efforts to produce a successful formula frustrated by frequent staff changes. Negotiations with the Society of Authors for a Minimum Terms Agreement promise a long haul.

Julia MacRae
See **Random House UK Ltd**

Mad Jack
See **Henderson Publishing Limited**

Madcap
See **André Deutsch Ltd**

Magi Publications

22 Manchester Street, London W1M 5PG
☎0171 486 0925   Fax 0171 486 0926
Publisher *Monty Bhatia*
Editor *Linda Jennings*
Approx. Annual Turnover £1 million

FOUNDED 1987. *Publishes* children's picture books only. About 24 titles a year. Unsolicited mss, synopses and ideas welcome, but please telephone first.
Royalties paid annually.

Magic Jewellery

See **Henderson Publishing Limited**

Mainstream Publishing Co. (Edinburgh) Ltd

7 Albany Street, Edinburgh EH1 3UG
☎0131 557 2959   Fax 0131 556 8720
Directors *Bill Campbell, Peter MacKenzie*
Approx. Annual Turnover £2.2 million

Publishes art, autobiography/biography, current affairs, health, history, illustrated and fine editions, photography and sport, politics and world affairs, popular paperbacks. Over 60 titles a year. Ideas for books considered, but they should be preceded by a letter, synopsis and s.a.e. or return postage.
Royalties paid twice-yearly.

Authors' Rating A Scottish company aiming for a British profile. Keen on finding authors who 'can develop with us'.

Mammoth Paperbacks

See **Reed Books**

Management Books 2000 Ltd

Cowcombe House, Cowcombe Hill,
Chalford, Gloucestershire GL6 8HPW
☎01285 760722   Fax 01285 760708
Managing Director *Nicholas Dale-Harris*
Approx. Annual Turnover £500,000

FOUNDED 1993 to develop a range of books for executives and managers working in the modern world of business, supplemented with information through other media like seminars, audio and video. *Publishes* business and management and sponsored titles. About 30 titles a year. Unsolicited mss, synopses and ideas for books welcome.

Manchester United Books

See **André Deutsch Ltd**

Manchester University Press

Oxford Road, Manchester M13 9NR
☎0161 273 5539   Fax 0161 274 3346
Publisher/Chief Executive *David Rodgers*
Approx. Annual Turnover £1.7 million

FOUNDED at the turn of the century and now Britain's third largest university press, with a list marketed and sold internationally. Originally based on history, MUP's list has expanded to cover the humanities, social sciences and academic books from A-level texts to research monographs. *Publishes* academic and educational books in literature, cultural and media studies, history, art and architecture, politics, international law, economics and modern languages. Also more general books, notably on genealogy, history and the North-west of England. About 120 titles a year, plus journals. Launched a new paperback imprint in 1997, **Mandolin**, to publish new work and reprints with a trade/mass-market appeal while retaining academic authority.

DIVISIONS
Humanities *Matthew Frost*; **History** *Vanessa Graham*; **Politics and Economics** *Nicola Viinikka*. Unsolicited mss welcome.
Royalties paid annually.

Mandarin

See **Random House UK Ltd**

Mandolin

See **Manchester University Press**

George Mann Books

PO Box 22, Maidstone, Kent ME14 1AH
☎01622 759591   Fax 01622 759591
Chairman & Managing Director *George Mann*

FOUNDED 1972, originally as library reprint publishers, but has moved on to other things with the collapse of the library market. *Publishes* original non-fiction and selected reprints. Until further notice, not considering new fiction for publication. Launched a new imprint called **Recollections** in 1992 for subsidised publication of books of an autobiographical/biographical nature, for which unlimited editorial advice and assistance can be made available.

IMPRINTS
George Mann; **Arnefold**; **Recollections**. No unsolicited mss; send preliminary letter with synopsis. Material not accompanied by return postage will neither be read nor returned.
Royalties paid twice-yearly.

Mansell
See **Cassell**

Manson Publishing Ltd
73 Corringham Road, London NW11 7DL
☎0181 905 5150   Fax 0181 201 9233
Chairman/Managing Director *Michael Manson*
Approx. Annual Turnover £600,000
FOUNDED 1992. *Publishes* scientific, technical, medical and veterinary. 20 titles in 1997. No unsolicited mss; synopses and ideas will be considered.
Royalties paid twice-yearly.

Marc
See **Monarch Publications**

Marshall Pickering
See **HarperCollins Publishers Ltd**

Marston House
Marston House, Marston Magna, Yeovil, Somerset BA22 8DH
☎01935 851331   Fax 01935 851331
Managing Director/Editorial Head *Anthony Birks-Hay*
Approx. Annual Turnover £200,000
FOUNDED 1989. Publishing imprint of book packager Alphabet & Image Ltd. *Publishes* fine art, architecture, ceramics. 4 titles a year.
Royalties paid twice-yearly, or flat fee in lieu of royalties.

Mask Noir
See **Serpent's Tail**

Kenneth Mason Publications Ltd
Dudley House, 12 North Street, Emsworth, Hampshire PO10 7DQ
☎01243 377977   Fax 01243 379136
Chairman *Kenneth Mason*
Managing Director *Piers Mason*
Approx. Annual Turnover £500,000
FOUNDED 1958. *Publishes* diet, health, fitness, nutrition and nautical. No fiction. 15 titles in 1996. Initial approach by letter with synopsis preferred. IMPRINT **Boatswain Press**.
Royalties paid twice-yearly (Jun/Dec) in first year, annually (Dec) thereafter.

Kevin Mayhew Ltd
Rattlesden, Bury St Edmunds, Suffolk IP30 0SZ
☎01449 737978   Fax 01449 737834
Chairman *Kevin Mayhew*

Managing Director *Gordon Carter*
Approx. Annual Turnover £3 million
FOUNDED in 1976. One of the leading sacred music and Christian book publishers in the UK. *Publishes* religious titles – liturgy, sacramental, devotional, also children's books and school resources. 200 titles in 1996. TITLES *Hymns Old & New (Anglican Edition); More Things to do in Children's Worship.* Unsolicited synopses and mss should be sent only after consultation.
IMPRINT **Palm Tree Press** *Kevin Mayhew* Bible stories, colouring/activity and puzzle books for children.
Royalties paid annually.

The Medici Society Ltd
34–42 Pentonville Road, London N1 9HG
☎0171 837 7099   Fax 0171 837 9152
Art Director *Charles Howell*
FOUNDED 1908. *Publishes* illustrated children's fiction, art and nature. About 6 titles a year. No unsolicited mss; send synopses with specimen illustrations only.
Royalties paid annually.

Melrose Press Ltd
3 Regal Lane, Soham, Ely, Cambridgeshire CB7 5BA
☎01353 721091   Fax 01353 721839
Chairman *Richard A. Kay*
Managing Director *Nicholas S. Law*
Approx. Annual Turnover £2 million
FOUNDED 1960. Took on its present name in 1969. *Publishes* biographical who's who reference only (not including *Who's Who*, which is published by **A. & C. Black**).
DIVISIONS **International Biographical Centre** *Jocelyn Timothy.* TITLES *International Authors and Writers Who's Who; International Who's Who in Music; Who's Who in Australasia and the Pacific Nations; International Who's Who in Poetry.*

Mentor
See **Christian Focus Publications**

Mercat Press
53 South Bridge, Edinburgh EH1 1YS
☎0131 556 6743   Fax 0131 557 8149
Chairman/Managing Director *D. Ainslie Thin*
Editorial Heads *Tom Johnstone, Seán Costello*
FOUNDED 1971 as an adjunct to the large Scottish-based bookselling chain of James Thin. Began by publishing reprints of classic Scottish

literature but has since expanded into publishing new non-fiction titles. In 1992 the company acquired the bulk of the stock of Aberdeen University Press, a victim of the collapse of the Maxwell empire. The backlist expanded greatly as a result and now stands at around 300 titles. New titles are added regularly. *Publishes* Scottish classics reprints and non-fiction of Scottish interest, mainly historical and literary. TITLES *The Scot's Herbal* Tess Darwin; *Scotland's Place-names* David Dorward; *Playing for Scotland: A History of the Scottish Stage* Donald Campbell; *The Scots Kitchen* F. Marian McNeill; *Scotichronicon* Walter Bower. Unsolicited synopses of non-fiction Scottish interest books, preferably with sample chapters, are welcome. No new fiction or poetry.
Royalties paid annually.

Merehurst Fairfax
Ferry House, 51–57 Lacy Road, London SW15 1PR
☎0181 780 1177   Fax 0181 780 1714
Chief Executive Officer *Graham Fill*
Publishing Director *Shirley Patton*
Approx. Annual Turnover £4.5 million
Owned by Australian media group J. B. Fairfax International Ltd. *Publishes* full-colour non-fiction: cake decorating, cookery, craft, gardening, homes and interiors, children's crafts and hobbies. About 60 titles a year. Synopses and ideas for books welcome; no unsolicited mss.
Royalties paid twice-yearly.

The Merlin Press Ltd
2 Rendlesham Mews, Rendlesham, Nr Woodbridge, Suffolk IP12 2SZ
☎01394 461313   Fax 01394 461314
Directors *Martin Eve, P. M. Eve, Julie Millard*
FOUNDED 1956. *Publishes* ecology, economics, history, philosophy, left-wing politics. AUTHORS Georg Lukács, Ernest Mandel, Istvan Meszaros, Ralph Miliband, E. P. Thompson. About 20 titles a year. No fiction.
IMPRINTS
  Green Print; **Seafarer Books** Sailing titles, with an emphasis on the traditional. No unsolicited mss; preliminary letter essential before making any type of submission.
Royalties paid twice-yearly.

Methuen
See **Random House UK Ltd**

Methuen & Co.
See **Routledge**

Methuen Children's Books
See **Reed Books**

Metro Books
Metro Publishing Ltd, 19 Gerrard Street, London W1V 7LA
☎0171 734 1411   Fax 0171 734 1811
Managing Director *Susanne McDadd*
Editorial Manager *Cheryl Lanyon*
FOUNDED 1995. *Publishes* general non-fiction – popular psychology, health, giftbooks and cookery. 15 titles in 1997. TITLES *Staying Sane* Raj Persaud; *Real Fast Vegetarian Food* Ursula Ferrigno; *Big Living* Angela Sandler; *Green & Easy* Clare Bradley. No unsolicited mss. Send outline, sample chapter and c.v. plus s.a.e. in the first instance.
Royalties paid twice-yearly.

Authors' Rating Big advances are out and ideas are likely to be developed in-house. But authors should be encouraged by the promise to fill out royalty statements with information on where titles are selling and at what discount. Draft marketing plans will be included with contracts and authors will be encouraged to attend marketing meetings.

Michelin Tyre plc
The Edward Hyde Building, 38 Clarendon Road, Watford, Hertfordshire WD1 1SX
☎01923 415000   Fax 01923 415052
FOUNDED 1900 as travel publisher. *Publishes* travel guides, maps and atlases, children's I-Spy books. Travel-related synopses and ideas welcome; no mss.

Midland Publishing Ltd
24 The Hollow, Earl Shilton, Leicester LE9 7NA
☎01455 847256   Fax 01455 841805
Director *N. P. Lewis*
Publishes aviation, military and railways. No wartime memoirs. No unsolicited mss; synopses and ideas welcome.
Royalties paid quarterly.

Millenium
See **The Orion Publishing Group Ltd**

Harvey Miller Publishers
Knightsbridge House, 8th Floor, 197 Knightsbridge, London SW7 1RB
☎0171 584 7676   Fax 0171 823 7969
Editorial Director *Mrs Elly Miller*
FOUNDED 1974. *Publishes* serious studies in the

history of art only. Approx. 6 titles a year. No unsolicited mss; synopses and ideas welcome.
Royalties paid annually.

Mills & Boon Ltd
See **Harlequin Mills & Boon Ltd**

Minerva
See **Random House UK Ltd**

Minerva Press Ltd
195 Knightsbridge, London SW7 1RE
☎0171 225 3113   Fax 0171 581 9237
Chairman/Managing Director R. *Hamblin*

FOUNDED in 1992, the Minerva imprint dates back to 1792. *Publishes* fiction and non-fiction; biography, poetry, children's and historical. Specialises in new authors. 250 titles in 1996. No 'adult' or sexually explicit material. Unsolicited mss, synopses and ideas for books welcome.
Royalties paid twice-yearly.

Authors' Rating Liable to ask authors to contribute towards costs of publication.

Mira
See **Harlequin Mills & Boon Ltd**

The MIT Press Ltd
Fitzroy House, 11 Chenies Street, London WC1E 7ET
☎0171 306 0603   Fax 0171 306 0604
Director F. *Urbanowski*
General Manager A. *Sexsmith*

Part of **The MIT Press**, USA. *Publishes* academic, architecture and design, art history and theory, bibliography, biography, business and industry, cinema and media studies, computer science, cultural studies and critical theory, economics, educational and textbooks, engineering, environment, linguistics, medical, music, natural history, philosophy, photography, physics, politics and world affairs, psychology, reference, scientific and technical, neurobiology and neuroscience. All mss go to the American office: 55 Hayward Street, Cambridge, Mass. 02142.

Mitchell Beazley
See **Reed Books**

Mitre
See **Monarch Publications**

Monarch Publications
Broadway House, The Broadway, Crowborough, East Sussex TN6 1HQ
☎01892 652364   Fax 01892 663329

Directors *Tony & Jane Collins*

Publish an independent list of Christian books across a wide range of concerns. About 30 titles a year. In 1994 took on *Renewal* and *Healing and Wholeness* magazines.

IMPRINTS **Monarch** Upmarket, social concern issues list covering a wide range of areas from psychology to future studies, politics, etc., all with a strong Christian dimension; **Marc** Leadership, mission and church growth titles; **Mitre** Creative writing imprint: humour and drama with a Christian dimension. Unsolicited mss, synopses and ideas welcome. 'Regretfully no poetry or fiction.'

Mosby International (a division of Times Mirror International Publishers Ltd)
Lynton House, 7–12 Tavistock Square, London WC1H 9LB
☎0171 388 7676   Fax 0171 391 6555
Managing Director *Fiona Foley*

Part of Times Mirror Co., Los Angeles. Acquired Wolfe Publishing in the late '80s, and acquired Gower Medical Publishing in 1993. Broadening its horizon from the core list of books and journals for nurses to a list which now includes colour atlases and texts in medicine, dentistry and veterinary science.

IMPRINTS **Mosby; Mosby Wolfe Publishing** TITLES *Immunology; A Colour Atlas & Text of Clinical Medicine; A Colour Atlas of Human Anatomy; Rheumatology; Head and Neck Surgery; 1995 Nursing Drug Reference*. Synopses and ideas for books welcome.
Royalties paid twice-yearly.

Motor Racing Publications
Unit 6, The Pilton Estate, 46 Pitlake, Croydon, Surrey CR0 3RY
☎0181 681 3363   Fax 0181 760 5117
Chairman/Editorial Head *John Blunsden*
Approx. Annual Turnover £500,000

FOUNDED soon after the end of World War II to concentrate on motor-racing titles. Fairly dormant in the mid '60s but was reactivated in 1968 by a new shareholding structure. John Blunsden later acquired a majority share and major expansion followed in the 70s. About 10–12 titles a year. *Publishes* motor-sporting history, classic car collection and restoration, road transport, motorcycles, off-road driving and related subjects.

IMPRINTS **Fitzjames Press; Motor Racing Publications** TITLES *Cars in the UK, Vol 2:*

1971 to 1995 G. Robson; *Morris Minor* G. Saddlestone; *Morgans to 1997* R. Bell; *Sporting Peugeot 205s* D. Thornton; *No Time to Lose: The fast moving world of Bill Ivy* A. Peck. Unsolicited mss, synopses and ideas in specified subject areas welcome.

Royalties paid twice-yearly.

Mowbray
See **Cassell**

Multi-Sensory Learning Ltd
34 Nene Valley Business Park, Oundle, Peterborough PE8 4HL
☎01832 274714   Fax 01832 275281
Senior Editor *Philippa Attwood*
Course Co-ordinator *Karen Robinson*

Part of **First and Best in Education Ltd**. *Publishes* materials and books related to dyslexia; the multi-sensory learning course for dyslexic pupils needing literacy skills development, plus numerous other items on assessment, reading, maths, music, etc. for dyslexics. Keen to locate authors able to write materials for dyslexic people and for teachers of dyslexics.

John Murray (Publishers) Ltd
50 Albemarle Street, London W1X 4BD
☎0171 493 4361   Fax 0171 499 1792
Chairman *John R. Murray*
Managing Director *Nicholas Perren*

FOUNDED 1768. Independent publisher. *Publishes* general trade books, educational (secondary school and college textbooks) and Success Studybooks.

DIVISIONS **General Books** *Grant McIntyre*; **Educational Books** *Nicholas Perren*. Unsolicited material discouraged.

Royalties paid annually.

Authors' Rating Investing heavily in education titles in anticipation of a lift in the school market. Biography and history sales have had a few knocks though quality remains high.

NAG Press Ltd
See **Robert Hale Ltd**

National Museums of Scotland (NMS Publishing)
Chambers Street, Edinburgh EH1 1JF
☎0131 247 4161   Fax 0131 247 4012
Managing Director *Mark Jones*
Approx. Annual Turnover £130,000

FOUNDED 1987 to *publish* non-fiction related to the National Museums of Scotland collections:

academic and general; children's – archaeology, history, decorative arts worldwide, history of science, technology, natural history and geology. 10 titles in 1996. **NMS Publishing** *Jenni Calder* TITLES *Scotland's Past in Action* series; *The Scottish Home; Domestic Culture in the Middle East; Agates; Harmony and Contrast: A Journey Through East Asian Art; Photography 1900; Fish Facts* (cartoon book). No unsolicited mss; only interested in synopses and ideas for books which are genuinely related to NMS collections.

Royalties paid twice-yearly.

Navigator Books
Moorhouse, Kingston, Ringwood, Hampshire BH24 3BJ
☎01425 476708   Fax 01425 480075
Managing Director *Philip Bristow*

FOUNDED 1964. *Publishes* fiction, nautical, war, travel, history. TITLES *Aquatic Mammals; Jump On Jump; On the Edge of Asia; Across Africa and Beyond; The Tale of the Golden Scale; Beating About the Nigerian Bush; A Colonial Odyssey; A Walk Around England; The Germans in Jersey; Old Time Characters of the Isle of Wight; Tales of Dinglewood Dell.* Prefers to hear from authors of completed works – send synopsis and sample chapter. 'Quick response to *all* submitted material.'

Royalties paid twice-yearly.

Authors' Rating Liable to ask authors to contribute towards cost of publication.

NCVO Publications
Regent's Wharf, 8 All Saints Street, London N1 9RL
☎0171 713 6161   Fax 0171 713 6300
Publications Manager *David Cameron*
Approx. Annual Turnover £140,000

FOUNDED 1992. Publishing imprint of the National Council for Voluntary Organisations, embracing former Bedford Square Press titles and NCVO's many other publications. The list reflects NCVO's role as the representative body for the voluntary sector. *Publishes* directories, management and trustee development, legal, finance and fundraising titles of primary interest to the voluntary sector. TITLES *The Voluntary Agencies Directory; Grants from Europe; The Good Trustee Guide: Planning Together.* No unsolicited mss as most projects are commissioned in-house.

Royalties paid twice-yearly.

Thomas Nelson & Sons Ltd

Nelson House, Mayfield Road, Walton on Thames, Surrey KT12 5PL
☎01932 252211   Fax 01932 246109

President *Rodrigue E. Gauvin*
Vice President Finance *Nick White*
Vice President Publishing *David Fothergill*
Approx. Annual Turnover £30 million

FOUNDED 1798. Part of the Thomson Corporation. Major educational publisher of printed and electronic product, from pre-school to Higher Education, with emphasis on requirements of National Curriculum, GCSE, A Level, GNVQ and NVQ. Publisher of *The Arden Shakespeare* imprint, and of a range of material for the Caribbean market. TITLES *GAIA: Geography, An Integrated Approach; The Wider World; Nelson English; Nelson Maths; Wellington Square; Route Nationale; Encore Tricolore; Zickzack Neu; World of Sport Examined; New Balanced Science; Bath Science; Foundations of Psychology* Royalties paid twice-yearly.

Authors' Rating Weaknesses in the school market have hit sales. The ELT division has been sold to Pearson.

Network Books

See **BBC Consumer Publishing**

The New Adventures

See **Virgin Publishing Ltd**

New English Library

See **Hodder Headline plc**

New Holland (Publishers) Ltd

24 Nutford Place, London W1H 6DQ
☎0171 724 7773   Fax 0171 724 6184

Chairman *Gerry Struik*
Managing Director *John Beaufoy*
Editorial Heads *Charlotte Parry-Crooke, Yvonne McFarlane*
Approx. Annual Turnover £4 million

FOUNDED 1956. Relaunched 1987 with new name and editorial identity. New directions and rapid expansion transformed the small specialist imprint into a publisher of illustrated books for the international market. In 1993, they diversified further with the acquisition of the **Charles Letts Publishing Division** list. *Publishes* non-fiction, specialising in natural history, travel, cookery, cake decorating, crafts, gardening and DIY. TITLES *Dive Sites of the Philippines; Wild Thailand; Complete Garden Bird Book; Globetrotter Travel Guide Series; Design and Make Bedroom Furnishings; The Illustrated Book of Herbs.* No unsolicited mss; synopses and ideas welcome.
Royalties paid twice-yearly.

Authors' Rating This South African-owned company produces superbly illustrated books. Authors need to know what looks good on the coffee table.

New Left Books Ltd

See **Verso**

Newleaf

See **Boxtree**

Nexus

See **Virgin Publishing Ltd**

Nexus Special Interests

Nexus House, Boundary Way, Hemel Hempstead, Hertfordshire HP2 7ST
☎01442 66551   Fax 01442 66998

Manager *Beverly Laughlin*

Argus Consumer Magazines and Argus Books were bought out by Nexus Media Communications in 1995 and the Nexus Special Interests imprint was established in the spring of that year. *Publishes* aviation, engineering, leisure and hobbies, modelling, electronics, health, wine and beer making, woodwork. Send synopses rather than completed mss.
Royalties paid twice-yearly.

NFER-NELSON Publishing Co. Ltd

Darville House, 2 Oxford Road East, Windsor, Berkshire SL4 1DF
☎01753 858961   Fax 01753 856830

Managing Director *Michael Jackson*

FOUNDED 1981. Jointly owned by the Thomson Corporation and the National Foundation for Educational Research. *Publishes* educational and psychological tests and training materials. Main interest is in educational, clinical and occupational assessment and training material. Unsolicited material welcome.
Royalties vary according to each contract.

Nicholson

See **HarperCollins Publishers Ltd**

James Nisbet & Co. Ltd

78 Tilehouse Street, Hitchin, Hertfordshire SG5 2DY
☎01462 438331   Fax 01462 431528

Chairman *E. M. Mackenzie-Wood*

FOUNDED 1810 as a religious publisher and expanded into more general areas from around 1850 onwards. The first educational list appeared in 1926 and the company now specialises in educational material and business studies. About 5 titles a year. No fiction, leisure or religion. No unsolicited mss; synopses and ideas welcome.
Royalties paid twice-yearly.

NMS Publishing
See **National Museums of Scotland**

No Exit Press
See **Oldcastle Books Ltd**

Nonesuch Press
See **Reinhardt Books Ltd**

Northcote House Publishers Ltd
Plymbridge House, Estover Road, Plymouth, Devon PL6 7PY
☎01752 202368   Fax 01752 202330
Managing Director *Brian Hulme*

FOUNDED 1985. Recently launched a new series of literary critical studies, in association with the British Council, called *Writers and their Work*. Publishes careers, education management, literary criticism, educational dance and drama. 30 titles in 1996. 'Well-thought-out proposals, including contents and sample chapter(s), with strong marketing arguments welcome.'
Royalties paid annually.

W. W. Norton & Co. Ltd
10 Coptic Street, London WC1A 1PU
☎0171 323 1579   Fax 0171 436 4553
Managing Director *R. A. Cameron*

Owned by US parent company. *Publishes* non-fiction and academic. No unsolicited material. Enquiries only in writing.

Notting Hill Electronic Publishers
31 Brunswick Gardens, London W8 4AW
☎0171 937 6003   Fax 0171 937 0003
Chairman *Andreas Whittam Smith*
Managing Director *Ben Whittam Smith*

FOUNDED 1994. Award-winning electronic publisher created by Andreas Whittam Smith, founder of *The Independent*. Publishes (on CD-ROM) arts, sport, popular science, food and wine. TITLES *International Athletics; Wine, Spirits & Beer; The Art of Singing; The Evolution of Life*. Welcomes synopses and ideas for CD-ROMs; no pornography or fiction.

Nottingham University Press
Manor Farm, Main Street, Thrumpton, Nottingham NG11 0AX
☎0115 9831011   Fax 0115 9831003
Managing Editor *Dr D. J. A. Cole*
Approx. Annual Turnover £150,000

Initially concentrated on agricultural and food sciences titles but now branching into new areas including engineering, lifesciences, medicine, law and sport. Sports books published under newly-formed subsidiary, **Castle Publications**. TITLES *Recent Developments in Pig Nutrition; Recent Developments in Ruminant Nutrition; Recent Advances in Animal Nutrition; Nutrition and Feeding of Poultry; Principles of Pig Science; Microorganisms in Ruminant Nutrition; Issues in Agricultural Bioethics*. **Castle Publications** *Titles The Mental Game of Golf; The Natural Sportsman; Worldwide Directory of Distilleries*.
Royalties paid twice-yearly.

Oak
See **Omnibus Press**

Oberon Books
521 Caledonian Road, London N7 9RH
☎0171 607 3637   Fax 0171 607 3629
Publishing Director *James Hogan*
Managing Director *Charles D. Glanville*

Publishes play texts (usually in conjunction with a production) and theatre books. *Specialises* in contemporary plays and translations of European classics. IMPRINTS **Oberon Books; Absolute Classics**. AUTHORS/TRANSLATORS Rodney Akland, Michel Azarna, Simon Bent, Ken Campbell, Barry Day, Marguerite Duras, Dic Edwards, Dario Fo, Jonathan Gems, Peter Gill, Graham Greene, Giles Havergal, Robert David MacDonald, Dino Mahoney, Louis Mellis, Adrian Mitchell, Gregory Motton, Stephen Mulrine, Jimmy Murphy, Meredith Oakes, Stewart Parker, David Pownall, Roland Rees, David Scinto, Colin Winslow, Charles Wood.

Octagon Press Ltd
PO Box 227, London N6 4EW
☎0181 348 9392   Fax 0181 341 5971
Managing Director *George R. Schrager*
Approx. Annual Turnover £100,000

FOUNDED 1972. *Publishes* philosophy, psychology, travel, Eastern religion, translations of Eastern classics and research monographs in series. 4–5 titles a year. Unsolicited material not welcome. Enquiries in writing only.
Royalties paid annually.

Oldcastle Books Ltd

18 Coleswood Road, Harpenden,
Hertfordshire AL5 1EQ
☎01582 761264   Fax 01582 712244
Managing Director *Ion S. Mills*

FOUNDED 1985. *Publishes* crime fiction and
gambling non-fiction. 20 titles in 1996. No
unsolicited mss; synopses and ideas for books
within the two areas of interest welcome.
    IMPRINTS **No Exit Press** TITLES *Burglar In
the Library* Lawrence Block; *No Beast So Fierce*
Eddie Bunker; **Oldcastle Books** TITLES
Biggest Game in Town Al Alvarez.
    Royalties paid twice-yearly.

Oldie Publications

45/46 Poland Street, London W1V 4AU
☎0171 734 2225   Fax 0171 734 2226
Chairman *Richard Ingrams*

FOUNDED in 1992. Book publishing arm of
The Oldie magazine. *Publishes* compilations
from the magazine, including cartoon books. 3
titles in 1996. TITLES *I Once Met; Dictionary For
Our Time.* Unsolicited synopses and ideas for
books welcome.

OM Publishing

See **STL Ltd**

Michael O'Mara Books Ltd

9 Lion Yard, Tremadoc Road, London
SW4 7NQ
☎0171 720 8643   Fax 0171 627 8953
Chairman *Michael O'Mara*
Managing Director *Lesley O'Mara*
Editorial Director *David Roberts*
Approx. Annual Turnover £5 million

FOUNDED 1985. Independent publisher.
Publishes general non-fiction, royalty, history,
humour, anthologies and reference. TITLES
Diana: Her True Story Andrew Morton; *The
Seven Wonders of the World* John Romer; *I
Don't Believe It!* Richard Wilson. Unsolicited
mss, synopses and ideas for books welcome.
    Royalties paid twice-yearly.

Omnibus Press

Book Sales/Music Sales Ltd, 8–9 Frith Street,
London W1V 5TZ
☎0171 434 0066   Fax 0171 734 2246
Editorial Head *Chris Charlesworth*

FOUNDED 1971. Independent publisher of
music books, rock and pop biographies, song
sheets, educational tutors, cassettes, videos and
software.

IMPRINTS **Amsco; Bobcat; Oak; Omnibus;
Proteus; Wise; Zomba.** Unsolicited mss, synopses and ideas for books welcome.
    Royalties paid twice-yearly.

Oneworld Publications

185 Banbury Road, Oxford OX2 7AR
☎01865 310597   Fax 01865 310598
Editorial Director *Juliet Mabey*

FOUNDED 1986. Distributed worldwide by
Penguin Books. *Publishes* adult non-fiction
across a range of subjects from world religions
and social issues to psychology and health. 20
titles in 1996. TITLE New series on world religions launched in 1994 with *A Short History of
Buddhism* and *A Short History of Islam.* AUTHORS
include Geoffrey Parrinder, Keith Ward,
William Montgomery Watt, Alfred Adler, Kahlil
Gibran. No unsolicited mss; synopses and ideas
welcome, but should be accompanied by s.a.e.
for return of material and/or notification of
receipt. No autobiographies, fiction or poetry.
    Royalties paid annually.

Onlywomen Press Ltd

40 St Lawrence Terrace, London W10 5ST
☎0181 960 7122   Fax 0181 960 2817
Editorial Director *Lilian Mohin*

FOUNDED 1974. *Publishes* radical feminist lesbian
books only: fiction, poetry and non-fiction
anthologies. About 6 titles a year. In 1995/96,
published the first three titles in a new crime
novel list, original paperbacks set in contemporary England with lesbian protagonists. TITLES
Burning Issues Maggie Kelly; *Dirty Work* Vivien
Kelly; *A Fearful Symmetry* Tash Fairbanks; *An
Antimacy of Equals: Lesbian Feminist Ethics* ed.
Lilian Mohin. Unsolicited mss, synopses and
ideas welcome. Submissions should be accompanied by s.a.e. for return of material and/or
notification of receipt.

Open Books Publishing Ltd

Beaumont House, Wells, Somerset BA5 2LD
☎01749 677276   Fax 01749 670760
Managing Director *Patrick Taylor*

FOUNDED 1974. *Publishes* general and gardening books. No unsolicited material. All books
are commissioned.
    Royalties paid twice-yearly.

Open University Press

Celtic Court, 22 Ballmoor, Buckingham,
Buckinghamshire MK18 1XW
☎01280 823388   Fax 01280 823233
Managing Director *John Skelton*

Approx. Annual Turnover £3 million

FOUNDED 1977 as an imprint independent of the Open University's course materials. *Publishes* academic and professional books in the fields of education, management, sociology, health studies, politics, psychology, women's studies. No economics or anthropology. Not interested in anything outside the social sciences. About 100 titles a year. No unsolicited mss; enquiries/proposals only.
Royalties paid annually.

Orbit
See **Little, Brown & Co. (UK)**

Orchard Books
See **The Watts Publishing Group**

The Orion Publishing Group Ltd
Orion House, 5 Upper St Martin's Lane, London WC2H 9EA
☎0171 240 3444   Fax 0171 240 4822
Chairman *Nicholas Barber*
Chief Executive *Anthony Cheetham*
Managing Director *Peter Roche*
Approx. Annual Turnover £31 million

FOUNDED 1992 by Anthony and Rosemary Cheetham and Peter Roche. Incorporates Weidenfeld & Nicolson, J. M. Dent and Chapmans Publishers.

DIVISIONS
Orion *Rosemary Cheetham, Jane Wood* Hardcover fiction and non-fiction. IMPRINTS **Millenium** *Caroline Oakley* Science fiction and fantasy; **Orion Media** *Trevor Dolby* Film, theatre, television, music, multimedia; **Orion Business** *Martin Liu.*
  Weidenfeld & Nicolson *Ion Trewin* General non-fiction, biography and autobiography, history and travel. IMPRINTS **J. M. Dent** *Hilary Laurie*; **Phoenix House** *Maggie McKernan* Literary fiction.
  Illustrated *Michael Dover* Illustrated non-fiction with a strong emphasis on the visual, and upmarket design, cookery, wine, gardening, art and architecture, natural history and personality-based books.
  Orion Children's Books *Judith Elliott* Children's fiction and non-fiction.
  Mass Market *Susan Lamb* IMPRINTS **Orion**; **Phoenix**; **Everyman** *Hilary Laurie.*

Authors' Rating On expansionist course while trying 'to preserve the intimacy of a small company', Orion has opened up three new divisions – media, business and military history. Current annual output of 250 titles likely to increase to 350 over the next year.

Osprey
See **Reed Books**

Peter Owen Ltd
73 Kenway Road, London SW5 0RE
☎0171 373 5628/370 6093
Fax 0171 373 6760
Chairman *Peter Owen*
Editorial Director *Antonia Owen*

FOUNDED 1951. *Publishes* biography, general non-fiction, English literary fiction and translations, sociology. 'No middlebrow romance, thrillers or children's.' AUTHORS Jane Bowles, Paul Bowles, Shusaku Endo, Anna Kavan, Fiona Pitt-Kethley, Anaïs Nin, Jeremy Reed, Peter Vansittart. 35–40 titles a year. Unsolicited synopses welcome for non-fiction material; mss should be preceded by a descriptive letter and synopsis with s.a.e..
  Royalties paid twice-yearly. *Overseas associates* worldwide.

Authors' Rating For ever looking for ways of cutting costs to maintain output in the highbrow market, Peter Owen has been described as 'a publisher of the old and idiosyncratic school'. He has seven Nobel prizewinners on his list.

Oxford Illustrated Press/ Oxford Publishing Co.
See **Haynes Publishing**

Oxford University Press
Great Clarendon Street, Oxford OX2 6DP
☎01865 556767   Fax 01865 556646
Chief Executive *James Arnold-Baker*
Approx. Annual Turnover £250 million

A department of the university, OUP grew from the university's printing works and developed into a major publishing business in the 19th century. *Publishes* academic books in all categories: student texts, scholarly journals, schoolbooks, ELT material, dictionaries, reference, music, bibles, electronic publishing, as well as paperbacks, poetry, general non-fiction and children's books. Around 3000 titles a year.

DIVISIONS
Academic *I. S. Asquith* TITLES *Concise Oxford Dictionary*; *Birds of the Western Palearctic*; **Educational** *F. E. Clarke* Courses for the National Curriculum; **ELT** *W. R. Andrewes* ELT courses and dictionaries.

IMPRINTS
Clarendon Press Monographs in humanities,

science and social science; **Oxford Paperbacks** Trade paperbacks; **Oxford Science Publications**; **Oxford Medical Publications**; **Oxford Electronic Publications**. OUP welcomes first-class academic material in the form of proposals or accepted theses.

Royalties paid twice-yearly. *Overseas subsidiaries* Sister company in USA; also branches in Australia, Canada, East Africa, Hong Kong, India, Japan, New Zealand, Pakistan, Singapore, South Africa. Offices in Argentina, Brazil, France, Germany, Greece, Italy, Mexico, Spain, Taiwan, Thailand, Turkey, Uruguay. Joint companies in Malaysia, Nigeria and Germany.

Authors' Rating By far the largest of the university presses, OUP is the market leader in dictionary publishing and in English Language Teaching. But the real strength of Oxford is its international network. It publishes in 12 countries and has offices and associated companies in 40 others.

Palm Tree Press
See **Kevin Mayhew Ltd**

G. J. Palmer & Sons Ltd
See **Hymns Ancient & Modern Ltd**

Pan Books Ltd
See **Macmillan Publishers Ltd**

Paper Tiger Books
See **Dragon's World**

Papermac
See **Macmillan Publishers Ltd**

Paragon Softcover Large Print
See **Chivers Press Ltd**

Partridge Press
See **Transworld Publishers Ltd**

The Paternoster Press
See **STL Ltd**

Pavilion Books Ltd
As we went to press, Pavilion Books had gone into receivership, its assets acquired by **Collins and Brown**. Pavilion will be run as a sister company from the Collins and Brown address.

Payback Press
See **Canongate Books Ltd**

Pelham Books/ Pelham Studio
See **Penguin Books Ltd**

Pen & Sword Books Ltd
See **Leo Cooper**

Penguin Books Ltd
27 Wrights Lane, London W8 5TZ
☎0171 416 3000   Fax 0171 416 3099
Chief Executive *Michael Lynton*
Managing Director *Anthony Forbes Watson*
Publisher, Children's *Philippa Milnes-Smith*

Owned by Pearson plc. For more than 60 years the publisher of one of the largest paperback lists in the English language, the Penguin list embraces fiction, non-fiction, poetry, drama, classics, reference and special interest areas. Reprints and new work.

DIVISIONS

General Adult fiction and non-fiction. Publisher *Tony Lacey*, Publishing Director *Juliet Annan* IMPRINTS **Hamish Hamilton Ltd**; **Penguin**; **Viking**. Non-fiction synopses and ideas welcome; no unsolicited fiction; no poetry.

Penguin Press Serious adult non-fiction, reference and classics. Director *Alastair Rolfe* IMPRINTS **Allen Lane**; **Arkana** Mind, body and spirit; **Buildings of England**; **Classics**; **Penguin Books**. Approach in writing only.

Michael Joseph Ltd Publishing Director *Tom Weldon* IMPRINTS **Michael Joseph** Popular fiction; **Pelham**; **Pelham Studio** Illustrated books; **ROC** Science fiction and fantasy. Unsolicited mss discouraged; synopses and ideas welcome.

Frederick Warne *Sally Floyer* Classic children's publishing and merchandising including *Beatrix Potter*™; *Flower Fairies*; *Orlando*; **Ventura** *Sally Floyer* Producer and packager of *Spot* titles by Eric Hill.

Children's Hardback IMPRINTS **Blackie** *Rosemary Stones* Mainly *Topsy & Tim* titles; **Dutton** *Rosemary Stones* Novelty, picture books and fiction; **Hamish Hamilton Children's** *Jane Nissen* Fiction and picture books. Unsolicited mss, synopses and ideas welcome; **Viking Children's** *Rosemary Stones*. Fiction, non-fiction, picture books and poetry. Unsolicited mss discouraged; synopses and ideas welcome.

Children's Paperbacks IMPRINTS **Puffin** *Philippa Milnes-Smith* Leading children's paperback list publishing in virtually all fields including fiction, non-fiction, poetry and picture books, media-related titles.

Royalties paid twice-yearly. *Overseas associates* worldwide.

Authors' Rating Everyone is hoping for a period of consolidation at Penguin after yet more redundancies and change at the top with Peter Mayer giving way to Disney-trained Michael Lynton. Reorganisation has led to the disappearance of the Signet imprint and from now on Michael Joseph titles will be paperbacked by Penguin. A major buy in to Rough Guides has increased the Penguin share of the travel book market to close on 10 per cent while Pearson's acquisition of Putnam in the US looks set to make Penguin the world's second largest English language publisher.

Petroc Press
See **Librapharm Ltd**

Phaidon Press Limited
Regent's Wharf, All Saints Street, London N1 9PA
☎0171 843 1000   Fax 0171 843 1010
Chairman *Richard Schlagman*
Managing Director *Paula Kahn*
Editorial Heads *David Jenkins, Pat Barylski, Iwona Blazwick*

Publishes quality books on the visual arts, including fine art, art history, architecture, design, photography, decorative arts, music and performing arts. Recently started producing videos. About 100 titles a year. Unsolicited mss welcome but 'only a small amount of unsolicited material gets published'.

Royalties paid twice-yearly.

Philip's
See **Reed Books**

Phillimore & Co. Ltd
Shopwyke Manor Barn, Chichester, West Sussex PO20 6BG
☎01243 787636   Fax 01243 787639
Chairman *Philip Harris*
Managing Director *Noel Osborne*
Approx. Annual Turnover £1 million

FOUNDED 1897 by W. P. W. Phillimore, Victorian campaigner for local archive conservation in Chancery Lane, London. Became the country's leading publisher of historical source material and local histories. Somewhat dormant in the 1960s, it was revived by Philip Harris in 1968. *Publishes* British local and family history, including histories of institutions, buildings, villages, towns and counties, plus guides to research and writing in these fields. About 70 titles a year. No unsolicited mss; synopses/ideas welcome for local or family histories.

IMPRINTS **Phillimore** *Noel Osborne* TITLES *Domesday Book; A History of Essex; Carlisle; The Haberdashers' Company; Channel Island Churches; Bolton Past; Warwickshire Country Houses.*

Royalties paid annually.

Phoenix/Phoenix House
See **The Orion Publishing Group Ltd**

Piatkus Books
5 Windmill Street, London W1P 1HF
☎0171 631 0710   Fax 0171 436 7137
Managing Director *Judy Piatkus*
Approx. Annual Turnover £4.75 million

FOUNDED 1979 by Judy Piatkus. The company is committed to continuing independence. *Specialises* in publishing books and authors 'who we feel enthusiastic and committed to as we like to build for long-term success as well as short-term!' *Publishes* self-help, biography, personal growth, business and management, careers, cookery, health and beauty, healing, mind, body and spirit, popular psychology and fiction. In 1996 launched a list of mass-market non-fiction and fiction titles. About 120 titles a year (70 of which are fiction).

DIVISIONS
Non-fiction *Gill Cornode* TITLES *Curry Club Cookery Range* Pat Chapman; *The 10 Day MBA* Steve Silbiger; *The Perfect CV* Tom Jackson; *The Reflexology Handbook* Laura Norman; *Creating Sacred Space with Feng Shui* Karen Kingston; *Fitness For Life* Susie Dinan and Craig Sharp.

Fiction *Judy Piatkus* TITLES *Her Father's House* Emma Sinclair; *Army Wives* Catherine Jones; *Monkey King* Patricia Chao; *Come the Day* Una Horne. Piatkus are expanding their range of books and welcome synopses and ideas.

Royalties paid twice-yearly.

Authors' Rating A small publisher which continues to do well despite hard times by focusing titles on clearly defined markets.

Picador
See **Macmillan Publishers Ltd**

Pictorial
See **Souvenir Press Ltd**

Picture Knight
See **Hodder Headline plc**

Picture Lions
See **HarperCollins Publishers Ltd**

Pimlico
See **Random House UK Ltd**

Pinter
See **Cassell**

Pitkin Guides
See **Reed Books**

Pitman Publishing
128 Long Acre, London WC2E 9AN
☎0171 447 2000   Fax 0171 240 5771
Managing Director *Rod Bristow*

Part of Pearson Professional. Publisher and supplier of business education and management development materials. Portfolio of products and services includes books, journals, directories, looseleafs, CD-ROMS aimed at business education and management development in both private and public sectors. About 250 titles a year.

IMPRINTS **Pitman Publishing; Financial Times; Institute of Management; NatWest Business Handbooks; Allied Dunbar; Investors Chronicle; Financial Adviser; Fairplace Institute of Banking & Finance; M&E Handbooks**. Unsolicited mss, synopses and ideas for books and other materials welcome.

Royalties paid annually.

Plenum Publishing Co. Ltd
New Loom House, 101 Back Church Lane, London E1 1LU
☎0171 264 1910   Fax 0171 264 1919
Chairman *Martin E. Tash* (USA)
Managing Director *Dr Ken Derham*
Editor *Joanna Lawrence*

FOUNDED 1966. A division of **Plenum Publishing**, New York. The London office is the editorial and marketing base for the company's UK and European operations. *Publishes* postgraduate, professional and research-level scientific, technical and medical monographs, conference proceedings and reference books. About 300 titles (worldwide) a year.

IMPRINTS **Consultants Bureau; IFI Plenum Data Company; Plenum Insight; Plenum Medical Company; Plenum Press; Human Science Press**. Proposals for new publications will be considered, and should be sent to the editor.

Royalties paid annually.

Pluto Press Ltd
345 Archway Road, London N6 5AA
☎0181 348 2724   Fax 0181 348 9133
Managing Director *Roger Van Zwanenberg*
Editorial Director *Anne Beech*

FOUNDED 1970. Has developed a reputation for innovatory publishing in the field of non-fiction. *Publishes* academic and scholarly books across a range of subjects including cultural studies, politics and world affairs, social sciences and socialist, feminist and Marxist books. About 50–60 titles a year. Synopses and ideas welcome if accompanied by return postage.

Point
See **Scholastic Ltd**

The Policy Press
University of Bristol, Rodney Lodge, Grange Road, Bristol BS8 4EA
☎0117 9738797   Fax 0117 9737308
Managing Director *Alison Shaw*
Approx. Annual Turnover £150,000

Incorporating the former SAUS Publications, The Policy Press *specialises* in the production of books, concise reports, practice guides, pamphlets and a journal. Material published is taken from research findings in policy studies, providing critical discussion of policy initiatives and their impact; also recommendations for policy change. 35–45 titles per year. No unsolicited mss; brief synopses and ideas welcome.

Polity Press
65 Bridge Street, Cambridge CB2 1UR
☎01223 324315   Fax 01223 461385

FOUNDED 1984. All books are published in association with **Blackwell Publishers**. *Publishes* archaeology and anthropology, criminology, economics, feminism, general interest, history, human geography, literature, media and cultural studies, medicine and society, philosophy, politics, psychology, religion and theology, social and political theory, sociology. Unsolicited mss, synopses and ideas for books welcome.

Royalties paid annually.

Polygon
See **Edinburgh University Press**

Pont Books
See **Gomer Press**

Pop Universal
See **Souvenir Press Ltd**

Portland Press Ltd
59 Portland Place, London W1N 3AJ
☎0171 580 5530   Fax 0171 323 1136
Chairman *Professor A.J. Turner*
Managing Director *G.D. Jones*
Editorial Director *Rhonda Oliver*
Approx. Annual Turnover £2.5 million
FOUNDED 1990 to expand the publishing activities of the Biochemical Society (1911). *Publishes* biochemisty and medicine for graduate, postgraduate and research students. Expanding the list to include schools and general readership. 11 titles in 1996. TITLES *Techniques in Apoptosis; Postgraduate Study in the Physical Sciences; Glossary of Biochemistry and Molecular Biology; Making Sense of Science* series includes *Planet Ocean* and *The Space Place*. Unsolicited mss, synopses and ideas welcome. No fiction.
Royalties paid twice-yearly. *Overseas subsidiary* Portland Press Inc.

T. & A. D. Poyser
See **Harcourt Brace and Company Limited**

Presentations
See **Souvenir Press Ltd**

Princeton University Press
See **University Presses of California, Columbia & Princeton Ltd**

Prion Books Ltd
Unit L, 32–34 Gordon House Road, London NW5 1LP
☎0171 482 4248   Fax 0171 482 4203
Managing Director *Barry Winkleman*
Formerly a packaging operation but began publishing under the Prion imprint in 1987. *Publishes* illustrated non-fiction: Americana, cinema and photography, cars, guidebooks, food and drink, sex, psychology and health. About 40 titles a year. Unsolicited mss, synopses and ideas welcome.
Royalties paid twice-yearly.

Professional Information Publishing
37–41 Mortimer Street, London W1N 7JX
☎0171 637 4383   Fax 0171 453 2247
Managing Director *Mary Ann Bonomo*
Owned by International Business Communications (Holdings) plc. *Publishes* a range of legal, tax, financial, management and business to business books, newsletters and directories, aimed at senior management and professional

practices. About 30 titles a year. Unsolicited synopses and ideas welcome, but initial approach in writing preferred.
Royalties paid twice-yearly.

Profile Books
62 Queen Anne Street, London W1M 9LA
☎0171 486 6010   Fax 0171 486 6010
Managing Director *Andrew Franklin*
FOUNDED 1996, taking on the publishing of **Economist Books** from Penguin. *Publishes* nonfiction including current affairs, history, politics, psychology, cultural criticism, business and management. 10 titles in 1996.
IMPRINTS **Profile Books** *Andrew Franklin*; **Economist Books** *Stephen Brough*. No unsolicited mss.
Royalties paid twice-yearly.

Authors' Rating Andrew Franklin, former publisher at Hamish Hamilton and the latest escapee from the conglomerates to go independent, promises to be 'author friendly, fast and fleet of foot'. But anyone who expects a large advance will be disappointed.

Proteus
See **Omnibus Press**

Puffin
See **Penguin Books Ltd**

Putnam Aeronautical Books
See **Brassey's (UK) Ltd**

Quadrille Publishing Ltd
Alhambra House, 27–31 Charing Cross Road, London WC2H 0LS
☎0171 839 7117   Fax 0171 839 7118
Chairman *Sue Thomson*
Managing Director *Alison Cathie*
Publishing Director *Anne Furniss*
FOUNDED in 1994 by four ex-directors of Conran Octopus, with a view to producing a small list of top-quality illustrated books. *Publishes* non-fiction, including cookery, gardening, interior design and decoration, craft, health and travel. 9 titles in 1996. TITLES *Country Living Needlework Collection; Tricia Guild in Town; Sauces* Michel Roux; *A Flower for Every Day* Nigel Colborn; *Hocus Pocus: Titania's Book of Spells*. No unsolicited mss; synopses and ideas for books welcome. No fiction or children's books.
Royalties paid twice-yearly.

Quantum
See **W. Foulsham & Co.**

Quartet Books

27 Goodge Street, London W1P 2LD
☎0171 636 3992   Fax 0171 637 1866
Chairman *Naim Attallah*
Managing Director *Jeremy Beale*
Publishing Director *Stella Kane*
Approx. Annual Turnover £1 million

FOUNDED 1972. Independent publisher. *Publishes* contemporary literary fiction including translations, popular culture, biography, music, history, politics and some photographic books. Unsolicited mss with return postage welcome; no poetry, romance or science fiction.
Royalties paid twice-yearly.

Authors' Rating Best known for translations of European and Middle Eastern literature, Quartet is clearing the decks of mediocre sellers to concentrate on popular titles like *Joy of Sex* and *Romance Reader* in cheaper format.

Queen Anne Press

See **Lennard Associates Ltd**

Quiller Press

46 Lillie Road, London SW6 1TN
☎0171 499 6529   Fax 0171 381 8941
Managing/Editorial Director *Jeremy Greenwood*

Specialises in sponsored books and publications sold through non-book trade channels as well as bookshops. *Publishes* architecture, biography, business and industry, children's, cookery, DIY, gardening, guidebooks, humour, reference, sports, travel, wine and spirits. About 15 titles a year. TITLES *The Coffee Makers* Edward Bramah; *Guide to Smoking in London* James Leavey; *French Entrée Guides* Patricia Finn; *The British Tradition – Simpson Style* David Wainwright; *Eton & Harrow at Lord's* Robert Titchener-Barrett. Most ideas originate in-house – unsolicited mss not welcome unless the author sees some potential for sponsorship or guaranteed sales.
Royalties paid twice-yearly.

Quotes Ltd/Quotes in Camera

See **The Barracuda Collection**

RAC Publishing

See **West One (Trade) Publishing Ltd**

Radcliffe Medical Press Ltd

18 Marcham Road, Abingdon, Oxon OX14 1AA
☎01235 528820   Fax 01235 528830
Managing Director *Andrew Bax*
Editorial Director *Gillian Nineham*
Editorial Manager *Jamie Etherington*

Approx. Annual Turnover £1.5 million

FOUNDED 1987. Medical publishers which began by specialising in books for general practice. *Publishes* clinical, management, health policy books and CD-ROM. 40 titles in 1996. Unsolicited mss, synopses and ideas welcome. No non-medical or medical books aimed at lay audience.
Royalties paid twice-yearly. *Overseas subsidiary* Radcliffe Medical Press Inc., New York.

The Ramsay Head Press

15 Gloucester Place, Edinburgh EH3 6EE
☎0131 225 5646   Fax 0131 225 5646
Managing Directors *Conrad Wilson, Mrs Christine Wilson*

FOUNDED 1968 by Norman Wilson OBE. A small independent family publisher. *Publishes* biography, cookery, Scottish fiction and nonfiction, plus the quarterly literary magazine *Books in Scotland*. About 3–4 titles a year. TITLES *Medusa Dozen* Tessa Ransford; *The Happy Land* Howard Denton & Jim C. Wilson. Synopses and ideas for books of Scottish interest welcome.
Royalties paid twice-yearly.

Random House UK Ltd

Random House, 20 Vauxhall Bridge Road, London SW1V 2SA
☎0171 973 9000   Fax 0171 233 6058
Chief Executive *Gail Rebuck*
Executive Chairman *Simon Master*

Random's increasing focus on trade publishing, both here and in the US, has been well rewarded, with sales continuing to grow over the last year. Random House UK Ltd is the parent company of three separate publishing divisions following the Group's reorganisation under Gail Rebuck. These are: General Books division, the Group's largest publishing division; Children's Books, Audio & New Media; Ebury Press Special Books division.

DIVISIONS
General Books Divided into two operating groups, allowing hardcover editors to see their books through to publication in paperback. The literary imprints Jonathan Cape, Methuen, Secker & Warburg and Chatto & Windus work side by side with paperback imprints Vintage and Pimlico to form one group; trade imprints Century, William Heinemann and Hutchinson go hand-in-hand with Arrow and Legend to form the other group.

IMPRINTS
Jonathan Cape Ltd ☎0171 840 8574 Fax

0171 233 6117 Publishing Director *Dan Franklin* Archaeology, biography and memoirs, current affairs, economics, fiction, history, philosophy, photography, poetry, politics, sociology and travel.

Methuen ☎0171 840 8629 Fax 0171 233 6117 Publishing Director *Michael Early* Plays, drama, humour, fiction, music, arts.

Secker & Warburg ☎0171 840 8649 Fax 0171 233 6117 Editorial Director *Geoff Mulligan* Principally literary fiction with some non-fiction.

William Heinemann ☎0171 840 8400 Fax 0171 233 6127 Publishing Director *Maria Rejt* Editorial Director *Lynne Drew* General non-fiction and fiction, especially crime, thrillers and women's fiction.

Chatto & Windus Ltd; Sinclair-Stevenson ☎0171 840 8522 Fax 0171 233 6123 Publishing Director *Jonathan Burnham* Archaeology, art, belles-lettres, biography and memoirs, cookery, crime, current affairs, essays, fiction, history, illustrated and fine editions, poetry, politics, psychoanalysis, translations and travel.

Century (including **Business Books**) ☎0171 840 8555 Fax 0171 233 6127 Publishing Director *Kate Parkin* General fiction and non-fiction, plus business management, advertising, communication, marketing, selling, investment and financial titles.

Hutchinson Books Ltd ☎0171 840 8565 Fax 0171 233 6129 Publishing Director *Sue Freestone* General fiction and non-fiction including notably belles-lettres, current affairs, politics, travel and history.

Arrow; **Mandarin** ☎0171 840 8516 Fax 0171 233 6127 Publishing Director *Andy McKillop* Mass-market paperback fiction and non-fiction.

Legend ☎0171 973 9700 Fax 0171 233 6127 Editorial Director *Andy McKillop* Science fiction and fantasy (hardback and paperback).

Pimlico ☎0171 840 8631 Fax 0171 233 6129 Publishing Director *Will Sulkin* Large-format quality paperbacks in the fields of history, biography, autobiography and literature.

Vintage; **Minerva** ☎0171 840 8531 Fax 0171 233 6127 Publisher *Caroline Michel* Quality paperback fiction and non-fiction. Vintage was founded in 1989 and has been described as one of the 'greatest literary success stories in recent British publishing'.

Children's Books ☎0171 973 9000 Fax 0171 233 6058 Chairman *Piet Snyman*. Managing Director *Ian Hudson* IMPRINTS **Hutchinson** Publishing Director *Caroline Roberts*; **Jonathan Cape** Publishing Director *Tom Maschler*; **Bodley Head** Publishing Director *Anne McNeil*; **Red Fox** and **Tellastory** Publishing Director *Pilar Jenkins*; **Julia MacRae** Publishing Director *Delia Huddy* Picture books, fiction, non-fiction, novelties and audio cassette (see entry under **Audio Books**). CD-ROM multimedia titles under the **Random House New Media** imprint.

Ebury Press Special Books ☎0171 840 8710 Fax 0171 233 6057 Managing Director *Amelia Thorpe*. Publishing Directors *Fiona MacIntyre, Julian Shuckburgh* IMPRINTS **Ebury Press**; **Barrie & Jenkins**; **Condé Nast Books**; **Studio Editions**; **Fodor's**; **Ebury Press Stationery** and the paperback imprints **Vermilion**; **Rider** and **Bracken Books**. Art, architecture, antiques, cookery, gardening, health and beauty, homes and interiors, photography, travel and guides, puzzles and games, sport, natural history, DIY, diaries, gift stationery, reference, TV tie-ins. About 150 titles a year. Unsolicited mss, synopses and ideas for books welcome.

Royalties paid twice-yearly for the most part.

Authors' Rating Buying the trade division of Reed Books has added some illustrious imprints to what was already a prestigious collection of famous names. The latest arrivals include Heinemann, Secker & Warburg, Methuen and Reed's paperback imprint Mandarin which is likely to be merged into Arrow/Vintage. Authors are reported to be happy with the move. Gail Rebuck is committed to general trade publishing 'not just as our core activity but as our entire activity'.

Random Publishing Co.
39 Brideoak Street, Manchester M8 0PN
☎0161 205 3500

Chairman *James Lansbury*
Senior Editor *Hope Dubé*

FOUNDED 1995. *Publishes* fiction and non-fiction in paperback format; memoirs, biography, autobiography, religion/inspirational, popular sciences, young children, health, Millennium. 'May consider some poetry.' No cookery, academic, manuals, playscripts or erotica. 20 books published to-date; 45 planned for 1997. No unsolicited mss; send synopsis and one sample chapter with return postage.
Royalties paid annually.

Authors' Rating Not to be confused with Random House. This is an entirely independent, smallish publisher hoping to grow larger before too long.

Ransom Publishing Ltd
Ransom House, 2 High Street, Watlington,
Oxfordshire OX9 5PS
☎01491 613711   Fax 01491 613733
Managing Director *Jenny Erhe*

FOUNDED 1995 by ex-McGraw-Hill publisher.
Partnerships formed with, among others,
Channel 4 and the BBC Natural History Unit.
Publishes educational and consumer multimedia
and study packs; all titles will link to the
Internet and be published on-line. 2 titles in
1996 but plans to expand list in 1997. TITLES
Lost Animals; Worlds of the Reef; Sahara Desert.
No unsolicited mss. Synopses and ideas for
books, as well as multimedia/Internet projects,
welcome. No science, geography, maths, gen-
eral reference or natural history.
  Royalties paid twice yearly.

Raven
See **Robinson Publishing Ltd**

RCB General Books
See **Richard Cohen Books Ltd**

Reader's Digest Association Ltd
11 Westferry Circus, Canary Wharf, London
E14 4HE
☎0171 715 8000   Fax 0171 715 8181
Managing Director *Neil McRae*
Editorial Head *Cortina Butler*
Approx. Annual Turnover £210 million

Publishes gardening, natural history, cookery, history, DIY, travel and word books. About 35
titles a year. TITLES *Family Encyclopedia of World
History; Know Your Rights; New Encyclopedia of
Garden Plants and Flowers; Treasures in Your Home;
Foods That Harm, Foods That Heal.* Unsolicited
mss, synopses and ideas for books welcome.

Reaktion Ltd
11 Rathbone Place, London W1P 1DE
☎0171 580 9928   Fax 0171 580 9935
Managing Director *Michael R. Leaman*

FOUNDED in Edinburgh in 1985 and moved to
its London location in 1988. *Publishes* art history,
design, architecture, history, cultural studies,
Asian studies, travel and photography. About 16
titles a year. TITLES *The Destruction of Art* Dario
Gamboni; *Monkey Painting* Thierry Lenain; *A
Short History of the Shadow* Victor I. Stoichita;
Painting the Soul Robin Cormack; *Hans Holbein*
Oskar Bätschmann & Pascal Griener. No unso-
licited mss; synopses and ideas welcome.
  Royalties paid twice-yearly.

Reardon and Rawes
11 Trowscoued Avenue, Cheltenham,
Gloucestershire GL53 7BP
☎01242 245259
Editor *Julian Rawes*

FOUNDED 1996. *Publishes* re-issues of out-of-
print titles in electronic/multimedia format.
Non-fiction historical titles only. 4 titles in
1996. TITLES *Picture of Bristol – A Guide* Rev.
John Evans; *Proverbs and Family Mottoes* J. A.
Mair; *Wessex to Essex* Rosemary Barham.
Unsolicited mss welcome.
  Royalties not paid.

Reardon Publishing
56 Upper Norwood Street, Leckhampton,
Cheltenham, Gloucestershire GL53 0DU
☎01242 231800
Managing Editor *Nicholas Reardon*

FOUNDED in the mid 1970s. Family-run publishing house specialising in local interest and
tourism in the Cotswold area. Member of the
Outdoor Writers Guild. *Publishes* walking
and driving guides, and family history for societies. 10 titles a year. TITLES *The Cotswold Way*
(video); *The Cotswold Way Map; Cotswold
Walkabout; Cotswold Driveabout; The Donnington
Way; The Haunted Cotswolds; The Cotswold
Way.* Unsolicited mss, synopses and ideas welcome with return postage only.
  Royalties paid twice-yearly.

Rebel Inc.
See **Canongate Books Ltd**

Recollections
See **George Mann Books**

Red Fox
See **Random House UK Ltd**

William Reed Directories
Merchant House, 4A Reading Road,
Pangbourne, Berkshire RG8 7LL
☎0118 9844111   Fax 0118 9841579
Editorial Manager *Mrs H. Turner*

FOUNDED 1991. *Specialises* in information
books, magazines and booklets for government
departments, national organisations, media/PR
agencies and blue-chip companies. Database
facility for publication of directories, yearbooks
and exhibition programmes. No unsolicited
mss. Preliminary letter essential.

Reed Books

Michelin House, 81 Fulham Road, London SW3 6RB

☎0171 581 9393   Fax 0171 225 9424

Chief Executive *John Holloran*
Approx. Annual Turnover £200 million

Reed Books (formerly the consumer books division of Reed International Books) has several offices; addresses and telephone numbers have been given if different from that above.

ILLUSTRATED NON-FICTION:

Hamlyn/Octopus Fax 0171 225 9528 Publishing Director *Laura Bamford* Popular non-fiction, particularly cookery, gardening, craft, sport, film tie-ins, rock 'n' roll, road atlases TITLES *Larousse Gastronomique; Sunday Times Chronicle of Sport; Hamlyn New Cookbook; Hamlyn Book of Gardening; Hamlyn Book of DIY & Decorating.*

Mitchell Beazley Fax 0171 225 9024 Publishing Director *Jane Aspden* Quality illustrated reference books, particularly wine, antiques, gardening, craft and interiors TITLES *Hugh Johnson's Pocket Wine Book; The New Joy of Sex; Miller's Antiques Price Guide.*

Osprey Second Floor, Unit 6, Spring Gardens, Tinworth Street, London SE11 5EH ☎0171 581 9393 Fax 0171 225 9869 Managing Director *Jonathan Parker* Militaria, aviation, automotive SERIES *Men-at-Arms; New Vanguard; Warrior; Aircraft of the Aces.* TITLES *Combat Aircraft; Stanley Classic Car Year Book; Osprey Companion to Military History; Spitfire – Flying Legend.*

Conran Octopus 37 Shelton Street, London WC2H 9HN ☎0171 240 6961 Fax 0171 836 9951 Publishing Director *John Wallace* Quality illustrated books, particularly interiors, design, cookery, gardening and crafts TITLES Terence Conran's *Essential House Book*; Gordon Ramsay's *Passion for Flavour*; Mary Keen *Making a Garden*; Cressida Bell *The Decorative Painter.*

Philip's Unit 6, Spring Gardens, Tinworth Street, London SE11 5EH ☎0171 581 9393 Fax 0171 225 9841 Publishing Director *John Gaisford* World atlases, globes, astronomy, road atlases, encyclopaedias, thematic reference TITLES *Philip's Atlas of the World; Philip's Modern School Atlas; Philip's Guide to the Stars and Planets; Ordnance Survey Motoring Atlas Britain; Michelin Motoring Atlas France; Philip's Concise Encyclopaedia; Philip's Atlas of World History.*

Pitkin Guides Healey House, Dene Road, Andover, Hampshire SP10 2AA ☎01264 334303 Fax 01264 334110 Managing Director *Ian Corsie* Illustrated souvenir guides.

CHILDRENS:

REED CHILDREN'S BOOKS Fax 0171 225 9731 Managing Director *Jane Winterbotham*, Publishing Director *Gill Evans.*

Heinemann Young Books Quality picture books, novelty books, novels and anthologies TITLES *Thomas The Tank Engine; The Jolly Postman; The Trouble With* series; **Methuen Children's Books** Quality picture books and fiction for babies to early teens TITLES *Winnie the Pooh; Tintin; The Wind in the Willows*; **Hamlyn** Illustrated non-fiction and reference books for children TITLES *Every Boy's/Girl's Handbook; Crime Files; In the Next 3 Seconds*; **Mammoth Paperbacks** Paperback imprint of the above hardback imprints; licensed characters and tie-ins TITLES *Barbie; Star Wars; Disney Playbooks.* No unsolicited mss.

Brimax Books Units 4/5, Studlands Park Industrial Estate, Exning Road, Newmarket, Suffolk CB8 7AU ☎01638 664611 Fax 01638 665220 Editorial Director *Ian Golding* Mass-market board and picture books for children age groups 1–10.

Royalties paid twice-yearly/annually, according to contract in all divisions.

Authors' Rating Having at last disposed of its trade division to Random House, Reed is almost free to concentrate on educational, professional and electronic publishing. Almost – because the children's books, reference and illustrated books are still waiting for new owners. A sign of future expansion was the purchase of Tolley, the tax and legal publisher, for around four times the price paid by Random for the general books. It just shows the value Reed puts on niche publishing as an eventual money spinner. Some academic writers complain of unfair distribution of income from subsidiary rights.

Reed Educational & Professional Publishing

Halley Court, Jordan Hill, Oxford OX2 8EJ

☎01865 311366   Fax 01865 314641

Chief Executive *William Shepherd*

Incorporating Butterworth-Heinemann, Heinemann Educational, Heinemann English Language Teaching and Ginn in the UK; Greenwood Publishing Group, Heinemann and Rigby in the USA; Rigby Heinemann in Australia.

This division has several different offices: addresses and telephone numbers have been given if different from that above.

Heinemann Educational Fax 01865 314140 Managing Director *Bob Osborne*, Primary: *Paul Shuter*, Secondary: *Kay Symons*. Textbooks/literature/other educational resources for primary and secondary school and further education. Mss, synopses and ideas welcome.

Heinemann English Language Teaching Fax 01865 414193 Managing Director *Mike Esplen*, Publishing Director *Sue Bale*. English language teaching books and materials.

Ginn & Co Prebendal House, Parson's Fee, Aylesbury, Bucks HP20 2QY ☎01296 394442 Fax 01296 393433 Managing Director *Nigel Hall*, Editorial Director *Jill Duffy*. Textbook/other educational resources for primary and secondary schools.

Butterworth Heinemann International Linacre House, Jordan Hill, Oxford OX2 8EJ ☎01865 310366 Fax 01865 310898 Managing Director *Philip Shaw*, Engineering & Technology: *Peter Dixon*, Business: *Kathryn Grant*, Medical: *Geoff Smaldon*, College: *Stephen Wellings*. Books and electronic products across business, technical, medical and open-learning fields for students and professionals.

Royalties paid twice-yearly/annually, according to contract in all divisions.

Reinhardt Books Ltd

Flat 2, 43 Onslow Square, London SW7 3LR ☎0171 589 3751

Chairman/Managing Director *Max Reinhardt* **Director** *Joan Reinhardt*

FOUNDED 1887 as H. F. L. (Publishers) and was acquired by Max Reinhardt in 1947. Changed its name to the present one in 1987. First publication under the new name was Graham Greene's *The Captain and the Enemy*. Also publishes under the **Nonesuch Press** imprint. AUTHORS include Mitsumasa Anno, Alistair Cooke and Maurice Sendak. New books are no longer considered.

Royalties paid according to contract.

Religious & Moral Educational Press (RMEP)

See **Hymns Ancient & Modern Ltd**

Richmond House Publishing Company

Douglas House, 3 Richmond Buildings, London W1V 5AE ☎0171 437 9556 Fax 0171 287 3463

Managing Director *Gloria Gordon* **Editorial Head** *Nicholas David Leigh*

Manager *Spencer Block*

Publishes directories for the theatre and entertainment industries. Synopses and ideas welcome.

Rider

See **Random House UK Ltd**

Right Way

See **Elliot Right Way Books**

Robinson Publishing Ltd

7 Kensington Church Court, London W8 4SP ☎0171 938 3830 Fax 0171 938 4214

Managing Director *Nicholas Robinson* **Editorial Director** *Mark Crean*

Publishes fiction – science fiction; horror, fantasy, historical whodunnits, romantic fiction; reference – anthologies, military, puzzles, games, health, self-help and popular psychology, children's. 50 titles in 1996. IMPRINTS **Raven**; **Scarlet** (romantic fiction, 4 titles per month) *Sue Curran*; **Robinson Children's Books** *Tom Keegan*. No unsolicited mss; synopses and ideas welcome.

Royalties paid twice-yearly.

Authors' Rating Now heavily into what was once the preserve of Mills & Boon. The new Scarlet series of romantic fiction is low priced and sold heavily through supermarkets and petrol stations.

Robson Books Ltd

Bolsover House, 5–6 Clipstone Street, London W1P 8LE ☎0171 323 1223 Fax 0171 636 0798

Managing Director *Jeremy Robson* **Editorial Head** *Kate Mills*

FOUNDED 1973. *Publishes* general non-fiction, including biography, cookery, gardening, guidebooks, health and beauty, humour, travel, sports and games. About 70 titles a year. Unsolicited mss, synopses and ideas for books welcome (s.a.e. essential).

Royalties paid twice-yearly.

Authors' Rating The hard-pressed gift buyers' favourite publisher. Strong on humour.

ROC

See **Penguin Books Ltd**

Rosendale Press Ltd

Premier House, 10 Greycoat Place, London SW1P 1SB ☎0171 222 8866 Fax 0171 799 1416

Chairman *Timothy S. Green*

Editorial Director *Maureen P. Green*

FOUNDED 1985. Independent publisher of non-fiction and illustrated books, namely food and drink, travel, business and family health. About 10 titles a year. TITLES *The Top 100 Pasta Sauces; Favourite Indian Food; The Vegetable Market Cookbook; The World of Gold; Eating Out in Barcelona and Catalunya; Understanding Your Baby.* Synopses and ideas for books considered within their specialist fields only.

Payment varies according to contract.

Round Hall
See **Sweet & Maxwell Ltd**

Roundhouse Publishing Group
PO Box 140, Oxford OX2 7FF
☎01865 512682   Fax 01865 559594
Editorial Head *Alan Goodworth*

ESTABLISHED 1991. *Publishes* cinema and media-related titles. TITLES *Cinema of Oliver Stone; Cinema of Stanley Kubrick; Shoot the Piano Player; Animating Culture; Toms, Coons, Mulattoes, Mammies and Bucks.* Represents a broad range of non-fiction publishing houses throughout the UK and Europe. No unsolicited mss.

Royalties paid twice-yearly.

Routledge
11 New Fetter Lane, London EC4P 4EE
☎0171 583 9855   Fax 0171 842 2298
Managing Director *David Hill*
Publishing Director *Peter Sowden*
Publishers *Gordon Smith, Claire L'Enfant, Alan Jarvis*
Approx. Annual Turnover (Group) £30 million

Publishes academic and professional books and journals in the humanities and sciences for the international market. Routledge was formed in 1987 through an amalgamation of Routledge & Kegan Paul, Methuen & Co., Tavistock Publications, and Croom Helm. Subsequent acquisitions include the Unwin Hyman academic list from **HarperCollins** (1991), *Who's Who* and historical atlases from **Dent/Orion** (1994) and archaeology and ancient history titles from **Batsford** (1996). *Publishes* addiction, anthropology, archaeology, Asian studies, biblical studies, business and management, classical heritage and studies, counselling, criminology, development and environment, dictionaries, economics, education, geography, health, history, Japanese studies, journals, language, linguistics, literary criticism, media and culture, Middle East, nursing, philosophy, politics, political economy, psychiatry, psychology, reference, social administration, social studies and sociology, therapy, theatre and performance studies, women's studies. No poetry, fiction, travel or astrology. About 750 titles a year. Send synopses with sample chapter and c.v. rather than complete mss.

Royalties paid annually.

Ryland Peters and Small Limited
Cavendish House, 51–55 Mortimer Street, London W1N 7TD
☎0171 436 9090   Fax 0171 436 9790
Managing Director *David Peters*

FOUNDED 1996 – first titles published in the autumn. *Publishes* highly illustrated lifestyle books – gardening, cookery, craft, interior design. No fiction. No unsolicited mss; synopses and ideas welcome.

Royalties paid twice-yearly.

Authors' Rating A new list of illustrated books of eye-catching quality.

Saint Andrew Press
Board of Communication, Church of Scotland, 121 George Street, Edinburgh EH2 4YN
☎0131 225 5722   Fax 0131 220 3113
Publishing Manager *Lesley Ann Taylor*
Approx. Annual Turnover £225,000

FOUNDED in 1954 to publish and promote the 17-volume series *The Daily Study Bible New Testament* by Professor William Barclay. Owned by the Church of Scotland Board of Communication. *Publishes* religious, Scottish local interest and some children's books. No fiction. 15 titles in 1996. No unsolicited mss; synopses and ideas preferred.

Royalties paid annually.

St Paul's Bibliographies
1 Step Terrace, Winchester, Hampshire SO22 5BW
☎01962 860524   Fax 01962 842409
Chairman/Managing Director *Robert Cross*
Approx. Annual Turnover £30,000

FOUNDED 1982. *Publishes* bibliographical reference books and works on the history of the book. 2–3 titles a year. TITLES *Antiquaries, Book Collectors and the Circle of Learning* ed. Robin Myers and Michael Harris; *A New Introduction to Bibliography* Philip Gaskell; *Julian Symons: Memoirs and Bibliography.* Unsolicited mss, synopses and ideas welcome if relevant to subjects covered.

Royalties paid twice-yearly.

St Pauls

191 Battersea Bridge Road, London SW11 3AS
☎0171 228 1656   Fax 0171 228 2656

Managing Director *Karamvelil Sebastian*

Publishing division of the Society of St Paul. Began publishing in 1914 but activities were fairly limited until around 1948. *Publishes* religious material only: theology, scripture, catechetics, prayer books, children's material and biography. Unsolicited mss, synopses and ideas welcome. About 50 titles a year.

Salamander Books Ltd

129–137 York Way, London N7 9LG
☎0171 267 4447   Fax 0171 267 5112

Managing Director *David Spence*

FOUNDED 1973. Independent publishing house. *Publishes* collecting, cookery, interiors, gardening, music, crafts, military and aviation, pet care, sport and transport. About 55 titles a year. Unsolicited synopses and ideas for books welcome.

Royalties outright fee paid instead of royalties.

Sangam Books Ltd

57 London Fruit Exchange, Brushfield Street, London E1 6EP
☎0171 377 6399   Fax 0171 375 1230

Executive Director *Anthony de Souza*

Traditionally an educational publisher of school and college level textbooks. Also *publishes* art, India, medicine, science, technology, social sciences, religion, plus some fiction in paperback.

Sapling

See **Boxtree**

W. B. Saunders & Co. Ltd/ Saunders Scientific Publications

See **Harcourt Brace and Company Ltd**

SAUS Publications

See **The Policy Press**

SB Publications

c/o 19 Grove Road, Seaford, East Sussex BN25 1TP
☎01323 893498

Managing Director *Steve Benz*
Approx. Annual Turnover £200,000

FOUNDED 1987. *Specialises* in local history, including themes illustrated by old picture postcards and photographs; also travel, guides (town, walking), maritime history and railways. 20 titles a year.

IMPRINTS **Brampton Publications** *Steve Benz* TITLES *Potteries Picture Postcards*; *Curiosities of East Sussex*; *A Dorset Quiz Book*. Also provides marketing and distribution services for local authors.

Royalties paid annually.

Scala Books

See **Philip Wilson Publishers Ltd**

Scarlet

See **Robinson Publishing Ltd**

Scarlet Press

5 Montague Road, London E8 2HN
☎0171 241 3702   Fax 0171 275 0031

Directors *Christine Considine, Avis Lewallen*

FOUNDED 1989. Independent publishing house. *Publishes* feminist non-fiction covering politics, autobiography, social policy, arts, leisure, history, lesbian and gay studies. No fiction or any 'non-woman-centred' material. About 8 titles a year. TITLES *Patient No More: The Politics of Breast Cancer* Sharon Batt; *Idols to Incubators: Reproduction Theory Through the Ages* Julia Stonehouse; *Stolen Lives: Trading Women into Sex and Slavery* Sietske Altink. Unsolicited mss, synopses and ideas welcome.

Royalties paid twice-yearly.

Sceptre

See **Hodder Headline plc**

Scholastic Ltd

Villiers House, Clarendon Avenue, Leamington Spa, Warwickshire CV32 5PR
☎01926 887799   Fax 01926 883331

Chairman *M. R. Robinson*
Managing Director *David Kewley*
Approx. Annual Turnover £52 million

FOUNDED 1964. Owned by US parent company. *Publishes* children's fiction and non-fiction and education for primary schools.

DIVISIONS

Scholastic Children's Books *David Fickling* Commonwealth House, 1–19 New Oxford Street, London WC1A 1NU ☎0171 421 9000 Fax 0171 421 9001 IMPRINTS **Scholastic Press** (hardbacks); **Adlib** (12+ fiction); **Hippo** (paperbacks); **Point** (paperbacks) TITLES *Postman Pat; Rosie & Jim; Tots TV; Horrible Histories; Goosebumps; Point Horror*.

Educational Publishing *Anne Peel* (Villiers House address) Professional books and classroom materials for primary teachers, plus magazines such as *Child Education, Junior Education, Art & Craft, Junior Focus, Infant Projects*.

Red House Book Clubs *David Teale,*
Victoria Birkett Cotswold Business Park, Witney,
Oxford OX8 5YT ☎01993 774171/771144
Fax 01993 776813 The Book Club group sells to
families at home through The Red House Book
Club and Book Parties, through Scholastic and
Red House School Book Clubs (four different
clubs catering for children from 4–15), and
through the Red House International Schools
Club.

Book Fairs *Will Oldham* (Villiers House
address) The Book Fair Division sells directly
to children, parents and teachers in schools
through 14,000 week-long book events held in
schools throughout the UK.

Royalties paid twice-yearly.

Authors' Rating Has held up well against
tough competition in a shrinking children's
market. Authors benefit from strong marketing.

SCM Press Ltd

9–17 St Albans Place, London N1 0NX
☎0171 359 8033   Fax 0171 359 0049
Managing Director *Rev. Dr John Bowden*
Approx. Annual Turnover £1 million

Publishes religion and theology from an open
perspective, with some ethics and philosophy.
About 40 titles a year. Relevant unsolicited mss
and synopses considered if sent with s.a.e..

Royalties paid annually.

Authors' Rating Leading publisher of religious ideas with well-deserved reputation for
fresh thinking. At SCM, 'questioning theology
is the norm'.

Scope International Ltd

Forestside House, Forestside, Rowlands
Castle, Hampshire PO9 6EE
☎01705 631468   Fax 01705 631777
Managing Director/Editorial Director
Richard Cawte

Publishes business, economics, finance, privacy,
tax haven and tax planning, antique porcelain.
IMPRINTS **Scope**. No unsolicted mss.
Approach in writing with ideas/proposals.
Additional material for existing reports wel-
come.

Royalties paid twice-yearly.

Scottish Academic Press

56 Hanover Street, Edinburgh EH2 2DX
☎0131 225 7483   Fax 0131 225 7662
Managing Editor *Dr Douglas Grant*

FOUNDED 1969. *Publishes* academic: architecture, education, geology, history, literature,
poetry, social sciences, theology.

Royalties paid annually.

Seafarer Books

See **The Merlin Press Ltd**

Search Press Ltd/Burns & Oates

Wellwood, North Farm Road, Tunbridge
Wells, Kent TN2 3DR
☎01892 510850   Fax 01892 515903
Managing Director *Countess de la Bédoyère*

FOUNDED 1847. Publishers to the Holy See.
Publishes (Search Press) full-colour art, craft,
needlecrafts; (Burns & Oates) theology, history, spirituality, reference.

DIVISIONS
Academic *Paul Burns* TITLES include
Butler's Lives of the Saints, new full edition, 12
volumes. **Craft** *Rosalind Dace* Books on papermaking and papercrafts, painting on silk, art
techniques and embroidery.

Royalties paid annually.

Secker & Warburg

See **Random House UK Ltd**

Sensation

See **Harlequin Mills & Boon Ltd**

Seren

First Floor, 2 Wyndham Street, Bridgend
CF31 1EF
☎01656 767834   Fax 01656 767834
Chairman *Cary Archard*
Managing Director *Mick Feltin*
Approx. Annual Turnover £100,000

FOUNDED 1981 as a specialist poetry publisher
but has now moved into general literary publishing with an emphasis on Wales. *Publishes*
poetry, fiction, literary criticism, drama, biography, art, history and translations of fiction.
25 titles in 1996.

DIVISIONS
Poetry *Amy Wack* AUTHORS Robert
Minhinnick, Tony Curtis, Sheenagh Pugh,
Duncan Bush, Deryn Rees-Jones. **Drama**
Brian Mitchell AUTHORS Edward Thomas,
Charles Way, Lucinda Coxon. **Fiction, Art,
Literary Criticism, History, Translations**
Mick Felton AUTHORS Christopher Meredith,
Leslie Norris, Gwyn Thomas.

IMPRINT
Border Lines Biographies TITLES *Bruce
Chatwin; Dennis Potter; Mary Webb; Wilfred*

Owen; Raymond Williams. Unsolicited mss, synopses and ideas for books welcome.

Royalties paid twice yearly.

Serpent's Tail
4 Blackstock Mews, London N4 2BT
☎0171 354 1949   Fax 0171 704 6467
Contact *Laurence O'Toole*
Approx. Annual Turnover £650,000

FOUNDED 1986. Won the *Sunday Times* Small Publisher of the Year Award (1989) and the Ralph Lewis Award for new fiction (1992). Serpent's Tail has introduced to British audiences a number of major internationally known writers. Noted for its strong emphasis on design – including flaps on paperback covers in the continental style – and an eye for the unusual. *Publishes* contemporary fiction, including works in translation, crime, popular culture and biography. No poetry, science fiction, horror, romance or fantasy. About 40 titles a year.

IMPRINTS
Serpent's Tail TITLES *Mr Clive and Mr Page* Neil Bartlett; *Hallucinating Foucault* Patricia Duncker; *Ocean of Sound* David Toop; **Mask Noir** TITLES *A Little Yellow Dog*; *Black Betty* Walter Mosley; *Wavewalker* Stella Duffy; *Acid Casuals* Nicholas Blincoe; **High Risk Books** *Rent Boy* Gary Indiana; *Spinsters* Pagan Kennedy; *Bombay Talkie* Armeena Meer. Send preliminary letter outlining proposal (include s.a.e. for reply). No unsolicited mss. Prospective authors who are not familiar with Serpent's Tail are advised to study the list before submitting anything.

Royalties normally paid yearly.

Authors' Rating Described by publisher Peter Ayrton as 'a reference point for outlaw culture', Serpent's Tail gives a voice to writers who are outside the political, sexual or racial mainstream.

Settle Press
10 Boyne Terrace Mews, London W11 3LR
☎0171 243 0695
Chairman/Managing Director *D. Settle*

FOUNDED 1981. *Publishes* travel and guidebooks. About 12 titles a year. **Travel/Tourist Guides** TITLES *City Break Series* (Paris, Rome, Vienna, etc.); *Where to Go Series* (Romania, Turkey, Greece, etc.); *Key To Series* (Far East, Africa, Caribbean, etc). Unsolicited synopses accepted but no mss.

Royalties paid by arrangement.

Severn House Publishers Ltd
9–15 High Street, Sutton, Surrey SM1 1DF
☎0181 770 3930   Fax 0181 770 3850
Chairman *Edwin Buckhalter*
Editorial *Sara Short*

FOUNDED 1974. A leader in library fiction publishing. *Publishes* hardback fiction: romance, science fiction, horror, fantasy, crime. About 130 titles a year. No unsolicited material. Synopses/proposals preferred through *bona fide* literary agents only.

Royalties paid twice-yearly. *Overseas associates* Severn House Publishers Inc., New York.

Sheffield Academic Press
Mansion House, 19 Kingfield Road, Sheffield S11 9AS
☎0114 2554433   Fax 0114 2554626
Managing Director *Mrs Jean R.K. Allen*
Approx. Annual Turnover £1.5 million

FOUNDED in 1976. Originally known as JSOT Press. Now the leading academic publisher of biblical titles. Recently expanded its list to include archaeology, literary studies, history and culture, languages. 110 titles in 1996. Unsolicited mss, synopses and ideas welcome. No fiction.
IMPRINTS **Sheffield Academic Press** *Jean Allen*; **Subis** *Duncan Chambers*.

Royalties paid annually

Sheldon Press
See **Society for Promoting Christian Knowledge**

Shepheard–Walwyn (Publishers) Ltd
Suite 34, 26 Charing Cross Road, London WC2H 0DH
☎0171 240 5992   Fax 0171 379 5770
Managing Director *Anthony Werner*
Approx. Annual Turnover £150,000

FOUNDED 1972. 'We regard books as food for the mind and want to offer a wholesome diet of original ideas and fresh approaches to old subjects.' *Publishes* general non-fiction in three main areas: Scottish interest; gift books in calligraphy and/or illustrated; history, political economy, philosophy. About 5 titles a year. Synopses and ideas for books welcome.

Royalties paid twice-yearly.

The Shetland Times Ltd
Prince Alfred Street, Lerwick, Shetland ZE1 0EP
☎01595 693622   Fax 01595 694637
Managing Director *Robert Wishart*

Publications Manager *Beatrice Nisbet*

FOUNDED 1872 as publishers of the local newspaper. Book publishing followed thereafter plus publication of monthly magazine, *Shetland Life*. *Publishes* anything with Shetland connections – local and natural history, music, crafts, maritime. 10 titles in 1996. Prefers material with a Shetland theme/connection.

Royalties paid annually.

Shire Publications Ltd

Cromwell House, Church Street, Princes Risborough, Buckinghamshire HP27 9AA
☎01844 344301   Fax 01844 347080
Managing Director *John Rotheroe*

FOUNDED 1967. *Publishes* original non-fiction paperbacks. About 25 titles a year. No unsolicited material; send introductory letter with detailed outline of idea.

Royalties paid annually.

Authors' Rating You don't have to live in the country to write books for Shire but it helps. With titles like *Church Fonts, Haunted Inns* and *Discovering Preserved Railways* there is a distinct rural feel to the list. Another way of putting it, to quote John Rotheroe, Shire specialises in 'small books on all manner of obscure subjects'.

Sidgwick & Jackson
See **Macmillan Publishers Ltd**

Sigma Press

1 South Oak Lane, Wilmslow, Cheshire SK9 6AR
☎01625 531035   Fax 01625 536800
Chairman/Managing Director *Graham Beech*

FOUNDED in 1980 as a publisher of technical books. Sigma Press now publishes mainly in the leisure area. *Publishes* outdoor, local heritage, myths and legends, sports, dance and exercise. Recently launched a popular science series. Approx. 55 titles in 1996. No unsolicited mss; synopses and ideas welcome.

DIVISIONS **Sigma Leisure** TITLES *Snowdonia Rocky Rambles; Peak District Memories; In Search of Swallows & Amazons*; **Sigma Press** TITLES *Scrooge's Cryptic Carol; Alice in Quantumland.*

Royalties paid twice-yearly.

Silhouette Desire
See **Harlequin Mills & Boon Ltd**

Simon & Schuster

West Garden Place, Kendal Street, London W2 2AQ
☎0171 316 1900   Fax 0171 402 0639
Managing Director *Nick Webb*
Editorial Directors *Joanna Frank, Martin Fletcher, Helen Gummer*

FOUNDED 1986. Offshoot of the leading American publisher. *Publishes* general fiction, including science fiction under its **Spectrum** imprint and non-fiction in hardback and paperback. The academic division is based in Hemel Hempstead. No academic or technical material.

Royalties paid twice-yearly.

Authors' Rating Best known in the States for its technology list, Simon & Schuster has made its British reputation with new fiction and children's books. But the company's single biggest advantage is being able to take in books from the American side of Simon & Schuster, an economic bonus that nonetheless makes it harder for British authors to gain a foothold.

Sinclair-Stevenson
See **Random House UK Ltd**

Skoob Books Ltd

11A–17 Sicilian Avenue, Southampton Row, London WC1A 2QH
☎0171 404 3063   Fax 0171 404 4398
Editorial office: 76A Oldfield Road, London N16 0RS ☎/Fax 0171 275 9811
Managing Director *I. K. Ong*
Editorial *M. Lovell*

Publishes Literary guides, cultural studies, esoterica/occult, new writing from the Orient. Unsolicited summaries with samples and s.a.e. welcome; no mss. TITLES *Where We Are* Lucien Stryk; *Skoob Directory of Secondhand Bookshops*; *The Necronomicon* George Hay; *Skoob Esoterica Anthology; Haunting the Tiger* K. S. Maniam.

Smith Gryphon Ltd

12 Bridge Wharf, 156 Caledonian Road, London N1 9UU
☎0171 278 2444   Fax 0171 833 5680
Chairman/Managing Director *Robert Smith*

FOUNDED 1990. Family-owned company. *Publishes* biography, autobiography, music (mostly rock), cinema, true crime, topical issues, finance and business, wine, food and cookery, and illustrated. 20 titles in 1997. TITLES *Diana in Private* Lady Colin Campbell; *The Diary of Jack the Ripper* Shirley Harrison; *Harry's Bar Cookbook* Arrigo Cipriani; *Parkhurst*

Tales Norman Parker; *Terminal Velocity* Steve Devereux. No unsolicited mss; ideas and synopses welcome.

Royalties paid twice-yearly.

Authors' Rating Living up to its early promise, Smith Gryphon favours concentration on a select group of strong sellers.

Colin Smythe Ltd

PO Box 6, Gerrards Cross, Buckinghamshire
SL9 8XA
☎01753 886000   Fax 01753 886469
Managing Director *Colin Smythe*
Approx. Annual Turnover £1.5 million
FOUNDED 1966. *Publishes* Anglo-Irish literature, drama, and criticism, history. About 15 titles a year. No unsolicited mss; send synopses and ideas for books in first instance.
Royalties paid annually/twice-yearly.

Society for Promoting Christian Knowledge (SPCK)

Holy Trinity Church, Marylebone Road,
London NW1 4DU
☎0171 387 5282   Fax 0171 388 2352
Director of Publishing *Simon Kingston*
FOUNDED 1698, SPCK is the third oldest publisher in the country.

IMPRINTS
Sheldon Press Editorial Director: *Joanna Moriarty* Popular medicine, health, self-help, psychology, business.

SPCK Senior Editor: *Alex Wright* Theology and academic; Senior Editor: *Rachel Boulding* Liturgy, prayer, spirituality; Editor: *Lucy Gasson* Biblical studies, educational resources, mission; Editor: *Naomi Starkey* Gospel and culture, worldwide; Editorial Director: *Joanna Moriarty* Pastoral care.

Triangle Editor: *Naomi Starkey* Popular Christian paperbacks.

Lynx Editor: *Robin Keeley* Parish resources, training and youthwork, textbooks.
Royalties paid annually.

Authors' Rating Religion with a strong social edge.

SoftbABCks

See **ABC – All Books for Children**

Solo Books Ltd

49–53 Kensington High Street, London
W8 5ED
☎0171 376 2166   Fax 0171 938 3165
Chairman/Managing Director *Don Short*

Approx. Annual Turnover (Group) £1.3 million

Publishing arm of **Solo Literary Agency** (see entry under **UK Agents**). *Publishes* biography and autobiography and celebrity books, some non-fiction and business titles. About 15 titles a year. No fiction. Unsolicited mss not welcome; approach in writing with synopses or ideas.
Royalties paid quarterly.

Solway

See **STL Ltd**

Sotheby's Publications

See **Philip Wilson Publishers Ltd**

Souvenir Press Ltd

43 Great Russell Street, London WC1B 3PA
☎0171 580 9307/8 & 637 5711/2/3
Fax 0171 580 5064
Chairman/Managing Director *Ernest Hecht*
Senior Editor *Tessa Harrow*

Independent publishing house. FOUNDED 1951. *Publishes* academic and scholarly, animal care and breeding, antiques and collecting, archaeology, autobiography and biography, business and industry, children's, cookery, crafts and hobbies, crime, educational, fiction, gardening, health and beauty, history and antiquarian, humour, illustrated and fine editions, magic and the occult, medical, military, music, natural history, philosophy, poetry, psychology, religious, sociology, sports, theatre and women's studies. About 55 titles a year. Souvenir's Human Horizons series for the disabled and their carers is one of the most preeminent in its field and recently celebrated 17 years of publishing for the disabled.

IMPRINTS
Condor; Pictorial; Presentations; Pop Universal; Human Horizons. TITLES *The Wrath of Grapes or The Hangover Companion* Andy Toper; *The Handbook of Chinese Horoscopes* Theodora Lau; *How to Get Your Message Across* Dr David Lewis; *Pulp Frictions* ed. Peter Haining; *The Rear View, A Brief and Elegant History of Bottoms Through the Ages* Jean-Luc Hennig; *Aloe Vera* Alasdair Barcroft; *The Sound of the City – The Rise of Rock and Roll* Charlie Gillett; *Time on Fire, My Comedy of Terrors* Evan Handler. Unsolicited mss considered but initial letter of enquiry preferred.
Royalties paid twice-yearly.

Authors' Rating Eclectic is the only word for Souvenir. Jokey books about knickers and bras share shelf space with translations of work by

Nobel Prize winners and the Human Horizon series for and about disabled people. Ernest Hecht is foremost a showman (his company takes its name from the souvenir theatre programmes he produced as his first publishing venture). His chaotic office with books everywhere has been described as Dada out of Dickens, but he is much loved by his authors.

SPCK
See **Society for Promoting Christian Knowledge**

Neville Spearman
See **The C. W. Daniel Co. Ltd**

Special Edition
See **Harlequin Mills & Boon Ltd**

Spectrum
See **Simon & Schuster**

Spellmount Ltd
The Old Rectory, Staplehurst, Kent TN12 0AZ
☎01580 893730   Fax 01580 893731

Managing Director *Jamie Wilson*
Approx. Annual Turnover £250,000

FOUNDED 1983. *Publishes* non-fiction in hardcover; primarily history and military history, biography. About 20 titles a year. Synopses/ideas for books in these specialist fields welcome, enclosing return postage.
   Royalties six-monthly for two years, then annually.

E & F N Spon
2–6 Boundary Row, London SE1 8HN
☎0171 865 0066   Fax 0171 522 9621

Managing Director *Geoffrey Burn*
Publishing Director *Phillip Read*

FOUNDED 1834 by the son and grandson of Baron de Spon, a refugee from the French Revolution, the company has always specialised in science and technology. In the 1950s, it became an imprint of Chapman & Hall and since 1987 has concentrated solely on construction-related titles. About 70 titles a year. *Publishes* architecture, building, civil and environmental engineering, landscape, planning & property (all built-environment), sports science, leisure & recreation management. TITLES *The Modern Steel House; Business Occupiers Handbook; Water Quality Assessment; Earthquake Engineering; Facilities Management; Coastal Recreation Management; Science and*

Skiing. Unsolicited mss, synopses and ideas welcome.
   Royalties paid annually.

Sporting & Leisure Press
See **The Barracuda Collection**

Stainer & Bell Ltd
PO Box 110, 23 Gruneisen Road, London N3 1DZ
☎0181 343 3303   Fax 0181 343 3024

Chairman *Bernard A. Braley*
Managing Directors *Carol Y. Wakefield, Keith M. Wakefield*
Publishing Manager *Nicholas Williams*
Approx. Annual Turnover £630,000

FOUNDED 1907 to publish sheet music. *Publishes* music and religious subjects related to hymnody. Unsolicited synopses/ideas for books welcome. Send letter enclosing brief précis.
   Royalties paid annually.

Harold Starke Publishers Ltd
Pixey Green, Stradbroke, Near Eye, Suffolk IP21 5NG
☎01379 388334   Fax 01379 388335

Directors *Harold K. Starke, Naomi Galinski*

Publishes adult non-fiction, medical and reference. No unsolicited mss.
   Royalties paid annually.

The Stationery Office Publishing
St Crispins, Duke Street, Norwich, Norfolk NR3 1PD
☎01603 622211   Fax 01603 695582

Chief Executive *Fred J. Perkins*
Managing Director *Robert Mackay*
Approx. Annual Turnover £55 million

Formerly HMSO, which was FOUNDED 1786. Became part of the private sector in October 1996. Publisher of material sponsored by Parliament, government departments and other official bodies. Also commercial publishing in the following broad categories: business and professional, environment, education, heritage. Unsolicited material may be considered if suitable and should be sent in the first instance to Mick Spencer, Editorial Manager.

Authors' Rating After privatisation, the Stationery Office was rationalised, streamlined and downsized. Not before time, some might say. As HMSO, the setup was losing money hand over fist. Now, there is a serious expectation of turning in a profit within the year. On the trade side, the Stationery Office produces some excellent popular history. There may be opportunities here for authors who would not automatically think of the publisher of the *Highway Code* as their natural home.

Patrick Stephens Ltd
See **Haynes Publishing**

Stevens
See **Sweet & Maxwell Ltd**

STL Ltd
PO Box 300, Kingstown Broadway, Carlisle, Cumbria CA3 0QS
☎01228 512512   Fax 01228 514949
Publishing Director *Pieter Kwant*
Editorial Manager *Mark Finnie*
Approx. Annual Turnover £2 million
Owns Paternoster Publishing with the following IMPRINTS:
The Paternoster Press FOUNDED 1935. *Publishes* religion and learned/church/life-related journals. Over 100 titles a year. TITLES *The New International Dictionary of New Testament Theology* (4 vols) ed. Colin Brown; *Acts in its 1st Century Setting* ed. Bruce Winter; *Calvin's Old Testament Commentaries.*
OM Publishing FOUNDED 1966. *Publishes* Christian books on evangelism, discipleship and mission. About 30 titles a year. TITLES *Operation World* Patrick Johnstone; *You Can Change the World* Jill Johnstone; and many titles by Elisabeth Elliot and A. W. Tozer.
Solway FOUNDED 1996. 'Tackling Christianity and Christian art from an original perspective.' About 10 titles a year. TITLES *After Eating the Apricot* John Goldingay; *Learning to Fly* Adrian Plass and Ben Ecclestone. Unsolicited mss, synopses and ideas for books welcome.
Royalties paid twice-yearly.

Studio Editions
See **Random House UK Ltd**

Subis
See **Sheffield Academic Press**

Summersdale Publishers
46 West Street, Chichester, West Sussex PO19 1RP
☎01243 771107   Fax 01243 786300
Manager *Alastair Williams*
Editor *Stewart Ferris*
FOUNDED 1990. *Publishes* non-fiction: cookery, biography, gardening, sport (including martial arts/self defence), humour, self-

improvement, travel, local interest, arts/entertainment. TITLES *During the War* Buster Merryfield; *Bestsellers* Richard Joseph; *500 Chat-up Lines and Put Downs*; *Two Feet, Four Paws – The Girl Who Walked Her Dog 4,500 Miles.* 40 titles in 1997. No unsolicited mss; initial approach by letter only.
Royalties paid.

Susquehanna University Press
See **Golden Cockerel Press**

Sutton Publishing Ltd
Phoenix Mill, Thrupp, Stroud, Gloucestershire GL5 2BU
☎01453 731114   Fax 01453 731117
Managing Director *David Hogg*
Publishing Director *Peter Clifford*
Approx. Annual Turnover £4 million
FOUNDED 1978. Owned by Guernsey Press. *Publishes* academic, archaeology, biography, countryside, history, regional interest, local history, pocket classics (lesser known novels by classic authors), transport. About 240 titles a year. Send synopses rather than complete mss.
Royalties paid twice-yearly.

Swan Hill Press
See **Airlife Publishing Ltd**

Sweet & Maxwell Ltd
100 Avenue Road, London NW3 3PF
☎0171 393 7000   Fax 0171 393 7010
Managing Director *Mike Boswood*
FOUNDED 1799. Part of The Thomson Corporation. *Publishes* legal and professional materials in all media, looseleaf works, journals, law reports and on CD-ROM. About 150 book titles a year, with live backlist of over 700 titles, 75 looseleaf services and more than 80 legal periodicals. Not interested in material which is non-legal. The legal and professional list is varied and contains many academic titles, as well as treatises and reference works in the legal and related professional fields.
IMPRINTS **Sweet & Maxwell; Sweet & Maxwell Asia; Stevens; W. Green (Scotland); Round Hall/Sweet & Maxwell (Ireland)** *Anthony Kinahan* (Managing Director). Ideas welcome. Writers with legal/professional projects in mind are advised to contact the company at the earliest possible stage in order to lay the groundwork for best design, production and marketing of a project.
Royalties and fees vary according to contract.

Take That Ltd
PO Box 200, Harrogate, North Yorkshire
HG1 2NA
☎01423 507545   Fax 01423 526035
Chairman/Managing Director *C. Brown*

FOUNDED 1986. Independent publisher of
computing, business, humour and gambling
titles (books and magazines). TITLES *Understand
Financial Risk in a Day; Complete Beginner's
Guide to the Internet; The Hangover Handbook;
Playing Lotteries For the Big Money.* About 10
titles a year. Unsolicited synopses for books
welcome; 'no novels, please'.
Royalties paid twice-yearly.

Tango Books
See **Sadie Fields Productions Ltd** under
UK Packagers

I. B. Tauris & Co. Ltd
Victoria House, Bloomsbury Square, London
WC1B 4DZ
☎0171 916 1069   Fax 0171 916 1068
Chairman/Publisher *Iradj Bagherzade*
Managing Director *Jonathan McDonnell*

FOUNDED   1984.   Independent   publisher.
Publishes general non-fiction and academic in the
fields of international relations, current affairs,
history, cultural studies, Middle East, East-West
relations, Russia and East European studies. Joint
projects with Cambridge University Centre for
Middle Eastern Studies, Institute for Latin
American Studies and Institute of Ismaili Studies.
Distributes The New Press (New York) out-
side North America. *Represents* **The Curzon
Press** in the UK. IMPRINTS **Tauris Parke
Books** Illustrated books on architecture, travel,
design and culture. **British Academic Press**
Academic monographs. Unsolicited mss, syn-
opses and ideas for books welcome.
Royalties paid twice-yearly.

Tavistock Publications
See **Routledge**

Taxation Publishing
See **Tolley Publishing Co. Ltd**

Taylor & Francis Group
1 Gunpowder Square, London EC4A 3DE
☎0171 583 0490   Fax 0171 583 9581
Chairman *Mrs Elnora Ferguson*
Managing Director *Anthony Selvey*
Approx. Annual Turnover £23 million

FOUNDED 1798 with the launch of *Philosophical
Magazine* which has been in publication ever
since (now a solid state physics journal). The
company is privately owned with strong academic connections among the major shareholders. **Falmer Press** (see entry) joined the group
in 1979 and it doubled its size in the late '80s
with the acquisition of Crane Russak in 1986
and Hemisphere Publishing Co in 1988. In
1995, acquired Erlbaum Associates Ltd, adding
to the growing list of psychology publications. In
1996, UCL Press Ltd was acquired, adding further to its portfolio of publications in science and
humanities. *Publishes* scientific, technical, education titles at university, research and professional levels. About 250 titles a year. Unsolicited
mss, synopses and ideas welcome.
Royalties paid yearly. *Overseas office* Taylor &
Francis Inc., Washington DC.

Teach Yourself
See **Hodder Headline plc**

Telegraph Books
1 Canada Square, Canary Wharf, London
E14 5DT
☎0171 538 6824   Fax 0171 538 6064
Owner *Telegraph Group Ltd*
Manager *Vicky Unwin*
Approx. Annual Turnover £1 million

Concentrates on Telegraph branded books in
association/collaboration with other publishers. Also runs Telegraph Books Direct, a direct
mail, 24-hour phone-line bookselling service
and off-the-page sales for other publishers'
books. *Publishes* general non-fiction: journalism, business and law, cookery, education,
gardening, wine, guides, sport, puzzles and
games, maps. 70 titles in 1996. Only interested
in books if a Telegraph link exists. No unsolicited material.
Royalties paid twice-yearly.

Tellastory
See **Random House UK Ltd**

Temple House Books
See **The Book Guild Ltd**

Test Your Child
See **Hodder Headline plc**

Thames and Hudson Ltd
30–34 Bloomsbury Street, London
WC1B 3QP
☎0171 636 5488   Fax 0171 636 4799
Managing Director *Thomas Neurath*
Editorial Head *Jamie Camplin*

Publishes art, archaeology, architecture and

design, biography, crafts, fashion, garden and landscape design, graphics, history, illustrated and fine editions, mythology, music, photography, popular culture, travel and topography. Over 150 titles a year. SERIES *World of Art; New Horizons; Chic Simple; Celtic Design; Sacred Symbols; Fashion Memoir.* TITLES *The Panorama of the Renaissance; Derek Jarman's Garden; The Shock of the New; Chronicle of the Roman Emperors; Style Surfing; The Book of Kells; The Most Beautiful Villages of the Dordogne; Multimedia Graphics; The Graphic Language of Neville Brody 1 & 2; The Body; David Bailey's Rock and Roll Heroes.* Send preliminary letter and outline before mss.

Royalties paid twice-yearly.

Authors' Rating A company that thrives on artistic excellence with a list that has more dip-into books than that of any other publisher.

Thistle Publishing
122 Bedford Court Mansions, Bedford Square, London WC1B 3AH
☎0171 636 4917   Fax 0171 436 1898
Managing Director *Andrew Lownie*

FOUNDED in 1996 to publish a three-volume collection of short stories by John Buchan. *Publishes* Scottish subjects only. No unsolicited material; approach with preliminary letter.

Stanley Thornes (Publishers) Ltd
Ellenborough House, Wellington Street, Cheltenham, Gloucestershire GL50 1YW
☎01242 228888   Fax 01242 221914
Managing Director *David Smith*
Approx. Annual Turnover £20 million

FOUNDED 1972. Part of the Wolters-Kluwer Group. Merged with Mary Glasgow Publications in 1992. *Publishes* secondary school and college curriculum textbooks and primary school resources. About 200 titles a year. Unsolicited mss, synopses and ideas for books welcome if appropriate to specialised list.

IMPRINT **Mary Glasgow Publications** foreign-language teaching materials and teacher support.

Royalties paid annually.

Thorsons
See **HarperCollins Publishers Ltd**

Times Books
See **HarperCollins Publishers Ltd**

Titan Books
42–44 Dolben Street, London SE1 0UP
☎0171 620 0200   Fax 0171 620 0032
Managing Director *Nick Landau*

Editorial Director *Katy Wild*

FOUNDED 1981. Now a leader in the publication of graphic novels and in film and television tie-ins. *Publishes* comic books/graphic novels, film and television titles. About 70–80 titles a year.

IMPRINTS
Titan Books; **Eros Plus** Erotic fiction. TITLES *Batman; Superman; Star Trek; Beginners Guide to Japanese Animation; Star Wars; Guide to Monster Make-up.* No unsolicited fiction or children's books please. Ideas for film and TV titles considered; send synopsis/outline with sample chapter. Author guidelines available.

Royalties paid twice-yearly.

Tolkien
See **HarperCollins Publishers Ltd**

Tolley Publishing Co. Ltd
Tolley House, 2 Addiscombe Road, Croydon, Surrey CR9 5AF
☎0181 686 9141   Fax 0181 686 3155
Chief Executive *Neville Cusworth*
Managing Director *Christine Durman*

Owned by Reed Elsevier Legal Division.

DIVISIONS **Tolley Publishing; Charles Knight Publishing; Taxation Publishing; Fourmat Publishing; Payroll Alliance.** Unsolicited mss, synopses and ideas welcome.

Transworld Publishers Ltd
61–63 Uxbridge Road, London W5 5SA
☎0181 579 2652   Fax 0181 579 5479
Chairman *Stephen Rubin*
Managing Director *Mark Barty-King*

FOUNDED 1950. A subsidiary of **Bantam, Doubleday, Dell Publishing Group Inc.**, New York, which is a wholly-owned subsidiary of Bertelsmann AG, Germany. *Publishes* general fiction and non-fiction, children's books, sports and leisure.

DIVISIONS
Adult Trade *Patrick Janson-Smith* **Adult Hardback** *Ursula Mackenzie* **Adult Paperback** *Larry Finlay* IMPRINTS **Bantam** *Francesca Liversidge;* **Bantam Press** *Sally Gaminara;* **Corgi, Black Swan** *Bill Scott-Kerr;* **Doubleday** *Marianne Velmans;* **Partridge Press** *Ursula Mackenzie.* AUTHORS Kate Atkinson, Bill Bryson, Catherine Cookson, Jilly Cooper, Nicholas Evans, Frederick Forsyth, Robert Goddard, Stephen Hawking, Terry Pratchett, James Redfield, Gerald Seymour, Danielle Steel, Joanna Trollope, Mary Wesley.

Children's & Young Adult Books
Philippa Dickinson IMPRINTS **Doubleday** (hardcover); **Picture Corgi; Corgi Pups; Young Corgi; Corgi Yearling; Corgi; Corgi Freeway; Bantam** (paperback). AUTHORS Ian Beck, Malorie Blackman, Helen Cooper, Peter Dickinson, Francine Pascal, K. M. Peyton, Terry Pratchett, Philip Pullman, Robert Swindells, Jacqueline Wilson. Unsolicited mss welcome only if preceded by preliminary letter.

Royalties paid twice-yearly. *Overseas associates* Transworld Australia/New Zealand, Trans-South Africa Book Distributors.

Authors' Rating Tops the *Guardian* fast-seller list with such as *The Horse Whisperer* (1 million+ copies sold). The books may be good but where Transworld really stands out is in the quality of its marketing and promotion. Authors rarely complain that they are ignored.

Trentham Books Ltd

Westview House, 734 London Road, Stoke on Trent, Staffordshire ST4 5NP
☎01782 745567   Fax 01782 745553
Chairman/Managing Director *Dr John Eggleston*
Editorial Head *Gillian Klein*
Approx. Annual Turnover £1 million

Publishes education (nursery, school and higher), social sciences, intercultural studies, design and technology education for professional readers *not* for children and parents. No fiction, biography or poetry. About 25 titles a year. Unsolicited mss, synopses and ideas welcome if relevant to their interests.

Royalties paid annually.

Triangle

See **Society for Promoting Christian Knowledge**

Trotman & Co. Ltd

12 Hill Rise, Richmond, Surrey TW10 6UA
☎0181 940 5668   Fax 0181 948 9267
Managing Director *Andrew Fiennes Trotman*
Publishing Director *Morfydd Jones*
Approx. Annual Turnover £3 million

Publishes general careers books, higher education guides, teaching support material, employment and training resources. About 70 titles a year. TITLES *Complete Degree Course Offers* (book and CD-ROM); *How to Complete Your UCAS Form; Students' Money Matters.* Unsolicited material welcome. Also in the educational resources market, producing recruitment brochures.

Royalties paid twice-yearly.

Two-Can Publishing Ltd

346 Old Street, London EC1V 9NQ
☎0171 684 4000   Fax 0171 613 3371
Chairman *Andrew Jarvis*
Marketing Director *Ian Grant*
Creative Director *Sara Lynn*
Approx. Annual Turnover £5 million

FOUNDED 1987 to publish innovative, high-quality material for children. *Publishes* books and magazines, including *Young Telegraph* (weekend supplement for 9–12-year-olds).

DIVISIONS **Books** *Ian Grant*; **Magazines** *Andrew Jarvis.* No unsolicited mss; send synopses and ideas in the first instance.

Royalties paid twice-yearly.

UCL Press Ltd

1 Gunpower Square, London EC4A 3DE
☎0171 583 0490   Fax 0171 583 0581
Chairman *Alexander Smith*
Publisher/Chief Executive *R. F. J. Jones*

FOUNDED 1991. Acquired by the **Taylor & Francis Group** in 1996. *Publishes* academic books only. About 80 titles a year. No unsolicited mss; synopses and ideas welcome.

Royalties paid annually.

University Presses of California, Columbia & Princeton Ltd

1 Oldlands Way, Bognor Regis, West Sussex PO22 9SA
☎01243 842165   Fax 01243 842167

Publishes academic titles only. US-based editorial offices. Over 200 titles a year. Enquiries only.

Unwin Hyman

See **HarperCollins Publishers Ltd**

Usborne Publishing Ltd

83–85 Saffron Hill, London EC1N 8RT
☎0171 430 2800   Fax 0171 430 1562
Managing Director *Peter Usborne*
Editorial Director *Jenny Tyler*
Approx. Annual Turnover £14 million

FOUNDED 1973. *Publishes* non-fiction, fiction, puzzle books, and music for children and young adults. Some titles for parents. Up to 100 titles a year. Also, **Usborne Books at Home** imprint. Based at Oasis Park, Eynsham, Oxford OX8 1TU. Books are written in-house to a specific format and therefore unsolicited mss are not normally welcome. Ideas which may be developed in-house are considered. Keen to hear from new illustrators and designers.

Royalties paid twice-yearly.

Authors' Rating 21 years in the business of 'making books that children want to read' has given the Usborne imprint a distinctive, busy look recognisable in the bookshops at several yards. Most of the writing is done by in-house editors.

Vallentine Mitchell
See **Frank Cass & Co Ltd**

Ventura
See **Penguin Books Ltd**

Vermilion
See **Random House UK Ltd**

Verso
6 Meard Street, London W1V 3HR
☎0171 437 3546   Fax 0171 734 0059
Chairman *Lucy Heller*
Managing Director *Colin Robinson*
Approx. Annual Turnover £2 million
Formerly New Left Books which grew out of the *New Left Review*. Publishes politics, history, sociology, economics, philosophy, cultural studies, feminism. TITLES *Theatres of Memory* Raphael Samuel; *The Enemy Within* Seumas Milne; *The Missionary Position* Christopher Hitchens; *City of Quartz* Mike Davis; *Senseless Acts of Beauty* George McKay; *Year 501* Noam Chomsky; *Ideology* Terry Eagleton; *The Politics of Friendship* Jacques Derrida; *The Motorcycle Diaries* Ernesto Che Guevara. No unsolicited mss; synopses and ideas for books welcome.
Royalties paid annually. *Overseas office* in New York.

Authors' Rating Dubbed by *The Bookseller* as 'one of the most successful small independent publishers'.

Viking/Viking Children's
See **Penguin Books Ltd**

Vintage
See **Random House UK Ltd**

Virago Press
Little, Brown & Co. (UK), Brettenham House, Lancaster Place, London WC2E 7EN
☎0171 911 8000   Fax 0171 911 8100
Publisher *Lennie Goodings*
Approx. Annual Turnover £2.75 million
FOUNDED 1973 by Carmen Callil, with the aim of publishing a wide range of books which illuminate and celebrate all aspects of women's lives. Bought by **Little, Brown & Co. (UK)**

in 1996. Most titles are published in paperback; a distinguished reprint list makes up one third of these, with two thirds original titles commissioned across a wide range of interest: autobiography, biography, crime, fiction, history, social issues, politics, psychology, women's studies. About 50 titles a year. TITLES *Oyster* Janette Turner Hospital; *Two or The Book of Twins and Doubles* Penelope Farmer. Send return postage with unsolicited material.
Royalties paid twice-yearly.

Authors' Rating Having changed the reading habits of a generation of British women, Virago has now latched on to Big Brother who, it is hoped, will provide the resources for major growth. A new list of raunchy, popular fiction may show the way.

Virgin Publishing
332 Ladbroke Grove, London W10 5AH
☎0181 968 7554   Fax 0181 968 0929
Chairman *Robert Devereux*
Managing Director *Robert Shreeve*
Approx. Annual Turnover £10 million
The Virgin Group's book publishing company. *Publishes* non-fiction, fiction and large-format illustrated books on entertainment and popular culture, particularly music, TV tie-ins and books about film, showbiz, sport, biography, autobiography and humour. Also developing a travel list. No poetry, short stories, individual novels, children's books or cartoons.

IMPRINTS
Non-fiction: **Virgin** *Rod Green* Sport, music biography, humour, film, TV tie-ins; *Carolyn Price* Illustrated books on all above subjects.
Fiction: **Virgin; The New Adventures**; **Crime & Passion**; **Idol**; **Black Lace**; **Nexus** Branded series of genre novels. Publisher *Peter Darvill-Evans*. Series editors: *Kerri Sharp* (erotica, crime), *Rebecca Levene* (science fiction).
Royalties paid twice-yearly.

Authors' Rating Aiming for the popular end of the market with some sure-fire hits like the Black Lace erotic fiction for women readers.

Vista
See **Cassell**

Volcano Press Ltd
PO Box 139, Leicester LE2 2YH
☎0116 2706714   Fax 0116 2706714
Chairman *F. Hussain*
Managing Director *A. Hussain*
FOUNDED 1992. *Publishes* academic non-fiction

in the following areas: Islam, women's studies, human rights, Middle East, strategic studies and cultural studies. About 15 titles a year. TITLES *The Sociology of Islamic Fundamentalism; Islam in Britain; Islamic Fundamentalism in Britain; Women in the Islamic Struggle*. No unsolicited mss; synopses and ideas welcome. No fiction, poetry or plays.

Royalties paid twice-yearly.

University of Wales Press
6 Gwennyth Street, Cathays, Cardiff CF2 4YD
☎01222 231919   Fax 01222 230908
Director *Ned Thomas*
Approx. Annual Turnover £350,000

FOUNDED 1922. *Publishes* academic and scholarly books in English and Welsh, particularly humanities, modern languages and social sciences, and scholarly Celtic works. 60 titles in 1996.

IMPRINTS
GPC Books; Gwasg Prifysgol Cymru; University of Wales Press. TITLES *Disraeli and the Rise of a New Imperialism* C. C. Eldridge; *Writers in a Landscape* Jeremy Hooker; *The Gododdin of Aneurin* John T. Koch. Unsolicited mss considered.

Royalties paid annually.

Walker Books Ltd
87 Vauxhall Walk, London SE11 5HJ
☎0171 793 0909   Fax 0171 587 1123

Editors *Vanessa Clarke, Jackie Goff, Caroline Royds, Sally Christie, Jacqui Bailey, Sally Foord-Kelcey, Lesley Ann Daniels, Sara Carroll*
Approx. Annual Turnover £23 million

FOUNDED 1979. *Publishes* illustrated children's books, children's fiction and non-fiction. About 300 titles a year. TITLES *Where's Wally?* Martin Handford; *Five Minutes' Peace* Jill Murphy; *Can't You Sleep, Little Bear?* Martin Waddell & Barbara Firth; *Guess How Much I Love You* Sam McBratney & Anita Jeram; *MapHead* Lesley Howarth. Unsolicited mss welcome.

Royalties paid twice-yearly.

Authors' Rating The leading publisher of children's books continues to grow apace largely thanks to a breakthrough in the US market. Authors praise the friendly and efficient editors and designers.

Ward Lock
See **Cassell**

Ward Lock Educational Co. Ltd
1 Christopher Road, East Grinstead, West Sussex RH19 3BT
☎01342 318980   Fax 01342 410980
Owner *Ling Kee (UK Ltd)*
Editor (Maths, Science, Geography) *Rose Hill*
Editor (English) *Diane Biston*

FOUNDED 1952. *Publishes* educational books (primary, middle, secondary, teaching manuals) for all subjects, specialising in maths, science, geography, reading and English.

Royalties paid annually.

Frederick Warne
See **Penguin Books Ltd**

Warner
See **Little, Brown & Co. (UK)**

Warner Chappell Plays Ltd
See entry under **UK Agents**

Waterline Books
See **Airlife Publishing Ltd**

Franklin Watts
See **The Watts Publishing Group**

The Watts Publishing Group
96 Leonard Street, London EC2A 4RH
☎0171 739 2929   Fax 0171 739 2318
Managing Director *Marlene Johnson*

Part of Hachette SA. *Publishes* general non-fiction, reference, information and children's (fiction, picture and novelty). About 300 titles a year.

IMPRINTS
Franklin Watts *Philippa Stewart* Non-fiction and information; **Orchard Books** *Francesca Dow* Children's fiction, picture and novelty books. Unsolicited mss, synopses and ideas for books welcome.

Royalties paid twice-yearly. *Overseas associates* in Australia and New Zealand, US and Canada.

Wayland Publishers Ltd
(incorporating **Macdonald Young Books**)
61 Western Road, Hove, East Sussex BN3 1JD
☎01273 722561   Fax 01273 329314
Director & General Manager *Roberta Bailey*
Editorial Director *Stephen White-Thomson*
Approx. Annual Turnover £6 million

Part of the Wolters Kluwer Group. FOUNDED

1969. *Publishes* a broad range of subjects for children, mainly colour-illustrated non-fiction and fiction for 5 years and upwards. About 400 titles a year. No unsolicited mss or synopses as all books are commissioned.

Royalties paid annually. *Overseas associates* Steck-Vaughn Company, USA.

Weidenfeld & Nicolson Ltd
See **The Orion Publishing Group Ltd**

Welsh Academic Press
See **Ashley Drake Publishing Ltd**

West One (Trade) Publishing Ltd
4 Great Portland Street, London W1N 5AA
☎0171 580 6886   Fax 0171 580 9788
Chairman *Martin Coleman*
Managing Director *Kevin Fitzgerald*
Approx. Annual Turnover £2 million

Publishes travel guides and cartography, including RAC publications. TITLES *RAC Inspected Hotels Guide to UK and Ireland; RAC Hotels in France.* Unsolicited synopses and ideas welcome.

Wharncliffe Publishing Ltd
47 Church Street, Barnsley, South Yorkshire S70 2AS
☎01226 734222   Fax 01226 734438
Chairman *Sir Nicholas Hewitt*
Publishing Manager *C. Hewitt*

Part of Barnsley Chronicle Holdings Ltd. Wharncliffe is the book and magazine publishing arm of an old-established, independently owned newspaper publishing and printing house. *Publishes* local and regional interest and activities, field sports and related material. Unsolicited mss, synopses and ideas welcome but return postage must be included with all submissions.

Royalties paid twice-yearly. *Associated company* **Leo Cooper/Pen & Sword Books Ltd.**

Which? Books/Consumers' Association
2 Marylebone Road, London NW1 4DF
☎0171 830 6000   Fax 0171 830 7660
Director *Sheila McKechnie*
Head of Publishing *Gill Rowley*

FOUNDED 1957. Publishing arm of the consumer organisation, a registered charity. *Publishes* non-fiction: information, reference and how-to books on travel, gardening, health, personal finance, consumer law, food, education, crafts, DIY. Titles must offer direct value or utility to the UK consumer. 25–30 titles a year.

IMPRINT **Which? Books** *Gill Rowley* TITLES *Good Food Guide; Good Skiing Guide; Good Walks Guide; Which? Travel Guides; Which? Consumer Guides.* No unsolicited mss; send synopses and ideas only.

Royalties paid twice-yearly; but owing to in-house editorial development of many titles, royalties are not always applicable.

Whittet Books Ltd
18 Anley Road, London W14 0BY
☎0171 603 1139   Fax 0171 603 8154
Managing Director *Annabel Whittet*

Publishes natural history, pets, horses, rural interest and transport. Unsolicited mss, synopses and ideas for books welcome.

Royalties paid twice-yearly.

Whurr Publishers Ltd
19B Compton Terrace, London N1 2UN
☎0171 359 5979   Fax 0171 226 5290
Chairman/Managing Director *Colin Whurr*
Approx. Annual Turnover £1 million

FOUNDED in 1987. Originally specialised in publishing books and journals on disorders of communication but now publishing in a number of academic and professional fields. *Publishes* speech and language therapy, nursing, psychology, psychotherapy, business and management, dyslexia. No fiction and general trade books. 12 titles in 1996. Unsolicited mss, synopses and ideas welcome within their specialist fields only.

Royalties paid twice-yearly.

John Wiley & Sons Ltd
Baffins Lane, Chichester, West Sussex PO19 1UD
☎01243 779777   Fax 01243 775878
Chairman *The Duke of Richmond*
Managing Director *Dr John Jarvis*
Publishing Director *Steven Mair*
Approx. Annual Turnover £45 million

FOUNDED 1807. US parent company. *Publishes* professional, reference trade and text books, scientific, technical and biomedical.

DIVISIONS

Behavioural & Professional Sciences *Richard Baggaley;* **Physical Sciences** *Dr Ernest Kirkwood;* **Life & Medical Sciences** *Mike Davis;* **Technology** *Rosemary Altoft;* **Wiley Chancery Law & Finance** *David Wilson;* **Earth & Environmental Sciences** *Helen Bailey;* **College Publishing Group** *Simon*

Plumtree. Unsolicited mss welcome, as are synopses and ideas for books.
Royalties paid annually.

Authors' Rating Voted best publisher by academic bookshops, Wiley's inexorable rise (it now publishes more titles than OUP) is tied to the success of its college division and to academic journals. Recent expansion has taken in VCH, a leading German professional and scientific publisher.

Neil Wilson Publishing Ltd
Suite 303a, The Pentagon Centre,
36 Washington Street, Glasgow G3 8AZ
☎0141 221 1117   Fax 0141 221 5363
Chairman *Gordon Campbell*
Managing Director/Editorial Director
  Neil Wilson
Approx. Annual Turnover £250,000

FOUNDED 1992. *Publishes* Scottish interest and history, biography, humour and hillwalking, whisky and beer; also cookery and Irish interest. About 10 titles a year. Unsolicited mss, synopses and ideas welcome. No fiction, politics, academic or technical.
Royalties paid twice-yearly.

Philip Wilson Publishers Ltd
143–149 Great Portland Street, London
W1N 5FB
☎0171 436 4490   Fax 0171 436 4403/4260
Chairman *Philip Wilson*
Managing Director *Antony White*

FOUNDED 1976. *Publishes* art, art history, antiques and collectables. 21 titles in 1996. DIVISIONS **Philip Wilson Publishers Ltd; Scala Books** *Anne Jackson;* **Flint River Press Ltd** *Bato Tomasevic;* **Sotheby's Publications** *Anne Jackson.*

Windrow & Greene Ltd
5 Gerrard Street, London W1V 7LJ
☎0171 287 4570   Fax 0171 494 0583
Managing Director *Alan Greene*
Editorial Director *Martin Windrow*

FOUNDED 1990 by ex-conglomerate refugees wanting to publish quality books in close consultation with authors. *Publishes* military history and hobbies, cars and motorcycling, aviation and transport, directories and specialist journals. About 28 titles a year. Unsolicited mss considered but synopses and ideas preferred in the first instance.
Royalties paid twice-yearly.

The Windrush Press
Little Window, High Street, Moreton in Marsh, Gloucestershire GL56 0LL
☎01608 652012/652025   Fax 01608 652125
Managing Director *Geoffrey Smith*
Editorial Head *Victoria Huxley*

FOUNDED 1987. Independent company. *Publishes* travel, biography, history, military history, humour. About 10 titles a year. TITLES *Reflections of Rifleman Harris; Lanzarote: A Windrush Island Guide; A Traveller's History of China.* Send synopsis and letter with s.a.e..
Royalties paid twice-yearly.

Windsor Large Print
See **Chivers Press Ltd**

Wise
See **Omnibus Press**

Woburn Press
See **Frank Cass & Co Ltd**

Oswald Wolff Books
See **Berg Publishers Ltd**

The Women's Press
34 Great Sutton Street, London EC1V 0DX
☎0171 251 3007   Fax 0171 608 1938
Publishing Director *Kathy Gale*
Approx. Annual Turnover £1 million

Part of the Namara Group. First title 1978. *Publishes* women only: quality fiction and non-fiction. Fiction usually has a female protagonist and a woman-centred theme. International writers and subject matter encouraged. Non-fiction: subjects of general interest, both practical and theoretical, to women generally; art books, feminist theory, health and psychology, literary criticism. About 50 titles a year.

IMPRINTS
Women's Press Crime; Women's Press Handbooks Series; Livewire Books for Teenagers Fiction and non-fiction series for young adults. Synopses and ideas for books welcome. No mss without previous letter, synopsis and sample material.
Royalties paid twice-yearly.

Woodhead Publishing Ltd
Abington Hall, Abington, Cambridge
CB1 6AH
☎01223 891358   Fax 01223 893694
Chairman *Alan Jessup*
Managing Director *Martin Woodhead*

Approx. Annual Turnover £1.1 million

FOUNDED 1989. *Publishes* engineering, materials technology, finance and investment, food technology, production and management. TITLES *The TWI Journal* (welding research); *Advanced Composites Letters; The International Grain/Nickel/Zinc/Tin/Silver Trade* series; *Base Metals Handbook; Foreign Exchange Options.* About 30 titles a year.

DIVISIONS

Woodhead Publishing *Martin Woodhead;* **Abington Publishing** (in association with the Welding Institute) *Patricia Morrison;* **Gresham Books** (in association with the Chartered Institute of Bankers). Unsolicited material welcome.

Royalties paid annually.

Woodstock Books

The School House, South Newington, Banbury, Oxon OX15 4JJ
☎01295 720598   Fax 01295 720717
Chairman/Managing Director *James Price*
Approx. Annual Turnover £150,000

FOUNDED 1989. *Publishes* literary reprints only. Main series: *Revolution and Romanticism, 1789–1834; Decadents, Symbolists, Anti-Decadents: Poetry of the 1890s; Hibernia: Literature and Nation in Victorian Ireland.* No unsolicited mss.

Wordsworth Editions Ltd

Cumberland House, Crib Street, Ware, Hertfordshire SG12 9ET
☎01920 465167   Fax 01920 462267
Editorial Office: 6 London Street, London W2 1HL ☎0171 706 8822 Fax 0171 706 8833
Directors *M. C. W. Trayler, E. G. Trayler*
Director/Editorial Head *C. M. Clapham*
Approx. Annual Turnover £7 million

FOUNDED 1987. *Publishes* reprints of English literature, paperback reference books, poetry, children's classics, classic erotica, military history, mind, body and spirit and American classics. About 150 titles a year. No unsolicited mss.

Authors' Rating A non-starter for living writers, Wordsworth is dedicated to high-run, low-cost editions of books everyone has heard of. The formula has proved a winner, particularly with young people, who don't mind paying a pound for required reading but resent the fiver charged by up-market publishers for essentially the same product.

World International Limited

Deanway Technology Centre, Wilmslow Road, Handforth, Cheshire SK9 3FB
☎01625 650011   Fax 01625 650040
Managing Director *Ian Findlay*
Creative Director *Michael Herridge*
Publishing Manager *Nina Filipek*

Part of the Egmont Group, Denmark. *Specialises* in children's books for home and international markets: activity, sticker, baby, early learning, novelty/character books and annuals. SERIES *Mr Men; Fun to Learn; I Can Learn; Learning Rewards.* 'Unsolicited material rarely used. World International does not accept responsibility for the return of unsolicited submissions.'

X Libris

See **Little Brown & Co. (UK)**

Y Ddraig Fach

See **Ashley Drake Publishing Ltd**

Y Lolfa Cyf

Talybont, Ceredigion SY24 5HE
☎01970 832304   Fax 01970 832782
Managing Director *Robat Gruffudd*
Editor *Elena Gruffudd*
Approx. Annual Turnover £500,000

FOUNDED 1967. Small company which publishes mainly in Welsh. It handles all its own typesetting and printing too. *Publishes* Welsh language publications; Celtic language tutors; English language books about Wales for the visitor; nationalism and sociology (English language). 30 titles in 1996. Expanding slowly. TITLES *Artists in Snowdonia* James Bogle; *The Welsh Learner's Dictionary* Heini Gruffudd; *Burning Down the Dosbarth* David Greenslade. Not interested in any English language books except political and Celtic. Write first with synopses or ideas.

Royalties paid twice-yearly.

Yale University Press (London)

23 Pond Street, London NW3 2PN
☎0171 431 4422   Fax 0171 431 3755
Managing Director/Editorial Director *John Nicoll*

FOUNDED 1961. Owned by US parent company. *Publishes* academic and humanities. About 160 titles (worldwide) a year. Unsolicited mss and synopses welcome if within specialised subject areas.

Royalties paid annually.

Roy Yates Books

Smallfields Cottage, Cox Green, Rudgwick,
Horsham, West Sussex RH12 3DE
☎01403 822299   Fax 01403 823012

Chairman/Managing Director *Roy Yates*
Approx. Annual Turnover £120,000

FOUNDED 1990. *Publishes* children's books
only. No unsolicited material as books are
adaptations of existing popular classics suitable
for translation into dual-language format.

Royalties paid quarterly.

Zed Books Ltd

7 Cynthia Street, London N1 9JF
☎0171 837 4014   Fax 0171 833 3960

Approx. Annual Turnover £1 million

FOUNDED 1976. *Publishes* international and
Third World affairs, development studies,
women's studies, environmental studies, cultural studies and specific area studies. No
fiction, children's or poetry. About 40 titles a
year.

DIVISIONS

Development & Environment *Robert
Molteno*; **Women's Studies, Cultural
Studies** *Louise Murray*. TITLES *The Development
Dictionary* ed. Wolfgang Sachs; *Staying Alive*
Vandana Shiva; *The Hidden Face of Eve* Nawal
el Saadawi. No unsolicited mss; synopses and
ideas welcome though.

Royalties paid annually.

Zomba

See **Omnibus Press**

Nothing Succeeds Like Sexcess

The book trade is enjoying a boom in sex. Shelves of popular fiction are built on the appeal of vicarious copulation. Publishers who once peddled sweet romantic dreams now think of sex all the time. And they get paid too. Their success story has its beginning in the vindication of *Lady Chatterley* nearly 40 years ago. The laughter of incredulity that echoed round the Old Bailey as prosecuting counsel paraded their Victorian morality was the starting signal for the permissive sixties. Thereafter, despite an Obscene Publications Act which to this day forbids the publication of 'anything that may deprave or corrupt' and some highly publicised cases arising from it, the printed word has been virtually immune from prosecution. Such has been the growth in erotic fiction, embracing sex in all its 57 varieties, that seemingly the only limit is the imagination of the writers.

The latest development is erotic fiction for women. Until recently it was assumed that only men wanted to read about sex. Women, it was said, were just not interested. This was the line adopted by some of the more vocal feminists who argued that erotica, or pornography as they preferred to call it, demeaned women. There were even calls to reintroduce stringent censorship.

But while it was true that women were not attracted to the soft core magazines, largely written by men for men, they responded with more enthusiasm to erotic fiction by and specifically for their own sex. In the wake of the bodice-ripper (sex in period costume) and the bonk buster (athletic gyrations in a contemporary setting) came the novels of untrammelled lust and wild passion with titles like *Her Hungry Heart*, *Going Too Far*, *Healing Passion* and *Led On By Compulsion*. New imprints were created to satisfy demand – Liaison (Hodder Headline), Black Lace (Virgin) and X Libris (Little Brown). Even dear old Mills and Boon, oblivious for so long to the sexual revolution, fell into line with its Temptation list.

Kerri Sharp, editor of Black Lace, has identified five categories of plot that have proved their value within the erotic genre:

1. **Initiation** In the male 'language', usually a young, innocent girl introduced to sex by an older protagonist (male) or (more rarely) a dominant lesbian. The loss of virginity is paramount to the plot. Variations include (a) strong class differences between innocent and debauched; (b) racial differences; (c) urban/rural differences. Mostly, the accent is on 'joy of discovery' often culminating in the innocent character transforming into a procurer at the end of the book – thereby setting up the basis for a sequel.

2. **Violation** Roots in Sade. The one most likely to fit into the body of literature considered art. Examples of the violation story include *Story of the Eye* by Georges Bataille, *The Story of O* by Pauline Reage and *The Image*

by Jean de Berg. These three books have found intellectual approval despite their obscene and amoral content, possibly due to the extreme forms of consciousness the characters experience in their pain and their pleasure. Obsessive sexuality is crucial to the narrative of the violation plot. The protagonist finds a sense of liberation in tirelessly debasing the object of desire. A popular choice for those interested in Gothic themes.

3. **Specialisation** An uncommon choice within male generated erotica. Equates sexual adroitness with the perfection of high art. Settings like the ballet school, the world of classical music or painting are popular. Accent heavily slanted towards seduction of pupil by teacher, or performer by wealthy patron (the latter more common when the seducer is female). Nearly always a European location or, possibly, Czarist Russia/18th century Vienna if historical. Detail of finery, architecture very evident. In filmic terms, *The Draughtsman's Contract* is a useful example.

4. **History** A vast area. They are sophisticated plots in that they attempt, like the speciality plots, to posit a sexual dynamism at the root of historical events: the French Revolution, medieval battles etc. They sexualise the past, real and fictional. Of all types of erotic novel the attention to detail is most important to this category. Clothing must be fetishised – armour, breeches, uniforms, corsets etc. and it's probably the area where one can have most artistic licence.

5. **Power relationships** These seem to form the basis of most extended erotic fantasies, both male and female. Unpalatable as it may be in a PC world, we like to imagine ourselves in sexualised situations where our dominance or submission is a factor. This is because, sexually, most people tend to want to surrender responsibility to someone else. They want exciting and experimental sex, but they don't want to be ashamed by having to ask for it. In fantasy, your man knows what you like without you having to explain.

By way of example, here is an extract from *Aria Appassionata* by Juliet Hastings. There are no prizes for guessing which category it falls into. The scene is a pasta bar on an off night. Tess has wandered in for a quick bite but having caught sight of the waiter, she takes a fancy to another sort of quickie. And what, just what, does she propose to do about it?

Abandoning her half-eaten pasta, Tess takes a deep breath and plunges in, 'Where can we go to make love?' she said. His lips were parted and his chest rose and fell with his quick breathing. For a moment he didn't speak. Then he said, 'Are you joking?' Tess shook her head. 'I'm serious. Try me.'

They wind up in the manager's office, of all places.

'Christ,' he hissed into her lips, and then his arms were around her, catching her under her haunches and lifting her. He pushed her back and up until her bottom was resting on the edge of the manager's desk and he was pressing against her, pushing her legs apart, reaching up under her skirt. She gave an urgent gasp of lust and heaved her hips up towards him, inviting him to touch her. His hand was shaking and his fingers fumbled before he got hold of her panties and pulled them aside, feeling inside them. Tess knew she was wet, but even so it was a delicious shock to feel his strong thick fingers sink without hesitation into her, penetrating her so firmly that her sex clenched around them as if to keep him there.

'God, you're wet,' Dean hissed. He felt with his other hand for his fly, unbuttoned it and unfastened the zip, and in one swift motion pulled his erect penis from his underpants and advanced upon her.

The latest recruit to Black Lace is Laura Thornton. She is an American, married to an Englishman and they have two young children. Her interest in erotic fiction started when she was at Oxford researching the influence of the Victorian Gothic novel. Having bought some Black Lace titles to wile away a train journey she recognised the plots as Gothic retreads and she thought, 'I can do better than this'. Two sample chapters led, seven months on, to a go-ahead for a full manuscript. *The Name of An Angel*, her first book, was published in August.

Being American helps to loosen up the inhibitions, Laura believes, but she doubts that the popular theme of the dominant woman commanding submissive men would go down in the States.

'American women are not so liberated as you might imagine,' she says. 'They share a rich vein of sentiment which is why romantic fiction still thrives. It is also one reason why women's erotic fiction still has a long way to go. So far it is only reaching a small proportion of the potential readership. But it is making an impact, not least in pointing readers towards a greater understanding of their own sexuality.'

Erotic fiction is by no means confined to specific imprints. The liberating tendency of the last few years has had its effect. Barely any work of popular fiction is deemed marketable unless the author delves beneath the sheets. There are those who make a right hash of it. If you want a literary example of bad sex just try reading Jeffrey Archer or Frederick Forsyth or, for that matter, Graham Greene. But this leaves plenty of scope for those who really know what they are writing about even if, in many cases, high sales and a loyal readership do not always gain recognition in the review pages.

One who has led the way is Anne Rice, 'the best erotic writer around' according to Maxim Jakubowski of Eros Plus who adds 'her Anne Roquelaure series has never been bested'. *Interview with the Vampire*, Anne Rice's break to fame, was followed by a succession of bestsellers like *The Mummy* where the erotic imagination gives a new twist to the familiar themes of horror and mysticism.

Literary editors may patronise a cult novelist but there is no way they can ignore Ruth Rendell and A.S. Byatt who are appearing in a new list from

Chatto & Windus called The Secret Chamber. 'I want to take the erotic back into mainstream fiction,' says editor Jonathan Burnham, 'and show that it can be done by serious writers.' Secker & Warburg have also broken the barrier with *Miami Purity* from American writer Vicki Hendricks whose ex-stripper heroine goes to the limits of sexual experience (and beyond, in some critics' eyes) without losing credibility.

Vicki Hendricks feels that sex is just one weapon among many in her literary armour. 'You have to have various strands going on at the same time in order to flesh out a story. It's not a straight line going forward.' Nevertheless she does believe that sex - or a lack of sexual control - motivates most human behaviour. 'Much as we'd like to think we're civilised human beings on many other levels, I think we're just sexual animals. That's why sex is an important vehicle for me. It drives the narrative.'

Interestingly, of those authors whose books are likely to be reviewed in the quality press, it is the writers on gay themes who seem best able to portray sex without descending to cliché or self parody. Alan Hollinghurst's *The Swimming Pool Library* and *The Folding Star* are recent examples of compelling novels which are at the same time erotic and, for heterosexual readers, weirdly disturbing.

Then again, gay liberation has created an erotic genre every bit as powerful as that aimed at heterosexual women and men. Publishers like Gay Men's Press do not see themselves as purveyors of erotica though, as director David Fernbach writes, 'there is certainly an erotic dimension in the work of several writers we publish, both the literary and the more popular'. The border line takes in semi-fictional work that leans towards the documentary like *Serbian Diaries* by Boris L. Davidovich, a university teacher in Belgrade whose diary of a city at war contains explicit portrayals of gay sex.

What chance is there for the newcomer to erotic fiction? Laura Thornton struck lucky but many wind up on the lower depths of the slush pile.

'The main reason I reject manuscripts which in all other respects are passable (grammar, punctuation etc.) is that they tend to be about "some people having sex" and not a lot more,' says Kerri Sharp. 'An element of shame or power dynamics is important. Descriptions of well-endowed couples happily bonking is dull, as is the more 1970's angle of "swinging" and "orgies". Cliched settings and characters in contemporary novels which have me groaning in despair are: women's "health clubs with a difference"; impossibly wealthy suitors (i.e. Arab princes); sex as therapy; contact magazines and the making of porno videos; yachts; fetish nightclubs.'

Mike Bailey, who makes the decisions at Delta and Liaison (Hodder Headline) believes that the beginner who can relax and not get too fussed by anatomical detail has every chance of emerging from the slush pile. Shyness and modesty however are guarantees of failure. Derek Parker, whose guide to *Writing Erotic Fiction* was published last year argues that reserve has no place in this genre: 'The writer must have fun. If you don't enjoy sex, there is no chance of portraying it in a way that will appeal.' The best erotica, he says, is pure fantasy: 'Everything is always for the best in the best of all possibly beds; there is no disease, no unwanted pregnancy and rape is a game.'

The same rules apply to the portrayal of sex on the screen except that here the medium is restricted to what can be done literally while with the printed word fantasy knows no boundaries. For now, the point is, in any case, academic since much of what appears on the page could not be translated to the screen or, for that matter, the stage without attracting the attention of the vice squad.

But this may change. The biggest threat to erotic books must be the steady relaxation of film censorship. Public opinion is changing to accommodate a liberated younger generation who laugh at the absurdity of the restraints imposed by their elders. When so much else is permissible why, for example, is it still illegal to show an erect penis on screen or even in a magazine? And how is it that raunchy greetings cards are exempt from this dictat?

But it is technology more than rational argument that is likely to do for censorship. The communication revolution has made visual erotica, pornography by any other name, available to anyone who can press a few buttons. Moreover, it may not be long before the book loses its monopoly on the far reaches of fantasy. Virtual reality is bringing us closer to an artificially created sensation that might rival the real thing. When that day comes, when fantasy and special effects coalesce, the erotic book may be thrown out of bed.

Erotic fiction publishers

UK

Black Lace (Kerri Sharp), Virgin Publishing
Delta (Mike Bailey), Hodder Headline
Eros Plus (Maxim Jakubowski), Titan Books
Liaison (Mike Bailey), Hodder Headline
New English Library (Nick Austin), Hodder Headline
Nexus (Peter Darvill-Evans), Virgin Publishing
Silver Moon Books, PO Box CR25, Leeds LS7 3TN (☎0891 310976)
Wordsworth Editions – reprints only of classic erotica
X-Libris (Helen Pisano), Little, Brown & Co.

US

Carroll & Graf Inc (Kent Carroll), 260 Fifth Avenue, New York, NY 10001
(☎001 212 889 8772)
Masquerade Books (Richard Kasak), 801 Second Avenue, New York,
NY 10017 (☎001 212 986 5100)

Irish Publishers

An Gúm

44 Sráid Uí Chonaill, Uacht, Dublin 1,
Republic of Ireland
☎00 353 1 8734700   Fax 00 353 1 8731140
Editors *Dónall ó Cuill, Máire Nic-Mhaoláin*

FOUNDED 1926. Publications branch of the Department of Education. Established to provide general reading, textbooks and dictionaries in the Irish language. *Publishes* educational, children's, music, lexicography and general. Little fiction or poetry. About 50 titles a year. Unsolicited mss, synopses and ideas for books welcome. Also welcomes reading copies of first and second level school textbooks with a view to translating them into the Irish language.
Royalties paid annually.

Anvil Books

45 Palmerston Road, Dublin 6,
Republic of Ireland
☎00 353 1 4973628
Managing Director *Rena Dardis*

FOUNDED 1964 with the emphasis on Irish history and biography. Expansion of the list followed to include more general interest Irish material and in 1982 The Children's Press was established, making Anvil the first Irish publisher of mass-market children's books of Irish interest. *Publishes* illustrated books, history, biography (particularly 1916–22), folklore, children's fiction (for ages 7–14) and quiz books. No adult fiction or illustrated books for children under 7. About 7 titles a year. Unsolicited mss, synopses and ideas for books welcome.

DIVISIONS
General TITLES *Guerilla Days in Ireland* Tom Barry; *The Workhouses of Ireland* John O'Connor; *The Norman Invasion of Ireland* Richard Roche. **The Children's Press** TITLES *Young Champions* Peter Regan; *The Secret of the Ruby Ring* Yvonne MacGrory; *Landscape with Cracked Sheep* Mary Arrigan.
Royalties paid annually.

Attic Press Ltd

29 Upper Mount Street, Dublin 2, Republic of Ireland
☎00 353 1 6616128   Fax 00 353 1 6616176
Publisher *Róisín Conroy*

FOUNDED 1988. Began life in 1984 as a forum for information on the Irish feminist movement. *Publishes* adult and teenage fiction, and non-fiction (history, women's studies, politics, biography). About 22 titles a year. A second imprint, **Basement Press**, was launched in 1994 to publish popular fiction and non-fiction (politics, entertainment and information) by men and women. Unsolicited mss, synopses and ideas for books welcome. Not interested in poetry or short stories.
Royalties paid twice yearly.

Basement Press
See **Attic Press**

Beacon
See **Poolbeg Press Ltd**

Blackwater Press

c/o Folens Publishers, Broomhill Business Park, Broomhill Road, Tallaght, Dublin 24, Republic of Ireland
☎00 353 1 4515311   Fax 00 353 1 4515308
Chairman *Dirk Folens*
Managing Director *John O'Connor*

Part of Folens Publishers. *Publishes* political, sports, fiction (*Anna O'Donovan*) and children's (*Deidre Whelan*). 26 titles in 1996.

Boole Press

26 Temple Lane, Temple Bar, Dublin 2, Republic of Ireland
☎00 353 1 6797655   Fax 00 353 1 6792469

A division of AIC Ltd, Dublin. *Publishes* scientific and technical, medical, and conference proceedings. About 2 titles a year.
Royalties paid every two years.

Brandon Book Publishers Ltd

Dingle, Co. Kerry, Republic of Ireland
☎00 353 66 51463   Fax 00 353 66 51234
Managing Director *Bernie Goggin*
Approx. Annual Turnover £450,000

FOUNDED 1982 and in the 15 years since its inception Brandon has earned itself something of a reputation for new fiction authors and for challenging, often contentious, non-fiction. *Publishes* politics, biography, local history, children's, commercial and literary fiction. About 15 titles a year. Not interested in educational, scientific and technical or instruction material. Submit outlines with sample mss in the first instance. Ideas welcome.

Royalties paid annually.

Edmund Burke Publisher

Cloonagashel, 27 Priory Drive, Blackrock, Co. Dublin, Republic of Ireland
☎00 353 1 2882159   Fax 00 353 1 2834080
Chairman *Eamonn De Búrca*
Approx. Annual Turnover £100,000

Small family-run business publishing historical and topographical and fine limited-edition books relating to Ireland. TITLES *The Irish Fiants of the Tudor Sovereigns; Irish Names of Places* Joyce; *History of the Kingdom of Kerry* Cusack; *Scot's Mercenary Forces in Ireland* G. A. Hayes-McCoy; *The Dean's Friend* Alan Harrison; *Manners and Customs of the Ancient Irish* Eugene O'Curry. Unsolicited mss welcome. No synopses or ideas.

Royalties paid twice yearly.

Butterworth Ireland Limited

26 Upper Ormond Quay, Dublin 7, Republic of Ireland
☎00 353 1 8731555   Fax 00 353 1 8731876
Chairman *P. Woods (UK)*
General Manager *Gerard Coakley*

Subsidiary of Butterworth & Co. Publishers, London, (Reed Elsevier is the holding company). *Publishes* solely law and tax books. Tax Editor *Susan Keegan*, Legal Editor *Louise Leavy*. 16 titles in 1996. Leading publisher of Irish law and tax titles. Unsolicited mss, synopses and ideas welcome for titles within the broadest parameters of tax and law.

Royalties paid twice yearly.

The Children's Press

See **Anvil Books**

Cló Iar-Chonnachta

Indreabhán, Connemara, Galway, Republic of Ireland
☎00 353 91 593307   Fax 00 353 91 593362
Chairman/Director *Micheál Ó Conghaile*
Editor *Nóirín Ní Ghrádaigh*
Approx. Annual Turnover £250,000

FOUNDED 1985. *Publishes* fiction, poetry, plays and children's, mostly in Irish but not exclusively. Also publishes cassettes of writers reading from their own works. 18 titles in 1996.

Royalties paid annually.

The Collins Press

Carey's Lane, The Huguenot Quarter, Cork, Republic of Ireland
☎00 353 21 271346   Fax 00 353 21 275489
Managing Director *Con Collins*
Editor *Maria O'Donovan*

FOUNDED 1989. *Publishes* archaeology, biography, fiction, general non-fiction, health, history, mind, body and spirit, poetry, photographic and travel guides. About 3 titles a year. Unsolicited mss, synopses and ideas for books welcome.

Royalties paid annually.

The Columba Press

Unit 55A Spruce Avenue, Stillorgan Industrial Park, Blackrock, Co. Dublin, Republic of Ireland
☎00 353 1 2942556   Fax 00 353 1 2942564
Chairman *Neil Kluepfel*
Managing Director *Seán O'Boyle*
Approx. Annual Turnover £750,000

FOUNDED 1985. Small company committed to growth. *Publishes* only religious titles. 28 titles in 1996. (Backlist of 225 titles.) TITLES *Nine Faces of God* Pat Collins; *Through the Year with George Otto Simms* Lesley Whiteside. Unsolicited ideas and synopses rather than full mss preferred.

Royalties paid twice yearly.

Cork University Press

University College, Cork, Co. Cork, Republic of Ireland
☎00 353 21 902980   Fax 00 353 21 273553
Managing Director *Sara Wilbourne*
Production Editor *Eileen O'Carroll*

FOUNDED 1925. Relaunched in 1992, the Press *publishes* academic and some trade titles. Plans to publish 20 titles in 1997. Two journals, *Graph* (annual), an interdisciplinary cultural review, and *The Irish Journal of Feminist Studies* (bi-annual), are now part of the list. Unsolicited synopses and ideas welcome for textbooks, academic monographs, belles lettres, illustrated histories and journals.

Royalties paid annually.

Flyleaf Press

4 Spencer Villas, Glenageary, Co. Dublin, Republic of Ireland
☎00 353 1 2806228   Fax 00 353 1 8370176
Managing Director *Dr James Ryan*

FOUNDED 1981 to publish natural history titles. Now concentrating on family history and Irish history as a background to family history. No fiction. TITLES *Irish Records; Longford and its*

People; Tracing Kerry Ancestors; Tracing Dublin's Ancestors. Unsolicited mss, synopses and ideas for books welcome.

Royalties paid twice yearly.

Four Courts Press Ltd
55 Prussia Street, Dublin 7,
Republic of Ireland
☎00 353 1 8388960   Fax 00 353 1 8388951
Chairman/Managing Director *Michael Adams*
Director *Martin Healy*
Approx. Annual Turnover £300,000

FOUNDED 1972. Has recently undergone major changes with the expansion of its list. Art, 17th/18th/19th and 20th century history have been added to its existing list of theology, philosophy, Celtic and medieval studies and law. Planning to expand into Scottish history. About 15 titles a year. Unsolicited mss, synopses and ideas for books welcome.

Royalties paid annually.

Gill & Macmillan
Goldenbridge, Inchicore, Dublin 8,
Republic of Ireland
☎00 353 1 4531005   Fax 00 353 1 4541688
Managing Director *M. H. Gill*
Approx. Annual Turnover £5 million

FOUNDED 1968 when M. H. Gill & Son Ltd and Macmillan Ltd formed a jointly owned publishing company. *Publishes* biography/autobiography, history, current affairs, literary criticism (all mainly of Irish interest), guidebooks, cookery, religion, theology, counselling/psychology. Also professional books in law and accountancy, and educational textbooks for secondary and tertiary levels. About 100 titles a year. Contacts: *Hubert Mahony* (educational); *Fergal Tobin* (general); *Ailbhe O'Reilly* (tertiary textbooks). Unsolicited synopses and ideas welcome. Not interested in fiction or poetry.

Royalties paid subject to contract.

Institute of Public Administration
57–61 Lansdowne Road, Dublin 4,
Republic of Ireland
☎00 353 1 2697011   Fax 00 353 1 2698644
Chairman *Frank Murray*
Director General *John Gallagher*
Publisher *Jim O'Donnell*
Approx. Annual Turnover £450,000

FOUNDED 1957 by a group of public servants, the Institute of Public Administration is the Irish public sector management development agency. The publishing arm of the organisation is one of its major activities. *Publishes* academic and professional books and periodicals: history, law, politics, economics and Irish public administration for students and practitioners. 9 titles in 1996. TITLES *Administration Yearbook & Diary; Measuring Civil Service Performance; Your Rights at Work; A Politics of the Common Good.* No unsolicited mss; synopses and ideas welcome. No fiction or children's publishing.

Royalties paid annually.

Irish Academic Press Ltd
44 Northumberland Road, Ballsbridge,
Dublin 4, Republic of Ireland
☎00 353 1 6688244   Fax 00 353 1 6686769
Chairman *Frank Cass (London)*
Managing Editor *Linda Longmore*
Approx. Annual Turnover £250,000

FOUNDED 1974. *Publishes* academic monographs and humanities. 14 titles in 1996. Unsolicited mss, synopses and ideas welcome.

Royalties paid annually.

Irish Management Institute
Sandyford Road, Dublin 16,
Republic of Ireland
☎00 353 1 2956911   Fax 00 353 1 2955150
Chief Executive *Barry Kenny*
Approx. Annual Turnover £8 million

FOUNDED 1952. The Institute is owned by its members (individual and corporate) and its major activities involve management education, training and development. The book publishing arm of the organisation was established in 1970. *Publishes* management practice, interpersonal skills and aspects of national macroeconomics. TITLES *The Economy of Ireland; Practical Finance; Pricing For Results; Personnel Management; Managing Your Business: A Guidebook for Small Business.* Unsolicited mss welcome provided that any case material is relevant to Irish management practice. Synopses and ideas also welcome.

Royalties paid annually.

The Lilliput Press
4 Rosemount Terrace, Arbour Hill, Dublin 7,
Republic of Ireland
☎00 353 1 6711647   Fax 00 353 1 6711647
Chairman *Vincent Hurley*
Managing Director *Antony Farrell*
Approx. Annual Turnover £200,000

FOUNDED 1984. *Publishes* non-fiction: literature, history, autobiography and biography, ecology, essays; criticism; fiction and poetry. About 20 titles a year. TITLES *Beckett in Dublin* (essays); *The Growth Illusion* (ecology); *The Great*

Famine (history); *Hazel, Lady Laverey* (biography); *My Generation – Rock 'n' Roll Remembered, An Imperfect History; The Irish Writers' Guide 1995–97*. Unsolicited mss, synopses and ideas welcome. No children's or sport titles.

Royalties paid annually.

Marino Books
See **Mercier Press Ltd**

Mercier Press Ltd
PO Box No 5, 5 French Church Street, Cork, Republic of Ireland
☎00 353 21 275040   Fax 00 353 21 274969
Chairman *George Eaton*
Managing Director *John F. Spillane*

FOUNDED 1944. One of Ireland's largest publishers with a list of approx 250 Irish interest titles and a smaller range of religious titles. *Publishes* alternative lifestyle, folklore, women's interest, popular psychology, dual language, children's, cookery, history, politics, poetry and fiction. No academic books. IMPRINTS **Mercier Press** *Mary Feehan* **Marino Books** *Jo O'Donoghue*. 25 titles in 1996. TITLES *The Course of Irish History; The Field; Irish High Crosses; Irish Myths & Legends; Mortally Wounded; The Great Irish Famine; A Short History of Ireland*. Unsolicited mss, synopses and ideas welcome.

Royalties paid annually.

The O'Brien Press Ltd
20 Victoria Road, Rathgar, Dublin 6, Republic of Ireland
☎00 353 1 4923333   Fax 00 353 1 4922777
Chairman/Managing Director *Michael O'Brien*
Editorial Director *Íde Ní Laoghaire*

FOUNDED 1974 to publish biography and books on the environment. In recent years the company has become a substantial force in children's publishing, concentrating mainly on juvenile novels and non-fiction in the craft and history areas. Also *publishes* business, adult fiction, crime, popular biography, music and travel. No poetry or academic. About 40 titles a year. Unsolicited mss (with return postage enclosed), synopses and ideas for books welcome.

Royalties paid annually.

Oak Tree Press
Merrion Building, Lower Merrion Street, Dublin 2, Republic of Ireland
☎00 353 1 6761600   Fax 00 353 1 6761644
Managing Director *Brian O'Kane*

FOUNDED 1992. Part of Cork Publishing.

Specialist publisher of business and professional books: accounting, finance, management and law, aimed at students and practitioners in Ireland and the UK. About 25 titles a year. TITLES *Accounting Standards; Winning Business Proposals; The European Handbook of Management Consultancy; Personal Finance; Understanding Services Management*. Unsolicited mss and synopses welcome; send to David Givens, General Manager, at the above address.

Royalties paid twice yearly.

On Stream Publications Ltd
Cloghroe, Blarney, Co. Cork, Republic of Ireland
☎00 353 21 385798   Fax 00 353 21 385798
Chairman/Managing Director *Roz Crowley*
Approx. Annual Turnover £100,000

FOUNDED 1992. Formerly Forum Publications. *Publishes* academic, fiction, cookery, wine, general health and fitness, local history, railways, photography and practical guides. About 6 titles a year. TITLES *The Merchants of Ennis; On-Farm Research – The Broad Picture; Suicide: The Irish Experience*. Synopses and ideas welcome. No children's books.

Royalties paid twice yearly.

Poolbeg Press Ltd
123 Baldoyle Industrial Estate, Baldoyle, Dublin 13, Republic of Ireland
☎00 353 1 832 1477   Fax 00 353 1 832 1430
Managing Director *Philip MacDermott*
Approx. Annual Turnover £1 million+

FOUNDED 1976 to publish the Irish short story and has since diversified to include all areas of fiction (literary and popular), children's fiction and non-fiction, and adult non-fiction: history, biography and topics of public interest. About 100 titles a year. Unsolicited mss, synopses and ideas welcome (mss preferred). No drama. IMPRINTS **Poolbeg** (paperback and hardback); **Children's Poolbeg**; **Beacon**.

Royalties paid bi-annually.

Real Ireland Design Ltd
27 Beechwood Close, Boghall Road, Bray, Co. Wicklow, Republic of Ireland
☎00 353 1 2860799   Fax 00 353 1 2829962
Managing Director *Desmond Leonard*

Producers of calendars, diaries, posters, greeting cards and books, servicing the Irish tourist industry. *Publishes* photography, cookery and tourism. About 2 titles a year. No fiction. Unsolicited mss, synopses and ideas welcome.

Royalties paid twice yearly.

Relay Publications

Tyone, Nenagh, Co. Tipperary,
Republic of Ireland
☎00 353 67 31734   Fax 00 353 67 31734

Managing Director *Donal A. Murphy*

FOUNDED 1980; in abeyance 1985–92. *Publishes*
regional history. 5 titles in 1996. Welcomes
unsolicited mss, ideas and synopses. Not interested in adult fiction.

Royalties paid twice yearly.

Roberts Rinehart Publishers

Trinity House, Charleston Road, Dublin 6,
Republic of Ireland
☎00 353 1 4976860   Fax 00 353 1 4976861

Chairman *Rick Rinehart*
Managing Director *Jack Van Zandt*
Approx. Annual Turnover £2 million

European branch of a US company first estab-
lished in 1983. Particularly active in the Irish-
American market. *Publishes* general non-
fiction, particularly arts, environment, nature,
Irish interest, photography, history and biogra-
phy; and colour illustrated children's books,
fiction and non-fiction. About 40 titles a year.
TITLES *Ireland: The Living Landscape; Legendary
Ireland; The Troubles; I am of Ireland; Under the
Black Flag; The People Who Hugged the Trees.*
No adult fiction.

Royal Dublin Society

Science Section, Ballsbridge, Dublin 4,
Republic of Ireland
☎00 353 1 6680866   Fax 00 353 1 6604014

President *Liam Connellan*

FOUNDED 1731 for the promotion of agriculture,
science and the arts, and throughout its history
has published books and journals towards this
end. Publishers hired on contract basis. *Publishes*
conference proceedings, biology and the history
of Irish science. TITLES *Agricultural Development
for the 21st Century; Kerry and Dexter Cattle and
Other Ancient Irish Breeds – A History; The Right
Trees in the Right Places; Agriculture & the
Environment; Water of Life; Science, Technology &
Relaism.*

Royalties not generally paid.

Royal Irish Academy

19 Dawson Street, Dublin 2, Republic of
Ireland
☎00 353 1 6762570   Fax 00 353 1 6762346

Executive Secretary *Patrick Buckley*
Approx. Annual Turnover £50,000

FOUNDED in 1785, the Academy, has been
publishing since 1787. Core publications are
journals but more books have been published in
the last 12 years. *Publishes* academic, Irish interest and Irish language. About 7 titles a year.
Welcomes mss, synopses and ideas of an academic standard.

Royalties paid once yearly, where applicable.

Tír Eolas

Newtownlynch, Doorus, Kinvara,
Co. Galway, Republic of Ireland
☎00 353 91 37452   Fax 00 353 91 37452

Publisher/Managing Director *Anne Korff*
Approx. Annual Turnover £50,000

FOUNDED 1987. *Publishes* books and guides on
ecology, archaeology, folklore and culture.
TITLES *The Book of the Burren; The Shannon
Floodlands; Not a Word of a Lie; The Book of
Aran; Women of Ireland, A Biographic Dictionary.*
Unsolicited mss, synopses and ideas for books
are welcome. No specialist scientific and
technical, fiction, plays, school textbooks or
philosophy.

Royalties paid annually.

Town House and Country House

Trinity House, Charleston Road, Ranelagh,
Dublin 6, Republic of Ireland
☎00 353 1 4972399   Fax 00 353 1 4970927

Managing Director *Treasa Coady*

FOUNDED 1980. *Publishes* commercial fiction,
art and archaeology, biography and environment. About 20 titles a year. TITLES *A Place of
Stones; Irish Painting; The Illustrated Archaeology
of Ireland; Lifelines.* Good production and
design standards. Unsolicited mss, synopses and
ideas welcome. No children's books.

Royalties paid twice yearly.

Veritas Publications

7–8 Lower Abbey Street, Dublin 1,
Republic of Ireland
☎00 353 1 8788177   Fax 00 353 1 8786507

Chairman *Diarmuid Murray*
Managing Director *Fr Sean Melody*

FOUNDED 1969 to supply religious textbooks
to schools and later introduced a more general
religious list. Part of the Catholic Communications Institute. *Publishes* religious books only.
About 20 titles a year. Unsolicited mss, synopses and ideas for books welcome.

Royalties paid annually.

Wolfhound Press

68 Mountjoy Square, Dublin 1,
Republic of Ireland
☎00 353 1 8740354   Fax 00 353 1 8720207
Managing Director *Seamus Cashman*
FOUNDED 1974. Member of **Clé** – the Irish
Book Publishers Association. *Publishes* art, biog-
raphy, children's, fiction, general non-fiction,
history, literature, literary studies and gift books.
About 30 titles a year. TITLES *Famine; Run With
the Wind; Leading Hollywood; Eye Witness Bloody
Sunday; Breakfast in Babylon.* Unsolicited mss
(with synopses and s.a.e.) and ideas welcome.

Royalties paid annually.

Multimedia –
The Revolution Falters

The multimedia bandwagon has stalled a few times in the past year; there has even been talk of an imminent, long-term breakdown. But all new technology carries a high risk warning and it would have been a near miracle if publishers had got the market right at the first try.

The problems started with the over-production of pricey CD-ROMs. It seems that in that wonderful way that book publishers have of assuming their markets are price insensitive (despite all the evidence to the contrary) they decided to make CD-ROMs luxury products selling at £50 or more. This looked good to the accountants who had been made nervous by multimedia's hefty development costs – two to three hundred thousand pounds and upwards for a single title. The sooner this investment outlay was back in a savings account the happier the money men would be. But as with so many high hopes in publishing, the sales forecasts did not live up to expectations. Customers were disinclined to lash out on the latest fad knowing, as many did, that US prices for CD-ROMs were in free fall and that before long the market here would be bound to follow.

Another misjudgement was the extent of the market. With the book trade going through a dodgy period, publishers were too quick in reckoning multimedia as an easy way of repackaging existing titles. But they soon found that on the overlap between books and CD-ROMs demand was concentrated on education, children's and reference material. General titles did not stand a chance.

Finally, there was the revelation that the domestic hardware was not all that it was cracked up to be. While some 30 per cent of UK homes were equipped with home computers, a survey by Book Marketing Ltd revealed that only seven per cent of households had computers with CD-ROM drives. Moreover, around half of the existing home computers were too old to be upgraded to incorporate multimedia.

By the end of 1996, the book publishers were pulling back from multimedia. Marshall Cavendish, Penguin and HarperCollins were among the first to cry 'Enough'. Then, more surprisingly, Dorling Kindersley, a notable cheerleader of multimedia, made redundancies in the wake of disappointing sales and the First Information Group, formed expressly to exploit multimedia, saw its share price collapse. In March, Bertelsmann closed its new media company. The only good news came from Random House which has created a niche market for its New Media children's titles (though, interestingly, Random House in the US has dropped its CD-ROM publishing programme) and more specialist companies like Europress, which has the potential for developing software with the technological know-how that holds down costs.

For the immediate future, the multimedia industry will be dominated by games, largely of American origin and produced on the expensive high risk, hit or miss principle adopted by Hollywood. But this is not to say that multimedia must remain solely the preserve of facile entertainment. Despite the disappearance of some famous names, the number of CD-ROM titles continues to increase year on year with general interest recreation and leisure and education, training and careers showing higher than average growth.

The technology shows no sign of losing the capacity to surprise. As home computers become more sophisticated and easier to handle, so too will the hardware with the soon to appear Digital Video Disk, capable of storing 10 times as much information as the CD-ROM. And, despite the temporary glitch in the multimedia market, the digital revolution continues. Surveying the world economy with an eye to the millennium, Peter Norman, Economics Editor of *The Financial Times* believes that 'Multimedia could prove to be as significant in the development of mankind as the harnessing of steam and the development of the railways in the 19th century or the exploitation and spread of electric power in the early years of this century'.

Where does this leave the writers? As an author who has worked on computer games and 'infotainment' titles, Chris Elliott reminds us that 'the written word is the mother of information technologies and only because it is so familiar do we tend to forget how powerful it is'. He goes on: 'in the new interactive age, successful titles will still need people who know their subject area, or have something worthwhile to say, and can communicate it better than most. They must understand the opportunities offered by the new technology but most important of all, they must know what they want to do and why it could only be done using this technology.' It means learning a new technique, not to mention a new language, for a whole new set of working relationships.

Having completed his second interactive screenplay for Disney, writer Michele Em set down his experiences for the benefit of his Writers' Guild colleagues.

An interactive script differs in a number of ways from a linear narrative script. The parameters are different from film or television. Depending on your target platform (CD-ROM, Sega Saturn, Genesis, floppy disk, on-line, to name a few), the limitations of playback are going to affect your dialogue. Sometimes your dialogue is going to be in text form for one platform and spoken for another.

It's tricky to write for text, but harder, as we all know, to write believable dialogue for actors to speak. The dialogue also needs to be brief. Very brief. In some cases, such as where the player addresses a character repeatedly, the same line may be heard over and over again. What starts out clever can become aggravating through no fault of yours. All too often, due in part to storage limitations, each and every line has to have a specific purpose, making it very difficult to casually build a character. Every line has to contain the information needed to move the story forward. After that it's in the hands of the actors.

If your dialogue is going to be shown on screen you must bear in mind such things as that there are only 80 characters to a line of 12-point type and that the text may be displayed even larger. Inform yourself about the issues pertinent to your work. The technical team, the producer and the designer won't necessarily have your time or craft in their minds. You need to look out for yourself. All they'll know is whether your dialogue worked for them or didn't. But they are not used to giving direction. So ask for it.

And a final word from Chris Elliott.

There is a lot of hype about multimedia at the moment and the danger is that people will become cynical and decide that this particular emperor has no new clothes, just a lot of old ones. He may have a huge wardrobe, but unlike in the fable, there is no shortage of people to comment on his dress sense. Someone has to provide this, to make sure that multimedia applications offer compelling advantages over conventional media and that they are as easy to use as the technology that people are used to. Someone has to make sure he's fit to appear in public and who better than us, as writers, to be the emperor's valet?

Audio Books

Abbey Home Entertainment
Warwick House, 106 Harrow Road, London
W2 1XD
☎0171 262 1012 Fax 0171 262 6020
Managing Director *Anne Miles*

Abbey were the instigators (previously as MSD Holdings) in the development of the spoken word. With over 20 years' experience in recording, marketing and distribution of audio, book and cassette, their catalogue includes major children's story characters such as *Thomas the Tank Engine, Rosie and Jim, Postman Pat, Rupert Bear* and *Winnie the Pooh. Specialises* in children's audio cassettes. 80 titles in 1996. Ideas from authors and agents welcome.

Argo
See **PolyGram Spoken Word**

BBC Radio Collection
Woodlands, 80 Wood Lane, London
W12 0TT
☎0181 576 2708 Fax 0181 749 0538
Owner *BBC Worldwide Publishing*
Spoken Word Publishing Director
Jan Paterson

ESTABLISHED in 1988 as The BBC Radio Collection, BBC Audio now releases material associated with BBC Radio and Television. *Publishes* comedy, science fiction, fiction, non-fiction and sound effects. TITLES *Hancock's Half Hour; Round the Horne; Alan Bennett's Diaries; Knowing Me, Knowing You; This Sceptred Isle.* Ideas for cassettes welcome although most releases start as BBC Radio programmes.

Bespoke Audio Ltd
Pepys Court, 84 The Chase, London
SW4 0NF
☎0171 627 8777 Fax 0171 498 6420
Managing Director *Bob Nolan*

FOUNDED in 1994 by ex-**PolyGram** executive. Part of Total Records. *Publishes* and distributes for other publishers such as **Macmillan** and **HarperCollins**; biography, children's, fiction, comedy. AUTHORS John Cole, Patrick O'Brian, Steve Turner, Sue Townsend. Ideas from authors and agents welcome.

Canongate Audio
14 High Street, Edinburgh EH1 1TE
☎0131 557 5111 Fax 0131 557 5211
Joint Managing Directors *Jamie Byng,*
Hugh Andrew

Part of **Canongate Books**. Purchased the Schiltron and Whigmaleerie lists in 1993. *Publishes* fiction, children's, humour, poetry, historical and Scottish titles. TITLES *The Driver's Seat* Muriel Spark, read by Judi Dench; *Lanark* read by the author, Alasdair Gray; *Parahandy* Neil Munro; *Scots Quair* Lewis Grassic Gibbon; Robert Louis Stevenson titles.

Cavalcade Story Cassettes
See **Chivers Audio Books**

Champs Elysées
See entry under **Magazines**

Chivers Audio Books
Windsor Bridge Road, Bath BA2 3AX
☎01225 335336 Fax 01225 448005
Managing Director *Julian Batson*

Part of **Chivers Press Ltd.** *Publishes* a wide range of titles, mainly for library consumption. Fiction, autobiography, children's and crime. 216 titles in 1996. TITLES *Taken on Trust* Terry Waite; *Brideshead Revisited* Evelyn Waugh; *If Only They Could Talk* James Herriot; *The Power and the Glory* Graham Greene; *Goggle-Eyes* Anne Fine; *The Incredible Journey* Sheila Burnford.

IMPRINTS **Chivers Audio Books, Chivers Children's Audio, Cavalcade Story Cassettes, Word-for-Word Audio Books, Sterling Audio Books.**

The Complete Listener Recorded Book Company
Field End Cottage Studios, 8 Apple Street, Oxenhope, Keighley, West Yorkshire
BD22 9LT
☎01535 645983
Managing Director *James D. Gillhouley*

FOUNDED 1989. One of the largest catalogues of unabridged classic titles in Europe and the only one to include the complete novels of the Brontë sisters, Henry Fielding and Charles Dickens. TITLES *War and Peace; Anna Karenina.* Recordings of contemporary works by new authors are undertaken by special arrangement. Please write for details.

Cover To Cover Cassettes Ltd
PO Box 112, Marlborough, Wiltshire
SN8 3UG
☎01672 562255   Fax 01672 564634
Managing Director *Helen Nicoll*

Publishes classic 19th-century fiction – Jane Austen, Charles Dickens, Anthony Trollope, plus children's titles – *Fantastic Mr Fox* Roald Dahl; *Worst Witch* Jill Murphy; *Sheep-Pig* Dick King-Smith; *In Your Garden* Vita Sackville-West (book/cassette). 10 titles in 1996.

CSA Telltapes Ltd
101 Chamberlayne Road, London NW10 3ND
☎0181 960 8466   Fax 0181 968 0804
Managing Director *Clive Stanhope*

FOUNDED 1989. *Publishes* fiction, children's, short stories, poetry, travel, biographies. 70 titles to-date. Tends to favour quality/classic/nostalgic literature for the 40+ age group. TITLES *Carry on Jeeves* P. G. Wodehouse; *Great Trials: Oscar Wilde*; *Billy Bunter of Greyfriars School* Frank Richards; *Lamb's Tales from Shakespeare I & II*; *Bitter Lemons* Lawrence Durrell; *The Picture of Dorian Gray* Oscar Wilde. Ideas for cassettes welcome.

CYP Limited
The Fairway, Bush Fair, Harlow, Essex
CM18 6LY
☎01279 444707   Fax 01279 445570
Managing Director *Mike Kitson*

FOUNDED 1978. *Publishes* children's material for those under 10 years of age; educational, entertainment, licensed characters (i.e. *Mr Men; Little Miss*). Ideas for cassettes welcome.

Faber Penguin Audiobooks
27 Wrights Lane, London W8 5TZ
☎0171 416 3000   Fax 0171 416 3289
3 Queen Square, London WC1N 3AU
☎0171 465 0045   Fax 0171 465 0108
Publishing Manager *Anna Hopkins (at Wrights Lane address)*
Rights Manager *Margaret Hulton (at Queen Square address)*

A joint venture between **Penguin Books** and **Faber & Faber**. *Publishes* 25–30 titles per year, drawing on the strength of Faber's authors. AUTHORS include Ted Hughes, Philip Larkin, Hanif Kureishi, Sylvia Plath, T.S. Eliot, Wendy Cope, William Golding, Seamus Heaney, Paul Muldoon.

Funny Business
See **PolyGram Spoken Word**

Golden Days of Radio
See **Hodder Headline Audio Books**

HarperCollins AudioBooks
77–85 Fulham Palace Road, London W6 8JB
☎0181 741 7070
Fax 0181 307 4517(adult)/307 4291(child.)

The Collins audio and video company was acquired in the mid-eighties but the video section was later sold. In 1990/91 HarperCollins overhauled the audio company, dividing the adult and children's tapes into two separate divisions.

ADULT DIVISION
Managing Director *Adrian Bourne*
Publisher *Rosalie George*

Publishes a wide range including popular and classic fiction, non-fiction, Shakespeare and poetry. 50 titles in 1996. TITLES *Human Croquet* Kate Atkinson; *Every Man for Himself* Beryl Bainbridge; *Alias Grace* Margaret Atwood; *Goodfellow MP* Michael Dobbs; *Sharpe's Tiger* Bernard Cornwell; *The Yellow Admiral* Patrick O'Brian.

CHILDREN'S DIVISION
Publishing Director *Gail Penston*
Senior Editor *Stella Paskins*

Publishes picture books/cassettes and story books/cassettes as well as single and double tapes for children aged 2–13 years. Fiction, songs, early learning, poetry etc. 60 titles in 1996. AUTHORS Roald Dahl, C. S. Lewis, Enid Blyton, Michael Rosen, Robert Westall, Jean Ure, Nick Butterworth, Colin and Jacqui Hawkins, Judith Kerr, Jonathan Langley.

Hodder Headline Audio Books
338 Euston Road, London NW1 3BH
☎0171 873 6000   Fax 0171 873 6024
Publisher *Rupert Lancaster*
Editor *Charlotte Barton*

LAUNCHED in 1994 with 50 titles. A strong list, especially for theatre, vintage radio, film tie-ins, poetry plus fiction, non-fiction, children's, religious. Approx 200 titles in 1996. AUTHORS Enid Blyton, John LeCarré, Mick Inkpen (*Kipper* books), Stephen King, Rosamunde Pilcher, Emma Tennant, Joanna Trollope, Terry Waite, Mary Wesley.

IMPRINT **Golden Days of Radio** series of classic vintage radio broadcasts.

Isis Audio Books

7 Centremead, Osney Mead, Oxford OX2 0ES
☎01865 250333   Fax 01865 790358
Managing Director *John Durrant*
Editorial Head *Veronica Babington Smith*

Part of **Isis Publishing Ltd.** *Publishes* fiction and a few non-fiction titles. AUTHORS Virginia Andrews, Barbara Taylor Bradford, Edwina Currie, Leslie Thomas, Douglas Adams, Terry Pratchett.

Ladybird Books Ltd

Beeches Road, Loughborough, Leicestershire
LE11 2NQ
☎01509 268021   Fax 01509 234672
Managing Director *Laurence James*

Part of the Penguin Group. Only *publishes* recordings of titles which appear on the Ladybird book list. 58 titles in 1996. TITLES *The Railway Children; Gulliver's Travels; Little Red Riding Hood; Puss in Boots; Farmyard Stories for Under Fives.*

Laughing Stock

PO Box 408, London SW11 5TA
☎0181 944 9455   Fax 0181 944 9466
Managing Director *Colin Collino*

FOUNDED 1991. Issues a wide range of comedy cassettes from family humour to alternative comedy. 12–16 titles per year. TITLES *Red Dwarf; Shirley Valentine* (read by Willy Russell); *Rory Bremner; Peter Cook Anthology; Sean Hughes; John Bird and John Fortune; Eddie Izzard.*

Listen for Pleasure

E.M.I. House, 43 Brook Green, London
W6 7EF
☎0171 605 5000   Fax 0171 605 5134
Director *Paul Holland*

Part of E.M.I. Records, the Listen for Pleasure label started in 1977 as part of Music for Pleasure. Also covers Virgin and E.M.I.. *Publishes* humour, comedy classics, children's, fiction and non-fiction, poetry. TITLES *Morecambe & Wise; The Goon Shows; The Railway Children; The Borrowers; An Evening with Johnners; The Beiderbecke Affair; All Creatures Great and Small; Under Milk Wood; Pride and Prejudice; Every Living Thing; Smith & Jones.* Welcomes original ideas for cassettes.

Macmillan Audio Books

25 Eccleston Place, London SW1W 9NF
☎0171 881 8000   Fax 0171 881 8001
Owner *Macmillan Publishers Ltd*
Manager *Gina Rozner*

FOUNDED 1995. *Publishes* adult fiction and auto-biography focusing mainly on lead book titles and releasing audio simultaneously with hard or paperback publication. Now moving into the children's audio market. About 25 titles a year. TITLES *The English Patient* Michael Ondaatje, read by Ralph Fiennes; *The Echo* Minette Walters, read by Bob Peck; *Birds of Prey* Wilbur Smith, read by Martin Shaw.

MCI Spoken Word

36–38 Caxton Way, Watford, Hertfordshire
WD1 8UF
☎01923 255558   Fax 01923 816880
Owner *VCI Plc*
Head of Spoken Word *Steve Crickmer*

Established in 1993 and now a rapidly expanding publisher of a wide range of audiobooks: comedy, children's, classics, thrillers & chillers, true crime, TV programmes. 150 titles to-date. TITLES *Inspector Morse; Barbie; Joe Pasquale, Eddie Izzard, Cracker; James Bond.*

Naxos AudioBooks

16 Wolsey Mews, London NW5 2DX
☎0171 482 4110   Fax 0171 482 4101
Owner *HNH International, Hong Kong*
Managing Director *Nicolas Soames*

FOUNDED 1994. Part of Naxos, the classical budget CD company. *Publishes* classic and modern fiction, non-fiction, children's and junior classics, drama and poetry. 100 titles by the end of 1996. TITLES *Paradise Lost* Milton; *Ulysses* Joyce; *Kim* Kipling; *Decline and Fall of the Roman Empire* Gibbon.

Penguin Audiobooks

27 Wrights Lane, London W8 5TZ
☎0171 416 3000   Fax 0171 416 3289
Owner *Penguin Books Ltd*
Publishing Manager *Anna Hopkins*

Launched in November 1993 and has rapidly expanded since then to reflect the diversity of **Penguin Books'** list. *Publishes* mostly fiction, both classical and contemporary, non-fiction and autobiography. Approx. 110 titles a year. Contemporary AUTHORS: Paul Theroux, Miss Reed, Dick Francis, Barbara Vine, William Boyd, Terry MacMillan, Stephen King, John Mortimer.

PolyGram Spoken Word

1 Sussex Place, Hammersmith, London
W6 9XS
☎0181 910 5000   Fax 0181 910 5400
Owner *PolyGram*

Product Manager *Alex Mitchison*

Part of PolyGram, the Spoken Word division has been operating for two years, publishing under the **Speaking Volumes**, **Funny Business** and **Argo** labels. *Publishes* comedy, biography, fiction, poetry and documentary titles. TITLES *Red Dwarf*, *Backwards* Rob Grant; *They Think It's All Over* Kenneth Wolstenholme; *Left Foot Forward* Garry Nelson; *You Can Read Me Like a Book* Maureen Lipman; The Multi Cast Radio One play *Independence Day UK*; *Billy Connolly's World Tour of Australia* from the BBC TV series. Ideas for new releases always welcome.

Random House Audiobooks

20 Vauxhall Bridge Road, London SW1V 2SA
☎0171 973 9000   Fax 0171 233 6127

Owner *Random House UK Ltd.*
Managing Director *Simon King*

The audiobooks division of Random House started early in 1991 and *publishes* fiction, non-fiction and self help. 35 adult titles in 1996. AUTHORS include John Grisham, Stephen Fry, P. G. Wodehouse, Frederick Forsyth, Patricia Cornwell, Michael Crichton and Anne Rice.

CHILDREN'S DIVISION IMPRINT **Tellastory** AUTHORS include Jane Hissey, Shirley Hughes, David McKee.

Reed Audio

Michelin House, 81 Fulham Road, London SW3 6RB
☎0171 581 9393   Fax 0171 589 8419

Owner *Reed Books*
Managing Director *Helen Fraser*
Executive Editor *Alexa Moore*

Publishes fiction and non-fiction. A list of over 150 titles includes AUTHORS Roddy Doyle, Michael Palin, Bruce Chatwin, Wilbur Smith, P. J. O'Rourke, David Nobbs, Antonia Fraser.

Simon & Schuster Audio

West Garden Place, Kendal Street, London W2 2AG
☎0171 316 1900   Fax 0171 262 3102

Audio Manager *Clare Ledingham*

Simon & Schuster Audio began by distributing their American parent company's audio products. Moved on to repackaging products specifically for the UK market and in 1994 became more firmly established in this market with a huge rise in turnover. *Publishes* adult fiction, self help, business, Star Trek titles. 3 titles per month. TITLES *From Potter's Field* Patricia Cornwell; *A Thousand Acres* James Smiley;

Shipping News E. Annie Proulx; *Popcorn* Ben Elton; *My Story* Duchess of York; *Star Trek, First Contact* J. M. Dillard.

Smith/Doorstop Cassettes

The Poetry Business, The Studio, Byram Arcade, Huddersfield, West Yorkshire HD1 1ND
☎01484 434840   Fax 01484 426566

Co-directors *Peter Sansom, Janet Fisher*

Publishes poetry, read and introduced by the writer. AUTHORS Simon Armitage, Sujata Bhatt, Carol Ann Duffy, Les Murray, Ian McMillan.

Soundings

Kings Drive, Whitley Bay, Tyne & Wear NE26 2JT
☎0191 253 4155   Fax 0191 251 0662

Managing Director *Derek Jones*

FOUNDED in 1982. *Publishes* fiction and non-fiction; crime, romance, young adults. 124 titles in 1996. Has 1100 titles recorded in their unabridged form on their list and planning to increase annual output to 150 titles. TITLES *Bees in My Bonnet* Angus McVicar; *A Ghost in Monte Carlo* Barbara Cartland; *The Branded Man* Catherine Cookson; *School for Love* Olivia Manning; *Gull on the Roof* Derek Tangye. Ideas for cassettes welcome.

Speaking Volumes

See **PolyGram Spoken Word**

Sterling Audio Books

See **Chivers Audio Books**

WALKfree Productions Ltd

56 Upper Norwood Street, Leckhampton, Cheltenham, Gloucestershire GL53 0DU
☎01242 579206

Managing Director *Mark Richards*
Publishing/Sales Director *Nicholas Reardon*

FOUNDED 1996. In association with the Ordnance Survey, produces *WALKfree Audio-Guides* which 'cultivate a new form of country walking experience in the countryside'. The audio tape is accompanied by a 16-page guide book containing an Ordnance Survey Travel-master map extract plus outline route maps. Each guide also offers advice on convenient places for refreshment and local contacts. 8 titles in 1996. TITLES The Cotswolds; Peak District; Hadrian's Wall.

Word-for-Word Audio Books

See **Chivers Audio Books**

Poetry – All The Same Thing?

Peter Finch

Not a hope. If you'd imagined contemporary poetry as a sort of cardigan-clad club bent on good works, rather like Oxfam, then think again. British poetry is as diverse, dislocated and devious as one could imagine it. The long fought cold war between form and content is over. In poetry today, as in postmodernism itself, anything goes. Rather than an academic-based Eng. Lit. centre with experimenters, amateurs, foreigners and other deviants banished to its fringes, poetry has now drawn everything in to the middle giving us a churning, multi-faceted, multi-cultural and multi-purpose whole. The Celtic republics are celebrated – Scottish poetry is where the action is, for the first time in years Welsh verse is acceptable in London, and the Irish mists are imitated by all. The rebels are tamed – nothing is now beyond the pale. Cambridge master of linguistic difficulty, J. H. Prynne, has his own fan club on the Internet; Iain Sinclair's Picador anthology, *Conductors of Chaos*, has gathered the innovators and poetry weirdos into one commercial pack and put them on sale from station bookstalls. Women's poetry invariably now gets there before that by men. 'The War Won By Women' was the title for a recent special number of *The Poetry Review*. The new mainstream poetry anthologies – Ted Hughes and Seamus Heaney's *The School Bag* and Jo Shapcott and Matthew Sweeney's *Emergency Kit* do all they can to blur the boundaries of what English poetry might be. Add to that the rise and rise of the local bard with newspapers, small publishers and regional radio stations all giving space to verse by the amateur and we have a *fin-de-siecle* British poetry of considerable diversity.

Poetry has now also become a kind of spectator sport. Already both the Forward and the T. S. Eliot annual prizes bestow considerable financial reward and public recognition on their chosen winners. With the Forward prize in particular there is an air of the horse race about who might come first. The BBC has its annual polls, mounted around National Poetry Day to find the Nation's Favourite Poem. Among all-comers the traditional emerged tops with Rudyard Kipling, Alfred Lord Tennyson and Walter De La Mare – readily remembered from school perhaps – drawing the most votes. But with the contemporary Jenny Joseph, Roger McGough and Stevie Smith were winners proving that the nation, after all, does have an ear. Bookselling chains and regional publishers have not been slow to imitate with polls of their own. The latest variant is the poetry slam – a down-market import from America where poets compete in public and are scored like ice-skaters by teams of judges bearing numbered cards. The slams are drawing huge crowds wherever they are mounted. A new audience looking for excitement but this time also listening to the words.

Poetry is also much more accessible (and acceptable) than ever before. *Poetry On The Underground* where short verses ride the tubes in place of adverts has been one of the great successes of the decade. Cassell's anthologies drawn from the project are huge best-sellers every time they appear. The scheme has been imitated first by London Buses and now by local transport companies everywhere. Waterstones, a serious commercial bookselling chain, has seen enough money in poetry to justify the publication of its own poetry catalogue – a splendid descriptive introduction to poetry with added new verse. No fuss, if you want more you can buy the actual books, just like that.

In some areas poetry has come to be regarded entirely as a branch of the entertainment industry. Pam Ayres, who has been around for years plugging middle-aged doggerel, still pulls the crowds and regularly sells her books into the top ten. John Hegley, John Cooper Clark, Henry Normal, Benjamin Zephaniah and others work a circuit of gleeful audiences totally outside the accepted literary world. This is poetry performed by stand-up comedians or motor-mouth reciters from punk bands. Catching the flavour the literati have given us Poetry International plus a heap of big-name headline events at grand venues such as the Albert Hall. Audiences have remained satisfyingly large.

There have been developments in cyberspace with Internet poetry and instant on-line access to the world's verse resources becoming increasingly common (see later in this article). In the market place there are still enormous best-sellers. **Faber**'s Auden collection *Tell Me The Truth About Love* which ties-in with the film *Four Weddings And A Funeral* has sold more than 200,000 copies. That's how many you shift if you are a top thriller writer. Realising that price is always a factor the **Everyman Library** published a range of paperback collections, mixing classics with contemporary writers, and sold them, dump-binned, at a pound a time. R. S. Thomas suddenly found himself moving out of the shops as fast as John Grisham. Reassuring information.

But, and there is always a but, the Arts Council of England survey into the state of verse still found that the majority of the population perceive poetry to be out-of-touch, gloomy, irrelevant, effeminate, high-brow and elitist. Modern poetry – despite its good press – remains for most people a difficult art. 'Most people ignore most poetry because most poetry ignores most people' to quote Adrian Mitchell. Most in the business realise that poetry has a problem with its image. Too few participants read and those who do, do not do so enough. At least half of those questioned in the survey admitted to having penned a poem at some time in their life but hardly any of them regarded this as actual participation in the art-form. What does it take, I wonder, for poetry to become real?

In the rush to mount the bandwagon publishers are now putting out far too many books and as a consequence reviewers are increasingly ignoring them. Attitudes among those surveyed suggest that in any event the book – the often daunting single collection – might not be the best vehicle to get poetry across. Posters, post-cards, appearances in daily newspapers or as fillers between programmes on television may offer better routes. All of this, however, ignores the fact that poetry is not quite the same thing as an episode of *Men Behaving Badly*. To get anything out of it the reader too has to do some work.

Are you up to this?

See if you are ready first. Are you personally convinced that your work is up to it? If you are uncertain, then most likely that will be the view of everyone else. Check your text for glips and blips. Rework it. Root out any clichés or archaic poetry expressions such as O, doeth, bewilld'd and the like. Drop any of what Peter Sansom calls 'spirit of the age' poetry words. Do without shards, lozenges, lambent patina, stippled seagulls. If you use them make the rhymes less obvious. If by this time your writing still sounds okay, then go ahead.

Commercial publishers

Despite the obvious possibilities of making something from poetry in the commercial marketplace the number of those conglomerate publishers involved continues to shrink. The latest to absent themselves include **Random House**'s new acquisition Christopher Sinclair-Stevenson's eponymous **Sinclair-Stevenson** which is now content to tick-over on its back list and, after some vacillation the great **Chatto and Windus.** Despite providing a number of winners in the annual Forward Prizes Chatto has nonetheless parted company with its poetry editor, Simon Armitage, and left verse to other members of the Random House group. Where it remains poetry is increasingly seen through rather old-fashioned eyes as the quality which enhances a publisher's list. Never there to make profit but rather to impart class. Compared to other lines, slim volumes are slow sellers. Their editors are almost always part-time or have other jobs within the company and are never allowed to publish everyone they would like.

The obvious exception to this approach is long-term market leader and envy of the whole business **Faber & Faber**. Here editor Christopher Reid, along with Jane Feaver who handles children's books, preside over a list which continues to be as important to the firm as when T.S. Eliot inaugurated it more than seventy years ago. And for Faber it all seems to work. Among their top fifty titles are nineteen poetry books including the much celebrated W.H. Auden. This is the imprint most poets would like to join. The greats of the twentieth century are here – Pound, Eliot, Plath, Hughes, Larkin. Seamus Heaney made half-a-million in sales when he won the Nobel prize. Wendy Cope shifts at least 70,000 copies each time she goes into print. Simon Armitage regularly sells into five figures. The imprint is built on distinctively designed class and the roster of contemporary poets are some of the best we have – Derek Walcott, Don Paterson, Glyn Maxwell, Andrew Motion, Tom Paulin, Hugo Williams, Paul Muldoon, Douglas Dunn. Reid will read all manuscripts submitted determined to continue publishing good poetry despite the vagaries of the market place. Send a brief covering letter and a sample of your writing (10-20 poems) not forgetting s.a.e. if you think this is where you'll fit in.

At the traditional centre for English verse, **Oxford University Press,** long regarded for its unbeatable anthologies and mainstream mix of Keats, Milton and Pope, there are changes. Poetry editor Jacqueline Simms who presides over a successful contemporary list which includes Sean O'Brien, Moniza Alvi, Fleur Adcock, D. J. Enright, and Penelope Shuttle along with recent rising stars Tobias Hill and Alice Oswald is now no longer considering unsolicited mss. OUP's 'Oxford Poets' series which runs to around ten new volumes annually has been totally redesigned. Output will maintain its high profile. New volumes will be actively commissioned. But the slush pile is no more. New poets will need to score elsewhere first.

The commercial editor most admired for his taste is **Cape**'s Robin Robertson. 'You can see a clear editorial mind at work,' says Poetry Society chairman Bill Swainson. The Cape list is by no means all things to all people. Robertson, himself a fine poet, moved into the editorial chair from **Secker & Warburg**, who abandoned their own poetry list when he went. He produces four to six titles annually – all books, no anthologies. Robertson reckons that poetry indicates the health of a trade list and points to successful cross-fertilisation at Cape where at least half a dozen of his poets are now also novelists (John Burnside, Adam Thorpe), short story writers (Matthew Sweeney) or essayists (Thomas Lynch). It is not enough for the books simply to appear either. Design is important. 'At £7 for 64 pages we must make it a beautiful thing.' Check them out, with their distinctive fold-in flaps these books look worth the money. Worth trying? Yes but potential contributors should never waste anyone's time by not looking at the list first.

At **The Harvill Press** poetry is part of the company's overall commitment to literature. Under poetry editor Bill Swainson the imprint manages around four titles each year with Paul Durcan and Raymond Carver cornering the sales but new writers would be better off starting elsewhere.

Among the other commercial houses former activity is now limited to nominal titles or back-list obligations. **Cassell** successfully exploit their best-selling 'Poems On The Underground' with a flood of spin-offs. The **Orion** group's **Everyman** imprint repackages the past at £1 per volume with a series which includes John Sketlon, Andrew Marvell, John Clare, and William Shakespeare. **Hutchinson** have Dannie Abse and the inspirational attractions of Helen Steiner Rice. **Methuen** stick to Brecht and John Hegley. Mainstream imprints may once have been the proving grounds for new voices but if recent activity is anything to go on that is certainly no longer the case.

The smaller operators

Not all commercial publishing is vast and conglomerate. Independents still exist and on their lists poetry still occurs. **Arcadia**, a new company are trying things out with the infamous Fiona Pitt-Kethley. Northern Ireland general publisher, **The Blackstaff Press**, continue to bring out one or two titles annually, mainly of Irish interest. Joan Newmann, Frank Ormsby and Ruth Carr's anthology of women poets are typical. Welsh family firm **Gwasg Gomer** do Jon Dressel, Nigel Jenkins and Chris Bendon. Former *Sunday Times* Small Publisher of the Year, **Polygon**, (which is an imprint of **Edinburgh University Press**) continues to mix Gaelic with English as part of its 'poetry for the new generation' policy. The press has at least half a dozen poets on the list including Meg Bateman, Rody Gorman, Liz Lochhead and W. N. Herbert. Try here if you are part of the Scottish renaissance.

Nominal dabbling

Poetry in the shape of single titles and the occasional anthology dots the lists of many UK publishers but this is hardly a declaration of interest or a desire to see more. **BBC Books** publish an anthology of the nation's favourite poems but you need to have been voted there to get in. **Marion Boyars** stick with Robert Creeley and Yevgeny Yevtushenko. **Element** track the mystical. **John Murray** have George Mackay Brown, **Weidenfeld & Nicolson** re-run W. B. Yeats. **Headline**, **Bloomsbury**, **Michael Joseph**, **Macmillan**, **Routledge**, **Deutsch** and others publish either generic anthologies or handy reprints of the classics. The occasional new voice that gets in arrives almost by mistake. Tokenism. For the beginner these are not the places to try and it is worth remembering that the editors of commercially produced anthologies do not accept unsolicited single poems. Some specialist interests are dealt with at **Lion** (Christian verse), **Peepal Tree** (Caribbean) and **Oscars** (gay) but it isn't a lot.

Universities

Apart from OUP activity is sparse in the UK. Reprints and literary studies at Cambridge, are the same as at Manchester. At the **University of Wales Press**, who publish a splendid series of collected works from Welsh poets, you need to be dead. American university presses such as **Nebraska**, **Nevada**, **Pittsburg**, **Ohio**, **Yale**, **Duke**, **Iowa**, **Syracuse** and **California** along with **W. W. Norton** do an increasing amount of verse but exclusively by Americans. No chances there. In Austria, however, the **University of Salzburg Press**, run these days exclusively from the pocket of James Hogg, has embarked on an extensive programme of substantial poetry volumes from the less commercial. Workmanlike, if not brilliantly designed, the books fill a niche unoccupied by anyone else. Peter Russell, John Gurney, Alexis Lykiard, Alison Bielski, and William Oxley are typical authors. In addition Hogg has revived *The Poet's Voice*, a literary magazine edited by Fred Beake and produced a number of anthologies drawn from the little mags including a best of both *Stride* and *Outposts*. Despite its Austrian location the poetry is exclusively British in origin.

Women

A spent force. Well hardly that, but as a commercial proposition poetry is not seen as the way ahead. Britain's leading feminist publishing house, **Virago**, now part of **Little Brown**, does little more than bring out the obvious (Margaret Atwood, Jean Binta Breeze, Merle Collins, Maya Angelou). As the direction for UK women poets? Not a hope. At **The Women's Press**, Virago's main competitor, the situation is much the same. Original good intentions sunk into a programme which endlessly publishes Alice Walker. Women poets are better served by the poetry specialists. More of them anon.

The mass market paperback

The cheap and popular end is where many poets imagine the best starting place to be. Mass-market paperback houses were founded to publish inexpensive reprints of cloth-covered originals and, despite a certain amount of innovation, to a large extent they still fulfil this role. Being neither cheap nor popular poetry does not really fit in. You do not see it among the twirlies on station bookstalls. Check the empires of **Arrow**, **Minerva**, **Corgi**, **Headline** and **Pan**. If you discount the inspirational, you won't find a book of verse between them. **Vintage** to their credit publish the occasional anthology and run reprints of Iain Sinclair but he is also a successful novelist. Elsewhere nothing, although there are two exceptions. At **Penguin**, where things are always different, poetry plays a significant part. With a commercial ear ever to the ground the company have correctly assessed the market for contemporary and traditional verse and systematically and successfully filled it. Reprinting important volumes pioneered by poetry presses such as **Anvil**, **Carcanet** and **Bloodaxe**, originating historic and thematic anthologies, reviving classic authors and producing a multitude of translations en route, Penguin continues to provide an almost unrivalled introduction to the world of verse. But appearances aside, this is most certainly no place for the beginner. 'As a large trade publisher, we publish only anthologies plus a handful of famous poets,' publishing director Tony Lacey told me. 'We leave the discovering of poets to the specialists. The smaller presses can take risks; we cannot.' Despite this, the company still originates a few titles with Craig Raine, Geoffrey Hill and Roger McGough serving as good examples. All sure fire sellers. The main thrust remains the re-packaging of proven bards such as James Fenton, Simon Armitage, Carol Ann Duffy and Dannie Abse backed with a programme of modern poets in translation along with larger sets from the likes of Allen Ginsberg and John Ashbery. Recently the revived *Penguin Modern Poets* series of poetry anthologies has kept the pot boiling. Trios of loosely-connected poets are repackaged and issued at affordable prices. Michael Donaghy/Andrew Motion/Hugo Williams and Helen Dunmore/Jo Shapcott/Matthew Sweeney are recent titles. Despite a forthcoming Robert Crawford and Simon Armitage anthology of post-war British poetry, Lacey sees the whole market for verse as small, despite the hype.

Penguin's nearest rival, **Picador**, the literary imprint from **Pan Macmillan**, has recently dipped its toe with an outgoing and very non-mainstream anthology of UK outsiders *Conductors of Chaos*. Emboldened by the success imprint editor Jon Riley has appointed Don Paterson as poetry talent scout to work with Tanya Stobbs, the in-house poetry editor, and intends moving ahead with two to four titles annually. 'Picador is a literary list, adding poetry to it will round out what we do,' Riley told me. Robin Robertson and Ruth Sharman launch the series and will be followed with books from Kathleen Jamie and Paul Farley. Worth trying here? 'Poets who haven't published in the magazines are discouraged,' is the official line. Watch this space.

The specialists

Despite having a tough time at the hands of the commercial giants poetry flourishes. Where? With the specialist independents, a host of semi-commercial operations scattered across the country. They are run by genuine poetry enthusiasts whose prime concern is not so much money as the furtherance of their art. Begun as classic small presses which soon outgrew the restraints of back-bedroom offices and under-the-stairs warehousing, they have emerged by stealth. A real force on the poetry scene most now have national representation of some sort, with a number using *Password*, the Arts Council subsidised poetry specialists who issue a very useful catalogue (23 New Mount Street, Manchester M4 4 DE). These presses have learned well how the business works. You can find them in Waterstones, you can see them in Dillons. Most (but not all) receive grant aid, without which their publishing programmes would be sunk. They are models of what poetry publishing should be – active, involving, alert and exciting. They promote their lists through readings, tours and broadcasts and they involve their authors in the production and sales of their books. Never before have new poets been faced with so many publishing opportunities. And if there is any criticism then this is it. Too many books jamming the market, flooding the bookshops and clogging the review pages of the press. Just how does the reader see through the flood? By the press's reputation I guess.

In the swing now for years and regarded by many as the only specialist with critical clout **Carcanet** is almost indistinguishable from its trade competitors. Although no longer exclusively a publisher of verse, it still gives poetry pre-eminence and has over 500 titles in print and reps in 42 countries. Managing Director Michael Schmidt agrees with Auden's observation that most people who read verse read it for some reason other than the poetry. He fights the tide with his own mainstream journal *PN Review*. Despite an IRA bombing of his Manchester offices his press continues its policy of serious quality. 'I am strongly aware of the anti-modernist slant in a lot of poetry publishing, and publish to balance this,' he comments. 'Most submissions we receive come from people ignorant of the list to which they are submitting. Nothing is more disheartening than to receive a telephone call asking whether Carcanet publishes poetry.' The press concentrates on producing substantial editions which make a poet's whole oeuvre available alongside cheaper selected poems and new titles by both the untried and the famous. Typical of their list are John Ash, Les Murray, Sophie Hannah, Miles Champion, Eavan Boland and best-seller, Elizabeth Jennings. Three major millennium projects under way at present involve the bringing back into print the entire outputs of Robert Graves, Hugh MacDiarmid and Ford Madox Ford, a total in excess of fifty volumes. Carcanet has an air of purpose about it. 'We avoid the technicolour and pyrotechnic media razzmatazz,' says Schmidt. New poets are welcome to submit but check both your own past performance as well Carcanet's list before you go ahead.

At the **Anvil Press**, founder Peter Jay celebrates thirty years of independent, alternative publishing. Founded as a small press in 1968 Anvil was an early alternative to the Fabers and OUPs of the poetry scene. Jay still sticks with his original coterie of poets and makes what personality cult he can of Harry Guest, Peter Levi, Anthony Howell and Heather Buck. With the assistance of Bill Swainson, Jay has recently gone into over-drive expanding his abiding interest in poetry in translation. The press is justly proud of its claim of keeping British poetry open to new work from all over the world. Four Nobel Laureates are among the authors on its list. Editions have a quiet style with as much attention paid to presentation inside the book as out. Anvil's runaway best-seller is Carol Ann Duffy who also edits their useful *Anvil New Poets* anthology. Typical poets include Dick Davis, Ruth Silcock, Sally Purcell and Dennis O'Driscoll.

Enitharmon Press represents quality, cares about presentation and like Anvil has a real concern for internal design. Its books, its splendid poet/artist limited edition collaborations and its occasional pamphlets are produced to the highest of standards. Enitharmon has little interest in fashion, preferring 'poetry of the human spirit' which exhibits 'moral imagination'. Owner Stephen Stuart-Smith continues a policy of publishing between eight and ten volumes annually by new, established and unjustly neglected poets. David Gasgoyne's *Selected Verse Translations* sells alongside Jeremy Reed's rich and subversive *Sweet Sister Lyric*. Enitharmon is 'wary of unsolicited mss – unless, of course, those manuscripts are of extraordinary brilliance.' Stuart-Smith considers the finding of such a work in the slush pile unlikely. Typical recent poets include Martyn Crucefix, Judith Kazantzis, Hilary Davies and Phoebe Hesketh. In a recent and rather uncharacteristic dash for publicity Enitharmon teamed with the Arts Council and the charity Barnados to publish *Poetry On The Ceiling*, a series of posters for display above dentist's chairs.

If the tumble of contemporary poetry has a centre anywhere these days then it is with Neil Astley's acclaimed **Bloodaxe Books.** Publishing fifty titles annually the press concerns itself exclusively with poetry and related titles. Picking up poets dropped by the commercial operators and selling on to the world's anthologists, this is certainly one of poetry's best proving grounds. Based in Newcastle-upon-Tyne and begun around fifteen years ago, the press is unhindered by a past catalogue of classical greats or an overly regional concern. It relentlessly pursues the new. Regarded by some as garish and fast, Bloodaxe is now the UK's only real rival to the otherwise unassailable Faber. Astley presents the complete service from thematic anthologies, world greats and selecteds to slim volumes by total newcomers. The press has its own range of excellent handbooks to the scene including Paul Hyland's *Getting Into Poetry* and Peter Sansom's *Writing Poems* along with an increasing range of critical volumes including Deryn Rees Jones's essays on new women poets, *Consorting With Angels*. Not that the media really support much of this activity. Astley reports that reviews are now taking so long to appear that by the time many of them do bookshops have returned the books as non-sellers. Many main titles get missed, newer names do not get a look in. Best-sellers include R. S. Thomas, Linda France's anthology *Sixty Women Poets*, Jenni Couzyn's *Contemporary Women Poets*, along with Lorca in translation. Still way out ahead is the decade-framing and expectedly controversial anthology, *The New Poetry*. With commendable concern to stay ahead Bloodaxe is already looking at the even newer generation with books from Tracey Herd, Roddy Lumsden, Elinor Brown and Jane Holland, all born in the 60s and 70s. This plus Maura Dooley's anthology *Making For Planet Alice*, thirty new women poets whose first collections have appeared since 1990. If the poets of earlier generations were teachers then the present ones earn their livings from playing snooker or pub quiz machines. The dominance of academia is over. Typical recent Bloodaxe poets include Helen Dunmore, Barry MacSweeney, Selima Hill and C.K. Williams. The press welcomes newcomers but since they receive at least 100 new collections a week, advise that you can increase your chance of an early answer by restricting yourself to sending a dozen of your best. If Bloodaxe want to see more, they'll ask. A simple way to taste the imprint's range is to try their anthology, *Poetry With An Edge*.

Seren Books (the Welsh for 'star') are by now a fully blown literary house publishing novels, short fiction, biographies and critical texts. Started by Cary Archard as an offshoot of the magazine *Poetry Wales* the imprint still maintains a solid interest in verse publishing at least six new single author volumes annually. In receipt of considerable Arts Council of Wales sponsorship the bias is towards work from Wales and the border regions. Poetry editor Amy Wack reads *everything* submitted but admits that she has only ever accepted one unsolicited manuscript in her entire tenure. Seren wants to see poems that 'are not afraid to reveal the "sad music of humanity": humour, bitterness, joy, sorrow, rage, lust'. Editions are quality productions with plenty of attention paid to design inside and out. Typical recent poets include Sheenagh Pugh, Duncan Bush, John Davies, Robert Minhinnick and Hilary Llewellyn-Williams. A good press sampler is their anthology, *Burning The Bracken*. They have also published their own guide to the scene, *The Poetry Business*.

Longer in the tooth than it once was, the stylish **Arc Publications** run by

Tony Ward from Lancashire has little interest in poetry's market forces. 'Our only criteria is that in the view of the editors the work is worthy of being published.' Using editors Michael Hulse and David Morley to catch his fishes Ward publishes around ten new titles annually. The view here is that despite the apparent vibrancy of the scene beginner poets still appear not to read contemporary work. Comprehension of literary tradition and, indeed, our native tongue, are missing. Ward suggests a crash course in book consumption, starting, naturally, with Arc. No bad thing. The books are as international, exciting and innovative as any. Typical poets include John Kinsella, Robert Gray, Geoff Hattersley, W.N. Herbert and best-seller Ivor Cutler.

Rupert Loydell's **Stride** began in 1982 as a wild small mag which took over the editor's life. The booklet series which spun from the magazine is now the main thrust and Stride faces the future as a fully fledged poetry publisher, producing well-designed full-size volumes the equal of any commercial operation he comes up against. Based in the south west the press has a list of well over 150 titles ranging from the totally unknown to the famous. Innovative poetry, 'reinvigorated and re-explored/invented forms', form the backbone although Loydell is certainly no opponent of more formal material, so long as it lives dangerously. The press runs individual collections, criticism, interviews and a range of excellent, alternative anthologies. This year it won a Ralph Lewis Award which Loydell reckons should keep the operation on the straight and narrow until 1999. Advice to prospective contributors? 'Research your market, target your work correctly, buy and read new writing.' Stride responds to submissions swiftly. Invariably within three weeks and often within three days. Best-sellers include the productive Peter Redgrove, David H.W. Grubb, American avant-gardist Robert Lax, Mary Maher and others. Check Stride's anthology *Ladder To The Next Floor* for a sampler of how the press got where it is or *The Stumbling Dance*, a collection of twenty-one new poets to see the kind of thing Loydell likes.

Peterloo Press, based in Cornwall and run by the redoubtable Harry Chambers, represents poetry without frills, without fuss and most definitely without the avant-garde. The press aims to publish quality work by new and neglected poets, some of them late starters (although if you have been flogging your stuff around the circuit for years and got nowhere then Chambers is unlikely to be your saviour); to co-publish with reputable presses abroad (Goose Lane in Canada, Storyline Press and the University of Pittsburgh in the States and Lagan Press in Ireland); and to establish a Peterloo list of succeeding volumes by a core of poets of proven worth. Chambers avoids anthologies and has finished with magazines and newsletters. The press sticks to books, running an active backlist of over two hundred titles. Bestsellers include U.A. Fanthorpe, John Mole, John Whitworth, John Latham and Dana Gioia. Recent additions are Sandy Soloman, Gary Geddes, Gabriel Fitzmorris and Ann Drysdale. Current plans include the establishment of a Peterloo centre in a converted chapel at Calstock, a venture not without its funding difficulties. Chambers runs his own poetry competition sponsored by Marks and Spencers (£4000 first prize) and insists that prospective contributors to his press have had at least six poems in reputable magazines. Send a full mss accompanied by a stamped envelope large enough to carry your mss back to you. Chambers currently takes twelve months to reply and is full to the year 2000.

There are other presses with less prodigious outputs but whose editions can still give the poetry world a run for its money. In Newcastle Peter Elfed Lewis's **Flambard Press** publishes books in the Bloodaxe style. With aid from Northern Arts the press sees a role as an outlet for new or neglected writers from the region. Cynthia Fuller, Geoffrey Holloway, Patricia Pogson, Peter Mortimer and Michael Blackburn are typical names. If you think you qualify send a small sample rather than a lifetime's output. In nearby Huddersfield, the self-styled poetry capital of Britain, Janet Fisher and Peter Sansom run **Smith/Doorstop** the poetry imprint of their enterprising **Poetry Business** (see **Organisations**). The press produce a mixture of pamphlets, full-length collections and stylish cassettes. Duncan Curry, Martin Stannard, Jo Haslam, Carcanet Press MD Michael Schmidt, and Irene Rawnsley are typical authors. Simon Armitage, Carol Ann Duffy and Ian Macmillan feature in the cassette series. From the appropriately named Coleridge Cottage in Somerset, Derrick Woolf runs the poetry publisher **Odyssey**, like Stride another outgrowth of a successful small mag. His editions have a south-west bias although this doesn't prevent him from casting his net where he wishes. Kerry Sowerby, Tilla Brading, Andy Brown and Tony Charles are on the list. As technology continues to make life easier for publishers it becomes harder to draw the line between the poetry specialists and the classic small presses. Maybe by now such a division does not exist at all.

The traditional outlets

Poetry has a place in our national press, albeit a small one. The *Independent* runs a daily poem, *The Guardian* features verse from times to time as do all the serious Sunday heavies. *The Times Literary Supplement* gives over considerable space on a regular basis; whole double page spreads devoted to the work of one poet or to a long single poem are not unusual although the paper does have its favourites. *The London Review Of Books* shows a similar interest although neither appear very keen to use unsolicited work from the mailbox. *The London Magazine*, another stalwart, has the reputation for being the fastest responder in the business (you walk to the post box, mail your poems, then return home to find them rejected and waiting for you on the mat). Auberon Waugh upholds stuffy tradition at *The Literary Review*. Among other weeklies and monthlies the situation is fluid. Poetry gets in when someone on the staff shows an interest. Check your targets along the shelves at W. H. Smith's. Some local newspapers and freesheets are responding to the perceived poetry boom by devoting pages to contributions from readers, mostly dire doggerel and largely unpaid, although it is publication. If your paper hasn't joined in yet try sending your work in the form of a letter to

Postbag. Start a trend. Much of this might sound quite reassuring for the poet but the truth is that were poetry to cease to exist overnight, then these publications would continue to publish without a flicker. Who, other than the poets, would notice?

Forward Press and the regional anthologies

Running in parallel with the high ground literary approach of much of the fore-mentioned poetry publishing is an empire largely unknown to the taste-makers and ignored by the critics. Ian and Tracy Walton's ground-floor **Forward Press** in Peterborough now turns over a million and a half annually, has more than 2000 titles in print, and reckons to account for around ten percent of all verse published in the UK. Depressed with 'twenty years of not being able to enjoy poetry' because it was inevitably obscure, the couple have moved from back kitchen to factory unit in the service of 180,000 active British verse scribblers. In the eight years since it was founded, Forward Press has certainly lived up to its claim to have 'de-mystified poetry' for a large section of the population. Publishing under a variety of imprints including **Poetry Now**, **Arrival Press**, **Anchor Books**, **Triumph House** and **Poetry Now Young Writers**, the operation receives thousands of contributions annually. Poets are sourced through free editorial copy in regional newspapers. 'Peterborough publishers are looking for contributions to their new poetry anthology *Anchor Books Inspirations From Yorkshire*' is a typical line. The contributors flow in their hundreds. 'It is a bit like amateur dramatics,' Ian told me, 'anyone can take part.'

Forward's outstanding success is built on its approachability. Perpetuating a poetry world's *Home and Away* image, the Walton's and their team of exclusively young editors include as many as two hundred and fifty poems in each antholo-gy. Submissions under thirty lines are preferred. Costs are kept down by using in-house printing equipment coupled to serviceable bindings. If you want to see your work in print, and for most contributors this is the whole *raison d'etre* for writing, then you have to buy the book. For many poets this will be their first published appearance and chances are they will buy more than a single copy. This is not a traditional vanity operation. No one is actually being ripped off nor are the publishers raking in exorbitant profits. Page for page, their titles are no more expensive than those of Cape or Faber and are cheaper than the output of some little presses. However distribution is patchy and not that many Forward titles make the shelves at Waterstones or Dillons. As for many of the small presses interested parties are encouraged to buy direct. Forward's critics, some of whom are quite vociferous, claim that quality is being neglected in exchange for quantity. Reduce your criteria for inclusion, include more poems, sell more copies. Undoubtedly the genuine literary achievement of appearing in one of these books is questionable. In mitigation though it must be said that for some people this will be a much-needed beginning and for others the only success they are going to get.

The Walton's have embellished their operation with a range of add-ons including contributor's badges for the young, signed participation certificates, framed versions of your poem printed along with money prizes for the best work. There is talk of royalty payments for contributors to successful anthologies although by definition this is never going to amount to very much.

Forward reckon now to have reached the UK limits for regular anthology publication and will no longer have to be as aggressive as they were. In addition to their schools and regional collections they regularly co-operate with national charities producing anthologies that directly benefit causes such as the National Anti-Vivisection Society and the Swindon Dyslexia Centre. They run three magazines, *Poetry Now, Triumph Herald* (which specialises in Christian verse) and *Rhyme Arrival* , have their own bookshop, **The Garret** in Warwick, a print and design service for self-publishers, and have just started **Poetry Now** *Introducing,* a series of books featuring the work of single authors. **Need2Know**, their how-to imprint has a range of titles for new writers, including poets, while their **Writers' Bookshop** imprint publishes guides to the small magazines of Britain, America and Australia. If *Poetry Now North West − Communicating Across The Barriers* sounds like your scene then send for the group's newsletters (1-2 Wainman Road, Woodston, Peterborough PE2 7BU) or ring them up (01733 230759). You'll find no dubious accommodation address dealing here, but on the other hand, few literary giants either.

Envious of Forward's success at catching the hearts and minds of most of the UK's poetry hobbyists a good number of rival operations have risen in their wake. Regional poetry anthologies, Best of Britain collections, compendiums of English, Scottish, Irish and Welsh verse abound. Contributions are sourced through notices on library walls, local free-sheets, local radio and through direct mail. These operations vary from the glossy **Hilton House Reflections** series to a number of pathetically produced and, one hopes, short-lived incarnations based in the non-metropolitan sticks. No actual rip-off occurs and contributors get in whether they purchase or not. But if you want to see your work then you must buy and the books can be mightily expensive. Before agreeing to contribute check the press's output. Do not submit blindly, research the back list. It is what Faber would demand of you. The rule applies to the whole poetry scene.

The small press and the little magazine

Hobbyist publishing ventures have been with us for quite a long time. Virginia Woolf began the **Hogarth Press** this way, quite literally on the kitchen table. But it was not until well after the Second War and the rise of the transatlantic mimeo revolution that amateur poetry magazine and pamphlet publication really took off. And recent advances have seen that revolution overturned again. Technologically literate poets are everywhere. Publishing has been stripped of its mystery. Access to laser printers and the computers that drive them are commonplace. Desk-Top Publishing and Word Processing software make it easy to originate. Disposable income has gone up. Poets in growing numbers are able and willing to establish competent one-person publishing operations, turning out neat professional-looking titles on a considerable scale.

These are the small presses and little magazines. They sell to new and often non-traditional markets rarely finding space on bookshop shelves, where they are regarded as unshiftable nuisances. Instead, small mags go hand-to-hand among friends at poetry readings, creative writing classes, literary functions, via subscriptions, and are liberally exchanged among all those concerned. The network is large. The question remains: is anyone out there not directly concerned with the business of poetry actually reading it? But that is another story.

Statistically, the small presses and the little magazines are the largest publishers of new poetry both in terms of range and circulation. They operate in a bewildering blur of shapes and sizes everywhere from Brighton to Birmingham and Aberystwyth to Aberdeen. Check at the **Association of Little Presses** (see **Organisations**) who produce a regular catalogue of member's output along with *PALPI*, a new publications listings magazine. Derrick Woolf's fine *Poetry Quarterly Review* (Coleridge Cottage, Nether Stowey, Somerset TA5 1NQ) carries regular reviews, as does Andy Cox's *Zene* (5 Martins Lane, Witcham, Ely, Cambs CB6 2LB). There are others. The **Small Press Centre** (see **Organisations**) also provides information.

This country's best poetry magazines all began as classic littles. Between them *PN Review, Ambit, Agenda, Outposts, Orbis, Poetry Review, Rialto, Acumen, Scratch, Staple, The North, Smiths Knoll, Envoi, Iron* and *Stand* do not come up to even half the circulation of journals like *Shooting Times* and *Practical Fishkeeping* – which says a lot about the way society values its poetry. Nonetheless, taken as a group, they will get to almost everyone who matters. They represent poetry as a whole. Read this group and you will get some idea of where the cutting edge is. In the second division in terms of kudos lie the regional or genre specialists such as *Lines Review* (Scottish poetry), *Poetry Ireland, The New Welsh Review, Poetry Wales, Queer Words* (the magazine of new lesbian and gay writing), *Psycopoetica* (psychologically based poetry), *Krax* (humorous verse), *Christian Poetry Review, Haiku Quarterly*, and *Poetry Manchester*. All these magazines are well produced, sometimes with the help of grants, and all represent a specific point of view. In Wales there is *Barddas* for poets using the strict meters and in Scotland *Lallans* for poets working in Lowland Scots. The vast majority of small magazines, however, owe no allegiance and range from fat irregulars like *Bete Noir* (reputed to be the worst responder in the UK), and *Angel Exhaust*, quality general round ups like *Oxford Poetry, The Oxford Review, Tears In The Fence*, and *Seam* (small enough to slide up your sleeve), to pamphlets like *The Yellow Crane* (interesting new poems), *The Cadmium Blue Literary Journal* (spearhead of the romantic renaissance), *Iota* (recent poetry), *The Wide Skirt* (at least 50% accepted from the mailbox), *Ramraid Extraordinaire Vol 2* (the cultural mosaic of the nineties), and *Pulsar* (personal thoughts & views). Some like *Prop* want to be both dynamic and eclectic, *The Whistle House* runs pseudonymously while *The News That Stays*

News is a private affair. If you can't find a magazine that suits you and your style then you can't be writing poetry. On the other hand if you are really sure you are then start your own.

Among the small presses there is a similar range. **Hippopotamus Press** publishes first collections and work by the neglected; Bob Cobbing's venerable **Writers Forum** sticks to mainstream experimental; John Harvey's **Slow Dancer** follows its owners taste publishing a mix of the new and the known in pamphlet form. In Hereford, **Spanner** manage Allen Fisher's prolific output adding unconventional support acts who would not get a look in elsewhere. **Dangaroo**, **Peepal Tree** and **Totem** have third world and ethnic concerns. **Staple First Editions** and **Rockingham Press** work at the edge of the mainstream. **Oscars Press** cover gay poetry. **Mudfog** excel at twenty-page pamphlets. **Spectacular Diseases** work with the new, as do **Words Worth** and **Microbrigade**. **Redbeck** follow David Tipton's reliable ear. **Y Lolfa** publish unofficial bards. For the new writer these kinds of presses are the obvious place to try first. Indeed it is where many have. Who put out T. S. Eliot's first? A small publisher. Dannie Abse, Peter Redgrove, James Fenton and Dylan Thomas, the same. R.S.Thomas, Ezra Pound and Edgar Allen Poem didn't even go that far – they published themselves.

Cash

A lot of writers new to the business are surprised to learn that their poetry will not make them much money. Being a poet is not really much of an occupation. You get better wages delivering papers. There will be the odd pound from the better heeled magazine, perhaps even as much as £40 or so from those periodicals lucky enough to be in receipt of a grant, but generally it will be free copies of the issues concerned, thank you letters and little more. Those with collections published by a subsidised, specialist publisher can expect a couple of hundred as an advance on royalties. Those using the small presses can look forward to a few dozen complimentary copies. The truth is that poetry itself is undervalued. You can earn money writing about it, reviewing it, lecturing on it or certainly by giving public recitations (£100 standard here, £800 if you are Tony Harrison, several thousand if you are Ted Hughes). In fact, most things in the poetry business will earn better money than the verse itself. Expect to spend a lot on stamps and a fair bit on sample copies. Most of the time all you'll get in return is used envelopes.

Readings

Since the great Beat Generation Albert Hall reading of 1964, there has been an ever-expanding phenomenon of poets on platforms, reading or reciting their stuff to an audience that can be anywhere between raptly attentive and fast asleep. Jaci

Stephen, writing in *The Daily Mirror*, reckoned readings to be like jazz. 'Both involve a small group of people making a lot of noise, and then, just when you think it's all over, it carries on.' But I believe there can be a magic in the spoken poem. The music lives, the images echo. Yet for some writers the whole thing has devolved so far as to become a branch of the entertainment industry; for others, it is an essential aspect of what they do. Whichever way you view it, it is certainly an integral part of the business and one in which the beginner is going to need to engage sooner or later. Begin by attending and see how others manage. Watch out for events advertised at your local library or ring your local arts board. Poets with heavy reputations can often turn out to be lousy performers while many an amateur can really shake it down. Don't expect to catch every image as you listen. Readings are not places for total comprehension but more for glancing blows. Treat it as fun and it will be. If you are trying things yourself for the first time, make sure you've brought your books along to sell, stand upright, drop the shoulders, gaze at a spot at the back of the hall and blow. If you end up pleased with your own performance then you could always enter the annual Speak-a-Poem competition. Check at **The Poetry Society** (see **Organisations)** for further details.

Competitions

Poetry competitions have been the vogue for more than a decade now with the most unlikely organisations sponsoring them. The notion here is that anonymity ensures fairness. Entries are made under pseudonyms so that if your name does happen to be Miroslav Holub, then this won't help you much. Results seem to bear this out too. The big competitions run biennially by the **Arvon Foundation** with the help of commercial sponsors, or the Poetry Society's National attract an enormous entry and usually throw up quite a number of complete unknowns among the winners. And why do people bother? Cash prizes can be large – thousands of pounds – but it costs at least a pound a poem to enter, and often much more than that. If it is cash you want, then the Lottery scratch-cards are a better bet. And there has been a trend for winners to come from places like Cape Girardeau, Missouri and Tibooburra, Australia. The odds are getting longer. Who won the last Arvon? I don't remember. But if you do fancy a try then it is a pretty innocent activity. You tie up a poem for a few months and you spend a couple of pounds. Winners' tips include reading the work of the judges to see how they do it, submitting non-controversial middle-of-the-road smiling things, and doing this just before the closing date so you won't have to wait too long. Try two or three of your best. Huge wodges are costly and will only convince the judges of your insecurity. Watch the small mags for details, write to your regional arts board, check out *Writer's Monthly, The New Writer, Poetry London Newsletter, Writer's News* or the listings in *Orbis* magazine, look on the notice board at your local library, or write for the regularly updated list from **The Poetry Library** in London (see **Organisations**).

Combining both competition and reading is a recent US import, **The**

Poetry Slam. Here all-comers are given the opportunity to strut their stuff for around three closely-timed minutes before a usually not all that literary crowd. Points are awarded for performance and audience reaction Scatology and street-wise crowd pleasing are more likely to get you through the rounds than closely-honed work. The ultimate winners get prizes, a slice of the door-take or a donated book. The events, which involve much shouting, can be a lot of fun. Slams have been seen in places as far apart as Cardiff and Sheffield and the craze is spreading. Call John O'Neill on 0181 533 0227 who organises the London based **Farrago UK Slam Poetry Championships** if you'd like to learn more.

Radio and TV

Taking National Poetry Day as a true celebration of poetry in all its forms the BBC, both television and radio, have seen verse as a vehicle for popular entertainment. There have been annual polls for the Nation's Favourite Poem which are shown on BBC1 plus an array of support programmes on radio including footballing poetry on Radio 5 along with rhyme and reason on Radio 2. Give poetry a focus and the media pick it up. Generally, though, coverage is slight. The regular slots are all on radio, naturally enough. It is so hard to make verse visually appealing. Some TV producers have tried, notably Peter Symes who produced both *Poet's News* and *Words On Film* for BBC2. Symes' approach is to avoid the poem illustrated and to concentrate instead on documentary-style collaborations between commissioned poet and film-maker. His great successes have all been with Tony Harrison although projects with Simon Armitage, Jackie Kay, Lem Sissay, Fred d'Aquir and others underline his open approach. 'The crucial thing,' he advises, 'is an ability to write to picture and not to rely on things the other way around.' If you have a project in mind, rather than a set of existing poems, then he would be delighted to hear from you. On Radio Four, Susan Roberts is editor for two regular programmes: *Poetry Please,* presented by Gareth Owen which runs listeners' requests (everything from John Donne to Carol Ann Duffy), and *Stanza*, a late night poetry performance and discussion slot fronted by Simon Armitage. Poets here include Les Murray, Seamus Heaney, Sharon Olds and Tessa Gallagher. In addition, there is *With Great Pleasure* where prominent figures from public life choose their favourite pieces. Newcomers can try their hands at sending in but most of the slots go to the better knowns. On Radio Three, Fiona McLean produces *Best Words*, an occasional poetry magazine programme. She also does *Young Poets*, a series of ten-minute programmes featuring the new. Other producers such as Piers Plowright, Elizabeth Burke, and Julian May at the *Kaleidoscope* programme all put out the occasional poetry feature. It is also worth listening out for the Sunday feature programme on Radio 3 which includes poetry in its range. Radio 1 puts poetry into its Mark Radcliffe show, showcasing poets like Simon Armitage and Ian Macmillan. Independent radio are trying verse as fillers. An enlarging but difficult market. If you are determined to put your verse on air then local radio offers better possibilities. Try sending in self-produced readings on cassette (if you are any good at it) or topical poetry which regional magazine programmes could readily use. Don't expect to be paid much.

Internet

Poetry's current development is its appearance in huge quantity on the Internet. For those without a connection this is rather like hearing that verse is now big on Mars. So what? Who reads it? Quite a large number of people, it turns out. Net surfing is very much on the up. What the Internet has done is not only to make the supply of free information overwhelming but also to destroy all idea of geographic location. When you log on half the time you have absolutely no idea to where you are connected. The language might be English but the site could be anywhere.

Poetry is an obvious Internet medium. It's textural, has thousands of users and is easy to put on screen. From slow beginnings in the academic archives – University of Virginia with its down-loadable copies of everything from *The Germ*, the world's first little mag to the complete *Hunting Of The Snark;* University of North Carolina's Sunsite with its Seamus Heaney mug-shot and playable recording of the man reading his own poems; University of Columbia's Project Bartleby with its unending Housmann, Keats, Graves, Frost and Eliot – verse is now everywhere. Most service providers offer free Web-space as part of their subscriptions so an increasing number of users are posting up their own poems, starting e-zines (the cyberspace equivalents of little mags) or launching fan pages for poets they admire. I've already checked out sites devoted to Jack Kerouac, Allen Ginsberg, William Shakespeare and, amazingly, J. H. Prynne.

The downside of this proliferation is the abysmal standard of much of work displayed. With something so free and easy dross gets in enormously among the gold. Not that different from the real poetry world? Perhaps not.

If you'd like to check out cyber-poetry then this can be readily done and cheaply at one of the many cyber cafes which have opened up and down the country. Five pounds an hour for unlimited use, advice is free, coffee costs extra. Most poetry pages contain links to others. The Web is truly a web. Important UK sites start with the Poetry Society at *www.bbc.co.uk/poetry_soc/* who have appointed their own official web-watcher, Peter Howard. His home page (*hphoward.demon.co.uk/poetry*) contains almost as much useful data of that of his employers. A Howard inspired development is hypertext poetry which hot-links poems and verse fragments situated throughout the Web into a somewhat inco-herent whole. To try, the links are on his site. The best UK e-zine is still Sean Woodward's **The Living Poet's Society** (see **Organisations**) although there are plenty of others on the rise. Yahoo's poetry page at *www.yahoo.com/ Arts/Humanities/Literature/Genres/Poetry/* holds a huge list. *Resources For Poets*, an

American site at *www.inkspot.com/~ohi/inkspot/genrepoetry.html* has connections to just about everything else you'd care to find plus a lot besides. Net fanatics will already be using the free on-line rhyming dictionary (*www.cs.cmu.edu/~dougb/ rhyme.html*), depositing their poems with *Isibongo* the South African mag at *www.uct.ac.za/projects/poetry/isibongo/isibongo.htm*, supporting Michael R. Brown's proposal for PTV, a 24–hour poetry television channel, or perhaps engaging in some of the wilder web poetry practises such as the composition of twenty conso-nant poetry. Check out *http://www.au.com/ammx/20cp.html* if that sounds like you.

The Net also hosts a variety of critique groups and workshops. These operate either as a news groups or via e-mail and are the on-line, larger and much more anarchic equivalents of the old-fashioned postal workshop. Chuck your stuff into one of these and wait for the world-wide response. *Resources For Poets* (see above) runs a list.

Chadwyck-Healey who have already brought out the entirety of English poetry published from 600 to 1900 on a set of CDs (*English Poetry: The Full Text Database*) have now enlarged their services to include 40,000 American poems along with a comprehensive database of *African-American Poetry 1760–1900*. These new products, designed principally for libraries, are offered on-line on payment of a subscription fee. Soon there will be nothing left to buy from your local book-store. Check the Internet Bookstore for a searchable poetry books database. The pen is dead, long live the keyboard. If not quite now then pretty soon.

Starting up

Probably the best place will be locally. Find out through the library or the near-est arts board which writers groups gather in your area and attend. There you will meet others of a like mind, encounter whatever locally produced magazines there might be and get a little direct feedback on your work. 'How am I doing?' is a big question for the emerging poet and although criticism is not all that hard to come by, do not expect it from all sources. Magazine editors, for example, will rarely have the time to offer advice. It is also reasonable to be suspicious of that offered by friends and relations – they will no doubt be only trying to please. Writers groups present the best chance for poets to engage in honest mutual criticism. But if you'd prefer a more detached, written analysis of your efforts and are willing to pay a small sum, then you could apply to *The Script,* the service operated nationally by the Poetry Society (22 Betterton Street, London WC2H 9BU), by The Arts Council of Wales (see **Arts Councils and Regional Arts Boards**) or to one of those run on an area basis by your local arts board. There are also a number of non-subsidised critical services which you will find advertised in writers' magazines.

If you have made the decision to publish your work – and I don't suppose you'd be reading this if you hadn't – then the first thing to do is some market research. I've already indicated how overstocked the business is with periodicals and publications, yet surprisingly you will not find many of these in your local W. H. Smith. Most new poetry still reaches its public by other routes. However, begin by reading a few newly published mainstream books. Ask at your booksellers for their recommendations. Check Waterstones or Dillons who both do a good job. *Waterstone's Guide to Poetry Books* edited by Nick Rennison is a decent map. Most shops these days carry a basic stock, but if you need a specialist then get hold of the Poetry Library's current list of shops with a specific interest in poetry. Enquire at the library. Try selecting a recent anthology of contemporary verse. To get a broad view of what's going on, not only should you read Hulse, Kennedy and Morley's Bloodaxe *The New Poetry* along with Ian Sinclair's *Conductors of Chaos* (Picador) and the recent Jo Shapcott and Matthew Sweeney set of poems for strange times *Emergency Kit* (Faber), but the annual *Forward Book of Poetry* (Faber); Mike Horovitz's *Grandchildren of Albion* (New Departures); Bob Cobbing's *Verbi Visi Voco* (Writer's Forum); Edward Lucie Smith's Penguin *British Poetry Since 1945*; and perhaps Seamus Heaney and Ted Hughes' *The Rattle Bag* (Faber) or their *The School Bag* (Faber); Jeni Couzyn's *The Bloodaxe Book of Contemporary Women Poets*; Linda France's *Sixty Women Poets* (Bloodaxe); William Oxley's *Completing the Picture* (Stride); *From the Other Side of the Century – A New American Poetry 1960-1990* edited by Douglas Messerli (Sun & Moon), and *Postmodern American Poetry,* a really splendid selection edited by Paul Hoover (Norton). These last two might be harder to find but will be worth the effort. Progress to the literary magazine. Write off to a number of the magazine addresses which follow this article and ask the price of sample copies. Enquire about subscriptions. Expect to pay a little but inevitably it will not be a lot. It is important that poets read not only to familiarise themselves with what is currently fashionable and to increase their own facility for self-criticism, but to help support the activity in which they wish to participate. Buy – this is vital for little mags, it is the only way in which they are going to survive. Read; if it's all a mystery to you, try Tony Curtis' *How to Study Modern Poetry* (Macmillan); Peter Sansom's excellent *Writing Poems* (Bloodaxe) or my own *The Poetry Business* (Seren). How real poets actually work can be discovered by reading C. B. McCully's the *Poet's Voice and Craft* (Carcanet) or *How Poets Work* (Seren). After all this, if you still think it's appropriate, try sending in.

How to do it

Increase your chances of acceptance by following simple, standard procedure:

❑ Type or computer print on a single side of the paper, A4 size, single-spacing with double between stanzas exactly as you'd wish your poem to appear when printed.

❑ Give the poem a title, clip multi-page works together, include your name and address at the foot of the final sheet. Avoid files, plastic covers, stiffeners and fancy clips of any sort.

❑ Keep a copy, make a record of what you send where and when, leave a space to note reaction.

❑ Send in small batches – six is a good number – with a brief covering letter saying who you are. Leave justification, apology and explanation for your writers group.

❑ Include a self-addressed, stamped envelope of sufficient size for reply and/or return of your work.

❑ Be prepared to wait some weeks for a response. Don't pester. Be patient. Most magazines will reply in the end.

❑ Never send the same poem to two places at the same time.

❑ Send your best. Work which fails to fully satisfy even the author is unlikely to impress anyone else.

Where?

Try the list which follows, sending for samples as suggested. The total market is vast – 200 or so addresses here – hundreds more in *Small Presses and Little Magazines of the UK and Ireland* (Oriel Bookshop, The Friary, Cardiff – £4 including postage for the latest edition), the *Small Press Guide* (which only covers journals – Writers' Bookshop, 7-11 Kensington High Street, London W8 5NP) and in *Light's List of Literary Magazines* which contains both UK and US addresses (John Light, The Lighthouse, 29 Longfield Road, Tring, Hertfordshire HP23 4DG), literally thousands and thousands worldwide in Christine Martin's *Poet's Market* (Writer's Digest Books) and Len Fulton's *Directory of Poetry Publishers* (Dustbooks) – the two main American directories.

Scams and cons

With poetry overpopulated by participants it is not surprising that the con artist should make an appearance. There are plenty of people out there taking money off beginner writers and offering very little in return. The traditional vanity anthology, once the staple of the trickster, appears to be in retreat. With this scam classified small ads ask poets to contribute to a forthcoming anthology of verse. All work submitted is accepted, poets are told they have 'unusual and high potential' and are then asked to 'contribute fifty pounds to help offset ever increasing publishing costs'. There are no value judgements made yet poets are led to believe that they have in some way succeeded. The scam has been around for decades. In the sixties, TV host Bernard Braden submitted cut-ups of the local newspaper, a shopping list, two Shakespearean sonnets and the scribblings of a six-year old. The lot were accepted. More recently, the National Poetry Foundation's Johnathon Clifford has tested the market by sending in grossly amateur items in the tradition of William McGonagall. He was amazed to receive a sheaf of letters praising him as a poet of real worth, suggesting that in 'partnership' they should go right ahead and publish his shining verses and could he find his way to stump up the odd £3000 to help pay the bills. If Clifford had been a real beginner he might have fallen for the deal, sold the family silver and invested in what sadly would have turned out to be a no-hope project where the books would languish unsold, unwanted and unread in a distant warehouse or more likely under the author's bed. Instead Clifford wrote up his experiences (*Vanity Press & The Proper Poetry Publishers*) and began a one-man campaign against the vanity industry of back-street operators, accommodation addresses, and abandoned value judgements. You get published by the vanity presses because you pay and not because you are any good. Clifford has chased doggedly after his foe recruiting supporters, including the Advertising Standards Authority, by the dozen. Traditional vanity operations now face a Clifford blitzkrieg everytime they peer over the parapet. Poets can once again sleep peacefully in their beds.

Wish that they could. Already variations and embellishments on the vanity press theme are surfacing. These include offers to put your poetry to music setting you off on the road to stardom, readings of your verse by actors with deep voices to help you break into the local radio market (there isn't one) and further requests for cash to have entries on you appear in leather-bound directories of world poets, Everyone appears, including your uncle. There is a huge rash of bogus competitions where entry fees bear no relation to final prize money and the advertised 'publication of winners in anthology form' often means shelling out more for what will turn out to be a badly printed abomination crammed full of weak work. Poets should look vary carefully at anything which offers framed certificates, scrolls or engraved wall hangings. They should also be wary of suggestions that they have come high in the State of Florida's Laureateship Contest (or some such like) and have been awarded a calligraphed testimonial. Presentation usually occurs at a three-day festival held in one of the state's most expensive hotels. To get your bit of paper you need to stay for all three days and it is you who has to settle the bill.

How do you spot the tricksters? They change their names and addresses at will. They bill themselves as Foundations, Societies, Libraries, National Associations, Guilds. They sound so plausible. If you have the slightest suspicion then check with the Poetry Society (see **Organisations**). In the poetry world genuine advertisements for contributions are rare. And if anyone asks you for money then forget it. It is not the way things should be done. (See Graham King's article, *What Price Vanity?*, on page 170.)

The next step

Once you have placed a few poems you may like to consider publishing a booklet. There are as many small presses around as there are magazines. Start with the upmarket professionals by all means – Jonathan Cape, Faber & Faber – but be prepared for compromise. The specialists and the small presses are swifter and more open to new work.

If all else fails you could do it yourself. Blake did, so did Walt Whitman. Modern technology puts the process within the reach of us all and if you can put up a shelf, there is a fair chance you will be able to produce a book to go on it. Read my *How to Publish Yourself* (Allison & Busby), *The Writer's Companion* (Macmillan) and Jonathan Zeitlyn's *Print: How You Can Do It Yourself* (Journeyman). Remember that publishing the book may be as hard as writing it but marketing and selling it is quite something else. If you are determined, have a look at Bill Godber, Robert Webb and Keith Smith's excellent *Marketing For Small Publishers* (Journeyman).

The listings

None of the lists of addresses which follow are exhaustive. Publishers come and go with amazing frequency. There will always be the brand new press on the look-out for talent and the projected magazine desperate for contributions. For up to the minute information check some of the **Organisations of Interest to Poets** in the lists which follow. Poetry has a huge market. It pays to keep your ear to the ground.

Poetry presses

Abbey Books See also **RJ Publications, Acorn Books, Maypole Books** *Rosemary J. Peel*, PO Box 58, Cleckheaton, West Yorkshire BD19 3YS

Acorn Books See also **RJ Publications, Abbey Books, Maypole Books** *Rosemary J. Peel*, PO Box 58, Cleckheaton, West Yorkshire BD19 3YS

Acumen Publications See also **Acumen** magazine, *Patricia Oxley*, 6 The Mount, High Furzeham, Brixham, Devon TQ5 8QY

Agenda Editions See also **Agenda** magazine, *William Cookson & others*, 5 Cranbourne Court, Albert Bridge Road, London SW11 4PE

Aireings Press See also **Aireings** magazine, *Jean Barker*, 24 Brudenell Road, Leeds, West Yorkshire LS6 1BD

Akros Publications *Duncan Glen*, 18 Warrender Park Terrace, Edinburgh EH9 1EF

Alfred David Editions 3a Palace Road, London SW2 3DY

Allardyce, Barnett, Publishers See under **Small Presses**

Aloes Books *Jim Pennington & others*, 110 Mount View Road, London N4 4JH

Alun Books (includes **Goldleaf & Barn Owl Press**) *Sally Jones*, 3 Crown Street, Port Talbot, West Glamorgan SA13 1BG

Amazing Colossal Press *Maureen Richardson*, PO Box 177, Nottingham NG3 5JT

Amra Imprint *Bill Griffiths*, 21 Alfred Street, Seaham, Co. Durham SR7 7LH

Anarcho Press *Stan Trevor*, Briagha, Badninish, Dornoch, Sutherland IV25 3JB

Anchor Books See also **Arrival** and **Forward Presses** and **Poetry Now** and **Rhyme Arrival** magazines, *Ian Walton*, 1-2 Wainman Road, Woodston, Peterborough, Cambs PE2 7BU

Ankle Books 153 Gwydir Street, Cambridge CB1 2LJ

Anvil Press Poetry (*anvil@cix.compulink.co.uk*) See under **UK Publishers**

Appliance Books *Tabitha Webb*, 1 Bolton Lane, Ipswich, Suffolk 1PX 2BX

Aramby Publishing See also **Wire Poetry Magazine**, *Mal Cieslak*, 1 Alanbrooke Close, Knaphill, Surrey GU21 2RU

Arcadia Books 6–9 Cynthia Street, London N1 9JF

Arc Publications See under **UK Publishers**

Argyll Publishing Glendaruel, Argyll PA22 3AE

Arrival Press See also **Anchor Books** and **Forward Press** and **Poetry Now** and **Rhyme Arrival** magazines, 1–2 Wainman Road, Woodston, Peterborough, Cambs PE2 7BU

Astrapost *Eric Ratcliffe*, 7 The Towers, Stevenage, Hertfordshire SG1 1HE

Avalanche Books *Deborah Gaye*, 125 Derricke Road, Stockwood, Bristol

Aylesford Press *D. A. Ashton*, 158 Moreton Road, Upton, Wirral, Cheshire LA9 4NZ

Bad Press *Philip Boxall*, Chisenhale Works, 64–84 Chisenhale Road, London E3 5QZ

Bander-Snatch Books *Graham Holter*, 6 Highgrove, 63 Carlisle Road, Eastbourne, East Sussex BN20 7BN

The Bay Press 7 Collingwood Terrace, Whitley Bay, North Yorks NE26 2NP

BB Books See also **Global Tapestry Journal** *Dave Cunliffe*, Springbank, Longsight Road, Copster Green, Blackburn, Lancs BB1 9EU

Bedlam Press *David Moody*, Church Green House, Old Church Lane, Pately Bridge, Harrogate, North Yorks HG3 5LZ

Beyond the Cloister *Hugh Hellicar*, Flat 1, 14 Lewes Crescent, Brighton, East Sussex

Big Little Poem Books *Robert Richardson*, 3 Park Avenue, Melton Mowbray, Leics LE13 0JB

Black Cat Communications 10 Lincoln Street, Brighton, East Sussex BN2 2UH

Black Cygnet Press *A. D. Burnett*, 33 Hastings Avenue, Merry Oaks, Durham DH1 3QG

The Black Gate Press *John Spence*, 25 York Close, Cramlington, Northumberland NE23 9TN

Black Hat *Lloyd Robson*, 18 Sapphire Street, Cardiff CF2 1PZ

Blackstaff Press See under **UK Publishers**

Blackwater Press 17 Holbrook Road, Leicester LE2 3LG

Blaxland Family Press *John Jarrett* 12 Matthews Road, Taunton, Somerset TA1 4NH

Bloodaxe Books See under **UK Publishers**

Blue Cage See also **Blue Cage** magazine, 98 Bedford Road, Birkdale, Southport, Merseyside PR8 4HL

Blue Nose Press 32 Northolme Road, London N5

Bradgate Press See also **Poetry Digest** magazine *Maureen Forrest*, 28 Stainsdale Green, Whitwick, Leics LE67 5PW

Brentham Press *Margaret Tims* 40 Oswald Road, St Albans, Herts AL1 3AW

Businesslike Publishing See under **Small Presses**

Carcanet Press (*pnr@carcanet.u-net.com*) See also **PN Review** and under **UK Publishers**

Carnivorous Arpeggio (Press) *George Messo* 329 Beverley Road, Hull, Humberside HU5 1LD

Chapman Press See under **UK Publishers**, also **Chapman** magazine

Cheerybite Publications 45 Burton Road, Little Neston, South Wirral L64 4AE

Chotriffid Books *K. V. Bailey*, 1 Val De Mer, Alderney, Channel Islands CN9 3YR

The Chrysalis Press 11 Convent Close, Kenilworth, Warwickshire CV8 2FQ

Chudbury Books *David Southall*, 5 Fairhaven, Yate BS17 4DS

Clocktower Press 27 Alfred Street, Stromness, Orkney KW16 3DF

Cloud *Michael Thorp*, 48 Biddleston Road, Heaton, Newcastle upon Tyne NE6 5SL

Coelecanth Press *Maurice Scully*, 21 Corrovorrin Grove, Ennis, Co Clare, Eire

The Collective (*blind.cwm@aol.com*) *John Jones*, Penlanlas Farm, Llantilio Pertholey, Y-fenni, Gwent NP7 7HN

Commonword See also **Crocus Books**, *Cathy Bolton*, Cheetwood House, 21 Newton Street, Manchester M1 1FZ

Company of Poets Books Oversteps, Froude Road, Salcombe, S. Devon TQ8 8LH

The Corbie Press 57 Murray Street, Montrose, Angus DD10 8JZ

Crabflower Pamphlets See also **The Frogmore Papers** magazine and press, *Jeremy Page*, 42 Morehall Avenue, Folkstone, Kent CT19 4EF

Creation Books 83 Clerkenwell Road, London EC1M 5RJ

Credo Publishing *Annie Manning*, 45 Melsted Road, Boxmoor, Hemel Hempstead, Herts HP1 1SX

Crescent Moon Publishing and Joe's Press See under **Small Presses**, and **Passion** magazine

Crocus Books (Imprint of **Commonword**) *Cathy Bolton*, Cheetwood House, 21 Newton Street, Manchester M1 1FZ

Curfew Press *John Citizen*, 112 Sunnyhill Road, Streatham, London SW16 2UL

Cwm Nedd Press *Robert King*, 16 Rhydhir, Neath Abbey, Neath, W Glamorgan SA10 7HP

Da'th Scholarly Dervices/Darengo Publications 31b Northbury Crescent, London SW16 4JS

Daft Lad Press *Chris Challis*, 34 Leicester Street, Leicester LE5 3YR

Damnation Publications (*kerry@peepal.demon.co.uk*) *Kerry Sowerby*, 2 Midland Road, Leeds, West Yorks LS6 1BQ

Dangaroo Press See also **Kunapipi** magazine, PO Box 20, Hebden Bridge, West Yorks HX7 5UZ

Day Dream Press See also **Haiku Quarterly**, *Kevin Bailey*, 39 Exmouth Street, Swindon, Wilts SN1 3PU

Dedalus Press/Peppercanister Books *John F. Deane*, 24 The Heath, Cypress Downs, Dublin 6, Eire

Deucalion Press *D. S. Savage*, 67 Church Street, Mevagissy, St Austell, Cornwall PL26 6SR

Diamond Press *G. Godbert*, 5 Berners Mansions, 34–36 Berners Street, London W1P 3DA

Dido Press *Diane Thomas*, 2 Pelham Street, London SW7 2NG

Diehard Publishers *Ian King & others*, Grindles Bookshop, 3 Spittal Street, Edinburgh EH3 9DY

Dilettante Publications Little Bystock, Bystock Close, Exeter, Devon EX4 4JJ

Direction Poetry *Peter Harrison*, 28 Nant Y Felin, Pentraeth, Anglesey LL75 8UY

Dissident Editions *Frederik Wolff*, 71 Ballyculter Road, Loughkeelan, Downpatrick, Co. Down BT30 7BD

Dog and Bone Publishers 175 Queen Victoria Drive, Scotstown, Glasgow G12 9BP

Dragonfly Press 2 Charlton Cottages, Barden Road, Speldhurst, Kent TN3 0LH

Dragonheart Press *Sean Woodward*, 11 Menin Road, Allestree, Derby DE22 2NL

Ellerton Press PO Box 354, Newcastle under Lyme ST5 4NH

Enitharmon Press See under **UK Publishers**

Equinox Press Sinodum House, Shalford, Braintree, Essex CM7 5MW

Equipage *Rod Mengham,* Jesus College, Cambridge CB5 8BL

Eros Press See also **Interactions** magazine, *Andrew Yardwell*, PO Box 250, St Helier, Jersey JE4 8TZ, Channel Islands

Farrago Collective Press 106 High Street, West Wickham, Kent BR4 0ND

Fatchance Press See also **Fatchance** magazine, Elm Court, East Street, Sheepwash, Beaworthy EX21 5NL

Feather Books See under **Small Presses**

57 Productions *Paul Besley*, 57 Effingham Road, Lee Green, London SE12 8NT

Fire River Poets 19 Green Close, Holford, Bridgwater, Somerset TA5 1SB

Firs Publications The Firs, Bryndu, Llannon, Llanelli, Dyfed SA14 6AP

First Class Publications PO Box 1799, London W9 2BZ

First Time Publications See also **First Time** magazine, *Josephine Austin*, 4 Burdett Place, George Street, Hastings, East Sussex TN34 3ED

Five Leaves Publications See under **Small Presses**

Five Seasons Press Wickton Court, Stoke Prior, Leominster, Herefordshire HR6 0LN

Flambard Press *Peter Elfed Lewis*, 4 Mitchell Avenue, Jesmond, Newcastle upon Tyne NE2 3LA

Forest Books *Brenda Walker* 20 Forest View, Chingford, London E4 7AY

Form Books *Harry Gilonis,* 42a Lowden Road, London SE24 0BH

Forward Press/Arrival Press See also **Anchor Books** press and **Poetry Now** and **Rhyme Arrival** magazines, *Ian Walton*, 1–2 Wainman Road, Woodston, Peterborough, Cambs PE2 7BU

Fox Press/Winter Sweet Press *Beryl Bron*, Oak Tree, Main Road, Colden Common, Nr Winchester, Hants SO21 1TL

The Frogmore Press See also **The Frogmore Papers** magazine, *Jeremy Page*, 42 Morehall Avenue, Folkestone, Kent CT19 4EF

Gallery Press *Peter Fallon*, Loughcrew, Oldcastle, County Meath, Eire

Gekko Press *Anne Bailey*, 30b Stanmer Street, Battersea, London SW11 3BG

Get Connected Press 342 Hartshill Road, Stoke on Trent, Staffs ST4 7NX

Gisgog Books *Natasha Vann*, 70 Sycamore Avenue, Boythorpe, Chesterfield, Derbyshire S40 2PS

Golgonooza Press *Brian Keeble*, 3 Cambridge Drive, Ipswich, Suffolk IP2 9EP

Gomer Press/Gwasg Gomer See under
    UK Publishers
Gorse Publications *Pat Earnshaw*, PO Box
    214, Shamley Green, Guildford, Surrey
    GU5 0SW
Green Branch Press Kencot Lodge, Kencot,
    Lechlade, Glos GL7 3QX
Green Lantern Press 9 Milner Road,
    Wisbech, Cambs PE12 2LR
Grevatt & Grevatt See under **Small Presses**
Greylag Press *Jim Vollmar*, 2 Grove Street,
    Higham Ferrars, Rushden, Northants
    NN10 8HX
Gruffyground Press *Anthony Baker*, Ladram,
    Sidcot, Winscombe, Somerset
    BS25 1PW
Gryphon Press *Barbara Beazeley*, 28 Prince
    Edwards Road, Lewes, East Sussex
    BN7 1BE
Hangman Books *Jack Ketch*, 2 May Road,
    Rochester, Kent ME1 2HY
Hard Pressed Poetry *Billy Mills*,
    11 Watermeadow Park, Old Bawn,
    Tallaght, Dublin 24, Eire
Hastings Arts Pocket Press/Pickpockets
    Margaret Rose, 25 St Mary's Terrace,
    Hastings, East Sussex TN34 3LS
Headland Publications *Gladys Mary Coles*,
    Ty Coch, Galltegfa, Ruthin, Clwyd
    LL15 2AR
Hearing Eye *John Rety*, Box 1, 99 Torriano
    Avenue, London NW5 2RX
Here Now *Tom Kelly*, 69 Wood Terrace,
    Jarrow, Tyne & Wear NE32 5LU
Heron Press 6 Bramfield Drive, Newcastle
    under Lyme, North Staffs ST5 0ST
Highcliff Press See under **Small Presses**
Hillside Books *Johan de Wit*, Flat 1, Sylva
    Court, 81 Putney Hill, London
    SW15 3NX
Hilltop Oress *Steve Sneyd*, 4 Nowell Place,
    Almondbury, Huddersfield, West Yorks
    HD5 9PD
Hilton House (Publishers) *Michael K.
    Moore*, 39 Long John Hill, Norwich,
    Norfolk NR1 2JP
Hippopotamus Press See also **Outposts**
    magazine *Roland John*, 22 Whitewell Road,
    Frome, Somerset BA11 4EL
Honno *Elin Ap Hywel*, Alisa Craig, Heol Y
    Cawl, Dinas Powys, S. Glamorgan
    CF6 4AH
Hub Editions *Colin Blundell,* 11 The
    Ridgway, Flitwick, Beds MK45 1DH
Hunter House – Anachoresis *J. E.
    Rutherford*, 36 Lisburn Street, Hillsborough,
    Co Down BT26 6AB

I*D Books *Clive Hopwood*, Connah's Quay
    Library, High Street, Connah's Quay,
    Deeside, Clwyd
Ibid Press See also **Ibid** magazine *Matthew
    Hollis*, Dept of English Literature,
    University of Edinburgh, David Hume
    Tower, George Square, Edinburgh
    EH8 9JX
Icon Press *Philip Brown*, 71 Northbourne
    Road, Eastbourne, East Sussex BN22 8QP
Ink Sculptors/Cult Productions *Patricia
    Scanlan*, 34 Waldemar Avenue, Fulham,
    London SW6 5NA
International Concrete Poetry Archive
    Paula Claire, 11 Dale Close, Thames Street,
    Oxford OX1 1TU
Intimacy Books See also **Intimacy** maga-
    zine *Adam McKeown*, 4 Bower Street,
    Maidstone, Kent ME16 8SD
Invisible Books *B. Oenney*, BM Invisible,
    London WC1N 3XX
Iron Press See also **Iron** magazine, *Peter
    Mortimer*, 5 Marden Terrace, Cullercoats,
    North Shields, Tyne & Wear NE30 4PD
Isle of Wight Poetry Society Spindrift,
    Heathfield Road, Freshwater, Isle of Wight
    PO40 9SH
Jackson's Arm Press See also **Sunk Island
    Publishing** under **Small Presses** *Michael
    Blackburn*, PO Box 74, Lincoln LN1 1QG
Jayol Publications 145 Saintfield Road,
    Lisburn, Co. Antrim BT27 6UH
Joe's Press See also **Passion** magazine and
    Crescent Moon Publishing under **Small
    Presses**
Jugglers Fingers Press See also
    Uncompromising Positions magazine,
    Cheryl Wilkinson, 92 Staneway, Leam Lane,
    Gateshead, Tyne & Wear NE10 8LS
Katabasis *Dinah Livingstone*, 10 St Martin's
    Close, London NW1 0HR
Kawabata Press Knill Cross House, Knill
    Cross, Millbrook, Nr Torpoint, Cornwall
    PL10 1DX
Kerin Publishers *Irene & Keith Thomas*, 29 Glan
    Yr Afon, Ebbw Vale, Gwent NP3 5NR
Kernow Poets Press See also **Links**
    magazine *Bill Headdon*, Bude Haven,
    18 Frankfield Rise, Tunbridge Wells, Kent
    TN2 5LF
Kettleshill Press PO Box 38, Wirral,
    Merseyside L20 6NS
King of Hearts *Aude Gotto*, 13–15 Fye
    Bridge Street, Norwich, Norfolk NR3 1LJ
Klinker Zoundz *Hugh Metcalf*, 10 Malvern
    House, Stamford Hill Estate, London
    N16 6RR

The KQBX Press *Malcolm Povey,*
124 Carberry Avenue, Bournemouth,
Dorset BH6 3LH

Kropotkin's Lighthouse Publications
Jim Huggon 59 Leiston Road, Knodishall,
Suffolk IP17 1UQ

K. T. Publications See also **The Third Half**
magazine, *Kevin Troop,* 16 Fane Close,
Stamford, Lincolnshire PE9 1HG

Language Alive (*cris@slang.demon.co.uk*) *Chris
Cheek,* 85 London Road South, Lowestoft,
Suffolk NR33 0AS

The Lansdowne Press 33 Lansdowne Place,
Hove, East Sussex BN3 1HF

Lapwing Publications *Dennis & Rene Greig,*
1 Ballysillan Drive, Belfast BT14 8HQ

Last Ever Melodic Scribble Press
35 Kearsey Road, Sheffield S2 4TE

Laurel Books 282 The Common, Holt,
Wiltshire BA14 6QJ

Libanus Press *Christopher Driver,* 6 Church
Road, London N6 4QT

Ligden Publishers See also **Pulsar** magazine,
Jill Meredith, 34 Linacre Close, Grange
Park, Swindon, Wiltshire SN5 6DA

The Lilliput Press 12 Christopher Close,
Norwich, Norfolk NR1 2PQ

Lobby Press *Richard Tabor,* Simonburn
Cottage, Sutton Montis, Yeovil, Somerset
BA22 7HF

Lomond Press *R. L. Cook,* Whitecraigs,
Kinnesswood, Kinross KY13 7JN

Lothian Press 43 Ickburgh Road, London
E5 8AF

The Lymes Press *Alex Crossley,* Greenfields,
Agger Hill, Finney Green, Newcastle
under Lyme, Staffs ST5 6AA

Magenta *Maggie O'Sullivan,* Middle Fold
Farm, Colden, Heptonstall, Hebden
Bridge, West Yorks HX7 7PG

Making Waves *Anthony Selbourne,* PO Box
226, Guildford, Surrey GU3 1EW

Malfunction Press See also
Bardonni/Stopgap/Songs magazine,
Peter E. Presford, Rose Cottage, 3 Tram
Lane, Buckley, Clwyd

Mammon Press *Fred Beake,* 12 Dartmouth
Avenue, Bath BA2 1AT

Mandeville Press *Peter Scupham & others,* Old
Hall, Norwich Road, South Burlingham,
Norfolk NR13 4EY

The Many Press *John Welch,* 15 Norcott
Road, London N16 7BJ

Marc Goldring Books PO Box 250,
St Helier, Jersey, Channel Islands JE4 5PU

Mariscat Press *Hamish Whyte & others,*
3 Mariscat Road, Glasgow G41 4ND

Maypole Books See also **RJ Publications,**
Abbey Books and **Acorn Books**
Rosemary J. Peel, PO Box 58, Cleckheaton,
West Yorks BD19 3YS

Maypole Editions See under **Small Presses**

Menard Press *Anthony Rudolf,* 8 The Oaks,
Woodside Avenue, London N12 8AR

Microbrigade See also **Garuda** magazine,
Ulli Freer, 7 Highwood Avenue, London
N12 8QL

MidNag Publications Leisure Dept,
Wansbeck Square, Ashington,
Northumberland NE63 9XL

Morning Star Publications *Alex Finlay,*
17 Gladstone Terrace, Edinburgh
EH9 1LS

Mr Pillow's Press See also **Apostrophe**
magazine, *Diana Andersson,* 41 Canute
Road, Faversham, Kent ME13 8SH

Mudfog 11 Limes Road, Linthorpe,
Middlesbrough TS5 7QR

Mushroom Press 48 Dryclough Road,
Beaumont Park, Huddersfield, West Yorks
HD4 5JA

National Poetry Foundation See also
Pause magazine, *Johnathon Clifford & others,*
27 Mill Road, Fareham, Hants
PO16 0TH

Naturama Publications 42 Pinner Court,
Pinner Road, Pinner, Middx HA5 5RJ

NDA Press *Natalie D'Arbeloff,* 6 Lady
Somerset Road, London NW5 1UT

New Albion Press *David Geall,* 42 Overhill
Road, London SE22 0PH

New Departures *Michael Horovitz,* PO Box
9819, London W11 2GQ

New Hope International *Gerald England,*
20 Werneth Avenue, Gee Cross, Hyde,
Cheshire SK14 5NL

New River Project See also **Writers Forum**
and **And** magazine, *Bob Cobbing & others,*
89a Petherton Road, London N5 2QT

North and South *Peterjon & Yasmin Skelt,*
23 Egerton Road, Twickenham,
Middlesex TW2 7SL

Northern House Poets See also **Stand**
magazine, 19 Haldane Terrace, Newcastle
upon Tyne NE2 3AN

Northgate Books *Joseph Clancy,* PO Box
106, Aberystwyth SY33 3ZZ

Oasis Books See also **Oasis** magazine *Ian
Robinson,* 12 Stevenage Road, London
SW6 6ES

Odyssey Poets See also **Poetry Quarterly
Review** magazine, *Derrick Woolf,*
Coleridge Cottage, Nether Stowey,
Somerset TA5 1NQ

Oldtown Books/Macprint *Graham Mawhinnes*, 185 Gulladuff Road, Bellaghy, Londonderry BT45 8LW

The Oleander Press, *Philip Ward*, 17 Stansgate Avenue, Cambridge CB2 2QZ

On the Wire Press 6 Orchard Court, Beverley Road, Barnes, London SW13 0NA

Orbis Books See also **Orbis** magazine, *Mike Shields*, 199 The Long Shoot, Nuneaton, Warwickshire CV11 6JQ

Oscars Press *Peter Daniels*, BM Oscars, London WC1N 3XX

The Other Press *Frances Presley* 19b Marriott Road, London N4 3QN

Oversteps Books Oversteps, Froude Road, Salcombe, South Devon TQ8 8LH

Parataxis *Drew Milne*, School of English Studies, Arts Building, University of Sussex, Falmer, Brighton, E Sussex BN1 9NQ

Pennine Pens (*100342.3424@compuserve.com* and *http://www.eclipse.co.uk/pens*) *Chris Ratcliffe*, 32 Windsor Road, Hebden Bridge, West Yorks HX7 8LF

Pennyworth Press *Douglas Evans*, 64 Rosehill Park, Emmer Green, Reading, Berks RG4 8XF

Penygraig Community Publishing Penygraig Community Project, 1 Cross Street, Penygraig, Rhondda

Peppercorn Books *Judith White*, 24 Cromwell Road, Ely, Cambs CB6 1AS

Pepsi Rejects *Julie Ann Devon*, 73 Manor Way, Peterlee, Co Durham SR8 5RS

Permanent Press *Robert Vas Dias*, 5b Compton Avenue, Canonbury, London N1 2XD

Perpetua Press 26 Norham Road, Oxford OX2 6SF

Peterloo Poets *Harry Chambers*, 2 Kelly Gardens, Calstock, Cornwall PL18 9SA

The Phlebas Press 7 The Stables, High Park, Oxenholme, Cumbria LA9 7RE

Phoenix Press *Bruce Barnes*, 37 Wilmer Road, Bradford BD9 4RX

Pig Press *Richard Caddel*, 7 Cross View Terrace, Durham DH1 4JY

Pikestaff Press *Robert Roberts*, Ellon House, Harpford, Sidmouth, Devon EX10 0NH

Pimp$ of the Alphabet *Glenn Carmichael*, 130c Lower Cheltenham Place, Montpelier, Bristol BS6 5LF

Piscean Press 60 Silam Road, Stevenage, Hertfordshire SG1 8BQ

Pleasure To Be Alive 52 Cissbury Road, Tottenham, London N15 5QA

Pocket Prints *Florence Williams*, 425 Footscray Road, New Eltham, London SE9 3UL

Poet and Printer *Alan Tarling*, 30 Grimsdyke Road, Hatch End, Pinner, Middlesex HA5 4PW

Poetical Histories *Peter Riley*, 27 Sturton Street, Cambridge CB1 2QG

The Poetry Bookshop *Alan Halsey*, West House, 22 Broad Street, Hay on Wye HR3 5DB

The Poetry Business See also **Smith/Doorstop Books** press and **The North** magazine, *Peter Sansom & others*, 51 Byram Arcade, Westgate, Huddersfield, West Yorks HD1 1ND

Poetry Life Publishing See also **Poetry Life Magazine**, 14 Pennington Oval, Lymington, Hants SO41 8BQ

Poetry Now Young Writers 1-2 Wainman Road, Woodston, Peterborough, Cambs PE2 7EB

Polygon See under **UK Publishers**, also **Edinburgh Review** under **Magazines**

Polyptoton – Sea Dream Music *Keith Dixon*, 236 Sebert Road, Forest Gate, London E7 0NP

Prebendal Publications PO Box 9313. London E17 8LX

Precious Pearl Press See also **Cadmium Blue Literary Journal, The People's Poetry** and **Romantic Heir** magazines, *Peter Thompson*, 71 Harrow Crescent, Romford, Essex RM3 7BJ

The Press Upstairs *Giles Goodland*, 360 Cowley Road, Oxford OX4 2AG

Prest Roots Press *P. E. Larkin*, 34 Alpine Court, Lower Ladyes Hill, Kenilworth, Warwickshire CV8 2GP

Pretani Press *Harris Adamson*, 78 Abbey Street, Bangor, Co. Down BT20 4JB

The Previous Parrot Press The Foundry, Church Hanborough, Near Witney, Oxford OX8 8AP

Priapus Press *John Cotton*, 37 Lombardy Drive, Berkhamstead, Herts HP4 2LQ

Prospero Illustrated Poets Clarion Publishing, Neatham Mill, Holybourne, Alton, Hampshire GU24 4NP

Providence Press Whitstable See also **Scriptor** magazine, *John & Lesley Dench*, 22 Plough Lane, Swalecliffe, Whitstable, Kent CT5 2NZ

Psychopoetica Publications See also **Psychopoetica** magazine, *Geoff Lowe*, Dept of Psychology, University of Hull, Hull HU6 7RX

Purple Sandpiper Press *E. Tanguy*, Misson
Beau Regard, Five Oaks, Jersey, Channel
Islands JE2 7GR

Pyramid Press The Hen Hoouse, Hawerby
Hall, Hawerby, Grimsby DN36 5PX

Quince Tree Press *D. R. & J. M. Carr*,
116 Hardwick Lane, Bury St Edmunds,
Suffolk IP33 2QJ

Rack Press *N. Murray*, The Rack,
Kinnerton, Presteigne, Powys LD8 2PF

Raunchland Publications See also **3x4**
magazine, *John Mingay*, 2 Henderson
Street, Kingseat, by Dunfermline, Fife
KY12 0TP

Raven Arts Press PO Box 1430, Finglass,
Dublin 11, Eire

Reality Street Editions *Ken Edwards &
others*, 4 Howard Court, Peckham Rye,
London SE15 3PH

Rebec Press 79 Bronwydd Road,
Carmarthen SA31 2AP

The Red Candle Press See also
Candelabrum Poetry Magazine,
9 Milner Road, Wisbech, Cambs
PE13 2LR

Red Sharks Press *Tôpher Mills*, 122 Clive
Street, Grangetown, Cardiff CF1 7JE

Redbeck Press *David Tipton*, 24 Aireville
Road, Frizinghall, Bradford, West Yorks
BD9 4HH

Rialto Publications See also **The Rialto**
magazine, *Michael Mackmin*, PO Box 309,
Aylsham, Norwich, Norfolk NR11 6LN

River Publishing Company, 39
Cumberland Street, London SW1V 4LU

RJ Publications See also **Abbey Books**,
Acorn Books, **Maypole Books**,
Rosemary J. Peel, PO Box 58, Cleckheaton,
West Yorks BD19 3YS

Road Books *Judy Kravis & others*, Garravagh,
Inniscarra, Co Cork, Eire

Rockingham Press *David Perman*, 11 Musley
Lane, Ware, Herts SG12 7EN

Rubicon Press 57 Cornwall Gardens,
London SW7 4BE

S.A.K.S. Publications 42 Chatsworth Road,
London E5 0LP

S. A. Publishing See also **The Zone**
magazine, *Tony Lee*, 13 Hazely Combe,
Arreton, Isle of Wight PO30 3AJ

S. Editions *Ray Seaford*, 11 Richmond
Avenue, Feltham, Middx TW14 9SG

Salmon Poetry *Jessie Lendennie* Knocksedan
House, Baldoyle Industrial Estate,
Baldoyle, Dublin 15, Eire

Satis *Matthew Mead*, Knoll Hill House,
Ampleforth, West End, York YO6 4DU

Scottish Cultural Press See under **Small
Presses**

Scottish Poetry Index Scottish Poetry
Library, Tweedale Court, 14 High Street,
Edinburgh EH1 1TE

Scratch Publications See also **Scratch**
magazine, *Mark Robinson*, 9 Chestnut Road,
Eaglescliffe, Stockton-on-Tees T
S16 0BA

Seren Books See under **UK Publishers** and
Poetry Wales magazine

Shearsman Books See also **Shearsman**
magazine, *Tony Frazer*, 47 Dayton Close,
Plymouth, Devon PL6 5DX

Shell Press See also **Unicorn** magazine, *Alex
Warner*, 12 Milton Avenue, Millbrook,
Stalybridge, Cheshire SK15 3HB

Ship of Fools See also **Pages** magazine,
Robert Sheppard, 78 Nicander Road,
Liverpool 18

Shoestring Press 19 Devonshire Avenue,
Beeston, Nottingham NG9 1BS

Skoob Books Publishing Ltd See under
UK Publishers

Slow Dancer Press *John Harvey*, Flat 2,
59 Parliament Hill, London
NW3 2TB

Smith/Doorstop Books See also **The
Poetry Business** press and **The North**
magazine, *Peter Sansom & others*, The
Studio, Byram Arcade, Westgate,
Huddersfield, West Yorks HD1 1ND

Sol Publications See also **Sol Poetry
Magazine**, *Malcolm E. Wright*, 58 Malvern,
Coleman Street, Southend on Sea, Essex
SS2 5AD

Somniloquence Publishing *Lee Freeman*,
25 Broadwater Road, Worthing, West
Sussex BN14 8AD

South Manchester Poets *Dave Tarrant*,
122 Peterburgh Road, Edgeley Park,
Stockport SK3 9RB

Spanner Press See also **Spanner** magazine,
Allen Fisher, 14 Hopton Road, Hereford
HR1 1BE

Spareman Press 65 Sycamore Avenue,
Newport, Gwent NP9 9AJ

Spectacular Diseases See also **Spectacular
Diseases** magazine, *Paul Green*, 83b London
Road, Peterborough, Cambs PE2 9BS

Spectrum *Chris Bendon*, 14 Maes Y Deri,
Lampeter SA48 7EP

Spike Press 57 Spencer Avenue, Earlsdon,
Coventry, Warwickshire CV5 6NQ

Spineless Press *Tim Allen*, 21 Overton
Gardens, Mannamead, Plymouth, Devon
PL3 5BX

Spout Publications Birstall Library, Market Street, Birstall, Batley, West Yorks WF17 9EN

Staple First Editions See also **Staple** magazine, Tor Cottage, 81 Cavendish Road, Matlock, Derbyshire DE4 3HD

Stingy Artist Book Co. *Bernard Hemensley*, 85 Goldcroft Road, Weymouth, Dorset DT4 0EA

Street Editions See **Reality Street Editions**

Stride Publications See also **Taxus Press**, *Rupert Loydell,* 11 Sylvlan Road, Exeter, Devon EX4 6EW

Sui Generis Publishing *Gavin Leigh*, 18e Marlborough Road, Roath, Cardiff CF2 5BX

Swan Books and Educational Services *Mrs E. O. Evans*, Sole Proprietor, Salama, 13 Henrietta Street, Swansea SA1 4HW

Swansea Poetry Workshop *Nigel Jenkins*, 124 Overland Road, Mumbles, Swansea SA3 4EU

Tabor Press *M. A. Duxbury-Hibbert*, 2 Holyhead Road, Llanerchymedd, Ynys Mon LL71 7AB

Talking Pen Press 12 Derby Crescent, Moorside, Consett, Co Durham DH8 8DZ

Talus Editions See also **Talus** magazine, *Hanne Bramness & others*, Dept of English, King's College, Strand, London WC2R 2LS

Taranis Books See also **West Coast Magazine** *Kenny MacKenzie*, 2 Hugh Miller Place, Edinburgh EH3 5JG

Taxus Press See also **Stride Publications**, 11 Sylvan Road, Exeter, Devon EX4 6EW

The Tenormen Press See also **Ostinato** magazine, *Stephen C. Middleton*, PO Box 552, London N8 7SZ

Tiger Bay Press *Olly Rees*, 34 Cedarville Gardens, London SW16 3DA

Torque Press *Peter Middleton*, 79 Welbeck Avenue, Southampton SO17 1SQ

Totem *Fiifi Annobil*, 13 Llanbradach Street, Cardiff CF1 7AD

Tracks See also **Dedalus Press** 23 The Heath, Cypress Downs, Dublin 6, Eire

Triple Cat Publishing *R. E. Field*, 3 Back Lane Cottages, Bucks Horn Oak, Farnham, Surrey GU10 4LN

Triumph House *Ian Walton*, 1-2 Wainman Road, Woodston, Peterborough, Cambs PE2 7BU

Tuba Press See also **Tuba** magazine, *Peter Ellison*, Tunley Cottage, Tunley, Nr Cirencester, Glos GL7 6LW

A Twist In The Tail *Paul Cookson*, PO Box 25, Retford, Nottinghamshire DN22 7ER

Two Rivers Press *Peter Hay*, 145 Liverpool Road, Reading, Berkshire RG1 3PN

Ulsterman Pamphlets See also **HU – The Honest Ulsterman** magazine, *Tom Clyde*, 14 Shaw Street, Belfast BT4 1PT

Underground Press *John Evans*, 9 Laneley Terrace, Maesycoed, Pontypridd, Mid Glamorgan CF37 1ER

Unusual Books 4 Colonel Road, Ammanford SA18 2HB

Vennel Press *Richard Price*, 8 Richmond Road, Staines, Middlesex TW18 2AB

Ver Poets *May Badman*, 'Haycroft', 61/63 Chiswell Green Lane, St Albans, Herts AL2 3AL. (See also under **Professional Associations**)

Vigil Publications See also **Vigil** magazine, *John Howard-Greaves*, 12 Priory Mead, Bruton, Somerset BA10 0DZ

Visual Associations *Michael Weller* 3 Queen Adelaide Court, Queen Adelaide Road, London SE20 7DZ

Wanda Publications See also **Doors** and **South** magazines, Word and Action, 61 West Borough, Wimborne, Dorset BH21 1LX

Weatherlight Press *David Keefe*, 34 Cornwallis Crescent, Clifton, Bristol BS8 4PH

Welford Court Press 1 Welford Court, Leicester LE2 6ER

Wellsweep Press *John Cayley*, 1 Grove End House, 150 Highgate Road, London NW5 1PD

Westwords *Dave Woolley*, 15 Trelawney Road, Peverall, Plymouth, Devon PL3 4JS

White Adder Press 1 Forth View, Rucklaw Mains, Stenton Dunbar, East Lothian EH42 6DA

White Box Publications *James Turner*, 114 Monks Road, Exeter, Devon EX4 7BQ

Wild Goose Publications Unit 15, Six Harmony Row, Glasgow GL51 3BA

Wild Hawthorn Press *Ian Hamilton Finlay*, Little Sparta, Dunsyre, Lanark ML11 8NG

Windows Publications See also **Windows Poetry Broadsheet** *Heather Brett*, Nature Haven, Legaginney, Ballinagh, Cavan, Eire

Woodman's Press See also **Rustic Rub** magazine, *Jay Woodman*, 14 Hillfield, Selby, N Yorkshire YO8 0ND

Words Worth Books See also **Words Worth** magazine, *Alaric Sumner*, BM Box 4515, London WC1N 3XX

Writers Forum See also **And** magazine & **New River Project** press *Bob Cobbing*, 89a Petherton Road, London N5 2QT

Wysiwyg Chapbooks *Ric Hool*, 89 Abertillery Road, Blaina, Gwent

Yorkshire Art Circus Ltd See under **Small Presses**

Zum Zum Books *Neil Oram*, Goshem, Bunlight, Drumnadrochit, Inverness-shire IV3 6AH

ZZZg Press *Chris Jones*, 106 Banbury Road, Oxford OX2 6JD

Poetry magazines

Many poetry magazines have links with or are produced by companies listed in **Poetry Presses**

Acid Rainbow Dada Dance *Dee Rimbaud*, Ground Floor Left, 35 Falkland Street, Glasgow G12 9QZ

Acumen See also **Acumen Publications**, *Patricia Oxley*, 6 The Mount, Higher Furzeham, Brixham, Devon TQ5 8QY

The Affectionate Punch *Andrew Tutty*, 35 Brundage Road, Manchester M22 0BY

Agenda See also **Agenda Editions** *William Cookson*, 5 Cranbourne Court, Albert Bridge Road, London SW11 4PE

Aireings See also **Aireings Press** *Jean Barker*, 3/24 Brudenell Road, Leeds, West Yorks LS6 1BD

Ambit *Martin Bax*, 17 Priory Gardens, London N6 5QY

Anarchist Angel *Liz Berry*, 5 Aylesford Close, Sedgley, Nr Dudley, West Midlands DY3 3QB

And See also **New River Project** and **Writers Forum** presses, *Bob Cobbing & others*, 89a Petherton Road, London N5 2QT

Angel Exhaust (*http//angel-exhaust.offworld.co.uk*) *Andrew Duncan & others*, 27 Sturton Street, Cambridge CB1 2QC

Anthem *Howard Roake*, 36 Cyril Avenue, Bobbers Mill, Nottingham NG8 5BA

Apostrophe See also **Mr Pillows Press** *Diana Andersson*, Orton House, 41 Canute Road, Faversham, Kent ME13 8SH

Aquarius *Eddie S. Linden*, Flat 10, Room A, 116 Sutherland Avenue, Maida Vale, London W9

The Arcadian *Mike Boland*, 11 Boxtree Lane, Harrow Weald, Middlesex HA3 6JU

Areopagus *Julian Barritt*, 101 May Tree Close, Badger Farm, Winchester SO22 4JF

The Argotist 417 Chesnut House, Mulberry Street, Liverpool L7 7EZ

At Last 16 Ramsay Lane, Kincardine-on-Forth, Fife FK10 4QY

Avaganda *Albert Benson*, 51a Rodney Street, Liverpool L1 9ER

Avon Literary Intelligencer (*dsr@maths.bath.ac.uk*) 20 Byron Place, Clifton, Bristol BS8 1JT

Bad Poetry Quarterly PO Box 6319, London E11 2EP

The Banshee *Rachel Fones*, 16 Rigby Close, Waddon Road, Croydon CR0 4JU

Bardonni/Stopgap/Songs See also **Malfunction Press** *Peter E. Presford*, Rose Cottage, 3 Tram Lane, Buckley, Clwyd

Barfly *Jon Summers*, 96 Brookside Way, West End, Southampton SO30 3GZ

Basically Insane *Gary Greenwood & others*, Number 20 Publications, 48 St Davids Crescent, Newport, Gwent NP9 3AW

Bête Noire *John Osborne*, American Studies Dept., The University of Hull, Cottingham Road, Hull HU6 7 RX

Beyond the Boundaries (Formerly **Mab Ser**) *John Sheppard*, 87 Station Street, Barry, S Glam CF63 4LX

Beyond the Brink *Ed Hackett*, PO Box 493, Sheffield S10 3YX

The Big Spoon 32 Salisbury Court, Belfast BT7 1DD

Blade *Jane Holland*, Maynrys, Glen Chass, Port St Mary, Isle of Man IM9 5PN

Blithe Spirit *Jackie Hardy*, Farnley Gate Farmhouse, Riding Mill, Northumberland NE44 6AA

Blue Cage See also **Blue Cage** press, *Paul Donnelly*, 98 Bedford Road, Birkdale, Southport, Merseyside PR8 4HL

Bogg *George Cairncross*, 31 Bellevue Street, Filey, North Yorks YO14 9HU

Borderlines *Dave Bingham*, 20 Hodgebower, Ironbridge, Shropshire TF8 7QG

Braquemard *David Allenby*, 20 Terry Street, Hull HU3 1UD

The Bridge *James Mawer*, 112 Rutland Street, Grimsby DN32 7NF

Butterfly & Bloomers *Maggie Allen*, 12 Wetmoor Lane, Wath-upon-Dearne, Rotherham S63 6DF

Cadmium Blue Literary Journal See also **The People's Poetry** and **Romantic Heir** magazines and **Precious Pearl Press** *Peter Thompson*, 71 Harrow Crescent, Romford, Essex RM3 7BJ

Candelabrum Poetry Magazine See also **The Red Candle Press** *M. L. McCarthy*, 9 Milner Road, Wisbech, Cambs PE13 2LR

Cascando *Emily Ormond*, PO Box 1499, London SW10 9TZ

Celtic Pen *Diarmuid O'Breaslain*, 36 Fruithill Park, Belfast B11 8GE

Cencrastus – The Curly Snake *Raymond Ross & others*, Unit 1, Abbeymount Techbase, 8 Easter Road, Edinburgh EH8 8EJ

Chapman See under **Magazines**

Christian Poetry Review *Val Newbrook*, Grendon House, 67 Walsall Road, Lichfield, Staffordshire WS13 8AD

Chronicles of Disorder *Wayne Dean-Richards*, 191 Pound Road, Oldbury, Warley, West Midlands B68 8NF

City Writings *David Wright*, 47 Thornbury Avenue, Shirley, Southampton SO1 5BZ

Civil Service Author See also **Businesslike Publishing** under **Small Presses**, *Iain R. McIntyre*, 'Bluepool', Strathoykel, Ardgay, Inverness-shire IV24 3DP

Cobweb Arts Security Press, St Patrick's College, Maynooth, Co Kildare, Eire

Connections *Jeanne Conn*, 165 Domonic Drive, New Eltham, London SE9 3LE

Critical Quarterly *Brian Cox & others*, University of Strathclyde, Glasgow G1 1XH

Cuirt Review *Trish Fitzpatrick*, Galway Arts Centre, 47 Dominick Street, Galway, Eire

Cyphers *Eilean NcChuilleanain*, 3 Selskar Terrace, Ranelagh, Dublin 6, Eire

D.A.M. (Disability Arts Magazine) *Kit Wells*, 11a Cleveland Avenue, Lupset Park, Wakefield, West Yorks WF2 8LE

Dandelion Arts Magazine *Jacqueline Gonzalez-Marina*, 24 Frosty Hollow, East Hunsbury, Northants NN4 0SY

The Dark Horse *Gerry Cambridge*, 19 Cunninghamhead Estate, By Kilmarnock, Ayrshire KA3 2PY

Data Dump *Steve Sneyd*, 4 Nowell Place, Almondsbury, Huddersfield, West Yorks HD5 9PB

Defying Gravity *C. Turner*, 60 Howard Close, Cambridge CB5 8QU

Distaff *J. Brice*, London Women's Centre, Wesley House, 4 Wild Court, Kingsway, London WC2

Dog *David Crystal*, 32b Breakspears Road, London SE4 1UW

Doors See also **Wanda Publications** and **South** magazine, Word and Action, 61 West Borough, Wimborne, Dorset BH21 1LX

The Echo Room *Brendan Cleary*, 45 Bewick Court, Princess Square, Newcastle upon Tyne NE1 8HG

Eco-runes *D. O'Ruie*, 68b Fivey Road, Ballymoney BT53 8JH, N. Ireland

Edible Society *Peter Godfrey*, 10 Lincoln Street, Brighton, East Sussex BN2 2UH

Edinburgh Review See under **Magazines**

Envoi *Roger Elkin*, 44 Rudyard Road, Biddulph Moor, Stoke-on-Trent, Staffs ST8 7JN

Erran Publishing See also **Poetic Hours** magazine, *Nick Clark*, 8 Dale Road, Carlton, Notts NG4 1GT

Exile *Herbert Marr*, 8 Snow Hill, Clare, Suffolk CO10 8QF

Fatchance See also **Fatchance Press**, *Louise Hudson & others*, Elm Court, East Street, Sheepwash, Beaworthy, Devon EX21 5NL

Figments 218 York Street, Belfast BT15 1GY

First Time See also **First Time Publications** *Josephine Austin*, 4 Burdett Place, George Street, Hastings, East Sussex TN34 3ED

Flaming Arrows *Leo Regan*, County Sligo V.e.c., Riverside, Sligo, Eire

Fragmente *Andrew Lawson & others*, Dept of English, University of Durham, Elvet Riverside, New Elvet, Durham DH1 3JT

The Frogmore Papers See also **The Frogmore Press** *Jeremy Page*, 6 Vernon Road, London N8 0QD

Full Moon *Barbara Parkinson*, Church Road, Killybegs, Co. Donegal, Eire

Gairm *Derek Thomson*, 29 Waterloo Street, Glasgow G2 6BZ

Garuda See also **Microbrigade Press**, *Ulli Freer*, 7 Highwood Avenue, London N12 8QL

Global Tapestry Journal See also **BB Books** *Dave Cunliffe*, Spring Bank, Longsight Road, Copster Green, Blackburn, Lancs BB1 9EU

Granite – new verse from Cornwall *Alan M. Kent*, South View, Wheal Bull, Foxhole, St Austell, Cornwall PL26 7UA

Haiku Quarterly See also **Day Dream Press** *Kevin Bailey*, 39 Exmouth Street, Swindon, Wilts SN1 3PU

Headlock *Tony Charles*, The Old Zion Chapel, The Triangle, Somerton, Somerset TA11 6QP

Heart Throb (Formerly **People to People**) *Mike Parker*, 95 Spencer Street, Birmingham B18 6DA

Helicon *Shelagh Nugent*, Cherrybite Publications, Linden Cottage, 45 Burton Road, Little Neston, South Wirral L64 4AE

Hjok-Finnie's Sanglines *Jim Inglis*, 8 Knockbain Road, Dingwall IV15 9NR

How Do I Love Thee? See also **Poetry Life Magazine**, 14 Pennington Oval, Lymington, Hants SO41 8BQ

Hrafnhoh *Joseph Biddulph*, 32 Stryd Ebeneser, Pontypridd CF 37 5PB

HU – The Honest Ulsterman See also **Ulsterman Pamphlets** press, *Tom Clyde*, 14 Shaw Street, Belfast BT4 1PR

Ibid See also **Ibid Press,** *Matthew Hollis*, Dept of English Literature, University of Edinburgh, David Hume Tower, George Square, Edinburgh EH8 9JX

Interactions See also **Eros Press** *Diane M. Moore*, PO Box 250, St Helier, Jersey JE4 8TZ, Channel Islands

The Interpreter's House *Merryn Williams*, 10 Farrell Road, Wootton, Beds MK43 9DU

Intimacy See also **Intimacy Books** *Adam McKeown*, Apartment C, Romney House, 1 Charles Street, Maidstone, Kent ME16 8EU

Involution *A. M. Horne*, Magdelene College, Cambridge CB3 0AG

Iota *David Holliday*, 67 Hady Crescent, Chesterfield, Derbyshire S41 0EB

Iron See also **Iron Press** *Peter Mortimer*, 5 Marden Terrace, Cullercoats, North Shields, Tyne & Wear NE30 4PD

Issue One/The Bridge *Ian Brocklebank*, 2 Tewkesbury Drive, Grimsby, South Humberside DN34 4TL

Journal of Contemporary Anglo-Scandinavian Poetry *Sam Smith*, 11 Heatherton Park, Bradford-on-Tone, Taunton, Somerset TA4 1EV

Krax See also **Rump Books** press, *Andy Robson*, 63 Dixon Lane, Wortley, Leeds, West Yorks LS12 4RR

Krino – the review *Gerald Dawe & others*, PO Box 65, Dun Laoghaire, Co. Dublin, Eire

Kunapipi See also **Dangaroo Press** *Anna Rutherford*, PO Box 20, Hebden Bridge, West Yorks HX7 5UZ

Lallans *Neil MacCullum*, 18 Redford Avenue, Edinburgh EH13 0BU

Lateral Moves *Ann White*, 5 Hamilton Street, Astley Bridge, Bolton, Lancs BL1 6RJ

Lines Review *Tessa Ransford*, Macdonald Publishing, Edgefield Street, Loanhead, Mid Lothian EH20 9SY

The Link *David Pollard*, Brumus Management, PO Box 317, Hounslow, Middlesex TW3 2SD

Links See also **Kernow Poets Press**, *Bill Headdon*, Bude Haven, 18 Frankfield Rise, Tunbridge Wells, Kent TN2 5LF

Lit Up *Jeremy Rogers*, 8a Mill Street, Torrington, Devon EX38 8HQ

London Magazine – See under **Magazines**

Mad Cow *J. Whittington*, 33 Kingsley Place, Highgate, London N6 5EA

Madam X (*colpress@ress.sonnet.co.uk*) *M. Lollopit*, Colophon Press, 18a Prentis Road, London SW16 1QD

The Magazine *Nancy Allison*, Open Studies, Dept of Continuing Education, University of Warwick, Coventry, Warwickshire CV4 7AL

Magma *Laurie Smith & others*, The Stukely Press, The City Lit, Stukely Street, Drury Lane, London WC2 B 5LJ

Magpie's Nest *Bal Saini*, 176 Stoney Lane, Sparkhill, Birmingham B12 8AN

Mana *Gerait Roberts & others*, 15 Llantwit Street, Cathays, Cardiff CF2 4AJ

Modern Poetry in Translation *Daniel Weissbort*, MPT, School of Humanities, King's College, Strand, London WC2R 2LS

Mosaic *L. Williamson*, 16 Vale Close, Eastwood, Nottingham

Navis *Robert Bush & others*, 211 Bedford Hill, London SW12 9HQ

Never Bury Poetry *Eileen Holroy*, 12a Kirkstall Gardens, Radcliffe, Manchester M26 0JQ

New Departures See also **New Departures** press *Michael Horovitz*, PO Box 9819, London W11 2GQ

New Hope International *Gerald England*, 20 Werneth Avenue, Gee Cross, Hyde, Cheshire SK14 5NL

New Poetry Quarterly *Simon Brittan*, 5 Stockwell, Colchester, Essex CO1 1HP

New Scottish Epoch *Neil Mathers*, 57 Murray Street, Montrose, Angus DD10 8JZ

New Welsh Review See under **Magazines**

The New Writer (incorporating **Acclaim** & **Quartos**) See under **Magazines**

Night Dreams *Anthony Barker*, 52 Denman Lane, Huncote, Leicester LE9 3BS

Nineties Poetry *Graham Ackroyd*, 33 Lansdowne Place, Hove, East Sussex BN3 1HF

The North Also see **Smith/Doorstep Books** & **The Poetry Business** presses *Peter Sansom & Janet Fisher*, The Studio, Byram Arcade, Westgate, Huddersfield, West Yorks HD1 1ND

Northwords *Tom Bryan*, 68 Strathkanaird, Ullapool, Rosshire IV26 2TN

Nova Poetica 14 Pennington Oval, Lymington, Hampshire SO41 8BQ

Oasis See also **Oasis Books**, *Ian Robinson*, 12 Stevenage Road, Fulham, London SW6 6ES

One *Wendy B. Cardy*, 48 South Street, Colchester, Essex CO2 7BJ

Orbis See also **Orbis Books** *Mike Shields*, 199 The Long Shoot, Nuneaton, Warwickshire CV11 6JQ

Ostinato See also **The Tenormen Press** *Stephen C. Middleton*, PO Box 522, London N8 7SZ

Other Poetry *Peter Bennet & others*, 8 Oakhurst Terrace, Benton, Newcastle upon Tyne NE12 9NY

Otter *R. Skinner*, Little Byspock, Richmond Road, Exeter, Devon

Outposts See also **Hippopotamus Press** *Roland John*, 22 Whitewell Road, Frome, Somerset BA11 4EL

Outreach *M. Brooks*, 7 Grayson Close, Stockbridge, Sheffield, S Yorks S30 5BJ

Oxford Poetry *Ian Sansom & others*, Magdalen College, Oxford OX1 4AU

Oxford Quarterly Review *Ernie Hibert*, St Catherine's College, Oxford OX1 3UJ

Pages See also **Ship of Fools** press *Robert Sheppard*, 78 Nicander Road, Liverpool 18

Paladin *Ken Morgan*, 66 Heywood Court, Tenby SA70 8BS

Passion See also **Crescent Moon Publishing and Joe's Press** under **Small Presses** *Jeremy Robinson*, 18 Chaddesley Road, Kidderminster, Worcs DY10 3AD

Pause See also **National Poetry Foundation** *Helen Robinson*, 27 Mill Road, Fareham, Hants PO16 0TH

Peace and Freedom *Paul Rance*, 17 Farrow Road, Whaplode Drove, Spalding, Lincs PE12 0TS

The Pen Magazine *Pam Probert*, 15 Berwyn Place, Penlan, Swansea, West Glamorgan SA5 5AX

The Penniless Press *Alan Dent*, 100 Waterloo Road, Ashton, Preston, Lancs PR2 1EP

Pennine Platform *Brian Merrikin Hill*, Ingmanthorpe Hall, Farm Cottage, Wetherby, West Yorks LS22 5EQ

The People's Poetry See also **Precious Pearl Press** and **Cadmium Blue Literary Journal** and **Romantic Heir** magazines, *Peter Thompson*, 71 Harrow Crescent, Romford, Essex RM3 7BJ

Planet *John Barnie*, PO Box 44, Aberystwyth

Plow/:/share(s) The Rectory, Castle Carrock, Carlisle CA4 9LZ

PN Review (*pnr@carcaneet.u-net.com*) See also **Carcanet Press** under **UK Publishers** *Michael Schmidt*, 4th Floor, Conavon Court, 12 Blackfriars Street, Manchester M3 5BQ

Poetic Hours See also **Erran Publishing** *Nick Clark*, 8 Dale Road, Carlton, Notts NG4 1GT

Poetry and Audience *Carolyn Fyffe*, School of English, University of Leeds, Leeds, West Yorks LS2 9JT

Poetry Digest *Alan Forrest*, Bradgate Press, 28 Stainsdale Green, Whitwick, Leics LE67 5PW

Poetry Ireland Review Bermingham Tower, Upper Yard, Dublin Castle, Dublin, Eire

Poetry Life Magazine See also **Poetry Life Publishing** *Adrian Bishop*, 14 Pennington Oval, Lymington, Hants SO41 8BQ

Poetry London Newsletter (*http://www.rmplc.co.uk/eduweb/sites/pooetry.index.html*) *P. Daniels*, 35 Benthal Road, London N16 7AR

Poetry Manchester *Sean Boustead*, 13 Napier Street, Swinton, Manchester M27 0JQ

Poetry Monthly *Martin Holroyd*, 39 Cavendish Road, Long Eaton, Nottingham NG10 4HY

Poetry Nottingham International *Cathy Grindrod*, 13 Bradmore Rise, Sherwood, Nottingham NG5 3BJ

Poetry Now See also **Anchor Books**, **Arrival** and **Forward Presses** and **Rhyme Arrival** magazine *Ian Walton*, 1-2 Wainman Road, Woodston, Peterborough, Cambs PE2 7BU

Poetry Quarterly Review See also **Odyssey Poets** *Derrick Woolf*, Coleridge Cottage, Nether Stowey, Somerset TA5 1NQ

Poetry Review *Peter Forbes*, Poetry Society, 22 Betterton Street, London WC2H 9BU

Poetry Wales See also **Seren Books** under **UK Publishers** First Floor, 2 Wyndham Street, Bridgend, Mid Glamorgan CF31 1EF

Pomes *Adrian Spendlow*, 23 Bright Street, York YO2 4XS

PPQ *Peter Taylor*, PO Box 1435, London W1A 9LB

Presence *Martin Lucas*, 188 Langthorne Road, London E11 4HS

The Present Tense *Michael Abbott*, 115 Princess Victoria Street, Clifton, Bristol

Prop 31 Central Avenue, Farnworth, Bolton, Lancs BL4 0AU

Psychopoetica See also **Psychopoetica Publications** *Geoff Lowe*, Dept. of Psychology, University of Hull, Hull HU6 7RX

Pulsar See also **Ligden Publishers** *David Pike*, 34 Lineacre, Grangepark, Swindon, Wilts SN5 6DA

Purge *Robert Hampson*, 11 Hillview Court, Hillview Road, Woking, Surrey GU22 7QN

Purple Patch *Geoff Stevens*, 8 Beaconview House, Charlemont Farm, West Bromwich B71 3PL

Queer Words *Michael Nobbs*, PO Box 23, Aberystwyth SY23 1AA

Ramraid Extraordinaire 57 Canton Court, Canton, Cardiff CF1 9BG

Raw Edge Magazine *Dave Reeves*, PO Box 4867, Birmingham B3 3HD

Reader's Feast *Jennifer Brown*, PO Box 879, Rhyl, Clwyd LL18 1TJ

The Reater *Shane Rhodes*, 1 Pilmar Lane, Roos, North Humberside HU12 0HP

Red Herring See also **MidNag Publications**, Arts Section, Central Library, The Willows, Morpeth, Northumberland NE61 1TA

The Red Shoes *Adrian Hodges*, 3 Ashfield Close, Bishops Cleeve, Cheltenham, Glos GL52 4LG

Reflections PO Box 70, Sunderland SR1 1DU

Rhyme Arrival See also **Poetry Now** magazine and **Anchor Books**, **Arrival** and **Forward Presses** *Trudi Ramm*, 1-2 Wainman Road, Woodston, Peterborough, Cambs PE2 7BU

The Rialto See also **Rialto Publications** *Michael Mackmin*, PO Box 309, Aylsham, Norwich, Norfolk NR11 6LN

A Riot of Emotions *Andrew Cocker*, Dark Diamonds Pubs. PO Box HK 31, Leeds, West Yorks LS11 9XN

Rivet *Eve Catchpole & others*, 74 Walton Drive, High Wycombe, Bucks HP13 6TT

Roisin Dubh Em, 16 Gotham Street, Leicester

Romantic Heir See also **Cadmium Blue Literary Journal**, *Peter Thompson*, The People's Poetry, 71 Harrow Crescent, Romford, Essex RM3 7BJ

Rustic Rub See also **Woodman's Press** *Jay Woodman*, 14 Hillfield, Selby, N. Yorkshire YO8 0ND

Scar Tissue *Tony Lee*, Pigasus Press, 13 Hazley Combe, Isle of Wight PO30 3AJ

Scratch See also **Scratch Publications** (*100626.374@compuserve.comhttp://our-world.compuserve.com.homepages/scratchhq*) *Mark Robinson*, 9 Chestnut Road, Eaglescliffe, Stockton-on-Tees TS16 0BA

Scriptor See also **Providence Press Whitstable** *John & Lesley Dench*, 22 Plough Lane, Swalecliffe, Whitstable, Kent CT5 2NZ

Sepia See also **Kawabata Press** *Colin David Webb*, Knill Cross House, Knill Cross, Millbrook, Torpoint, Cornwall PL10 1DX

Shearsman See also **Shearsman Books** *Tony Frazer*, 47 Dayton Close, Plymouth, Devon PL6 5DX

Sheffield Thursday *E. A. Markham*, School of Cultural Studies, Sheffield Hallam University, 36 Collegiate Crescent, Sheffield S10 2BP

Skald *Zoe Skoulding*, 2 Park Street, Bangor, Gwynedd LL57 2AY

Smiths Knoll *Roy Blackman & others* 49 Church Road, Little Glemham, Woodbridge, Suffolk IP13 0BJ

Smoke *Dave Ward*, The Windows Project, 40 Canning Street, Liverpool L8 7NP

Sol Poetry Magazine See also **Sol Publications** *Malcolm E. Wright*, 24 Fowler Close, Southchurch, Southend-on-Sea, Essex SS1 2RD

Sound & Language 85 London Road South, Lowestoft, Suffolk NR33 0AS

The Source *Kelly Lemaitre*, 19 Cumberland Street, Edinburgh EH3 6RT

South See also **Wanda Publications** and **Doors** magazine, Word and Action, 61 West Borough, Wimborne, Dorset BH21 1LX

Southfields *Raymond Friel & others*,
98 Gresenhall Road, Southfields, London
SW18 5QJ

Spanner See also **Spanner Press**, *Allen Fisher*,
14 Hopton Road, Hereford HR1 1BE

Spear *Jacqueline Jones*, 2 Fforest Road,
Lampeter

Spectacular Diseases See also **Spectacular
Diseases** press *Paul Green*, 83b London
Road, Peterborough, Cambs PE2 9BS

Spokes *Alister Wisker*, 319a Hills Road,
Cambridge CB2 2QT

Stand See also **Northern House Poets**
Jon Silkin & others, 179 Wingrove Road,
Newcastle-upon-Tyne NE4 9DA

Staple See also **Staple First Editions** *Bob
Windsor* Tor Cottage, 81 Cavendish Road,
Matlock, Derbyshire DE4 3HD

The Steeple *Patrick Cotter*, Three Spires Press,
Killeen, Blackrock Village, Cork City, Eire

Still 49 Englands Lane, London NW3 4YD

Stone Soup 37 Chesterfield Road, London
W4 3HQ

The Storehouse Carad, The Old Pantydwr
Stores, West Street, Rhayader, Powys
LD6 5AF

Story Cellar *Sara Waddington*, 26 Cippenham
Lane, Slough, Berkshire SL1 5BS

Super-Trouper *Andrew Savage*, 81 Castlerigg
Drive, Burnley, Lancs BB12 8AT

Swagmag *Peter Thabit Jones*, Dan-y-Bryn,
74 Cwm Level Road, Brynhyfred,
Swansea SA5 9DY

The Swansea Review, *Glyn Pursglove*, Dept
of English, University College Swansea,
Singleton Park, Swansea SA2 8PP

Symphony Bemerton Press, 9 Hamilton
Gardens, London NW8 9PU

Symtex & Grimmer *Chris Jones*,
106 Banbury Road, Oxford OX2 6JU

Tabla *Stephen James Ellis & others*,
7 Parliament Hill, London NW3 2SY

Talus See also **Talus Editions** *Marzia Balzani
& others*, Dept of English, King's College,
Strand, London WC2R 2LS

Tandem *Michael J. Woods*, 13 Stephenson
Road, Barbourne, Worcester WR1 3EB

Target *Bryn Fortey*, 212 Caerleon Road,
Newport, Gwent NP9 7GC

Tears In The Fence *David Caddy*, 38 Hod
View, Stourpaine, Nr Blandford Forum,
Dorset DT11 8TN

10th Muse *Andrew Jordan*, 33 Hartington
Road, Southampton SO2 0EW

The Third Alternative *Andy Cox*,
5 St Martin's Lane, Witcham, Ely, Cambs
CB4 2LB

The Third Half See also **K.T. Publications**
Kevin Troop, 16 Fane Close, Stamford,
Lincs PE9 1HG

Threads *Geoff Lynas*, 32 Irvin Avenue,
Saltburn, Cleveland TS12 1QH

3x4 See also **Raunchland Publications**,
John Mingay, 2 Henderson Street, Kingseat,
By Dunfermline, Fife KY12 0TP

Thumbscrew *Tim Kendall* PO Box 657,
Oxford OX2 6PH

Time Haiku *K. K. Facey*, 105 Kings Head
Hill, London E4 7JG

Tongue to Boot *Miles Champion*, 5 Abbots
Court, Thackeray Street, London W8 5ES

Tops *Anthony Cooney*, Rose Cottage,
17 Hadassah Grove, Liverpool L17 8XH

Track Marks *Dee Rimbaud*, Triangle Arts
Centre, West Pilton Bank, Pilton,
Edinburgh EH44 HN

Triumph Herald (a magazine of **Forward
Press**) Chris Walton, 1-2 Wainman Road,
Woodston, Peterborough, Cambs PE2 7BU

Tuba See also **Tuba Press** *Charles Graham*,
Tunley Cottage, Tunley, Nr Cirencester,
Glos GL7 6LW

Uncompromising Positions See also
Jugglers Fingers Press *Cheryl Wilkinson*,
92 Staneway, Leam Lane, Gateshead, Tyne
& Wear NE10 8LS

Under Surveillance 60 Arnold Street,
Brighton, East Sussex BN2 2XT

Unicorn See also **Shell Press** *Alex Warner*,
12 Milton Avenue, Millbrook, Stalybridge,
Cheshire SK15 3HB

Urges *Ian Hunter*, Huntiegouke Press,
32 Caneluk Avenue, Carluke ML8 4LZ

Various Artists *Tony Lewis Jones*,
65 Springfield Avenue, Horfield, Bristol
BS7 9QS

Verse *Andrew Zawacki* University College,
Oxford OX1

Vertical Images *Brian Docherty*,
10a Dickenson Road, London N8 9ET

Vigil See also **Vigil Publications** *John
Howard-Greaves*, 12 Priory Mead, Bruton,
Somerset BA10 0DZ

Walking Naked *Sean Boustead*, 13 Napier
Street, Swinton, Manchester M27 3JQ

West Coast Magazine See also **Taranis
Books** *Joe Murray*, Em-dee Productions,
Unit 7, 29 Brand Street, Glasgow G51 1DN

Weyfarers *Martin Jones*, Guildford Poets Press,
1 Mountside, Guildford, Surrey GU2 5JD

The Whistle House *J. Wistlin*, 4 Hamilton
Road, Windle, Merseyside WA10 6HG

The Wide Skirt *Geoff Hattersley*, 1a Church
Street, Penistone, South Yorks S30 6AR

Windows Poetry Broadsheet See also
Windows Publications *Heather Brett &
others*, Nature Haven, Legaginney,
Ballinagh, Cavan, Eire

Wire Poetry Magazine See also **Aramby
Publishing** *Mal Cieslak*, 1 Alanbrooke
Close, Knaphill, Surrey GU21 2RU

Wits End *Jean Turner*, 27 Pheasants Close,
Winnersh, Wokingham, Berks RG11 5LS

Words Worth See also **Words Worth
Books** *Alaric Sumner*, BM Box 4515,
London WC1N 3XX

Working Titles *Claire Williamson*, 5 Hillside,
Clifton Wood, Bristol BS8 4TD

Writer's Viewpoint *Belinda Rance*, PO Box
514, Eastbourne, E Sussex BN23 6RE

Writing Women *Linda Anderson & others*,
Unit 14, Hawthorn House, Forth Banks,
Newcastle upon Tyne NE1 3SG

Yellow Crane (Formerly **The Cardiff
Poet**) *Jonathan Brookes* Flat 6,
23 Richmond Crescent, Roath, Cardiff
CF2 3AH

Zed 2 0 *Duncan Glen*, Akros Publications,
18 Warrender Park Terrace, Edinburgh
EH9 1EF

Zimmerframe Pileup *Stephen Jessener*, Loose
Hand Press, 54 Hillcrest Road,
Walthamstow, London E17 4AP

The Zone See also **S. A. Publishing**, *Tony
Lee*, 13 Hazely Combe, Arreton, Isle of
Wight PO30 3AJ

Organisations of interest to poets

A survey of some of the societies, groups and other bodies in the UK which may
be of interest to practising poets. Organisations not listed should send details to
The Editor, *The Writer's Handbook*, 34 Ufton Road, London N1 5BX for inclusion in future editions.

Apples & Snakes

Unit 7, Theatre Place, 489a New Cross Road,
London SE14 6TQ
☎0181 692 0393
e-mail: apples@snakes.demon.co.uk

Contacts *Ruth Harrison, Malika Booker*

A unique, independent promotional organisation for poetry and poets - furthering poetry
as an innovative and popular medium and
cross-cultural activity. A&S organises an annual
programme of over 150 events (including their
London season which actively pushes new
voices), tours, residencies and festivals as well as
operating a Poets-in-Education Scheme and a
non-profit booking agency for poets.

The Arvon Foundation

See entry under **Professional Associations**

The Association of Little Presses

See entry under **Professional Associations**

The British Haiku Society

44 Ramsgill Drive, Newbury Park, Ilford,
Essex IG2 7TR
☎0181 924 3186

Secretary *Susan Rowley*

Formed in 1990. Promotes the appreciation

and writing within the British Isles of haiku,
senyru, tanka, and renga by way of tutorials,
workshops, exchange of poems, critical comment and information. *Publishes* a quarterly
journal, *Blithe Spirit*, and administers the annual
James W. Hackett Award for haiku.

The Eight Hand Gang

5 Cross Farm, Station Road, Padgate,
Warrington WA2 0QG
Secretary *John F. Haines*

An association of British SF poets. *Publishes* a
newsletter, *Handshake*, of SF poetry and information available free in exchange for a s.a.e..

The Little Magazine Collection
and Poetry Store

University College London, Gower Street,
London WC1E 6BT
☎0171 380 7796

Housed at University College London Library,
these are the fruits of Geoffrey Soar and David
Miller's interest in UK and US alternative publishing, with a strong emphasis on poetry. The
Little Magazines Collection runs to over 3500
titles mainly in the more experimental and
avant-garde areas. The Poetry Store consists of

over 11,000 small press items, mainly from the '60s onwards, again with some stress on experimental work. In addition, there are reprints of classic earlier little magazines, from Symbolism through to the present. Anyone who is interested can consult the collections, and it helps if you have some idea of what you want to see. Bring evidence of identity for a smooth ride. The collections can be accessed by visiting the Manuscripts and Rare Books Room at University College at the above address between 10.00am and 5.00pm on weekdays. Most items are available on inter-library loans.

The Living Poets Society

Dragonheart Press, 11 Menin Road, Allestree, Derby DE22 2NL
e-mail: lpoets@drci.co.uk
President *Sean Woodward*

Established to encourage poets of any age and location to share their work through new electronic media, the Society offers inclusion in the electronic journal *Living Poets*, freely available on the Internet at http://dougal.derby.ac.uk/lpoets. Membership is £10 per annum with reduced lifetime and junior membership. Sean Woodward also runs the Dragonheart Press which publishes poetry in a variety of formats including HTML, ASCII and Amiga Hyperbook. The annual Dragonheart Press Poetry Competition includes electronic publication as part of its prizes.

The National Convention of Poets and Small Presses/Poets and Small Press Festival

The Old Zion Temple, The Triangle, Somerton, Somerset TA11 6QP
Contact *Tony Charles*

An accessible, some might say disorganised, weekend jamboree of writers and poetry publishers held at a different venue each year. The quasi-amateur status of the event is celebrated and it can be good fun for those with enough stamina to last out the marathon readings. There is no central organising committee - bids to host future conventions being made in person at the event itself. So far it has visited Liverpool, Hastings, Corby, Dartford, Stamford, Norwich, North Shields, Exeter, Stockton-on-Tees, Middlesborough and Huddersfield. Write to Tony Charles for information on the next convention.

National Poetry Foundation

27 Mill Road, Fareham, Hampshire PO16 0TH
☎/Fax 01329 822218

A charitable poetry organisation (Registered Charity No: 283032) founded by Johnathon Clifford and administered by a board of trustees from the address above. With the financial assistance of Rosemary Arthur who has so far put over £42,000 into the kitty, the NPF attempts to encourage new writers through a criticism scheme and a series of well produced poetry books. Subscription costs £20 which, in addition, gives members access to *Pause*, the organisation's internal magazine. The NPF has an interest in the professional poetry recital as a fund-raising device for the furtherance of its work. Eight small mags and a number of individual poets have to date benefited from NPF financial aid. Grants are small, unrenewable and directed at that sector of the poetry community traditionally ignored by other bodies. A good history of the NPF, together with information on poetry and the poetry scene can be found in Johnathon Clifford's self-published *Metric Feet & Other Gang Members*, available from the same address.

The National Small Press Centre

BM Bozo, London WC1N 3XX
Liaison Officers *John & Lesley Dench*

A point of focus for small, self and independent publishers. Offers advice surgeries, book ordering services, publicity, help with origination and design, mounts exhibitions and workshops, holds a comprehensive reference library. Publishes a handbook along with regular newsletters. An outgrowth of the former Small Press Group, the Centre was originally housed at Middlesex University but is currently relocating. Contact the liaison officers for more information.

The New Writer

PO Box 60, Cranbrook, Kent TH17 2ZR
☎01559 371108

Editor *Suzanne Ruthven*
Publisher *Merric Davidson*

The contemporary writing magazine resulting from the merging of *Quartos* and *Acclaim* magazines. Includes a poets' showcase edited by Abi Hughes-Edwards along with news and views from the poetry scene. Subscriptions £29.50 for ten issues. Best single source of information on poetry competitions. Offers an inexpensive critical service for poets, currently £12.00 for six poems. Send two first-class stamps for free back issue. (See entry under **Magazines**.)

The Northern Poetry Library

Central Library, The Willows, Morpeth, Northumberland NE61 1TA
☎01670 511156/512385 Fax 01670 518012

Membership available to everyone in Cleveland, Cumbria, Durham, Northumberland and Tyne and Wear. Associate membership available for all outside the region. Over 13,000 books and magazines for loan including virtually all poetry published in the UK since 1968. Access to English Poetry, the full text database of all English Poetry from 600–1900. Postal lending available too. In association with MidNag publishes *Red Herring*, a poetry magazine.

The Poetry Bookshop

Westhouse, Broad Street, Hay-on-Wye HR3 5DB
☎01497 820305

Contact *Alan Halsey*

Holds a large stock of modern and contemporary poetry - British, Irish, American, translations, concrete, etc. - mostly second-hand but including some new small press material and poetry magazines. Deals extensively by post.

The Poetry Book Society

Book House, 45 East Hill, London SW18 2QZ
☎0181 870 8403   Fax 0181 877 1615

Director *Clare Brown*

Can't choose? This is one way to increase your reading of mainstream poetry. For an annual fee of £30, members receive quarterly a new volume of verse selected by experts and a quarterly bulletin. Members are also entitled to buy from a vast selection of PBS recommendations, all at 25% discount, to have free tickets to PBS readings and have a right to an advisory vote in any poetry prizes organised by the Society. If that's not enough, Charter Membership costing £120 will bring you 20 new books annually, while the Associate form of membership, at £10, gives just the four bulletins and the discount offers on books. The PBS also administers the annual **T. S. Eliot Prize** for the best new collection of poetry.

The Poetry Business

The Studio, Byram Arcade, Westgate, Huddersfield, West Yorkshire HD1 1ND
☎01484 434840   Fax 01484 426566

Administrators *Peter Sansom, Janet Fisher*

The Business publishes *The North* magazine, and books, pamphlets and cassettes under the Smith/Doorstop imprint. It runs an annual competition and organises monthly writing Saturdays. Send an s.a.e. for full details.

Poetry Ireland

Bermingham Tower, Upper Yard, Dublin Castle, Dublin, Republic of Ireland
☎00 353 1 6714632   Fax 00 353 1 6714634
e-mail: poetry@iol.ie

Director *Theo Dorgan*
General Manager *Niamh Morris*

The national poetry organisation for Ireland, supported by Arts Councils both sides of the border. Publishes a quarterly magazine *Poetry Ireland Review* and a bi-monthly newsletter of upcoming events and competitions, as well as organising tours and readings by Irish and foreign poets and the National Poetry Competition of the Year, open to poets working in both Irish and English. Administers the Austin Clarke Library, a collection of over 6000 volumes and is Irish partner in the European Poetry Translation Network.

The Poetry Library

Royal Festival Hall, Level 5, London SE1 8XX
☎0171 921 0943/0664/0940
Fax 0171 921 0939

Librarian *Mary Enright*

Founded by the Arts Council in 1953. A collection of 45,000 titles of modern poetry since 1912, from Georgian to Rap, representing all English-speaking countries and including translations into English by contemporary poets. Two copies of each title are held, one for loan and one for reference. A wide range of poetry magazines and ephemera from all over the world are kept along with cassettes, records and videos for consultation, with many available for loan. There is a children's poetry section with a teachers' resource collection. An information service compiles lists of poetry magazines, competitions, publishers, groups and workshops, which are available from the Library on receipt of a large s.a.e. It also has a noticeboard for lost quotations, through which it tries to identify lines or fragments of poetry which have been sent in by other readers. General enquiry service available. Membership is free, proof of identity and address are essential to join. Open 11.00am to 8.00pm, Tuesday to Sunday. Beside the Library is The Voice Box, a performance space especially for literature. For details of current programme ring 0171 921 0906.

Poetry London Newsletter

35 Benthal Road, London N16 7AR
e-mail: pdaniels@easynet.co.uk

Contacts *Peter Daniels* (subscriptions),
Katherine Gallagher (promotions),
Pascale Petit (poetry editor),
Tamar Yoseloff (reviews)

Published three times a year, and now with a new look, PLN includes poetry by new and established writers, reviews of recent collections and anthologies, features on issues relating to poetry, and an encyclopaedic listings section of virtually everything to do with poetry in the capital and the South East. The magazine also carries a limited coverage of events elsewhere.

The Poetry Society

22 Betterton Street, London WC2H 9BU
☎0171 240 4810   Fax: 0171 240 4818
e-mail: poetrysoc@dial.pipex.com

Chairman *Mary Enright*
Director *Chris Meade*

FOUNDED in 1909, which ought to make it venerable, the Society exists to help poets and poetry thrive in Britain. At one time notoriously strife-ridden, it has been undergoing a renaissance lately, reaching out from its Covent Garden base to promote the national health of poetry in a range of imaginative ways. Membership costs £27.50 for individuals. Friends membership is £10. Current activities include:

● A quarterly, recently redesigned magazine of new verse, views and criticism, *Poetry Review*, edited by Peter Forbes.
● A quarterly newsletter, *Poetry News*.
● Promotions, events and co-operation with Britain's many literature festivals, poetry venues and poetry publishers.
● Competitions and awards including the annual **National Poetry Competition** with a substantial first prize.
● A mss diagnosis service, The Script, which gives detailed reports on submissions. Reduced rates for members.
● Seminars, fact sheets, training courses, ideas packs.
● An education service, run in conjunction with W. H. Smith which annually puts over 1500 children in direct contact with poets. *Publishes* the excellent *Poetry Society Resources* files for primary level, and provides specialist information and advice on all aspects of poetry in education. Recently published are The *Young Poetry Pack*, an informative and colourful guide to reading, writing and performing

poetry along with poetry posters for Keystages 2 & 3. Many of Britain's most popular poets – including Michael Rosen, Roger McGough and Jackie Kay – contribute, offering advice and inspiration.
● The Café Ltd serving delicious food & drink to members, friends and guests, part of The Poetry Place, a venue for many poetry activities – readings, poetry clinic, workshops and poetry launches.
● A poetry website at http://www.poetrysociety.co.uk redesigned to provide a full on-line service of information and poetry.
● Current developments at the Society include a virtual residency by Jo Shapcott.

Poeziecentrum

Hoornstraat 11, B-9000 Ghent, Belgium
☎00 32 9 225 22 25   Fax 00 32 9 225 90 54
Manager *Willy Tibergien*

Taking over some of the activities of the now defunct European Centre For The Promotion of Poetry, Poezicentrum (Poetry Centre) aims to document everything to do with poetry and poetry activity. It has an archive of literary periodicals, press cuttings, information on poets, a non-book poetry collection and other data. Poeziecentrum has its own press publishing collections along with the bi-monthly journal *Poezierant*. The emphasis is on suppressed genres. The Centre is keen to expand its activities on an international level by developing a European Poetry Network of activity and exchange. Like-minded organisations are asked to make contact.

Point

Apdo 119, E-03590 Altea, Spain
☎00 34 6 584 2350   Fax 00 34 6 584 2350
Brusselsesteenweg 356, B-9402 Ninove, Belgium
☎00 32 54 32 4748   Fax 00 32 54 32 4660
e-mail: elpoeta@ctv.es
website: www.ctv.es/USERS/elpoeta

Director *Germain Droogenbroodt*

Founded as Poetry International in 1984, Point has offices in Spain and Belgium. A multilingual publisher of contemporary verse from established poets, the organisation has brought out more than 50 titles in at least eight languages, including English. Editions run the original work alongside a verse translation into Dutch made in co-operation with the poet. Point also organises an annual international poetry festival in Altea, Spain.

Regional Arts Boards

For a full list of addresses see Arts Councils and Regional Arts Boards. Most are of invaluable interest to poets as a source of information on local activities, poetry groups, competitions, publications, readings and creative writing weekends. Many publish a magazine of their own, a number run critical services for writers. Some provide fellowships for poets, paying for school visits or for poets' workshops to be established. Service varies from region to region depending on demand and the influence and interest of the local literature officer.

Scottish Poetry Library

Tweeddale Court, 14 High Street, Edinburgh EH1 1TE
☎0131-557 2876
e-mail: spl/queries@presence.co.uk
Librarian *Penny Duce*

Freely open to the public; membership scheme £10 p.a. A comprehensive collection of work by Scottish poets in Gaelic, Scots and English, plus the work of international poets, including books, tapes, videos and magazines. Borrowing is free to all. Services include: a postal lending scheme, for which there is a small fee, and a mobile library which can visit schools and other centres by arrangement. Members receive a newsletter and support the Library, whose work includes exhibitions, bibliographies, publications, information and promotion in the field of poetry. Also available is an online catalogue and computer index to poetry and poetry periodicals.

The Stationery Office Oriel Bookshop

The Friary, Cardiff CF1 4AA
☎01222 395548

Publishes at regular intervals *Small Presses and Little Magazines of the UK and Ireland - An*

Address List (currently into its thirteenth edition - £4.00 including p&p), specialises in twentieth century poetry, operates a mail order service, hosts poetry readings and provides information on local competitions, workshops, groups and literary activities.

Survivors' Poetry

Diorama Arts Centre, 34 Osnaburgh Street, London NW1 3ND
Administration *Clare Douglas*
    (☎0171 916 5317 Fax 0171 916 0830)
Outreach *Alison Smith* (☎0171 916 6637)
London Events *Frank Bangay*
    (☎0171 916 0825)

Arts Council-funded literature/performance project managed by and for poets who have survived the mental-health system. Organises regular poetry workshops and performances in London and throughout the UK. Also runs performance training workshops led by established writers. Has published three full-length anthologies of Survivors' work. Through its Outreach Project has established twenty groups in a UK-wide network which spreads from Portsmouth to Glasgow

Ty Newydd

Llanystumdwy, Cricieth, Gwynedd LL52 0LW
☎01766 522811   Fax: 01766 523095
Director *Sally Baker*

Run by the Taliesin Trust, an independent, Arvon-style residential writers centre in North Wales. Programme has a regular poetry content. Fees start at £100 for weekends and £255 for week-long courses. Tutors to date have included Gillian Clarke, Wendy Cope, Roger McGough, Carol Ann Duffy, Liz Lochhead, Peter Finch and Paul Henry. (See entry under **Writers' Courses, Circles and Workshops**.)

Small Presses

Aard Press
c/o Aardverx, 31 Mountearl Gardens, London SW16 2NL
Managing Editor D. Jarvis, Dawn Redwood

FOUNDED 1971. *Publishes* artists' bookworks, experimental/visual poetry, 'zines, eonist literature, topographics ephemera and international mail-art documentation. TITLES: *Eos – The Arts & Letters of Transkind* (TG & M-A 'zine); *I, Jade Green, Jade's Ladies, Jade AntiJade* (thrillers) A. K. Ashe. AUTHORS/ARTISTS: Dawn Redwood, Petal Jeffery, Phaedra Kelly, Barry Edgar Pilcher (Eire), D. Jarvis, Y. Kumykov (Russia), Harry Fox. No unsolicited material or proposals.
Royalties not paid. No sale-or-return deals.

ABCD
See **Allardyce, Barnett, Publishers**

Agneau 2
See **Allardyce, Barnett, Publishers**

AK Press/AKA Books
PO Box 12766, Edinburgh EH8 9YE
☎0131 555 5165   Fax 0131 555 5215
Managing Editor Alexis McKay

AK Press grew out of the activities of AK Distribution which distributes a wide range of radical (anarchist, feminist, etc.) literature (books, pamphlets, periodicals, magazines), both fiction and non-fiction. *Publishes* politics, history, situationist work, occasional fiction in both book and pamphlet form. About 12 titles a year. TITLES *Pen and the Sword* Edward W. Said; *Chronicles of Dissent* Noam Chomsky; *Some Recent Attacks* James Kelman; *Scum Manifesto* Valerie Solanus; *Tales From the Clit* ed. Cherie Matrix. Unsolicited mss, proposals and synopses welcome if they fall within AK's specific areas of interest.
Royalties paid.

The Alembic Press
Hyde Farm House, Marcham, Abingdon, Oxon OX13 6NX
☎01865 391391   Fax 01865 391322
Owner Claire Bolton

FOUNDED 1976. Publisher of hand-produced books by traditional letterpress methods. Short print-runs. *Publishes* bibliography, book arts and printing, miniatures and occasional poetry. Book design and production service to like-minded authors wishing to publish in this manner. No unsolicited mss.

Allardyce, Barnett, Publishers
14 Mount Street, Lewes, East Sussex BN7 1HL
☎01273 479393   Fax 01273 479393
Publisher Fiona Allardyce
Managing Editor Anthony Barnett

FOUNDED 1981. *Publishes* art, literature and music, with past emphasis on contemporary English poets. About 3 titles a year.
IMPRINTS **Agneau 2**, **ABCD**, **Allardyce Book**. TITLES *Poems* Andrea Zanzotto; *Desert Sands: The Recordings and Performances of Stuff Smith* Anthony Barnett; *The Black Heralds* César Vallejo. Unsolicited mss and synopses cannot be considered.

Amate Press
See **IKON Productions Ltd**

Anglo-Saxon Books
Frithgarth, Thetford Forest Park, Hockwold cum Wilton, Norfolk IP26 4NQ
☎01842 828430   Fax 01842 828430
Managing Editor Tony Linsell

FOUNDED 1990 to promote a greater awareness of and interest in early English history and culture. Originally concentrated on Old English texts but now also publishes less academic, more popular titles. Seeking titles for all periods of English history. *Publishes* English history, culture, language and society before 1066. About 5–10 titles a year. TITLES *A Handbook of Anglo-Saxon Food; English Martial Arts; The Rebirth of England and English: The Vision of William Barnes.* Unsolicited synopses welcome but return postage necessary.
Royalties paid.

AVERT
AIDS Education and Research Trust, 11 Denne Parade, Horsham, West Sussex RH12 1JD
☎01403 210202   Fax 01403 211001
Managing Editor Annabel Kanabus

Publishing arm of the AIDS Education and Research Trust, a national registered charity

established 1986. *Publishes* books and leaflets about HIV infection and AIDS. About 3 titles a year. TITLES *AIDS: The Secondary Scene; Guidelines for Management of Children with HIV Infection*. Unsolicited mss, synopses and ideas welcome.
Royalties paid accordingly.

M. & M. Baldwin
24 High Street, Cleobury Mortimer, Near Kidderminster, Worcestershire DY14 8BY
☎01299 270110   Fax 01299 270110
Managing Editor *Dr Mark Baldwin*
FOUNDED 1978. *Publishes* local interest/history and inland waterways books. Up to 5 titles a year. TITLES *Idle Women; West Midland Wanderings; Canal Coins*. Unsolicited mss, synopses and ideas for books welcome.
Royalties paid.

Bardon Enterprises
20 Queen's Keep, Palmerston Road, Southsea, Hampshire PO5 3NX
☎01705 874900   Fax 01705 874900
Managing Director *W. B. Henshaw*
FOUNDED 1996. *Publishes* music and academic books. 1 title in 1996. TITLES *Bibliography of Organ Music; Dictionary of Musical Terms*. Unsolicited mss, synopses and ideas welcome. No pictorial books.

Barnworks Publishing
St Annes Cottage, Bury, Pulborough, West Sussex RH20 1PA
☎01798 831410   Fax 01798 831410
Managing Editor *Hazel Kelly*
Publishes interesting lives. 2 titles in 1996. TITLES *Together They Fly; French Resistance in Sussex; Appleford: A Berkshire Village*. 'We will accept more mss for vanity publishing, offering advice, editing, format suggestions and aid with distribution.' Telephone in the first instance.
Royalties paid.

BB Books
See under **Poetry Presses**

Birlinn Ltd
14 High Street, Edinburgh EH1 1TE
☎0131 556 6660   Fax 0131 558 1500
Managing Editor *Hugh Andrew*
FOUNDED 1992. *Publishes* humour, Scottish interest and history. 17 titles in 1996. TITLES *Scottish Folklore* Raymond Lamont-Brown; *Island Going* Robert Atkinson; *Drove Roads of Scotland* A. R. B. Haldane. No unsolicited mss; synopses and ideas welcome.
Royalties paid.

Black Cat Books
See **Neil Miller Publications**

The Bonaventura Press
Bagpath, Tetbury, Gloucestershire GL8 8YG
☎01453 860827   Fax 01453 860487
Managing Editor *Janet Sloss*
FOUNDED 1995 as a self-publishing venture. Synopses and ideas concerning the British connection with Menorca welcome. Shared cost publishing considered in certain circumstances. TITLES *Richard Kane, Governor of Minorca; Archive Annie or How to Solve the Mysteries of Historical Research*.

The Book Castle
12 Church Street, Dunstable, Bedfordshire LU5 4RU
☎01582 605670   Fax 01582 662431
Managing Editor *Paul Bowes*
FOUNDED 1986. *Publishes* non-fiction of local interest (Bedfordshire, Hertfordshire, Buckinghamshire, Northamptonshire, the Chilterns). 6+ titles a year. About 40 titles in print. TITLES *Chiltern Walks* series; *The Hill of the Martyr; Journeys into Bedfordshire*. Unsolicited mss, synopses and ideas for books welcome.
Royalties paid.

The Book Gallery
Bedford Road, St. Ives, Cornwall TR26 1SP
☎01736 793545
Directors *David & Tina Wilkinson*
FOUNDED 1991. *Publishes* limited edition monographs by and about writers/painters associated with the so-called Newlyn and St Ives schools of painting. Topics include Sven Berlin, Kit Barker, Arthur Caddick, Guido Morris, Leach Pottery. Ideas welcome.
Royalties not paid; flat fee.

Book-in-Hand Ltd
20 Shepherds Hill, London N6 5AH
☎0181 341 7650   Fax 0181 341 7650
Contact *Ann Kritzinger*
Print production service for self-publishers. Includes design and editing advice to give customers a greater chance of selling in the open market. Also runs an editing service called Scriptmate.

Bookmarque Publishing
26 Cotswold Close, Minster Lovell,
Oxfordshire OX8 5SX
☎01993 775179

Managing Editor *John Rose*

FOUNDED 1987. Publishing business with aim of filling gaps in motoring history of which it is said 'there are many!' *Publishes* motoring history, motor sport and general titles. About 8 titles a year (increasing). All design and photo-typesetting of books done in-house. TITLES *The First Motor Racing in Britain – Bexhill-on-Sea 1902; The History of Oxford Airport; Fairthorpe Cars*. Unsolicited mss, synopses and ideas welcome on transport titles. S.a.e. required for reply or return of material or for advice on publishing your work. No novels or similar.
Royalties paid.

Bozo
BM Bozo, London WC1N 3XX
Managing Editors *John & Cecilia Nicholson*

FOUNDED 1981. Began by producing tiny pamphlets (*Patriotic English Tracts*) and has gained a reputation for itself as 'one of England's foremost pamphleteers'. *Publishes* historical analyses, apocalyptic rants, wry/savage humour and political 'filth'. Considerable expansion of titles is underway. No unsolicited mss, synopses or ideas.
Royalties not paid.

Brentham Press
See under **Poetry Presses**

Brilliant Publications
The Old School Yard, Leighton Road,
Northall, Dunstable, Bedfordshire LU6 2HA
☎01525 222844   Fax 01525 221250

Publisher *Priscilla Hannaford*

FOUNDED 1993. *Publishes* books for primary and special needs teachers. About 8–10 titles a year. SERIES *How to be Brilliant at ...* for 7–11-year-olds; *How to Sparkle at ...* for 5–7-year-olds. Submit synopsis and sample pages in the first instance.
Royalties paid twice yearly.

Brinnoven
9 Thomson Green, Livingston, West Lothian
EH54 8TA
☎01506 442846   Fax 01506 442846

Proprietor *William Murray*

FOUNDED 1991. *Publishes* Scottish interest titles specialising in local history, dialects, languages and traditional/folk music. About 3–5 titles a year. Unsolicited mss, synopses and ideas welcome but return postage must be included.
Royalties and fees paid.

Business Innovations Research
Tregeraint House, Zennor, St Ives, Cornwall
TR26 3DB
☎01736 797061   Fax 01736 797061

Managing Director *John T. Wilson*

Publishes business books and newsletters, home study courses, and guidebooks. Production service available to self-publishers.

Businesslike Publishing
'Bluepool', Strathoykel, Ardgay,
Inverness-shire IV24 3DP
☎01549 441211

Managing Editor *Iain R. McIntyre*

FOUNDED 1989. Provides a printing and publishing service for members of the **Society of Civil Service Authors**. *Publishes* magazines, collections of poetry, short stories (not individual poems or short stories) and Scottish history. About 6 titles a year. TITLES *From Scotland's Past; Happy Days in Rothesay; Tales of a Glasgow Childhood* – 2nd printing (non-fiction); *Childhood Days in Glasgow; To Freedom Born* – 2nd printing (Doric Scots poetry); *Focus* (poetry anthology series). Ideas/synopses accepted. No unsolicited mss.
Royalties generally not paid but negotiable in some circumstances.

Chapter Two
13 Plum Lane, Plumstead Common, London
SE18 3AF
☎0181 316 5389   Fax 0181 854 5963

Managing Editor *E. N. Cross*

FOUNDED 1976. Chapter Two's chief activity is the propagation of the Christian faith through the printed page. *Publishes* exclusively on Plymouth Brethren. About 12 titles a year. No unsolicited mss, synopses or ideas: enquiries only.
Royalties not paid.

Charlewood Press
7 Weavers Place, Chandlers Ford, Eastleigh,
Hampshire SO53 1TU
☎01703 261192

Managing Editors *Gerald Ponting, Anthony Light*

FOUNDED 1987. Publishes local history booklets on the Fordingbridge area, researched and written by the two partners and leaflets on local walks. TITLES: *Breamore – A Short History &*

Guide; Tudor Fordingbridge; The Tragedies of the Dodingtons; Victorian Fordingbridge. No unsolicited mss.

Royalties not paid.

The Cheverell Press
Manor Studios, Manningford Abbots, Pewsey, Wiltshire SN9 6HS
☎01672 563163   Fax 01672 564301

Managing Editor *Sarah de Larrinaga*

Publishes careers, media and performing arts. No fiction.

IMPRINTS
The Cheverell Press, First Hand Books. TITLES *The Guide to Drama Training in the UK 1996/7; The Guide to Careers and Training in the Performing Arts; How to Become a Working Actor; Guide to Careers; Training in the Media.* Currently using researchers/writers on a fee basis, rather than royalties. No unsolicited mss. Started as a self–publisher and has produced a self-publishers information pack. Write for details.

Chrysalis Press
11 Convent Close, Kenilworth, Warwickshire CV8 2FQ
☎01926 855223   Fax 01926 856611

Managing Editor *Brian Boyd*

FOUNDED 1994. *Publishes* fiction, literary criticism and biography. TITLES *Two Tales; Challenge and Renewal: D.H. Lawrence and the Thematic Novel.* No unsolicited mss.

Royalties paid.

CNP Publications
Roseland, Gorran, St Austell, Cornwall
☎01726 843501   Fax 01726 843501

Managing Editor *Dr James Whetter*

FOUNDED 1975. *Publishes* poetry, political essays, local Cornish interest/biography and Celtic design. 1–2 titles a year. TITLES *An Baner Kernewek (The Cornish Banner)* – quarterly local-interest magazine; Cornish history published under the **Lyfrow Trelyspen** imprint – *Cornish Weather and Cornish People in the 17th Century; The Bodrugans: A Study of a Cornish Medieval Knightly Family.* Unsolicited mss, synopses and ideas welcome.

Royalties not paid.

Condor Books
78 Highland Road, Earlsdon, Coventry, West Midlands CV5 6GR
☎01203 714359

Contact *Alvaro Graña*

Condor Books was created by pan-pipes expert Alvaro Graña to publish his book *How to Make and Play Pan-Pipes*.

Copperfield Books
Hillbrook House, Lyncombe Vale Road, Bath BA2 4LS
☎01225 442835   Fax 01225 319755

Managing Director *John Brushfield*

Publishes paperback fiction and general non-fiction. 1 title in 1996. No unsolicited mss; 'we only commission books to our own specification'.

Corvus Press
See **ignotus press**

The Cosmic Elk
68 Elsham Crescent, Lincoln LN6 3YS
☎01522 691146

Managing Editor *Heather Hobden*

FOUNDED 1988. Academic, specialised and local interests, in science, history and the history of science. Books, leaflets, posters, handbooks, booklets to accompany exhibitions, videos or CD-ROMs; tutorial notes, etc.. A4 card and comb bindings. Illustrated and colour. TITLES: *John Harrison and the Problem of Longitude; The Telescope Revolution; Law or War – the Legal Aspects of the Cuban Missile Crisis; Life and Death According to the Traditional Beliefs of the Yakuts; First Scientific Ideas on the Universe; The Planets Handbook; Chinese Astronomy and its Influence; The Hampton Court Clock; History of Yakutia.*

Creation Books
83 Clerkenwell Road, London EC1R 5AR
☎0171 430 9878   Fax 0171 242 5527

Managing Editor *James Williamson*

FOUNDED 1990 to publish books of extreme thought and imagination – surreal, pulp, horror, avant-garde, underground film, art, erotica. 20 titles in 1996. Royalties paid annually.

Royalties paid annually.

Crescent Moon Publishing and Joe's Press
PO Box 393, Maidstone, Kent ME14 5XU
Managing Editor *Jeremy Robinson*

FOUNDED 1988 to publish critical studies of figures such as D. H. Lawrence, Thomas Hardy, André Gide, Powys, Rilke, Leonardo Da Vinci, Mark Rothko, Cavafy and Robert Graves. *Publishes* literature, criticism, media, art, feminism, painting, poetry, travel, guide-

books, cinema and some fiction. Literary magazine, *Passion*, launched February 1994. Quarterly. Twice-yearly anthology of American poetry, *Pagan America*. About 15–20 titles a year. TITLES *Samuel Beckett Goes into the Silence; Jackie Collins and the Blockbuster Novel; Vincent Van Gogh; The Poetry of Cinema; Wild Zones: Pornography, Art and Feminism; Andrea Dworkin.* Unsolicited mss, synopses and ideas welcome but approach in writing only with s.a.e..
Royalties negotiable.

Crocus Books
See under **Poetry Presses**

Daniels Medica
4 Hines Close, Barton, Cambridge CB3 7BB
☎01223 262490   Fax 01223 262490
Publisher *Dr Victor G. Daniels*

Educational materials and training packs for the pharmaceutical industry.

Dark Diamonds Publications
PO Box HK 31, Leeds, West Yorkshire LS11 9XN
☎0113 2453868
Managing Editor *Andrew Cocker*

FOUNDED 1987. Member of the Small Press Group of Great Britain. *Publishes* 2–3 titles a year. Print runs average 1000 copies. Limited funds. TITLES *Cacophony* – music magazine; *Dark Diamonds* – journal covering social and political subjects. Mainly concerned with environmental development and human rights issues. Unsolicited articles and illustrations on the above subject matter welcome. *A Riot of Emotions* magazine features art and poetry, and carries reviews of small press publications and independent music releases. Unsolicited poetry/short story mss welcome (2000 words maximum). Also unsolicited art (b&w illustrations only) welcome. Return postage must be included with all unsolicited contributions. Unsolicited material for review also welcome. Free copy to all contributors. Contributors' guidelines and current catalogue available (send s.a.e.).
Royalties not paid.

Delectus
27 Old Gloucester Street, London WC1N 3XX
☎0181 963 0979   Fax 0181 963 0502
Contact *Michael R. Goss*

FOUNDED 1990. *Publishes* classic erotic and horror fiction. Unsolicited mss, synopses and ideas not welcome.
Royalties paid annually.

Diamond Press
See under **Poetry Presses**

Dog House Publications
18 Marlow Avenue, Eastbourne, East Sussex BN22 8SJ
☎01323 729214
Managing Editor *Silvia Kent*

FOUNDED 1990. Publishes books and booklets on dog behaviour and related subjects. Unsolicited mss, synopses and ideas welcome but must be relevant. Mss must be practical and informed; 'we get too many doggie sob stories and poetry!' TITLES: *Dynamic Dog Psychology; Trance Training; Behaviour Counsellors' Handbook.* Branching out into other doggie subjects, e.g. health and general new age dog care and training.
Royalties paid.

The Dragonby Press
15 High Street, Dragonby, Scunthorpe DN15 0BE
☎01724 840645
Managing Editor *Richard Williams*

FOUNDED 1987 to publish affordable bibliography for reader, collector and dealer. About 3 titles a year. TITLES *Collins Crime Club: A Checklist.* Unsolicited mss, synopses and ideas welcome for bibliographical projects only.
Royalties paid.

Dragonfly Press
Courtyard Mews, Southover, Burwash, East Sussex TN19 7JB
☎01435 882580
Managing Editor *C. Bell*

FOUNDED 1989. *Publishes* local history, literary fiction, poetry and how-to titles. 1–2 titles a year. TITLES *The Writer's Guide to Self-Publishing; Organisation and Time Management for Square Pegs; Common Sense for Creative Writers; Saheli Kitchen* (ethnic cookery book). No unsolicited material accepted. Commissions only.
Royalties paid where applicable.

Education Now Publishing Cooperative Ltd
113 Arundel Drive, Bramcote Hills, Nottingham NG9 3FQ
☎0115 9257261   Fax 0115 9257261
Managing Editors *Dr Roland Meighan, Philip Toogood*

A non-profit research and writing group set up in reaction to 'the totalitarian tendencies of the 1988 Education Act'. Its aim is to widen the terms of the debate about education and its choices. *Publishes* reports on positive educational initiatives such as flexi-schooling, mini-schooling, small schooling, home-based education and democratic schooling. 4–5 titles a year. TITLES *Beyond Authoritarian School Management* Lynn Davies; *Developing Democratic Education* Clive Harber; *Flexischooling* Roland Meighan. No unsolicited mss or ideas. Enquiries only.

Royalties generally not paid.

Educational Heretics Press
113 Arundel Drive, Bramcote Hills, Nottingham NG9 3FQ
☎0115 9257261   Fax 0115 9257261
Directors *Janet & Roland Meighan*

Non-profit venture which aims to question the dogmas of schooling in particular and education in general. TITLES *Alice Miller: The Unkind Society, Parenting and Schooling* Chris Shute; *Rules, Routines and Regimentation* Ann Sherman; *John Holt: Personalised Education and the Reconstruction of Schooling* Roland Meighan. No unsolicited material. Enquiries only.

Royalties not paid but under review.

EKO Fund
Wedgwood Memorial College, Barlaston, Staffs ST12 9DG
☎01782 372105   Fax 01782 372393
Managing Editor *Brian W. Burnett*

FOUNDED January 1996 to publish modern, lively books and magazines in and about Esperanto. Unsolicited mss, synopses and ideas welcome. *Royalties* paid.

Enable Business Services
150 Sadler Road, Radford, Coventry CV6 2LN
☎070209 21158   Fax 070209 21158
Contact *Simon Stevens*

Enable Business Services aims to provide publications for all types of businesses, to assist them in all areas of development such as the fields of disability access and the Internet. Unsolicited material is 'always welcome, especially in terms of business related ideas and suggestions'.

estamp
204 St Albans Avenue, London W4 5JU
☎0181 994 2379   Fax 0181 994 2379
Contact *Silvie Turner*

Independent publisher of fine art books on printmaking, papermaking and artists' book–making. Books are designed and written for artists, craftspeople and designers. TITLES *British Printmaking*

Studios; About Prints; Europe for Printmakers; British Artists Books; Which Paper?. Approach in writing in first instance.

Feather Books
Fair View, Old Coppice, Lyth Bank, Shrewsbury, Shropshire SY3 0BW
☎01743 872177   Fax 01743 872177
Managing Editor *Rev. John Waddington-Feather*

FOUNDED 1980 to publish writers' group work. All material has a strong Christian ethos. *Publishes* poetry (mainly, but not exclusively, religious). 10 titles a year. TITLES *The Quill Hedgehog Series; The Poetry Church Magazine; Feather Books Poets Series; Feather Books Songs & Hymns Series*. No unsolicited mss, synopses or ideas. All correspondence to include s.a.e. please.

Ferry Publications
See entry under **Stop Press**

Field Day Publications
Foyle Arts Centre, Old Foyle College, Lawrence Hill, Derry BT48 7NJ
☎01504 360196   Fax 01504 365419

Specialises in work of Irish interest. Pamphlets, essays, playscripts. Usually commissioned. TITLES *Revising the Rising; Field Day Anthology of Irish Writing*.

First Hand Books
See **The Cheverell Press**

Fisher Miller Publishing
11 Ramsholt Close, North Waltham, Basingstoke, Hampshire RG25 2DG
☎01256 397482/781050
Fax 01256 397482/782850
Managing Editor *Janey Fisher*

ESTABLISHED 1994 as a result of enquiries from an author whose book was too esoteric to warrant publication by a commercial publisher. 'We are a service publisher, passing on the costs of publishing direct to the author to facilitate self-publishing to professional standards.' Unsolicited mss, synopses and ideas welcome. TITLES *The Hibiscus Years; Pika-Don; Eight Hundred Years of Physics Teaching* all by George Bishop.

Royalties not paid.

Fitzgerald Publishing
PO Box 804, London SE13 5JJ
☎0181 690 0597
Managing Editor *Tim Fitzgerald*
General Editor *Andrew Smith*

FOUNDED 1974. *Specialises* in scientific studies of

insects and spiders. 1–2 titles a year. TITLES *Stick Insects of Europe & The Mediterranean; Baboon Spiders of Africa; Tarantula Classification and Identification Guide.* Unsolicited mss, synopses and ideas for books welcome. Also considers video scripts for video documentaries. New video documentary: *Desert Tarantulas.*
Royalties paid.

Five Leaves Publications
PO Box 81, Nottingham NG5 4ER
☎0115 9603355
Contact *Ross Bradshaw*

FOUNDED 1995 (taking over the publishing programme of Mushroom Bookshop), producing 6–8 titles a year. *Publishes* fiction, poetry, politics and Jewish Interest. TITLES *The Dybbuk of Delight: an Anthology of Jewish Women's Poetry* eds. Sonja Lyndon and Sylvia Paskin; *The Shallow Grave: a Memoir of the Spanish Civil War* Walter Gregory; *The Slow Mirror and Other Stories: New Fiction by Jewish Writers* ed. Sonja Lyndon and Sylvia Paskin. Publisher of several books by Michael Rosen. No unsolicited mss; titles normally commissioned.
Royalties and fees paid.

Flying Witch Publications
See **ignotus press**

Forth Naturalist & Historian
University of Stirling, Stirling FK9 4LA
☎01259 215091   Fax 01786 464994
Also at: 30 Dunmar Drive, Alloa,
Clackmannanshire FK10 2EH
Honorary Editors *Lindsay Corbett, Neville Dix*

FOUNDED 1975 by the collaboration of Stirling University members and the Central Regional Council to promote interests and publications on central Scotland. Aims to provide a 'valuable local studies educational resource for mid-Scotland schools, libraries and people'. *Publishes* naturalist, historical and environmental studies and maps. TITLES *The Forth Naturalist & Historian from 1976* (annual publication); *Postcards of the Past; Central Scotland: Land, Wildlife, People* (a new survey); *The Ochil Hills: Landscapes, Wildlife, Heritage, Walks; Airthrey and Bridge of Allan; Alloa Tower and The Erskines of Mar; Central Scotland.* In preparation: *Lure of Loch Lomond; Alloa in Days of Prosperity 1830–1914;* 1890s maps 25″ to the mile – 24 of Central Scotland areas/places with historical notes. Welcomes papers, mss and ideas relevant to central Scotland. Promotes annual environment/heritage symposia.
Royalties not paid.

Freedom Publishing
PO Box 4, Topsham, Exeter, Devon
EX3 0YR
☎0976 213181
Proprietors *Scott and Charmiene Leland*

FOUNDED 1995. *Publishes* works connected with the topics of 'personal awakenings to truth, self-awareness and non-duality'. New authors who are not considered 'mainstream' are especially welcome. About 4 titles a year. TITLES *The Mountain Path; Araminta's Message: A Fairytale; One Year in India; I Married a Dolphin.* Unsolicited mss, synopses and ideas (with s.a.e.) welcome. Shared funding, shared profits.

The Frogmore Press
See under **Poetry Presses**

Frontier Publishing
Windetts, Kirstead, Norfolk NR15 1BR
☎01508 558174   Fax 01508 550194
Managing Editor *John Black*

FOUNDED 1983. *Publishes* travel, photography and literature. 2–3 titles a year. TITLES *Travellers on a Trade Wind; From Dot to Cleopatra; Eye on the Hill: Horse Travels in Britain; Euphonics: A Poet's Dictionary of Sounds; Broken China; The Green Book of Poetry.* No unsolicited mss; synopses and ideas welcome.
Royalties paid.

Full House Productions
12 Sunfield Gardens, Bayston Hill,
Shrewsbury, Shropshire SY3 0LA
☎01743 874059
Managing Editor *Judith A. Shone*

FOUNDED 1993 by writer/producer Judith Shone in order to supply professionally written pantomime scripts to small production companies such as operatic societies, amateur dramatic societies and other performing groups – village halls etc. *Publishes* a complete low-cost 'panto-pack' consisting of scripts, posters and tickets. Future plans are to expand into publication of plays and sketches. All titles are written and published in-house. 11 titles to date; 3 planned for 1997.

Galactic Central Publications
Imladris, 25A Copgrove Road, Leeds, West Yorkshire LS8 2SP
Managing Editor *Phil Stephensen-Payne*

FOUNDED 1982 in the US. *Publishes* science fiction bibliographies. About 4 titles a year. TITLES *Gene Wolfe: Urth-Man Extraordinary;*

Andre Norton: Grand Master of Witch World. All new publications originate in the UK. Unsolicited mss, synopses and ideas welcome.

The Gargoyle's Head
Chatham House, Gosshill Road, Chislehurst, Kent BR7 5NS
☎0181 467 8475 Fax 0181 295 1967
Managing Editor *Jennie Gray*
FOUNDED 1990. *Publishes* a quarterly magazine and newsletter plus books and supplements on Gothic and macabre subjects. History, literary criticism, reprints of forgotten texts, biography, architecture, art etc., usually with a gloomy and black-hued flavour. About 4 titles a year. Synopses and ideas welcome. (Also see **The Gothic Society** under **Literary Societies**).
Royalties flat fee.

Gateway Books
The Hollies, Wellow, Bath BA2 8QJ
☎01225 835127 Fax 01225 840012
Publisher *Alick Bartholomew*
FOUNDED 1983. *Publishes* mind, body and spirit, alternative health. 7 titles in 1996. No unsolicited mss; synopses and ideas for books welcome but 'authors should check our list first'. No fiction, children's or poetry.
Royalties paid annually.

Geological Society Publishing House
Unit 7, Brassmill Enterprise Centre, Brassmill Lane, Bath BA1 3JN
☎01225 445046 Fax 01225 442836
Managing Editor *Mike Collins*
Publishing arm of the Geological Society which was founded in 1807. *Publishes* under-graduate and postgraduate texts in the earth sciences. 25 titles a year. Unsolicited mss, synopses and ideas welcome.
Royalties not paid.

Get a Grip
See **Working Books Ltd**

Global Books
See **Neil Miller Publications**

Global Publishing Ltd
70 Mount Pleasant Road, London NW10 3EJ
☎0181 830 0126 Fax 0181 830 0126
Chief Executive *Dr I. O. Azuonye*
FOUNDED 1993. *Publishes* contemporary issues, politics, economics, personal development,

general fiction, education and humour. 4 titles a year. TITLE *If We Elect Her President in November of the Year 2000* Ikechukwu O. Azuonye. Welcomes synopses and sample chapters with return postage. Reading fee charged.
Royalties paid twice yearly. *Distributors* Access Publishers Network.

Glosa
PO Box 18, Richmond, Surrey TW9 2AU
☎0181 948 8417
Managing Editors *Wendy Ashby, Ronald Clark*
FOUNDED 1981. *Publishes* textbooks, dictionaries and translations for the teaching, speaking and promotion of Glosa (an international, auxiliary language); also a newsletter and journal. Rapid growth in the last couple of years. TITLES *Glosa 6000 Dictionary; Introducing Euro-Glosa; Eduka-Glosa; Central Glosa; Glosa 1000 – Chinese; Glosa 1000 – Swahili Dictionary.* In 1994 launched *Sko-Glosa*, a new publication for and by younger students of Glosa to be distributed to schools in different countries. Also in 1994 published several fairy stories and activity pages for school children who are learning Glosa in school. Unsolicited mss and ideas for Glosa books welcome.

Gothic Press
PO Box 542, Highgate, London N6 6BG
Managing Editor *Robin Crisp*
Specialist publisher of Gothic titles in quality, case editions. Mostly non-fiction at present. *Publishes* mysticism, supernatural, history, biography, Gothic novels. TITLES *Dracula: The Story Continues; The Highgate Vampire; Mad, Bad and Dangerous to Know; From Satan to Christ; The Grail Church.* No unsolicited mss; synopses and ideas may be welcome.
Royalties paid annually.

Grant Books
The Coach House, New Road, Cutnall Green, Droitwich, Worcestershire WR9 0PQ
☎01299 851588 Fax 01299 851446
Managing Editor *H. R. J. Grant*
FOUNDED 1978. *Publishes* golf-related titles only: course architecture, history, biography, etc., but no instructional material. New titles and old, plus limited editions. About 4 titles a year. TITLES *The Parks of Musselburgh – Golfers, Architects, Club-makers; Some Essays on Golf Course Architecture; The Amateur: The Stories of the Amateur Championship 1885–1995; The Golf Courses of James Braid; Golf with a View: Broadway Golf Club 1895–1995; The Murdoch*

Golf Library; Aspects of Collecting Golf Books; The Architectural Side of Golf; British Professional Golfers – A Register, 1887–1930. Unsolicited mss, synopses and ideas welcome.
Royalties paid.

Grevatt & Grevatt
9 Rectory Drive, Newcastle upon Tyne
NE3 1XT
Chairman/Editorial Head *Dr S. Y. Killingley*
FOUNDED 1981. Alternative publisher of works not normally commercially viable. Three books have appeared with financial backing from professional bodies. *Publishes* academic titles and conference reports, particularly language, linguistics and religious studies. Some poetry also. Dr Killingley is editor of the Linguistic Association's *British Linguistic Newsletter.* TITLES *Overhearing the Incoherent: Selected Poems; The Sanskrit Tradition in the Modern World,* a series of rewritten conference/lecture proceedings launched 1988. New title: *Sound, Speech and Silence: Selected Poems.* No unsolicited mss. Synopses and ideas should be accompanied by s.a.e..
Royalties paid annually (after first 500 copies).

Grey Seal Books
28 Burgoyne Road, London N4 1AD
☎0181 340 6061   Fax 0181 342 8102
Chairman *John E. Duncan*
FOUNDED 1990. *Publishes* comparative religion, Islam and future studies. About 6 titles a year. No unsolicited mss; synopses and ideas welcome. *Royalties* paid annually.

GRM Publications
34 Holmwood Avenue, Meanwood, Leeds,
West Yorkshire LS6 4NJ
☎0113 27524565   Fax 0113 27524565
Managing Editors *Graham Wade,*
   Elizabeth Wade
FOUNDED 1996. Publishes monographs on music, especially relating to the classical guitar repertoire. About 5 titles a year. TITLES *Distant Sarabandes: The Solo Guitar Music of Joaquín Rodrigo; The Guitarist's Guide to Associated Board Examinations.*

GSSE
11 Malford Grove, Gilwern, Abergavenny,
Gwent NP7 0RN
☎01873 830872
Owner/Manager *David P. Bosworth*
Publishes newsletters and booklets describing classroom practice (at all levels of education and training). Ideas welcome – particularly

from practising teachers, lecturers and trainers describing how they use technology in their teaching. TITLES *OLS News* (quarterly newsletter); series: *IT in the Classroom* (first title: *Databases in the School*).
Royalties paid by arrangement.

Guildhall Press
41 Great James Street, Derry BT48 7DF
☎01504 364413   Fax 01504 372949
Managing Editor *Adrian Kerr*
FOUNDED 1979 to produce local history material. Government funding has helped establish the press as a community publishing house with increased output across a wide range of subjects. Interested in joint ventures with similar organisations to increase output and gain commercial experience. About 6 titles a year. TITLES *Seeing is Believing, Murals in Derry* Oona Woods; *The Road to Bloody Sunday* Dr Raymond McClean; *Perceptions: Cultures in Conflict* Adrian Kerr; *The Wile Big Derry Phrasebook* Seamus McConnell. Unsolicited mss, synopses and ideas welcome.
Royalties negotiable.

Happy House
3b Castledown Avenue, Hastings, East Sussex
TN34 3RJ
☎01424 434778
FOUNDED 1992 as a self-publishing venture for Dave Arnold/Martin Honeysett collaboration of poetry and cartoons. TITLES *Out to Lunch; Under the Wallpaper; Before and After the Shrink; Fragile Balance; Zen Haiku.*

Haunted Library
Flat 1, 36 Hamilton Street, Hoole, Chester,
Cheshire CH2 3JQ
☎01244 313685
Managing Editor *Rosemary Pardoe*
FOUNDED 1979. *Publishes* a twice-yearly ghost story magazine and booklets in the antiquarian tradition of M. R. James. The magazine publishes stories, news and articles. 2–3 titles a year. TITLE *Ghosts & Scholars.* No unsolicited mss.
Royalties not paid.

Heart of Albion Press
2 Cross Hill Close, Wymeswold,
Loughborough, Leicestershire LE12 6UJ
☎01509 880725
Managing Editor *R. N. Trubshaw*
FOUNDED 1990 to publish books and booklets on the East Midlands area. *Publishes* mostly

local history. About 4–6 titles a year. TITLES *Little-known Leicestershire & Rutland; User-Friendly Dictionary of Old English.* No unsolicited mss but synopses and ideas welcome. *Royalties* negotiable.

Hedgerow Publishing Ltd

325 Abbeydale Road, Sheffield, South Yorkshire S7 1FS
☎0114 2554873   Fax 0114 2509400
Managing Editor *T. Hale*

FOUNDED 1988. Publisher of local interest postcards and greeting cards. Expanded into book publishing in 1990 with the emphasis on tourist-orientated material. Ideas for books relevant to the South Yorkshire and Northern Peak District areas will be considered. Interested in photographic submissions of colour transparencies of local views. Outright purchase only. Telephone *before* sending.
Royalties negotiable.

Highcliff Press

23 Avon Drive, Guisborough, Cleveland TS14 8AX
☎01287 637274
Managing Editor *Robert Sampson*

FOUNDED 1994. *Publishes* fiction, short prose, prose poems and poetry. TITLES *Lady on a Stained Glass Fire-Escape* Pete Faulkner; *For Everything Must be Returned* Andrew Fox; *Between the Falling Rain* and *Images* Robert Sampson. Unsolicited mss welcome.

Hilmarton Manor Press

Calne, Wiltshire SN11 8SB
☎01249 760208   Fax 01249 760379
Chairman/Managing Director *Charles Baile de Laperriere*

Publishes fine art reference only. *Royalties* paid.

Hisarlik Press

4 Catisfield Road, Enfield Lock, Middlesex EN3 6BD
☎01992 700898   Fax 0181 292 6118
Managing Editors *Dr Jeffrey Mazo, Georgina Clark-Mazo*

FOUNDED 1991. *Publishes* academic books and journals on folklore, local history and medieval studies. TITLES *With Disastrous Consequences: London Disasters 1830–1917; The Maiden Who Rose From The Sea and Other Finnish Folktales; From Sagas to Society: Comparative Approaches to Early Iceland.* No unsolicited mss; synopses and ideas welcome. *Royalties* paid.

Horseshoe Publications

PO Box 37, Kingsley, Warrington, Cheshire WA6 8DR
☎01928 787477 (Afternoons and evenings)
Managing Editor *John C. Hibbert*

FOUNDED 1994. Initially to publish work of Cheshire writers. Poetry, short stories and own writing. Shared cost publishing considered in certain circumstances. Reading fee on full mss £25. TITLES *One Boy's War; The Reincarnate; Windmills; The Travellers Series.* Unsolicited mss, synopses and ideas in the realm of commercial fiction welcome. S.a.e. for return.

ignotus press

BCM-Writer, 27 Old Gloucester Street, London WC1X 3XX
☎01559 371108   Fax 01559 371108
Publisher *Suzanne Ruthven*

Specialises in full length esoteric non-fiction and fiction of all traditions although writers are advised to send s.a.e. for authors' guidelines before submitting material for consideration. All mss are checked for accuracy and knowledge of subject by specialists who will reject sword-n-sorcery and idealistic New Age material.

IMPRINTS **Corvus Press** *Christine Sempers* Non-fiction paperbacks and booklets relating to self-help, healing, herb lore and primitive native traditions. **Flying Witch Publications** *Frances Denton* Non-fiction paperbacks and booklets on idigenous craft and arts/craft covering Anglo Saxon, Nordic and Celtic traditions.
Royalties paid.

IKON Productions Ltd

Manor Farm House, Manor Road, Wantage, Oxfordshire OX12 8NE
☎01235 767467   Fax 01235 767467
Publisher *Clare Goodrick-Clarke*

FOUNDED 1988. *Publishes* religion countryside and self-help. TITLES *The English Religious Tradition and the Genius of Anglicanism; Setting Your Sights: A Guide to Job Hunting and Interview Technique.* Also **Amate Press** imprint. No unsolicited mss. Please write first.

Intellect Books

E.F.A.E., Earl Richards Road North, Exeter, Devon EX2 6AS
☎01392 475110   Fax 01392 475110
Publisher *Masoud Yazdani*
Assistant Publisher *Robin Beecroft*

FOUNDED 1984. *Publishes* books and journals on

social implications of computing, language learning and European studies. 10 titles in 1996. TITLES *Women and Computers; English Language in Europe; Forms of Representation; Signs, Symbols and Icons.* Unsolicited synopses and ideas welcome. *Royalties* paid.

Iolo
38 Chaucer Road, Bedford MK40 2AJ
☎01234 270175   Fax 01234 270175
Managing Director *Dedwydd Jones*

Publishes Welsh theatre-related material and campaigns for a Welsh National Theatre. SERIES *Black Books on the Welsh Theatre.* Ideas on Welsh themes welcome; approach in writing.

JAC Publications
28 Bellomonte Crescent, Drayton, Norwich, Norfolk NR8 6EJ
☎01603 861339
Managing Editor *John James Vasco*

Publishes World War II Luftwaffe history only. TITLES *Zerstörer: The Messerschmitt 110 and its Units in 1940* John J. Vasco and Peter D. Cornwell. Unsolicited mss welcome. No synopses or ideas.
Royalties paid.

Jackson's Arm
See **Sunk Island Publishing**

John Jones Publishing Ltd
Borthwen, Wrexham Road, Ruthin, Denbighshire LL15 1DA
☎01824 707255
Managing Editor *John Idris Jones*

FOUNDED 1989. *Publishes* inexpensive books and booklets in English with a Welsh background. Interested in short, illustrated texts for the tourist and schools market. Approach in writing with s.a.e..
Royalties paid.

Katabasis
See under **Poetry Presses**

Richard Kay Publications
80 Sleaford Road, Boston, Lincolnshire PE21 8EU
☎01205 353231
Managing Editor *Richard Kay*

FOUNDED 1970. Non-profit motivated publisher of local interest (Lincolnshire) material: dialect, history, autobiography and biography, philosophy, medico-political and contemporary dissent

on current affairs. About 6 titles a year. TITLES *Herbert Ingram, Esq., MP, Founder of the Illustrated London News; Now the Day is Over: The Life and Times of Rev. Sabine Baring-Gould; William Brewster: The Father of New England; Woods and Doggeybaw – A Lincolnshire Dialect Dictionary.* No unsolicited mss; synopses and ideas welcome.
Royalties paid if appropriate.

Kittiwake Press
3 Glantwymyn Village Workshops, Nr. Machynlleth, Montgomeryshire SY20 8LY
☎01650 511314   Fax 01650 511602
Managing Editor *David Perrott*

FOUNDED 1986. Owned by Perrott Cartographics. *Publishes* guidebooks only, with an emphasis on good design/production. TITLES *Western Islands Handbook; Outer Hebrides Handbook; Local Walks Guides.* Unsolicited mss, synopses and ideas welcome. Specialist cartographic and electronic publishing services available. *Royalties* paid.

Lily Publications
PO Box 9, Narberth, Pembrokeshire SA68 0YT
☎01834 891461   Fax 01834 891463
Managing Editor *Miles Cowsill*

FOUNDED 1991. *Publishes* holiday guides and specialist books. TITLES *Premiere Guide to Pembrokeshire 1997; Cardiganshire 1997/8; Brecon Beacons and Heart of Wales Guide 1997; Isle of Man 1996/7,* tourist guide to the island; *Isle of Man – A Photographic Journey.* Unsolicited mss, synopses and ideas welcome. Sister company **Lily Publications (Isle of Man) Ltd.**, PO Box 1, Portland House, Ballasalla, Isle of Man. Tel/fax 01624 823848.
Royalties paid.

Logaston Press
Logaston, Woonton, Almeley, Herefordshire HR3 6QH
☎01544 327344
Managing Editors *Andy Johnson,*
  Ron Shoesmith

FOUNDED 1985. *Publishes* walking guides, social history, rural issues and local history for Wales, the Welsh Border and West Midlands. 6–8 titles a year. TITLES *A View from Hereford's Past; Castles and Moated Sites of Herefordshire; Castles of Radnorshire; Prehistoric Sites of Monmouthshire; Arthurian Links with Herefordshire; The Man in the Moone.* Unsolicited mss, synopses and ideas welcome. Return postage appreciated.
Royalties paid.

Luath Press Ltd
Barr, Ayrshire KA26 9TN
☎01465 861636   Fax 01465 861625
Managing Editor *T. W. Atkinson*
FOUNDED 1980 to publish books of Scottish interest. *Publishes* guidebooks and books with a Scottish connection. About 6 titles a year. TITLES *Seven Steps in the Dark* (autobiography of a Scottish miner); *Mountain Days and Bothy Nights*. Unsolicited mss, synopses and ideas welcome.
Royalties paid.

Lyfrow Trelyspen
See **CNP Publications**

Madison Publishing Ltd
83 Albert Palace Mansions, Lurline Gardens, London SW11 4DH
☎0973 224536   Fax 0171 622 4679
Managing Director *Nathan Andrew Iyer*
FOUNDED 1995. *Publishes* British fiction. TITLE *Domino Run*. No unsolicited mss. Synopses (no more than 2pp) and ideas welcome.

Mandrake of Oxford
PO Box 250, Oxford OX1 1AP
☎01865 243671
Managing Editor *Kris Morgan*
Publishes occult, surreal, magical art, sexology, heretical and radically new ideas. 3–5 titles a year. TITLE *Rune Magician Trilogy* Jan Fries. No mss; send synopsis first with return postage.
Royalties paid.

Marine Day Publishers
64 Cotterill Road, Surbiton, Surrey KT6 7UN
☎0181 399 7625   Fax 0181 399 1592
Managing Editor *Anthony G. Durrant*
FOUNDED 1990. Part of The Marine Press Ltd. *Publishes* local history. 1 title a year. TITLES *Malden Old & New; Malden Old & New Revisited; Kingston and Surbiton Old & New; All Change*. Unsolicited synopses and ideas welcome; no mss.
Royalties not paid.

Matching Press
1 Watermans End, Matching Green, Harlow, Essex CM17 0RQ
☎01279 731308
Publisher *Patrick Streeter*
FOUNDED 1993. *Publishes* biography, autobiography, social history and fiction. Enquiries welcome. *Royalties* paid.

Maverick Publishing
47 Allerton Walk, Manchester M13 9TG
☎0161 272 7271   Fax 0161 272 7271
Managing/Editorial Director *Chancery Stone*
Art/Production *Max Scratchman*
FOUNDED 1996. *Publishes* fiction, erotica, art and photography. No romance, children's, mainstream or poetry unless 'deeply sinister or wildly warped'. 4 titles in 1997. Please send s.a.e. for guidelines before submitting mss or samples.

Maypole Editions
22 Mayfair Avenue, Ilford, Essex IG1 3DQ
☎0181 252 0354
Contact *Barry Taylor*
Publisher of fiction and poetry in the main. About 3 titles a year. TITLES *Snorting Mustard; Metallum Damnantorum; Love Sonnets; Chocolate Rose; Memoriam; Neon Lilly Tiger; Memento Mori, No Bodyguard*. Plays: *Laurel Trireme; Frog; Piraeus Pelican*. Unsolicited mss welcome, especially plays and poetry, provided return postage is included. Poems should be approximately 30 lines long, broadly covering social concerns, ethnic minorities, feminist issues, romance, lyric. No politics. The annual collected anthology is designed as a small press platform for first-time poets and a permanent showcase for those already published.

Meadow Books
22 Church Meadow, Milton under Wychwood, Chipping Norton, Oxfordshire OX7 6JG
☎01993 831338
Managing Director *C. O'Neill*
FOUNDED 1990. Published a social history of hospitals. TITLES *A Picture of Health; More Pictures of Health* Cynthia O'Neill.

Mercia Cinema Society
19 Pinder's Grove, Wakefield, West Yorkshire WF1 4AH
☎01924 372748
Managing Editor *Brian Hornsey*
FOUNDED 1980 to foster research into the history of picture houses. *Publishes* books and booklets on the subject, including cinema circuits and chains. Books are often tied in with specific geographical areas. TITLES *Cinemas of Lincoln; How to Research the History of Cinemas; Cinemas of Exeter; Cinemas of Essex; Cinema Story – The Rise, Fall and Revival of Wakefield Cinemas; Essoldo*. Unsolicited mss, synopses and ideas.
Royalties not paid.

Meridian Books

40 Hadzor Road, Oldbury, Warley, West
Midlands B68 9LA
☎0121 429 4397

Managing Editor *Peter Groves*

FOUNDED 1985 as a small home-based enterprise
following the acquisition of titles from Tetradon
Publications Ltd. *Publishes* local history, walking
and regional guides. 4–5 titles a year. TITLES *In
the Footsteps of the Gunpowder Plotters* Conall
Boyle; *The Navigation Way: A Hundred Mile
Towpath Walk* Peter Groves & Trevor Antill; *The
Monarch's Way, Books 1, 2 & 3* Trevor Antill.
New titles 1996: *Heart of England Hillwalks* John
Newson; *Country Walks in Warwickshire and
Worcestershire* Des Wright. Unsolicited mss, syn-
opses and ideas welcome if relevant. Send s.a.e. if
mss is to be returned.

Royalties paid.

Merton Priory Press Ltd

67 Merthyr Road, Whitchurch, Cardiff
CF4 1DD
☎01222 521956   Fax 01222 521956

Managing Director *Philip Riden*

FOUNDED 1993. *Publishes* academic and mid-
market history, especially local and industrial
history; also distributes for small publishers
working in the same field. About 6 titles a year.
Full catalogue available.

Royalties paid twice yearly.

Neil Miller Publications

Mount Cottage, Grange Road, Saint
Michael's, Tenterden, Kent TN30 6EE

Managing Editor *Neil Miller*

FOUNDED 1994. *Publishes* tales with a twist,
comedy, suspense, mystery, fantasy, science fiction, horror and the bizarre under the **Black
Cat Books** imprint. **Global Books** romance
tales. Also *publishes* paperbacks: classics, rare
tales, tales of the unexpected. New authors
always welcome. Evaluation and critique service
available for large mss. 'We will help and advise
on anything well written and researched.' Write
in the first instance with s.a.e. for information
package.

Minimax Books Ltd

Broadgate House, Church Street,
Deeping St James, Peterborough,
Cambridgeshire PE6 8HD
☎01778 347609   Fax 01778 341198

Chairman *Bob Lavender*
Managing Director *Lynn Green*

Approx. Annual Turnover £40,000

FOUNDED in the early 1980s. *Publishes* books of
local interest and history. No academic or
technical. *Royalties* paid twice yearly.

Minority Rights Group

379 Brixton Road, London SW9 7DE
☎0171 978 9498   Fax 0171 738 6265

Head of Publications *Angela Warren*

FOUNDED in the late 1960s, MRG works to
raise awareness of minority issues worldwide.
Publishes books, reports and educational material
on minority rights. 8–10 titles a year. TITLES *The
Kurds; Afro-Latins; Burundi; North Caucasus.*

Morton Publishing

PO Box 23, Gosport, Hampshire PO12 2XD

Managing Editor *Nik Morton*

FOUNDED 1994. *Publishes* fiction – genre novellas, max. 20,000 words; short story anthologies –
max. 4000 words per story. TITLES *Auguries 18* (a
science fiction/fantasy/horror anthology); *A Sign
of Grace* and *Silenced in Darkness* both by Robert
W. Nicholson. Unsolicited synopses and ideas
for books welcome. *Royalties* paid annually.

Need2Know

1–2 Wainman Road, Woodston,
Peterborough PE2 7BU
☎01733 230759   Fax 01733 230751

Managing Editor *Kerrie Pateman*

FOUNDED 1995 'to fill a gap in the market for
self-help books', Need2Know is an imprint of
Forward Press Ltd. (see under **Poetry
Presses**). *Publishes* self-help, reference guides
for people in difficult situations. TITLES *Make
the Most of Being a Carer; Stretch Your Money;
Make the Most of Retirement; Buying a House;
Help Yourself to a Job.* 26 titles in 1996. No mss.
Unsolicited synopses and ideas for books welcome in the first instance as it is important to
ensure the project fits in with the series and
that the subject is not already covered.

Payment Advance paid and six monthly payments thereafter.

New Arcadian Press

13 Graham Grove, Burley, Leeds,
West Yorkshire LS4 2NF
☎0113 2304608

Managing Editor *Patrick Eyres*

FOUNDED 1981 to publish artist-writer collaborations on landscape and garden themes
through *The New Arcadian Journal* (limited edition collector's items). TITLES *Castle Howard;*

The Wentworths; A Cajun Chapbook; Hearts of Oak; Sons of the Sea; Naumachia; Landfall; The Political Temples of Stowe. No unsolicited mss, synopses or ideas. *Royalties* not paid.

New Millennium
292 Kennington Road, London SE11 4LD
☎0171 582 1477   Fax 0171 582 4084
Managing Editor *Tom Deegan*

New Millennium is the imprint of the Professional Authors' & Publishers' Association (see entry under **Professional Associations**, established in 1993 'to provide self-publishing writers with an alternative to the vanity trade'. *Publishes* general fiction and non-fiction. 48 titles in 1996. TITLES *George Meek; Travels With My Daughter; Silent Unseen; The Call of Nepal.* Unsolicited mss, synopses and ideas welcome but a reading fee is charged.

Nimbus Press
18 Guilford Road, Leicester LE2 2RB
☎0116 2706318   Fax 0116 2706318
Managing Editor *Clifford Sharp*

FOUNDED in 1991 to encourage churches to use drama in worship. *Publishes* Christian drama and discussion booklets on Christian themes. TITLES *The Good Church Guide; Looking for a King; Is this Your Life?.* 7 titles in 1996. No unsolicited mss. Synopses and ideas for plays of less than 25 minutes' length, suitable for production in a church, and plays for children welcome.
Royalties paid.

Norvik Press Ltd
School of Modern Languages & European Studies, University of East Anglia, Norwich, Norfolk NR4 7TJ
☎01603 593356   Fax 01603 250599
Managing Editors *James McFarlane, Janet Garton, Michael Robinson*

Small academic press. *Publishes* the journal *Scandinavica* and books related to Scandinavian literature. About 4 titles a year. TITLES *A Sudden Liberating Thought* Kjell Askildsen; *From Baltic Shores* ed Christopher Moseley; *Days with Diam* Svend Åge Madsen; *My Son on the Galley* Jacob Wallenberg; *A Century of Swedish Narrative* eds. Sarah Death & Helena Forsås-Scott; *A Fighting Pig's Too Tough to Eat* Suzanne Brøgger; *Magic Circles* Kerstin Ekman; *Modus Vivendi* Gunnar Ekelöf; *Five Swedish Poets* Robin Fulton. Interested in synopses and ideas for books within its *Literary History and Criticism* series. No unsolicited mss.
Royalties paid.

Nyala Publishing
4 Christian Fields, London SW16 3JZ
☎0181 764 6292
Fax 0181 764 6292/0115 9819418
Editorial Head *J. F. J. Douglas*

FOUNDED 1996. Publishing arm of Geo Group. *Publishes* biography, travel and general non-fiction. No unsolicited mss; synopses and ideas considered. *Royalties* paid twice-yearly.

Oast Books
See **Parapress Ltd**

Octave Books
See **Parapress Ltd**

Open Gate Press
51 Achilles Road, London NW6 1DZ
☎0171 431 4391   Fax 0171 431 5088
Managing Directors *Jeannie Cohen, Elisabeth Petersdorff*

FOUNDED 1989 to provide a forum for psychoanalytic social and cultural studies. *Publishes* psychology, philosophy, social sciences, politics. SERIES *Psychoanalysis and Society.* Synopses and ideas for books welcome.
Royalties paid twice yearly.

Oriflamme Publishing
60 Charteris Road, London N4 3AB
☎0171 281 8501   Fax 0171 281 8501
Managing Editor *Tony Allen*

FOUNDED 1982, originally to publish science fiction and fantasy but now concentrating on a range of educational textbooks, mainly English and mathematics. Some fiction and special interest also. About 7 titles a year. SERIES *The Rules of Maths; Help Yourself to English; The Rules of English.* No unsolicited mss; synopses/ideas welcome but must be brief.
Royalties paid.

Palladour Books
Hirwaun House, Aberporth, Nr. Cardigan, Ceredigion SA43 2EU
☎01239 811658   Fax 01239 811658
Managing Editors *Jeremy Powell/Anne Powell*

FOUNDED 1986. Started with a twice-yearly issue of catalogues on the literature and poetry of the First World War. Occasional catalogues on Second World War poetry have also been issued. TITLES *A Deep Cry*, a literary pilgrimage to the battlefields and cemeteries of First World War British soldier–poets killed in Northern France and Flanders; *The Fierce Light: The Battle of the*

Somme: July – November 1916. No unsolicited mss.
Royalties not paid.

Parapress Ltd
12 Dene Way, Speldhurst, Tunbridge Wells, Kent TN3 0NX
☎01892 862860   Fax 01892 863861
Managing Director *Ian W. Morley-Clarke*

FOUNDED 1993. *Publishes* autobiography, biography, diaries, journals of military personnel, composers and sportsmen. Also books on local history. About 12 titles a year. Largely self-publishing. IMPRINT: **Oast Books** Literary and local guides; **Parapress** Militaria; **Octave Books** Music biographies.

Parthian Books
41 Skelmuir Road, Cardiff CF2 2PR
☎01222 460164   Fax 01222 460164
Chairman *Gillian Griffiths*
Managing Director *Richard Davies*
Approx. Annual Turnover £30,000

FOUNDED in 1993. *Publishes* contemporary Welsh fiction in English. TITLES *Work, Sex & Rugby* Lewis Davies; *Tilting at Windmills.* 3–4 books per year. No unsolicited; synopses and ideas welcome.
Royalties paid annually.

Partizan Press
816–818 London Road, Leigh on Sea, Essex SS9 3NH
☎01702 73986   Fax 01702 73986
Managing Editor *David Ryan*

Caters for the growing re-enactment and war-gaming market. *Publishes* military history and local history, with particular regard to the 17th and 18th centuries. About 30 titles a year. TITLES *Winchester in the Civil War; Eye & Eye Witnesses; Discovery of Witchcraft.* Unsolicited mss welcome.
Royalties paid.

Paupers' Press
27 Melbourne Road, West Bridgford, Nottingham NG2 5DJ
☎0115 9815063   Fax 0115 9815063
Managing Editor *Colin Stanley*

FOUNDED 1983. *Publishes* extended essays in booklet form (about 15,000 words) on literary criticism and philosophy. About 6 titles a year. TITLES *A Report on the Violent Male* A. E. van Vogt; *Mozart's Journey to Prague: A Playscript* Colin Wilson; *More on the Word Hoard: The*

Poetry of Seamus Heaney Stephen Wade; *Proportional Representation: A Debate on the Pitfalls of our Electoral System* Gregory K. Vincent; *Sex and Sexuality in Ian McEwan's Work* Christina Byrnes; *Sex and the Intelligent Teenager* Colin Wilson. Limited hardback editions of bestselling titles. No unsolicited mss but synopses and ideas for books welcome. *Royalties* paid.

Peepal Tree Press Ltd
17 King's Avenue, Leeds, West Yorkshire LS6 1QS
☎0113 2451703   Fax 0113 2468368
Managing Editor *Jeremy Poynting*

FOUNDED 1985. *Publishes* fiction, poetry, drama and academic studies. *Specialises* in Caribbean, Black British and South Asian writing. About 18 titles a year. In-house printing and finishing facilities. AUTHORS Kamau Brathwaite, Cyril Dabydeen, Beryl Gilroy, Velma Pollard, Jan Shinebourne and **Forward Poetry Prize** winner Kwame Dawes. 'Please send an A5 s.a.e. with a 38p stamp for a copy of our submission guidelines.' Write or 'phone for a free catalogue.
Royalties paid.

The Penniless Press
100 Waterloo Road, Ashton, Preston, Lancashire PR2 1EP
Managing Editor *Alan Dent*

Publishes quarterly magazine with literary, philosophical, artistic and political content, including reviews of poetry, fiction, non-fiction and drama. Prose of up to 3000 words welcome. No mss returned without s.a.e..
Payment Free copy of magazine.

Pentaxion Ltd
180 Newbridge Street, Newcastle upon Tyne NE1 2TE
☎0191 232 6189   Fax 0191 232 6190
Managing Editor *Adrian Spooner*

Publishes academic, medical, arts and professional studies. 11 titles in 1996. TITLES *Reflection and Action for Health Care Professionals; The Law of Evidence; Venice Sketchbook.* No unsolicited mss; synopses and ideas welcome. 'Under certain circumstances we will enter into joint ventures with authors.' *Royalties* paid.

Pigasus Press
13 Hazely Combe, Arreton, Isle of Wight PO30 3AJ
☎01983 865668
Editor *Tony Lee*

FOUNDED 1989 (formerly S. A. Publishing).

Publishes science fiction and horror short stories in magazines, genre poetry anthologies and media review newsletters. TITLES Magazine: *The Zone*; Newsletters: *Dragon's Breath* (monthly small press review); *Videovista* (bi-monthly review); SF poetry anthologies: *The Others Amongst Us*. Fiction and articles for SF magazines welcome. Send s.a.e. for contributor's guidelines.

Pipers' Ash Ltd

'Pipers' Ash', Church Road, Christian Malford, Chippenham, Wiltshire SN15 4BW
☎01249 720563

Managing Editor *Mr A. Tyson*

FOUNDED 1976 to publish technical manuals for computer-controlled systems. Later broadened the company's publishing activities to include individual collections of contemporary short stories, science fiction short stories, poetry, short novels, local histories, children's fiction and non-fiction. 17 titles in 1996. TITLES *The Hour Glass* Sarah Collett; *Free Spirit* Val Ryrie; *The Keelmen* Jackie Crawford. Periodicals (published quarterly): *Poet of the Season*; *Contemporary Short Stories*; *Science Fiction Short Stories*. No unsolicited mss. Synopses and ideas welcome; 'new authors with potential will be actively encouraged'.
Royalties paid annually.

Planet

PO Box 44, Aberystwyth, Ceredigion SY23 5BS
☎01970 611255

Managing Editor *John Barnie*

FOUNDED 1985 as publishers of the arts and current affairs magazine *Planet: The Welsh Internationalist* and branched out into book publishing in 1995. 1 title in 1996. TITLES *Graffit: Narratives* poems by Mike Jenkins; *Them & Other Stories* (trans. from Galician) by Xosé Luís Méndez Ferrín; *A Barrel of Stones – In Search of Serbia* Peter Morgan. All books so far have been commissioned. Unsolicited synopses and ideas welcome. *Royalties* paid.

Playwrights Publishing Co.

70 Nottingham Road, Burton Joyce, Nottinghamshire NG14 5AL
☎0115 9313356

Managing Editors *Liz Breeze, Tony Breeze*

FOUNDED 1990. *Publishes* one-act and full-length plays. TITLES *Birthmarks* Mark Jenkins; *Lifestyles* Silvia Vaughan; *Undercoats* Roger Pinkham. Unsolicited scripts welcome. No synopses or ideas. Reading fees: £15 one act; £30 full length. *Royalties* paid.

Polymath Publishing

Manor Farm, Thornton Steward, Ripon, North Yorkshire HG4 4BB
☎01677 460058   Fax 01677 460059

Owner *Charles Knevitt*

FOUNDED 1989. *Publishes* general interest and technical architecture and construction industry books, postcard books, calendars, etc., also cartoon anthologies. TITLES *From Pecksniff to The Prince of Wales: 150 Years of Punch Cartoons on Architecture, Planning and Development 1851–1991*; *The Responsive Office: People and Change*; *Seven Ages of the Architect: The Very Best of Louis Hellman 1967–92*; *Shelter: Human Habitats From Around the World*; re-issue of *Community Architecture* (Penguin 1987). Synopses and ideas welcome.
Royalties negotiable.

David Porteous Editions

PO Box 5, Chudleigh, Newton Abbot, Devon TQ13 0YZ
☎01626 853310   Fax 01626 853663

Publisher *David Porteous*

FOUNDED 1992 to produce high quality colour illustrated books on hobbies and leisure for the UK and international markets. *Publishes* crafts, hobbies, art techniques and needlecrafts. No poetry. 3–4 titles a year. TITLES *Flower Painting* Paul Riley; *Paper Craft* Dette Kim; *Nursery Cross Stitch* Julie Hasler. Unsolicited mss, synopses and ideas welcome if return postage included.
Royalties paid twice yearly.

Power Publications

1 Clayford Avenue, Ferndown, Dorset BH22 9PQ
☎01202 875223   Fax 01202 875223

Contact *Mike Power*

FOUNDED 1989. *Publishes* local interest, pub walk guides and mountain bike guides. 2–3 titles a year. TITLES *Pub Walks in Cornwall/Hampshire/New Forest* (every county along the south coast); *Mountain Bike Guides to the New Forest, Hampshire, Dorset and Chilterns*; *Ferndown: A Look Back*; *Famous Women in Dorset*; *Penstemons*; *A Century of Cinema in Dorset*; *Ancient Stones of Dorset*. Unsolicited mss, synopses and ideas welcome.
Royalties paid.

Praxis Books

Sheridan, Broomers Hill Lane, Pulborough, West Sussex RH20 2DU
☎01798 873504

Proprietor *Rebecca Smith*

FOUNDED 1992. *Publishes* travel, memoirs, re-issues of Victorian fiction, general interest. 11 titles to date. TITLES *In Search of Life's Meaning* R. Matley and R. Smith; *The Poet's Kit* Katherine Knight; *A Book of Folklore* Sabine Baring-Gould; *By Way of Beachy Head* Joyce Tombs. Unsolicited mss accepted with s.a.e.. No fiction or humour. Editing service available. Shared funding, shared proceeds.

Previous Parrot Press
The Foundry, Church Hanborough, Nr. Witney, Oxford OX8 8AB
☎01993 881260   Fax 01993 883080
Managing Editor *Dennis Hall*

Publishes limited editions with a strong emphasis on illustration. About 3 titles a year. TITLES *An Avian Alphabet* Nyr Indictor, illus. Elizabeth Rashley; *Newhaven – Dieppe* written and illus. by Frank Martin; *The Return of A. J. Raffles* Graham Green, illus. Annie Newnham.

Prism Press Book Publishers Ltd
The Thatched Cottage, Parway Lane, Hazelbury Bryan, Sturminster Newton, Devon DT10 2DP
☎01258 817164   Fax 01258 817635
Managing Director *Julian King*

FOUNDED 1974. *Publishes* alternative medicine, conservation, environment, psychology, health, mysticism, philosophy, politics and cookery. About 6 titles a year. TITLES *Boundaries of the Soul* June Singer; *Beyond the Warning* Antony Milne; *Beyond Therapy* Guy Claxton. Synopses and ideas welcome.
Royalties paid twice-yearly. *Overseas associates* Prism Press USA.

Pulp Faction
PO Box 12171, London N19 3HB
☎0171 263 2090   Fax 0171 263 2090
Contact *Editor*

FOUNDED 1994. *Publishes* book form collections of underground/offbeat short fiction along with artwork and graphic fiction. TITLE *Technopagan, Fission, Allnighter.* Flat fee paid for short stories. (Website www: http://pulpfact.demon.co.uk should be checked for themes of future compilations and deadlines.) **Pulp Books** Set up in 1996 to publish new contemporary fiction with an urban/underground slant. About 6 titles a year. TITLES *Call Me*; *Their Heads Are Anonymous.* 'A good first stop for ambitious new writers.' Send synopsis/sample chapters from a novel. Postage must be included for return of mss or response. No telephone queries.
Royalties paid.

QED Books
1 Straylands Grove, York YO3 0EB
☎01904 424381   Fax 01904 424381
Managing Editor *John Bibby*

Publishes and *distributes* resource guides and learning aids, including laminated posters, for mathematics and science. TITLES *Fun Maths Calendar; Maths Resource Guides; Maths and Art; Joy of Maths; Geometer's Sketchpad*™. Synopses (3pp) and ideas for books welcome. QED arranges publicity for other small presses and has many contacts overseas. Also provides publishing services for other publishers.
Royalties by agreement.

QueenSpark Books
Brighton Media Centre, 11 Jew Street, Brighton, East Sussex BN1 1UT
☎01273 748348

A community writing and publishing group run mainly by volunteers who work together to write and produce books. Since the early 1970s they have published 40 titles: local autobiographies, humour, poetry, history and politics. Free writing workshops and groups held on a regular basis. New members welcome.

Redstone Press
7A St Lawrence Terrace, London W10 5SU
☎0171 352 1594   Fax 0171 352 8749
Managing Editor *Julian Rothenstein*

FOUNDED 1987. *Publishes* art and literature. About 5 titles a year. No unsolicited mss; synopses and ideas welcome but familiarity with Redstone's list advised in the first instance.
Royalties paid.

Regentlane Ltd
Devonshire Road Industrial Estate, Millom, West Cumbria LA18 4JS
☎01229 770465   Fax 01229 770339
Managing Editor *Alan Bryant*

FOUNDED 1992. *Publishes* local and national guide books, autobiographies and travel-orientated books. 20 titles in 1996. SERIES: *Travellers' Guide; Festivals, Galas and Events of Britain; Towns and Villages of Britain.* Unsolicited mss welcome; no synopses or ideas. *Royalties* paid.

Rivers Oram Press
144 Hemingford Road, London N1 1DE
☎0171 607 0823   Fax 0171 609 2776
Managing Director *Elizabeth Fidlon*

FOUNDED 1990. *Publishes* radical political and

social sciences. No fiction, children's or cookery. *Royalties* paid annually.

The Robinswood Press

30 South Avenue, Stourbridge,
West Midlands DY8 3XY
☎01384 397475　　　Fax 01384 440443

Managing Editor *Christopher J. Marshall*

FOUNDED 1985. *Publishes* education, particularly remedial and Steiner-based. About 3–5 titles a year. TITLES *Waldorf Education, An Introduction; Take Time; Phonic Rhyme Time; The Extra Lesson* (exercises for children with learning difficulties); *Stories for the Festivals; Spotlight on Words; The Eden Mission.* Unsolicited mss, synopses and ideas welcome. *Royalties* paid.

Romer Publications

Smith Yard, Unit 5, 29A Spelman Street,
London E1 6LQ
☎0171 247 3581　　　Fax 0171 247 3581

PO Box 10120, NL–1001 EC, Amsterdam,
The Netherlands ☎/Fax 00 31 20 6769442

Managing Editor *Hubert de Brouwer*

FOUNDED 1986. *Publishes* children's books but main tenet remains critical reflection on origins and legitimacy of established institutions. Specialises in history, education and law. TITLES *The Children's Kosher Funbook* Rabbi L. Book; *The Decline of the House of Herod* Hubert de Brouwer; *African Mythology for Children* Impendoh Dan Iyan; *Dominic Dormouse Goes to Town* Anthony Wall. Will consider sound, coherent and quality mss, synopses or ideas appropriate to its list.
Royalties paid.

Sawd Books

Plackett's Hole, Bicknor, Sittingbourne, Kent ME9 8BA
☎01795 472262　　　Fax 01795 422633

Managing Editor *Susannah Wainman*

FOUNDED 1989 to supply the local interests of the people of Kent. *Publishes* local interest, cookery, gardening and general non-fiction. About 3 titles a year. No unsolicited mss; synopses and ideas welcome (include s.a.e.). No fiction. *Royalties* paid.

Scottish Cultural Press

Unit 14, Leith Walk Business Centre,
130 Leith Walk, Edinburgh EH6 5DT
☎0131 555 5950　　　Fax 0131 555 5018

Chair/Managing Editor *Jill Dick*

Children's Press Administrator *Avril Gray*

FOUNDED 1992. Began publishing in 1993. *Publishes* Scottish interest titles, including cultural, literature, poetry, archaeology, local history, children's fiction and non-fiction. Pre-publication consultancy.

IMPRINTS
Scottish Cultural Press, **Scottish Children's Press**. TITLES *Teach Yourself Doric; John Buchan's Collected Poems; A World of Folk Tales from Multi-Cultural Scotland; A–Z Scots Words for Younger Children; A Doric Dictionary; Scottish Contemporary Poets Series; Scottish Burgh Surveys Series; Classic Children's Games.* Unsolicited mss, synopses and ideas welcome provided return postage is included.
Royalties paid.

Serif

47 Strahan Road, London E3 5DA
☎0181 981 3990　　　Fax 0181 981 3990

Managing Editor *Stephen Hayward*

FOUNDED 1994. *Publishes* cookery, Irish studies and modern history; no fiction. TITLES *Gifts* Nuruddin Farah; *The Crowd in History* George Rudé; *The Alice B. Toklas Cookbook; The Crime Studio* Steve Aylett. Ideas and synopses welcome; no unsolicited mss.
Royalties paid.

Sherlock Publications

6 Bramham Moor, Hill Head, Fareham,
Hampshire PO14 3RU
☎01329 667325

Managing Editor *Philip Weller*

FOUNDED to supply publishing support to a number of Sherlock Holmes societes. *Publishes* Sherlock Holmes studies only. About 14 titles a year. TITLES *Elementary Holmes; Alphabetically, My Dear Watson; Anonymously, My Dear Lestrade; The Annotated Sherlock Holmes Cases.* No unsolicited mss; synopses and ideas are welcome.
Royalties not paid.

Silent Books Ltd

58 Carey Street, London WC2A 2JB
☎0171 405 7484　　　Fax 0171 405 7459

Managing Director *Brian H. W. Hill*

FOUNDED 1985. *Publishes* general art titles, gardening, cookery, community care and books for the gift market, 'all high quality productions'. No fiction. About 12 titles a year. Unsolicited mss, synopses and ideas welcome.

Silver Link Publishing Ltd

Unit 5, Home Farm Close, Church Street,
Wadenhoe, Peterborough PE8 5TE
☎01832 720440   Fax 01832 720531

Managing Editor *William Adams*

FOUNDED 1985 in Lancashire, changed hands in
1990 and now based in Northamptonshire.
Small independent company specialising in nostalgia titles including illustrated books on railways, trams, ships and other transport subjects,
also, under the Past and Present Publishing
imprint, post-war nostalgia on all aspects of social
history. TITLES: *British Railways Past and Present*
series; *British Roads Past and Present* series; *British
Counties, Towns and Cities Past and Present* series;
Daily Life In Britain Past and Present series; *Classic
Steam; Railway Heritage; Maritime Heritage; A
Nostalgic Look at ...* photographic collections;
Silver Link Library of Railway Modelling. Un-
solicited synopses and ideas welcome.
   Fees paid.

Spacelink Books

115 Hollybush Lane, Hampton, Middlesex
TW12 2QY
☎0181 979 3148

Managing Director *Lionel Beer*

FOUNDED 1986. Named after a UFO magazine
published in the 1960/70s. *Publishes* non-fiction
titles connected with UFOs, Fortean phenomena and paranormal events. TITLE *The Moving
Statue of Ballinspittle and Related Phenomena.* No
unsolicited mss; send synopses and ideas.
Publishers of *TEMS News* for the Travel and
Earth Mysteries Society. Distributor of wide
range of related titles and magazines.
   Royalties and fees paid according to contract.

Spindlewood

70 Lynhurst Avenue, Barnstaple, Devon
EX31 2HY
☎01271 71612   Fax 01271 25906

Managing Director *Michael Holloway*

FOUNDED 1980. *Publishes* children's books. 4
titles in 1996. No unsolicited mss; send synopsis with sample chapter or two.
   Royalties paid according to contract.

Springboard

See **Yorkshire Art Circus Ltd**

Richard Stenlake Publishing

Ochiltree Sawmill, The Lade, Ochiltree,
Ayrshire KA18 2NX
☎01290 423114   Fax 01290 423114

Publishes local history, transport, Scottish,
industrial and poetry. 21 titles in 1996. Unsolicited mss, synopses and ideas welcome if
accompanied by s.a.e. *Royalties* paid annually.

Stepney Books Publications

19 Tomlins Grove, Bow, London E3 4NX
☎0181 980 2987

Contact *Jenny Smith*

FOUNDED 1976. A community publishing project run on a part-time basis. Heavily reliant on
fundraising and grants for each new publication
of which there is one about every 18 months.
Publishes history and autobiography of Tower
Hamlets in London. TITLES *Memories of Old
Poplar; In Letters of Gold; Outside the Gate;
Children of the Green.* Unsolicited material considered but 'any publication we undertake to
do can take years to get to press whilst we raise
the money to fund it'.

Stride Publications

See under **Poetry Presses**

Sunk Island Publishing

PO Box 74, Lincoln LN1 1QG
☎01522 575660   Fax 01522 520394

Managing Editor *Michael Blackburn*

FOUNDED 1989. *Publishes* occasional paper-
back fiction. TITLES *Hallowed Ground* Robert
Edric; *Radio Activity* John Murray; *Winterman's
Company* David Lightfoot. Also publishes
poetry under the **Jackson's Arm** imprint.
TITLES *Unlike the Buddha* Nigel Planer; *The
Constructed Space – A Celebration of W. S.
Graham* ed. Duncan & Davidson.
   Royalties by arrangement, on publication.

T.C.L. Publications

23 Castle Rise, Ridgewood, Uckfield, East
Sussex TN22 5UN
☎01825 769019

Managing Editor *Duncan Haws*

FOUNDED 1966 as Travel Creatours Limited
(TCL). *Publishes* nautical books only – the
Merchant Fleet series (31 vols.). 2 titles in 1996.
TITLES *White Star Line; Elder Dempster Line;
Cunard Line; French Line; Holland America Line.*
Unsolicited mss welcome, 'provided they are
in our standard format and subject matters'. No
unsolicited synopses or ideas.
   Royalties paid.

Tamarind Ltd

PO Box 296, Camberley, Surrey GU15 4WD
☎01276 683979   Fax 01276 685365

Managing Editor *Verna Wilkins*

FOUNDED 1987 to publish material in which Black children are given an unselfconscious, positive profile. *Publishes* a series of picture books and other educational material (puzzles, recipes, maps) with the emphasis on a balance between education and fun. Titles include 4 tie-ins with BBC Education.

Tarquin Publications
Stradbroke, Diss, Norfolk IP21 5JP
☎01379 384218   Fax 01379 384289
Managing Editor *Gerald Jenkins*

FOUNDED 1970 as a hobby which gradually grew and now *publishes* mathematical, cut-out models, teaching and pop-up books. Other topics covered if they involve some kind of paper cutting or pop-up scenes. 9 titles in 1997. TITLES *Make Shapes; Sliceforms; The Chemical Helix; High Fashion in Stuart Times; The Paper Jeweller; Dragon Mobiles*. No unsolicited mss; letter with 1–2 page synopses welcome. *Royalties* paid.

Tarragon Press
Moss Park, Ravenstone, Whithorn DG8 8DR
☎01988 850368   Fax 01988 850304
Director/Editorial Head *David Sumner*

FOUNDED 1987. *Publishes* medical and scientific for the layperson. About 3 titles a year. Unsolicited mss, synopses and ideas for books welcome. *Royalties* paid annually.

Tartarus Press
5 Birch Terrace, Hangingbirch Lane, Horam, East Sussex TN21 0PA
☎01435 813224
Managing Director *Raymond Russell*

FOUNDED 1987. *Publishes* fiction, short stories, essays. Also books by and about Arthur Machen. About 4 titles a year. TITLES Short story collections: *Worming the Harpy and Other Bitter Pills* Rhys Hughes; *Ritual and Other Stories* Arthur Machen. Essays: *The Secret of the Sangraal and Other Writings* Arthur Machen. Reference: *The Tartarus Press Guide to First Edition Prices*. Letters: *Containing a Number of Things* Starrett & Millard.

Thames Publishing
14 Barlby Road, London W10 6AR
☎0181 969 3579   Fax 0181 969 1465
Publishing Manager *John Bishop*

FOUNDED 1970. *Publishes* music, and books about English music and musicians, particularly of this century but not pop. About 4 titles a year. No unsolicited mss; send synopses and ideas in first instance.

Tuckwell Press Ltd
The Mill House, Phantassie, East Linton, East Lothian EH40 3DG
☎01620 860164   Fax 01620 860164
Managing Director *John Tuckwell*

FOUNDED 1995. *Publishes* history, literature, ethnology, with a bias towards Scottish and academic texts, also north of England. 50 titles in print. No unsolicited mss but synopses and ideas welcome if relevant to subjects covered. *Royalties* paid annually.

Two Heads Publishing
9 Whitehall Park, London N19 3TS
☎0171 561 1606   Fax 0171 561 1607
Contact *Charles Frewin*

Independent publisher of sport, particularly football and cricket, and guides with a London focus. Synopses and ideas welcome; write in the first instance.
Royalties paid quarterly.

Underhill Press
8 Herriot Way, Thirsk, North Yorkshire YO7 1FL
☎01845 526749   Fax 01845 524347
Managing Editor *Peter Pack*

Publishing arm of the Learning Resources Development Group. Began by publishing conference and seminar proceedings but has since expanded. *Publishes* further and higher education material with particular reference to the management of learning resources; alternative systems of delivering learning; information strategy and IT in colleges; independent and distance learning; new developments in college management. 2–3 titles a year. TITLES *Product & Performance; Citing Your References; Bridging the Gap; Funding and Performance; College Learning Resources: Are They Really Worth It?*. Ideas and synopses welcome. No unsolicited mss.
Payment negotiable.

UNKN
Highfields, Brynymor Road, Aberystwyth, Dyfed SY23 2HX
☎01970 627337   Fax 01970 627337
Managing Editor *Niall Quinn*
Publisher *Siobhán O'Rourke*

FOUNDED 1995 originally to promote the work of writers (primarily poets) engaged in the production of experimental and marginal text – its core commitment. TITLES *However Introduced to the Soles*. Unsolicited mss welcome. Critiques also offered.

Wakefield Historical Publications

19 Pinder's Grove, Wakefield, West Yorkshire
WF1 4AH
☎01924 372748

Managing Editor *Kate Taylor*

FOUNDED 1977 by the Wakefield Historical Society to publish well-researched, scholarly works of regional (namely West Riding) historical significance. 1–2 titles a year. TITLES *Aspects of Medieval Wakefield; Landscape Gardens in West Yorkshire 1680–1880; Coal Kings of Yorkshire; The Aire and Calder Navigation; Right Royal – Wakefield Theatre 1776–1994.* Unsolicited mss, synopses and ideas for books welcome.

Royalties not paid.

Paul Watkins Publishing

18 Adelaide Street, Stamford, Lincolnshire
PE9 2EN
☎01780 56793   Fax 01780 56793

Proprietor *Shaun Tyas*

Publishes non-fiction – medieval, academic, biography, nautical, local history. No fiction. 5 titles in 1996. Unsolicited mss, synopses and ideas for books welcome.

Royalties paid twice yearly.

Westwood Press

44 Boldmere Road, Sutton Coldfield, West Midlands B73 5TD
☎0121 354 5913   Fax 0121 355 6920

Managing Editor *Reg Hollins*

FOUNDED 1955 as a general printer and commenced local publication in the 1970s. *Publishes* local history of the Birmingham area only and specialised printing 'Know How' publications. TITLES *A History of Boldmere; The Book of Brum; Up the Terrace – Down Aston and Lozells.* No unsolicited mss; synopses and ideas welcome.

Royalties paid.

Whittles Publishing

Roseleigh House, Latheronwheel, Caithness
KW5 6DW
☎01593 741240   Fax 01593 741360

Managing Editor *Dr Keith Whittles*

FOUNDED 1986 to offer freelance commissioning and consulting. Started publishing a few years ago in the field of civil engineering and surveying. Also general books with a marine/Scottish theme. 6 titles in 1996. TITLES *Sprayed Concrete; The Geological Interpretation of Well Logs; Rock Lighthouses of Britain.* Unsolicited mss, synopses and ideas welcome on appropriate themes.

Royalties paid annually.

Whyld Publishing Co-op

Moorland House, Kelsey Road, Caistor, Lincolnshire LN7 6SF
☎01472 851374   Fax 01472 851374

Managing Editor *Janie Whyld*

Having taken over former ILEA titles on anti-sexist work with boys, Janie Whyld has gone on to publish a specialist list of educational materials for teachers, trainers and students, with an emphasis on equal opportunities and interpersonal skills. About 2 titles a year. Now moving into 'paperless publishing'. TITLES *Anti-Sexist Work with Boys and Young Men; Equal Opportunities in Training and Groupwork; Using Counselling Skills to Help People Learn; NVQs and the Assessment of Interpersonal Skills; Teaching Assertiveness in Schools and Colleges; The Essence of Yin and Yang; Multicultural Stories.* Mss, synopses/ideas which meet these requirements welcome.

Royalties nominal.

Working Books Ltd

3 Quadrant Court, Middle Street, Taunton, Somerset TA1 1SJ
☎01823 3349946   Fax 01823 3348970

Directors *E. Ephraums, G. Jones*

FOUNDED in 1993. *Publishes* highly illustrated and informative practical photography books covering conventional processes and digital imaging techniques. Launched motorsports imprint **Get a Grip** in 1996. About 7 titles a year. Unsolicited mss, synopses and ideas for books welcome. *Royalties* paid annually.

Works Publishing

12 Blakestones Road, Slaithwaite, Huddersfield, West Yorkshire HD7 5UQ
☎01484 842324/0589 076334
Fax 01484 842324

Managing Editor *Dave W. Hughes*

One-man operation publishing two magazines: *Works* (science fiction) and *The Modern Dance* (music review). Stories and poems welcome for *Works* but no submissions for *Modern Dance*. Unsolicited mss (with s.a.e.) welcome; no synopses/ideas. Advertising rates, single issue rates, guidelines and subscription rates are all available for an s.a.e. *Royalties* not paid. Complimentary copy of magazine.

Yorkshire Art Circus Ltd

School Lane, Glass Houghton, Castleford, West Yorkshire WF10 4QH
☎01977 550401   Fax 01977 512819

Books Coordinator *Reini Schühle*

FOUNDED 1986. *Specialises* in new writing by

first-time authors. *Publishes* autobiography, community books, fiction and local interest (Yorkshire, Humberside). No local history, children's, poetry, reference or nostalgia. TITLES *Shells On a Woven Cord* partnership with MAMA East African Women's Group (bilingual text); *The Story of A House, Askham Grange Women's Open Prison* ed Brian Lewis and Harry Crewe; *On Earth To Make the Numbers Up* Evelyn Haythorne; *Future Conditional* Jo Hatton; *The White Room* Karen Maitland; *The Books Starts Here – How to Publish Your Story* Reini Schühle and Karl Woolley. Unsolicited mss discouraged; authors should send for fact sheet first. **Springboard** fiction imprint launched 1993 mainly for Yorkshire/Humberside-based writers. Write or ring for free catalogue.

Royalties paid.

What Price Vanity?

Graham King investigates a paying business

AUTHORS!
Are you looking for a publisher?
If your book deserves publication, please write to ...

AUTHORS WANTED.
American publisher seeks manuscripts for UK and USA. Please call...

POETS – We urgently require poems for a new anthology
to be published shortly. Send us...

These are typical siren signals of the vanity publishers. Although their tiny advertisements don't say so, the unwritten rule is that a prospective author must put up money before they'll agree to publish a book. It's a big business, sometimes barely operating within the law.

For an aspiring author or the terminally rejected author, the vanity press is the last stop before literary oblivion. Even publication by a vanity press is near-oblivion, for books issued by it seldom get reviewed, are rarely stocked by bookshops, and sell only in extremely small numbers.

Yet it must be said that the principle of vanity publishing *is* defensible, and that there are no doubt vanity practitioners who run respectable businesses satisfying what they perceive as a market need – for a profit, naturally. They claim they've been given a bad press by the crooks in their line of business.

What, then, is vanity publishing exactly? Publishing has always been a hybrid trade. Until the beginning of the 19th century, soliciting funds in advance to pay for publication of a book was a practice common at all levels of literature. Publishers would typically invite wealthy would-be patrons to lavish dinners, after which they would offer or auction shares in a proposed book. The publishing historian Frank Mumby cites, as examples, Henry Fielding's *Tom Jones*, a 26th share of which fetched £8, while a one-hundredth share of Johnson's *Lives of the Poets* fetched £11, and a 1/60th share in Johnson's *Dictionary* sold for £5. Today, many commercial publishing houses will happily accept an arrangement with a major sponsor - say, a bank, an airline, a motor manufacturer - in which the sponsor agrees to buy a substantial quantity of a book often with payment in advance. Such books, often written by arrangement to enhance the standing of such firms, are sent out free as gifts to important customers. This is considered to be an acceptable form of subsidy publishing, and few publishers are inclined to turn away such opportunities.

Another type of subsidy is co-publishing, a simple arrangement where author and publisher (usually a small press) put up the money between them and share the profits after all costs have been met. And still another is the straightforward transaction in which the author gives a cheque to the publisher to cover his bottom line.

The difference between subsidy publishing and vanity publishing is often deliberately confused by the vanity presses themselves, but it is quite clear: the vanity press is in it for profit without risk and the merit or marketability of the work is not a factor at all. A poorly written book of reminiscences, a few bad poems, or an ill-thought-out inspirational tract, the vanity presses will take them all. For decades, they have provided a home for such works as Betty Isaac's *A Breast for Life*, an account of the author's battle with breast cancer; *How to Knurl* by Wesley E. McColgan; *Mr Wisdom's Smidgens of Wisdom*, Richard Snyder's *65 Buttercream Flowers*, R. Lee Eddy III's *What You Should Know about Marriage, Divorce, Annulment, Separation and Community Property in Louisiana*, and Joyce Richard's *Diderot's Dilemma: His Evaluation Regarding the Possibility of Moral Freedom in a Deterministic Universe* – all Exposition Press titles of the 1970s. There is nothing intrinsically wrong with paying to have a book published, of course, providing the author knows what he is buying, and that is the difficulty of vanity publishing. To understand the pitfalls it is worth following what happens when someone responds to a vanity ad.

One of the most buoyant activities on the vanity front is the publication of poetry. In a rambling but engaging autobiography, American vanity publisher Edward Uhlan – self-styled Dean of Subsidy Publishing and the Rogue of Publishers' Row – recounted how he started his business by taking money from poets in the mid-1930s. He may not have invented the idea, but the techniques he describes are still typical today. Uhlan remembered that when he had been the editor of his high school magazine, many students vied with each other to have their poetry accepted, often offering bribes to improve their chances. It seemed to him that a fact of literary life was staring him in the face, that poets would pay, and he decided there could be a business in it. For three months he haunted the New York Public Library, hunting down the names of anyone who had written poetry, from back issues of magazines, newspapers, and directories. Then with $15 severance pay from his previous employer – it was now in the middle of the Depression and there were no jobs at all – he bought 600 letter-headed sheets to announce a poetry contest, offering a $25 Liberty Bond for the best poems submitted. He followed this letter with another, this time offering to print the poems in an anthology provided the poet subscribed $4 a copy or $5 for two copies. For an extra 50 cents the poet could have his or her name stamped in gold on the cover.

'With the mailing of the letters I was in business,' Uhlan recalled. 'I called my enterprise the Adastra Publishing Company and I altered my name to Igor Ulianov, feeling that this would be more to the taste of the recherché clientele I was trying to lure.' Three weeks later, he received his first cheque for $5 from the wife of an Oregon doctor, and from then on the money flowed.

Sixty years later, the *modus operandi* of the paid-for poetry publisher is the same, even to the gold-blocked personalised cover. And so is the ethical argument. 'If anyone had brought up the question of ethics,' Uhlan reasoned, 'I would have argued then, as I would argue now, that in such a matter ethics and honesty are synonymous: people were willing to pay me for a specified service, and if I performed that service to their satisfaction the moderate profits I made were certainly ethical - and deserved.'

Uhlan's argument for the vanity option is fine providing the publisher lives up to performing the agreed service to the satisfaction of his clients. Unfortunately, for thousands of disgruntled vanity authors, the reverse is more often the case. What actually goes on behind the doors of some vanity houses amounts to plain fraud. According to Martin Baron, formerly an editor for a vanity publisher, vanity publishing is to legitimate publishing as loansharking is to banking. During his time at a vanity house, Baron witnessed all the cunning of the craft. Because the author pays, the unscrupulous vanity publisher will accept *any* manuscript. Last year, Johnathon Clifford, founder of the National Poetry Foundation, set out to prove the point by composing the worst poem he could think of using words plucked at random from the Yellow Pages. His submission to the International Library of Poetry was immediately taken up for publication in an anthology. There was just one proviso. Mr Clifford was invited to buy the 'classic quality hardbound volume' in which his poem was to appear for a 'discount price' of £50.

Because he invests not a penny in a book, but instead is geared to make a profit from it anyway, there is no incentive for the vanity publisher to make it saleable. This simple fact escapes most starry-eyed authors because it is effectively disguised in the contract he signs. This usually binds the author to pay 30% of the fee upfront, 30% on receipt of proofs, and the remainder upon publication. This is the nitty-gritty part. But the rest of the contract will positively glow with promise: what will be paid to the author for subsequent reprintings, subsidiary and foreign rights, and so on. He will also note with joy that the vanity publisher offers him royalties of up to 40% of the retail price of his book's first printing, when he has been told that commercial publishers offer only 10 to 15%. There are a couple of fallacies here. First, vanity books might sell in dozens, possibly hundreds - but never, with rare exceptions, in thousands. There have been some books that failed, to the author's dismay although not the publisher's, to sell a single copy. So the vanity house, having been paid to print, say, 1,500 copies of a book, is well protected against it selling more than a small proportion of the edition. In any case, if in the unlikely event of royalties becoming payable, the author is merely receiving 40% of his own money.

Other fairly standard clauses in a vanity contract include a quota of 'free' copies to the author; if he requires more, he has to pay for them. In reality, he is paying for them *twice*! The stock of unsold books usually remains the property of the publisher, so if there is a chance to remainder them later, he takes the proceeds. Then there is a fine-print definition of printing or publishing a book. In vanity-speak, this does not necessarily include the binding of a book. Unless otherwise directed, only a certain number of an edition will actually be bound; the rest will remain as flat printed sheets until required, which is probably never. Of an edition of 1,500 copies, perhaps as few as 200 will emerge from the bindery. If these are sold and there are cash orders for more (including the author's cash orders), the requisite number will be bound, but no more.

Another impressive-looking clause in a typical contract has the publisher offering to publish a second edition at his own expense – providing the entire original edition is sold first. As the clever combination of quantity and retail price will virtually ensure this will never happen, the offer is purely hypothetical.

The services a vanity house provides – which the author pays for – include such things as editing, design, sending out review copies, marketing and sometimes advertising. These services sound better than they really are. It is almost impossible to improve a really bad idea or wretched writing, so no great effort is expended here. But the vanity client is really let down when the day of publication arrives. As Martin Baron observes,

'It is at this point, just as the book is about to be published, that the author's interest in its fate is at its most intense. Authors are keenly interested in the promotion and distribution of their books, and vanity authors especially so. It is the vanity author's only chance of recovering the thousands of pounds he has paid the publisher, and it is just here, when for the first time the circle broadens to include others in addition to the author and publisher, that the fraud of vanity publishing becomes the more obvious. It is not now the author who must be convinced, but the reviewers, booksellers and the reading public.'

A vanity publisher will usually undertake to distribute a certain number of review copies, but this task is pretty academic; vanity books are invariably consigned to the wastebasket on sight, although the regional press might run notices if there is some local interest in the book. It is equally rare for a vanity book to be advertised, and if it is it is usually an additional cost to the author.

Finally, and crucially, we arrive at the distribution and marketing operation. For most vanity books, neither exists. Again, unless the book reflects local interest or occupies some marketable niche – say, a book about hospital humour designed for sale at hospital gift shops or nearby bookstores – retailers will not be interested. Most vanity books are therefore sold through the vanity house's mail order operation, with most of the work – circularising friends, common interest groups – by the author. As Baron sourly observes, 'Only a vanity publisher sells vanity books.' In practice, unless the vanity house has an efficient and proven distribution and sales set-up, the author might as well take all the copies, because if they are to be sold he is going to have to do it himself.

There is rarely any other comeback. It is true that in June 1996 there was a milestone judgement in the West London County Court which required Excalibur Press to repay money advanced for the publication of a book. Joanna Steans got back her £2,100 because, as she bravely conceded, 'the book is of such poor quality that it is unsaleable'. But few authors would be prepared to follow her on that route.

A slender hope for circumventing the vanity publishers rests on the new desk-top technology and the opportunities it provides for self-publishing. Even so, self-publication is for the few. It demands time and at least some knowledge of editing, printing, book design, publicity and marketing. Many authors simply do not have either the time, energy or inclination to embark upon it and that is one of the reasons why the vanity presses are big business. Moreover, it is recession-proof: when trade publishers cut back their output, more authors beat a path to vanity's door. A vanity press is founded, as any proprietor knows, on the solid rock of the human ego.

UK Packagers

The Albion Press Ltd
Spring Hill, Idbury, Oxfordshire OX7 6RU
☎01993 831094   Fax 01993 831982
Chairman/Managing Director Emma
  Bradford

FOUNDED 1984 to produce high-quality illustrated titles. *Commissions* illustrated trade titles,
particularly children's, English literature, social
history and art. About 4 titles a year. TITLES
Christmas Fairy Tales Isabelle Brent; *Tales of
Heartsease Wood* Neil Philip & Tracey
Williamson; *Odin's Family* Neil Philip & Mary
Clare Foa. Unsolicited synopses and ideas for
books not welcome.
  Royalties paid; fees paid for introductions and
partial contributions.

Alphabet & Image Ltd
See **Marston House** under **UK Publishers**

Andromeda Oxford Ltd
11–15 The Vineyard, Abingdon, Oxfordshire
OX14 3PX
☎01235 550296   Fax 01235 550330
Managing Director Mark Ritchie
Approx. Annual Turnover £7 million

FOUNDED 1986. *Commissions* adult and junior
international illustrated reference, both single
volume and series. About 30 titles a year.

DIVISIONS
Adult Books *Graham Bateman* (Editorial
Director); **Children's Books** *Derek Hall*
(Editorial Director); **Andromeda Interactive**
(CD-ROMs) TITLES *Encyclopedia of World
Geography; Cultural Atlases; Science Encyclopedia;
Atlas of World History; Factfiles; Interactive Space
Encyclopedia; Complete Shakespeare; Classic Library;
Medical Science* on CD-ROM. Approach by
letter in the first instance.

Archival Facsimiles Ltd
The Old Bakery, 52 Crown Street, Banham,
Norwich, Norfolk NR16 2HW
☎01953 887277   Fax 01953 888361
Chief Executive *Cris de Boos*

FOUNDED 1986. Specialist private publishers
for individuals and organisations. Produces
scholarly reprints for the **British Library**
among others, plus high-quality limited edition
publications for academic/business organisations in Europe and the USA, ranging from
leather-bound folios of period print reproduc-
tions to small illustrated booklets. *Publishes*
Antarctic exploration titles (about 2 a year)
under the **Erskine Press** imprint. No unsolicited mss. Ideas welcome.
  Royalties paid twice yearly.

AS Publishing
73 Montpelier Rise, London NW11 9DU
☎0181 458 3552   Fax 0181 458 0618
Managing Director *Angela Sheehan*

FOUNDED 1987. *Commissions* children's illustrated non-fiction. No unsolicited synopses or
ideas for books, but approaches welcome from
experienced authors, editors and illustrators in
this field.
  Fees paid.

BCS Publishing Ltd
1 Bignell Park Barns, Kirtlington Road,
Chesterton, Bicester, Oxon OX6 8TD
☎01869 324423   Fax 01869 324385
Managing Director *Steve McCurdy*
Approx. Annual Turnover £350,000

Commissions general interest non-fiction for
international co-edition market.

Belitha Press Ltd
London House, Great Eastern Wharf, Parkgate
Road, London SW11 4NQ
☎0171 978 6330   Fax 0171 223 4936
Editorial Director *Mary-Jane Wilkins*

FOUNDED 1980. *Commissions* children's non-
fiction in all curriculum areas. About 50 titles a
year. All titles are expected to sell in at least
four co-editions. TITLES *Built for Speed; Rebels
With a Cause; Travelling Through Time; Body
Works; All About Colour; Introducing Composers;
Take It Apart; Touch/Shape/Pattern; The World
in the Time Of...* (8 titles exploring history and
culture around the world at different times);
The World's Top Ten; Who Am I? (a series of
puzzle books for young children). No unsolicited mss. Synopses and ideas for books welcome from experienced children's writers.

Bellew Publishing Co. Ltd
See entry under **UK Publishers**

Bender Richardson White

PO Box 266, Uxbridge, Middlesex UB9 5BD
☎01895 832444   Fax 01895 835213

Partners *Lionel Bender, Kim Richardson, Ben White*

FOUNDED 1990 to produce illustrated non-fiction for children aged 7–14 for publishers in the UK and abroad. 20 titles in 1996. Unsolicited material not welcome.

Fees paid.

David Bennett Books Ltd

15 High Street, St Albans, Hertfordshire AL3 4ED
☎01727 855878   Fax 01727 864085

Managing Director *David Bennett*

FOUNDED 1989. Producer of children's books: picture and novelty books, interactive and board books, baby gifts and non-fiction. Synopses and ideas for books welcome. No fiction or poetry.

Payment both fees and royalties.

BLA Publishing Ltd

1 Christopher Road, East Grinstead, West Sussex RH19 3BT
☎01342 318980   Fax 01342 410980

Owner *Ling Kee (UK) Ltd*

Packagers of multi-volume encyclopedias for younger readers, and information book series on various topics. Now only producing a minimal number of books.

Payment varies according to contract (reference books tend to be flat fees; royalties for single author or illustrator).

Book Packaging and Marketing

3 Murswell Lane, Silverstone, Towcester, Northamptonshire NN12 8UT
☎01327 858380   Fax 01327 858380

Contact *Martin F. Marix Evans*

FOUNDED 1989. Essentially a project management service, handling books demanding close designer/editor teamwork or complicated multi-contributor administration, for publishers, business 'or anyone who needs one'. Mainly illustrated adult non-fiction including travel, historical, home reference, military and coffee-table books. No fiction or poetry. 3–5 titles a year. Proposals considered; and writers are often required for projects in development. TITLES *Royal College of Nursing Manual of Family Health; Pregnant and Fit; Canals of England; Contemporary Photographers*, 3rd ed.; *Michelin's Paris in Your Pocket; The Battles of the Somme 1916-18; Britain's Military Heritage.*

Payment Authors contract direct with client publishers; fees paid on first print usually and royalties on reprint but this depends on publisher.

Breslich & Foss Ltd

20 Wells Mews, London W1P 3FJ
☎0171 580 8774   Fax 0171 580 8784

Director *Paula Breslich*

Approx. Annual Turnover £1.5 million

Packagers of non-fiction titles only, including art, children's, crafts, gardening and health. Unsolicited mss welcome but synopses preferred. Include s.a.e. with all submissions.

Royalties paid twice yearly.

Brown Wells and Jacobs Ltd

Forresters Hall, 25–27 Westow Street, London SE19 3RY
☎0181 771 5115   Fax 0181 771 9994

Managing Director *Graham Brown*

FOUNDED 1979. *Commissions* non-fiction, novelty, pre-school and first readers, natural history and science. About 40 titles a year. Unsolicited synopses and ideas for books welcome.

Fees paid.

Calmann & King Ltd

71 Great Russell Street, London WC1B 3BN
☎0171 831 6351   Fax 0171 831 8356

Chairman *Robin Hyman*

Managing Director *Laurence King*

Approx. Annual Turnover £4 million

FOUNDED 1976. *Commissions* books on art, the decorative arts, design, architecture, graphic design, carpets and textiles. About 30 titles a year. Unsolicited synopses and ideas for books welcome.

Royalties paid twice yearly.

Cameron Books (Production) Ltd

PO Box 1, Moffat, Dumfriesshire DG10 9SU
☎01683 220808   Fax 01683 220012

Directors *Ian A. Cameron, Jill Hollis*

Approx. Annual Turnover £350,000

Commissions natural history, social history, decorative arts, fine arts including environmental art, collectors' reference, educational reference, gardening, cookery, conservation, countryside, film and design. About 6 titles a year. Unsolicited synopses and ideas for books welcome.

Payment varies with each contract.

Candle Books

See **Angus Hudson Ltd**

Chancerel International Publishers Ltd

120 Long Acre, London WC2E 9PA
☎0171 240 2811   Fax 0171 836 4186
Managing Director *W. D. B. Prowse*

FOUNDED 1976. *Commissions* educational books, and *publishes* language-teaching materials in most languages. Language teachers/writers often required as authors/consultants, especially native speakers other than English.

Payment generally by flat fee but royalties sometimes.

Philip Clark Ltd

53 Calton Avenue, Dulwich, London
SE21 7DF
☎0181 693 5605   Fax 0181 299 4647
Managing Director *Philip Clark*

Founder member of the **Book Packagers Association**. *Commissions* heavily illustrated titles on a variety of subjects. TITLES include *Travellers Wine Guides* series (first edition sold over 100,000 copies in several languages; second edition published in 1997/8).

Fees paid.

Concorde House Books

See **Angus Hudson Ltd**

Roger Coote Publishing

Gissing's Farm, Fressingfield, Eye, Suffolk
IP21 5SH
☎01379 588044   Fax 01379 588055
Director *Roger Goddard-Coote*

FOUNDED 1993. Packager of high-quality children's and adult non-fiction for trade, school and library markets. About 24 titles a year. No fiction.

Fees paid; no royalties.

Diagram Visual Information Ltd

195 Kentish Town Road, London
NW5 8SY
☎0171 482 3633   Fax 0171 482 4932
Managing Director *Bruce Robertson*

FOUNDED 1967. Producer of library, school, academic and trade reference books. About 10 titles a year. Unsolicited synopses and ideas for books welcome.

Fees paid; no payment for sample material/submissions for consideration.

Dorling Kindersley Ltd

See under **UK Publishers**

Eddison Sadd Editions

St Chad's House, 148 King's Cross Road,
London WC1X 9DH
☎0171 837 1968   Fax 0171 837 2025
Managing Director *Nick Eddison*
Editorial Director *Ian Jackson*
Approx. Annual Turnover £3.5 million

FOUNDED 1982. Produces a wide range of popular illustrated non-fiction, with books published in 25 countries. Ideas and synopses are welcome but titles must have international appeal.

Royalties paid twice yearly; flat fees paid when appropriate.

Erskine Press

See **Archival Facsimiles Ltd**

Expert Publications Ltd

Sloe House, Halstead, Essex CO9 1PA
☎01787 474744   Fax 01787 474700
Chairman *Dr. D. G. Hessayon*

FOUNDED 1993. Produces the Expert series of books by Dr. D. G. Hessayon. TITLES *The Flowering Shrub Expert; The Greenhouse Expert; The Flower Arranging Expert; The Container Expert; The Bulb Expert.* No unsolicited material.

First Rank Publishing

23 Ditchling Rise, Brighton, East Sussex
BN1 4QL
☎01273 279934   Fax 01273 297128
Contact *Byron Jacobs, Andrew Kinsman*

FOUNDED 1996. Packagers and publishers of sports, games and leisure books. 12–15 titles a year. Also providers of editorial, production and typesetting services. No unsolicited mss but ideas and synopses welcome.

Royalties usually fees.

Geddes & Grosset Ltd

See entry under **UK Publishers**

Angus Hudson Ltd

Concorde House, Grenville Place, Mill Hill,
London NW7 4JN
☎0181 959 3668   Fax 0181 959 3678
Chairman *Angus R. M. Hudson*
Managing Director *Nicholas Jones*
Approx. Annual Turnover £2.5 million

FOUNDED 1977. Management buyout from Maxwell Communications in 1989. Leading packager of religious co-editions. *Commissions* Christian books for all ages and co-editioning throughout the world. About 60 titles in 1996.

IMPRINTS **Candle Books**; **Concorde**

House Books. Prototype dummies complete with illustrations welcome for consideration. No mss on their own, please.
Royalties paid.

Lexus Ltd
205 Bath Street, Glasgow G2 4HZ
☎0141 221 5266   Fax 0141 226 3139
Managing/Editorial Director *P. M. Terrell*
FOUNDED 1980. Compiles bilingual reference, language and phrase books. About 20 titles a year. TITLES *Rough Guide Phrasebooks; Collins Italian Concise Dictionary; Harrap Study Aids; Hugo's Phrase Books; Harrap Shorter French Dictionary* (revised); *Impact Specialist Bilingual Glossaries; Oxford Student's Japanese Learner*. No unsolicited material. Books are mostly commissioned. Freelance contributors employed for a wide range of languages.
Payment generally flat fee.

Lionheart Books
10 Chelmsford Square, London
NW10 3AR
☎0181 459 0453   Fax 0181 451 3681
Senior Partner *Lionel Bender*
Partner *Madeleine Samuel*
Designer *Ben White*
Approx. Annual Turnover £250,000
A design/editorial packaging team. Titles are primarily commissioned from publishers. Highly illustrated non-fiction for children aged 8–14, mostly natural history, history and general science. About 20 titles a year.
Payment generally flat fee.

Market House Books Ltd
2 Market House, Market Square, Aylesbury, Buckinghamshire HP20 1TN
☎01296 84911   Fax 01296 437073
Directors *Dr Alan Isaacs, Dr John Daintith*
FOUNDED 1970. Formerly Laurence Urdang Associates. *Commissions* dictionaries, encyclopedias and reference. About 15 titles a year. TITLES *Concise Medical Dictionary; Brewer's 20th Century Phrase and Fable; Oxford Dictionary for Science Writers and Editors; Concise Dictionary of Business; Concise Dictionary of Finance; Bloomsbury Thesaurus; Larousse Thematica* (6 volume encyclopedia); *Collins English Dictionary; The Macmillan Encyclopedia; Grolier Bibliographical Encyclopedia of Scientists* (10 vols); *Oxford Dictionary for the Business World*. Unsolicited material not welcome as most books are compiled in-house.
Fees paid.

Marshall Cavendish Books
119 Wardour Street, London W1V 3TD
☎0171 734 6710   Fax 0171 439 1423
Head of Books *Ellen Dupont*
Approx. Annual Turnover £3 million
A division of Marshall Cavendish Partworks Ltd. FOUNDED 1968. Primarily partwork material in book form but also originates its own material. Freelance editorial services sought on occasions. *Fees* paid, not royalties.

Marshall Editions Ltd
170 Piccadilly, London W1V 9DD
☎0171 629 0079   Fax 0171 834 0785
Publisher *Barbara Anderson*
Editorial Director *Sophie Collins*
FOUNDED 1977. *Commissions* non-fiction, including thematic atlases, leisure, self-improvement, health and visual information for children. TITLES *The Human Body Explained; Revelations: The Medieval World; The Robot Zoo; The Natural History of Evolution; Your Personal Trainer*.

MM Productions Ltd
16–20 High Street, Ware, Hertfordshire
SG12 9BX
☎01920 466003   Fax 01920 466003
Chairman/Managing Director *Mike Moran*
Packager and publisher. TITLES *MM Publisher Database; MM Printer Database* (available in UK, European and international editions).

Oyster Books Ltd
Unit 4, Kirklea Farm, Badgworth, Axbridge, Somerset BS26 2QH
☎01934 732251   Fax 01934 732514
Managing Director *Jenny Wood*
FOUNDED 1985. Packagers of quality books and book/toy/gift items for children of pre-school age to ten years. About 20 titles a year. Most material is created in-house.
Payment usually fees.

Parke Sutton Ltd
Orchard House, Grange Farm, Ashwellthorpe, Norfolk NR16 1ET
☎01508 489212   Fax 01508 489212
Director *Ian S. McIntyre*
FOUNDED 1982. Produces newspapers, magazines and reference books for organisations and training offices; and packages books for publishers. Unsolicited synopses and ideas for books welcome. S.a.e. essential. *Royalties* paid twice yearly; fees sometimes paid rather than royalties.

Playne Books Limited

Chapel House, Trefin, Haverfordwest,
Pembrokeshire SA62 5AU
☎01348 837073   Fax 01348 837063

Director *Gill Davies*
Design & Production *David Playne*

FOUNDED 1987. *Commissions* highly illustrated
and practical books on any subject. Currently
developing a new list for young children.
Unsolicited synopses and ideas for books welcome.

Royalties paid 'on payment from publishers'.
Fees sometimes paid instead of royalties.

Mathew Price Ltd

The Old Glove Factory, Bristol Road,
Sherborne, Dorset DT9 4HP
☎01935 816010   Fax 01935 816310

Chairman/Managing Director *Mathew Price*
Approx. Annual Turnover £1 million

Commissions high-quality, full-colour picture
books and fiction for young children; also novelty and non-fiction. Unsolicited synopses and
ideas for books welcome.

Fees sometimes paid instead of royalties.

Quarto Publishing

The Old Brewery, 6 Blundell Street, London
N7 9BH
☎0171 700 6700/333 0000
Fax 0171 700 4191/700 0077

Chairman *Laurence Orbach*

FOUNDED 1976. Britain's largest book packager. *Commissions* illustrated non-fiction,
including painting, graphic design, visual arts,
history, cookery, gardening, crafts. *Publishes*
under the Apple imprint. Unsolicited syn-
opses/ideas for books welcome.

Payment flat fees paid.

Sadie Fields Productions Ltd

3D West Point, 36–37 Warple Way, London
W3 0RG
☎0181 746 1171   Fax 0181 746 1170

Directors *David Fielder, Sheri Safran*

FOUNDED 1981. Quality children's books with
international co-edition potential: pop-ups,
three-dimensional, novelty, picture and board
books, 1500 words maximum. About 30 titles
a year. Approach with preliminary letter and
sample material in the first instance. *Publishes* in
the UK under the **Tango Books** imprint.

Royalties based on a per-copy-sold rate and
paid in stages.

Salariya Book Company Ltd

25 Marlborough Place, Brighton, East Sussex
BN1 1UB
☎01273 603306   Fax 01273 693857

Managing Director *David Salariya*

FOUNDED 1989. Children's information books
– fiction, history, art, music, science, architecture, education and picture books. No unsolicited material.

Payment by arrangement.

Savitri Books Ltd

115J Cleveland Street, London W1P 5PN
☎0171 436 9932   Fax 0171 580 6330

Managing Director *Mrinalini S. Srivastava*
Approx. Annual Turnover £200,000

FOUNDED 1983. Keen to work 'very closely with
authors/illustrators and try to establish long-term
relationships with them, doing more books with
the same team of people'. *Commissions* high-
quality, illustrated non-fiction, crafts, New Age
and nature. About 7 titles a year. Unsolicited
synopses and ideas for books 'very welcome'.

Royalties 10–15% of the total price paid by
the publisher.

Sheldrake Press

188 Cavendish Road, London SW12 0DA
☎0181 675 1767   Fax 0181 675 7736

Publisher *Simon Rigge*
Approx. Annual Turnover £250,000

Commissions illustrated non-fiction: history,
travel, style, cookery and stationery. TITLES *The
Victorian House Book; The Shorter Mrs Beeton; The
Power of Steam; The Railway Heritage of Britain;
Wild Britain; Wild France; Wild Spain; Wild Italy;
Wild Ireland; The Kate Greenaway Baby Book.*
Synopses and ideas for books welcome, but not
interested in fiction.

Fees or royalties paid.

Templar Publishing

Pippbrook Mill, London Road, Dorking,
Surrey RH4 1JE
☎01306 876361   Fax 01306 889097

Managing Director/Editorial Head
     Amanda Wood
Approx. Annual Turnover £5 million

FOUNDED 1981. A division of The Templar
Company plc. *Commissions* novelty and gift
books, children's illustrated non-fiction, educational and story books, children's illustrated
non-fiction. 100–175 titles a year. Synopses
and ideas for books welcome.

Royalties by arrangement.

Toucan Books Ltd

Fourth Floor, 32–38 Saffron Hill, London
EC1N 8BS
☎0171 404 8181   Fax 0171 404 8282
Managing Director *Robert Sackville-West*
Approx. Annual Turnover £1,400,000

FOUNDED 1985. Specialises in international co-editions and fee-based editorial, design and production services to film. *Commissions* illustrated non-fiction only. About 20 titles a year. TITLES *The Eventful Century; The Earth, Its Wonders, Its Secrets; Leith's Cookery Bible; Charles II; The Complete Photography Course; Journeys into the Past* series; *People and Places.* Unsolicited synopses and ideas for books welcome. No fiction or non-illustrated titles.

Royalties twice yearly; fees paid in addition to or instead of royalties.

Touchstone Publishing Ltd

Gissing's Farm, Fressingfield, Eye, Suffolk
IP21 5SH
☎01379 588044   Fax 01379 588055
Chairman/Managing Director *Roger Goddard-Coote*
Editorial Director *Edwina Conner*

FOUNDED 1989. Packager of children's non-fiction for trade, school and library markets. About 8 titles a year. No fiction, textbooks or adult material. Synopses and ideas welcome. Include s.a.e. for return.

Fees paid; no royalties.

Victoria House Publishing Ltd

King's Court, Parsonage Lane, Bath BA1 1ER
☎01225 463401   Fax 01225 460942
Managing Director *Clyde Hunter*
Approx. Annual Turnover £9.5 million

Part of the Reader's Digest Group. Trade imprint: Reader's Digest Children's Books. *Commissions* children's projects in novelty or interactive formats – acetate, pop-up, toy add-ons. Also religious list. About 50 titles a year.

Royalties or flat fee according to contract.

Wordwright Books

25 Oakford Road, London NW5 1AJ
☎0171 284 0056   Fax 0171 284 0041
Contact *Charles Perkins*

FOUNDED by ex-editorial people 'so good writing always has a chance with us'. *Commissions* illustrated non-fiction: social history and comment, military history, women's issues, sport. *Specialises* in military and social history, natural history, science, art, cookery, and gardening. About 4–6 titles a year. Unsolicited synopses/ideas (a paragraph or so) welcome for illustrated non-fiction.

Payment usually fees but royalties (twice-yearly) paid for sales above a specified number of copies.

Working Partners Ltd

4 Furber Street, London W6 0HE
☎0181 741 4387   Fax 0181 563 9965
Contact *Ben Baglio, Rod Ritchie*

Specialises in children's mass-market series fiction books. Creators of *Animal Ark; Mystery Club; Little Sister; Internet Detectives; Puppy Patrol; Sheltie.* No unsolicited mss.

Payment both fees and royalties by arrangement.

Zöe Books Ltd

15 Worthy Lane, Winchester, Hampshire
SO23 7AB
☎01962 851318   Fax 01962 843015
Managing Director *Imogen Dawson*
Director *Bob Davidson*

FOUNDED 1990. *Specialises* in full-colour information and reference books for schools and libraries. *Publishes* about 30 titles a year. Tends to generate own ideas but happy to hear from freelance writers and editors of information books. Does *not* publish picture books or fiction.

Fees paid.

Book Clubs

Artists' Choice
PO Box 3, Huntingdon, Cambridgeshire
PE18 0QX
☎01832 710201   Fax 01832 710488
Specialises in books for the amateur artist at all levels of ability.

BCA (Book Club Associates)
87 Newman Street, London W1P 4EN
☎0171 637 0341   Fax 0171 291 3525
With two million members, BCA is Britain's largest book club organisation. Consists of 19 book clubs, catering for general and specific interests: Ancient & Medieval History Book Club, The Arts Guild, The Book Club of Ireland, Book of the Month Club, Discovery The Book Club for Children, Classical Music Direct, The English Book Club, Executive World, Fantasy and Science Fiction, History Guild, Home Computer Club, The Literary Guild, Military and Aviation Book Society, Music Direct, Mystery and Thriller Guild, The New Home & Garden Guild, Quality Paperbacks Direct, Railway Book Club, World Books.

Bookmarks Club
265 Seven Sisters Road, Finsbury Park, London N4 2DE
☎0181 802 6145   Fax 0181 802 3835
New and recent books of interest to Socialists at discount prices. Write, phone or fax for latest list.

Books for Children (Time-Life Entertainment Group Ltd)
4 Furzeground Way, Stockley Park, Uxbridge, Middlesex UB11 1DP
☎0181 606 3061   Fax 0181 606 3099
Hardcover and paperback books for children from newly-born to teenage. Also occasional adult fiction and non-fiction – cookery, family interest, parenting guides.

The Bookworm Club
Heffers Booksellers, 20 Trinity Street, Cambridge CB2 1TY
☎01223 568650   Fax 01223 568591
Sells paperback books for children through schools.

Cygnus Book Club
PO Box 15, Llandeilo, Carmarthenshire
SA19 6YX
☎01550 777693   Fax 01550 777569
'Books which make people think.' Information books on spirituality, complementary healthcare, environmental issues, plus some management and education titles.

The Folio Society
44 Eagle Street, London WC1R 4FS
☎0171 400 4200   Fax 0171 400 4242
Fine editions of classic titles and reference; also some children's classics.

Letterbox Library
Children's Book Cooperative,
Unit 2D/2nd Floor, Leroy House,
436 Essex Road, London N1 3QP
☎0171 226 1633   Fax 0171 226 1768
Hard and softcover, non-sexist and multicultural books for children from one to teenage.

Poetry Book Society
See under **Organisations of Interest to Poets**

Readers Union Ltd
Brunel House, Newton Abbot, Devon
TQ12 2DW
☎01626 336424   Fax 01626 664463
Has ten book clubs, all dealing with specific interests: Country Sports Book Society, The Craft Club, Craftsman Book Society, Creative Living Book Club, Creative Books Plus, Equestrian Book Society, Gardeners Book Society, Needlecrafts with Cross Stitch, Focal Point, Ramblers & Climbers Book Society.

Red House Book Clubs
See **Scholastic Ltd** under **UK Publishers**

Scholastic School Book Club
See **Scholastic Ltd** under **UK Publishers**

The Softback Preview (Time-Life UK)
4 Furzeground Way, Stockley Park, Uxbridge, Middlesex UB11 1DP
☎0181 606 3073   Fax 0181 606 3099
Mainly serious non-fiction.

The Women's Press Book Club

The Women's Press, 34 Great Sutton Street, London EC1V 0DX
☎0171 251 3007
Fax 0171 608 1938

'Best women writers from more than 70 publishers.' Fiction, biography and autobiography; popular mind, body and spirit; health and self-help; also a collection of women's studies, social issues and current affairs.

UK Agents

★ = Members of the **Association of Authors' Agents**

The Agency (London) Ltd★

24 Pottery Lane, Holland Park, London
W11 4LZ
☎0171 727 1346   Fax 0171 727 9037

Contact *Stephen Durbridge, Sheila Lemon, Leah Schmidt, Sebastian Born, Julia Kreitman, Bethan Evans, Hilary Delamere*

FOUNDED 1995. *Handles* children's fiction, TV, film, theatre, radio scripts. No adult fiction or non-fiction. Unsolicited TV, film and radio scripts welcome. Send letter with s.a.e.. No reading fee. CLIENTS include William Boyd, Andrew Davies, Jimmy McGovern, Sam Mendes. *Commission* Home 10%; USA various.

Aitken & Stone Ltd★

29 Fernshaw Road, London SW10 0TG
☎0171 351 7561   Fax 0171 376 3594

Contact *Gillon Aitken, Brian Stone, Antony Harwood*

FOUNDED 1984. *Handles* fiction and non-fiction. No plays or scripts unless by existing clients. Send preliminary letter, with synopsis and return postage, in the first instance. No reading fee. CLIENTS Pat Barker, Agatha Christie, Sebastian Faulks, Germaine Greer, Alan Hollinghurst, Susan Howatch, V. S. Naipul, Caryl Phillips, Piers Paul Read, Paul Theroux. *Commission* Home 10%; US 15%; Translation 20%.

Jacintha Alexander Associates

See **Lucas Alexander Whitley**

Darley Anderson Literary, TV & Film Agency★

Estelle House, 11 Eustace Road, London
SW6 1JB
☎0171 385 6652   Fax 0171 386 5571

Contact *Darley Anderson, Kerith Biggs (Crime/ Foreign Rights), Gabi Chase (Film/TV Scripts), Elizabeth Wright (Contemporary Women's Fiction/Erotica)*

Run by an ex-publisher with a sympathetic touch and a knack for spotting and encouraging talent who is known to have negotiated a £150,000 UK advance and a TV mini-series deal for one first-time novelist and a £150,000 advance and a $150,000 US advance for another first-time novelist. *Handles* commercial fiction & non-fiction; also scripts for film, TV and radio. No academic books or poetry. *Special interests* Fiction: all types of thrillers and all types of women's fiction including contemporary, 20th-century romantic sagas, erotica, women in jeopardy; also crime (cosy/hard-boiled/historical), horror, fantasy, comedy and Irish novels. Non-fiction: celebrity autobiographies, biographies, 'true life' women in jeopardy, popular psychology, self-improvement, diet, health, beauty and fashion, humour/cartoons, gardening, cookery, inspirational and religious. Send letter and outline with first 3 chapters; return postage/s.a.e. essential. CLIENTS Tessa Barclay, Paul Carson, Lee Child, Martina Cole, Joseph Corvo, Debbie Frank, Joan Jonker, Martica Heaner, Beryl Kingston, Frank Lean, Deborah McKinlay, Lesley Pearse, Allan Pease, Adrian Plass, Ben Richards, Fred Secombe, Jane Walmsley. *Commission* Home 15%; US & Translation 20%; *Overseas associates* Renaissance-Swanson Film and Literary Agency (LA/Hollywood); and leading foreign agents throughout the world.

Anubis Literary Agency

79 Charles Gardner Road, Leamington Spa, Warwickshire CV31 3BG
☎01926 832644   Fax 01926 832644

Contact *Steve Calcutt, Val Bissell, Maggie Heavey, Liam Martin*

FOUNDED 1994. *Handles* mainstream adult fiction, especially historical, horror, crime and women's. Also literary fiction. No children's books, poetry, short stories, journalism, academic or non-fiction. No unsolicited mss; send a covering letter and brief (one-page) synopsis (s.a.e. essential). No reading fee. *Commission* Home 15%; USA & Translation 20%.

Yvonne Baker Associates

8 Temple Fortune Lane, London NW11 7UD
☎0181 455 8687   Fax 0181 458 3143

Contact *Yvonne Baker*

FOUNDED 1987. *Handles* scripts for TV, theatre, film and radio. Books extremely rarely. No poetry. Approach by letter giving as much detail as possible, including s.a.e.. No reading fee. *Commission* Home 10%; US & Translation 20%.

Blake Friedmann Literary✓ Agency Ltd★

37–41 Gower Street, London
WC1E 6HH
☎0171 631 4331   Fax 0171 323 1274

Contact *Carole Blake* (books), *Julian Friedmann* (film/TV), *Conrad Williams* (original scripts/radio)

FOUNDED 1977. *Handles* all kinds of fiction from genre to literary; a varied range of specialised and general non-fiction, plus scripts for TV, radio and film. No poetry, juvenile, science fiction or short stories unless from existing clients. *Special interests* commercial women's fiction, literary thrillers. Unsolicited mss welcome but initial letter with synopsis and first two chapters preferred. Letters should contain as much information as possible on previous writing experience, aims for the future, etc. No reading fee. CLIENTS include Ted Allbeury, Jane Asher, Teresa Crane, Barbara Erskine, Maeve Haran, John Harvey, Ken Hom, Glenn Meade, Lawrence Norfolk, Joseph O'Connor, Michael Ridpath, Robyn Sisman. *Commission* Books: Home 15%; US & Translation 20%. Radio/TV/Film: 15%. *Overseas associates* throughout Europe, Asia and the US.

David Bolt Associates

12 Heath Drive, Send, Surrey
GU23 7EP
☎01483 721118   Fax 01483 721118

Contact *David Bolt*

FOUNDED 1983. *Handles* fiction and general non-fiction. No books for small children or verse (except in special circumstances). No scripts. *Special interests* fiction, African writers, biography, history, military, theology. Preliminary letter with s.a.e. essential. Reading fee for unpublished writers. Terms on application. CLIENTS include Chinua Achebe, David Bret, Eilis Dillon, Arthur Jacobs, James Purdy, Joseph Rhymer, Colin Wilson. *Commission* Home 10%; US & Translation 19%.

BookBlast Literary Agency

21 Chesterton Road, London W10 5LY
☎0181 968 3089   Fax 0181 932 4087

Director *Georgia de Chamberet*

HANDLES traditional and underground literature. Also authors from the African diaspora, Asia, Europe. No poetry, plays, light romance, science fiction, horror, travel, fantasy, children's, cookery, gardening, health. No reading fee.

No unsolicited mss. Will suggest revisions. Preliminary letter, biographical information and s.a.e. essential, also names of agents and publishers previously contacted. *Commission* Home 10%; USA 15%; Translation 20%.

Alan Brodie Representation Ltd (incorporating **Michael Imison Playwrights Ltd**)

211 Piccadilly, London W1V 9LD
☎0171 917 2871   Fax 0171 917 2872

Contact *Alan Brodie*

FOUNDED 1989. *Handles* theatre, film and TV scripts. No books. Preliminary letter and c.v. essential. No reading fee but s.a.e. required. *Commission* Home 10%; Overseas 15%.

Rosemary Bromley Literary Agency

Avington, Near Winchester, Hampshire
SO21 1DB
☎01962 779656   Fax 01962 779656

Contact *Rosemary Bromley*

FOUNDED 1981. *Handles* non-fiction. Also scripts for TV and radio. No poetry or short stories. *Special interests* natural history, leisure, biography and cookery. No unsolicited mss. Send preliminary letter with full details. Enquiries unaccompanied by return postage will not be answered. CLIENTS include Elisabeth Beresford, Linda Birch, Gwen Cherrell, Teresa Collard, estate of Fanny Cradock, Cécile Curtis, Glenn Hamilton, Jacynth Hope-Simpson, David Rees, Judy Strafford, Keith West, Ron Wilson, John Wingate. *Commission* Home 10%; US 15%; Translation 20%; Illustration 20%.

Felicity Bryan★

2A North Parade, Banbury Road, Oxford
OX2 6PE
☎01865 513816   Fax 01865 310055

Contact *Felicity Bryan*

FOUNDED 1988. *Handles* fiction of various types and non-fiction with emphasis on history, biography, science and current affairs. No scripts for TV, radio or theatre. No crafts, how-to, science fiction or light romance. No unsolicited mss. Best approach by letter. No reading fee. CLIENTS include John Charmley, Liza Cody, John Julius Norwich, Rosamunde Pilcher, Miriam Stoppard, Roy Strong. *Commission* Home 10%; US & Translation 20%. *Overseas associates* Lennart Sane, Scandinavia; Andrew Nurnberg, Europe; **Curtis Brown Ltd**, US.

Peter Bryant (Writers) ✓
94 Adelaide Avenue, London
SE4 1YR
☎0181 691 9085   Fax 0181 692 9107
Contact *Peter Bryant*

FOUNDED 1980. *Special interests* animation, children's fiction and TV sitcoms. Also *handles* drama scripts for theatre, radio, film and TV. No reading fee for these categories but return postage essential for all submissions. CLIENTS include Isabelle Amyes, Roy Apps, Joe Boyle, Andrew Brenner, Lucy Daniel, Jimmy Hibbert, Jan Page, Ruth Silvestre, Peter Symonds. *Commission* 10%. *Overseas associates* Hartmann & Stauffacher, Germany.

Bycornute Books
76A Ashford Road, Eastbourne,
East Sussex BN21 3TE
☎01323 726819   Fax 01323 649053
Contact *Ayeshah Haleem*

FOUNDED 1987. *Handles* illustrated books on art, archaeology, cosmology, symbolism and metaphysics, both ancient and modern. No scripts. No unsolicited mss. Send introductory letter outlining proposal. No reading fee. *Commission* 10%.

Campbell Thomson & McLaughlin Ltd★
1 King's Mews, London WC1N 2JA
☎0171 242 0958   Fax 0171 242 2408
Contact *John McLaughlin, Charlotte Bruton*

FOUNDED 1931. *Handles* book-length mss (excluding children's, science fiction and fantasy). No plays, film scripts, articles, short stories or poetry. No unsolicited mss. Send preliminary letter with synopsis and s.a.e. in the first instance. No reading fee. *Overseas associates* Fox Chase Agency, Philadelphia; Raines & Raines, New York.

Carnell Literary Agency★
Danescroft, Goose Lane, Little Hallingbury,
Hertfordshire CM22 7RG
☎01279 723626
Contact *Pamela Buckmaster*

FOUNDED 1951. *Handles* fiction and general non-fiction, specialising in science fiction and fantasy. No poetry. No scripts except from published authors. No unsolicited mss and no phone calls. *Commission* Home 10%; US & Translation 19%. Works in conjunction with agencies worldwide.

Casarotto Ramsay Ltd
National House, 60–66 Wardour Street,
London W1V 3HP
☎0171 287 4450   Fax 0171 287 9128
Film/TV/Radio *Jenne Casarotto, Greg Hunt, Tracey Smith, Rachel Swann, Charlotte Kelly*
Stage *Tom Erhardt, Mel Kenyon*
(**Books** *Handled by* **Lutyens and Rubinstein**)

Took over the agency responsibilities of Margaret Ramsay Ltd in 1992, incorporating a strong client list, with names like Alan Ayckbourn, Caryl Churchill, Willy Russell and Muriel Spark. *Handles* scripts for TV, theatre, film and radio, plus general fiction and non-fiction. No poetry or books for children. No unsolicited material without preliminary letter. CLIENTS include J. G. Ballard, Edward Bond, Simon Callow, David Hare, Terry Jones, Neil Jordan, Willy Russell, David Yallop. *Commission* Home 10%; US & Translation 20%. *Overseas associates* worldwide.

Celia Catchpole
56 Gilpin Avenue, London SW14 8QY
☎0181 255 7200   Fax 0181 878 0594
Contact *Celia Catchpole*

FOUNDED 1996. *Handles* children's books – artists and writers. No TV, film, radio or theatre scripts. No unsolicited mss. Approach by phone in the first instance. *Commission* Home 10–15%; USA & Translation 20%. Works with associate agents abroad.

Chapman & Vincent ✓
The Mount, Sun Hill, Royston,
Hertfordshire SG8 9ATZ
☎01763 247474   Fax 01763 243033
Contact *Jennifer Chapman, Gilly Vincent*

A new, small agency whose clients come mainly from personal recommendation and write original non-fiction and quality fiction – usually with TV and film potential which the agents help to develop as necessary (although they do not handle scripts). Since the agency aims to look after only a small number of writers, it is not actively seeking clients but 'we are enthusiasts who are happy to consider really original work'. No poetry, children's, romantic fiction, science fiction or avant-garde prose. No reading fee but in the case of non-fiction a fully-developed idea is required for consideration together with confirmation that a ms is 50% complete; for fiction, send a synopsis and two sample chapters. Write, please do not telephone, and enclose s.a.e.. Do not send complete ms in the first instance. CLIENTS include Leslie Geddes-Brown, Sara George, Rowley Leigh, Dorit Peleg. *Commission* Home 15%; US & Europe 20%.

Mic Cheetham Literary Agency
138 Buckingham Palace Road, London
SW1W 9SA
☎0171 730 3027   Fax 0171 730 0037
Contact *Mic Cheetham*
ESTABLISHED 1994. *Handles* general and literary fiction, crime and science fiction, and non-fiction. No scripts apart from existing clients. No children's, illustrated books or poetry. No unsolicited mss. Approach in writing with publishing history, first two chapters and return postage. No reading fee. CLIENTS include Iain Banks, Anita Burgh, Laurie Graham, Janette Turner Hospital, Glyn Hughes, Antony Sher. *Commission* Home 10%; USA & Translation 20%. Works with **The Marsh Agency** for all translation rights.

Judith Chilcote Agency★
8 Wentworth Mansions, Keats Grove, London NW3 2RL
☎0171 794 3717   Fax 0171 794 7431
Contact *Judith Chilcote*
FOUNDED 1990. *Handles* commercial fiction, royal books, TV tie-ins, health, beauty and fitness, sport, cinema, self-help, popular psychology, biography and autobiography, cookery and current affairs. No academic, science fiction, children's, short stories or poetry. No unsolicited mss. Send letter with c.v., synopsis, three chapters and s.a.e. for return. No reading fee. CLIENTS include Jane Alexander, Vanessa Feltz, Dr Patricia Macnair, Maureen Paton, Douglas Thompson. *Commission* Home 15%; Overseas 20–25%. *Overseas associates* in the US and abroad.

Teresa Chris Literary Agency
43 Musard Road, London W6 8NR
☎0171 386 0633
Contact *Teresa Chris*
FOUNDED 1989. *Handles* general, commercial and literary fiction, and non-fiction: health, business, travel, cookery, sport and fitness, gardening etc. *Specialises* in crime fiction and commercial women's fiction. No scripts. Film and TV rights handled by co-agent. No poetry, short stories, fantasy, science fiction or horror. Unsolicited mss welcome. Send query letter with sample material (*s.a.e. essential*) in first

instance. No reading fee. CLIENTS include Prof. Eysenck, John Malcolm, Marguerite Patten. *Commission* Home 10%; US 15%; Translation 20%. *Overseas associates* Thompson & Chris Literary Agency, California; representatives in most other countries.

Serafina Clarke★
98 Tunis Road, London W12 7EY
☎0181 749 6979   Fax 0181 740 6862
Contact *Serafina Clarke, Amanda White*
FOUNDED 1980. *Handles* fiction: romance, horror, thrillers, literary; and non-fiction: travel, cookery, gardening and biography. Only deals in scripts by authors already on its books. *Special interests* gardening, history, country pursuits. No unsolicited mss. Introductory letter with synopsis (and return postage) *essential*. No reading fee. *Commission* Home 15%; US & Translation 20%. *Represents* Permanent Press, US; Second Chance Press, US.

Mary Clemmey Literary Agency★
6 Dunollie Road, London NW5 2XP
☎0171 267 1290   Fax 0171 267 1290
Contact *Mary Clemmey*
FOUNDED 1992. *Handles* fiction and non-fiction – high-quality work with an international market. No science fiction, fantasy or children's books. TV, film, radio and theatre scripts from existing clients only. No unsolicited mss. Approach by letter giving a description of the work in the first instance. S.a.e. essential. No reading fee. CLIENTS include Paul Gilroy, Sheila Kitzinger, Ray Shell; US & Canadian clients: The Bukowski Agency, **Frederick Hill Associates**, Lynn C. Franklin Associates Ltd, The Miller Agency, Roslyn Targ Literary Agency Inc. *Commission* Home 10%; USA & Translation 20%. *Overseas Associate* Elaine Markson Literary Agency, New York.

Jonathan Clowes Ltd★
10 Iron Bridge House, Bridge Approach, London NW1 8BD
☎0171 722 7674   Fax 0171 722 7677
Contact *Brie Burkeman, Isobel Pilsworth*
FOUNDED 1960. Pronounced 'clewes'. Now one of the biggest fish in the pond, and not really for the untried unless they are true highflyers. Fiction and non-fiction, plus scripts. No textbooks or children's. *Special interests* situation comedy, film and television rights. No unsolicited mss; authors come by recommendation or by successful follow-ups to preliminary

letters. CLIENTS include David Bellamy, Len Deighton, Carla Lane, Doris Lessing, David Nobbs, and the estate of Kingsley Amis. *Commission* Home/US 15%; Translation 19%. *Overseas associates* **Andrew Nurnberg Associates**; Sane Töregard Agency.

Elspeth Cochrane Agency
11–13 Orlando Road, London SW4 0LE
☎0171 622 0314/4279   Fax 0171 622 5815
Contact *Elspeth Cochrane, Nicholas Turrell*

FOUNDED 1960. *Handles* fiction, non-fiction, biographies, screenplays. Subjects have included Marlon Brando, Sean Connery, Clint Eastwood, Lord Olivier. Also scripts for all media, with special interest in drama. No unsolicited mss. Preliminary letter, synopsis and s.a.e. is essential in the first instance. CLIENTS include David Pinner, Royce Ryton, Robert Tanitch. *Commission* 12½% ('but this can change; the percentage is negotiable, as is the sum paid to the writer').

Rosica Colin Ltd
1 Clareville Grove Mews, London SW7 5AH
☎0171 370 1080   Fax 0171 244 6441
Contact *Joanna Marston*

FOUNDED 1949. *Handles* all full-length mss, plus theatre, film, television and sound broadcasting. Preliminary letter with return postage essential; writers should outline their writing credits and whether their mss have previously been submitted elsewhere. May take 3–4 months to consider full mss; synopsis preferred in the first instance. No reading fee. *Commission* Home 10%; US 15%; Translation 20%.

Combrógos Literary Agency
10 Heol Don, Whitchurch, Cardiff CF4 2AU
☎01222 623359   Fax 01222 529202
Contact *Meic Stephens*

FOUNDED 1990. *Specialises* in books about Wales or by Welsh authors, including novels, short stories, poetry, biography and general. Good contacts in Wales and London. Also editorial services, arts and media research. No unsolicited manuscripts; preliminary letter (s.a.e. essential). *Commission* 10%.

Jane Conway-Gordon★
1 Old Compton Street, London W1V 5PH
☎0171 494 0148   Fax 0171 287 9264
Contact *Jane Conway-Gordon*

FOUNDED 1982. Works in association with **Andrew Mann Ltd**. *Handles* fiction and general

non-fiction, plus occasional scripts for TV/radio/theatre. No poetry or science fiction. Unsolicited mss welcome; preliminary letter and return postage essential. No reading fee. *Commission* Home 10%; US & Translation 20%. *Overseas associates* **Ellen Levine, Literary Agency, Inc.**, New York; plus agencies throughout Europe and Japan.

Rupert Crew Ltd★
1A King's Mews, London WC1N 2JA
☎0171 242 8586   Fax 0171 831 7914
Contact *Doreen Montgomery, Caroline Montgomery*

FOUNDED 1927. International representation, handling volume and subsidiary rights in fiction and non-fiction properties. No plays or poetry, journalism or short stories. Preliminary letter essential. No reading fee. *Commission* Home 10–15%; Elsewhere 20%.

The Croft Agency
13 Croft Road, Caister–on–Sea, Great Yarmouth, Norfolk NR30 5EJ
☎01493 721919
Contact *John Laity, Betty Laity*

FOUNDED 1975. *Handles* Fiction – crime, suspense and drama, murder mysteries and novels with 'social issues'. No poetry, children's, science fiction or supernatural. No unsolicited mss; approach with initial letter and s.a.e. for agency conditions. All mss will be read; minor revisions suggested free of charge. Reading fee starting from £10. CLIENTS John Collins, Catherine Hill, B. M. Rogers. *Commission* Home 10%; USA 15%; Translation 20%.

Cruickshank Cazenove Ltd
97 Old South Lambeth Road, London SW8 1XU
☎0171 735 2933   Fax 0171 820 1081
Contact *Harriet Cruickshank*

FOUNDED 1983. *Specialises* in plays and screenplays only. No unsolicited mss. Preliminary letter with synopsis and s.a.e. essential. *Commission* Home 10%; US & Translation varies according to contract. *Overseas associates* Various.

Curtis Brown Group Ltd★ ✓
Haymarket House, 28/29 Haymarket, London SW1Y 4SP
☎0171 396 6600   Fax 0171 396 0110
Contact *Address material to the company*

Long-established literary agency, whose first sales were made in 1899. Merged with John

Farquharson, forming the Curtis Brown Group Ltd in 1989. *Handles* a wide range of subjects including fiction, general non-fiction, children's and specialist, scripts for film, TV, theatre and radio. Send synopsis with covering letter and c.v. rather than complete mss. No reading fee. *Commission* Home 10%; US 20%; Translation 20%. *Overseas associates* in Australia, Canada and the US.

Judy Daish Associates Ltd
2 St Charles Place, London W10 6EG
☎0181 964 8811   Fax 0181 964 8966
Contact *Judy Daish, Sara Stroud, Deborah Harwood*

FOUNDED 1978. Theatrical literary agent. *Handles* scripts for film, TV, theatre and radio. No books. Preliminary letter essential. No unsolicited mss.

Caroline Davidson Literary Agency
5 Queen Anne's Gardens, London W4 1TU
☎0181 995 5768   Fax 0181 994 2770
Contact *Caroline Davidson*

FOUNDED 1988. *Handles* fiction and non-fiction, including architecture, art, biography, cookery, crafts, design, fitness, gardening, history, investigative journalism, medicine, music, natural history, photography, reference, science, TV tie-ins, travel. Many highly illustrated books. Finished first novels positively welcomed. No occult, short stories, plays or poetry. Writers should telephone or send an initial letter giving details of the project together with c.v. and s.a.e.. CLIENTS Robert Baldock, Elizabeth Bradley, Lynda Brown, Andrew Dalby, Emma Donoghue, Willi Elsener, Anissa Helou, Paul Hillyard, Mary Hollingsworth, Tom Jaine, Bernard Lavery, Huon Mallalieu, J. P. McEvoy, Gaitri Pagrach-Chandra, Rena Salaman, Roland Vernon, S4C, the Welsh Channel Four. *Commission* US, Home, Commonwealth, Translation 12½%; occasionally more (20%) if sub-agents have to be used.

Merric Davidson Literary Agency
12 Priors Heath, Goudhurst, Cranbrook, Kent TN17 2RE
☎01850 212626   Fax 01850 212626
Contact *Merric Davidson*

FOUNDED 1990. *Handles* fiction and general non-fiction. No scripts. No children's, academic, short stories or articles. Particularly keen on contemporary fiction. No unsolicited mss. Send preliminary letter with synopsis and biographical details. S.a.e. essential for response.

No reading fee. CLIENTS include Valerie Blumenthal, Louise Doughty, Elizabeth Harris, Alison Habens, Alison MacLeod, Allis Moss, Mark Pepper. *Commission* Home 10%; US 15%; Translation 20%.

Felix de Wolfe
Manfield House, 1 Southampton Street, London WC2R 0LR
☎0171 379 5767   Fax 0171 836 0337
Contact *Felix de Wolfe*

FOUNDED 1938. *Handles* quality fiction only, and scripts. No non-fiction or children's. No unsolicited mss. No reading fee. CLIENTS Jan Butlin, Robert Cogo-Fawcett, Brian Glover, Sheila Goff, Jennifer Johnston, John Kershaw, Bill MacIlwraith, Angus Mackay, Gerard McLarnon, Braham Murray, Julian Slade, Malcolm Taylor, David Thompson, Paul Todd, Dolores Walshe. *Commission* Home 12½%; US 20%.

Dorian Literary Agency
Upper Thornehill, 27 Church Road, St Marychurch, Torquay, Devon TQ1 4QY
☎01803 312095   Fax 01803 312095
Contact *Dorothy Lumley*

FOUNDED 1986. *Handles* mainstream and commercial full-length adult fiction; specialities are women's (including contemporary and sagas), crime and thrillers; horror, science fiction and fantasy. Also limited non-fiction: primarily self-help and media-related subjects; plus scripts for TV and radio. No poetry, children's, theatrical scripts, short stories, academic or technical. Introductory letter with synopsis/outline and first chapter (with return postage) only please. No reading fee. CLIENTS include Stephen Jones, Brian Lumley, Amy Myers, Dee Williams. *Commission* Home 10%; US 15%; Translation 20–25%. Works with agents in most countries for translation.

Anne Drexl
8 Roland Gardens, London SW7 3PH
☎0171 244 9645
Contact *Anne Drexl*

FOUNDED 1988. *Handles* commercially orientated full-length mss for women's fiction, general, family sagas and crime. Ideas welcome for business-related books, how-to, DIY, hobbies and collecting. Strong interest too in juvenile fiction, including children's games and activity books. Writers should approach with preliminary letter and synopsis (including s.a.e.). No reading fee but may ask for a contribution to admin. costs. *Commission* Home 12½%; US &

Translation 20% (but varies depending on agent used).

Toby Eady Associates Ltd

9 Orme Court, London W2 4RL
☎0171 792 0092 Fax 0171 792 0879

Contact *Toby Eady, Alexandra Pringle, Victoria Hobbs*

Handles fiction, and non-fiction. No scripts. No unsolicited mss. Approach by letter first. No reading fee. CLIENTS include Nuha Al-Radi, Elspeth Barker, Sister Wendy Beckett, Ronan Bennett, Julia Blackburn, John Carey, Jung Chang, Bernard Cornwell, Nell Dunn, Patricia Duncker, Geoff Dyer, Lucy Ellmann, Esther Freud, Kuki Gallmann, Alasdair Gray, Sean Hardie, Tobias Hill, Michael Hofmann, Tim Jeal, Rana Kabbani, Que Lei Lei, Karl Miller, Tim Pears, Sun Shuyun, Amir Taheri, Barbara Trapido, Hong Ying. *Commission* Home 10%; US & Translation 20%. *Overseas associates* La Nouvelle Agence; Mohr Books; The English Agency, Tokyo; Jan Michael; Rosemarie Buckman.

Eddison Pearson Literary Agents

44 Inverness Terrace, London W2 3JA
☎0171 727 9113 Fax 0171 727 9143

Contact *Clare Pearson, Tom Eddison*

FOUNDED 1995. *Handles* literary fiction, non-fiction and poetry; children's fiction and picture books; also TV, film, theatre and radio scripts. Unsolicited mss with s.a.e welcome. No reading fee. *Commission* Home 10%; USA 15%; Translation from 15%.

Edwards Fuglewicz

49 Great Ormond Street, London WC1N 3HZ
☎0171 405 6725 Fax 0171 405 6726

Contact *Ros Edwards, Helenka Fuglewicz*

FOUNDED 1996. *Handles* adult and children's fiction; non-fiction: biography, current affairs, business books, music and film. No scripts. Unsolicited mss welcome; approach in writing in the first instance with covering letter giving publishing history and brief c.v. (enclose s.a.e. and postage for return of mss). No reading fee. *Commission* Home 10%; USA & Translation 20%.

Faith Evans Associates★

27 Park Avenue North, London N8 7RU
☎0181 340 9920 Fax 0181 340 9410

Contact *Faith Evans*

FOUNDED 1987. Small, selective agency. *Handles* fiction and non-fiction. No scripts, unsolicited mss or phone enquiries. CLIENTS include Melissa Benn, Eleanor Bron, Midge Gillies, Saeed Jaffrey, Helena Kennedy, Cleo Laine, Seumas Milne, Roger Mugford, Christine Purkis, Sheila Rowbotham, Lorna Sage, Hwee Hwee Tan, Marion Urch, Elizabeth Wilson, Andrea Weiss. *Commission* Home 15%; US & Translation 20%. *Overseas associates* worldwide.

John Farquharson★

See **Curtis Brown Group Ltd**

Film Rights Ltd

See **Laurence Fitch Ltd**

Laurence Fitch Ltd ✓

483 Southbank House, Black Prince Road, Albert Embankment, London SE1 7ST
☎0171 735 8171

Contact *Brendan Davis*

In association with Film Rights Ltd. FOUNDED 1952 (incorporating the London Play Company, FOUNDED 1922). *Handles* scripts for theatre, film, TV and radio only. No unsolicited mss. Send synopsis with sample scene(s) in the first instance. No reading fee. CLIENTS include Judy Allen, Hindi Brooks, John Chapman & Ray Cooney, John Graham, Glyn Robbins, Gene Stone, and the estate of Dodie Smith. *Commission* 10%. *Overseas associates* worldwide.

Jill Foster Ltd ✓

9 Barb Mews, Brook Green, London W6 7PA
☎0171 602 1263 Fax 0171 602 9336

Contact *Jill Foster, Alison Finch, Ann Foster*

FOUNDED 1976. *Handles* scripts for TV, drama and comedy. No fiction, short stories or poetry. No unsolicited mss; approach by letter in the first instance. No reading fee. CLIENTS include Colin Bostock-Smith, Jan Etherington and Gavin Petrie, Rob Gittins, Paul Hines, Julia Jones, Chris Ralling, Peter Tilbury, Susan Wilkins. *Commission* Home 12½%; US & Translation 15%.

Fox & Howard Literary Agency

4 Bramerton Street, London SW3 5JX
☎0171 352 8691 Fax 0171 352 8691

Contact *Chelsey Fox, Charlotte Howard*

FOUNDED 1992. *Handles* general non-fiction: biography, popular history, current affairs, reference, business, self-help, health and mind, body and spirit. No scripts. No poetry, plays, short stories, children's, science fiction, fantasy and horror. No unsolicited mss; send letter, synopsis and sample chapter with s.a.e. for response. No reading fee. CLIENTS Sir Rhodes Boyson, Bruce King, Tony Clayton Lea, Betty Parsons, Geoffrey Regan, Jane Struthers. *Commission* Home 10%; US & Translation 20%.

French's

9 Elgin Mews South, London W9 1JZ
☎0171 266 3321   Fax 0171 286 6716
Contact *John French*

FOUNDED 1973. *Handles* fiction and non-fiction; and scripts for all media. No religious or medical books. No unsolicited mss. 'For unpublished authors we offer a reading service at £50 per mss, exclusive of postage.' Interested authors should write in the first instance. *Commission* Home 10%.

Vernon Futerman Associates★✓

159a Goldhurst Terrace, London NW6 3EU
☎0171 625 9601   Fax 0171 625 9601
All submissions to: 17 Deanhill Road, London SW14 7DQ
☎0181 286 4860   Fax: 0181 286 4861
Academic/Politics/Current Affairs *Vernon Futerman*
Educational/Art *Alexandra Groom*
Fiction/Show Business/TV, Film & Theatre Scripts *Guy Rose*

FOUNDED 1984. *Handles* fiction and non-fiction, including academic, art, educational, politics, history, current affairs, show business; also scripts for film, TV and theatre. No short stories, science fiction, crafts or hobbies. No unsolicited mss; send preliminary letter with detailed synopsis and s.a.e.. No reading fee. CLIENTS Sir Martin Ewans KCMG, Susan George, Stephen Lowe, V. Grosvenor Myer, Prof. Wu Ningkun, Judy Upton, Russell Warren Howe, Ernie Wise. *Commission* Literature: Home 12½%; Overseas: 17½%. Drama/Screenplays: Home 15%; Overseas & Translation 20%. *Overseas associates* USA, South Africa, France (Lora Fountain), Germany/Scandinavia (Brigitte Axster).

Jüri Gabriel ✓

35 Camberwell Grove, London SE5 8JA
☎0171 703 6186   Fax 0171 703 6186
Contact *Jüri Gabriel*

Handles quality fiction, non-fiction and scripts for film, TV and radio. Jüri Gabriel worked in television, wrote books for 20 years and is chairman of **Dedalus** publishers. No short stories, articles, verse or books for children. Unsolicited mss ('2-page synopsis and 3 sample chapters in first instance, please') welcome if accompanied by return postage and letter giving sufficient information about author's writing experience, aims etc. CLIENTS include Nigel Cawthorne, Diana Constance, Stephen Dunn, Pat Gray, James Hawes, Robert Irwin, Mark Lloyd, David Madsen, David Miller, Prof. Cedric Mims, John Outram, Ewen Southby-Tailyour, Dr Terence White, John Wyatt, Dr Robert Youngson. *Commission* Home 10%; US & Translation 20%.

Eric Glass Ltd

28 Berkeley Square, London W1X 6HD
☎0171 629 7162   Fax 0171 499 6780
Contact *Janet Glass*

FOUNDED 1934. *Handles* fiction, non-fiction and scripts for publication or production in all media. No poetry. No unsolicited mss. No reading fee. CLIENTS include Marc Camoletti, Charles Dyer, Wolf Mankowitz, Jack Popplewell and the estates of Rodney Ackland, Jean Cocteau, William Douglas Home, Philip King, Robin Maugham, Beverley Nichols, Jean-Paul Sartre. *Commission* Home 10%; US & Translation 20% (to include sub-agent's fee). *Overseas associates* in the US, Australia, France, Germany, Greece, Holland, Italy, Japan, Poland, Scandinavia, South Africa, Spain.

Christine Green Authors' Agent★

40 Doughty Street, London WC1N 2LF
☎0171 831 4956   Fax 0171 405 3935
Contact *Christine Green*

FOUNDED 1984. *Handles* fiction (general and literary) and general non-fiction. No scripts, poetry or children's. No unsolicited mss; initial letter and synopsis preferred. No reading fee but return postage essential. *Commission* Home 10%; US & Translation 20%.

Greene & Heaton Ltd★

37 Goldhawk Road, London W12 8QQ
☎0181 749 0315   Fax 0181 749 0318
Contact *Carol Heaton, Judith Murray*

A small agency that likes to involve itself with its authors. *Handles* fiction (no science fiction or fantasy) and general non-fiction. No original scripts for theatre, film or TV. No unsolicited mss without preliminary letter. CLIENTS include Geraldine Bedell, Bill Bryson, Kate Charles, Jan Dalley, Colin Forbes, Jane Green, P. D. James, Mary Morrissy, Conor Cruise O'Brien, William Shawcross. *Commission* Home 10%; US & Translation 20%.

Gregory & Radice Authors' Agents*

3 Barb Mews, London W6 7PA
☎0171 610 4676   Fax 0171 610 4686

Contact *Jane Gregory, Dr Lisanne Radice* (Editorial), *Pippa Dyson* (Film/TV)

FORMED 1987, incorporating the former Jane Gregory Agency established 1982. *Handles* fiction and non-fiction. *Special interest* crime, thrillers, literary and commercial fiction, politics. Particularly interested in books with international sales potential. No plays, film or TV scripts, science fiction, poetry, academic or children's. No reading fee. No unsolicited mss, but preliminary letter with synopsis and first three chapters (plus return postage) welcome. *Commission* Home 15%; Newspapers 20%; US & Translation 20%; Radio/TV/Film 15%. Is well represented throughout Europe, Asia and USA.

David Grossman Literary Agency Ltd

118b Holland Park Avenue, London W11 4UA
☎0171 221 2770   Fax 0171 221 1445

Contact *Address material to the company*

FOUNDED 1976. *Handles* full-length fiction and general non-fiction – good writing of all kinds and anything healthily controversial. No verse or technical books for students. No original screenplays or teleplays (only works existing in volume form are sold for performance rights). Generally works with published writers of fiction only but 'truly original, well-written novels from beginners' will be considered. Best approach by preliminary letter giving full description of the work. All material must be accompanied by return postage. No approaches or submissions by fax. No unsolicited mss. No reading fee. *Commission* Rates vary for different markets. *Overseas associates* throughout Europe, Asia, Brazil and the US.

The Guidelines Partnership, Publishing Consultants & Agents

4 Shelton Park, Shrewsbury, Shropshire SY3 8BL
☎01743 340559   Fax 01743 340619

Contact *Mr G. Black, Mrs L. Black*

FOUNDED 1986. Strong links with major publishing houses throughout the world. *Handles* educational materials, particularly study guides, for most age groups and across all subject areas, e.g. Longman GCSE and A Level Revise Guides. No fiction. Unsolicited mss only welcome subject to prior letter enclosing c.v. and s.a.e.. Approach by letter enclosing s.a.e.. No reading fee. *Commission* Home 10–15%; USA & Translation by negotiation.

Margaret Hanbury Literary Agency*

27 Walcot Square, London SE11 4UB
☎0171 735 7680   Fax 0171 793 0316

Contact *Margaret Hanbury*

Personally-run agency representing quality fiction and non-fiction. No plays, scripts, poetry, children's books, fantasy, horror. No unsolicited mss; preliminary letter with s.a.e. essential. *Commission* Home 15%; Overseas 20%.

Roger Hancock Ltd

4 Water Lane, London NW1 8NZ
☎0171 267 4418   Fax 0171 267 0705

Contact *Material should be addressed to the Company*

FOUNDED 1961. *Special interests* drama and light entertainment. Scripts only. No books. Unsolicited mss not welcome. Initial phone call required. No reading fee. *Commission* 10%.

A. M. Heath & Co. Ltd*

79 St Martin's Lane, London WC2N 4AA
☎0171 836 4271   Fax 0171 497 2561

Contact *Michael Thomas, Bill Hamilton, Sara Fisher, Sarah Molloy*

FOUNDED 1919. *Handles* fiction and general non-fiction. No dramatic scripts or poetry. Preliminary letter and synopsis essential. No reading fee. CLIENTS include Christopher Andrew, Anita Brookner, Marika Cobbold, Lesley Glaister, Graham Hancock, Hilary Mantel, Hilary Norman, Adam Thorpe, Elizabeth Walker. *Commission* Home 10–15%; US & Translation 20%; Film & TV 15%. *Overseas associates* in the US, Europe, South America, Japan.

Hermes The Agency

Hermes House, 4 Queens Close, Old Windsor, Berkshire SL4 2PP
☎01753 861631   Fax 01494 728851

Contact *Susan Wells*

FOUNDED 1993. *Handles* full-length fiction. *Specialises* in the high-concept/techno-thriller genre – typescripts and screenplays. Unsolicited, fully revised mss accepted with return postage and packaging. Also enclose c.v., synopsis and copies of all publisher rejections. No reading fee.

No telephone calls. CLIENTS include Sam Christopher. *Commission* Home 10–15%; US & Translation 20%; Motion Picture 20%.

David Higham Associates Ltd★ (incorporating Murray Pollinger)
5–8 Lower John Street, Golden Square, London W1R 4HA
☎0171 437 7888   Fax 0171 437 1072
Scripts *Elizabeth Cree, Nicky Lund, Georgina Ruffhead*
Books *Susie Alkin-Sneath, Sara Menguc, Caroline Walsh*
FOUNDED 1935. *Handles* fiction and general non-fiction: biography, history, current affairs, art, music, etc. Also scripts. Preliminary letter with synopsis essential in first instance. No reading fee. CLIENTS include John le Carré, Stephen Fry, James Herbert, Alice Walker. *Commission* Home 10%; US & Translation 20%.

Vanessa Holt Ltd★
59 Crescent Road, Leigh-on-Sea, Essex SS9 2PF
☎01702 73787/714698   Fax 01702 471890
Contact *Brenda White*
FOUNDED 1989. *Handles* general adult fiction and non-fiction. No scripts, poetry, academic or technical. *Specialises* in commercial and crime fiction. No unsolicited mss. Approach by letter in first instance, 'although agency taking on few new clients at present'; s.a.e. essential. No reading fee. *Commission* Home 10%; US & Translation 20%. *Overseas associates* in the US, Europe, South America and Japan.

Valerie Hoskins
20 Charlotte Street, London W1P 1HJ
☎0171 637 4490   Fax 0171 637 4493
Contact *Valerie Hoskins*
FOUNDED 1983. *Handles* scripts for film, TV and radio. *Special interests* feature films and TV. No unsolicited scripts; preliminary letter of introduction essential. No reading fee. *Commission* Home 12½%; US 20% (maximum).

Tanja Howarth Literary Agency★
19 New Row, London WC2N 4LA
☎0171 240 5553/836 4142
Fax 0171 379 0969
Contact *Tanja Howarth*
FOUNDED 1970. Interested in taking on both fiction and non-fiction from British writers. No children's books, plays or poetry, but all other subjects considered providing the treatment is intelligent. No unsolicited mss. Prelim-

inary letter preferred. No reading fee. Also an established agent for foreign literature, particularly from the German language. *Commission* Home 15%; Translation 20%.

ICM
Oxford House, 76 Oxford Street, London W1N 0AX
☎0171 636 6565   Fax 0171 323 0101
Contact *Ian Amos, Sue Rodgers, Amanda Davis, Jessica Sykes, Cathy King*
FOUNDED 1973. *Handles* film, TV and theatre scripts. No books. No unsolicited mss. Preliminary letter essential. No reading fee. *Commission* 10%. *Overseas associates* ICM, New York/Los Angeles.

IMG
Pier House, Strand on the Green, Chiswick, London W4 3NN
☎0181 233 5000   Fax 0181 233 5001
Contact *Jean Cooke (London), Julian Bach, David Chalfant (New York)*
Part of the Mark McCormack Group. Offices in New York. *Handles* celebrity books, sports-related books, commercial fiction (New York), non-fiction, how-to business books. No TV, film, radio, theatre, children's books, poetry and academic. No unsolicited mss; send letter with c.v., synopsis, three chapters and s.a.e.. CLIENTS include Ross Benson, Tony Buzan, Pat Conroy, Mark McCormack, professional sports stars, classical musicians, broadcasting personalities. *Commission* Home & USA 15%; Translation 25%.

Michael Imison Playwrights Ltd
See **Alan Brodie Representation Ltd**

International Copyright Bureau Ltd
22A Aubrey House, Maida Avenue, London W2 1TQ
☎0171 724 8034   Fax 0171 724 7662
Contact *Joy Westendarp*
FOUNDED 1905. *Handles* scripts for TV, theatre, film and radio. No books. Preliminary letter for unsolicited material essential. *Commission* Home 10%; US & Translation 19%. *Overseas agents* in New York and most foreign countries.

International Scripts
1 Norland Square, London W11 4PX
☎0171 229 0736   Fax 0171 792 3287
Contact *Bob Tanner, Pat Homsey, Jill Lawson*
FOUNDED 1979 by Bob Tanner. *Handles* all

types of books and scripts for all media. No poetry or short stories. Preliminary letter required. CLIENTS include Masquerade (USA), Lifetime Books (USA), Barrons (USA), Ed Gorman, Peter Haining, Julie Harris, Robert A. Heinlein, Anna Jacobs, Dean R. Koontz, Richard Laymon, Mary Ryan, John Spencer, A. N. Steinberg. *Commission* Home 15%; US & Translation 20–25%. *Overseas associates* include Ralph Vicinanza, USA; Thomas Schluck, Germany; Yanez, Spain; Eliane Benisti, France.

Heather Jeeves Literary Agency★
9 Dryden Place, Edinburgh
EH9 1RP
☎0131 668 3859   Fax 0131 668 3859
Contact *Heather Jeeves*

FOUNDED 1989. *Handles* general trade fiction and non-fiction, specialising in crime and cookery. Scripts for TV, film, and theatre are handled through **Casarotto Ramsay Ltd.** Not interested in academic, fantasy, science fiction, romances, poetry, short stories, sports, military history or freelance journalism. *No* unsolicited mss. Approach in the first instance in writing describing the project and professional experience. Return postage essential. No reading fee. CLIENTS include Debbie Bliss, Lindsey Davis, Elspeth Huxley, Susan Kay, Sue Lawrence, Mark Timlin. *Commission* Home 10%; US 15–20%; Translation 20%. *Overseas associates* throughout Europe and in the US.

John Johnson (Authors' Agent) Limited★
Clerkenwell House, 45/47 Clerkenwell Green, London EC1R 0HT
☎0171 251 0125   Fax 0171 251 2172
Contact *Andrew Hewson, Margaret Hewson, Elizabeth Fairburn*

FOUNDED 1956. *Handles* general fiction and non-fiction. No science fiction, technical or academic material. Scripts from existing clients only. No unsolicited mss; send a preliminary letter and s.a.e. in the first instance. No reading fee. *Commission* Home 10%; USA 15–20%; Translation 20%.

Jane Judd Literary Agency★
18 Belitha Villas, London N1 1PD
☎0171 607 0273   Fax 0171 607 0623
Contact *Jane Judd*

FOUNDED 1986. *Handles* general fiction and non-fiction: women's fiction, crime, fantasy, thrillers, literary fiction, cookery, humour,

pop/rock, biography, investigative journalism, health, women's interests and travel. 'Looking for good sagas/women's read but not Mills & Boon-type.' No scripts, academic, gardening or DIY. Approach with letter, including synopsis, first chapter and return postage. Initial telephone call helpful in the case of non-fiction. CLIENTS include Patrick Anthony, John Brunner, Jillie Collings, Andy Dougan, Jill Mansell, Lester Piggott, Jonathon Porritt, Rosie Rushton. *Commission* Home 10%; US & Translation 20%.

Juvenilia
Avington, Near Winchester, Hampshire
SO21 1DB
☎01962 779656   Fax 01962 779656
Contact *Rosemary Bromley*

FOUNDED 1973. *Handles* young/teen fiction and picture books; non-fiction and scripts for TV and radio. No poetry or short stories unless part of a collection or picture book material. No unsolicited mss. Send preliminary letter with full details of work and biographical outline in first instance. Preliminary letters unaccompanied by return postage will not be answered. Phone calls not advised. CLIENTS include Paul Aston, Elisabeth Beresford, Linda Birch, Denis Bond, Nicola Davies, Linda Dearsley, Terry Deary, Steve Donald, Gaye Hicyilmaz, Tom Holt, Phil McMylor, Elizabeth Pewsey, Saviour Pirotta, Kelvin Reynolds, Peter Riley, Malcolm Rose, Cathy Simpson, Margaret Stuart Barry, Keith West, Jennifer Zabel. *Commission* Home 10%; US 15%; Translation 20%; Illustration 20%.

Michelle Kass Associates★✓
36–38 Glasshouse Street, London
W1R 5RH
☎0171 439 1624   Fax 0171 734 3394
Contact *Michelle Kass*

FOUNDED 1991. *Handles* fiction, TV, film, radio and theatre scripts. Approach with explanatory letter in the first instance. No reading fee. *Commission* Home 10%; US & Translation 15–20%.

Frances Kelly★
111 Clifton Road, Kingston upon Thames, Surrey KT2 6PL
☎0181 549 7830   Fax 0181 547 0051
Contact *Frances Kelly*

FOUNDED 1978. *Handles* non-fiction, including illustrated: biography, history, art, self-help, food & wine, complementary medicine and therapies, New Age; and academic non-fiction in all disciplines. No scripts except for existing clients. No unsolicited mss. Approach by letter with brief description of work or synopsis, together with c.v. and return postage. *Commission* Home 10%; US & Translation 20%.

Paul Kiernan
13 Embankment Gardens, London
SW3 4LW
☎0171 352 5562   Fax 0171 351 5986
Contact *Paul Kiernan*
FOUNDED 1990. *Handles* fiction and non-fiction, including autobiography and biography, plus specialist writers like cookery or gardening. Also scripts for TV, film, radio and theatre (TV and film scripts from book-writing clients only). No unsolicited mss. Preferred approach is by letter or personal introduction. Letters should include synopsis and brief biography. No reading fee. CLIENTS include K. Banta, Lord Chalfont, Ambassador Walter J. P. Curley, Sir Paul Fox. *Commission* Home 15%; US 20%.

Knight Features
20 Crescent Grove, London SW4 7AH
☎0171 622 1467   Fax 0171 622 1522
Contact *Peter Knight, Gaby Martin,*
Ann King-Hall, Andrew Knight, Giovanna
Farrell-Vinay
FOUNDED 1985. *Handles* motor sports, cartoon books for both adults and children, puzzles, factual and biographical material, and scripts (on a very selective basis). No poetry, science fiction or cookery. No unsolicited mss. Send letter accompanied by c.v. and s.a.e. with synopsis of proposed work. Reading fee charged. CLIENTS include Michael Crozier, Frank Dickens, Christopher Hilton, Frederic Mullally. *Commission* dependent upon authors and territories. *Overseas associates* United Media, US; Auspac Media, Australia.

Cat Ledger Literary Agency★
33 Percy Street, London W1P 9FG
☎0171 436 5030   Fax 0171 631 4273
Contact *Cat Ledger*
FOUNDED 1996. *Handles* non-fiction: popular culture – film, music, sport, travel, humour, biography, politics; investigative journalism; fiction (non-genre). No scripts. No children's, poetry, fantasy, science fiction, romance. No unsolicited mss; approach with preliminary letter, synopsis and s.a.e.. No reading fee. *Commission* Home 10%; US & Translation 20%.

Barbara Levy Literary Agency★
64 Greenhill, Hampstead High Street, London
NW3 5TZ
☎0171 435 9046   Fax 0171 431 2063
Contact *Barbara Levy, John Selby*
FOUNDED 1986. *Handles* general fiction, non-fiction and scripts for TV and radio. No unsolicited mss. Send detailed preliminary letter in the first instance. No reading fee. *Commission* Home 10%; US 20%; Translation by arrangement, in conjunction with **The Marsh Agency**. *US associate* Arcadia Ltd, New York.

Limelight Management
54 Marshall Street, London W1V 1LR
☎0171 734 1218   Fax 0171 287 1998
Contact *Fiona Lindsay, Linda Shanks*
FOUNDED 1991. *Handles* general non-fiction and fiction books; cookery, gardening, wine, art and crafts, health, historical and romantic. No TV, film, radio or theatre. Not interested in science fiction, short stories, plays, children's. *Specialises* in illustrated books. Unsolicited mss welcome; send preliminary letter (s.a.e. essential). No reading fee. *Commission* Home 12½%; USA & Translation 20%.

The Christopher Little Literary Agency (1979)★
48 Walham Grove, London SW6 1QR
☎0171 386 1800   Fax 0171 381 2248
Fiction/Non-fiction *Christopher Little,*
Patrick Walsh
Office Manager *Emma Bowles*
FOUNDED 1979. *Handles* commercial and literary full-length fiction, non-fiction, and film/TV scripts. *Special interests* crime, thrillers, autobiography, popular science and narrative, and investigative non-fiction. Also makes a particular speciality out of packaging celebrities for the book market and representing book projects for journalists. Rights representative in the UK for six American literary agencies. No reading fee. Send detailed letter ('giving a summary of present and future intentions together with track record, if any'), synopsis and/or first two chapters and s.a.e. in first instance. CLIENTS include Felice Arena, Simon Beckett, Marcus Berkmann, Colin Cameron, Harriet Castor, Linford Christie, Storm Constantine, Michael Cordy, Mike Dash, Frankie Dettori, Ginny Elliot, Simon Gandolfi, Brian Hall, Paula Hamilton, Damon Hill, Tom Holland, Clare Latimer, Alastair MacNeill, Sanjida O'Connell, Samantha Phillips, A. J. Quinnell, Alvin Rakoff, Candace Robb, Peter

Rosenberg, Vivienne Savory, Simon Singh, Alan Smith, John Spurling, David Thomas, Laura Thompson, James Whitaker. *Commission* Home 15%; US, Translation, Motion Picture 20%.

London Independent Books
26 Chalcot Crescent, London NW1 8YD
☎0171 706 0486   Fax 0171 724 3122
Proprietor *Carolyn Whitaker*

FOUNDED 1971. A self-styled 'small and idiosyncratic' agency. *Handles* fiction and non-fiction reflecting the tastes of the proprietors. All subjects considered (except computer books and young children's), providing the treatment is strong and saleable. Scripts handled only if by existing clients. *Special interests* boats, travel, travelogues, commercial fiction. No unsolicited mss; letter, synopsis and first two chapters with return postage the best approach. No reading fee. *Commission* Home 15%; US & Translation 20%.

Lucas Alexander Whitley*
Elsinore House, 77 Fulham Palace Road, London W6 8JA
☎0181 600 3800   Fax 0181 600 3810
Contact *Mark Lucas, Julian Alexander, Araminta Whitley, Roger Houghton, Kirstan Romano, Alexa de Ferranti, Tom Bancroft*

FOUNDED 1996. *Handles* full-length general and literary fiction and non-fiction. No plays, poetry, textbooks. Film and TV scripts handled for established clients only. Preliminary letter with s.a.e. essential. *Commission* Home 15%; US & Translation 20%. *Overseas associates* worldwide.

Lutyens and Rubinstein*
231 Westbourne Park Road, London W11 1EB
☎0171 792 4855   Fax 0171 792 4833
Partners *Sarah Lutyens, Felicity Rubinstein*
Submissions *Susannah Godman*

FOUNDED 1993. *Handles* adult fiction and non-fiction books. No TV, film, radio or theatre scripts. Unsolicited mss accepted; send introductory letter, c.v., two chapters and return postage for all material submitted. No reading fee. *Commission* Home 10%; USA & Translation 20%.

Duncan McAra
28 Beresford Gardens, Edinburgh EH5 3ES
☎0131 552 1558   Fax 0131 552 1558
Contact *Duncan McAra*

FOUNDED 1988. *Handles* fiction (thrillers and

literary fiction) and non-fiction, including art, architecture, archaeology, biography, film, military, travel. Preliminary letter, synopsis and sample chapter (including return postage) essential. No reading fee. *Commission* Home 10%; Overseas by arrangement.

Bill McLean Personal Management
23B Deodar Road, London SW15 2NP
☎0181 789 8191
Contact *Bill McLean*

FOUNDED 1972. *Handles* scripts for all media. No books. No unsolicited mss. Phone call or introductory letter essential. No reading fee. CLIENTS include Dwynwen Berry, Jane Galletly, Tony Jordan, Bill Lyons, John Maynard, Michael McStay, Les Miller, Jeffrey Segal, Frank Vickery, Mark Wheatley. *Commission* Home 10%.

McLean and Slora Agency
20A Eildon Street, Edinburgh EH3 5JU
☎0131 556 3368
25 Colinton Road, Edinburgh EH10 5DR
☎0131 447 8001
Contact *Barbara McLean, Annie Slora*

FOUNDED 1996. *Handles* literary fiction; some non-fiction including biography and cookery. *Specialises* in books of Scottish interest. No science fiction or scripts. No unsolicited mss. Send preliminary letter, synopsis, sample chapter(s); s.a.e. essential. No initial reading fee. CLIENTS Tom Bryan, John Herdman, Ruari McLean. *Commission* Home 10%; USA & Translation 20%.

Eunice McMullen Children's Literary Agent Ltd
38 Clewer Hill Road, Windsor, Berkshire SL4 4BW
☎01753 830348   Fax 01753 833459
Contact *Eunice McMullen*

FOUNDED 1992. *Handles* all types of children's material from picture books to teenage fiction. Particularly interested in younger children's fiction and illustrated texts. Has a strong list of picture book author/illustrators. Send preliminary letter with s.a.e., outline and biographical details in the first instance. No unsolicited scripts. CLIENTS include Wayne Anderson, Reg Cartwright, Mark Foreman, Simon James, Graham Oakley, Sue Porter, James Riordan, Susan Winter, David Wood. *Commission* Home 10%; US 15%; Translation 20%.

Andrew Mann Ltd★
1 Old Compton Street, London
W1V 5PH
☎0171 734 4751   Fax 0171 287 9264
Contact *Anne Dewe, Tina Betts*

In association with **Jane Conway-Gordon**.
FOUNDED 1975. *Handles* fiction, general non-fiction and film, TV, theatre, radio scripts. No unsolicited mss. Preliminary letter, synopsis and s.a.e. essential. No reading fee. *Commission* Home 10%; US & Translation 19%. *Overseas associates* various.

Manuscript ReSearch
PO Box 33, Bicester, Oxfordshire
OX6 7PP
☎01869 323447   Fax 01869 324096
Contact *Graham Jenkins*

FOUNDED 1988. *Handles* fiction: thrillers, literary novels, crime and general; children's books and scripts for TV and radio. No technical, religious, science fiction, poetry or short stories unless from established clients. *Special interests* revision/rewriting scripts for selected clients. Optional criticism service available, including professional line-by-line editing and laser printing. Approach by letter with s.a.e. in first instance. No reading fee. CLIENTS include Tom Barrat, Margaritte Bell, Richard Butler, Nicholai Kollantoy, Roscoe Howells, Val Manning, Peter Pook, Kev Shannon. *Commission* Home 10%; US 20%.

The Marsh Agency★
138 Buckingham Palace Road, London
SW1W 9SA
☎0171 730 1124   Fax 0171 730 0037
Contact *Paul Marsh, Susanna Nicklin*

FOUNDED 1994. *Handles* translation rights only. No TV, film, radio or theatre. No unsolicited mss. CLIENTS include several British and American agencies and publishers. *Commission* 10%.

M. C. Martinez Literary Agency
60 Oakwood Avenue, Southgate, London
N14 6QL
☎0181 886 5829
Contact *Mary Caroline Martinez, Francoise Budd*

FOUNDED 1988. *Handles* high-quality fiction, children's books, arts and crafts, interior design, alternative health/complementary medicine, cookery, travel, autobiography, biography, popular music, sport and business. Also scripts for films, TV and radio. *Specialises* in fiction, children's and alternative health. No unsolicited mss. Phone call in the first instance before sending letter with synopsis; s.a.e. essential. (Possible change of address; telephone first before sending submissions.) No reading fee but may charge an admin. fee where appropriate. DTP service available. *Commission* Home 15%; US, Overseas & Translation 20%; Performance Rights 20%. *Overseas associates* various.

MBA Literary Agents Ltd★
62 Grafton Way, London W1P 5LD
☎0171 387 2076/4785   Fax 0171 387 2042
Contact *Diana Tyler, John Richard Parker, Meg Davis, Ruth Needham*

FOUNDED 1971. *Handles* fiction and non-fiction. No poetry or children's fiction. Also scripts for film, TV, radio and theatre. CLIENTS include Campbell Armstrong, Jeffrey Caine, Glenn Chandler, Neil Clarke, Maggie Furey, Valerie Georgeson, Andrew Hodges, Roy Lancaster, Paul J. McAuley, Anne McCaffrey, Anne Perry, Elspeth Sandys, Sir Roger Penrose, Iain Sinclair, Tom Vernon, Douglas Watkinson, Freda Warrington, Richard Weston, Valerie Windsor and the estate of B. S. Johnson. No unsolicited mss. No reading fee. Preliminary letter with outline and s.a.e. essential. *Commission* Home 10%; US & Translation 20%; Theatre/TV/Radio 10%; Film 10–15%. *Overseas associates* in the US, Japan and throughout Europe. Also rights representative in the UK for the Donald Maass Agency and **Susan Schulman Agency**, New York.

Richard Milne Ltd
15 Summerlee Gardens, London N2 9QN
☎0181 883 3987   Fax 0181 883 3987
Contact *R. M. Sharples, K. N. Sharples*

FOUNDED 1956. *Specialises* in drama and comedy scripts for radio, film and television. Not presently in the market for new clients as 'fully committed handling work by authors we already represent'. No unsolicited mss. *Commission* Home 10%; US 15%; Translation 25%.

Jay Morris & Co., Authors' Agents
PO Box 70, Blackpool FY1 2GE
☎01253 296988   Fax 01253 291774
Contact *Toby Tillyard-Burrows, Dr Phillida Kanta*

FOUNDED 1994. *Handles* full-length mainstream commercial adult fiction, also racy sagas, gay erotica, horror, children's fantasy, women in power (not women's issues), thrillers and crime. No academic, articles, non-fiction, Aga sagas or romance. Approach in the first instance by letter only, no faxes, enclosing synopsis and s.a.e.. Reading fee of £35 may be requested. CLIENTS include Piers de Villias, Jonathan Douglas, Saxon Hollis, Hon. Joy Parker-Dixon, Elika Rise. *Commission* Home 10%; US & Translation 15%. *Overseas associates* in New York, San Francisco, Hawaii.

William Morris Agency UK Ltd★
31–32 Soho Square, London W1V 6HH
☎0171 434 2191   Fax 0171 437 0238
Film/TV *Steve Kenis, Jane Annakin, Alan Radcliffe*
Stage *Alan Radcliffe*
Books *Stephanie Cabot*

FOUNDED 1965. Worldwide theatrical and literary agency with offices in New York, Beverly Hills and Nashville and associates in Munich and Sydney. *Handles* film, TV, stage, radio scripts; fiction and general non-fiction. No unsolicited material without preliminary letter. No reading fee. *Commission* Film/TV/Theatre/UK Books 10%; US Books & Translation 20%.

Michael Motley Ltd★
42 Craven Hill Gardens, London W2 3EA
☎0171 723 2973   Fax 0171 262 4566
Contact *Michael Motley*

FOUNDED 1973. *Handles* all subjects, except short mss (e.g. journalism), poetry and original dramatic material. *Special interest* literary fiction and crime novels. Mss will be considered but must be preceded by a preliminary letter with specimen chapters and s.a.e.. No reading fee. CLIENTS include Simon Brett, Doug Nye, K. M. Peyton, Annette Roome, Barry Turner. *Commission* Home 10%; US 15%; Translation 20%. *Overseas associates* in all publishing centres.

William Neill-Hall Ltd
53 Effingham Road, Surbiton, Surrey KT6 5LA
☎0181 398 7420   Fax 0181 398 7420
Contact *William Neill-Hall*

FOUNDED 1995. *Handles* general non-fiction, cartoons, religion, academic. No TV, film, theatre or radio scripts; no fiction or poetry. *Specialises* in religion, sport, history, current affairs and humour. No unsolicited mss. Approach by phone or letter. No reading fee. CLIENTS Mary Batchelor, Mark Bryant, George Carey (Archbishop of Canterbury), Richard Foster, Jennifer Rees Larcombe, Heather Pinchen. *Commission* Home 10%; USA 15%; Translation 20%.

The Maggie Noach Literary Agency★
21 Redan Street, London W14 0AB
☎0171 602 2451   Fax 0171 603 4712
Contact *Maggie Noach*

FOUNDED 1982. Pronounced 'no-ack'. *Handles* a wide range of books including commercial, well-written fiction, general non-fiction and some children's. No scientific, academic or specialist non-fiction. No romantic fiction, poetry, plays, short stories or books for the very young. Recommended for promising young writers but *very* few new clients taken on as it is considered vital to give individual attention to each author's work. Unsolicited mss not welcome. Approach by letter (*not by telephone*), giving a brief description of the book and enclosing a few sample pages. Return postage essential. No reading fee. *Commission* Home 15%; US & Translation 20%.

Andrew Nurnberg Associates Ltd★
Clerkenwell House, 45–47 Clerkenwell Green, London EC1R 0HT
☎0171 417 8800   Fax 0171 417 8812
Directors *Andrew Nurnberg, Klaasje Mul, Sarah Nundy*

FOUNDED in the mid-1970s. *Specialises* in foreign rights, representing leading authors and agents. Branches in Moscow, Bucharest, Budapest, Prague, Sofia, Warsaw and Riga. *Commission* Home 15%; US & Translation 20%.

Alexandra Nye
Cauldhame Cottage, Sheriffmuir, Dunblane, Perthshire FK15 0LN
☎01786 825114
Contact *Alexandra Nye*

FOUNDED 1991. *Handles* fiction and topical non-fiction. *Special interests* literary fiction, historicals, thrillers. No children's, horror or crime. No scripts, poetry or plays. Preliminary approach by letter, with synopsis and sample chapter, preferred (s.a.e. essential for return). Reading fee for supply of detailed report on mss. CLIENTS include Dr Tom Gallagher, Harry Mehta, Robin Jenkins. *Commission* Home 10%; US 20%; Translation 15%.

David O'Leary Literary Agents

10 Lansdowne Court, Lansdowne Rise,
London W11 2NR
☎0171 229 1623   Fax 0171 727 9624

Contact *David O'Leary*

FOUNDED 1988. *Handles* fiction, both popular and literary, and non-fiction. Areas of interest include thrillers, history, popular science, Russia and Ireland (history and fiction), TV drama and documentaries. No poetry, science fiction or children's. No unsolicited mss but happy to discuss a proposal. Ring or write in the first instance. No reading fee. CLIENTS include James Barwick, Alexander Keegan, James Kennedy, Jim Lusby, Charles Mosley, Edward Toman. *Commission* Home 10%; US 10%. *Overseas associates* Lennart Sane, Scandinavia/Spain/South America; Tuttle Mori, Japan.

Deborah Owen Ltd★

78 Narrow Street, Limehouse, London
E14 8BP
☎0171 987 5119/5441   Fax 0171 538 4004

Contact *Deborah Owen*

FOUNDED 1971. Small agency specialising in representing authors direct around the world. *Handles* international fiction and non-fiction (books which can be translated into a number of languages). No scripts, poetry, science fiction, children's or short stories. No unsolicited mss. No new authors at present. CLIENTS include Penelope Farmer, Amos Oz, Ellis Peters, Delia Smith. *Commission* Home 10%; US & Translation 15%.

Mark Paterson & Associates★

10 Brook Street, Wivenhoe, Colchester,
Essex CO7 9DS
☎01206 825433   Fax 01206 822990

Contact *Mark Paterson, Mary Swinney, Penny Tyndale-Hardy*

FOUNDED 1961. World rights representatives of authors and publishers handling many subjects, with specialisation in psychoanalysis and psychotherapy. CLIENTS range from Balint, Bion, Casement and Ferenczi, through to Freud and Winnicott; plus Hugh Brogan, Peter Moss and the estates of Sir Arthur Evans, Hugh Schonfield and Dorothy Richardson. No scripts, poetry, children's, articles, short stories or 'unsaleable mediocrity'. No unsolicited mss, but preliminary letter and synopsis with s.a.e. welcome. *Commission* 20% (including sub-agent's commission).

John Pawsey

60 High Street, Tarring, Worthing,
West Sussex BN14 7NR
☎01903 205167   Fax 01903 205167

Contact *John Pawsey*

FOUNDED 1981. Experience in the publishing business has helped to attract some top names here, but the door remains open for bright, new talent. *Handles* non-fiction: biography, politics, current affairs, show business, gardening, travel, sport, business and music; and fiction; will consider any well-written novel except science fiction, fantasy and horror. *Special interests* sport, current affairs and popular fiction. No drama scripts, poetry, short stories, journalism or academic. Preliminary letter with s.a.e. essential. No reading fee. CLIENTS include Jonathan Agnew, Emily Bell, Dr David Lewis, David Rayvern Allen, Caroline Fabre, Elwyn Hartley Edwards, Peter Hobday, Jon Silverman. *Commission* Home 10–15%; US & Translation 19%. *Overseas associates* in the US, Japan, South America and throughout Europe.

Maggie Pearlstine Associates Ltd★

31 Ashley Gardens, Ambrosden Avenue,
London SW1P 1QE
☎0171 828 4212   Fax 0171 834 5546

Contact *Maggie Pearlstine*

FOUNDED 1989. Small, selective agency. *Handles* commercial fiction, general and illustrated non-fiction: home and leisure, health, biography, history and politics. No children's or poetry. Deals only with scripts and short stories by existing clients. No unsolicited mss. Best approach first by letter with synopsis, sample material and s.a.e. for response. No reading fee. CLIENTS David Aaronovich, John Biffen, Matthew Baylis, Kate Bingham, James Cox, John Drews, Glorafilia, Prof Roger Gosden, Roy Hattersley, Prof Lisa Jardine, Charles Kennedy, Prof Nicholas Lowe, Sara Morrison, Prof Lesley Regan, Jackie Rowley, Polly Sellar, Lady Henrietta Spencer-Churchill, Jack Straw, Dr Thomas Stuttaford, Brian Wilson, Prof the Lord Winston, Tony Wright. Translation rights handled by **Aitken & Stone Ltd**. *Commission* Home 12½% (fiction), 10% (non-fiction); US & Translation 20%; TV, Film & Journalism 20%.

Penman Literary Agency

185 Daws Heath Road, Benfleet, Essex
SS7 2TF
☎01702 557431

Contact *Mark Sorrell*

FOUNDED 1950. Under new management since October 1993. *Handles* all types of fiction and non-fiction. No plays. Send preliminary letter, synopsis and sample chapters with s.a.e.. No reading fee. *Commission* Home 10%; Overseas 15–20%.

Peters Fraser & Dunlop Group Ltd★
503–504 The Chambers, Chelsea Harbour, Lots Road, London SW10 0XF
☎0171 344 1000Fax 0171 352 7356/351 1756
Managing Director *Anthony Baring*
Books *Michael Sissons, Pat Kavanagh, Caroline Dawnay, Sarah Leigh, Robert Kirby, Charles Walker, Rosemary Canter*
Serial *Pat Kavanagh*
Film/TV *Anthony Jones, Tim Corrie, Norman North, Charles Walker, Vanessa Jones, St. John Donald, Rosemary Scoular, Natasha Galloway, Henrietta Lees*
Actors *Maureen Vincent, Ginette Chalmers, Dallas Smith, Lindy King*
Theatre *Kenneth Ewing, St John Donald, Nicki Stoddart*
Children's *Rosemary Canter*
Multimedia *Rosemary Scoular*

FOUNDED 1988 as a result of the merger of A. D. Peters & Co. Ltd and Fraser & Dunlop, and was later joined by the June Hall Literary Agency. *Handles* all sorts of books including fiction and children's, plus scripts for film, theatre, radio and TV material. No third-rate DIY. No unsolicited mss. Prospective clients should write 'a full letter, with an account of what he/she has done and wants to do'. Enclose s.a.e.. No reading fee. CLIENTS include Julian Barnes, Alan Bennett, A. S. Byatt, Alan Clark, Margaret Drabble, Clive James, Robert McCrum, John Mortimer, Douglas Reeman, Ruth Rendell, Anthony Sampson, Gerald Seymour, Tom Stoppard, Joanna Trollope Evelyn Waugh. *Commission* Home 10%; US & Translation 20%.

Laurence Pollinger Limited
18 Maddox Street, London W1R 0EU
☎0171 629 9761   Fax 0171 629 9765
Contacts *Gerald J. Pollinger, Heather Chalcroft*
Negotiating Editor *Juliet Burton*
Children's Books *Lesley Hadcroft*
FOUNDED 1958. A successor of Pearn, Pollinger & Higham. *Handles* all types of books including children's. No pure science, academic or technological. Good for crime and romantic fiction. CLIENTS include the estates of H. E. Bates, W. Heath Robinson, William Saroyan, John

Cowper Powys, D. H. Lawrence and other notables. Unsolicited mss welcome if preceded by letter. A contribution of £20 is requested towards editorial costs. *Commission* Home & US 15%; Translation 20%.

Murray Pollinger★
See **David Higham Associates Ltd**

Shelley Power Literary Agency Ltd★
Le Montaud, 24220 Berbiguières, France
☎00 33 55329 6252   Fax 00 33 55329 6254
Contact *Shelley Power*
FOUNDED 1976. Shelley Power works between London and France. This is an English agency with London-based administration/accounts office and the editorial office in France. *Handles* general commercial fiction, quality fiction, business books, self-help, true crime, investigative exposés, film and entertainment. No scripts, short stories, children's or poetry. Preliminary letter with brief outline of project (plus s.a.e.) essential. No reading fee. CLIENTS include Michael Beer, Paul Fifield, Sutherland Lyall, Shirley McLaughlin, Clive Reading, Richard Stern, Madge Swindells, Roger Wilkes. *Commission* Home 10%; US & Translation 19%.

PVA Management Limited
Hallow Park, Worcester WR2 6PG
☎01905 640663   Fax 01905 641842
Managing Director *Paul Vaughan*
FOUNDED 1978. *Handles* mainly non-fiction, plus some fiction and scripts. Please send synopsis and sample chapters together with return postage. *Commission* 15%.

Radala & Associates
17 Avenue Mansions, Finchley Road, London NW3 7AX
☎0171 794 4495   Fax 0171 431 7636
Contact *Richard Gollner, Neil Hornick, Anna Swan, Andy Marino*
FOUNDED 1970. *Handles* quality fiction, non-fiction, drama, performing and popular arts, psychotherapy, writing from Eastern Europe. Also provides editorial services, initiates in-house projects and can recommend independent professional readers if unable to read or comment on submissions. No poetry or screenplays. Prospective clients should send a shortish letter plus synopsis (maximum 2pp), first two chapters (double-spaced, numbered pages) and s.a.e. for return. *Commission* Home 10%; US 15–20%; Translation 20%. *Overseas associates*

Writers House, Inc. (Al Zuckerman), New York; plus agents throughout Europe.

Rogers, Coleridge & White Ltd★
20 Powis Mews, London W11 1JN
☎0171 221 3717   Fax 0171 229 9084

Contacts *Deborah Rogers, Gill Coleridge, Patricia White*
Foreign Rights *Ann Warnford-Davis*

FOUNDED 1967. *Handles* fiction, non-fiction and children's books. No poetry, plays or technical books. No unsolicited mss, please and no submissions by fax. Rights representative in UK and translation for several New York agents. *Commission* Home 10%; US 15%; Translation 20%. *Overseas associates* ICM, New York.

Hilary Rubinstein Books
32 Ladbroke Grove, London W11 3BQ
☎0171 792 4282   Fax 0171 221 5291

Contact *Hilary Rubinstein*

FOUNDED 1992. *Handles* fiction and non-fiction. No poetry or drama. Approach in writing in the first instance. No reading fee but return postage, please. CLIENTS include Eric Lomax, Elisabeth Maxwell, Donna Williams. *Commission* Home 10%; US & Translation 20%. *Overseas associates* **Ellen Levine Literary Agency** New York; **Andrew Nurnberg Associates** (European rights).

Uli Rushby-Smith and Shirley Stewart
72 Plimsoll Road, London N4 2EE
☎0171 354 2718   Fax 0171 354 2718

Contacts *Uli Rushby-Smith, Shirley Stewart*

FOUNDED 1993. *Handles* fiction and non-fiction, commercial and literary, both adult and children's. Film and TV rights handled in conjunction with a sub-agent. No plays, poetry, science fiction or fantasy. Approach with an outline, two or three sample chapters and explanatory letter in the first instance (s.a.e. essential). No reading fee. *Commission* Home 10%; US & Translation 20%. Represents UK rights for **Curtis Brown (New York)** and Henry Holt & Co. Inc.

Rosemary Sandberg Ltd
6 Bayley Street, London WC1B 3HB
☎0171 304 4110   Fax 0171 304 4109

Contact *Rosemary Sandberg*

FOUNDED 1991. In association with **Ed Victor Ltd.** *Handles* children's picture books and nov-els; women's interests e.g. cookery. *Specialises* in children's writers and illustrators and women's fiction. No unsolicited mss as client list is currently full. *Commission* Home 10-15%; US 15%; Translation 15-20%.

Tessa Sayle Agency★ ✓
11 Jubilee Place, London SW3 3TE
☎0171 823 3883   Fax 0171 823 3363

Books *Rachel Calder*
Film/TV *Jane Villiers*

Handles fiction: literary novels rather than category fiction; non-fiction: current affairs, social issues, travel, biographies, historical; and drama (TV, film and theatre): contemporary social issues or drama with comedy, rather than broad comedy. No poetry, children's, textbooks, science fiction, fantasy, horror or musicals. No unsolicited mss. Preliminary letter essential, including a brief biographical note and a synopsis. No reading fee. CLIENTS Books: Stephen Amidon, Peter Benson, Pete Davies, Marele Day, Margaret Forster, Georgina Hammick, Paul Hogarth, Andy Kershaw, Phillip Knightley, Rory MacLean, Ann Oakley, Kate Pullinger, Ronald Searle, Gitta Sereny, William Styron, Mary Wesley. Drama: William Corlett, Shelagh Delaney, Marc Evans, John Forte, Stuart Hepburn, David Hilton, Geoff McQueen, Chris Monger, Ken Russell, Dom Shaw, Sue Townsend. *Commission* Home 10%; US & Translation 20%. *Overseas associates* in the US, Japan and throughout Europe.

Script, Literary and Film Agency
3 Buchanan's Wharf (South), Ferry Street, Bristol BS1 6HJ
☎0117 9221951   Fax 0117 9077412

Contact *Andrew Boswell*

FOUNDED 1996. *Handles* film scripts mainly and some TV scripts. Unsolicited mss welcome; send s.a.e. for details of services provided. An editorial service is available for a fee. *Commission* Home 15%; US 20%.

Seifert Dench Associates ✓
24 D'Arblay Street, London W1V 3FH
☎0171 437 4551   Fax 0171 439 1355

Contact *Linda Seifert, Elizabeth Dench*

FOUNDED 1972. *Handles* scripts for TV and film. Unsolicited mss will be read, but a letter with sample of work and c.v. (plus s.a.e.) is preferred. CLIENTS include Peter Chelsom, Tony Grisoni, Michael Radford, Stephen Volk. *Commission* Home 12½-15%. *Overseas associates* William Morris/Sanford Gross and C.A.A., Los Angeles.

The Sharland Organisation Ltd ✓
9 Marlborough Crescent, London
W4 1HE
☎0181 742 1919   Fax 0181 995 7688
Contact *Mike Sharland, Alice Sharland*

FOUNDED 1988. *Specialises* in national and international film and TV negotiations. Also negotiates multimedia, interactive TV deals and computer game contracts. *Handles* scripts for film, TV, radio and theatre; also non-fiction. Markets books for film and handles stage, radio, film and TV rights for authors. No scientific, technical or poetry. No unsolicited mss. Preliminary enquiry by letter or phone essential. *Commission* Home 15%; US & Translation 20%. *Overseas associates* various.

Vincent Shaw Associates ✓
20 Jay Mews, Kensington Gore, London
SW7 2EP
☎0171 581 8215   Fax 0171 225 1079
Contact *Vincent Shaw*

FOUNDED 1954. *Handles* TV, radio, film and theatre scripts. Unsolicited mss welcome. Approach in writing enclosing s.a.e.. No phone calls. *Commission* Home 10%; US & Translation by negotiation. *Overseas associates* Herman Chessid, New York.

Sheil Land Associates Ltd★ ✓
43 Doughty Street, London WC1N 2LF
☎0171 405 9351   Fax 0171 831 2127

Contact *Anthony Sheil, Sonia Land,*
 Vivien Green, Robert Kirby, Simon Trewin,
 John Rush (film/drama/TV)
Foreign & US *Laura Susijn, Susy Behr*

FOUNDED 1962. Incorporates the Richard Scott Simon Agency. *Handles* full-length general and literary fiction, biography, travel, cookery and humour, UK and foreign estates. Also theatre, film, radio and TV scripts. One of the UK's more dynamic agencies, Sheil Land represents over 270 established clients and welcomes approaches from new clients looking either to start or to develop their careers. Known to negotiate sophisticated contracts with publishers. Preliminary letter with s.a.e. essential. No reading fee. CLIENTS include Peter Ackroyd, Melvyn Bragg, John Banville, Catherine Cookson, Josephine Cox, Nick Fisher, John Fowles, Susan Hill, HRH The Prince of Wales, Michael Ignatieff, John Keegan, Bernard Kops, Richard Mabey, James Roose-Evans, Eddy Shah, Tom Sharpe, Rose Tremain, John Wilsher. *Commission* Home 10%; US & Translation 20%. *Overseas associates* Georges Borchardt, Inc. (Richard Scott Simon). UK representatives for **Farrar, Straus & Giroux, Inc**. US Film and TV representation: CAA, **H.N. Swanson**, and others.

Caroline Sheldon Literary Agency★
71 Hillgate Place, London W8 7SS
☎0171 727 9102
Contact *Caroline Sheldon*

FOUNDED 1985. *Handles* adult fiction, in particular women's, both commercial and literary novels. Also full-length children's fiction. No TV/film scripts unless by book-writing clients. Send letter with all relevant details of ambitions and four chapters of proposed book (enclose large s.a.e.). No reading fee. *Commission* Home 10%; US & Translation 20%.

The Shennan Agency
64 Ashton Lane, Glasgow G12 8SJ
☎0141 357 6440   Fax 0141 357 6446
Contact *Francis Shennan*

FOUNDED 1988. *Specialises* in journalism: strong features, business and finance, for newspapers and magazines, including *Daily Mail, The Express, The Scotsman, The Herald, Scotland on Sunday, Investors Chronicle*. Writers must be accurate, reliable, able to substantiate stories and have full rights to sell. No reading fee but a rewrite fee if it is necessary. No unsolicited faxes. Keep copies as no mss returned. Disks preferred – 3.5in or 5.25in, stored as ASCII (Text Only) files – with good photographs (and the rights to them) plus c.v. of writer. Associate company of Top Table Speakers Agency (other associates sought). *Commission* Home 25%; Foreign 40% plus translation costs.

Jeffrey Simmons
10 Lowndes Square, London SW1X 9HA
☎0171 235 8852   Fax 0171 235 9733
Contact *Jeffrey Simmons*

FOUNDED 1978. *Handles* biography and autobiography, cinema and theatre, fiction (both quality and commercial), history, law and crime, politics and world affairs, parapsychology and sport (but not exclusively). No science fiction/fantasy, children's books, cookery, crafts, hobbies or gardening. Film scripts handled only if by book-writing clients. *Special interests* personality books of all sorts and fiction from young writers (i.e. under 40) with a future. Writers become clients by personal introduction or by letter, enclosing a synopsis if possible, a brief biography, a note of any previously published books, plus a list of any publishers and agents who have already seen the mss. CLIENTS include Michael Bentine, Billy Boy, Clive Collins, Doris Collins, Euphrosyne Doxiadis, Fred Lawrence Guiles, Jim Haskins, Sanda Miller, Keith Wright. *Commission* Home 10–15%; US 15%; Translation 20%.

Simpson Fox Associates

52 Shaftesbury Avenue, London W1V 7DE
☎0171·434 9167   Fax 0171 494 2887

Contact *Georgina Capel*

ESTABLISHED 1973. *Handles* literary and commercial fiction, general non-fiction, and film/play scripts. No children's books. Approach with synopsis and sample chapter, with s.a.e., in the first instance. CLIENTS Niall Ferguson, Suzanne Moore, Andrew Roberts, Peter York. *Commission* Home, US & Translation 15%.

Carol Smith Literary Agency

22 Adam & Eve Mews, Kensington High Street, London W8 6UJ
☎0171 937 4874   Fax 0171 938 5323

Contact *Carol Smith, Petra Lewis, Zoë Waldie*

FOUNDED 1976. *Handles* full-length fiction and non-fiction. *Specialises* in commercial contemporary novels. Welcomes beginners. No telephone calls; send first three chapters and synopsis with preliminary letter. Return postage essential. No reading fee. Mss submissions by invitation only. *Commission* Home 10%; Overseas & Translation 20%.

Solo Literary Agency Ltd

49–53 Kensington High Street, London W8 5ED
☎0171 376 2166   Fax 0171 938 3165

Chairman *Don Short*
Senior Executive/Accounts *John Appleton*

FOUNDED 1978. *Handles* non-fiction. *Special interests* celebrity autobiographies, unauthorised biographies, sports and adventure stories, wildlife, nature & ecology, crime, fashion, beauty & health. Also some fiction but only from established authors. No unsolicited mss. Preliminary letter essential. CLIENTS include Peter Essex, Derek Shuff, Rick Sky. Also *specialises* in worldwide newspaper syndication of photos, features and cartoons. Professional contributors only.

Commission Books: Home 15%; US 20%; Translation 20–30%; Journalism 50%.

Elaine Steel

110 Gloucester Avenue, London NW1 8JA
☎0181 348 0918/0171 483 2681   Fax 0181 341 9807

Contact *Elaine Steel*

FOUNDED 1986. *Handles* scripts and screenplays. No technical or academic. Initial phone call preferred. CLIENTS include Les Blair, Anna Campion, Michael Eaton, Brian Keenan, Troy Kennedy Martin, Rob Ritchie, Snoo Wilson. *Commission* Home 10%; US & Translation 15–20%.

Abner Stein★

10 Roland Gardens, London SW7 3PH
☎0171 373 0456   Fax 0171 370 6316

Contact *Abner Stein*

FOUNDED 1971. Mainly represents US agents and authors but *handles* some full-length fiction and general non-fiction. No scientific, technical, etc. No scripts. Send letter and outline in the first instance rather than unsolicited mss. *Commission* Home 10%; US & Translation 20%.

Micheline Steinberg Playwrights' Agent

409 Triumph House, 187–191 Regent Street, London W1R 7WF
☎0171 287 4383   Fax 0171 287 4384

Contact *Micheline Steinberg*

FOUNDED 1988. *Specialises* in plays for stage, TV, radio and film. Best approach by preliminary letter (with s.a.e.). Dramatic associate for **Laurence Pollinger Limited**. *Commission* Home 10%; Elsewhere 15%.

Peter Tauber Press Agency

94 East End Road, London N3 2SX
☎0181 346 4165

Contact *Peter Tauber, Robert Tauber*

Handles non-fiction: auto/biographies of the famous; innovative, provable diet books; solutions to important historical or scientific mysteries. Fiction: high-quality contemporary women's fiction, horror and thrillers. Prefers new fiction authors to have some writing background such as press, media or advertising. No poetry, short stories, plays, children's or foreign books. Send letter, synopsis, author c.v., copies of all previous rejections, a fully stamped addressed envelope. 'Failure to comply with these exact terms will result in no reply.' *Commission* 20%.

J. M. Thurley

213 Linen Hall, 162–168 Regent Street, London W1R 5TA
☎0171 437 9545/6   Fax 0171 287 9208

Contact *Jon Thurley, Patricia Preece*

FOUNDED 1976. *Handles* full-length fiction, non-fiction, TV and films. Particularly interested in strong commercial and literary fiction. Will provide creative and editorial assistance to promising writers. No unsolicited mss; approach by letter in the first instance with synopsis and first three chapters plus return postage. No reading fee. *Commission* Home 10% (15% where editorial and creative input are involved); US & Translation 15%.

Lavinia Trevor Agency★

7 The Glasshouse, 49A Goldhawk Road, London W12 8QP
☎0181 749 8481   Fax 0181 749 7377

Contact *Lavinia Trevor*

FOUNDED 1993. *Handles* general fiction and non-fiction. No poetry, academic or technical work. No TV, film, radio, theatre scripts. Approach with a preliminary letter and first 50–100 typewritten pages, including s.a.e.. No reading fee. *Commission* Rate by agreement with author.

Jane Turnbull★

13 Wendell Road, London W12 9RS
☎0181 743 9580   Fax 0181 749 6079

Contact *Jane Turnbull*

FOUNDED 1986. *Handles* fiction and non-fiction. No science fiction, sagas or romantic fiction. *Specialises* in literary fiction, history, current affairs, health and diet. No unsolicited mss. Approach with letter in the first instance. No reading fee. CLIENTS include Kirsty Gunn, Penny Junor, Kevin McCloud, Monty Roberts, Judith Wills. Translation rights handled by **Aitken & Stone Ltd**. *Commission* Home 10%; USA & Translation 20%.

Ed Victor Ltd★

6 Bayley Street, Bedford Square, London WC1B 3HB
☎0171 304 4100   Fax 0171 304 4111

Contact *Ed Victor, Graham Greene, Maggie Phillips, Sophie Hicks*

FOUNDED 1976. *Handles* a broad range of material from Iris Murdoch to Jack Higgins, Erich Segal to Stephen Spender. Leans towards the more commercial ends of the fiction and non-fiction spectrums. No scripts, no academic. Takes on very few new writers. After trying his hand at book publishing and literary magazines, Ed Victor, an ebullient American, found his true vocation. Strong opinions, very pushy and works hard for those whose intelligence he respects. Loves nothing more than a good title auction. Preliminary letter essential, setting out very concisely and clearly what the book aims to do. No unsolicited mss. CLIENTS include Douglas Adams, Josephine Hart, Jack Higgins, Erica Jong, Kathy Lette, Iris Murdoch, Erich Segal, Will Self, Sir Stephen Spender and the estates of Raymond Chandler, and Irving Wallace. *Commission* Home 15%; US 15%; Translation 20%.

Cecily Ware Literary Agents ✓

19C John Spencer Square, London N1 2LZ
☎0171 359 3787   Fax 0171 226 9828

Contact *Cecily Ware, Gilly Schuster, Warren Sherman*

FOUNDED 1972. Primarily a film and TV script agency representing work in all areas: drama, children's, series/serials, adaptations, comedies, etc. Also radio and occasional general fiction. No unsolicited mss or phone calls. Approach in writing only. No reading fee. *Commission* Home 10%; US 10–20% by arrangement.

Warner Chappell Plays Ltd

129 Park Street, London W1Y 3FA
☎0171 514 5236   Fax 0171 514 5201

Contact *Michael Callahan*

Formerly the English Theatre Guild, Warner Chappell are now both agents and publishers of scripts for the theatre. No unsolicited mss; introductory letter essential. No reading fee. CLIENTS include Ray Cooney, John Godber, Peter Gordon, Debbie Isitt, Arthur Miller, Sam Shepard, John Steinbeck. *Overseas representatives* in the US, Canada, Australia, New Zealand, India, South Africa and Zimbabwe.

Watson, Little Ltd★

Capo Di Monte, Windmill Hill, London NW3 6RJ
☎0171 431 0770   Fax 0171 431 7225

Contact *Sheila Watson, Mandy Little*

Handles fiction and non-fiction. *Special interests* popular science, psychology, self-help and business books. No scripts. Not interested in authors who wish to be purely academic writers. Send preliminary ('intelligent') letter rather than unsolicited synopsis. *Commission* Home 10%; US & Translation 19%. *Overseas associates* worldwide.

A. P. Watt Ltd*

20 John Street, London WC1N 2DR
☎0171 405 6774   Fax 0171 831 2154

Directors *Caradoc King, Linda Shaughnessy, Rod Hall, Nick Marston, Derek Johns*

FOUNDED 1875. The oldest-established literary agency in the world. *Handles* full-length typescripts, including children's books, screenplays for film and TV, and plays. No poetry, academic or specialist works. No unsolicited mss accepted. CLIENTS include Evelyn Anthony, Quentin Blake, Martin Gilbert, Nadine Gordimer, Michael Holroyd, Alison Lurie, Jan Morris, Graham Swift, and the estates of Wodehouse, Graves and Maugham. *Commission* Home 10%; US & Translation 20%. *Overseas associates* Scovil Chichak Galen Literary Agency, Inc., US.

John Welch, Literary Consultant & Agent

Milton House, Milton, Cambridge CB4 6AD
☎01223 860641   Fax 01223 440575

Contact *John Welch*

FOUNDED 1992. *Handles* military history, aviation, history, biography and some sport. No poetry, children's books or scripts for radio, TV, film or theatre. No unsolicited mss. Has a fairly full hand of authors but is prepared to consider one or two more. Send letter with c.v., synopsis, two chapters and s.a.e. for return. Consultancy fees may apply for unpublished authors. CLIENTS include Alexander Baron, Michael Calvert, Paul Clifford, David Rooney, Norman Scarfe, Jason Woolgar, David Wragg. *Commission* Home 10%.

Dinah Wiener Ltd*

27 Arlington Road, London
NW1 7ER
☎0171 388 2577   Fax 0171 388 7559

Contact *Dinah Wiener*

FOUNDED 1985. *Handles* fiction and general non-fiction: auto/biography, popular science, cookery. No scripts, children's or poetry. Approach with preliminary letter in first instance, giving full but brief c.v. of past work and future plans. Mss submitted must include s.a.e. and be typed in double-spacing. CLIENTS include Catherine Alliott, T. J. Armstrong, Christiaan Barnard, Joy Berthoud, Malcolm Billings, Guy Burt, David Deutsch, Robin Gardiner, Phillip Hall, Tania Kindersley, Daniel Snowman, Harry Tait, Peta Tayler, Michael Thornton, Marcia Willett, Angela Wright. *Commission* Home 15%; US & Translation 20%.

Michael Woodward Creations Ltd

Parlington Hall, Aberford, West Yorkshire
LS25 3EG
☎0113 2813913   Fax 0113 2813911

Contact *Michael Woodward, Janet Woodward*

FOUNDED 1979. International licensing company with own in-house studio. Worldwide representation. Current properties include *Rambling Ted, Teddy Tum Tum, Railway Children, Oddbods, Angel Babies, Kit 'n' Kin*. New artists should forward full-concept synopses with sample illustrations. Scripts or stories not accepted without illustration/design or concept mock-ups. No standard commission rate; varies according to contract.

Agent Power

*How the wheeler-dealers of publishing
are strengthening their power base.*

Ten to fifteen per cent of income is a lot of money to hand over which makes
one wonder why so many writers, penny-pinching people in the main, put such
value on agents. The quick answer is that a good agent brings in the work, a
function that prompted one eminent member of the profession to deny emphat-
ically that he took fifteen per cent of his clients' income. 'On the contrary,' he
said. 'They take 85 per cent of mine.'

But work creation is only part of the story. An author who is big enough to
have the publishers queuing up at his front door may still value the services of an
agent. Think how handy it is to have someone to front up for you, to say to a
publisher what you can hardly say for yourself, that you are the best thing since
sliced bread and that you deserve an advance on your next book that is at least
the equal of the National Debt. An agent who knows his stuff can play one publisher off against another to receive the best deal. More, he can cut through the
small print of a contract to home in on the money-making clauses. This is more
difficult than it sounds. The simple agreement to publish, a two- or three-page
document much favoured by publishers of the old school, has typically grown to
15 pages or more. This is to encompass book club deals, promotion budgets,
cover design, the timing of publication, print number and subsidiary rights – the
latter capable of attracting earnings long after the book is out of print. The sheer
range of potential subsidiary rights is mind-boggling – overseas publication (the
publisher will try for world rights but when an agent is acting, US and translation rights are nearly always held back), film and television adaptations, audio
cassettes, video, information retrieval, to mention only the most obvious. A
book does not have to be a bestseller to earn advances and royalties in several
countries, languages and formats, sums which in themselves may be quite small
but which can add up to a healthy income. A writer acting on his own behalf is
unlikely to realise all the possibilities.

Advances, it has to be said, are well down on the boom years of the late eighties
and early nineties. But there is still big money to be made by authors with a talent
to amuse and as Andrew Wylie, who represents Norman Mailer, Susan Sontag,
Philip Roth and Salman Rushdie, will tell you, 'Any nitwit can show that if a publisher pays six million for something they'll move heaven and earth to sell the book
and if the publisher pays six thousand heaven and earth will have to move for the
book to sell'.

Cautious as they now are, you might think that publishers would run a mile
from an agent who came on waving a big stick. But publishers need products to
sell and in a period of self doubt when they are not sure which way the market

will turn, there is a tendency to rely on agents as their talent scouts. There is no question that a new writer who has caught the interest of an agent has the best chance of getting into print simply because a publisher knows that the manuscript has already gone through a rigorous selection process.

Note the word 'rigorous'. To get on to an agent's client list, the fledgling writer must be able to show that he is capable of paying his way. He can do this by coming up with the big idea (Carole Blake of Blake Friedman discovered Michael Ridpath's thriller *Free to Trade* on her slush pile, a chance find that made Mr Ridpath's fortune) or, more probably, by showing a body of work in evidence of talent that is bursting to take off. Neither the one book writer nor the occasional writer ('I like to keep my hand in') is welcome.

Most agents actively seek new writers but few sign up clients as a result of receiving unsolicited material. Rather they exercise their skills in talent spotting by reading first novels, literary magazines and review sections of the national press or rely on word of mouth recommendations from social and professional contacts. This fact of life often goes unrecognised by budding authors. Unsolicited manuscripts clog the agents' post. An average intake is 30–50 packages a month but two respondents are in the 80–100 category and one agent tops 150. Of these, less than two per cent show real promise. An agent who receives 20–30 unsolicited manuscripts a month reports 'less than five strong leads in fourteen years'.

Most agents want to see a synopsis and maybe a sample chapter rather than completed manuscripts. Expect to wait a minimum of two to three weeks for a response. Constructive criticism is reserved for submissions that hint at potential or, as one agent concedes, 'when the writer is a friend of an existing client'.

A writer in need of an agent can narrow the field by identifying those agents who cover a particular interest. Some agencies do not deal with plays or television scripts, for example, though they may have outside associates who handle this side of the business for their established clients.

The famous names exercise the heaviest clout, of course, but the most powerful agencies are not necessarily suitable for a beginner who may feel the need for the close personal contact offered by a smaller agency. On the other hand, the smaller agency may already have taken on its full quota of newcomers.

As an indication of quality, one of the best guides is membership of the Association of Authors' Agents. To qualify, an agent must have been in business for three or more years and bring in average commission totalling not less than £25,000 a year. The Association's code of practice rules that all monies due to clients should be paid within 21 days of cheques being cleared. Another organisation that sets up high standards is the Personal Managers' Association which represents agents who act on behalf of playwrights and screenwriters (not to mention directors, producers and actors). Where a client's interests overlap (a playwright may turn to novel writing, or a novelist may become a top flight television dramatist) two or more specialist agencies may cooperate on a shared commission basis. Advice frequently given by the agented to the agentless is to seek out the opinion of authors who have been through the mill and learn from their experiences. Writers' circles and seminars organised by the Society of Authors and The Writers' Guild are fruitful sources of gossip.

It is useful to know from the start what agents charge for their services. Ten per cent is standard but an increasing number go for 15 per cent and a few pitch as high as 17½ or 20 per cent – plus VAT. A VATable author can reclaim the tax. Others must add 17½ per cent of the commission to calculate the agent's deduction from earnings. Reading fees are condemned by writers' associations and spurned by leading agents. It has been argued, by writers as well as agents that a reading fee is a guarantee of serious intent; that if an agent is paid to assess the value of a manuscript, he is bound to give it professional attention. Sadly, this is not necessarily the case. While there are respectable agents who deserve a reading fee, the regular charging of fees can too easily end up as a means of exploiting the naive. But some agents do invoice certain administrative costs such as photocopying.

Do not be disappointed if an agent, or even several agents give the thumbs down. They may be overloaded with clients. But even if this is not so, remember that all writing is in the realm of value judgement. Where one agent fails to see talent, another may be more perceptive. The best advice is to keep trying.

When a writer does strike lucky, the first priority is to arrive at a clear understanding as to the scope of mutual commitment. Will the agent handle all freelance work including, for example, journalism, personal appearances on radio and television, lecturing – or just plays and scripts, or books? Will the agent take a percentage of all earnings including those he does not negotiate? This is a touchy subject. Some writers think of their agency as an employment exchange. Any work they find themselves should not be subject to commission. But this is to assume a clear dividing line between what the agent does and what the writer achieves on his own account. In reality the distinction is not always apparent.

Understanding the market: what's needed, by whom, in what form, and in which media, is all part of an agent's job. Once he knows what his client can do, he is able to promote his talents to the people most likely to want to buy. Eventually, offers come out of the blue – an invitation to write for a newspaper, say, an editing job or a chance to present a television programme. It is at this point that the writer is tempted to bypass his agent. 'Why should I pay him, he didn't get me the work?' But the chances are that he did, by making the author a saleable property in the first place.

If a writer is persuaded that his agent is no good, or no good for him, he should look elsewhere. Actors do it all the time but writers seem curiously reluctant to jump from one agency to another. The distinction may have less to do with degrees of apathy or generosity of spirit than with the competitive nature of the agency business. Theatrical agents are by and large a tougher breed. They have to be because there are so many of them chasing a limited amount of business. Literary agents are altogether a more gentlemanly crowd. Since they rarely go in for poaching each other's clients, there is little incentive for authors to switch allegiance. But times are changing. With the rise of the trans-Atlantic publisher, American agents are showing a greater interest in writers whose appeal extends beyond the domestic market. Their eagerness to compete for top-flight clients is already having an impact with certain high profile authors making it known that they would not be averse to a move.

A writer who has yet to make his reputation and is thus unlikely to be head-hunted needs to think carefully before dumping his agent. It is one thing if the agent is incompetent (and in a profession without qualifications or necessary training there are bound to be duds) but quite another if the writer is expecting too much, too quickly.

An agent combines the skills of a salesman, an accountant and a lawyer. If asked to provide his own job definition, he would probably call himself a professional adviser. (Not, he would hasten to add, a teacher. An agent does not expect to tell anyone *how* to write.)

Yet another way of defining an agent is to think of him as a partner. The relationship between writer and agent, assuming they get on well together, invariably lasts longer than any connection with individual editors, publishers, producers or directors.

To a confused world, the agent brings a welcome note of stability.

But the writer who handles his own affairs is not entirely alone. After years of vigorous campaigning, the writers' unions have negotiated a Minimum Terms Agreement (MTA) with several leading publishers including BBC Books, Bloomsbury, Faber, HarperCollins, Hodder Headline, Methuen, Penguin, Random House, Sinclair-Stevenson and Transworld.

A copy of the MTA, which can be obtained from either the Society of Authors or The Writers' Guild (free of charge to members who send a stamped, addressed envelope), is a useful standard against which to judge a publisher's offer. When it comes to signing on the bottom line, you may feel you have had to give way on a few points, but if the general principles of the MTA are followed, the chances of securing a reasonable deal are much enhanced.

Whatever you concede, do not give way on the delivery date of the completed work. Agree only to a duration of work that is within your scope. It is so easy to submit to a publisher's plea to shave off a few weeks here and there only to find that keeping to an over-tight schedule can bring on a nervous breakdown.

Also, contracts often require the author to submit two copies of the typescript. However, publishers will usually agree to one copy, a saving if the author does not have word processing equipment. It should also be possible to negotiate a fee if the author supplies the material on disk, marked up for the typesetter.

Probably the most important break from tradition contained in the MTA is the clause allowing for the length of licence granted by the author to the publisher to be negotiable. The custom is for the licence to run for the duration of copyright (i.e. the author's lifetime plus 70 years). The writers' unions have pressed for a 20-year licence and some publishers have agreed to this but an acceptable compromise is a review procedure which permits the contract to be revised every ten years. This gives the author the opportunity to claim, for example, improved royalties if the book has been a success.

Other basic principles covered by the MTA include:

- ❏ *Accounting*. Once the advance has been earned, a publisher must immediately pay over to the author income from the sale of subsidiary rights.
- ❏ *Indexing*. The cost of indexing should not fall entirely on the author. At the very least, the cost should be shared equally with the publisher.
- ❏ *Free Copies*. The author should receive 12 free copies of a hardback and 20 free copies of a paperback with the option of buying further copies at a 45% or 50% discount.
- ❏ *Print-run*. The author is entitled to know the size of print-runs.
- ❏ *Proofs*. The author is required to read, correct and return proofs within a specified time, usually 14 days. Corrections have to be paid for and it is often the case that an author has to bear the share of the cost of late amendments. The best advice is, having made a decision, stick to it.
- ❏ *Reversion of Rights*. As well as the author being able to recover rights after a book goes out of print (when fewer than 50 copies of the hardback or 150 copies of the paperback remain in stock), the author may also pull out of the contract if sales fall below certain figures. This gives the author the opportunity to leave a publisher if a book is not being properly marketed.

The MTA offers some valuable guarantees on author involvement in the publication of their books. For example:

The contract should specify the length of the typescript, the number and type of illustrations, and so on. Clarification at the outset can prevent misunderstanding and dispute at a later stage.

Before signing the contract there should be full discussion on the availability of illustrations, the costs involved, and who is to pay for them. Normally, the publishers will make a substantial contribution and if illustrations have to be specially prepared, as for art books and some children's books, the normal arrangement is for the publisher to foot the entire bill.

There must be full consultation on the placing of illustrations, the jacket design, blurb, catalogue copy, the distribution of review copies, and publication date.

Royalties

An author's earnings from a book comes from royalties, his share of the sale price as determined by the publisher. The standard hardback royalty scale is 10% to 2,500 copies, 12½% on the next 2,500 copies and 15% thereafter. On certain small reprints the royalty may revert to 10%.

On home (mass market) paperback sales, the minimum royalty should be 7½% of the published price, rising to 10% after 30,000 copies.

Overseas royalties

Here again, generalisations can be misleading – there are so many different ways in which publishers handle export sales. But as a rule of thumb, if the royalty is calculated on net receipts (when the publisher has sold in bulk at a special price), the percentages should not be less than the home royalty percentages. If the royalty is calculated on the British published price, it should be not less than half the home royalty. Whatever the basis, a rising scale is usually adopted.

Translation rights

These rights should never be underplayed. They can sometimes produce a large proportion of the income from a book. If the author uses an agent, he will almost certainly exclude translation rights from the publishing contract and market them himself. If no agent is involved, the publisher is probably in a better position than the author to market the rights effectively. The publisher's percentage of the proceeds should not normally exceed 20%, any sub-agents' commission being paid out of this share.

US editions

More complications arise. All depends on how the publisher deals with this potentially most lucrative of markets. If the publisher has a subsidiary or parent company in the US, the royalty percentages should be much the same as those for home sales. But the calculation may be based on the US published price.

When an American publisher is licensed to produce a separate edition, normal US royalties should be paid. The MTA recommends that an author should receive 85% of these.

A third and, for the author, the least attractive option, is for the UK publisher to sell unbound copies to an American distributor. Since the deal rarely covers more than the manufacturing cost, there is not much leeway for a payment to the author. The time to sort this out is when the contract is negotiated.

Subsidiary rights

By way of example, the author should get 90% from the first serial rights, TV and radio dramatisations, and film and dramatic rights. Other percentages to the author include: anthology and quotation rights, not less than 50%; TV and radio readings, 75%; merchandising, 80%; sound and video recording rights, not less than 75%.

Bear in mind that the royalty percentages noted here do not necessarily apply to all books. For example, heavily illustrated books are excluded and there are occasions when publishers pay lower royalties on such as long works of fiction published in short print-runs for libraries.

Book clubs

If a publisher sells copies to a book club for an all-in price (a 'royalty inclusive' deal), the author should receive at least 10% of the publisher's receipts. But on a royalty exclusive deal, when royalties are paid on sales, the author should receive at least 50% of the royalties paid by the book club. The MTA suggested split is 60:40.

Cheap editions and remainders

There should be no cheap edition at less than two-thirds of the original price, remainder sales or destruction of stock within at least one year (and preferably two) of first publication without an author's written consent. The publisher should give the author first refusal on purchasing remainder stock and pay him 10% of the net receipts. If surplus copies are to be pulped, the author should be offered the chance to obtain free copies within 28 days of the notification.

Electronic editions and audio or video cassettes

The right to publish in electronic form (as a database or CD) or as an audio or video cassette should be listed separately. Royalties and other terms must be agreed with the author.

Accounts

Whether the contract provides for royalty statements to be sent to the author twice yearly or only once – twice is usual (except with academic and educational publishers, shame on them) and should certainly apply for the first two years from publication – the monies due should be paid within three months of the date to which accounts are made up. Once the advance has been earned, money from 'sub licences' over, say, £100, should be paid over to the author on receipt. In fact, publishers will normally do this on request, even if the contract does not specifically require it.

Example:

(a) The Publishers shall make up accounts at 30 June and 31 December and shall render such accounts and pay all monies due to the Author by the succeeding 1 October and 1 April respectively.

(b) Any sum of £100 or more due to the Author in respect of sub-licensed rights shall be paid to the Author within one month of receipt if the advance has been earned.

(c) Each statement of account shall report the number of copies printed, the number of free copies distributed, the number of copies sold during the previous accounting period, the total sales to date, the list price, the royalty rate, the amount of royalties, the number of returned copies, the gross amount received pursuant to each licence granted by the Publishers, and itemised deductions. Each statement of account shall be accompanied by copies of statements received from sub-licensees.

(d) The Author or his authorised representative shall have the right upon written request to examine the Publishers' books of account in so far as they relate to the work, which examination shall be at the cost of the Author unless errors exceeding £50 shall be found to his disadvantage in which case the costs shall be paid by the Publishers.

Authors who are registered for VAT should inform the publishers of their VAT registration number on signature of the contract.

If provision is made for the publishers to 'make a reserve against returns' (ie hold back a percentage of the royalties due to an author in anticipation of unsold copies of the work being returned by booksellers), the reserve should be limited to not more that 10–15% of the royalties on the hardback edition, or 20–25% of the paperback royalties. The publishers should only be entitled to withhold any reserve at the first accounting date following publication or reissue of the work and the balance should be repaid to the author not more than 12 months later.

Competing works

It is only reasonable that an author should be deterred from publishing with another firm a book which is virtually an abridged or expanded version of the work covered by the contract. The difficulty is in choosing a form of words that leaves the author – particularly the specialist author – free to publish other books on his particular subject.

Example:

The Author shall not prepare any work which may be an expansion or an abridgement or of a nature similar to the said work published in such a style and at such a price as to be likely to affect prejudicially the sales of the said work.

It is often wise to exchange letters setting out the interpretation of any clause relating to competing works.

Assignment of contract

It is advisable to have in writing that the publishers shall not assign the rights granted to them in the contract or the benefit of the contract without the author's written consent.

And finally ...

As a spot check on the acceptability of a contract, confirm five essential points before signature.

First, there should be an unconditional commitment to publish the book within a specified time, say, 12 months from delivery of the typescript or, if the typescript is already with the publisher, from signature of the agreement. It is also as well for the approximate published price to be noted.

The obligation to publish should not be subject to approval or acceptance of the manuscript. Otherwise what looks like a firm contract may be little more than an unenforceable declaration of intent to publish. It is equally important to watch that the words 'approval' or 'acceptance' do not appear in the clause relating to the advance payment. For example, if the advance, or part of it, is payable 'on delivery and approval' of the script, this might qualify the publisher's obligation to publish the work.

This point about the publisher's commitment to publishing a book is of vital importance, particularly since publishers' editors change jobs with increasing frequency. An author who has started a book with enthusiastic support from his editor may, when he delivers it, find he is in the hands of someone with quite different tastes and ideas. The publisher should be satisfied themselves at the outset that the author is capable of writing the required book – if necessary by seeing and approving a full synopsis and sample chapter. Provided the book, when delivered, follows the length and outline agreed, the publishers should be under a contractual obligation to publish it, subject, possibly, to reasonable and specified changes to the typescript.

Second, there should be a proper termination clause. This should operate if the publisher breaks the contract or if the book goes out-of-print. When rights revert to the author it should be without prejudice to any claims for monies due. Occasionally, a termination clause is made dependent on the author refunding any unearned advance or on fulfilling some other obligation. Any such proviso should be struck out.

Third, the contract should not contain any unreasonable restrictions on future work. If an option clause is unavoidable it should be limited to one book on terms to be mutually agreed (not 'on the same terms') and enforceable only within a specified time limit, say, six weeks after delivery of a novel, or of submission of a synopsis and specimen chapter in the case of non-fiction.

Next, get it in writing. A recent article in *The Author* says it all:

> 'Your editor may be wonderful. Your faith in human nature may be undented. It may seem pedantic, pushy, bossy. But if you ever agree something important with a publisher which is not in your contract – be it regarding deadlines, amendments, publicity or, especially, money – follow up the meeting or conversation with a friendly letter, confirming the salient points. If things go wrong and all you have is the memory of an airy promise on the telephone that the publisher has since "forgotten", you will be in a much stronger position if you can produce a copy of a letter as evidence of that promise.'

Finally, the author should not be expected to contribute towards the cost of publication. Every writers' organisation warns against subsidised or vanity publishing. It is expensive (some vanity publishers charge up to £8000 for a modest print run), the quality of production is often inferior to that offered by conventional publishers, and the promises of vigorous marketing and impressive sales are rarely borne out by experience. (See *What Price Vanity?* on page 170.)

National Newspapers

Daily Express

Ludgate House, 245 Blackfriars Road, London
SE1 9UX
☎0171 928 8000   Fax 0171 620 1654
Owner *United Newspapers*
Editor *Richard Addis*
Circulation 1.23 million

Now being run as a seven-day publication with *The Express* published Monday to Friday, *The Express on Saturday* and *The Express on Sunday* (see entry), with editors working for each publication. The general rule of thumb is to approach in writing with an idea; all departments are prepared to look at an outline without commitment. Ideas welcome but already receives many which are 'too numerous to count'.

   News Editor *Alastair McCall*
   Diary Editor *John McEntee (William Hickey)*
   Features Editor *Jack Wright*
   Literary Editor *Maggie Pringle*
   Sports Editor *Dean Morse*

Planning Editor (News Desk) should be circulated with copies of official reports, press releases, etc., to ensure news desk cover at all times.

Saturday magazine **Editor** *Katie Bowen-Bravery*

Daily Mail

Northcliffe House, 2 Derry Street,
Kensington, London W8 5TT
☎0171 938 6000   Fax 0171 937 4463
Owner *Lord Rothermere*
Editor *Paul Dacre*
Circulation 2.18 million

In-house feature writers and regular columnists provide much of the material. Photo-stories and crusading features often appear; it's essential to hit the right note to be a successful *Mail* writer. Close scrutiny of the paper is strongly advised. Not a good bet for the unseasoned. Accepts news on savings, building societies, insurance, unit trusts, legal rights and tax.

   News Editor *Ian MacGregor*
   Diary Editor *Nigel Dempster*
   Features Editor *Veronica Wadley*
   Sports Editor *Cameron Kelleher*

Femail *Ted Verity*

Weekend: Saturday supplement **Editor** *Aileen Doherty*

Daily Mirror

1 Canada Square, Canary Wharf, London
E14 5AP
☎0171 293 3000   Fax 0171 293 3409
Owner *Mirror Group Newspapers*
Editor *Piers Morgan*
Circulation 2.38 million

No freelance opportunities for the inexperienced, but strong writers who understand what the tabloid market demands are always needed.

   News Editor *Eugene Duffy*
   Features Editor *Tina Weaver*
   Political Editor *John Williams*
   Showbusiness Diary Editor *Matthew Wright*
   Sports Editor *David Balmforth*
   Women's Page *Jane Johnson*

Daily Record

Anderston Quay, Glasgow G3 8DA
☎0141 248 7000   Fax 0141 242 3145/6
Owner *Mirror Group Newspapers*
Editor *Terry Quinn*
Circulation 729,391

Mass-market Scottish tabloid. Freelance material is generally welcome.

   News Editor *Murray Morse*
   Features Editor *Alan Rennie*
   Education *Tom Little*
   Political Editor *Tom Brown*
   Women's Page *Julia Clarke*

Daily Sport

19 Great Ancoats Street, Manchester M60 4BT
☎0161 236 4466   Fax 0161 236 4535
Owner *Sport Newspapers Ltd*
Editor *Jeff McGowan*
Circulation 235,000

Tabloid catering for young male readership. Unsolicited material welcome; send to News Editor.

   News/Feature Editor *Tony Hoare*
   Sports Editor *Marc Smith*

Daily Star

Ludgate House, 245 Blackfriars Road, London
SE1 9UX
☎0171 928 8000   Fax 0171 922 7960
Owner *United Media*
Editor *Philip Walker*

Circulation 671,286

In competition with *The Sun* for off-the-wall news and features. Freelance opportunities almost non-existent. Most material is written in-house or by regular outsiders.

News Editor *Hugh Whittow*
Features Editor *Brian Dunlea*
Entertainments *Pat Codd*
Sports Editor *Phil Rostron*
Women's Page *Karen Livermore*

The Daily Telegraph

1 Canada Square, Canary Wharf, London
E14 5DT
☎0171 538 5000   Fax 0171 538 6242

Owner *Conrad Black*
Editor *Charles Moore*
Circulation 1.12 million

Unsolicited mss not generally welcome – 'all are carefully read and considered, but only about one in a thousand is accepted for publication'. As they receive about 20 weekly, this means about one a year. Contenders should approach the paper in writing, making clear their authority for writing on that subject. No fiction.

News Editor *Martin Newland* Tip-offs or news reports from *bona fide* journalists. Must phone the news desk in first instance. Maximum 200 words. *Payment* minimum £10 (tip).

Arts Editor *Sarah Crompton*
Business Editor *Roland Gribben*
Diary Editor *David Rennie* Always interested in diary pieces; contact *Peterborough* (Diary column).

Education *John Clare*
Environment *Charles Clover*
Features Editor/Women's Page *Corinna Honan* Most material supplied by commission from established contributors. New writers are tried out by arrangement with the features editor. Approach in writing. Maximum 1500 words.

Literary Editor *John Coldstream*
Political Editor *George Jones*
Sports Editor *David Welch* Occasional opportunities for specialised items.
Payment by arrangement.

Telegraph Magazine: Saturday colour supplement. **Editor** *Emma Soames*. **Young Telegraph** (see entry under **Magazines**).

The European

200 Gray's Inn Road, London WC1X 8NE
☎0171 418 7777   Fax 0171 713 1840

Owner *The Barclay Brothers*
Editor-in-Chief *Andrew Neil*

Circulation 153,006

LAUNCHED May 1990. Three-section colour weekly aimed at a European weekend market. News and current affairs, business, sport, European affairs, society and politics, plus European arts and lifestyle section, *The European Magazine*. Freelance contributions from recognised experts in their field will be considered. First approach in writing.

News/Features *David Meilton*
Business *Tim Castle*

The European Magazine *Andrew Harvey*
Payment by arrangement.

Express on Sunday

Ludgate House, 245 Blackfriars Road, London
SE1 9UX
☎0171 928 8000   Fax 0171 620 1656

Owner *United Newspapers*
Editor *Richard Addis*
Circulation 1.18 million

FOUNDED 1918. Unsolicited mss are generally welcome. Approach in writing with ideas.

News Editor *Alistair McCall* Occasional news features by experienced journalists only. All submissions must be preceded by ideas.

Features Editor *Jack Wright*
Literary Editor *Maggie Pringle*
Sports Editor *Dean Morse*

Express on Sunday Magazine: colour supplement. **Editor** *Katie Bowen-Bravery*. No unsolicited mss. All contributions are commissioned. Ideas in writing only.
Payment negotiable.

Financial Times

1 Southwark Bridge, London SE1 9HL
☎0171 873 3000   Fax 0171 873 3076

Owner *Pearson*
Editor *Richard Lambert*
Circulation 306,464

FOUNDED 1888. Business and finance-orientated certainly, but by no means as featureless as some suppose. All feature ideas must be discussed with the department's editor in advance. Not snowed under with unsolicited contributions – they get less than any other national newspaper. Approach in writing with ideas in the first instance.

News Editor *Julia Cuthbertson*
Features Editor *John Willman*
Arts/Literary Editor *Annalena McAfee*
City/Financial Editor *Jane Fuller*
Diary Editor *Michael Cassell*
Education *Simon Targett*

Environment *Leyla Boulton*
Political Editor *Robert Peston*
Small Businesses *Katherine Campbell*
Sports Editor *Peter Aspden*
Women's Page *Lucia van der Post*

The Guardian
119 Farringdon Road, London EC1R 3ER
☎0171 278 2332Fax 0171 837 2114/833 8342
Owner *The Scott Trust*
Editor *Alan Rusbridger*
Circulation 400,348

Of all the nationals *The Guardian* probably offers the greatest opportunities for freelance writers, if only because it has the greatest number of specialised pages which use freelance work. But mss must be directed at a specific slot.

News Editor *Harriet Sherwood* No opportunities except in those regions where there is presently no local contact for news stories.

Arts Editor *Claire Armitstead*
City/Financial Editor *Alex Brummer*
On Line Science, computing and technology. A major part of Thursday's paper, almost all written by freelancers. Expertise essential – but not a trade page; written for 'the interested man in the street' and from the user's point of view. Computing/communications (Internet) articles should be addressed to *Jack Schofield*; science articles to *Tim Radford*. Mss on disk or by e-mail (online@guardian.co.uk).

Diary Editor *Matthew Norman*
Education Editor *John Carvel* Expert pieces on modern education welcome. Maximum 1000 words.

Environment *John Vidal*
Features Editor *Roger Alton* Receives up to 30 unsolicited mss a day; these are passed on to relevant page editors.

Guardian Society *Malcolm Dean* Focuses on social change in the 90s – the forces affecting us, from environment to government policies. Top journalists and outside commentators on nine editorial pages.

Literary Editor *Stephen Moss*
Media Editor *John Mulholland* Approximately six pieces a week, plus diary. Outside contributions are considered. All aspects of modern media, advertising, PR, consumer trends in arts/entertainments. Background insight important. Best approach is a note, followed by phone call.

Political Editor *Mike White*
Sports Editor *Mike Averis*
Women's Page *Clare Longrigg* Now runs three days a week. Unsolicited ideas used if

they show an appreciation of the page in question. Maximum 800–1000 words.

Guardian Weekend Saturday issue. **Editor** *Deborah Orr*. **The Guide** *Ben Olins*.

The Herald (Glasgow)
195 Albion Street, Glasgow G1 1QP
☎0141 552 6255   Fax 0141 552 2288
Owner *Scottish Television Plc*
Acting Editor *Harry Reid*
Circulation 106,192

The oldest national newspaper in the English-speaking world, The Herald, which dropped its 'Glasgow' prefix in February 1992, was bought by Scottish Television in 1996. Lively, quality, national Scottish daily broadsheet. Approach with ideas in writing or by phone in first instance.

News Editor *Colin McDiarmid*
Arts Editor *Keith Bruce*
Business Editor *Ronald Dundas*
Diary *Tom Shields*
Education *Barclay McBain*
Environment *Liz Buie*
Sports Editor *Iain Scott*
Women's Page *Jackie McGlone*

The Independent
1 Canada Square, Canary Wharf, London E14 5AP
☎0171 293 2000   Fax 0171 293 2435
Owner *Mirror Group Newspapers*
Editor *Andrew Marr*
Circulation 261,316

FOUNDED October 1986. The first new quality national in over 130 years. Particularly strong on its arts/media coverage, with a high proportion of feature material. Theoretically, opportunities for freelancers are good. However, unsolicited mss are not welcome; most pieces originate in-house or from known and trusted outsiders. Ideas should be submitted in writing.

News Editor *David Felton*
Features Editor *David Robson*
Arts Editor *Mark Pappenheim*
Business Editor *Jeremy Warner*
City/Financial Editor *Peter Rodgers*
Education *Judith Judd*
Environment *Nicholas Schoon*
Literary Editor *Boyd Tonkin*
Political Editor *Donald Macintyre*
Sports Editor *Paul Newman*

The Independent Magazine: Saturday supplement. **Editor** *Michael Watts*

Independent on Sunday

1 Canada Square, Canary Wharf, London
E14 5AP
☎0171 293 2000   Fax 0171 293 2435

Owner *Mirror Group Newspapers*
Editor *Rosie Boycott*
Circulation 281,660

FOUNDED 1986. Regular columnists contribute most material but feature opportunites exist. Approach with ideas in first instance.

News Editor *Mike McCarthy*
Arts Editor *Simon O'Hagan*
Commissioning Editor, Features
  Caroline Roux
City/Financial Editor *Ian Griffiths*
Environment *Geoffrey Lean*
Political Editor *Stephen Castle*
Sports Editor *Paul Newman*

Review supplement. **Editor** *Laurence Earle.*

International Herald Tribune

181 avenue Charles de Gaulle, 92200 Neuilly-sur-Seine, France
☎0033 1 4143 9300   Fax 0033 1 4143 9338

Editor *Michael Getler*
Circulation 195,185

Published in France, Monday to Saturday, and circulated in Europe, the Middle East, North Africa, the Far East and the USA. General news, business and financial, arts and leisure. Use regular freelance contributors. Query letter to features editor in first instance.

Features Editor *Katherine Knorr*
News Editor *Walter Wells*

The Mail on Sunday

Northcliffe House, 2 Derry Street, Kensington, London W8 5TS
☎0171 938 6000   Fax 0171 937 3829

Owner *Lord Rothermere*
Editor *Jonathon Holborrow*
Circulation 2.12 million

Sunday paper with a high proportion of newsy features and articles. Experience and judgement required to break into its band of regular feature writers.

News Editor *Tom Henry*
City/Financial Editor *Bill Kay*
Diary Editor *Nigel Dempster*
Features Editor *Andy Bull*
Literary Editor *Paula Johnson*
Political Editor *Joe Murphy*
Sports Editor *Roger Kelly*

Night & Day: review supplement. **Editor** *Simon Kelner*

You – The Mail on Sunday Magazine: colour supplement. Many feature articles, supplied entirely by freelance writers. **Editor** *Dee Nolan*
Features Editor *Jane Phillimore*
Arts Editor *Liz Galbraith*

Morning Star

1–3 Ardleigh Road, London N1 4HS
☎0171 254 0033   Fax 0171 254 5950

Owner *Peoples Press Printing Society*
Editor *John Haylett*
Circulation 9,000

Not to be confused with the *Daily Star*, the *Morning Star* is the farthest left national daily. Those with a penchant for a Marxist reading of events and ideas can try their luck, though feature space is as competitive here as in the other nationals.

News/Arts/Features/Women's Page
  Paul Corry
Political Editor *Mike Ambrose*
Sports Editor *Amanda Kendal*

The News of the World

1 Virginia Street, London E1 9XR
☎0171 782 4000Fax 0171 488 4433 (Features)

Owner *News International plc*
Editor *Phil Hall*
Circulation 4.5 million

Highest circulation Sunday paper. Freelance contributions welcome. Features Department welcomes tips and ideas. Approach by fax in first instance with follow-up phone call.

Assistant Editor (News) *Gary Thompson*
Features Editor *Ray Levine*
Sports Editor *Mike Dunn*
Women's Page *Vicky Bubb*

Sunday Magazine: colour supplement. **Editor** *Judy McGuire*. Showbiz interviews and strong human-interest features make up most of the content, but there are no strict rules about what is 'interesting'. Unsolicited mss and ideas welcome.

The Observer

119 Farringdon Road, London EC1R 3ER
☎0171 278 2332   Fax 0171 713 4250

Owner *Guardian Newspapers Ltd*
Editor *Will Hutton*
Circulation 454,658

FOUNDED 1791. Acquired by Guardian Newspapers from Lonrho in May 1993. Occupies the middle ground of Sunday newspaper politics. Unsolicited material is not generally welcome, 'except from distinguished, established writers'. Receives far too many unsolicited offerings already. No news, fiction or special page opportunities. The newspaper runs annual competitions which change from year to year. Details are advertised in the newspaper.

News Editor *Paul Dunn*
Arts Editor *Jane Ferguson*
Business Editor *Ben Laurance*
City Editor *Heather Connon*
Education Correspondent *Martin Bright*
Features Editor *Lisa O'Kelly*
Literary Editor *Robert McCrum*

Life: arts and lifestyle supplement. **Editor** *Justine Picardie*.

The People
1 Canada Square, Canary Wharf, London E14 5AP
☎0171 293 3000   Fax 0171 293 3810
Owner *Mirror Group Newspapers*
Editor *Len Gould*
Circulation 2 million

Slightly up-market version of *The News of the World*. Keen on exposés and big-name gossip. Interested in ideas for investigative articles. Phone in first instance.

News Editor *Danny Buckland*
City/Financial Editor *Cathy Gunn*
Features Editor/Women's Page *Tom Petrie*
Political Editor *Nigel Nelson*
Sports Editor *Ed Barry*

Yes! Magazine. **Editor** *Tom Petrie*. Approach by phone with ideas in first instance.

Scotland on Sunday
20 North Bridge, Edinburgh EH1 1YT
☎0131 225 2468   Fax 0131 220 2443
Owner *The Barclay Brothers*
Editor *Brian Groom*
Circulation 103,688

Scotland's top-selling quality broadsheet. Welcomes ideas rather than finished articles.

News Editor *William Paul*
Features Editor *Stewart Hennessey*
Political Editor *Kenneth Farquharson*

Scotland on Sunday Magazine: colour supplement. **Editor** *Fiona Macleod*. Features on personalities, etc.

The Scotsman
20 North Bridge, Edinburgh EH1 1YT
☎0131 225 2468   Fax 0131 226 7420
Owner *The Barclay Brothers*
Editor *Martin Clarke*

Circulation 77,057

Scotland's national newspaper. Many unsolicited mss come in, and stand a good chance of being read, although a small army of regulars supply much of the feature material not written in-house.

News Editor *Ian Stewart*
City/Financial Editor *Martin Flanagan*
Education *Matt Wells*
Environment *Christopher Cairn*
Features Editor *Robert Campbell*
Literary Editor *Catherine Lockerbie*
Women's Page *Gillian Glover*

Weekend **Editor** *Maggie Lennon*. Includes book reviews, travel articles, etc.

The Sun
1 Virginia Street, London E1 9XP
☎0171 782 4000   Fax 0171 488 3253
Owner *News International plc*
Editor *Stuart Higgins*
Circulation 4 million

Highest circulation daily with a populist outlook; very keen on gossip, pop stars, TV soap, scandals and exposés of all kinds. No room for non-professional feature writers; 'investigative journalism' of a certain hue is always in demand, however.

News Editor *Glenn Goodey*
Features Editor *Mike Ridley*
Sports Editor *Paul Ridley*
Women's Page *Jane Moore*

Sunday Business
3 Cavendish Square, London W1M 0BB
☎0171 468 6000   Fax 0171 436 3797
Owner *Martin Lavell*
Editor *David Rydell*
Circulation 50,000

LAUNCHED April 1996. New national newspaper dedicated entirely to business. Consists of two sections: *Trading Week* and *News Review*.

Features/Business Editor *Greg Herbert*
Political Editor *Adam Sherwin*

Sunday Life
124–144 Royal Avenue, Belfast BT1 1EB
☎01232 264300   Fax 01232 554507
Owner *Trinity International Holdings plc*
Editor *Martin Lindsay*
Circulation 101,120

Deputy Editor *Dave Culbert*
Sports Editor *Jim Gracey*

Sunday Mail

Anderston Quay, Glasgow G3 8DA
☎0141 248 7000   Fax 0141 242 3587
Owner *Mirror Group Newspapers*
Editor *Jim Cassidy*
Circulation 847,776

Popular Scottish Sunday tabloid.
News Editor *Brian Steel*
Features Editor *Rob Bruce*
Political Editor *Angus McLeod*
Women's Page *Melanie Reid*

Sunday Mail 2: weekly supplement. **Editor** *Jeanette Harkess.*

Sunday Mirror

1 Canada Square, Canary Wharf, London
E14 5AP
☎0171 293 3000   Fax 0171 293 3939
Owner *Mirror Group Newspapers*
Editor *Bridget Rowe*
Circulation 2.40 million

Receives anything up to 100 unsolicited mss weekly. In general terms, these are welcome, though the paper patiently points out it has more time for contributors who have taken the trouble to study the market. Initial contact in writing preferred, except for live news situations. No fiction.
News Editor *Andy Byrne* The news desk is very much in the market for tip-offs and inside information. Contributors would be expected to work with staff writers on news stories.
City/Financial Editor *Diane Boliver*
Features Editor *Shan Lancaster* 'Anyone who has obviously studied the market will be dealt with constructively and courteously.' Cherishes its record as a breeding ground for new talent.
Sports Editor *Bill Bradshaw*

Personal: colour supplement. **Editor** *Paul Bennett.*

Sunday Post

2 Albert Square, Dundee DD1 9QJ
☎01382 223131   Fax 01382 201064
Owner *D. C. Thomson & Co. Ltd*
Editor *Russell Reid*
Circulation 904,504

The highest circulation Scottish Sunday paper. Contributions should be addressed to the editor.
News Editor *Iain MacKinnon*

Sunday Post Magazine: monthly colour supplement. **Editor** *Maggie Dun.*

Sunday Sport

19 Great Ancoats Street, Manchester M60 4BT
☎0161 236 4466   Fax 0161 236 4535
Owner *David Sullivan*
Editor *Jon Wise*
Circulation 335,000

FOUNDED 1986. Sunday tabloid catering for a particular sector of the male 18–35 readership. As concerned with 'glamour' as with human interest, news, features and sport. Regular short story competition (maximum 1000 words). Unsolicited mss welcome; receives about 90 a week. Approach by phone in the case of news and sports items, by letter for features. All material should be addressed to the news editor.
News Editor *Mark Harris* Off-beat news, human interest, preferably with photographs.
Features Editor *Mark Harris* Regular items: glamour, showbiz and television, as well as general interest.
Sports Editor *Marc Smith* Hard-hitting sports stories on major soccer clubs and personalities, plus leading clubs/people in other sports. Strong quotations to back up the news angle essential.
Payment negotiable and on publication.

Sunday Telegraph

1 Canada Square, Canary Wharf, London
E14 5DT
☎0171 538 5000   Fax 0171 513 2504
Owner *Conrad Black*
Editor *Dominic Lawson*
Circulation 890,000

Right-of-centre quality Sunday paper (meaning it has the least tendency to bend its ear to the scandals of the hour). Traditionally formal, it has pepped up its image to attract a younger readership. Unsolicited material from untried writers is rarely ever used. Contact with idea and details of track record.
News Editor *Chris Anderson*
City/Financial Editor *Neil Bennett*
Features Editor *Rebecca Nicolson*
Arts Editor *John Preston*
Literary Editor *Miriam Gross*
Diary Editor *Sunny Tucker*
Sports Editor *Colin Gibson*
Women's Page *Rebecca Nicolson*

Sunday Telegraph Magazine Rebecca Tyrrel

The Sunday Times

1 Pennington Street, London E1 9XW
☎0171 782 5000   Fax 0171 782 5658
Owner *News International plc*
Editor *John Witherow*

Circulation 1.28 million

FOUNDED 1820. Tendency to be anti-establishment, with a strong crusading investigative tradition. Approach the relevant editor with an idea in writing. Close scrutiny of the style of each section of the paper is strongly advised before sending mss. No fiction. All fees by negotiation.

News Editor *Mark Skipworth* Opportunities are very rare.

News Review Editor *Sarah Baxter* Submissions are always welcome, but the paper commissions its own, uses staff writers or works with literary agents, by and large. The features sections where most opportunities exist are *Style* and *The Culture*.

   Arts Editor *Helen Hawkins*
   Economics Editor *David Smith*
   Education *Judith O'Reilly*
   Environment *Jonathan Leake*
   Literary Editor *Geordie Greig*
   Sports Editor *Jeff Randall*
   Style Editor *Jeremy Langmead*

Sunday Times Magazine: colour supplement. **Editor** *Robin Morgan*. No unsolicited material. Write with ideas in first instance.

The Times

1 Pennington Street, London E1 9XN
☎0171 782 5000   Fax 0171 488 3242
Owner *News International plc*
Editor *Peter Stothard*
Circulation 793,920

Generally right-wing (though features can range in tone from diehard to libertarian). *The Times* receives a great many unsolicited offerings. Writers with feature ideas should approach by letter in the first instance. No fiction.

   News Editor *Graham Duffill*
   Arts Editor *Richard Morrison*
   Business/City/Financial Editor *Patience Wheatcroft*
   Diary Editor *Andrew Yates*
   Education *John O'Leary*
   Environment *Nick Nuttall*
   Associate Editor *Brian MacArthur*
   Literary Editor *Erica Wagner*
   Political Editor *Phil Webster*
   Sports Editor *David Chappell*

Weekend Times **Editor** *Gill Morgan*

The Times Magazine: Saturday supplement. **Editor** *Nicholas Wapshott*
   Features Editor *Sandra Parsons*

Wales on Sunday

Thomson House, Havelock Street, Cardiff CF1 1WR
☎01222 223333   Fax 01222 583725
Owner *Trinity International Holdings plc*
Editor *Alan Edmunds*
Circulation 57,379

LAUNCHED 1989. Tabloid with sports supplement. Does not welcome unsolicited mss.
   News Editor *Alistair Milburn*
   Features/Women's Page *Mike Smith*
   Sports Editor *Richard Morgans*

Regional Newspapers

Regional newspapers are listed in alphabetical order under town. Thus the *Evening Standard* appears under 'L' for London; the *Lancashire Evening Post* under 'P' for Preston.

Aberdeen

Evening Express (Aberdeen)
PO Box 43, Lang Stracht, Mastrick, Aberdeen
AB9 8AF
☎01224 690222   Fax 01224 699575
Owner *Northcliffe Newspapers Group Ltd*
Editor *Geoff Teather*
Circulation 67,742

Circulates in Aberdeen and the Grampian region. Local, national and international news and pictures, family finance and property news. Unsolicited mss welcome 'if on a controlled basis'.
   News Editor *Jonathan Brocklebank* Freelance news contributors welcome.
   Payment £30–60.

The Press and Journal
PO Box 43, Lang Stracht, Mastrick, Aberdeen
AB9 8AF
☎01224 690222   Fax 01224 663575
Owner *Northcliffe Newspapers Group Ltd*
Editor *Derek Tucker*
Circulation 107,138

Circulates in Aberdeen, Grampians, Highlands, Tayside, Orkney, Shetland and the Western Isles. A well-established regional daily which is said to receive more unsolicited mss a week than the *Sunday Mirror*. Unsolicited mss are nevertheless welcome; approach in writing with ideas. No fiction.
   News Editor *David Knight* Wide variety of hard or off-beat news and features relating especially, but not exclusively, to the North of Scotland.
   Sports Editor *Jim Dolan*
   Women's Page *Kate Yuill*
   Payment by arrangement.

Barrow in Furness

North West Evening Mail
Abbey Road, Barrow in Furness, Cumbria
LA14 5QS
☎01229 821835   Fax 01229 840164

Owner *CN Group Ltd*
Editor *Donald Martin*
Circulation 20,673

All editorial material should be addressed to the editor.
   Assistant Editor *Bill Myers*.
   Sports Editor *Leo Clarke*.

Basildon

Evening Echo
Newspaper House, Chester Hall Lane, Basildon, Essex SS14 3BL
☎01268 522792   Fax 01268 282884
Owner *Newsquest Media Group*
Editor *Martin McNeill*
Circulation 45,000

Relies almost entirely on staff and regular outside contributors, but will very occasionally consider material sent on spec. Approach the editor in writing with ideas. Although the paper is Basildon-based, its largest circulation is in the Southend area.

Bath

The Bath Chronicle
33/34 Westgate Street, Bath BA1 1EW
☎01225 444044   Fax 01225 445969
Owner *Newsquest (Wessex) Ltd*
Editor *David Gledhill*
Circulation 17,720

   Deputy Editor *John McCready*
   News Editor *Paul Wiltshire*
   Features Editor *Andrew Knight*
   Sports Editor *Neville Smith*

Local news and features especially welcomed.

Belfast

Belfast Telegraph
Royal Avenue, Belfast BT1 1EB
☎01232 264000   Fax 01232 554506
Owner *Trinity International Holdings Plc*
Editor *Edmund Curran*

Circulation 133,132

Weekly business supplement.

Deputy Editor *Jim Flanagan*
News Editor *Janet Devlin*
Features Editor *John Caruth*
Sports Editor *John Laverty*
Business Editor *Rosie Cowan*

The Irish News

113/117 Donegall Street, Belfast BT1 2GE
☎01232 322226   Fax 01232 337505

Owner *Irish News Ltd*
Editor *Tom Collins*
Circulation 45,906

All material to appropriate editor (phone to check), or to the news desk.

Deputy Editor *Noel Doran*
Head of Content *Ben Webster, Fiona McGarry*
Arts Editor *Colin McAlpin*
Sports Editor *Stephen O'Reilly*
Women's Page *Ann Molloy*

Ulster News Letter

46–56 Boucher Crescent, Belfast BT12 6QY
☎01232 680000   Fax 01232 664412

Owner *Century Newspapers Ltd*
Editor *Geoff Martin*
Circulation 33,753

Supplements: *Farming Life* (weekly); *Shopping News; Belfast Newsletter.*

Deputy Editor *Mike Chapman*
Assistant Editor *Billy Kennedy*
News Editor *Harry Robinson*
Features Editor *Geoff Hill*
Sports Editor *Brian Millar*
Fashion & Lifestyle/Property Editor *Sandra Chapman*
Business Editor *David Kirk*
Agricultural Editor *David McCoy*

Birmingham

Birmingham Evening Mail

28 Colmore Circus, Queensway, Birmingham B4 6AX
☎0121 236 3366   Fax 0121 233 0271

Owner *Midland Independent Newspapers Plc*
Editor *Ian Dowell*
Circulation 197,532

Freelance contributions are welcome, particularly topics of interest to the West Midlands and Women's Page pieces offering original and lively comment.

News Editor *Norman Stinchcombe*

Features Editor *Paul Cole*
Women's Page *Briony Jones*

Birmingham Post

28 Colmore Circus, Queensway, Birmingham B4 6AX
☎0121 236 3366
Fax 0121 233 0271/625 1105

Owner *Midland Independent Newspapers Plc*
Editor *Nigel Hastilow*
Circulation 26,090

One of the country's leading regional newspapers. Freelance contributions are welcome. Topics of interest to the West Midlands and pieces offering lively, original comment are particularly welcome.

News Editor *Chris Russon*
Features Editor *Peter Bacon*
Women's Page *Ros Dodd*

Sunday Mercury (Birmingham)

28 Colmore Circus, Queensway, Birmingham B4 6AZ
☎0121 236 3366   Fax 0121 625 1105
Owner *Birmingham Post & Mail Ltd*
Editor *Peter Whitehouse*
Circulation 145,472

News Editor *Bob Haywood*
Features Editor *James Windle*
Sports Editor *Roger Skidmore*

Blackburn

Lancashire Evening Telegraph

Newspaper House, High Street, Blackburn, Lancashire BB1 1HT
☎01254 678678   Fax 01254 680429

Owner *Newsquest Media Group Ltd*
Editor *Peter Butterfield*
Circulation 45,381

News stories and feature material with an East Lancashire flavour (a local angle, or written by local people) welcome. Approach in writing with an idea in the first instance. No fiction.

News/Features/Women's Page Editor *Nick Nunn*

Blackpool

Evening Gazette (Blackpool)

PO Box 20, Preston New Road, Blackpool, Lancashire FY4 4AU
☎01253 839999   Fax 01253 694152

Owner *United Newspapers*
Managing Editor *Philip Welsh*

Circulation 44,578

Unsolicited mss welcome in theory. Approach in writing with an idea. Supplements: *Monday Green* (sport); *Eve* (women, Tuesday); *Wheels* (motoring, Wednesday); *Property* (Thursday); *Sevendays* (entertainment & leisure, Saturday).
Head of Content *Ian Hamilton*
Sports Editor *Jonathan Lee*

Bolton

Bolton Evening News
Newspaper House, Churchgate, Bolton, Lancashire BL1 1DE
☎01204 522345   Fax 01204 365068
Owner *Newsquest Media Group Ltd*
Editor *Andrew Smith*
Circulation 43,837

Business, children's page, travel, local services, motoring, fashion and cookery.
News Editor *Melvyn Horrocks*
Features Editor/Women's Page *Angela Kelly*

Bournemouth

Evening Echo
Richmond Hill, Bournemouth, Dorset BH2 6HH
☎01202 554601   Fax 01202 292115
Owner *Southern Newspapers Plc*
Editor *Mike Woods*
Circulation 46,808

FOUNDED 1900. Has a strong features content and invites specialist articles, particularly on unusual and contemporary subjects but only with a local angle. Supplements: business, gardening, family matters, motoring. Regular features on weddings, property, books, local history, green issues, the Channel coast. All editorial material should be addressed to the **News Editor** *Andy Bissell*.
Payment on publication.

Bradford

Telegraph & Argus (Bradford)
Hall Ings, Bradford, West Yorkshire BD1 1JR
☎01274 729511   Fax 01274 723634
Owner *Newsquest Media Group Ltd*
Editor *Perry Austin-Clarke*
Circulation 57,213

No unsolicited mss – approach in writing with samples of work. No fiction.
Head of Content *Jan Brierley* Local features

and general interest. Showbiz pieces. 600–1000 words (maximum 1500).
Sports Editor *Peter Rowe*
Women's Editor *Sharon Dale*

Brighton

Evening Argus
Argus House, Crowhurst Road, Hollingbury, Brighton, East Sussex BN1 8AR
☎01273 544544   Fax 01273 505703
Owner *Newsquest (Sussex) Ltd*
Editor *Adrian Faber*
Circulation 64,264
News Editor *Claire Byrd*
Sports Editor *Chris Giles*
Women's Page *Winifred Blackmore*

Bristol

Evening Post
Temple Way, Bristol BS99 7HD
☎0117 9343000   Fax 0117 9343575
Owner *Bristol Evening Post Plc*
Editor *Mike Lowe*
Circulation 84,939
News Editor *Rob Stokes*
Features Editor *Matthew Shelley*
Sports Editor *Chris Bartlett*

Western Daily Press
Temple Way, Bristol BS99 7HD
☎0117 9343000   Fax 0117 9343574
Owner *Bristol Evening Post & Press Ltd*
Editor *Ian Beales*
Circulation 60,451
News Editor *Steve Hughes*
Features Editor *Jane Riddiford*
Sports Editor *Bill Beckett*
Women's Page *Lynda Cleasby*

Burton upon Trent

Burton Mail
65–68 High Street, Burton upon Trent, Staffordshire DE14 1LE
☎01283 512345   Fax 01283 515351
Owner *Burton Daily Mail Ltd*
Editor *Brian Vertigen*
Circulation 20,030

Fashion, health, wildlife, environment, nostalgia, financial/money (Monday); consumer, motoring (Tuesday); women's world, rock (Wednesday); property (Thursday); motoring, farming, what's on (Friday); what's on, leisure (Saturday).

News/Features Editor *Andrew Parker*
Sports Editor *Rex Page*
Women's Page *Sue Grief*

Cambridge
Cambridge Evening News
Winship Road, Milton, Cambridge
CB4 6PP
☎01223 434434   Fax 01223 434415
Owner *Cambridge Newspapers Ltd*
Editor *Robert Satchwell*
Circulation 41,906

News Editor *John Conlon*
Sports Editor *Alex Martin*
Women's Page *Angela Singer*

Cardiff
South Wales Echo
Thomson House, Cardiff CF1 1XR
☎01222 223333   Fax 01222 583624
Owner *Trinity International Holdings Plc*
Editor *Robin Fletcher*
Circulation 77,618

Circulates in South and Mid Glamorgan and Gwent.

News Editor *Jeremy Clifford*
Features *Martin Wells*
Sports Editor *Terry Phillips*

The Western Mail
Thomson House, Havelock Street, Cardiff
CF1 1WR
☎01222 223333   Fax 01222 583652
Owner *Trinity International Holdings Plc*
Editor *Neil Fowler*
Circulation 64,172

Circulates in Cardiff, Merthyr Tydfil, Newport, Swansea and towns and villages throughout Wales. Mss welcome if of a topical nature, and preferably of Welsh interest. No short stories or travel. Approach in writing to the editor. 'Usual subjects already well covered, e.g. motoring, travel, books, gardening. We look for the unusual.' Maximum 1000 words. Opportunities also on women's page. Supplements: Television Wales; Arena; Welsh Homes; Country and Farming; Business; Sport.

Head of News & Features *Simon Irwin*
Sports Editor *Mark Tattersall*

Carlisle
News & Star
Newspaper House, Dalston Road, Carlisle, Cumbria CA2 5UA
☎01228 23488   Fax 01228 512828
Owner *Cumbrian Newspaper Group Ltd*
Editor *Keith Sutton*
Circulation 26,795

News Editor *Nick Turner*
Head of Content *Steve Johnston*
Sports Editor *John Reynolds*
Women's Page *Jane Loughran*

Chatham
Kent Today
395 High Street, Chatham, Kent
ME4 4PQ
☎01634 830600   Fax 01634 829484
Owner *Kent Messenger Group*
Editor *C. Stewart*
Circulation 24,148

Assistant Editor (Production) *Neil Webber*
Community Editor *David Jones*
Sports Editor *Mike Rees*
Women's Page *Helen Daly*
Business Editor *Trevor Sturgess*

Cheltenham
Gloucestershire Echo
1 Clarence Parade, Cheltenham, Gloucestershire GL50 3NZ
☎01242 271900   Fax 01242 271803
Owner *Northcliffe Newspapers Group Ltd*
Editor *Anita Syvret*
Circulation 26,387

All material, other than news, should be addressed to the editor.

News Editor *Chris Bishop*

Chester
Chronicle Newspapers (Chester)
Chronicle House, Commonhall Street, Chester CH1 2BJ
☎01244 340151   Fax 01244 340165
Owner *Trinity International Holdings Plc*
Editor-in-Chief *Bob Adams*

All unsolicited feature material will be considered.

Colchester

Evening Gazette (Colchester)
Oriel House, 43–44 North Hill, Colchester,
Essex CO1 1TZ
☎01206 761212   Fax 01206 769523
Owner *Essex County Newspapers*
Editor *Irene Kettle*
Circulation 29,525

Unsolicited mss not generally used. Relies
heavily on regular contributors.
    Features Editor *Iris Clapp*

Coventry

Coventry Evening Telegraph
Corporation Street, Coventry CV1 1FP
☎01203 633633   Fax 01203 550869
Owner *Midland Independent Newspapers*
Editor *Dan Mason*
Circulation 83,838

Unsolicited mss are read, but few are published. Approach in writing with an idea. No
fiction. All unsolicited material should be
addressed to the editor. Maximum 600 words
for features.
    News Editor *Peter Mitchell*
    Features Editor *Paul Simoniti*
    Sports Editor *Roger Draper*
    Women's Page *Barbara Argument*
    Payment negotiable.

Darlington

The Northern Echo
Priestgate, Darlington, Co. Durham
DL1 1NF
☎01325 381313   Fax 01325 380539
Owner *North of England Newspapers*
Editor *Andrew Smith*
Circulation 72,499

FOUNDED 1870. Freelance pieces welcome but
telephone first to discuss submission.
    News Editor *Tony Metcalf* Interested in
reports involving the North-east or North
Yorkshire. Preferably phoned in.
    Features Editor *Chris Lloyd* Background
pieces to topical news stories relevant to the
area. Must be arranged with the features editor
before submission of any material.
    Business Editor *Colin Tapping*
    Sports Editor *Kevin Dinsdale*
    Payment and length by arrangement.

Derby

Derby Evening Telegraph
Northcliffe House, Meadow Road, Derby
DE1 2DW
☎01332 291111   Fax 01332 253027
Owner *Northcliffe Newspapers Group Ltd*
Editor *Keith Perch*
Circulation 63,478

Weekly business supplement.
    News Editor *Robert Irvine*
    Features Editor/Women's Page *Nigel
    Poulson*
    Sports Editor *Steve Nicholson*
    Motoring Editor *Bob Maddox*

Doncaster

The Doncaster Star
40 Duke Street, Doncaster, South Yorkshire
DN1 3EA
☎01302 344001   Fax 01302 329072
Owner *Sheffield Newspapers Ltd*
Editor *Allan Tunningley*
Circulation 7,916

All editorial material to be addressed to the editor.
    Sports Editor *Steve Hossack*
    Women's Page *Jane Stapleton*

Dundee

The Courier and Advertiser
80 Kingsway East, Dundee DD4 8SL
☎01382 223131   Fax 01382 454590
Owner *D. C. Thomson & Co. Ltd*
Editor *Adrian Arthur*
Circulation 103,768

Circulates in Dundee, Tayside, Fife and parts
of Central and Grampian. Features welcome
on a wide variety of subjects, not solely of
local/Scottish interest. Two pages devoted to
features each weekend, supplied by freelancers
and in-house. Finance, insurance, agriculture,
EU topics, motoring, women, modern homes.
Only rule of thumb is to keep it short.
Maximum 500 words.
    News Editor *Steve Bargeton*
    Features Editor/Women's Page *Shona
Lorimer*
    Sports Editor *Graham Dey*

Evening Telegraph & Post
80 Kingsway East, Dundee DD4 8SL
☎01382 223131   Fax 01382 454590
Owner *D. C. Thomson & Co. Ltd*
Editor *Alan Proctor*

Editor *Harold Pirie*
Circulation 35,458

Circulates in Tayside, Dundee and Fife. All material should be addressed to the editor.

East Anglia

East Anglian Daily Times
See under **Ipswich**

Eastern Daily Press
See under **Norwich**

Edinburgh

Evening News
20 North Bridge, Edinburgh EH1 1YT
☎0131 225 2468   Fax 0131 225 7302

Owner *European Press Holdings Ltd*
Editor *John C. McGurk*
Circulation 86,650

FOUNDED 1873. Circulates in Edinburgh, Fife, Central and Lothian. Coverage includes: lifestyle and entertainments (daily); motoring column (Friday); gardening, computers, book reviews, DIY, historical memories, shopping, fashion, nature, show business, and *The Doctor* (health). Unsolicited feature material welcome. Approach the appropriate editor by telephone.
    News Editor *David Lee*
    Features Editor *Helen Martin* Weekender magazine supplement of broad general/historical interest. Occasional Platform pieces (i.e. sounding off, topical or opinion pieces). Maximum 1000 words.
    Sports Editor *Paul Greaves*
    Payment NUJ/house rates.

Exeter

Express & Echo
Heron Road, Sowton, Exeter, Devon
EX2 7NF
☎01392 442211
Fax 01392 442294/442287 (editorial)

Owner *Express & Echo Publications Ltd*
Editor *John Meehan*
Circulation 30,812

Weekly supplements: *Business Week; Property Echo; Wheels; Weekend Echo.*
    News Editor *Marc Astley*
    Features Editor/Women's Page *Sue Kemp*
    Sports Editor *Jerry Charge*

Glasgow

Evening Times
195 Albion Street, Glasgow G1 1QP
☎0141 552 6255   Fax 0141 553 1355

Owner *Scottish Television Plc*
Editor *John D. Scott*
Circulation 138,066

Circulates in the Strathclyde region. Supplements: *Job Search; Home Front; Inspirations* (women's section); *Time Out* (leisure); *TGIF* (weekend preview).
    News Editor *Ally McLaws*
    Features Editor *Russell Kyle*
    Sports Editor *David Stirling*
    Women's Page *Agnes Stevenson*

The Herald (Glasgow)
See **National Newspapers**

Gloucester

The Citizen
St John's Lane, Gloucester GL1 2AY
☎01452 424442   Fax 01452 307238

Owner *Northcliffe Newspapers Group Ltd*
Editor *Spencer Feeney*
Circulation 37,087

All editorial material to be addressed to the **News Editor** *Chris Hill.*

Gloucestershire Echo
See under **Cheltenham**

Greenock

Greenock Telegraph
2 Crawfurd Street, Greenock PA15 1LH
☎01475 726511   Fax 01475 783734

Owner *Clyde & Forth Press Ltd*
Editor *Ian Wilson*
Circulation 20,618

Circulates in Greenock, Port Glasgow, Gourock, Kilmacolm, Langbank, Bridge of Weir, Inverkip, Wemyss Bay, Skelmorlie, Largs. Unsolicited mss considered 'if they relate to the newspaper's general interests'. No fiction. All material to be addressed to the editor.

Grimsby

Grimsby Evening Telegraph
80 Cleethorpe Road, Grimsby, N. E. Lincs
DN31 3EH
☎01472 360360   Fax 01472 372257

Owner *Northcliffe Newspapers Group Ltd*

Editor *Peter Moore*
Circulation 71,167

Sister paper of the *Scunthorpe Evening Telegraph*. Unsolicited mss generally welcome. Approach in writing. No fiction. Monthly supplement: *Business Telegraph*. All material to be addressed to the **News Editor** *S. P. Richards*. Particularly welcome hard news stories – approach in haste by telephone.
   Special Publications Editor *B. Farnsworth*

Guernsey

Guernsey Evening Press & Star
Braye Road, Vale, Guernsey, Channel Islands GY1 3BW
☎01481 45866   Fax 01481 48972

Owner *Guernsey Press Co. Ltd*
Editor *Graham Ingrouille*
Circulation 15,891

Special pages include children's and women's interest, gardening and fashion.
   News Editor *Dave Edmonds*
   Sports Editor *Rob Batiste*
   Women's Page *Kay Leslie*

Halifax

Evening Courier
PO Box 19, Halifax, West Yorkshire HX1 2SF
☎01422 365711   Fax 01422 330021

Owner *Johnston Press Plc*
Editor *Edward Riley*
Circulation 31,937

   News Editor *John Kenealy*
   Features Editor *William Marshall*
   Sports Editor *Ian Rushworth*
   Women's Page *Diane Crabtree*

Hartlepool

Mail (Hartlepool)
New Clarence House, Wesley Square, Hartlepool TS24 8BX
☎01429 274441   Fax 01429 869024

Owner *Northeast Press Ltd*
Editor *Christopher Cox*
Circulation 26,460

   Deputy Editor *Harry Blackwood*
   News Editor *Neil Hunter*
   Features Editor *Bernice Saltzer*
   Sports Editor *Roy Kelly*
   Women's Page *Margaret O'Rourke*

Huddersfield

Huddersfield Daily Examiner
Queen Street South, Huddersfield, West Yorkshire HD1 2TD
☎01484 430000   Fax 01484 423722

Owner *Trinity International Holdings Plc*
Editor *John Williams*
Editor *Richard Mallinson*
Circulation 37,694

Home improvement, home heating, weddings, dining out, motoring, fashion, services to trade and industry.
   Deputy Editor *Melvyn Briggs*
   News Editor *Neil Atkinson*
   Features Editor *Andrew Flynn*
   Sports Editor *John Gledhill*
   Women's Page *Hilarie Stelfox*

Hull

Hull Daily Mail
Blundell's Corner, Beverley Road, Hull, North Humberside HU3 1XS
☎01482 327111   Fax 01482 584353

Owner *Northcliffe Newspapers Group Ltd*
Editor *Michael Wood*
Circulation 89,156

   News/Features Editor *Mark Woodward*
   Sports Editor *Chris Harvey*
   Women's Page *Jo Davison*

Ipswich

East Anglian Daily Times
30 Lower Brook Street, Ipswich, Suffolk IP4 1AN
☎01473 230023   Fax 01473 211391

Owner *Eastern Counties Newspaper Group*
Editor *Terry Hunt*
Circulation 47,463

FOUNDED 1874. Unsolicited mss generally not welcome; three or four received a week and almost none are used. Approach in writing in the first instance. No fiction. Supplements: Job Quest (Wednesday); Business (Wednesday); Property (Thursday); Motoring (Friday); Leisure Guide (Saturday).
   News Editor *Mark Hindle* Hard news stories involving East Anglia (Suffolk, Essex particularly) or individuals resident in the area are always of interest.
   Features Editor *Robyn Bechelet* Mostly in-house, but will occasionally buy in when the subject is of strong Suffolk/East Anglian interest. Photo features preferred (extra payment).

Special advertisement features are regularly run. Some opportunities here. Max. 1000 words.
Sports Editor *Nick Garnham*
Women's Page *Robyn Bechelet*

Evening Star
30 Lower Brook Street, Ipswich, Suffolk IP4 1AN
☎01473 230023   Fax 01473 225296
Owner *Eastern Counties Newspaper Group*
Editor *Nigel Pickover*
Circulation 30,391

Deputy Editor *Russell Cook*
Sports Editor *Mike Horne*

Jersey
Jersey Evening Post
PO Box 582, Jersey, Channel Islands JE4 8XQ
☎01534 611611   Fax 01534 611622
Owner *Jersey Evening Post Ltd*
Editor *Chris Bright*
Circulation 23,194

Special pages: gardening, motoring, farmers and growers, property, boating, computer and office, young person's (16–25), women, food and drink, personal finance, rock and classical reviews.
News Editor *Sue Le Ruez*
Features Editor *Rob Shipley*
Sports Editor *Ron Felton*

Kent
Kent Messenger
See under *Maidstone*

Kent Today
See under *Chatham*

Kettering
Evening Telegraph
Northfield Avenue, Kettering, Northamptonshire NN16 9TT
☎01536 81111   Fax 01536 85983
Owner *Johnston Press Plc*
Editor *David Rowell*
Circulation 36,118

Business Telegraph (weekly); *Guide* supplement (Thursday/Saturday), featuring TV, gardening, videos, films, eating out; two monthly supplements, *Home & Garden* and *Car Driver*.
News Editor *Helen O'Neill*
Business Editor *Tony Bacon*
Sports Editor *Ian Davidson*

Lancashire
Lancashire Evening Post
See under *Preston*

Lancashire Evening Telegraph
See under *Blackburn*

Leamington Spa
Leamington Spa Courier
32 Hamilton Terrace, Leamington Spa, Warwickshire CV32 4LY
☎01926 888222   Fax 01926 451690
Owner *Central Counties Newspapers*
Editor *Martin Lawson*
Circulation 13,410

One of the Leamington Spa Courier Series which also includes the *Warwick Courier* and *Kenilworth Weekly News*. Unsolicited feature articles considered, particularly matter with a local angle. Telephone with idea first.
News Editor *Mark Sanderson*

Leeds
Yorkshire Evening Post
Wellington Street, Leeds, West Yorkshire LS1 1RF
☎0113 2432701   Fax 0113 2388536
Owner *Yorkshire Post Newspapers Ltd*
Editor *Christopher Bye*
Circulation 101,810

Evening sister of the *Yorkshire Post*.
News Editor *David Helliwell*
Features Editor *Anne Pickles*
Sports Editor *Ian Ward*
Women's Page *Carmen Bruegmann*

Yorkshire Post
Wellington Street, Leeds, West Yorkshire LS1 1RF
☎0113 2432701   Fax 0113 2388537
Owner *Yorkshire Post Newspapers Ltd*
Editor *Tony Watson*
Circulation 76,771

A serious-minded, quality regional daily with a generally conservative outlook. Three or four unsolicited mss arrive each day; all will be considered but initial approach in writing preferred. All submissions should be addressed to the editor. No fiction.
Assistant Editor (News) *John Furbisher*
Features Editor *Mick Hickling* Open to suggestions in all fields (though ordinarily commissioned from specialist writers).

Sports Editor *Bill Bridge*
Women's Page *Jill Armstrong*

Leicester
Leicester Mercury
St George Street, Leicester LE1 9FQ
☎0116 2512512   Fax 0116 2530645
Owner *Northcliffe Newspapers Group Ltd*
Editor *Nick Carter*
Circulation 117,416

News Editor *Simon Orrell*
Features Editor *Mark Clayton*

Lincoln
Lincolnshire Echo
Brayford Wharf East, Lincoln LN5 7AT
☎01522 525252   Fax 01522 545759
Owner *Northcliffe Newspapers Group Ltd*
Editor *Cliff Smith, OBE*
Circulation 30,124

Best buys, holidays, motoring, dial-a-service, restaurants, sport, leisure, home improvement, record review, gardening corner, stars. All editorial material to be addressed to the **Assistant Editor** *Mike Gubbins.*

Liverpool
Daily Post
PO Box 48, Old Hall Street, Liverpool L69 3EB
☎0151 227 2000   Fax 0151 236 4682
Owner *Liverpool Daily Post & Echo Ltd*
Editor *Alastair Machray*
Circulation 72,776

Unsolicited mss welcome. Receives about six a day. Approach in writing with an idea. No fiction. Local, national/international news, current affairs, profiles – with pictures. Maximum 800–1000 words.
Features Editor *Mark Davies*
Sports Editor *Len Capeling*
Women's Page *Margaret Kitchen*

Liverpool Echo
PO Box 48, Old Hall Street, Liverpool L69 3EB
☎0151 227 2000   Fax 0151 236 4682
Owner *Liverpool Daily Post & Echo Ltd*
Editor *John Griffith*
Circulation 160,861

One of the country's major regional dailies. Unsolicited mss welcome; initial approach with ideas in writing preferred.

News Editor *Tony Storey*
Features Editor *Janet Tansley* Maximum 1000 words.
Sports Editor *Ken Rogers*
Women's Editor *Sue Lee*

London
Evening Standard
Northcliffe House, 2 Derry Street, London W8 5EE
☎0171 938 6000   Fax 0171 937 2648
Owner *Lord Rothermere*
Editor *Max Hastings*
Circulation 440,000

Long-established evening paper, serving Londoners with both news and feature material. Genuine opportunities for London-based features. Produces a weekly colour supplement, *ES The Evening Standard Magazine* and weekly listings magazine *Hot Tickets.*
Deputy Editor *Peter Boyer*
Associate Editor (Features) *Nicola Jeal*
News Editor *Stephen Clackson*
Features Editor *Bernice Davison*
Sports Editor *Michael Herd*
Editor, *ES Adam Edwards*
Editor, *Hot Tickets Miles Chapman*

Maidstone
Kent Messenger
6 & 7 Middle Row, Maidstone, Kent ME14 1TG
☎01622 695666   Fax 01622 757227
Owner *Kent Messenger Group*
Editor *Ron Green*
Circulation 42,000

Very little freelance work is commissioned.

Manchester
Manchester Evening News
164 Deansgate, Manchester M60 2RD
☎0161 832 7200   Fax 0161 834 3814
Owner *Manchester Evening News Ltd*
Editor *Michael Unger*
Circulation 183,543

One of the country's major regional dailies. Initial approach in writing preferred. No fiction. Property (Tuesday); holiday feature (Saturday); Lifestyle (Friday/Saturday).
News Editor *Lisa Roland*
Features Editor *Diane Robinson* Regional news features, personality pieces and showbiz profiles considered. Maximum 1200 words.

Sports Editor *Neville Bolton*
Women's Page *Diane Cooke*
Payment based on house agreement rates.

Middlesbrough
Evening Gazette
Borough Road, Middlesbrough, Cleveland
TS1 3AZ
☎01642 245401   Fax 01642 232014
Owner *Trinity International Holdings plc*
Editor *Ranald Allan*
Circulation 69,000

Special pages: business, motoring, home, computing.
News Editor *Tony Beck*
Features Editor *Alan Sims*
Sports Editor *Allan Boughey*
Women's Page *Kathryn Armstrong*
Crime *Damian Bates*
Environment *Iain Laing*
Consumer *Karen Bell*
Health *Amanda Todd*
Councils *Sandy McKenzie*

Mold
Evening Leader
Mold Business Park, Wrexham Road, Mold,
Clwyd CH7 1XY
☎01352 707707   Fax 01352 752180
Owner *North Wales Newspapers*
Editor *Reg Herbert*
Circulation 30,976

Circulates in Wrexham, Clwyd, Deeside and
Chester. Special pages/features: motoring,
travel, arts, women's, children's, photography,
local housing, information and news for the
disabled, music and entertainment.
Features Page *Debra Greenhouse*
News Editor *Nick Bourne*
Women's Page *Gail Cooper*
Sports Editor *Allister Syme*

Newcastle upon Tyne
Evening Chronicle
Thomson House, Groat Market, Newcastle
upon Tyne, Tyne & Wear NE1 1ED
☎0191 232 7500   Fax 0191 232 2256
Owner *Trinity International Holdings Plc*
Editor *Alison Hastings*
Circulation 118,360

Receives a lot of unsolicited material, much of

which is not used. Family issues, gardening,
pop, fashion, cooking, consumer, films and
entertainment guide, home improvements,
motoring, property, angling, sport and holidays. Approach in writing with ideas.
News Editor *David Bourn*
Features Editor *Jane Pikett* Limited opportunities due to full-time feature staff. Maximum
1000 words.
Sports Editor *Paul New*
Women's Interests *Kay Jordan*

The Journal
Thomson House, Groat Market, Newcastle
upon Tyne, Tyne & Wear NE1 1ED
☎0191 232 7500   Fax 0191 232 2256
Owner *Trinity International Holdings Plc*
Editor *Mark Dickinson*
Circulation 55,373

Daily platforms include farming and business.
Monthly full-colour business supplement: *The
Journal Northern Business Magazine.*
Assistant Editor *Tom Patterson*
Sports Editor *Nick Crockford*
Arts & Entertainment Editor *David
Whetstone*
Environmental Editor *Tony Henderson*

Sunday Sun
Thomson House, Groat Market, Newcastle
upon Tyne, Tyne & Wear NE1 1ED
☎0191 201 6330   Fax 0191 230 0238
Owner *Trinity International Holdings Plc*
Editor *Chris Rushton*
Circulation 123,962

All material should be addressed to the appropriate editor (phone to check), or to the editor.
Associate Editor *Carole Watson*
Sports Editor *David Lamont*

Newport
South Wales Argus
Cardiff Road, Maesglas, Newport, Gwent
NP9 1QW
☎01633 810000   Fax 01633 462202
Owner *South Wales Argus Ltd*
Editor *Gerry Keighley*
Circulation 33,524

Circulates in Newport, Gwent and surrounding areas.
News Editor *Jeremy Flye*
Features Editor/Women's Page *Lesley
Williams*
Sports Editor *Carl Difford*

Northampton
Chronicle and Echo
Upper Mounts, Northampton NN1 3HR
☎01604 231122   Fax 01604 233000
Owner *Northampton Mercury Co. Ltd*
Editor *Mark Edwards*
Circulation 29,672

Unsolicited mss are 'not necessarily unwelcome but opportunities to use them are rare'. Some three or four arrive weekly. Approach in writing with an idea. No fiction. Supplements: *Sports Chronicle* (Monday); *Property Week* (Wednesday); *What's On Guide* (Thursday); *Weekend Motors* (Friday).
  News Editor *Steve Scoles*
  Features Editor/Women's Page *Ruth Supple*
  Sports Editor *Steve Pitts*

Northern Ireland
Belfast Telegraph, Northern Ireland
See under *Belfast*

The Irish News, Northern Ireland
See under *Belfast*

Sunday Life (Belfast), Northern Ireland
See **National Newspapers**

Norwich
Eastern Daily Press
Prospect House, Rouen Road, Norwich,
Norfolk NR1 1RE
☎01603 628311   Fax 01603 612930
Owner *Eastern Counties Newspapers*
Editor *Peter Franzen*
Circulation 79,880

Unsolicited mss welcome. Approach in writing with ideas. News (if relevant to Norfolk), and features up to 900 words. Other pieces by commission only. Supplements: what's on (daily); employment (twice-weekly); motoring (weekly); business (weekly); property pages (weekly); women's interests (monthly); arts focus (monthly); plus agriculture, horse and rider, boating, golf and wildlife.
  News Editor *Paul Durrant*
  Features Editor *Colin Chinery*
  Sports Editor *David Thorpe*
  Women's Page *Sarah Hardy*

Evening News
Prospect House, Rouen Road, Norwich,
Norfolk NR1 1RE
☎01603 628311   Fax 01603 612930
Owner *Eastern Counties Newspapers*
Editor *Bob Crawley*
Circulation 39,689

Includes special pages on local property, motoring, children's page, pop, fashion, arts, entertainments and TV, gardening, local music scene, home and family.
  Assistant Editor *Roy Strowger*
  Deputy Editor *Celia Sutton*
  Features Editor *Derek James*

Nottingham
Evening Post Nottingham
Forman Street, Nottingham NG1 4AB
☎0115 9482000   Fax 0115 9644027
Owner *Northcliffe Newspapers Group Ltd*
Editor *Graham Glen*
Circulation 100,000

Unsolicited mss welcome. Send ideas in writing. Supplements: motoring, business, holidays and travel supplements; financial, employment and consumer pages.
  News Editor *Judy Rees*
  Head of Content *Jon Grubb* Good local interest only. Maximum 800 words. No fiction.
  Sports Editor *Mick Holland*

Oldham
Evening Chronicle
PO Box 47, Union Street, Oldham,
Lancashire OL1 1EQ
☎0161 633 2121   Fax 0161 655 2111
Owner *Hirst Kidd & Rennie Ltd*
Editor *Philip Hirst*
Circulation 34,672

'We welcome the good but not the bad.' Motoring, food and wine, women's page, business page.
  News Editor *Mike Attenborough*
  Women's Page *Ralph Badham*

Oxford
Oxford Mail
Osney Mead, Oxford OX2 0EJ
☎01865 244988   Fax 01865 243382
Owner *Oxford & County Newspapers*
Editor *Chris Cowley*
Circulation 35,000

Unsolicited mss are considered but a great many unsuitable offerings are received. Approach in writing with an idea, rather than by phone. No fiction. All fees negotiable.

Head of Content *Anne Harrison*

Paisley

Paisley Daily Express
14 New Street, Paisley PA1 1YA
☎0141 887 7911   Fax 0141 887 6254

Owner *Scottish & Universal Newspapers Ltd*
Editor *Norman Macdonald*
Circulation 8,270

Circulates in Paisley, Linwood, Renfrew, Johnstone, Elderslie, Raiston and Barrhead. Unsolicited mss welcome only if of genuine local (Paisley) interest. The paper does not commission work, and will consider submitted material. Maximum 1000–1500 words. All submissions to the editor.

Features Editor/Women's Page *Anne Dalrymple*
Sports Editor *Matthew Vallance*

Plymouth

Evening Herald
17 Brest Road, Derriford Business Park, Derriford, Plymouth, Devon PL6 5AA
☎01752 765500   Fax 01752 765527

Owner *Northcliffe Newspapers Group Ltd*
Editor *Rachael Campey*
Circulation 55,036

All editorial material to be addressed to the editor or the **News Editor** *Anthony Abbott*.

Sunday Independent
Burrington Way, Plymouth, Devon PL5 3LN
☎01752 206600   Fax 01752 206164

Owner *Southern Newspapers Plc*
Editor *Anna Jenkins*
Circulation 40,000

Fashion, what's on, gardening, computers, DIY, business, motors and motorcycles, furniture, food and wine, out and about, property, photography, hobbies, health and beauty, kitchens. All editorial should be addressed to the editor.

Western Morning News
17 Brest Road, Derriford Business Park, Derriford, Plymouth, Devon PL6 5AA
☎01752 765500   Fax 01752 765535

Owner *Northcliffe Newspapers Group Ltd*

Editor *Barrie Williams*
Circulation 50,556

Unsolicited mss welcome, but must be of topical and local interest. Special pages include a motoring supplement, West country matters, books, antiques, lifestyle and arts.

News Editor *Jason Clark*
Sports Editor *Rick Cowdery*
All other editorial material to be addressed to the editor.

Portsmouth

The News
The News Centre, Hilsea, Portsmouth, Hampshire PO2 9SX
☎01705 664488   Fax 01705 673363

Owner *Portsmouth Printing & Publishing Ltd*
Editor *Geoffrey Elliott*
Circulation 76,348

Unsolicited mss not generally welcome. Approach by letter.

News Editor *Mark Acheson*
Features Editor *Rachel Hughes* General subjects of S.E. Hants interest. Maximum 600 words. No fiction.
Sports Editor *Colin Channon* Sports background features. Maximum 600 words.
Women's Page *Seren Boyd*

Preston

Lancashire Evening Post
Olivers Place, Eastway, Fulwood, Preston, Lancashire PR2 9ZA
☎01772 254841   Fax 01772 880173

Owner *United Newspapers Publications Ltd*
Editor *Neil Hodgkinson*
Circulation 65,000

Unsolicited mss are not generally welcome; many are received and not used. All ideas in writing to the editor.

Reading

Evening Post
Tessa Road, Reading, Berkshire RG1 8NS
☎0118 9575833   Fax 0118 9599363

Owner *Guardian Media Group*
Editor *Kim Chapman*
Circulation 24,000

Unsolicited mss welcome; one or two received every day. Fiction rarely used. Interested in local news features, human interest, well-researched investigations. Special sections include women's page (Tuesday & Wednesday); motoring and motorcycling (Tuesday); business (Thursday); travel (Thursday); gardening (Friday); rock music (Friday); children's page (Friday).

Features Editor *Kate Magee*

News Editor *Phil Pledger* Topical subjects, particularly of Thames Valley interest. Maximum 800 words.

Women's Page *Kate Magee*

Scarborough

Scarborough Evening News
17–23 Aberdeen Walk, Scarborough, North Yorkshire YO11 1BB
☎01723 363636   Fax 01723 354092

Owner *Yorkshire Regional Newspapers Ltd*
Editor *David Penman*
Circulation 16,939

Special pages include property (Monday); motoring (Tuesday/Friday).

News Editor *Damian Holmes*
Motoring *Dennis Sissons*
Sports Editor *Charles Place*

All other material should be addressed to the editor.

Scotland

Daily Record (Glasgow)
See **National Newspapers**

Scotland on Sunday (Edinburgh)
See **National Newspapers**

The Scotsman (Edinburgh)
See **National Newspapers**

Sunday Mail (Glasgow)
See **National Newspapers**

Sunday Post (Dundee)
See **National Newspapers**

Scunthorpe

Scunthorpe Evening Telegraph
Doncaster Road, Scunthorpe,
N. E. Lincs DN15 7RQ
☎01724 273273   Fax 01724 273101

Owner *Northcliffe Newspapers Group Ltd*
Editor *P. L. Moore*
Circulation 24,810

All correspondence should go to the news editor.

Assistant Editor *D. H. Stephens*
News Editor *Jane Manning*

Sheffield

The Star
York Street, Sheffield, South Yorkshire S1 1PU
☎0114 2767676   Fax 0114 2725978

Owner *Sheffield Newspapers Ltd*
Editor *Peter Charlton*
Circulation 102,749

Unsolicited mss not welcome, unless topical and local.

Joint News Editors *Bob Westerdale/Alison Hurndall* Contributions only accepted from freelance news reporters if they relate to the area.

Features Editor *Jim Collins* Very rarely require outside features, unless on specialised subject.

Sports Editor *Derek Fish*
Women's Page *Fiona Firth*
Payment negotiable.

Shropshire

Shropshire Star
See under **Telford**

South Shields

Gazette
Chapter Row, South Shields, Tyne & Wear
NE33 1BL
☎0191 455 4661   Fax 0191 456 8270

Owner *Northeast Press Ltd*
Editor *Rob Lawson*
Circulation 24,177

News Editor *Nigel Green*
Sports Editor *John Cornforth*
Women's Page *Joy Yates*

Southampton

The Southern Daily Echo
Newspaper House, Test Lane, Redbridge,
Southampton, Hampshire SO16 9JX
☎01703 424777   Fax 01703 424770

Owner *Southern Newspapers Ltd*
Editor *Mike Woods*
Circulation 64,101

Unsolicited mss 'tolerated'. Approach the editor in writing with strong ideas; staff supply almost all the material.

Stoke on Trent
The Sentinel
Sentinel House, Etruria, Stoke on Trent,
Staffordshire ST1 5SS
☎01782 289800   Fax 01782 280781
Owner *Staffordshire Sentinel Newspapers Ltd*
Editor *Sean Dooley*
Circulation 95,334

Weekly sports final supplement. All material
should be sent to the **News Editor** *Michael
Wood.*

Sunderland
Sunderland Echo
Echo House, Pennywell, Sunderland, Tyne &
Wear SR4 9ER
☎0191 534 3011   Fax 0191 534 5975
Owner *North East Press Ltd*
Editor *Ian Holland*
Circulation 59,177

All editorial material to be addressed to the
news editor.

Swansea
South Wales Evening Post
Adelaide Street, Swansea, West Glamorgan
SA1 1QT
☎01792 650841   Fax 01792 469665
Owner *Northcliffe Newspapers Group Ltd*
Editor *George Edwards*
Circulation 66,566

Circulates throughout South West Wales.
  News Editor *Jonathan Isaacs*
  Features Editor *Andy Pearson*
  Sports Editor *David Evans*

Swindon
Evening Advertiser
100 Victoria Road, Swindon, Wiltshire
SN1 3BE
☎01793 528144   Fax 01793 542434
Owner *Newsquest (Wiltshire) Ltd*
Editor *Kevin Mochrie*
Circulation 25,168

Copy and ideas invited. 'All material must be
strongly related or relevant to the town of
Swindon, borough of Thamesdown or the
county of Wiltshire.' Little scope for freelance
work. Fees vary depending on material.

Head of Content *Pauline Leighton*
Sports Editor *Alan Johnson*
Women's Page *Shirley Mathias*

Telford
Shropshire Star
Ketley, Telford, Shropshire TF1 4HU
☎01952 242424   Fax 01952 254605
Owner *Shropshire Newspapers Ltd*
Editor *Andy Wright*
Circulation 94,160

No unsolicited mss; approach the editor with
ideas in writing in the first instance. No news or
fiction.
  News Editor *Sarah-Jane Smith*
  Features Editor *Alun Owen* Limited
opportunities; uses mostly in-house or syndi-
cated material. Maximum 1200 words.
  Sports Editor *Peter Byram*
  Women's Page *Sharon Walters*

Torquay
Herald Express
Harmsworth House, Barton Hill Road,
Torquay, Devon TQ2 8JN
☎01803 676000   Fax 01803 676299/676228
Owner *Northcliffe Newspapers Group Ltd*
Editor *J. C. Mitchell*
Circulation 29,609

Drive scene, property guide, Monday sports,
special pages, rail trail, Saturday surgery, nature
and conservation column. Supplements:
Gardening, Healthcare News (all quarterly);
Visitors Guide and *Antiques & Collectables* (fortnightly); *Devon Days Out* (every Saturday in
summer and at Easter and May Bank Holidays).
Unsolicited mss generally not welcome. All
editorial material should be addressed to the
editor in writing.

Wales
South Wales Argus
See under *Newport*

South Wales Echo
See under *Cardiff*

South Wales Evening Post
See under *Swansea*

Wales on Sunday
See **National Newspapers**

Western Mail
See under *Cardiff*

West of England

Express & Echo
See under *Exeter*

Western Daily Press
See under *Bristol*

Western Morning News
See under *Plymouth*

Weymouth

Dorset Evening Echo
57 St Thomas Street, Weymouth, Dorset
DT4 8EU
☎01305 784804   Fax 01305 760387

Owner *Southern Newspapers plc*
Editor *David Lee*
Circulation 21,386

Farming, by-gone days, films, arts, showbiz, brides, teens page, children's page, and video.
  News Editor *Paul Thomas*
  Sports Editor *Jack Wyllie*

Wolverhampton

Express & Star
Queen Street, Wolverhampton,
West Midlands WV1 3BU
☎01902 313131   Fax 01902 319721

Owner *Midlands News Association*
Editor *Warren Wilson*
Circulation 204,231

  Deputy Editor *Richard Ewels*
  News Editor *David Evans*
  Features Editor *Garry Copeland*
  Sports Editor *Steve Gordos*
  Women's Page *Shirley Tart*

Worcester

Evening News
Berrow's House, Hylton Road, Worcester
WR2 5JX
☎01905 748200   Fax 01905 748009

Owner *Newsquest (Midlands South) Ltd*
Editor *Andrew Martin*
Circulation 23,588

Pulse pop page (Thursday/Friday/Saturday); leisure (Wednesday); property (Thursday). Weekly supplements: *Midweek News*; *Motoring News*; *Weekend News and Entertainment*.
  News Editor *Nick Watson*
  Features Editor/Women's Page *Mark Higgitt*
  Sports Editor *Paul Ricketts*

York

Evening Press
PO Box 29, 76–86 Walmgate, York
YO1 1YN
☎01904 653051   Fax 01904 612853

Owner *York & County Press*
Editor *Elizabeth Page*
Circulation 43,634

Unsolicited mss not generally welcome, unless submitted by journalists of proven ability. *Business Press Pages* (Wednesday); *Women's Press Extra* (monthly section); *Property Press* (Thursday); *8 Days* leisure and entertainments supplement (Saturday).
  News Editor *Claire Timms*
  Picture Editor *Martin Oates*
  Sports Editor *Martin Jarred*
  Payment negotiable.

Yorkshire

Yorkshire Evening Post
See under *Leeds*

Yorkshire Post
See under *Leeds*

Copyright in Time and Space

Writers with an eye to the future should be grateful to the European Union. Heavy negotiations in Brussels have produced a Community directive which extends copyright protection from 50 years to 70 years after the author's death. There is no inherent logic to this figure. It is just that of all the member states, Germany offers the longest period of protection which has now been adopted as the common standard. By the same reasoning, the Italians are having to change their copyright on musical recordings from 30 to 50 years to match the British law.

The bad news is that whatever the law says it may prove increasingly difficult, if not impossible, to enforce it. Concern started when every office, school and college acquired its own photocopier. Hardly anyone thought twice before reproducing articles, chapters from books or even whole books. Savings showed up on library budgets. Why buy six or sixty copies of a publication when you can make do with one? The irony, as noted by Mark Rose (*Authors and Owners: The Invention of Copyright*) was that the photocopier was a direct descendent of the printing press, the starting point for copyright law. Thus, copyright's 'technological foundation has turned, like a vital organ grown cancerous, into an enemy'.

But now we have the new, new technology – Internet – and, with it, the information highways which have no clear ownership and are almost impossible to police. Nicholas Negroponte, the media guru at Massachusetts Institute of Technology, predicts that the new technology will eradicate the traditional constraints on the copying of material at the click of a mouse:

'Most people worry about copyright in terms of the ease of making copies. In the digital world, not only the ease is at issue, but also the fact that the digital copy is as perfect as the original and, with some fancy computing, even better. In the same way that bit strings can be error-corrected, a copy can be cleaned up, enhanced, and have noise removed. The copy is perfect ...'

But, in the digital world it is not just a matter of copying being easier and copies more faithful.

'We see a new a new kind of fraud, which may not be fraud at all. When I read something on the Internet and, like a clipping from a newspaper, wish to send a copy of it to somebody else or to a mailing list of people, this seems harmless. But, with less than a dozen keystrokes, I could redeliver that material to literally thousands of people all over the world.'

Duplication is not only efficient, it is incredibly cheap which is why, after initial enthusiasm, hardly any publishers are making money from the Internet.

Even if this changes in the future and some rational economic model is laid on top of the Internet, it may cost a penny or two to distribute a million bits to a million people. It certainly will not cost anything like postage. Negroponte concludes: 'Copyright law is totally out of date. It is a Gutenberg artefact. Since it is a reactive process, it will probably have to break down completely before it is corrected.'

There is no shortage of statistics to underline his message. In the Far East it is reckoned that over 90 per cent of all videocassettes sold are pirated. Unauthorised printing of books in China, Russia and a motley of smaller nations is said to be depriving British publishers and their authors of £200 million a year. As for the dear old photocopier, a luxury product just ten years ago, it is now responsible for some 300 billion pages of illegally reproduced material.

What is to be done? On one side are those who argue for abandoning traditional ideas of copyright. Rather than try to tighten up the current law (which may, in any case, be impracticable) a more liberal regime would best serve the interests of education, economic growth and civilisation. Their case is illustrated by the long running dispute between America and China. It may be galling for the US to have its finest brains picked clean by a repressive regime but if we want to bring the Chinese into the family of democracies, should we not be delighted by their enthusiasm for Western technology and, by extension, Western culture?

So what that they lift ideas that should be making money for their originators. Owners of intellectual property could look to other sources of income. This is how publishers reacted to the photocopying threat, by hiking up the price of academic and reference books and journals. In this way, the cost of illicit copying was built into the overheads.

Owners of electronic rights are beginning to think the same way.

'Maybe the price of software will reduce and the price of manuals increase', says Francis Pritchard, an academic specialising in computer law. 'People who create works must find other ways of earning money from their creations than simply by charging for copies. Take the "shareware" business as an example; software developers make their products freely available, and ask people who use it regularly to send them a small fee. Shareware might not make developers multi-billionaires, like Bill Gates, the Microsoft founder. Yet some earn comfortable livings, even when only five per cent of users pay up.'

Naturally this is not a strategy that appeals to writers who want to hold their market value. After all, it is only recently that the potential for making money from copyright has taken off. As Michael Sissons, writing in *The Author* points out, 'A generation ago the main constraint on the earnings of writers was in fact the inhibition on the transmission of the written word to the consumer. Paperbacks were in their infancy, bookshops were still, in the main, Dickensian shambles, the processes of production, distribution, reprinting and marketing were antique. Today the book is a more attractive and desirable object for the consumer, it can be produced and reprinted far quicker, and the computer has revolutionised the distributive and retail processes.'

But that is only part of the story. The time has long since gone when authors had to rely exclusively on royalties from their books in print. Nowadays there is a kaleidoscope of revenue-earning opportunities – translation rights, serial rights, rights of quotation, anthology, merchandising, bookclub rights, film and TV adaptation rights, dramatisation rights, and, not least, electronic publishing and copying.

The success of the CLA – Copyright Licensing Agency – in making copying profitable for writers shows what can be achieved. Set up in 1982 as a negotiating arm of the Authors' Licensing and Collecting Society (ALCS) and the Publishers' Licensing Society (PLS), the CLA has forged agreements with education and commerce on a licensing scheme for reprographic rights which now brings in over £14 million a year. Whether or not a similar scheme can be applied to electronic rights depends largely on developing an effective policing system. If Negroponte is right in believing that the superhighway is also a freeway, then a large area of copyright will be unenforceable. But reports are already filtering through the technological grapevine of new metering systems which will allow publishers to monitor and record the use of its information on Internet and other networks. In early 1997, WIPO (the World Intellectual Property Organisation, the UN's agency responsible for administering copyright conventions) required member states to outlaw devices aimed at bypassing technical measures to prevent unauthorised copying. The digital debate is set to run and run.

Meanwhile, back on earth, there is much that the individual writer can do to guard against the pirating of what is, or what might turn out to be, a valuable property. The best advice is always to check the small print.

Any publisher who offers a deal that is dependent on exclusive rights must be regarded with suspicion. The chances are that he has in mind a nice little earner that does not require him to pay the author a single penny beyond a basic fee or royalty. This is what happens to contributors to academic and specialist journals who are invariably asked to assign their copyright as a condition of publication. The reasons given are wildly imaginative, ranging from conditions in the US where a publisher must assert copyright over a whole journal to prevent pirating (not true) to the need to regularise applications to reproduce. The latter is a real cheek since under the current CLA rules, all the money collected for the photocopying of articles from British journals and periodicals is taken by the publishers. Yet more outrageously, money set aside specifically for British authors by overseas collecting societies including those of Norway, the Netherlands and Germany is purloined along the way by the publishers.

The response is to argue that authors receive all that they are entitled to under contracts freely entered into but this is to subscribe to the naive view that academic writers are in any position to argue. In reality, their need to publish is closely linked to career advancement. When an offer comes they jump at it. But this does not excuse the injustice of having the ownership of their intellectual property taken from them at the earliest possible stage of publication. The ALCS, the Society of Authors and the Writers' Guild are united in their efforts to secure a remedy.

Even those who make a living out of writing and are skilled in the devious ways of publishing can lose out simply by ignoring the subsidiary clauses of a contract or, if reading them, by not realising the long term implications. In 1984, Random House of New York announced a revised standard contract demanding all electronic publishing rights from authors including rights for technologies not yet invented. The sad litany of rights carelessly discarded would make a sizeable volume in itself.

Once surrendered, there is no going back. As Nicola Solomon, a lawyer specialising in copyright law, warns, 'an assignment of copyright is binding ... it is not contingent on an agreed fee or royalties being paid. If a publisher fails to pay, your only remedy ... is to sue for the unpaid debt but you will not be able to regain copyright.'

Never say never. There must be occasions when the surrender of copyright is justified. A writer who works to order, adapting material provided for a company training course, say, or a sponsored history to be used as a promotional tool, would be pushing his luck to argue for more than a set fee.

Another moot point arises when it is not altogether clear who it is that has first claim to copyright. The most obvious example is the journalist – say, a columnist whose by-line appears twice weekly in a national newspaper. If he is on the payroll, with all the rights and responsibilities of an employee, then copyright on his articles is assumed to belong to his employer – 'unless otherwise agreed'. In other words, if the journalist is a self-assertive type who is ready to bargain with his editor he may well emerge with a contract which secures his copyright beyond the first printing. A scribe with less muscle might prefer to rely on his editor's sense of decency in handing over a share of any supplementary fees. It does happen on most national papers, but over the rest of the printed media those who commission work invariably demand exclusive copyright, including syndication rights. This applies to free-lancers who, technically speaking, are entitled to copyright, as well as to regular employees. The journalists' unions urge members to resist but the need to make a living in a highly competitive market weakens the resolve of all but the star turns.

Film and television

In late 1992 the European Commission's Rental and Lending Directive declared the 'author' of a film to have the right to sanction (or stop) rental and to be paid ' "equitable" remuneration'. But who is the 'author'? Under British law, he is generally assumed to be the producer, an interpretation which naturally offends writers and directors. The European Community, on the other hand, takes it lead from France where the primary author of a film is the director while others, including the scriptwriter, can be named as co-authors. Producers have done their worst to frustrate the change, threatening expensive legal action and claiming that equitable remuneration should be deemed to have been paid under whatever financial arrangements have been made to set up a project. But in late 1996, Parliament gave the go-ahead for scriptwriters and authors whose work has been filmed or broadcast to receive payments for the rental of their works even when they have assigned all rights to a third party. Checking who owes what to whom is made easier by signing up with the ALCS which acts as a collecting agency on behalf of its members.

Problems remain, however. Lending is horrendously difficult to control. It has been known for years that the loss of income attributed to domestic sound and video recorders runs into billions. With the advance of technology, the problem is bound to worsen. Before long we will have video on demand, an almost limitless choice of programming available to any home at a push of the remote control. In some versions of this futuristic state, a viewer will rarely summon up a whole programme. Instead they will want segments of programmes, selected from the whole menu and patched together by the computer. Sailing enthusiasts could choose great sailing moments from half a dozen programmes and English students could choose the gravedigger scene from six different productions of *Hamlet*. The entire system would be *a la carte*.

'We are at the threshold of something very new and very strange,' says Chris Barlas in a recent ALCS newsletter. 'The digital media will enable us to do things with other people's work that only a couple of years ago would have been quite impossible. I've seen programmes that let children incorporate clips of film into school essays, programmes that take dictation and print the words on a screen, programmes that electronically read books in a variety of voices. The technology is mind boggling.'

Extent of copyright

Copyright applies to all written work, unpublished as well as published. For works not published during the author's lifetime, the period of copyright runs from the date of publication. For a published work of joint authorship, protection extends from the end of the year of the death of the author who dies last.

In most books a copyright notice appears on one of the front pages. In its simplest form this is the symbol © followed by the name of the copyright owner and the year of first publication. The assertion of copyright may be emphasised by the phrase 'All rights reserved', and in case there are any lingering doubts the reader may be warned that 'No part of this publication may be reproduced or transmitted in any form or by any means without permission'.

But this is to overstate the case. It is perfectly legitimate for a writer to quote from someone else's work for 'purposes of criticism or review' as long as 'sufficient acknowledgement' is given. What he must not do is to lift 'a substantial part' of. In one case, four lines from a thirty-two line poem were held to amount to 'a substantial part'. On the other hand, even a 'substantial' quotation from a copyright work may be acceptable if a student or critic is engaged in 'fair dealing with a literary work for the purposes of research or music study'.

Commonsense suggests basing the assessment on the length and importance of the quotation; the amount quoted in relation to the text as a whole; the extent to which the work competes with the work quoted; and the extent to which the words quoted are saving a writer time and trouble.

Some years ago the Society of Authors and the Publishers' Association stated that they would usually regard as 'fair dealing' the use of a single extract of up to 400 words, or a series of extracts (of which none exceeds 300 words) to a total of 800 words from a prose work, or of extracts to a total of 40 lines from a poem, provided that this did not exceed a quarter of the poem.

With the 1988 Copyright Designs and Patents Act, the European concept of 'moral rights' was introduced into British law. The most basic is the right of paternity which entitles authors to be credited as the creators of their work. However, paternity must be asserted in writing and is not retrospective. No right of paternity attaches to authors of computer programs or to writers who create works as part of their employment or journalists or as contributors to a 'collective work' such as an encyclopedia, dictionary or year book.

A second moral right is that of integrity. In theory, this opens the way to forceful objections to any 'derogatory treatment' if derogatory amounts to 'distortion or mutilation ... or is otherwise prejudicial to the honour or reputation of the author'. Mis-correction of grammar by an illiterate editor does not qualify. In the absence of test cases, all things are possible, but relying on lawyers' gossip it seems that a book would have to be savaged beyond recognition for an injunction to be granted.

Those most likely to have their right of integrity infringed are film directors (specifically mentioned in the 1988 Act) and visual artists who might, for example, suffer the attentions of an airbrusher. For those in the writing trade, the Society of Authors urges 'locking the stable door before the horse bolts by ensuring that your contract does not permit the publishers to make significant editorial changes without your agreement' though with the virtual abandonment of hard copy in favour of disks, changes can be introduced without the author noticing – until it is too late.

Moral rights may 'be waived by written agreement or with the consent of the author'. There are cases where the concession is justified. For example, a ghost writer who has chosen to be anonymous may reasonably be expected to waive moral rights.

Titles and Trademarks

Technically, there is no copyright in a title. But where a title is inseparable from the work of a particular author, proceedings for 'passing off' are likely to be successful. Everything depends on the nature of the rival works, the methods by which they are exploited and the extent to which the title is essentially distinctive.

The risks of causing offence multiply when a unique image is involved. In a recent full-page advertisement promoting the services of The Patent Office the *Mr Men* characters created by Roger Hargreaves (60 million books sold to date) are offered as an example of a registered trademark that protects the author against literary and other predators. The interesting feature of trademarks is that unlike copyright, they go on for ever. The Coca-Cola and Kodak marks, for example, are well over 100 years old. Neither of these have close literary associations but what about Thomas the Tank Engine, who now has his own trademark, or Mickey Mouse? The official British artist of the Gulf war, John Keene, has faced legal threats from the Disney Corporation for having painted a picture of the devastation of a Kuwait beach which included a Mickey Mouse doll.

In theory it should be easier to preserve copyright in fictional characters than on titles. But in broadcasting, a frequent source of dispute is the lifting of characters from one series to another when there are two or more writers involved. Sometimes royalties are paid; other times, not. Production companies are liable to take possession of fictional characters unless their originators make a fuss.

The singularity of letters

The copyright status of a letter is something of a curiosity. The actual document belongs to the recipient, but the copyright remains with the writer and after his or her death, to the writer's estate. This has caused difficulty for some biographers who have assumed that it is the owners of letters who are empowered to give permission to quote from them. This only applies if the writer has assigned copyright. Even then, the way may not be smooth. Witness the frustration of Eric Jacobs, the biography of Sir Kingsley Amis, who found himself unable to quote from letters written by the novelist because the Bodleian Library, which has the bulk of the Amis papers, would not concede any part of the copyright Sir Kingsley has invested in them. The matter was resolved only when the letter writer himself requested permission to quote from his own correspondence.

It is dangerous to assume that letters which are not in themselves of great intrinsic value are fair game for a biographer. Copyright owners do not have to look far for reasons to assert their rights and may not be swayed by appeals for liberality. The author Diana Souhami spent five years researching a book detailing the 'strange romance' of Greta Garbo and Cecil Beaton which fell victim to a failure to gain permission to use letters Garbo wrote to her friend Mimi Pollak. Cape had to pulp the entire hardback edition.

Copyright in lectures and speeches

Even if a speaker talks without notes, copyright exists in a lecture as soon as it is recorded (in writing or otherwise) but not until then. The copyright belongs to the person who spoke the words, whether or not the recording was made by, or with the permission of, the speaker.

This means that nobody may make substantial use of a transcript of a lecture without permission. There is one important exception: Where a record of spoken words is made to report current events, it is not an infringement of copyright to use or copy the record for that purpose provided that the record is a direct record of the spoken words and the making of the record was not prohibited by the speaker.

Copyright on ideas

Writers trying to sell ideas should start on the assumption that it is almost impossible to stake an exclusive claim. So much unsolicited material comes the way of publishers and script departments, duplication of ideas is inevitable.

Frequent complaints of plagiarism have led publishers and production companies to point out the risks whenever they acknowledge an unsolicited synopsis or script, warning correspondents, 'it is often the case that we are currently considering or have already considered ideas that may be similar to your own'. Having something in print to wave at the judge helps to assert a charge of plagiarism. Recently, Guy Lyon Playfair scored a triumph with a little help from Willesden County Court. His case related to a BBC programme called *Ghostwatch* which, he argued, was inspired by and, to a significant extent, based on his book *This House is Haunted*. He listed 20 close similarities between book and film. The BBC offered an out of court settlement. Another BBC settlement was with the writer Tony Collins, who said an episode of the award-winning police series *Between the Lines* took its storyline from *Open Verdict*, his nonfiction book about deaths among defence scientists. Collins had sent a dramatisation to the BBC in 1992. Two years later the episode called *The Lone Soldier* appeared under the name of another writer. 'It has taken two years of fighting a completely intransigent BBC before it made one offer, then another and finally a fourth, which I accepted,' said Collins.

In America, the columnist Art Buchwald finally won his case against Paramount Pictures after a seven-year fight. The studio, he claimed, had taken his synopsis and turned it into the Eddie Murphy film *Coming to America*. 'In America they are now so worried about being sued that any writer offering an idea or script must sign a document waiving rights and simply accept the risk of not being able to sue,' says Mark Le Fanu, general secretary of the Society of Authors. 'I haven't heard of that in Britain yet, but it might happen.'

A writer who is nervous of the attention of rivals is best advised to maintain a certain reticence in dealings with the media. He should, for example, resist the urge to give out all his best ideas at an expensive lunch or in a brain-storming session with an ever so friendly producer who just might be able to slot your programme into his overcrowded schedule. It is flattering to be invited to hold forth but the experience can be costly unless there is an up front fee.

At the same time, remember that there is no such thing as an entirely original plot. To succeed in an action for infringement of copyright on an idea or on the bare bones of a plot, the copying of 'a combination or series of dramatic events' must be very close indeed. Proceedings have failed because incidents common to two works have been stock incidents or revolving around stock characters common to many works. Recently, The Patent Office has been collecting views on possible amendments to copyright law to give specific protection to programme formats. But so far there is not even a consensus on whether there is a problem to be overcome.

Permissions

A quotation of a 'substantial' extract from a copyright work or for any quotation of copyright material, however short, for an anthology must be approved by the publishers of the original work. It is in the author's interest to deal with permissions as early as possible. Last-minute requests just before a book goes to press can lead to embarrassing difficulties if fees are too high or if permission is refused.

Whenever copyright is an issue, a contract must specify the territory permissions should cover. The difference between British Commonwealth and the World can be a yawning gap in fees. Some publishers have a standard letter for clearing permissions which may help to speed up negotiations. But rights departments are notoriously slow in responding to requests from individuals who are unclear as to what they want or who give the impression of writing in on spec.

Difficulties can arise when the identity of a copyright holder is unclear. The publisher of the relevant book may have gone out of business or been absorbed into a conglomerate, leaving no records of the original imprint. Detective work can be yet more convoluted when it comes to unpublished works. When copyright holders are hard to trace, the likeliest source of help is the Writers and their Copyright Holders project, otherwise known as WATCH. A joint enterprise of the universities of Texas and Reading, WATCH has created a database of English language authors whose papers are housed in archives and manuscript repositories. The database is available free of charge on the Internet.

If, despite best efforts, a copyright owner cannot be found, there are two options; either to cut the extract or to press ahead with publication in the hope that if the copyright holder does find out he will not object or will not demand an outrageous fee. The risk can be minimised by open acknowledgement that every effort to satisfy the law has been made.

Anthology and quotation rates

Prose

The rate suggested by the Society of Authors and the Publishers Association is
£82-96 per 1,000 words for world rights. The rate for the UK and Commonwealth or the USA alone is usually half of the world rate. For an individual
country: one quarter of the world rate. Where an extract is complete in itself (eg
a chapter or short story) publishers sometimes charge an additional fee at half the
rate applicable for 1,000 words. This scale generally covers one edition only. An
additional fee may be payable if the material is used in a reset or offset edition or
in a new format or new binding (eg a paperback edition) and will certainly be
required if the publisher of an anthology sub-licenses publication rights to
another publisher.

Fees vary according to the importance of the author quoted, the proportion
of the original work that the user intends to quote and its value to the
author/publisher requesting permission. The expected size of the print-run
should also be taken into consideration. Fees for quotations in scholarly works
with print-runs of under 1,000 copies are usually charged at half the normal rate.

Poetry

For anthology publication in the UK and Commonwealth a minimum fee of
£36 should be charged for the first 10 lines; thereafter £1.80 per line for the
next 20 lines and £1.20 a line subsequently but the rates for established poets
may well be significantly higher.

US Copyright

The US Copyright Act of 1909 provided for two separate terms of copyright, a
period of twenty-eight years from publication followed by a renewal period of a
further twenty-eight years. A new copyright act, which came into force in
January 1978, made changes in the duration of copyright protection and set out
rules for the transition of existing works.

Copyrights registered before 1950 and renewed before 1978 were automatically extended by the new act until December of the seventy-fifth year of the
original date of registration. This meant that all copyrights in their second term
were extended for nineteen years. But copyrights registered after 1950 and
before December 1977 had to be renewed. Strictly speaking, this should no
longer be necessary. Following a Congressional amendment, if copyright has
already been secured, the period of protection is extended automatically. But
there may still be advantages in renewing copyright protection in a work's
twenty-eigth year (i.e. by 31 December 1997 for works published in this
country in 1969), particularly for works that have gone out of print. Copyright
renewal, along with registration (if the work was not registered with the Library

of Congress in the first place) costs $20. Further information and the appropriate forms are available from the Copyright Office, Library of Congress, Washington DC 20559, USA.

For any queries on British copyright contact: The Intellectual Property Policy Directorate, Copyright Enquiries, Room 4/5, Hazlitt House, 45 Southampton Buildings, London WC2A 1AR (☎0171-438 4778).

Magazines

Abraxas

57 Eastbourne Road, St Austell, Cornwall
PL25 4SU
☎01726 64975 Fax 01726 64975

Owner *Paul Newman*
Editors *Paul Newman, Pamela Smith-Rownsley*

FOUNDED 1991. QUARTERLY incorporating the *Colin Wilson Newsletter*. Aims at being a periodical, but sometimes turns out to be a spasmodical. Unsolicited mss welcome after a study of the magazine – initial approach by phone or letter preferred.

Features Essays, translations and reviews. Issues have had Colin Wilson remembering R.D. Laing and appraising the work of Jacques Derrida and Michel Foucault; Paul Newman on *Little Grey Gropers from Mars* or 'Close Encounters of a Fourth Kind', and Ted Brown appraising 'Frozen Atlantis'. *Abraxus* welcomes provocative, lively articles on little-known literary figures (e.g. David Lindsay/E. H. Visiak/Laura Del Rivo/P. D. Ouspensky/Brocard Sewell) and new slants on psychology, existentialism and ideas. Maximum length 2000 words. *Payment* nominal if at all.

Fiction One story per issue. Favours compact, obsessional stories – think of writers like Kafka, Borges or Wolfgang Borchert – of not more than 2000 words.

Poetry Double-page spread – slight penchant for the surreal but open to most styles – has published D. M. Thomas, Zofia Ilinksa, Kenneth Steven and John Ellison.
Payment free copy of magazine.

Acclaim

See **The New Writer**

Accountancy

40 Bernard Street, London WC1N 1LD
☎0171 833 3291 Fax 0171 833 2085

Owner *Institute of Chartered Accountants in England and Wales*
Editor *Brian Singleton-Green*
Circulation 70,232

FOUNDED 1889. MONTHLY. Written ideas welcome.

Features *Brian Singleton-Green* Accounting/tax/business-related articles of high technical content aimed at professional/managerial readers. Maximum 2000 words.
Payment by arrangement.

Accountancy Age

32–34 Broadwick Street, London W1A 2HG
☎0171 316 9000 Fax 0171 316 9250

Owner *VNU Business Publications*
Editor *Andrew Pring*
Circulation 70,000

FOUNDED 1969. WEEKLY. Unsolicited mss welcome. Ideas may be suggested in writing provided they are clearly thought out.

Features *Harriot Lane Fox* Topics right across the accountancy, business and financial world. Maximum 2000 words.
Payment negotiable.

Active Life

Aspen Specialist Media, Christ Church, Cosway Street, London NW1 5NJ
☎0171 262 2622 Fax 0171 706 4811

Owner *Aspen Specialist Media*
Editor *Helene Hodge*

FOUNDED 1990. BI-MONTHLY magazine aimed at over 50s. General consumer interests including travel, finance, property and leisure. Opportunities for freelancers in all departments, including fiction. Approach in writing with synopsis of ideas. Authors' notes available on receipt of s.a.e..

Acumen

See under **Poetry, Little Magazines**

African Affairs

Dept of Politics, University of Reading, Whiteknights, PO Box 218, Reading, Berkshire RG6 6AA
☎01734 318501 Fax 01734 753833

Owner *Royal African Society*
Editors *Peter Woodward, David Killingray*
Circulation 2250

FOUNDED 1901. QUARTERLY learned journal publishing articles on contemporary developments on the African continent. Unsolicited mss welcome.

Features Should be well researched and written in a style that is immediately accessible to the intelligent lay reader. Maximum 8000 words.

Payment up to £40 per 1000 words for non-academics; no payment for academics.

Air International

PO Box 100, Stamford, Lincolnshire PE9 1XQ
☎01780 55131   Fax 01780 57261
Owner *Key Publishing Ltd*
Editor *Malcolm English*

FOUNDED 1971. MONTHLY. Civil and military aircraft magazine. Unsolicited mss welcome but initial approach by phone or in writing preferred.

Airforces Monthly

PO Box 100, Stamford, Lincolnshire PE9 1XQ
☎01780 55131   Fax 01780 57261
Owner *Key Publishing Ltd*
Editor *David Oliver*
Circulation 24,749

FOUNDED 1988. MONTHLY. Modern military aircraft magazine. Unsolicited mss welcome but initial approach by phone or in writing preferred.

Amateur Gardening

Westover House, West Quay Road, Poole, Dorset BH15 1JG
☎01202 680586   Fax 01202 674335
Owner *IPC Magazines Ltd*
Editor *Graham Clarke*
Circulation 55,126

FOUNDED 1884. WEEKLY. New contributions are welcome provided that they have a professional approach. Of the 20 unsolicited mss received each week, 90% are returned as unsuitable. All articles/news items are supported by colour pictures (which may or may not be supplied by the author).

Features Topical and practical gardening articles. Maximum 800 words.

News Compiled and edited in-house generally.

Payment negotiable.

Amateur Golf

129A High Street, Dovercourt, Harwich, Essex CO12 3AX
☎01255 507526   Fax 01255 556221
Publisher *Fore Golf Publications Ltd*
Editor *Paul Baxter*
Circulation 13,000

MONTHLY journal of the English Golf Union. UK coverage of amateur golf interests, club

events and international matches. Unsolicited mss considered. Approach with ideas in writing to John Lelean, Features Editor, PO Box 12, Wetherby, West Yorkshire LS22 6SR (☎01937 583181).

Features Golf course management, new developments and equipment, golf holidays, profiles and general amateur golf concerns. Maximum 1500 words.

Amateur Photographer

King's Reach Tower, Stamford Street, London SE1 9LS
☎0171 261 5100   Fax 0171 261 5404
Owner *IPC Magazines Ltd*
Group Editor *Keith Wilson*
Circulation 32,164

WEEKLY. For the competent amateur with a technical interest. Freelancers are used but writers should be aware that there is ordinarily no use for words without pictures.

Amateur Stage

83 George Street, London W1H 5PL
☎0171 486 1732   Fax 0171 224 2215
Owner *Platform Publications Ltd*
Editor *Charles Vance*

Some opportunity here for outside contributions. Topics of interest include amateur premières, technical developments within the amateur forum and items relating to landmarks or anniversaries in the history of amateur societies. Approach in writing only (include s.a.e for return of mss).

No payment.

Ambit

See under **Poetry, Little Magazines**

The American

114–115 West Street, Farnham, Surrey GU9 7HL
☎01252 713366/721267   Fax 01252 737938
Owner *British American Newspapers Ltd*
Editor *David J. Williams*
Circulation 15,000

FOUNDED 1976. FORTNIGHTLY community newspaper for US citizens resident in the UK and as such requires a strong American angle in every story. 'We are on the look-out for items on business and commerce, diplomacy and international relations, defence and "people" stories.' Maximum length 'five minutes read'. First approach in writing with samples of previous work.

Payment 'modest but negotiable'.

Amiga Format

30 Monmouth Street, Bath BA1 2AP
☎01225 442244   Fax 01225 732341

Owner *Future Publishing*
Editor *Nick Veitch*
Circulation 42,655

FOUNDED 1988. MONTHLY. Specialist computer magazine dedicated to Commodore Amiga home computers, offering reviews, features and product information of specific interest to Amiga users. Unsolicited material welcome. Contact by phone with ideas.

News *Ben Vost* Amiga-specific exclusives and product information. Length 500–1000 words.

Features *Nick Veitch* Computer-related features (i.e. CD-ROMs, games, virtual reality) with Amiga-specific value. Maximum 10,000 words.

Special Pages *Ben Vost* Hardware and software reviews. Maximum 3000 words.

Payment £100 per 1000 words.

Animal Action

Causeway, Horsham, West Sussex
RH12 1HG
☎01403 264181   Fax 01403 241048

Owner *RSPCA*
Editor *Michaela Miller*
Circulation 70,000

BI-MONTHLY. RSPCA youth membership magazine. Articles (pet care, etc.) are written in-house. Good-quality animal photographs welcome.

The Antique Dealer and Collectors' Guide

PO Box 805, Greenwich, London
SE10 8TD
☎0181 691 4820   Fax 0181 691 2489

Owner *Statuscourt Ltd*
Publisher *Philip Bartlam*
Circulation 12,500

FOUNDED 1946. MONTHLY. Covers all aspects of the antiques and fine art worlds. Unsolicited mss welcome.

Features Practical but readable articles on the history, design, authenticity, restoration and market aspects of antiques and fine art. Maximum 2000 words. *Payment* £76 per 1000 words.

News *Philip Bartlam* Items on events, sales, museums, exhibitions, antique fairs and markets. Maximum 300 words.

Antique Interiors International

10–11 Lower John Street, London W1R 3PE
☎0171 434 9180   Fax 0171 287 3828

Owner *Antique Publications*
Editor-in-Chief *Alistair Hicks*
Managing Editor *Christopher Gower*
Circulation 22,000

FOUNDED 1986. QUARTERLY. Amusing coverage of antiques, art and interiors. Unsolicited mss not welcome. Approach by phone or in writing in the first instance. Interested in freelance contributions on international art news items.

Apollo Magazine

1 Castle Lane, London SW1E 6DR
☎0171 233 6640   Fax 0171 630 7791

Owner *Paul Z. Josefowitz*
Editor *Robin Simon*

FOUNDED 1925. MONTHLY. Specialist articles on art and antiques, exhibition and book reviews, exhibition diary, information on dealers and auction houses. Unsolicited mss welcome. Interested in specialist, usually new research in fine arts, architecture and antiques. Approach in writing. Not interested in crafts or practical art or photography.

Aquarist & Pondkeeper

Caxton House, Wellesley Road, Ashford,
Kent TN24 8ET
☎01233 636349   Fax 01233 631239

Owner *M. J. Publications Ltd*
Editor *Dick Mills*
Circulation 20,000

FOUNDED 1924. MONTHLY. Covers all aspects of aquarium and pondkeeping: conservation, herpetology (study of reptiles and amphibians), news, reviews and aquatic plant culture. Unsolicited mss welcome. Ideas should be submitted in writing first.

Features Good opportunities for writers on any of the above topics or related areas. 1500 words (maximum 2500), plus illustrations. 'We have stocks in hand for up to two years, but new material and commissioned features will be published as and when relevant.' Average lead-in 4–6 months.

News Very few opportunities.

Architects' Journal

151 Rosebery Avenue, London EC1R 4QX
☎0171 505 6700   Fax 0171 505 6701

Owner *EMAP Architecture*
Editor *Paul Finch*

Circulation 18,000

WEEKLY trade magazine dealing with all aspects of the industry. No unsolicited mss. Approach in writing with ideas.

Architectural Design

42 Leinster Gardens, London W2 3AN
☎0171 402 2141　　　Fax 0171 723 9540
Owner *Academy Group Ltd*
Editor *Maggie Toy*
Circulation 12,000

FOUNDED 1930. BI-MONTHLY. Theoretical architectural magazine. Unsolicited mss not generally welcome. Copy tends to come from experts in the field.

The Architectural Review

151 Rosebery Avenue, London EC1R 4QX
☎0171 505 6725　　　Fax 0171 505 6701
Owner *EMAP Construct*
Editor *Peter Davey*
Circulation 20,000

MONTHLY trade magazine dealing with all aspects of the industry. No unsolicited mss. Approach in writing with ideas.

Arena

Block A, Exmouth House, Pine Street,
London EC1R 0JL
☎0171 837 7270　　　Fax 0171 837 3906
Owner *Wagadon Ltd/Condé Nast Publications*
Editor *Ekow Eshun*
Circulation 86,850

Style and general interest magazine for men. Intelligent feature articles and profiles, plus occasional fiction.

Features Fashion, lifestyle, film, television, politics, business, music, media, design, art, architecture and theatre.

Payment £200–250 per 1000 words.

Art & Craft

Villiers House, Clarendon Avenue,
Leamington Spa, Warwickshire CV32 5PR
☎01926 887799　　　Fax 01926 883331
Owner *Scholastic Ltd*
Editor *Sian Morgan*
Circulation 16,000

FOUNDED 1936. MONTHLY aimed at a specialist market – the needs of primary school teachers and pupils. Ideas and synopses considered for commission.

Features The majority of contributors are primary school teachers with good art and craft skills and familiar with the curriculum.

News Handled by in-house staff. No opportunities.

Art Monthly

Suite 17, 26 Charing Cross Road, London WC2H 0DG
☎0171 240 0389　　　Fax 0171 497 0726
Owner *Brittania Art Publications*
Editor *Patricia Bickers*
Circulation 5000

FOUNDED 1976. TEN ISSUES YEARLY. News and features of relevance to those interested in modern and contemporary visual art. Unsolicited mss welcome. Contributions should be addressed to the editor, accompanied by an s.a.e..

Features Alongside exhibition reviews: usually 750–1000 words and almost always commissioned. Interviews and articles of up to 1500 words on art theory, individual artists, contemporary art history and issues affecting the arts (e.g. funding and arts education). Book reviews of 750–1000 words.

News Brief reports (250–300 words) on art issues.

Payment negotiable.

The Art Newspaper

27-29 Vauxhall Grove, London SW8 1SY
☎0171 735 3331　　　Fax 0171 735 3332
Owner *Umberto Allemandi & Co. Publishing*
Editor *Anna Somers Cocks*
Circulation 30,000

FOUNDED 1990. MONTHLY. Tabloid format with up-to-date information on the international art market, news, museums, exhibitions, archaeology, conservation, books and current debate topics. Length 250–2000 words. No unsolicited mss. Approach with ideas in writing. Commissions only.

Payment £120 per 1000 words.

The Artist

Caxton House, 63–65 High Street,
Tenterden, Kent TN30 6BD
☎0158076 3673　　　Fax 0158076 5411
Owner *Irene Briers*
Editor *Sally Bulgin*
Circulation 17,500

FOUNDED 1931. MONTHLY.

Features *Sally Bulgin* Art journalists, artists, art tutors and writers with a good knowledge of art materials are invited to write to the editor with ideas for practical and informative features about art, materials, techniques and artists.

Artscene
Dean Clough Industrial Park, Halifax, West
Yorkshire HX3 5AX
☎01422 322527   Fax 01422 322518
Owner *Yorkshire and Humberside Arts*
Editor *Victor Allen*
Circulation 25,000

FOUNDED 1973. MONTHLY. Listings magazine
for Yorksire and Humberside. No unsolicited
mss. Approach by phone with ideas.

    Features Profiles of artists (all media) and
associated venues/organisers of events of interest. Topical relevance vital. Maximum length
1500 words. *Payment* £100 per 1000 words.

    News Artscene strives to bring journalistic
values to arts coverage – all arts 'scoops' in the
region are of interest. Maximum length 500
words. *Payment* £100 per 1000 words.

Asian Times
See **Caribbean Times/Asian Times**

Attitude
Northern & Shell Tower, City Harbour,
London E14 9GL
☎0171 308 5090   Fax 0171 308 5075
Owner *Northern & Shell Plc*
Editor *James Collard*
Circulation 50,000

FOUNDED 1994. MONTHLY. Style magazine
aimed primarily, but not exclusively, at gay
men. Fashion and cultural coverage. Unsolicited mss not welcome. No phone calls. Brief
summaries of proposed features, together with
details of previously published work, should be
sent by post or fax only. 'It sounds obvious, but
anyone wanting to contribute to the magazine
should read it first.'

Audit
19 Rutland Street, Cork, Republic of Ireland
☎00 353 21313855   Fax 00 353 21313496
Editor *Ken Ebbage* (01707 373355)
Circulation 1000

BI-MONTHLY with a specialist, professional
readership   and   world-wide   circulation.
Features tend to be commissioned. Approach
in writing with ideas. Maximum 3000 words.
No unsolicited mss. *Payment* £250.

The Author
84 Drayton Gardens, London SW10 9SB
☎0171 373 6642
Owner *The Society of Authors*
Editor *Derek Parker*

Manager *Kate Pool*
Circulation 7000

FOUNDED 1890. QUARTERLY journal of **The
Society of Authors**. Unsolicited mss not welcome.

Auto Option Europe
8 Spencer Street, Skelmanthorpe,
Huddersfield HD8 9BE
☎01484 864520   Fax 01484 866332
Owner *First Call Marketing Ltd*
Editor *Ewan Scott*

FOUNDED 1996. Rolling motoring publication
on the Internet (http://www.auto-option.co.
uk/newhome.htm). Items on insurance, tests,
4x4, travelogue, security, news, technical, new
developments. Approach by phone in the first
instance.

    Features   4x4,   travelogue,   sports   cars.
750–1500 words.

    News 'Always looking for material'. 200
words maximum.

    Payment 'All fees are negligible (£3 per 1000
visits).'

Autocar
38–42 Hampton Road, Teddington,
Middlesex TW11 0JE
☎0181 943 5013   Fax 0181 943 5653
Owner *Haymarket Magazines Ltd*
Editor-in-Chief *Steve Cropley*
Circulation 75,000

FOUNDED 1895. WEEKLY. All news stories, features, interviews, scoops, ideas, tip-offs and
photographs welcome.

    Features *Colin Goodwin*

    News *Julian Rendell*

    Payment from £175 per 1000 words/nego-
tiable.

Baby Magazine
The Publishing House, Highbury Station
Road, Islington, London N1 1SE
☎0171 226 2222   Fax 0171 359 5225
Owner *Highbury House Communications*
Editor *Lucy Bowman*
Circulation 79,000

TEN ISSUES ANNUALLY. For parents-to-be and
parents of children up to five years old. No
unsolicited mss.

    Features Send synopsis of feature with cov-
ering letter in the first instance. Unsolicited
material is not returned.

Back Brain Recluse (BBR)
PO Box 625, Sheffield S1 3GY
Owner *Chris Reed*
Editor *Chris Reed*
Circulation 3000

International speculative fiction magazine providing opportunity for new writers. 'We strongly recommend familiarity with our guidelines for contributors, and with recent issues of *BBR*, before any material is submitted.' All correspondence must be accompanied by s.a.e. or international reply coupons.
Payment £5 per 1000 words.

Badminton
Connect Sports, 14 Woking Road, Cheadle Hulme, Cheshire SK8 6NZ
☎0161 485 2728/0171 938 7399 (editorial)
Fax 0161 485 2728

Owner *Mrs S. Ashton*
Editor *William Kings*

BI-MONTHLY. Specialist badminton magazine, with news, views, product information, equipment reviews, etc. Unsolicited material will be considered. Approach the editor by phone with an idea.
Features *William Kings* Open to approaches and likes to discuss ideas in the first instance. Interested in badminton-related articles on health, fitness, psychology, clothing, accessories, etc.
Payment £60.

The Badminton Times
PO Box 3443, London SE8 5BG
☎0181 692 6302   Fax 0181 692 6302
Editor *Mr R. Richardson*

FOUNDED 1980. QUARTERLY. Events, players, fashion and footwear, rackets, facilities, technique and tactics.

Balance
British Diabetic Association, 10 Queen Anne Street, London W1M 0BD
☎0171 323 1531   Fax 0171 637 3644
Owner *British Diabetic Association*
Editor *Maggie Gibbons*
Circulation 170,000

FOUNDED 1935. BI-MONTHLY. Unsolicited mss are not accepted. Writers may submit a brief proposal in writing. Only topics relevant to diabetes will be considered.
Features *Maggie Gibbons* Medical, diet and lifestyle features written by people with diabetes

or with an interest and expert knowledge in the field. General features are mostly based on experience or personal observation. Maximum 1500 words. *Payment* NUJ rates.
News *Maggie Gibbons* Short pieces about activities relating to diabetes and the lifestyle of diabetics. Maximum 150 words.
Young Balance *Jackie Mace* Any kind of article written by those under 18 and with personal experience of diabetes. *Payment* varies.

The Banker
149 Tottenham Court Road, London W1P 9LL
☎0171 896 2507   Fax 0171 896 2586
Owner *Pearson Professional*
Editor *Stephen Timewell*
Circulation 14,520

FOUNDED 1926. MONTHLY. News and features on banking, finance and capital markets worldwide and technology.

BBC Gardeners' World Magazine
Woodlands, 80 Wood Lane, London W12 0TT
☎0181 576 3959   Fax 0181 576 3986
Owner *BBC Worldwide Publishing*
Editor *Adam Pasco*
Circulation 293,041

FOUNDED 1991. MONTHLY. Gardening advice, ideas and inspiration. No unsolicited mss. Approach by phone or in writing with ideas.

BBC Good Food
Woodlands, 80 Wood Lane, London W12 0TT
☎0181 576 2000   Fax 0181 576 3825
Owner *BBC Worldwide Publishing*
Editor *Mitzie Wilson*
Circulation 393,633

FOUNDED 1989. MONTHLY food and drink magazine with television and radio links. No unsolicited mss.

BBC Homes & Antiques
Woodlands, 80 Wood Lane, London W12 0TT
☎0181 576 3490   Fax 0181 576 3867
Owner *BBC Worldwide Publishing*
Editor *Judith Hall*
Circulation 171,674

FOUNDED 1993. MONTHLY traditional home interest magazine with a strong bias towards antiques and collectables. Opportunities for freelancers are limited; most features are commissioned from regular stable of contributors. No fiction, health and beauty, fashion or general showbusiness. Approach with ideas by phone or in writing.

Features *Judith Hall* At-home features: inspirational houses – people-led items. Pieces commissioned on recce shots and cuttings. Guidelines available on request. Celebrity features: 'at homes or favourite things' – send cuttings of relevant work published. Maximum 1500 words.

Special Pages Regular feature on memories of childhood homes. Maximum 800 words.

Payment negotiable.

BBC Music Magazine

Room A1004, Woodlands, 80 Wood Lane, London W12 0TT

☎0181 576 3283   Fax 0181 576 3292

Owner *BBC Worldwide Publishing*
Editor *Fiona Maddocks*
Circulation 68,104

FOUNDED 1992. MONTHLY. All areas of classical music. Not interested in unsolicited material. Approach with ideas only, by fax or in writing.

BBC Vegetarian Good Food

Room AG176, Woodlands, 80 Wood Lane, London W12 0TT

☎0181 576 3767   Fax 0181 576 3825

Owner *BBC Worldwide Publishing*
Editor *Gilly Cubitt*
Circulation 78,958

FOUNDED 1992. MONTHLY magazine containing recipes, health and environment features. Unsolicited mss not welcome. Approach in writing with ideas.

BBC Wildlife Magazine

Broadcasting House, Whiteladies Road, Bristol BS8 2LR

☎0117 973 8402   Fax 0117 946 7075

Owner *BBC Worldwide Publishing*
Editor *Rosamund Kidman Cox*
Circulation 116,537

FOUNDED 1963 (formerly *Wildlife*, originally *Animals*). MONTHLY. Unsolicited mss not welcome.

Features Most features commissioned from writers with expert knowledge of wildlife or conservation subjects. Unsolicited mss are usually rejected. Maximum 3500 words. *Payment* £120–350.

News Most news stories commissioned from known freelancers. Maximum 800 words. *Payment* £40–100.

Bedfordshire Magazine

34 Spring Road, Kempston, Bedfordshire MK42 8LP

☎01234 266839

Owner *White Crescent Press*
Editor *Ann Collett-White*
Circulation 2400

FOUNDED 1947. QUARTERLY. Unsolicited material welcome on Bedfordshire. No general interest articles. Approach by phone or in writing in the first instance.

Features History, biography, natural history and arts. No consumer features.

News Very little.

Fiction Occasional stories and poems of county interest only.

Special Pages Primarily historical material on Bedfordshire. Maximum 1500 words.

Payment nominal.

Bee World

18 North Road, Cardiff CF1 3DY

☎01222 372409   Fax 01222 665522

Owner *International Bee Research Association*
Editor *Dr P. A. Munn*
Circulation 1700

FOUNDED 1919. QUARTERLY. High-quality factual journal, including peer-reviewed articles, with international readership. Features on apicultural science and technology. Unsolicited mss welcome. It is recommended that authors write to the Editor for guidelines before submitting mss.

Bella

H. Bauer Publishing, Shirley House, 25–27 Camden Road, London NW1 9LL

☎0171 284 0909   Fax 0171 485 3774

Owner *H. Bauer Publishing*
Editor-in-Chief *Jackie Highe*
Circulation 1.2 million

FOUNDED 1987. WEEKLY. General interest women's magazine. Contributions welcome.

Features *Sharon Bexley* Maximum 1200–1500 words. Send s.a.e. for guidelines.

Fiction *Linda O'Byrne* Maximum 1200–2000 words. Send s.a.e. for guidelines.

Payment about £300 per 1000 words/varies.

Best

Portland House, Stag Place, London SW1E 5AU

☎0171 245 8700   Fax 0171 245 8825

Owner *G & J (UK)*
Editor *Juli Ackhurst*

Circulation 554,744

FOUNDED 1987. WEEKLY women's magazine and stablemate of the magazine *Prima*. Multiple features, news, short stories on all topics of interest to women. Important for would-be contributors to study the magazine's style which differs from many other women's weeklies. Approach in writing with s.a.e..

Features Maximum 1500 words. No unsolicited mss.

Fiction 'Five-Minute Story' slot; unsolicited mss accepted. Maximum 1400 words.

Payment £100.

Best of British

Ian Beacham Publishing, 200 Eastgate, Deeping St James, Peterborough, Cambridgeshire PE6 8RD

☎01778 347003   Fax 01778 347003

Owner *Ian Beacham Publishing*
Editor *Ian Beacham*

FOUNDED 1994. BI-MONTHLY magazine celebrating all things British, both past and present. Study of the magazine is advised in the first instance. All preliminary approaches should be made in writing.

The Big Issue

Fleet House, 57–61 Clerkenwell Road, London EC1M 5NP

☎0171 418 0418   Fax 0171 418 0427

Publisher *Andrew Jaspan*
Editor-in-Chief *A. John Bird*
Associate Editor *Becky Gardiner*
Features Editor *Simon Rogers*
Arts Editor *Tina Jackson*
News Editor *Jane Cassidy*
Circulation 142,937

FOUNDED 1991. WEEKLY. An award-winning campaigning and street-wise general interest magazine sold in London and the south of England. Separate regional editions sold in Manchester, Scotland, Wales and Ireland.

Features *Simon Rogers* Interviews, campaigns, comment, opinion and social issues reflecting a twenty-something informed audience. Balance includes social issues but mixed with arts and cultural features. Freelance writers used each week – commissioned from a variety of writers. Best approach is to fax or post synopses to features editor with examples of work in the first instance. Maximum 1200 words. *Payment* £150 for 1000 words.

News *Jane Cassidy* Hard-hitting exclusive stories with emphasis on social injustice. Not interested in re-runs of other people's stories. Emphasis on magazine's publication area.

Arts *Tina Jackson* Interested in comment, interviews and analysis ideas. Reviews written in-house. Send synopses to arts editor.

Fiction Annual short story season covering variety of subjects – not only homelessness. Send stories/synopses to arts editor.

BIG!

Mappin House, 4 Winsley Street, London W1N 7AR

☎0171 436 1515   Fax 0171 312 8246

Owner *EMAP Metro*
Editor *Dominic Smith*
Circulation 180,114

FOUNDED 1990. FORTNIGHTLY celebrity/entertainment magazine for teenage girls. Interested in interviews with celebrities from the worlds of pop, film and television. 1500 words maximum; approach by phone in the first instance.

Birds

The Lodge, Sandy, Bedfordshire SG19 2DL

☎01767 680551   Fax 01767 692365

Owner *Royal Society for the Protection of Birds*
Editor *R. A. Hume*
Circulation 524,124

QUARTERLY magazine which covers not only wild birds but also wildlife and related conservation topics. No interest in features on pet birds or 'rescued' sick/injured/orphaned ones. Mss or ideas welcome. On the look-out for photo features (colour transparencies) from photographers. Especially interested in unusual bird behaviour. 'No captive birds, please.'

Birdwatch

310 Bow House, 153–159 Bow Road, London E3 2SE

☎0181 983 1855   Fax 0181 983 0246

Owner *Solo Publishing*
Editor *Dominic Mitchell*
Circulation 16,500

FOUNDED 1992. MONTHLY high-quality magazine featuring illustrated articles on all aspects of birds and birdwatching, especially in Britain. No unsolicited mss. Approach in writing with synopsis of 100 words maximum. Annual **Birdwatch Bird Book of the Year** award (see entry under **Prizes**).

Features *Dominic Mitchell* Unusual angles/personal accounts, if well-written. Articles of an educative or practical nature suited to the readership. Maximum 2000–3000 words.

Fiction *Dominic Mitchell* Very little opportunity although occasional short story published. Maximum 1500 words.

News *Tim Harris* Very rarely use external material.

Payment £40 per 1000 words.

Black Beauty & Hair

Hawker Consumer Publications Ltd, 13 Park House, 140 Battersea Park Road, London SW11 4NB

☎0171 720 2108   Fax 0171 498 3023

Owner *Hawker Consumer Publications Ltd*
Editor *Irene Shelley*
Circulation 22,017

QUARTERLY with two annual specials: Bridal issue in March, hairstyle book in October. Black beauty and fashion magazine with emphasis on humorous but authoritative articles relating to clothes, hair, lifestyle, sexual politics, women's interests, etc. Unsolicited contributions welcome.

Features Beauty and fashion pieces welcome from writers with a sound knowledge of the Afro-Caribbean beauty scene plus bridal features. Minimum 1000 words.

Payment £95 per 1000 words.

Boat International

5–7 Kingston Hill, Kingston upon Thames, Surrey KT2 7PW

☎0181 547 2662   Fax 0181 547 1201

Owner *Edisea Ltd*
Editor *Nicholas Jeffery*
Circulation 30,000

FOUNDED 1983. MONTHLY. Unsolicited mss welcome. Approach with ideas in writing and s.a.e..

Features Maximum 2000 words.
News Maximum 300 words.
Payment £100 per 1000 words.

Book and Magazine Collector

43–45 St. Mary's Road, London W5 5RQ
☎0181 579 1082   Fax 0181 566 2024

Owner *John Dean*
Editor *Crispin Jackson*
Circulation 12,000

FOUNDED 1984. MONTHLY. Contains articles about collectable authors/publications/subjects. Unsolicited mss welcome, but write first with ideas. Must be bibliographical and include a full bibliography and price guide. Not interested in purely biographical features.

Features Maximum length 4000 words.
Payment £30 per 1000 words.

The Book Collector

PO Box 12426, London W11 3GW
☎0171 792 3492   Fax 0171 792 3492

Owner *The Collector Ltd*
Editor *Nicolas J. Barker*

FOUNDED 1950. QUARTERLY magazine on bibliography and the history of books, book-collecting, libraries and the book trade.

Bookdealer

Suite 34, 26 Charing Cross Road, London WC2H 0DH
☎0171 240 5890   Fax 0171 379 5770

Editor *Barry Shaw*

WEEKLY trade paper which acts almost exclusively as a platform for people wishing to buy or sell rare/out-of-print books. Twelve-page editorial only; occasional articles and book reviews by regular freelance writers.

Books

43 Museum Street, London WC1A 1LY
☎0171 404 0304   Fax 0171 242 0762

Editor *Liz Thomson*
Circulation 115,000

Formerly *Books and Bookmen*. Consumer magazine dealing chiefly with features about authors and reviews of books. Carries few commissioned pieces. *Payment* negotiable.

Books in Wales

See **Llais Llyfrau**

The Bookseller

12 Dyott Street, London WC1A 1DF
☎0171 420 6000
Fax 0171 420 6103 (Editorial)

Owner *J. Whitaker & Sons Ltd*
Editor *Louis Baum*

Trade journal of the publishing and book trade – the essential guide to what is being done to whom. Trade news and features, including special features, company news, publishing trends, etc. Unsolicited mss rarely used as most writing is either done in-house or commissioned from experts within the trade. Approach in writing first.

Features *Jenny Bell*
News *Ms Danuta Kean*

Brides and Setting Up Home

Vogue House, Hanover Square, London W1R 0AD
☎0171 499 9080   Fax 0171 460 6369

Owner *Condé Nast Publications Ltd*

Editor *Sandra Boler*
Circulation 63,543

BI-MONTHLY. Much of the magazine is produced in-house, but a good, relevant feature on
cakes, jewellery, music, flowers, etc. is always
welcome. Maximum 1000 words. Prospective
contributors should telephone with an idea in
the first instance.

British Birds

Fountains, Park Lane, Blunham, Bedford
MK44 3NJ
☎01767 640025   Fax 01767 640025
Owner *British Birds Ltd*
Editor *Dr J. T. R. Sharrock*
Circulation 10,000

FOUNDED 1907. MONTHLY ornithological
magazine published by non-profit-making
company. Features annual *Reports on Rare Birds
in Great Britain*, bird news from official national
correspondents throughout Europe and sponsored competitions for Bird Photograph of the
Year, Bird Illustrator of the Year and Young
Ornithologists of the Year. Unsolicited mss
welcome from ornithologists only.

Features Well-researched, original material
relating to Western Palearctic birds welcome.
Maximum 6000 words.

News *Bob Scott/Wendy Dickson* Items ranging from conservation to humour. Maximum
200 words.

Payment only for photographs, drawings and
paintings.

British Chess Magazine

The Chess Shop, 69 Masbro Road, London
W14 OLS
☎0171 603 2877   Fax 0171 371 1477
Owner *Murray Chandler*
Editor *Murray Chandler*

FOUNDED 1881. MONTHLY. Emphasis on tour-
naments, the history of chess and chess-related
literature. Approach in writing with ideas.
Unsolicited mss not welcome unless from qualified chess experts and players.

British Medical Journal

BMA House, Tavistock Square, London
WC1H 9JR
☎0171 387 4499   Fax 0171 383 6418
Owner *British Medical Association*
Editor *Professor Richard Smith*

No market for freelance writers.

British Railway Modelling

The Maltings, West Street, Bourne,
Lincolnshire PE10 9PH
☎01778 393313   Fax 01778 394748
Owner *Warners Group Holdings Plc*
Editor *David Brown*
Assistant Editor *Jarrod Cotter*
Circulation 17,594

FOUNDED 1993. MONTHLY. A general magazine for the practising modeller. No unsolicited
mss but ideas are welcome. Interested in features on quality models, from individual items
to complete layouts. Approach in writing.

Features articles on practical elements of
the hobby, e.g. locomotive construction, kit
conversions etc. Layout features and articles on
individual items which represent high standards
of the railway modelling art. Maximum length
6000 words (single feature). *Payment* up to £40
per published page.

News news and reviews containing the
model railway trade, new products etc.
Maximum length 1000 words. *Payment* up to
£40 per published page.

Broadcast

33-39 Bowling Green Lane, London
EC1R 0DA
☎0171 505 8014   Fax 0171 505 8050
Owner *EMAP Business Communications*
Editor *Matt Baker*
Circulation 12,372

FOUNDED 1960. WEEKLY. Opportunities for
freelance contributions. Write to the relevant
editor in the first instance.

Features *Mark McNulty* Any broadcasting
issue. Maximum 1500 words.

News *Jacey Lamerton* Broadcasting news.
Maximum 350 words.

Payment £180 per 1000 words.

Brownie

17-19 Buckingham Palace Road, London
SW1W 0PT
☎0171 834 6242   Fax 0171 828 8317
Owner *The Guide Association*
Editor *Marion Thompson*
Circulation 30,000

FOUNDED 1962. MONTHLY. Aimed at Brownie
members aged 7-10.

Articles Crafts and simple make-it-yourself
items using inexpensive or scrap materials.

Fiction Brownie content an advantage. No
adventures involving unaccompanied children in

dangerous situations – day or night. Maximum 600 words.

Payment £50 per 1000 words pro rata.

Building

Builder House, 40 Marsh Wall, London E14 9TP
☎0171 560 4141   Fax 0171 560 4004

Owner *The Builder Group*
Editor *Adrian Barrick*
Circulation 23,000

FOUNDED 1842. WEEKLY. Features articles on aspects of the modern building industry. Unsolicited mss are not welcome but freelancers with specialist knowledge of the industry are often used.

Features Focus on the modern industry. No building history required. Maximum 1000 words.

News Maximum 300 words.
Payment by arrangement.

The Burlington Magazine

14–16 Duke's Road, London WC1H 9AD
☎0171 388 1228   Fax 0171 388 1230

Owner *The Burlington Magazine Publications Ltd*
Editor *Caroline Elam*

FOUNDED 1903. MONTHLY. Unsolicited contributions welcome on the subject of art history provided they are previously unpublished. All preliminary approaches should be made in writing.

Exhibition Reviews Usually commissioned, but occasionally unsolicited reviews are published if appropriate. Maximum 1000 words.

Articles Maximum 4500 words. *Payment* £100 (maximum).

Shorter Notices Maximum 2000 words. *Payment* £50 (maximum).

Business Brief

PO Box 582, Five Oaks, St Saviour, Jersey JE4 8XQ
☎01534 611600   Fax 01534 611610

Owner *Michael Stephen Publishers*
Editor *Simon Petulla*
Circulation 4,100

FOUNDED 1989. MONTHLY magazine covering business developments in the Channel Islands and how they affect the local market. Interested in business-orientated articles only – 800 words maximum.

Payment £8 per 100 words.

Business Life

Haymarket House, 1 Oxendon Street, London SW1Y 4EE
☎0171 925 2544   Fax 0171 839 4508

Owner *Premier Magazines*
Editor *Sandra Harris*
Editorial Assistant *Catherine Flanagan*
Circulation 193,000

MONTHLY. Glossy business travel magazine with few opportunities for freelancers. Distributed on BA European routes, TAT and Deutsche BA only. Unsolicited mss not welcome. Approach with ideas in writing only.

Business Traveller

Compass House, 22 Redan Place, London W2 4SZ
☎0171 229 7799   Fax 0171 229 9441

Owner *Perry Publications*
Editor *Gillian Upton*
Circulation 55,386

MONTHLY. Consumer publication. Opportunities exist for freelance writers but unsolicited contributions tend to be 'irrelevant to our market'. Would-be contributors are advised to study the magazine first. Approach in writing with ideas. *Payment* varies.

Camcorder User

57–59 Rochester Place, London NW1 9JU
☎0171 485 0011   Fax 0171 482 6269

Owner *W. V. Publications*
Editor *Christine Morgan*
Circulation 21,797

FOUNDED 1988. MONTHLY magazine dedicated to camcorders, with features on creative technique, shooting advice, new equipment, accessory round-ups and interesting applications on location. Unsolicited mss, illustrations and pictures welcome. *Payment* negotiable.

Campaign

174 Hammersmith Road, London W6 7JP
☎0171 413 4036   Fax 0171 413 4507

Owner *Haymarket Publishing Ltd*
Editor *Stefano Hatfield*
Circulation 15,918

FOUNDED 1968. WEEKLY. Lively magazine serving the advertising and related industries. Freelance contributors are best advised to write in the first instance.

Features Articles of 1500–2000 words.

News Relevant news stories of up to 300 words.

Payment negotiable.

Camping and Caravanning

Greenfields House, Westwood Way,
Coventry, Warwickshire CV4 8JH
☎01203 694995   Fax 01203 694886

Owner *Camping and Caravanning Club*
Editor *Peter Frost*
Circulation 133,160

FOUNDED 1901. MONTHLY. Interested in journalists with camping and caravanning knowledge. Write with ideas for features in the first instance.

Features Outdoor pieces in general, plus items on specific regions of Britain. Maximum 1200 words. Illustrations to support text essential.

Camping Magazine

Star Brewery, Castle Ditch Lane, Lewes, East Sussex BN7 1YJ
☎01273 477421   Fax 01273 477421

Owner *Garnett Dickinson Publishing*
Editor *John Lloyd*

FOUNDED 1961. MONTHLY magazine with features on walking and camping. Aims to reflect this enjoyment by encouraging readers to appreciate the outdoors and to pursue an active camping holiday, whether as a family in a frame tent or as a lightweight backpacker. Articles that have the flavour of the camping lifestyle without being necessarily expeditionary or arduous are always welcome. Study of the magazine is advised in the first instance. Ideas welcome. Contact editor by phone before sending mss.

Payment negotiable.

Canal and Riverboat

c/o Burrows Design Works, Jonathan Scott Hall, Thorne Road, Norwich, Norfolk NR1 1UH
☎01603 623856   Fax 01603 623856

Owner *A. E. Morgan Publications Ltd*
Editor *Chris Cattrall*
Circulation 26,000

Covers all aspects of waterways, narrow boats and cruisers. Contributions welcome. Make initial approach in writing.

Features *Chris Cattrall* Waterways, narrow boats and motor cruisers, cruising reports, practical advice, etc. Unusual ideas and personal comments are particularly welcome. Maximum 2000 words. *Payment* around £50 per page.

News *Chris Cattrall* Items of up to 300 words welcome on the Inland Waterways System, plus photographs if possible. *Payment* £15.

Car Mechanics

Kelsey Publishing, 77 High Street, Beckenham, Kent BR3 1AN
☎0181 658 3531   Fax 0181 650 8035

Owner *Kelsey Publishing*
Editor *Peter Simpson*
Circulation 35,000

MONTHLY. Practical guide to DIY, maintenance and repair of post–1978 cars. Unsolicited mss, with good-quality colour prints or transparencies, welcome 'at sender's risk'. Ideas preferred. Initial approach by letter or phone strongly recommended.

Features Good, technical, entertaining and well-researched material welcome, especially anything presenting complex matters clearly and simply.

Payment by arrangement.

Caravan Life

The Maltings, West Street, Bourne, Lincolnshire PH10 9PH
☎01778 391166   Fax 01778 394748

Editor *Stuart Craig*
Circulation 15,809

FOUNDED 1987. Magazine for experienced caravanners and enthusiasts providing practical and useful information and product evaluation. Opportunities for caravanning, relevant touring and travel material with good-quality colour photographs.

Caravan Magazine

Link House, Dingwall Avenue, Croydon, Surrey CR9 2TA
☎0181 686 2599   Fax 0181 781 6044

Owner *Link House Magazines Ltd*
Editor *Barry Williams*
Circulation 21,792

FOUNDED 1933. MONTHLY. Unsolicited mss welcome. Approach in writing with ideas. All correspondence should go direct to the editor.

Features Touring with strong caravan bias and technical/DIY features. Maximum 1500 words.

Payment by arrangement.

Caribbean Times/Asian Times

3rd Floor, Tower House, 141–149 Fonthill Road, London N4 3HF
☎0171 281 1191   Fax 0171 263 9656

Owner *Arif Ali*
Editor *Arif Ali*

Two WEEKLY community papers for the Asian, African and Caribbean communities in Britain.

Caribbean Times has a circulation of 22,500 and was founded in 1981; *Asian Times* was founded two years later and has a circulation of 33,000. Interested in general, local and international issues relevant to these communities. Approach in writing with ideas for submission.

Carmarthenshire Life
Merlins Bridge, Haverfordwest,
Pembrokeshire SA61 1XF
☎01437 763133 ext. 223   Fax 01437 760482
Owner *Southern Newspapers*
Editor *David Fielding*

FOUNDED 1995. MONTHLY county magazine with articles on local history, issues, characters, off-beat stories with good colour or b&w photographs. No country diaries, short stories or poems. Most articles are commissioned from known freelancers but 'always prepared to consider ideas from new writers'. No mss. Send cuttings of previous work (published or not) and synopsis to the editor.

Cars and Car Conversions Magazine
Link House, Dingwall Avenue, Croydon,
Surrey CR9 2TA
☎0181 686 2599   Fax 0181 781 6042
Owner *Link House Magazines Ltd*
Editor *Steve Bennett*
Circulation 46,537

FOUNDED 1965. MONTHLY. Unsolicited mss welcome but prospective contributors are advised to make initial contact by telephone.
    Features Technical articles on current motorsport and unusual sport-orientated road cars. Length by arrangement.
    Payment negotiable.

Cat World
Avalon Court, Star Road, Partridge Green,
West Sussex RH13 8RY
☎01403 711511   Fax 01403 711521
Owner *Ashdown Publishing*
Editor *Joan Moore*
Circulation 19,000

FOUNDED 1981. MONTHLY. Unsolicited mss welcome but initial approach in writing preferred.
    Features Lively, first-hand experience features on every aspect of the cat. Breeding features and veterinary articles by acknowledged experts only. Maximum 1000 words.
    News Short, concise, factual or humorous items concerning cats. Maximum 100 words.
    Poems Maximum 50 words.

Catholic Herald
Lamb's Passage, Bunhill Row, London
EC1Y 8TQ
☎0171 588 3101   Fax 0171 256 9728
Editor *Debra Jones*
Deputy Editor *Piers McGrandle*
Literary Editor *Damian Thompson*
Circulation 22,000

WEEKLY. Interested not only in straight Catholic issues but also in general humanitarian matters, social policies, the Third World, the arts and books. *Payment* by arrangement.

The Celtic Review
Celtic Publications, 53 Waterloo Road,
Ramsey, Isle of Man IM8 1DZ
☎01624 817060   Fax 01624 817060
Owner *Robert Watson*
Editor *Robert Watson*
Circulation 5000

FOUNDED 1996. QUARTERLY Celtic magazine featuring anything to do with Scotland, Ireland, Wales, Cornwall, Isle of Man, Brittany and other Celtic countries. Unsolicited mss welcome on Celtic/Gaelic subjects; ancient or modern history; fiction and book reviews welcome if on a Celtic theme – maximum 2000 words for fiction. *Payment* negotiable/free magazine for news items.

Certified Accountant
19 Rutland Street, Cork, Republic of Ireland
☎00 353 21313 855   Fax 00 353 21313 496
Editor *Brian O'Kane*
Circulation 59,000

MONTHLY. Specialist, professional readership with world-wide circulation. Unsolicited mss welcome though most features tend to be commissioned. Make initial contact in writing. No fiction.
    Features Maximum 1750 words. *Payment* £135 per 1000 words.

Challenge
PO Box 300, Kingstown Broadway, Carlisle,
Cumbria CA3 0QS
☎01228 512512 (ext. 2305) Fax 01228 593388
Owner *Challenge Publishing*
Editor *Donald Banks*
Circulation 80,000

FOUNDED 1958. MONTHLY Christian newspaper which welcomes contributions. Send for sample copy of writers' guidelines in the first instance.
    Fiction Short children's stories. Maximum 600 words.

News Items of up to 500 words (preferably with pictures) 'showing God at work', and human interest photo stories. 'Churchy' items not wanted. Stories of professional sportsmen who are Christians always wanted but check first to see if their story has already been used.

Women's Page Relevant items of interest welcome.

Payment negotiable.

Champs-Elysées

119 Altenburg Gardens, The Conservatory, Bakery Place, London SW11 1JQ
☎0171 738 9323   Fax 0171 738 0707

Owner *Wes Green*
European Editor *David Ralston*

FOUNDED 1984. MONTHLY audio magazine for advanced speakers of French, German, Italian and Spanish issued in two parts: Part One is an hour-long programme (original stories, interviews and songs) in one of the above languages on cassette; Part Two is a booklet comprising a complete transcript with a glossary of difficult words plus features in English relating to topics covered on the tape. Interested in receiving ideas for unusual, well-researched features (for online use) for a sophisticated and well-educated readership.

Features European culture and travel. 1500 words maximum. *Payment* £200 per 1000 words. Approach in writing in the first instance.

Chapman

4 Broughton Place, Edinburgh EH1 3RX
☎0131 557 2207   Fax 0131 556 9565

Owner *Joy M. Hendry*
Editor *Joy M. Hendry*
Circulation 2000

FOUNDED 1970. QUARTERLY. Scotland's quality literary magazine. Features poetry, short works of fiction, criticism, reviews and articles on theatre, politics, language and the arts. Unsolicited material welcome if accompanied by s.a.e.. Approach in writing unless discussion is needed. Priority is given to full-time writers.

Features Topics of literary interest, especially Scottish literature, theatre, culture or politics. Maximum 5000 words.

Fiction Short stories, occasionally novel extracts if self-contained. Maximum 6000 words. *Payment* £15 per 1000 words.

Special Pages Poetry, both UK and non-UK in translation (mainly, but not necessarily, European). *Payment* £8 per published page.

(*Payment* can be had in each category in equivalent copies at discount rate.)

Chapter One

See **Alliance of Literary Societies** under **Professional Associations**

Chat

King's Reach Tower, Stamford Street, London SE1 9LS
☎0171 261 6565   Fax 0171 261 6534

Owner *IPC Magazines Ltd*
Editor-in-Chief *Iris Burton*
Circulation 526,365

FOUNDED 1985. WEEKLY general interest magazine for women. Unsolicited mss considered (receives about 100 a week). Approach in writing with ideas. Not interested in contributors 'who have never bothered to read *Chat* and don't therefore know what type of magazine it is'.

Features *Karen Swayne* Human interest and humour. Maximum 1000 words. *Payment* up to £300 maximum.

Fiction *Shelley Silas* Maximum 1000 words.

Cheshire Life

2nd Floor, Oyston Mill, Strand Road, Preston, Lancashire PR1 8UR
☎01772 722022   Fax 01772 760905

Owner *Life Magazines*
Editor *Patrick O'Neill*
Circulation 11,000

FOUNDED 1934. MONTHLY. Homes, gardens, personalities, business, farming, conservation, heritage, books, fashion, arts, science – anything which has a Cheshire connection somewhere.

Child Education

Villiers House, Clarendon Avenue, Leamington Spa, Warwickshire CV32 5PR
☎01926 887799   Fax 01926 883331

Owner *Scholastic Ltd*
Editor *Gill Moore*
Circulation 59,900

FOUNDED 1923. MONTHLY magazine aimed at nursery, pre-school playgroup, infant and first teachers. Articles from teachers, relating to education for 4–7-year age group, are welcome. Maximum 1200 words. Approach in writing with synopsis. No unsolicited mss.

Choice

Apex House, Oundle Road, Peterborough, Cambridgeshire PE2 9NP
☎01733 555123   Fax 01733 898487

Owner *EMAP/Bayard Presse*
Editor *Sue Dobson*

Circulation 98,015

MONTHLY full-colour, lively and informative magazine for people aged 50 plus which helps them get the most out of their lives, time and money after full-time work.

Features Real-life stories, hobbies, interesting (older) people, British heritage and countryside, involving activities for active bodies and minds, health, competitions. Unsolicited mss read (s.a.e. for return of material); write with ideas and copies of cuttings if new contributor. No phone calls, please.

Rights/News All items affecting the magazine's readership are written by experts. Areas of interest include pensions, state benefits, health, money, property, legal, and caring for elderly relatives.

Payment by arrangement.

Church Music Quarterly
151 Mount View Road, London N4 4JT
☎0181 341 6408   Fax 0181 340 0021

Owner *Royal School of Church Music*
Editor *Trevor Ford*
Associate Editor *Marianne Barton*
Circulation 13,700

QUARTERLY. Contributions welcome. Telephone in the first instance.

Features *Trevor Ford* Articles on church music or related subjects considered. Maximum 2000 words.

Payment £60 per page.

Church of England Newspaper
10 Little College Street, London SW1P 3SH
☎0171 976 7760   Fax 0171 976 0783

Owner *Parliamentary Communications Ltd*
Editor *Colin Blakely*
Circulation 11,600

FOUNDED 1828. WEEKLY. Almost all material is commissioned but unsolicited mss considered.

Features *Andrew Carey* Preliminary enquiry essential. Maximum 1200 words.

News *Emma Watkins* Items must be sent promptly and should have a church/Christian relevance. Maximum 200–400 words.

Payment negotiable.

Church Times
33 Upper Street, London N1 0PN
☎0171 359 4570   Fax 0171 226 3073

Owner *Hymns Ancient & Modern*
Editor *Paul Handley*
Circulation 38,000

FOUNDED 1863. WEEKLY. Unsolicited mss considered.

Features *Paul Handley* Articles and pictures (any format) on religious topics. Maximum 1600 words. *Payment* £100 per 1000 words.

News *Paul Handley* Occasional reports (commissions only) and up-to-date photographs.

Payment by arrangement.

Classic Boat
Link House, Dingwall Avenue, Croydon, Surrey CR9 2TA
☎0181 686 2599   Fax 0181 781 6535

Owner *Boating Publications Ltd*
Editor *Nic Compton*
Circulation 14,611

FOUNDED 1987. MONTHLY. Traditional boats and classic yachts old and new; maritime history. Unsolicited mss, particularly if supported by good photos, are welcome. Sail and power boat pieces considered. Approach in writing with ideas. Interested in well-researched stories on all nautical matters. News reports welcome. Contributor's notes available (s.a.e.).

Features Boatbuilding, boat history and design, events, yachts and working boats. Material must be well-informed and supported where possible by good-quality or historic photos. Maximum 3000 words. Classic is defined by excellence of design and construction – the boat need not be old and wooden! *Payment* £75–100 per published page.

News Discarded famous classic boats, events, boatbuilders, etc. Maximum 500 words. *Payment* according to merit.

Classic Cars
Abbots Court, 34 Farringdon Lanr, London EC1R 3AU
☎0171 216 6240   Fax 0171 216 6270

Owner *EMAP National Publications*
Editor *Robert Coucher*
Circulation 86,006

FOUNDED 1973. MONTHLY classic car magazine containing entertaining and informative articles about old cars and associated personalities.

Classical Guitar
Olsover House, 43 Sackville Road, Newcastle upon Tyne NE6 5TA
☎0191 276 0448   Fax 0191 276 1623

Owner *Ashley Mark Publishing Co.*
Editor *Colin Cooper*

FOUNDED 1982. MONTHLY.

Features *Colin Cooper* Usually written by staff writers. Maximum 1500 words. *Payment* by arrangement.

News *Thérèse Wassily Saba* Small paragraphs and festival concert reports welcome. *No payment.*

Reviews *Chris Kilvington* Concert reviews of up to 250 words are usually written by staff reviewers.

Classical Music
241 Shaftesbury Avenue, London
WC2H 8EH
☎0171 333 1742   Fax 0171 333 1769
Owner *Rhinegold Publishing Ltd*
Editor *Keith Clarke*

FOUNDED 1976. FORTNIGHTLY. A specialist magazine using precisely targeted news and feature articles aimed at the music business. Most material is commissioned but professionally written unsolicited mss are occasionally published. Freelance contributors may approach in writing with an idea but should familiarise themselves beforehand with the style and market of the magazine.

Payment negotiable.

Classical Piano
241 Shaftesbury Avenue, London
WC2H 8EH
☎0171 333 1724   Fax 0171 333 1769
Owner *Rhinegold Publishing*
Editor *Jessica Duchen*
Circulation 11,000

FOUNDED 1993. BI-MONTHLY magazine containing features, profiles, technical information, news, reviews of interest to those with a serious amateur or professional concern with pianos or their playing. No unsolicited material. Approach with ideas in writing only.

Climber
7th Floor, The Plaza Tower, East Kilbride, Glasgow G74 1LW
☎01355 246444   Fax 01355 263013
Owner *Scottish Television*
Editor *Tom Prentice*
Circulation 16,000

FOUNDED 1962. MONTHLY. Unsolicited mss welcome (they receive about ten a day). Ideas welcome.

Features Freelance features are accepted on climbing, mountaineering and hill-walking in the UK and abroad, but the standard of writing must be extremely high. Maximum 2000 words. *Payment* negotiable.

News No freelance opportunities as all items are handled in-house.

Club International
2 Archer Street, London W1V 8JJ
☎0171 734 9191   Fax 0171 734 5030
Owner *Paul Raymond*
Editor *Robert Swift*
Circulation 180,000

FOUNDED 1972. MONTHLY. Features and short humorous items aimed at young male readership aged 18–30.

Features Maximum 1000 words.
Shorts 200–750 words.
Payment negotiable.

Coin News
Token Publishing Ltd, PO Box 14, Honiton, Devon EX14 9YP
☎01404 831878   Fax 01404 831895
Owner *J. W. Mussell and Carol Hartman*
Editor *J. W. Mussell*
Circulation 10,000

FOUNDED 1964. MONTHLY. Contributions welcome. Approach by phone in the first instance.

Features Opportunity exists for well-informed authors 'who know the subject and do their homework'. Maximum 2500 words.

Payment £20 per 1000 words.

Commerce Magazine
Station House, Station Road, Newport Pagnell, Milton Keynes MK16 0AG
☎01908 614477   Fax 01908 616441
Owner *Holcot Press Group*
Group Editor *Steve Brennan*
Circulation 25,000

MONTHLY. Ideas welcome. Approach by phone or in writing first.

Features *Isabelle Morgan* By-lined articles frequently used. Generally 750–800 words with photos.

News Handled in-house.

Special Pages Throughout the year – media and marketing; building and construction; finance and professional; office update. *No payment.*

Company
National Magazine House, 72 Broadwick Street, London W1V 2BP
☎0171 439 5000   Fax 0171 439 5117
Owner *National Magazine Co. Ltd*
Editor *Fiona McIntosh*
Circulation 272,160

MONTHLY. Glossy women's magazine appealing to the independent and intelligent young woman. A good market for freelancers: 'We look for great newsy features relevant to young British women'. Keen to encourage bright, new, young talent, but uncommissioned material is rarely accepted. Feature outlines are the only sensible approach in the first instance. Maximum 1500–2000 words. Features to *Rachel Loos*.

Payment £250 per 1000 words.

Company Clothing Magazine
Willowbrook House, The Green, Leire, Lutterworth, Leicestershire LE17 5HL
☎01455 202088   Fax 01455 202692

Owner *Company Clothing Information Services Ltd*
Editor *Carole Bull*
Circulation 13,000

Only UK magazine dedicated to the corporate clothing industry. Unsolicited mss welcome on any aspect of business clothing and workwear.

Complete Car
Compass House, 22 Redan Place, London W2 4SZ
☎0171 229 7799   Fax 0171 221 7846

Owner *Perry Motorpress Ltd*
Editor-in-Chief *Wolfgang Koenig*
Circulation 48,042

FOUNDED 1994. MONTHLY car magazine. Unsolicited mss are rarely, if ever, used. Prospective contributors are advised to make initial approach in writing 'once they have read the magazine from cover to cover at least once'.

Computer Weekly
Quadrant House, The Quadrant, Sutton, Surrey SM2 5AS
☎0181 652 3122   Fax 0181 652 8979

Owner *Reed Business Information*
Editor *Helena Sturridge*
Circulation 120,000

FOUNDED 1966. Freelance contributions welcome.

Features *Ian Mitchell* Always looking for good new writers with specialised industry knowledge. Previews and show features on industry events welcome. Maximum 1500 words.

News *Karl Schneider* Some openings for regional or foreign news items. Max. 300 words.
Payment Up to £50 for stories/tips.

Computing, The IT Newspaper
32–34 Broadwick Street, London W1A 2HG
☎0171 316 9158   Fax 0171 316 9160

Owner *VNU Business Publications Ltd*
Editor *Peter Kirwan*

Circulation 114,000
WEEKLY newspaper.
    Associate Editor *Eira Hayward*
    Features *Janine Milne*
    News *Ambrose McNevin*
    Unsolicited technical articles welcome. Please enclose s.a.e. for return.
    Payment negotiable.

Contemporary Review
Cheam Business Centre, 14 Upper Mulgrave Road, Cheam, Surrey SM2 7AZ
☎0181 643 4846   Fax 0181 241 7507

Owner *Contemporary Review Co. Ltd*
Editor *Dr Richard Mullen*

FOUNDED 1866. MONTHLY. One of the first periodicals to devote considerable space to the arts. Covers a wide spectrum of interests, including home affairs and politics, literature and the arts, history, travel and religion. No fiction. Maximum 3000 words.
    Literary Editor *Dr James Munson* Monthly book section with reviews which are always commissioned.
    Payment £5 per page.

Cosmopolitan
National Magazine House, 72 Broadwick Street, London W1V 2BP
☎0171 439 5000   Fax 0171 439 5016

Owner *National Magazine Co. Ltd*
Editor *Mandi Norwood*
Circulation 461,080

MONTHLY. Designed to appeal to the mid-twenties, modern-minded female. Popular mix of articles, with emphasis on relationships and careers, and hard news. Known to have a policy of not considering unsolicited mss but always on the look-out for 'new writers with original and relevant ideas and a strong voice'. Send short synopsis of idea. All would-be writers should be familiar with the magazine.
    Payment about £200 per 1000 words.

Cotswold Life
Beshara House, Northway Trading Estate, Northway Lane, Tewkesbury, Gloucestershire GL20 8JH
☎01684 854410   Fax 01684 854458

Owner *Beshara Press*
Editor *John Drinkwater*
Circulation 10,000

FOUNDED 1968. MONTHLY. News and features on life in the Cotswolds. Most news written in-house but contributions welcome for features.

Features Interesting places and people, reminiscences of Cotswold life in years gone by, and historical features on any aspect of Cotswold life. Approach in writing in the first instance. Maximum 1500–2000 words.
Payment by negotiation after publication.

Country

Hill Crest Mews, London Road, Baldock, Hertfordshire SG7 6JN
☎01462 490206   Fax 01462 893565
Owner *The Country Gentlemen's Association*
Editor *Barry Turner*
Circulation 25,000

FOUNDED 1893. SUBSCRIPTION MONTHLY. News and features covering rural events, countryside, leisure, heritage, homes and gardens. Some outside contributors. Approach in writing in the first instance.
Payment by arrangement.

Country Garden & Smallholding

Broad Leys Publishing Company, Buriton House, Station Road, Newport, Saffron Walden, Essex CB11 3PL
☎01799 540922   Fax 01799 541367
Owner *D. and K. Thear*
Editor *Helen Sears*
Circulation 21,000

FOUNDED 1975. MONTHLY journal dealing with practical country living. Unsolicited mss welcome; around 30 are received each week. Articles should be detailed and practical, based on first-hand knowledge and experience of smallholding.

Country Homes and Interiors

King's Reach Tower, Stamford Street, London SE1 9LS
☎0171 261 6451   Fax 0171 261 6895
Owner *Home Interest Group/IPC Magazines Ltd*
Editor *Katherine Hadley*
Circulation 112,111

FOUNDED 1986. MONTHLY. The best approach for prospective contributors is with an idea in writing as unsolicited mss are not welcome.

Features *Dominic Bradbury* Monthly personality interviews of interest to an intelligent, affluent readership (women and men), aged 25–44. Maximum 1200 words. Also hotel reviews, leisure pursuits and weekending pieces in England and abroad. Length 750 words.

Houses *Sarah Whelan* Country-style homes with excellent design ideas. Length 1000 words.
Payment negotiable.

Country Life

King's Reach Tower, Stamford Street, London SE1 9LS
☎0171 261 7058   Fax 0171 261 5139
Owner *IPC Magazines Ltd*
Editor *Clive Aslet*
Circulation 42,804

ESTABLISHED 1897, *Country Life* features articles which relate to the countryside, wildlife, rural events, sports and pursuits, and are of interest to country dwellers. Strong informed material rather than amateur enthusiasm. 'No responsibility can be taken for transparencies/artwork submitted.' *Payment* from £120 per 1000 words.

Country Living

National Magazine House, 72 Broadwick Street, London W1V 2BP
☎0171 439 5000   Fax 0171 439 5093
Owner *National Magazine Co. Ltd*
Editor *Susy Smith*
Circulation 175,657

Magazine aimed at country dwellers and town dwellers who love the countryside. Covers people, conservation, wildlife, houses (gardens and interiors) and country businesses. No unsolicited mss. *Payment* negotiable.

Country Origins

PO Box 4, Nairn IV12 4HU
☎01667 454441   Fax 01667 454401
Owner *David St John Thomas*
Editor *Hilary Gray*

FOUNDED 1995. QUARTERLY magazine offering a factual look at yesterday's countryside, incorporating family history. No unsolicited mss.

Country Sports

The Old Town Hall 367 Kennington Road, London SE1 4PT
☎0171 582 5432   Fax 0171 793 8484
Owner *British Field Sports Society*
Editor *Graham Downing*
Circulation 84,000

FOUNDED 1996. QUARTERLY magazine on country sports and conservation issues. No unsolicited mss.

Country Walking

Bretton Court, Bretton, Peterborough, Cambridgeshire PE3 8DZ
☎01733 264666   Fax 01733 465939
Owner *EMAP Plc*
Editor *Lynne Maxwell*
Circulation 50,027

FOUNDED 1987. MONTHLY magazine containing

walks, features related to walking and things you see, country crafts, history, nature, photography etc, plus pull-out walks guide containing 27 routes every month. Very few unsolicited mss accepted. An original approach to subjects welcomed. Not interested in book or gear reviews, news cuttings or poor-quality pictures. Approach by phone with ideas.

Features *Lynne Maxwell* Reader's story (maximum 1000 words). Health-related features (500–1000 words).

Special Pages *Lynne Maxwell* 'Down your way' section walks. Accurately and recently researched walk and fact file. Points of interest along the way and pictures to illustrate. Please contact for guidelines (unsolicited submissions not often accepted for this section).

Payment not negotiable.

Country-Side

BNA, 48 Russell Way, Higham Ferrers, Northamptonshire NN10 8EJ
☎01933 314672   Fax 01933 314672

Owner *British Naturalists' Association*
Editor *Dr D. Applin*
Circulation *c.* 20,000

FOUNDED 1905. BI-MONTHLY. Conservation and natural history magazine. Unsolicited mss and ideas for features welcome on conservation, environmental and natural history topics. Approach in writing with ideas. Maximum 1400 words. *Payment* £50 (with pictures).

The Countryman

Sheep Street, Burford, Oxon OX18 4LH
☎01993 822258   Fax 01993 822703

Owner *Link House Magazines Limited*
Editor *Tom Quinn*
Circulation 50,000

FOUNDED 1927. SIX ISSUES YEARLY. Unsolicited mss with s.a.e. welcome; about 120 received each week. Contributors are strongly advised to study the magazine's content and character in the first instance. Approach in writing with ideas. Articles supplied with top quality illustrations (colour transparencies, archive b&w prints and line drawings) are far more likely to be used.

The Countryman's Weekly
(incorporating **Gamekeeper and Sporting Dog**)

Yelverton, Devon PL20 7PE
☎01822 855281   Fax 01822 855372

Publisher *Vic Gardner*
Editor *Jayne Willcocks*

FOUNDED 1895. WEEKLY. Unsolicited material welcome.

Features On any country sports topic. Maximum 1000 words.

Payment rates available on request.

County

70–72 St Mark's Road, Maidenhead, Berkshire SL6 6DW
☎01628 789444   Fax 01628 789396

Owner *Mr and Mrs Watts*
Editor *Mrs Ashlyn Watts*
Circulation 50,000

FOUNDED 1986. QUARTERLY lifestyle magazine featuring homes, interiors, gardening, fashion and beauty, motoring, leisure and dining. Welcome unsolicited mss. All initial approaches should be made in writing.

The Cricketer International

Third Street, Langton Green, Tunbridge Wells, Kent TN3 0EN
☎01892 862551   Fax 01892 863755

Owner *Ben G. Brocklehurst*
Editor *Peter Perchard*
Circulation 40,000

FOUNDED 1921. MONTHLY. Unsolicited mss considered. Ideas in writing only. No initial discussions by phone. All correspondence should be addressed to the editor.

Cumbria and Lake District Magazine

Dalesman Publishing Co. Ltd, Stable Courtyard, Broughton Hall, Skipton, North Yorkshire BD23 3AE
☎01756 701381   Fax 01756 701326

Owner *Dalesman Publishing Co. Ltd*
Editor *Terry Fletcher*
Circulation 15,600

FOUNDED 1951. MONTHLY. County magazine of strong regional and countryside interest, focusing on the Lake District. Unsolicited mss welcome. Maximum 1000 words. Approach in writing or by phone with feature ideas.

Cycle Sport

King's Reach Tower, Stamford Street, London SE1 9LS
☎0171 261 5588   Fax 0171 261 5758

Owner *IPC Magazines Ltd*
Editor *Andrew Sutcliffe*
Circulation 23,477

Magazine dedicated to professional cycle racing.

Cycling Today

67–71 Goswell Road, London
EC1V 7EN
☎0171 410 9410   Fax 0171 410 9440

Owner *Stonehart Group*
Editor *Roger St Pierre*
Circulation 20,800

Previously *New Cyclist*. MONTHLY general interest cycling magazine. Unsolicited feature proposals welcome. Not interested in personal accounts such as how you began cycling.
Features Almost any cycling subject. Touring pieces on Mac-compatible (Word for Windows) disk with hard copy and high-quality transparencies. Submissions welcomed from writers and illustrators with specialist knowledge: e.g. sports medicine, bike mechanics. NB It may take them some time to reply. Maximum 2000 words.

Cycling Weekly

King's Reach Tower, Stamford Street,
London SE1 9LS
☎0171 261 5588   Fax 0171 261 5758

Owner *IPC Magazines Ltd*
Editor *Andrew Sutcliffe*
Circulation 33,762

FOUNDED 1891. WEEKLY. All aspects of cycle sport covered. Unsolicited mss and ideas for features welcome. Approach in writing with ideas. Fiction rarely used.
Features Cycle racing, technical material and related areas. Maximum 2000 words. Most work commissioned but interested in seeing new work. *Payment* £60–100 per 1000 words (quality permitting).
News Short news pieces, local news, etc. Maximum 300 words. *Payment* £15 per story.

The Dalesman

Stable Courtyard, Broughton Hall, Skipton,
North Yorkshire BD23 3AE
☎01756 701381   Fax 01756 701326

Owner *Dalesman Publishing Co. Ltd*
Editor *Terry Fletcher*
Circulation 55,000

FOUNDED 1939. Now the biggest-selling regional publication of its kind in the country. MONTHLY magazine with articles of specific Yorkshire interest. Unsolicited mss welcome; receive approximately ten per day. Initial approach in writing preferred. Maximum 2000 words. *Payment* negotiable.

Dance & Dancers

214 Panther House, 38 Mount Pleasant,
London WC1X 0AP
☎0171 837 2711   Fax 0171 837 2711

Owner *Dance & Dancers Ltd*
Editor *John Percival*

FOUNDED 1950. MONTHLY magazine covering ballet and modern dance throughout the world. Some opportunity here for 'good writers with good knowledge of dance', but preliminary discussion is strongly advised. *Payment* nominal.

Dance Theatre Journal

Laban Centre for Movement & Dance, Laurie
Grove, London SE14 6NH
☎0181 692 4070   Fax 0181 694 8749

Owner *Laban Centre for Movement & Dance*
Editor *Ann Nugent*

FOUNDED 1982. THRICE-YEARLY. Interested in features on every aspect of the contemporary dance scene, particularly issues such as the funding policy for dance, critical assessments of choreographers' work and the latest developments in the various schools of contemporary dance. Unsolicited mss welcome. Length 1000–3000 words. *Payment* varies 'according to age and experience'.

The Dancing Times

Clerkenwell House, 45–47 Clerkenwell
Green, London EC1R 0EB
☎0171 250 3006   Fax 0171 253 6679

Owner *The Dancing Times Ltd*
Editor *Mary Clarke*

FOUNDED 1910. MONTHLY. Freelance suggestions welcome from specialist dance writers and photographers only. Approach in writing.

Darts World

9 Kelsey Park Road, Beckenham, Kent
BR3 6LH
☎0181 650 6580   Fax 0181 650 2534

Owner *World Magazines Ltd*
Editor *A. J. Wood*
Circulation 24,500

Features Single articles or series on technique and instruction. Maximum 1200 words.
Fiction Short stories with darts theme of no more than 1000 words.
News Tournament reports and general or personality news required. Maximum 800 words.
Payment negotiable.

Dateline Magazine
25 Abingdon Road, London W8 6AL
☎01869 324100   Fax 01869 324529

Owner *John Patterson*
Editors *Peter Bennett, Nicky Boult*
Circulation 23,000

FOUNDED 1976. MONTHLY magazine for single people. Unsolicited mss welcome.

Features Anything of interest to, or directly concerning, single people. Maximum 2500 words.

News Items required at least six weeks ahead. Maximum 2500 words.

Payment from £45 per 1000 words; £10 per illustration/picture used (black & white preferred at present).

Day by Day
Woolacombe House, 141 Woolacombe Road, Blackheath, London SE3 8QP
☎0181 856 6249

Owner *Loverseed Press*
Editor *Patrick Richards*
Circulation 24,000

FOUNDED 1963. MONTHLY. News commentary and digest of national and international affairs, with reviews of the arts (books, plays, art exhibitions, films, opera, musicals) and county cricket reports among regular slots. Unsolicited mss welcome (s.a.e. essential). Approach in writing with ideas. Contributors are advised to study the magazine in the first instance.

News *Ronald Mallone* Interested in themes connected with non–violence and social justice only. Maximum 600 words.

Features No scope for freelance contributions here.

Fiction *Michael Gibson* Very rarely published.

Poems *Michael Gibson* Short poems in line with editorial principles considered. Maximum 20 lines.

Payment negotiable.

Decanter
Priory House, 8 Battersea Park Road, London SW8 4BG
☎0171 627 8181   Fax 0171 738 8688

Editor *Jonathan Goodall*
Circulation 32,000

FOUNDED 1975. Glossy wines and spirits magazine. Unsolicited material welcome but an advance telephone call is appreciated. No fiction.

News/Features All items and articles should concern wines, spirits, food and related subjects.

Derbyshire Life and Countryside
Heritage House, Lodge Lane, Derby DE1 3HE
☎01332 347087   Fax 01332 290688

Owner *B. C. Wood*
Editor *Vivienne Irish*
Circulation 12,427

FOUNDED 1931. MONTHLY county magazine for Derbyshire. Unsolicited mss and photographs of Derbyshire welcome, but written approach with ideas preferred.

Descent
51 Timbers Square, Roath, Cardiff, South Glamorgan CF2 3SH
☎01222 486557   Fax 01222 486557

Owner *Ambit Publications*
Editor *Chris Howes*
Assistant Editor *Judith Calford*

FOUNDED 1969. BI-MONTHLY magazine for cavers and mine enthusiasts. Submissions welcome from freelance contributors who can write accurately and knowledgeably on any aspect of caves, mines or underground structures.

Features General interest articles of under 1000 words welcome, as well as short foreign news reports, especially if supported by photographs/illustrations. Suitable topics include exploration (particularly British, both historical and modern), expeditions, equipment, techniques and regional British news. Maximum 2000 words.

Payment on publication according to page area filled.

Desire Direct
192 Clapham High Street, London SW4 7UD
☎0171 627 5155   Fax 0171 627 5808

Owner *Moondance Media Ltd*
Editor *Ian Jackson*

FOUNDED 1994. SIX ISSUES YEARLY. Britain's first erotic magazine for both women and men, celebrating sex and sensuality with a mix of articles, columns, features, reviews, fiction and poetry.

Features 1200–1600 words.

Fiction 1500–1600 words.

For sample copy of magazine plus contributors' guidelines and rates, please enclose 2x first class stamps.

Director

Mountbarrow House, Elizabeth Street,
London SW1W 9RB
☎0171 730 8320   Fax 0171 235 5627
Consulting Editor *Carol Kennedy*
Deputy Editor *François Hecht*
Circulation 40,000

1991 Business Magazine of the Year. Published
by The Director Publications Ltd. for the members of the Institute of Directors. Wide range of
features from political and business profiles and
management thinking to employment and financial issues. Also book reviews. Regular contributors used. Send letter with synopsis/published
samples rather than unsolicited mss. Strictly no
'lifestyle' writing. *Payment* negotiable.

Dirt Bike Rider (DBR)

PO Box 100, Stamford, Lincolnshire PE9 1XQ
☎01780 755131   Fax 01780 757261
Owner *Key Publishing Ltd*
Editor *Roddy Brooks*
Circulation 19,836

FOUNDED 1981. MONTHLY. Off-road dirt bikes
(motor-cross, endurance, trial and trail).

Disability Now

12 Park Crescent, London W1N 4EQ
☎0171 636 5020   Fax 0171 436 4582
Publisher *SCOPE* (formerly The Spastics
Society)
Editor *Mary Wilkinson*
Circulation 30,000

FOUNDED 1984. MONTHLY. Leading publication for disabled people in the UK, reaching
people with a wide range of physical disabilities,
as well as their families, carers and relevant professionals. No unsolicited material but freelance
contributions welcome. Approach in writing.

Features Covering new initiatives and services, personal experiences and general issues of
interest to a wide national readership. Maximum
1200 words. Disabled contributors welcome.

News Maximum 300 words.

Special Pages Possible openings for cartoon-
ists.

Payment by arrangement.

Disabled Driver

DDMC, Cottingham Way, Thrapston,
Northamptonshire NN14 4PL
☎01832 734724   Fax 01832 733816
Owner *Disabled Drivers' Motor Club*
Circulation 14,500 plus

BI-MONTHLY publication of the Disabled

Drivers' Motor Club. Includes information for
members, members' letters. Approach in writing with ideas. Unsolicited mss welcome.

Dog World

9 Tufton Street, Ashford, Kent
TN23 1QN
☎01233 621877   Fax 01233 645669
Owner *Dog World Ltd*
Editor *Simon Parsons*
Circulation 28,365

FOUNDED 1902. WEEKLY newspaper for
people who are seriously interested in pedigree
dogs. Unsolicited mss occasionally considered
but initial approach in writing preferred.

Features Well-researched historical items or
items of unusual interest concerning dogs. Max.
1000 words. Photographs of unusual 'doggy'
situations occasionally of interest. *Payment* up to
£50; photos £15.

News Freelance reports welcome on court
cases and local government issues involving dogs.

Dragon's Breath

See **Pigasus Press** under **Small Presses**

The Ecologist

Agriculture House, Bath Road, Sturminster
Newton, Dorset DT10 1DU
☎01258 473476   Fax 01258 473748
Owner *Ecosystems Ltd*
Co-Editors *Nicholas Hildyard, Sarah Sexton*
Circulation 9000

FOUNDED 1970. BI-MONTHLY. Unsolicited mss
welcome but initial approach in writing preferred.

Features Contents tend to be academic, but
accessible to the general reader, looking at the
social, political, economic and gender aspects of
environmental and related issues. Writers are
advised to study the magazine for style. Maximum 5000 words.

Payment £20 per 1000 words.

The Economist

25 St James's Street, London SW1A 1HG
☎0171 830 7000   Fax 0171 839 2968
Owner *Pearson/individual shareholders*
Editor *Bill Emmott*
Circulation 620,000

FOUNDED 1843. WEEKLY. Worldwide circulation. Approaches should be made in writing
to the editor. No unsolicited mss.

The Edge
1 Nichols Court, Belle Vue, Chelmsford,
Essex CM2 0BS
Editor *Graham Evans*

BI-MONTHLY magazine. Looking for 'non-mainstream fiction, modern horror and imaginative fiction'. Sample copy £2, cheques payable to The Edge. Writers' guidelines available on request. Send s.a.e..

Edinburgh Review
22 George Square, Edinburgh EH8 9LF
☎0131 650 4218   Fax 0131 662 0053
Owner *Polygon Books*
Editors *Gavin Wallace, Robert Alan Jamieson*
Circulation 1500

FOUNDED 1969. ANNUAL. Articles and fiction on Scottish and international literary, cultural and philosophical themes. Unsolicited contributions are welcome (1600 are received each year), but prospective contributors are strongly advised to study the magazine first. Allow up to three months for a reply.
  Features Interest will be shown in accessible articles on philosophy and its relationship to literature or visual art.
  Fiction Scottish and international. Maximum 6000 words.

Electrical Times
Quadrant House, The Quadrant, Sutton,
Surrey SM2 5AS
☎0181 652 3115   Fax 0181 652 8972
Owner *Reed Business Information*
Editor *Steve Hobson*
Circulation 13,000

FOUNDED 1891. MONTHLY. Aimed at electrical contractors, designers and installers. Unsolicited mss welcome but initial approach preferred.

Elle
20 Orange Street, London WC2H 7ED
☎0171 957 8838   Fax 0171 930 0184
Owner *EMAP Elan Publications*
Editor *Marie O'Riordan*
Circulation 205,623

FOUNDED 1985. MONTHLY fashion glossy. Prospective contributors should approach the relevant editor in writing in the first instance, including cuttings.
  Features Maximum 2000 words.
  News/Insight Short articles on current/cultural events with an emphasis on national, not London-based, readership. Max. 500 words.
  Payment about £250 per 1000 words.

Embroidery
PO Box 42B, East Molesley, Surrey KT8 9BB
☎0181 943 1229   Fax 0181 977 9882
Owner *Embroiderers' Guild*
Editor *Maggie Grey*
Circulation 14,500

FOUNDED 1933. QUARTERLY. Features articles on embroidery techniques, historical and foreign embroidery, and specific artists' work with illustrations. Also reviews. Unsolicited mss welcome. Maximum 1000 words.
  Payment negotiable.

Empire
Mappin House, 4 Winsley Street, London
W1N 7AR
☎0171 436 1515   Fax 0171 312 8249
Owner *EMAP Metro Publications*
Editor *Ian Nathan*
Circulation 161,503

FOUNDED 1989. Launched at the Cannes Film Festival. MONTHLY guide to the movies which aims to cover the world of films in a 'comprehensive, adult, intelligent and witty package'. Although most of *Empire* is devoted to films and the people behind them, it also looks at the developments and technology behind television and video. Wide selection of in-depth features and stories on all the main releases of the month, and reviews of over 100 films and videos. Contributions welcome but must approach in writing first.
  Features Short, behind-the-scenes features on films.
  Payment by agreement.

The Engineer
30 Calderwood Street, London SE18 6QH
☎0181 855 7777   Fax 0181 316 3040
Owner *Miller Freeman*
Editor *Adele Kimber*
Circulation 38,000

FOUNDED 1856. News magazine for engineers and their managers.
  Features Most outside contributions are commissioned but good ideas are always welcome. Maximum 2000 words.
  News Some scope for specialist regional freelancers, and for tip-offs. Maximum 500 words.
  Techscan Technology news from specialists, and tip-offs. Maximum 500 words.
  Payment by arrangement.

English Nature

English Nature, Northminster House, Peterborough, Cambridgeshire PE1 1UA
☎01733 455193   Fax 01733 455188

Owner *English Nature*
Editor *Martin Tither*
Circulation 13,500

FOUNDED 1992. BI-MONTHLY magazine which explains the work of English Nature, the government adviser on wildlife policies. No unsolicited material.

Epicurean

Monocle Publications, PO Box 161, Newport, Gwent NP6 1YQ
Owner *Monocle Publications*
Editor *Mr I. Evren*
Circulation 5000

ESTABLISHED 1996. QUARTERLY erotic literary magazine aimed at an adult market. No pornography but imaginative text that celebrates erotica. Unsolicited material welcome. Approach in writing in the first instance.
Features Thoughtful articles with a sensual and erotic theme. 500–4000 words.
Fiction Literary, elegant and sensual stories sought. 500–4000 words.
Special Pages Reviews, comic strips, letters, all on a sensual theme. Poetry – maximum 40 lines.
Payment contributor copies.

ES (Evening Standard magazine)
See entry under **Regional Newspapers**

Esquire

National Magazine House, 72 Broadwick Street, London W1V 2BP
☎0171 439 5000   Fax 0171 439 5067

Owner *National Magazine Co. Ltd*
Editor *Peter Howarth*
Circulation 111,007

FOUNDED 1991. MONTHLY. Quality men's general interest magazine. No unsolicited mss or short stories.

Essentials

King's Reach Tower, Stamford Street, London SE1 9LS
☎0171 261 6970   Fax 0171 261 5262

Owner *IPC Magazines*
Editor *Sue James*
Circulation 319,810

FOUNDED 1988. MONTHLY women's interest magazine. Unsolicited mss (not originals) welcome if accompanied by s.a.e.. Initial approach in writing preferred. Prospective contributors should study the magazine thoroughly before submitting anything. No fiction.
Features Maximum 2000 words (double-spaced on A4).
Payment negotiable, but minimum £100 per 1000 words.

Essex Countryside

Griggs Farm, West Street, Coggeshall, Essex CO6 1NT
☎01376 562578   Fax 01376 562581

Owner *Market Link Publishing Ltd*
Editor *Andy Tilbrook*
Circulation 15,000

FOUNDED 1952. MONTHLY. Unsolicited material of Essex interest welcome. No general interest material.
Features Countryside, culture and crafts in Essex. Maximum 1500 words.
Payment £40.

European Medical Journal

Publishing House, Trinity Place, Barnstaple, Devon EX32 9HJ
☎01271 328892   Fax 01271 328768

Owner *Dr Vernon Coleman*
Editor *Dr Vernon Coleman*
Circulation 21,000

FOUNDED 1991. MONTHLY critical medical review.

Eventing

King's Reach Tower, Stamford Street, London SE1 9LS
☎0171 261 5388   Fax 0171 261 5429

Owner *IPC Magazines Ltd*
Editor *Kate Green*

FOUNDED 1984. MONTHLY. Specialist horse trials magazine. Opportunities for freelance contributions.
Payment NUJ rates.

Evergreen

PO Box 52, Cheltenham, Gloucestershire GL50 1YQ
☎01242 577775   Fax 01242 222034

Editor *R. Faiers*
Circulation 75,000

FOUNDED 1985. QUARTERLY magazine featuring articles and poems about Britain. Unsolicited contributions welcome.
Features Britain's natural beauty, towns and villages, nostalgia, wildlife, traditions, odd cus-

toms, legends, folklore, crafts, etc. Length 250–2000 words.

Payment £15 per 1000 words; poems £4.

Executive Travel

Church Street, Dunstable, Bedfordshire
LU5 4HB
☎01582 695097   Fax 01582 695095

Owner *Reed Travel Group*
Editor *Mike Toynbee*
Circulation 43,378

FOUNDED 1979. MONTHLY. Aimed specifically at frequent corporate travellers.

Executive Woman Magazine

2 Chantry Place, Harrow, Middlesex
HA3 6NY
☎0181 420 1210   Fax 0181 420 1691

Owner *Saleworld*
Editor *Angela Giveon*
Circulation 75,000

FOUNDED 1987. BI-MONTHLY magazine for female executives in the corporate field and female entrepreneurs. Unsolicited material welcome. Initial approach by phone or in writing.

Features New and interesting business issues and 'Women to Watch'. No health, stress, beauty, fashion or arts items. Maximum 850–1600 words.

Legal/Financial Opportunities for lawyers/accountants to write on issues in their field. Maximum 850 words.

Payment negotiable.

Express on Sunday Magazine

See under **National Newspapers (Express on Sunday)**

The Face

3rd Floor, Block A, Exmouth House, Pine Street, London EC1R 0JL
☎0171 837 7270   Fax 0171 837 3906

Owner *Wagadon Ltd*
Editor *Richard Benson*
Fashion Editor *Ashley Heath*
Circulation 113,028

FOUNDED 1980. Magazine of the style generation, concerned with who's what and what's cool. Profiles, interviews and stories. No fiction. Acquaintance with the 'voice' of *The Face* is essential before sending mss on spec.

Features *Craig McLean/Ashley Heath* New contributors should write to the features editor with their ideas. Maximum 3000 words. *Payment* £150 per 1000 words.

Diary No news stories.

Family Circle

King's Reach Tower, Stamford Street,
London SE1 9LS
☎0171 261 5000   Fax 0171 261 5929

Owner *IPC Magazines Ltd*
Editor *Sue James*
Circulation 300,204

FOUNDED 1964. THIRTEEN ISSUES YEARLY. Little scope for freelancers as most material is produced in-house. Unsolicited material is rarely used, but it is considered. Prospective contributors are best advised to send written ideas to the relevant editor.

Style *Amanda Cooke*
Food and Drink *Sally Mansfield*
Features *Gillian Drummond* Very little outside work commissioned.
Fiction *Dee Remmington* Short stories of 1000–1500 words.
Home *Caroline Rodrigues*
Payment not less than £100 per 1000 words.

Family Tree Magazine

61 Great Whyte, Ramsey, Huntingdon,
Cambridgeshire PE17 1HL
☎01487 814050   Fax 01487 711361

Owner *Armstrong Boon & Marriott (Publishing)*
Editorial Director *J.M. Armstrong*
Circulation 39,000

FOUNDED 1984. MONTHLY. News and features on matters of genealogy. Unsolicited mss considered. Keen to receive articles about unusual sources of genealogical research. Not interested in own family histories. Approach in writing with ideas. All material should be addressed to *Avril Cross*.

Features Any genealogically related subject. Maximum 3000 words. No puzzles or fictional articles.

Payment £25 per 1000 words (news and features).

Fancy Fowl/Turkeys

Andover Road, Highclere, Newbury,
Berkshire RG20 9PH
☎01635 253239   Fax 01635 254146

Owner *Fancy Fowl Publications Ltd*
Editor *Shirley Murdoch*
Circulation 3000

FOUNDED 1981. Two publications, one specialising in rare poultry and waterfowl, the other in commercial turkey production. *Fancy Fowl* MONTHLY catering for those interested in keeping and exhibiting rare and pure breeds of poultry and waterfowl. Interested in news (maximum 300 words) and features (maximum

800 words) in line with the magazine's content. *Payment* £30 per 1000 words. *Turkeys* BI-MONTHLY aiming to deal with all aspects of turkey breeding, growing, processing and marketing at an international level. Specialist technical information from qualified contributors will always be considered. Length by arrangement. No unsolicited mss. Approach in writing with ideas, or by phone. *Payment* £70 per 1000 words.

Farmers Weekly

Quadrant House, Sutton, Surrey SM2 5AS
☎0181 652 4911   Fax 0181 652 4005
Owner *Reed Business Information*
Editor *Stephen Howe*
Circulation 98,268

WEEKLY. 1996 Business Magazine of the Year. For practising farmers. Unsolicited mss considered.

Features A wide range of material relating to farmers' problems and interests: specific sections on arable and livestock farming, farm life, practical and general interest, machinery and business.
News General farming news.
Payment negotiable.

Farming News

Miller Freeman, 30 Calderwood Street, London SE18 6QH
☎0181 855 7777   Fax 0181 854 6795
Owner *Miller Freeman plc*
Editor *Donald Taylor*
Circulation 74,000

News and features of direct concern to the industry.

Fast Car

Berwick House, 8–10 Knoll Rise, Orpington, Kent BR6 0PS
☎01689 874025   Fax 01689 896847
Owner *SPL*
Editor *Ian Strachan*
Circulation 85,000

FOUNDED 1987. FOUR-WEEKLY. Concerned with the modification of road and race vehicles, with technical data and testing results. No kit-car features, race reports or road-test reports of standard cars.
Features Innovative ideas in line with the magazine's title. Generally about four pages in length.
News Any item in line with magazine's title. Copy should be as concise as possible.
Payment negotiable.

The Field

King's Reach Tower, Stamford Street, London SE1 9LS
☎0171 261 5198   Fax 0171 261 5358
Owner *IPC Magazines*
Editor *J. Young*
Circulation 31,147

FOUNDED 1853. MONTHLY magazine for those who are serious about the British countryside and its pleasures. Unsolicited mss (and transparencies) welcome but initial approach should be made in writing.
Features Exceptional work on any subject concerning the countryside. Most work tends to be commissioned.
Payment varies.

Film and Video Maker

Church House, 102 Pendlebury Road, Swinton, Manchester M27 4BF
☎0161 794 8282   Fax 0161 794 8282
Owner *Film Maker Publications*
Editor *Mrs Liz Donlan*
Circulation 2600

FOUNDED in the 1930s. BI-MONTHLY magazine of the Institute of Amateur Cinematographers. Reports news and views of the Institute. Unsolicited mss welcome but all contributions are unpaid.

Film Review

Visual Imagination Ltd, 9 Blades Court, Deodar Road, London SW15 2NU
☎0181 875 1520   Fax 0181 875 1588
Owner *Visual Imagination Ltd*
Editor *David Richardson*
Circulation 50,000

MONTHLY. Reviews, profiles, interviews and special reports on films. Unsolicited material considered.

First Down

The Spendlove Centre, Enstone Road, Charlbury, Oxford OX7 3PQ
☎01608 811266   Fax 01608 811380
Owner *Independent UK Sports Publishing*
Editor *Tony Evans*
Circulation 25,000

FOUNDED 1986. WEEKLY American football tabloid paper. Features and news.

The First Word Bulletin

See entry under **Stop Press**

Fishkeeping Answers

Apex House, Oundle Road, Peterborough,
Cambridgeshire PE2 9NP
☎01733 898100   Fax 01733 898487

Owner *EMAP Apex Publications Ltd*
Editor *Karen Youngs*
Circulation 15,522

FOUNDED 1992. BI-MONTHLY. Concerned
with all aspects of keeping fish. Unsolicited
mss, synopses and ideas welcome. Approach by
phone or in writing with ideas. No fiction.

Features Specialist answers to specific fishkeeping problems, breeding, plants, health, etc;
aquatic plants and ponds; plus coldwater fish,
marine and tropical, and herptiles. 1500 words.
Quality fish photographs welcome.

Flight International

Quadrant House, The Quadrant, Sutton,
Surrey SM2 5AS
☎0181 652 3882   Fax 0181 652 3840

Owner *Reed Business Information*
Editor *Allan Winn*
Circulation 60,000

FOUNDED 1909. WEEKLY. International trade
magazine for the aerospace industry, including
civil, military and space. Unsolicited mss considered. Commissions preferred – phone with
ideas and follow up with letter. E-mail, modem
and disk submissions encouraged.

Features *Forbes Mutch* Technically informed
articles and pieces on specific geographical
areas with international appeal. Analytical, in-
depth coverage required, preferably supported
by interviews. Maximum 1800 words.

News *Andrew Chuter* Interested in pieces
from particular geographical areas on specific
technical developments. Maximum 350 words.
Payment NUJ rates.

Flora International

46 Merlin Grove, Eden Park, Beckenham,
Kent BR3 3HU
☎0181 658 1080

Owner *Maureen Foster*
Editor *Russell Bennett*
Circulation 15,000

FOUNDED 1974. BI-MONTHLY magazine for
flower arrangers and florists. Unsolicited mss
welcome. Approach in writing with ideas. Not
interested in general gardening articles.

Features Fully illustrated (preferably b&w
photos/illustrations or colour transparencies).
Flower arranging, flower gardens and flowers.
Floristry items written with practical knowledge and well illustrated are particularly wel-

come. Maximum 2000 words.

Profiles/Reviews Personality profiles and
book reviews.
Payment £40 per 1000 words.

FlyPast

PO Box 100, Stamford, Lincolnshire PE9 1XQ
☎01780 55131   Fax 01780 57261

Owner *Key Publishing Ltd*
Editor *Ken Delve*
Circulation 41,742

FOUNDED 1981. MONTHLY. Historic aviation,
mainly military, Second World War period up
to c.1970. Unsolicited mss welcome.

Focus

See **Science Fiction Association** under
Professional Associations

Folk Roots

PO Box 337, London N4 1TW
☎0181 340 9651   Fax 0181 348 5626

Owner *Southern Rag Ltd*
Editor *Ian A. Anderson*
Circulation 14,000

FOUNDED 1979. MONTHLY. Features on folk and
roots music, and musicians. Max. 3000 words.

For Women

Fantasy Publications, 4 Selsdon Way, London
E14 9EL
☎0181 538 8969   Fax 0181 987 0756

Circulation 60,000

FOUNDED 1992. MONTHLY general interest
women's magazine: celebrity interviews, beauty,
health and sex, erotic fiction and erotic photography. No homes and gardens articles.
Approach in writing in the first instance.

Features Relationships and sex. Maximum
2500 words. *Payment* £150 per 1000 words.

Fiction Erotic short stories. Maximum 2000
words. *Payment* £125 total.

Fortean Times: The Journal of Strange Phenomena

PO Box 2409, London NW5 4NP
☎0171 485 5002   Fax 0171 485 5002

Owners/Editors *Bob Rickard/Paul Sieveking*
Circulation 50,000

FOUNDED 1973. MONTHLY. Accounts of strange
phenomena and experiences, curiosities, mysteries, prodigies and portents. Unsolicited mss
welcome. Approach in writing with ideas. No
fiction, poetry, rehashes or politics.

Features Well-researched material on cur-
rent/historical mysteries or first-hand accounts of

oddities. Maximim 3000 words, preferably with good relevant photos/illustrations.

News Concise copy with full source references essential.

Payment negotiable.

Foundation: The Review of Science Fiction

c/o Dept. of History, University of Reading, Whiteknights, Reading, Berkshire RG6 6AA
☎0118 9263047

Owner *Science Fiction Foundation*
Editor *Professor Edward James*

THRICE-YEARLY publication devoted to the critical study of science fiction. *Payment* None.

France Magazine

Dormer House, Digbeth Street, Stow-on-the-Wold, Gloucestershire GL54 1BN
☎01451 831398   Fax 01451 830869

Owner *Centralhaven*
Editor *Philip Faiers*
Circulation 60,000

FOUNDED 1989. QUARTERLY magazine containing all things of interest to Francophiles – in English. No unsolicited mss. Approach with ideas in writing.

Freelance Market News

Sevendale House, 7 Dale Street, Manchester M1 1JB
☎0161 237 1827   Fax 0161 228 3533

Editor *Angela Cox*
Circulation 3000

MONTHLY. News and information on the freelance writers' market, both inland and overseas. Includes market information on competitions, seminars, courses, overseas openings, etc. Short articles (700 words max.). Unsolicited contributions welcome. *Payment* £35 per 1000 words.

The Freelance

NUJ, Acorn House, 314 Gray's Inn Road, London WC1X 8DP
☎0171 278 7916   Fax 0171 278 1812

BI-MONTHLY published by the **National Union of Journalists**. Contributions welcome.

Garden Answers (incorporating Practical Gardening)

Apex House, Oundle Road, Peterborough, Cambridgeshire PE2 9NP
☎01733 898100   Fax 01733 898433

Owner *EMAP Apex Publications Ltd*
Managing Editor *Adrienne Wild*

Circulation 111,807

FOUNDED 1982. MONTHLY. 'It is unlikely that unsolicited manuscripts will be used, as articles are usually commissioned and must be in the magazine style.' Prospective contributors should approach the editor in writing. Interested in hearing from gardening writers on any subject, whether flowers, fruit, vegetables, houseplants or greenhouse gardening.

Garden News

Apex House, Oundle Road, Peterborough, Cambridgeshire PE2 9NP
☎01733 898100   Fax 01733 898433

Owner *EMAP Apex Publications Ltd*
Editor *Jim Ward*
Circulation 73,107

FOUNDED 1958. Britain's biggest-selling, full-colour gardening WEEKLY. News and advice on growing flowers, fruit and vegetables, plus colourful features on all aspects of gardening for the committed gardener. News and features welcome, especially if accompanied by top-quality photos or illustrations. Contact the editor before submitting any material.

The Garden, Journal of the Royal Horticultural Society

Apex House, Oundle Road, Peterborough, Cambridgeshire PE2 9NP
☎01733 898100   Fax 01733 890657

Owner *The Royal Horticultural Society*
Editor *Ian Hodgson*
Circulation 214,733

FOUNDED 1866. MONTHLY journal of the Royal Horticultural Society. Covers all aspects of the art, science and practice of horticulture and garden making. 'Articles must have depth and substance'; approach by letter with a synopsis in the first instance.

Gardens Illustrated

John Brown Publishing Ltd, The Boathouse, Crabtree Lane, London SW6 6LU
☎0171 470 2400   Fax 0171 381 3930

Owner *John Brown Publishing Ltd*
Editor *Rosie Atkins*
Circulation 48,070

FOUNDED 1993. BI-MONTHLY. 'Britain's fastest growing garden magazine' with a world-wide readership. The focus is on garden design, with a strong international flavour. Unsolicited mss are rarely used and it is best that prospective contributors approach the editor with ideas in writing, supported by photographs.

Gay Times

Worldwide House, 116–134 Bayham Street, London NW1 0BA
☎0171 482 2576   Fax 0171 284 0329

Owner *Millivres Ltd*
Editor *David Smith*
Circulation 57,000

Covers all aspects of gay life, plus general interest likely to appeal to the gay community, art reviews and news. Regular freelance writers used. Unsolicited contributions welcome. *Payment* negotiable.

Gibbons Stamp Monthly

Stanley Gibbons, 5 Parkside, Ringwood, Hampshire BH24 3SH
☎01425 472363   Fax 01425 470247

Owner *Stanley Gibbons Holdings plc*
Editor *Hugh Jefferies*
Circulation 22,000

FOUNDED 1890. MONTHLY. News and features. Unsolicited mss welcome. First approach in writing or by telephone to avoid disappointment.

Features *Hugh Jefferies* Unsolicited material of specialised nature and general stamp features welcome. Maximum 3000 words but longer pieces can be serialised. *Payment* £20–50 per 1000 words.

News *Michael Briggs* Any philatelic news item. Maximum 500 words. *No payment.*

Girl About Town

9 Rathbone Street, London W1P 1AF
☎0171 636 6651   Fax 0171 255 2352

Owner *Independent Magazines*
Editor-in-Chief *Bill Williamson*
    News/Style Pages *Dee Pilgrim*
Circulation 100,000

FOUNDED 1972. Free WEEKLY magazine for women aged 16 to 26. Unsolicited mss may be considered. No fiction.

Features Standards are 'exacting'. Commissions only. Some chance of unknown writers being commissioned and unsolicited material is considered. Maximum 1500 words.

Payment negotiable.

Golf Monthly

King's Reach Tower, Stamford Street, London SE1 9LS
☎0171 261 7237   Fax 0171 261 7240

Owner *IPC Magazines Ltd*
Editor *Colin Callander*
Circulation 70,470

FOUNDED 1911. MONTHLY. Player profiles, golf instruction, general golf features and columns. Not interested in instruction material from outside contributors. Unsolicited mss welcome. Approach in writing with ideas.

Features Maximum 1500–2000 words.
Payment by arrangement.

Golf Weekly

Bretton Court, Bretton, Peterborough, Cambridgeshire PE3 8DZ
☎01733 264666   Fax 01733 267198

Owner *EMAP Pursuit Ltd*
Managing Editor *Bob Warters*
Circulation 20,000

FOUNDED 1890. WEEKLY. Unsolicited material welcome from full-time journalists only. For features, approach in writing in first instance; for news, fax or phone.

Features Maximum 1500 words.
News Maximum 300 words.
Payment negotiable.

Golf World

Mappin House, 4 Winsley Street, London W1N 7AR
☎01733 264666   Fax 0171 817 9630

Owner *EMAP Pursuit Ltd*
Editor *David Clarke*
Circulation 82,610

FOUNDED 1962. MONTHLY. No unsolicited mss. Approach in writing with ideas.

Good Food Retailing

PO Box 1525, Gillingham, Dorset SP8 5TA
☎01963 371271   Fax 01963 371270

Owner *Robert Farrand*
Editor *Robert Farrand*
Circulation 4200

FOUNDED 1980. TEN ISSUES YEARLY. Serves the speciality food retail trade. Small budget for freelance material.

Good Health Magazine

Shadwell House, 65 Lower Green Road, Rusthall, Tunbridge Wells, Kent TN4 8TW
☎01892 535300   Fax 01892 535311

Owner *Pantile Publications Ltd*
Editor *Jack Hay*

FOUNDED 1997. MONTHLY. Aimed primarily at women and their families, covering all aspects of maintaining a healthy lifestyle, featuring health expert writers and professional practitioners. The magazine gives advice on all aspects of family health, including allergies, diet, emotions, fitness, hair, skin and body care, with emphasis on real-life experiences. Features and casebooks: variable length – average article 1200 words.

Payment negotiable.

Good Holiday Magazine

91 High Street, Esher, Surrey KT10 9QD
☎01372 468140   Fax 01372 470765
Editor *John Hill*
Circulation 100,000

FOUNDED 1985. QUARTERLY aimed at better-off holiday-makers rather than travellers. World-wide destinations including Europe and domestic. Any queries regarding work/commissioning must be in writing. Copy must be precise and well-researched – the price of everything from coffee and tea to major purchases included along with exchange rates, etc. *Payment* negotiable.

Good Housekeeping

National Magazine House, 72 Broadwick Street, London W1V 2BP
☎0171 439 5000   Fax 0171 439 5591
Owner *National Magazine Co. Ltd*
Editor-in-Chief *Pat Roberts Cairns*
Circulation 489,239

FOUNDED 1922. MONTHLY glossy. No unsolicited mss. Write with ideas in the first instance to the appropriate editor.

Features *Hilary Robinson* Most work is commissioned but original ideas are always welcome. Send short synopsis, plus relevant cuttings, showing previous examples of work published. No unsolicited mss.

Fiction *Hilary Robinson* No unsolicited mss.

Entertainment *Linda Gay* Reviews and previews on film, television, theatre and art.

Good Motoring

Station Road, Forest Row, East Sussex RH18 5EN
☎01342 825676   Fax 01342 824847
Owner *Guild of Experienced Motorists*
Editor *Derek Hainge*
Circulation 53,000

FOUNDED 1932. QUARTERLY motoring and travel magazine. Occasional general features. 1500 words maximum. Prospective contributors should approach in writing only.

Good Ski Guide

91 High Street, Esher, Surrey KT10 9QD
☎01372 468140   Fax 01372 470765
Editor *John Hill*
Circulation 40,000

FOUNDED 1976. QUARTERLY. Unsolicited mss welcome from writers with a knowledge of skiing and ski resorts. Prospective contributors are best advised to make initial contact in writing as ideas and work need to be seen before any discussion can take place.

Payment negotiable.

Good Taste

PO Box 5, Fleet Street, Ashton-under-Lyne OL6 7FA
☎0161 339 2228   Fax 0161 339 4271
Owner *S & D Communications*
Editor *Sinclair Newton*
Circulation 20,000

FOUNDED 1996. MONTHLY north west of England lifestyle magazine.

Features *Sinclair Newton* Travel, food and drink. 500–1000 words.

News *Sinclair Newton* Diary stories and news information. 100 words maximum.

Fiction *David Hart* Only if relevant to the magazine and previously unpublished.

Promotional features with potential advertisers also welcome. 1000 words maximum. Approach in writing or by fax in the first instance.

Payment by arrangement.

GQ

Vogue House, Hanover Square, London W1R 0AD
☎0171 499 9080   Fax 0171 495 1679
Owner *Condé Nast Publications Ltd*
Editor *James Brown*
Deputy Editor *Simon Hills*
Circulation 148,574

FOUNDED 1988. MONTHLY men's style magazine. No unsolicited material. Write or fax with an idea in the first instance.

Granta

2–3 Hanover Yard, Noel Road, London N1 8BE
☎0171 704 9776   Fax 0171 704 0474
Editor *Ian Jack*
Deputy Editor *Robert Winder*

QUARTERLY magazine of new writing, including fiction, autobiography, politics, history, reportage published in paperback book form. Highbrow, diverse and contemporary, with a thematic approach. Unsolicited mss (including fiction) considered. A lot of material is commissioned. Important to read the magazine first to appreciate its very particular fusion of cultural and political interests. No reviews. No poetry.

Payment negotiable.

The Great Outdoors
See **TGO**

Guardian Weekend
See under **National Newspapers (The Guardian)**

Guiding
17–19 Buckingham Palace Road, London SW1W 0PT
☎0171 834 6242   Fax 0171 828 8317
Owner *The Guide Association*
Editor *Nora Warner*
Circulation 31,000

FOUNDED 1914. MONTHLY. Unsolicited mss welcome provided topics relate to the movement and/or women's role in society. Ideas in writing appreciated in first instance.
Features Topics that can be useful in the Guide programme, or special interest features with Guide link. Maximum 1200 words.
News Guide activities. Maximum 100–150 words.
Special Pages Outdoor activity, information pieces, Green issues. Maximum 1200 words.
Payment £70 per 1000 words.

Hair
King's Reach Tower, Stamford Street, London SE1 9LS
☎0171 261 6975   Fax 0171 261 7382
Owner *IPC Magazines Ltd*
Editor *Annette Dennis*
Circulation 168,500

FOUNDED 1980. BI-MONTHLY hair and beauty magazine. No unsolicited mss, but always interested in good photographs. Approach with ideas in writing.
Features *Sharon Christal* Fashion pieces on hair trends. Maximum 1000 words.
Payment negotiable.

Hairflair
2 Coral Row, Plantation Wharf, London SW11 3UF
☎0171 738 9911   Fax 0171 738 9922
Owner *Hair & Beauty Ltd*
Editor *Rebecca Barnes*
Circulation 62,930

FOUNDED 1982. MONTHLY. Original and interesting hair-related features written in a young, lively style to appeal to a readership aged 16–35 years. Unsolicited mss not welcome, but as the magazine is expanding new ideas are encouraged. Write to the editor.

Features Hair and beauty. Maximum 1000 words.
Payment negotiable.

Harpers & Queen
National Magazine House, 72 Broadwick Street, London W1V 2BP
☎0171 439 5000   Fax 0171 439 5506
Owner *National Magazine Co. Ltd*
Editor *Fiona Macpherson*
Circulation 93,186

MONTHLY. Up-market glossy combining the Sloaney and the streetwise. Approach in writing (not phone) with ideas.
Features *Anthony Gardner/Samantha Weinberg* Ideas only in the first instance.
Fiction *Samantha Weinberg* Only literary fiction welcome. Maximum 3000 words.
News Snippets welcome if very original.
Payment negotiable.

Health & Fitness Magazine
Nexus Media, Nexus House, Azalea Drive, Swanley, Kent BR8 8HY
☎01322 660070   Fax 01322 615636
Owner *Nexus Media*
Editor *Sharon Walker*
Circulation 65,000

FOUNDED 1983. MONTHLY. Will consider ideas; approach in writing in the first instance.

Health Education
MCB University Press, 60–62 Toller Lane, Bradford, West Yorkshire BD8 9BY
☎01274 777700   Fax 01274 785200/785201
Owner *MCB University Press*
Editor *Sharon Kingman*
Circulation 2000

FOUNDED 1992. SIX ISSUES YEARLY. Health education magazine with an emphasis on schools and young people. Professional readership. Most work is commissioned but ideas are welcome.

Hello!
Wellington House, 69–71 Upper Ground, London SE1 9PQ
☎0171 334 7404   Fax 0171 334 7412
Owner *Hola!* (Spain)
Editor *Maggie Koumi*
Circulation 536,724

WEEKLY. Owned by a Madrid-based publishing family, *Hello!* has grown faster than any other British magazine since its launch here in 1988 and continues to grow despite the recession.

The magazine is printed in Madrid, with editorial offices both there and in London. Major colour features plus regular news pages. Although much of the material is provided by regulars, good proposals do stand a chance. Approach with ideas in the first instance. No unsolicited mss.

Features Interested in celebrity-based features, with a newsy angle, and exclusive interviews from generally unapproachable personalities.

Payment by arrangement.

Here's Health
20 Orange Street, London WC2H 7ED
☎0171 957 8383   Fax 0171 957 8857
Owner *EMAP Elan Publications*
Editor *Sheena Miller*
Circulation 42,558

FOUNDED 1956. MONTHLY. Full-colour magazine dealing with alternative medicine, nutrition, natural health, wholefoods, supplements, organics and the environment. Prospective contributors should bear in mind that this is a specialist magazine with a pronounced bias towards alternative/complementary medicine, using expert contributors on the whole.

Features Length varies.
Payment negotiable.

Heritage
4 The Courtyard, Denmark Street,
Wokingham, Berkshire RG40 2AZ
☎01189 771677   Fax 01189 772903
Owner *Bulldog Magazines*
Editor *Sian Ellis*
Circulation 70,000

FOUNDED 1984. BI-MONTHLY. Unsolicited mss welcome. Interested in complete packages of written features with high-quality transparencies – words or pictures on their own also accepted. Not interested in poetry, fiction or non-British themes. Approach in writing with ideas.

Features British villages, tours, towns, castles, gardens, traditions, crafts, historical themes and people. Maximum length 1200 words. *Payment* approx. £100 per 1000 words.

News Small pieces – usually picture stories in Diary section. Limited use. Maximum length 100–150 words. *Payment* £20.

Heritage Scotland
5 Charlotte Square, Edinburgh EH2 4DU
☎0131 243 9386   Fax 0131 243 9309
Owner *National Trust for Scotland*
Editor *Peter Reekie*

Circulation 140,660

FOUNDED 1983. QUARTERLY magazine containing heritage/conservation features. No unsolicited mss.

Hi-Fi News & Record Review
Link House, Dingwall Avenue, Croydon,
Surrey CR9 2TA
☎0181 686 2599   Fax 0181 781 6046
Owner *Link House Magazines Ltd*
Editor *Steve Harris*
Circulation 25,000

FOUNDED 1956. MONTHLY. Write in the first instance with suggestions based on knowledge of the magazine's style and subject. All articles must be written from an informed technical or enthusiast viewpoint. *Payment* negotiable, according to technical content.

High Life
Haymarket House, 1 Oxendon Street,
London SW1Y 4EE
☎0171 925 2544   Fax 0171 839 4508
Owner *Premier Magazines*
Editor *Mark Jones*
Circulation 295,000

FOUNDED 1973. MONTHLY glossy. British Airways in-flight magazine. Almost all the content is commissioned. No unsolicited mss. Few opportunities for freelancers.

Home & Country
104 New Kings Road, London SW6 4LY
☎0171 731 5777   Fax 0171 736 4061
Owner *National Federation of Women's Institutes*
Editor *Amber Tokeley*
Circulation 68,000

FOUNDED 1919. MONTHLY. Official full-colour journal of the Federation of Women's Institutes, containing articles on a wide range of subjects of interest to women. Strong environmental country slant with crafts and cookery plus gardening appearing every month. Unsolicited mss, photos and illustrations welcome. *Payment* by arrangement.

Home & Family
Mary Sumner House, 24 Tufton Street,
London SW1P 3RB
☎0171 222 5533   Fax 0171 222 1591
Owner *MU Enterprises Ltd*
Editor *Margaret Duggan*
Circulation 85,826

FOUNDED 1976. QUARTERLY. Unsolicited mss

considered. No fiction or poetry.

Features Family life, social problems, marriage, Christian faith, etc. Maximum 1000 words.

Payment 'modest'.

Home Wine and Beer Maker

304 Northridge Way, Hemel Hempstead, Hertfordshire HP1 2AB
☎01442 67228   Fax 01442 67228
Owner *Homebrew Publications*
Editor *Evelyn Barrett*
Circulation 150,000

FOUNDED 1986. QUARTERLY. Articles on all aspects of home wine and beer making and the use of homemade wine in cooking, etc. Unsolicited mss welcome.

Homes & Gardens

King's Reach Tower, Stamford Street, London SE1 9LS
☎0171 261 5000   Fax 0171 261 6247
Owner *IPC Magazines Ltd/Reed Publishing*
Editor *Julia Watson*
Circulation 165,533

FOUNDED 1919. MONTHLY. Almost all published articles are specially commissioned. No fiction or poetry. Best to approach in writing with an idea.

Horse & Pony Magazine

Bretton Court, Bretton, Peterborough, Cambridgeshire PE3 8DZ
☎01733 264666   Fax 01733 465939
Owner *EMAP Pursuit Publications*
Editor *Andrea Oakes*
Circulation 54,260

Magazine for young (aged 10–16) owners and 'addicts' of the horse. Features include pony care, riding articles and celebrity pieces. Some interest in freelancers but most feature material is produced by staff writers.

Horse and Hound

King's Reach Tower, Stamford Street, London SE1 9LS
☎0171 261 6315   Fax 0171 261 5429
Owner *IPC Magazines Ltd*
Editor *Arnold Garvey*
Circulation 68,104

WEEKLY. The oldest equestrian magazine on the market, now re-launched with modern make-up and colour pictures throughout. Contains regular veterinary advice and instructional articles, as well as authoritative news and comment on fox hunting, international showjumping, horse trials, dressage, driving and cross-country riding. Also weekly racing and point-to-points, breeding reports and articles. The magazine includes junior sections for the Pony Club. Regular books and art reviews, and humorous articles and cartoons are frequently published. Plenty of opportunities for freelancers. Unsolicited contributions welcome.

Now also publishes a sister monthly publication, *Eventing*, which covers the sport of horse trials comprehensively.

Payment NUJ rates.

Horse and Rider

Haslemere House, Lower Street, Haslemere, Surrey GU27 2PE
☎01428 651551   Fax 01428 653888
Owner *D. J. Murphy (Publishers) Ltd*
Editor *Alison Bridge*
Editorial Assistant *Sarah Muir*
Circulation 40,404

FOUNDED 1949. MONTHLY. Adult readership, largely horse-owning. News and instructional features, which make up the bulk of the magazine, are almost all commissioned. New contributors and unsolicited mss are occasionally used. Approach the editor in writing with ideas.

Horticulture Week

174 Hammersmith Road, London W6 7JP
☎0171 413 4595   Fax 0171 413 4518
Owner *Haymarket Magazines Ltd*
Editor *Vicky Browning*
Circulation 11,200

FOUNDED 1841. WEEKLY. Specialist magazine involved in the supply of business-type information. No unsolicited mss. Approach in writing in first instance.

Features No submissions without prior discussion. *Payment* negotiable.

News *Maja Pawinska* Information about horticultural businesses – nurseries, garden centres, landscapers and parks departments in the various regions of the UK. No gardening stories.

House & Garden

Vogue House, Hanover Square, London W1R 0AD
☎0171 499 9080   Fax 0171 629 2907
Owner *Condé Nast Publications Ltd*
Editor *Susan Crewe*
Circulation 167,846

FOUNDED 1947. MONTHLY. Most feature material is produced in-house but occasional specialist features are commissioned from qualified freelancers, mainly for the interiors or wine and food sections.

Features *Liz Elliot* Suggestions for features, preferably in the form of brief outlines of proposed subjects, will be considered.

House Beautiful

National Magazine House, 72 Broadwick Street, London W1V 2BP
☎0171 439 5000   Fax 0171 439 5595

Owner *National Magazine Co. Ltd*
Editor *Caroline Atkins*
Circulation 332,115

FOUNDED 1989. MONTHLY. Lively magazine offering sound, practical information and plenty of inspiration for those who want to make the most of where they live. Over 100 pages of easy-reading editorial. Regular features about decoration, DIY and home finance. Approach in writing with synopses or ideas in the first instance.

House Buyer

96 George Lane, South Woodford, London E18 1AD
☎0181 532 9299/01403 822059
Fax 0181 532 9329/01403 822059

Owner *Dalton's Weekly Plc*
Editor *Con Crowley*
Circulation 18,000

FOUNDED 1955. MONTHLY magazine with features and articles for house buyers, including retirement homes, mortgage information, etc. A 32-page section includes details of over 200,000 new homes throughout the UK. Unsolicited mss will neither be read nor returned.

i-D Magazine

Universal House, 251–255 Tottenham Court Road, London W1P 0AE
☎0171 813 6170   Fax 0171 813 6179

Owner *Levelprint*
Editor *Avril Mair*
Circulation 45,000

FOUNDED 1980. MONTHLY lifestyle magazine for both sexes aged 16–24. Very hip. 'We are always looking for freelance non-fiction writers with new or unusual ideas.' A different theme each issue – past themes include Green politics, taste, films, sex, love and loud dance music – means it is advisable to discuss feature ideas in the first instance.

Ideal Home

King's Reach Tower, Stamford Street, London SE1 9LS
☎0171 261 6474   Fax 0171 261 6697

Owner *IPC Magazines Ltd*
Editor-in-chief *Sally O'Sullivan*
Circulation 200,784

FOUNDED 1920. MONTHLY glossy. Unsolicited feature articles are welcome if appropriate to the magazine (one or two are received each week). Prospective contributors wishing to submit ideas should do so in writing to the editor. No fiction.

Features Furnishing and decoration of houses, kitchens or bathrooms; interior design, soft furnishings, furniture and home improvements, lifestyle, travel, etc. Length to be discussed with editor.

Payment negotiable.

The Illustrated London News

20 Upper Ground, London SE1 9PF
☎0171 805 5562   Fax 0171 805 5911

Owner *James Sherwood*
Editor *Alison Booth*
Circulation 47,547

FOUNDED 1842. BI-ANNUAL: the Christmas and Summer issues, plus the occasional special issue to coincide with particular events. Although the *ILN* covers issues concerning the whole of the UK, its emphasis remains on the capital and its life. Travel, wine, restaurants, events, cultural and current affairs are all covered. There are few opportunities for freelancers but all unsolicited mss are read (receives about 20 a week). The best approach is with an idea in writing. Particularly interested in articles relating to events and developments in contemporary London, and about people working in the capital. All features are illustrated, so ideas including picture opportunities are particularly welcome.

Image Magazine

Upper Mounts, Northampton NN1 3HR
☎01604 231122   Fax 01604 233000

Owner *Northampton Mercury Co.*
Editor *Peter Hall*
Circulation 12,000

FOUNDED 1905. MONTHLY general interest regional magazine. No unsolicited mss. Approach by phone or in writing with ideas. No fiction.

Features Local issues, personalities, businesses, etc., of Northamptonshire, Bedfordshire, Buckinghamshire interest. Maximum 500 words. *Payment* £60.

News No hard news as such, just monthly diary column.

Other Regulars on motoring, fashion, lifestyle, sport, travel, history, and picture files. Maximum 500 words. *Payment* £60.

In Britain

Haymarket House, 1 Oxendon Street,
London SW1Y 4EE
☎0171 925 2544   Fax 0171 976 1088

Owner *Premier Magazines*
Editor *Andrea Spain*
Circulation 40,000

MONTHLY. Travel magazine of the British Tourist Authority. Articles vary from 1000 to 1500 words. Approach in writing with ideas and samples – not much opportunity for unsolicited work.

Independent Magazine

See under **National Newspapers (The Independent)**

Infusion

16 Trinity Churchyard, Guildford, Surrey
GU1 3RR
☎01483 562888   Fax 01483 302732

Publisher *Bond Clarkson Russell*
Editor *Lorna Swainson*
Circulation 800,000

FOUNDED 1986. THREE ISSUES YEARLY. Sponsored by the Tea Council. Features all subjects related to tea. All editorial features are commissioned. Approach with ideas only in writing.

Interzone: Science Fiction & Fantasy

217 Preston Drove, Brighton, East Sussex
BN1 6FL
☎01273 504710

Owner *David Pringle*
Editor *David Pringle*
Circulation 10,000

FOUNDED 1982. MONTHLY magazine of science fiction and fantasy. Unsolicited mss are welcome 'only from writers who have a knowledge of the magazine and its contents'. S.a.e. essential for return.

Fiction 2000–6000 words. *Payment* £30 per 1000 words.

Features Book/film reviews, interviews with writers and occasional short articles. Length by arrangement. *Payment* negotiable.

Investors Chronicle

Greystoke Place, Fetter Lane, London
EC4A 1ND
☎0171 405 6969   Fax 0171 405 5276

Owner *Pearson Professional*
Editor *Ceri Jones*
Surveys Editor *Faith Glasgow*
Circulation 59,182

FOUNDED 1860. WEEKLY. Opportunities for freelance contributors in the survey section only. All approaches should be made in writing. Over forty surveys are published each year on a wide variety of subjects, generally with a financial, business or investment emphasis. Copies of survey list and synopses of individual surveys are obtainable from the surveys editor.

Payment negotiable.

Jane's Defence Weekly

Sentinel House, 163 Brighton Road,
Coulsdon, Surrey CR5 2NH
☎0181 700 3700   Fax 0181 763 1007

Owner *Jane's Information Group*
Publishing Director *Robert Hutchinson*
Editor *Carol Reed*
Circulation 21,016

FOUNDED 1984. WEEKLY. No unsolicited mss. Approach in writing with ideas in the first instance.

Features Current defence topics (politics, strategy, equipment, industry) of worldwide interest. No history pieces. Maximum 2000 words.

Jazz Journal International

1–5 Clerkenwell Road, London EC1M 5PA
☎0171 608 1348   Fax 0171 608 1292

Owner *Jazz Journal Ltd*
Editor-in-Chief *Eddie Cook*
Circulation 10,000

FOUNDED 1948. MONTHLY. A specialised jazz magazine, mainly for record collectors, principally using expert contributors whose work is known to the editor. Unsolicited mss not welcome, with the exception of news material (for which no payment is made). It is not a gig guide, nor a free reference source for students.

Jersey Now

Michael Stephen Publishers, PO Box 582,
Five Oaks, St Saviour, Jersey, Channel Islands
JE4 8XQ
☎01534 611600   Fax 01534 611610

Owner *Michael Stephen Publishers*
Production Manager *Simon Petulla*

Circulation 10,000

FOUNDED 1984. SEASONAL lifestyle magazine with features on homes, leisure, motoring, fashion, beauty, health, local issues and travel. No fiction. No unsolicited mss. Approach by phone in the first instance.

Jewish Chronicle

25 Furnival Street, London EC4A 1JT
☎0171 405 9252   Fax 0171 405 9040

Owner *Kessler Foundation*
Editor *Edward J. Temko*
Circulation 50,000

WEEKLY. Unsolicited mss welcome if 'the specific interests of our readership are borne in mind by writers'. Approach in writing, except for urgent current news items. No fiction. Maximum 1500 words for all material.

   Features *Gerald Jacobs*
   Leisure/Lifestyle *Alan Montague*
   Home News *Barry Toberman*
   Foreign News *Joseph Millis*
   Supplements *Angela Kiverstein*
   Payment negotiable.

Jewish Quarterly

PO Box 2078, London W1A 1JR
☎0171 629 5004(admin)/
0181 361 6372(edit)
Fax 0181 361 6372

Publisher *Jewish Literary Trust Ltd*
Editor *Elena Lappin*

FOUNDED 1953. QUARTERLY illustrated magazine featuring Jewish literature and fiction, politics, art, music, film, poetry, history, dance, community, autobiography, Hebrew, Yiddish, Israel and the Middle East, Judaism, interviews, Zionism, philosophy and holocaust studies. Features a major books and arts section. Unsolicited mss welcome but letter or phone call preferred in first instance.

Jewish Telegraph

Jewish Telegraph Group of Newspapers, 11 Park Hill, Bury Old Road, Prestwick, Manchester M25 0HH
☎0161 740 9321   Fax 0161 740 9325

Editor *Paul Harris*
Circulation 16,000

FOUNDED 1950. WEEKLY publication with local, national and international news and features. Unsolicited features on Jewish humour and history welcome.

The Journal Magazines (Norfolk, Suffolk, Cambridgeshire)

The Old Eagle, Market Place, Dereham, Norfolk NR19 2AP
☎01362 699699   Fax 01362 699606

Owner *Hawksmere Plc*
Editor *Pippa Bastin*
Circulation 9000 each

FOUNDED 1990. MONTHLY magazines covering items of local interest – history, people, conservation, business, places, food and wine, fashion, homes and sport.
   Features 750 words maximum, plus pictures. Approach the editor by phone with ideas in the first instance.
   Payment £75.

Just Seventeen

20 Orange Street, London WC2H 7ED
☎0171 957 8383   Fax 0171 930 5728

Owner *EMAP Elan Publications*
Editor *Sam Baker*
Circulation 130,030

FOUNDED 1983. MONTHLY. Top of the mid-teen market, with news, articles and quizzes of interest to girls aged 12–17. Ideas are sought in all areas. Prospective contributors should send ideas to the relevant editorial department, then follow up with a phone call.
   Beauty *Jessie Cartner-Morley*
   Features *Sarah Pyper*
   Music *Kate Hodges*
   News *Sarra Manning*
   Payment by arrangement.

Kennel Gazette

Kennel Club, 1–5 Clarges Street, Piccadilly, London W1Y 8AB
☎0171 493 6651   Fax 0171 495 6162

Owner *Kennel Club*
Editor *Charles Colborn*
Circulation 10,000

FOUNDED 1873. MONTHLY concerning dogs and their breeding. Unsolicited mss welcome.
   Features Maximum 2500 words.
   News Maximum 500 words.
   Payment £70 per 1000 words.

Kent Life

Datateam Publishing, Fairmeadow, Maidstone, Kent ME14 1NG
☎01622 687031   Fax 01622 757646

Publisher *Datateam Publishing*
Editor *Roderick Cooper*

Circulation 10,000

FOUNDED 1962. MONTHLY. Strong Kent interest plus fashion, food, books, wildlife, motoring, property, sport, interiors with local links. Unsolicited mss welcome. Interested in anything with a genuine Kent connection. No fiction or non-Kentish subjects. Approach in writing with ideas. Maximum length 1500 words. *Payment* negotiable.

Keyboard Review

30 Monmouth Street, Bath BA1 2BW
☎01225 442244   Fax 01225 732353
Owner *Future Publishing*
Editor *Cliff Douse*
Circulation 18,000

FOUNDED 1985. MONTHLY. Broad-based keyboard magazine, covering organs, pianos, keyboards, synthesisers, MIDI keyboard, add-ons such as samplers and modules, and their players. Approach by phone or in writing with ideas.

The Lady

39–40 Bedford Street, Strand, London WC2E 9ER
☎0171 379 4717   Fax 0171 497 2137
Owner *T. G. A. Bowles*
Editor *Arline Usden*
Circulation 53,068

FOUNDED 1885. WEEKLY. Unsolicited mss are accepted provided they are not on the subject of politics or religion, or on topics covered by staff writers, i.e. fashion and beauty, health, cookery, household, gardening, finance and shopping.

Features Well-researched pieces on British and foreign travel, historical subjects or events; interviews and profiles and other general interest topics. Maximum 1000 words for illustrated articles; 900 words for one-page features; 450 words for first-person 'Viewpoint' pieces. All material should be addressed to the editor. Photographs supporting features may be supplied as colour transparencies or b&w prints.

Lakeland Walker

8 Faircroft, 37 St Andrews Grove, London N16 5NJ
☎0181 809 2338
Owner *Raven Marketing Group*
Editors *Les Douglas, David Sharp*
FOUNDED 1996. QUARTERLY. News and features relating to the Lake District and walking in the area – wildlife, local history, places to visit, local transport. Maximum 1000–1500 words. Unsolicited material welcome.

Land Rover World Magazine

Link House, Dingwall Road, Croydon, Surrey CR9 2TA
☎0181 686 2599   Fax 0181 781 6042
Owner *Link House Magazines Ltd*
Editor *Alan Kidd*
Circulation 30,000

FOUNDED 1993. MONTHLY. Incorporates *Practical Land Rover World*. Unsolicited mss welcome, especially if supported by high-quality illustrations. 'Editorial policy is to encourage and support unknown writers and beginners wherever possible.'

Features *Alan Kidd* All articles with a Land Rover theme of interest. Potential contributors are strongly advised to examine previous issues before starting work.

Payment negotiable.

Learning Resources Journal/ Learning Resources News

5 White Hart Lane, Wistaston, Crewe, Cheshire CW2 8EX
☎01270 68550
Owner *Learning Resources Development Group*
Editor *David Scott*

THRICE-YEARLY publications. The Journal publishes articles by those involved in the management of resourses in modern academic libraries and custom-built learning resource centres. The problems of identifying the resources needed to maintain the curriculum in higher, further and school level education are discussed. The main aim of the News is to provide information on the availability of resource management tools, products and services. Resource managers and providers are encouraged to send information about their work/products to the editor.

Leisure Vehicle Times

Fawkham Green Post Office, Longfield, Kent DA3 8NL
☎0956 974890
Owner *PhD Publishing*
Editor *Dave Randle*
Circulation 70,000

FOUNDED 1997. Initially a QUARTERLY colour magazine for leisure motorists, published as a supplement to *Vintage Times* (see entry) to achieve accurate targeting of readership and ready-made circulation. Preliminary approach by phone or letter with ideas.

Let's Go Coarse Fishing Magazine

Temple Building, Railway Terrace, Rugby, Warwickshire CV21 3EJ

☎01788 535218   Fax 01788 541845

Owner *Chrisreel Ltd*
Editor *John Hunter*
Circulation 50,000

FOUNDED 1985. MONTHLY. Unsolicited mss welcome but initial approach by phone or in writing preferred.

Features Any general coarse angling interest accepted. Length 1000–2000 words plus photos.
Reviews Product reviews welcome (include photos).
Payment variable.

Lexikon

PO Box 754, Stoke-on-Trent, Staffordshire ST1 4BU

☎01782 205060   Fax 01782 285331

Editors *Francis Anderson, Roger Stapenhill*

'Sharp, discerning prose, giving writers in the UK and abroad the opportunity to share their work and exchange new ideas.' Poetry, short stories, critical articles, book reviews plus regular competitions with cash prizes. Maximum of 2000 words for short stories; maximum of 150 lines for poetry. *Payment* complimentary copies.

Liberal Democrat News

4 Cowley Street, London SW1P 3NB

☎0171 222 7999   Fax 0171 222 7904

Owner *Liberal Democrats*
Editor *David Boyle*

FOUNDED 1988. WEEKLY. As with the political parties, this is the result of the merger of *Liberal News* (1946) and *The Social Democrat* (1981). Political and social topics of interest to party members and their supporters. Unsolicited contributions welcome.

Features Maximum 800 words.
News Maximum 350 words.
No payment.

Lincolnshire Life

County Life Ltd, PO Box 81, Lincoln LN1 1HD

☎01522 527127   Fax 01522 560035

Publisher *A.L. Robinson*
Executive Editor *Jez Ashberry*
Circulation 10,000

FOUNDED 1961. MONTHLY county magazine featuring geographically relevant articles. Maximum 1000–1500 words. Contributions supported by three or four good-quality photo-graphs are always welcome. Approach in writing. *Payment* varies.

The List

14 High Street, Edinburgh EH1 1TE

☎0131 558 1191   Fax 0131 557 8500

Owner *The List Ltd*
Publisher *Robin Hodge*
Editor *Kathleen Morgan*
Circulation 15,000

FOUNDED 1985. FORTNIGHTLY. Events guide covering Glasgow and Edinburgh. Interviews and profiles of people working in film, theatre, music and the arts. Maximum 1200 words. Not interested in anything not related to events or to life in Central Scotland. No unsolicited mss. Phone with ideas. News material tends to be handled in-house. *Payment* £100.

Literary Review

44 Lexington Street, London W1R 3LH

☎0171 437 9392   Fax 0171 734 1844

Owner *Namara Group*
Editor *Auberon Waugh*
Circulation 15,000

FOUNDED 1979. MONTHLY. Publishes book reviews (commissioned), features and articles on literary subjects. Prospective contributors are best advised to contact the editor in writing. Unsolicited mss not welcome. Runs a monthly competition, the Literary Review Grand Poetry Competition, on a given theme. Open to subscribers only. Details published in the magazine. *Payment* varies.

Living France

The Picture House, 79 High Street, Olney, Buckinghamshire MK46 4EF

☎01234 713203   Fax 01234 711507

Editor *Trevor Yorke*

FOUNDED 1989. TEN ISSUES YEARLY. A Francophile magazine catering for those with a passion for France, French culture and lifestyle. Editorial covers all aspects of holidaying, living and working in France. Property section for those owning or wishing to buy a property in France. No unsolicited mss; approach in writing with an idea.

Llais Llyfrau/Books in Wales

Cyngor Llyfrau Cymru/Welsh Books Council, Castell Brychan, Aberystwyth, Ceredigion SY23 2JB

☎01970 624151   Fax 01970 625385

Owner *Cyngor Llyfrau Cymru/Welsh Books Council*

Editors R. Gerallt Jones, Katie Gramich,
Lorna Herbert

FOUNDED 1961. QUARTERLY bilingual magazine containing articles of relevance to the
book trade in Wales plus reviews of new books
and comprehensive lists of recent titles. A complete section devoted to children's books
appears every quarter. No unsolicited mss. All
initial approaches should be made in writing.

Features R. Gerallt Jones (Welsh)/Katie
Gramich (English) Each edition features a
writer's diary in Welsh and English, plus articles on books, publishing, the media etc. Most
items commissioned. Articles on the literature
of Wales are welcome, in either language.

Special pages Lorna Herbert Children's
Books section – latest Welsh-language and
Welsh-interest books reviewed.

Payment £30 maximum.

Logos
5 Beechwood Drive, Marlow,
Buckinghamshire SL7 2DH
☎01628 477577   Fax 01628 477577

Owner Whurr Publishers Ltd
Editor Gordon Graham
Associate Editor Betty Graham

FOUNDED 1990. QUARTERLY. Aims to 'deal in
depth with issues which unite, divide, excite and
concern the world of books,' with an international perspective. Each issue contains 6–8
articles of between 3500–7000 words. Hopes to
establish itself as a forum for contrasting views.
Suggestions and ideas for contributions are welcome, and should be addressed to the editor.
'Guidelines for Contributors' available. Contributors write from their experience as authors,
publishers, booksellers, librarians, etc. No payment.

London Magazine
30 Thurloe Place, London SW7 2HQ
☎0171 589 0618

Owner Alan Ross
Editor Alan Ross
Deputy Editor Jane Rye
Circulation 4500

FOUNDED 1954. BI-MONTHLY paperback journal providing an eclectic forum for literary talent, thanks to the dedication of Alan Ross. The
Times once said that 'London Magazine is far and
away the most readable and level-headed, not to
mention best value for money, of the literary
magazines'. Today it boasts the publication of
early works by the likes of William Boyd,
Graham Swift and Ben Okri among others. The
broad spectrum of interests includes art, memoirs, travel, poetry, criticism, theatre, music, cinema, short stories and essays, and book reviews.
Unsolicited mss welcome; s.a.e. essential. About
150–200 unsolicited mss are received weekly.

Fiction Maximum 5000 words.
Payment £100 maximum.
Annual Subscription £28.50 or $67.

London Review of Books
28 Little Russell Street, London WC1A 2HN
☎0171 209 1101   Fax 0171 209 1102

Owner LRB Ltd
Editor Mary-Kay Wilmers
Circulation 21,717

FOUNDED 1979. FORTNIGHTLY. Reviews,
essays and articles on political, literary, cultural
and scientific subjects. Also poetry. Unsolicited
contributions welcome (approximately 50
received each week). No pieces under 2000
words. Contact the editor in writing. Please
include s.a.e.. Payment £100 per 1000 words;
poems £50.

Looking Good
Upper Mounts, Northampton NN1 3HR
☎01604 231122   Fax 01604 233000

Owner Herald Newspapers Ltd
Editor Ruth Supple
Circulation 6000

FOUNDED 1984. QUARTERLY county lifestyle
magazine of Northamptonshire. Contributions
are not required as all work is done in-house.

Looks
20 Orange Street, London WC2H 7ED
☎0171 957 8383   Fax 0171 930 4091

Owner EMAP Women's Group Magazines
Editor Wendy Rigg
Circulation 179,007

MONTHLY magazine for young women aged
15–22, with emphasis on fashion, beauty and
hair, as well as general interest features, including celebrity news and interviews, giveaways,
etc. Freelance writers are occasionally used in
all areas of the magazine. Contact the editor
with ideas. Payment varies.

Loving Holiday Special
PO Box 435A, Surbiton, Surrey KT6 6YT
Owner Perfectly Formed Publishing Ltd
Editor Jo Pink
Circulation 40,000

ANNUAL. Unclichéd love stories for women
under 30. Story lengths 1000-4000 words.

Write for a style guide (January/February only) before putting pen to paper.

M & E Design

Quadrant House, The Quadrant, Sutton, Surrey SM2 5AS

☎0181 652 3115   Fax 0181 652 8972

Owner *Reed Business Information*
Editor *Steve Hobson*
Circulation 13,000

FOUNDED 1996. SIX ISSUES YEARLY. Aimed at mechanical and electrical consulting engineers and designers.

Machine Knitting Monthly

PO Box 1479, Maidenhead, Berkshire SL6 8YX

☎01628 783080   Fax 01628 33250

Owner *Machine Knitting Monthly Ltd*
Editor *Sheila Berriff*

FOUNDED 1986. MONTHLY. Unsolicited mss considered 'as long as they are applicable to this specialist publication. We have our own regular contributors each month but we're always willing to look at new ideas from other writers.' Approach in writing in first instance.

Management Today

17 Hammersmith Road, London W6 7JP

☎0171 413 4566   Fax 0171 413 4138

Owner *Haymarket Business Publications Ltd*
Editor *Charles Skinner*
Circulation 103,000

General business topics and features. Ideas welcome. Send brief synopsis to the editor.
Payment about £300 per 1000 words.

Map Collector

48 High Street, Tring, Hertfordshire HP23 5BH

☎01442 891004   Fax 01442 827712

Owner *Valerie G. Scott*
Editor *Valerie G. Scott*
Circulation 2500

FOUNDED 1977. QUARTERLY magazine dedicated to the history of cartography and study of early maps. Articles, book reviews, news items and guide to prices. Not interested in modern mapping.
   Features Articles on early maps particularly welcome. Maximum 2500 words.
   News Events and exhibitions of early maps. Maximum 300 words.
   Payment NUJ rates.

marie claire

2 Hatfields, London SE1 9PG

☎0171 261 5240   Fax 0171 261 5277

Owner *European Magazines Ltd*
Editor *Juliet Warkentin*
Circulation 457,034

FOUNDED 1988. MONTHLY. An intelligent glossy magazine for women, with strong international features and fashion. No unsolicited mss. Approach with ideas in writing. No fiction.
   Features *Lorraine Butler* Detailed proposals for feature ideas should be accompanied by samples of previous work.

Marketing Week

St Giles House, 50 Poland Street, London W1V 4AX

☎0171 439 4222   Fax 0171 434 1439

Owner *Centaur Communications*
Editor *Stuart Smith*
Circulation 39,000

WEEKLY trade magazine of the marketing industry. Features on all aspects of the business, written in a newsy and up-to-the-minute style. Approach with ideas in the first instance.
   Features *Tom O'Sullivan*
   Payment negotiable.

Match

Bretton Court, Bretton, Peterborough, Cambridgeshire PE3 8DZ

☎01733 260333   Fax 01733 465206

Owner *EMAP Pursuit Publications*
Editor *Chris Hunt*
Circulation 190,434

FOUNDED 1979. Popular WEEKLY football magazine aimed at 10–15-year-olds. Most material is generated in-house by a strong news and features team. Some freelance material used if suitable, apart from photographs. No submissions without prior consultation with editor, either by phone or in writing.
   Features/News Good and original material is always considered. Maximum 500 words.
   Payment negotiable.

Matrix

See **British Science Fiction Association** under **Professional Associations**

Maxim

19 Bolsover Street, London W1P 7HJ

☎0171 631 1433   Fax 0171 917 7663

Owner *Dennis Publishing*
Editor *Gill Hudson*

Circulation 150,261

ESTABLISHED 1995. MONTHLY glossy men's lifestyle magazine featuring sex, travel, health, finance, motoring and fashion. No fiction or poetry. Approach in writing in the first instance, sending outlines of ideas only together with examples of published work. Some scope for first-person accounts.

Mayfair

2 Archer Street, Piccadilly Circus, London
W1V 8JJ
☎0171 734 9191   Fax 0171 734 5030
Owner *Paul Raymond Publications*
Editor *Steve Shields*
Circulation 331,760

FOUNDED 1966. THIRTEEN ISSUES YEARLY. Unsolicited material accepted if suitable to the magazine. Interested in features and humour aimed at men aged 20–30. For style, length, etc., writers are advised to study the magazine. 'No more romantic fiction, we beseech you!'

Mayfair Times

102 Mount Street, London W1X 5HF
☎0171 629 3378   Fax 0171 629 9303
Owner *Mayfair Times Ltd*
Editor *Stephen Goringe*
Circulation 20,000

FOUNDED 1985. MONTHLY. Features on Mayfair of interest to both residential and commercial readers. Unsolicited mss welcome.

Medal News

Token Publishing Ltd, PO Box 14, Honiton,
Devon EX14 9YP
☎01404 831878   Fax 01404 831895
Owners *J. W. Mussell, Carol Hartman*
Editor *Diana Birch*
Circulation 2500

FOUNDED 1989. MONTHLY. Unsolicited material welcome but initial approach by phone or in writing preferred.

Features Only interested in articles from well-informed authors 'who know the subject and do their homework'. Maximum 2500 words.

Payment £20 per 1000 words.

Media Week

33–39 Bowling Green Lane, London
EC1R 0DA
☎0171 505 8341   Fax 0171 505 8363
Owner *EMAP Media*
Editor *Susannah Richmond*

Circulation 13,944

FOUNDED 1986. WEEKLY trade magazine. UK and international coverage on all aspects of commercial media. No unsolicited mss. Approach in writing with ideas.

Melody Maker

King's Reach Tower, Stamford Street,
London SE1 9LS
☎0171 261 6229   Fax 0171 261 6706
Owner *IPC Magazines Ltd*
Editor *Allan Jones*
Circulation 46,895

WEEKLY. Freelance contributors used on this tabloid magazine competitor of the *NME*. Opportunities exist in reviewing and features.

Features *Paul Lester* A large in-house team, plus around six regulars, produce most feature material.

Reviews *Saron O'Connell* (Live), *Everett True* (Albums) Sample reviews, whether published or not, welcome on pop, rock, soul, funk, etc.

Payment negotiable.

Metropolitan

19 Victoria Avenue, Didsbury, Manchester
M20 2GY
☎0161 434 6290
Publishers *John Ashbrook, Elizabeth Baines, Ailsa Cox*
Editors *Elizabeth Baines, Ailsa Cox*
Circulation 1500

FOUNDED 1993. BI-ANNUAL magazine devoted to the short story, with the occasional novel extract (usually of a forthcoming novel), author interview or cultural commentary. A platform for new talent alongside names such as Colum McCann, Russell Hoban and Livi Michael.

Features Usually commissioned, but open to proposals. Approach in writing with idea, c.v. and s.a.e..

Fiction Stories of high literary standard engaging with contemporary issues. Unsolicited mss welcome. S.a.e. essential. Maximum length 6000 words (2500 ideal).

No poetry please.

Payment negotiable (depending on grants). Annual subscription £8.

MG (My Guy) Magazine

PO Box 435a, Surbiton, Surrey KT6 6YT
☎0181 255 3151   Fax 0181 390 5832
Owner *Perfectly Formed Publishing*
Editor *Frank Hopkinson*

Circulation 45,000

FOUNDED 1979. MONTHLY teen magazine for teenage girls. No freelance contributions.

MiniWorld Magazine

Link House, Dingwall Road, Croydon, Surrey CR9 2TA

☎0181 686 2599   Fax 0181 781 1158

Owner *Link House Magazines Ltd*
Editor *Monty Watkins*
Circulation 50,000

FOUNDED 1991. MONTHLY car magazine devoted to the Mini. Unsolicited material welcome but prospective contributors are advised to make initial contact by phone.

    Features Restoration, tuning tips, technical advice and sporting events. Readers' cars and product news. Length by arrangement.

    Payment negotiable.

Mizz

King's Reach Tower, Stamford Street, London SE1 9LS

☎0171 261 6319   Fax 0171 261 6032

Owner *IPC Magazines Ltd*
Editor *Jeanette Baker*
Circulation 138,381

FOUNDED 1985. FORTNIGHTLY magazine for the 15–17-year-old girl. Freelance articles welcome on real life, human interest stories and emotional issues. All material should be addressed to the features editor.

    Features *Julie Burniston* Approach in writing, with synopsis, for feature copy; send sample writing with letter for general approach. No fiction.

The Modern Dance

See **Works Publishing** under **Small Presses**

Mojo

Mappin House, 4 Winsley Street, London W1N 7AR

☎0171 436 1515   Fax 0171 312 8926

Owner *EMAP-Metro*
Editor *Mat Snow*
Circulation 64,589

FOUNDED 1993. MONTHLY magazine containing features, reviews and news stories about rock music and its influences. Receives about five mss per day.

    Features Amateur writers discouraged except as providers of source material, contacts, etc. *Payment* negotiable.

    News All verifiable, relevant stories considered. *Payment* approx. £150 per 1000 words.

    Reviews Write to Reviews Editor with relevant specimen material. *Payment* approx. £150 per 1000 words.

Moneywise

RD Publications Ltd, 10 Old Bailey, London EC4M 7NB

☎0171 409 5274   Fax 0171 409 5261

Owner *Reader's Digest Association*
Editor *Matthew Vincent*
Circulation 122,444

FOUNDED 1990. MONTHLY. Unsolicited mss with s.a.e. welcome but initial approach in writing preferred.

More!

20 Orange Street, London WC2H 7ED

☎0171 957 8383   Fax 0171 930 4637

Owner *EMAP Elan Publications*
Editor *Tony Cross*
Features Editor *Nigel May*
Circulation 430,696

FOUNDED 1988. FORTNIGHTLY women's magazine aimed at the working woman aged 18–24. Features on sex and relationships plus news. Most items are commissioned; approach features editor with idea. Prospective contributors are strongly advised to study the magazine's style before submitting anything.

Mother and Baby

Victory House, Leicester Place, London WC2H 7BP

☎0171 437 9011   Fax 0171 434 0656

Owner *EMAP Elan Publications*
Editor *Sharon Parsons*
Circulation 100,632

FOUNDED 1956. MONTHLY. Unsolicited mss welcome, about practical baby and childcare. Personal 'viewpoint' pieces are considered. Approaches may be made by telephone or in writing.

Motor Boat and Yachting

King's Reach Tower, Stamford Street, London SE1 9LS

☎0171 261 5333   Fax 0171 261 5419

Owner *IPC Magazines Ltd*
Editor *Alan Harper*
Circulation 22,365

FOUNDED 1904. MONTHLY for those interested in motor boats and motor cruising.

    Features *Alan Harper* Cruising features and practical features especially welcome. Illustrations (mostly colour) are just as important as text. Maximum 3000 words. *Payment* £100 per 1000 words or by arrangement.

News *Dennis O'Neill* Factual pieces. Maximum 200 words. *Payment* up to £50 per item.

Motorcaravan Motorhome Monthly (MMM)

14 Eastfield Close, Andover, Hampshire SP10 2QP
Fax 01264 324794

Owner *Sanglier Publications Ltd*
Editor *Mike Jago*
Circulation 23,259

FOUNDED 1966. MONTHLY. 'There's no money in motorcaravan journalism but for those wishing to cut their first teeth...' Unsolicited mss welcome if relevant, but ideas in writing preferred in first instance.

Features Caravan site reports – contact the editor for questionnaire. Maximum 500 words.

Travel Motorcaravanning trips (home and overseas). Maximum 2000 words.

News Short news items for miscellaneous pages. Maximum 200 words.

Fiction Must be motorcaravan-related and include artwork/photos if possible. Maximum 2000 words.

Special pages DIY – modifications to motorcaravans. Maximum 1500 words.

Owner Reports Contributions welcome from motorcaravan owners. Contact the Editor for requirements. Maximum 2000 words.

Payment varies.

Ms London

7–9 Rathbone Street, London W1P 1AF
☎0171 636 6651   Fax 0171 255 2352

Owner *Independent Magazines*
Editor-in-Chief *Bill Williamson*
Editor *Cathy Howes*
Circulation 85,000

FOUNDED 1968. WEEKLY. Aimed at working women in London, aged 18–35. Unsolicited mss must be accompanied by s.a.e.. Because the magazine is purely London-orientated, there is a real bias towards London-based writers who are in touch with the constantly changing trends and attitudes of the capital.

Features Content is varied and ambitious, ranging from stage and film interviews to fashion, careers, relationships, homebuying and furnishing. Approach with ideas first and sample of published writing. Material should be London-angled, sharp and sophisticated in content. Max. 1500 words. *Payment* about £125 per 1000 words.

News Handled in-house but follow-up feature ideas welcome.

Music Week

8 Montague Close, London SE1 9UR
☎0171 620 3636   Fax 0171 401 8035

Owner *Miller Freeman Entertainment*
Editor-in-Chief *Steve Redmond*
Editor *Selina Webb*
Circulation 13,900

WEEKLY. Britain's only weekly music business magazine also includes dance industry title *Record Mirror*. No unsolicited mss. Approach in writing with ideas.

Features *Selina Webb* Analysis of specific music business events and trends. Maximum 2000 words.

News Music industry news only. Maximum 350 words.

Musical Option

2 Princes Road, St Leonards on Sea, East Sussex TN37 6EL
☎01424 715167   Fax 01424 712214

Owner *Musical Option Ltd*
Editor *Denby Richards*
Circulation 5000

FOUNDED 1877. QUARTERLY with free supplement in intervening months. Classical music content, with topical features on music, musicians, festivals, etc., and reviews (concerts, festivals, opera, ballet, jazz, CDs, CD-Roms, videos, books and printed music). International readership. No unsolicited mss; commissions only. Ideas always welcome though; approach by phone or fax, giving telephone number. It should be noted that topical material has to be submitted six months prior to events. Not interested in review material, which is already handled by the magazine's own regular team of contributors.

Payment Negotiable.

Musical Times

☎0171 482 5697   Fax 0171 482 5697

Owner *The Musical Times Publications Ltd*
Editor *Antony Bye*

FOUNDED 1844. Scholarly journal with a practical approach to its subject. All material is commissioned.

My Weekly

80 Kingsway East, Dundee DD4 8SL
☎01382 464276   Fax 01382 452491

Owner *D. C. Thomson & Co. Ltd*

Editor *Harrison Watson*
Circulation 394,480

A traditional women's WEEKLY. D. C. Thomson has long had a policy of encouragement and help to new writers of promise. Ideas welcome. Approach in writing.

Features Particularly interested in human interest pieces (1000–1500 words) which by their very nature appeal to all age groups.

Fiction Three stories a week, ranging in content from the emotional to the off-beat and unexpected. 1500–4000 words. Also serials.

Payment negotiable.

The National Trust Magazine
36 Queen Anne's Gate, London SW1H 9AS
☎0171 222 9251   Fax 0171 222 5097

Owner *The National Trust*
Editor *Gina Guarnieri*
Circulation 2.3 million

FOUNDED 1968. THRICE-YEARLY. Conservation of historic houses, coast and countryside in England, Northern Ireland and Wales. No unsolicited mss. Approach in writing with ideas.

Natural World
20 Upper Ground, London SE1 9PF
☎0171 805 5555   Fax 0171 805 5911

Publishers *Illustrated London News Group on behalf of The Wildlife Trusts*
Editor *Linda Bennett*
Circulation 153,000

FOUNDED 1981. THRICE-YEARLY. Unsolicited mss welcome if of high quality and relevant to ideals of the magazine. Ideas in writing preferred. No poetry.

Features Popular but accurate articles on British wildlife and the countryside, particularly projects associated with the local wildlife trusts. Maximum 1500 words.

News Interested in national wildlife conservation issues, particularly those involving local nature conservation or wildlife trusts. Maximum 300 words.

Payment negotiable.

The Naturalist
c/o University of Bradford, Bradford, West Yorkshire BD7 1DP
☎01274 384212   Fax 01274 384231

Owner *Yorkshire Naturalists' Union*
Editor *Prof. M. R. D. Seaward*
Circulation 5000

FOUNDED 1875. QUARTERLY. Natural history, biological and environmental sciences for a professional and amateur readership. Unsolicited mss welcome. Particularly interested in material – scientific papers – relating to the north of England.

No payment.

Nature
Porters South, 4–6 Crinan Street, London N1 9XW
☎0171 833 4000

Owner *Macmillan Magazines Ltd*
Editor *Philip Campbell*
Circulation 55,438

Covers all fields of science, with articles and news on science policy only. No features. Little scope for freelance writers.

Needlecraft
30 Monmouth Street, Bath BA1 2BW
☎01225 442244   Fax 01225 732398

Owner *Future Publishing*
Editor *Rebecca Bradshaw*
Circulation 57,011

FOUNDED 1991. MONTHLY. Needlework projects with full instructions covering cross-stitch, needlepoint, embroidery, patchwork quilting and lace. Will consider ideas or sketches for projects covering any of the magazine's topics. Initial approaches should be made in writing.

Features on the needlecraft theme. Discuss ideas before sending complete mss. Maximum 1000 words.

Technical pages on 'how to' stitch, use different threads, etc. Only suitable for experienced writers.

Payment negotiable.

New Beacon
224 Great Portland Street, London W1N 6AA
☎0171 388 1266   Fax 0171 388 0945

Owner *Royal National Institute for the Blind*
Editor *Ann Lee*
Circulation 6000

FOUNDED 1917. MONTHLY (except August). Published in print, braille and on tape and disk. Unsolicited mss welcome. Approach with ideas in writing. Personal experiences by writers who have a visual impairment (partial sight or blindness), and authoritative items by professionals or volunteers working in the field of visual impairment welcome. Maximum 1500 words.

Payment negotiable.

New Christian Herald

Herald House, 96 Dominion Road,
Worthing, West Sussex BN14 8JP
☎01903 821082   Fax 01903 821081

Owner *Herald House Ltd*
Editor *Russ Bravo*
Circulation 20,000

WEEKLY. Evangelical, inter-denominational Christian newspaper aimed at committed Christians. News, bible-based comment and incisive features. Contributors' guidelines available. *Payment* Herald House rates.

New Humanist

Bradlaugh House, 47 Theobald's Road,
London WC1X 8SP
☎0171 430 1371   Fax 0171 430 1271

Owner *Rationalist Press Association*
Editor *Jim Herrick*
Circulation 1500

FOUNDED 1885. QUARTERLY. Unsolicited mss welcome. No fiction.

Features Articles with a humanist perspective welcome in the following fields: religion (critical), humanism, human rights, philosophy, current events, literature, history and science. 2000–4000 words. *Payment* nominal, but negotiable.

Book reviews 750–1000 words, by arrangement with the editor.

New Impact

Anser House, PO Box 1448, Marlow,
Bucks SL7 3HD
☎01628 481581   Fax 01628 481581

Owner *D. E. Sihera*
Editor *Elaine Sihera*
Circulation 10,000

FOUNDED 1993. BI-MONTHLY. Promotes training enterprise and diversity from a minority ethnic perspective. Unsolicited mss welcome. Interested in training, arts, features, personal achievement, small business features, profiles or personalities especially for a multicultural audience. Not interested in anything unconnected to training or business. Approach in writing with ideas.

Promotes the British Diversity Awards each November.

News Local training/business features – some opportunities. Maximum length 250 words. *Payment* negotiable.

Features Original, interesting pieces with a deliberate multicultural/equal opportunity focus. Personal/professional successes and achievements welcome. Maximum length 1500 words. *Payment* negotiable.

Fiction Short stories, poems – especially from minority writers. Maximum length 1500 words. *Payment* negotiable.

Special Pages Interviews with personalities – especially Asian, Afro-Caribbean. Maximum length 1200 words. *Payment* negotiable.

New Internationalist

55 Rectory Road, Oxford OX4 1BW
☎01865 728181   Fax 01865 793152

Owner *New Internationalist Trust*
Co-Editors *Vanessa Baird, Chris Brazier, David Ransom, Nikki van der Gaag*
Circulation 70,000

Radical and broadly leftist in approach, but unaligned. Concerned with world poverty and global issues of peace and politics, feminism and environmentalism, with emphasis on the Third World. Difficult to use unsolicited material as they work to a theme each month and features are commissioned by the editor on that basis. The way in is to send examples of published or unpublished work; writers of interest are taken up. Unsolicited material for shorter articles could be used in the magazine's regular *Update* section.

New Moon Magazine

28 St Albans Lane, London NW11 7QE
☎0181 731 8031   Fax 0181 381 4033

Owner *New Moon Publishing*
Editor *Simon Goodman*
Circulation 8000

FOUNDED 1990. MONTHLY Jewish magazine covering arts, entertainment, politics, religion, and relationships for an audience that is mostly aged 20–40 and single. No fiction or poetry.

Features *Victoria Stagg Elliott* Opportunities exist primarily with celebrity interviews and general features. Not many opportunities for outside contributors but 'always open to a good idea'. Maximum 4000 words. Approach with ideas in writing in the first instance. *Payment* by arrangement.

New Musical Express

Floor 25, King's Reach Tower, Stamford Street, London SE1 9LS
☎0171 261 6472   Fax 0171 261 5185

Owner *IPC Magazines Ltd*
Editor *Steve Sutherland*
Circulation 111,211

Britain's best-selling musical WEEKLY. Freelancers used, but always for reviews in the first instance. Specialisation in areas of music (or film, which is also covered) is a help.

Reviews: Books *Stephen Dalton* **Film** *Stephen Dalton* **LPs** *John Robinson* **Live** *Ted Kessler*. Send in examples of work, either published or specially written samples.

New Scientist

King's Reach Tower, Stamford Street, London SE1 9LS
☎0171 261 5000   Fax 0171 261 6464
Owner *IPC Magazines Ltd*
Editor *Alun Anderson*
Circulation 120,744

FOUNDED 1956. WEEKLY. No unsolicited mss. Approach in writing or by phone with an idea.

Features *Jeremy Webb* Commissions only, but good ideas welcome. Maximum 3500 words.

News *Peter Aldhous* Mostly commissions, but ideas for specialist news welcome. Maximum 1000 words.

Reviews *Maggie McDonald* Reviews are commissioned.

Forum *Richard Fifield* Unsolicited material welcome if of general/humorous interest and related to science. Maximum 1000 words.

Payment £200+ per 1000 words.

New Statesman

Victoria Station House, 191 Victoria Street, London SW1E 5NE
☎0171 828 1232   Fax 0171 828 1881
Owner *Geoffrey Robinson*
Editor *Ian Hargreaves*
Deputy Editor *Jane Taylor*
Circulation 25,000

WEEKLY magazine, the result of a merger (May 1988) of *New Statesman* and *New Society*. Coverage of news, book reviews, arts, current affairs, politics and social reportage. Unsolicited contributions with s.a.e. will be considered. No short stories.

Books *Peter Wilby*
Arts *Laura Cummings*

New Welsh Review

Chapter Arts Centre, Market Road, Cardiff CF5 1QE
☎01222 665529   Fax 01222 665529
Owner *New Welsh Review Ltd*
Editor *Robin Reeves*
Circulation 1000

FOUNDED 1988. QUARTERLY Welsh literary magazine in the English language. Welcomes material of literary and cultural interest to Welsh readers and those with an interest in Wales. Approach in writing in the first instance.

Features Maximum 3000 words. *Payment* £20 per 1000 words.

Fiction Maximum 5000 words. *Payment* £60 average.

News Maximum 400 words. *Payment* £5–15.

New Woman

20 Orange Street, London WC2H 7ED
☎0171 957 8383   Fax 0171 930 7246
Owner *Hachette/EMAP Magazines Ltd*
Editor *Dawn Bébe*
Circulation 216,765

MONTHLY women's interest magazine. Relaunched and redesigned under new editor. Aimed at women aged 25–35. An 'entertaining, informative and intelligent' read. Main topics of interest include men, sex, love, health, careers, beauty and fashion. Uses mainly established freelancers but unsolicited ideas submitted in synopsis form will be considered. Welcomes ideas from male writers for humorous 'men's opinion' pieces.

Features/News *Emma Marlin* Articles must be original and look at subjects or issues from a new or unusual perspective.

Fashion *Corinna Kitchen*

The New Writer

PO Box 60, Cranbrook, Kent TN17 2ZR
☎01580 212626   Fax 01580 212041
Publisher *Merric Davidson*
Editor *Suzanne Ruthven*

FOUNDED 1996. Published MONTHLY following the merger between *Acclaim* and *Quartos* magazines. TNW continues to offer practical 'nuts and bolts' advice on poetry and prose but with the emphasis on *forward-looking* articles and features on all aspects of the written word that demonstrate the writer's grasp of contemporary writing and current editorial/publishing policies. Plenty of news, views, competitions, reviews and regional gossip in the Newsletter section; writers' guidelines available with s.a.e..

Features Unsolicited mss welcome. Interested in lively, original articles on writing in its broadest sense. Approach with ideas in writing in the first instance. No material is returned unless accompanied by s.a.e.. *Payment* £20 per 1000 words.

Fiction Publishes short-listed entries from the **Ian St James Awards** and subscriber-only submissions. *Payment* £10 per story.

Poetry Unsolicited poetry welcome. Both

short and long unpublished poems, providing they are original and interesting. *Payment £3* per poem.

Newcastle Life
See **North East Times**

19
King's Reach Tower, Stamford Street, London SE1 9LS
☎0171 261 6410   Fax 0171 261 7634
Owner *IPC Magazines Ltd*
Acting Editor *Lee Kynaston*
Circulation 187,740

MONTHLY women's magazine aimed at 16–20-year-olds. A little different from the usual teen magazine mix: *19* are now aiming for a 50/50 balance between fashion/lifestyle aspects and newsier, meatier material, e.g. women in prison, boys, abortion, etc.. 40% of the magazine's feature material is commissioned, ordinarily from established freelancers. 'But we're always keen to see bold, original, vigorous writing from people just starting out.'
Features Approach in writing with ideas.

North East Times
Tattler House, Beech Avenue, Fawdon, Newcastle upon Tyne NE3 4LA
☎0191 284 4495   Fax 0191 285 9606
Owner *Chris Robinson (Publishing) Ltd*
Editor *Chris Robinson*
Circulation 10,000

MONTHLY county magazine incorporating *Newcastle Life*. No unsolicited mss. Approach with ideas in writing. Not interested in any material that is not applicable to ABC1 readers.

The North
See **Poetry, Little Magazines**

Nursing Times
Porters South, Crinan Street, London N1 9XW
☎0171 843 4600   Fax 0171 843 4633
Owner *Macmillan Magazines Ltd*
Editor *Jane Salvage*
Circulation 80,670

A large proportion of *Nursing Times*' feature content is from unsolicited contributions sent on spec. Pieces on all aspects of nursing and health care, both practical and theoretical, written in a lively and contemporary way, are welcome. Commissions also.
Payment varies/NUJ rates apply to commissioned material from union members only.

Office Secretary
Brookmead House, Thorney Leys Business Park, Witney, Oxfordshire OX8 7GE
☎01993 775545
Owner *Trade Media Ltd*
Editor *Danusia Hutson*
Circulation 60,000

FOUNDED 1986. QUARTERLY. Features articles of interest to secretaries and personal assistants aged 25–60. No unsolicited mss.
Features Informative pieces on current affairs, health, food, fashion, hotel, travel, motoring, office and employment-related topics. Length 1000 words.
Payment by negotiation.

OK! Weekly
The Northern & Shell Tower, City Harbour, London E14 9GL
☎0171 308 5391   Fax 0171 301 5082
Owner *Richard Desmond*
Editor *Sharon Ring*
Circulation 120,978

FOUNDED 1996. WEEKLY celebrity-based magazine. Welcomes interviews and pictures on well known personalities, and ideas for general features. Approach by phone or fax in the first instance.

The Oldie
45–46 Poland Street, London W1V 4AU
☎0171 734 2225   Fax 0171 734 2226
Owner *Oldie Publications Ltd*
Editor *Richard Ingrams*
Circulation 45,000

FOUNDED 1992. MONTHLY general interest magazine with a strong humorous slant for the older person. Synopses and ideas welcome; approach in writing in the first instance.

OLS (Open Learning Systems) News
11 Malford Grove, Gilwern, Abergavenny, Gwent NP7 0RN
☎01873 830872   Fax 01873 830872
Owner *David P. Bosworth*
Editor *David P. Bosworth*
Circulation 800

FOUNDED 1980. QUARTERLY dealing with the application of open, flexible, distance learning and supported self-study at all educational/training levels. Interested in open-access learning and the application of educational technology to learning situations. Case studies particularly welcome. Not interested in theory of education alone, the emphasis is strictly on applied policies and trends.

Features Learning programmes (how they are organised); student/learner-eye views of educational and training programmes with an open-access approach. Approach the editor by phone or in writing.

No payment for 'news' items. Focus items will negotiate.

On the Ball

Moondance Publications, The Design Works, William Street, Gateshead, Tyne and Wear NE10 0JP

☎0191 420 8383 Fax 0191 420 4950

Owner *Moondance Publications Ltd*
Editor *Joanne Smith*
Circulation 30,000

FOUNDED 1996. MONTHLY. Sole magazine for women footballers. Contributions welcome.

Features *Joanne Smith* International reports, player and team profiles, diet, health and fitness, tactics, training advice, fund-raising, play improvement. 1500 words maximum.

News *Wilf Frith* Match reports, team news, transfers, injuries, results and fixtures. 600 words maximum.

Payment negotiable.

Opera

1A Mountgrove Road, London N5 2LU

☎0171 359 1037 Fax 0171 354 2700

Owner *Opera Magazine Ltd*
Editor *Rodney Milnes*
Circulation 11,500

FOUNDED 1950. MONTHLY review of the current opera scene. Almost all articles are commissioned and unsolicited mss are not welcome. All approaches should be made in writing.

Opera Now

241 Shaftesbury Avenue, London WC2H 8EH

☎0171 333 1740 Fax 0171 333 1769

Publisher *Rhinegold Publishing Ltd*
Editor-in-Chief *Graeme Kay*
Assistant Editor *Antonia Carling*

FOUNDED 1989. BI-MONTHLY. News, features and reviews for those interested in opera. No unsolicited mss. All work is commissioned. Approach with ideas in writing.

Options

King's Reach Tower, Stamford Street, London SE1 9LS

☎0171 261 5000 Fax 0171 261 7344

Owner *IPC Magazines Ltd*

Editor *Maureen Rice*
Circulation 146,692

'Invest in yourself' is the motto of this women's magazine with an emphasis on practical and self-help articles. Almost all material is written by a regular team of freelancers, but new writers are encouraged. *Payment* about £250 per 1000 words.

Orbis

See under **Poetry, Little Magazines**

Parents

Victory House, Leicester Place, London WC2H 7BP

☎0171 437 9011 Fax 0171 434 0656

Owner *EMAP Elan Publications*
Acting Editor *Liz Bestic*
Circulation 46,628

FOUNDED 1976. MONTHLY. Features commissioned from outside contributors. No unsolicited mss. Approach with ideas in the first instance. Age span: from pregnancy to four years.

Paris Transcontinental

Institut des Pays Anglophones, Sorbonne Nouvelle, 5 rue de l'Ecole de Médecine, Paris, France 75006

☎00 33 1 69018635

Owner *Claire Larrière*
Editor-in-chief *Claire Larrière*
Editors *Devorah Goldberg, Albert Russo*
Circulation 550

FOUNDED 1990. BI-ANNUAL. French magazine which publishes original short stories in English from around the world. No poetry, non-fiction or artwork. All themes. A good style, originality and strength. The magazine purports to be a forum for writers of excellent stories whose link is the English language and the short story. Length 2500-4500 words. Original short stories only. No translations: stories must be written in English. Stories should be submitted along with a few lines about yourself and your work (about 100 words only) and must be accompanied by International Reply Coupons

Payment two copies of the magazine.

PC Week

32–34 Broadwick Street, London W1A 2HG

☎0171 316 9000 Fax 0171 316 9355

Owner *VNU Business Publications*
Editor *Simon Hill*
Circulation 50,000

FOUNDED 1986. WEEKLY news, analysis and opinion on the corporate desktop market.

Welcomes reviews of PC software products; brief synopsis in the first instance. Approach by e-mail, fax or in writing.

Features *Cliff Saran* Most articles are commissioned. Maximum 2000 words.

News *Tracey Snell* Maximum 800 words.

Pembrokeshire Life

Merlins Bridge, Haverfordwest, Pembrokeshire SA61 1XF
☎01437 763133 (ext. 223) Fax 01437 760482

Owner *Southern Newspapers*
Editor *David Fielding*

FOUNDED 1991. MONTHLY county magazine with articles on local history, issues, characters, off-beat stories with good colour or b&w photographs. No country diaries, short stories, poems. Most articles are commissioned from known freelancers but 'always prepared to consider ideas from new writers'. No mss. Send cuttings of previous work (published or not) and synopsis to the editor.

The People's Friend

80 Kingsway East, Dundee DD4 8SL
☎01382 462276/223131   Fax 01382 452491

Owner *D. C. Thomson & Co. Ltd*
Editor *Sinclair Matheson*
Circulation 462,077

The *Friend* is basically a fiction magazine, with two serials and several short stories each week. FOUNDED in 1869, it has always prided itself on providing 'a good read for all the family'. All stories should be about ordinary, identifiable characters with the kind of problems the average reader can understand and sympathise with. 'We look for the romantic and emotional developments of characters, rather than an over-complicated or contrived plot. We regularly use period serials and, occasionally, mystery/adventure.'

Short Stories Can vary in length from 1000 words or less to as many as 4000.

Serials Long-run serials of 10–15 instalments or more preferred. Occasionally shorter.

Articles Short fillers welcome.

Payment on acceptance.

Period Living & Traditional Homes

Lisa House, 52–55 Carnaby Street, London W1V 3PF
☎0171 287 5377   Fax 0171 287 4180

Owner *EMAP Elan*
Editor *Clare Weatherall*
Circulation 84,386

FOUNDED 1992. Formed from the merger of *Period Living* and *Traditional Homes*. Covers interior decoration in a period style, period house profiles, traditional crafts, renovation of period properties, antiques and profiles of collectors.

Features *Clare Weatherall*
Payment varies according to length/type of article.

Personal

See under **National Newspapers (Sunday Mirror)**

Personal Finance

4 Tabernacle Street, London EC2A 4LU
☎0171 638 1916   Fax 0171 638 3128

Owner *Charterhouse Communications Plc*
Editor *John Givens*
Circulation 50,000

ESTABLISHED 1994. MONTHLY finance magazine.

Features All issues relating to personal finance, particularly investment, insurance, banking, mortgages, savings, borrowing, health care and pensions. No corporate articles or personnel issues. Telephone the editor with ideas in the first instance. No unsolicited mss. Maximum 1500–2000 words. *Payment* £150–£200.

News Most items written in-house. However some pieces may be considered. Maximum 300 words. *Payment* negotiable.

The Philosopher

4 Wellington Road, Ilkley, West Yorkshire LS29 8HR

Owner *The Philosophical Society*
Editor *Martin Cohen*

FOUNDED 1913. BI-ANNUAL journal of the Philosophical Society of Great Britain. Analytical philosophy in the Anglo-American tradition. Wide range of interests, but leaning towards articles that present philosophical investigation which is relevant to the individual and to society in our modern era. Accessible to the non-specialist. Will consider articles and book reviews. No 'new age' philosophy, pseudo-science, amateur essays on 'philosophy of life'. Notes for Contributors available; send s.a.e.. As well as short philosophical papers, will accept:

News about lectures, conventions, philosophy groups. Ethical issues in the news. Maximum 1000 words.

Reviews of philosophy books (maximum 600 words); discussion articles of individual philosophers and their published works (maximum 2000 words)

Payment free copies.

Picture Postcard Monthly

15 Debdale Lane, Keyworth, Nottingham
NG12 5HT
☎0115 9374079　　　　Fax 0115 9376197
Owners *Brian & Mary Lund*
Editor *Brian Lund*
Circulation 4300

FOUNDED 1978. MONTHLY. News, views, clubs,
diary of fairs, sales, auctions, and well-researched
postcard-related articles. Might be interested in
general articles supported by postcards. Unsolicited mss welcome. Approach by phone or in
writing with ideas.

Pilot

The Clock House, 28 Old Town, Clapham,
London SW4 0LB
☎0171 498 2506　　　　Fax 0171 498 6920
Owner/Editor *James Gilbert*
Circulation 30,669

FOUNDED 1968. MONTHLY magazine for private
plane pilots. No staff writers; the entire magazine
is written by freelancers – mostly regulars.
Unsolicited mss welcome but ideas in writing
preferred. Perusal of any issue of the magazine
will reveal the type of material bought. 700
words of 'Advice to would-be contributors' sent
on receipt of s.a.e. (mark envelope 'Advice').

　　Features *James Gilbert* Many articles are unsolicited personal experiences/travel accounts from
pilots of private planes; good photo coverage is
very important. Maximum 5000 words. *Payment*
£100–700 (first rights). Photos £26 each.

　　News *Mike Jerram* Contributions need to be as
short as possible. See *Pilot Notes* in the magazine.

The Pink Paper

72 Holloway Road, London N7 8NZ
☎0171 296 6210　　　　Fax 0171 296 0026
Owner *Chronos Group*
Editor *Paul Clements*
Circulation 55,000

FOUNDED 1987. WEEKLY. Only national newspaper for lesbians and gay men covering politics, social issues, health, the arts and all areas of
concern to lesbian/gay people. Unsolicited mss
welcome. Initial approach by phone with an
idea preferred. Interested in profiles, reviews,
in–depth features and short news pieces.

　　News Maximum 300 words.

　　Listings/Arts & Reviews *Tim Teeman*
Maximum 200 words/**Books** *Tim Teeman*
　　Payment by arrangement.

Planet: The Welsh Internationalist

See **Planet** under **Small Presses**

Plays and Players

Northway House, 1379 High Road, London
N20 9LP
☎0181 343 8515　　　　Fax 0181 446 1410
Owner *Mineco Designs*
Editor *Sandra Rennie*
Circulation 10,000

Theatre MONTHLY which publishes a mixture
of news, reviews, reports and features on all the
performing arts. Rarely uses unsolicited material
but writers of talent are taken up. Almost all
material is commissioned.

PN Review

See under **Poetry, Little Magazines**

Poetry Ireland Review

See under **Poetry, Little Magazines**

Poetry Review

See under **Poetry, Little Magazines**

Poetry Wales

See under **Poetry, Little Magazines**

The Polish Gazette (Gazeta)

PO Box 1945, Edinburgh EH4 1AB
☎0131 315 2002
Owner *Gazeta Ltd*
Editor *Maria Rayska*

FOUNDED 1995. QUARTERLY. The only English
language publication in the UK for the Polish
community, friends of Poland, and businesses
dealing with Poland. Approach in writing with
ideas for articles.

　　Features *Tony Keniston* Travel, business,
autobiography. 600 words maximum.

　　News *Maria Rayska* General, local and international news of interest to the Polish community in Britain: Poland, exhibitions, events, etc.
　　Payment by arrangement.

Pony

D.J. Murphy (Publishers) Ltd, Haslemere
House, Lower Street, Haslemere, Surrey
GU27 2PE
☎01428 651551　　　　Fax 01428 653888
Owner *D. J. Murphy (Publishers) Ltd*
Editor *Janet Rising*
Circulation 38,000

FOUNDED 1948. Lively MONTHLY aimed at
10–16-year-olds. News, instruction on riding,
stable management, veterinary care, interviews.
Approach in writing with an idea.

　　Features welcome. Maximum 900 words.

　　News Written in-house. Photographs and

illustrations (serious/cartoon) welcome.
Payment £65 per 1000 words.

Popular Crafts
Nexus House, Boundary Way, Hemel
Hempstead, Hertfordshire HP2 7ST
☎01442 66551   Fax 01442 66998
Owner *Nexus Special Interests*
Editor *Carolyn Schulz*
Circulation 32,000

FOUNDED 1980. MONTHLY. Covers crafts of all
kinds. Freelance contributions welcome – copy
needs to be lively and interesting. Approach in
writing with an outline of idea.
    Features Project-based under the following
headings: homecraft; needlecraft; popular craft;
kidscraft; news and columns. Any craft-related
material: projects to make, with full instructions/
patterns supplied; profiles of crafts people; news
of craft group activities or individual successes;
articles on collecting crafts; personal experiences
and anecdotes.
    Payment on publication.

PR Week
174 Hammersmith Road, London W6 7JP
☎0171 413 4520   Fax 0171 413 4509
Owner *Haymarket Business Publications Ltd*
Editor *Stephen Farish*
Circulation 20,000

FOUNDED 1984. WEEKLY. Contributions accepted from experienced journalists. Approach in
writing with an idea.
    Features *Kate Nicholas*
    News *Steve Bevan*
    Payment £185 per 1000 words.

Practical Boat Owner
Westover House, West Quay Road, Poole,
Dorset BH15 1JG
☎01202 680593   Fax 01202 674335
Owner *IPC Magazines*
Editor *Rodger Witt*
Circulation 55,462

FOUNDED 1967. MONTHLY magazine of practical information for cruising boat owners.
Receives about 1500 mss per year. Interested
in hard facts about gear, equipment, pilotage
from experienced yachtsmen.
    Features Technical articles about mainte-
nance, restoration, modifications to cruising
boats, power and sail up to 45ft, or reader
reports on gear and equipment. European
pilotage articles and cruising guides. Approach
in writing with synopsis in the first instance.
    Payment negotiable.

Practical Caravan
60 Waldegrave Road, Teddington, Middlesex
TW11 8LG
☎0181 943 5629   Fax 0181 943 5798
Owner *Haymarket Magazines Ltd*
Editor *Rob McCabe*
Deputy Editor *John Rawlings*
Circulation 47,037

FOUNDED 1967. MONTHLY. Contains caravan
reviews, travel features, investigations, products, park reviews. Unsolicited mss welcome
on travel relevant only to caravanning/touring
vans. No motorcaravan or static van stories.
Approach with ideas by phone.
    Features *John Rawlings* Must refer to cara-
vanning, towing. Written in friendly, chatty
manner. Features with pictures/transparencies
preferred (to include caravans where possible).
Maximum length 2000 words. *Payment* negotiable (usually £120 per 1000 words).

Practical Fishkeeping
Apex House, Oundle Road, Peterborough,
Cambridgeshire PE2 9NP
☎01733 898100   Fax 01733 898487
Owner *EMAP Apex Publications Ltd*
Managing Editor *Steve Windsor*
Circulation 30,012

MONTHLY. Practical articles on all aspects of fishkeeping. Unsolicited mss welcome. Approach in
writing with ideas. Quality photographs of fish
always welcome. No fiction or verse.

Practical Gardening
See **Garden Answers**

Practical Motorist
Frogham, Fordingbridge, Hampshire
SP6 2HW
☎01425 654255   Fax 01425 653458
Owner *Crownwheel Publishing Co. Ltd*
Editor *Ewan Scott*
Circulation 26,000

FOUNDED 1934. MONTHLY. Practical aspects of
maintaining the modern car. Unsolicited articles with photos, drawings, artwork, etc. welcome but prospective contributors should
make initial telephone contact.
    Payment by arrangement.

Practical Parenting
King's Reach Tower, Stamford Street,
London SE1 9LS
☎0171 261 5058   Fax 0171 261 6542
Owner *IPC Magazines Ltd*

Editor-in-Chief *Jayne Marsden*
Circulation 81,849

FOUNDED 1987. MONTHLY. Practical advice on pregnancy, birth, babycare and childcare up to five years. Submit ideas in writing with synopsis or send mss on spec. Interested in feature articles of up to 3000 words in length, and in readers' experiences/personal viewpoint pieces of between 750–1000 words. Humorous articles on some aspect of parenthood may also stand a chance. All material must be written for the magazine's specifically targeted audience and in-house style.

Payment negotiable.

Practical Photography

Apex House, Oundle Road, Peterborough, Cambridgeshire PE2 9NP
☎01733 898100   Fax 01733 894472

Owner *EMAP Apex Publications Ltd*
Editor *Martyn Moore*
Circulation 80,966

MONTHLY. All types of photography, particularly technique-orientated pictures. No unsolicited mss. Preliminary approach may be made by telephone. Always interested in new ideas.

Features Anything relevant to the world of photography, but not 'the sort of feature produced by staff writers'. Features on technology and humour are two areas worth exploring. Bear in mind that there is a three-month lead-in time. Maximum 2000 words.

News Only 'hot' news applicable to a monthly magazine. Maximum 400 words. *Payment* varies.

Practical Wireless

Arrowsmith Court, Station Approach, Broadstone, Dorset BH18 8PW
☎01202 659910   Fax 01202 659950

Owner *P.W. Publishing*
Editor *Rob Mannion*
Circulation 27,000

FOUNDED 1932. MONTHLY. News and features relating to amateur radio, radio construction and radio communications. Unsolicited mss welcome. Guidelines available (send s.a.e.). Approach by phone with ideas in the first instance. Copy should be supported where possible by artwork, either illustrations, diagrams or photographs.

Payment £54–70 per page.

Practical Woodworking

Boundary Way, Hemel Hempstead, Hertfordshire HP2 7ST
☎01442 66551   Fax 01442 66636

Owner *Nexus Special Interests Ltd*
Editor *Peter Roper*
Circulation 41,000

FOUNDED 1965. MONTHLY. Contains articles relating to woodworking – projects, techniques, new products, tips, letters etc. Unsolicited mss welcome. No fiction. Approach with ideas in writing or by phone.

News Anything related to woodworking. *Payment* £60 per published page.

Features Projects, techniques etc. *Payment* £60 per published page.

Prediction

Link House, Dingwall Avenue, Croydon, Surrey CR9 2TA
☎0181 686 2599   Fax 0181 781 1159

Owner *Link House Magazines Ltd*
Editor *Jo Logan*
Circulation 35,000

FOUNDED 1936. MONTHLY. Covering astrology and occult-related topics. Unsolicited material in these areas welcome (about 200–300 mss received every year). Writers' guidelines available on request.

Astrology Pieces, ranging from 800–2000 words, should be practical and of general interest. Charts and astro data should accompany them, especially if profiles.

Features *Jo Logan* Articles on mysteries of the earth, alternative medicine, psychical/occult experiences and phenomena are considered. 800–2000 words. *Payment* £25–100 and over.

News & Views Items of interest to readership welcome. Maximum 300 words. *No payment.*

Press Gazette

33–39 Bowling Green Lane, London EC1R 0DA
☎0171 505 8000   Fax 0171 505 8220

Owner *EMAP Media*
Editor *Roy Farndon*
Circulation 9,500

WEEKLY magazine for all journalists – in regional and national newspapers, magazines, broadcasting, and on-line – containing news, features and analysis of all areas of journalism, print and broadcasting. Unsolicited mss welcome; interested in profiles of magazines, broadcasting companies and news agencies, personality profiles, technical and current affairs relating to the world of journalism. Approach with ideas by phone, fax or in writing.

Prima
Portland House, Stag Place, London SW1E 5AU
☎0171 245 8700   Fax 0171 630 5509
Owner *Gruner & Jahr (UK)*
Editor *Lindsay Nicholson*
Circulation 565,051
FOUNDED 1986. MONTHLY women's magazine.
Features Coordinator *June Walton* Mostly practical and written by specialists, or commissioned from known freelancers. Unsolicited mss not welcome.

Private Eye
6 Carlisle Street, London W1V 5RG
☎0171 437 4017   Fax 0171 437 0705
Owner *Pressdram*
Editor *Ian Hislop*
Circulation 190,000
FOUNDED 1961. FORTNIGHTLY satirical and investigative magazine. Prospective contributors are best advised to approach the editor in writing. News stories and feature ideas are always welcome, as are cartoons. All jokes written in-house.
Payment in all cases is 'not great', and length of piece varies as appropriate.

Prospect
4 Bedford Square, London WC1B 3RA
☎0171 255 1281   Fax 0171 255 1279
Owner *Prospect Publishing Limited*
Editor *David Goodhart*
Circulation 20,000
FOUNDED1995. MONTHLY. Essays, reviews and research on current/international affairs and cultural issues. No news features. No unsolicited mss. Approach in writing with ideas in the first instance.

Psychic News
Clock Cottage, Stansted Hall, Stansted, Essex CM24 8UD
☎01279 817050   Fax 01279 817051
Owner *Psychic Press 1995 Ltd*
Editor *Lyn Guest de Swarte*
Circulation 15,000
FOUNDED 1932. *Psychic News* is the world's only WEEKLY spiritualist newspaper. It covers subjects such as psychic research, hauntings,

ghosts, poltergeists, spiritual healing, survival after death, and paranormal gifts. Unsolicited material considered.

Publishing News
43 Museum Street, London WC1A 1LY
☎0171 404 0304   Fax 0171 242 0762
Editor *Fred Newman*
WEEKLY newspaper of the book trade. Hardback and paperback reviews and extensive listings of new paperbacks and hardbacks. Interviews with leading personalities in the trade, authors, agents and features on specialist book areas.

Punch
Trevor House, 100 Brompton Road, London SW3 1ER
☎0171 225 6846   Fax 0171 225 6845
Owner *Liberty Publishing*
Editor *Paul Spike*
FOUNDED in 1841, this WEEKLY humorous magazine was RELAUNCHED in 1996. Ideas are welcome; approach in writing in the first instance.
Payment negotiable.

Q
Mappin House, 4 Winsley Street, London W1N 7AR
☎0171 436 1515   Fax 0171 323 0680
Owner *EMAP Metro Publications*
Editor *Andrew Collins*
Circulation 212,607
FOUNDED 1986. MONTHLY. Glossy aimed at educated rock music enthusiasts of all ages. Few opportunities for freelance writers. Unsolicited mss are strongly discouraged. Prospective contributors should approach in writing only.

Quartos Magazine
See **The New Writer**

QWF (Quality Women's Fiction)
80 Main Street, Linton, Nr Swadlincote, Derbyshire DE12 6QA
☎01283 761042
Editor *Jo Good*
BI-MONTHLY small press magazine FOUNDED in 1994 as a show-case for the best in women's short story writing – original and thought-provoking, with forthright female characters. Features two regular article slots: *Against All Odds* and *A Guided Tour Around the New Man*.

Will only consider stories that are previously unpublished and of less than 3000 words; articles must be less than 500 words. Include covering letter and brief biography with mss. Also runs a script appraisal service and regular short story competitions. For further details, contact the editor at the above address (enclose s.a.e.).

Radio Times
Woodlands, 80 Wood Lane, London W12 0TT
☎0181 576 3066　　　Fax 0181 576 3160
Owner *BBC Worldwide Publishing*
Editor *Sue Robinson*
Deputy Editor *Liz Vercoe*
Circulation 1,406,417

WEEKLY. UK's leading broadcast listings magazine. The majority of material is provided by freelance and retained writers, but the topicality of the pieces means close consultation with editors is essential. Very unlikely to use unsolicited material. Detailed BBC, ITV, Channel 4, Channel 5 and satellite television and radio listings are accompanied by feature material relevant to the week's output. *Payment* by arrangement.

RAIL
Apex House, Oundle Road, Peterborough, Cambridgeshire PE2 9NP
☎01733 898100 ext. 6949　Fax 01733 894472
Owner *EMAP Apex Publications*
Managing Editor *Nigel Harris*
Circulation 31,892

FOUNDED 1981. FORTNIGHTLY magazine dedicated to modern railway. News and features, and topical newsworthy events. Unsolicited mss welcome. Approach by phone with ideas. Not interested in personal journey reminiscences. No fiction.

Features By arrangement with the editor. Traction-related subjects of interest. Maximum 2000 words. *Payment* varies/negotiable.

News Any news item welcomed. Maximum 500 words. *Payment* varies (up to £100 per 1000 words).

The Railway Magazine
King's Reach Tower, Stamford Street, London SE1 9LS
☎0171 261 5533/5821　　Fax 0171 261 5269
Owner *IPC Magazines Ltd*
Editor *Nick Pigott*
Circulation 32,564

FOUNDED 1897. MONTHLY. Articles, photos and short news stories of a topical nature, covering modern railways, steam preservation and railway history, welcome. Maximum 2000

words, with sketch maps of routes, etc., where appropriate. Unsolicited mss welcome. Maximum 2000 words.
Payment negotiable.

Rambling Today
1–5 Wandsworth Road, London SW8 2XX
☎0171 582 6878　　　Fax 0171 587 3799
Owner *Ramblers' Association*
Editor *Annabelle Birchall*
Circulation 90,000

QUARTERLY. Official magazine of the Ramblers' Association, available to members only. Unsolicited mss welcome. S.a.e. required for return.

Features Freelance features are invited on any aspect of walking in Britain and abroad. Length 900–1300 words, preferably with good photographs. No general travel articles.

Reader's Digest
Berkeley Square House, Berkeley Square, London W1X 6AB
☎0171 629 8144　　　Fax 0171 408 0748
Owner *Reader's Digest Association Ltd*
Editor-in-Chief *Russell Twisk*
Circulation 1.5 million

In theory, a good market for general interest features of around 2500 words. However, 'a tiny proportion' comes from freelance writers, all of which are specially commissioned. Toughening up its image with a move into investigative journalism. Opportunities exist for short humorous contributions to regular features – 'Life's Like That', 'Humour in Uniform'. Issues a helpful booklet called 'Writing for Reader's Digest' available by post at £2.50. *Payment* up to £200.

Record Collector
43–45 St Mary's Road, Ealing, London W5 5RQ
☎0181 579 1082　　　Fax 0181 566 2024
Owner *Johnny Dean*
Editor *Peter Doggett*

FOUNDED 1979. MONTHLY. Detailed, well-researched articles welcome on any aspect of record collecting or any collectable artist in the field of popular music (1950s–1990s), with complete discographies where appropriate. Unsolicited mss welcome. Approach with ideas by phone. *Payment* negotiable.

Record Mirror
See **Music Week**

Red Wing

151 Mill Road, Hamilton, Lanarkshire
ML3 8JA
☎01698 457431

Editors *Paul Nicoll, Stephen Mungall*

FOUNDED 1995. QUARTERLY independent,
radical left-wing magazine with short stories,
poetry, philosophy, news review, art, political
and cultural analysis. Unsolicited mss 'very welcome'; approach in writing in the first instance.
  Features 1500 words maximum.
  News 1000 words maximum.
  Fiction 3000 words maximum.
  Payment none.

Reincarnation International

Phoenix Research Publications, PO Box
10839, London SW13 0ZG
☎0181 241 2184   Fax 0181 241 2184

Publisher *Reincarnation International Ltd*
Editor *Roy Stemman*
Circulation 3000

QUARTERLY. The only publication in the
world dealing with all aspects of reincarnation
– from people who claim to recall their past
lives spontaneously to the many thousands who
have done so through hypnotic regressions. It
also examines reincarnation in the light of various religious beliefs and the latest discoveries
about the mind and how it works.

Report

ATL, 7 Northumberland Street, London
WC2N 5DA
☎0171 930 6441   Fax 0171 930 1359

Owner *Association of Teachers and Lecturers*
Editor *Nick Tester*
Circulation 150,000

FOUNDED 1978. EIGHT ISSUES YEARLY during
academic terms. Contributions welcome. All
submissions should go directly to the editor.
Articles should be no more than 800 words and
must be of practical interest to the classroom
teacher and F. E. lecturers.

Resident Abroad

Greystoke Place, Fetter Lane, London
EC4A 1ND
☎0171 405 6969   Fax 0171 831 2181

Owner *Financial Times*
Editor *Cristina Nordenstahl*
Circulation 17,919

FOUNDED 1979. MONTHLY magazine aimed at
British expatriates. Unsolicited mss considered,
if suitable to the interests of the readership.

Features Up to 1200 words on finance,
property, employment opportunities and other
topics likely to appeal to readership, such as living conditions in countries with substantial
British expatriate populations. No 'lighthearted
looks' at anything.
  Fiction Rarely published, but exceptional,
relevant stories (no longer than 1000 words)
might be considered.
  Payment negotiable.

Riding

2 West Street, Bourne, Lincolnshire
PE10 9NE
☎01778 393747   Fax 01778 425453

Owner *Equestrian Publications Ltd*
Editor *Steve Moore*

Aimed at an adult, horse-owning audience.
Most of the writers on *Riding* are freelance with
the emphasis on non-practical and lifestyle-
orientated features. New and authoritative writers always welcome. *Payment* negotiable.

Right Now!

BCM Right, London WC1N 3XX
☎0181 692 7099   Fax 0181 692 7099

Owner *Right Now!*
Editor *Derek Turner*
Circulation 1500

FOUNDED 1993. QUARTERLY right-wing
conservative commentary. Welcomes well-
documented disputations, news stories and
elegiac features about British heritage ('the
more politically incorrect, the better!').
Generally, no fiction and poems. Approach in
writing in the first instance. *No payment*.

Rugby News & Monthly

7–9 Rathbone Street, London W1P 1AF
☎0171 636 6651   Fax 0171 255 2352

Owner *Independent Magazines Ltd*
Editor *Graeme Gillespie*
Circulation 25,000

FOUNDED 1987 and incorporated *Rugby Monthly*
magazine in July 1994. Contains news, views
and features on the UK and the world rugby
scene, with special emphasis on clubs, schools,
fitness and coaching. Welcomes unsolicited
material.

Rugby World

23rd Floor, King's Reach Tower, Stamford
Street, London SE1 9LS
☎0171 261 6830   Fax 0171 261 5419

Owner *IPC Magazines Ltd*

Editor *Alison Kervin*
Circulation 38,799

MONTHLY. Features of special rugby interest only. Unsolicited contributions welcome but s.a.e. essential for return of material. Prior approach by phone or in writing preferred.

Runner's World
7–10 Chandos Street, London W1M 0AD
☎0171 291 6000   Fax 0171 291 6080
Owner *Rodale Press*
Editor *Steven Seaton*
Circulation 44,604

FOUNDED 1979. MONTHLY magazine giving practical advice on all areas of distance running including product and training, travel features, up-to-date athletics profiles and news. Personal running-related articles, famous people who run or off-beat travel articles are welcome. No elite athletics or training articles. Approach in writing in the first instance.

Saga Magazine
The Saga Building, Middelburg Square, Folkestone, Kent CT20 1AZ
☎01303 711523   Fax 01303 712699
Owner *Saga Publishing Ltd*
Editor *Paul Bach*
Circulation 738,675

FOUNDED 1984. MONTHLY. 'Saga Magazine sets out to celebrate the role of older people in society. It reflects their achievements, promotes their skills, protects their interests, and campaigns on their behalf. A warm personal approach, addressing the readership in an up-beat and positive manner, required.' It has a hard core of celebrity commentators/writers (Clement Freud, Michael Parkinson, Keith Waterhouse) as regular contributors. Articles mostly commissioned or written in-house but genuine exclusives always welcome. Length 1000–1200 words (max.1600).

Sailing Today
30 Monmouth Street, Bath BA1 2BW
☎01225 442244   Fax 01225 732248
Owner *Future Publishing*
Editor *Philip Dunn*

FOUNDED 1997. MONTHLY magazine featuring family cruising under sail with an emphasis on enjoyment and practical aspects. Most articles are commissioned but will consider cruise stories with photos. Approach by telephone or in writing in the first instance.
    Features/News *Colin Jarman. Payment* by agreement.

Sailplane and Gliding
281 Queen Edith's Way, Cambridge CB1 4NH
☎01223 247725   Fax 01223 413793
Owner *British Gliding Association*
Editor *Gillian Bryce-Smith*
Circulation 8400

FOUNDED 1930. BI-MONTHLY for gliding enthusiasts. A specialist magazine with very few opportunities for freelancers. *No payment.*

Sainsbury's The Magazine
20 Upper Ground, London SE1 9PD
☎0171 633 0266   Fax 0171 401 9423
Owner *New Crane Publishing*
Editor *Michael Wynn Jones*
Food Editor *Delia Smith*
Circulation 416,880

FOUNDED 1993. MONTHLY featuring a main core of food and cookery, health, beauty, fashion, home, gardening and news. No unsolicited mss. Approach in writing with ideas only in the first instance.

The Salisbury Review
33 Canonbury Park South, London N1 2JW
☎0171 226 7791   Fax 0171 354 0383
Owner *Claridge Press*
Editor *Roger Scruton*
Managing Editor *Merrie Cave*
Circulation 1700

FOUNDED 1982. QUARTERLY magazine of conservative thought. Editorials and features from a right-wing viewpoint. Unsolicited material welcome.
    Features Maximum 4000 words.
    Reviews Maximum 1000 words.
    No payment.

Scotland on Sunday Magazine
See under **National Newspapers (Scotland on Sunday)**

The Scots Magazine
2 Albert Square, Dundee DD1 9QJ
☎01382 223131   Fax 01382 322214
Owner *D. C. Thomson & Co. Ltd*
Editor *John Methven*
Circulation 70,000

FOUNDED 1739. MONTHLY. Covers a wide field of Scottish interests ranging from personalities to wildlife, climbing, reminiscence, history and folklore. Outside contributions welcome; 'staff delighted to discuss in advance by letter'.

Scottish Accent

1 Watergate, Perth PH1 5TE
☎01250 884288   Fax 01250 884288
Owner *Accent Publishing Ltd*
Editor *Maggie Campbell*

FOUNDED 1996. BI-MONTHLY. General women's interest features with a Scottish perspective. Unsolicited mss welcome but only material which is based on a study of the magazine's style and content.

Features *Maggie Campbell* Fashion, beauty, travel, cookery and family matters which relate to Scotland. Max. 1800 words. *Payment* NUJ rates.

The Scottish Farmer

The Plaza Tower, The Plaza, East Kilbride G74 1LW
☎01355 246444   Fax 01355 263013
Owner *Caledonian Magazines Ltd*
Editor *Alasdair Fletcher*
Circulation 23,086

FOUNDED 1893. WEEKLY. Farmer's magazine covering most aspects of Scottish agriculture. Unsolicited mss welcome. Approach with ideas in writing.

Features *Alasdair Fletcher* Technical articles on agriculture or farming units. 1000–2000 words.

News *John Duckworth* Factual news about farming developments, political, personal and technological. Maximum 800 words.

Weekend Family Pages Rural and craft topics.

Payment £10 per 100 words; £25 per photo.

Scottish Field

Special Publications, Royston House, Caroline Park, Edinburgh EH5 1QJ
☎0131 551 2942   Fax 0131 551 2938
Owner *Oban Times*
Editor *Archie Mackenzie*

FOUNDED 1903. MONTHLY. Scotland's quality lifestyle magazine. Unsolicited mss welcome but writers should study the magazine first.

Features Articles of general interest on Scotland and Scots abroad with good photographs or, preferably, colour slides. Approx 1000 words.

Payment negotiable.

Scottish Golfer

c/o The Scottish Golf Union, Drumoig, Leuchars, St Andrews, Fife KY16 0BE
Owner *Scottish Golf Union*

Editor *Martin Dempster*
Circulation 30,000

FOUNDED MID-1980s. MONTHLY. Features and results, in particular the men's events. No unsolicited mss. Approach in writing with ideas.

Scottish Home & Country

42A Heriot Row, Edinburgh EH3 6ES
☎0131 225 1934   Fax 0131 225 8129
Owner *Scottish Women's Rural Institutes*
Editor *Stella Roberts*
Circulation 14,000

FOUNDED 1924. MONTHLY. Scottish or rural-related issues. Unsolicited mss welcome but reading time may be from 2–3 months. Commissions are rare and tend to go to established contributors only.

Scottish Rugby Magazine

11 Dock Place, Leith, Edinburgh EH6 6LU
☎0131 554 0540   Fax 0131 554 0482
Owner *Hiscan Ltd*
Editor *Kevin Ferrie*
Circulation 19,200

FOUNDED 1990. MONTHLY. Features, club profiles, etc. Approach in writing with ideas.

Scouting Magazine

Baden Powell House, Queen's Gate, London SW7 5JS
☎0171 584 7030   Fax 0171 590 5124
Owner *The Scout Association*
Editor *David Easton*
Circulation 30,000

MONTHLY magazine for adults connected to or interested in the Scouting movement. Interested in Scouting-related features only. No fiction. *Payment* by negotiation.

Screen

The John Logie Baird Centre, University of Glasgow, Glasgow G12 8QQ
☎0141 330 5035   Fax 0141 330 8010
Owner *The John Logie Baird Centre*
Editors *Annette Kuhn, John Caughie, Simon Frith, Norman King, Karen Lury, Jackie Stacey*
Editorial Assistant *Caroline Beven*
Circulation 1500

QUARTERLY refereed academic journal of film and television studies for a readership ranging from undergraduates to media professionals. There are no specific qualifications for acceptance of articles. Straightforward film reviews are not normally published. Check the magazine's style and market in the first instance.

Screen International

33–39 Bowling Green Lane, London
EC1R 0DA
☎0171 505 8080   Fax 0171 505 8117

Owner *EMAP Business Communications*
Editor *Boyd Farrow*

International trade paper of the film, video and television industries. Expert freelance writers are occasionally used in all areas. No unsolicited mss. Approach with ideas in writing.

   Features *Mike Goodridge*
   Payment negotiable on NUJ basis.

Sea Breezes

Units 28–30, Spring Valley Industrial Estate, Braddan, Isle of Man IM2 2QS
☎01624 626018   Fax 01624 661655

Owner *Print Centres*
Editor *Captain A. C. Douglas*
Circulation 14,500

FOUNDED 1919. MONTHLY. Covers virtually everything relating to ships and seamen. Unsolicited mss welcome; they should be thoroughly researched and accompanied by relevant photographs. No fiction, poetry, or anything which 'smacks of the romance of the sea'.

   Features Factual tales of ships, seamen and the sea, Royal or Merchant Navy, sail or power, nautical history, shipping company histories, epic voyages, etc. Length 1000–4000 words. 'The most readily acceptable work will be that which shows it is clearly the result of first-hand experience or the product of extensive and accurate research.'
   Payment £7 per page (about 500 words).

Sex

47 Allerton Walk, Manchester M13 9TG
☎0161 272 7271   Fax 0161 272 7271

Owner *Maverick Publishing*
Editor *Chancery Stone*

MONTHLY. Seeks 'erudite and controversial features on sex, particularly anything that challenges current accepted thinking'. Magazine has a firm anti-censorship stance. Fiction required. 'Positively no "I confess ..." or men's mag format erotica. Aimed at both sexes and all sexualities, so balance please.' Also seeking art and photographic items. Mss and ideas welcome. Send s.a.e. for gudelines quoting features, fiction or visual arts.

   Art/Production *Max Scratchman*
   Payment negotiable on NUJ basis.

She Magazine

National Magazine House, 72 Broadwick Street, London W1V 2BP
☎0171 439 5000   Fax 0171 439 5350

Owner *National Magazine Co. Ltd*
Editor *Alison Pylkkanen*
Circulation 221,481

Glossy MONTHLY for the thirtysomething woman, addressing her needs as an individual, a partner and a parent. Talks to its readers in an intelligent, humorous and sympathetic way. Features should be about 1500 words long. Approach with ideas in writing. No unsolicited material. *Payment* NUJ rates.

Shoot Magazine

King's Reach Tower, Stamford Street, London SE1 9LS
☎0171 261 6287   Fax 0171 261 6019

Owner *IPC Magazines Ltd*
Editor *David C. Smith*
Circulation 119,205

FOUNDED 1969. WEEKLY football magazine. No unsolicited mss. Present ideas for news, features or colour photo-features to the editor by telephone.

   Features Hard-hitting, topical and off-beat. Length 400–1000 words.
   News Items welcome, especially exclusive gossip and transfer speculation. Maximum 150 words.
   Payment NUJ rates (negotiable for exclusive material).

Shooting and Conservation (BASC)

Marford Mill, Rossett, Wrexham, Clwyd LL12 0HL
☎01244 570881   Fax 01244 571678

Owner *The British Association for Shooting and Conservation (BASC)*
Editor *Robin Peel*
Circulation 111,000

QUARTERLY. Unsolicited mss welcome.
   Features/Fiction Good articles and stories on shooting, conservation and related areas are always sought. Maximum 1500 words.
   Payment negotiable.

Shooting Times & Country Magazine

King's Reach Tower, Stamford Street, London SE1 9LS
☎0171 261 6180   Fax 0171 261 7179

Owner *IPC Magazines*
Editor *John Gregson*

Circulation 29,266

FOUNDED 1882. WEEKLY. Covers shooting, fishing and related countryside topics. Unsolicited mss considered. Maximum 1100 words. *Payment* negotiable.

Shropshire Magazine

77 Wyle Cop, Shrewsbury, Shropshire SY1 1UT
☎01743 362175

Owner *Leopard Press Ltd*
Editor *Pam Green*

FOUNDED 1950. MONTHLY. Unsolicited mss welcome; ideas in writing preferred.

Features Personalities, topical items, historical (e.g. family) of Shropshire; also general interest: homes, weddings, antiques, etc. Maximum 1000 words.

Payment negotiable 'but modest'.

Sight & Sound

British Film Institute, 21 Stephen Street, London W1P 1PL
☎0171 255 1444   Fax 0171 436 2327

Owner *British Film Institute*
Editor *Philip Dodd*

FOUNDED 1932. MONTHLY. Topical and critical articles on international cinema, with regular columns from the USA and Europe. Length 1000–5000 words. Relevant photographs appreciated. Also book, film and video release reviews. Unsolicited material welcome. Approach in writing with ideas. *Payment* by arrangement.

The Sign

See **Hymns Ancient & Modern Ltd** under **UK Publishers**

Ski Survey

The White House, 57–63 Church Road, Wimbledon, London SW19 5DQ
☎0181 401 2000   Fax 0181 401 2001

Owner *Ski Club of Great Britain*
Editor *Gill Williams*
Circulation 19,675

FOUNDED 1903. FIVE ISSUES YEARLY. Features from established ski writers only.

The Skier and The Snowboarder Magazine

48 London Road, Sevenoaks, Kent TN13 1AP
☎01732 743644   Fax 01732 743647

Owner *Mountain Marketing Ltd*
Editor *Frank Baldwin*
Circulation 20,000

SEASONAL. From September to May. FIVE ISSUES YEARLY. Outside contributions welcome.

Features Various topics covered, including race reports, resort reports, fashion, equipment update, dry slope, school news, new products, health and safety. Crisp, tight, informative copy of 1000 words or less preferred.

News All aspects of skiing news covered.

Payment negotiable.

Slimming

Victory House, 14 Leicester Place, London WC2H 7BP
☎0171 437 9011   Fax 0171 434 0656

Owner *EMAP Elan Publications*
Editor *Christine Michael*
Circulation 150,140

FOUNDED 1969. TEN ISSUES YEARLY. Leading magazine about slimming, diet and health. Opportunities for freelance contributions on general health (diet-related); psychology related to health and fitness; celebrity interviews. Best to approach with an idea in writing.

Payment negotiable.

Smallholder

Hook House, Wimblington March, Cambridgeshire PE15 0QL
☎01354 741182   Fax 01354 741182

Owner *The Bailey Newspaper Group Dursley Glos.*
Editor *Liz Wright*
Circulation 18,000

FOUNDED 1982. MONTHLY. Outside contributions welcome. Send for sample magazine and schedule before submitting anything. Follow up with samples of work to the editor so that style can be assessed for suitability. No poetry or humorous but unfocused personal tales.

Features New writers always welcome, but must have high level of technical expertise – 'not textbook stuff'. Length 750–1500 words.

News All agricultural and rural news welcome. Length 200–500 words.

Payment negotiable ('but modest').

Smash Hits

Mappin House, Winsley Street, London W1N 7AR
☎0171 436 1515   Fax 0171 636 5792

Owner *EMAP Metro Publications*
Editor *Gavin Reeve*
Circulation 268,685

FOUNDED 1979. FORTNIGHTLY. Top of the mid-teen market. Unsolicited mss are not accepted, but prospective contributors may approach in writing with ideas.

Snooker Scene

Cavalier House, 202 Hagley Road, Edgbaston, Birmingham B16 9PQ
☎0121 454 2931 Fax 0121 452 1822
Owner *Everton's News Agency*
Editor *Clive Everton*
Circulation 16,000

FOUNDED 1971. MONTHLY. No unsolicited mss. Approach in writing with an idea.

Somerset Magazine

23 Market Street, Crewkerne, Somerset TA18 7JU
☎01460 78000 Fax 01460 76718
Owner *Smart Print Publications Ltd*
Editor *Roy Smart*
Circulation 6000

FOUNDED 1990. MONTHLY magazine with features on any subject of interest (historical, geographical, arts, crafts) to people living in Somerset. Length 1000–1500 words, preferably with illustrations. Unsolicited mss welcome but initial approach in writing preferred.
Payment negotiable.

The Spectator

56 Doughty Street, London WC1N 2LL
☎0171 405 1706 Fax 0171 242 0603
Owner *The Spectator (1828) Ltd*
Editor *Frank Johnson*
Circulation 56,313

FOUNDED 1828. WEEKLY political and literary magazine. Prospective contributors should write in the first instance to the relevant editor. Unsolicited mss welcome, but over twenty are received every week and few are used.
Features *Anne McElvoy*
Arts *Elizabeth Anderson*
Books *Mark Amory*
Payment nominal.

Sport Magazine

English Sports Council, 16 Upper Woburn Place, London WC1H 0QP
☎0171 273 1591 Fax 0171 383 0273
Owner *English Sports Council*
Editor *Louise Fyfe*
Circulation 15000

FOUNDED 1949. BI-MONTHLY. Covering sports development, policies and politics, plus new ideas and innovations in the world of sport. Approach by phone with ideas.
News/Features On any of the areas mentioned above. Features should be 750–1000 words.
Payment £120 per 1000 words.

The Sporting Life

1 Canada Square, Canary Wharf, London E14 5AP
☎0171 293 3291 Fax 0171 293 3758
Owner *Mirror Group Newspapers Ltd*
Editor *Tom Clarke*
Circulation 95,181

DAILY newspaper of the horse-racing world. Always on the look-out for specialised, well-informed racing writers – not necessarily established sports writers. No unsolicited mss. Phone or write with an idea in first instance. 'The talented will be taken up and used again.'
Associate Editor *Alastair Down*
Deputy Editor *Ben Newton*

Sports in the Sky

Freestyle Publications, Alexander House, Ling Road, Tower Park, Poole, Dorset BH12 4NZ
☎01202 735090 Fax 01202 733969
Owner *Mark Nuttall*
Editor *Gethin James*

FOUNDED 1996. MONTHLY magazine highlighting the excitement of aerial sports such as skydiving, paragliding, hang-gliding, ballooning and microlighting. Features, equipment reviews, profiles and flight guides. Unsolicited mss welcome; approach in writing in the first instance. Not interested in 'my first parachute jump' stories.

Springboard – Writing To Succeed

30 Orange Hill Road, Prestwich, Manchester M25 1LS
☎0161 773 5911
Owner/Editor *Leo Brooks*
Circulation 200

FOUNDED 1990. QUARTERLY. *Springboard* is not a market for writers but a forum from which they can find encouragement and help. Provides articles, news, market information, competition/folio news directed at helping writers to achieve success. Free to subscribers: a copy of *The Curate's Egg* – a collection of poetry submitted.

The Squash Times

PO Box 3443, London SE8 5BG
☎0181 692 6302 Fax 0181 692 6302
Editor *Mr R. Richardson*

FOUNDED 1980. QUARTERLY. Events, players, fashion and footwear, rackets, facilities, technique and tactics.

Staffordshire Life

The Publishing Centre, Derby Street, Stafford
ST16 2DT
☎01785 257700   Fax 01785 253287

Owner *The Staffordshire Newsletter*
Editor *Philip Thurlow-Craig*
Circulation 20,000

FOUNDED 1982. EIGHT ISSUES YEARLY. Full-colour county magazine devoted to Staffordshire, its surroundings and people. Contributions welcome. Approach in writing with ideas.
   Features Maximum 1200 words.
   Fashion Copy must be supported by photographs.
   Payment NUJ rates.

The Stage (incorporating Television Today)

47 Bermondsey Street, London SE1 3XT
☎0171 403 1818   Fax 0171 357 9287

Owner *The Stage Newspaper Ltd*
Editor *Brian Attwood*
Circulation 42,000

FOUNDED 1880. WEEKLY. No unsolicited mss. Prospective contributors should write with ideas in the first instance.
   Features Preference for middle-market, tabloid-style articles. 'Puff pieces', PR plugs and extended production notes will not be considered. Maximum 800 words.
   News News stories from outside London are always welcome. Maximum 300 words.
   Payment £100 per 1000 words.

Stand Magazine

See under **Poetry, Little Magazines**

Staple Magazine

See under **Poetry, Little Magazines**

Stone Soup

37 Chesterfield Road, London W4 3HQ
☎0181 742 7554   Fax 0181 742 7554

Editors *Igor Klikovac, Ken Smith*
Associate Editors *Srdja Pavlovic, Vesna*
   Domany-Hardy
Circulation 3000

THRICE-YEARLY international magazine for new writing – mainly poetry and theory, combined with some fiction and criticism. Edited by English poet Ken Smith and Bosnian poet Igor Klikovac, the magazine is printed bilingually, in English and languages of former Yugoslavia but it also attracts a broad audience across Europe. It tends to bring the most interesting work from Eastern Europe and combines it with well-established authors from the West. Contributors for the first three issues include Edward W. Said, Umberto Eco, Jean Baudrillard, Noam Chomsky, Hanif Kureishi, Adam Zagajewski and Alain Bosquet. Most work is commissioned. Approach in writing, mss should be sent in duplicate, preferably on disk, with s.a.e. supplied.

The Strad

7 St. John's Road, Harrow, Middlesex
HA1 2EE
☎0181 863 2020   Fax 0181 863 2444

Owner *Orpheus Publications Ltd*
Editor *Joanna Pieters*
Circulation 12,000

FOUNDED 1890. MONTHLY for classical string musicians, makers and enthusiasts. Unsolicited mss welcome 'though acknowledgement not guaranteed'.
   Features Profiles of string players, teachers, luthiers and musical instruments, also relevant research. Maximum 2000 words.
   Reviews *Juliette Barber*.
   Payment £100 per 1000 words.

Student Outlook

87 Kirkstall Road, London SW2 4HE
☎0181 671 7920

Owner/Editor *I. J. Hensall*
Circulation 80,000

FOUNDED 1990. THRICE-YEARLY (one for each academic term). Student-related topics across a broad range of interests, including music, film, books, 'Campus News' and 'Planet News' (politics from a green perspective). Unsolicited mss welcome from both students and ex-students who are not long out of student life. 'Student Outlook' and 'Planet News' are currently only Internet publications. The former is at http://www.student.uk.com and the latter at http://www.pro-net.co.uk/planetnews. Articles of up to 800 words can be e-mailed to student@mail.pro-net.co.uk.

Suffolk and Norfolk Life

Barn Acre House, Saxtead Green, Suffolk
IP13 9QJ
☎01728 685832   Fax 01728 685842

Owner *Today Magazines Ltd*
Editor *Kevin Davis*
Circulation 17,000

FOUNDED 1989. MONTHLY. General interest,

local stories, historical, personalities, wine, travel, food. Unsolicited mss welcome. Approach by phone or in writing with ideas. Not interested in anything which does not relate specifically to East Anglia.

Features *Kevin Davis* Maximum 1500 words, with photos.

News *Kevin Davis* Maximum 1000 words, with photos.

Special Pages *Sue Wright* Study the magazine for guidelines. Maximum 1500 words.

Payment £25 (news); £30 (other).

Suffolk Countryside
Griggs Farm, West Street, Coggeshall, Essex CO6 1NT
☎01376 562578   Fax 01376 562578
Owner *Market Link Publishing*
Editor *Andy Tilbrook*

FOUNDED 1995. MONTHLY. Unsolicited material of Suffolk interest welcome. No general interest material.

Features Countryside, culture and crafts in Suffolk. Maximum 1500 words.

Payment £40.

Sunday Magazine
See under **National Newspapers (News of the World)**

Sunday Mail Magazine
See under **National Newspapers (Sunday Mail, Glasgow)**

Sunday Mirror Magazine
See **Personal**

Sunday Post Magazine
See under **National Newspapers (Sunday Post, Glasgow)**

Sunday Times Magazine
See under **National Newspapers (The Sunday Times)**

Superbike Magazine
Link House, Dingwall Avenue, Croydon, Surrey CR9 2TA
☎0181 686 2599   Fax 0181 781 1164
Owner *Alan Morgan*
Editor *Grant Leonard*
Circulation 46,000

FOUNDED 1977. MONTHLY. Dedicated to all that is best and most exciting in the world of high-performance motorcycling. Unsolicited mss, synopses and ideas welcome.

Surrey County Magazine
PO Box 154, South Croydon, Surrey CR2 0XA
☎0181 657 8568   Fax 0181 657 8568
Owner *Datateam Publishing*
Editor *Theo Spring*
Circulation 9500

FOUNDED 1970. MONTHLY. County matters for Surrey dwellers. News, views, history and comment. Interested in product information for an A/AB readership. Unsolicited mss welcome. Approach by phone or in writing with ideas.

Sussex Life
30–32 Teville Road, Worthing, West Sussex BN11 1UG
☎01903 218719   Fax 01903 820193
Owner *Sussex Life Ltd*
Editor *Trudi Linscer*
Circulation 35,000

FOUNDED 1965. MONTHLY. Sussex and general interest magazine. Regular supplements on education, caring for the elderly and homes and gardens. Interested in investigative, journalistic pieces relevant to the area and celebrity profiles. No historical pieces. Unsolicited mss, synopses and ideas in writing welcome. Maximum 500 words.

Payment £15 per 500 words and picture.

Swimming Times
Harold Fern House, Derby Square, Loughborough, Leicestershire LE11 5AL
☎01509 234433   Fax 01509 235049
Owner *Amateur Swimming Association*
Editor *P. Hassall*
Circulation 20,000

FOUNDED 1923. MONTHLY about competitive swimming and associated subjects. Unsolicited mss welcome.

Features Technical articles on swimming, water polo, diving or synchronised swimming. Length and payment negotiable.

The Tablet
1 King Street Cloisters, Clifton Walk, London W6 0QZ
☎0181 748 8484   Fax 0181 748 1550
Owner *The Tablet Publishing Co Ltd*
Editor *John Wilkins*
Circulation 19,428

FOUNDED 1840. WEEKLY. Quality international Roman Catholic magazine featuring articles of interest to concerned laity and clergy. Unsolicited material welcome (1500 words) if relevant to magazine's style and market. All approaches should be made in writing. *Payment* from about £50.

Take a Break
Shirley House, 25–27 Camden Road, London NW1 9LL
☎0171 284 0909

Owner *H. Bauer*
Editor *John Dale*
Circulation 1.3 million

FOUNDED 1990. WEEKLY. True-life feature magazine. Approach with ideas in writing.

News/Features Always on the look-out for good, true-life stories. Maximum 1200 words. *Payment* negotiable.

Fiction Sharp, succinct stories which are well told and often with a twist at the end. All categories, provided it is relevant to the magazine's style and market. Maximum 1000 words. *Payment* negotiable.

Talking Business
237 Kennington Lane, London SE11 5QY
☎0171 582 0536   Fax 0171 582 4917

Owner *Square One Publishing Ltd*
Editor *Peter Dean*
Circulation 6,500

FOUNDED 1994. MONTHLY. News, reviews, features and charts covering the expanding audiobooks market. Interested in considering business-oriented material and personality profiles. Approach in writing in the first instance.

The Tatler
Vogue House, Hanover Square, London W1R 0AD
☎0171 499 9080   Fax 0171 409 0451

Owner *Condé Nast Publications Ltd*
Editor *Jane Procter*
Circulation 88,235

Up-market glossy from the Condé Nast stable. New writers should send in copies of either published work or unpublished material; writers of promise will be taken up. The magazine works largely on a commission basis: they are unlikely to publish unsolicited features, but will ask writers to work to specific projects.

Features *Tina Gaudoin*

The Tea Club Magazine
PO Box 221, Guildford, Surrey GU1 3YT
☎01483 562888   Fax 01483 302732

Publisher *Bond Clarkson Russell*
Editor *Lorna Swainson*

FOUNDED 1992 by The Tea Council. THRICE YEARLY. Specialist focus on tea and tea-related topics. All editorial features are commissioned. Approach with ideas only.

Telegraph Magazine
See under **National Newspapers (The Daily Telegraph)**

The Tennis Times
PO Box 3443, London SE8 5BG
☎0181 692 6302   Fax 0181 692 6302

Editor *Mr R. Richardson*

FOUNDED 1980. QUARTERLY. Events, players, fashion and footwear, rackets, facilities, technique and tactics.

TGO (The Great Outdoors)
The Plaza Tower, East Kilbride, Glasgow G74 1LW
☎01355 246444   Fax 01355 263013

Owner *Caledonian Magazines Ltd*
Editor *Cameron McNeish*
Circulation 22,000

FOUNDED 1978. MONTHLY. Deals with walking, backpacking and countryside topics. Unsolicited mss are welcome.

Features Well-written and illustrated items on relevant topics. Maximum 2000 words. Colour photographs only please.

News Short topical items (or photographs). Maximum 300 words.

Payment £100–200 for features; £10–20 for news.

that's life!
2nd Floor, 1–5 Maple Place, London W1P 5FX
☎0171 462 4700   Fax 0171 636 1824

Owner *H. Bauer Publishing Ltd*
Editor *Janice Turner*
Circulation 480,500

FOUNDED 1995. WEEKLY. True-life stories, puzzles, fashion, cookery and fun. Interested in considering true-life stories. Approach by phone or in writing in the first instance.

Features *Karen Jones* Maximum 1600 words. *Payment* £650.

Fiction *Emma Fabian* 1200. *Payment* £200–£300.

Theologia Cambrensis
Church in Wales Centre, Woodland Place, Penarth, Cardiff CF64 2EX
☎01222 705278   Fax 01222 712413

Owner *The Church in Wales*

Editor Dr John Herbert

FOUNDED 1988. THRICE YEARLY. Concerned exclusively with theology and news of theological interest. Includes religious poetry, letters and book reviews (provided they have a scholarly bias). No secular material. Unsolicited mss welcome. Approach in writing with ideas.

The Third Alternative

5 Martins Lane, Witcham, Ely, Cambridgeshire CB6 2LB
☎01353 777931

Owner TTA Press
Editor Andy Cox

FOUNDED 1993. Quarterly magazine of horror, fantasy, science fiction and slipstream fiction, plus poetry, features and art. Publishes talented newcomers alongside award-winning authors. Unsolicited mss welcome if accompanied by s.a.e. or International Reply Coupons. Guidelines are available but potential contributors are also advised to study the magazine. Winner of the 1996 British Fantasy Award.

This England

PO Box 52, Cheltenham, Gloucestershire GL50 1YQ
☎01242 577775   Fax 01242 222034

Owner This England Ltd
Editor Roy Faiers
Circulation 180,000

FOUNDED 1968. QUARTERLY, with a strong overseas readership. Celebration of England and all things English: famous people, natural beauty, towns and villages, history, traditions, customs and legends, crafts, etc. Generally a rural basis, with the 'Forgetmenots' section publishing readers' recollections and nostalgia. Up to one hundred unsolicited pieces received each week. Unsolicited mss/ideas welcome. Length 250– 2000 words. *Payment* £25 per 1000 words.

Time

Brettenham House, Lancaster Place, London WC2E 7TL
☎0171 499 4080   Fax 0171 322 1230

Owner Time Warner, Inc.
Editor Christopher Redman
Circulation 5.46 million

FOUNDED 1923. WEEKLY current affairs and news magazine. There are few opportunities for freelancers on *Time* as almost all the magazine's content is written by staff members from various bureaux around the world. No unsolicited mss.

Time Out

Universal House, 251 Tottenham Court Road, London W1P 0AB
☎0171 813 3000   Fax 0171 813 6001

Publisher Tony Elliott
Editor Dominic Wells
Circulation 106,031

FOUNDED 1968. WEEKLY magazine of news and entertainment in London.

Features Elaine Paterson 'Usually written by staff writers or commissioned, but it's always worth submitting an idea by phone if particularly apt to the magazine.' Maximum 2500 words.

News Tony Thompson Despite having a permanent team of staff news writers, sometimes willing to accept contributions from new journalists 'should their material be relevant to the issue'.

Payment £164 per 1000 words.

The Times Educational Supplement

Admiral House, 66–68 East Smithfield, London E1 9XY
☎0171 782 3000   Fax 0171 782 3200

Owner News International
Editor Caroline St John-Brooks
Circulation 139,862

FOUNDED 1910. WEEKLY. New contributors are welcome and should phone with ideas for news or features; write for reviews.

Arts and Books Heather Neill

Media & Resources Janette Wolf Unsolicited reviews are not accepted. Anyone wanting to review should write, sending examples of their work and full details of their academic and professional background to either the literary editor or the media and resources editor. Maximum 1200 words.

Opinion Caroline St John-Brooks 'Platform': a weekly slot for a well-informed and cogently argued viewpoint. Maximum 1200 words. 'Second Opinion': a shorter comment on an issue of the day by somebody well placed to write on the subject. Maximum 700 words.

Further Education Ian Nash Includes training and college management.

Primary Diane Hofkins

School Management Bob Doe Weekly pages on practical issues for school governors and managers. Maximum 1000 words.

Features Sarah Bayliss Longer articles on contemporary practical subjects of general interest to the TES reader. Maximum 1000–1500 words; longer or multi-part features are rarely accepted.

Extra *Joyce Arnold* Subjects covered include: science, travel, music, modern languages, home economics, school visits, primary education, history, geography, mathematics, health, life skills, environmental education, technology, special needs. Articles should relate to current educational practice. Age-range covered is primary to sixth form. Maximum 1000–1300 words. *Payment* by arrangement.

Update a monthly magazine section devoted to Primary (*Diane Hofkins*); IT/Multimedia (*Merlin John*); School management (*Bob Doe*).

The Times Educational Supplement Scotland

37 George Street, Edinburgh EH2 2HN
☎0131 220 1100   Fax 0131 220 1616

Owner *Times Supplements Ltd*
Editor *Willis Pickard*
Circulation 7000

FOUNDED 1965. WEEKLY. Unsolicited mss welcome.

Features Articles on education in Scotland. Maximum 1200 words.

News Items on education in Scotland. Maximum 600 words.

The Times Higher Education Supplement

Admiral House, 66–68 East Smithfield, London E1 9XY
☎0171 782 3000   Fax 0171 782 3300/1

Owner *News International*
Editor *Auriol Stevens*
Circulation 27,000

FOUNDED 1971. WEEKLY. Unsolicited mss are welcome but most articles and *all* book reviews are commissioned. 'In most cases it is better to write, but in the case of news stories it is all right to phone.'

Books *Andrew Robinson*

Features *Sian Griffiths* Most articles are commissioned from academics in higher education.

News *Clare Sanders-Smith* Freelance opportunities very occasionally.

Science *Kam Patel*
Science Books *Andrew Robinson*
Foreign *David Jobbins*
Payment NUJ rates.

The Times Literary Supplement

Admiral House, 66–68 East Smithfield, London E1 9XY
☎0171 782 3000   Fax 0171 782 3100

Owner *Times Supplements*

Editor *Ferdinand Mount*
Circulation 34,500

FOUNDED 1902. WEEKLY review of literature. Contributors should approach in writing and be familiar with the general level of writing in the *TLS*.

Literary Discoveries *Alan Jenkins*
Poems *Mick Imlah*

News *Ferdinand Mount* News stories and general articles concerned with literature, publishing and new intellectual developments anywhere in the world. Length by arrangement.

Payment by arrangement.

Titbits

2 Caversham Street, London SW3 4AH
☎0171 351 4995   Fax 0171 351 4995

Owner *Sport Newspapers Ltd*
Editor *Leonard Holdsworth*
Circulation 150,000

FOUNDED 1895. MONTHLY. Consumer magazine for men covering show business and general interests. Unsolicited mss and ideas in writing welcome. Maximum 3000 words. News, features, particularly photofeatures (colour), and fiction. *Payment* negotiable.

To & Fro

PO Box 1479, Maidenhead, Berkshire SL6 8YX
☎01628 783080   Fax 01628 33250

Owner *RPA Publishing*
Editor *Anne Smith*

FOUNDED 1978. BI-MONTHLY. Specialist machine knitting magazine. Interested in material related to machine knitting only. Unsolicited mss and ideas welcome. Contact the editor in writing in the first instance.

Today's Golfer

Bretton Court, Bretton, Peterborough, Cambridgeshire PE3 8DZ
☎01733 264666   Fax 01733 465221

Owner *EMAP Pursuit Publishing*
Editor *Neil Pope*
Deputy Editor *David Ayres*
Circulation 54,028

FOUNDED 1988. MONTHLY. Golf instruction, features, player profiles and news. Most features written in-house but unsolicited mss will be considered. Approach in writing with ideas. Not interested in instruction material from outside contributors.

Features/News *Kevin Brown* Opinion, player profiles and general golf-related features.

Today's Runner

Bretton Court, Bretton, Peterborough,
Cambridgeshire PE3 8DZ
☎01733 264666   Fax 01733 465206

Owner *EMAP Pursuit Publishing Ltd*
Editor *Victoria Tebbs*
Circulation 26,075

FOUNDED 1985. MONTHLY. Instructional articles on running, fitness, and lifestyle, plus running-related activities and health.

Features Specialist knowledge an advantage. Opportunities are wide, but approach with ideas in first instance.

News Opportunities for people stories, especially if backed up by photographs.

Top of the Pops Magazine

Room A1047, Woodlands, 80 Wood Lane,
London W12 0TT
☎0181 576 2756   Fax 0181 576 2694

Owner *BBC Worldwide Publishing*
Editor *Peter Loraine*
Circulation 292,824

FOUNDED 1995. MONTHLY teenage pop music magazine with a lighthearted and humorous approach. No unsolicited material apart from pop star interviews.

Top Santé Health and Beauty

Presse Publishing, 17 Radley Mews,
Kensington, London W8 6JP
☎0171 938 3033   Fax 0171 938 5464

Owner *Presse Publishing*
Editor *Jane Garton*
Circulation 160,489

FOUNDED 1993. MONTHLY magazine covering all aspects of health and beauty. Unsolicited mss not generally accepted. Not interested in anything except health and beauty. Approach in writing with ideas.

Total Football

30 Monmouth Street, Bath BA1 2BW
☎01225 442244   Fax 01225 732248

Owner *Future Publishing*
Editor *Richard Jones*
Circulation 39,416

FOUNDED 1995. MONTHLY. News, features and reviews covering all aspects of domestic and international football. Contributions welcome.

Features *Richard Jones/Alex Murphy* New and interesting angles; particularly funny pieces and fan-based articles. 2000 words maximum. *Payment* negotiable.

News *Richard Jones/Alex Murphy* Unusual stories from all areas of the game – tabloid style. 500 words maximum. *Payment* £75 per 500 words.

Special Pages Celebrity interviews. 500 words maximum. *Payment* £75 per 500 words.

Tourism Times

Michael Stephen Publishers, PO Box 582,
Five Oaks, St Saviour, Jersey JE4 8XQ
☎01534 611600   Fax 01534 611610

Owner *The Guiton Group*
Editor *Harry McRandle*
Circulation 5000

FOUNDED 1993. BI-ANNUAL travel trade newspaper of the Jersey Tourist industry. Contributions from travel experts welcome; interesting tourism stories which relate to the Channel Islands – 1000 words maximum. Approach by phone in the first instance.

Townswoman

Media Associates, 8 Capitol House, Heigham Street, Norwich, Norfolk NR2 4TE
☎01603 616005   Fax 01603 767397

Owner *Townswomen's Guilds*
Editor *Moira Eagling*
Circulation 30,000

FOUNDED 1933. MONTHLY. No unsolicited mss. Few opportunities as in-house editorial staff are strong.

Traditional Woodworking

The Well House, High Street, Burton on Trent, Staffordshire DE14 1JQ
☎01283 564290   Fax 01283 561077

Owner *Waterways World*
Editor *Helen Adkins*

FOUNDED 1989. MONTHLY. Features workshop projects, techniques, reviews of the latest woodworking tools and equipment, general articles on woodworking and furniture making. All news stories and test reports written in-house.

Features Technique features, instructions, plans and cutting lists for making furniture. Maximum 2000 words. *Payment* negotiable. Approach in writing in the first instance.

Trail

Bretton Court, Bretton, Peterborough,
Cambridgeshire PE3 8DZ
☎01733 264666   Fax 01733 465939

Owner *EMAP Pursuit Publishing Ltd*
Editor *David Ogle*

Circulation 30,653

FOUNDED 1990. MONTHLY. Gear reports, where to walk and practical advice for the hill-walker and long distance walker. Approach by phone or in writing in the first instance.

Features *David Ogle* Very limited requirement for overseas articles, 'written to our style'. Ask for guidelines. Maximum 2000 words.

Big requirement for guided walks articles. Specialist writers only. Ask for guidelines. Max. 750–2000 words (depending on subject).

Payment £60 per 1000 words.

Traveller

45–49 Brompton Road, London SW3 1DE
☎0171 581 4130   Fax 0171 581 1357

Owner *I. M. Wilson*
Editor *Miranda Haines*
Circulation 35,359

FOUNDED 1970. QUARTERLY.

Features Six colour features per issue – copy must be accompanied by good-quality colour transparencies. Articles welcome on off-beat cultural or anthropological subjects. Western Europe rarely covered. No general travel accounts. Maximum 2000 words.

Payment £125 per 1000 words.

Trout Fisherman

Bretton Court, Bretton, Peterborough, Cambridgeshire PE3 8DZ
☎01733 264666   Fax 01733 465436

Owner *EMAP Pursuit Publications*
Editor *Chris Dawn*
Circulation 35,003

FOUNDED 1977. MONTHLY instructive magazine on trout fishing. Most of the articles are commissioned, but unsolicited mss and quality colour transparencies welcome.

Features Maximum 2500 words.
Payment varies.

Turkeys

See **Fancy Fowl**

TV Times

King's Reach Tower, Stamford Street, London SE1 9LS
☎0171 261 5000   Fax 0171 261 7777

Owner *IPC Magazines*
Editor *Liz Murphy*
Circulation 981,811

FOUNDED 1955. WEEKLY magazine of listings and features serving the viewers of independent television, BBC, satellite and radio. Almost no freelance contributions used, except where the writer is known and trusted by the magazine. No unsolicited contributions.

Twinkle

2 Albert Square, Dundee DD1 2QJ
☎01382 223131 ext. 4149 Fax 01382 322214

Owner *D. C. Thomson & Co. Ltd*
Editor *David Robertson*
Circulation 65,000

FOUNDED 1968. WEEKLY magazine for 5–7-year-olds. Mainly picture stories but some text-based pieces. Will consider unsolicited material but would-be contributors are advised to study the magazine first. 500–600 words maximum for text-based stories.

Ulster Tatler

39 Boucher Road, Belfast BT12 6UT
☎01232 681371   Fax 01232 381915

Owner/Editor *Richard Sherry*
Circulation 12,000

FOUNDED 1965. MONTHLY. Articles of local interest and social functions appealing to Northern Ireland's ABC1 population. Welcomes unsolicited material; approach by phone or in writing in the first instance.

Features *Noreen Dorman* Maximum 1500 words. *Payment* £50.

Fiction *Richard Sherry* Maximum 3000 words. *Payment* £150.

The Universe

St James's Buildings, Oxford Street, Manchester M1 6FP
☎0161 236 8856   Fax 0161 236 8530

Owner *Gabriel Communications Ltd*
Editor *Joe Kelly*
Circulation 90,000

Occasional use of new writers, but a substantial network of regular contributors already exists. Interested in a very wide range of material: all subjects which might bear on Christian life. Fiction not usually accepted. *Payment* negotiable.

Vector

See **British Science Fiction Association** under **Professional Associations**

The Vegan

Donald Watson House, 7 Battle Road, St Leonards on Sea, East Sussex TN37 7AA
☎01424 427393   Fax 01424 717064

Owner *Vegan Society*
Editor *Richard Farhall*
Circulation 5000

FOUNDED 1944. QUARTERLY. Deals with the

ecological, ethical and health aspects of veganism. Unsolicited mss welcome. Maximum 2000 words.

Payment negotiable.

Veteran Car

Jessamine Court, 15 High Street, Ashwell, Hertfordshire SG7 5NL
☎01462 742818   Fax 01462 742997

Owner *The Veteran Car Club of Great Britain*
Editor *Elizabeth Bennett*
Circulation 1500

FOUNDED 1938. BI-MONTHLY magazine which exists primarily for the benefit of members of The Veteran Car Club of Great Britain. It is concerned with all aspects of the old vehicle hobby – events, restoration, history, current world news, legislation, etc., relating to pre-1919 motor cars. Most professional writers who contribute to the magazine are Club members. No budget for paid contributions.

Vintage Times

PhD Publishing, Navestock Hall, Navestock, Essex RM4 1HA
☎01708 370380/370053

Owner *PhD Publishing*
Editor *David Hoppit*
Circulation 60,000

FOUNDED 1994. QUARTERLY lifestyle magazine 'for over-40s who have not quite given up hope of winning Wimbledon'. Preliminary approach by phone or in writing with ideas.

Vogue

Vogue House, Hanover Square, London W1R 0AD
☎0171 499 9080   Fax 0171 408 0559

Owner *Condé Nast Publications Ltd*
Editor *Alexandra Shulman*
Circulation 201,187

Condé Nast Magazines tend to use known writers and commission what's needed, rather than using unsolicited mss. Contacts are useful.

Features *Louise Chunn* Upmarket general interest rather than 'women's'. Good proportion of highbrow art and literary articles, as well as travel, gardens, food, home interest and reviews. No fiction.

The Voice

370 Coldharbour Lane, London SW9 8PL
☎0171 737 7377   Fax 0171 274 8994

Owner *Vee Tee Ay Media Resources*
Editor *Annie Stewart*

Circulation 50,060

FOUNDED 1982. WEEKLY newspaper, particularly aimed at the black British community. Copy for consideration welcome but 'publication is not guaranteed'. Initial approach in writing preferred. Opportunities in both features and news – especially from the regions.

Payment from £100 per 1000 words/negotiable.

The War Cry

101 Queen Victoria Street, London EC4P 4EP
☎0171 236 5222   Fax 0171 236 3491

Owner *The Salvation Army*
Editor *Captain Charles King*
Circulation 80,000

FOUNDED 1879. WEEKLY magazine containing Christian comments on current issues. Unsolicited mss welcome if appropriate to contents. No fiction or poetry. Approach by phone with ideas.

News relating to Christian Church or social issues. Maximum length 500 words. *Payment* £20 per article.

Features Magazine-style articles of interest to the 'man/woman-in-the-street'. Maximum length 500 words. *Payment* £20 per article.

The Water Gardener

9 Tufton Street, Ashford, Kent TN23 1QN
☎01233 621877   Fax 01233 645669

Owner *Dog World Publishing*
Editor *Yvonne Rees*
Circulation 23,568

FOUNDED 1994. Nine issues per year. Everything relevant to water gardening. Will consider in-depth features on aspects of the subject; write with idea in the first instance. Maximum 2000 words.

Payment by negotiation.

Waterways World

The Well House, High Street, Burton on Trent, Staffordshire DE14 1JQ
☎01283 564290   Fax 01283 561077

Owner *Waterways World Ltd*
Editor *Hugh Potter*
Circulation 22,408

FOUNDED 1972. MONTHLY magazine for inland waterway enthusiasts. Unsolicited mss welcome, provided the writer has a good knowledge of the subject. No fiction.

Features *Hugh Potter* Articles (preferably illustrated) are published on all aspects of inland waterways in Britain and abroad, including recreational and commercial boating on rivers and canals.

News *Regan Milnes* Maximum 500 words.
Payment £37 per 1000 words.

Waymark
Woodlands, West Lane, Sutton in Craven, Keighley, West Yorkshire BD20 7AS
☎01535 637957   Fax 01535 637576

Editor *Stephen Jenkinson*
Circulation 500

FOUNDED 1986. QUARTERLY journal of the Institute of Public Rights of Way Officers. Glossy, spot colour magazine for countryside access managers in England and Wales, employed throughout the public and private sectors. Also available to non-members by subscription.

News Most produced in-house but some opportunities for original/off-beat items. Maximum 300 words.

Features Ideas welcome on any topic broadly relating to the British countryside and public access to it. Controversial, thought provoking pieces readily considered. Maximum 1000 words.

Special Pages Cartoons or brief humorous items on an access or countryside/environmental theme welcome. Send ideas in writing with s.a.e. initially.

Payment negotiable, up to £25.

Wedding and Home
King's Reach Tower, Stamford Street, London SE1 9LS
☎0171 261 7471   Fax 0171 261 7459

Owner *IPC Magazines Ltd*
Editor *Christine Prunty*
Circulation 42,945

BI-MONTHLY for women planning their wedding, honeymoon and first home. Most features are written in-house or commissioned from known freelancers. Unsolicited mss are not welcome, but approaches may be made in writing.

Weekly News
Albert Square, Dundee DD1 9QJ
☎01382 223131   Fax 01382 201390

Owner *D. C. Thomson & Co. Ltd*
Editor *David Hishmurgh*
Circulation 365,000

FOUNDED 1855. WEEKLY. Newsy, family-orientated magazine designed to appeal to the busy housewife. 'We get a lot of unsolicited stuff and there is great loss of life among them.' Usually commissions, but writers of promise

will be taken up. Series include showbiz, royals and television. No fiction. *Payment* negotiable.

West Lothian Life
Ballencrieff Cottage, Ballencrieff Toll, Bathgate, West Lothian EH48 4LD
☎01506 632728   Fax 01506 632728

Owner *Pages Editorial & Publishing Services*
Editor *Susan Coon*

QUARTERLY county magazine for people who live, work or have an interest in West Lothian. Includes three or four major features (1500 words) on successful people, businesses or initiatives. A local walk takes up the centre spread. Regular articles by experts on collectables, property, interior design, photography, cookery and local gardening, plus news items, letters and a competition. Freelance writers used exclusively for main features. Phone first to discuss content and timing.

Payment by arrangement.

What Car?
38–42 Hampton Road, Teddington, Middlesex TW11 0JE
☎0181 943 5044   Fax 0181 943 5959

Owner *Haymarket Motoring Publications Ltd*
Editor *Mark Payton*
Circulation 148,137

MONTHLY. The car buyer's bible, *What Car?* concentrates on road test comparisons of new cars, news and buying advice on used cars, as well as a strong consumer section. Some scope for freelancers. Testing is only offered to the few, and general articles on aspects of driving are only accepted from writers known and trusted by the magazine. No unsolicited mss.

Payment negotiable.

What Hi-Fi?
60 Waldegrave Road, Teddington, Middlesex TW11 8LG
☎0181 943 5000   Fax 0181 943 5798

Owner *Haymarket Magazines Ltd*
Publishing Editor *Rahiel Nasir*
Circulation 74,087

FOUNDED 1976. MONTHLY. Features on hi-fi and new technology. No unsolicited contributions. Prior consultation with the editor essential.

Features General or more specific on hi-fi and new technology pertinent to the consumer electronics market.

Reviews Specific product reviews. All material is now generated by in-house staff. Freelance writing no longer accepted.

What Investment

3rd Floor, 4–8 Tabernacle Street, London
EC2A 4LU
☎0171 638 1916   Fax 0171 638 3128
Owner *Charterhouse Communications*
Editor *Keiron Root*
Circulation 37,000

FOUNDED 1983. MONTHLY. Features articles
on a variety of savings and investment matters.
Unsolicited mss welcome. All approaches
should be made in writing.
  Features Length 1200–1500 words (maximum 2000).
  Payment NUJ rates minimum.

What Mortgage

4–8 Tabernacle Street, London EC2A 4LU
☎0171 638 1916   Fax 0171 638 3128
Owner *Charterhouse Communications*
Editor *Nia Williams*
Circulation 30,000

FOUNDED 1982. MONTHLY magazine on property purchase, choice and finance. No unsolicited mss; prospective contributors may make
initial contact with ideas either by telephone or
in writing.
  Features Up to 1500 words on related topics are considered. Particularly welcome are
new angles, new ideas or specialities relevant to
mortgages.
  Payment £150 per 1000 words.

What Satellite TV

WV Publications, 57–59 Rochester Place,
London NW1 9JU
☎0171 485 0011   Fax 0171 482 6269
Owner *WV Publications*
Editor *Geoff Bains*
Circulation 65,000

FOUNDED 1986. MONTHLY including news,
technical information, equipment tests, programme background, listings. Contributions
welcome; 'a phone call first saves everyone's
time'.
  Features *Geoff Bains* Unusual installations
and users. In-depth guides to popular/cult
shows. Technical tutorials.
  News *Mark Newman* Industry and programming. 250 words maximum.

What's New in Building

Miller Freeman House, 30 Calderwood Street,
London SE18 6QH
☎0181 855 7777   Fax 0181 854 8058
Owner *Miller Freeman plc*
Editor *Mark Pennington*

Circulation 31,496

MONTHLY. Specialist magazine covering new
products for building. Unsolicited mss not generally welcome. The only freelance work available is rewriting press release material. This is
offered on a monthly basis of 25–50 items of
about 150 words each.
  Payment £5.25 per item.

What's On in London

180–182 Pentonville Road, London N1 9LB
☎0171 278 4393   Fax 0171 837 5838
Owner *E. G. Shaw*
Editor *Michael Darvell*
Circulation 40,000

FOUNDED 1935. WEEKLY entertainment-based
guide and information magazine. Features, listings and reviews. Always interested in well-thought-out and well-presented mss. Articles
should have London/Home Counties connection, except during the summer when they can
be of much wider tourist/historic interest, relating to unusual traditions and events. Approach
the editor by telephone in the first instance.
  Features *Graham Hassell*
  Art *Ria Higgins*
  Cinema *David Clark*
  Pop Music *Danny Scott*
  Classical Music *Michael Darvell*
  Theatre *Neil Smith*
  Events *Roger Foss*
  Payment by arrangement.

Wine

Quest Magazines Ltd., 652 Victoria Road,
South Ruislip, Middlesex HA4 0SX
☎0181 842 1010   Fax 0181 841 2557
Owner *Wilmington Publishing*
Editor *Susan Vumback Low*
Circulation 35,000

FOUNDED 1983. MONTHLY. No unsolicited mss.
  News/Features Wine, food and food/
wine-related travel stories. Prospective contributors should approach in writing.

Wisden Cricket Monthly

25 Down Road, Merrow, Guildford, Surrey
GU1 2PY
☎01483 570358   Fax 01483 33153
Owner *Wisden Cricket Magazines Ltd*
Editor *Tim de Lisle*
Circulation 33,000

FOUNDED 1979. MONTHLY. Very few uncommissioned articles are used, but would-be contributors are not discouraged. Approach in
writing. *Payment* varies.

Woman

King's Reach Tower, Stamford Street,
London SE1 9LS
☎0171 261 5000   Fax 0171 261 5997

Owner *IPC Magazines Ltd*
Editor *Carole Russell*
Circulation 828,114

Long-running, popular women's magazine which boasts a readership of over 2.5 million. No unsolicited mss. Most work commissioned. Approach with ideas in writing.
    Features *Mandie Appleyard* Max. 1250 words.
    Books *Gillian Carter*

Woman and Home

King's Reach Tower, Stamford Street,
London SE1 9LS
☎0171 261 5000   Fax 0171 261 7346

Owner *IPC Magazines Ltd*
Editor *Jan Henderson*
Circulation 352,811

FOUNDED 1926. MONTHLY. No unsolicited mss. Prospective contributors are advised to write with ideas, including photocopies of other published work or details of magazines to which they have contributed. S.a.e. essential for return of material. Most freelance work is specially commissioned.

Woman's Journal

King's Reach Tower, Stamford Street,
London SE1 9LS
☎0171 261 6220   Fax 0171 261 7061

Owner *IPC Magazines Ltd*
Editor *Deirdre Vine*
Circulation 134,929

MONTHLY. Original, entertaining feature ideas welcome, with samples of previous work.
    Features *Jane Dowdeswell* Major features are generally commissioned, but new fresh ideas on all subjects welcome. Maximum 2000 words. *Payment* negotiable.
    Design and Homes *Sue Price*
    Fashion *Alex Parnell*
    Food *Katie Stewart*
    Health *Cherry Maslen*

Woman's Own

King's Reach Tower, Stamford Street,
London SE1 9LS
☎0171 261 5474   Fax 0171 261 5346

Owner *IPC Magazines Ltd*
Editor *Keith McNeill*
Circulation 808,311

WEEKLY. Prospective contributors should contact the features editor *in writing* in the first instance before making a submission.
    Features *Keith Richmond*
    Fiction No unsolicited fiction.

Woman's Realm

King's Reach Tower, Stamford Street,
London SE1 9LS
☎0171 261 5000
Fax 0171 261 5326/261 7678 (Features)

Owner *IPC Magazines Ltd*
Editor *Kathy Watson*
Deputy Editor *Linda Belcher*
Circulation 250,261

FOUNDED 1958. WEEKLY. Some scope here for freelancers. Write to the appropriate editor.
    Features *Sally Morgan* General, real-life; practical and human interest.
    Fiction Two short stories used every week, a one-pager (up to 1200 words), plus a longer one (2500 words). Unsolicited mss not accepted.

Woman's Weekly

King's Reach Tower, Stamford Street,
London SE1 9LS
☎0171 261 5000   Fax 0171 261 6322

Owner *IPC Magazines Ltd*
Editor *Olwen Rice*
Circulation 696,212

Mass-market women's WEEKLY.
    Features *Frances Quinn* Inspiring, positive human interest stories, especially first-hand experiences, of up to 1200 words. Freelancers used regularly but tend to be experienced magazine journalists. Synopses and ideas should be submitted in writing.
    Fiction *Gaynor Davies* Short stories 1000–2500 words; serials 12,000–30,000 words. Guidelines for serials: 'a strong emotional theme with a conflict not resolved until the end'; short stories should have warmth and originality.

Woodworker

Nexus House, Boundary Way, Hemel Hempstead, Hertfordshire HP2 7ST
☎01442 66551   Fax 01442 66998

Owner *Nexus Special Interests*
Editor *Mark Ramuz*
Circulation 45,000

FOUNDED 1901. MONTHLY. Contributions welcome; approach with ideas in writing.
    Features Articles on woodworking with good photo support appreciated. Maximum 2000 words. *Payment* £40–60 per page.

News Stories and photos (b&w) welcome. Maximum 300 words. *Payment £10–25 per story.*

Words Worth
14 Langcliffe Drive, Heelands, Milton Keynes MK13 7LA
Owner *Speakeasy Press*
Editor *Michael I. Puckwood*

FOUNDED 1996. BI-ANNUAL literary magazine with poetry, short stories and features. Unsolicited mss welcome; approach in writing with ideas.

Working Titles
See under **Poetry, Little Magazines**

Works Magazine
See **Works Publishing** under **Small Presses**

World Fishing
Nexus House, Swanley, Kent BR8 8HY
☎01322 660070   Fax 01322 666408
Owner *Nexus Media Ltd*
Editor *Martin Gill*
Circulation 5746

FOUNDED 1952. MONTHLY. Unsolicited mss welcome; approach by phone or in writing with an idea.

News/Features Technical or commercial nature relating to the commercial fishing and fish processing industries worldwide. Maximum 1000 words.
Payment by arrangement.

World of Bowls
22–26 Market Road, London N7 9PW
☎0171 607 8585   Fax 0171 700 1408
Owner *HBP Ltd*
Editor *Chris Mills*
Circulation 16,000

MONTHLY on all aspects of flat green bowling. Welcomes personality pieces. Approach in writing in the first instance.

Features Unusual, off-the-wall bowling features. Maximum 1000 words.

News Hard news stories. Maximum 200 words. *Payment* by negotiation.

The World of Interiors
Vogue House, Hanover Square, London W1R 0AD
☎0171 499 9080   Fax 0171 493 4013
Owner *Condé Nast Publications Ltd*
Editor *Min Hogg*
Circulation 73,307

FOUNDED 1981. MONTHLY. Best approach by phone or letter with an idea, preferably with reference snaps or guidebooks.

Features *Sarah Howell* Most feature material is commissioned. 'Subjects tend to be found by us, but we are delighted to receive suggestions of houses unpublished elsewhere, and would love to find new writers.'

World Soccer
King's Reach Tower, Stamford Street, London SE1 9LS
☎0171 261 5737   Fax 0171 261 7474
Owner *IPC Magazines Ltd*
Editor *Keir Radnedge*
Circulation 53,744

FOUNDED 1960. MONTHLY. Unsolicited material welcome but initial approach by phone or in writing preferred. News and features on world soccer.

Writers' Monthly
235–239 High Road, London N22 4HF
☎0181 365 8101   Fax 0181 829 9766
Owner *The Writer Ltd*
Editor *Alan Williams*

FOUNDED 1984. MONTHLY. For writers and aspiring writers. 'Publishers and agents use the magazine to find new writers and help them publish their works.' Articles on writing for television, theatre, radio, newspapers and magazines. Regular features include publisher/ agency profile, poets' press, author interviews, regular short story and poetry competitions. (NB Does not publish short stories other than their short story competition results.) Unsolicited mss from new and established writers welcome.

Features On any aspect of writing. Maximum 2200 words.
Payment negotiable.

Xenos
29 Prebend Street, Bedford MK40 1QN
☎01234 349067

Editor *Stephen Copestake*

FOUNDED 1990. BI-MONTHLY. Science fiction, fantasy, horror, occult, humour, mystery and suspense short story digest. Devoted to a very wide definition of 'fantasy'. 'We favour an optimistic emphasis and demand real plots/characterisation. No mood pieces; purely romantic stories, blood and gore, navel-gazing angst or pornographic/experimental material.' No poetry. Length 2000–10,000 words; anything outside this range will not be read. All stories printed are evaluated by readers and their comments printed in the Evaluations section of the subsequent issue. All submissions receive free and prompt analysis by the editor, plus suggestions for revision if appropriate. All submissions must be accompanied by s.a.e. or IRCs and be well presented. No submissions by e-mail. Annual competition with cash prizes (see entry under **Prizes**). Single issue £3.45; annual subscription £16.50. Special services: 'Writers' Tips', a bi-monthly listing of writing markets; £10 per annum.

Yachting Monthly

King's Reach Tower, Stamford Street, London SE1 9LS
☎0171 261 6040   Fax 0171 261 7555
Owner IPC Magazines Ltd
Editor Geoff Pack
Circulation 41,003

FOUNDED 1906. MONTHLY magazine for yachting enthusiasts. Unsolicited mss welcome, but many are received and not used. Prospective contributors should make initial contact in writing.
    Features Paul Gelder A wide range of features concerned with maritime subjects and cruising under sail; well-researched and innovative material always welcome, especially if accompanied by colour transparencies. Max. 2750 words.
    Payment £90–£110 per 1000 words.

Yachting World

King's Reach Tower, Stamford Street, London SE1 9LS
☎0171 261 6800   Fax 0171 261 6818
Owner IPC Magazines Ltd
Editor Andrew Bray
Circulation 36,365

FOUNDED 1894. MONTHLY with international coverage of yacht racing, cruising and yachting events. Will consider well researched and written sailing stories. Preliminary approaches should be by phone for news stories and in writing for features. Payment by arrangement.

Yes Magazine

See under **National Newspapers (The People)**

You – The Mail on Sunday Magazine

See under **National Newspapers (The Mail on Sunday)**

You and Your Wedding

Silver House, 31–35 Beak Street, London W1R 3LD
☎0171 437 2998 (editorial)Fax 0171 287 8655
Owner AIM Publications Ltd
Editor Carole Hamilton
Circulation 58,000

FOUNDED 1985. BI-MONTHLY. Anything relating to weddings, setting up home, and honeymoons. No unsolicited mss. Ideas may be submitted in writing only, especially travel features. No phone calls.

Young Telegraph

346 Old Street, London EC1V 9NQ
☎0171 684 4000   Fax 0171 613 3372
Editor Damian Kelleher
Circulation 1.25 million

FOUNDED 1990. WEEKLY colour supplement for 8–12-year-olds. Unsolicited mss and ideas in writing welcome.
    Features Kitty Melrose Usually commissioned. Any youth-orientated material. Maximum 500 words.
    News Richard Mead Short, picture-led articles always welcome. Maximum 80 words.
    Payment by arrangement.

Young Writer

Glebe House, Weobley, Hereford HR4 8SD
☎01544 318901   Fax 01544 318901
Editor Kate Jones

Describing itself as 'The Magazine for Children with Something to Say', Young Writer is issued three times a year, at the back-to-school times of September, January and April. A forum for young people's writing – fiction and non-fiction, prose and poetry – the magazine is an introduction to journalism for young writers. Payment from £20 to £100 for freelance articles.

Your Cat Magazine

Apex House, Oundle Road, Peterborough, Cambridgeshire PE2 9NP
☎01733 898100   Fax 01733 898487
Owner EMAP Apex
Editor Sue Parslow

FOUNDED 1994. MONTHLY magazine giving practical information on the care of cats and kittens, pedigree and non-pedigree, plus a wide range of general interest items on cats. Will consider 'true life' cat stories (maximum 900 words) and quality fiction. Send synopsis in the first instance. 'No articles written as though by a cat.'

Your Garden Magazine

IPC Magazines Ltd., Westover House,
West Quay Road, Poole, Dorset BH15 1JG
☎01202 680603   Fax 01202 674335

Owner *IPC Magazines Ltd*
Editor *Michael Pilcher*
Circulation 58,935

FOUNDED 1993. MONTHLY full colour glossy
for all gardeners. Welcomes good, solid gardening advice that is well written. Receives
approx 50 mss per month but only five per
cent are accepted. Always approach in writing
in the first instance.

Features *Michael Pilcher* Good gardening
features, preferably with a new slant. Small gardens only. Maximum 1000 words. Photographs
welcome.

Payment negotiable – all rights preferred.

Yours Magazine

Apex House, Oundle Road, Peterborough,
Cambridgeshire PE2 9NP
☎01733 555123   Fax 01733 898487

Owner *Choice Publications - Bayard Presse*
Editor *Neil Patrick*
Circulation 234,845

FOUNDED 1973. MONTHLY. Aimed at a readership aged 55 and over.

Features Best approach by letter with outline in first instance. Maximum 1000 words.

News Short, newsy items of interest to
readership welcome. Length 300–500 words.

Fiction One or two short stories used in
each issue.

Payment negotiable.

ZENE

5 Martins Lane, Witcham, Ely,
Cambridgeshire CB6 2LB
☎01353 777931

Owner *TTA Press*
Editor *Andy Cox*

FOUNDED 1994. Features detailed contributors'
guidelines of international small press and semi-
professional publications, plus varied articles,
news, views, reviews and interviews.

Features Unsolicited articles, maximum
1000 words, welcome on any aspect of small
press publishing: market information, writing,
editing, illustrating, interviews and reviews. All
genres.

The Zone

See **Pigasus Press** under **Small Presses**

News Agencies

AP–Dow Jones News Service
10 Fleet Place, London EC4M 7RB
☎0171 832 9105   Fax 0171 832 9101

A real-time financial and business newswire operated by The Associated Press, the US news agency, and Dow Jones & Co., publishers of *The Wall Street Journal*. No unsolicited material.

Associated Press News Agency
12 Norwich Street, London EC4A 1BP
☎0171 353 1515
Fax 0171 353 8118 (Newsdesk)

Material is either generated in-house or by regulars. Hires the occasional stringer. No unsolicited mss.

National News Press and Photo Agency
109 Clifton Street, London EC2A 4LD
☎0171 417 7707   Fax 0171 216 4111

All press releases welcome. Most work is ordered or commissioned. Coverage includes courts, tribunals, conferences, general news, etc – words and pictures – as well as PR.

PA News Ltd
292 Vauxhall Bridge Road, London SW1V 1AE
☎0171 963 7000
Fax 0171 963 7192 (24-hr Newsdesk)
No unsolicited mss. They will be returned unread with an apology. Most material is produced in-house though occasional outsiders may be used. A phone call to discuss specific material may lead somewhere 'but this is rare'.

Reuters Ltd
85 Fleet Street, London EC4P 4AJ
☎0171 250 1122

No unsolicited mss.

Solo Syndication Ltd
49–53 Kensington High Street, London W8 5ED
☎0171 376 2166   Fax 0171 938 3165

FOUNDED 1978. *Specialises* in world-wide newspaper syndication of photos, features and cartoons. Professional contributors only.

Worldwide Media Limited
PO Box 3821, London NW2 4DQ
☎0181 452 6241   Fax 0181 452 7258

FOUNDED 1995. Supplies magazines around the world with well-written feature articles, mostly of which focus on women's interest and health topics. Commissions a large proportion of the features it syndicates. 'Often looking for freelance writers to research and write specific pieces.'

National and Regional Television

BBC Television
Television Centre, Wood Lane, London `
W12 7RJ
☎0181 743 8000

Chief Executive, BBC Broadcast
Will Wyatt
Chief Executive, BBC Production
Ronald Neil
BBC Broadcast, Director of Television/Controller, BBC1
To be appointed
Controller, BBC2 *Mark Thompson*
BBC Production, Director of Programmes *Alan Yentob*

Over the last year, the BBC has udergone a major restructuring with two new directorates, BBC Production and BBC Broadcast being formed in October 1996. As part of the restructuring network television and radio have been brought together for the first time as bi-media departments

The Production Directorate includes all the programme-making departments involved in non-news programmes for national and international output. The bi-media department includes all the BBC drama producers (TV, Radio and World Service) in England as well as Entertainment, Music, Arts and Factual areas.

BBC Broadcast is responsible for Television, Radio, Regional Broadcasting and Education. The bi-media divisions within BBC Production are BBC Arts, BBC Children's Programmes, BBC Consumer and Leisure, BBC Documentaries and History, BBC Drama, BBC Education Production, BBC Entertainment, BBC Events, BBC Music, BBC Science, BBC Sport and BBC Topical Features. Division address given if different from above.

BBC ARTS
EM07 East Tower, Television Centre, Wood Lane, London W12 9RJ
☎0181 895 6770/6500 Fax 0181 895 6586

Head of BBC Arts *Kim Evans*
Editor, Arts Features *Keith Alexander*
Series Editor, Omnibus *Gillian Greenwood*
Series Editor, Arena *Anthony Wall*
Editor, The Works, Face to Face, Late Review *Mike Poole*
Editor, Home Front, The Bookworm, Looking Good *Daisy Goodwin*

BBC CHILDREN'S PROGRAMMES
Head of BBC Children's Programmes
Anna Home
Executive Producer, Drama
Richard Langridge
Executive Producer, Entertainment
Chris Pilkington
Executive Producer, Factual Programmes
Eric Rowan
Editor, Blue Peter *Oliver MacFarlane*
Producer, Grange Hill *Stephen Andrew*
Editor, Live & Kicking *Christopher Bellinger*
Editor, Newsround *Susie Staples*

BBC CONSUMER AND LEISURE
Head of BBC Consumer and Leisure
Anne Morrison
Editor, Watchdog *Steve Anderson*
Series Producer, Crimewatch UK
Seetha Kumar

BBC DOCUMENTARIES AND HISTORY
White City, 201 Wood Lane, London
W12 7TS
☎0181 752 5252 Fax 0181 752 6060

Head of BBC Documentaries *Paul Hamann*
Editor, Inside Story *Olivia Lichtenstein*
Editor, Modern Times *Stephen Lambert*
Editor, Reputations *Janice Hadlow*
Editor, Timewatch *Laurence Rees*

BBC DRAMA
Head of BBC Drama *To be appointed*
Head of Serials *Michael Wearing*
Head of Series *Jo Wright*
Head of Single Drama and Films *David Thompson*

BBC EDUCATION PRODUCTION
Head of BBC Education Production
Marilyn Wheatcroft

BBC ENTERTAINMENT
Head of BBC Entertainment *Paul Jackson*
Head of Comedy *Geoffrey Perkins*
Head of Light Entertainment *Michael Leggo*
Bi-media Script Editor *Bill Dare*
Head of Comedy Entertainment
Jon Plowman
Head of Independent Production
Kevin Lygo

BBC EVENTS
Head of BBC Events *Philip Gilbert*

BBC Music

Head of Classical Music *Roger Wright*
(Room 4105 Broadcasting House
☎0171 765 1810)

Head of Music Entertainment *Trevor Dann*
(114 Yalding House, London W1A 1AA
☎0171 765 4321)

BBC Science

201 Wood Lane, London W12 7TS
☎0181 752 6178

Head of BBC Science *Jana Bennett*
Acting Editor, Tomorrow's World
Phil Dolling
Editor, Horizon *John Lynch*
Editor, QED *Lorraine Heggessey*

BBC Sport

Controller, TV Sport *Jonathan Martin*
Head of Sport *Brian Barwick*
Editor, Match of the Day/Sportsnight
Niall Sloane
Editor, Grandstand *David Gordon*

BBC Topical Features

Broadcasting House, London W1A 1AA
☎0171 580 4468

Head of BBC Topical Features
Anne Winder

Currently only radio programmes but due to develop into a bi-media department.

BBC News and Current Affairs

BBC Television Centre, Wood Lane, London W12 7RJ
☎0181 743 8000

Chief Executive, News and Current Affairs *Tony Hall*
Head of Weekly News & Current Affairs
Mark Damazer
Head of News Programmes *Peter Bell*
Head of News Gathering *Richard Sambrook*
Head of Political Programmes
Samir Shah
Editor, Foreign Affairs Unit *John Simpson*
Editor, Business & Economics Unit
Peter Jay
News Editor, Breakfast News *Tim Orchard*
News Editor, One O'Clock News
Jon Barton
News Editor, Six O'Clock News
Nikki Clarke
News Editor, Nine O'Clock News
Malcolm Balen
News Editor, Newsnight *Peter Horrocks*
Editor, Public Eye *Mark Wakefield*
Editor, Panorama *Steve Hewlett*

Editor, The Money Programme *Jane Ellison*
Editor, Ceefax *Peter Clifton*
Head of Subtitling *Ruth Griffiths*

News and current affairs broadcasting across television and radio were unified as a single operation in 1987.

Ceefax

Room 7013, Television Centre, Wood Lane, London W12 7RJ
☎0181 576 1801

The BBC's main news and information service, broadcasting hundreds of pages on both BBC1 and BBC2. It is on the air at all times when transmitters are broadcasting.

Subtitling

Room 1468, BBC White City, Wood Lane, London W12 7RJ
☎0181 752 7054/0141 330 2345 ext. 2128

A rapidly expanding service available via Ceefax page 888. Units based in both London and Glasgow.

BBC Educational Directorate

BBC White City, 201 Wood Lane, London W12 7TS
☎0181 752 5252

Director of Education *Jane Drabble*
Head of Educational Policy *Lucia Jones*
Head of Educational Publishing
Juliet Waugh
**Head of Commissioning, Schools &
Colleges** *Frank Flynn*
**Head of Commissioning, Education for
Adults** *Glenwyn Benson*
Head of Learning Channels *Paul Gerhardt*
**Head of Open University Production
Centre** *Roger Waugh;* **Head of
Programmes** *Dr Clive Holloway* (Walton
Hall, Milton Keynes, MK7 6BH
☎01908 655544 Fax 01908 376324)

The educational programme-making and publishing activities of the BBC were brought together in 1993 under the aegis of the Educational Directorate. This incorporates radio and television broadcasting of schools and college programmes, education for adults, and the Marketing division, which produces a range of multimedia products and promotion activity. It also produces programmes and audiovisual material on behalf of and in partnership with the Open University and is responsible for The Learning Zone, which broadcasts education, training and information programmes from midnight during the week.

BBC Religious Broadcasting

New Broadcasting House, PO Box 27,
Oxford Road, Manchester M60 1SJ
☎0161 200 2020   Fax 0161 244 3183

Head of Religious Broadcasting *Rev.*
Ernest Rea

Regular programmes for television include
Songs of Praise; Everyman; Heart of the Matter.
Radio output includes *Good Morning Sunday;*
Sunday Half Hour; Choral Evensong; Seeds of
Faith.

BBC Northern Ireland

Broadcasting House, Ormeau Avenue, Belfast
BT2 8HQ
☎01232 338000

Controller *Patrick Loughrey*
Head of Broadcasting *Anna Carragher*
Head of Production *Paul Evans*
Head of News & Current Affairs
   Tony Maddox
Head of Drama *Robert Cooper*
Chief Producer, Features
   Charlie Warmington
Chief Producer, Sport *Terry Smyth*
Chief Producer, Agriculture *Veronica Hughes*
Chief Producer, Music & Arts
   Ian Kirk-Smith
Chief Producer, Youth & Community
   Fedelma Harkin
Chief Producer, Education *Michael McGowan*
Chief Producer, Topical Programmes
   Bruce Batten
Chief Producer, Religion *Bert Tosh*

Regular programmes include *Friday Live; Hearts*
and Minds and *Country Times* .

BBC Scotland

Broadcasting House, Queen Margaret Drive,
Glasgow G12 8DG
☎0141 339 8844

Controller *John McCormick*
Head of Production *Colin Cameron*
Head of Bi-Media News, Current Affairs
   & TV Sport *Kenneth Cargill*
Head of Arts & Entertainment *Mike*
   Bolland
Head of Drama *Andrea Calderwood*
Head of Broadcasting *Ken MacQuarrie*
Head of Education & Religious
   Broadcasting *Andrew Barr*

Headquarters of BBC Scotland with centres in
Aberdeen, Dundee, Edinburgh and Inverness.
Regular programmes include the nightly
Reporting Scotland plus *Friday Sportscene;*
Frontline Scotland and *Landward* (bi-monthly
farming news).

Aberdeen

Broadcasting House, Beechgrove Terrace,
Aberdeen AB9 2ZT
☎01224 625233

News, plus some features, but most programmes are made in Glasgow. Second TV
centre, also with regular radio broadcasting.

Dundee

Nethergate Centre, 66 Nethergate, Dundee
DD1 4ER
☎01382 202481

News base only; contributors' studio.

Edinburgh

Broadcasting House, Queen Street, Edinburgh
EH2 1JF
☎0131 469 4200

Religious, arts and science programming base.
Bi-media news operation.

Inverness

7 Culduthel Road, Inverness 1V2 4AD
☎01463 221711

News features for Radio Scotland. HQ for
Radio Nan Gaidheal, the Gaelic radio service
serving most of Scotland (see **National**
Radio).

BBC Wales

Broadcasting House, Llandaff, Cardiff
CF5 2YQ
☎01222 322000   Fax 01222 552973/322666

Controller *Geraint Talfan Davies*
Head of Broadcast (Welsh Language)
   Gwynn Pritchard
Head of Broadcast (English Language)
   Dai Smith
Head of News & Current Affairs
   Aled Eurig
Head of Drama *Karl Francis*
Series Producer, Pobol y Cwm
   Glenda Jones
Head of Sport *Arthur Emyr*
Head of Production *John Geraint*

Headquarters of BBC Wales, with regional
television centres in Bangor and Swansea. All
Welsh language programmes are transmitted by
S4C and produced in Cardiff or Swansea.
Regular programmes include *Wales Today;*
Wales on Saturday; and *Pobol y Cwm* (Welsh-
language drama series).

Bangor
Broadcasting House, Meirion Road, Bangor,
Gwynedd LL57 2BY
☎01248 370880   Fax 01248 351443
Head of Production *Marian Wyn Jones*
News only.

Swansea
Broadcasting House, 32 Alexandra Road,
Swansea, West Glamorgan SA1 5DZ
☎01792 654986   Fax 01792 468194
Senior Producer *Geraint Davies*

BBC Midlands & East
Broadcasting Centre, Pebble Mill Road,
Birmingham B5 7QQ
☎0121 414 8888   Fax 0121 414 8634
Controller, English Regions *Nigel Chapman*
Head of Network Production *Rod Natkiel*
Head of Local Programmes *Laura Dalgleish*
Editor, News & Current Affairs *Peter Lowe*

Home of the Pebble Mill Studio. Regular programmes include *Midlands Today* and *The Midlands Report*. Output for the network includes: *The Clothes Show; Telly Addicts; Top Gear; The Really Useful Show; Style Challenge; Call My Bluff; Gardener's World; Kilroy*. Openings exist for well-researched topical or local material.
     BBC Midlands & East serves opt-out stations in Nottingham and Norwich.

BBC East Midlands (Nottingham)
East Midlands Broadcasting Centre, York House, Mansfield Road, Nottingham NG1 3JA
☎0115 9550500
Head of Local Programmes *Richard Lucas*
Local news programmes such as *East Midlands Today*

BBC East (Norwich)
St Catherine's Close, All Saint's Green,
Norwich, Norfolk NR1 3ND
☎01603 619331   Fax 01603 667865
Head of Centre *Arnold Miller*
Editor, News & Current Affairs *David Holdsworth*

Regular slots include *Look East* (regional magazine) and *Matter of Fact*.

BBC North
New Broadcasting House, Oxford Road,
Manchester M60 1SJ
☎0161 200 2020
Head of Youth & Entertainment Features
   John Whiston

Editor, News & Current Affairs *Richard Porter*

Headquarters of BBC North, incorporating the former North East and North West divisions. Leeds and Newcastle continue to make their own programmes, each having its own head of centre. Regular programmes include *Rough Guides; The Travel Show; Great Railway Journeys; Red Dwarf; Mastermind*.

Leeds
Broadcasting Centre, Woodhouse Lane,
Leeds, West Yorkshire LS2 9PX
☎01132 441188
Head of Centre *Martin Brooks*
Acting Editor, News & Current Affairs
   John Lilley
Regional Political Editor *Geoff Talbott*
Series Producer, Close Up North *Ian Lundall*

Newcastle upon Tyne
Broadcasting Centre, Barrack Road,
Newcastle Upon Tyne NE99 2NE
☎0191 232 1313
Head of Centre *Olwyn Hocking*
**Editor, News and Current Affairs/
   News Editor, Look North** *Ian Cameron*
Producers, Look North *Iain Williams, Brid Fitzpatrick, Andrew Lambert, Fiona MacBeth*
Producer, North of Westminster
   Michael Wild

BBC West/BBC South/BBC South West/BBC South East

BBC West (Bristol), Broadcasting House,
Whiteladies Road, Bristol BS8 2LR
☎0117 9732211

The four regional television stations, BBC West, BBC South, BBC South West and BBC South East produce more than 1,100 hours of television each year, including nightly news magazine programmes, as well as regular 30-minute local current affairs programmes and parliamentary programmes. The leisure programme *Out + About* is also produced regionally. The region operates a comprehensive local radio service. The four stations all have a 'bi-media' approach – which means that both radio and television share their resources – as well as a range of correspondents specialising in health, education, business, local government and the environment.

BBC West (Bristol)
(address/telephone number as above)

Head of Regional and Local Programmes
John Conway (Responsible for BBC West,
Radio Bristol, Somerset Sound, Radio
Gloucestershire and BBC Wiltshire Sound)
Editor, News *Ian Cameron*
Series Producer, Close Up West *James
Macalpine*

BBC South (Southampton)
Broadcasting House, Havelock Road,
Southampton, Hampshire SO14 7PU
☎01703 226201

**Acting Head of Regional and Local
Programmes** *Andy Griffee* (Responsible for
BBC South, BBC Solent and Southern
Counties Radio)
Acting Editor, News & Current Affairs
Craig Henderson

BBC South West (Plymouth)
Broadcasting House, Seymour Road,
Mannamead, Plymouth, Devon PL3 5BD
☎01752 229201

Head of Regional and Local Programmes
Roy Roberts (Responsible for BBC South
West, Radio Devon, Radio Cornwall,
Radio Guernsey and Radio Jersey)
Editor, News *Roger Clark*
Editor, Current Affairs *Simon Willis*

BBC South East (Elstree)
Elstree Centre, Clarendon Road,
Borehamwood, Hertfordshire WD6 1JF
☎0181 953 6100

Head of Regional and Local Programmes
Michèle Romaine (Responsible for BBC
South East, Radio Kent, Thames Valley FM
and GLR)
Editor, News & Current Affairs *Jane Mote*
Editor, First Sight *Alison Rooper*

BBC Bristol
Broadcasting House, Whiteladies Road,
Bristol BS8 2LR
☎0117 9732211

Head of Features *Jeremy Gibson* (bi-media)
Head of Natural History Unit *Alastair
Fothergill* (bi-media)

BBC Bristol is the home of the BBC's Natural
History Unit, producing programmes like
*Wildlife on One; The Natural World; The Private
Life of Plants; Incredible Journeys*; and *The Really
Wild Show* for BBC1 and BBC2. It also pro-
duces natural history programmes for Radio 4
and Radio 5 Live. The features department pro-
duces a wide range of television programmes,
including *999; Antiques Roadshow; The Great
Antiques Hunt; 10x10; Picture This; Vets' School;
Under the Sun.*

Independent Television

Anglia Television
Anglia House, Norwich, Norfolk NR1 3JG
☎01603 615151   Fax 01603 631032
London office: 48 Leicester Square, London
WC2H 7FB
☎0171 321 0101   Fax 0171 930 8499
**Managing Director/Director of
Programmes** *Graham Creelman*
Controller of News *Mike Read*

Anglia Television is a major producer of programmes for the ITV network and Channel 4.
These include *The Time ... The Place* and the
Survival wildlife documentaries, Britain's best-
selling programme export. Network dramas for
1997 include *Pale Horse; The Man Who Made
Husbands Jealous* and *Touching Evil.*

Border Television plc
Television Centre, Durranhill, Carlisle,
Cumbria CA1 3NT
☎01228 25101   Fax 01228 41384
Chairman & Chief Executive *James Graham
OBE*
Head of Programmes *Neil Robinson*

Border's programming concentrates on documentaries rather than drama. Most scripts are
supplied in-house but occasionally there are
commissions. Apart from notes, writers should
not submit written work until their ideas have
been fully discussed.

Carlton Television
101 St Martin's Lane, London WC2N 4AZ
☎0171 240 4000   Fax 0171 240 4171
Chairman *Nigel Walmsley*
Chief Executive *Clive Jones*
Director of Programmes *Andy Allan*

Carlton Television comprises: Carlton Broad-
casting which is responsible for the ITV licence
for London and the South East, plus **Central
Broadcasting** and **Westcountry** (see entries);
Carlton Productions (see entry under **Film,
TV and Video Production Companies**);
Carlton Sales which sells airtime and sponsor-
ship. Also runs two facilities operations: Carlton
Studios in Nottingham, supplying studios and
related services and Carlton 021, the largest com-
mercial operator of Outside Broadcast Services in
Europe.

Central Broadcasting

Central House, Broad Street, Birmingham
B1 2JP
☎0121 643 9898   Fax 0121 643 4897

Chairman *Nigel Walmsley*
Managing Director *Ian Squires*

Part of **Carlton Television**. Responsible for the ITV licence for East, West and South Midlands. Regular programmes include *Central Weekend; Tuesday Specials; Crime Stalker.*

Channel 4

124 Horseferry Road, London
SW1P 2TX
☎0171 396 4444   Fax 0171 306 8356

Chief Executive *Michael Jackson*
Director of Programmes *John Willis*
Controller, Factual Programmes
  Karen Brown
Head of Drama *David Aukin*
Controller, Arts & Entertainment
  Stuart Cosgrove

COMMISSIONING EDITORS
Independent Film & Video (Acting Editor) *Robin Gutch*
Arts *Janey Walker*
Television Drama *Peter Ansorge*
Entertainment *Graham K. Smith*
Documentaries *Peter Moore*
News & Current Affairs *David Lloyd*
Comedy *Seamus Cassidy*
Sport *Mike Miller*
Youth *David Stevenson*
Multicultural Programmes
  Farrukh Dhondy
Religion & Features *Peter Grimsdale*
Head of Purchased Programmes
  Mairi MacDonald

When Channel 4 started broadcasting as a national TV channel in November 1982, it was the first new TV service to be launched in Britain for 18 years. Under the 1981 Broadcasting Act it was required to cater for tastes and audiences not previously served by the other broadcast channels, and to provide a suitable proportion of educational programmes. Channel 4 does not make any of its own programmes; they are commissioned from the independent production companies, from the ITV sector, or co-produced with other organisations. The role of the commissioning editors is to sift through proposals for programmes and see interesting projects through to broadcast. Regulated by the ITC.

Channel 5

22 Long Acre, London WC2E 9LY
☎0171 550 5555   Fax 0171 421 7260

Chairman *Greg Dyke*
Chief Executive *David Elstein*
Head of Programmes *Dawn Airey*
Controller of Children's Programmes
  Nick Wilson
Controller of Features & Arts *Michael Attwell*
Controller of News, Current Affairs & Documentaries *Tim Gardam*
Controller of Drama *Corinne Hollingworth*

Channel 5 Broadcasting Ltd, led by Greg Dyke of Pearson TV, won the franchise for Britain's third commercial terrestrial television station in 1995 with a bid of £22.02 million. The station, describing itself as 'intelligent and stylish and a force for change in popular contemporary culture', came on air on 30 March 1997. Regular programmes include *Family Affairs* (Monday to Friday soap opera) and *The Jack Docherty Show* (late-night chat show), plus mainstream drama, films, sport and entertainment.

Channel Television

The Television Centre, La Pouquelaye,
St Helier, Jersey, Channel Islands JE1 3ZD
☎01534 816816   Fax 01534 816817

Also at: The TV Centre, St George's Place,
St Peter Port, Guernsey ☎01481 723451
Managing Director *John Henwood*
Director of Television *Michael Lucas*

After its successful debut on ITV in 1996, *Island*, Channel's 'teen drama' went to a second series. Also in 1996, a broadcast pilot, *Escape From the Black Hole*, was recorded in the Jersey studio. The series is a new entertainment format for children shot 'in the dark' using the unique BVS technology. Two comedies in development. Previous commission for ITV and Ch4 include one-off documentaries, factual series and animation programmes.

GMTV

The London Television Centre, Upper Ground, London SE1 9TT
☎0171 827 7000   Fax 0171 827 7001

Managing Director *Christopher Stoddart*
Director of Programmes *Peter McHugh*
Managing Editor *John Scammell*

Winner of the national breakfast television franchise. Jointly owned by Scottish Television, Carlton, Granada, The Guardian and Disney. GMTV took over from TV-AM on 1 January 1993, with live programming from 6 am to 9.25 am. Regular news headlines, current affairs, topical features, showbiz and lifestyle, sports and business, quizzes and competitions, travel and weather reports.

Grampian Television plc
Queen's Cross, Aberdeen AB15 4XJ
☎01224 846846   Fax 01224 846800
Director of Programmes/Head of Documentaries & Features
George W. Mitchell, MA
Head of News & Current Affairs
Alistair Gracie
Head of Gaelic Robert Kenyon

Extensive regional news and reports including farming, fishing and sports, interviews and leisure features, various light entertainment, Gaelic and religious programmes, and live coverage of the Scottish political, economic and industrial scene. Serves the area stretching from Fife to Shetland. Regular programmes include *Gaelic News; Criomagan* (Gaelic Diary); and *Reflections*.

Granada Television
Granada TV Centre, Quay Street, Manchester M60 9EA
☎0161 832 7211   Fax 0161 953 0283
London office: Stornoway House,
13 Cleveland Row, London SW1A 1GG
☎0171 451 3000

Director of Programmes Peter Salmon
Director of Production Max Graesser
Managing Editor of Factual Programming Ian McBride
Executive Producer GSB and Lifestyle Programmes GTV Ian Hunt
Controller of Drama Gub Neal
Controller of Drama Serials Carolyn Reynolds
Controller of Factual Programmes Charles Tremayme
Controller of Comedy Andy Harries
Head of Music Iain Rousham

Opportunities for freelance writers are not great but mss from professional writers will be considered. All mss should be addressed to the head of scripts. Regular programmes include *Coronation Street; World in Action*; and *This Morning*.

HTV Group plc
Television Centre, Culverhouse Cross, Cardiff CF5 6XJ
☎01222 590590   Fax 01222 599108
Chief Executive Christopher Rowlands
Group Director of Broadcasting Ted George

HTV (Wales)
(address/telephone number as above)
Deputy Director of Broadcasting
Menna Richards

HTV (West)
Television Centre, Bath Road, Bristol BS4 3HG
☎0117 9722722   Fax 0117 9722400
Director of Programmes Jeremy Payne

Harvest Entertainment
(Bristol address/telephone and fax as above)
Managing Director, Programmes
Stephen Matthews
Controller of Children's Programmes
Dan Maddicott
Controller of Factual Programmes
Tom Archer
Director of Programmes, Partridge Films
Michael Rosenberg

HTV's Rights Division is involved in the creation, development and maximisation of the full range of media rights, including television, theatrical, video, book and music publishing, interactive and merchandising. Drama, children's, factual and natural history programming is produced for national and international markets, including *Wycliffe, The Famous Five* and *The Slow Norris*.

ITN (Independent Television News Ltd)
200 Gray's Inn Road, London WC1X 8XZ
☎0171 833 3000

Editor-in-Chief Richard Tait
Editor, ITN Programmes for ITV
Nigel Dacre

Provider of the main national and international news for ITV and Channel 4. Programmes on ITV: *Lunchtime News; Early Evening News; News at Ten; ITN Morning News*, plus regular news summaries, and three programmes a day at weekends. Programmes on Channel 4: in-depth news analysis programmes, including *Channel 4 News* and *The Big Breakfast News*. ITN also provides the news, sport and business news for *ITN's World News*, the first international English-language news programme. Regulated by the ITC.

LWT (London Weekend Television)
The London Television Centre, Upper Ground, London SE1 9LT
☎0171 620 1620
Chief Operating Officer Charles Allen

Managing Director *Eileen Gallagher*
Director of Programmes *Simon Shaps*
Controller of Entertainment *Nigel Lythgoe*
Controller of Drama *Sally Head*
Controller of Arts *Melvyn Bragg*
Acting Controller of Factual and
   Regional Programmes *Jim Allen*

Makers of current affairs, entertainment and drama series such as *Blind Date, Surprise Surprise, The Knock, London's Burning*; also *The South Bank Show* and *Jonathan Dimbleby*. Provides a large proportion of ITV's drama and light entertainment, and also BSkyB and Channel 4.

Meridian Broadcasting

Television Centre, Southampton, Hampshire
SO14 0PZ
☎01703 222555   Fax 01703 335050

London office: Ludgate House, 245 Blackfriars Road, London SE1 9UY
☎0171 921 5000

Managing Director *Mary McAnally*
Director of Broadcasting *Richard Platt*
Controller of Programmes *Richard Simons*
Director of News Strategy *Jim Raven*
Controller of Drama *Simon Lewis*
Controller of Children's Programmes
   Richard Morss

Meridian's newly refurbished studios in Southampton provide a base for network and regional productions. Regular regional programmes include the award-winning news service, *Meridian Tonight; Countryways* and *The Pier.*

S4C

Parc Ty Glas, Llanishen, Cardiff
CF4 5DU
☎01222 747444   Fax 01222 754444

Chief Executive *Huw Jones*
Director of Programmes *Deryk Williams*

The Welsh 4th Channel, established by the Broadcasting Act 1980, is responsible for a schedule of Welsh and English programmes on the Fourth Channel in Wales. Known as S4C, the service is made up of about 30 hours per week of Welsh language programmes and more than 85 hours of English language output from Channel 4. Ten hours a week of the Welsh programmes are provided by the BBC; the remainder are purchased from HTV and independent producers. Drama, comedy and documentary are all part of S4C's programming.

Scottish Television

Cowcaddens, Glasgow G2 3PR
☎0141 300 3000   Fax 0141 300 3030

London office: 20 Lincoln's Inn Field, London
WC2A 3ED
☎0171 446 7000   Fax 0171 446 7010

Director of Broadcasting *Blair Jenkins*
Controller of Drama *Robert Love*
Controller of Entertainment *Sandy Ross*
Head of Features *Agnes Wilkie*
Head of Current Affairs *Alan Smart*
Head of News & Sport *Mark Smith*
Head of General Factual Programmes
   (Social action, Arts, Religion)
   Denis Mooney

An increasing number of STV programmes such as *Taggart* and *Doctor Finlay* are now networked nationally. Programme coverage includes drama, religion, news, sport, outside broadcasts, special features, entertainment and the arts, education and Gaelic programmes. STV produces many one-offs for ITV and Channel 4.

Teletext Ltd

101 Farm Lane, Fulham, London SW6 1QJ
☎0171 386 5000   Fax 0171 386 5002

Managing Director *Peter van Gelder*
Editor *Graham Lovelace*

On 1 January 1993 Teletext Ltd took over the electronic publishing service, previously the domain of Oracle, servicing both ITV and Channel 4. Transmits a wide range of news pages and features, including current affairs, sport, TV listings, weather, travel, holidays, finance, games, competitions, etc. Provides a regional service to each of the ITV regions.

Tyne Tees Television

Television Centre, Newcastle upon Tyne
NE1 2AL
☎0191 261 0181   Fax 0191 261 2302

London office: 15 Bloomsbury Square,
London WC1A 2LJ
☎0171 405 8474   Fax 0171 242 2441

Managing Director (Broadcasting) *Tony Brill*
Director of Programmes *Peter Mitchell*
Head of News & Current Affairs *Graeme Thompson*
Head of Young People's Programmes
   Lesley Oakden
Head of Entertainment *Christine Williams*
Head of Training & Community Affairs
   Annie Wood

Head of Sport *Roger Tames*
Head of Features *Malcolm Wright*

Programming covers religion, politics, news and current affairs, regional documentaries, business, entertainment, sport and arts. Regular programmes include *North East Tonight with Mike Neville; Quayside* and *Around the House* (politics).

UTV (Ulster Television)

Havelock House, Ormeau Road, Belfast
BT7 1EB
☎01232 328122   Fax 01232 246695

Controller of Programming *A. Bremner*
Head of News & Current Affairs
   Rob Morrison
Director of Outside Broadcasts
   Robert Lamrock
Director of Gardening/Heritage
   Ruth Johnston

Regular programmes on news and current affairs, sport, education, music, light entertainment, arts, politics and health.

Westcountry

Langage Science Park, Western Wood Way, Plymouth, Devon PL7 5BG
☎01752 333333   Fax 01752 333444

Chief Executive *Sir John Banham*
Director of News & Sport *Richard Myers*

Part of **Carlton Television**. Came on air in 1 January 1993. News, current affairs, documentary and religious programming. Regular programmes include *Westcountry Live; Westcountry Focus; Westcountry Showcase*.

Yorkshire Television

The Television Centre, Leeds, West Yorkshire
LS3 1JS
☎0113 2438283   Fax 0113 2445107

Chief Executive *Bruce Gyngell*
Managing Director (Broadcasting)
   Richard Gregory
Managing Director (Productions)
   David Holdgate
Group Controller, Drama *Keith Richardson*
Group Controller, Entertainment
   David Reynolds
Group Controller, Factual Programmes
   Chris Bryer
Head of Regional Production *Mike Best*
Head of News & Current Affairs
   Clare Morrow
Head of Children's and Education
   Patrick Titley
Head of Religion *Pauline Duffy*

Drama series, situation comedies, film productions and long-running series like *Emmerdale* and *Heartbeat*. Always looking for strong writing in these areas, but prefers to find it through an agent. Documentary/current affairs material tends to be supplied by producers; opportunities in these areas are rare but adaptations of published work as a documentary subject are considered. Especially interested in developing sit-com ideas. In theory opportunity exists within series, episode material. Best approach is through a good agent.

Cable and Satellite Television

Asianet

Elliott House, Victoria Road, London
NW10 6NY
☎0181 930 0930   Fax 0181 930 0546

Chief Executive *Dr Banad Viswanath*
Managing Director *Deepak Viswanath*

Broadcasting since September 1994, Asianet transmits entertainment to the Asian community 24 hours a day in English, Hindi, Gujarati, Punjabi, Bengali and Urdu.

British Sky Broadcasting Ltd (BSkyB)

Grant Way, Isleworth, Middlesex
TW7 5QD
☎0171 705 3000   Fax 0171 705 3030

Chief Executive & Managing Director
   Sam Chisholm
General Manager, Broadcasting
   Elisabeth Murdoch
Head of Programming *James Baker*
Head of Sky Channels *Les Sampson*
Director of Broadcasting *Tim Riordan*
Director of Programme Acquisitions
   Jeremy Boulton

Sky Broadcasting is distributed via cable and DTH satellite to more than six million homes in the UK and Eire, offering a choice of more than 40 channels. The channels available have been progressively extended since the service was launched in 1989: in addition to the 12 Sky channels, BSkyB is a partner in 13 joint venture channels and also offers the Disney channel plus 15 other independent channels in its multi-channel package.

Sky One

Family entertainment with some of the most talked-about shows on television from *The Simpsons* to *The X-Files*.

Sky Two
'Hottest youth entertainment' from home and abroad.

Sky News
Award-winning 24-hour news service, offering breaking news, hourly bulletins and expert comment.

Sky Sports 1/Sky Sports 2/Sky Sports 3
Over 1000 hours of sport a month across three channels, including FA Premier League Football, England internationals, domestic and international cricket, Rugby Union from around the world and Rugby Super League.

Sky Movies and The Movie Channel
Over 400 different movies every month on these two 24-hour premium channels, including around 30 British television premières.

Sky Movies Gold
Classic and popular movies from 70 years of cinema.

PREMIUM CHANNELS
Sky Movies, The Movie Channel and Sky Sports 1.

PREMIUM BONUS CHANNELS
Sky Movies and The Disney Channel available when you subscribe to both Sky Movies and The Movie Channel. Sky Sports 2 and Sky Sports 3 available when you subscribe to Sky Sports 1.

SKY MULTI-CHANNELS PACKAGE
Sky 1, Sky 2, Sky News, Sky Soap, Sky Travel, TLC, QVC, The Discovery Channel, Bravo, MTV, VH-1, CMT, The Family Channel, UK Gold, UK Living, TCC, Nickelodeon, CNBC, EBN, The History Channel, The Sci-Fi Channel, The Paramount Channel, The Weather Channel, Sky Scottish, Fox Kids, The Computer Channel, and seven channels from Granada Sky Broadcasting (Granada Plus, Men & Motors, Talk TV, TV High Street, Food & Wine, Health & Beauty, Home & Garden).

Channel One Television Ltd
60 Charlotte Street, London W1P 2AX
☎0171 209 1234   Fax 0171 209 1235
Also at: The Television Centre, Bath Road, Bristol BS4 3HG
☎0117 9722551   Fax 0117 9722492

Managing Director *Julian Aston*

Head of Programmes *Barbara Gibbon*
Owned by Daily Mail & General Trust plc. 24-hour, news-led channel.

Cable News Network International
CNN House, 19–22 Rathbone Place, London W1P 1DF
☎0171 637 6700   Fax 0171 637 5854
Bureau Chief *Charles Hoff*
Managing Director CNN Financial News Europe *Albie Bozzo*

LAUNCHED in 1985 as the international sister network to CNN. Wholly-owned subsidiary of Time Warner Inc. Distributes 24-hour news to 184 million households in more than 210 countries and territories. Four and a half hours of programming are originated and produced daily in London: *World News, World Business Today* and *World View*, plus 14 two-minute business news updates.

European Business News (EBN)
10 Fleet Place, London EC4M 7RB
☎0171 653 9300   Fax 0171 653 9333
Managing Director *Michael Connor*

24-hour European financial and corporate news broadcasting.

L!VE TV
24th Floor, One Canada Square, Canary Wharf, London E14 5AP
☎0171 293 3900   Fax 0171 293 3820
Managing Director *Kelvin MacKenzie*
Head of Programming *Nick Ferrari*

24-hour cable channel with an emphasis on upbeat and lively entertainment and information programming. Owned by Mirror Group Newspapers.

Maxat Ltd
200 Gray's Inn Road, London WC1X 8XZ
☎0171 430 4400   Fax 0171 430 4321
Chief Executive *Sarah Williams*

European satellite providing sports, news-gathering and uplink services to, for example, the BBC, ITN, ABC, NBC, MTV and UK Gold.

MTV Networks Europe Inc
Hawley Crescent, London NW1 8TT
☎0171 284 7777   Fax 0171 284 7788
President, International *William Roedy*

ESTABLISHED 1987. Europe's 24-hour music and youth entertainment channel, available on cable and via satellite. Transmitted from London in English across Europe.

NBC Europe
4th Floor, 3 Shortlands, Hammersmith, London W6 8BX
☎0181 600 6600 Fax 0181 563 9080
President & Managing Director *Roger L. Ogden*
Director of Programming *Kim Montour*

Launched in 1987 and relaunched under NBC ownership in 1993. 24-hour European broad-based news, information and entertainment service in English (with occasional programmes and advertisements in Dutch and German).

Travel (Landmark Travel Channel)
66 Newman Street, London W1P 3LA
☎0171 636 5401 Fax 0171 636 6424
Launched in February 1994. Broadcasts pro-grammes and information on the world of travel. Destinations reports, lifestyle pro-grammes plus food and drink, sport and leisure pursuits.

UK Living/UK Gold
The Quadrangle, 180 Wardour Street, London W1V 4AE
☎0171 306 6100 Fax 0171 306 6101
Chief Executive *Bruce Steinberg*
Programme Director, UK Living *Liz Howell*
Programme Director, UK Gold *Andrew Keyte*

UK Living broadcasts from 6.00 am to midnight daily. Women's magazine programmes, gameshows, soaps and films. UK Gold broadcasts from 6.00 am to 2.00 am daily. Vintage drama and light entertainment programmes.

National and Regional Radio

BBC and Independent

BBC Radio

Broadcasting House, London W1A 1AA
☎0171 580 4468   Fax 0171 636 9786

**Director, BBC Radio/Controller, Radio
1** *Matthew Bannister*
Controller, Radio 2 *James Moir*
Controller, Radio 3 *Nicholas Kenyon*
Controller, Radio 4 *James Boyle*
Controller, Radio 5 Live *Roger Mosey*

See entry for **BBC Television** for details of the major structural reorganisation which has created new bi-media departments. Religious and educational broadcasting comes under the aegis of separate directorates established to handle bi-media output in these areas – see entries **BBC Religious Broadcasting** and **BBC Educational Directorate** under **National and Regional Television** section. Radio 1 is the popular music-based station; Radio 2 broadcasts popular light entertainment with celebrity presenters; Radio 3 is devoted mainly to classical and contemporary music; Radio 4 is the main news and current affairs station while broadcasting a wide range of other programmes such as consumer matters, wildlife, science, gardening, etc. It also produces the bulk of drama, comedy, serials and readings. Radio 5 Live, which won the 1996 Sony Radio Award for UK Station of the Year, is the 24-hour news and sport station.

BBC ARTS

EM07 East Tower, Television Centre, Wood Lane, London W12 9RJ
☎0181 895 6770/6500   Fax 0181 895 6586

Head of BBC Arts *Kim Evans*
Editor, Arts Features *Keith Alexander*
Editor, Kaleidoscope, Night Waves
John Boundy
Editor, World Service Arts Radio
Jenny Bowen

At the time of going to press, BBC Arts was mainly concerned with television programmes but it is in the process of developing as a bi-media department with Radio 3 likely to profit from the restructuring.

BBC RADIO DRAMA

Head of BBC Radio Drama *Kate Rowland*

BBC Radio Drama is produced by the Radio Drama Department (with production centres in London, Birmingham and Manchester) and by production teams in Edinburgh, Belfast and Cardiff. The Department (part of the bi-media BBC Drama department within the BBC Production Directorate) has now been divided into seven production teams:

Chief Producer (Manchester) *To be appointed*
Editor, The Archers and Midlands Drama (Pebble Mill) *Vanessa Whitburn*
World Service Drama (London) *Gordon House*
Readings and Features (London) *Paul Kent*
Series/Serials Development *Marilyn Imrie*
Comedy Drama Development (London) *To be appointed*
Short-form & Event Development (London) *Jeremy Mortimer*

The Radio Drama Department produces drama and readings for broadcast on Radios 2, 3, 4, 5-Live and the World Service. Writers interested in proposing dramatisations of extant work should check with the Radio Drama Department to ensure that the work has not already been dramatised for radio. All mss should be accompanied bt s.a.e. Response time to mss is approx. 3–4 months. Commissioning cycles for Radio Drama are set by the Network commissioners, who are also responsible for all independent commissioning. For further information, contact BBC Radio Drama, Room 6057 at the Broadcasting House address above.

BBC MUSIC

Head of Classical Music *Roger Wright*
(Room 4105 Broadcasting House
☎0171 765 1810)
Head of Music Entertainment *Trevor Dann*
(114 Yalding House, London W1A 1AA
☎0171 765 4321)

Regular programmes include *Music in Mind; Composer of the Week; In Tune* (music, arts, interviews); *Impressions* (jazz magazine).

BBC SPORT

Head of Radio Sport *Bob Shennan*
Sports Editor *Gordon Turnbull*

Sports news and commentaries across Radio 1, 4 and 5 Live, with the majority of output on Radio 5 Live. Regular programmes include

Sports on Five and *6-0-6* (presented by David Mellor).

BBC TOPICAL FEATURES
Head of BBC Topical Features *Anne Winder*
A new bi-media department under the restructuring operation. Regular radio programmes include *Woman's Hour; Desert Island Discs; Loose Ends; Does He Take Sugar?*.

BBC News and Current Affairs (Radio)

Broadcasting House, London W1A 1AA
☎0171 580 4468

Managing Director, Radio & Television
   Tony Hall
Head of News Programmes, News &
   Current Affairs *Peter Bell*
Head of Political Programmes, News &
   Current Affairs *Samir Shah*
Head of News Gathering, News &
   Current Affairs *Richard Sambrook*
Editor, Radio News Programmes
   Steve Mitchell
Editor, General News Service *Dave Dunford*
Foreign Editor *Vin Ray*
Home Editors *Peter Mayne*

BBC Radio news and current affairs broadcasting comes under the aegis of BBC News & Current Affairs, a bi-media directorate established in 1987 to unify news and current affairs across both radio and television.

PROGRAMME EDITORS
Today *Jon Barton*
The World at One/The World This
   Weekend *Kevin Marsh*
PM *Margaret Budy*
The World Tonight *Anne Koch*
Contributions from outside writers to existing
   series welcome.

BBC Religious Broadcasting

See entry under **National and Regional Television**

BBC World Service

PO Box 76, Bush House, Strand, London WC2B 4PH
☎0171 240 3456   Fax 0171 379 6729
Managing Director *Sam Younger*
Director, World Service News &
   Programme Commissioning *Bob Jobbins*

The World Service broadcasts in English and 44 other languages. The English service is round-the-clock, with news and current affairs as the main component. With 143 million listeners, excluding countries where research is not possible, it reaches a bigger audience than its five closest competitors combined. The World Service is increasingly available throughout the world on local FM stations, via satellite and on-line as well as through short-wave frequencies. Coverage includes world business, politics, people/events/opinions, development issues, the international scene, developments in science and technology, sport, religion, music, drama, the arts. BBC World Service broadcasting is financed by a grant-in-aid voted by Parliament amounting to £152.4 million for 1997/98.

If you have an idea for a feature programme or series, please direct your enquiry to: Radio News Features 0171 257 2203.

BBC Radio Nan Gaidheal

See **BBC Radio Scotland**

BBC Northern Ireland

Broadcasting House, 25–27 Ormeau Avenue, Belfast BT2 8HQ
☎01232 338000   Fax 01232 338800
Controller, Northern Ireland *Patrick Loughrey*
Head of Broadcasting *Anna Carragher*
Head of Production *Paul Evans*
Senior Drama Producer *Roland Jaquarello*
Head of News *Tony Maddox*
Local stations: Radio Foyle and Radio Ulster
   (see **Local Radio**).

BBC Radio Scotland

Broadcasting House, Queen Margaret Drive, Glasgow G12 8DG
☎0141 339 8844

Broadcasting House, 5 Queen Street, Edinburgh EH2 1JF
☎0131 225 3131

Broadcasting House, Beechgrove Terrace, Aberdeen AB9 2ZT
☎01224 625233

Broadcasting House, Inverness, 7 Culduthel Road, Inverness IV2 4AD
☎01463 720720

Controller, Scotland *John McCormick*
Head of Production *Colin Cameron*
Head of Broadcast *Ken MacQuarrie*
Head of Bi-Media News, Current Affairs
   & TV Sport *Kenneth Cargill*
Executive Producer, Radio Nan Gaidheal
   (Stornoway) *Marion MacKinnon*
Editor, Radio Nan Gaidheal (Inverness)
   Ishbel MacLennan
Editor, Programme Development
   Mike Shaw

Editor, Drama (Edinburgh) *Patrick Rayne*
Executive Producer, Sport *Douglas Wernham*

Produces a full range of news and current affairs programmes, plus comedy, drama, documentaries, short stories, talks and features. Emphasis is on speech-based programmes, reflecting Scottish culture. BBC Radio Scotland provides a national service, primarily from its centres in Glasgow, Edinburgh, Inverness and Aberdeen. Regular programmes include *Good Morning Scotland; People & Power, News After Noon; Mr Anderson's Fine Tunes* and *Storyline*. Community stations: Highland, Selkirk, Dumfries, Orkney and Shetland (see **Local Radio**).

Radio Nan Gaidheal, the Gaelic radio service, broadcasts about 32 hours a week. The main production centre is at 52 Church Street, Stornoway, Isle of Lewis HS1 2LS, ☎01851 705000 (general and youth programmes).

BBC Wales

Broadcasting House, Llandaff, Cardiff
CF5 2YQ
☎01222 572888   Fax 01222 552973

Broadcasting House, 32 Alexandra Road, Swansea, West Glamorgan SA1 5DZ
☎01792 654986   Fax 01792 468194

Broadcasting House, Meirion Road, Bangor, Gwynedd LL57 2BY
☎01248 370880   Fax 01248 351443

Controller, Wales *Geraint Talfan Davies*
Head of Production *John Geraint*
Head of Programmes (English) *Dai Smith*
Head of Programmes (Welsh)
    Gwynn Pritchard
Editor, Radio Wales *Nick Evans*
Editor, Radio Cymru *Aled Glynne-Davies*
Senior Drama Producer *Foz Allan*
Head of Bi-Media News/Current Affairs
    Aled Eurig

Two national radio services now account for nearly 200 hours of programmes per week. Radio Wales transmits a wide mix of output in the English language, whilst Radio Cymru broadcasts a comprehensive range of programmes in Welsh. Regular programmes include *Good Morning Wales; Meet for Lunch; Bore Nwydd* and *Post Prynhawn*.

BFBS (British Forces Broadcasting Service)

Bridge House, North Wharf Road, London
W2 1LA
☎0171 724 1234

Controller of Programmes *Charly Lowndes*

Classic FM

Academic House, 24–28 Oval Road, London
NW1 7DQ
☎0171 284 3000   Fax 0171 713 2630

Chief Executive *Ralph Bernard*
Programme Controller *Michael Bukht*
Head of News *Clare Carson*

Classic FM, Britain's first independent national commercial radio station, started broadcasting in September 1992. It plays accessible classical music 24 hours a day and broadcasts news, weather, travel, business information, charts, music and book event guides, political/celebrity/general interest talks, features and interviews. Classic has gone well beyond its expectations, attracting 4.7 million listeners a week.

Talk Radio UK

76 Oxford Street, London W1N 0TR
☎0171 636 1089   Fax 0171 636 1053

Managing Director *Travis Baxter*
Programme Director *Jason Bryant*

LAUNCHED in February 1995, Talk Radio is the third national commercial radio station. Broadcasts 24 hours a day with a mix of news, opinions, entertainment, weather, traffic and sport based on studio interviews, celebrity chat and 'the views of the Great British listening audience'.

Virgin Radio

30 Leicester Square Square, London
WC2H 7LA
☎0171 766 6000   Fax 0171 766 6100

Chief Executive *David Campbell*
Managing Director *John Pearson*
Programme Director *Mark Story*

Britain's second national commercial station was acquired by **Capital Radio** in 1997. More male, rock-orientated listeners likely as a result of the new ownership.

BBC Local Radio

BBC Regional Broadcasting

Room 715, Henry Wood House, 3 & 6 Langham Place, London W1A 1AA
☎0171 580 4468

There are 39 local BBC radio stations in England transmitting on FM and medium wave. These present local news, information and entertainment to local audiences and reflect the life of the communities they serve. They have their own newsroom which supplies local bulletins and national news service. Many have specialist producers. A comprehensive list of programmes for each is unavailable and would soon be out of date. For general information on programming, contact the relevant station direct.

BBC Asian Network

BBC Pebble Mill, Birmingham B5 7SH
☎0121 414 8558   Fax 0121 472 3174
Also at: Epic House, Charles Street, Leicester LE1 3SH
☎0116 2516688   Fax 0116 2511463
Managing Editor *Vijay Sharma*

Commenced broadcasting in November 1996 to a Midlands audience with programmes in English, Bengali, Gujerati, Hindi, Punjabi and Urdu.

BBC Radio Berkshire

See **Thames Valley FM**

BBC Radio Bristol

PO Box 194, Bristol BS99 7QT
☎0117 9741111   Fax 0117 9732549
Managing Editor *Michael Hapgood*
Wide range of feature material used.

BBC Radio Cambridgeshire

PO Box 96, 104 Hills Road, Cambridge CB2 1LD
☎01223 259696   Fax 01223 460832
Managing Editor *Nigel Dyson*
Assistant Editor *Andrew Wilson*
Short stories are broadcast occasionally.

BBC Radio Cleveland

Broadcasting House, PO Box 95FM, Middlesbrough, Cleveland TS1 5DG
☎01642 225211   Fax 01642 211356
Managing Editor David Peel
Assistant Editor *John Allard*

Material used is almost exclusively local to Cleveland, Co. Durham and North Yorkshire, and written by local writers. Contributions welcome for *House Call* (Saturdays 1.05–2 pm, presented by Bill Hunter). Poetry and the occasional short story are included.

BBC Radio Cornwall

Phoenix Wharf, Truro, Cornwall TR1 1UA
☎01872 75421   Fax 01872 75045
News Editor *Pauline Causey*

On air from 1983 serving Cornwall and the Isles of Scilly. The station broadcasts a news/talk format 18 hours a day on 103.9/95.2 FM.

Chris Blount's afternoon programme includes interviews with local authors and arts-related features on Cornish themes.

BBC Coventry & Warwickshire

25 Warwick Road, Coventry CV1 2WR
☎01203 559911   Fax 01203 520080
Managing Editor *Peter Davies*
Senior Editor *Conal O'Donnell*

News, current affairs, public service information and community involvement, relevant to its broadcast area: Coventry and Warwickshire. Occasionally uses the work of local writers, though cannot handle large volumes of unsolicited material. Any material commissioned will need to be strong in local interest and properly geared to broadcasting.

BBC Radio Cumbria

Annetwell Street, Carlisle, Cumbria CA3 8BB
☎01228 592444   Fax 01228 511195
Managing Editor *John Watson*

Few opportunities for writers apart from *Write Now*, a weekly half-hour regional local writing programme, shared with Radio Merseyside, Radio GMR Talk and Radio Lancashire. Contact *Jenny Collins* on 0151–708 5500.

BBC Radio Derby

PO Box 269, Derby DE1 3HL
☎01332 361111   Fax 01332 290794
Managing Editor *Mike Bettison*

News and information (the backbone of the station's output), local sports coverage, daily magazine and phone-ins, minority interest, Asian and West Indian weekly programmes.

BBC Radio Devon

PO Box 5, Broadcasting House, Seymour Road, Plymouth, Devon PL3 5YQ
☎01752 260323   Fax 01752 234599
Managing Editor *Bob Bufton*

Short stories – up to 1000 words from local authors only – used weekly on the Sunday afternoon show (2.05–3.30 pm) and on Friday's *Late Night Sou' West* (10.05pm–midnight). Contact *Debbie Peers*.

BBC Essex

198 New London Road, Chelmsford, Essex CM2 9XB
☎01245 262393   Fax 01245 492983
Managing Editor *Margaret Hyde*

Provides no regular outlets for writers but

mounts special projects from time to time; these are well publicised on the air.

BBC Radio Foyle
8 Northland Road, Londonderry BT48 7JT
☎01504 378600   Fax 01504 378666
Station Manager *Jim Sheridan*
News Producers *Jim Lindsay, Felicity McCall, Paul McFadden*
Arts/Book Reviews *Frank Galligan, Stephen Price, Colum Arbuckle*
Features *Michael Bradley, Marie Louise Kerr, Danny Kelly*

Radio Foyle broadcasts about seven hours of original material a day, seven days a week to the north west of Northern Ireland. Other programmes are transmitted simultaneously with Radio Ulster. The output ranges from news, sport, and current affairs to live music recordings and arts reviews. Provides programmes as required for Radio Ulster and the national networks and also provides television input to nightly BBC NI News Magazine programme.

BBC Radio Gloucestershire
London Road, Gloucester GL1 1SW
☎01452 308585   Fax 01452 306541
Managing Editor *Jenny Lacey*

News and information covering the large variety of interests and concerns in Gloucestershire. Leisure, sport and music, plus African-Caribbean and Asian interests. Regular book reviews and interviews with local authors.

BBC GLR
PO Box 94.9, 35c Marylebone High Street, London W1A 4LG
☎0171 224 2424   Fax 0171 935 0821
Managing Editor *Steve Panton*
Assistant Editor (News) *Martin Shaw*
Assistant Editor (General Programmes) *Jude Howells*

Greater London Radio was launched in 1988. It broadcasts news, information, travel bulletins, sport and rock music to Greater London and the Home Counties.

BBC GMR Talk
PO Box 951, Manchester M60 1SD
☎0161 244 3002   Fax 0161 228 6110 (admin)
Editor *Karen Hannah*
Contacts *Jim Clarke, Sally Wheatman*

Programmes of interest to writers are: *GM Arts*, a weekly arts and events programme on a Thursday evening, 6.30–7.30pm; and James H.

Reeve's afternoon programme, Monday to Friday 1.00pm to 4.00pm, includes coverage of leisure, entertainment and arts. *Write Now*, a weekly half-hour regional local writing programme is shared with Radio Merseyside, Radio Cumbria and Radio Lancashire. Contact *Jenny Collins* on 0151–708 5500. GMR Talk is predominately a talk station and often carries interviews with new, as well as established, local writers.

BBC Radio Guernsey
Commerce House, Les Banques, St Peter Port, Guernsey, Channel Islands GY1 2HS
☎01481 728977   Fax 01481 713557
Managing Editor *Bob Lloyd-Smith*

BBC Hereford & Worcester
Hylton Road, Worcester WR2 5WW
☎01905 748485   Fax 01905 748006
Also at: 43 Broad Street, Hereford HR4 9HH
☎01432 355252   Fax 01432 356446
Managing Editor *James Coghill*
Senior Producer (Programme) *Denzil Dudley*

Interested in short stories, plays or dramatised documentaries with a local flavour.

BBC Radio Humberside
9 Chapel Street, Hull, North Humberside HU1 3NU
☎01482 323232   Fax 01482 326038
Managing Editor *John Lilley*
Assistant Editor *Barrie Stephenson*

Occasionally broadcasts short stories by local writers and holds competitions for local amateur authors and playwrights.

BBC Radio Jersey
18 Parade Road, St Helier, Jersey, Channel Islands JE2 3PL
☎01534 870000   Fax 01534 832569
Station Manager *Bob Lloyd-Smith*
Senior Producer *Su Loyd*

Local news, current affairs and community items.

BBC Radio Kent
Sun Pier, Chatham, Kent ME4 4EZ
☎01634 830505   Fax 01634 830573
Managing Editor *David Farwig*

Occasional commissions are made for local interest documentaries and other one-off programmes.

BBC Radio Lancashire

Darwen Street, Blackburn, Lancashire BB2 2EA
☎01254 262411   Fax 01254 680821

Editor *Steve Taylor*

Journalism-based radio station, interested in interviews with local writers. Also *Write Now*, a weekly half-hour regional local writing programme, shared with Radio Cumbria, Radio Merseyside and Radio GMR Talk. Contact *Jenny Collins* on 0151–708 5500.

BBC Radio Leeds

Broadcasting House, Woodhouse Lane, Leeds, West Yorkshire LS2 9PN
☎0113 2442131   Fax 0113 2420652

Acting Managing Editor *Ashley Peatfield*

One of the country's biggest local radio stations, BBC Radio Leeds was also one of the first, coming on air in the 1960s as something of an experimental venture. The emphasis is on speech, with a comprehensive news, sport and information service as the backbone of its daily output. For the past three years, BBC Radio Leeds has been a finalist for the title of Sony Regional Station of the Year. Has also won two Gold Sonys for best presentation. For the past four years, it has won the National Award for best speech-based religious affairs programmes.

BBC Radio Leicester

Epic House, Charles Street, Leicester LE1 3SH
☎0116 2516688   Fax 0116 2511463(News)/2513632(Management)

Managing Editor *Liam McCarthy*

The first local station in Britain. Concentrates on speech-based programmes in the morning and on a music/speech mix in the afternoon. Leicester runs a second station (on AM) for the large Asian community.

BBC Radio Lincolnshire

PO Box 219, Newport, Lincoln LN1 3XY
☎01522 511411   Fax 01522 511726

Managing Editor *David Wilkinson*
Assistant Editor *Mike Curtis*

Unsolicited material considered only if locally relevant. Maximum 1000 words: straight narrative preferred, ideally with a topical content.

BBC Radio Manchester

See **BBC GMR Talk**

BBC Radio Merseyside

55 Paradise Street, Liverpool L1 3BP
☎0151 708 5500   Fax 0151 794 0988

Editor *Mick Ord*

Write Now, a weekly 25-minute regional writers' programme, is produced at Radio Merseyside and also broadcast on BBC Radio Cumbria, Radio GMR Talk and Radio Lancashire. Short stories (maximum 1200 words), plus poetry and features on writing. Contact *Jenny Collins* on 0151–708 5500.

BBC Radio Newcastle

Broadcasting Centre, Newcastle upon Tyne NE99 1RN
☎0191 232 4141

Editor *Tony Fish*
Assistant Editor *Andrew Hartley*

'We welcome short stories of about 10 minutes duration for consideration for broadcast in our afternoon programme. We are *only* interested in stories by local writers.' Afternoon programme producer: *Sarah Miller*.

BBC Radio Norfolk

Norfolk Tower, Surrey Street, Norwich, Norfolk NR1 3PA
☎01603 617411   Fax 01603 633692

Assistant Editor *David Clayton*

Good local material welcome for features/documentaries, but must relate directly to Norfolk.

BBC Radio Northampton

Broadcasting House, Abington Street, Northampton NN1 2BH
☎01604 239100   Fax 01604 230709

Managing Editor *Claire Paul*
Assistant Editor *Mike Day*

No literary outlets although books of local interest are reviewed on air occasionally.

BBC Radio Nottingham

PO Box 222, Nottingham NG1 3HZ
☎0115 9550500   Fax 0115 9550501

Editor, News & Programmes *Peter Hagan*
Assistant Editor *Antony Bellekom*

Rarely broadcasts scripted pieces of any kind but interviews with authors form a regular part of the station's output.

BBC Radio Scotland (Dumfries)

Elmbank, Lover's Walk, Dumfries DG1 1NZ
☎01387 268008   Fax 01387 252568

News Editor *Willie Johnston*

Senior Producer *Glenn Cooksley*

Previously Radio Solway. The station mainly outputs news bulletins (four daily). Recent changes have seen the station become more of a production centre with programmes being made for Radio Scotland as well as BBC Radio 2 and 5 Live. Freelancers of a high standard, familiar with Radio Scotland, should contact the producer.

BBC Radio Scotland (Orkney)
Castle Street, Kirkwall KW15 1DF
☎01856 873939   Fax 01856 872908
Senior Producer *John Fergusson*

Regular programmes include *Around Orkney* (weekday news programme); *Bruck* (magazine programme); *Yesterday's Yarns* (local archive material).

BBC Radio Oxford
See **Thames Valley FM**

BBC Radio Scotland (Selkirk)
Municipal Buildings, High Street,
Selkirk TD7 4BU
☎01750 21884   Fax 01750 22400
Senior Producer *Carol Wightman*

Formerly BBC Radio Tweed. Produces weekly travel and holiday programme, *The Case for Packing*.

BBC Radio Sheffield
60 Westbourne Road, Sheffield S10 2QU
☎0114 2686185   Fax 0114 2664375
Editor *Barry Stockdale*
Assistant Editor *David Holmes*

BBC Radio Scotland (Shetland)
Brentham House, Lerwick, Shetland ZE1 0LR
☎01595 694747   Fax 01595 694307
Senior Producer *Mary Blance*

Regular programmes include *Good Evening Shetland*. An occasional books programme highlights the activities of local writers and writers' groups.

BBC Radio Shropshire
2–4 Boscobel Drive, Shrewsbury, Shropshire
SY1 3TT
☎01743 248484   Fax 01743 271702
Managing Editor *Barbara Taylor*
Assistant Editor *Eric Smith, Bob Calver*

Unsolicited literary material very rarely used, and then only if locally relevant.

BBC Solent
Broadcasting House, Havelock Road,
Southampton, Hampshire SO14 7PW
☎01703 631311   Fax 01703 339648
Managing Editor *Chris Van Schaick*

BBC Somerset Sound
14 Paul Street, Taunton, Somerset
TA1 3PF
☎01823 252437   Fax 01823 332539
Senior Producer *Richard Greenaway*

Informal, speech-based programming, with strong news and current affairs output and regular local-interest features, including local writing. Poetry and short stories on *3 Til Tea* programme.

BBC Southern Counties Radio
Broadcasting Centre, Guildford, Surrey
GU2 5AP
☎01483 306306   Fax 01483 304952
Programme Controller *Chris Van Schaick*

Formerly known as BBC Radio Sussex and Surrey.

BBC Radio Stoke
Cheapside, Hanley, Stoke on Trent,
Staffordshire ST1 1JJ
☎01782 208080   Fax 01782 289115
Managing Editor *Phil Ashworth*
Assistant Editor *Mervyn Gamage*

Emphasis on news, current affairs and local topics. Music represents one fifth of total output. Unsolicited material of local interest is welcome – send to assistant editor.

BBC Radio Suffolk
Broadcasting House, St Matthews Street,
Ipswich, Suffolk IP1 3EP
☎01473 250000   Fax 01473 210887
Managing Editor *Ivan Howlett*
Assistant Editor *Kevin Burch*

Strongly speech-based, dealing with news, current affairs, community issues, the arts, agriculture, commerce, travel, sport and leisure. Programmes frequently carry interviews with writers.

BBC Radio Sussex and Surrey
See **BBC Southern Counties Radio**

Thames Valley FM
269 Banbury Road, Oxford OX2 7DW
☎01865 311444   Fax 01865 311915
Managing Editor *Steve Egginton*

Formed from a merger of BBC Radio Berkshire and BBC Radio Oxford. No opportunities at present as the outlet for short stories has been discontinued for the time being though the station frequently carries interviews with authors and offers books as prizes.

BBC Three Counties Radio

PO Box 3CR, Hastings Street, Luton, Bedfordshire LU1 5XL
☎01582 441000   Fax 01582 401467
Managing Editor *David Robey*
Assistant Editor *Jeff Winston*

Encourages freelance contributions from the community across a wide range of radio output, including interview and feature material. The station *very* occasionally broadcasts drama. Stringent local criteria are applied in selection. Particularly interested in historical topics (five minutes maximum).

BBC Radio Ulster

Broadcasting House, Ormeau Avenue, Belfast BT2 8HQ
☎01232 338000   Fax 01232 338800
Head of Broadcasting *Anna Carragher*

Programmes broadcast from 6.30 am–midnight weekdays and from 7.55 am–midnight at weekends. Radio Ulster has won seven Sony awards in recent years. Programmes include: *Good Morning Ulster, John Bennett, Gerry Anderson, Talkback, Newsbreak, Afternoon Spin, Just Jones, Evening Extra* and *Across the Line*.

BBC Radio Wales

The Old School House, Glanrafon Road, Mold, Clwyd CH7 1PA
☎01352 700367
Fax 01352 759821/750919
Senior Broadcast Journalist *Tracy Cardwell*
Producers, Factual Programmes *Gavin McCarthy, Jane Morris*

Broadcasts regular news bulletins Monday to Friday and until lunchtime on Saturday; *The Big Idea* and *Gravel's Travels* network programmes Friday (6–7.30 pm); *Adam Walton* on Saturday evening.

BBC Wiltshire Sound

Broadcasting House, Prospect Place, Swindon, Wiltshire SN1 3RW
☎01793 513626   Fax 01793 513650
Managing Editor *Sandy Milne*

Regular programmes include: *Wake Up Wiltshire; Wiltshire Today; Wiltshire at One*.

BBC Radio WM

PO Box 206, Birmingham B5 7SD
☎0121 414 8484   Fax 0121 472 3174
Acting Managing Editor *Andy Conroy*

This is a news and current affairs station with no interest in short stories or plays.

BBC Radio York

20 Bootham Row, York YO3 7BR
☎01904 641351   Fax 01904 610937
Managing Editor *Geoff Sargieson*
Assistant Editor *Jane Sampson*

A regular outlet for short stories of up to 10 minutes duration. They must be locally written or based (i.e. North Yorkshire).

Independent Local Radio

Radio Authority

Holbrook House, 14 Great Queen Street, London WC2B 5DG
☎0171 430 2724

The Radio Authority authorises Independent Radio licences and acts as a regulator of services. The number of Independent Radio stations continues to increase with new licences being advertised on a regular basis.

96.3 Aire FM/Magic 828

PO Box 2000, 51 Burley Road, Leeds, West Yorkshire LS3 1LR
☎0113 2452299   Fax 0113 2421830
Programme Director *Jim Hicks*

Music-based programming. 96.3 Aire FM caters for the 15–40–year–old listener while Magic 828 aims at the 25–44 age group with classic oldies.

Amber Radio

PO Box 4000, Norwich, Norfolk NR3 1DB
☎01603 630621   Fax 01603 666252
Programme Controller *Dave Brown*

Part of East Anglian Radio plc. Broadcasts classic hits of the '60s and '70s and easy listening; national and local news.

Beacon FM/WABC

267 Tettenhall Road, Wolverhampton, West Midlands WV6 0DQ
☎01902 757211   Fax 01902 838266
Programme Director, Beacon Radio *Colin Wilsher*
Programme Director, WABC *Dave Myatt*

No outlets for unsolicited literary material at present.

The Breeze
See **Essex FM**

96.4 BRMB-FM/1152 XTRA-AM
Radio House, Aston Road North,
Birmingham B6 4BX
☎0121 359 4481   Fax 0121 359 1117

Programme Controller, BRMB/XTRA
  Clive Dickens
News Editor *Robyn Dangerfield*
Music-based stations; no outlets for writers.

Radio Borders
Tweedside Park, Tweedbank, Galashiels
TD1 3TD
☎01896 759444   Fax 01896 759494

Programme Controller *Rod Webster*
Head of News *Kevin Young*

Radio Broadland
St Georges Plain, 47–49 Colegate, Norwich,
Norfolk NR3 1DB
☎01603 630621   Fax 01603 666252

Programme Controller *Dave Brown*

Part of GWR Group plc. Popular music programmes only.

Brunel Classic Gold/GWR FM (East)/GWR FM (West)
Brunel: PO Box 2020, Bristol BS99 7SN
☎0117 9843201   Fax 0117 9843202

GWR FM (East): PO Box 2000, Swindon,
Wiltshire SN4 7EX
☎01793 440300   Fax 01793 440302

GWR FM (West): PO Box 2000, Bristol
BS99 7SN
☎0117 9843200   Fax 0117 9843202

**Programme Controller, Brunel Classic
  Gold** *Jana Rangooni*
Programme Controller, GWR FM (East)
  Scott Williams
Programme Controller, GWR FM (West)
  Dirk Antony

Very few opportunities. Almost all material originates in-house. Part of the GWR Group plc.

Capital FM/Capital Gold
30 Leicester Square, London WC2H 7LA
☎0171 766 6000   Fax 0171 766 6100

Head of News & Talks *Patrick Johnston*

Britain's largest commercial radio station. Main
outlet is news and showbiz programme each
weekday evening at 7 pm called *The Way It Is*.
This covers current affairs, showbiz, features

and pop news, aimed at a young audience. The
vast majority of material is generated in-house.

Central FM
PO Box 103, Stirling FK7 7JY
☎01786 451188   Fax 01786 461883

Managing Director *Grant Millard*

Broadcasts music, sport and local news to
Central Scotland 24 hours a day.

Century Radio
Century House, PO Box 100, Church Street,
Gateshead NE8 2YY
☎0191 477 6666   Fax 0191 477 5660

Programme Controller *John Simons*

Music, talk, news and interviews, 24 hours a
day.

CFM
PO Box 964, Carlisle, Cumbria
CA1 3NG
☎01228 818964   Fax 01228 819444

Head of Programming *Simon Grundy*
Head of Production *Simon Monk*
News Editor *Gill Garston*
Music, news and information station.

Cheltenham Radio
Regent Arcade, Cheltenham, Gloucestershire
GL50 1JZ
☎01242 699555   Fax 01242 699666

Programme Controller *Peter MacFarlane*

Music-based programmes, broadcasting 24
hours a day.

City FM/Radio City 1548 AM
8–10 Stanley Street, Liverpool L1 6AF
☎0151 227 5100   Fax 0151 471 0330

Managing Director *Lynne Wood*
Programme Director *Tony McKenzie*

Opportunities for writers are very few and far
between as this is predominantly a music
station.

Radio Clyde/Clyde 1 FM/ Clyde 2
Clydebank Business Park, Clydebank
G81 2RX
☎0141 306 2272   Fax 0141 306 2265

Director *Alex Dickson, OBE,AE,FIMgt*

Programmes usually originate in-house or by
commission. All documentary material is made
in-house. Good local news items always considered.

Coast FM

41 Conwy Road, Colwyn Bay, Clwyd
LL28 5AB
☎01492 534555   Fax 01492 534248
Programme Director *Terry Underhill*
Programme Controller *Kevin Howard*

Programmes include an hour of Welsh language items each weekday. Broadcasts 24 hours a day.

Cool FM

See **Downtown Radio**

Downtown Radio/Cool FM

Newtownards, Co. Down, Northern Ireland
BT23 4ES
☎01247 815555   Fax 01247 815252
Programme Head *John Rosborough*

Downtown Radio first ran a highly successful short story competition in 1988, attracting over 400 stories. The competition is now an annual event and writers living within the station's transmission area are asked to submit material during the winter and early spring. The competition is promoted in association with Eason Shops. For further information, write to *Derek Ray* at the station.

Essex FM/The Breeze

Radio House, Clifftown Road, Southend on Sea, Essex SS1 1SX
☎01702 333711   Fax 01702 345224
Programme Controller *Paul Chantler*

Music-based stations. No real opportunities for writers' work as such, but will occasionally interview local authors of published books. Contact *Heather Bridge* (Programming Secretary) in the first instance.

Fame 1521 AM

See **Mercury FM 102.7/Fame 1521 AM**

FM 103 Horizon

Broadcast Centre, Crownhill, Milton Keynes, Buckinghamshire MK8 0AB
☎01908 269111   Fax 01908 564893
Programme Controller *Liz Rhodes*

Part of the GWR Group plc. Music and news.

Forth FM/Max AM

Forth House, Forth Street, Edinburgh
EH1 3LF
☎0131 556 9255   Fax 0131 558 3277
Director of Programming *Tom Steele*
News Editor *David Johnston*

News stories welcome from freelancers. Max AM, launched 1990, is aimed at the 35+ age group. Although music-based, it includes a wide range of specialist general interest programmes.

FOX FM

Brush House, Pony Road, Cowley, Oxford
OX4 2XR
☎01865 871000   Fax 01865 871037 (news)
Managing Director *Mark Flanagan*
Head of News *Karen Thorpe*

Backed by an impressive list of shareholders including the Blackwell Group of Companies and Capital Radio Plc. No outlet for creative writing; however, authors soliciting book reviews should contact *David Freeman* at the station.

Galaxy 101

Broadcast Centre, Portland Square, Bristol
BS2 8RZ
☎0117 9240111   Fax 0117 9245589
Programme Controller *Simon Dennis*

Dance music, 24 hours a day. Occasionally interviews local authors and features books about local places. Contact the Programme Controller in the first instance.

GEM AM

29–31 Castle Gate, Nottingham NG1 7AP
☎0115 9527000   Fax 0115 9129302
Managing Director *Chris Hughes*

Part of the GWR Group plc. Music and news.

Gemini Radio FM/AM

Hawthorn House, Exeter Business Park,
Exeter, Devon EX1 3QS
☎01392 444444   Fax 01392 444433
Programme Controller (FM) *Kevin Kane*
Programme Controller (AM) *Mike Allen*

Took over the franchise previously held by DevonAir Radio in January 1995. Part of Orchard Media Group. Occasional outlets for poetry and short stories on the AM wavelength. Contact *Mike Allen*.

Great North Radio (GNR)

See **Metro FM**

Great Yorkshire Gold

900 Herries Road, Sheffield S6 1RH
☎0114 2852121   Fax 0114 2853159
Programme Director *Dave Shearer*

Music, news and features, 24 hours a day.

GWR FM (East)
See **Brunel Classic Gold/GWR FM**

Hallam FM
Radio House, 900 Herries Road, Sheffield
S6 1RH
☎0114 2853333   Fax 0114 2853159
Programme Director *Dave Shearer*

Heart FM
1 The Square, 111 Broad Street, Birmingham
B15 1AS
☎0121 626 1007   Fax 0121 696 1007
Managing Director *Phil Riley*
Programme Director *Paul Fairburn*

Commenced broadcasting in September 1994.
Music, regional news and information.

102.7 Hereward FM/
Classic Gold 1332 AM
PO Box 225, Queensgate Centre,
Peterborough, Cambridgeshire PE1 1XJ
☎01733 460460   Fax 01733 281445
Programme Controller, Hereward FM
   Adrian Cookes
Programme Controller, Classic Gold
   Rob Jones

Not usually any openings offered to writers as
all material is compiled and presented by in-
house staff.

Invicta FM/Invicta Supergold
PO Box 100, Whitstable, Kent
CT5 3QX
☎01227 772004   Fax 01227 771558
Programme Controller *Paul Jackson*

Music-based station, serving listeners in Kent.

Isle of Wight Radio
Dodnor Park, Newport, Isle of Wight
☎01983 822557   Fax 01983 821690
Programme Director *Andy Shier*

Part of the Local Radio Company, Isle of
Wight Radio is the island's only radio station
broadcasting local news, music and general
entertainment.

Key 103
See **Piccadilly 1152**

LBC
See **News Direct 97.3 FM/
LBC 1152 AM**

Leicester Sound 105.4 FM
Granville House, Granville Road, Leicester
LE1 7RW
☎0116 2561300   Fax 0116 2561305
Station Director *Carlton Dale*
Programme Controller *Steve Fountain*
News Editor *Peter Beame*

Predominantly a music station. Very occasionally, unsolicited material of local interest –
'targeted at our particular audience' – may be
broadcast.

1458 Lite AM
PO Box 1458, Quay West, Trafford Park,
Manchester M17 1FL
☎0161 872 1458   Fax 0161 872 0206
Head of Programming *Simon Wynne*

Music-based programmes, 24 hours a day.

Magic 1161
See **Viking FM**

Magic 828
See **96.3 Aire FM**

Marcher Gold
Marcher Sound Ltd., The Studios, Mold
Road, Wrexham LL11 4AF
☎01978 752202   Fax 01978 759701
Programme Controller *Kevin Howard*

Occasional features and advisory programmes.
Hour-long Welsh language broadcasts are aired
weekdays at 6.00 pm.

Max AM
See **Forth FM**

Mercia FM/Mercia Classic Gold
Mercia Sound Ltd., Hertford Place, Coventry
CV1 3TT
☎01203 868200   Fax 01203 868202
Station Director *Ian Rufus*
Programme Controller *Steve Dawson*

Music-based station.

Mercury FM 102.7/Fame 1521 AM
Broadfield House, Brighton Road, Crawley,
West Sussex RH11 9TT
☎01293 519161   Fax 01293 560927
Programme Director *Carole Straker*

Mercury FM plays contemporary music targeting 25–44 years. Fame 1521 plays hits from the
'60s to '90s, targeting 35 years-plus. Both services carry local, national and international
news.

Metro FM/Great North Radio (GNR)

Swalwell, Newcastle upon Tyne NE99 1BB
☎0191 420 0971 (Metro)/420 3040 (GNR)
Fax 0191 488 9222

Programme Controller, Metro *Sean Marley*
Programme Director, GNR *Jim Brown*

Very few opportunities for writers, but phone-in programmes may interview relevant authors.

Moray Firth Radio

PO Box 271, Scorguie Place, Inverness
IV3 6SF
☎01463 224433   Fax 01463 243224

Managing Director/Programme Controller *Thomas Prag*
Programme Organiser *Ray Atkinson*
Book Reviews *May Marshall*

Book reviews every Monday afternoon at 2.20 pm. Also fortnightly arts programme called *The North Bank Show* which features interviews with authors, etc. The station was hoping to revive *Playsearch*, the competition for writing short radio dramas, in 1997.

New Chiltern FM/Classic Gold

Chiltern Road, Dunstable, Bedfordshire
LU6 1HQ
☎01582 666001   Fax 01582 661725

Programme Controller, FM *Trevor James*
Programme Controller, Classic Gold *Jana Rangooni*

Part of the GWR Group plc. Music-based programmes, broadcasting 24 hours a day.

News Direct 97.3 FM/LBC 1152 AM

200 Gray's Inn Road, London WC1X 8XZ
☎0171 973 1152
Fax 0171 312 8470 (FM)/8565 (AM)

Editor (FM) *Chris Mann*
Programme Controller (AM) *Charles Golding*

News Direct 97.3 FM – 24-hour rolling news station; LBC 1152 AM – news, views and entertainment for London.

Northants 96 FM/Classic Gold 1557

19–21 St Edmunds Road, Northampton
NN1 5DY
☎01604 795600   Fax 01604 795601

Programme Controller *Terry Doyle*

Music and news, 24 hours a day.

NorthSound Radio

45 King's Gate, Aberdeen AB15 4EL
☎01224 632234   Fax 01224 631511

Programme Controller *John Martin*

Features and music programmes 24 hours a day.

Ocean FM/South Coast Radio

Whittle Avenue, Segensworth West, Fareham, Hampshire PO15 5PA
☎01489 589911   Fax 01489 589453

Programme Controller *Steve Power*
News Editor *Karen Woods*

Music-based programming only.

Orchard FM

Haygrove House, Shoreditch, Taunton, Somerset TA3 7BT
☎01823 338448   Fax 01823 321044

Programme Controller *Bob McCreadie*
News Editor *Dominic Cotter.*

Music-based programming only.

Piccadilly 1152/Key 103

Castlequay, Castlefield, Manchester M15 4NJ
☎0161 288 5000   Fax 0161 288 5001

Programme Director *John Dash*

Music-based programming with some opportunities for comedy writers.

Plymouth Sound FM/AM

Earl's Acre, Alma Road, Plymouth, Devon
PL3 4HX
☎01752 227272   Fax 01752 670730

Programme Controller *Peter Greig*

Music-based station. No outlets for writers.

Premier Radio

Glen House, Stag Place, London SW1E 5AG
☎0171 233 6705   Fax 0171 233 6706

Station Director *Peter Kerridge*

Broadcasts programmes that reflect the beliefs and values of the Christian faith, 24 hours a day.

Q103.FM

PO Box 103, Vision Park, Chivers Way, Histon, Cambridge CB4 4WW
☎01223 235255   Fax 01223 235161

Station Director *Alistair Wayne*

Part of GWR Group plc. Music and news.

Radio 1521 AM

Carn Business Park, Craigavon, Co Armagh
BT63 5RH
☎01762 330033   Fax 01762 391896

Managing Director *Ivan Tinman*

Commenced broadcasting in April 1996 with predominantly music-based programmes.

RAM FM
Market Place, Derby DE1 3AA
☎01332 292945   Fax 01332 292229
Programme Controller Rob Wagstaff
Part of the GWR Group plc. Music-based programming only.

Red Dragon FM/Touch Radio
Radio House, West Canal Wharf,
Cardiff CF1 5XJ
☎01222 384041   Fax 01222 384014
Programme Controller Simon Walkington
News Editor Andrew Jones
Music-based programming only.

Red Rose 999 AM/Rock FM
PO Box 301, St Paul's Square, Preston,
Lancashire PR1 1YE
☎01772 556301   Fax 01772 201917
Programme Director Paul Jordan
Music-based stations. No outlets for writers.

Sabras Sound
Radio House, 63 Melton Road, Leicester
LE4 6PN
☎0116 2610666   Fax 0116 2667776
Programme Controller Don Kotak
Programmes for the Asian community, broadcasting 24 hours a day.

Scot FM
Number 1 Shed, Albert Quay, Leith,
Edinburgh EH6 7DN
☎0131 554 6677   Fax 0131 554 2266
Also at: Anderston Quay, Glasgow
G3 8DA
☎0141 204 1003   Fax 0141 204 1067
Managing Director Norman L. Quirk
Programme Controller Jeff Graham
Commenced broadcasting in September 1994 to the central Scottish region. Music and talk shows, sport and phone-ins.

Severn Sound FM/Severn Sound Supergold
67 Southgate Street, Gloucester GL1 2DQ
☎01452 423791
Fax 01452 529446/423008 (news)
Station Director Penny Holton
Programme Controller Andy Westgate
Part of the GWR Group plc. Music and news.

SGR FM 97.1/96.4
Alpha Business Park, Whitehouse Road,
Ipswich, Suffolk IP1 5LT
☎01473 461000   Fax 01473 741200
Managing Director Mike Stewart
Programme Controller Mark Pryke
Features Producer Nigel Rennie
Music-based programming.

Signal Cheshire
Regent House, 1st Floor, Heaton Lane,
Stockport, Cheshire SK4 1BX
☎0161 480 5445   Fax 0161 474 1806
Programme Controller Paul Allen
Strong local flavour to programmes. Part of the Signal Network.

Signal One/Signal Gold/Signal Stafford
Stoke Road, Stoke on Trent, Staffordshire
ST4 2SR
☎01782 747047   Fax 01782 744110
Programme Director John Evington
Head of News Paul Sheldon
Music-based station. No outlets for writers. Part of the Radio Partnership.

South Coast Radio
See **Ocean FM**

South West Sound
See **West Sound**

Southern FM
PO Box 2000, Brighton, East Sussex
BN41 2SS
☎01273 430111   Fax 01273 430098
Programme Controller Mark Sadler
News Manager Phil Bell
Music, news, entertainment and competitions.

Spectrum Radio
80 Silverthorne Road, Battersea, London
SW8 3XA
☎0171 627 4433   Fax 0171 627 3409
Managing Director Wolfgang Bucci
Programmes for a broad spectrum of ethnic groups in London.

Spire FM
City Hall Studios, Malthouse Lane, Salisbury,
Wiltshire SP2 7QQ
☎01722 416644   Fax 01722 415102
Station Director Ian Axton

Music, news current affairs, quizzes and sport. Won the Sony Award for the best local radio station in 1994.

Sun. City 103.4
PO Box 1034, Sunderland, Tyne & Wear
SR1 3YZ
☎0191 567 3333   Fax 0191 567 0888
General Manager *Jon Hewson*
Music-based programmes only.

Sunrise FM
Sunrise House, 30 Chapel Street, Bradford,
West Yorkshire BD1 5DN
☎01274 735043   Fax 01274 728534
Programme Controller, Chief Executive
& Chairman *Usha Parmar*

Programmes for the Asian community in Bradford. Part of the Sunrise Radio Group.

Sunshine 855
South Shropshire Communications Ltd.,
Sunshine House, Waterside, Ludlow,
Shropshire SY8 1GS
☎01584 873795   Fax 01584 875900
Station Manager & Programme
Controller *Mark Edwards*

Music, news and information broadcast 24 hours a day.

Swansea Sound 1170 M/Wave
Victoria Road, Gowerton, Swansea SA4 3AB
☎01792 511170   Fax 01792 511171
Head of Programmes *Rob Pendry*
Head of News *Lynn Courtney*

Interested in a wide variety of material, though news items must be of local relevance. An explanatory letter, in the first instance, is advisable.

Tay FM/Radio Tay AM
Radio Tay Ltd., PO Box 123, Dundee
DD1 9UF
☎01382 200800   Fax 01382 593252
Managing Director *Sandy Wilkie*
Programme Director *Ally Ballingall*

Wholly-owned subsidiary of Scottish Radio Holdings. Unsolicited material is assessed. Short stories and book reviews of local interest are welcome. Send to the programme controller.

TFM Radio
Yale Crescent, Stockton-on-Tees, Cleveland
TS17 6AA
☎01642 615111   Fax 01642 674402

Programme Director *Graham Ledger*
Music, sport and information, 24 hours a day.

Touch Radio
See **Red Dragon FM**

TRENT FM
29–31 Castlegate, Nottingham NG1 7AP
☎0115 9527000   Fax 0115 9129302
Managing Director *Chris Hughes*
Part of the GWR Group plc.

2CR-FM (Two Counties Radio)
5–7 Southcote Road, Bournemouth, Dorset
BH1 3LR
☎01202 259259   Fax 01202 255244
Acting Programme Controller *Tom Hardy*

Wholly-owned subsidiary of the GWR Group Plc. Serves Dorset and Hampshire. All reviews/topicality/press releases to The Producer, Morning Crew, 2CRFM at the above address. '*The 2CRFM Breakfast Show* focuses on any material that touches the lives of our listeners.'

2-Ten FM/Classic Gold 1431
PO Box 210, Reading, Berkshire RG31 7RZ
☎0118 9254400   Fax 0118 9254456
Programme Controller *Andrew Phillips*

A subsidiary of the GWR Group plc. Music-based programming.

Viking FM/Magic 1161
Commercial Road, Hull, North Humberside
HU1 2SA
☎01482 325141   Fax 01482 587067
Managing Director *Dee Ford*
Programme Controller *Mark Matthews*
News Co-ordinator *Stephen Edwards*
Features Producer *Paul Bromley*
Music-based programming.

WABC
See **Beacon Radio**

Wessex FM
Radio House, Trinity Street, Dorchester,
Dorset DT1 1DJ
☎01305 250333   Fax 01205 250052
Programme Manager *Phil Miles*

Music, local news, information and features. These include motoring, cooking, reviews of theatre, cinema, books, videos, local music. Expert phone-ins on gardening, antiques, pets, legal matters, DIY and medical issues.

West Sound/South West Sound/ West FM

Radio House, 54 Holmston Road, Ayr
KA7 3BE
☎01292 283662
Fax 01292 283665/262607 (news)

Programme Controller *Gordon McArthur*
News Editor *Robin Bulloch*

West FM broadcasts music programmes. West Sound and South West Sound programmes tend to be more speech orientated.

Radio Wyvern

PO Box 22, 5–6 Barbourne Terrace, Worcester WR1 3JZ
☎01905 612212

Managing Director *Norman Bilton*

Programme Controller *Stephanie Denham*
Part of the GWR Group plc since spring 1997.

Radio XL 1296 AM

KMS House, Bradford Street, Birmingham
B12 0JD
☎0121 753 5353   Fax 0121 753 3111

Station Manager *Barry Curtis*

Asian broadcasting for the West Midlands, 24 hours a day.

1152 XTRA-AM

See **96.4 BRMB-FM**

Film, TV and Video Production Companies

Absolutely Productions Ltd

6–7 Fareham Street, London W1V 3AH
☎0171 734 9824   Fax 0171 734 8284
Executive Producer *Miles Bullough*

TV and radio production company specialising in comedy and entertainment. OUTPUT *Absolutely* Series 1–4 (Ch4); *mr don and mr george* (Ch4); *Squawkietalkie* (comedy wildlife programme for Ch4); *The Preventers* (ITV); *Scotland v England* (Ch4); *Barry Welsh is Coming* (HTV).

Action Time Ltd

Wrendal House, 2 Whitworth Street West, Manchester M1 5WX
☎0161 236 8999   Fax 0161 236 8845
Chairman *Stephen Leahy*
Director of Programming *Trish Kinane*

Major producers and licensers of TV quiz and game entertainment shows such as *Catchphrase; Here's One I Made Earlier; Crazy Cottage; Backdate; Body Heat; A Game of War; Jeopardy; Spellbound*. Action Time has co-production partners in Spain, Sweden, Denmark, Norway, Ireland and India.

Alomo Productions

1 Stephen Street, London W1P 1PJ
☎0171 691 6000   Fax 0171 691 6081
Bought by Pearson in 1996. Major producers of television drama and comedy. OUTPUT *Goodnight Sweetheart; Birds of a Feather; Love Hurts; The New Statesman; Grown Ups*. Scripts not welcome unless via agents but new writing is encouraged.

Anglia TV Entertainment

See **United Film and Television Productions**

Antelope (UK) Ltd

2 Bloomsbury Place, London WC1A 2QA
☎0171 209 0099   Fax 0171 209 0098
Managing Director *Mick Csáky*
Head of Non-Fiction *Krishan Arora*
Head of Production *Carol Rodger*

Film, television and video productions for drama, documentary and corporate material. OUTPUT *Cyberspace* (ITV); *Brunch* (Ch5); *The Pier* (weekly arts and entertainment programme); *Placido Domingo* (ITV); *Baden Powell – The Boy Man; Howard Hughes – The Naked Emperor* (Ch4 'Secret Lives' series); *Hiroshima*. No unsolicited mss – 'we are not reading any new material at present'.

Apex Television Production & Facilities Ltd

Button End Studios, Harston, Cambridge CB2 5NX
☎01223 872900   Fax 01223 873092
Contact *Bernard Mulhern*

Video producer: drama, documentary, commercials and corporate. Largely corporate production for a wide range of international companies. Many drama-based training programmes and current-affairs orientated TV work. No scripts. All work is commissioned against a particular project.

Arena Films Ltd

2 Pelham Road, London SW19 1SX
☎0181 543 3990   Fax 0181 540 3992
Producer *David Conroy*

Film and TV drama. Scripts with some sort of European connection or tie-in particularly welcome. Open-minded with regard to new writing.

Arlington Productions Limited

Pinewood Studios, Iver Heath, Buckinghamshire SL0 0NH
☎01753 651700   Fax 01753 656050
Contact *Kevin Francis, Gillian Garrow*

Television drama. OUTPUT *The Masks of Death* (TVM); *Murder Elite* (TVM); *A One-Way Ticket to Hollywood* (Entertainment doc). Prefers to see synopsis in the first instance. 'We try to encourage new writing.'

Michael Barratt Ltd

Profile House, 5–7 Forlease Road, Maidenhead, Berkshire SL6 1RP
☎01628 770800   Fax 01628 770144
Contact *Michael Barratt*

Corporate and educational video, and TV programmes. Also a wide range of publishing work including company newspapers, brochures and training manuals. Unsolicited scripts and ideas welcome 'if they are backed by commercial realism – like sources of funding for development. However, straightforward notification of availability, special writing skills, contact addresses, etc, will find a place in the company records.' Also trades as MBL Publishing Ltd.

Bazal Productions
See **Broadcast Communications**

Beckmann Communications Ltd
Britannia House, 1 Glenthorne Road, London W6 0LF
☎0181 748 9898   Fax 0181 748 4250
Contact *David Willoughby*

London office of Isle of Man-based company. Video and television documentary. OUTPUT *Practical Guide to Europe* (travel series); *Maestro* (12-part series on classical composers); *Wars in Peace* (co-production with ITN). One-page proposals considered. No scripts.

Behr Cinematography
22 Redington Road, London NW3 7RG
☎0171 794 2535   Fax 0171 794 2535
Contact *Arnold Behr, Betty Burghes*

Documentary, educational, corporate film and/or video, often for voluntary organisations. No actors, except for voice-overs. No unsolicited mss. S.a.e. appreciated from applicants needing a reply.

Paul Berriff Productions Ltd
The Chestnuts, Woodfield Lane, Hessle, North Humberside HU13 0EW
☎01482 641158   Fax 01482 649692
Contact *Paul Berriff*

Television documentary. OUTPUT *Rescue* (13-part documentary for ITV); *M25: The Magic Roundabout* ('First Tuesday'); *Animal Squad Undercover* (Ch4); *Evidence of Abuse* (BBC1 'Inside Story'); *Lessons of Darkness* (BBC2 'Fine Cut'); *The Nick* (Ch4 series); *Confrontation on E Wing* (BBC 'Everyman'); *Astronauts* (Ch4 series).

BFI Production
29 Rathbone Street, London W1P 1AG
☎0171 636 5587   Fax 0171 580 9456
Head of Production *Ben Gibson*

Part of the **British Film Institute**. Produces a range of projects from short films and videos to feature-length films, acting as executive producer and co-investor. Feature treatments or screenplays are accepted for consideration, generally low-budget and innovative. Unsolicited mss have a two-month turnaround period. OUTPUT includes *Gallivant; Stella Does Tricks; Smalltime*. Runs a New Directors Scheme (advertised annually).

Martin Bird Productions
Saucelands Barn, Coolham, Horsham, West Sussex RH13 8QG
☎01403 741620   Fax 01403 741647
Contact *Alastair Martin-Bird*

Makers of film and video specialising in programmes covering equestrianism and the countryside. No unsolicited scripts, but always looking for new writers who are fully acquainted with the subject.

Black Coral Productions Ltd
PO Box 333, Woodford Green, Essex IG9 6DB
☎0181 880 4860   Fax 0181 504 3338
Contacts *Lazell Daley, Isabelle Tracy*

Producers of drama and documentary film and television. Committed to the development of new writing. Offers a script evaluation service for which a fee is payable, with a particular interest in short and feature-length dramas. Runs courses in: *Writing for Short Film Production, Foundation and Intermediate; Screenwriting, Foundation, Intermediate and Advanced; Working with Writers, Actors and Directors, Foundation and Intermediate; Script Reading, Foundation; Script Editing, Foundation and Intermediate; Writing for TV/Radio Drama, Foundation and Intermediate*. TV Intermediate courses carry 50% concessionary places.

Blue Heaven Productions Ltd
45 Leather Lane, London EC1N 7TJ
☎0171 404 4222   Fax 0171 404 4266
Contact *Graham Benson, Christine Benson*

Film and television drama and occasional documentary. OUTPUT *The Ruth Rendell Mysteries; Crime Story: Dear Roy, Love Gillian; Ready When You Are/Screen Challenge* (three series for Meridian Regional); *The Man who Made Husbands Jealous* (Anglia Television Entertainment/Blue Heaven). Scripts considered but treatments or ideas preferred in the first instance. New writing encouraged.

Bond Clarkson Russell Ltd
16 Trinity Churchyard, Guildford, Surrey GU1 3RR
☎01483 562888   Fax 01483 302732
Contact *Peter Bond, Chris Russell, Nigel Mengham*

Corporate literature, film, video and multi-media producer of a wide variety of material, including conference videos, for blue-chip companies in the main. No scripts. All work is commissioned.

Matt Boney Associates
Woodside, Holdfast Lane, Grayswood,
Haslemere, Surrey GU27 2EU
☎01428 656178
Contact *Matt Boney*

Writer/director for video and television: commercials, documentaries, skiing and travel. No unsolicited mss.

Box Clever Productions
The Maples Centre, 144 Liverpool Road,
London N1 1LA
☎0171 619 0606   Fax 0171 700 2248
Contact *Claire Walmsley*

Broadcast TV, film and video documentaries, specialising in social and current affairs. Sister company of Boxclever Communication Training, specialising in media interview skills. OUTPUT documentaries for BBC and Ch4; corporate videos for the European Commission, public sector and voluntary organisations. No unsolicited scripts; outlines and proposals only.

British Lion Screen Entertainment Ltd
Pinewood Studios, Iver, Buckinghamshire
SL0 0NH
☎01753 651700   Fax 01753 656391
Chief Executive *Peter R. E. Snell*

Film production. OUTPUT has included *A Man for All Seasons; Treasure Island; A Prayer for the Dying; Lady Jane; The Crucifer of Blood; Death Train.* No unsolicited mss. Send synopses only.

Broadcast Communications
46/47 Bedford Square, London WC1B 3DP
☎0171 462 9000   Fax 0171 462 9001
Chief Executive *Tom Barnicoat*
Director of Factual Programming
   Peter Bazalgette
Director of Music and Entertainment
   Malcolm Gerrie

Television division of *The Guardian Media Group*. One of Britain's largest independent producers, responsible for nearly 1000 hours of programming for all the UK's terrestrial networks as well as cable and satellite. It has four production companies, wholly owned. These are: Bazal Productions, Initial Film and

Television, Hawkshead and Lomond Television. Broadcast specialises in leisure – from music and entertainment to practical pursuits such as cooking and gardening.

Caledonian Television Ltd
Caledonian House, Phoenix Crescent,
Strathclyde Business Park, Strathclyde
ML4 3UJ
☎01698 845522   Fax 01698 845811
Contact *Russell Galbraith, Jock Brown*

Film, video and TV: documentary and corporate. Send preliminary letter in the first instance.

Caravel Film Techniques Ltd
The Great Barn Studios, Cippenham Lane,
Slough, Berkshire SL1 5AU
☎01753 534828   Fax 01753 571383
Contact *Nick See*

Film, video and TV: documentary, commercials and corporate. OUTPUT Promos for commercial TV, documentaries BBC & ITV, sales and training material for corporate blue chip companies. No unsolicited scripts. Prepared to review mostly serious new writing.

Carlton Productions
35–38 Portman Square, London W1H 9FH
☎0171 486 6688   Fax 0171 486 1132
Director of Programmes *Andy Allan*
Director of Drama & Co-production
   Jonathan Powell
Controller of Entertainment and Comedy
   John Bishop
Controller of Factual Programmes
   Steve Clark

Makers of independently produced TV drama for ITV. OUTPUT *She's Out; Kavanagh QC; Morse; Boon; Gone to the Dogs; The Guilty; Tanamera; Soldier, Soldier; Seekers; Sharpe; Peak Practice, Cadfael, Faith.* 'We try to use new writers on established long-running series.' Scripts welcome from experienced writers and agents only.

Carnival (Films & Theatre) Ltd
12 Raddington Road, Ladbroke Grove,
London W10 5TG
☎0181 968 0968/1818/1717
Fax 0181 968 0155/0177
Contact *Brian Eastman*

Film, TV and theatre producers. OUTPUT Film: *The Mill on the Floss* (BBC); *Firelight* (Hollywood Pictures/Wind Dancer Productions); *Shadowlands* (Savoy/Spelling); *In Hitler's Shadow* (Home Box Office); *Under Suspicion* (Columbia/Rank

/LWT); *Wilt* (Rank/LWT); *Whoops Apocalypse* (ITC). Television: *The Fragile Heart* (Ch4); *Crime Traveller* (BBC); *Poirot* (LWT); *Bugs* (BBC); *Anna Lee* (LWT); *All or Nothing At All* (LWT); *Head Over Heels* (Carlton); *The Big Battalions* (Ch4); *Jeeves & Wooster* I–IV (Granada); *Traffik* (Ch4); *Forever Green* (LWT); *Porterhouse Blue* (Ch4); *Blott on the Landscape* (BBC). Theatre: *What a Performance; Juno & the Paycock; Murder is Easy; Misery; Ghost Train; Map of the Heart; Shadowlands; Up on the Roof.*

Cartwn Cymru

Screen Centre, Llantrisant Road, Cardiff
CF5 2PU
☎01222 575999   Fax 01222 575919

Contact *Naomi Jones*

Animation production company. OUTPUT *Toucan 'Tecs* (YTV/S4C); *Funnybones* (S4C/BBC); *Turandot: Operavox* (S4C/BBC); *Testament: The Bible in Animation* (BBC2/S4C). In production: *The Jesus Story* (S4C)

Pearl Catlin Associates

Production Centre, The Clock House, Summersbury Drive, Shalford, Guildford, Surrey GU4 8JQ
☎01483 567932   Fax 01483 302646

Contact *Pearl Catlin, Peter Yolland, Paul Bernard*

Film and video: drama, documentary, children's, feature films. Interested in creative ideas for all kinds of programmes; s.a.e. with all material necessary.

CCC Wadlow

3rd Floor South, Harling House, 47–51 Great Suffolk Street, London SE1 0BL
☎0171 450 4720   Fax 0171 450 4734

Head of Productions *Sarah Dent*

Film and video, multimedia and graphic design: corporate and commercials. CLIENTS include Bovis; Camelot; De La Rue plc; Del Monte Foods International; East Midlands Electricity; Hill & Norton; Knowlton; Lloyds of London; Nationwide Building Society; P&O; M&C Saatchi; Samaritans. 'We are very keen to hear from new writers, but please send c.v.s rather than scripts.'

Celador Productions Ltd

39 Long Acre, London WC2E 9JT
☎0171 240 8101   Fax 0171 836 1117

Contact *Paul Smith, Nic Phillips*

Primarily light entertainment programming for all broadcast television and radio channels, including game shows, variety, documentaries and sitcoms. OUTPUT *Talking Telephone Numbers; Everybody's Equal; The Hypnotic World of Paul McKenna; The South Bank Show – Cliff Richard; Schofield's TV Gold* (all for ITV); *Canned Carrott; Carrott's Commercial Breakdown; The Detectives; Auntie's Bloomers; Gibberish; Digging The Dancing Queens* (all for BBC); *Classic Country* (BSB) and Sky TV's London link for the Oscar Awards.

Central Office of Information Film & Video

Hercules Road, London SE1 7DU
☎0171 261 8667   Fax 0171 261 8776

Contact *Geoff Raison*

Film, video and TV: drama, documentary, commercials, corporate and public information films. OUTPUT includes government commercials and corporate information, plus a monthly magazine for overseas use. No scripts. New writing commissioned as required.

Channel X Communications Ltd

22 Stephenson Way, London NW1 2HD
☎0171 387 3874   Fax 0171 387 0738

Contact *Alan Marke*

FOUNDED 1986 by Jonathan Ross and Alan Marke to develop Ross's first series *The Last Resort*. Now producing comedy series and documentary. Actively developing narrative comedy and game shows. OUTPUT *Unpleasant World of Penn & Teller; XYZ; Jo Brand – Through The Cakehole; Sean's Show; The Smell of Reeves & Mortimer; Fantastic Facts; One for the Road; Funny Business; Shooting Stars.*

Chatsworth Television Ltd

97–99 Dean Street, London W1V 5RA
☎0171 734 4302   Fax 0171 437 3301

Head of Drama Development *Stephen Jeffrey-Poulter*

Drama and light entertainment TV producers. All unsolicited drama scripts will be considered. Mainly interested in contemporary, factually based or comedy drama material, but *not* sitcoms. S.a.e. must accompany *all* submissions.

Childsplay Productions Ltd

8 Lonsdale Road, London NW6 6RD
☎0171 328 1429   Fax 0171 328 1416

Contact *Kim Burke*

Television: drama, children's (not pre-school) and educational. OUTPUT includes *Streetwise; All Change; Picture Box; Miles Better; Eye of the Storm; Pirates.*

Circus Films
See **Elstree (Production) Co. Ltd.**

Claverdon Films Ltd
28 Narrow Street, London E14 8DQ
☎0171 702 8700   Fax 0171 702 8701
Contact *Mike Bluett, Tony Palmer*

Film and TV: drama and documentary.
OUTPUT *Menuhin; Maria Callas; Testimony; In From the Cold; Pushkin; England, My England* (by John Osborne); *Kipling.* Unsolicited material is read, but please send a written outline first.

The Clear Picture Co.
PO Box 12, Bakewell, Derbyshire DE45 1ZP
☎0114 2492201   Fax 0114 2492225
Contact *Shaun Gilmartin, Judy Laybourn*

Television documentaries, sport and corporate programmes. OUTPUT includes programmes for Carlton Television, Central Television, YTV and Sky Sports. No drama. 'We use in-house writers on most projects. However, we do occasionally use freelance talent from across a range of skills.'

Cleveland Productions
5 Rainbow Court, Oxhey, Near Watford, Hertfordshire WD1 4RP
☎01923 254000   Fax 01923 254000
Contact *Michael Gosling*

Communications in sound and vision A/V production and still photography specialists in education and sport.

Collingwood & Convergence Productions Ltd
10–14 Crown Street, Acton, London W3 8SB
☎0181 993 3666   Fax 0181 993 9595
Producers *Christopher O'Hare, Terence Clegg*
Development Director *Helen Stroud*

Film and TV. Convergence Productions produces live action, drama documentaries; Tony Collingwood Productions specialises in children's animation. OUTPUT Convergence: *Coral Browne: Caviar to the General* (Ch4 documentary); *On the Road Again* (8-part documentary series for BBC and Discovery Channel UK); *The Last Executioner* (feature film developed with the support of the European Script Fund); 60-minute programme for Ch4's 'Witness', *Better Dead Than Gay* and a half-hour documentary for Ch4's 'Without Walls', *The True Story of Marco Polo.* In development: a documentary on Harry S. Truman. Collingwood: *RARG* (award-winning animated film); two series of *Captain Zed and the Zee Zone* (ITV); *Daisy-Head Mayzie* (Dr Seuss animated series for Turner Network and Hanna-Barbera); *Oscar's Orchestra* (13-part animated series for BBC and Time Warner); *Dennis and Gnasher* (13-episode animated series for HIT Entertainment and D. C. Thomson).

Complete Communications
Communications House, Garsington Road, Cowley, Oxford OX4 2NG
☎01865 384004/383073   Fax 01865 749854
Contact *A. M. Black, Ms C. Richman, Mrs V. Andrews-Semple*

Video production for corporate, commercial and documentary work, plus satellite/business production. No unsolicited mss. Samples of work are kept on file. Freelancers used.

Creative Channel Ltd
Channel TV, Television Centre, La Pouquelaye, St Helier, Jersey, Channel Islands JE1 3ZD
☎01534 816888   Fax 01534 816889
Managing Director *Gordon de Ste Croix*

Part of the Channel Television Group. Producers of TV commercials and corporate material: information, promotional, sales, training and events coverage. OUTPUT *Exploring Guernsey* and *This is Jersey* (video souvenir travel guides); promotional videos for all types of businesses in the Channel Islands and throughout Europe; plus over 300 commercials a year. No unsolicited mss; new writing/scripts commissioned as required. Interested in hearing from local writers resident in the Channel Islands.

Creative Film Makers Ltd
Pottery Lane House, 34A Pottery Lane, London W11 4LZ
☎0171 229 5131   Fax 0171 229 4999
Contact *Michael Seligman, Nicholas Seligman*

Corporate and sports documentaries, commercials and television programmes. OUTPUT *The World's Greatest Golfers*, plus various corporate and sports programmes for clients like Nestlé, Benson & Hedges, Wimpey, Bouygues. 'Always open to suggestions but have hardly ever received unsolicited material of any value.' Keen nevertheless to encourage new writers.

Creative Film Productions
68 Conway Road, London N14 7BE
☎0181 447 8187   Fax 0181 886 3054
Contact *Phil Davies*

OUTPUT Animation: *Joey* (Ch4). Drama: *Billy* (ITV); *Baby Love* (feature). Documentary: short series about food (BBC). Corporate: *A Little Time* (for Parkinson's Disease Society). Will consider ideas for five-minute adult animation.

The Creative Partnership
13 Bateman Street, London W1V 5TB
☎0171 439 7762   Fax 0171 437 1467
Contact *Christopher Fowler, Jim Sturgeon*

Producers of commercials and marketing campaigns for feature films. OUTPUT includes campaigns for *Secrets and Lies; Romeo and Juliet; Goldeneye; Trainspotting*. No scripts. 'We train new writers in-house, and find them from submitted c.v.s. All applicants must have previous commercial writing experience.' Freelance writers employed for special projects.

Cricket Ltd
1 Lower James Street, London W1R 3PN
☎0171 287 4848   Fax 0171 413 0654
Creative Director *Andrew Davies*
Head of Production (Film & Video)
   Jonathan Freer

Film and video, live events and conferences, print and design, and business television. 'Communications solutions for business clients wishing to influence targeted external and internal audiences.'

Croft Television and Graphics Ltd
Croft House, Progress Business Centre, Whittle Parkway, Slough SL1 6DQ
☎01628 668735   Fax 01628 668791
Contact *Keith Jones, Terry Adlam*

Producers of video and TV for drama, documentary, commercials, corporate, training and children's educational programmes. Any form of visual communication and entertainment. Fresh and creative new writing encouraged.

Cromdale Films Ltd
12 St Paul's Road, London N1 2QN
☎0171 226 0178
Contact *Ian Lloyd*

Film, video and TV: drama and documentary. OUTPUT *The Face of Darkness* (feature film); *Drift to Dawn* (rock music drama); *The Overdue Treatment* (documentary); *Russia, The Last Red Summer* (documentary). Initial phone call advised before submission of scripts.

Crown Business Communications Ltd
United House, 9 Pembridge Road, London W11 3JY
☎0171 727 7272   Fax 0171 727 9940

Contact *Nicky Havelaar*

Leading producers of videos, conferences and multi-media programmes for business. Interested in talented scriptwriters with experience in the field of business.

Dancetime Ltd
See **Table Top Productions**

Dareks Production House
58 Wickham Road, Beckenham, Kent BR3 6RQ
☎0181 658 2012   Fax 0181 325 0629
Contact *David Crossman*

Independent producers of corporate and broadcast television.

Dibgate Productions Ltd
Studio 4, Parkstead Lodge, 31 Upper Park Road, London NW3 2UL
☎0171 722 5634
Contact *Nicholas Parsons*

Documentary and travel films; plus comedy shorts for cinema and television. OUTPUT has included *A Fair Way to Play; Mad Dogs and Cricketers; Relatively Greek; Viva Menorca; Terribly British*.

Directors Video Company
Suite 11-13, Askew Crescent, London W12 9DP
☎0181 740 6359
Contact *Frances Jacobs, Tony Barton*

Corporate video; drama and documentary. OUTPUT Mostly corporate identity programmes, recruitment and new product launches. Writers 'with new ideas and showreels of video scripts' are particularly welcome.

Diverse Fiction Limited
Gorleston Street, London W14 8XS
☎0171 603 4567   Fax 0171 603 2148
Contact *Laurence Bowen*

Producer of film and TV drama. Recent OUTPUT includes: *The Hello Girls; Stone, Scissors, Paper; Dual Balls* and *Prairie Doves*.

Diverse Production Limited
Gorleston Street, London W14 8XS
☎0171 603 4567   Fax 0171 603 2148
Contact *Roy Ackerman, Narinder Minhas*

Broadcast television production with experience in popular prime-time formats, strong documentaries (one-offs and series), investigative journalism, science, business and history films, travel series, arts and music, talk shows, schools and education. 'We have always been committed to editorial and visual originality.' Recent OUTPUT includes *Secret Lives; Omnibus; Cutting Edge; Equinox; Modern Times; Dispatches; Without Walls; Panorama; The Big Idea; Empires and Emperors* and the *Little Picture Show*.

Drake A-V Video Ltd
89 St Fagans Road, Fairwater, Cardiff CF5 3AE
☎01222 560333   Fax 01222 554909
Contact *Ian Lewis*

Corporate A-V film and video, mostly promotional, training or educational. Scripts in these fields welcome. Other work includes interactive multimedia and CD-ROM production.

The Drama House Ltd
1 Hertford Place, London W1P 5RS
☎0171 388 9140   Fax 0171 388 3511
Contact *Jack Emery*

Television producers. OUTPUT *Breaking the Code* (BBC1); *Witness Against Hitler* (BBC1); *Suffer the Little Children* (BBC2 'Stages'); *A Curse on the House of Windsor* (Ch4 'Without Walls' dramadocumentary); *Call to Prayer* (BBC1 4-part documentary series). Scripts (synopses preferred) welcome but only read and returned if accompanied by full postage. Interested in developing contacts with new and established writers.

Charles Dunstan Communications Ltd
42 Wolseley Gardens, London W4 3LS
☎0181 994 2328   Fax 0181 994 2328
Contact *Charles Dunstan*

Producers of film, video and TV for documentary and corporate material. OUTPUT *Renewable Energy* for broadcast worldwide in *Inside Britain* series; National Power Annual Report video *The Electric Environment*. No unsolicited scripts.

Eagle and Eagle Ltd
15 Marlborough Road, London W4 4EU
☎0181 995 1884   Fax 0181 995 5648
Contact *Robert Eagle, Catharine Alen-Buckley*

Film, video and TV: drama, documentary and children's programmes. No unsolicited scripts.

East Anglian Productions
Studio House, 21–23 Walton Road, Frinton on Sea, Essex CO13 0AA
☎01255 676252   Fax 01255 850528
Contact *Ray Anderson*

Film, video and TV: drama and documentary,

children's television, comedy, commercials and corporate.

Eclipse Presentations Ltd
Walters Farm Road, Tonbridge, Kent TN9 1QT
☎01732 365107   Fax 01732 362600
Contact *Brian Adams*

Practitioners in audio and visual communications. *Specialises* in corporate videos, conferences, PR events and award ceremonies, safety, sales and marketing, and training.

Edinburgh Film & Video Productions
Nine Mile Burn, by Penicuik, Midlothian EH26 9LT
☎01968 672131   Fax 01968 672685
Contact *R. Crichton*

Film, TV drama and documentary. OUTPUT *Sara; Moonacre; Torch; Silent Mouse; The Curious Case of Santa Claus; The Stamp of Greatness*. No unsolicited scripts at present.

Elstree (Production) Co. Ltd
Shepperton Studios, Studios Road, Shepperton, Middlesex TW17 0QD
☎01932 572680/1   Fax 01932 572682
Contact *Greg Smith*

Produces feature films and TV drama/situation comedy. OUTPUT *Othello* (BBC); *Great Expectations* (Disney Channel); *Porgy & Bess* (with Trevor Nunn); *Old Curiosity Shop* (Disney Channel/RHI); *London Suite* (NBC/Hallmark). Co-owner of Circus Films with Trevor Nunn for feature film projects.

Enigma Productions Ltd
13–15 Queen's Gate Place Mews, London SW7 5BG
☎0171 581 0238   Fax 0171 584 1799
Head of Development *Jane Wittekind*
Chairman *Sir David Puttnam*

Backed by Warner Bros. OUTPUT *Memphis Belle*; *Meeting Venus; Being Human; War of the Buttons*; *Le Confessional* by Robert Lepage. In development: *Fade Out* (drama set in Prague in the 1940s); *Shackleton* (true story of the Antarctic explorer); *Serenade* (musical romantic comedy); *The Scarlet Pimpernel; Lorna Doone; A Very Long Engagement* (based on novel by Sebastien Japrisot about the First World War); *The Ginger Boy* (based on 'Son of Adam' by Denis Forman). Unsolicited submissions accepted only from a recognised agent or motion picture lawyer.

Essential Film & TV Productions Ltd

5 Anglers Lane, London NW5 3DG
☎0171 482 1992   Fax 0171 485 4287
Creative Director *Christopher Skala*

TV situation comedy and drama. OUTPUT *Surgical Spirit* (Granada); *Porkpie* (Ch4); *Agony Again* (BBC); *Desmonds* (Ch4).

Excalibur Productions

13–15 Northgate, Heptonstall, West Yorkshire HX7 7ND
☎01422 844595   Fax 01422 843871
Contact *Jay Jones*

Most recent productions are medical documentaries such as an investigation into diabetes control sponsored by Bayer Diagnostics, collaborative literary and cultural projects such as *The Boys From Savoy* with David Glass, and corporates for clients such as South Yorkshire Supertram and Datacolor International. Interested in ideas, scripts and possible joint development for broadcast, sell-through and experimental arts.

Farnham Film Company Ltd

34 Burnt Hill Road, Lower Bourne, Farnham, Surrey GU10 3LZ
☎01252 710313   Fax 01252 725855
Contact *Ian Lewis*

Television and film: children's drama and documentaries. Unsolicited mss welcome. 'Always looking for new material which is commercially viable.'

Farrant Partnership

91 Knatchbull Road, London SE5 9QU
☎0171 733 0711   Fax 0171 738 5224
Contact *James Farrant*

Corporate video productions.

Filmit Productions

2 Tunstall Road, London SW9 8BN
☎0171 738 4175   Fax 0171 738 3787
Contact *John Samson*

Television documentaries and corporate work. OUTPUT *A Polite Enquiry; The Gulf Between Us; Loyalty on the Line; Who Let Our Children Die* (all documentaries for Ch4); *Free for All; Speak Out* (Ch4 series). Unsolicited scripts welcome. Keen to discover and nurture new writing talent.

First Creative Group Ltd

The Stables, Mellings Farm, Benson Lane, Catforth, Preston, Lancashire PR4 0HY
☎01772 690450   Fax 01772 690964
Contact *M. Mulvihill*

Film, video and TV productions for documentary, corporate and multimedia material. Unsolicited scripts welcome. Open to new writing.

First Information Group

Knightsbridge House, 197 Knightsbridge, London SW7 1RB
☎0171 393 3000   Fax 0171 393 3033
Contact *Michael Rodd*

Multi-media for business and industry including video, computer and on-line services. No unsolicited material but always interested in c.v.s and personal profiles.

Fitting Images Ltd

Alfred House, 127A Oatlands Drive, Weybridge, Surrey KT13 9LB
☎01932 840056   Fax 01932 858075
Managing Director *Sue Fleetwood*

Promotional, training, medical/pharmaceutical; contacts from experienced writers of drama and comedy welcome. We are also interested in broadcast projects.

Flashback Communication Ltd

25 Greenhead Street, Glasgow G40 1ES
☎0141 554 6868   Fax 0141 554 6869
Contact *Chris Attkins*

Video and TV producers: drama, documentary, corporate, training and education, and sell-throughs. OUTPUT includes dramatised training videos and TV programmes or inserts for the ITV network, BBC and stations worldwide. Proposals considered; no scripts. New talent encouraged. Interested in fresh ideas and effective style.

Flicks Films Ltd

101 Wardour Street, London W1V 3TD
☎0171 734 4892   Fax 0171 287 2307
Managing Director/Producer *Terry Ward*

Film and video: children's animated series and specials. OUTPUT *The Mr Men; Little Miss; Bananaman; The Pondles; Junglies; Nellie the Elephant; See How They Work With Dig and Dug.* Scripts specific to their needs will be considered. 'Always willing to read relevant material.'

Focus Films Ltd

The Rotunda Studios, Rear of 116–118 Finchley Road, London NW3 5HT
☎0171 435 9004/5   Fax 0171 431 3562
Contact *David Pupkewitz, Lisa Disler, Malcolm Kohill (Head of Development)*

Film and TV producers. Drama OUTPUT

CrimeTime (medium–budget feature thriller); *Diary of a Sane Man* (experimental feature for Ch4); *Othello* (Ch4 drama). Projects in development include *Johnny Riff; The 51st State; Spindrift; The Complete History of the Breast.* No unsolicited scripts.

Folio Productions

60 Charlotte Street, London W1P 2AX
☎0171 436 3310   Fax 0171 436 3117
Contact *Charles Thompson*

Film, TV and video: documentary and corporate work. OUTPUT includes programmes for *Dispatches, Cutting Edge, Secret History* and *Black Bag* (Ch4); plus a 7–part commando series for ITV. Scripts and ideas welcome, including work from new writers.

Forge Productions Ltd

14 Ceylon Road, London W14 0PY
☎0171 602 1867   Fax 0171 602 1867
Contact *Ralph Rolls*

TV, video and radio: documentaries, features, specialising in the arts, literature and poetry. OUTPUT includes *Everyman: Celtic Britain* for BBC1; religious programmes for the BBC, including four programmes on Islamic communities in the UK; 13–part TV series on the paranormal for European 'Discovery'; *Kaleidoscope* feature for Radio 4. New writers encouraged but no unsolicited mss.

Mark Forstater Productions Ltd

27 Lonsdale Road, London NW6 6RA
☎0171 624 1123   Fax 0171 624 1124
Production *Mark Forstater, Rosie Homan*

Active in the selection, development and production of material for film and TV. OUTPUT *Monty Python and the Holy Grail; The Odd Job; The Grass is Singing; Xtro; Forbidden; Separation; The Fantasist; Shalom Joan Collins; The Silent Touch; Grushko; The Wolves of Willoughby Chase; Between the Devil and the Deep Blue Sea; Doing Rude Things.* No unsolicited mss.

Friday Productions Ltd

23a St. Leonards Terrace, London SW3 4QG
☎0171 730 0608   Fax 0171 730 0608
Contact *Georgina Abrahams*

Film and TV productions for drama material. OUTPUT *Goggle Eyes; Harnessing Peacocks; The December Rose.* No unsolicited scripts. New writing encouraged especially from under-represented groups.

Gaia Communications

Sanctuary House, 35 Harding Avenue, Eastbourne, East Sussex BN22 8PL
☎01323 734809   Fax 01323 734809
Producer *Robert Armstrong*
Script Editor *Loni Webb*

Video and TV corporate and documentary. OUTPUT *Discovering* (tourist and local knowledge series); *Holistic* (therapies & general information). 'Open to new ideas'; synopsis only on first contact.

Gala International Ltd

25 Stamford Brook Road, London W6 0XJN
☎0181 741 4200   Fax 0181 741 2323
Producer *David Lindsay*

TV commercials, promos, epics, film and TV documentaries.

John Gau Productions

Burston House, 1 Burston Road, Putney, London SW15 6AR
☎0181 788 8811   Fax 0181 789 0903
Contact *John Gau*

Documentaries and series for TV, plus corporate video. OUTPUT includes *The Great Sell-Off* (BBC2); *Korea* series (BBC1); *Reaching for the Skies* (BBC2); *Voyager* (Central); *The Power and The Glory* (BBC2); *The Team – A Season With McLaren* (BBC2); *The Great Outdoors* (Ch4); *Lights, Camera, Action!: A Century of the Cinema* (ITV network); *The Triumph of the Nerds* (Ch4). Open to ideas from writers.

Noel Gay Television

1 Albion Court, Albion Place, Hammersmith, London W6 0QT
☎0181 600 5200   Fax 0181 600 5222
Contact *Charles Armitage*

The association with Noel Gay (agency/management and music publishing) makes this one of the most securely financed independents in the business. Recent OUTPUT and confirmed productions for 1997: *I-Camcorder* (Ch4); *10%ers – Series 2* (Carlton/ITV); *Call Up the Stars* (BBC1); *Smeg Outs* (BBC video); *Les Bubb* (BBC Scotland); *Red Dwarf – Series 7&8; Red Dwarf Christmas Special* (BBC); *Making of Red Dwarf* (BBC video); *Dave Allen* (ITV). Joint ventures and new companies include a partnership with Odyssey, a leading Indian commercials, film and TV producer, and international networks; a joint venture with Reed Consumer Books to develop book and magazine ideas for film, video and television, and the Noel Gay Motion Picture Company, whose 1996 credits include *Trainspotting* (with Ch4 and Figment Films), and *Killer Tongue*, a co-production with Iberoamericana. Other associate NGTV companies are Grant Naylor Productions, Rose Bay Film Productions, Pepper Productions and Jane Davies Casting.

Geofilms Ltd
12 Thame Lane, Culham, Oxford OX14 3DS
☎01235 555422   Fax 01235 530581
Contact *Ms Martine Benoit*

Film, video and TV productions for documentary, corporate and education material. OUTPUT *Equinox: The Bermuda Triangle; Dispatches: Power Connection* (Ch4); *Horizon: Magma Chamber; Antenna: Hot Ice* (BBC2); also training programmes for the Resource Industry. Unsolicited scripts welcome relating to earth sciences and the environment.

Goldcrest Films International Ltd
65–66 Dean Street, London W1V 6PL
☎0171 437 8696   Fax 0171 437 4448
Chairman *John Quested*
Chief Executive Officer *Guy Collins*

FOUNDED in the late 70s. Formerly part of the Brent Walker Leisure Group but independent since 1990 following management buy-out led by John Quested. The company's core activities are film production and worldwide distribution. Scripts via agents only.

The Good Film Company
2nd Floor, 14–15 D'Arblay Street, London W1V 3FP
☎0171 734 1331   Fax 0171 734 2997
Contact *Yanina Barry*

Commercials and pop videos. CLIENTS include Hugo Boss, Cadbury's, Wella, National Express Coaches, Camel Cigarettes, Tunisian Tourist Board. No unsolicited mss.

Granada Film
The London Television Centre, Upper Ground, South Bank, London SE1 9LT
☎0171 737 8681   Fax 0171 737 8682
Contact *Pippa Cross, Tessa Gibbs, David Blaikley*

Films and TV films. OUTPUT *My Left Foot; Jack & Sarah; August* (features); *Some Kind of Life* (TV). No unsolicited scripts. Supportive of new writing but often hard to offer real help as Granada are developing mainstream commercial projects which usually requires some status in talent areas.

Grasshopper Enterprises Ltd
50 Peel Street, London W8 7PD
☎0171 229 1181   Fax 0171 229 2070
Contact *Joy Whitby*

Children's programmes and adult drama. No unsolicited mss.

Green Umbrella Ltd
The Production House, 147A St Michaels Hill, Bristol BS2 8DB
☎0117 9731729   Fax 0117 9467432

Television documentary makers. OUTPUT includes episodes for *The Natural World* and *Wildlife on One*. Unsolicited scripts relating to natural history subjects are welcome.

✹Howard Hall
6 Foster Road, Abingdon, Oxfordshire OX14 1YN
☎01235 533981/0860 775438
Fax 01235 533981
Contact *Howard Hall*

Film, video and TV: drama, documentary, commercials and corporate programmes. OUTPUT includes drama training programmes, satellite programmes, commercials, and programmes for broadcast channels. Scripts welcome. 'Always looking for new writers. We need a store of good writers in different fields of work.' Howard Hall has written two books: *Corporate Video Directing* (Focal Press) and *Careers in Film and Video* (**Kogan Page**).

Hammer Film Productions Ltd
Millennium Studios, Elstree Way, Borehamwood, Hertfordshire WD6 1SF
☎0181 207 4011   Fax 0181 905 1127
Contact *Roy Skeggs, Graham Skeggs*

Feature films. No unsolicited scripts.

Hammerwood Film Productions
110 Trafalgar Road, Portslade, East Sussex BN41 1GS
☎01273 277333   Fax 01273 822247
Contact *Ralph Harvey, Karen King, Petra Ginman*

Film, video and TV drama. OUTPUT *Sacre Bleu; Operation Pandora* (on-going TV series, episodes are invited); *Boadicea – Queen of the Iceni* (co-production with Pan-European Film Productions). 1997 project: *Maison D'Amour*. Most material is written in-house. 'We do not have the time to read scripts but will always read 2–3-page synopses/plot outlines. Anything of interest will be followed up.' Hammerwood are also distributors with a stock of 5000 movies and TV programmes.

Hand Pict Productions Ltd
4 Picardy Place, Edinburgh EH1 3JT
☎0131 558 1543   Fax 0131 556 0792
Contact *George Cathro*

Television production for drama and documentary material. OUTPUT *The Ken Fine Show* (6-part series for Scottish Television); *Face Value* (Ch4); *Et in Stadia Ego* ('Without Walls', Ch4); *Blood Ties* (arts documentary for BBC Wales); *Blackfish* (current affairs for Ch4); *The Boat Band* (BBC). Unsolicited scripts welcome but pressure of work and programmes in production can lead to delays in response. Encourages new writing.

HandMade Films Ltd
15 Golden Square, London W1R 3AG
☎0171 434 3132   Fax 0171 434 3143

Feature films. OUTPUT has included *The Life of Brian; Withnail and I; Mona Lisa; The Missionary; Time Bandits; The Lonely Passion of Judith Hearne; The Raggedy Rawney; Long Good Friday; A Private Function; How To Get Ahead in Advertising; Nuns on the Run.* New projects for release in 1997 include *Intimate Relations* and *Sweet Angel Mine.* Recently completed films include *The Wrong Guy; The Assistant; The James Gang; Dinner at Fred's.* No unsolicited mss at present.

Hartswood Films Ltd
Twickenham Film Studios, The Barons, St Margarets, Middlesex TW1 2AW
☎0181 607 8736   Fax 0181 607 8744
Contact *Beryl Vertue, Elaine Cameron*

Film and TV production for drama and light entertainment. OUTPUT *Men Behaving Badly* (BBC, previously Thames); *Is It Legal?* (Carlton); *The English Wife* (Meridian); *A Woman's Guide to Adultery* (Carlton); *My Good Friend* (ITV); *Code Name Kyril* (HTV). No unsolicited scripts. New writing read if recommended by agents.

Hat Trick Productions Ltd
10 Livonia Street, London W1V 3PH
☎0171 434 2451   Fax 0171 287 9791
Contact *Denise O'Donoghue*

Television programmes. OUTPUT includes *A Very Open Prison; Clive Anderson Talks Back; Confessions; Drop the Dead Donkey; Eleven Men Against Eleven; Father Ted; Game On; Have I Got News For You; Room 101; The Peter Principle; Whose Line is it Anyway?.*

Hawkshead
See **Broadcast Communications**

Hawthornden Films
Cambridge Court, Cambridge Road, Frinton on Sea, Essex CO13 9HN
☎01255 676381   Fax 01255 676381
Contact *Timothy Foster*

Active in European film co-production in the Netherlands, France and Italy. Mainstream connections in the USA. Also documentaries.

Head to Head Communication Ltd
The Hook, Fiveways Business Centre, Plane Tree Crescent, Feltham, Middlesex TW13 7AQ
☎0181 893 7766   Fax 0181 893 2777
Contact *Bob Carson*

Producers of business and corporate communication programmes and events.

Jim Henson Productions Ltd
30 Oval Road, Camden, London NW1 7DE
☎0171 428 4000   Fax 0171 428 4001
Contact *Angus Fletcher*

Feature films and TV: family entertainment and children's. OUTPUT *Gulliver's Travels; Buddy; Muppet Treasure Island; The Muppet Christmas Carol; Labyrinth; The Witches* (films); *Dinosaurs* (ABC); *Muppet Tonight* (BBC/Sky); *The Muppet Show* (ITV); *The Storyteller* (Ch4); *Dr Seuss; The Secret Life of Toys* (BBC); *The Animal Show* (BBC). Scripts via agents only.

Hightimes Productions Ltd
5 Anglers Lane, London NW5 3DG
☎0171 482 5202   Fax 0171 485 4254
Contact *A. C. Mitchell, A. Humphreys*

Television comedies. OUTPUT *Trouble in Mind* (situation comedy, 9 episodes LWT); *Me & My Girl* (situation comedy, 5 series, LWT package); *The Zodiac Game* (game show, 2 series, Anglia package); *Guys 'n' Dolls* (light entertainment, 13 episodes, BSB). Unsolicited scripts welcome. New writing encouraged where possible.

Philip Hindin
66 Melbourne Way, Bush Hill Park, Enfield, Middlesex EN1 1XQ
☎0181 366 2978   Fax 0181 366 2978
Contact *P. Hindin*

Producers of quiz-panel game shows for TV and theatre. No unsolicited material but always interested in new ideas/writing, e.g. *Call My Bluff; Password.*

Holmes Associates

38–42 Whitfield Street, London
W1P 5RF
☎0171 813 4333   Fax 0171 637 9024
Contact *Andrew Holmes, Alison Carter,*
Ian Benson

Prolific originators, producers and packagers of documentary, drama and music television and films. OUTPUT has included *The Shadow of Hiroshima* (Ch4 'Witness'); *The House of Bernarda Alba* (Ch4/WNET/Amaya); *Piece of Cake* (drama mini-series for LWT); *Well Being* and *Signals* (Ch4); *The Cormorant* (BBC/Screen 2); *John Gielgud Looks Back* (Ch4); *Four Up Two Down* and *Rock Steady* (Ch4); *Timeline* (with MPT, TVE Spain & TRT Turkey). Now concentrating on TV drama and feature films through development company Devco. Unsolicited drama/film scripts will be considered but may take some time for response.

Hourglass Pictures Ltd

117 Merton Road, Wimbledon, London
SW19 1ED
☎0181 540 8786   Fax 0181 542 6598
Director *Martin Chilcott*

Film and video: documentary, drama and commercials. OUTPUT includes television science documentaries; public relations material for government and industrial bodies; health and social issues for the World Health Organisation; product promotion for pharmaceutical companies. Open to new writing.

Hourglass Productions Limited

Television: 4 The Heights, London
SE7 8JH
☎0181 858 6870   Fax 0181 858 6870
Film: Charlton House, Charlton Road,
London SE7 8RE   ☎0181 319 8949
Producer/Director *John Walsh, MD*
Producer/Head of Finance *David Walsh, ACA*
Producer/Head of Development
Maura Walsh

Award-winning producers of drama, documentaries. OUTPUT *Monarch* (major feature film marking the 450th anniversary of the death of King Henry VIII); *Ray Harryhausen: Movement Into Life*; *The Comedy Store*; *Spiritual World*; *Sceptic & The Psychic*; *The Sleeper*. We prefer to receive mss through agents but do consider unsolicited material. Currently in development with feature film and documentary projects including *The Frozen Four, a.k.a. Otto Palindrome*; *Part Time Love*. Co-production enquiries welcome.

Hubner Video & Film Ltd

79 Dean Street, London W1V 5MA
☎0171 439 4060   Fax 0171 287 1072
Contact *Martin Hubner, Christine Fontaine*

Film commercials, corporate videos and documentaries, and feature film scripts. CLIENTS Associated Newspapers, Gateway Supermarkets, De Beers Diamonds, Bentalls, British Gas, IBM, Nat West, Audi, Parkfield/Ford (USA). Unsolicited scripts or outlines for feature films and documentaries welcome. Material is read and discussed before being forwarded if promising to TV/film companies or agents for production packaging.

Alan Hydes Associates

East Royd House, Woodlands Drive,
Apperley Bridge, West Yorkshire BD10 0PA
☎0113 2503467   Fax 0113 2503467
Contact *Alan Hydes*

Film, video and TV: drama and corporate work, including children's TV programmes, promotional, recruitment and security films for the Halifax Building Society. Also news agency facilities for national press and television. No unsolicited scripts. Interested in new ideas for conversion to drama.

Icon Films

56 Kingsdown Parade, Bristol BS6 5UQ
☎0117 9248535   Fax 0117 9420386
Contact *Harry Marshall*

Film and TV documentaries. OUTPUT *The Elephant Men* (WNET/Ch4); *The Living Edens – Bhutan, The Last Shangri La* (ABC/Kane); *Joanna Lumley in Bhutan* (BBC); *Lost Civilisations – Tibet* (Time Life for NBC). Specialises in documentaries. Open-minded to new filmmakers. Proposals welcome.

Ideal Image Ltd

Cherrywood House, Crawley Down Road,
Felbridge, Surrey RH19 2PP
☎01342 300566   Fax 01342 312566
Contact *Alan Frost*

Producers of documentary and drama for film, video, TV and corporate clients. OUTPUT *The Devils' Year* (documentary on the Red Devils); *Just Another Friday* (corporate drama).

Illuminations Films

19–20 Rheidol Mews, Rheidol Terrace,
London N1 8NU
☎0171 226 0266   Fax 0171 359 1151
Contact *Keith Griffiths*

Film and TV drama. OUTPUT includes projects

with directors like Jan Svankmajer, the Brothers Quay, G. F. Newman, Chris Petit and Patrick Keiller. 'We try to promote new talent and develop work by young writers new to the screen and experienced writers looking for new and imaginative ways to express their ideas.'

In Video Productions Ltd

16 York Place, Edinburgh EH1 3EP
☎0131 557 2151   Fax 0131 557 5465
Contact *Catherine Ann G. Reid*

Film, video and TV production for documentary, commercials, corporate and title sequences material. Unsolicited scripts welcome.

INCA (Independent Communications Associates) Ltd

3 Neal Street, Covent Garden, London WC2H 9PU
☎0171 460 4713   Fax 0171 460 4666
Managing Director *William Woollard*

Television documentary and corporate work. OUTPUT includes science, technology and medical documentaries for programmes such as *Equinox* and *Horizon*; also educational, current affairs, music, arts and light entertainment. Proposals for documentary programmes or series welcome. Positive policy towards new writing.

Initial Film and Television

See **Broadcast Communications**

Interesting Television Ltd

Oakslade Studios, Station Road, Hatton, Warwickshire CV35 7LH
☎01926 843777
Senior Producer *John Pluck*

Producers of broadcast television documentaries and feature series on film and video for ITV and BBC TV. Currently looking towards cable, satellite and home video to broaden its output. Ideas for television documentaries particularly welcome. Send a treatment in the first instance, particularly if the subject is 'outside our area of current interest'. OUTPUT has included television programmes on heritage, antiques, gardening, science and industry; also projects on heritage, health and sports for the home video front.

Isis Productions

14–15 Vernon Street, London W14 0RG
☎0171 602 0959   Fax 0171 610 5212
Director *Nick de Grunwald*

Director *Jamie Rugge-Price*
Production coordinator *Farne Sinclair*

Formed in 1991 and maintaining an earlier link with **Oxford University Press**, Isis Productions focuses on the production of music and documentary programmes, and co-produces children's programmes under its Rocking Horse banner. Current: *Classic Albums* (major international series on the making of the greatest records in rock history, including films on Grateful Dead, Stevie Wonder, Jimi Hendrix, Paul Simon, The Band. Co-produced with Daniel Television, BBC, NCRV, VH-1 and Castle Communications). *Energize!* – kids-in-sport magazine series for Westcountry TV (Rocking Horse). OUTPUT *Behind the Reporting Line* (behind-the-scenes look at foreign news gathering with Foreign Editor John Simpson for BBC2); *Dido and Aeneas* (film of Purcell's opera for BBC2/Thirteen WNET/ZDF-Arte/NVC Arts); *The Score* (classical music magazine series, co-produced with After Image for BBC2); *The Making of Sgt Pepper* (60-min film for Buena Vista International/LWT – winner of Grand Prix at MIDEM); *Mine Eyes Have Seen the Glory* (3-part documentary series for Ch4, co-produced with Cutting Edge/WTTW Chicago).

Kay Communications Ltd

Gauntley Court Studios, Gauntley Court, Nottingham NG7 5HD
☎0115 9781333   Fax 0115 9783734
Contact *John Alexander*

Makers of industrial video programmes and training programmes. Scripts written in-house. No unsolicited mss.

King Rollo Films Ltd

Dolphin Court, High Street, Honiton, Devon EX14 8LS
☎01404 45218   Fax 01404 45328
Contact *Clive Juster*

Film, video and TV: children's animated series. OUTPUT *Mr Benn; King Rollo; Victor & Maria; Towser; Play-It-Again; The Adventures of Spot; Not Now, Bernard; The Hill and the Rock; Two Can Toucan; The Sad Story of Veronica Who Played the Violin; Elmer; I Want a Cat; Oscar Got the Blame; Super Dooper Jezebel; I'm Coming to Get You; I Want My Potty; The Adventures of Ric; It's Fun to Learn With Spot; Art; Buddy & Pip; Spot's Magical Christmas; Fred; Philipp; Jakob.* Generally works from existing published material 'although there will always be the odd exception'. Proposals or phone calls in the first instance. No scripts.

Kingfisher Television Productions Ltd

Carlton Studios, Lenton Lane, Nottingham NG7 2NA

☎0115 9645262   Fax 0115 9645263

Contact *Tony Francis*

Broadcast television production.

Lagan Pictures Ltd

7 Rugby Court, Agincourt Avenue, Belfast BT7 1PN

☎01232 326125

Producer/Director *Stephen Butcher*
Producer *Alison Grundle*

Film, video and TV: drama, documentary and corporate. OUTPUT *A Force Under Fire* (Ulster TV). In development: *Smallholdings* (one-off drama); *Into the Bright Light of Day* (drama-doc). 'We are always interested in hearing from writers originating from or based in Northern Ireland or anyone with, preferably unstereo-typical, projects relevant to Northern Ireland. We do not have the resources to deal with unsolicited mss, so please phone or write with a brief treatment/synopsis in the first instance.'

Landseer Film and Television Productions Ltd

140 Royal College Street, London NW1 0TA

☎0171 485 7333   Fax 0171 485 7573

Contact *Kate Greening*

Film and video production: documentary, drama, music and arts, children's and current affairs. OUTPUT *Winter Dreams* (BBC2); *Sunny Stories – Enid Blyton* ('Arena'); *J. R. R. Tolkien* (Tolkien Partnership); *Kenneth MacMillan at 60* (BBC); *Discovering Delius* (Delius Trust); *Should Accidentally Fall* (BBC/Arts Council); *Nobody's Fool* ('South Bank Show' on Danny Kaye for LWT); *Mister Abbott's Broadway* ('Omnibus' BBC); *Hear My Chanson* ('South Bank Show'); *Gounod's Faust* (Ch4); *Swinger* (BBC2/Arts Council); *Auld Lang Syne* (BBC Scotland).

Helen Langridge Associates

75 Kenton Street, London WC1N 1NN

☎0171 833 2955   Fax 0171 837 2836

Managing Directors *Helen Langridge,*
Mike Wells

Film, video and TV: drama, music videos and commercials.

Lawson Productions Ltd

Newton Park, Wicklow, Co Wicklow Republic of Ireland

☎00 353 404 69497   Fax 00 353 404 69092

Contact *Sarah Lawson*

Film and TV: drama and comedy. OUTPUT has included *That's Love* (UK and US); *Home to Roost* (US version); *The Dawning* with Anthony Hopkins; *Life After Life* (ITV) with George Cole; *Natural Lies* (BBC); *Seekers* (ITV). Interested in new talent but no unsolicited mss unless via agents.

Lightarama Ltd

12a Wellfield Avenue, London N10 2EA

☎0181 444 8315   Fax 0181 444 8315

Contact *Alexis Key*

Video and TV production for commercials and corporate material and also special effects (light-ing). OUTPUT Mercedes Benz training pro-gramme; Renault UK training programme; British Gas special effects; Discovery Channel, new idents, lighting effects; Video London Sound Studios Ltd; French to English translation of French Natural History series; IPSEN International Ltd, brochure and communication consultancy. No unsolicited scripts but c.v.s welcome. Interested in new and creative ideas.

Lilyville Productions Ltd

7 Lilyville Road, London SW6 5DP

☎0171 371 5940   Fax 0171 736 9431

Contact *Tony Cash*

Drama and documentaries for TV. OUTPUT *Poetry in Motion* (series for Ch4); *South Bank Show: Ben Elton & Vanessa Redgrave*; *Musique Enquête* (drama-based French language series, Ch4); *Landscape and Memory* (arts documentary series for the BBC); Jonathan Miller's produc-tion of the *St Matthew Passion* for the BBC; major documentary on the BeeGees for the *South Bank Show*. Scripts with an obvious appli-cation to TV may be considered. Interested in new writing for documentary programmes.

Little Dancer Ltd

Avonway, Naseby Road, London SE19 3JJ

☎0181 653 9343   Fax 0181 653 9343

Contact *Robert Smith, Sue Townsend*

Television and cinema, both shorts and full-length features.

Living Tape Productions

See **Videotel Productions**

Lomond Television
See **Broadcast Communications**

Lucida Productions
Studio 303, 296–302 Borough High Street,
London SE1 1JS
☎0171 407 4114   Fax 0171 407 4115
Contact *Paul Joyce*

Television and cinema: arts, adventure, current
affairs, documentary, drama and music. OUTPUT
has included *Motion and Emotion: The Films of
Wim Wenders 1989; Dirk Bogarde – By Myself;
Sam Peckinpah – Man of Iron; The Making of Naked
Lunch; Kris Kristofferson – Pilgrim; Wild One:
Marlon Brando; Reel Women*. Currently in devel-
opment for documentary and drama projects.

Main Communications
City House, 16 City Road, Winchester,
Hampshire SO23 8SD
☎01962 870680   Fax 01962 870699
Contact *Eben Wilson*

Multimedia marketing, communications, electronic and publishing company for film, video
and TV: drama, documentary and commercials.
OUTPUT includes marketing communications,
educational, professional and managerial distance
learning, documentary programmes for broadcast
TV and children's material. Interested in proposals for television programmes, and in ideas for
video sell-throughs, interactive multimedia and
business information texts and programming.

Malone Gill Productions Ltd
Canaletto House, 39 Beak Street, London
W1R 3LD
☎0171 287 3970   Fax 0171 287 8146
Contact *Georgina Denison*

Mainly documentary but also some drama.
OUTPUT includes *Vermeer* (South Bank Show);
Highlanders (ITV); *Storm Chasers* (Ch4); *Nature
Perfected* (Ch4); *The Feast of Christmas* (Ch4); *The
Buried Mirror: Reflections on Spain and the New
World* by Carlos Fuentes (BBC2/Discovery
Channel); *Nomads* (Ch4/ITEL). Bronze medal
winner, New York Film Festival 1991, first at
Rencontres Internationales de l'Environnement
et de la Nature, Paris, 1992. Approach by letter
with proposal in the first instance.

Mike Mansfield Television Ltd
5–7 Carnaby Street, London W1V 1PG
☎0171 494 3061   Fax 0171 494 3057
Contact *Lucy Dickson*

Television for BBC, ITV network, Ch4 and

Ch5. OUTPUT includes *Animal Country; Just a
Minute; The James Whale Show; The Exchange;
The Entertainers; HRH the Princess of Wales Concert
of Hope; Cue the Music; Helter Skelter; Funky
Bunker*.

Bill Mason Films Ltd
Orchard House, Dell Quay, Chichester, West
Sussex PO20 7EE
☎01243 783558
Contact *Bill Mason*

Film and video: documentaries only. OUTPUT
*Racing Mercedes; The History of Motor Racing;
The History of the Motor Car*. No need for out-
side writing; all material is written in-house.
The emphasis is on automotive history.

Maverick Television
The Custard Factory, Gibb Street,
Birmingham B9 4AA
☎0121 771 1812   Fax 0121 771 1550
Contact *Jonnie Turpie*

FOUNDED 1994. High quality and innovative
Hi-8 programming in both documentary and
drama. Now expanding into light entertain-
ment and more popular drama. OUTPUT
includes *Going for a Song* (antiques panel game,
BBC1); *Blazed* (Ch4 drama); *Trade Secrets*
(BBC2); *Video Diaries* (BBC1); *Wingnut and the
Sprog* (Ch4 drama); *Michelle's Story* (a Comic
Relief special, BBC1).

Maya Vision Ltd
43 New Oxford Street, London WC1A 1BH
☎0171 836 1113   Fax 0171 836 5169
Contact *Rebecca Dobbs*

Film and TV: drama and documentary.
OUTPUT *Saddam's Killing Fields* (for 'View-
point', Central TV); *3 Steps to Heaven* (feature
film for BFI/Ch4); *A Place in the Sun* (drama for
Ch4/Arts Council); *Barcelona* (for 'Omnibus',
BBC1); *North of Vortex* (drama for Ch4/Arts
Council); *A Bit of Scarlet* (feature film for
BFI/Ch4); *In the Footsteps of Alexander the Great*
(BBC1 documentary); *Out* (several pieces for
Ch4's lesbian and gay series). No unsolicited
material; commissions only.

MediSci Healthcare Communications
Stoke Grange, Fir Tree Avenue, Stoke Poges,
Buckinghamshire SL2 4NN
☎01753 516644   Fax 01753 516965
Contact *Peter Fogarty, Caroline Witts,
Christine Lowe*

Corporate: medical programmes and training

packages for health care professionals. Health care ideas welcome. No unsolicited mss.

Melendez Films
1–17 Shaftesbury Avenue, London W1V 7RL
☎0171 434 0220   Fax 0171 434 3131
Contact *Steven Melendez, Graeme Spurway*

Independent producers working with TV stations. Animated films aimed mainly at a family audience, produced largely for the American market, and prime-time network broadcasting. Also develops and produces feature films (eight so far). OUTPUT has included *Peanuts* (half-hour TV specials); *The Lion, the Witch and the Wardrobe; Babar the Elephant* (TV specials); *Dick Deadeye or Duty Done*, a rock musical based on Gilbert & Sullivan operettas; and a video of fairytales *Happily Ever After, Jules Feiffer Series*. 'Three of the above walked in through the door.' Synopsis with completed script only. Enclose s.a.e. for return.

Melrose Film Productions
16 Bromells Road, London SW4 0BL
☎0171 627 8404   Fax 0171 622 0421
Contact *Vincent Thompson*

Producers of generic management and staff training films, and interactive programmes.

Mentorn Films
138–140 Wardour Street, London W1V 3AV
☎0171 287 4545   Fax 0171 287 3728
Contact *Tom Gutteridge, John Needham*

FOUNDED in 1985 by ex-BBC arts producer Tom Gutteridge. Producer of successful peak-time show *Challenge Anneka* and Emmy award-winning drama *The Bullion Boys*. Co-producer of Gerry Anderson's *Space Precinct*. Film, video and television: cinema, documentary, drama, music and arts.

Mersey Television Company Ltd
Campus Manor, Childwall Abbey Road, Liverpool L16 0JP
☎0151 722 9122   Fax 0151 722 1969
Contact *Prof. Phil Redmond*

The best known of the independents in the North of England. Makers of television programmes: drama and fiction serials for popular consumption only. OUTPUT *Brookside; Hollyoaks; And the Beat Goes On* (all for Ch4).

MMW Productions Ltd
26 Woodsford Square, London W14 8DP
☎0171 602 0657   Fax 0171 602 8556
Contact *Max Morgan-Witts*

Film, video and TV: drama, documentary, corporate and sell-through videos. Literary: joint-author 10 non-fiction books including re-published *Voyage of the Damned; Enola Gay; Guernica*. Scandinavian publishers' representative.

MNV
8 Dereham Road, Hingham, Norfolk NR9 4HU
☎01953 851067/0973 222843
Fax 01953 851067
Contact *Michael Norman*

Video production: corporate, training and communications. Also video publishing and conference television. No unsolicited mss but interested in new writers.

Alan More Films
Suite 205–206, Pinewood Studios, Pinewood Road, Iver, Buckinghamshire SL0 0NH
☎01753 656789   Fax 01753 656844
Contact *Alan More, Judith More*

Film, video and TV: documentary, commercials and corporate. No scripts. No need of outside writers.

The Morrison Company
302 Clive Court, Maida Vale, London W9 1SF
☎0171 289 7976   Fax 0171 681 1031
Contact *Don Morrison*

Film and video: drama, documentary and commercials. Unsolicited mss welcome.

Newgate Company
13 Dafford Street, Larkhall, Bath, Somerset BA1 6SW
☎01225 318335
Contact *Jo Anderson*

A commonwealth of established actors, directors and playwrights, Newgate originally concerned itself solely with theatre writing (at the Bush, Stratford, Roundhouse, etc.) However, in the course of development, several productions have fed into a list of ongoing drama for BBC TV/Ch4. Now looking to develop this co-production strand for film and television projects with other 'Indies'.

Northlight Productions Ltd
The Media Village, Grampian Television, Queen's Cross, Aberdeen AB15 4XJ
☎01224 646460   Fax 01224 646450
Contact *Robert Sproul-Cran*

Film, video and TV: drama, documentary and

corporate work. OUTPUT ranges from high-end corporate fund-raising videos for the National Museum of Scotland to *Anything But Temptation*, a feature film currently in development; *Calcutta Chronicles* (5-part documentary series for Ch4) and two schools series for Ch4. Scripts welcome. Has links with EAVE (European Audio-Visual Entrepreneurs) and Media 95.

Open Media
Ground Floor, 9 Leamington Road Villas, London W11 1HS
☎0171 229 5416   Fax 0171 221 4842
Contact *Alice Kramers Pawsey, Sebastian Cody*

Broadcast television: OUTPUT *After Dark; The Secret Cabaret; James Randi Psychic Investigator; Opinions; Is This Your Life?; Don't Quote Me; Brave New World; The Talking Show; Natural Causes.*

Open Mind Productions
6 Newburgh Street, London W1V 1LH
☎0171 437 0624   Fax 0171 434 9256
Directors *Chris Ellis, Roland Tongue*

Video and TV production, including documentary and educational. OUTPUT *Investigating Britain* (BBC); *Living Proof* (Ch4); *The Geography Programme: Images of the Earth* (for BBC Schools TV); *Eureka: The Earth in Space; Geography, Start Here: The Local Network; Rat-a-tat-tat; One Last Lie* (for Ch4 Schools). No unsolicited material. Currently developing children's drama series. 'We are a small company interested in programmes that reflect our name. We want to produce more drama and multi-media resources.' Chris Ellis, a writer himself, is a guest lecturer on scriptwriting with BBC TV Training and the London Media Workshop.

Orbit Ltd
Four Rivers, Ash Island, Hampton Court, Surrey KT8 9AX
☎0181 979 0196   Fax 0181 979 0196
Contact *Michael Custance*

Film and TV drama. OUTPUT *Murder in Paradise* (ABC Network/CBC/ITV); *Party Time; Writing Game* (both Ch4 plays); *Voices in the Garden* ('Screen 2' BBC/Atenne 2/Gaumont); *Small Stages* (5x90mins series of fringe plays for Ch4). No unsolicited mss. Involved with TAPS – Teddington Arts Performance Showcase (for new TV writers).

Orpheus Productions
6 Amyand Park Gardens, Twickenham, Middlesex TW1 3HS
☎0181 892 3172   Fax 0181 892 4821
Contact *Richard Taylor*

Television documentaries and corporate work. OUTPUT has included programmes for BBC Current Affairs, Music and Arts, and the African-Caribbean Unit as well as documentaries for the Shell Film Unit and Video Arts. Unsolicited scripts are welcomed with caution. 'We have a preference for visually stirring documentaries with quality writing of the more personal and idiosyncratic kind, not straight reportage.'

Ovation Productions
One Prince of Wales Passage, 117 Hampstead Road, London NW1 3EF
☎0171 387 2342   Fax 0171 380 0404
Contact *John Plews*

Corporate video and conference scripts. Unsolicited mss not welcome. 'We talk to new writers from time to time.'

Oxford Scientific Films Ltd
Lower Road, Long Hanborough, Oxfordshire OX8 8LL
☎01993 881881   Fax 01993 882808
Also at: 45–49 Poland Street, London W1N 7TD
☎0171 494 0720   Fax 0171 287 9125
Managing Director *Karen Goldie-Morrison*

Established independent media company with specialist knowledge and expertise in award-winning natural history films and science-based programmes. Film, video and TV: documentaries, TV commercials, multimedia, and educational films. Scripts welcome. Operates an extensive stills and film footage library specialising in wildlife and special effects (see **Picture Libraries**).

Pace Productions Ltd
12 The Green, Newport Pagnell, Buckinghamshire MK16 0JW
☎01908 618767   Fax 01908 617641
Contact *Chris Pettit*

Film and video: drama, documentary, corporate and commercials.

Pacesetter Productions Ltd
The Gardener's Lodge, Cloisters Business Centre, 8 Battersea Park Road, London SW8 4BH
☎0171 720 4545   Fax 0171 720 4949
Contact *Timothy Spencer*

Film and video producers of drama, documentary and corporate work. OUTPUT *History of the Telephone; Pictures from the Past; The Wheatfield; Merchant of Wood Street* (the latter two feature films in development). CLIENTS include British Telecom, British Gas, Midland Bank, Lloyds Bank. No unsolicited scripts.

Barry Palin Associates Ltd
143 Charing Cross Road, London
WC2H 0EE
☎0171 439 0039   Fax 0171 494 1305
Contact *Barry Palin*

Film, video and TV production for drama, documentary, commercials and corporate material. OUTPUT *Harmfulness of Tobacco* Anton Chekhov short story – BAFTA Best Short Film Award-winner (Ch4); Corporate: Kraft Jacobs Suchard. Unsolicited scripts welcome. New writing encouraged.

Paper Moon Productions
Wychwood House, Burchetts Green Lane, Littlewick Green, Nr. Maidenhead, Berkshire
SL6 3QW
☎01628 829819   Fax 01628 825949
Contact *David Haggas*

Television and video: medical and health education documentaries. OUTPUT includes *Shamans and Science*, a medical documentary examining the balance between drugs discovered in nature and those synthesised in laboratories. Unsolicited scripts welcome. Interested in new writing 'from people who really understand television programme-making'.

Parallax Pictures Ltd
7 Denmark Street, London WC2H 8LS
☎0171 836 1478   Fax 0171 497 8062
Contact *Sally Hibbin*

Feature films/television drama. OUTPUT *Riff-Raff; Bad Behaviour; Raining Stones; Ladybird, Ladybird; I.D.; Land and Freedom; The Englishman Who Went up a Hill But Came Down a Mountain; Bliss; Jump the Gun; Carla's Song.*

Philip Partridge Productions Ltd
The High Street, South Woodchester, Near Stroud, Gloucestershire GL5 5EL
☎01453 872743   Fax 01453 872743
Contact *Phil Partridge*

Film and TV producers for drama and comedy material. OUTPUT *Once Upon a Time in the North* Tim Firth six 30-minute comedies on film (BBC1). Unsolicited scripts welcome

'providing writers are patient while they're read'. Particularly interested in developing new writing with writers who are totally committed.

PBF Motion Pictures
The Little Pickenhanger, Tuckey Grove, Ripley, Surrey GU23 6JG
☎01483 225179   Fax 01483 224118
Contact *Peter B. Fairbrass*

Film, video and TV: drama, documentary, commercials and corporate. Also televised chess series and chess videos. OUTPUT *Grandmaster Chess* (in association with Thames TV); *Glue Sniffing; RN Special Services; Nightfrights* (night-time TV chiller series). CLIENTS include GEC-Marconi, Coca Cola, MoD, Marks & Spencer, various government departments, British Consulate. No scripts; send one-page synopsis only in the first instance. Good scripts which relate to current projects will be followed up, otherwise not, as PBF do not have the time to reply to proposals which do not interest them. Only good writing stands a chance.

Pearson Television Ltd
1 Stephen Street, London W1P 1PJ
☎0171 691 6000
Chief Executive *Greg Dyke*
Managing Director, UK Production
   Alan Boyd
Head of Drama *Mal Young*
Head of Comedy *Tony Charks*

Uk's largest independent production and distribution company. OUTPUT includes *The Bill; Birds of a Feather; Goodnight Sweetheart; This Is Your Life; Strike It Lucky; Mosley; Neighbours; Wish You Were Here …?*

Pelicula Films
7 Queen Margaret Road, Glasgow G20 6DP
☎0141 945 3333   Fax 0141 946 8345
Contact *Mike Alexander*

Television producers. Makers of drama documentaries and music programmes for Ch4 and the BBC. OUTPUT *As an Eilean (From the Island); The Shetland Sessions; The Trans-Atlantic Sessions; Songroads; Follow the Moonstone.*

Penumbra Productions Ltd
Flat 3, 80 Brondesbury Road, London
NW6 6RX
☎0171 328 4550   Fax 0171 328 3844
Contact *H. O. Nazareth*

Film, video, TV and radio: drama, documentary and information videos on health, housing, arts and political documentaries. OUTPUT includes *Will It Be a Likeness?* (Radio 3 play); *Repomen* ('Cutting Edge', Ch4); *Doctors and Torture* ('Inside Story', BBC); *Bombay & Jazz* (BBC2); *Awaaz* (information video in eight languages for Kings Fund/Manchester Council for Community Relations); *When Shura Met Hobie* (BBC Radio 3). In development: *Slave Brides* (for TV/cinema). Film treatments, drama proposals and documentary synopses welcome. Keen to assist in the development of new writing but only interested in social issue-based material.

PHI Television Ltd

Wood Farm, Peasenhall, Suffolk IP17 2HG
☎01728 660252   Fax 01728 660306
Contact *David Holmans*

Television drama, games and light entertainment. OUTPUT *Operation Julie; Treasure Hunt; Bullseye; Jangles*. No scripts in the first instance. Send one-page outlines only.

Picture Palace Films Ltd

53A Brewer Street, London W1R 3FD
☎0171 734 6630   Fax 0171 734 8574
Contact *Malcolm Craddock*

FOUNDED 1971. Leading independent producer of TV drama. OUTPUT *Sharpe's Rifles* (14 x 2-hour films for Carlton TV); *Little Napoleons* (4-part comedy drama for Ch4); *The Orchid House* (4-part drama serial for Ch4); plus episodes of *Eurocops; Tandoori Nights; 4 Minutes; When Love Dies; Ping Pong* (feature film). Material will only be considered if submitted through an agent.

Phil Pilley Productions

Ferryside, Felix Lane, Shepperton, Middlesex TW17 8NG
☎01932 246455   Fax 01932 246455
Contact *Phil Pilley*

Programmes for TV and video, mainly sports, including documentaries for the BBC, ITV, Ch4 and the US. Also books, newspapers and magazine features, mainly sports. Unsolicited ideas and synopses welcome.

Planet 24 Ltd

The Planet Building, Thames Quay, 195 Marsh Wall, London E14 9SG
☎0171 345 2424   Fax 0171 345 9400
Executive Producer/Managing Director
  Charles Parsons

Television and radio producers of light enter-tainment, comedy and music programmes. OUTPUT TV: *The Big Breakfast; The Word; The Messiah* (live recording); *Hotel Babylon; Gaytime TV; Delicious.* Radio: *Entertainment Superhighway; Straight Up; Rock Wives; Pulp.* Unsolicited scripts welcome.

Platinum Film & TV Production Ltd

79 Islip Street, London NW5 2DL
☎0171 916 9091   Fax 0171 916 5238
Contact *Terry Kelleher*

Television documentaries, including drama-doc-umentary. OUTPUT *South Africa's Black Economy* (Ch4); *Murder at the Farm* (Thames TV); *The Biggest Robbery in the World* (major investigative true-crime drama-documentary for Carlton TV). Scripts and format treatments welcome.

Portman Productions

167 Wardour Street, London W1V 3TA
☎0171 468 3400   Fax 0171 468 3499
Head of Development *Katherine Butler*

Television drama. Synopses in the first instance, please.

Premiere Productions Ltd

3 Colville Place, London W1P 1HN
☎0171 255 1650
Contact *Henrietta Williams*

Film and video: drama and corporate, includ-ing dramatised training videos. Currently look-ing for feature film scripts, with Anglo/American/East European themes. Preference for stories with humour. No horror or sci-fi. Please enclose a list of previous sub-missions and return postage.

Primetime plc

Seymour Mews House, Seymour Mews, Wigmore Street, London W1H 9PE
☎0171 935 9000   Fax 0171 935 1992
Contact *Richard Price, Simon Willock*

Television distribution and packaging, plus international co-productions. OUTPUT *An Evening with Sir Peter Ustinov; Porgy and Bess* (BBC, Homevale, Greg Smith); *Re:Joyce* (BBC); *The CIA* (BBC/A&E/NRK); *José Carreras – A Life* (LWT); *Othello* (BBC); *Ustinov on the Orient Express* (A&E/CBC/NOB/JMP); *Ethan Frome* (American Playhouse). Works closely with associated US company, Primetime Entertainment and in the music and arts area through Anglo-German company Euro-Arts-Primetime. OUTPUT *Who could ask for anything more?* (Ira Gershwin tribute); *The Gold and Silver Gala* (a celebration of Placido Domingo's 25th anniversary and 50th anniversary of the Royal Opera House company). No unsolicited scripts.

Prospect Pictures
Prospect House, 150 Great Portland Street, London W1N 6BB
☎0171 636 1234   Fax 0171 636 1236
Contact *Milla Harrison-Hansley*

Drama, documentary and corporate video and TV. Actively looking for projects from new writers; 'using our development fund for new drama'. Welcomes treatments and synopses of scripts.

Red Lion Communications Ltd
12 Sherwood Street, London W1V 7RD
☎0171 734 5364   Fax 0171 494 0608
Contact *Mike Kilcooley*

Video producers: commercials, training and corporate work, including product launch videos, in-house training, open learning, multimedia programmes, etc. 'We are always on the lookout for new, well thought through ideas for broadcast.'

Red Rooster Film and Television Entertainment
29 Floral Street, London WC2E 9DP
☎0171 379 7727   Fax 0171 379 5756
Contact *Jill Green*

Film and TV drama. OUTPUT *The Sculptress; Wilderness; Crocodile Shoes; Body & Soul; The Life and Times of Henry Pratt; Smokescreen*. No unsolicited scripts. Encourages new writers; 'recommend that they find an agent'.

Renaissance Vision
15 Capitol House, Heigham Street, Norwich, Norfolk NR2 4TE
☎01603 767272   Fax 01603 768163
Contact *B. Gardner*

Video: full range of corporate work (training, sales, promotional, etc.). Producers of educational and special-interest video publications. Willing to consider good ideas and proposals.

Richmond Films & Television Ltd
5 Dean Street, London W1V 5RN
☎0171 734 9313   Fax 0171 287 2058
Contact *Sandra Hastie*

Film and TV: drama and comedy. OUTPUT *Press Gang; The Lodge; The Office; Wavelength*.

'We will accept *two pages only* consisting of a brief treatment of your project (either screenplay or TV series) which includes its genre and its demographics. Please tell us also where the project has been submitted previously and what response you have had. If we are interested in reading a longer treatment or the script you will then be contacted. Only projects/scripts with s.a.e. will be returned.'

Roberts & Wykeham Films
7 Barb Mews, Hammersmith, London W6 7PA
☎0171 602 4897   Fax 0171 602 3016
Contact *S. Wykeham*

Television documentaries and packaging. OUTPUT Ch4 'Dispatches': *The Saudi Tapes; Trail of Red Mercury; Mandela's Nuclear Nightmare;* BBC 'Everyman': *Road Back to Hell*. No unsolicited scripts.

Rocking Horse
See **Isis Productions**

Rose Bay Film Productions
1 Albion Court, Albion Place, London W6 0QT
☎0181 600 5200   Fax 0181 600 5222
Contact *Matthew Steiner, Simon Usiskin*

Film and TV production for drama, entertainment and documentary. Unsolicited scripts welcome.

Sands Films
119 Rotherhithe Street, London SE16 4NF
☎0171 231 2209   Fax 0171 231 2119
Contact *Richard Goodwin, Christine Edzard*

Film and TV drama. OUTPUT *Little Dorrit; The Fool; As You Like It; A Dangerous Man; The Long Day Closes; A Passage to India*. In development: *Buddenbrooks*. No unsolicited scripts.

Scala Productions
39–43 Brewer Street, London W1R 3FD
☎0171 734 7060   Fax 0171 437 3248
Contact *Stephen Woolley, Nik Powell, Rachel Wood*

Production company set up by ex-Palace Productions Nik Powell and Stephen Woolley, who have an impressive list of credits including *Company of Wolves; Absolute Beginners; Mona Lisa; Scandal; Crying Game; Backbeat; Hollow Reed; Neon Bible*. Productions include: *B. Monkey; Dead Heart; 24:7; Little Voice*. In development: *St Agnes' Stand; Skintight; Jonathan Wild; Mort; The Lost Son; Wise Children*.

Schwops Productions
34 Ashton Road, Luton, Bedfordshire
LU1 3QE
☎01582 412622   Fax 01582 412095
Contact *Maureen Brown*

Video producer of drama, documentary and
corporate material. Areas of interest include
music, travel, ballet, medical and training
material. Also distribution, facilities, duplication, and sell-through videos. Open-minded to
new writing. Scripts welcome.

Scope Productions Ltd
Keppie House, 147 Blythswood Street,
Glasgow G2 4EN
☎0141 332 7720   Fax 0141 332 1049
TV Commercials *Sharon Fullarton*
Corporate *Bill Gordon*

Corporate film and video; broadcast documentaries and sport; TV commercials. Unsolicited
mss, realistic scripts/ideas welcome.

Screen First Ltd
The Studios, Funnells Farm, Down Street,
Nutley, East Sussex TN22 3LG
☎01825 712034   Fax 01825 713511
Contact *M. Thomas, P. Madden*

Television dramas, documentaries, arts and animation programmes. OUTPUT *Secret Passions*
series I, II, III, IV (presenting new animation
for Ch4). Developing major drama series. No
unsolicited scripts.

Screen Ventures Ltd
49 Goodge Street, London W1P 1FB
☎0171 580 7448   Fax 0171 631 1265
Contact *Christopher Mould, Caroline Furness*

Film and TV sales and production: documen-
tary, music videos and drama. OUTPUT
Woodstock Diary; Vanessa Redgrave (LWT
'South Bank Show'); *Mojo Working; Burma:
Dying for Democracy* (Ch4); *Genet* (LWT 'South
Bank Show'); *Dani Dares* (Ch4 series on strong
women); *Amandla* (HBO).

Securicor Media Services
15 Carshalton Road, Sutton, Surrey SM1 4LE
☎0181 770 7000   Fax 0181 722 2672
Contact *Paul Fahey, Gill Arney*

Television producers of drama, documentary
and corporate material. OUTPUT includes promotional, information and training videos for
the Securicor Group and selected clients. Also
audio, print design and production.

Seventh House Films
1 Hall Farm Place, Bawburgh, Norwich,
Norfolk NR9 3LW
☎01603 749068   Fax 01603 749069
Contact *Clive Dunn, Angela Rule*

Documentary for film, video and TV. OUTPUT
A Pleasant Terror (life and ghosts of M. R.
James); *Piano Pieces* (musical excursion explor-
ing different aspects of the piano); *Rockin' the
Boat* (memories of pirate radio); *White Knuckles*
(on the road with a travelling funfair); *King
Romance* (life of Henry Rider Haggard); *A Drift
of Angels* (three women and the price of art);
Bare Heaven (the life and fiction of L. P.
Hartley); *A Swell of the Soil* (life of Alfred
Munnings); *Light Out of the Sky* (the art and life
of Edward Seago). 'We welcome programme
proposals with a view to collaborative co-production. Always interested in original and
refreshing expressions for visual media.'

Sianco Cyf
Tŷr Drindod, Y Sgwâr, Porthaethwy,
Ynys Môn LL59 5EE
☎01248 715005   Fax 01248 715006
Contact *Siân Teifi*

Children's, youth and education programmes.
Children's drama.

Signals, Essex Media Centre
21 St Peter's Street, Colchester, Essex
CO1 1EW
☎01206 560255   Fax 01206 369086
Coordinator *Caroline Norbury*

Promotion and documentary work for the voluntary and arts sectors. Specialists in media
education projects. No unsolicited mss.

Siriol Productions
3 Mount Stuart Square, Butetown, Cardiff
CF1 6RW
☎01222 488400   Fax 01222 485962
Contact *Andrew Offiler*

Animated series, mainly for children. OUTPUT
includes *The Hurricanes; Tales of the Toothfairies;
Billy the Cat*, as well as the feature films, *Under
Milkwood* and *The Princess and the Goblin*. Write
with ideas and sample script in the first
instance.

Skyline Film & TV Productions Ltd
46 Bedford Square, London WC1B 3DP
☎0171 462 9999   Fax 0171 462 9998
Contact *Emma James*

Television programmes, educational, drama and feature films. Suppliers of programmes to all major broadcasters. Always interested in new ideas/talent; written submissions only, please.

Sleeping Giant Films
56–58 Clerkenwell Road, London
EC1M 5PX
☎0171 490 5060   Fax 0171 490 5060
Contact *Harriet Pacaud*

Documentary film producer. OUTPUT includes *Kirkby's Kingdom*, the story of a Yorkshire smallholder whose land is threatened by property developers. Interested in original ideas with strong visual potential on environmental, natural history, arts and cultural themes. No fiction-based material. Happy to look at documentary ideas. Commentary writers used.

Smith & Watson Productions
The Gothic House, Fore Street, Totnes,
South Devon TQ9 5EH
☎01803 863033   Fax 01803 864219
Contact *Chris Watson, Nick Smith*

Film, video and TV: documentaries, drama, party political broadcasts (for the Liberal Democrats), and commercials. In production: *The Lads* (ITV series). Unsolicited mss welcome. Interested in new writing.

Solo Vision Ltd
49–53 Kensington High Street, London
W8 5ED
☎0171 376 2166   Fax 0171 938 3165
Contact *Don Short*

Video and TV: documentary, game shows, and corporate work. OUTPUT *Starmate* (the astrology game); *Surrogate Grandmother* (documentary, LWT/Cable USA); plus video packaging.

Specific Films
25 Rathbone Street, London W1P 1AG
☎0171 580 7476   Fax 0171 494 2676
Contact *Michael Hamlyn, Clare Wise*

FOUNDED 1976. OUTPUT includes *Mr Reliable* (feature film co-produced by PolyGram and the AFFC); *The Adventures of Priscilla, Queen of the Desert* a full-length feature film co-produced with Latent Image (Australia) and financed by PolyGram and AFFC; *U2 Rattle and Hum* (full-length feature film – part concert film/part cinema verité documentary); and numerous pop promos for major international artists. First-Look deal with PolyGram Filmed Entertainment.

Spectel Productions Ltd
165 Main Road, Baxterley, Atherstone,
Warwickshire CV9 2JX
☎01827 714746   Fax 01827 714746
Contact *David Webster*

Film and video: documentary and corporate; also video publishing. No unsolicited scripts.

Spellbound Productions Ltd
90 Cowdenbeath Path, Islington, London
N1 0LG
☎0171 278 0052   Fax 0171 278 0052
Contact *Paul Harris*

Film and television drama. OUTPUT includes *Leave to Remain* for 'Film on 4'. Unsolicited scripts welcome. Please enclose s.a.e. for return of material. Keen to support and encourage new writing.

SPI 1980 Ltd
27 Old Gloucester Street, London WC1N 3XX
☎0171 435 1007
Contact *Victor Schonfeld*

Drama, arts, current affairs, documentary, films for TV and cinema. OUTPUT includes *It's a Boy!; MoneyLove; Shattered Dreams, Picking Up the Pieces; The Animals Film; Courage Along the Divide; And I Don't Have to Do the Dishes*. Send a brief letter prior to submission of unsolicited material.

The Spice Factory
52 The Old Steine, Brighton, East Sussex
BN1 1NH
☎01273 728686   Fax 01273 821567
Head of Development *Anney Wyner*
Joint Managing Directors *Michael Cowan,*
    Jason Piette

Film and TV drama and PC games. Developing and producing TV series. Produced US feature films, *Killer Tongue* and *Dying to Go Home*. Very interested in new writers; unsolicited mss welcome.

'Spoken' Image Ltd
The Design Centre, 44 Canal Street,
Manchester M1 3WD
☎0161 236 7522   Fax 0161 236 0020
Contact *Geoff Allman, Steve Jones, Steve Foster,*
    Phil Griffin

Film, video and TV production for documentary and corporate material. Specialising in high-quality brochures and reports, exhibitions, conferences, film and video production for broadcast, industry and commerce.

Unsolicited scripts welcome. Interested in educational, and historical new writing, mainly for broadcast programmes.

Straight Forward Film & Television Productions Ltd
Crescent Studios, 18 High Street, Holywood, Co. Down BT18 9AD
☎01232 427697   Fax 01232 422289
Contact *Joy Hines, John Nicholson, Ian Kennedy*

Northern Ireland–based production company specialising in documentary, feature and lifestyle series. Unsolicited mss welcome. New work in drama and documentary fields welcome, particularly those with a strong Irish theme, contemporary or historical. OUTPUT *Close to Home* (Ch4 documentary on abortion laws in N. Ireland); *Greenfingers* (BBC/RTE gardening series); *Places Apart* (BBC Northern Ireland series); *The Last Colony* (Ch4 documentary on the Troubles); *Adventure Ireland* (BBC N. Ireland holiday series). In production: *Just Jones* (BBC Radio Ulster daily show); *Missing* (BBC N. Ireland documentary).

Strawberry Productions Ltd
36 Priory Avenue, London W4 1TY
☎0181 994 4494   Fax 0181 742 7675
Contact *John Black*

Film, video and TV: drama and documentary; corporate and video publishing.

Swanlind Communication
The Wharf, Bridge Street, Birmingham B1 2JR
☎0121 616 1701   Fax 0121 616 1520
Chief Executive *Peter Stack*

Producer of business television and internal communication strategies.

Table Top Productions
1 The Orchard, Chiswick, London W4 1JZ
☎0181 742 0507   Fax 0181 742 0507
Contact *Alvin Rakoff*

TV and film. OUTPUT *Paradise Postponed* (TV mini-series); *A Voyage Round My Father; The First Olympics 1896; Dirty Tricks; A Dance to the Music of Time*. No unsolicited mss. Also Dancetime Ltd.

Talisman Films Ltd
5 Addison Place, London W11 4RJ
☎0171 603 7474   Fax 0171 602 7422
Contact *Alan Shallcross*

Drama for film and TV: developing the full range of drama – TV series, serials and single films, as well as theatric features. 'We will only consider material submitted via literary agents.' Interested in supporting and encouraging new writing.

TalkBack Productions
36 Percy Street, London W1P 0LN
☎0171 323 9777   Fax 0171 637 5105
Managing Director *Peter Fincham*

Independent TV production company set up in 1981 by comedians Mel Smith and Griff Rhys Jones. Specialises in comedy, comedy drama and drama; also corporate and training films. OUTPUT *Smith and Jones; Murder Most Horrid; Bonjour la Classe; Demob; The Day Today; Paris; Knowing Me Knowing You with Alan Patridge; Milner; Loose Talk; In Search of Happiness; They Think It's All Over.*

Teamwork Productions
Gate House, Walderton, Chichester, West Sussex PO18 9ED
☎01705 631384/0410 483149
Contact *Rob Widdows*

Video and TV producer of documentary, corporate and commercial work. OUTPUT includes motor racing coverage, motor sport productions and corporate motor sport videos. Good ideas will always be considered. No scripts.

Telemagination Ltd
41 Buckingham Palace Road, London SW1W 0PP
☎0171 828 5331   Fax 0171 828 7631
Contact *John M. Mills*

Producers of television animation. OUTPUT includes *The Animals of Farthing Wood*, 39 half-hour episodes for children's television. Unsolicited outlines welcome either in writing or by phone. No new writings considered unless the outlines have been discussed first.

Televideo Productions
The Riverside, Furnival Road, Sheffield, South Yorkshire S4 7YH
☎0114 2491500   Fax 0114 2491505
Contact *Graham King*

Video and television: TV news and sports coverage, documentary and corporate work; sell-through videos (distributed on own label). OUTPUT includes *The Premier Collection* (football club videos); varied sports coverage for cable, satellite and terrestrial broadcasters plus a wide range of corporate work from drama-based material to documentary.

Teliesyn
Helwick House, 19 David Street, Cardiff
CF1 2EH
☎01222 667556   Fax 01222 667546
Chief Executive *Michael Esthop*

Film and video: produces drama, documentary, music and social action in English and Welsh. Celtic Film Festival, BAFTA Cymru, Grierson and Indie award winner. OUTPUT *Branwen* (90 minute feature film for S4C); *Reel Truth* (drama doc series on the history of early film for S4C and Ch4); *Subway Cops and the Mole Kings* (Ch4); *Dragon's Song* (music series for schools, Ch4); *Codi Clawr Hanes II* (a second drama-documentary series on women's history for S4C). Will consider unsolicited mss only if accompanied by synopsis and c.v. Encourages new writing wherever possible, in close association with a producer.

Tern Television Productions Ltd
73 Crown Street, Aberdeen AB11 6EX
☎01224 211123   Fax 01224 211199
Also at: 74 Victoria Crescent Road, Glasgow
G12 9JN   ☎0141 337 2892
Contact *David Strachan, Gwyneth Hardy, Nick Ibbotson*

Broadcast, video, corporate and training. Specialises in religious and factual entertainment. Currently developing drama. Unsolicited mss welcome.

Thames Television Ltd
See **Pearson Television Ltd**

Theatre of Comedy Co.
See **Theatre Producers**

Huw Thomas & Associates
17 Brunswick Gardens, London W8 4AS
☎0171 727 9953   Fax 0171 727 9931
Contact *Anne E. Thomas*

Video and TV: documentary and corporate; also media training. CLIENTS include Lloyd's of London, Nestlé, Morgan Crucible. No unsolicited scripts.

Tiger Aspect Productions
5 Soho Square, London W1V 5DE
☎0171 434 0672   Fax 0171 287 1448
Contact *Charles Brand*

Television producers for documentary programmes, drama and comedy – variety, sitcom and comedy drama. OUTPUT *Mr Bean; The Thin Blue Line; The Vicar of Dibley; Howard Goodall's Organ Works; Deacon Brodie; Hospital.*

Only considers material submitted via an agent or from writers with a known track record.

Tonfedd
Uned 33, Cibyn, Caernarfon, Gwynedd
LL55 2BD
☎01286 676800   Fax 01286 676466
Contact *Hefin Elis*

Light entertainment, music.

Alan Torjussen Productions Ltd
17 Heol Wen, Cardiff CF4 6EG
☎01222 624669   Fax 01222 624669
Contact *Alan Torjussen*

Film, video and TV production for drama, documentary, commercials and corporate material. Particularly interested in all types of documentary, education, schools and drama. Background includes work in the Welsh language. Unsolicited scripts welcome, particularly if about Wales by Welsh writers (includes Welsh language scripts). Also original ideas for comedy and documentary/dramas.

Transatlantic Films Production and Distribution Company
184 Kensington Church Street, London
W8 4DP
☎0171 727 0132   Fax 0171 727 2293
Contact *Revel Guest*

Producers of TV documentaries. OUTPUT *History's Turning Points* 26x30-mins programmes on decisive moments in world history (The Learning Channel); *Greek Fire* 10 x 30 mins on Greek culture (Ch4); *Four American Composers* 4 x 1 hour (Ch4); *The Horse in Sport* 8 x 1 hour (Ch4); *A Year in the Life of Placido Domingo.* No unsolicited scripts. Interested in new writers to write 'the book of the series', e.g. for *Greek Fire* and *The Horse in Sport*, but not usually drama script writers.

Turning Point Productions
Pinewood Studios, Pinewood Road,
Iver Heath, Buckinghamshire SL0 0NH
☎01753 630666   Fax 01753 650855
Contact *Adrian Bate*

Television drama producer. OUTPUT includes *Red Fox* (LWT mini-series). Very keen to nurture new writing talent. No unsolicited scripts.

TurnOver Titles
c/o Camerson AV, Unit 8A, Intec 2, Wade
Road, Basingstoke, Hampshire RG24 8NE
☎01256 350022   Fax 01256 350046
Contact *Paul Friend*

A television production company. Looking to produce and develop original scripts and ideas. Mainly interested in sitcoms and drama series, also radical and cult ideas for low budget programming. Write in the first instance, please.

Twentieth Century Fox Productions Ltd

Twentieth Century House, 31–32 Soho Square, London W1V 6AP
☎0171 437 7766   Fax 0171 434 2170

London office of the American giant.

Two Four Productions Ltd

Quay West Studios, Old Newnham, Plymouth, Devon PL7 5BH
☎01752 345424   Fax 01752 344224

Managing Director *Charles Wace*
Corporate Director *Charles Boydell*

Video and television: drama, documentary, commercials and corporate. OUTPUT includes *Close to Home: Journey for Life* (current affairs for Ch4); *The West at Work* (business magazine for Westcountry Television); *Great Westerners* (documentary for HTV); *The Church in Crisis* (current affairs programme for BBC2 South West); *On the Moor* (a 6-part documentary filmed inside Dartmoor Prison); *HMP Dartmoor* (ITV network); *Soul Mates* and *The Right Thing* (two 13-part series for satellite television); and *Westcountry Focus* (a series of weekly business programmes for Westcountry Television). Currently in production: *Collectors' Lot* (Ch4). Ideas welcome.

Two Sides TV Ltd

53A Brewer Street, London W1R 3FD
☎0171 439 9882   Fax 0171 287 2289

Managing Director *Catherine Robins*

Broadcast TV including children's programmes such as *The Adventures of Captain Zeelig; Bug Alert!* for ITV. Always looking for fresh new children's writing with a humorous edge. Also documentaries ('Equinox', 'Under the Sun') for Ch4 and BBC.

UBA Ltd

21 Alderville Road, London SW6 2EE
☎01984 623619   Fax 01984 623733

Contact *Peter Shaw*

Quality feature films and TV for an international market. OUTPUT *Windprints; The Lonely Passion of Judith Hearne* (co-production with **HandMade Films Ltd**); *Taffin; Castaway; Turtle Diary; Sweeney Todd; Keep the Aspidistra*

Flying. In development: *Hunting the Devil; A Witch in New York; Kinder Garden; Paul Robeson; Rebel Magic; No Man's Land; Murdering Shakespeare.* Prepared to commission new writing whether adapted from another medium or based on a short outline/treatment. Concerned with the quality of the script (*Turtle Diary* was written by Harold Pinter) and breadth of appeal. 'Exploitation material' not welcome.

United Film and Television Productions

48 Leicester Square, London WC2H 7FB
☎0171 389 8555   Fax 0171 930 8499

Managing Director *Vernon Lawrence*
Controller of Drama *Simon Lewis*
Head of Drama Development *Sue Hogg*

Television drama. RECENT OUTPUT Jane Austen's *Emma*; *No Child of Mine* by Peter Kosminsky (drama-doc); *Where the Heart Is* by Ashley Pharoah (6x60min series); *Touching Evil* by Paul Abbott (6x60min series).

United International Pictures (UK)

Mortimer House, 37–41 Mortimer Street, London W1A 2JL
☎0171 636 1655   Fax 0171 636 4118

UK office of American giant; distributes for MGM, Paramount and Universal.

United Media Ltd

68 Berwick Street, London W1V 3PE
☎0171 287 2396   Fax 0171 287 2398

Contact *Mr N. Mackie*

Film, video and TV: drama. OUTPUT *To the Lighthouse* (TV movie with BBC); *Jamaica Inn* (HTV mini-series); *The Krays* (feature film with Fugitive/Rank). Unsolicited scripts welcome but synopses preferred in the first instance. 'We encourage new writing if we see commercially orientated talent.'

Vanson Productions

2 Cairns Way, London SW11 1ES
☎0171 223 1919/801 7020
Fax 0171 223 1919

Contact *Yvette Vanson*

OUTPUT *The Stephen Lawrence Story* and *Violence and the Censors*(both for Ch4); *Cock o' the North* (Granada arts documentary). Vanson Productions are currently working on a major disaster thriller with **Working Title Films**; a new screenplay by Edna O'Brien; *Hot House* (feature film with Japanese co-producer); a children's TV series with World Productions;

Mighty Belfast; and a science fiction series (in development with Channel 5).

Vera Productions

30–38 Dock Street, Leeds, West Yorkshire LS10 1JF
☎0113 2428646   Fax 0113 2451238
Contact *Alison Garthwaite, Catherine Mitchell*

Documentary, corporate, promotional, training and campaigning videos and multimedia. OUTPUT *There's More to Drugs Than Dying; Children Who Foster; I Want to be an Astronaut; Video 28* (lesbians' response to Section 28 of the Local Government Bill); *International Women's Day; Gender on the Timetable.* Unsolicited mss welcome from women only. 'We do not produce drama or comedy.'

Video Arts (Production) Ltd

Dumbarton House, 68 Oxford Street, London W1N 0LH
☎0171 637 7288   Fax 0171 580 8103
Contact *Margaret Tree*

Film and video, CDi and CD-ROM: training, corporate and educational.

Video Enterprises

12 Barbers Wood Road, High Wycombe, Buckinghamshire HP12 4EP
☎01494 534144 (mobile: 0831 875216)
Fax 01494 534144
Contact *Maurice R. Fleisher*

Video and TV, mainly corporate: business and industrial training, promotional material and conferences. No unsolicited material 'but always ready to try out good new writers'.

Video Newsreels

Church Cottage, Ruscombe, Nr Twyford, Berkshire RG10 9UB
☎01734 321123   Fax 01734 321333
Contact *Gerry Clarke*

Corporate video production: sales and training. OUTPUT has included staff-training videos for British Airways and Midland Bank. Unsolicited mss welcome.

Video Presentations

PO Box 281, Wimbledon, London SW19 3DD
☎0181 542 7721   Fax 0181 543 0855
Contact *John Holloway*

Corporate video. CLIENTS include the Post Office, IBM, British Gas, Freemans, Eastern Electricity.

Videotel Productions/ Living Tape Productions

Ramillies House, 1–2 Ramillies Street, London W1V 1DF
☎0171 439 6301   Fax 0171 437 0731
Contact *Robert Wallace*

Film, video and TV of a broadly educational nature but not exclusively so. Unsolicited mss welcome in the education and training fields only. 'We would like to support new writers who can put up with the ego-bashing they are likely to get from industrial and commercial sponsors.' OUTPUT has included *Oceans of Wealth* (British Gas, DTI & Ch4); *Response to Marine Chemical Spills* (for industrial consortium); *Dealing with Violence and Aggression at Work* (NHS, THF); *Defence against Drug Traffickers* (SKULD); *Alcohol, Beware!* (Mobil); *Responsible Chemical Manufacturing* (consortium of chemical companies); *Hospital Security* (NAHAT); *The Office* (BBC/EBS Trust); *More than Meets the Eye* (DOH, EBS Trust).

Brian Waddell Productions Ltd

Strand Studios, 5/7 Shore Road, Holywood, Co. Down BT18 9HX
☎01232 427646   Fax 01232 427922
Contacts *Brian Waddell, Maureen Gallagher*

Producers of a wide range of television programmes in leisure activities, the arts, music, children's, comedy, travel/adventure and documentaries. Currently developing several drama projects. Interested in encouraging new writers, particularly within Ireland.

Wall to Wall Television

8–9 Spring Place, London NW5 3ER
☎0171 485 7424   Fax 0171 267 5292
Contact *Jane Root, Alex Graham*

Documentary, features and drama. OUTPUT includes *Plotlands; It's Not Unusual; Nightmare: The Birth of Horror* (BBC); *Baby It's You; A Taste of the Times; Weekly Planet* (Ch4). Material is produced in-house; occasional outside ideas accepted. Continued expansion of drama production means more opportunities for writers.

The Walnut Partnership

Crown House, Armley Road, Leeds, West Yorkshire LS12 2EJ
☎0113 2456913   Fax 0113 2439614
Contact *Geoff Penn*

A film and video production company specialising in business communication.

Warner Sisters Film & TV Ltd

Canalot Studios, 222 Kensal Road, London
W10 5BN
☎0181 960 3550   Fax 0181 960 3880

Chief Executives *Lavinia Warner, Jane*
  Wellesley, Anne-Marie Casey, Dorothy Viljoen

FOUNDED 1984. Drama and comedy. TV and
feature films. OUTPUT includes *Selling Hitler;*
Rides; Dangerous Lady; Life's a Gas; She-Play; A
Village Affair; Dressing for Breakfast; The Spy that
Caught a Cold; The Bite. Developing a wide
range of TV and feature projects including *Jilting*
Joe.

Wave Communication Group

Wave Studios, 12 Park Street, Lytham,
Lancashire FY8 5LU
☎01253 796399   Fax 01253 794532

Contact *Roy Turner*

Corporate film and video, including sell-
throughs, sponsored, tourism-based programmes,
and technical and specialist videograms. Unsolicited scripts not normally welcome. Keen to
support new writing talent. 'We welcome contact with new writers whom we assess on track
record or sample writing.'

Western Eye Business Television

Easton Business Centre, Felix Road, Easton,
Bristol BS5 0HE
☎0117 9415854   Fax 0117 9415851

Contact *Steve Spencer*

Corporate video production for Royal Mail,
Motorola, HNE Healthcare, BT. Looking for
experienced writers in the above field.

Michael White Productions Ltd

48 Dean Street, London W1V 5HL
☎0171 734 7707   Fax 0171 734 7727

Contact *Michael White*

High-output company whose credits include
Widow's Peak; White Mischief; Nuns on the Run
(co-production with **HandMade Films Ltd**);
The Comic Strip Series. Also theatre projects,
including *Fame; Me and Mamie O'Rourke; She*
Loves Me; Crazy for You. Contributions are
passed by Michael White to a script reader for
consideration.

WitzEnd Productions

1 Stephen Street, London W1P 1PJ
☎0171 691 6000   Fax 0171 691 6081

Bought by Pearson in 1996. Producers of television drama and comedy. OUTPUT *Pie in the*
Sky; Lovejoy; Tracey Ullman: A Class Act; We
Know Where You Live. Scripts not welcome
unless via agents but new writing is encouraged.

The Word Business

56 Leyborne Park, Kew, Richmond, Surrey
TW9 3HA
☎0181 948 8346   Fax 0181 948 8346

Contact *John Mabbett*

Copywriter, scriptwriter, producer of corporate video material, generally low-budget projects. No unsolicited scripts. Writing is handled
in-house.

Workhouse Television

Granville House, St Peter Street, Winchester,
Hampshire SO23 8BP
☎01962 626400   Fax 01962 626401

Television Manager *Carol Wade*

Video and TV: documentary, light entertain-
ment, magazine programmes and corporate
work. OUTPUT *Dear Nick* (ITV); *Lifeschool*
A–Z (BBC); *Big Day Out* (BBC); *Parents*
Talking; DIY; Cash in Hand (The Learning
Channel); *Time Off; Tale of Three Seaside Towns*
(Meridian); *Mastercraft* (Westcountry TV);
Wizadora (network). Corporate clients include
BZW, Barclays, Price Waterhouse, Nuclear
Electric.

Working Title Films Ltd

Oxford House, 76 Oxford Street, London
W1N 9FD
☎0171 307 3000   Fax 0171 307 3001/2/3

Co-Chairmen (Films) *Tim Bevan,*
  Eric Fellner
Head of Development (Films)
  Debra Hayward
Development Executive (Films)
  Natascha Wharton
Television *Simon Wright*

Affiliated to PolyGram Filmed Entertainment.
Feature films, TV drama; also family/children's
entertainment and TV comedy. OUTPUT Films:
Bean; The Borrowers; The Matchmaker; Fargo;
Dead Man Walking; Loch Ness; French Kiss; Four
Weddings and a Funeral; The Hudsucker Proxy;
The Tall Guy; A World Apart; Wish You Were
Here; My Beautiful Laundrette. Television: *Zig and*
Zag's Million Quid Vid; The Borrowers I & II;
Armisted Maupin's Tales of the City; News Hounds;
Echoes. No unsolicited mss at present, but keen
to encourage new writing nevertheless via New
Writers Scheme – contact Natascha Wharton.

Worldview Pictures

10 Cameron House, 12 Castlehaven Road,
London NW1 8QW
☎0171 916 4696   Fax 0171 916 1091

Contact *Stephen Trombley, Bruce Eadie*

Documentaries and series for TV, plus theatrical.
OUTPUT *Nuremberg* (Discovery/Ch4); *Raising
Hell: The Life of A. J. Bannister; The Execution
Protocol* (both Discovery/BBC/France 2); *Drancy:
A Concentration Camp in Paris; The Lynchburg
Story* (both for Discovery/Ch4/ France 2).

Worldwide Television News

The Interchange, Oval Road, London
NW1 7DZ
☎0171 410 5200   Fax 0171 413 8302

Contact *Gerry O'Reilly*

Video and TV: documentary, news, features,
sport and entertainment. OUTPUT *Earthfile*
(weekly environmental series); *Roving Report*
(weekly current affairs series); *Earth Works* (children's environmental series); *The Adventures of
Dodo* (children's animation); *America Exposed*
(documentary series); *Crime International* (real-
ity-based crime show); plus many one-off
specials. Unsolicited material welcome.

Wortman Productions UK

48 Chiswick Staithe, London W4 3TP
☎0181 994 8886

Producer *Neville Wortman*

Film, video and TV production for drama,
documentary, commercials and corporate
material. OUTPUT *House in the Country* John
Julius Norwich (ITV series); *Ellington* (Jazz
series); *'C'm on to My House* (TV feature series);
Theatre (CD-ROM); *Celebration Theatre
Company for the Young – The Winter's Tale*. Send
outline treatments 2–3 pages and s.a.e. and a
couple of pages of dialogue if appropriate.
Open to new writing.

Zenith Productions Ltd

43–45 Dorset Street, London W
1H 4AB
☎0171 224 2440   Fax 0171 224 3194

Script Executive *Ming Ho*

Feature films and TV. OUTPUT Films: Hal
Hartley's *Amateur*, Nicole Holofcener's *Walking
and Talking*. Television: *Inspector Morse; Hamish
Macbeth; Rhodes; Bodyguards*. No unsolicited
scripts.

The Zoom Production Company

102 Dean Street, London W1V 5RA
☎0171 434 3895   Fax 0171 734 2751

Managing Director *Mark Bergin*

Film and video production for corporate
clients. Full spectrum of corporate communications in both public and private sectors.

Theatre Producers

Aba Daba

30 Upper Park Road, London NW3 2UT
☎0171 722 5395   Fax 0171 722 5395
Contact *Aline Waites, Robin Hunter*

Plays and satirical pantomimes performed at venues like the Water Rats, Underneath the Arches and the Canal Café in London. The company writes all its own material but would be happy to consider some of the great piles of unsolicited mss they receive, were it not for the fact that there is absolutely no money available for outsiders.

Actors Touring Company

Alford House, Aveline Street, London
SE11 5DQ
☎0171 735 8311
Fax 0171 735 1031 attn ATC
Artistic Director *Nick Philippou*

'Actors Touring Company takes old stories and works with living writers to produce new theatre.' Collaborations with writers are based on adaptation and/or translation work and unsolicited mss will only be considered in this category. 'We endeavour to read mss but do not have the resources to do so quickly.' As a small-scale company, all plays must have a cast of six or less.

Almeida Theatre Company

Almeida Street, Islington, London N1 1TA
☎0171 226 7432   Fax 0171 704 9581
Artistic Directors *Ian McDiarmid,*
  Jonathan Kent

FOUNDED 1980. Now in its ninth year as a full-time producing theatre, presenting a year-round theatre and music programme in which international writers, composers, performers, directors and designers are invited to work with British artists on challenging new and classical works. Previous productions: *Butterfly Kiss; The Rules of the Game; Medea; No Man's Land; The Rehearsal; Bajazet; Galileo; Moonlight; The School for Wives; Hamlet; Tartuffe; Who's Afraid of Virginia Woolf; Ivanov; Ubu Roi*. No unsolicited mss: 'our producing programme is very limited and linked to individual directors and actors'.

Alternative Theatre Company Ltd

Bush Theatre, Shepherds Bush Green,
London W12 8QD
☎0171 602 3703   Fax 0171 602 7614
Literary Manager *Joanne Reardon*

FOUNDED 1972. Trading as The Bush Theatre. Produces about six new plays a year (principally British) and hosts up to four visiting companies also producing new work: 'we are a writer's theatre'. Previous productions: *Kiss of the Spiderwoman* Manuel Puig; *More Light* Snoo Wilson; *Raping the Gold* Lucy Gannon; *Handful of Stars* Billy Roche; *Boys Mean Business* Catherine Johnson; *The Pitchfork Disney* Philip Ridley; *Phoenix* Roy MacGregor; *Democracy* John Murrell; *Beautiful Thing* Jonathan Harvey; *Killer Joe* Tracy Letts. Scripts are read by a team of associates, then discussed with the management, a process which takes about three months. The theatre offers a small number of commissions, recommissions to ensure further drafts on promising plays, and a guarantee against royalties so writers are not financially penalised even though the plays are produced in a small house.

Annexe Theatre Company Ltd

The Bishops House, Porterfield Road,
Kilmacolm PA13 4PD
☎01505 874111   Fax 01505 874111
Artistic Director *Paula Macgee*
Associate Director *Wendy Seager*
Administrator *Gaynor Holmes*
  Literary Manager *Chris Ballance*

FOUNDED 1986. Touring productions, play readings and workshops for writers. Interested in considering new work from Scottish writers. Writers' pack available. All scripts are read and reports given; writers are encouraged through re-writes, one-to-one meetings; playwrights with potential are invited to join the company's Development Programme. In 1996, Annexe staged its second highly successful writers' conference, a full scale production of a new play and a series of play readings.

Yvonne Arnaud Theatre

Millbrook, Guildford, Surrey GU1 3UX
☎01483 440077   Fax 01483 564071
Contact *James Barber*

New work always considered, but a response can be slow in coming. Credits include: *Laughter on the 23rd Floor* Neil Simon; *A Passionate Woman* Kay Mellor; *Communicating Doors* Alan Ayckbourn; *The Weekend* Michael Palin; *Indian Ink* Tom Stoppard; *Home* David Storey; *Cellmates* Simon Gray.

The Base Theatre Company
The Base, 59 Bethwin Road, London SE5 0XY
☎0171 701 6396   Fax 0171 703 3796
Artistic Director *To be appointed*

FOUNDED 1983. Plays to a predominantly Black audience with two productions each year. New writers encouraged. The company's own venue, The Base, houses incoming shows, workshops and training.

Birmingham Repertory Theatre
Broad Street, Birmingham B1 2EP
☎0121 236 6771   Fax 0121 236 7883
Artistic Director *Bill Alexander*
Associate Directors *Gwenda Hughes,*
   Tony Clark
Literary Manager *Ben Payne*

The Birmingham Repertory Theatre aims to provide a platform for the best work from new writers from both within and beyond the West Midlands region along with a programme which also includes classics and 'discovery' plays. The Rep is committed to a policy of integrated casting and to the production of new work which reflects the diversity of contemporary experience. The commissioning of new plays takes place across the full range of the theatre's activities: in the Main House, the Studio (which is a dedicated new writing space) and the touring work of the Youth, Community and Education Department. 'Writers are advised that the Rep is very unlikely to produce an unsolicited script. We usually assess unsolicited submissions on the basis of whether it indicates a writer with whom the theatre may be interested in working. The theatre runs a programme of writers' attachments every year in addition to its commissioning policy and maintains close links with *Stagecoach* (the regional writers' training agency) and the **MA in Playwriting Studies** at the University of Birmingham.' For more information contact the Literary Manager.

Black Theatre Co-op
Unit 3P Leroy House, 436 Essex Road, London N1 3QP
☎0171 226 1225   Fax 0171 226 0223
Artistic Director *Felix Cross*

FOUNDED 1978. Plays to a mixed audience, approximately 65% female. Usually tours nationally twice a year. 'Committed in the first instance to new writing by Black British writers and work which relates to the Black culture and experience throughout the Diaspora, although anything considered.' Unsolicited mss welcome.

Bootleg Theatre Company
23 Burgess Green, Bishopdown, Salisbury, Wiltshire SP1 3El
☎01722 421476
Contact *Colin Burden*

FOUNDED 1984. Tries to encompass as wide an audience as possible and has a tendency towards plays with socially relevant themes. A good bet for new writing since unsolicited mss are very welcome. 'Our policy is to produce new and/or rarely seen plays and anything received is given the most serious consideration.' Actively seeks to obtain grants to commission new writers for the company. Playwrights whose work has been performed include Tony Marchant, Barrie Keeffe, Sam Snape and Mike Harris. 1997 production: Michael Burnham's *Hanging Hanratty* (tour following successful London run). Future productions include *The Boys Are Back in Town* by Trevor Suthers and new work by Kate Grayson, Sean Gilbert and Amy Roberts.

Borderline Theatre Company
Darlington New Church, North Harbour Street, Ayr KA8 8AA
☎01292 281010   Fax 01292 263825
Chief Executive *Eddie Jackson*
Artistic Director *Leslie Finlay*

FOUNDED 1974. A touring company taking shows to main-house theatres in city centres and small venues in outlying districts, plus the Edinburgh Festival, Mayfest and, occasionally, London. Mainly new and contemporary work, plus revivals: *George's Marvellous Medicine* Roald Dahl (a spectacular children's show); *Misterio Buffo* Dario Fo (one-man show with Robbie Coltrane); *The Odd Couple* Neil Simon; *Trumpets and Raspberries* Dario Fo; *Shanghied* Liz Lochhead; plus pantomime and children's plays. Synopsis with cast size preferred in the first instance. Borderline try to include one new work every season. 'We are looking for writing which is stimulating, relevant and, above all, entertaining, which will lend itself to dynamic physical presentation.'

Bristol Express Theatre Company

16 Frederick Street, Totterdown, Bristol
BS4 3AZ
☎0117 9717279

Director *Andy Jordan*

A non-funded, professional, sometimes middle-scale national touring company which has a continuing commitment to the discovery, development and encouragement of new writing, principally through its research and development programme *The Play's The Thing!* This consists of public/private staged and rehearsed readings; workshops and full-scale productions. Previous productions: *Child's Play* Jonathan Wolfman; *Winter Darkness* Allan Cubitt; *Prophets in the Black Sky* John Matshikiza; *Lunatic & Lover* Michael Meyer; *Heaven* Sarah Aicher; *Syme* Michael Bourdages; *Gangster Apparel* Richard Vetere. 'We look for plays that are socially/emotionally/theatrically/politically significant, analytical and challenging. The company is keen to produce work which attempts to mix genres (and create new ones!), is eloquent and honest, while remaining accessible and entertaining.'

Bristol Old Vic Company

Theatre Royal, King Street, Bristol BS1 4ED
☎0117 9493993   Fax 0117 9493996

Bristol Old Vic is committed to the commissioning and production of new writing in both the Theatre Royal (650 seats) and the New Vic Studio (150 seats). Plays must have the potential to attract an audience of significant size in either auditorium. 'We are eager to discover plays which possess genuine theatricality, are assured in characterisation and dramatic structure, recognise the power of emotion, and display a sense of humour.' The theatre will read and report on unsolicited scripts, and asks for a fee of £10 per script to cover the payments to readers.

Bush Theatre

See **Alternative Theatre Company**

Carnival (Films & Theatre) Ltd

See entry under **Film, TV and Video Production Companies**

Cheek By Jowl

Alford House, Aveline Street, London
SE11 5DQ

Produces only one show per year which is almost always classical. Unable to accept scripts. 'We have no mechanism for reading plays and beg writers to save their time and resources by not sending them to us.'

Chester Gateway Theatre Trust Ltd

Hamilton Place, Chester, Cheshire CH1 2BH
☎01244 344238   Fax 01244 317277

Artistic Director *Deborah Shaw*

FOUNDED 1968. Plays to a broad audience across a wide range of work, classical to contemporary, including Shakespeare, John Godber, Tennessee Williams, Alan Ayckbourn, Arthur Miller, Pinter, etc. An emphasis on new writing with eleven world premières in the last two years. Small-cast material, children's and young people, large-scale youth theatre, people with learning difficulties, plays by women and adaptations of novels. We budget on 70% capacity in a 440-seat theatre. Anything with a cast of over eight is unlikely to reach production. The smaller the cast the better. Scripts welcome but reading will take some time. Please send synopsis first. Winner of *The Stage* Award for Special Achievement in Regional Theatre in 1996.

Churchill Theatre

High Street, Bromley, Kent BR1 1HA
☎0181 464 7131   Fax 0181 290 6968

Artistic Director *To be appointed*

Produces a broad variety of popular plays, both new and revivals. Previous productions: *Phantom of the Opera* Ken Hill; *Don't Dress for Dinner* Marc Camoletti (adap. Robin Hawdon); *A Slight Hangover* Ian Ogilvy; *The Heiress* Henry James; *The Father* Strindberg; *The Prime of Miss Jean Brodie; The Hot Mikado*. Most productions go on either to tour or into the West End.

Citizens Theatre

Gorbals, Glasgow G5 9DS
☎0141 429 5561   Fax 0141 429 7374

Artistic Director *Giles Havergal*

No formal new play policy. The theatre has a play reader but opportunities to do new work are limited.

Michael Codron Plays Ltd

Aldwych Theatre Offices, Aldwych, London
WC2B 4DF
☎0171 240 8291   Fax 0171 240 8467

General Manager *Gareth Johnson*

Michael Codron Plays Ltd manages the Aldwych Theatre in London's West End. The plays it produces don't necessarily go into the Aldwych, but always tend to be big-time West End fare. Previous productions: *Hapgood; Uncle*

Vanya; The Sneeze; Rise and Fall of Little Voice; Arcadia; Dead Funny. No particular rule of thumb on subject matter or treatment. The acid test is whether 'something appeals to Michael'. Straight plays rather than musicals.

Colchester Mercury Theatre Limited

Balkerne Gate, Colchester, Essex CO1 1PT
☎01206 577006   Fax 01206 769607
Contact *Pat Trueman, Artistic Director*
Administrator *David Fairclough*

Repertory theatre with a wide-ranging audience. OUTPUT in 1996 included *The Woman in Black; The Last Yankee; Northanger Abbey; Golden Girls; Noises Off.* Expects to commission more new work in the future. Unsolicited scripts not welcome as there is a lack of appropriate staff to process them correctly. The theatre has a Writer in Residence, shared with the University of Essex MA in Theatre Studies Course.

The Coliseum, Oldham

Fairbottom Street, Oldham, Lancashire OL1 3SW
☎0161 624 1731   Fax 0161 624 5318
Chief Executive *Kenneth Alan Taylor*

The policy of the Coliseum is to present high quality work that is unashamedly 'popular'. Has a special interest in new work that has a Northern flavour, however this does not rule out other plays. In his first season, Kenneth Alan Taylor presented a new Mike Harding play and a new musical version of *Alfie.* Unsolicited scripts are all read but will only be returned if a large s.a.e. is included. Unfortunately, the Studio is not in use in 1997 but hopefully will re-open in 1998.

Communicado Theatre Company

12A Castle Terrace, Edinburgh EH1 2DP
☎0131 228 5465   Fax 0131 221 9003
Artistic Director *Gerard Mulgrew*

FOUNDED 1982. Scottish touring company which aims to present dynamic and challenging theatre to the widest range of audience in Scotland and internationally. 'We encourage new writing, especially, but not exclusively, of Scots origin. Unfortunately there are no facilities for dealing with unsolicited scripts.' Productions have included: *The House with the Green Shutters* adapt. Gerard Mulgrew; *Carmen 1936* Stephen Jeffreys; *The Hunchback of Notre Dame* adapt. Andrew Dallmeyer; *Mary Queen of Scots Got Her Head Chopped Off* Liz Lochhead; *Blood Wedding* trans. David Johnston; *Cyrano de Bergerac* trans. Edwin Morgan; *Crying Wolf* Gerald Mangan; *Sacred Hearts* Sue Glover; *Tall Tales for Cold Dark Nights; Tales of the Arabian Nights* both by Gerard Mulgrew.

Contact Theatre Company

Oxford Road, Manchester M15 6JA
☎0161 274 3434   Fax 0161 273 6286
Artistic Director *Benjamin Twist*

FOUNDED 1972. Plays to a young audience (up to 25). Limited opportunities for new plays without a specific marketing 'hook' for young people. Send s.a.e. for writers' guidelines before submitting script. Recent new productions: *Rupert Street Lonely Hearts Club* Jonathan Harvey; *Tell Me* Matthew Dunster (both world premières). Work by black, female and young writers, and work which creates opportunities for black and female performers, is particularly welcome. Commissions work and runs an annual **Young Playwrights Festival** (see entry under **Festivals**).

Crucible Theatre

55 Norfolk Street, Sheffield S1 1DA
☎0114 2760621   Fax 0114 2701532
Contact *Catriona Murray, Assistant Director*

All unsolicited scripts are seen by a reader and a small number may go on to a rehearsed reading/workshop. Finished scripts are always preferred to synopses or ideas. Scripts sent by a recognised theatre agent, director or actor are given more attention. Scripts only returned if accompanied by s.a.e..

Cwmni Theatr Gwynedd

Deiniol Road, Bangor, Gwynedd LL57 2TL
☎01248 351707   Fax 01248 351915
Artistic Director *Graham Laker*

FOUNDED 1984. A mainstream company, performing in major theatres on the Welsh circuit. Welsh-language work only at present. Classic Welsh plays, translations of European repertoire and new work, including adaptations from novels. New Welsh work always welcome; work in English considered if appropriate for translation (i.e. dealing with issues relevant to Wales). 'We are keen to discuss projects with established writers and offer commissions where possible.' Other activities include the hosting of an annual new writing festival in March.

Derby Playhouse
Eagle Centre, Derby DE1 2NF
☎01332 363271   Fax 01332 294412
Artistic Director *Mark Clements*

FOUNDED 1948. Plays to a mixed audience. Previous productions include *Assassins* Stephen Sondheim; *Our Boys* Jonathan Lewis; *Ham* Mark Chatterton première; *Comic Cuts* Jack Shepherd première; *Gym and Tonic* John Godber. 'We have a discreet commissioning budget and hold several readings a season. Productions of unsolicited scripts are rare and initially we prefer treatments to mss. Writers are welcome to send details of rehearsed readings and productions as an alternative means of introducing th⸱ theatre to their work. Scripts from East Midlands writers are also submitted to a separate regional reading panel.'

Druid Theatre Company
Chapel Lane, Galway, Republic of Ireland
☎00 353 91 568660   Fax 00 353 91 563109
Contact *Literary Manager*

FOUNDED 1975. Plays to a wide-ranging audience, urban and rural, from young adults to the elderly. National and international theatre with an emphasis on new Irish work, though contemporary European theatre is commonplace in the repertoire. Currently has six writers under commission and is commissioning more. Enclose s.a.e. for return of scripts.

The Dukes
Moor Lane, Lancaster LA1 1QE
☎01524 67461   Fax 01524 846817
Artistic Director *Ewan Marshall*

FOUNDED 1971. The only producing house in Lancashire. Wide target market. Plays in 322-seater end-on auditorium plus 198-seater in-the-round studio. Promenade performances in the summer months in Williamson Park. No unsolicited mss.

Dundee Repertory Theatre
Tay Square, Dundee DD1 1PB
☎01382 227684   Fax 01382 228609
Artistic Director *Hamish Glen*

FOUNDED 1939. Plays to a varied audience. Translations and adaptations of classics, and new local plays. Most new work is commissioned. Interested in contemporary plays in translation and in new Scottish writing. No scripts except by prior arrangement.

Eastern Angles Theatre Company
Sir John Mills Theatre, Gatacre Road, Ipswich, Suffolk IP1 2LQ
☎01473 218202   Fax 01473 250954
Contact *Ivan Cutting*

FOUNDED 1982. Plays to a rural audience for the most part. New work only: some commissioned, some devised by the company, some researched documentaries. Unsolicited mss welcome. 'We are always keen to develop and produce new writing, especially that which is germane to a rural area.' Involved in **Eastern Arts**' Write Lines project.

Edinburgh Royal Lyceum Theatre
See **Royal Lyceum Theatre Company**

English Stage Company Ltd
See **Royal Court Theatre**

English Touring Theatre
New Century Building, Hill Street, Crewe CW1 1BX
☎01270 501800   Fax 01270 501888
Artistic Director *Stephen Unwin*

FOUNDED 1993. National touring company visiting middle-scale receiving houses and arts centres throughout England. Mostly mainstream. Largely classical programme, but with increasing interest to tour one modern English play per year. Strong commitment to education and community Outreach work. No unsolicited mss.

Everyman Theatre
5–9 Hope Street, Liverpool L1 9BH
☎0151 708 0338   Fax 0151 709 0398
Contact *Artistic Director*

Currently offers a script-reading service and commissions new work.

Field Day Theatre Company
Foyle Arts Centre, Old Foyle College, Lawrence Hill, Derry BT48 7NJ
☎01504 360196   Fax 01504 365419

ESTABLISHED 1980, Field Day is a touring company which tends to commission plays from Irish writers. No unsolicited mss.

Robert Fox Ltd
6 Beauchamp Place, London SW3 1NG
☎0171 584 6855   Fax 0171 225 1638
Contact *Robert Fox*

Producers and co-producers of work suitable for West End production. Previous productions:

Another Country; Chess; Lettice and Lovage; Madhouse in Goa; Burn This; When She Danced; The Ride Down Mount Morgan; Me & Mamie O'Rouke; The Importance of Being Earnest; The Seagull; Goosepimples; Vita & Virginia; The Weekend; Three Tall Women; Skylight; Who's Afraid of Virginia Woolf. Scripts, while usually by established playwrights, are always read.

Gate Theatre Company Ltd
11 Pembridge Road, London W11 3HQ
☎0171 229 5387   Fax 0171 221 6055
Literary Manager *Mark Sparrow*

FOUNDED 1979. Plays to a mixed, London-wide audience, depending on production. Aims to produce British premières of plays which originate from abroad and translations of neglected classics. Most work is with translators. Previous productions: *The Boat Plays; The Robbers* Schiller; *The Ballad of Wolves and Silver Face; Cat and Mouse (Sheep)* Gregory Motton; *Services, or They All Do It* Elfriede Jelinek(trans. Nick Grindell). Positively encourages writers from abroad to send in scripts or translations. All unsolicited scripts are read but it is unlikely that new British, Irish or North American plays will have any future at the theatre due to emphasis on plays originating from abroad. Always enclose s.a.e. if play needs returning.

Gay Sweatshop
The Holborn Centre, Three Cups Yard, Sandland Street, London WC1R 4PZ
☎0171 242 1168   Fax 0171 242 3143
Artistic Directors *James Neale-Kennerley, Lois Weaver*

FOUNDED 1975. Plays to a wide audience, particularly those interested in lesbian/gay theatre and sexual politics. Previous productions: *Threesome* Claire Dowie, David Greenspan & Phyllis Nagy; *Kitchen Matters* Bryony Lavery; *Raising the Wreck* Sue Frumin; *Compromised Immunity* Andy Kirby; *This Island's Mine* Philip Osment; *Stupid Cupid* Phil Willmott; *Fucking Martin* adapted by Malcolm Sutherland from the novel by Dale Peck. Also experimental performance club *One Night Stands*, annual *Queerschool* for gay and lesbian theatre practitioners; also festivals of new work presented as staged rehearsed readings: *Gay Sweatshop x 10; GS x 12.* Committed to encouraging new work by gay, lesbian, black and disabled playwrights. Work submitted generally includes representation of those sections of the community which are under-represented in mainstream theatre. Unsolicited scripts welcome.

Geese Theatre Company
See **MAC - The Centre for Birmingham**

Graeae Theatre Company
Interchange Studios, Dalby Street, London NW5 3NQ
☎0171 267 1959   Fax 0171 267 2703
Minicom 0171 267 3164
Administrative Director *Kevin Dunn*
Associate Director *Amanda Colleran*

Europe's premier theatre company of disabled people, the company tours nationally and internationally with innovative theatre productions highlighting both historical and contemporary disabled experience. Graeae also runs T.I.E. and educational programmes available to schools, youth clubs and day centres nationally, provides vocational training in theatre arts (including playwriting) and runs London's only fully accessible Young People's Theatre Programme (called 'The Works') for the disabled community. Unsolicited scripts – particularly from disabled writers - welcome. New work examining disability issues is commissioned.

Greenwich Theatre Ltd
Crooms Hill, London SE10 8ES
☎0181 858 4447   Fax 0181 858 8042
Artistic Director *Matthew Francis*

Policy of encouraging new writing under severe threat because of standstill funding. No literary department; no budget for script readers. 'We still aim to produce two new plays or adaptations in a year. We are happy for writers to let us know about their more recent work but we urge them to ring or write before sending us a script. We hope this situation will improve through the course of 1997.'

Hampstead Theatre
Swiss Cottage Centre, Avenue Road, London NW3 3EX
☎0171 722 9224   Fax 0171 722 3860
Literary Manager *Ben Jancovich*

Produces new plays and the occasional modern classic. Scripts are initially assessed by a team of script readers and their responses are shared with management in monthly script meetings. The literary manager and/or artistic director then read and consider many submissions in more detail. It can therefore take 2–3 months to reach a decision. Writers produced in the past ten years include Marguerite Duras, Terry Eagleton, Brad Fraser, Michael Frayn, Brian Friel, William Gaminara, Beth Henley, Stephen Jeffreys, Terry

Johnson, Tony Kushner, Doug Lucie, Frank McGuinness, Rona Munro, Jennifer Phillips, Stephen Poliakoff, Philip Ridley, Martin Sherman and Michael Wall.

Harrogate Theatre Company

Oxford Street, Harrogate, North Yorkshire HG1 1QF

☎01423 502710   Fax 01423 563205

Contact *Artistic Director*

FOUNDED 1950. Describes its audience as 'eclectic, all ages and looking for innovation'. Previous productions: *The Marriage of Figaro* (commissioned adaptation of Beaumarchais, Mozart, Da Ponte); *Barber of Seville* (commissioned translation and adaptation of Beaumarchais, Rossini and Sterbini); *School for Wives*; *A Man with Connections*; *Don Juan*; *The Baltimore Waltz* Paula Vogel (European première); *Hot 'n' Throbbing* Paula Vogel (European première); *My Children! My Africa!*; *Wings* (Kopit, Lunden & Perlman European première); new adaptations of *The Government Inspector* and *The Turn of the Screw*; European premières of adaptations/translations by David Mamet of *The Cherry Orchard*, *Uncle Vanya* and *Three Sisters*; *Marisol* Jose Rivera; *Lulu* Angela Carter world première. Always struggling to produce new work.

Haymarket Theatre Company

Haymarket Theatre, Wote Street, Basingstoke, Hampshire RG21 1NW

☎01256 55844   Fax 01256 57130

Theatre Director *Adrian Reynolds*

Beautifully refurbished theatre with full rehearsal facilities on-site. At least seven in-house productions annually plus Christmas musical. One new play each year. Programme in 1997: *Aspects of Love* Andrew Lloyd Webber; *Misery* Stephen King; *Twelfth Night* William Shakespeare; *Life Goes On* new play by Adrian Hodges; *All My Sons* Arthur Miller; *Don't Dress for Dinner* Marc Camoletti.

The Hiss & Boo Company

24 West Grove, Walton on Thames, Surrey KT12 5NX

☎01932 248931   Fax 01932 248946

Contact *Ian Liston*

Particularly interested in new thrillers, comedy thrillers, comedy and melodrama – must be commercial full-length plays. Also interested in plays/plays with music for children. No one-acts. Previous productions: *Sleighrider*; *Beauty*

and the Beast; *An Ideal Husband*; *Mr Men's Magical Island*; *Mr Men and the Space Pirates*; *Nunsense*; *Corpse!*; *Groucho: A Life in Revue*; *See How They Run*; *Christmas Cat and the Pudding Pirates*; *Pinocchio*. No unsolicited scripts; no telephone calls. Send synopsis and introductory letter in the first instance.

Hull Truck Theatre Company

Spring Street, Hull HU2 8RW

☎01482 224800   Fax 01482 581182

General Manager *Simon Stallworthy*

John Godber, of *Teechers*, *Bouncers*, *Up 'n' Under* fame, the artistic director of this high-profile Northern company since 1984, has very much dominated the scene in the past with his own successful plays. The emphasis is still on new writing but Godber's work continues to be toured extensively. Most new plays are commissioned. Previous productions: *Dead Fish* Gordon Steel; *Off Out* Gill Adams; *Fish and Leather* Gill Adams; *Happy Families* John Godber. The company now reads all unsolicited scripts and aims to respond within three months. Bear in mind the artistic policy of Hull Truck, which is 'accessibility and popularity'. In general they are not interested in musicals, or in plays with casts of more than eight.

Humberside Theatre in Education

Humberside Cultural Enterprise Centre, Middleton Street, Springbank, Hull HU3 1NB

☎01482 324256   Fax 01482 326190

Artistic Director *John Hazlett*

FOUNDED 1983. Full-time company playing to Humberside schools, with a strong tradition of devising its own work. Previous productions: *Natural Forces* (for 13–14-year-olds); *The Wrong Side of the River* by Mary Cooper (for 15–18-year-olds); *Whose Voices?* by John Hazlett, Linda Taylor and Carol Bush (for 10–12-year-olds); *Festival* devised by the company for rural schools and communities; Shakespeare's *A Midsummer Night's Dream*; *Bellies* by Linda Taylor, Carol Bush and Janet Gordon; *Beauty and the Gaze* Linda Taylor; *Our Bodies* devised by the company; *Stoneface* by Linda Taylor.

Pola Jones Associates Ltd

14 Dean Street, London W1V 5AH

☎0171 439 1165   Fax 0171 437 3994

Contact *Andre Ptaszynski, Andrew Fell*

FOUNDED 1982. Comedy and musicals preferred. Previous productions have included: *Neville's Island*; *The Nerd*, with Rowan Atkinson;

Progress Doug Lucie; *The Gambler*, with Mel Smith. Current productions include: *Crazy for You* and *Tommy*. Also produces comedy for TV: *Tygo Road; Joking Apart; Chalk*. Unsolicited scripts welcome.

Stephen Joseph Theatre

Westborough, Scarborough, North Yorkshire YO11 1JW
☎01723 370540   Fax 01723 360506
Artistic Director *Alan Ayckbourn*
Director/Literary Manager *Connal Orton*

A two-auditoria complex housing a 165-seat end stage theatre/cinema (the McCarthy) and a 400-seat theatre-in-the-round (the Round). Positive policy on new work. For obvious reasons, Alan Ayckbourn's work features quite strongly but with a new writing programme now in place, plays from other sources are actively encouraged. Previous première productions include: *Woman in Black* (adap. Stephen Mallatratt); *The Ballroom* Peter King; *Neville's Island* and *The End of the Food Chain* Tim Firth; *Penny Blue* Vanessa Brooks; *White Lies* Robert Shearman; *All Things Considered* Ben Brown. Plays should have a strong narrative and be accessible. Submit to Connal Orton enclosing an s.a.e. for return of mss.

Bill Kenwright Ltd

55–59 Shaftesbury Avenue, London W1V 8JA
☎0171 439 4466   Fax 0171 437 8370
Contact *Bill Kenwright*

Presents both revivals and new shows for West End and touring theatres. Although new work tends to be by established playwrights, this does not preclude or prejudice new plays from new playwrights. Scripts should be addressed to Bill Kenwright with a covering letter and s.a.e.. 'We have enormous amounts of scripts sent to us although we very rarely produce unsolicited work. Scripts are read systematically. Please do not phone; the return of your script or contact with you will take place in time.'

King's Head Theatre

115 Upper Street, London N1 1QN
☎0171 226 8561   Fax 0171 226 8507

The first pub theatre since Shakespearean times and the first venue in the UK for dinner theatre, the King's Head produces some strong work, including previously neglected work by playwrights such as Terence Rattigan and Vivian Ellis. Noël Coward's work also has a strong presence; the company is committed to its contribution to the reappraisal of his work

and in 1995 toured *Cavalcade*. Previous productions: *Noël and Gertie; The Famous Five; Philadelphia, Here I Come!; Accapulco; Elegies for Angels, Punks and Raging Queens; A Day in the Death of Joe Egg*. Unsolicited submissions are not encouraged.

Knightsbridge Theatrical Productions Ltd

21 New Fetter Lane, London EC4A 1JJ
☎0171 583 8687   Fax 0171 583 1040
Contact *Mrs S. H. Gray*

Straight plays and musicals suitable for production in the West End only. No unsolicited scripts.

Komedia

14–17 Manchester Street, Brighton, East Sussex BN2 1TF
☎01273 694583   Fax 01273 563515
Contact *David Lavender*

FOUNDED in 1994, Komedia promotes, produces and presents new work. Mss of new plays welcome.

Leeds Playhouse

See **West Yorkshire Playhouse**

Leicester Haymarket Theatre

Belgrave Gate, Leicester LE1 3YQ
☎0116 2530021   Fax 0116 2513310
Artistic Director *Paul Kerryson*

'We aim for a balanced programme of original and established works.' Recent productions include: *Edward II* with Eddie Izzard; *King Lear* with Kathryn Hunter as Lear; Sondheim's *Sweeney Todd*. A script-reading panel has been established, and new writing is welcome. An Asian initiative has been set up to promote Asian work and Asian practitioners. Future productions include a new commission for Clare McIntyre – the British première of *Dance Like a Man*, the première of *Jasma Odan*, and a Sondheim musical.

Library Theatre Company

St Peter's Square, Manchester M2 5PD
☎0161 234 1913   Fax 0161 228 6481
Artistic Director *Christopher Honer*

Produces new and contemporary work, as well as occasional classics. No unsolicited mss. Send outline of the nature of the script first. Encourages new writing through the commissioning of new plays and through a programme of staged readings to help writers' development.

Live Theatre Company

7–8 Trinity Chare, Newcastle upon Tyne
NE1 3DF
☎0191 261 2694   Fax 0191 232 2224

Artistic Director *Max Roberts*
General Manager *Jane Tall*

FOUNDED 1973. The company has recently won a revenue-funding franchise from Northern Arts to continue to produce work at both its newly refurbished and fully developed 200-seat venue, The Live Theatre, and to tour extensively regionally and nationally. Company policy is to produce high-quality accessible theatrical productions: particularly for those audiences currently alienated from traditional arts and theatre venues. The company is particularly interested in promoting new writing. As well as full-scale productions the company organises workshops, rehearsed readings and other new writing activities. The company also enjoys a close relationship with Northern Playwrights Society. Recent plays include *Close the Coalhouse Door* Alan Plater; *Only Joking* Steve Chambers; *Blow Your House Down* Sarah Daniels; *The Grass House* Pauline Hadaway; *Your Home in the West* Rod Wooden; *Seafarers* Tom Hadaway; *Up and Running* Phil Woods; *Buffalo Girls* by Karin Young; *Two* Jim Cartwright; *Cabaret*, and an ambitious cycle of plays – the *Tyneside Mysteries* involving 12 writers.

Liverpool Everyman

See **Everyman Theatre**

Liverpool Playhouse

Williamson Square, Liverpool L1 1EL
☎0151 709 8478   Fax 0151 709 7113

Artistic Director *Richard Williams*

Regional theatre very active in promoting new writing, with an impressive record of first plays. Previous productions: *Self-Catering: A Short History of the World* Andrew Cullen; *Weldon Rising* Phyllis Nagy; *At Fifty She Discovered the Sea* Denise Chalem; *Boy* Shaun Duggan; *The Dark Side* Liam Lloyd; *Home for the Holidays* Cheryl Martin; *A Message for the Broken Hearted* Gregory Motton; *Somewhere* Judith Johnson. Scripts welcome.

London Bubble Theatre Company

3–5 Elephant Lane, London SE16 4JD
☎0171 237 4434   Fax 0171 231 2366

Artistic Director *Jonathan Petherbridge*

Produces workshops, plays and events for a mixed audience of theatregoers and non-

theatregoers, wide-ranging in terms of age, culture and class. Previous productions: *Measure for Measure; The Good Person of Sezuan; Brainpower*. Unsolicited mss welcome but 'our reading service is extremely limited and there can be a considerable wait before we can give a response'. Produces at least one new show a year which is invariably commissioned.

Lyric Theatre Hammersmith

King Street, London W6 0QL
☎0181 741 0824   Fax 0181 741 7694

Chief Executive *Sue Storr*
Artistic Director *Neil Bartlett*
Administrative Producer *Simon Mellor*

Theatre with a long tradition of putting on new work: *The Message* devised in association with Tony Harrison; *Sarrasine* Balzac; *The Letter* Somerset Maugham. Interested in developing projects with writers, translators and adaptors. Treatments, synopses and c.v.s only. No longer able to produce in its 110-seat studio owing to reduced funding but the studio continues to host work, including new, by some of the best touring companies in the country.

MAC – The Centre for Birmingham

Cannon Hill Park, Birmingham B12 9QH
☎0121 440 4221   Fax 0121 446 4372

Programme Director *Dorothy Wilson*

Home of the Geese Theatre Company and a host of other arts/performance-related organisations based in Birmingham. Details on Geese available from the Centre.

Cameron Mackintosh

1 Bedford Square, London WC1B 3RA
☎0171 637 8866   Fax 0171 436 2683

Successful West End producer of musicals. Credits include *Cats; Les Misérables; Phantom of the Opera; Miss Saigon; Oliver!*. Unsolicited scripts are read and considered (there is no literary manager, however) but chances of success are slim.

Made In Wales

Chapter, Market Road, Canton, Cardiff
CF5 1QE
☎01222 484017   Fax 01222 484016

Artistic Director *Jeff Teare*
Administrator *Jan Kreishan*

Varied audience. Works with Welsh and Wales-based writers and actors to create new and exciting plays which reflect the authentic Anglo-

Welsh voice, whilst not being parochially Welsh. Formed in 1982, since when it has premièred 32 new plays. The company also runs a programme of development work for playwrights at different levels of experience throughout the year. This includes workshops, rehearsed readings and a free script-reading service.

Major Road Theatre Company

29 Queens Road, Bradford, West Yorkshire BD8 7BS
☎01274 480251   Fax 01274 548528
Artistic Director *Graham Devlin*
General Manager *Sue Cullen*

FOUNDED 1973. Each show has a very specific target audience which varies considerably from show to show. Previous productions include: *The Bottle Imp* Robert Louis Stevenson (middle-scale tour, commissioned by the Warwick Arts Centre); *Final Cargo* Noel Greig (small-scale touring theatre); *Four Note Opera* Tom Johnson (small-scale contemporary opera); *Leaves of Life* Mick Eaton (community show – cast of 100); *Bow Down* Harrison Birtwistle (music-theatre tour); *Wonderland* Mick Martin (young people's touring show). Would prefer a synopsis of unsolicited mss first. Regularly commissions new work, interested in innovative, non-naturalistic work.

Man in the Moon Theatre Ltd

392 Kings Road, Chelsea, London SW3 5UZ
☎0171 351 2876   Fax 0171 351 1873
Artistic Director *Leigh Shine*
Administrator *Genene Cooper*

FOUNDED 1982. Fringe theatre. In 1996, awarded the Guinness Ingenuity Award for creativity and innovation. Often tries to fit new plays into seasons such as 'Nationalism' and 'Family Values' and very keen to do rehearsed readings. Unsolicited scripts welcome; 'interested in submissions from first-time writers or writers in the initial stages of their career'. No unfinished scripts or treatments.

Manchester Library Theatre

See **Library Theatre Company**

Method & Madness

25 Short Street, London SE1 8LJ
☎0171 401 9797   Fax 0171 401 9777
Artistic Director *Mike Alfreds*

Method & Madness tend to form long-term relationships with authors and 'unlikely to be in a position to produce another writer's new work until the year 2000'. Limited script-reading facilities. Unsolicited mss may not be read. Letters and synopses welcome; scripts only returned with s.a.e..

Midland Arts Centre

See **MAC – The Centre for Birmingham**

N.T.C. Touring Theatre Company

The Playhouse, Bondgate Without, Alnwick, Northumberland NE66 1PQ
☎01665 602586   Fax 01665 605837
Contact *Gillian Hambleton*

FOUNDED 1978. Formerly Northumberland Theatre Company. Recent winner of one of only two drama production franchises in the Northern region. Predominantly rural, small-scale touring company, playing to village halls and community centres throughout the Northern region, the Scottish Borders and countrywide. Recently expanded into touring middle-scale theatre venues throughout the North. Productions range from established classics to new work and popular comedies, but must be appropriate to their audience. Unsolicited scripts welcome provided they are suitable for touring. The company encourages new writing and commissions when possible. Financial constraints restrict casting to a *maximum* of seven.

New Victoria Theatre

Etruria Road, Newcastle under Lyme, Staffordshire ST5 0JG
☎01782 717954   Fax 01782 712885
Theatre Director *Peter Cheeseman*

FOUNDED 1962. Plays to a fairly broad-based audience which tends to vary from one production to another. A high proportion are not regular theatre-goers and new writing has been one of the main ways of contacting new audiences. Artistic Director Peter Cheeseman reports: 'Recently (last four years) combined effect of recession and local authority grant cuts with Arts Council funding at standstill has seriously affected new play production. Staff, including actors and marketing staff, have been reduced. Contingency funding necessary for risk of presenting new plays has been almost eliminated. Paradoxically, commission money is available but not the funding levels to support new play production. It is hoped this situation is only temporary, as new plays have always been an important element of work.' Recent new plays: *Nice Girls*, documentary; *Come On Stan* Rony Robinson; *The Good Companions* (adaptation from Priestley) Bob Eaton; *The Tinderbox* Peter Whelan. Unsolicited scripts welcome provided they are accompanied by s.a.e. for return.

Newpalm Productions

26 Cavendish Avenue, London N3 3QN
☎0181 349 0802   Fax 0181 346 8257
Contact *Phil Compton*

Rarely produces new plays (*As Is* by William M. Hoffman, which came from Broadway to the Half Moon Theatre, was an exception to this). National tours of productions such as *Noises Off*, *Seven Brides for Seven Brothers* and *Rebecca*, at regional repertory theatres, are more typical examples of Newpalm's work. Unsolicited mss, both plays and musicals, are, however, welcome; scripts are preferable to synopses.

Northampton Royal Theatre

See **Royal Theatre**

Northcott Theatre

Stocker Road, Exeter, Devon EX4 4QB
☎01392 56182   Fax 01392 499641
Artistic Director *John Durnin*

FOUNDED 1967. The Northcott is the Southwest's principal subsidised repertory theatre, situated on the University of Exeter campus. Describes its audience as 'geographically diverse, conservative in taste, with a core audience of AB1s (40–60 age range)'. Continually looking to broaden the base of its audience profile, targeting younger and/or non-mainstream theatregoers in the 16–35 age range. Aims to develop, promote and produce quality new writing which reflects the life of the region and addresses the audience it serves. Generally works on a commission basis but occasionally options existing new work. Unsolicited mss welcome – current turnaround on script reading service approximately three months and no mss can be returned unless a correct value s.a.e. is included with the original submission. Primarily interested in non-domestic, larger scale work that avoids TV naturalism (both original work and adaptation/translation welcome). Recently produced new work includes *Breaking Bread Together* Rob Shearman; *A Curlew's Cry* Paul McClure; *Northanger Abbey* Cathy Turner.

Northern Stage Company

Newcastle Playhouse, Barras Bridge,
Newcastle upon Tyne NE1 7RH
☎0191 232 3366   Fax 0191 261 8093
Artistic Director *Alan Lyddiard*

A young company which involves itself in the production of new work, including co-pro-

ductions with other local companies. Writers' workshops are likely to be arranged. Before submitting unsolicited scripts, please contact Rosie Hunter, Programme and Planning Coordinator.

Norwich Puppet Theatre

St James, Whitefriars, Norwich, Norfolk NR3 1TN
☎01603 615564   Fax 01603 617578
Artistic Director *Luis Boy*
General Manager *Tim Smith*

Plays to a young audience (aged 3–12), with occasional shows for adult audiences interested in puppetry. Christmas/summer season shows, plus school tours. Unsolicited mss welcome if relevant.

Nottingham Playhouse

Nottingham Theatre Trust, Wellington Circus, Nottingham NG1 5AF
☎0115 9474361   Fax 0115 9475759
Artistic Director *Martin Duncan*

Aims to make innovation popular, and present the best of world theatre, working closely with the communities of Nottingham and Nottinghamshire. Unsolicited mss will be read. It normally takes about six months, however, and 'we have never yet produced an unsolicited script. All our plays have to achieve a minimum of 60 per cent audiences in a 732-seat theatre. We have no studio.' Also see **Roundabout** - the Nottingham Playhouse's theatre-in-education company.

Nuffield Theatre

University Road, Southampton, Hampshire SO17 1TR
☎01703 315500   Fax 01703 315511
Artistic Director *Patrick Sandford*
Script Executive *Penny Gold*

Well-known as a good bet for new playwrights, the Nuffield gets an awful lot of scripts. They do a couple of new main stage plays every season. Previous productions: *Exchange* by Yri Trifonov (trans. Michael Frayn) which transferred to the Vaudeville Theatre; *The Floating Light Bulb* Woody Allen (British première); new plays by Claire Luckham: *Dogspot; The Dramatic Attitudes of Miss Fanny Kemble;* and by Claire Tomalin: *The Winter Wife.* Open-minded about subject and style, producing musicals as well as straight plays. Also opportunities for some small-scale fringe work. Scripts preferred to synopses in the case of writers new to theatre. All will, eventually, be read 'but please be patient. We do not have a large team of paid readers. We read everything ourselves.'

Octagon Theatre Trust Ltd

Howell Croft South, Bolton, Lancashire
BL1 1SB
☎01204 529407   Fax 01204 380110
Artistic Director *Lawrence Till*
Administrative Director *Amanda Belcham*

FOUNDED 1967. Audience is made up of a wide age range. Productions include Shakespeare, 'Northern' plays, European plays, new plays, 1960s plays. Unsolicited mss considered, but may take up to six months for reply. Interested in good theatrical pieces that connect with the audience – socially, politically, emotionally and often geographically, with casts of about six. No thin comedies or epic plays with casts over eight.

The Old Vic

Waterloo Road, London SE1 8NB
☎0171 928 2651   Fax 0171 261 9161
Director *Sir Peter Hall, CBE*
Director, New Plays *Dominic Dromgoole*
General Manager *Andrew Leigh*

The Peter Hall Company at The Old Vic produces annual seasons of 12 plays in 44 weeks, doing six classics and six new plays. Christmas sees the annual eight-week visit of *The Wind in the Willows*. Unsolicited scripts will be read (address to Dominic Dromgoole) but expect a three-month turn-around.

Orange Tree Theatre

1 Clarence Street, Richmond, Surrey TW9 2SA
☎0181 940 0141   Fax 0181 332 0369
Artistic Director *Sam Walters*

One of those theatre venues just out of London which are good for new writing, both full-scale productions and rehearsed readings (although these usually take place in The Room, above the Orange Tree pub). Productions, from August 1996: *Bodies* James Saunders; *What the Heart Feels* new play by Stephen Bill; *Family Circles* Alan Ayckbourn; *Inheritors* Susan Glaspell; *The Power of Darkness* Leo Tolstoy, trans. Anthony Clark; *Love Me Slender* Vanessa Brooks. The Room: *Clowns* Christina Reid; *Bitter Lemon* Jaime Salom; *Death of an Elephant* Trevor Preston; *Trifles* Susan Glaspell; *Edwin* John Mortimer; *A Village Wooing* George Bernard Shaw. Unsolicited mss are read, but patience (and s.a.e.) required.

Orchard Theatre

108 Newport Road, Barnstaple, Devon
EX32 9BA
☎01271 71475   Fax 01271 71825
Artistic Director *Bill Buffery*

FOUNDED 1969. Plays appealing to a wide age range, which tour some 60 or 70 cities, towns and villages throughout Devon, Cornwall, Dorset, Somerset and Gloucestershire. Programme includes classics, new adaptations, outstanding modern work and newly commissioned plays. OUTPUT *A Doll's House; East o' the Sun and West o' the Moon; Halfway to Paradise; La Ronde; An Enemy of the People.* Unsolicited mss are usually unsuccessful simply because the theatre is committed to several commissioned new plays at any one time.

Oxford Stage Company

3rd Floor, 15–19 George Street, Oxford
OX1 2AU
☎01865 723238   Fax 01865 790625
Artistic Director *John Retallack*

A middle-scale touring company producing established and new plays. At least one new play or new adaptation a year. Special interest in new writing for young people aged 13–18. Due to forthcoming projects not considering new scripts at present.

Paines Plough – New Writing New Theatre

4th Floor, 43 Aldwych, London WC2B 4DA
☎0171 240 4533   Fax 0171 240 4534
Artistic Director *Vicky Featherstone*
Literary Manager *Mark Ravenhill*

Tours new plays nationally. Works with writers to develop their skill and voices through courses, workshops, free script-reading service and surgeries. Encourages writers to bridge the gap between arthouse and commercial plays with entertaining and provocative work for audiences beyond the London fringe and West End. Welcomes new scripts from writers. For script-reading service send two s.a.e.s for response and return of script to Mark Sparrow, Literary Associate.

Palace Theatre, Watford

Clarendon Road, Watford, Hertfordshire
WD1 1JZ
☎01923 235455   Fax 01923 819664
Artistic Director *Giles Croft*

An important point of policy is the active commissioning of new plays. Previous productions:

Woman Overboard Adrian Mitchell; *Diplomatic Wives* Louise Page; *Over A Barrel* Stephen Bill; *The Marriage of Figaro*; *The Barber of Seville* (adap. Ranjit Bolt); Jon Canter's *The Baby*; Lou Stein's musical adaptation of *La Celestina* by Fernando de Rojas, entitled *Salsa Celestina*; *Borders of Paradise* by Sharman Macdonald; *Elton John's Glasses* by David Farr. Also supports local writers via Education Department (tel: 01923 810307).

Perth Repertory Theatre Ltd
185 High Street, Perth PH1 5UW
☎01738 472700   Fax 01738 624576
Artistic Director *Michael Winter*
General Manager *Paul McLennan*

FOUNDED 1935. A wide range of productions, including musicals, classics, new plays, comedy, etc. for a loyal audience. Unsolicited mss are read when time permits, but the timetable for return of scripts is lengthy. New plays staged by the company are invariably commissioned under the SAC scheme.

Plymouth Theatre Royal
See **Theatre Royal**

Q20 Theatre Company
Ivy Lea, Fyfe Lane, Baildon, Shipley,
West Yorkshire BD17 6DP
☎01274 591417/581316   Fax 01274 591417
Director *John Lambert*

Produces shows mainly for school and community venues. Particularly interested in plays for children. Q20 writes a lot of its own material and rarely has the resources to pay outside professional contributors. Write initially with ideas.

Queen's Theatre, Hornchurch
Billet Lane, Hornchurch, Essex RM11 1QT
☎0078 456118   Fax 01708 452348
Artistic Director *Marina Caldarone*

FOUNDED 1953. Nothing too adventurous for this mainly white, middle-class audience. Modern work, translations or classics are difficult to sell without a household name in the production. Marina Caldarone, however, wishes to broaden the company's repertoire. Committed to producing at least one new work per season (two a year), and keen to set up a complementary studio company which would develop new work. 'We try to offer as broad a repertoire as we can within our economic limitations.' Eight shows a year, including one musical and one Christmas/panto

slot. Always interested in 'the well-made play' and now encouraging the submission of more experimental work as well as translations, adaptations, and classics. Has an established tradition of successful comedies and musicals which have transferred to the West End, e.g. *Blood Brothers*. Unsolicited mss welcome; all are assessed but this can take some considerable time.

The Questors Theatre
12 Mattock Lane, Ealing, London W5 5BQ
☎0181 567 0011   Fax 0181 567 8736
Artistic Director *Spencer Butler*
Theatre Manager *Elaine Orchard*
Production Secretary *Christine Greening*

FOUNDED 1929. Attracts an intelligent, discerning, wide age range audience looking for something different, innovative, daring. Recent productions include: *The Lion in Winter* James Goldman; *The Revengers' Comedies* Alan Ayckbourn; *The Journalist* Arnold Wesker (UK première); *Here Comes a Chopper* Ionesco. Unsolicited mss welcome. All new plays are carefully assessed. Scripts received are acknowledged and all writers receive a written response to their work. Occasionally unsolicited plays receive productions, others rehearsed readings.

The Really Useful Group Ltd
20 Tower Street, London WC2H 9NS
☎0171 240 0880   Fax 0171 240 1204
Contact *Tania Slayter*

Commercial/West End theatre producers whose output has included *Jesus Christ Superstar; Sunset Boulevard; Joseph and the Amazing Technicolor Dreamcoat; Cats; Phantom of the Opera; Starlight Express; Daisy Pulls It Off; Lend Me a Tenor; Arturo Ui* and *Aspects of Love*.

Red Ladder Theatre Company
Cobden Avenue, Lower Wortley, Leeds, West Yorkshire LS12 5PB
☎0113 2792228   Fax 0113 2310660
Artistic Director/Literary Manager
   Kully Thiarai
Administrator *Ann Cross*

FOUNDED 1968. Commissioning company touring 2–3 shows a year with a strong commitment to new work and new writers. Aimed at an audience of young people aged between 14–25 years who have little or no access to theatre. Performances held in youth clubs and similar venues (not schools) where young people choose to meet. Recent productions: 1996: *End of Season* Noël Greig, an international collaboration with Theatre Direct of Canada;

1997: *Kaahini* a new play by Asian writer Maya Chowdhry. 'The company is currently developing its writing policy which will be available to writers interested in working for the company. Whilst unsolicited scripts are not discouraged, the company is particularly keen to enter into a dialogue with writers with regard to creating new work for young people.'

Red Shift Theatre Company

9 The Leathermarket, Weston Street, London SE1 3ER
☎0171 378 9787   Fax 0171 378 9789
Contact *Jonathan Holloway, Artistic Director*
General Manager *Deborah Rees*

FOUNDED 1982. Small-scale touring company which plays to a theatre-literate audience. Unlikely to produce an unsolicited script as most work is commissioned. Welcomes contact with writers – 'we try to see their work ... and welcomes receipt of c.v.s and treatments'. Occasionally runs workshops bringing new scripts, writers and actors together. These can develop links with a reservoir of writers who may feed the company. Interested in new plays with subject matter which is accessible to a broad audience and concerns issues of importance; also new translations and adaptations. 1996 productions: *Bartleby* Herman Melville; *Les Misérables* Victor Hugo.

Roundabout Theatre in Education

College Street Centre for Performing Arts, College Street, Nottingham NG1 5AQ
☎0115 9476202   Fax 0115 9539055
Contact *Kitty Parker*

FOUNDED 1973. Theatre-in-Education company of the Nottingham Playhouse. Plays to a young audience aged 5–18 years of age. Some programmes are devised or adapted in-house, some are commissioned. Unable to resource the adequate response required for unsolicited scripts. 'We are committed to the encouragement of new writing as and when resources permit.'

Royal Court Theatre/English Stage Company Ltd

St Martin's Lane, London WC2N 4BG
☎0171 565 5050   Fax 0171 565 5002
Literary Manager *Graham Whybrow*

The English Stage Company was founded by George Devine in 1956 to put on new plays. John Osborne, John Arden, Arnold Wesker, Edward Bond, Caryl Churchill, Howard Barker and Michael Hastings are all writers this theatre has discovered. Christopher Hampton and David Hare have worked here in the literary department. The aim of the Royal Court is to develop and perform the best in new writing for the theatre, encouraging writers from all sections of society to address the problems and possibilities of our times.

Royal Exchange Theatre Company

St Ann's Square, Manchester M2 7DH
☎0161 833 9333   Fax 0161 832 0881
Literary Manager *Alan Pollock*

FOUNDED 1976. The Royal Exchange has developed a new writing policy, which they find is attracting a younger audience to the theatre. The company produces plays by young dramatists like Iain Heggie, Michael Wall, Alex Finlayson, Rod Wooden, Simon Burke and Randhi McWilliams; also English and foreign classics, modern classics, adaptations and new musicals. The Royal Exchange receives 500–2000 scripts a year. These are read by Alan Pollock and a team of readers. Only a tiny percentage is suitable, but a number of plays are commissioned each year.

Royal Lyceum Theatre Company

Grindlay Street, Edinburgh EH3 9AX
☎0131 229 7404   Fax 0131 228 3955
Artistic Director *Kenny Ireland*
General Manager *Nikki Axford*

FOUNDED 1965. Repertory theatre which plays to a mixed urban Scottish audience. Produces classic, contemporary and new plays. Would like to stage more new plays, especially Scottish. No full-time literary staff to provide reports on submitted scripts.

Royal National Theatre

South Bank, London SE1 9PX
☎0171 928 2033   Fax 0171 620 1197
Literary Manager *Jack Bradley*

The majority of the National's new plays come about as a result of direct commission or from existing contacts with playwrights. There is no quota for new work, though so far more than a third of plays presented have been the work of living playwrights. Writers new to the theatre would need to be of exceptional talent to be successful with a script here, though the Royal National Theatre Studio acts as a bridge between the theatre and helps a limited number of playwrights, through readings, workshops and discussions. In some cases a new play is presented for a shorter-than-usual run in the Cottesloe Theatre. Scripts considered (send s.a.e).

Royal Shakespeare Company

Barbican Centre, London EC2Y 8BQ
☎0171 628 3351   Fax 0171 374 0818

Literary Manager *Colin Chambers*

The literary department receives around 500 unsolicited mss a year, most of which are totally unsuitable for the RSC. Committed to new plays but the work produced is usually commissioned by the company. Bear in mind that the RSC is not interested in straightforwardly biographical plays or singlemindedly topical writing, and have no use for reworkings of Shakespeare or musicals. RSC actors organise festivals in which new work is often a prominent feature.

Royal Theatre

15 Guildhall Road, Northampton
NN1 1EA
☎01604 38343   Fax 01604 602408

Artistic Director *Michael Napier Brown*

Describes its audience as 'wide-ranging in terms of taste, with a growing population which is encouraging a more adventurous and innovative programme'. Produces at least three new works each year. The studio theatre, theatre-in-education, community touring and youth theatre tend to produce the majority of new work, but there are normally two main-house premières each year. Previous productions: *Oleanna; An Old Man's Love; Mail Order Bride; Keely and Du; The Winter's Tale; Top Girls; Shaken not Stirred.* Unsolicited scripts welcome and always read.

Shared Experience Theatre

Soho Laundry, 9 Dufours Place, London
W1V 1FE
☎0171 434 9248   Fax 0171 287 8763

Artistic Director *Nancy Meckler*
Associate Director *Polly Teale*

FOUNDED 1975. Varied audience depending on venue, since this is a touring company. Recent productions have included: *The Birthday Party* Harold Pinter; *Sweet Sessions* Paul Godfrey; *Anna Karenina* (adap. Helen Edmundson); *Trilby & Svengali* (adap. David Fielder); *Mill on the Floss* (adap. Helen Edmundson); *The Danube* Maria Irene Fornes; *Desire Under the Elms* Eugene O'Neill; *War and Peace* (adap. Helen Edmundson); *The Tempest* William Shakespeare. No unsolicited mss. Primarily not a new writing company but 'we are interested in innovative new scripts'.

Sherman Theatre Company

Senghennydd Road, Cardiff CF2 4YE
☎01222 396844   Fax 01222 665581

Artistic Director *Phil Clark*

FOUNDED 1973. Theatre for Young People, with main house and studio. Encourages new writing; has produced 50 new plays in the last five years. Previous productions: *Erogenous Zones, Roots & Wings* Frank Vickery; *Fern Hill, A Long Time Ago* Mike Kenny; *A Spell of Cold Weather* Charles Way; *101 Dalmations* adap. Glyn Robbins. In 1996, the company presented six new plays live on stage and broadcast on BBC Radio Wales, and a new series of one-act lunchtime plays on stage and then filmed for HTV Wales. Priority will be given to Wales-based writers.

Show of Strength

Hebron House, Sion Road, Bedminster,
Bristol BS3 3BD
☎0117 9637634 ext 239   Fax 0117 9631770

Artistic Directors *Alan Coveney,*
     Sheila Hannon
Contact *Sheila Hannon*

FOUNDED 1986. Plays to an informal, younger than average audience. Aims to stage at least one new play each season with a preference for work from Bristol and the South West. Will read unsolicited scripts but a lack of funding means they are unable to provide written reports. Interested in full-length stage plays; 'we are undeterred by large casts'. OUTPUT *A Busy Day* Fanny Burney; *A Man and Some Women* Githa Sowerby; *Blue Murder* Peter Nichols and *Rough Music* James Wilson (both world premières). Also, three rehearsed readings of new work each season.

Snap People's Theatre Trust

Unit A, Causeway Business Centre,
Bishop's Stortford, Hertfordshire
CM23 2UB
☎01279 504095/503066   Fax 01279 501472

Contact *Andy Graham, Mike Wood*

FOUNDED 1979. Plays to young people in four age groups (5–7; 7–11; 11–14; 15–21), and to the thirty-something age group. Classic adaptations and new writing. Writers should make an appointment to discuss possibilities rather than submit unsolicited material. New writing encouraged. 'Projects should reflect the writer's own beliefs, be thought-provoking, challenging and accessible.'

Soho Theatre Company
21 Dean Street, London W1V 6NE
☎0171 287 5060   Fax 0171 287 5061
Artistic Director *Abigail Morris*
Literary Manager *Paul Sirett*

A new writing theatre company. The company produces around four new shows a year. Previous productions: *Brothers of the Brush* Jimmy Murphy; *Kindertransport* Diane Samuels; *Waking* Lin Coghlan; *Gabriel* Moira Buffini. The system for dealing with unsolicited mss is as follows: scripts go out to a team of readers; those they find interesting are passed on to the artistic director, who invites writers of promise to join the workshop series. Presents the **Verity Bargate Award** annually.

The Sphinx
25 Short Street, London SE1 8LJ
☎0171 401 9993   Fax 0171 501 9995
Artistic Director *Sue Parrish*

FOUNDED 1973. Formerly Women's Theatre Group. Tours new plays by women nationally to studio theatres and arts centres. Synopses and ideas are welcome.

Barrie Stacey Productions
9 Denmark Street, London WC2
☎0171 836 4128/6220   Fax 0171 836 2949
Contact *Barrie Stacey*

Touring company, much of the work being Barrie Stacey's own but not exclusively so. Previous productions: *Adventures of Pinocchio; Snow White and the Seven Dwarfs; West End to Broadway Songbook; Tales From the Jungle Book* Barrie Stacey. Always interested in two/three-handers for production, and in film synopses. Fast, experienced scriptwriters in-house.

The Steam Industry
Finborough Theatre, 118 Finborough Road, London SW10 9ED
☎0171 244 7439   Fax 0171 835 1853
Artistic Director *Phil Willmott*
Contact *The Literary Manager*

Since June 1994, the Finborough Theatre has been a base for The Steam Industry who produce in and out of the building. Their output is diverse and prolific and includes a high percentage of new writing alongside radical adaptations of classics and musicals. The space is also available for a number of hires per year and the hire fee is sometimes waived to encourage innovative work. Unsolicited scripts are welcome but due to minimal resources it can take up to six

months to respond. Send s.a.e. with material. The company regularly workshops new scripts at Monday-night play-readings. Previous productions include: *Born Bad; The Oedipus Table; Succulence; Mermaid Sandwich; Illyria*. The venue has presented new works by Anthony Neilson, Jack Bradley, Clare Bayley, Philip Kingston, Mark Ravenhill and Kate Dean.

Stoll Moss Theatres Ltd
Manor House, 21 Soho Square, London W1V 5FD
☎0171 494 5200   Fax 0171 434 1217
Contact *Nica Burns, Peter Cregeen*

Influential theatrical empire, with ten theatres under its umbrella: Apollo; Cambridge; Duchess; Garrick; Gielgud; Her Majesty's; London Palladium; Lyric Shaftesbury Avenue; Queen's and Theatre Royal Drury Lane.

Swan Theatre
The Moors, Worcester WR1 3EF
☎01905 726969   Fax 01905 723738
Artistic Director *Jenny Stephens*

Repertory company producing a wide range of plays to a mixed audience coming largely from the City of Worcester and the county of Hereford & Worcester. A writing group meets at the theatre. Unsolicited scripts discouraged.

Swansea Little Theatre Ltd
Dylan Thomas Theatre, Maritime Quarter, Gloucester Place, Swansea, West Glamorgan SA1 1TY
☎01792 473238
Contact *The Secretary*

A wide variety of plays, from pantomime to the classics. New writing encouraged. New plays considered by the Artistic Committee.

Tabard Theatre Company
2 Bath Road, London W4 1LW
☎0181 995 6035   Fax 0181 747 8256
Artistic Director *Kate Bone*

FOUNDED 1985. Interested in new good writing for a mixed audience. Synopses and ideas welcome (s.a.e. essential). Previous productions include: Shakespeare (*Henry V, Richard III*); new writing – *Hungry Ghosts* P. Kingston; *Theodora* Clare L. Price; *Sell Out* Tony Corkran.

Talawa Theatre Company Ltd
23/25 Great Sutton Street, London EC1V 0DN
☎0171 251 6644   Fax 0171 251 5969
Artistic Director *Yvonne Brewster*

Administrator *Oscar Watson*

FOUNDED 1985. Plays to an ABC audience of 60% black, 40% white across a wide age range depending upon the nature of productions and targeting. Previous productions include all-black performances of *The Importance of Being Earnest* and *Antony and Cleopatra*; plus Jamaican pantomime *Arawak Gold; The Gods Are Not to Blame; The Road* Wole Soyinka; *Beef, No Chicken* Derek Walcott; *Flying West* Pearl Cleage; *Othello* William Shakespeare. Restricted to new work from Black writers only. Occasional commissions, though these tend to go to established writers. 'Interested in the innovative, the modern classic with special reference to the African diasporic experience.' Runs a Black Women's Writers' project funded by **London Arts Board** for three years.

Theatr Clwyd

Mold, Clwyd CH7 1YA
☎01352 756331   Fax 01352 758323

Repertory company with a lively programming policy attracting audiences of all ages. The company has touring commitments within Wales and tours across Britain. Productions of classics and revivals have predominated but an international interest in contemporary drama is being developed. Previous productions: *India Song* Marguerite Duras; *The Choice* Claire Luckham; *Barnaby and the Old Boys* Keith Baxter; *Self Portrait* Sheila Yeger; *HRH* Snoo Wilson; *Full Moon* by Caradog Prichard, adapt. Helena Kaut-Howson and John Owen. Unsolicited material is unlikely to be considered for production, but special consideration is given to Welsh writers and scripts with Welsh themes.

Theatre of Comedy Company

210 Shaftesbury Avenue, London WC2H 8DP
☎0171 379 3345   Fax 0171 836 8181
Contact *Andrew Welch (Chief Executive)*

FOUNDED 1983 to produce new work as well as classics and revivals. Interested in strong comedy in the widest sense – Chekhov comes under the definition as does farce. Also has a light entertainment division, developing new scripts for television, namely situation comedy and series. A good bet for new work.

Theatre Royal, Plymouth

Royal Parade, Plymouth, Devon PL1 2TR
☎01752 668282/222200   Fax 01752 671179
Contact *Liz Turgeon, Grahame Morris*

Stages small-, middle- and large-scale drama

including musicals and music theatre. Commissions and produces new plays. Unsolicited scripts are read and reported on.

Theatre Royal Stratford East

Gerry Raffles Square, London E15 1BN
☎0181 534 7374   Fax 0181 534 8381
Associate Director *Kerry Michael*

Lively East London theatre, catering for a very mixed audience, both local and London-wide. Produces plays, musicals, youth theatre and local community plays/events, all of which is new work. Special interest in Asian and Black British work. Unsolicited scripts are welcome.

Theatre Royal Windsor

Windsor, Berkshire SL4 1PS
☎01753 863444   Fax 01753 831673
Artistic Director *Mark Piper*

FOUNDED 1938. Plays to a middle–class, West End–type audience. Produces thirteen plays a year and 'would be disappointed to do fewer than two new plays in a year; always hope to do half a dozen'. Modern classics, thrillers, comedy and farce. Only interested in scripts along these lines.

Theatre Workshop Edinburgh

34 Hamilton Place, Edinburgh EH3 5AX
☎0131 225 7942   Fax 0131 220 0112
Artistic Director *Robert Rae*

Plays to a young, broad-based audience with much of the work targeted towards particular groups or communities. OUTPUT has included adaptations of Gogol's *The Nose* and Aharon Appelfeld's *Badenheim 1939* – two community performance projects. Particularly interested in new work for children and young people. Frequently engages writers for collaborative/devised projects. Commissions a significant amount of new writing for a wide range of contexts, from large-cast community plays to small-scale professional tours. Favours writers based in Scotland, producing material relevant to a contemporary Scottish audience. Member of Scottish Script Centre to whom it refers senders of unsolicited scripts.

Thorndike Theatre (Leatherhead) Ltd

Church Street, Leatherhead, Surrey KT22 8DF
☎01372 376211   Fax 01372 362595
Artistic Director *Bill Kenwright*

West End and touring for an audience described as fairly conservative. 70% of the company's work goes out on tour; children's and family plays. Out of a total of ten in-house productions each year, five new plays are sought. Previous productions: *The Master Builder* Ibsen; *Emily Needs Attention* Feydeau; *Private Lives* Coward; *Chapter Two* Neil Simon; *Nicholas Nickleby* Dickens, adapt. David Hare.

Tiebreak Touring Theatre
Heartsease High School, Marryat Road,
Norwich, Norfolk NR7 9DF
☎01603 435209   Fax 01603 435184
Artistic Director *David Farmer*

FOUNDED 1981. Specialises in high-quality theatre for children and young people, touring schools, youth centres, museums and festivals. Previous productions: *Frog and Toad; Love Bites; Singing in the Rainforest; Boadicea – The Movie; Dinosaurs on Ice; Touch Wood; The Invisible Boy; My Friend Willy; The Ugly Duckling; Almost Human.* New writing encouraged. Interested in low-budget, small-cast material only. School, educational and socially relevant material of special interest. Scripts welcome.

Torch Theatre
St Peter's Road, Milford Haven,
Pembrokeshire SA73 2BU
☎01646 694192   Fax 01646 698919
Artistic Director *Mike James*

FOUNDED 1976. Plays to a mixed audience hard to attract to new work on the whole. Committed to new work but financing has become somewhat prohibitive. Small-cast pieces with broad appeal welcome. Previous productions: *Frankie and Tommy; School for Wives; Tess of the d'Urbervilles.* The repertoire runs from Ayckbourn to Friel. Scripts sometimes welcome.

Traverse Theatre
Cambridge Street, Edinburgh EH1 2ED
☎0131 228 3223   Fax 0131 229 8443
Artistic Director *Philip Howard*
Literary Associate *Ella Wildridge*

The Traverse is the best-known theatre in Scotland for new writing; indeed it has a policy of putting on nothing but new work by new writers. Also has a strong international programme of work in translation and visiting companies. Previous productions: *Knives in Hens* David Harrower; *The Collection* Mike Cullen; *Europe* David Greig; *Widows* Ariel Dorfman; *Passing Places* Stephen Greenhorn.

No unsolicited scripts. Writers welcome to make contact by phone or in writing.

Trestle Theatre Company
47–49 Wood Street, Barnet, Hertfordshire
EN5 4BS
☎0181 441 0349   Fax 0181 449 7036
Artistic Directors *Joff Chafer, Toby Wilsher*

FOUNDED 1981. Physical, mask theatre for mostly student-based audiences (18–36 years). All work is devised by the company. Scripts which have the company's special brand of theatre in mind will be considered. No non-physical-based material. New writing welcome.

Tricycle Theatre
269 Kilburn High Road, London
NW6 7JR
☎0171 372 6611   Fax 0171 328 0795
Artistic Director *Nicolas Kent*

FOUNDED 1980. Plays to a very mixed audience, in terms of both culture and class. Previous productions: *Two Trains Running* August Wilson; *The Day the Bronx Died* Michael Henry Brown; *Half the Picture* Richard Norton-Taylor and John McGrath; *Nativity* Nigel Williams; *Playboy of the West Indies* Mustapha Matura; *Joe Turner's Come and Gone* and *The Piano Lesson* August Wilson; *Pecong* Steve Carter; *A Love Song for Ulster* Bill Morrison; *Three Hotels* Jon Robin Baitz; *Nuremberg* adapt. from transcripts of the trials by Richard Norton-Taylor; *Srebrenica* adapt. Nicolas Kent. New writing welcome from women and ethnic minorities (particularly Black and Irish). Looks for a strong narrative drive with popular appeal, not 'studio' plays. Also runs workshops for writers.

Tron Theatre Company
63 Trongate, Glasgow G1 5HB
☎0141 552 3748   Fax 0141 552 6657
Artistic Director *Irina Brown*

FOUNDED 1981. Plays to a broad cross-section of Glasgow and beyond, including international tours (Toronto 1990 & 1996; New York 1991; Montreal 1992). Recent productions: *The Trick is to Keep Breathing* Janice Galloway/ Michael Boyd; *Endgame* Beckett; *Good* C. P. Taylor; *Macbeth*; *Lavochkin-5* (*La Funf in der Luft*) Alexei Shipenko, trans. Iain Heggie/Irina Brown. Interested in ambitious plays by Scottish and international writers. No unsolicited mss.

Umoja Theatre Company
See **The Base Theatre Company**

Unicorn Arts Theatre for Children

Arts Theatre, 6–7 Great Newport Street, London WC2H 7JB
☎0171 379 3280   Fax 0171 836 5366
Artistic Director *Tony Graham*

FOUNDED 1947 as a touring company, and took up residence in the Arts Theatre in 1967. Plays mainly to children between the ages of 4–12. Previous productions: *A Midsummer Night's Dream* and *Stig of the Dump.* Runs the **Unicorn Arts Theatre National Young Playwrights' Competition** annually (for children between the ages of 6 and 16).

Charles Vance Productions

83 George Street, London W1H 5PL
☎0171 486 1732   Fax 0171 224 2215
Contact *Charles Vance, Jill Streatfeild*

In the market for medium-scale touring productions and summer-season plays. Hardly any new work and no commissions but writing of promise stands a good chance of being passed on to someone who might be interested in it. Occasional try-outs for new work in the Sidmouth repertory theatre. Send s.a.e. for return of mss.

Warehouse Theatre, Croydon

Dingwall Road, Croydon CR0 2NF
☎0181 681 1257   Fax 0181 688 6699
Artistic Director *Ted Craig*
Writers' Workshop Manager *Sheila Dewey*

South London's new writing theatre, seating 100. Produces six new plays a year and co-produces with companies who share a commitment to new work. Continually building upon a tradition of discovering and nurturing new writers, with activities including a monthly writers' workshop and the annual **International Playwriting Festival**. Previous productions: *Sugar Hill Blues* Kevin Hood; *Playing Sinatra* Bernard Kops; *Eva and the Cabin Boys* Sheila Dewey; *The Astronomers Garden* Kevin Hood; *Groping in the Dark* James Martin Charlton; *Trouble Sleeping* Nick Ward; *Dinner with the Borgias* Roy Smiles. Unsolicited scripts welcome but it is more advisable to submit plays through the theatre's International Playwriting Festival. The theatre is committed to productions at least nine months in advance.

Watermill Theatre

Bagnor, Newbury, Berkshire RG20 8AE
☎01635 45834   Fax 01635 523726
Contact *Jill Fraser*

The Watermill tries to put on one new piece of work each year. Previous productions: *Couch Grass & Ribbon* Adam Thorpe; *Deadwood* Alex Jones; *Hindsight* Richard Everett; *The Great Big Radio Show* Philip Glassboron and David Rhind-Tutt; *The Ugly Duckling* George Stiles & Anthony Drene; *Goodbye Mr Chips* adapt. Norman Coaler; *Laura* (musical) Michael Heath.

Watford Palace Theatre

See **Palace Theatre**

West Yorkshire Playhouse

Playhouse Square, Leeds, West Yorkshire LS2 7UP
☎0113 2442141   Fax 0113 2448252
Literary Co-ordinator *Alfred Hickling*

Committed to programming new writing as part of its overall policy. Before sending an unsolicited script please phone or write. The Playhouse does readings, workshops and script surgeries on new plays with writers from all over Britain and also has strong links with local writers and Yorkshire Playwrights. The theatre has writers-in-residence. Premières include: *The Gulf Between Us* Trevor Griffiths; *A Passionate Woman* Kay Mellor; *Fathers Day* Maureen Lawrence; *The Beatification of Area Bay* Wole Soyinka; *The Winter Guest* Sharman Macdonald.

Whirligig Theatre

14 Belvedere Drive, Wimbledon, London SW19 7BY
☎0181 947 1732   Fax 0181 879 7648
Contact *David Wood*

One play a year in major theatre venues, usually a musical for primary school audiences and weekend family groups. Interested in scripts which exploit the theatrical nature of children's tastes. Previous productions: *The See-Saw Tree; The Selfish Shellfish; The Gingerbread Man; Save the Human; The Old Man of Lochnagar; The Ideal Gnome Expedition; Dreams of Anne Frank.*

Michael White Productions Ltd

See **Film, TV and Video Production Companies**

White Bear Theatre Club

138 Kennington Park Road, London SE11 4DJ
Administration: 3 Dante Road, Kennington, London SE11 4RB
☎0171 793 9193   Fax 0171 277 0526
Contact *Michael Kingsbury, Julia Parr*
Administrator *Vanessa Cornford*

FOUNDED 1988. OUTPUT primarily new work for an audience aged 20–35. Unsolicited scripts welcome, particularly new work with a keen eye on contemporary issues, though not agit-prop. Holds readings throughout the year. Recent production: *I Only Have Eyes For You* Barry Keefe. In the process of trying to set up a Lambeth New Play Award. Over the past 18 months, seven productions have been named as *Time Out* Critics' Choice.

Windsor Theatre Royal
See **Theatre Royal Windsor**

Wolsey Theatre Company
Civic Drive, Ipswich, Suffolk IP1 2AS
☎01473 218911   Fax 01473 212946
Artistic Director *Andrew Manley*
Contact *Eileen Kidd*

FOUNDED 1979. Tries to do one new play a year in the main house and studio. New writing encouraged. Unsolicited mss welcome. Previous productions: *Me and My Girl; Lady Windermere's Fan; The Tempest; The Devil's Cardinal; The Secret Garden; Noel and Gertie.*

Women's Theatre Group
See **The Sphinx**

York Theatre Royal
St Leonard's Place, York YO1 2HD
☎01904 658162   Fax 01904 611534
Artistic Director *Damian Cruden*

Not a new writing theatre in the main. Previous productions: *Into the Woods; Macbeth; Tom Jones* (musical version adapted by John Doyle). No scripts.

The Young Vic
66 The Cut, London SE1 8LZ
☎0171 633 0133   Fax 0171 928 1585
Artistic Director *Tim Supple*

FOUNDED 1970. The Young Vic produces adventurous and demanding work for an audience with a youthful spirit. The main house is one of London's most exciting spaces and seats up to 500. In addition, a smaller, entirely flexible space, The Young Vic Studio, seats 100 and is used for experiment, performance, rehearsals and installations. 'We are not able to produce many new scripts at the moment; nor are we able to develop or read unsolicited scripts with the care they deserve. However, we are always happy to receive work.'

Festivals

Aldeburgh Poetry Festival

Goldings, Goldings Lane, Leiston, Suffolk
IP16 4EB
☎01728 830631   Fax 01728 832029
Contact *Michael Laskey*

Now in its ninth year, an annual international festival of contemporary poetry held over one weekend each November in Aldeburgh and attracting large audiences. Regular features include a two-week residency leading up to the festival, poetry readings, a children's event, workshops, a public masterclass, a lecture, a performance spot and the festival prize for the year's best first collection (see entry **Prizes**).

Arundel Festival

The Arundel Festival Society Ltd, The Mary Gate, Arundel, West Sussex BN18 9AT
☎01903 883690   Fax 01903 884243
Administrator *Ms Julie Young*

Annual festival held at the end of August for ten days. Events include poetry, prose readings and lectures, open-air Shakespeare in Arundel Castle, concerts with internationally known artists, jazz, visual arts and active fringe.

Bath Fringe Festival

The Bell, 103 Walcot Street, Bath BA1 5BW
☎01225 480079   Fax 01225 427441
Chair *David Stevenson*

FOUNDED 1981. Complementing the international music festival, the Fringe presents theatre, poetry, jazz, blues, comedy, cabaret, storytelling, carnival and more in venues, parks and streets of Bath during late May and early June.

BBC Radio Young Playwrights' Festival

See **FIRST BITE**

Belfast Festival at Queen's

Festival House, 25 College Gardens, Belfast BT9 6BS
☎01232 667687   Fax 01232 663733
Executive Director *Robert Agnew*

FOUNDED 1964. Annual three-week festival held in November. Organised by Queen's University in association with the **Arts Council of Northern Ireland**, the festival covers a wide variety of events, including literature. Programme available in September.

Birmingham Readers and Writers Festival

Festival Office, Central Library, Chamberlain Square, Birmingham B3 3HQ
☎0121 235 4244   Fax 0121 233 9702
Festival Director *Jonathan Davidson*
Festival Organiser *Matthew Gidley*

FOUNDED 1983. Annual ten-day festival held in May in arts venues and libraries in Birmingham. Concerned with all aspects of contemporary reading and writing, with visiting authors, workshops, performances, cabaret, conferences and special programmes for young people.

Black Literature Festival

See **Bradford Festival**

Book Now!

Langholm Lodge, 146 Petersham Road, Richmond, Surrey TW10 6UX
☎0181 831 6138   Fax 0181 940 7568
Director *Nigel Cutting*

FOUNDED 1992. Annual festival which runs throughout the month of November, administered by the Arts Section of Richmond Council. Principal focus is on poetry and serious fiction, but events also cover biography, writing for theatre, children's writing. Programme includes readings, discussions, workshops, debates, exhibitions, schools events. Writers to appear at past festivals include A. S. Byatt, Penelope Lively, Benjamin Zephaniah, Sir Dirk Bogarde, Roger McGough, Rose Tremain, John Mortimer and Sean Hughes.

Bradford Festival

The Windsor Baths, 11 Great Horton Road, Bradford, West Yorkshire BD7 1AA
☎01274 309199   Fax 01274 724213
Director *Dusty Rhodes*

FOUNDED 1987. June/July; two weeks. The 'largest, award-winning annual community arts festival in the country'. Includes the Mela ('bazaar' or 'fair' in Urdu) which reflects the city's cultural mix. Music, dance, street theatre, spectacle and the annual Black Literature Festival.

Brighton Festival
Festival Office, 21–22 Old Steine, Brighton, East Sussex BN1 1EL
☎01273 713875   Fax 01273 622453
Contact *General Manager*
FOUNDED 1967. For 24 days every May, Brighton hosts England's largest mixed arts festival. Music, dance, theatre, film, opera, literature, comedy and exhibitions. Literary enquiries will be passed to the literature officer. Deadline October for following May.

Bury St Edmunds Festival
Borough Offices, Angel Hill, Bury St Edmunds, Suffolk IP33 1XB
☎01284 757080   Fax 01284 757091
Contact *Kevin Appleby, Festival Manager*
FOUNDED 1986. ANNUAL 17-day spring festival in various venues throughout this historic East Anglian town and outlying areas. Programme features classical music concerts and recitals, lunchtime jazz, theatre, comedy, walks, talks and exhibitions. 1997 highlights included The Dubliners, the Orchestra of the Age of Enlightenment, John Hegley and Alan Price.

Buxton Festival
1 Crescent View, Hall Bank, Buxton, Derbyshire SK17 6EN
☎01298 70395   Fax 01298 72289
Contact *General Manager*
FOUNDED 1979. Annual two-and-a-half-week festival held in July. Rarely performed operas are staged in Buxton Opera House and the programme is complemented by a wide variety of other musical events, including recitals, Young Artists series, festival masses, chamber music and cabarets. Also, the Buxton Jazz Festival.

Canterbury Festival
Christ Church Gate, The Precincts, Canterbury, Kent CT1 2EE
☎01227 452853   Fax 01227 781830
Festival Director *Mark Deller*
FOUNDED 1984. Annual two-week festival held in October. A mixed programme of events including talks by visiting authors, readings and storytelling, walks, concerts in the cathedral, jazz, master classes, drama, visual arts, opera, film, cabaret and dance.

Cardiff Literature Season
The Welsh Academy, 3rd Floor, Mount Stuart House, Mount Stuart Square, Cardiff CF1 6DQ
☎01222 492025   Fax 01222 492930
Director *Kevin Thomas*
Contact *Margaret Harlin*
FOUNDED 1986. Annual festival of literature, primarily for children, held in the autumn.

The Cheltenham Festival of Literature
Town Hall, Imperial Square, Cheltenham, Gloucestershire GL50 1QA
☎01242 521621   Fax 01242 256457
Festival Organiser *Sarah Smyth*
FOUNDED 1949. Annual festival held in October. The first purely literary festival of its kind, this festival has over the past decade developed from an essentially local event into the largest and most popular in Europe. A wide range of events including talks and lectures, poetry readings, novelists in conversation, exhibitions, discussions, cabaret and a large bookshop.

Chester Literature Festival
8 Abbey Square, Chester CH1 2HU
☎01244 319985   Fax 01244 341200
Chairman *John Elsley*
FOUNDED 1989. Annual festival during October, organised by local bookshops, writers' groups and Chester Arts Association. Major events sponsored by publishers. Authors taking part in the 1996 festival included Sir Roy Strong, Ned Sherrin, John Nichol, Liza Clayton, Willy Russell, Brian Patten and Beryl Bainbridge.

Contact Young Playwrights' Festival
Oxford Road, Manchester M15 6JA
☎0161 274 3434
Contact *Sally Abbott*
Associate Director (Community & Education) *Benedict Ayrton*
FOUNDED 1986 and open to young people aged between 11 and 25 living in the Northwest of England. The next festival will be held in March 1998 in the Contact Studio Theatre with a deadline for scripts of 15 September. All of the finalists are taken on a residential writing course in the Lake District with professional writers and directors who help them to develop their work. All scripts submitted to the festival receive a critical analysis.

Dartington Literary Festival
See **Ways With Words**

The Festival of Dover
Dover District Council, White Cliffs Business Park, Dover, Kent CT16 3PD
☎01304 872058   Fax 01304 872062
Festival Organiser *Lisa Webb*

Two-week festival held in May. The sixth Festival in 1997 was entitled 'New Horizons' which provided a platform for a celebration of global cultures and experiences by combining community and professional talent from all over the world. The programme featured exhibitions, concerts, dance, drama, walks, talks and workshops.

Dublin International Writers' Festival
An Chomhairle Ealaíon (The Arts Council), 70 Merrion Square, Dublin 2
☎00 353 1 6611840   Fax 00 353 1 6761302
Festival Director *Laurence Cassidy*

Biennial festival held in September. Features conference sessions, public interviews, debates, readings and exhibitions, with some of the world's leading authors in attendance.

Durham Literary Festival
Durham City Arts, Byland Lodge, Hawthorn Terrace, Durham City DH1 4TD
☎0191 386 6111 ext. 338 Fax 0191 386 0625
Secretary *Paul Rubinstein*

FOUNDED 1989. Annual 2–3-week event, end of May–beginning of June, held at various locations in the city. Workshops, plus performances, cabaret, and other events.

Edinburgh Book Festival
Scottish Book Centre, 137 Dundee Street, Edinburgh EH11 1BG
☎0131 228 5444   Fax 0131 228 4333
Director *Jan Fairley*

FOUNDED 1983. Held during the first fortnight of the Edinburgh International Festival. Now established as Britain's biggest book event, the programme includes discussions, readings and lectures by writers of national and international reputation, with an extensive programme for children.

Exeter Festival
Festival Office, Civic Centre, Exeter, Devon EX1 1JN
☎01392 265200   Fax 01392 265366

Festival Organiser *Lesley Maynard*
Artistic Director *Paul Patterson*

FOUNDED 1980. Annual two-week festival with a variety of events including concerts, theatre, dance and exhibitions.

First Bite – BBC Radio Young Writers' Festival
Room 6067, Broadcasting House, London W1A 1AA
Contact *Jonquil Panting*

FOUNDED 1988 – formerly the Young Playwright's Festival. Takes place every 2/3 years. Open to writers aged 16 – 30 (inclusive) who are new to radio. Plays and stories in five categories. For more details contact the above.

Glasgow Mayfest
See **Mayfest**

Greenwich and Docklands International Festival
6 College Approach, London SE10 9HY
☎0181 305 1818   Fax 0181 305 1188
Director *Bradley Hemmings*

FOUNDED 1970. Annual summer festival. Features a wide variety of events, including world music, theatre, dance, classical music, jazz, comedy, art, literature and free open-air events.

Guildford Book Festival
Old Coach House, Cuilfail, Lewes, East Sussex BN7 2BEA
☎01273 478943   Fax 01273 478943
Book Festival Organiser *Joan König*

FOUNDED 1989. A ten-day celebration of books and writing held annually, during the autumn half-term, throughout the town. The programme includes literary lunches; poetry readings; a writer-in-residence; children's events; the Annual University Poetry Lecture; writing workshops and bookshop events.

Harrogate International Festival
The Festival Office, Royal Baths, Harrogate, North Yorkshire HG1 2RR
☎01423 562303   Fax 01423 521264
Festival Director *William Culver Dodds*
Administrator *Fiona Goh*
Marketing Coordinator *Emily Till*

FOUNDED 1966. Annual two-week festival at the end of July and beginning of August. Events include international symphony orchestras, chamber concerts, ballet, celebrity recitals, contemporary dance, opera, drama, jazz, comedy plus an international street theatre festival.

The Hay Festival
See **The Sunday Times Hay Festival**

Huddersfield Poetry Festival
c/o The Word Hoard, 46/47 Byram Arcade, Westgate, Huddersfield, West Yorkshire HD1 1ND
☎01484 452070   Fax 01484 455049
Contact *Dianne Darby*

Twice-yearly event consisting of a spring season, concentrated in April, of around six events over as many weeks, and three weekend writing courses and performances in October, each exploring particular themes. Also occasional one-off events. Though very interested in local writers, the festival has a cosmopolitan outlook and features related performing arts including music, theatre and the visual arts.

Hull Literature Festival
Festival Office, 79 Ferensway, Hull HU2 8LE
☎01759 303454   Fax 01759 303454
Director *David Porter*

FOUNDED 1992. Annual festival running in November.

Ilkley Literature Festival
Festival Office, Manor House Museum, Ilkley, West Yorkshire LS29 9DT
☎01943 601210
Director *David Porter*

FOUNDED 1973. Three festivals a year of 4–5 days' duration. Previous guests have included Tony Harrison, Sarah Dunant, Irina Ratushinskaya, Colin Thubron. Also presents children's events, storytellers, theatre and music, and creative writing workshops. Runs an open poetry competition. Telephone to join free mailing list.

International Playwriting Festival
Warehouse Theatre, Dingwall Road, Croydon CR0 2NF
☎0181 681 1257   Fax 0181 688 6699

FOUNDED 1985. Annual competition for full-length unperformed plays, judged by a panel of theatre professionals. Finalists given rehearsed readings during the festival week in November. Entries welcomed from all parts of the world. Scripts, plus two stamped addressed envelopes (one script-sized), should reach the **Warehouse Theatre** by July, accompanied by an entry form (available from the theatre). Previous winners produced at the theatre include: Kevin Hood *Beached;* Anne Aylor *Children of the Dust;* Mark Bunyan *Dinner;* Ellen Fox *Conversations with George Sandburgh After a Solo Flight Across the Atlantic;* Guy Jenkin *Fighting for the Dunghill;* James Martin Charlton *Fat Souls;* Peter Moffat *Iona Rain;* Dino Mahoney *YoYo.*

Kent Literature Festival
The Metropole Arts Centre, The Leas, Folkestone, Kent CT20 2LS
☎01303 255070
Acting Festival Director *Ann Fearey*

FOUNDED 1980. Annual week-long festival held at the end of September which aims to bring the best in modern writing to a large audience. Visiting authors and dramatic presentations are a regular feature along with creative writing workshops, seminars, discussions and children's/family events. Also runs the Kent Young Writers of the Year Award and **Short Story Competition**.

King's Lynn, The Fiction Festival
19 Tuesday Market Place, King's Lynn, Norfolk PE30 1JW
☎01553 691661 (office hours) or 761919   Fax 01553 691779
Contact *Anthony Ellis*

FOUNDED 1989. Annual weekend festival held in March. Over the weekend there are readings and discussions, attended by guest writers of which there are usually eight. Previous guests have included Beryl Bainbridge, Malcolm Bradbury, Marina Warner, William Golding, Hilary Mantel, Elizabeth Jane Howard.

King's Lynn, The Poetry Festival
19 Tuesday Market Place, King's Lynn, Norfolk PE30 1JW
☎01553 691661 (office hours) or 761919   Fax 01553 691779
Contact *Anthony Ellis*

FOUNDED 1985. Annual weekend festival held at the end of September, with guest poets (usually eight). Previous guests have included Carol Ann Duffy, Paul Durcan, Gavin Ewart, Peter Porter, Stephen Spender. Events include readings and discussion panels.

Lancaster LitFest
67 Church Street, Lancaster LA1 1ET
☎01524 62166   Fax 01524 841216

FOUNDED 1978. Regional literature development agency, organising workshops, readings, residencies, publications. Year-round programme of literature-based events; and annual festival in October.

City of London Festival

230 Bishopsgate, London EC2M 4QD
☎0171 377 0540　　　Fax 0171 377 1972

Director *Michael MacLeod*

FOUNDED 1962. Annual three-week festival held in June and July. Features over forty classical and popular music events alongside poetry and prose readings, street theatre and open-air extravaganzas, in some of the most outstanding performance spaces in the world.

London New Play Festival

34 Osnabrook Street, London NW1 3ND
☎0171 209 2326

Artistic Director *Phil Setren*
Workshop Director *Christopher Preston*

FOUNDED 1989. Open to full-length and one-act plays which are assessed for originality, form, etc by a reading committee. Deadline for scripts is the end of January; details can be obtained from **The Writers' Guild**. In 1996, four plays were produced and a number of writers were commissioned for short pieces which were performed at the Young Vic Studio, Riverside Studios and the Lyric Hammersmith Studio in the autumn. Offers writers workshops and discussions, and runs The Writers Group.

Ludlow Festival

Castle Square, Ludlow, Shropshire SY8 1AY
☎01584 875070　　　Fax 01584 877673

Contact *Festival Administrator*

FOUNDED 1959. Annual two-week festival held in the last week of June and first week of July with an open-air Shakespeare production held at Ludlow Castle and a varied programme of events including recitals, opera, dance, popular and classical concerts, literary and historical lectures.

Manchester Festival of Writing

Manchester Central Library, St Peter's Square, Manchester M2 5PD
☎0161 234 1901

Contact *Tang Lin*

FOUNDED 1990. An annual event organised by Manchester Libraries and Commonword community publishers. It consists of a programme of practical writing workshops on specific themes/genres run by well-known writers. Attendance at all workshops is free to Manchester residents.

Mayfest

129 High Street, Glasgow G1 1PH
☎0141 552 8444　　　Fax 0141 552 6612

Director *Paul Bassett*

FOUNDED 1982. Glasgow's largest annual arts festival providing entertainment to national and international audiences. It encompasses music, dance, theatre, comedy, visual arts, film, special events, including the May Day celebrations, and a late night club.

National Student Drama Festival

See **University College, Scarborough** under **Writers' Courses**

Norfolk and Norwich Festival

16 Princes Street, Norwich, Norfolk NR3 1AE
☎01603 614921　　　Fax 01603 632303

Festival Director *Marcus Davey*

FOUNDED 1772, this performing arts festival is the second oldest in the UK. Held annually in October (8th–19th in 1997), it features performers from all over the world. The 'Book at Lunchtime' series has become a popular feature in recent years and there are also poetry and story-telling events.

North East Lincolnshire Literature Festival – Fishing for Words

Arts Development, North East Lincolnshire Council, Knoll Street, Cleethorpes, Lincolnshire DN35 8LN
☎01472 323000　　　Fax 01472 323005

Festival Programmer *Camilla Goddard*

Annual festival held in February/March. Reflecting the fishing heritage of the area, the festival aims to make literature accessible to all ages and abilities through a varied and unusual programme. In its launch year (1997), the festival featured Sue Townsend, Fleur Adcock and crime writer Ann Granger. Visitors could make their own medieval bindings and listen to Elizabethan sonnets accompanied by lutes and spinets.

Royal Court Young Writers' Festival

Royal Court Young People's Theatre, 309 Portobello Road, London W10 5TD
☎0181 960 4641　　　Fax 0181 960 1434

Contact *Festival Organiser*

Open to young people up to the age of 23 in targeted regions. Focuses on the process of playwriting: writers and directors from the Royal Court visit parts of Britain with five centres in each area, leading a workshop on playwriting. A second visit extends this process to the point at which young people attending are invited to submit work for the festival. Intensive work on the final draft of plays precedes production at the Royal Court Theatre Upstairs, before going on tour in the participating areas.

Salisbury Festival

Festival Office, 75 New Street, Salisbury, Wiltshire SP1 2PH
☎01722 323883   Fax 01722 410552
Director *Helen Marriage*

FOUNDED 1972. Annual festival held at the end of May/beginning of June. The 1997 Festival included a Literary Day. Participants included Edmund White, Michael Ondaatje, Nina Bawden, Penelope Lively, Michael Dodd, Tim Renton.

Scottish Young Playwrights Festival

Scottish Youth Theatre, Old Athenaeum Theatre, 179 Buchanan Street, Glasgow G1 2JZ
☎0141 332 5127   Fax 0141 333 1021
Artistic Director *Mary McCluskey*

The Scottish Young Playwrights project operates throughout Scotland. In every region an experienced theatre practitioner runs regular young writers' workshops aimed at developing the best possible scripts from initial ideas. A representative selection of scripts is then selected to form a showcase. The festival is mounted at the Old Athenaeum Theatre in December, in conjunction with the Royal Scottish Academy of Music and Drama. Scripts will be workshopped, revised and developed culminating in an evening presentation. Scripts are welcome throughout the year from young people aged 15–25 who are native Scots and/or resident in Scotland; synopses of unfinished scripts also considered. No restriction on style, content or intended media, but work must be original and unperformed. Further details from above.

Stratford-upon-Avon Poetry Festival

The Shakespeare Centre, Henley Street, Stratford-upon-Avon, Warwickshire CV37 6QW
☎01789 204016   Fax 01789 296083
Festival Director *Roger Pringle*

FOUNDED 1953. Annual festival held on Sunday evenings during July and August. Readings by poets and professional actors.

The Sunday Times Hay Festival

Festival Office, Hay-on-Wye HR3 5BX
☎01497 821217   Fax 01497 821066
Festival Director *Peter Florence*

FOUNDED 1988. Annual May festival sponsored by *The Sunday Times*. Guests have included Salman Rushdie, Toni Morrison, Stephen Fry, Joseph Heller, Carlos Fuentes, Maya Angelou, Amos Oz, Arthur Miller.

Warwick & Leamington Festival

Warwick Arts Society, Northgate, Warwick CV34 4JL
☎01926 410747   Fax 01926 407606
Festival Director *Richard Phillips*

FOUNDED 1980. Annual festival lasting 12 days in the first half of July. Basically a chamber and early music festival, with some open-air, large-scale concerts in Warwick Castle, the Festival also promotes plays by Shakespeare in historical settings. Large-scale education programme. Interested in increasing its literary content, both in performances and workshops, organised in conjunction with Pauline Prior-Pitt.

Ways with Words

Droridge Farm, Dartington, Totnes, Devon TQ9 6JQ
☎01803 867311   Fax 01803 863688
Festival Director *Kay Dunbar*

Ways with Words runs a major literature festival at Dartington Hall in south Devon in July each year. Features over 100 writers giving lectures, readings, interviews, discussions, performances, master classes and workshops.

Ways with Words also runs literary weekends in Southwold (Suffolk), Bath, York and Bury St Edmunds, plus writing, reading and painting courses in the UK and abroad.

Writearound

Cleveland Arts, Gurney House, Gurney Street, Middlesbrough, Cleveland TS1 1JL
☎01642 262424
Contact *Mark Robinson*

FOUNDED 1989. Annual festival with a commitment to local writers. Held during October, featuring workshops and readings, plus guest writers and opportunities for new writers. Publishes anthologies of poetry by local children. Contact above for further information. Programmes available in August.

Two Minds With a Single Thought

The Art of Translation

The ideal translator is also a gifted writer. He needs to have a feeling and fascination for language and the talent to convey the essence of the original work, echoing its style and tone. A word for word literal interpretation is bound to fail. Formal qualifications are not essential. Some translators start with the advantage of being raised in a bilingual family, others acquire linguistic skills by working overseas. A university education in modern languages can be helpful but is not in itself a badge of competence, let alone proof of style and inspiration.

Because the translator is a creative artist in his own right, copyright law recognises the 'original' nature of his work with copyright protection that is distinct from the copyright of the author. This opens up the possibility of a recurring income over many years, even when the duration of the author's copyright is exhausted. For example, a writer knowledgeable in Russian might produce a marvellous new Chekhov translation thus bringing a play back into copyright for the benefit of the translator.

The downside to any such enterprise is that there can be no exclusive right to the translation of a particular work. Where one translator has trod profitably, another may soon follow in his footsteps. Working from the same source text, the result is likely to be two different but equally valid renditions. Nonetheless, for a popular book or play, the possibilities for argument between translators as to who owns what are legion. In the theatre, such disputes are further complicated by the tendency of some translators to rely rather too heavily on existing English language versions of a play to achieve their own interpretation. It has been known for a 'translator' to possess only the haziest notion of the language he was supposed to be working from. His defence was that he had a good dictionary.

Ideas for translating books or plays invariably start with a publisher or producer. It follows that the best chance of a commission comes from sending out sample material. But it is open to anyone to offer proposals. A writer who is bilingual in, say, French or German should watch the reviews and publishing lists for likely projects. The trick here is to secure an understanding with a prospective partner before trying to negotiate a commission. This is at least some protection against a publisher who might thank you profusely for the idea before sending it off to one of his regular panel of translators.

Knowledge of a rare language can help though it is no longer enough to be conversant with one of the minority European languages like Dutch or Danish. The use of English in these countries is now so extensive that writers are inclined to do their own translations or compose in English as the first language. Also, much depends on fashion. A few years ago, French dramatists seemed to lose their appeal. Now, the trend is moving back in their favour with a demand for translation of new work and new translations of the classics.

Payment for translation can be by royalty or by fee. If it is in the form of a lump sum, it should not be for the translation but for a specified use of the translator's work, for example, for the right to print 5000 copies for sale in the UK. Such an arrangement makes fair allowance for additional fees to be paid if further copies are sold or if the licence is extended to include America. For the translation of a book, the Model Contract drawn up by the Translators Association recommends that there should be an advance payment on account of royalties and a share of the proceeds from the sale of subsidiary rights such as serialisation. In the case of a play, the translator should receive a percentage of the gross box office receipts. The translator should be able to obtain additional payment if asked to edit a literary work as well as translate it; and there should be an additional fee for the preparation of an index for the translated edition. When translations are borrowed from public libraries, the translator receives a 30 per cent share of the full Public Lending Right payment.

Usually the rights owner, either author or publisher, accepts lower royalties on the translated edition, say, a 7½ per cent royalty on sales of a translated book compared with 10 per cent on sales in its original language. On a theatre production the original author might receive 6 per cent instead of 10 per cent. The author may also forego a share of secondary rights, e.g. of the proceeds from the sale of American rights. This means that some or all of the payment received by the translator is money that would otherwise have been paid to the original author. To that extent, the author is the person who is paying the translator.

Sometimes the foreign author of a work is so keen to see it translated that he will offer to pay the translation costs directly. In this case, a written contract between author and translator should specify the respective rights and set out how any proceeds from publication or production are to be divided.

Bursaries and prizes

A number of residential bursaries are offered by The British Centre for Literary Translation at the Department of Modern Languages and European History, The University of East Anglia, Norwich NR4 1TJ. For up-to-date information about bursaries abroad, contact the Cultural Attaché of the relevant embassy or bodies such as the French Institute, the Goethe Institut and the Italian Institute. The Arts Council offers bursaries to theatre translators under its Theatre Translation Schemes. The Translators Association administers several prizes for already published translations and the Arts Council sometimes contributes towards the cost of producing translations.

The Translators Association

The Translators Association is a subsidiary group within the Society of Authors. Published translators can apply for full membership. Translators in the making may apply for Associate Membership either when they have received an offer for a full-length translation or if they have had occasional translations of shorter material, e.g. articles, short stories and poems, published or performed commercially.

The Association's Model Contract, with explanatory notes, is available free to members; and the Association also issues Guidelines for translators of dramatic works. The Association's journal, *In Other Words*, contains a wide variety of articles, reviews and information.

European Publishers

Austria

Paul Neff Verlag KG
Hackingerstrasse 52,
1140 Vienna
☎00 43 222 9406115
Fax 00 43 222 947641288
FOUNDED 1829. *Publishes* art, biography, general fiction, music and dance.

Springer-Verlag KG
Mölkerbastei 5, PO Box 367, 1011 Vienna
☎00 43 222 5339614 Fax 00 43 222 6381586
FOUNDED 1924. *Publishes* environmental studies, engineering (general), dentistry, medicine, nursing and general science.

Verlag Carl Ueberreuter
Alserstrasse 24, Postfach 306,
A-1090 Vienna
☎00 43 222 404440 Fax 00 43 222 404445
FOUNDED 1548. *Publishes* fiction and general non-fiction: art, government, history, economics, political science, general science, science fiction, fantasy, music and dance.

Paul Zsolnay Verlag GmbH
Prinz-Eugenstrasse 30, Postfach 142,
A-1041 Vienna
☎00 43 222 50576610 Fax 00 43 222 5057661-10
FOUNDED 1923. *Publishes* biography, fiction, general non-fiction, history, poetry.

Belgium

Facet NV
Willem Linnigstr 13, 2060 Antwerp
☎00 32 3 2274028 Fax 00 32 3 2273792
FOUNDED 1976. *Publishes* children's books.

Uitgeverij Lannoo NV
Kasteelstr 97, B-8700 Tielt
☎00 32 51 424211 Fax 00 32 51 401152
FOUNDED 1909. *Publishes* general non-fiction, art, biography, economics, gardening, health, history, management, nutrition, photography, poetry, government, political science, religion, travel.

Standaard Uitgeverij
Belgiëlei 147a, 2018 Antwerp
☎00 32 3 2395900 Fax 00 32 3 2308550
FOUNDED 1919. *Publishes* education, fiction, humour.

Denmark

Forlaget Apostrof ApS
Berggreensgade 24, Postboks 2580,
DK-2100 Copenhagen
☎00 45 31 208420 Fax 00 45 31 208453
FOUNDED 1980. *Publishes* essays, fiction, humour, literature, literary criticism, general non-fiction, psychology, psychiatry.

Aschehoug Fakta
7 Vognmagergade, PO Box 2179,
DK-1017 Copenhagen 0
☎00 45 33 919222 Fax 00 45 33 918218
FOUNDED 1977. *Publishes* cookery, health, how-to, maritime and nutrition.

Borgens Forlag A/S
Valbygardsvej 33, DK-2500 Valby
☎00 45 36 462100 Fax 00 45 36 441488
FOUNDED 1948. *Publishes* fiction, general non-fiction, art, computer science, crafts, education, games, hobbies, health, nutrition, religion, social sciences, sociology.

Forum Publishers
Snaregade 4, DK-1205 Copenhagen K
☎00 45 33 147714 Fax 00 45 33 147791
FOUNDED 1940. *Publishes* fiction and mysteries.

GEC Gads Forlagsaktieselskab
Vimmelskaftet 32, DK-1161
Copenhagen K
☎00 45 33 150558 Fax 00 45 33 110800
FOUNDED 1855. *Publishes* general non-fiction, biological sciences, cookery, crafts, games, economics, education, English as a second language, environmental studies, gardening, history, hobbies, law, mathematics, natural history, physics, plants, travel.

Gyldendalske Boghandel-Nordisk Forlag A/S

Forlag A/S
Klareboderne 3, DK-1001 Copenhagen K
☎00 45 33 110775   Fax 00 45 33 110323
FOUNDED 1770. *Publishes* fiction, art, biography, dance, dentistry, education, history, how-to, medicine, music, poetry, nursing, philosophy, psychology, psychiatry, general and social sciences, sociology.

Hekla Forlag

Valbygaardsvej 33, DK-2500 Valby
☎00 45 36 462100   Fax 00 45 36 441488
FOUNDED 1979. *Publishes* general fiction and non-fiction.

Høst & Søns Publishers Ltd

Købmagergade 62, Box 2212,
DK-1018 Copenhagen
☎00 45 33 153031   Fax 00 45 33 155155
FOUNDED 1836. *Publishes* arts, crafts, environmental studies, games, hobbies, language, linguistics, regional interests, travel.

Lademann A/S

Gerdasgade 37, 2500 Valby
☎00 45 36 441120   Fax 00 45 36 442236
FOUNDED 1954. *Publishes* general non-fiction.

Lindhardt og Ringhof

Frederiksborggade 1, 2th,
DK-1360 Copenhagen
☎00 45 33 695000   Fax 00 45 33 695001
FOUNDED 1971. *Publishes* fiction and general non-fiction.

Nyt Nordisk Forlag Arnold Busck A/S

Busck A/S
Købmagergade 49, DK-1150 Copenhagen K
☎00 45 33 111103   Fax 00 45 33 934490
FOUNDED 1896. *Publishes* fiction, art, biography, dance, dentistry, history, how-to, music, philosophy, religion, medicine, nursing, psychology, psychiatry, general and social sciences, sociology.

Politikens Forlag A/S

Vestergade 26, DK-1456 Copenhagen K
☎00 45 33 470707   Fax 00 45 33 470708
FOUNDED 1946. *Publishes* general non-fiction, art, crafts, dance, history, hobbies, music, natural history, sports, travel.

Samlerens Forlag A/S

Snaregade 4, DK-1205 Copenhagen K
☎00 45 33 131023   Fax 00 45 33 144314
FOUNDED 1942. *Publishes* essays, fiction, government, history, literature, literary criticism, political science.

Det Schønbergske Forlag A/S

Landemaerket 5, DK-1119 Copenhagen K
☎00 45 33 113066   Fax 00 45 33 330045
FOUNDED 1857. *Publishes* art, biography, fiction, history, humour, philosophy, poetry, psychology, psychiatry, travel

Spektrum Forlagsaktieselskab

4 Snaregade, DK-1205 Copenhagen K
☎00 45 33 147714   Fax 00 45 33 147791
FOUNDED 1990. *Publishes* general non-fiction.

Tiderne Skifter Forlag A/S

51 Pilestrade, 1001 Copenhagen K
☎00 45 33 325772   Fax 00 45 33 144205
FOUNDED 1979. *Publishes* fiction, literature and literary criticism, essays, photography, behavioural sciences.

Wangels Forlag AS

Gerdasgade 37, 2500 Valby
☎00 45 36 441120   Fax 00 45 36 441162
FOUNDED 1946. *Publishes* fiction.

Finland

Gummerus Publishers

Erottajankatu 5C, PO Box 2,
SF-00130 Helsinki
☎00 358 9 584301   Fax 00 358 9 58430200
FOUNDED 1872. *Publishes* fiction and general non-fiction.

Karisto Oy

Paroistentie 2, PO Box 102,
SF-13101 Hämeenlinna
☎00 358 3 6161551   Fax 00 358 3 6161565
FOUNDED 1900. *Publishes* fiction and general non-fiction.

Kirjayhtymä Oy

Eerikinkatu 28, PO Box 207,
SF-00180 Helsinki
☎00 358 9 6944522   Fax 00 358 9 6947265
FOUNDED 1958. *Publishes* fiction and general non-fiction.

Otava Kustannusosakeyhtiö
Uudenmaankatu 8–12, PO Box 134,
00120 Helsinki
☎00 358 9 19961   Fax 00 358 9 643136
FOUNDED 1890. *Publishes* fiction, general non-fiction, art, biography, history, how-to.

Werner Söderström Osakeyhtiö (WSOY)
Bulevardi 12, PO Box 222, 00121 Helsinki
☎00 358 9 61681   Fax 00 358 9 6168405
FOUNDED 1878. *Publishes* fiction, general non-fiction, education.

Tammi Publishers
Urho Kekkosen katu 4–6 E, PO Box 410,
FIN-00100 Helsinki
☎00 358 9 6937621   Fax 00 358 9 69376266
FOUNDED 1943. *Publishes* fiction, general non-fiction.

France

Editions Arthaud SA
26 rue Racine, F-75278 Paris
☎00 33 1 4051 3100   Fax 00 33 1 4329 2148
FOUNDED 1890. *Publishes* art, history, literature, literary criticism, esays, sport, travel.

Editions Belfond
216 blvd St-Germain, 75343 Paris
☎00 33 1 4544 3823   Fax 00 33 1 4544 9804
FOUNDED 1963. *Publishes* fiction, literature, literary criticism, essays, mysteries, romance, poetry, general non-fiction, art, biography, dance, health, history, how-to, music, nutrition.

Editions Bordas
17 rue Rémy-Dumoncel,
75661 Paris Cedex 14
☎00 33 1 4279 6200   Fax 00 33 1 4322 8518
FOUNDED 1946. *Publishes* education and general non-fiction.

Editions Calmann-Lévy SA
3 rue Auber, 75009 Paris
☎00 33 1 4742 3833   Fax 00 33 1 4742 7781
FOUNDED 1836. *Publishes* fiction, science fiction, fantasy, biography, history, humour, philosophy, psychology, psychiatry, social sciences, sociology, sports, economics.

Editions Denoël Sàrl
9 rue du Cherche-Midi, 75006 Paris
☎00 33 1 4439 7373   Fax 00 33 1 4439 7390
FOUNDED 1932. *Publishes* art, economics, fiction, science fiction, fantasy, government, history, philosophy, political science, psychology, psychiatry, sports.

Librairie Arthème Fayard
75 rue des Saints-Pères, 75006 Paris
☎00 33 1 4544 3845   Fax 00 33 1 4222 4017
FOUNDED 1854. *Publishes* biography, fiction, history, dance, music, philosophy, religion, social sciences, sociology, general science, technology.

Librairie Ernest Flammarion
26 rue Racine, F–75278 Paris Cedex 06
☎00 33 1 4051 3100   Fax 00 33 1 4329 2148
FOUNDED 1875. *Publishes* general fiction and non-fiction.

Editions Gallimard
5 rue Sébastien-Bottin, 75341 Paris Cedex 07
☎00 33 1 4954 4200   Fax 00 33 1 4544 9919
FOUNDED 1911. *Publishes* fiction, poetry, art, biography, dance, history, music, philosophy.

Société des Editions Grasset et Fasquelle
61 rue des Saints-Pères, 75006 Paris
☎00 33 1 4439 2200   Fax 00 33 1 4222 6418
FOUNDED 1907. *Publishes* fiction and general non-fiction, essays, literature, literary criticism, philosophy.

Hachette Livre
83 ave Marceau, 75116 Paris
☎00 33 1 4069 1600   Fax 00 33 1 4220 3993
FOUNDED 1826. *Publishes* fiction and general non-fiction, architecture and interior design, art, economics, education, general engineering, government, history, language and linguistics, political science, philosophy, general science, self-help, social science, sociology, sports, travel.

Editions Robert Laffont
24 ave Marceau, 75381 Paris Cedex 08
☎00 33 1 5367 1400   Fax 00 33 1 5367 1414
FOUNDED 1941. *Publishes* fiction and non-fiction.

Librairie Larousse
17 rue de Montparnasse,
75298 Paris Cedex 06
☎00 33 1 4439 4400   Fax 00 33 1 4439 4343
FOUNDED 1852. *Publishes* general and social sciences, sociology, language, linguistics, technology.

Editions Jean-Claude Lattès
17 rue Jacob, F–75006 Paris
☎00 33 1 4441 7400   Fax 00 33 1 4325 3047
FOUNDED 1968. *Publishes* fiction and general non-fiction, biography, dance, music, religion (Catholic and Jewish).

Les Editions Magnard Sàrl
122 blvd Saint-Germain, 75264 Paris Cedex 06
☎00 33 1 4329 4100   Fax 00 33 1 4331 6613
FOUNDED 1933. *Publishes* education.

Michelin et Cie (Services de Tourisme)
46 ave de Breteuil, F–75324 Paris Cedex 07
☎00 33 1 4566 1234   Fax 00 33 1 4566 1163
FOUNDED 1900. *Publishes* travel.

Les Editions de Minuit SA
7 rue Bernard-Palissy, 75006 Paris
☎00 33 1 4439 3920   Fax 00 33 1 4544 8236
FOUNDED 1942. *Publishes* fiction, essays, literature, literary criticism, philosophy, social science, sociology.

Fernand Nathan
9 rue Méchain, 75676 Paris
☎00 33 1 4587 5000   Fax 00 33 1 4331 2169
FOUNDED 1881. *Publishes* education, history, philosophy, psychology, psychiatry, general and social sciences, sociology.

Les Presses de la Cité
12 ave d'Italie, 75013 Paris
☎00 33 1 4416 0500   Fax 00 33 1 4416 0505
FOUNDED 1947. *Publishes* literature, literary criticism, essays, science fiction, fantasy, anthropology, biography, history, how-to, military science, travel.

Presses Universitaires de France (PUF)
108 blvd St-Germain, 75006 Paris 06
☎00 33 1 4634 1201   Fax 00 33 1 4634 6541
FOUNDED 1921. *Publishes* art, biography, dance, dentistry, government, general engineering, geography, geology, history, law, medicine, music, nursing, philosophy, psychology, psychiatry, religion, political and social sciences, sociology.

Editions du Seuil
27 rue Jacob, 75261 Paris Cedex 06
☎00 33 1 4046 5050   Fax 00 33 1 4329 0829
FOUNDED 1935. *Publishes* fiction, literature, literary criticism, essays, poetry, art, biography, dance, government, history, how-to, music, photography, philosophy, political science, psychology, psychiatry, religion, general and social sciences, sociology.

Les Editions de la Table Ronde
7 rue Corneille, 75006 Paris
☎00 33 1 4326 0395   Fax 00 33 1 4407 0930
FOUNDED 1944. *Publishes* fiction and general non-fiction, biography, history, psychology, psychiatry, religion.

Librairie Vuibert SA
63 blvd St-Germain, 75005 Paris
☎00 33 1 4441 7350   Fax 00 33 1 4325 7586
FOUNDED 1877. *Publishes* biological and earth sciences, chemistry, chemical engineering, economics, law, mathematics, physics.

Germany

Verlag C. H. Beck (OHG)
Wilhelmstr 9, 80801 Munich
☎00 49 89 381890   Fax 00 49 89 38189398
FOUNDED 1763. *Publishes* general non-fiction, anthropology, archaeology, art, dance, economics, essays, history, language, law, linguistics, literature, literary criticism, music, philosophy, social sciences, sociology, theology.

Bertelsmann-Lexikon Verlag GmbH
Carl-Bertelsmann-Str, Postfach 1300, 33310 Gütersloh
☎00 49 5241 801   Fax 00 49 5241 75166
Publishes fiction and non-fiction, anthropology, art, biography, business, economics, film, history, how-to, law, management, marketing, medicine, dentistry, nursing, radio, television, video, technology, travel.

Carlsen Verlag GmbH
Völckersstr 14–20, Postfach 500380, 22703 Hamburg
☎00 49 40 3910090   Fax 00 49 40 39100962
FOUNDED 1953. *Publishes* humour and general non-fiction.

Deutscher Taschenbuch Verlag GmbH & Co. KG (dtv)
Friedrichstr 1a, Postfach 400422, 80704 Munich
☎00 49 89 3817060   Fax 00 49 89 346428
FOUNDED 1961. *Publishes* fiction and general non-fiction; art, biography, computer science,

dance, history, how-to, music, poetry, psychiatry, psychology, philosophy, religion, medicine, dentistry, nursing, social sciences, literature, literary criticism, essays, humour, travel.

Droemersche Verlagsanstalt Th. Knaur Nachfolger
Rauchstr 9–11, 81673 Munich
☎00 49 89 92710   Fax 00 49 89 9271168
FOUNDED 1901. *Publishes* fiction, general non-fiction, cookery, how-to, self-help, travel and general science.

Econ-Verlag GmbH
Kaiserswerthestr 282, Postfach 300321,
40403 Düsseldorf
☎00 49 211 43596   Fax 00 49 211 4359786
Publishes general non-fiction and fiction, economics, general science.

Falken-Verlag GmbH
Schöne Aussicht 21, Postfach 1120,
65521 Niederhausen
☎00 49 6127 7020   Fax 00 49 6127 702133
FOUNDED 1923. *Publishes* computer science, crafts, cookery, education, games, gardening, health, history, hobbies, how-to, humour, nutrition, photography, sports.

S Fischer Verlag GmbH
Hedderichstr 114, Postfach 700355,
60553 Frankfurt am Main
☎00 49 69 60620   Fax 00 49 69 6062214
FOUNDED 1886. *Publishes* fiction, general non-fiction, essays, literature, literary criticism.

Carl Hanser Verlag
Kolbergerstr 22, Postfach 860420,
81631 Munich
☎00 49 89 998300   Fax 00 49 89 984809
FOUNDED 1928. *Publishes* general non-fiction, poetry, computer science, economics, electronics, electrical, mechanical and general engineering, environmental studies, management, mathematics, medicine, nursing, dentistry, philosophy, physics.

Wilhelm Heyne Verlag
Türkenstr 5–7, 80333 Munich
☎00 49 89 286350   Fax 00 49 89 2800943
FOUNDED 1934. *Publishes* fiction, mystery, romance, humour, science fiction, fantasy, astrology, biography, cookery, film, history, how-to, occult, psychology, psychiatry, video.

Hoffmann und Campe Verlag
Harvestehuder Weg 42, Postfach 130444,
20139 Hamburg
☎00 49 40 441880   Fax 00 49 40 44188-290
FOUNDED 1781. *Publishes* fiction and general non-fiction; art, biography, dance, history, music, poetry, philosophy, psychology, psychiatry, science, social sciences, sociology.

Ernst Klett Verlag
Rotebühlstr 77, Postfach 106016,
70049 Stuttgart
☎00 49 711 66720   Fax 00 49 711 628053
FOUNDED 1844. *Publishes* education.

Gustav Lübbe Verlag GmbH
Scheidtbachstr 29–31, Postfach 200127,
51431 Bergisch Gladbach
☎00 49 2202 1210   Fax 00 49 2202 36727
FOUNDED 1963. *Publishes* fiction and general non-fiction, archaeology, biography, history, how-to.

Mosaik Verlag GmbH
Neumarkter Str 18, Postfach 800360,
81603 Munich 80
☎00 49 89 431890   Fax 00 49 89 43189627
Publishes animals, antiques, architecture and interior design, child care and development, cookery, crafts, economics, finance, film, gardening, games, hobbies, health, house and home, human relations, nutrition, pets, self-help, sports, video, wine and spirits, women's studies.

Pestalozzi-Verlag Graphische Gesellschaft mbH
Am Pestalozziring 14, 91058 Erlangen
☎00 49 9131 60600
Fax 00 49 9131 773090
FOUNDED 1844. *Publishes* crafts, games, hobbies.

Rowohlt Taschenbuch Verlag GmbH
Hamburger Str 17, Postfach 1349,
21465 Reinbeck
☎00 49 40 72720   Fax 00 49 40 7272319
FOUNDED 1953. *Publishes* fiction and general non-fiction; archaeology, art, computer science, crafts, education, essays, games and hobbies, gay and lesbian, government, history, literature, literary criticism, philosophy, political science, psychology, psychiatry, religion, general science, social sciences, sociology.

Springer-Verlag GmbH & Co KG

Heidelberger Platz 3, Postfach 311340,
10643 Berlin 33

☎00 49 30 82787   Fax 00 49 30 8214091

FOUNDED 1842. *Publishes* biological sciences,
chemistry, computer science, dentistry, economics, general engineering, environmental
studies, law, mathematics, medicine, nursing,
philosophy, psychology, psychiatry, physics,
general science, technology.

Suhrkamp Verlag

Lindenstr 29–35, Postfach 101945,
60019 Frankfurt am Main

☎00 49 69 756010   Fax 00 49 69 75601522

FOUNDED 1950. *Publishes* biography, fiction,
philosophy, poetry, psychology, psychiatry,
general science.

K. Thienemanns Verlag

Blumenstr 36, 70182 Stuttgart

☎00 49 711 210550   Fax 00 49 711 2105539

FOUNDED 1849. *Publishes* fiction and general
non-fiction.

Verlag Ullstein GmbH

Charlottenstr 76, 10969 Berlin

☎00 49 30 25913500
Fax 00 49 30 25913590

FOUNDED 1903. *Publishes* fiction, architecture
and interior design, art, biography, dance, education, ethnology, geography, geology, government, health, history, how-to, military science,
music, nutrition, poetry, political science, general science, social sciences, sociology, travel.

Italy

Adelphi Edizioni SpA

Via S. Giovanni sul Muro 14,
20121 Milan

☎00 39 2 72000975   Fax 00 39 2 89010337

FOUNDED 1962. *Publishes* fiction, art, biography, dance, music, philosophy, psychology,
psychiatry, religion, general science.

Bompiana

Via Mecenate 91, 20138 Milan

☎00 39 2 50951   Fax 00 39 2 5065361

FOUNDED 1929. *Publishes* fiction and general
non-fiction, art, drama, theatre and general science.

Bulzoni Editore SRL (Le Edizioni Universitarie d'Italia)

Via Dei Liburni 14, 00185 Rome

☎00 39 6 4455207   Fax 00 39 6 4450355

FOUNDED 1969. *Publishes* fiction, literature, literary criticism, essays, art, drama, engineering,
film, law, language, linguistics, philosophy, general science, social sciences, sociology, theatre,
video.

Nuova Casa Editrice Licinio Cappelli GEM srl

Via Farini 14, I–40124 Bologna

☎00 39 51 239060   Fax 00 39 51 239286

FOUNDED 1851. *Publishes* fiction, art, biography,
drama, film, government, history, music and
dance, medicine, nursing, dentistry, philosophy,
poetry, political science, psychology, psychiatry,
religion, general science, social sciences, sociology, theatre, video.

Gruppo Editoriale Fabbri SpA

Via Mecenate 91, 20138 Milan

☎00 39 2 50951   Fax 00 39 2 5065361

FOUNDED 1945. *Publishes* art, crafts, dance,
environmental studies, games, hobbies, history,
music, medicine, nursing, dentistry, outdoor
recreation, general science.

Garzanti Editore

Via Senato 25, 20121 Milan

☎00 39 2 77871   Fax 00 39 2 76009233

FOUNDED 1861. *Publishes* fiction, literature, literary criticism, essays, art, biography, history,
poetry, government, political science.

Giunti Publishing Group

Via Bolognese 165, 50139 Florence

☎00 39 55 66791   Fax 00 39 55 6679298

FOUNDED 1840. *Publishes* fiction, literature, literary criticism, essays, art, chemistry, chemical
engineering, education, history, how-to, language arts, linguistics, mathematics, psychology,
psychiatry, general science. Italian publishers of
National Geographical Society books.

Gremese Editore SRL

Via Agnelli 88, 00151 Rome

☎00 39 6 65740507   Fax 00 39 6 65740509

FOUNDED 1978. *Publishes* fiction and non-
fiction; art, astrology, cookery, crafts, dance,
drama, environmental studies, fashion, games,
hobbies, essays, literature, literary criticism,
music, occult, photography, sport, travel,
theatre, film, video.

Istituto Geografico de Agostini SpA
Via Giovanni da Verrazzano 15, 28100
Novara
☎00 39 321 471830   Fax 00 39 321 471286
FOUNDED 1901. *Publishes* art, essays, gardening, geology and geography, history, literature, literary criticism, regional interests, religion.

Longanesi & C
Corso Italia 13, 20122 Milan
☎00 39 2 8692640   Fax 00 39 2 72000306
FOUNDED 1946. *Publishes* fiction, art, biography, dance, history, how-to, medicine, nursing, dentistry, music, philosophy, psychology, psychiatry, religion, general and social sciences, sociology.

Arnoldo Mondadori Editore SpA
Via Mondadori, 20090 Segrate (Milan)
☎00 39 2 75421   Fax 00 39 2 75422302
FOUNDED 1907. *Publishes* fiction, mystery, romance, art, biography, dance, dentistry, history, how-to, medicine, music, poetry, philosophy, psychology, psychiatry, religion, nursing, general science, education.

Società Editrice Il Mulino
Str Maggiore 37, 40125 Bologna
☎00 39 51 256011   Fax 00 39 51 256034
FOUNDED 1954. *Publishes* dance, drama, economics, government, history, law, language, linguistics, music, philosophy, political science, psychology, psychiatry, social sciences, sociology, theatre.

Gruppo Ugo Mursia Editore SpA
Via Tadino 29, 20124 Milan
☎00 39 2 29403030   Fax 00 39 2 29525557
FOUNDED 1922. *Publishes* fiction, poetry, art, biography, education, history, maritime, philosophy, religion, sport, general and social sciences, sociology.

RCS Rizzoli Libri SpA
Via Mecenate 91, 20138 Milan
☎00 39 2 50950   Fax 00 39 2 508012131
FOUNDED 1909. *Publishes* fiction, art, biography, crafts, dance, economics, games, hobbies, medicine, nursing, dentistry, music, religion, social sciences, sociology.

Societa Editrice Internazionale – SEI
Corso Regina Margherita 176, 10152 Turin
☎00 39 11 52271   Fax 00 39 11 5211320
FOUNDED 1908. *Publishes* literature, literary criticism, essays, education, geography, geol-

ogy, history, mathematics, philosophy, physics, religion, psychology, psychiatry.

Sonzogno
Via Mecenate 91, 20138 Milan
☎00 39 2 50951   Fax 00 39 2 5065361
FOUNDED 1818. *Publishes* fiction, mysteries, and general non-fiction.

Sperling e Kupfer Editori SpA
Via Borgonuovo 24, 20121 Milan
☎00 39 2 290341   Fax 00 39 2 6590290
FOUNDED 1899. *Publishes* fiction and general non-fiction, biography, economics, health, how-to, management, nutrition, general science, sport, travel.

Sugarco Edizioni SRL
Via Fermi 9, 21040 Carnago (Varese)
☎00 39 331 985511   Fax 00 39 331 985385
FOUNDED 1956. *Publishes* fiction, biography, history, how-to, philosophy.

Todariana Editrice
Via Gardone 29, 20139 Milan
☎00 39 2 55213405   Fax 00 39 2 55213405
FOUNDED 1967. *Publishes* fiction, poetry, science fiction, fantasy, literature, literary criticism, essays, language arts, linguistics, psychology, psychiatry, social sciences, sociology, travel.

The Netherlands

De Boekerij BV
Herengracht 540, 1017 CG Amsterdam
☎00 31 20 5353135   Fax 00 31 20 5353130
FOUNDED 1986. *Publishes* fiction and general non-fiction, film, video, mysteries, romance, science fiction and fantasy.

A.W. Bruna Uitgevers BV
Postbus 40203, 3504 AA Utrecht
☎00 31 30 2470411   Fax 00 31 30 2410018
FOUNDED 1868. *Publishes* fiction and general non-fiction; computer science, history, philosophy, psychology, psychiatry, general and social science, sociology.

Uitgeverij BZZTÔH
Laan van Meerdervoort 10, 2517 AJ The Hague
☎00 31 70 3632934   Fax 00 31 70 3631932
FOUNDED 1970. *Publishes* fiction, mysteries, general non-fiction, animals, astrology, biography, cookery, dance, humour, music, occult, pets, religion (Buddhist), romance, travel.

Elsevier Science BV
Sara Burgerhartstraat 25, PO Box 2400,
1000 CK Amsterdam
☎00 31 20 4853911   Fax 00 31 20 48552457
FOUNDED 1946. Parent company – Reed
Elsevier. *Publishes* sciences (all fields), management and professional, medicine, nursing, dentistry, economics, engineering (computer and general), mathematics, physics, psychology, psychiatry, social sciences, sociology, technology.

Uitgeverij Hollandia BV
Beukenlaan 20, Postbus 70, 3740 AB Baarn
☎00 31 2154 18941   Fax 00 31 2154 21917
FOUNDED 1899. *Publishes* fiction, maritime, travel.

Uitgeversmaatschappij J. H. Kok BV
Gildestraat 5, PO Box 130, 8260 AC Kampen
☎00 31 5202 92555   Fax 00 31 5202 27331
FOUNDED 1894. *Publishes* fiction, poetry, art, biography, crafts, education, environmental studies, games, history, hobbies, how-to, psychology, psychiatry, religion, general and social sciences, sociology, medicine, nursing, dentistry.

M & P Publishing House
Schoutlaan 4, 6002 EA Weert
☎00 31 4950 36880   Fax 00 31 4950 21145
FOUNDED 1974. *Publishes* general non-fiction.

Meulenhoff International
Herengracht 507, PO Box 100,
1000 AC Amsterdam
☎00 31 20 5533500   Fax 00 31 20 6258511
Publishes international co-productions, art and general non-fiction. Specialises in Dutch and translated literature, science fiction, non-fiction and children's.

Uitgeverij Het Spectrum BV
Montalbaendreef 2, Postbus 2073,
3500 GB Utrecht
☎00 31 30 650650   Fax 00 31 30 620850
FOUNDED 1935. *Publishes* science fiction, fantasy, literature, literary criticism, essays, mystery, crime, general non-fiction, computer science, history, astrology, occult, management, environmental studies, travel.

Time-Life Books BV
Ottho Heldringstr 5, 1066 AZ Amsterdam
☎00 31 20 5104911   Fax 00 31 20 6175077
Publishes art, cookery, gardening, history, how-to, general science, parapsychology, behavioural sciences, biological sciences.

Unieboek BV
Postbus 97, 3990 DB Houten
☎00 31 3403 77660   Fax 00 31 3403 77660
FOUNDED 1891. *Publishes* fiction, general non-fiction, architecture and interior design, government, political science, literature, literary criticism, essays, archaeology, cookery, history.

Uniepers BV
Postbus 69, 1390 AB Abcoude
☎00 31 294 285111   Fax 00 31 294 283013
FOUNDED 1961. *Publishes* (mostly in co-editions) antiques, anthropology, architecture and interior design, art, culture, dance, history, music, nature, natural history.

Veen Uitgevers Group
Postbus 14095, 3508 SC Utrecht
☎00 31 30 349211   Fax 00 31 20 349208
FOUNDED 1887. A member of the Wolters Kluwer Group. *Publishes* general non-fiction, fiction, essays, Dutch and foreign literature, literary criticism, travel, business,

Wolters Kluwer NV
Stadhouderskade 1, PO Box 818,
1000 AV Amsterdam
☎00 31 20 6070400   Fax 00 31 20 6070490
FOUNDED 1889. *Publishes* education, medical, technical encyclopedias, trade books and journals, law and taxation, periodicals.

Norway

H. Aschehoug & Co (W. Nygaard) A/S
Sehestedsgate 3, Postboks 363,
0102 Sentrum, Oslo
☎00 47 22 400400   Fax 00 47 22 206395
FOUNDED 1872. *Publishes* fiction and general non-fiction, general and social science, sociology.

J. W. Cappelens Forlag A/S
Maribosgaten 13, Postboks 350, 0101 Sentrum, Oslo
☎00 47 22 365000   Fax 00 47 22 365040
FOUNDED 1829. *Publishes* fiction, general non-fiction, religion.

N. W. Damm og Søn A/S
Tordenskioldsgt 6b, 0055 Oslo
☎00 47 22 471100   Fax 00 47 22 471149
FOUNDED 1845. *Publishes* fiction and general non-fiction.

Ex Libris Forlag A/S
Nordregt 22, Postboks 2130 Grünerløkka, 0505 Oslo
☎00 47 22 384450   Fax 00 47 22 385160
FOUNDED 1982. *Publishes* fiction, general non-fiction, cookery, health, nutrition, humour, human relations.

Gyldendal Norsk Forlag A/S
Sehestedsgt 4, Postboks 6860, 0130 St Olaf, Oslo
☎00 47 22 034100   Fax 00 47 22 034105
FOUNDED 1925. *Publishes* fiction, science fiction, fantasy, art, dance, biography, government, political science, history, how-to, music, social sciences, sociology, poetry, philosophy, psychology, psychiatry, religion.

Hjemmets Bokforlag AS
Tordenskioldsgate 6B, N-0055 Oslo
☎00 47 22 471000   Fax 00 47 22 471098
FOUNDED 1969. *Publishes* fiction and general non-fiction.

NKS-Forlaget
Postboks 5853, 0308 Oslo
☎00 47 22 596000   Fax 00 47 22 596300
FOUNDED 1971. *Publishes* accountancy, childcare, English as a second language, health, nutrition and mathematics, natural history, general and social sciences, sociology.

Tiden Norsk Forlag
PO Box 8813, Youngstorget, 0028 Oslo
☎00 47 22 429520   Fax 00 47 22 426458
FOUNDED 1933. *Publishes* fiction, general non-fiction.

Portugal

Bertrand Editora Lda
Indexed as: Bertrand Editora Lda
Rua Anchieta 29 – 1, 1200 Lisbon
☎00 351 1 3420084   Fax 00 351 1 3468286
FOUNDED 1727. *Publishes* art, essays, literature, literary criticism, social sciences, sociology.

Editorial Caminho SARL
Al Santo Antonio dos Capuchos 6B, 1100 Lisbon
☎00 351 1 3152683   Fax 00 351 1 534346
FOUNDED 1977. *Publishes* fiction, government, political science.

Livraria Civilizacão (Américo Fraga Lamares & Ca Lda)
Rua Alberto Aires de Gouveia 27, 4000 Porto
☎00 351 2 2002286   Fax 00 351 2 2012382
FOUNDED 1921. *Publishes* fiction, art, economics history, social and political science, government, sociology.

Publicações Dom Quixote Lda
Rua Luciano Cordeiro 116-2, 1098 Lisbon
☎00 351 1 3158079   Fax 00 351 1 574595
FOUNDED 1965. *Publishes* fiction, poetry, education, history, philosophy, general and social sciences, sociology.

Publicações Europa-America Lda
Apdo 8, Estrada Lisbon-Sintra Km 14, 2726 Mem Martins
☎00 351 1 9211461   Fax 00 351 1 9217940
FOUNDED 1945. *Publishes* fiction, poetry, art, biography, dance, education, general engineering, history, how-to, music, philosophy, medicine, nursing, dentistry, psychology, psychiatry, general and social sciences, sociology, technology.

Gradiva – Publicações Lda
Rua Almeida e Sousa 21 r/c Esq, 1350 Lisbon
☎00 351 1 3974067   Fax 00 351 1 3953471
FOUNDED 1981. *Publishes* fiction, science fiction, fantasy, education, history, human relations, philosophy, general science.

Livros Horizonte Lda
Rua das Chagas 17 - 1 Dto, 1121 Lisbon
☎00 351 1 3466917   Fax 00 351 1 3426921
FOUNDED 1953. *Publishes* art, education, history, psychology, psychiatry, social sciences, sociology.

Editorial Verbo SA
Rua Carlos Testa 1, 1000 Lisbon
☎00 351 1 3562131   Fax 00 351 1 3562139
FOUNDED 1959. *Publishes* education, history, general science.

Spain

Editorial Alhambra SA
Fernandez de la Hoz 9, 28010 Madrid
☎00 34 1 5940020   Fax 00 34 1 5921220
FOUNDED 1942. *Publishes* art, education, history, language arts, linguistics, medicine and nursing, dentistry, general science, psychology, psychiatry, philosophy.

Alianza Editorial SA
Juan Ignacio Luca de Tena 15,
28027 Madrid
☎00 34 1 7416600   Fax 00 34 1 7414343
FOUNDED 1965. *Publishes* fiction, poetry, art, history, mathematics, dance, music, philosophy, government, political and social sciences, sociology, general science.

Ediciones Anaya SA
Juan Ignacio Luca de Tena 15,
28027 Madrid
☎00 34 1 3938800   Fax 00 34 1 7426631
FOUNDED 1959. *Publishes* education.

Editorial Don Quijote
Compãs del Porvenir 6, 41013 Seville
☎00 34 958 4235080
FOUNDED 1981. *Publishes* fiction, literature, literary criticism, poetry, essays, drama, theatre, history.

EDHASA (Editora y Distribuidora Hispano – Americana SA)
Av Diagonal 519, 08029 Barcelona
☎00 34 3 4395104   Fax 00 34 3 4194584
FOUNDED 1946. *Publishes* fiction, literature, literary criticism, essays, history.

Editorial Espasa-Calpe SA
Apdo 547, Carretera de Irún Km 12,
200, 28049 Madrid
☎00 34 1 358 9689   Fax 00 34 1 358 9364
FOUNDED 1925. *Publishes* fiction, science fiction, fantasy, English as a second language, general non-fiction, biography, history, self-help, social sciences, sociology.

Ediciones Grijalbo SA
Aragò 385, 08013 Barcelona
☎00 34 3 4587000   Fax 00 34 3 4580495
FOUNDED 1942. *Publishes* fiction, general non-fiction, art, biography, history, government, political science, philosophy, psychology, psychiatry, religion, social sciences, sociology, technology.

Grupo Editorial CEAC SA
C/Peru 164, 08020 Barcelona
☎00 34 3 3073004   Fax 00 34 3 2660067
Formerly Editorial Timun Mas SA. *Publishes* education, technology, science fiction, fantasy.

Ediciones Hiperión SL
Calle Salustiano Olózaga 14, 28001 Madrid
☎00 34 1 5576015   Fax 00 34 1 4358690
FOUNDED 1976. *Publishes* fiction, literature, literary criticism, essays, poetry, religions (Islamic and Jewish).

Editorial Laia SA
Guitard 43, 08014 Barcelona
☎00 34 3 3215562   Fax 00 34 3 3217975
FOUNDED 1972. *Publishes* literature, literary criticism, essays, general non-fiction, education, psychology, psychiatry, social sciences, sociology.

LaSal (Edicions de les Dones)
Riereta 13, 08001 Barcelona
☎00 34 3 3298450
FOUNDED 1978. *Publishes* women's studies only.

Editorial Molino
Calabria 166 baixos, 08015 Barcelona
☎00 34 3 2260625   Fax 00 34 3 2266998
FOUNDED 1933. *Publishes* cookery, education, fiction.

Mondadori España SA
Aragó 385, 08013 Barcelona
☎00 34 1 4587000   Fax 00 34 1 4159033
FOUNDED 1987. *Publishes* fiction, general non-fiction, biography, history, general science.

Editorial Planeta SA
Córcega 273–279, 08008 Barcelona
☎00 34 3 4154100   Fax 00 34 3 2177140
FOUNDED 1952. *Publishes* fiction and general non-fiction.

Plaza y Janés SA
Enrique Granados 86–88, 08008 Barcelona
☎00 34 3 4151100   Fax 00 34 3 4156976
FOUNDED 1959. *Publishes* fiction and general non-fiction.

Santillana SA
Elfo 32, 28027 Madrid
☎00 34 1 3224500   Fax 00 34 1 3224475
FOUNDED 1964. *Publishes* fiction, essays, literature, literary criticism, travel.

Editorial Seix Barral SA
Córcega 270, 4, 08008 Barcelona
☎00 34 3 2186400   Fax 00 34 3 2184773
FOUNDED 1945. *Publishes* fiction, poetry, drama, theatre.

Tusquets Editores
Iradier 24 bajos, 08017 Barcelona
☎00 34 3 4174170   Fax 00 34 3 4176703
FOUNDED 1969. *Publishes* fiction, art, biography, eroticism, essays, history, literature, literary criticism, social sciences, sociology.

Ediciones Versal SA
Calabria 108, 08015 Barcelona
☎00 34 3 3257404   Fax 00 34 3 4236898
FOUNDED 1984. *Publishes* general non-fiction, biography, literature, literary criticism, essays.

Editorial Luis Vives (Edelvives)
Dr Federico Rubio y Gali 1, 28039 Madrid
☎00 34 976 5347000 Fax 00 34 976 5531919
FOUNDED 1890. *Publishes* education.

Sweden

Bokförlaget Bonnier Alba AB
Box 3159, S-103 63 Stockholm
☎00 46 8 6968660   Fax 00 46 8 6968361
FOUNDED 1981. *Publishes* fiction, general non-fiction, art, cookery.

Albert Bonniers Förlag AB
Box 3159, Sveavägen 56, S-103 63 Stockholm
☎00 46 8 6968660   Fax 00 46 8 6968361
FOUNDED 1837. *Publishes* fiction and general non-fiction.

Bokförlaget Bra Böcker AB
Södra Vägen, S-26380 Höganäs
☎00 46 42 339000   Fax 00 46 42 330504
FOUNDED 1965. *Publishes* fiction, geography, geology, history.

Brombergs Bokförlag AB
Industrigaton 4A, Box 12886, 11298 Stockholm
☎00 46 8 6503390   Fax 00 46 8 6500160
FOUNDED 1973. *Publishes* fiction, general non-fiction, government, political science, general science.

Bokförlaget Forum AB
Box 14115, Riddargatan 23,
S-104 41 Stockholm
☎00 46 8 6604122   Fax 00 46 8 6615885

FOUNDED 1944. *Publishes* fiction and general non-fiction.

Bokförlaget Natur och Kultur
Karlavägen 31, Box 27323, S-102 54
Stockholm
☎00 46 8 4538600   Fax 00 46 8 4538790
FOUNDED 1922. *Publishes* fiction and general non-fiction, biography, history, psychology, psychiatry, general science.

Norstedts Förlag AB
Box 2052, S-103 12 Stockholm
☎00 46 8 7893000   Fax 00 46 8 7893038
FOUNDED 1823. *Publishes* fiction and general non-fiction.

AB Rabén och Sjögren Bokförlag
PO Box 45022, S-104 30 Stockholm
☎00 46 8 4570300   Fax 00 46 8 4570331
FOUNDED 1942. *Publishes* fiction and general non-fiction.

Richters Förlag AB
Ostra Förstadsgatan 46, 205 75 Malmö
☎00 46 40 933708   Fax 00 46 40 930820
FOUNDED 1942. *Publishes* fiction.

Tiden
Box 45022, S-104 30 Stockholm
☎00 46 8 4570300   Fax 00 46 8 4570332
FOUNDED 1912. *Publishes* fiction, general non-fiction, poetry, history, government, political science, social sciences, sociology, psychology, psychiatry.

B Wählströms Bokförlag AB
Box 30022, S-104 25 Stockholm
☎00 46 8 6198600   Fax 00 46 8 6189761
FOUNDED 1911. *Publishes* fiction and general non-fiction.

Switzerland

Arche Verlag AG, Raabe und Vitali
Postfach 112, CH-8030 Zurich
☎00 41 1 2522410   Fax 00 41 1 2611115
FOUNDED 1944. *Publishes* literature and literary criticism, essays, biography, fiction, poetry, travel.

Artemis Verlags AG
Munstergasse 9, CH-8024 Zurich
☎00 41 1 2521100   Fax 00 41 1 2624792
FOUNDED 1943. *Publishes* art, architecture and

interior design, biography, history, philosophy, political science, government, travel.

Diogenes Verlag AG

Sprecherstr 8, CH–8032 Zurich
☎00 41 1 2528111   Fax 00 41 1 2528407
FOUNDED 1952. *Publishes* fiction, essays, literature, literary criticism, mysteries, art, drama, theatre, philosophy.

Langenscheidt AG Zürich-Zug

Postfach 328, CH–8021 Zurich
☎00 41 1 2115000   Fax 00 41 1 2122149
Publishes languages and linguistics.

Larousse (Suisse) SA

3 Route du Grand-Mont, CH–1052 Le Mont-sur-Lausanne
☎00 41 22 369140
Publishes dictionaries, reference and textbooks.

Neptun-Verlag

Morellstr 6, Postfach 307,
CH–8280 Kreuzlingen
☎00 41 72 727262   Fax 00 41 72 642023
FOUNDED 1946. *Publishes* history and travel.

Orell Füssli Verlag

Nuschderstr 22, CH–8022 Zurich
☎00 41 1 2113630   Fax 00 41 1 4667412
FOUNDED 1519. *Publishes* art, biography, eco-

nomics, educational, geography, geology, history, how-to.

Editions Payot Lausanne

33 ave de la Gare, CP 528, CH–1001 Lausanne
☎00 41 21 3290266   Fax 00 41 21 3290264
FOUNDED 1875. *Publishes* general non-fiction, anthropology, dance, education, history, law, medicine, nursing, dentistry, music, literature, literary criticism, essays, general science.

Verlag Rot-Weiss AG

Frutigenstr 6, Postfach 1308, CH–3601 Thun
☎00 41 33 256060   Fax 00 41 33 256066
FOUNDED 1988. *Publishes* cookery, dictionaries, encyclopedias, travel.

Sauerländer AG

Laurenzenvorstadt 89, CH–5001 Aarau
☎00 41 64 268626   Fax 00 41 64 245780
FOUNDED 1807. *Publishes* biography, education, history, poetry, medicine, nursing, dentistry, general science, social sciences, sociology.

Scherz Verlag AG

Theaterplatz 4–6, CH–3000 Berne 7
☎00 41 31 3277117   Fax 00 41 31 3277171
FOUNDED 1939. *Publishes* fiction and general non-fiction; biography, history, psychology, psychiatry, philosophy, parapsychology.

European Television Companies

Austria

ORF (Austrian Broadcasting Corporation)
Würzburggasse 30, A–1136 Vienna
☎00 43 1 87 8780   Fax 00 43 1 87 8782250

Belgium

BRTN
Auguste Reyerslaan 52, B–1043 Brussels
☎00 32 2 741 3111   Fax 00 32 2 734 9351

Radio-Télévision Belge de la Communauté Française (RTBF)
52 Boulevard Auguste Reyers,
1044 Brussels
☎00 32 2 737 2111   Fax 00 32 2 737 6812

RTL – TV1
Avenue Ariane 1, 1201 Brussels
☎00 32 2 778 6811   Fax 00 32 2 778 6812

Vlaamse Televisie Maatschappu (VTM)
Medialaan 1, 1800 Vilvoorde
☎00 32 2 255 3211   Fax 00 32 2 252 3787

Denmark

Danmarks Radio–TV
TV Centre - Morkhojvej 170, DK–2860 Søborg
☎00 45 35 20 3040   Fax 00 45 35 20 3939

Kanal 2
Mileparken 20A, DK–2740 Skovlunde
☎00 45 42 91 6699   Fax 00 45 42 84 1360

TV–2 Danmark
Sortedam Dossering 55A, DK–2100 Copenhagen
☎00 45 31 37 2200   Fax 00 45 31 37 5622

Eire

Radio Telefis Eireann (RTE – RTE 1)
Donnybrook, Dublin 4
☎00 353 1 208 3111   Fax 00 353 1 208 3082

Teilefis na Gaeilge
4 Argyle Square, Donnybrook, Dublin 4
☎00 353 1 667 0944   Fax 00 353 1 667 0946

Finland

MTV Finland
Ilmalankatu 2, SF–00240 Helsinki
☎00 358 9 15001   Fax 00 358 9 1500707

TV3 Finland
Ilmalankatu 2C, SF–00240 Helsinki
☎00 358 9 15001   Fax 00 358 9 1500712

Ylesradio (YLE)/TV1/TV2 – Finnish Broadcasting Company
PO Box 10, SF–0241 Helsinki
☎00 358 9 14801   Fax 00 358 9 14803391

France

France 2
22 ave Montaigne, 75387 Paris
☎00 33 1 44 21 42 42
Fax 00 33 1 44 21 51 45

France 3
116 ave du Président Kennedy, 75790 Paris
☎00 33 1 42 30 22 22
Fax 00 33 1 46 47 92 94

La Sept Arte
50 ave Théophile Gautier, 75016 Paris
☎00 33 1 44 14 77 77
Fax 00 33 1 44 14 77 00

M6
16 Cours Albert Premier, 75008 Paris
☎00 33 1 44 21 66 66
Fax 00 33 1 44 63 78 52

Arte Geie
2S rue de le Fonderie, 67080 Strasbourg
☎00 33 3 88 14 22 22
Fax 00 33 3 88 22 22 00

Canal Plus
85–89 Quai André Gitroën, 75015 Paris
☎00 33 1 44 25 10 00
Fax 00 33 1 44 25 12 34

La Cinquième
10 rue Horace-Vesnet, 92136 Issey
Les Moulineaux
☎00 33 1 41 46 55 55
Fax 00 33 1 41 08 02 22

RFO
5 ave du Recteur Poincaré, 75016 Paris
☎00 33 1 42 15 71 00
Fax 00 33 1 42 15 74 37

TF1
1 Quai du Pont du Jour, 92656 Boulogne
☎00 33 1 41 41 12 34
Fax 00 33 1 41 41 28 40

Germany

ARD – Das Erste
Arnulfstrasse 42, 80335 Munich
☎00 49 89 59 0001   Fax 00 49 89 59 003249

ZDF (Zweites Deutsches Fernsehen)
ZDF-Strasse, PO Box 4040, 55100 Mainz
☎00 49 61 31 70 2060
Fax 00 49 61 31 70 2052

Italy

RAI (Radiotelevisione Italiana)
Viale Mazzini 14, 00195 Rome
☎00 39 6 361 3608   Fax 00 39 6 323 1010

RTI (Reli Televisive Italiane)
Viale Europa 48, 20093 Cologno Monzese
☎00 39 2 22 5141   Fax 00 39 2 22 5146599

Telepiu
Via Piranesi 46, 20137 Milan
☎00 39 2 700 27367   Fax 00 39 2 700 27204

The Netherlands

AVRO
Postbus 2, 1200 JA Hilversum
☎00 31 35 671 79 11
Fax 00 31 35 671 75 17

IKON
Postbus 10009, 1201 DA Hilversum
☎00 31 35 672 72 72
Fax 00 31 35 621 51 00

NCRV
Bergweg 30, 1217 SC Hilversum
☎00 31 35 671 99 11
Fax 00 31 35 671 92 85

Nederlandse Omroep Stichting (NOS)
Postbus 26444, 1202 JJ Hilversum
☎00 31 35 677 92 22
Fax 00 31 35 677 26 49

TROS
Postbus 11, 1200 LL Hilversum
☎00 31 35 671 57 15
Fax 00 31 35 671 52 36

Veronica (VOO)
Laapersveld 75, 1213 VB Hilversum
☎00 31 35 671 67 16
Fax 00 31 35 624 97 71

VPRO
Postbus 11, 1200 JC Hilversum
☎00 31 35 671 29 11
Fax 00 31 35 671 22 54

Norway

NRK (Norwegian Broadcasting Corporation)
Bjørnstjerne Bjørnsons Place 1, N–0340 Oslo
☎00 47 22 45 9050   Fax 00 47 22 45 9645

TV 1000 Norge
Karl Johans Gate 12J, 0154–Oslo
☎00 47 24 41 1000   Fax 00 47 24 42 2715

TV2
Verftsgaten 2C, N–5002 Bergen
☎00 47 55 90 8070   Fax 00 47 55 90 8137

Portugal

Radiotelevisão Portuguesa (RTP)
Av 5 de Outubro 197, 1094 Lisbon
☎00 35 11 793 1774   Fax 00 35 11 793 1758

SIC (Sociedade Independente de Comunicacão)
Estrada da Outurela 119, Carnaxide
☎00 35 11 417 9550   Fax 00 35 11 417 3136

TVI (Televisão Independente)
Edificio Altejo 6, rua Matigna, 1900–Lisbon
☎00 35 11 861 1600   Fax 00 35 11 868 7968

Spain

Canal Plus Spain
Gran Via 32, E–28013 Madrid
☎00 34 1 396 5500   Fax 00 34 1 396 4253

RTVE (Radiotelevision Española)
Edificio Prado del Rey – 3a planta,
E–28223 Madrid
☎00 34 1 581 7000   Fax 00 34 1 581 7757

RTVM (Radiotelevision Madrid)
Zurbano 71, E–28010 Madrid
☎00 34 1 592 4100   Fax 00 34 1 592 4576

Telecino
Plaza Pablo Ruiz Picasso, Edificio Torre
Picasso, E–28020 Madrid
☎00 34 1 396 6100   Fax 00 34 1 555 0044

Antena 3
Avda. Isla Graciosa, E–28700 Madrid
☎00 34 1 623 0500   Fax 00 34 1 652 7144

Sweden

SVT (Sveriges Television)
Oxenstiernsgatan 26–34, S–10510 Stockholm
☎00 46 8 784 0000   Fax 00 46 8 784 1500

TV4
Storangskroken 10, S–11579 Stockholm
☎00 46 8 644 4400   Fax 00 46 8 644 4440

Schweizer Fernsehen DRS
Fernsehen DRS/SRG Fernsehenstrasse 1–4,
CH–8052 Zurich
☎00 41 1 305 66 11   Fax 00 41 1 305 56 60

Switzerland

TSR (Télévision Suisse Romande)
Quai Ernest Ansermet 20,
CH–1205 Geneva
☎00 41 22 708 99 11
Fax 00 41 22 708 98 07

Television Suisse – RTSI
Postfach 235, CH–6903 Lugarno
☎00 41 91 803 51 11
Fax 00 41 91 803 53 55

US Publishers

International Reply Coupons (IRCs) For return postage, send IRCs, available from the Post Office. Letters 60 pence; mss according to weight.

ABC–Clio, Inc.
Suite 350, 501 South Cherry Street, Denver CO 80222
☎001 303 333 3003   Fax 001 303 333 4037
President *Heather Cameron*
Editorial Director *Rolf A Janke*

FOUNDED 1955. *Publishes* non-fiction: reference, including mythology, native American studies, government and politics, history, military and war, women's studies/issues, current world issues. About 35–40 titles a year. No unsolicited mss; synopses and ideas welcome.
Royalties paid annually. *UK subsidiary* **ABC-Clio Ltd**, Oxford.

Abingdon Press
201 Eighth Avenue South, Box 801, Nashville TN 37202–0801
☎001 615 749 6404   Fax 001 615 749 6512

Editorial Director *Harriett Jane Olson*

Publishes non-fiction: religious (lay and professional), children's religious and academic texts. About 100 titles a year. Approach in writing only with synopsis and samples. IRCs essential.

William Abrahams
See **Penguin USA**

Harry N. Abrams, Inc.
100 Fifth Avenue, New York NY 10011
☎001 212 206 7715   Fax 001 212 645 8437
Publisher/Editor-in-chief *Paul Gottlieb*

Publishes illustrated books: art, architecture, design, nature, entertainment. No fiction. Submit completed mss (no dot matrix), together with sample illustrations.

Academy Chicago Publishers
363 W. Erie Street, Chicago IL 60610
☎001 312 751 7300   Fax 001 312 751 7306
Senior Editor *Anita Miller*

FOUNDED 1975. *Publishes* fiction: mystery and mainstream; non-fiction: history, women's studies. No romance, children's, young adult, religious, sexist or avant-garde. 15 titles in 1996.

IMPRINT **Cassandra Editions** ('Lost' Women Writers). Send first three chapters only, accompanied by IRCs; no synopses or ideas.

Royalties paid twice-yearly. *Distributed* in the UK and Europe by Gazelle, Lancaster.

Ace Science Fiction
See **Berkley Publishing Group**

Adams Media Corporation
260 Center Street, Holbrook MA 02343
☎001 617 767 8100   Fax 001 617 767 0994
President *Robert L. Adams*

FOUNDED 1980. *Publishes* general non-fiction: careers, business, personal finance, relationships, parenting and maternity, self-improvement, reference, cooking, sports, games and humour. TITLES *Adams Streetwise Small Business Start-up; The New Living Heart; Small Miracles; The Everything Baby Names Book; The Lost Lennon Interviews; Knock 'em Dead with Great Answers to Tough Interview Questions.* Ideas welcome.

Addison-Wesley Longman Inc.
General Publishing Group, One Jacob Way, Reading MA 01867
☎001 617 944 3700   Fax 001 617 944 8243
Publisher *David Goehring*
Contact *Editorial Department*

Publishes general non-fiction, business, science, health, parenting/childcare, psychology, current affairs, biography/memoir, social science/history/politics, narrative non-fiction, children's. No fiction. About 125 titles a year. Approach in writing or by phone in first instance, then submit synopsis and one sample chapter.
Royalties paid.

University of Alabama Press
Box 870380, Tuscaloosa AL 35487
☎001 205 348 5180   Fax 001 205 348 9201
Director *Nicole Mitchell*

Publishes academic books in the fields of American history, American literature, history of science and technology, linguistics, archaeology, rhetoric and speech communication, Judaic studies, political science and public administration, religion in America with special emphasis on Southern regional studies. About 40 titles a year.

Aladdin Books
See **Simon & Schuster Children's Publishing Division**

University of Alaska Press
1st Floor, Gruening Building, PO Box 756240, University of Alaska, Fairbanks AK 99775-6240
☎001 907 474 6389   Fax 001 907 474 5502
Manager Debbie Van Stone
Managing Editor Carla Helfferich
Acquisitions Pam Odom

Traces its origins back to 1927 but was relatively dormant until the early 1980s. Publishes scholarly works about Alaska and the North Pacific rim, with a special emphasis on circumpolar regions. 5–10 titles a year. No fiction or poetry.

DIVISIONS
Ramuson Library Historical Translation Series Marvin Falk TITLES The Great Russian Navigator, A. I. Chirikov; Journals of the Priest Ioann Veniaminov in Alaska, 1923 to 1836. **Oral Biography Series** William Schneider TITLES The Life I've Been Living; Kusiq: An Eskimo Life History from the Arctic Coast of Alaska. **Monograph Series** Carla Helfferich TITLES Intertidal Bivalves: A Guide to the Common Marine Bivalves of Alaska. **Classic Reprint Series** Terrence Cole TITLES Fifty Years Below Zero, A Lifetime of Adventure in the Far North; The Thousand-Mile War, World War II in Alaska and the Aleutians. **Lanternlight Library** Informal non-fiction covering Northern interest. TITLES Aleutian Echoes; Bear Man of Admiralty Island: A Biography of Allen E. Hasselborg. Unsolicited mss, synopses and ideas welcome.

AMACOM
1601 Broadway, New York NY 10019-7406
☎001 212 903 8917   Fax 001 212 903 8083
Publisher Hank Kennedy

Owned by American Management Association. Publishes business books only, including general management, business communications, sales and marketing, small business, finance, computers and information systems, human resource management and training, career/personal growth skills, research development, project management and manufacturing, quality/customer service titles. 65–70 titles a year. TITLES Corporate Executions; The Great Transition; Knock Your Socks Off Answers; Straight Talk About Gays in the Workplace; Diary of a Small Business Owner. Proposals welcome.
Royalties paid twice-yearly.

University Press of America, Inc.
4720 Boston Way, Lanham MD 20706
☎001 301 459 3366   Fax 001 301 459 2118
Publisher James E. Lyons

FOUNDED 1975. Publishes scholarly monographs, college and graduate level textbooks. No children's, elementary or high school. About 450 titles a year. Submit outline or request proposal questionnaire.
Royalties paid annually. Distributed Oxford Publicity Partners, Oxford.

Anchor
See **Bantam Doubleday Dell Publishing Group, Inc.**

Anvil
See **Krieger Publishing Co., Inc.**

Ann Arbor Paperbacks
See **University of Michigan Press**

Archway
See **Pocket Books**

University of Arizona Press
1230 North Park Avenue, Suite 102, Tucson AZ 85719-4140
☎001 520 621 1441   Fax 001 520 621 8899
Director Stephen Cox
Senior Editor Joanne O'Hare

FOUNDED 1959. Publishes academic non-fiction, particularly with a regional/cultural link, plus Native-American and Hispanic literature. About 50 titles a year.

Arkana
See **Penguin USA**

University of Arkansas Press
McIlroy House, 201 Ozark Avenue, Fayetteville AR 72701
☎001 501 575 3246   Fax 001 501 575 6044
Director Miller Williams

FOUNDED 1980. Publishes scholarly monographs, poetry and general trade including essays, etc. Particularly interested at present in scholarly works in history, politics, sociology and literary criticism. About 30 titles a year. TITLES Movement and Modernism: Yeats, Eliot, Lawrence, Williams, and Early Twentieth Century Dance Terri Mester; Breaking the Silence: The Little Rock Women's Emergency Committee to Open Our Schools, 1958–1963 Sara Murphy; Postmodernism and a Sociology of the Absurd Stanford Lyman.
Royalties paid annually.

Aspect
See **Warner Books Inc.**

Atheneum Books for Young Readers
See **Simon & Schuster Children's Publishing Division**

Atheneum Publishers
See **Simon & Schuster Trade Division**

Atlantic Disk Publishers, Inc.
PO Box 2902, Stanford CT 06906–0902

Exec. Editor/Publisher *Rejeena Bennett*
Editor-in-Chief/Publisher *Wayne Ray*

Publishes mass-market fiction as well as non-fiction on DOS, IBM compatible/readable disks and CD-ROM. 100 titles in 1996. IMPRINT **HMS Press**.
Royalties Pays 35%. No advances.

Atlantic Monthly Press
See **Grove/Atlantic Inc**

AUP (Associated University Presses)
AUP New Jersey titles are handled in the UK by **Golden Cockerel Press** (see **UK Publishers**).

Avery Publishing Group, Inc.
120 Old Broadway, Garden City Park, New York NY 11040
☎001 516 741 2155   Fax 001 516 742 1892
Managing Editor *Rudy Shur*

FOUNDED 1976. *Publishes* adult trade non-fiction, specialising in childbirth, childcare, alternative health, self-help, New Age and natural cooking. About 50 titles a year. TITLES *Smart Medicine for a Healthier Child* Janet Zand, Rachel Walton and Robert Rountree; *Secrets of Fat-Free Cooking* Sandra Woodruff; *How to Teach Your Baby to Read* Glenn Doman. No unsolicited mss; synopses and ideas welcome if accompanied by s.a.e..
Royalties paid twice-yearly.

Avon Books
1350 Avenue of the Americas, New York NY 10019
☎001 212 261 6800   Fax 001 212 261 6895
Senior Vice President/Publisher *Lou Aronica*

FOUNDED 1941. A division of the Hearst Corporation. *Publishes* mass-market and trade paperbacks, adult, young adult and children's. Fiction: contemporary and historical romance, science fiction and fantasy, action and adventure, suspense and thrillers, mystery and westerns. Non-fiction (all types): how-to, popular psychology, self-help, health, history, war, sports, business and economics, biography and politics. No textbooks. 414 titles in 1996. IMPRINTS **AvoNova**; **Camelot**; **Confident**; **Equinox**; **Flare**. Submit query letter only in first instance.

AvoNova
See **Avon Books**

Back Bay Books
See **Little, Brown & Co. Inc.**

Bad Boy
See **Masquerade Books**

Baker Book House
PO Box 6287, Grand Rapids MI 49516-6287
☎001 616 676 9185   Fax 001 616 676 9573
President *Richard Baker*
Director of Publications *Allan Fisher*

FOUNDED 1939. Began life as a used-book store and began publishing in earnest in the 1950s, primarily serving the evangelical Christian market. *Publishes* religious non-fiction and fiction; children's books; college/seminary textbooks and academic; Bible reference and professional (pastors and church leaders) books. About 190 titles a year.

DIVISIONS/IMPRINTS
Trade *Allan Fisher* TITLES *The Hope at Hand* David Bryant; *Real Presence* Leanne Payne. **Children's** *Betty De Vries*. **Academic & Reference** *Jim Weaver* TITLES *God in Three Persons* Millard Erickson; *20th Century Dictionary of Christian Biography*. **Professional Books** *Paul Engle* TITLES *Marketplace Preaching* Calvin Miller. No unsolicited mss. Send for proposal outlines specifying whether you will be proposing a trade, professional or academic book. **Chosen Books** *Jane Campbell* FOUNDED 1971. *Publishes* charismatic adult non-fiction for a Christian market. TITLES *Healing Evangelism* Don Dunkerley; *Angels All Around* Sarah Hornsby. About 10 titles a year. Synopses or ideas welcome. **Fleming H. Revell**; **Spire Books** *William J. Petersen* Adult fiction and non-fiction for evangelical Christians. A family-owned business until 1978, Fleming H. Revell was one of the first Christian publishers to take the step into secular publishing. TITLES *The Dual-Earner Marriage* Jack and Judy Balswick; *The Search for Lost Fathering* James Schaller. About 40 titles a year. Synopses or ideas welcome.
Royalties paid twice-yearly.

Balch Institute Press
See **Golden Cockerel Press** under
UK Publishers

Ballantine/Del Rey/Fawcett/
Ivy/One World Books
201 East 50th Street, New York NY 10022
☎001 212 572 2620   Fax 001 212 572 4912
President *Linda Grey*
Publisher *Clare Ferraro*
FOUNDED 1952. Division of **Random House,
Inc.** *Publishes* fiction and non-fiction, science
fiction. 465 titles in 1996.
   IMPRINTS **Ballantine Books**; **Del Rey**;
Fawcett Columbine; **Fawcett Crest**;
Fawcett Gold Medal; **Fawcett Juniper**;
House of Collectibles; **One World**.

Banner Books
See **University Press of Mississippi**

Bantam Doubleday Dell
Publishing Group, Inc.
1540 Broadway, New York NY 10036
☎001 212 354 6500   Fax 001 212 302 7985
Chairman/CEO *Jack Hoeft*
President/COO *Erik Engstrom*
**Snr. Vice-President/Publisher, Bantam
   Books** *Irwyn Applebaum*
**Snr. Vice-President/Publisher,
   Doubleday** *Arlene Friedman*
**Snr. Vice-President/Publisher, Dell
   Publishing** *Carole Baron*
Snr. Vice-President/Publisher *William T.
   Shinker*
**Vice President/Publisher, Books for
   Young Readers** *Craig Virden*
Publishes general commercial fiction: mysteries,
westerns, romance, war, science fiction and fan-
tasy, crime and thrillers, adventure; non-fiction,
including New Age, crime and adventure,
African-American/Latino, feminist, gay/lesbian
studies; young readers and children's.

DIVISIONS/IMPRINTS
Bantam Books; **Doubleday**; **Dell Publishing
Broadway Books**; **Books for Young
Readers)**; **International Division**; **Anchor**;
Island; **Spectra**; **Currency**; **Main Street**;
Loveswept; **New Age Books**. Most work
comes through agents. No unsolicited mss.

Barron's Educational Series
250 Wireless Boulevard, Hauppauge NY 11788
☎001 516 434 3311   Fax 001 516 434 3723
Chairman/President *Manuel H. Barron*

Managing Editor *Grace Freedson*
FOUNDED 1942. *Publishes* adult non-fiction,
children's fiction and non-fiction, test preparation materials and language materials/tapes,
cookbooks, gardening, pets, business, art and
painting. No adult fiction. 200 titles a year.
Unsolicited mss, synopses and ideas for books
welcome.
   Royalties paid twice-yearly.

Basic Books
See **HarperCollins Publishers, Inc.**

Beacon Press
25 Beacon Street, Boston MA 02108
☎001 617 742 2110   Fax 001 617 723 3097
Director *Helene Atwan*
Publishes general non-fiction. About 50 titles a
year. Approach in writing, or submit synopsis
and sample chapters (with IRCs) to the editorial department.

Bedford Books
See **St Martin's Press, Inc.**

Beech Tree Books
See **William Morrow & Co., Inc.**

Berkley Publishing Group
200 Madison Avenue, New York NY 10016
☎001 212 951 8800   Fax 001 212 213 6706
Senior VP/Editor-in-Chief *Leslie Gelbman*
FOUNDED 1954. Subsidiary of **The Putnam
Berkley Group**. *Publishes* paperbacks: general
interest fiction and non-fiction. About 700
titles a year. IMPRINTS **Ace Science Fiction &
Fantasy** Submit synopsis and first three chap-
ters; **Berkley Books**; **Berkley Prime Crime**;
Boulevard; **Charter/Diamond**; **Jove**.
   Royalties paid twice-yearly.

H. & R. Block
See **Simon & Schuster Trade Division**

Boulevard
See **Berkley Publishing Group**

Boyds Mills Press
815 Church Street, Honesdale PA 18431
☎001 717 253 1164   Fax 001 717 253 0179
Publisher *Kent Brown Jr*
Editorial Director *Larry Rosler*
A subsidiary of Highlights for Children, Inc.
FOUNDED 1990 as a publisher of children's
trade books. *Publishes* children's fiction, non-

fiction and poetry. About 50 titles a year. TITLES *The Animals' Song* David Harrison; *Bicycle Riding* Sandra Olson Liatsos; *Read for Me, Mama* Vashanti Rahaman; *Lichee Treet* Ching Yeung Russell; *Rattlesnake Dance* Jennifer Owings Dewey. Unsolicited mss, synopses and ideas for books welcome. No romance or fantasy novels.

Royalties paid twice-yearly.

Bradford Books
See **The MIT Press**

Brassey's, Inc.
1313 Dolley Madison Boulevard, Suite 401, McLean VA 22101
☎001 703 442 4535   Fax 001 703 442 9848
Managing Director *Jim Sutton*
Editorial Director *Don McKeon*

FOUNDED 1983. Associated with **Brassey's** of London. *Publishes* non-fiction titles on defence and military affairs, national and international, current affairs, foreign policy, history, biography, intelligence and sports. About 30 titles a year. TITLES *The US Military Online: A Directory for Internet Access to the Department of the Defense* William Arkin; *Touchdown: The Favorite Football Stories of Great College Coaches* Larry S. Roseberry and Ted Royal; *The Vietnam War: The Story and Photographs* Donald M. Goldstein, et al; *The World Factbook: 1997–98* The Central Intelligence Agency. No unsolicited mss; synopses and ideas welcome.

Royalties paid annually.

Browndeer Press
See **Harcourt Brace Children's Books Division**

Bulfinch Press
See **Little, Brown & Co., Inc.**

Buzz Books
See **St Martin's Press, Inc.**

University of California Press
2120 Berkeley Way, Berkeley CA 94720
☎001 510 642 4247   Fax 001 510 643 7127
Director *James H. Clark*

Publishes scholarly and scientific non-fiction; some fiction and poetry in translation. 300 titles in 1996. Preliminary letter with outline preferred.

Camelot
See **Avon Books**

Carol Publishing Group
120 Enterprise Avenue, Secaucus NJ 07094
☎001 201 866 0490   Fax 001 201 866 8159
Publisher *Steven Schragis*

FOUNDED 1989. *Publishes* some fiction but mostly non-fiction: biography and autobiography, history, science, humour, how-to, illustrated and self-help. About 150 titles a year.

Carolrhoda Books, Inc.
241 First Avenue North, Minneapolis MN 55401
☎001 612 332 3344   Fax 001 612 332 7615
Editorial Director *Amy Gelman*
Submissions Editor *Rebecca Poole*

Publishes children's: nature, biography, history, beginners' readers, world cultures, photo essays and historical fiction. Please send s.a.e. for author guidelines.

Cassandra Editions
See **Academy Chicago Publishers**

Charlesbridge Publishing
85 Main Street, Watertown MA 02172–4411
☎001 617 926 0329   Fax 001 617 926 5720
Chairman *Brent Farmer*
Managing Editor *Elena Wright*

FOUNDED 1980 as an educational publisher focusing on teaching thinking processes. *Publishes* children's educational programmes (pre-kindergarten through to grade 8, and remedial through to adult), non-fiction picture books and multicultural fiction for 3- to 12-year-olds. 40 titles in 1996. TITLES include *Sir Cumference and the First Round Table, A Math Adventure* Cindy Neuchwander; *Alice in Pastaland, A Math Adventure* Alexandra Wright; *Checker Power, A Game of Problem Solving* Bob Pike (each book has a teacher manual of lessons and games). Complete mss or proposal welcome with self-addressed envelope and IRCs. Mss should be paged, with suggested illustrations described for each page.

Charter/Diamond
See **Berkley Publishing Group**

University of Chicago Press
5801 South Ellis Avenue, Chicago IL 60637–1496
☎001 312 773 7700   Fax 001 312 773 9756

FOUNDED 1891. *Publishes* academic non-fiction only. 266 titles in 1996.

Children's Press
See **Grolier, Inc.**

Chosen Books
See **Baker Book House**

Chronicle Books
85 Second Street, Sixth Floor, San Francisco CA 94105
☎001 415 537 3730   Fax 001 415 537 4440
President and Publisher *Jack Jensen*
Associate Publisher *Christine Carswell*
Publishing Director *Caroline Herter*
Associate Publishers *Nion McEvoy, Victoria Rock*

FOUNDED 1966. Division of Chronicle Publishing. *Publishes* art and design, food and cookery, gardening, nature, photography, leisure and travel, adult fiction and short stories, children's, and stationery/gift items. About 200 titles a year.

DIVISIONS
Art *Annie Barrows* **Children's** *Victoria Rock* **Cooking/Gardening** *Bill LeBond* **Fiction** *Jay Schaefer* **Giftworks** *Caroline Herter/Debra Lande* **Multimedia/Humour** *Nion McEvoy* **Nature/Novelty** *Leslie Bruynesteyn.* Query or submit outline/synopsis and sample chapters and artwork.
Royalties paid twice-yearly.

Clarion Books
215 Park Avenue South, New York NY 10003
☎001 212 420 5800   Fax 001 212 420 5855
VP/Editor-in-Chief *Dorothy Briley*
Executive Editor *Dinah Stevenson*

Clarion Books began in 1965 as an imprint of Seabury Press. The Clarion name was inaugurated in 1974 and acquired by **Houghton Mifflin Co.** in 1979. *Publishes* children's and young adult books. TITLES *Tuesday* David Wiesner; *Piggie Pie!* Margie Palatini; *Midwife's Apprentice* Karen Cushman; *Walt Whitman* Catherine Reef. About 60 titles a year. No novelty, series or genre fiction. Unsolicited mss, synopses and ideas welcome with return postage. Synopses should be accompanied by sample chapter(s).
Royalties paid twice-yearly.

Clarkson Potter
See **Crown Publishing Group**

Classic Reprint
See **University of Alaska Press**

Cobblehill Books
See **Penguin USA**

Confident
See **Avon Books**

Contemporary Books
See **NTC/Contemporary Publishing Company**

Crown Publishing Group
201 East 50th Street, New York NY 10022
☎001 212 572 6117   Fax 001 212 572 6161
President/Publisher *Chip Gibson*

FOUNDED 1933. Division of **Random House, Inc.** *Publishes* popular trade fiction and non-fiction. 256 titles in 1996.
IMPRINTS **Clarkson Potter** *Lauren Shakely*; **Harmony** *Leslie Meredith*; **Living Language**; *Kathy Mintz* **Crown Trade Paperbacks** *Adrienne Ingrum.*

Currency
See **Bantam Doubleday Dell Publishing Group, Inc.**

DAW Books, Inc.
375 Hudson Street, 3rd Floor, New York NY 10014-3658
☎001 212 366 2096/Submissions 366 2095
Fax 001 212 366 2090
Publishers *Elizabeth R. Wollheim, Sheila E. Gilbert*
Submissions Editor *Peter Stampfel*

FOUNDED 1971 by Donald and Elsie Wollheim as the first mass-market publisher devoted to science fiction and fantasy. *Publishes* science fiction/fantasy, and some horror. No short stories, anthology ideas or non-fiction. Unsolicited mss, synopses and ideas for books welcome. About 36 titles a year. TITLES *Titles Otherland* Tad Williams; *Storm Breaking* Mercedes Lackey; *The Mageborn Traitor* Melanie Rawn.
Royalties paid twice-yearly.

Dearborn Financial Publishing, Inc.
155 N. Wacker Drive, Chicago IL 60606-1719
☎001 312 836 4400   Fax 001 312 836 1021
President *Dennis Blitz*
Chairman *Robert C. Kyle*
Vice Presidents *Carol Luitjens* (Textbook, Course, Training-Securities)

A niche publisher serving the financial services industries. Formerly part of Longman. *Publishes* real estate, insurance, financial planning, securities, commodities, investments, banking, professional education, motivation and reference titles, investment reference and how-to books for the consumer (individual investor) and small business owner. About 150 titles a year.

DIVISIONS/IMPRINTS
Trade/Professional *Scott Kyle* TITLES *Money Lessons for a Lifetime; If You're Clueless About Mutual Funds; Century 21 Guide to Remodelling Your Home.* **Textbook: Real Estate Education Company** *Carol Luitjens* TITLES *Modern Real Estate Practice* (14th ed.); *Real Estate Math* (5th ed.); *Realty Bluebook* (31st ed.). **Course: Dearborn/R&R Newkirk** *Carol Luitjens* Insurance titles. TITLES *Solutions Handbook; Variable Contracts; Distributions from Qualified Plans.* **Training-Securities** *Carol Luitjens* TITLES *PassTrak Series 6 Principles & Practices; One Track Professional Sales Assistant.* **Upstart Publishing Co., Inc.** *Jere Calmes* TITLES *Anatomy of a Business Plan, 4th ed.; Small Steps, Smart Choices.* **Commodity Trend Service** *Dennis Blitz* TITLES *Futures Charts.* **Vernon Publishing, Inc.** *Tim Honaker* TITLES *Personal Financial Plan; Financial Need Analysis II.* **Enterprise** *Kevin Shanley* TITLES *The Complete Book of Corporate Forms; The Executive's Business Letter Book.* Unsolicited mss, synopses and ideas welcome.
Royalties paid twice-yearly.

Del Rey
See **Ballantine/Del Rey/Fawcett/Ivy/One World Books**

Dell Publishing
See **Bantam Doubleday Dell Publishing Group, Inc.**

Michael di Capua Books
See **HarperCollins Publishers**

Dial Books for Young Readers
375 Hudson Street, New York
NY 10014–3657
☎001 212 366 2800   Fax 001 212 366 2020
Queries *Manuscript Reader*
FOUNDED 1961. Part of **Penguin USA**. *Publishes* children's books, including picture books, beginners' readers, fiction and non-fiction for junior and young adults. 70 titles a year.
IMPRINTS **Dial Easy-to-Read** Hardback and softcover editions; **Puffin Pied Piper/ Puffin Pied Piper Giant** Softcover only. No unsolicited mss; queries only, with IRCs.
Royalties paid twice-yearly.

Dimensions for Living
Box 801, Nashville TN 37203–0801
☎001 615 749 6000   Fax 001 615 749 6512
Acquisitions Editor *Sally Sharpe*
FOUNDED 1992. *Publishes* non-fiction books for laity (inspirational, Christian living and self-help). 16 titles in 1996.

Doubleday
See **Bantam Doubleday Dell Publishing Group, Inc.**

Lisa Drew
See **Simon & Schuster Trade Division**

Thomas Dunne Books
See **St Martin's Press, Inc.**

Sanford J. Durst Publications
11 Clinton Avenue, Rockville Centre,
New York NY 11570
☎001 516 766 4444   Fax 001 516 766 4520
Owner *Sanford J. Durst*
FOUNDED 1975. *Publishes* non-fiction: numismatic and related, philatelic, legal and art. Also children's books. About 12 titles a year.
Royalties paid twice-yearly.

Dutton/Dutton Children's Books
See **Penguin USA**

Dutton/Signet
See **Penguin USA**

Eaglebrook
See **William Morrow and Co., Inc.**

William B. Eerdmans Publishing Co.
255 Jefferson Avenue SE, Grand Rapids
MI 49503
☎001 616 459 4591   Fax 001 616 459 6540
President *William B. Eerdmans Jr*
Vice President/Editor-in-Chief *Jon Pott*
FOUNDED 1911 as a theological and reference publisher. Gradually began publishing in other genres with authors like C. S. Lewis, Dorothy Sayers and Malcolm Muggeridge on its lists. *Publishes* religious: theology, biblical studies, ethical and social concern, social criticism and children's.
DIVISIONS
Children's *Amy De Vries* **Other** *Jon Pott* TITLES *People of the Book David Jeffrey; The Man Who Created Narnia Michael Coren; Between*

Noon and Three Robert Farrar Capon; *Bioethics: A Primer for Christians* Gilbert Meilaender; *Saint Francis* Brian Wildsmith. Unsolicited mss, synopses and ideas welcome.
Royalties paid twice-yearly.

Enterprise
See **Dearborn Financial Publishing, Inc.**

Equinox
See **Avon Books**

M. Evans & Co., Inc.
216 East 49th Street, New York
NY 10017
☎001 212 688 2810   Fax 001 212 486 4544
Chairman *George C. de Kay*

FOUNDED 1954 as a packager. Began publishing in 1962. Best known for its popular psychology and medicine books, with titles like *Body Language, Open Marriage, Pain Erasure* and *Aerobics*. *Publishes* general non-fiction and western fiction. TITLES *The Arthritis Breakthrough* Henry Scammell; *Total Concentration* Harold Levinson; *Born in Blood* and *Dungeon, Fire and Sword* John J. Robinson; *Dr Atkins' Diet Revolution* Robert Atkins. About 40 titles a year. No unsolicited mss; query first. Synopses and ideas welcome.
Royalties paid twice-yearly.

Everyman's Library
See **Alfred A. Knopf, Inc.**

Faber & Faber, Inc.
53 Shore Road, Winchester MA 08190
☎001 617 721 1427   Fax 001 617 729 2783
Chairman *Tom Kelleher*
Approx. Annual Turnover $4.5 million

Part of the UK-based company. *Publishes* fiction and non-fiction for adults. About 100 titles a year. No unsolicited mss.
Royalties paid twice-yearly.

Facts On File, Inc.
11 Penn Plaza, New York NY 10001
☎001 212 967 8800   Fax 001 212 967 9196
President *Beverly A. Balaz*
Publisher *Laurie E. Likoff*

Started life in the early 1940s with News Digest subscription series to libraries. Began publishing on specific subjects with the Checkmark Books series and developed its current reference and trade book programme in the 1970s. *Publishes* general trade, young adult trade and academic reference for the school and library markets.

Specialises in single subject encyclopedias. About 135 titles a year. No fiction, cookery or popular non-fiction.

DIVISIONS
General Reference *Laurie Likoff* TITLES *Literary A–Z Series; Eyewitness History Series*. **Academic Reference** *Eleanora Von Dehsen* TITLES *Maps on File; Encyclopedia of Black Women in America*. **Young Adult** *Nicole Bowen* TITLES *Global Profiles Series; American Historic Places*. **Electronic Publishing** *Antonio Gomez* TITLES *Understanding Drugs and Alcohol CD-ROM; The American Indian Multimedia CD-ROM*. Unsolicited synopses and ideas welcome; no mss. Send query letter in the first instance.
Royalties paid twice-yearly.

Farrar, Straus & Giroux, Inc.
19 Union Square West, New York NY 10003
☎001 212 741 6900   Fax 001 212 633 9385
President/Chief Executive *Roger W. Straus III*
Snr Vice-President/Editor-in-Chief *Jonathan Galassi*

FOUNDED 1946. *Publishes* general fiction, non-fiction, juveniles. About 190 titles a year.

DIVISIONS
Children's Books *Margaret Ferguson*. Publishes fiction and non-fiction, books and novels for children and young adults. Approximately 100 titles a year. Submit synopsis and sample chapters (copies of artwork/photographs as part of package). **Hill & Wang** *Elisabeth Sifton*
IMPRINTS **MIRASOL Libros Juveniles**; **Noonday Press** *Elisabeth Dyssegaard*; **North Point Press**; **Sunburst Books**.

Fawcett
See **Ballantine/Del Rey/Fawcett/Ivy/One World Books**

Donald I. Fine Books
See **Penguin USA**

Fireside
See **Simon & Schuster Trade Division**

Flare
See **Avon Books**

Fodor's Travel Publications
See **Random House, Inc.**

Forge
See **St Martin's Press, Inc.**

The Free Press
See **Simon & Schuster Trade Division**

Samuel French, Inc.
45 West 25th Street, New York NY 10010
☎001 212 206 8990   Fax 001 212 206 1429

Senior Editor *William Talbot*
Editor *Lawrence Harbison*

FOUNDED 1830. *Publishes* plays in paperback: Broadway and off-Broadway hits, light comedies, mysteries, one-act plays and plays for young audiences. Unsolicited mss welcome. No synopses. About 80 titles a year.

Royalties paid annually (books); twice-yearly (amateur productions); monthly (professional productions). *Overseas associates* in London, Toronto and Sydney.

The Globe Pequot Press
PO Box 833, 6 Business Park Road,
Old Saybrook CT 06475
☎001 860 395 0440   Fax 001 860 395 1418

President *Linda Kennedy*
Associate Publisher *Michael K. Urban*

Publishes regional and international travel, how-to, personal finance, and outdoor recreation. About 100 titles a year.

IMPRINTS **Voyager Books**. TITLES include the *Off The Beaten Path* series, of which there are currently 50 titles, e.g. *Ohio: Off the Beaten Path*. Also publishes the *Recommended Country Inns* guides. Unsolicited mss, synopses and ideas welcome, particularly for travel and outdoor recreation books.

Royalties paid.

Greenwillow Books
See **William Morrow and Co., Inc.**

Griffin Trade Paperbacks
See **St Martin's Press**

Grolier, Inc.
Sherman Turnpike, Danbury CT 06816
☎001 203 797 3500   Fax 001 203 797 3197

Chairman/Chief Executive Officer *Arnaud Lagardere*

FOUNDED 1895. *Publishes* juvenile non-fiction, encyclopedias, speciality reference sets, children's fiction and picture books, professional and scholarly. Aout 600 titles a year.

DIVISIONS **Children's Press**; **Grolier Educational Corp.**; **Grolier Reference**; **Orchard Books**; **Scarecrow Press, Inc.** (see entry); **Franklin Watts** (see entry).

Grosset & Dunlap
See **Putnam & Grosset Group**

Grove/Atlantic Inc.
841 Broadway, New York NY 10003–4793
☎001 212 614 7850   Fax 001 212 614 7886

President/Publisher *Morgan Entrekin*
Senior Editor *Anton Mueller*

FOUNDED 1952. *Publishes* general fiction and non-fiction. 70 titles in 1996.

IMPRINTS **Atlantic Monthly Press**; **Grove Press**.

Gulliver Books
See **Harcourt Brace Children's Books Division**

Harcourt Brace Children's Books Division
525 B Street, Suite 1900, San Diego
CA 92101–4495
☎001 619 231 6616   Fax 001 619 699 6777

Vice President/Publisher *Louise Pelan*

A division of Harcourt Brace & Company. *Publishes* fiction, poetry and non-fiction covering a wide range of subjects: biography, environment and ecology, history, travel, science and current affairs for children and young adults. About 200 titles a year.

IMPRINTS **Browndeer Press**; **Gulliver Books**; **Gulliver Green® Books** Ecology and environment; **Harcourt Brace Children's Books**; **Harcourt Brace Paperbacks**; **Odyssey Paperbacks** Novels; **Red Wagon Books** For ages 6 months to 3 years; **Voyager Paperbacks** Picture books; **Silver Whistle**. No unsolicited mss.

Hard Candy
See **Masquerade Books**

Harlequin Historicals
See **Silhouette Books**

Harmony
See **Crown Publishing Group**

HarperCollins Publishers, Inc.
10 East 53rd Street, New York
NY 10022
☎001 212 207 7000   Fax 001 212 207 7797

President/Chief Executive Officer *Anthea Disney*

FOUNDED 1817. Owned by News Corporation. *Publishes* general fiction, non-fiction and college textbooks in hardcover, trade paperback and mass-market formats.

DIVISIONS/IMPRINTS
Adult Trade *Jack McKeown* President/Publisher; **Harper Business** *Kirsten Sandberg* Editor; **Harper Reference** *Linda Cunningham* Vice President/Associate Publisher/Editorial Director; **HarperCollins Children's Books** *Marilyn Kriney* Senior Vice President/Publisher; **Harper Paperbacks & Audio** *Geoff Hannell* Senior Vice President/Publisher; **Basic Books** *John Donatich* Vice President/Publisher; **Michael di Capua Books** *Michael di Capua* Vice President/Publisher; **Regan Books** *Judith Regan* President/Publisher.

Subsidiaries **Scott, Foresman & Co** (see entry); **Zondervan Publishing House** (see entry).

Harvard University Press
79 Garden Street, Cambridge MA 02138
☎001 617 495 2611   Fax 001 617 496 4677
Editor-in-Chief *Aida D. Donald*

Publishes scholarly non-fiction only: general interest, science and behaviour, social science, history, humanities, psychology, political science, sociology, economics, business, classics, religion. 120 new titles a year and 80–90 paperbacks. Free book catalogue available.

Harvest House Publishers
1075 Arrowsmith, Eugene OR 97402
☎001 541 343 0123   Fax 001 541 342 6410
President *R. C. Hawkins Jr*
Editorial Director *Carolyn McCready*

Publishes Christian living, fiction, children's and contemporary issues. TITLE *Israel, My Beloved* Kay Arthur; *Beyond the Garden Gate* Thomas Kinkade; *Secrets of the Dead Sea Scrolls* Randall Price. Unsolicited mss, synopses and ideas for books welcome, with IRCs; no children's books, gift books or juvenile fiction at present.

Royalties paid annually.

Hearst Books/Hearst Marine Books
See **William Morrow & Co., Inc.**

Hill & Wang
See **Farrar, Straus & Giroux, Inc**

Hippocrene Books, Inc.
171 Madison Avenue, New York NY 10016
☎001 212 685 4371   Fax 001 212 779 9338
President/Editorial Director *George Blagowidow*

FOUNDED 1971. *Publishes* general non-fiction and reference books. Particularly strong on foreign language dictionaries, language studies, military history and international cookbooks. No fiction. Send brief summary, table of contents and one chapter for appraisal. S.a.e. essential for response. For manuscript return include sufficient postage cover (IRCs).

HMS Press
See **Atlantic Disk Publishers, Inc.**

Holiday House, Inc.
425 Madison Avenue, New York NY 10017
☎001 212 688 0085   Fax 001 212 421 6134
Vice President/Editor-in-Chief *Regina Griffin*

Publishes children's general fiction and non-fiction (pre-school to secondary). About 50 titles a year. TITLES *Wicked Jack* Connie Wooldridge, illus. Will Hillenbrand; *The Life and Death of Crazy Horse* Russell Freedman. Submit synopsis and three sample chapters for novels and chapter books; complete mss (without artwork) for picture books. Mss will not be returned without return postage.

Henry Holt and Company, Inc.
115 West 18th Street, New York NY 10011
☎001 212 886 9200   Fax 001 212 633 0748
President/CEO *Michael Naumann*

FOUNDED 1866. Henry Holt is one of the oldest publishers in the United States. *Publishes* fiction, by both American and international authors, biographies, and books on history and politics, ecology and psychology. AUTHORS include: Robert Frost, Sue Grafton, Thomas Pynchon and Salman Rushdie.

Houghton Mifflin Co.
222 Berkeley Street, Boston MA 02116
☎001 617 351 5000
Contact *Submissions Editor*

FOUNDED 1832. *Publishes* literary fiction and general non-fiction, including autobiography, biography and history. Also school and college textbooks; children's fiction and non-fiction. Average 100 titles a year. Queries only for adult material; synopses, outline and sample chapters for children's non-fiction; complete mss for children's fiction. IRCs required with all submissions/queries.

DIVISIONS **Riverside Publishing Co.**; **Clarion Books** (see entry).

House of Collectibles
See **Ballantine/Del Rey/Fawcett/Ivy/ One World Books**

Hudson River Editions
See **Simon & Schuster Trade Division**

University of Illinois Press
1325 South Oak Street, Champaign
IL 61820-6903
☎001 217 333 0950   Fax 001 217 244 8082

Editorial Director *Richard L. Wentworth*

Publishes non-fiction, scholarly and general, with special interest in Americana, women's studies and African–American studies. Poetry – three volumes a year. About 110–120 titles a year.

Indiana University Press
601 North Morton Street, Bloomington
IN 42404-3797
☎001 812 855 4203   Fax 001 812 855 7931

Director *John Gallman*

Publishes scholarly non-fiction in the following subject areas: African studies, anthropology, Asian studies, Black studies, environment and ecology, film, folklore, history, Jewish studies, literary criticism, medical ethics, Middle East studies, military, music, philanthropy, philosophy, politics, religion, semiotics, Russian and East European studies, Victorian studies, women's studies. Query in writing in the first instance.

University of Iowa Press
Kuhl House, 119 West Park Road, Iowa City
IA 52242
☎001 319 335 2000   Fax 001 319 335 2055

Director *Paul Zimmer*

FOUNDED 1969 as a small scholarly press publishing about five books a year. Now publishing about 35 a year in a variety of scholarly fields, plus local interest, short stories, autobiography and poetry. No unsolicited mss; query first. Unsolicited ideas and synopses welcome.
Royalties paid annually.

Iowa State University Press
2121 South State Avenue, Ames IA 50010
☎001 515 292 0140   Fax 001 515 292 3348

Director *Linda Speth*

FOUNDED 1934 as an offshoot of the university's journalism department. *Publishes* agriculture, aviation, economics, rural sociology, food, consumer science, journalism and veterinary medicine.
Royalties paid annually; sometimes twice yearly.

Island
See **Bantam Doubleday Dell Publishing Group, Inc.**

Ivy
See **Ballantine/Del Rey/Fawcett/Ivy/ One World Books**

Jove
See **Berkley Publishing Group**

University Press of Kansas
2501 West 15th Street, Lawrence
KS 66049–3904
☎001 913 864 4154   Fax 001 913 864 4586

Director *Fred M. Woodward*

FOUNDED 1946. Became the publishing arm for all six state universities in Kansas in 1976. *Publishes* scholarly books in American history, women's studies, presidential studies, social and political philosophy, political science, military history and environmental. About 50 titles a year. Proposals welcome.
Royalties paid annually.

Jean Karl Books
See **Simon & Schuster Children's Publishing Division**

Kent State University Press
Kent OH 44242-0001
☎001 330 672 7913   Fax 001 330 672 3104

Director *John T. Hubbell*
Editor-in-Chief *Julia Morton*

FOUNDED 1965. *Publishes* scholarly works in history and biography, literary studies and general non-fiction. 25–30 titles a year. Queries welcome; no mss.
Royalties paid annually.

Martin Kessler Books
See **Simon & Schuster Trade Division**

Alfred A. Knopf Inc.
201 East 50th Street, New York NY 10022
☎001 212 751 2600   Fax 001 212 572 2593

President/Editor-in-Chief *Sonny Mehta*

FOUNDED 1915. Division of **Random House, Inc.** *Publishes* fiction and non-fiction, poetry, juvenile. 151 titles in 1996. IMPRINT **Everyman's Library**

Krieger Publishing Co., Inc.
PO Box 9542, Melbourne FL 32902–9542
☎001 407 724 9542   Fax 001 407 951 3671

Chairman *Robert E. Krieger*

President *Donald E. Krieger*
Editorial Head *Mary Roberts*

FOUNDED 1970. *Publishes* education and communications, history, medical science, psychology, chemistry, physical and natural sciences, reference, space sciences, technology and engineering.

IMPRINTS **Anvil**; **Exploring Community History Series**; **Open Forum**; **Orbit**; **Professional Practices in Adult Education and Human Resource Development**; **Public History**. Unsolicited mss welcome. Not interested in synopses/ideas.

Royalties paid yearly.

Lanternlight Library
See **University of Alaska Press**

Lehigh University Press
See **Golden Cockerel Press** under **UK Publishers**

Lerner Publications Co.
241 First Avenue North, Minneapolis
MN 55401
☎001 612 332 3344   Fax 001 612 332 7615

Editorial Director *Gar Willets*

Publishes children's and young adults: art, nature, biography, history, world cultures, world and US geography, aviation, sports, fiction, mysteries, physical science. 70 titles in 1996. Please send IRCs for author guidelines.

Little Simon
See **Simon & Schuster Children's Publishing Division**

Little, Brown and Co., Inc.
1271 Avenue of the Americas, New York
NY 10020
☎001 212 522 8700

Children's & Bulfinch editorial at: 34 Beacon Street, Boston, MA 02108
☎001 617 227 0730

Publisher *Sarah Crichton*

Division of Time Warner, Inc. FOUNDED 1837. *Publishes* contemporary popular fiction and literary fiction. Also non-fiction: distinctive cookbooks, biographies, history, poetry, art, photography, science, sport, and children's. About 100 titles a year.

IMPRINTS **Back Bay Books**; **Bulfinch Press**. No unsolicited mss. Query letter in the first instance.

Living Language
See **Crown Publishing Group**

Llewellyn Publications
PO Box 64383, St Paul MN 55164–0383
☎001 612 291 1970   Fax 001 612 291 1908

President/Publisher *Carl L. Weschcke*
Acquisitions Manager *Nancy J. Mostad*

Division of Llewellyn Worldwide Ltd. FOUNDED 1901. *Publishes* self-help and how-to: astrology, alternative health, tantra, Fortean studies, tarot, yoga, Santeria, dream studies, metaphysics, magic, witchcraft, herbalism, shamanism, organic gardening, women's spirituality, graphology, palmistry, parapsychology. Also fiction with an authentic magical or metaphysical theme. About 72 titles a year. TITLES *Time Travel* J. H. Brennan; *Crystal Ascension* Catherine Bowman; *Feng Shui for Beginners* Richard Webster; *Soul Healing* Dr Bruce Goldberg. Unsolicited mss welcome; proposals preferred. IRCs essential in all cases. Books are distributed in the UK by Airlift Book Co.

Lodestar Books
See **Penguin USA**

Lothrop, Lee & Shepard
See **William Morrow and Co., Inc.**

Louisiana State University Press
Baton Rouge LA 70893
☎001 504 388 6294   Fax 001 504 388 6461

Director *L. E. Phillabaum*

Publishes non-fiction: Southern history, American history, Southern literary criticism, American literary criticism, biography, political science, music (jazz) and Latin American studies. About 70 titles a year. Send IRCs for mss guidelines.

Loveswept
See **Bantam Doubleday Dell Publishing Group, Inc.**

Lyons & Burford, Publishers
31 West 21st Street, New York NY 10010
☎001 212 620 9580   Fax 001 212 929 1836

Chairman *Nick Lyons*
Managing Director *Peter Burford*

Publishes outdoor, nature, sports, gardening and angling titles, plus cookery and art. About 75 titles a year. No unsolicited mss; synopses and ideas welcome.

Royalties paid twice-yearly.

Margaret K. McElderry Books
See **Simon & Schuster Children's Publishing Division**

McFarland & Company, Inc., Publishers
PO Box 611, Jefferson NC 28640
☎001 910 246 4460   Fax 001 910 246 5018
President/Editor-in-Chief Robert Franklin
Vice President Rhonda Herman
Editors Steve Wilson, Virginia Tobiassen, isa Camp

FOUNDED 1979. A reference and upper-end speciality market press publishing scholarly books in many fields: international studies, performing arts, popular culture, sports, women's studies, music and fine arts, business, history, war memoirs and librarianship. *Specialises* in general reference. Especially strong in cinema studies. No fiction, poetry, children's, New Age or inspirational works. About 130 titles a year. TITLES *Heads of States and Governments*; *International Holidays*; *African Placenames*; *Opera Companies and Houses*; *Christopher Lee and Peter Cushing*; *The Sexual Harassment of Women*; *The Recreation Handbook*. No unsolicited mss; send query letter first. Synopses and ideas welcome.
Royalties paid annually.

McGraw-Hill, Inc.
1221 Avenue of the Americas, New York NY 10020
☎001 212 512 2000
Contact Submissions Editor

FOUNDED 1873. US parent of the UK-based **McGraw-Hill Book Co. Europe**. *Publishes* a wide range of educational, professional, business, science, engineering and computing books.
DIVISIONS **Legal Information Group**; **Macmillan/McGraw-Hill School Publishing Group**; **Osborne/McGraw-Hill**; **Professional Publishing Group**.

Macmillan/McGraw-Hill School Publishing Group
See **McGraw-Hill, Inc.**

Main Street
See **Bantam Doubleday Dell Publishing Group, Inc.**

Masquerade Books
801 Second Avenue, New York NY 10017
☎001 212 661 7878   Fax 001 212 986 7355
Publisher Richard Kasak

FOUNDED 1989. *Publishes* erotic fiction. 130 titles in 1996. IMPRINTS **Badboy; Hard Candy; Rhinoceros; Masquerade; Rosebud**.

University of Massachusetts Press
PO Box 429, Amherst MA 01004–0429
☎001 413 545 2217   Fax 001 413 545 1226
Director Bruce Wilcox
Senior Editor Clark Dougan

FOUNDED 1964. *Publishes* scholarly, general interest, African-American, ethnic, women's and gender studies, cultural criticism, architecture and environmental design, literary criticism, poetry, philosophy, biography, history, sociology. Unsolicited mss considered but query letter preferred in the first instance. Synopses and ideas welcome. 46 titles in 1996.
Royalties paid annually.

Mentor
See **Penguin USA**

Meridian
See **Penguin USA**

The University of Michigan Press
PO Box 1104, 839 Greene Street, Ann Arbor MI 48106
☎001 313 764 4392   Fax 001 313 936 0456
Director Colin Day

FOUNDED 1930. *Publishes* non-fiction, textbooks, literary criticism, theatre, economics, political science, history, classics, anthropology, law studies, women's studies, and English as a second language. 140 titles in 1996.

IMPRINTS
University of Michigan Press LeAnn Fields Specialises in monographs in anthropology, economics, classics, women's studies, theatre, political science. **Ann Arbor Paperbacks** TITLES *The Legacy of Tiananmen – China in Disarray* James A. R. Miles; *James Joyce and the Art of Mediation* David Weir; *Discovering American Culture* Cheryl L. Delk. No unsolicited mss.
Royalties paid twice-yearly.

The Millbrook Press, Inc.
2 Old New Milford Road, PO Box 335, Brookfield CT 06804
☎001 203 740 2220   Fax 001 203 775 5643
President Jean Reynolds
Editorial Director Jean Reynolds
Managing Editor Colleen Seibert

FOUNDED 1989. *Publishes* mainly non-fiction,

children's and young adult, for trade, school and public library. About 120 titles a year.

Royalties paid twice-yearly.

Minstrel Books
See **Pocket Books**

MIRASOL Libros Juveniles
See **Farrar, Straus & Giroux, Inc**

University Press of Mississippi
3825 Ridgewood Road, Jackson
MS 39211-6492
☎001 601 982 6205   Fax 001 601 982 6217

Chairman Dr *Thomas Richardson*
Managing Director Dr *Richard Abel*
Associate Director/Editor-in-Chief
Seetha A-Srinivasan
Approx. Annual Turnover $1.5 million

FOUNDED 1970. The non-profit book publisher partially supported by the eight State universities. *Publishes* scholarly and trade titles in literature, history, American culture, Southern culture, African-American, women's studies, popular culture, folklife, ethnic, performance, art and photography, and other liberal arts. About 50 titles a year. TITLES *Anabasis* Ellen Gilchrist; *Country Music Culture; Punk and Neo-Tribal Body Art.*

IMPRINTS
Muscadine Books *JoAnne Prichard* Regional trade titles. TITLES *The New Orleans Garden; The Crawfish Book; The Catfish Book.* **Banner Books** Paperback reprints of significant fiction and non-fiction. TITLES *Savage Holiday* Richard Wright; *Dark Princess* W. E. B. DuBois. Send letter of enquiry, prospectus, table of contents and sample chapter prior to submission of full mss.

Royalties paid annually. *Represented* worldwide. UK representatives: **Roundhouse Publishing Ltd** (see entry under **UK Publishers**).

University of Missouri Press
2910 LeMone Boulevard, Columbia
MO 65201-8227
☎001 573 882 7641   Fax 001 573 884 4498

Director/Editor-in-Chief *Beverly Jarrett*

Publishes academic: history, literary criticism, intellectual history and related humanities disciplines and short stories – usually four volumes a year. TITLES *Shades of Blue and Gray, An Introductory Military History of the Civil War* Herman Hattaway; *Orphan Trains to Missouri* Michael D. Patrick and Evelyn Goodrich

Trickel; *The Catholic Imagination in American Literature* Ross Labrie. Best approach is by letter. Send one short story for consideration, and synopses for academic work. About 50 titles a year.

The MIT Press
55 Hayward Street, Cambridge MA 02142
☎001 617 253 5646   Fax 001 617 258 6779

Managing Editor *Michael Sims*

Publishes scholarly and professional, technologically sophisticated books, including computer science and artificial intelligence, economics, architecture, cognitive science, neuroscience, environmental studies, linguistics and philosophy. 244 titles in 1996. IMPRINT **Bradford Books**.

Monograph Series
See **University of Alaska Press**

Moorings
See **Ballantine/Del Rey/Fawcett/Ivy/ One World Books**

William Morrow & Co., Inc.
1350 Avenue of the Americas, New York
NY 10019
☎001 212 261 6500   Fax 001 212 261 6595

Vice-President/Associate Publisher
Jacqueline Deval

FOUNDED 1926. *Publishes* fiction, poetry and general non-fiction. Approach in writing only. No unsolicited mss or proposals for adult books. Proposals read only if submitted through a literary agent. About 600 titles a year.

IMPRINTS
Hearst Books/Hearst Marine Books *Ann Bramson*; **Quill Trade Paperbacks** *Toni Sciarra*; **Morrow Junior Books** *David Reuther*, **Lothrop, Lee & Shepard** *Susan Pearson*; **Greenwillow Books** *Susan Hirschman*; **Eaglebrook** *Joann Davis*; **Mulberry Books/ Beech Tree Books** (trade paperbacks) *Paulette Kaufmann*; **Rob Weisbach Books** *Rob Weisbach*.

Mulberry Books
See **William Morrow and Co., Inc.**

Muscadine Books
See **University Press of Mississippi**

Mysterious Press
See **Warner Books Inc.**

University of Nevada Press
MS 166, Reno NV 89557-0076
☎001 702 784 6573   Fax 001 702 784 6200
Director *Ronald Latimer*
Editor-in-Chief *Margaret Dalrymple*
FOUNDED 1960. *Publishes* serious fiction, Native American studies, natural history, Western Americana, Basque studies and regional studies. About 40 titles a year including reprints. Unsolicited material welcome if it fits in with areas published, or offers a 'new and exciting' direction.
Royalties paid twice-yearly.

New Age Books
See **Bantam Doubleday Dell Publishing Group, Inc.**

University Press of New England
23 South Main Street, Hanover
NH 03755-2048
☎001 603 643 7100   Fax 001 603 643 1540
Chair/Director *Thomas L. McFarland*
Editorial Director *Philip Pochoda*
FOUNDED 1970. A scholarly book publisher sponsored by six institutions of higher education in the region: Brandeis, Dartmouth, Middlebury, Tufts, Wesleyan and the University of New Hampshire. *Publishes* general and scholarly non-fiction; plus poetry through the Wesleyan Poetry Series and Hardscrabble Books fiction of New England. About 75 titles a year.
IMPRINTS **Wesleyan University Press** Interdisciplinary studies, history, literature, women's studies, government and public issues, biography, poetry, natural history and environment. Unsolicited material welcome.
Royalties paid annually. *Overseas associates:* UK – University Presses Marketing; Europe – Trevor Brown Associates.

University of New Mexico Press
1720 Lomas Boulevard NE, Albuquerque
NM 87131-1591
☎001 505 277 2346   Fax 001 505 277 9270
Director *Elizabeth C. Hadas*
Editor *Larry Durwood Ball*
Publishes scholarly and regional books. No fiction, how-to, children's, humour, self-help, technical or textbooks. 94 titles in 1996.

Noonday Press
See **Farrar, Straus & Giroux, Inc**

North Point Press
See **Farrar, Straus & Giroux, Inc**

University of North Texas Press
PO Box 13856, Denton TX 76203
☎001 817 565 2142   Fax 001 817 565 4590
Director *Frances B. Vick*
Associate Director/Editorial Director
   Charlotte M. Wright
FOUNDED 1987. *Publishes* folklore, ecology, regional interest, contemporary, social issues, history, military, women's issues, writing and publishing reference, and Western literature. Publishes the Vassar Miller Poetry Prize winner each year. About 14 titles a year. No unsolicited mss. Approach by letter in the first instance. Synopses and ideas welcome.
Royalties paid annually.

W. W. Norton & Company
500 Fifth Avenue, New York NY 10110
☎001 212 354 5500   Fax 001 212 869 0856
FOUNDED 1923. *Publishes* quality fiction and non-fiction, college textbooks, professional and medical books. About 300 titles a year. No unsolicited mss.

NTC/Contemporary Publishing Company
4255 West Touhy Avenue, Lincolnwood
IL 60646–1975
☎001 847 679 5500   Fax 001 847 679 2494
Publisher *Christine Albritton*
Editorial Director *John Nolan*
FOUNDED 1947. *Publishes* general adult non-fiction and adult education books. 100 titles in 1996. Submissions require s.a.e. for response.

Odyssey Paperbacks
See **Harcourt Brace Children's Books Division**

University of Oklahoma Press
1005 Asp Avenue, Norman
OK 73019-0445
☎001 405 325 5111   Fax 001 405 325 4000
Editor-in-Chief *John N. Drayton*
FOUNDED 1928. *Publishes* general scholarly non-fiction only: American Indian studies, history of American West, classical studies, literary theory and criticism, anthropology, archaeology, natural history, political science and women's studies. About 100 titles a year.

One World
See **Ballantine/Del Rey/Fawcett/Ivy/ One World Books**

Onyx
See **Penguin USA**

Open Forum
See **Krieger Publishing Co., Inc.**

Orbit
See **Krieger Publishing Co., Inc.**

Orchard Books
See **Grolier, Inc.**

Osborne/McGraw Hill
2600 Tenth Street, Berkeley CA 94710
☎001 510 549 6600   Fax 001 510 549 6603
Publisher *Brandon A. Nordin*
Editor-in-Chief *Scott Rogers*
FOUNDED 1970. Osborne has been publishing computer books for over 20 years and has grown to become a leader in its field. *Publishes* computer software and microcomputer titles. About 85 titles a year. TITLES *Internet Yellow Pages; Windows 95 series; Busy People series.* Co-publisher of Oracle Press, Corel Press, AT&T and America Online.
Royalties paid twice-yearly.

Pantheon Books/Schocken Books
201 East 50th Street, New York NY 10022
☎001 212 751 2600   Fax 001 212 572 6030
Senior Editor (Pantheon) *Shelley Wanger*
Editor Director (Shocken) *Arthur Samuelson*
FOUNDED 1942. Division of **Random House, Inc.** *Publishes* Fiction and non-fiction, Jewish interest (Shocken Books). 78 titles in 1996.

Paragon House
2700 University Avenue, Suite 47, St Paul MN 55114–1016
☎001 612 644 3087   Fax 001 612 644 0997
Executive Director *Gordon L. Anderson*
FOUNDED 1982. *Publishes* non-fiction: reference and academic. Subjects include history, religion, philosophy, New Age, Jewish interest, health, political science, international relations, psychology.
Royalties paid twice-yearly.

Pelican Publishing Company
1101 Monroe Street, Box 3110, Gretna LA 70053
☎001 504 368 1175
Editor-in-Chief *Nina Kooij*
Publishes general non-fiction: popular history, cookbooks, travel, art, business, children's, edi-

torial cartoon, architecture and motivational. About 670 titles a year. Initial enquiries required for all submissions.

Pelion Press
See **Rosen Publishing Group, Inc.**

Penguin USA
375 Hudson Street, New York NY 10014
☎001 212 366 2000   Fax 001 212 366 2666
President *Marvin Brown*
Owned by Pearson. *Publishes* fiction and non-fiction in paperback; adult and children's. About 1000 titles a year. IMPRINTS: **Arkana; Mentor; Meridian; Onyx; Penguin Classics** *K. Court;* **Penguin Audio** *Mark Stafford;* **Plume** *Arnold Dolin;* **Puffin** *Tracy Tang;* **ROC Books** *Laura Gilman;* **Signet; Signet Classics; Topaz** *Michaela Hamilton;* **Viking** *Barbara Grossman;* **Viking Studio** *Michael Fragnito;* **Frederick Warne.**
DIVISIONS
Dutton/Signet *Elaine Koster* FOUNDED 1852. IMPRINTS **William Abrahams; Dutton; Donald I. Fine Books; Truman M. Talley. Dial Books for Young Readers** *Phyllis J. Fogelman* (see entry); **Dutton Children's Books** *Christopher Franceschelli/Lucia Monfried* FOUNDED 1852. *Publishes* picture books, fiction and non-fiction, board and novelty books. IMPRINTS **Cobblehill Books** *Rosanne Lauer,* **Ladybird Books** *Joan Powers;* **Lodestar Books** *Virginia Buckley;* **Looney Tunes Books** *Liane Onish;* **Viking Children's Books** *Regina Hayes.*
Royalties paid twice-yearly.

University of Pennsylvania Press
423 Guardian Drive, Philadelphia PA 19104–6097
☎001 215 898 1671   Fax 001 215 898 0404
Director *Eric Halpern*
FOUNDED 1896. *Publishes* serious non-fiction: scholarly, reference, professional, textbooks and semi-popular trade. No original fiction or poetry. TITLES include *Sculpture* Rawson; *Potter's Dictionary; Ellen Terry, Player in Her Time; Sensuous Scholarship; Postmodern Fairy Tales.* About 70 titles a year. No unsolicited mss but synopses and ideas for books welcome.
Royalties paid annually.

Perigee Books
See **Putnam Berkley Publishing Group**

Philomel Books
See **Putnam & Grosset Group**

Picador USA
See **St Martin's Press, Inc.**

Players Press
PO Box 1132, Studio City CA 91614-0132
☎001 818 789 4980
Chairman *William-Alan Landes*
Managing Director *David Cole*
Editorial Head *Robert W. Gordon*

FOUNDED 1965 as a publisher of plays; now publishes across the entire range of performing arts: plays, musicals, theatre, film, cinema, television, costume, puppetry, plus technical theatre and cinema material. 55–65 titles a year. TITLES *Principles of Stage Combat Handbook*; *Stage Crafts Handbook*; *Scenes for Acting & Directing, vol 2*; *Performance One – Monologues for Women*; *Period Costume for Stage and Screen – Medieval to 1500*; *Three Sisters*. No unsolicited mss; synopses/ideas welcome. Send query letter.

Royalties paid twice-yearly. *Overseas subsidiaries* in Canada, Australia and the UK.

Plenum Publishing
233 Spring Street, New York NY 10013
☎001 212 620 8000   Fax 001 212 463 0742
Executive Editor, Plenum Trade Books
Linda Greenspan Regan

FOUNDED 1946. *Publishes* quality non-fiction for the intelligent layman and the professional: trade science, social sciences, health, psychology, anthropology and criminology. Over 300 titles a year. Queries only. DIVISION **Plenum Trade** About 15–20 titles a year.

Plume
See **Penguin USA**

Pocket Books
1230 Avenue of the Americas, New York NY 10020
☎001 212 698 7000   Fax 001 212 698 7007
President/Publisher *Gina Centrello*

FOUNDED 1939. A division of Simon & Schuster Consumer Group. *Publishes* trade paperbacks and hardcovers; mass-market, reprints and originals. IMPRINTS **Archway**; **Minstrel Books**; **Pocket Star Books**; **Washington Square Press**.

Price, Stern, Sloan
See **Putnam & Grosset Group**

Public History
See **Krieger Publishing Co., Inc.**

Puffin
See **Penguin USA**

Puffin Pied Piper
See **Dial Books for Young Readers**

Putnam & Grosset Group
200 Madison Avenue, New York NY 10016
☎001 212 951 8700   Fax 001 212 532 3693
Chairman *Margaret Frith*
President *Douglas Whiteman*
President & Publisher, G. P. Putnam's Sons *Nancy Paulsen*
President & Publisher, Grosset & Dunlap *Jane O'Connor*

The children's book division of the **Putnam Berkley Publishing Group** (see entry).
IMPRINTS
G. P. Putnam's Sons *Refna Wilkin* Executive Editor; **Philomel Books** *Patricia Lee Gauch* Editorial Director; **Grosset & Dunlap** *Lana Bergen* Executive Editor; **Price, Stern, Sloan** 11150 Olympic Boulevard, Los Angeles, CA 90064, *Frances Baggetta* Publisher. All imprints *publish* picture books, activity books, fiction and non-fiction for children.

Putnam Berkley Publishing Group
200 Madison Avenue, New York NY 10016
☎001 212 951 8400   Fax 001 212 213 6706
President *David Shanks*

FOUNDED 1838. *Publishes* general fiction and non-fiction, including children's. Also business, how-to, nutrition and general fiction under the **Berkley** imprints. **Putnam & Grosset Group** is the children's book division (see entry).

DIVISIONS
Berkley Mass-market paperback division (see entry). **Perigee Books** *John Duff* Trade paperback division. Non-fiction: cookbooks, crafts, humour, music & dance, health, nutrition, psychology, self-help, social sciences and sociology, biography, child care and development, behavioural sciences, business, human relations, education. **Putnam** Hardcover division, includes **G. P. Putnam Sons**, **Grosset/Putnam** and **Jeremy P. Tarcher** imprints. **Riverhead Books** *Susan J. Petersen* Paperbacks – fiction and non fiction, including spirituality, religion, biography, African-American works and travel.

Royalties paid twice-yearly.

Questar
See **Warner Books Inc.**

Quill Trade Paperbacks
See **William Morrow and Co., Inc.**

Rabbit Ears
See **Simon & Schuster Children's Publishing Division**

Rand McNally & Co.
8255 North Central Park Avenue, Skokie IL 60076
☎001 847 329 8100   Fax 001 847 673 0539
Executive Editor *Jon Leverenz*
FOUNDED 1856. *Publishes* world atlases and maps, road atlases of North America and Europe, city and state maps of the United States and Canada, educational wall maps, atlases and globes, plus children's products. Includes electronic publications. 30 titles in 1996.

Random House, Inc.
201 East 50th Street, New York NY 10022
☎001 212 751 2600   Fax 001 212 572 8700
Chairman/Chief Executive Officer *Alberto Vitale*
FOUNDED 1925. *Publishes* trade fiction: adventure, confessional, experimental, fantasy, historical, horror, humour, mainstream, mystery and suspense; and non-fiction: biography, history, economics, politics, health, business, sports, humour, food and cookery, self-help, Americana, nature and environment, psychology, religion, sociology. Plus children's fiction: adventure, confessional (young adult), fantasy, historical, horror, humour, mystery, picture books, science fiction, suspense, young adult; and children's non-fiction: biography, humour, illustrated, nature and the environment, leisure, science and sport. 3346 titles in 1996. Submissions via agents preferred.

DIVISIONS
Juvenile & Merchandise Group (☎940 7682. Fax 940 7640) IMPRINTS **Random House Juvenile** *Alice Jonaitis* Editor; **Knopf Juvenile** *Arthur Levine* Editor-in-Chief; **Crown Juvenile** *Tracy Gates* Senior Editor; **Bullseye Books** *Lisa Banim* Executive Editor. **Crown Publishing Group** (see entry). **Ballantine/Del Rey/Fawcett/Ivy Books** (see entry). **Alfred A. Knopf, Inc.** (see entry).
Pantheon Books/Shocken Books (see entry). **Random House Adult Trade Books** (☎572 2120. Fax 572 4949) *Harold Evans* President/Publisher. **Times Books** (see entry);

Villard Books Fiction and non-fiction; **Vintage Books** Trade paperbacks.
Other divisions: **Random House Reference and Information Publishing**; **Fodor's Travel Publications, Inc.**
Royalties paid twice-yearly.

Rawson Associates
See **Simon & Schuster Trade Division**

Red Wagon Books
See **Harcourt Brace Children's Books Division**

Regan Books
See **HarperCollins Publishers, Inc.**

Fleming H. Revell
See **Baker Book House**

Rhinoceros
See **Masquerade Books**

Riverhead Books
See **Putnam Berkley Publishing Group**

Riverside Publishing Co.
See **Houghton Mifflin Co.**

ROC Books
See **Penguin USA**

Rosebud
See **Masquerade Books**

The Rosen Publishing Group, Inc.
29 East 21st Street, New York NY 10010
☎001 212 777 3017   Fax 001 212 253 6915
President *Roger Rosen*
Editorial Director *Patra McSharry Sevastiades*
Managing Editor *Jane Kelly Kosek*
Editors *Gina Ng, Jennifer Croft, Michele Drohan, Erica Smith, Gary van Wyk*
Reference Editors *Margaret Haerens, Christine Slovey*
Publishes non-fiction books (supplementary to the curriculum, reference and self-help) for a young adult audience. Reading levels are years 7–12 and 4–6 (books for teens with literacy problems). Areas of interest include health, religion, careers, self-esteem, sexuality, drug abuse prevention, personal safety, African studies and a wide variety of other multicultural titles. About 150 titles a year.

IMPRINTS
Pelion Press Music titles; **Power Kids Press** *Gina Strazzabosco-Hayn, Helen Packard* Non-

fiction books for Reception up to Year 4 that are supplementary to the curriculum. Subjects include conflict resolution, character building, health, safety, drug abuse prevention, history, self-help, religion and multicultural titles. 144 titles a year. For all imprints, write with outline and sample chapters.

Rutgers University Press

Bldg 4161, PO Box 5062, Livingston
Campus, New Brunswick NJ 08903–5062
☎001 732 445 7762   Fax 001 732 445 7039

Editor-in-Chief *Leslie Mitchner*

FOUNDED 1936. *Publishes* scholarly books, regional and social sciences. Unsolicited mss, synopses and ideas for books welcome. No original fiction or poetry. About 70 titles a year.
Royalties paid annually.

St Martin's Press, Inc.

175 Fifth Avenue, New York NY 10010
☎001 212 674 5151   Fax 001 212 420 9314

Chairman/Chief Executive *John Sargent*
President/Publisher (Trade Division)
  Sally Richardson

FOUNDED 1952. A subsidiary of **Macmillan Publishers** (UK), St Martin's Press made its name and fortune by importing raw talent from the UK to the States and has continued to buy heavily in the UK. *Publishes* general fiction, especially mysteries and crime; and adult non-fiction: history, self-help, political science, travel, biography, scholarly, popular reference, college textbooks. 1600 titles in 1996.
  IMPRINTS **Picador USA**; **Griffin Trade Paperbacks**; **St Martin's Paperbacks (Mass)**; **Thomas Dunne Books**; **Wyatt Books**; **Tor**; **Forge**; **Bedford Books**; **Buzz Books**.

Scarecrow Press, Inc.

4720 Boston Way, Lanham Maryland 20706
☎001 301 459 3366   Fax 001 301 459 2118

Editorial Director *Shirley Lambert*

FOUNDED 1950 as a short-run publisher of library reference books. Acquired by **University Press of America, Inc.** in 1995. *Publishes* reference, scholarly and monographs (all levels) for libraries. Reference books in all areas except sciences, specialising in the performing arts, music, cinema and library science. About 165 titles a year. Publisher for the Medical Library Association, Society of American Archivists, Children's Literature Association, Institute of Jazz Studies of Rutgers – the State University of New Jersey, the American Theological Library Association.

Also publisher of *VOYA* (Voice of Youth Advocates); six issues a year. Unsolicited mss welcome but material will not be returned unless requested and accompanied by return postage. Unsolicited synopses and ideas for books welcome.
  Royalties paid annually.

Schocken Books

See **Pantheon Books**

Scholastic, Inc.

555 Broadway, New York NY 10012
☎001 212 343 6100   Fax 001 212 343 6390

Vice President/Publisher *Barbara Marcus*
Executive Editor (picture books) *Dianne Hess*
Executive Editor (middle grade, young adult, non-fiction) *Ann Reit*
Executive Editor (middle grade, young adult, fiction) *Regina Griffin*

FOUNDED 1920. *Publishes* picture books and fiction for middle grade (8–12-year-olds) and young adults: family stories, friendship, humour, fantasy, mysteries and school. Also non-fiction: biography and multicultural subjects. 500 titles in 1996. Mss with outlines and three sample chapters welcome.

Anne Schwartz Books

See **Simon & Schuster Children's Publishing Division**

Scott, Foresman–Addison Wesley

1900 E Lake Avenue, Glenview IL 60025
☎001 847 729 3000   Fax 001 847 486 3999

President, School Publishing Group *Pat Donaghy*

FOUNDED 1896. Merged with **Addison-Wesley Longman Publishing Co.** in 1996. *Publishes* elementary and secondary education materials. 1300 titles in 1996.

Scribner

See **Simon & Schuster Trade Division**

Signet/Signet Classics

See **Penguin USA**

Silhouette Books

300 East 42nd Street, New York NY 10017
☎001 212 682 6080   Fax 001 212 682 4539

Editorial Director *Isabel Swift*

FOUNDED 1979 as an imprint of **Simon & Schuster** and was acquired by a wholly owned subsidiary of Toronto-based Harlequin

Enterprises Ltd in 1984. *Publishes* category, contemporary romance fiction and historical romance fiction only. Over 360 titles a year across a number of imprints.

IMPRINTS
Silhouette Romance *Melissa Senate*; **Silhouette Desire** *Lucia Macro;* **Silhouette Special Edition** *Tara Gavin*; **Silhouette Intimate Moments** *Leslie Wainger*, **Silhouette Yours Truly** *Leslie Wainger*, **Harlequin Historicals** *Tracy Farrell*. **Steeple Hill** *Tara Gavin* New imprint launched in 1997 to publish *Love Inspired* a line of inspirational contemporary romances with stories designed to 'lift readers' spirits and gladden their hearts'. No unsolicited mss. Submit query letter in the first instance or write for detailed submission guidelines/tip sheets.

Royalties paid twice-yearly. *Overseas associates* worldwide.

Silver Whistle
See **Harcourt Brace Children's Books Division**

Simon & Schuster Children's Publishing Division
1230 Avenue of the Americas, New York NY 10020
☎001 212 698 7200   Fax 001 212 605 3068
President and Publisher *Rick Richter*

A division of the Simon & Schuster Consumer Group. *Publishes* pre-school to young adult, picture books, hardcover and paperback fiction, non-fiction, trade, library and mass-market titles.

IMPRINTS
Aladdin Books *Ellen Krieger* Picture books, paperback fiction and non-fiction reprints and originals, and limited series for ages pre-school to young adult; **Atheneum Books for Young Readers** *Jonathan Lanman* Picture books, hardcover fiction and non-fiction books across all genres for ages 3 to young adult. Two lines within this imprint are **Jean Karl Books** quality fantasy-fiction; and **Anne Schwartz Books** distinct picture books and high-quality fiction; **Little Simon** *Robin Corey* Mass-market novelty books (pop-ups, board books, colouring & activity) and merchandise (book and audiocassette) for ages birth through 8; **Margaret K. McElderry Books** *Margaret K. McElderry* Picture books, hardcover fiction and non-fiction trade books for children ages 3 to young adult; **Rabbit Ears** *Robin Corey*

Children's audiocassettes of tales narrated by celebrities, featuring soundtracks by popular musicians and illustrations by acclaimed artists, packaged with companion books in hardcover, paperback, and mini-book formats. Entire programme derived from the videos produced by the entertainment company, Rabbit Ears; **Simon & Schuster Books for Young Readers** *Stephanie Owens Lurie* Picture books, hardcover fiction and non-fiction for children ages 3 to young adult. **Simon Spotlight** *Robin Corey* New imprint devoted exclusively to children's media tie-ins and licensed properties.

For submissions to all imprints: send envelope (US size 10) for guidelines, attention: *Manuscript Submissions Guidelines*.

Simon & Schuster Trade Division
1230 Avenue of the Americas, New York NY 10020
☎001 212 698 7000   Fax 001 212 698 7007
President/Publisher *Carolyn K. Reidy*
Snr Vice President/Editor-in-Chief
   Michael V. Korda

A division of the Simon & Schuster Consumer Group. *Publishes* fiction and non-fiction.

DIVISIONS
The Free Press *Paula Barker Duffy* VP & Publisher, *Adam Bellow;* **Fireside/Touchstone** *Mark Gompertz* VP & Publisher, *Trish Todd*; **Scribner** *Susan Moldow* VP & Publisher, *Nan Graham*; **Simon and Schuster** *Michele Martin* VP & Associate Publisher, *Michael V. Korda, Alice Mayhew.*

IMPRINTS **H. & R. Block**; **Lisa Drew Books**; **Fireside**; **The Free Press**; **Hudson River Editions**; **Martin Kessler Books**; **Rawson Associates**; **Scribner**, **Scribner Paperback Fiction** ; **Atheneum Publishers**; **S&S Aguilar-Libros eñ Espanol**; **Simon & Schuster**; **Touchstone**. No unsolicited mss.

Royalties paid twice-yearly.

Simon Spotlight
See **Simon & Schuster Children's Publishing Division**

Southern Illinois University Press
PO Box 3697, Carbondale IL 62902
☎001 618 453 2281   Fax 001 618 453 1221
Director *Rick Stetter*

FOUNDED 1953. *Publishes* scholarly non-fiction books and educational materials. 50 titles a year.

Royalties paid annually.

Spectra
See **Bantam Doubleday Dell Publishing Group, Inc.**

Spire Books
See **Baker Book House**

Stackpole Books
5067 Ritter Road, Mechanicsburg PA 17055
☎001 717 796 0411   Fax 001 717 796 0412
President M. David Detweiler
Vice President/Editorial Director Judith Schnell

FOUNDED 1933. Publishes outdoor sports, nature, photography, gardening, military reference, history, fishing, woodworking and carving. 75 titles in 1997.
Royalties paid twice-yearly.

Stanford University Press
Stanford CA 94305-2235
☎001 415 723 9434   Fax 001 415 725 3457
Director Norris Pope

Publishes non-fiction: scholarly works in all areas of the humanities, social sciences, political sciences, natural sciences, history and literature. About 100 titles a year. No unsolicited mss; query in writing first.

Steeple Hill
See **Silhouette Books**

Sterling Publishing Co. Inc.
387 Park Avenue South, 5th Floor, New York NY 10016-8810
☎001 212 532 7160   Fax 001 212 213 2495
President/Editor Burton Hobson
Contact Sheila Barry

FOUNDED 1949. Publishes non-fiction: reference and information books, science, nature, arts and crafts, architecture, home improvement, history, photography, humour, health, wine and food, social sciences, sports, music, psychology, occult, woodworking, pets, hobbies, business, military science, gardening, puzzles. 449 titles in 1996.

Stonehenge Press
See **Time-Life Inc.**

Sunburst Books
See **Farrar, Straus & Giroux, Inc**

Susquehanna University Press
See **Golden Cockerel Press** under **UK Publishers**

Syracuse University Press
1600 Jamesville Avenue, Syracuse NY 13244-5160
☎001 315 443 5541   Fax 001 315 443 5545
Director Robert Mandel

FOUNDED 1943. Publishes scholarly books in the following areas: contemporary Middle East studies, international affairs, Irish studies, Iroquois studies, women and religion, Jewish studies, peace studies. About 50 titles a year. TITLES Intellectual Life in Arab East M. Buheiry; Middle Eastern Lives M. Kramer. SERIES TITLES include Irish Studies; Modern Jewish History; New York Classics; Syracuse Studies on Peace and Conflict Resolution; Utopianism and Communitarianism; Writing About Women. Also co-publishes with a number of organisations such as the American University of Beirut. No unsolicited mss. Send query letter with IRCs.
Royalties paid annually.

Truman M. Talley
See **Penguin USA**

Jeremy P. Tarcher
See **Putnam Berkley Publishing Group**

Temple University Press
Broad and Oxford Streets, Philadelphia PA 19122
☎001 215 204 8787   Fax 001 215 204 4719
Editor-in-Chief Michael Ames

Publishes scholarly non-fiction: American history, Latin American studies, gay and lesbian studies, ethnic studies, psychology, Asian American studies, anthropology, law, cultural studies, sociology, women's studies, health care and disability, philosophy, public policy, labour studies, urban and environmental studies, photography and Black studies. About 60 titles a year. Authors generally academics. Write in first instance.

University of Tennessee Press
293 Communications Building, Knoxville TN 37996
☎001 615 974 3321   Fax 001 615 974 3724
FOUNDED in 1940. Publishes scholarly and regional non-fiction. 35 titles in 1996.
Royalties paid twice-yearly.

University of Texas Press
PO Box 7819, Austin TX 78713-7819
☎001 512 471 7233/Editorial: 471 4278
Fax 001 512 320 0668
Director Joanna Hitchcock

Assistant Director/Executive Editor
Theresa J. May

Publishes scholarly non-fiction: anthropology, archaeology, cultural geography, Latin/ Mexican/Native American studies, politics, biology and earth sciences, environmental, American/ Texan urban studies, Texana, women's, film, cultural, media, literary studies, Middle Eastern studies, regional cookbooks, natural history, Latin American/Middle Eastern literature in translation, art and architecture, classics. Unsolicited material welcome in above subject areas only. About 90 titles a year and 12 journals. TITLES *A John Graves Reader* John Graves; *Journey Through Kurdistan* Mary Ann Bruni; *Twentieth Century Latin American Poetry: A Bilingual Anthology* ed. Stephen Tapscott.
Royalties paid annually.

Time-Life Inc.

2000 Duke Street, Alexandria VA 22314
☎001 703 838 7000   Fax 001 703 838 7474

President/Chief Executive *George Artandi*

FOUNDED 1961. *Publishes* non-fiction: art, cooking, crafts, food, gardening, health, history, home maintenance, nature, photography, science. No unsolicited mss. About 300 titles a year.

DIVISIONS/IMPRINTS **Time-Life Books; Time-Life Education; Time-Life Music; Time-Life International; Time-Life Video & Television; Stonehenge Press**.

Times Books

201 East 50th Street, New York NY 10022
☎001 212 572 2120   Fax 001 212 940 7464

Publisher *Peter Bernstein*

FOUNDED 1959. A division of **Random House**. *Publishes* general non-fiction only. 67 titles in 1996. Unsolicited mss not considered. Letter essential.

Topaz

See **Penguin USA**

Tor

See **St Martin's Press, Inc.**

Touchstone

See **Simon & Schuster Trade Division**

Tyndale House Publishers, Inc.

351 Executive Drive, Carol Stream
IL 60188
☎001 630 668 8300   Fax 001 630 668 8311

Chairman *Kenneth N. Taylor*

President *Mark D. Taylor*

FOUNDED 1962 by Kenneth Taylor. Non-denominational religious publisher of around 100–150 titles a year for the evangelical Christian market. Books cover a wide range of categories from home and family to inspirational, theology, doctrine, Bibles, general reference and fiction. Also produces video material, calendars and audio books for the same market. No poetry. TITLES *New Living Translation; Left Behind; Tribulation Force; Walking With the Savior; Home with a Heart*. No unsolicited mss; they will be returned unread. Synopses and ideas considered. Send query letter summarising contents of books and length. Include a brief biography, detailed outline and sample chapters. IRCs essential for response or return of material. No audio cassettes, disks or video tapes in lieu of mss. Response time around 6–12 weeks. No phone calls. Send s.a.e. for free catalogue and full submission guidelines.
Royalties paid annually.

Upstart Publishing Co., Inc.

See **Dearborn Financial Publishing, Inc.**

Van Nostrand Reinhold

115 Fifth Avenue, New York NY 10003
☎001 212 254 3232   Fax 001 212 477 2719

President/CEO *Marianne J. Russell*

FOUNDED 1848. A division of International Thomson Publishing, Inc. *Publishes* professional and reference information products in the following fields: culinary arts/hospitality, architecture/design, environmental sciences and business technology. 110 titles in 1996.

Vernon Publishing Inc.

See **Dearborn Financial Publishing, Inc.**

Viking/Viking Studio/ Viking Children's Books

See **Penguin USA**

Villard Books

See **Random House, Inc.**

Vintage Books

See **Random House, Inc.**

Voyager Books

See **The Globe Pequot Press**

Voyager Paperbacks

See **Harcourt Brace Children's Books Division**

Walker & Co.

435 Hudson Street, New York
NY 10014
☎001 212 727 8300   Fax 001 212 727 0984
Contact *Submissions Editor*
FOUNDED 1959. *Publishes* fiction: mystery, westerns and children's; and non-fiction. Unsolicited submissions are welcome as follows: **Mystery** *Michael Seidman* 60–70,000 words. Send first three chapters and 3-5 page synopsis. **Westerns** *Jacqueline Johnson* 65,000 words, strong plot and character development. 50–75 pages plus short synopsis, or complete mss. **Trade non-fiction** *George Gibson* Permissions and documentation must be available with mss. Submit prospectus first, with sample chapters and marketing analysis. **Books for Young Readers** *Emily Easton* Fiction and non-fiction. Query before sending non-fiction proposals. Especially interested in young science, photoessays, historical fiction for middle grades, biographies, current affairs, and YA non-fiction.

Frederick Warne
See **Penguin USA**

Warner Books Inc.

1271 Avenue of the Americas, New York
NY 10020
☎001 212 522 7200   Fax 001 212 522 7991
Executive Editor *Joann Davis*
FOUNDED 1961. *Publishes* fiction and non-fiction, audio books, gift books, electronic and multimedia products. 330 titles in 1996.
IMPRINTS **Aspect** *Betsy Mitchell*; **Mysterious Press** *William Malloy*; **Questar**. Query or submit outline with sample chapters and letter.

Washington Square Press
See **Pocket Books**

Washington State University Press

Cooper Publications Building, Pullman
WA 99164-5910
☎001 509 335 3518   Fax 001 509 335 8568
Director *Thomas H. Sanders*
FOUNDED 1928. Revitalised in 1984 to publish hardcover originals, trade paperbacks and reprints. *Publishes* mainly on the history, prehistory and culture of the Northwest United States (Washington, Idaho, Oregon, Montana, Alaska) and British Columbia, but works that focus on national topics or other regions may also be considered. 8–10 titles a year. TITLES *Iron in Her Soul: Elizabeth Gurley Flynn and the American Left*; *Grand Coulee: Harnessing a Dream*; *Confederate Raider in the North Pacific*; *Raise Hell and Sell Newspapers: Alden J. Blethen and 'The Seattle Times'*; *Fighting the Odds: The Life of Senator Frank Church*; *Fields of Toil: A Migrant Family's Journey*. Unsolicited mss welcome. No synopses or ideas.
Royalties paid annually.

Franklin Watts

(A Division of Grolier Publishing),
Sherman Turnpike, Danbury CT 06813
☎001 203 797 3500   Fax 001 203 797 6986
Vice President/Publisher *John W. Selfridge*
FOUNDED 1942 and acquired by **Grolier** in 1975. *Publishes* non-fiction: curriculum-based material for ages 5–18 across a wide range of subjects, including history, social sciences, natural and physical sciences, health and medicine, biography. Over 100 titles a year. No unsolicited mss. Synopses and ideas considered. Address samples to 'Submissions' and include IRCs if response required. Be prepared for a three-month turnaround.
Royalties paid twice-yearly.

Rob Weisbach Books
See **William Morrow & Co., Inc.**

Wesleyan University Press
See **University Press of New England**

J. Weston Walch, Publisher

321 Valley Street, PO Box 658, Portland
ME 04104-0658
☎001 207 772 2846   Fax 001 207 772 3105
President *Suzanne Austin*
Editor-in-Chief *Joan Whitney*
Acquisitions Editors, *Kate O'Halloran, Elizabeth Isele, Lisa French*
FOUNDED 1927. *Publishes* supplementary educational materials for secondary schools across a wide range of subjects, including art, business, technology, careers, literacy, mathematics, science, music, social studies, special needs, etc. Always interested in ideas from secondary school teachers who develop materials in the classroom. About 70 titles a year. Unsolicited mss, synopses and ideas welcome.
Royalties paid twice-yearly.

Wyatt Books
See **St Martin's Press, Inc.**

Zondervan Publishing House

5300 Patterson Avenue SE, Grand Rapids
MI 49530
☎001 616 698 6900   Fax 001 616 698 3421

President/Chief Executive *Bruce E. Ryskamp*
FOUNDED 1931. Subsidiary of **HarperCollins Publishers, Inc.** *Publishes* Protestant religion, Bibles, books, audio & video, computer software, calendars and speciality items.

US Agents

Adler & Robin Books, Inc.

3000 Connecticut Avenue, Suite 317,
Washington DC 20008
☎001 202 986 9275   Fax 001 202 986 9485
President/Agent *Bill Adler Jr*
Senior Agent *Lisa Swayne*

FOUNDED 1988. *Handles* popular adult fiction
and non-fiction. Unsolicited synopses and
queries welcome. Send letter with outline or
proposal and sample chapters if possible.
Electronic submissions accepted. No reading
fee. CLIENTS H. Michael Fruse, Richard
Laermer, Arthur J. Magida, W. S. Penn.
Commission Home 15%; UK 20%.

The Ahearn Agency, Inc.

2021 Pine Street, New Orleans LA 70118
☎001 504 861 8395   Fax 001 504 866 6434
President *Pamela G. Ahearn*

FOUNDED 1992. *Handles* general and genre fiction, and non-fiction. Particularly interested in
women's fiction, suspense fiction and historical
romance. No children's books, poetry, autobiography, plays, screenplays or short fiction.
Reading fee charged to unpublished authors.
Send brief query letter with s.a.e. for reply in
the first instance. CLIENTS include John Ames,
Meagan McKinney, Laura Joh Rowland, Marc
Vargo. *Commission* Home 15%; Translation
and UK 20%. *Overseas associates* in Europe and
Latin America.

Marcia Amsterdam Agency

Suite 9A, 41 West 82nd Street, New York
NY 10024
☎001 212 873 4945
Contact *Marcia Amsterdam*

FOUNDED 1969. *Specialises* in mainstream fiction, horror, suspense, humour, young adult,
TV and film scripts. No poetry, books for the
8–10 age group or how-to. No unsolicited
mss. First approach by letter only and enclose
IRCs. No reading fee for outlines and synopses. CLIENTS include George Burt, James
Hatfield, Ruby Jean Jensen, Robert Leininger,
William H. Lovejoy, Isaac Millman, Patricia
Rowe, Joyce Sweeney. *Commission* Home
15%; Dramatic 10%; Foreign 20%.

Bart Andrews & Associates

7510 Sunset Boulevard 100, Los Angeles
CA 90046
☎001 213 271 9916
Contact *Bart Andrews*

FOUNDED 1982. General non-fiction: show
business, biography and autobiography, film
books, trivia, TV and nostalgia. No scripts. No
fiction, poetry, children's or science. No books
of less than major commercial potential.
Specialises in working with celebrities on autobiographies. No unsolicited mss. 'Send a brilliant
letter (with IRCs for response) extolling your
manuscript's virtues. Sell me!' CLIENTS include
J. Randy Taraborrelli, Wayne Newton, Bart
Andrews. No reading fee. *Commission* Home &
Translation 15%. *Overseas associates* **Abner Stein**,
London.

Joseph Anthony Agency

15 Locust Court Road, 20 Mays Landing,
New Jersey NJ 08330
☎001 609 625 7608
Contact *Joseph Anthony*

FOUNDED 1964. *Handles* all types of novel and
scripts for TV: 2-hour mini-series, screenplays
and ½-hour sitcoms. No poetry, short stories
or pornography. *Specialises* in action, romance
and detective novels. Last sale to **Silhouette
Books** by writer Karen Alaire. Unsolicited mss
welcome. Return postage essential. Reading
fee charged to new writers: novels $85; screen-
plays $100. CLIENTS include Ed Adair, Robert
Long, Joseph McCullough, Sandi Wether.
Signatory of the Writer's Guild of America.
Commission Home 15%; Dramatic &
Translation 20%.

The Artists Group

10100 Santa Monica Boulevard, Suite 2490,
Los Angeles CA 90067
☎001 310 552 1100   Fax 001 213 277 9513
Contact *Robert Malcolm, Hal Stalmaster*

FOUNDED 1978. Screenplays and plays for film
and TV. No unsolicited mss. Write with list of
credits, if any. No reading fee. *Commission*
10%.

Author Aid Associates
340 East 52nd Street, New York NY 10022
☎001 212 758 4213/980 9179

President/Editorial Director *Arthur Orrmont*

FOUNDED 1967. *Handles* fiction and non-fiction, both children's and adult, scripts for film, TV and theatre. No cookbooks, computing. No unsolicited mss. Advance query essential. Reading fee charged to new/unpublished authors. *Commission* Home 15%; Dramatic & Translation 20%.

Malaga Baldi Literary Agency
2112 Broadway, Suite 403, New York NY 10023
☎001 212 579 5075

Contact *Malaga Baldi*

FOUNDED 1986. *Handles* quality fiction and non-fiction. No scripts. No westerns, men's adventure, science fiction/fantasy, romance, how-to, young adult or children's. Writers of fiction should send mss with covering letter, including IRCs for return of mss and stamped addressed postcard for notification of receipt. Allow ten weeks minimum for response. For non-fiction, approach in writing with a proposal, table of contents and two sample chapters. No reading fee. CLIENTS include Margaret Erhart, Daniel Harris, Felice Picano, Daniel Pool, David J. Skal. *Commission* 15%. *Overseas associates* **Abner Stein**, **Marsh & Sheil Ltd**, London; Japan Uni.

The Balkin Agency, Inc.
PO Box 222, Amherst MA 01004
☎001 413 548 9835   Fax 001 413 548 9836

Contact *Richard Balkin*

FOUNDED 1973. *Handles* adult non-fiction only. No reading fee for outlines and synopses. *Commission* Home 15%; Foreign 20%.

Maximilian Becker Agency
See **Aleta M. Daley**

Meredith Bernstein Literary Agency, Inc.
2112 Broadway, Suite 503A, New York NY 10023
☎001 212 799 1007   Fax 001 212 799 1145

Contact *Meredith Bernstein, Elizabeth Cavanaugh*

FOUNDED 1981. Fiction and non-fiction of all types. Send query letter first; unpublished authors welcome. IRCs essential for response.

CLIENTS include Marilyn Campbell, Georgina Gentry, Patricia Ireland, David Jacobs, Nancy Pickard. *Commission* Home & Dramatic 15%; Translation 20%. *Overseas associates* **Abner Stein**, London; Lennart Sane, Holland, Scandinavia and Spanish language; Thomas Schluck, Germany; Bardon Chinese Media Agency; William Miller, Japan; Frederique Porretta, France; Agenzia Letteraria, Italy.

Reid Boates Literary Agency
PO Box 328, 69 Cooks Crossroad, Pittstown NJ 08867-0328
☎001 908 730 8523   Fax 001 908 730 8931

Contact *Reid Boates*

FOUNDED 1985. *Handles* general fiction and non-fiction. *Specialises* in journalism and media, serious self-help, biography and autobiography, true crime and adventure, popular science, current affairs, trade reference and quality fiction. No scripts. No science fiction, fantasy, romance, western, gothic, children's or young adult. Enquire by letter with IRCs in first instance. No reading fee. CLIENTS include Dr James Rippe, Stephen Singular, Jon Winokur and the estate of Ava Gardner. *Commission* Home & Dramatic 15%; Translation 20%. *Overseas associates* **David Grossman Literary Agency Ltd**, **The Marsh Agency** (Paul Marsh), London; Japan Uni.

Georges Borchardt, Inc.
136 East 57th Street, New York NY 10022
☎001 212 753 5785   Fax 001 212 838 6518

FOUNDED 1967. Works mostly with established/published authors. *Specialises* in fiction, biography, and general non-fiction of unusual interest. Unsolicited mss not read. *Commission* Home, UK, Dramatic 15%; Translation 20%. *UK associates* **Sheil Land Associates Ltd** (Richard Scott Simon), London.

Brandt & Brandt Literary Agents, Inc.
1501 Broadway, New York NY 10036
☎001 212 840 5760   Fax 001 212 840 5776

Contact *Carl D. Brandt, Gail Hochman, Marianne Merola, Charles Schlessiger*

FOUNDED 1914. *Handles* non-fiction and fiction. No poetry or children's books. No unsolicited mss. Approach by letter describing background and ambitions. No reading fee. *Commission* Home & Dramatic 15%; Foreign 20%. *UK associates* **A. M. Heath & Co. Ltd**.

Pema Browne Ltd

Pine Road, HCR Box 104B, Neversink NY 12765

☎001 914 985 2936 Fax 001 914 985 7635

Contact *Pema Browne, Perry Browne*

FOUNDED 1966. *Handles* mass-market mainstream and hardcover fiction: romance, men's adventure, horror, humour, westerns, children's picture books and young adult; non-fiction: how-to, politics, religion and reference; also scripts for film. No unsolicited mss; send query letter with IRCs. Also handles illustrators' work. CLIENTS include Eilene Hehl, Valerie Mangrum, Catherine Toothman. *Commission* Home & Translation 15%; Dramatic 10%; Overseas authors 20%.

Sheree Bykofsky Associates, Inc.

11 East 47th Street, New York NY 10017

☎001 212 308 1253

Contact *Sheree Bykofsky*

FOUNDED 1985. *Handles* adult fiction and non-fiction. No scripts. No children's, young adult, horror, science fiction, romance, westerns, occult or supernatural. *Specialises* in popular reference, self-help, psychology, biography and highly commercial or highly literary fiction. No unsolicited mss. Send query letter first with brief synopsis or outline and writing sample (1–3 pp) for fiction. IRCs essential for reply or return of material. No phone calls. No reading fee. CLIENTS include Joy Behar, Richard Carlson & Benjamin Shield, Martin Edelston, Glenn Ellenbogen, Merrill Furman, Don Gabor, Alan Lakein, Ed Morrow. *Commission* Home 15%; UK (including sub-agent's fee) 25%. Member A.A.R.

Maria Carvainis Agency, Inc.

235 West End Avenue, New York NY 10023

☎001 212 580 1559 Fax 001 212 877 3486

Contact *Maria Carvainis*

FOUNDED 1977. *Handles* fiction: literary and mainstream, contemporary women's, mystery, suspense, fantasy, historical, children's and young adult novels; non-fiction: business, finance, women's issues, political and film biography, medicine, psychology and popular science. No film scripts unless from writers with established credits. No science fiction. No unsolicited mss; they will be returned unread. Queries only, with IRCs for response. No reading fee. *Commission* Domestic & Dramatic 15%; Translation 20%.

Martha Casselman, Literary Agent

PO Box 342, Calistoga CA 94515-0342

☎001 707 942 4341

Contact *Martha Casselman*

FOUNDED 1979. *Handles* all types of non-fiction. No fiction at present. Main interests: food/cookery, biography, current affairs, popular sociology. No scripts, textbooks, poetry, coming-of-age fiction or science fiction. Especially interested in cookery with an appeal to the American market for possible co-publication in UK. Send queries and brief summary, with return postage. No mss. If you do not wish return of material, please state so. Also include, where applicable, any material on previous publications, reviews, brief biography. No proposals via fax. No reading fee. *Commission* Home 15%.

The Catalog Literary Agency

PO Box 2964, Vancouver WA 98668

☎001 360 694 8531

Contact *Douglas Storey*

FOUNDED 1986. *Handles* popular, professional and textbook material in all subjects, especially business, health, money, science, technology, computers, electronics and women's interests; also how-to, self-help, mainstream fiction and children's non-fiction. No genre fiction. No scripts, articles, screenplays, plays, poetry or short stories. No reading fee. No unsolicited mss. Query with an outline and sample chapters and include IRCs. CLIENTS include Don Brown, Malcolm S. Foster, Deborah Wallace. *Commission* 15%.

The Linda Chester Literary Agency

Rockefeller Center, 660 Fifth Avenue, 37th Floor, New York NY 10103

☎001 219 439 0881 Fax 001 212 439 9858

Contact *Joanna Pulcini*

FOUNDED 1978. *Handles* literary and commercial fiction and non-fiction in all subjects. No scripts, children's or textbooks. No unsolicited mss. No reading fee for solicited material. *Commission* Home & Dramatic 15%; Translation 25%.

Connie Clausen & Associates

250 East 87th Street, Apt. 16H, New York NY 10128

☎001 212 427 6135 Fax 001 212 996 7111

Founder *Connie Clausen*
Principal Associate *Stedman Mays*

Junior Associate *Kristina Richards*

Handles non-fiction work such as memoirs, bi-ography, true crime, true stories, how-to, psychology, spirituality, relationships, style, health/nutrition, fashion/beauty, women's issues, humour and cookbooks. No fiction. Books include Quentin Crisp's *Resident Alien; What the IRS Doesn't Want You to Know* Marty Kaplin and Naomi Weiss; *A Flat Stomach ASAP: The Fastest Way to Perfect Abs* Ellington Darden. Send query letter only. Include IRCs.

UK associates **David Grossman Literary Agency Ltd**.

Hy Cohen Literary Agency Ltd
PO Box 43770, Up. Montclair NJ 07043
☎001 201 783 9494   Fax 001 201 783 9867

President *Hy Cohen*

FOUNDED 1975. Fiction and non-fiction. No scripts. Unsolicited mss welcome, but synopsis with sample 100 pp preferred. IRCs essential. No reading fee. *Commission* Home & Dramatic 10%; Foreign 20%. *Overseas associates* **Abner Stein**, London.

Ruth Cohen, Inc.
Box 7626, Menlo Park CA 94025
☎001 415 854 2054

President *Ruth Cohen*

FOUNDED 1982. Works mostly with established/published authors but will consider new writers. *Specialises* in high-quality children's, young adult and women's fiction, plus genre fiction: mystery and historical romance. No poetry, short stories or film scripts. No unsolicited mss. Send opening 10 pp with synopsis. Include enough IRCs for return postage or materials will not be returned. No reading fee. *Commission* Home & Dramatic 15%; Foreign 20%.

Frances Collin Literary Agent
PO Box 33, Wayne PA 19087–0033
☎001 610 254 0555   Fax 001 610 254 5029

Contact *Frances Collin*

FOUNDED 1948. Successor to Marie Rodell. *Handles* general fiction and non-fiction. No scripts. No unsolicited mss. Send query letter only, with IRCs for reply, for the attention of Marsha Kear. No reading fee. Rarely accepts non-professional writers or writers not represented in the UK. *Overseas associates* worldwide.

Don Congdon Associates, Inc.
156 Fifth Avenue, Suite 625, New York NY 10010–7002
☎001 212 645 1229   Fax 001 212 727 2688

Contact *Don Congdon, Michael Congdon, Susan Ramer*

FOUNDED 1983. *Handles* fiction and non-fiction. No academic, technical, romantic fiction, or scripts. No unsolicited mss. Approach by letter in the first instance. No reading fee. *Commission* Home 10%; UK & Translation 19%. *Overseas associates* **The Marsh Agency** (Europe), **Abner Stein** (UK), Michelle Lapautre (France), Tuttle Mori Agency (Japan).

The Connor Literary Agency
2911 West 71st Street, Rockfield MN 55423
☎001 612 866 1486   Fax 001 612 869 4074

Contact *Marlene Connor, John Lynch*

FOUNDED 1985. *Handles* general non-fiction, contemporary women's fiction, popular fiction, Black fiction and non-fiction, how-to, mysteries and crafts. Particularly interested in illustrated books. No unsolicited mss; send query letter in the first instance. Previously published authors preferred. CLIENTS include Simplicity Pattern Company, *Essence Magazine*, Bonnie Allen, Ron Elmore, Nadezda Obradovic. *Commission* Home 15%; UK & Translation 25%. *Overseas associates* in England, Spain, Japan, France and Germany.

Richard Curtis Associates, Inc
171 East 74th Street, Second Floor, New York NY 10021
☎001 212 772 7363   Fax 001 212 772 7393

Contact *Richard Curtis*

FOUNDED 1969. *Handles* genre and mainstream fiction, plus commercial non-fiction. Scripts rarely. *Specialises* in electronic rights and multi-media.

Curtis Brown Ltd
10 Astor Place, New York NY 10003
☎001 212 473 5400

Book Rights *Laura Blake, Ellen Geiger, Peter L. Ginsberg, Emilie Jacobson, Ginger Knowlton, Perry Knowlton, Jennifer McDonald, Marilyn E. Marlow, Andrew Pope, Clyde Taylor, Maureen Walters, Mitchell Walters*
Film, TV, Audio Rights *Timothy Knowlton, Jess Taylor*
Translation *Dave Barbor*

FOUNDED 1914. *Handles* general fiction and non-fiction. Also some scripts for film, TV and theatre. No unsolicited mss; queries only, with IRCs for reply. No reading fee. *Overseas associates* representatives in all major foreign countries.

Aleta M. Daley/Maximilian Becker Agency

444 East 82nd Street, New York NY 10028
☎001 212 744 1453   Fax 001 212 249 2088

Contact *Aleta M. Daley*

FOUNDED 1950. *Handles* non-fiction and fiction; also scripts for film and TV. No unsolicited mss. Send query letter in the first instance with sample chapters or a proposal. No reading fee, but handling fee is charged to cover postage, telephone, etc. *Commission* Home 15%; UK 20%.

Joan Daves Agency

21 West 26th Street, New York
NY 10010-1003
☎001 212 685 2663   Fax 001 212 685 1781

Director *Jennifer Lyons*
Assistant *Edward Lee*

FOUNDED 1952. Literary fiction and non-fiction. No romance or textbooks. No scripts. Send query letter in the first instance. 'A detailed synopsis seems valuable only for non-fiction work. Material submitted should specify the author's background, publishing credits and similar pertinent information.' No reading fee. CLIENTS include Frederick Franck, Frank Browning, Suzy McKee Charnas, Mike Maples, Elizabeth Holtzman, Melvin Jules Bukret, Jeff Weinstein and the estates of Isaac Babel, Heinrich Böll and Martin Luther King Jr. *Commission* Home 15%; Dramatic 10–25%; Foreign 20%.

Elaine Davie Literary Agency

620 Park Avenue, Rochester NY 14607
☎001 716 442 0830

President *Elaine Davie*

FOUNDED 1986. *Handles* all types of adult fiction and non-fiction, specialising in books by and for women. Particularly interested in commercial genre fiction. No scripts. No short stories, anthologies, poetry or children's. Submit synopsis and sample chapters or complete mss together with IRCs. No reading fee.
    Commission Home 15%; Dramatic & Translation 20%.

Anita Diamant Literary Agency

Suite 1105, 310 Madison Avenue, New York
NY 10017
☎001 212 687 1122

Contact *John Talbot, Robin Rue*

FOUNDED 1917. *Handles* fiction and non-fiction. No academic, children's, science fiction and fantasy, poetry, articles, short stories, screenplays or teleplays. Works in association with Hollywood film agent. No unsolicited mss. Write with description of work, short synopsis and details of publishing background. No reading fee. CLIENTS include V. C. Andrews, Frederic Bean, Linda Howard, William W. Johnstone, Janice Kaiser, Richard Lederer, Mark McGarrity, Andrew Neiderman, Duane Schultz, Richard S. Wheeler. *Commission* Home & Dramatic 15%; Translation 20%. *Overseas associates* **A. M. Heath & Co. Ltd**, London.

Sandra Dijkstra Literary Agency

1155 Camino del Mar, Suite 515–C,
Del Mar CA 92014
☎001 619 755 3115

Contact *Debra Ginsberg*

FOUNDED 1981. *Handles* quality and commercial non-fiction and fiction, including some genre fiction. No scripts. No westerns, contemporary romance or poetry. Willing to look at children's projects. *Specialises* in quality fiction, mystery/thrillers, psychology, self-help, science, health, business, memoirs, biography. Dedicated to promoting new and original voices and ideas. For fiction: send brief synopsis (1 page) and first 50 pages; for non-fiction: send proposal with overview, chapter outline, author biog. and two sample chapters. All submissions should be accompanied by IRCs. No reading fee. *Commission* Home 15%; Translation 20%. *Overseas associates* **Abner Stein**, London; Ursula Bender, Agence Hoffman, Germany; Monica Heyum, Scandinavia; Luigi Bernabo, Italy; M. Casanovas, Spain; Caroline Van Gelderen, Netherlands; M. Kling (La Nouvelle Agence), France; William Miller, The English Agency, Japan.

Dykeman Associates, Inc.

4115 Rawlins, Dallas TX 75219-3661
☎001 214 528 2991   Fax 001 214 528 0241

Contact *Alice Dykeman*

FOUNDED 1974. *Handles* non-fiction, namely celebrity profiles and biographies, fiction and movie scripts. No unsolicited mss; send outline or synopsis. Reading fee of $60 charged for manuscripts (not movie scripts). *Commission* 15%.

Jane Dystel Literary Management

One Union Square West, Suite 904, New
York NY 10003
☎001 212 627 9100   Fax 001 212 627 9313

Contact *Jane Dystel, Miriam Goderich, Eliza Scott*

FOUNDED 1975. *Handles* non-fiction and fiction. *Specialises* in politics, history, biography, cookbooks, current affairs, celebrities, commercial and literary fiction. No reading fee. CLIENTS include Lorene Cary, Thomas French, Dan Gearino, Lynne Rossetto Kasper, Gus Lee, Alice Medrich, Thomas Moran, Barack Obama, Mary Russell, Elaine St James, Michael Tucker.

Educational Design Services, Inc.
PO Box 253, Wantagh NY 11793
☎001 718 539 4107/516 221 0995

President Bertram Linder
Vice President Edwin Selzer

FOUNDED 1979. Specialises in educational material and textbooks for sale to school markets. IRCs must accompany submissions. Commission Home 15%; Foreign 25%.

Elek International Rights Agents
457 Broome Street, New York NY 10013
☎001 212 431 9368   Fax 001 212 966 5768

Contact Nicola Nonhoff

FOUNDED 1979. Handles adult non-fiction and children's picture books. No scripts, novels, psychology, New Age, poetry, short stories or autobiography. No unsolicited mss; send letter of enquiry with IRCs for reply; include résumé, credentials, brief synopsis. No reading fee. CLIENTS Tedd Arnold, Dr Robert Ballard, Patrick Brogan, Robert Bateman, Laura Cornell, Chris Dodd, Sally Placksin. Commission Home 15%; Dramatic & Foreign 20%. Through wholly-owned subsidiary The Content Company Inc., licenses and manages clients' intellectual property for development into electronic formats – CD-ROM/CD-I/DVD/On-Line/CD-Plus, etc.

Ann Elmo Agency, Inc.
60 East 42nd Street, New York NY 10165
☎001 212 661 2880/1 Fax 001 212 661 2883

Contact Lettie Lee, Mari Cronin, Andree Abecassis

FOUNDED in the 1940s. Handles literary and romantic fiction, mysteries and mainstream; also non-fiction in all subjects, including biography and self-help. Some children's (8–12-year-olds) and young adult. Query letter with outline of project in the first instance. No reading fee. Commission Home 15–20%. Overseas associates **John Johnson Ltd**, London.

Frieda Fishbein Associates
PO Box 723, Bedford NY 10506
☎001 914 234 7232   Fax 001 914 234 4196

President Janice Fishbein

Associates Heidi Carlson, Douglas Michael

FOUNDED 1925. Eager to work with new/unpublished writers. Specialises in historical romance, historical adventure, male adventure, mysteries, thrillers, family sagas, 'non-reporting' and how-to. Also plays and screenplays. No poetry, magazine articles, short stories or young children's. First approach with query letter. No reading fee for outlines at our request or for published authors working in the same genre. CLIENTS include Gary Bohlke, Lisa Dillman, Herbert Fisher, Jeanne Mackin, William Seebring, Robert Simpson, Alicen White. Commission Home & Dramatic 10%; Foreign 20%.

Flannery, White & Stone Literary Agency
1675 Larimer Street, Suite 410, Denver CO 80202
☎001 303 571 4001   Fax 001 303 534 0577

Contact Robin Ann Barrett, Connie Solowiej

FOUNDED 1987. Handles literary and mainstream fiction, children's, general non-fiction and business. No poetry, theatre or radio. No pornography. Call or write with query in first instance. No unsolicited mss. Commission Home 15%; Dramatic & Translation 20%.

ForthWrite Literary Agency
3579 E. Foothill Boulevard, Suite 327, Pasadena CA 91107
☎001 818 795 2646   Fax 001 818 795 5311

Contact Wendy Keller

FOUNDED 1988. Specialises in non-fiction: business (marketing, management and sales), alternative health, popular psychology, history (English and Scottish), self-help, home and health, crafts, computer, how-to, animal care. Handles electronic, foreign (translation and distribution) and resale rights for previously published books. Send query letter with IRCs. Commission Home & Dramatic 15%; Translation 20%.

Robert A. Freedman Dramatic Agency, Inc.
Suite 2310, 1501 Broadway, New York NY 10036
☎001 212 840 5760

President Robert A. Freedman
Vice President Selma Luttinger

FOUNDED 1928 as Brandt & Brandt Dramatic Department, Inc.. Took its present name in 1984. Works mostly with established authors. Specialises in plays, film and TV scripts. Unsolicited mss not read. *Commission* Dramatic 10%.

Max Gartenberg, Literary Agent
521 Fifth Avenue, Suite 1700, New York NY 10175
☎001 212 860 8451   Fax 001 201 535 5033
Contact *Max Gartenberg*
FOUNDED 1954. Works mostly with established/published authors. *Specialises* in non-fiction and trade fiction. Query first. CLIENTS include Linda Davis, Ralph Hickok, Charles Little, Howard Owen, David Roberts, Ralph Sawyer. *Commission* Home & Dramatic 10%; 15% on initial sale, 10% thereafter; Foreign 15/20%.

Gelfman Schneider Literary Agents, Inc.
250 West 57th Street, Suite 2515, New York NY 10107
☎001 212 245 1993   Fax 001 212 245 8678
Contact *Deborah Schneider, Jane Gelfman*
FOUNDED 1919 (London), 1980 (New York). Formerly John Farquharson Ltd. Works mostly with established/published authors. *Specialises* in general trade fiction and non-fiction. No poetry, short stories or screenplays. No reading fee for outlines. Submissions must be accompanied by IRCs. *Commission* Home 15%; Dramatic 15%; Foreign 20%. *Overseas associates* **Curtis Brown Group Ltd**, London.

Lucianne Goldberg Literary Agents, Inc.
255 West 84th Street, New York NY 10024
☎001 212 799 1260
Editorial Director *Kathrine Butler*
FOUNDED 1974. *Handles* fiction and non-fiction. No unsolicited mss. Send query letter describing work in the first instance. *Commission* Home 10%; UK 20%. *Overseas associate* Peter Knight, London.

Sanford J. Greenburger Associates, Inc.
15th Floor, 55 Fifth Avenue, New York NY 10003
☎001 212 206 5600   Fax 001 212 463 8718
Contact *Heide Lange, Faith Hamlin, Beth Vesel, Theresa Park*
Handles fiction and non-fiction. No unsolicited mss. First approach with query letter, sample chapter and synopsis. No reading fee.

The Charlotte Gusay Literary Agency
10532 Blythe Avenue, Los Angeles CA 90064
☎001 310 559 0831   Fax 001 310 559 2639
Contact *Charlotte Gusay*
FOUNDED 1988. *Handles* fiction, both literary and commercial, plus non-fiction: children's and adult humour, parenting, gardening, women's and men's issues, feminism, psychology, memoirs, biography, travel. No science fiction, horror, short pieces or collections of stories. No unsolicited mss; send query letter first, then if your material is requested, send succinct outline and first three sample chapters for fiction, or proposal for non-fiction. No response without IRCs. No reading fee. *Commission* Home 15%; Dramatic 10%; Translation & Foreign 25%.

Joy Harris Literary Agency
See **Robert Lantz**

John Hawkins & Associates, Inc.
71 West 23rd Street, Suite 1600, New York NY 10010
☎001 212 807 7040   Fax 001 212 807 9555
Contact *John Hawkins, William Reiss*
FOUNDED 1893. *Handles* film and TV rights and software. No unsolicited mss; send queries with 1–3 page outline and 1 page c.v.. IRCs necessary for response. No reading fee. *Commission* Apply for rates.

Heacock Literary Agency, Inc.
1523 Sixth Street, Suite 14, Santa Monica CA 90401
☎001 310 393 6227/451 8523
Fax 001 310 451 8524
President *Rosalie G. Heacock*
FOUNDED 1978. Works with a small number of new/unpublished authors. *Specialises* in non-fiction on a wide variety of subjects: new ideas, new ways of solving problems, futurism, art criticism and techniques, health, nutrition, beauty, women's studies, popular psychology, crafts, celebrity biographies. No unsolicited mss. Queries with IRCs only. No reading fee. *Commission* Home 15% on first $50,000 each year, 10% thereafter; Foreign 15% if sold direct, 25% if agent used.

The Jeff Herman Agency, Inc.
140 Charles Street, Suite 15A, New York NY 10014
☎001 212 941 0540   Fax 001 212 941 0614
Contact *Jeffrey H. Herman*

Handles non-fiction, textbooks and reference and commercial fiction. No scripts. No unsolicited mss. Query letter with IRCs in the first instance. No reading fee. Jeff Herman publishes a useful reference guide to the book trade called *The Insider's Guide to Book Editors, Publishers & Literary Agents* (Prima). *Commission* Home 15%; Translation 10%.

Susan Herner Rights Agency, Inc.
PO Box 303, Scarsdale NY 10583
☎001 914 725 8967   Fax 001 914 725 8969
Contact *Susan N. Herner, Sue P. Yuen*

FOUNDED 1987. Adult fiction and non-fiction in all areas. No children's books. *Handles* film and TV rights and software. Send query letter with outline and sample chapters. No reading fee. *Commission* Home 15%; Dramatic & Translation 20%. *Overseas associates* **David Grossman Literary Agency Ltd**, London.

Frederick Hill Associates
1842 Union Street, San Francisco CA 94123
☎001 415 921 2910   Fax 001 415 921 2802
Contact *Fred Hill, Bonnie Nadell*

FOUNDED 1979. General fiction and non-fiction. No scripts. Send query letter detailing past publishing history if any. IRCs required. CLIENTS include Katherine Neville, Richard North Patterson, Randy Shilts. *Commission* Home & Dramatic 15%; Foreign 20%. *Overseas associates* **Mary Clemmey Literary Agency**, London.

Hull House Literary Agency
240 East 82nd Street, New York NY 10028
☎001 212 988 0725   Fax 001 212 794 8758
President *David Stewart Hull*
Associate *Lydia Mortimer*

FOUNDED 1987. *Handles* commercial fiction, mystery, biography, military history and true crime. No scripts, poetry, short stories, romance, science fiction and fantasy, children's or young adult. No unsolicited mss; send single-page letter describing project briefly, together with short biographical note and list of previous publications if any. IRCs essential. No reading fee. *Commission* Home 15%; Translation 20%.

IMG Literary
22 East 71st Street, New York NY 10021–4911
☎001 212 772 8900   Fax 001 212 772 2617
Contact *David Chalfant (Vice President), Meghan Sercombe*

FOUNDED 1986. *Handles* non-fiction and fiction. No science fiction, fantasy, poetry or photography. No scripts. Query first. Submissions should include brief synopsis (typed), sample chapters (50 pp maximum), publishing history, etc. Send IRCs for return. CLIENTS include Pat Conroy, Jan Morris, Arnold Palmer, Dianne Pugh, Tiger Woods. *Commission* Home & Dramatic 15%; Foreign 20%. *Overseas associates* worldwide.

Kidde, Hoyt & Picard Literary Agency
333 East 51st Street, New York NY 10022
☎001 212 755 9461/9465
Fax 001 212 223 2501
Chief Associate *Katharine Kidde*
Associate *Laura Langlie*

FOUNDED 1981. *Specialises* in mainstream and literary fiction, romantic fiction (historical and contemporary), and quality non-fiction in humanities and social sciences (biography, history, current affairs, the arts). No reading fee. Query first, include s.a.e.. CLIENTS include Michael Cadnum, Bethany Campbell, Jim Oliver, Patricia Robinson. *Commission* 15%.

Daniel P. King
5125 North Cumberland Boulevard, Whitefish Bay WI 53217
☎001 414 964 2903   Fax 001 414 964 6860
President *Daniel P. King*

FOUNDED 1974. *Specialises* in mystery and non-fiction books on crime and espionage. Also handles mainstream fiction including crime/mystery and science fiction. Scripts handled by representative office in Beverly Hills, California. No unsolicited mss. Send synopsis or sample chapter first or (and preferably) a concise letter (1–2 pages) describing the book. No reading fee unless an author wants a critique on his material. CLIENTS include John Bonnet, Ella Griffiths, Cyril Joyce. *Commission* Home & Dramatic 10%; Foreign 20%.

Kirchoff/Wohlberg, Inc.
866 United Nations Plaza, Suite 525, New York NY 10017
☎001 212 644 2020   Fax 001 212 223 4387
Authors' Representative *Elizabeth Pulitzer-Voges*

FOUNDED 1930. *Handles* books for children and young adults, specialising in children's picture books. No adult material. No scripts for TV, radio, film or theatre. Send letter of enquiry with synopsis or outline and IRCs for reply or return. No reading fee.

Paul Kohner, Inc.

9300 Wilshire Boulevard, Suite 555, Beverly Hills CA 90212

☎001 310 550 1060   Fax 001 310 276 1083

Contact *Gary Salt, Beth Bohn*

FOUNDED 1938. *Handles* a broad range of books for subsidiary rights sales to film and TV. Few direct placements with publishers as film and TV scripts are the major part of the business. *Specialises* in true crime, biography and history. Non-fiction preferred to fiction for the TV market but anything 'we feel has strong potential' will be considered. No short stories, poetry, science fiction or gothic. Unsolicited material will be returned unread, if accompanied by s.a.e.. Approach via a third-party reference or send query letter with professional résumé. No reading fee. CLIENTS Ed McBain, Tony Huston, John Katzenbach, Charles Marowitz, Alan Sharp, Donald Westlake. *Commission* Home & Dramatic 10%; Publishing 15%.

Barbara S. Kouts, Literary Agent

PO Box 560, Bellport NY 11713

☎001 516 286 1278   Fax 001 516 286 1538

Contact *Barbara S. Kouts*

FOUNDED 1980. *Handles* fiction, non-fiction and children's. No romance, science fiction or scripts. No unsolicited mss. Query letter in the first instance. No reading fee. CLIENTS include Hal Gieseking, Nancy Mairs, Robert San Souci. *Commission* Home 10%; Foreign 20%.

Peter Lampack Agency, Inc.

551 Fifth Avenue, Suite 1613, New York NY 10176

☎001 212 687 9106   Fax 001 212 687 9109

Contact *Peter Lampack, Sandra Blanton*

FOUNDED in 1977. *Handles* commercial fiction: male action and adventure, contemporary relationships, historical, mysteries and suspense, literary fiction; also non-fiction from recognised experts in a given field, plus biographies, autobiographies. Also handles theatrical, motion picture, and TV rights from book properties. No original scripts or screenplays, series or episodic material. Best approach by letter in first instance. Include s.a.e.. 'We will respond within three weeks and invite the submission of manuscripts which we would like to examine.' No reading fee. CLIENTS include J. M. Coetzee, Clive Cussler, Martha Grimes, Judith Kelman, Johanna Kingsley, Jessica March, Doris Mortman, David Osborn, Gerry Spence, Fred Mustard Stewart. *Commission* Home & Dramatic 15%; Translation & UK 20%.

Robert Lantz/Joy Harris Literary Agency, Inc.

156 Fifth Avenue, Suite 617, New York NY 10010

☎001 212 924 6269   Fax 001 212 924 6609

Contact *Joy Harris*

Handles adult non-fiction and fiction. No unsolicited mss. Query letter in the first instance. No reading fee. *Commission* Home & Dramatic 15%; Foreign 20%. *Overseas associates* Michael Meller, Germany; **Abner Stein**, London; Tuttle Mori, Japan/China; Eliane Benisti, France.

The Lazear Agency, Inc.

430 First Avenue North, Suite 416, Minneapolis MN 55401

☎001 612 332 8640   Fax 001 612 332 4648

Contact *Christi Cardenas, Cheryl Kissel, Jonathon Lazear, Wendy Lazear, Jeff McGuiness, Susie Moncur*

FOUNDED 1984. *Handles* fiction: mysteries, suspense, young adult and literary; also true crime, addiction recovery, biography, travel, business, and scripts for film and TV, CD-ROM and CD-I, broad band interactive television. Children's books from previously published writers. No poetry or stage plays. Approach by letter, with description of mss, short autobiography and IRCs. No reading fee. CLIENTS include Noah Adams, Andrei Codrescu, Al Franken, Jane Goodall, Merrill Lynch, Harvey Mackay, Gary Paulsen, The Pillsbury Co., Will Weaver, Bailey White. *Commission* Home & Dramatic 15%; Translation 20%.

L. Harry Lee Literary Agency

PO Box 203, Rocky Point NY 11778

☎001 516 744 1188

Contacts *Charles Rothery* (science fiction), *Sue Hollister Barr* (adventure/humour/westerns), *Patti Roenbeck* (romance/mainstream/mystery/suspense), *Diane Clerke* (historical/fantasy), *Cami Calligros* (horror/erotica), *Colin James* (mainstream), *Frank Killen* (military/war); *Katie Polk* (mystery/detective), *Mary Lee Gaylor* (mainstream/contemporary), *James Kingston* (motion pictures), *Stacy Parker/Anastassia Evereaux* (TV, episodic), *Vito Brenna* (plays)

FOUNDED 1979. *Handles* adventure, westerns, horror, romance, mainstream/contemporary, science fiction, humour, detective, military, war, historical, erotica, fantasy, occult, suspense, plays, literature. Also scripts for film, TV and theatre: handles a lot of material which goes into motion pictures/TV. No gay, lesbian, feminist, confessional, religious, poetry, how-to, children's, biographies, cookery, picture or textbooks. Strictly fiction. Keen on comedy and currently looking for comedy screenplays. No unsolicited mss; query letter first with IRCs, details (a page or two), on project and one-page autobiography. Response time two weeks. Critique fee charged depending on appraisal ($250 screenplays; $130 novels, first 70–75 pp; $1.10 per page plays). CLIENTS include Luis Anguilar, James Colaneri, Steve Blower, Anastassia Evereaux, Dennis Glover, James G. Kingston, John Lubas, Charlie Purpura, Bill Tyman, Fay Van. *Commission* Novels 15%; Film & Drama 10%.

Levant & Wales, Literary Agency, Inc.
108 Hayes Street, Seattle WA 98109
☎001 206 284 7114   Fax 001 206 284 0190

Contact *Elizabeth Wales, Adrienne Reed*

FOUNDED 1988. *Handles* quality fiction and non-fiction. No scripts except via sub-agents. No genre fiction, westerns, romance, science fiction or horror. Special interest in 'Pacific Rim', West, West Coast, and Pacific Northwest clients. No unsolicited mss; send query letter with publication list and writing sample. No reading fee. *Commission* Home 15%; Dramatic & Translation 20%.

Ellen Levine, Literary Agency, Inc.
Suite 1801, 15 East 26th Street, New York NY 10010-1505
☎001 212 899 0620   Fax 001 212 725 4501

Contact *Diana Finch, Elizabeth Kaplan, Louise Quayle, Ellen Levine*

FOUNDED 1980. *Handles* all types of books. No scripts. No unsolicited mss, nor any other material unless requested. No telephone calls. First approach by letter; send US postage or IRCs for reply, otherwise material not returned. No reading fee. *Commission* Home 15%; Foreign 20%. *Overseas associates* **A. M. Heath & Co. Ltd**, London.

Ray Lincoln Literary Agency
Elkins Park House, Suite 107-B,
7900 Old York Road, Elkins Park PA 19027
☎001 215 635 0827

Contact *Mrs Ray Lincoln*

FOUNDED 1974. *Handles* adult and children's fiction and non-fiction: biography, science, nature and history. Scripts as spin-offs from book mss only. No poetry or plays unless adaptations from published book. Keenly interested

in adult biography, in all types of children's books (age five and upwards, not illustrated), in fine adult fiction, science and nature. No unsolicited mss; send query letter first, including IRCs for response. If interested, material will then be requested. No reading fee. Postage fee for projects handled by the agency. *Commission* Home & Dramatic 15%; Translation 20%.

Literary & Creative Artists Agency
3543 Albemarle Street NW,
Washington DC 20008
☎001 202 362 4688   Fax 001 202 362 8875

Contact *Muriel G. Nellis, Jane F. Roberts, Elizabeth Pokempner, Jennifer Steinbach, Jennifer Engle*

FOUNDED 1981. *Specialises* in a broad range of non-fiction. No poetry, pornography, academic or educational textbooks. No unsolicited mss; query letter in the first instance. Include IRCs for response. No reading fee. *Commission* Home 15%; Dramatic 20%; Translation 20–25%.

Sterling Lord Literistic, Inc.
65 Bleecker Street, New York NY 10012
☎001 212 780 6050

Contact *Peter Matson, Sterling Lord*

FOUNDED 1979. *Handles* all genres, fiction and non-fiction, plus scripts for TV, radio, film and theatre. Unsolicited mss will be considered. Prefers letter outlining all non-fiction. No reading fee. *Commission* Home 15%; UK & Translation 20%. *Overseas associates* **Peters Fraser & Dunlop Group Ltd**, London.

Richard P. McDonough, Literary Agent
551 Franklin Street, Cambridge MA 02139
☎001 617 354 6440   Fax 001 617 354 6607

Contact *Richard P. McDonough*

FOUNDED 1986. General non-fiction and literary fiction. No scripts. No genre fiction. No unsolicited mss; query first with three sample chapters and include IRCs. No reading fee. CLIENTS John Dufresne, Robert Gordon, Jane Holtz Kay, Mary Leonhardt, Thomas Lynch, M. R. Montgomery, William Sullivan. *Commission* 15%.

McIntosh & Otis, Inc.
310 Madison Avenue, New York NY 10017
☎001 212 687 7400   Fax 001 212 687 6894

President *Eugene H. Winick*
Adult Books *Sam Pinkus*
Children's *Dorothy Markinko, Renée Cho*
Motion Picture/Television *Evva Pryor*

FOUNDED 1928. Adult and juvenile literary

fiction and non-fiction. No textbooks or scripts. No unsolicited mss. Query letter indicating nature of the work plus details of background. IRCs for response. No reading fee.

Commission Home & Dramatic 15%; Foreign 20%. *Overseas associates* **A. M. Heath & Co. Ltd**, London.

Denise Marcil Literary Agency, Inc.

685 West End Avenue, Suite 9C, New York NY 10025
☎001 212 932 3110

President *Denise Marcil*

FOUNDED 1977. *Specialises* in non-fiction: money, business, spirituality and inspirational, health, popular reference, childcare, parenting, self-help and how-to; and commercial fiction, especially women's, and thrillers. Query letters only, with IRCs. CLIENTS include Rosanne Bittner, Arnette Lamb, Carla Neggers, Dr William Sears. *Commission* Home & Dramatic 15%; Foreign 20%.

Betty Marks

176 East 77th Street, Apt. 9F, New York NY 10021
☎001 212 535 8388

Contact *Betty Marks*

FOUNDED 1969. Works mostly with established/published authors. *Specialises* in journalists' non-fiction and novels. No unsolicited mss. Query letter and outline in the first instance. *Commission* Home 15%; Foreign 20%. *Overseas associates* **Abner Stein**, London; Mohrbooks, Germany; International Editors, Spain & Portugal; Rosemary Buchman, Europe; Tuttle Mori, Japan.

The Evan Marshall Agency

6 Tristam Place, Pine Brook NJ 07058–9445
☎001 201 882 1122   Fax 001 201 882 3099

Contact *Evan Marshall*

FOUNDED 1987. *Handles* general adult fiction and non-fiction, and scripts for film and television. No unsolicited mss; send query letter first. Handling fee charged to unpublished authors. *Commission* Home 15%; UK & Translation 20%.

Mews Books Ltd

c/o Sidney B. Kramer, 20 Bluewater Hill, Westport CT 06880
☎001 203 227 1836   Fax 001 203 227 1144

Contact *Sidney B. Kramer, Fran Pollak*

FOUNDED 1970. *Handles* adult fiction and non-

fiction, children's, pre-school and young adult. No scripts, short stories or novellas (unless by established authors). *Specialises* in cookery, medical, health and nutrition, scientific non-fiction, children's and young adult. Also handles electronic rights to published books. Unsolicited material welcome. Presentation must be professional. Partial submissions should include summary of plot/characters, one or two sample chapters, personal credentials and brief on target market. No reading fee. If material is accepted, agency asks $350 circulation fee (4–5 publishers), which will be applied against commissions (waived for published authors). Charges for photocopying, postage expenses, telephone calls and other direct costs. Principal agent is an attorney and former publisher. Offers consultation service through which writers can get advice on a contract or on publishing problems.

Commission Home 15%; Film & Translation 20%. *Overseas associates* **Abner Stein**, London.

Robert P. Mills

See **Richard Curtis Associates, Inc.**

Maureen Moran Agency

PO Box 20191, Parkwest Station, New York NY 10025
☎001 212 222 3838   Fax 001 212 222 3838

Contact *Maureen Moran*

Formerly Donald MacCampbell, Inc.. *Handles* novels only. No scripts, non-fiction, science fiction, westerns or suspense. *Specialises* in romance. No unsolicited mss; approach by letter. No reading fee. *Commission* US Book Sales 10%; First Novels US 15%.

Howard Morhaim Literary Agency

841 Broadway, Suite 604, New York NY 10003
☎001 212 529 4433   Fax 001 212 995 1112

Contact *Howard Morhaim*

FOUNDED 1979. *Handles* general adult fiction and non-fiction. No scripts. No children's or young adult material, poetry or religious. No unsolicited mss. Send query letter with synopsis and sample chapters for fiction; query letter with outline or proposal for non-fiction. No reading fee. *Commission* Home 15%; UK & Translation 20%. *Overseas associates* worldwide.

Henry Morrison, Inc.

PO Box 235, Bedford Hills NY 10507
☎001 914 666 3500   Fax 001 914 241 7846

Contact *Henry Morrison, Joan Gurgold*

FOUNDED 1965. *Handles* general fiction, crime

and science fiction, and non-fiction. No scripts unless by established writers. Unsolicited material welcome; but send query letter with outline of proposal (1–5 pp) in the first instance. No reading fee. CLIENTS Beverly Byrne, Joe Gores, Robert Ludlum. *Commission* Home 15%; UK & Translation 20%.

Ruth Nathan Agency
53 East 34th Street, Suite 207, New York NY 10016
☎001 212 481 1185   Fax 001 212 481 1185

FOUNDED 1984. *Specialises* in illustrated books, fine art & decorative arts, historical fiction with emphasis on Middle Ages, true crime, showbiz. Query first. No unsolicited mss. No reading fee. *Commission* 15%.

B. K. Nelson Literary Agency
84 Woodland Road, Pleasantville NY 10570–1322
☎001 914 741 1322   Fax 001 914 741 1324
President *Bonita K. Nelson*

FOUNDED 1979. *Specialises* in business, self-help, how-to, political, autobiography, celebrity biography. Major motion picture and TV documentary success. No unsolicited mss. Letter of inquiry. Reading fee charged. *Commission* 20%. Lecture Bureau for Authors founded 1994; Foreign Rights Catalogue established 1995; BK Nelson Infomercial Marketing Co. 1996, primarily for authors and endorsements.

New Age World Services & Books
62091 Valley View Circle #2, Joshua Tree CA 92252
☎001 619 366 2833   Fax 001 619 366 2890
Contact *Victoria E. Vandertuin*

FOUNDED 1957. New Age fiction and non-fiction, young adult fiction and non-fiction, and poetry. No scripts, drama, missionary, biography, sports, erotica, humour, travel or cookbooks. *Specialises* in New Age, self-help, health and beauty, meditation, yoga, channelling, how-to, metaphysical, occult, psychology, theology, religion, lost continents, time travel. Unsolicited mss and queries welcome. Reading fee charged. *Commission* Home 15%; Foreign 20%.

New England Publishing Associates, Inc.
Box 5, Chester CT 06412
☎001 203 345 7323   Fax 001 203 345 3660
Contact *Elizabeth Frost-Knappman, Edward W. Knappman*

FOUNDED 1983. *Handles* non-fiction and (clients only) fiction. *Specialises* in current affairs, history, science, women's studies, reference, psychology, biography, true crime. No textbooks or anthologies. No scripts. Unsolicited mss considered but query letter or phone call preferred first. No reading fee. CLIENTS include Lary Bloom, Kathryn Cullen-DuPont, Hartford Curant, Sharon Edwards, Elizabeth Lewin, Philip Ginsburg, Michael Golby, William Gross, Dandi Mackall, Mike Nevins, William Packard, John Philpin, Art Plotnik, Carl Rollyson, Robert Sherrill, Orion Magazine, Claude Summers, Ian Tattersall, Ann Waldron. *Commission* Home 15%. *Overseas associates* throughout Europe and Japan; Scott-Ferris, UK. Dramatic rights: **Renaissance**, Los Angeles.

The Betsy Nolan Literary Agency
224 West 29th Street, 15th Floor, New York NY 10001
☎001 212 967 8200   Fax 001 212 967 7292
Contact *Betsy Nolan, Carla Glasser, Donald Lehr*

FOUNDED 1980. *Specialises* in non-fiction: popular culture, music, gardening, biography, childcare, cooking, how-to. Some literary fiction, film & TV rights. No unsolicited mss. Send query letter with synopsis first. No reading fee. *Commission* Home 15%; Foreign 20%.

The Otte Co
9 Goden Street, Belmont MA 02178–3002
☎001 617 484 8505
Contact *Jane H. Otte, L. David Otte*

FOUNDED 1973. *Handles* adult fiction and non-fiction. No scripts. No unsolicited mss. Approach by letter. No reading fee. *Commission* Home 15%; Dramatic 7½%; Foreign 20%.

Richard Parks Agency
138 East 16th Street, Suite 5B, New York NY 10003
☎001 212 254 9067
Contact *Richard Parks*

FOUNDED 1989. *Handles* general trade fiction and non-fiction: literary novels, mysteries and thrillers, commercial fiction, science fiction, biography, pop culture, psychology, self-help, parenting, medical, cooking, gardening, etc. No scripts. No technical or academic. No unsolicited mss. Fiction read by referral only. No reading fee. CLIENTS include Scott Campbell, Jo Coudert, Jonathan Lethem, Abraham Rodriguez Jr, Audrey Schulman. *Commission* Home 15%; UK & Translation 20%. *Overseas associates* **Marsh & Sheil Ltd, Barbara Levy Literary Agency**.

Penmarin Books

PO Box 286, 58 Oak Grove Avenue,
Woodacre CA 94973
☎001 415 488 1628   Fax 001 415 488 1123
Contact *Hal Lockwood*

FOUNDED 1987. *Specialises* in non-fiction. No
poetry or children's; no school, scholarly or
academic books. Unsolicited mss welcome;
initial approach in writing preferred: send pro-
fessional/personal background details, project
outline or synopsis (2–3 pp), sample of past or
current writing (5–8 pp) and pre-paid return
postage. No reading fee for initial reading.
Commission 15%.

James Peter Associates, Inc.

PO Box 772, Tenafly NJ 07670
☎001 201 568 0760   Fax 001 201 568 2959
Contact *Bert Holtje*

FOUNDED 1971. Non-fiction only. 'Many of
our authors are historians, psychologists, physicians – all are writing trade books for general
readers.' No scripts. No fiction or children's
books. *Specialises* in history, popular culture,
business, health, biography and politics. No
unsolicited mss. Send query letter first, with
brief project outline, samples and biographical
information. No reading fee. CLIENTS include
Jim Wright, Alan Axelrod, Charles Phillips,
David Stutz, Carol Turkington. A member of
the Association of Author's Representatives.
Commission 15%.

Stephen Pevner, Inc.

248 West 73rd Street, 2nd Floor, New York
NY 10023
☎001 212 496 0474   Fax 001 212 496 0796
Contact *Stephen Pevner*

FOUNDED 1991. *Handles* pop culture, novels
and film-related books. Also handles TV, film,
theatre and radio scripts. Approach in writing
with synopsis (include first chapters for a novel).
No reading fee. *Commission* Home 15%.

Alison J. Picard Literary Agent

PO Box 2000, Cotuit MA 02635
☎001 508 477 7192   Fax 001 508 420 0762
Contact *Alison Picard*

FOUNDED 1985. *Handles* mainstream and literary
fiction, contemporary and historical romance,
children's and young adult, mysteries and
thrillers; plus non-fiction. No short stories unless
suitable for major national publications, and no
poetry. Rarely any science fiction and fantasy.
Particularly interested in expanding non-fiction

titles. Approach with written query. No reading
fee. *Commission* 15%. *Overseas associates* **A. M.
Heath & Co. Ltd**, London.

Pinder Lane & Garon-Brooke Associates Ltd

159 West 53rd Street, New York NY 10019
☎001 212 489 0880   Fax 001 212 586 9346
Executive Agents *Dick Duane, Robert Thixton*
Vice President *Jean Free*
Agent *Nancy Coffey*

FOUNDED 1951. Fiction and non-fiction: his-
tory and historical romance, suspense/thrillers,
political intrigue, horror/occult, self-help. No
category romance, westerns or mysteries. No
unsolicited mss. First approach by query letter.
No reading fee. CLIENTS include Virginia
Coffman, Lolita Files, Curtis Gathje, Eric
Harry, Chris Heimerdinger, Patricia Matthews,
Michael Pinson, Rosemary Rogers, Richard
Steinberg, Major Chris Stewart. *Commission*
Home 15%; Dramatic 10–15%; Foreign 30%.
Overseas associates **Abner Stein**, London;
Translation: Bernard Kurman.

Arthur Pine Associates, Inc.

250 West 57th Street, New York NY 10107
☎001 212 265 7330   Fax 001 212 265 4650
Contact *Richard S. Pine, Lori Andiman,
Sarah Piel*

FOUNDED 1970. *Handles* fiction and non-fiction
(adult books only). No scripts, children's, autobiographical (unless celebrity), textbooks or scientific. No unsolicited mss. Send query letter
with synopsis, including IRCs in first instance.
All material must be submitted to the agency on
an exclusive basis with s.a.e.. *Commission* 15%.

PMA Literary & Film Management, Inc.

132 West 22nd Street, 12th Floor, New York
NY 10011
☎001 212 929 1222   Fax 001 212 206 0238
President *Peter Miller*
Vice President *Jennifer Robinson*
Associates *Eric Wilinski, Yuri Skujins, John
Stryder, Giselle Dean Miller, Talaya Delaney*
Director of Foreign Rights *Jody Saltzman*

FOUNDED 1976. Commercial fiction, non-fiction and screenplays. *Specialises* in books with
motion picture and television potential, and in
true crime. No poetry, pornography, non-commercial or academic. No unsolicited mss.
Approach by letter with one-page synopsis.
Editing service available for unpublished authors

(non–obligatory). Fee recoupable out of first monies earned. CLIENTS Ann Benson, Vincent T. Bugliosi, Jay R. Bonansinga, Wensley Clarkson, Michael Eberhardt, Christopher Cook Gilmore, John Glatt, Chris Rogers, Ted Sennett, Rob Thomas, Gene Walden, Steven Yount. *Commission* Home 15%; Dramatic 10–15%; Foreign 20–25%.

Susan Ann Protter Literary Agent

Suite 1408, 110 West 40th Street, New York NY 10018–3616
☎001 212 840 0480

Contact *Susan Protter*

FOUNDED 1971. *Handles* general fiction, mysteries, thrillers, science fiction and fantasy; nonfiction: history, general reference, biography, true crime, science, health and parenting. No romance, poetry, westerns, religious, children's or sport manuals. No scripts. First approach with letter, including IRCs. No reading fee. CLIENTS include Lydia Adamson, Terry Bisson, David G. Hartwell, John G. Cramer, Kathleen McCoy PhD, Lynn Armistead McKee, Rudy Rucker, Barbara C. Unell. *Commission* Home & Dramatic 15%; Foreign 25%. *Overseas associates* **Abner Stein**, London; agents in all major markets.

Puddingstone Literary/ SBC Enterprises, Inc.

11 Mabro Drive, Denville NJ 07834–9607
☎001 201 366 3622

Contact *Alec Bernard, Eugenia Cohen*

FOUNDED 1972. Works with new/unpublished writers as well as with established ones. *Handles* trade fiction, non-fiction, film and telemovies. No unsolicited mss. Send query letter with IRCs. No reading fee. *Commission* varies.

Quicksilver Books, Literary Agents

50 Wilson Street, Hartsdale NY 10530
☎001 914 946 8748

President *Bob Silverstein*

FOUNDED 1973. *Handles* literary fiction and mainstream commercial fiction: blockbuster, suspense, thriller, contemporary, mystery and historical; and general non-fiction, including self-help, psychology, holistic healing, ecology, environmental, biography, fact crime, New Age, health, nutrition, enlightened wisdom and spirituality. No scripts, science fiction and fantasy, pornographic, children's or romance. UK material being submitted must have universal appeal for the US market. Unsolicited material welcome but must be accompanied by

IRCs for response, together with biographical details, covering letter, etc. No reading fee. CLIENTS include John Harricharan, Vasart Lad, Ted Libbey, Dorothy Nolte, Arthur Reber, Barrymore Scherer, Grace Speare, Melvin van Peebles. *Commission* Home & Dramatic 15%; Translation 20%.

Helen Rees Literary Agency

308 Commonwealth Avenue, Boston MA 02115
☎001 617 262 2401   Fax 001 617 236 0133

Contact *Joan Mazmanian*

FOUNDED 1982. *Specialises* in books on health and business; also handles biography, autobiography and history; quality fiction. No scholarly, academic or technical books. No scripts, science fiction, children's, poetry, photography, short stories, cooking. No unsolicited mss. Send query letter with IRCs. No reading fee. CLIENTS Donna Carpenter, Alan Dershowitz, Alexander Dubcek, Harry Figgie Jr, Senator Barry Goldwater, Sandra Mackey, Price Waterhouse. *Commission* Home 15%; Foreign 20%.

Renaissance

8523 Sunset Boulevard, Los Angeles CA 90069
☎001 310 289 3636   Fax 001 310 289 3637

President *Joel Gotler*
Literary Associates *Steven Fisher, Alan Nevins, Irv Schwartz, Brian Lipson*

FOUNDED 1934. Fiction and non-fiction; film and TV rights. No unsolicited mss. Send query letter with IRCs in the first instance. No reading fee. *Commission* Home 10–15%.

Rights Unlimited, Inc.

101 West 55th Street, Suite 2D, New York NY 10019
☎001 212 246 0900   Fax 001 212 246 2114

Contact *Bernard Kurman*

FOUNDED 1985. *Handles* adult fiction, nonfiction. No scripts, poetry, short stories, educational or literary works. Unsolicited mss welcome; query letter with synopsis preferred in the first instance. No reading fee. CLIENTS Charles Berlitz, Gyo Fujikawa, Norman Lang. *Commission* Home 15%; Translation 20%.

Rosenstone/Wender

3 East 48th Street, 4th Floor, New York NY 10017
☎001 212 832 8330   Fax 001 212 759 4524

Contact *Phyllis Wender, Susan Perlman Cohen, Hannah M. Wallace*

FOUNDED 1981. *Handles* fiction, non-fiction,

children's and scripts for film, TV and theatre. No material for radio. No unsolicited mss. Send letter outlining the project, credits, etc. No reading fee. *Commission* Home 15%; Dramatic 10%; Foreign 20%. *Overseas associates* La Nouvelle Agence, France; Andrew Nurnberg, Netherlands; The English Agency, Japan; Mohrbooks, Germany; Ole Licht, Scandinavia.

Shyama Ross 'The Write Therapist'

2000 North Ivar Avenue, Suite 3, Hollywood CA 90068
☎001 213 465 2630   Fax 001 213 465 8597
Contact *Shyama Ross*

FOUNDED 1979. *Handles* non-fiction trade books: New Age, health and fitness, philosophy, psychology, trends, humour, business, mysticism; also fiction: thrillers, romance, suspense, mystery, contemporary. No scripts. Story analyst for screenplays. No Christian evangelical, travel, sleazy sex or children's. *Specialises* in humour, how-to, mainstream fiction, healing and women's issues. New writers welcome. Query by letter with brief outline of contents and background (plus IRCs). Fee charged ($120 for up to 50,000 words) for detailed analysis of mss. Professional editing also available (rates per page or hour). *Commission* Home & Film rights 15%; Translation 20%.

Jane Rotrosen Agency

318 East 51st Street, New York NY 10022
☎001 212 593 4330   Fax 001 212 935 6985
Contact *Meg Ruley, Andrea Cirillo, Ruth Kagle*

Handles commercial fiction: romance, horror, mysteries, thrillers and fantasy and popular non-fiction. No scripts, educational, professional or belles lettres. No unsolicited mss; send query letter in the first instance. No reading fee. *Commission* Home 15%; UK & Translation 20%. *Overseas associates* worldwide and film agents on the West Coast.

Victoria Sanders Literary Agency

241 Avenue of the Americas, New York NY 10014
☎001 212 633 8811   Fax 001 212 633 0525
Contact *Victoria Sanders, Diane Dickensheid*

FOUNDED 1993. *Handles* general trade fiction and non-fiction, plus ancillary film and television rights. CLIENTS Connie Briscoe, Yolanda Joe, Alexander Smalls, Colin Kersey, J. M. Redmann. *Commission* Home & Dramatic 15%; Translation 20%.

Sandum & Associates

144 East 84th Street, New York NY 10028
☎001 212 737 2011
Contact *Howard E. Sandum*

FOUNDED 1987. *Handles* all categories of general adult non-fiction, plus occasional fiction. No scripts. No children's, poetry or short stories. No unsolicited mss. Third-party referral preferred but direct approach by letter, with synopsis, brief biography and IRCs, is accepted. No reading fee. CLIENTS include James Cowan, Bro. Victor d'Arvila-Latourrette, Barbara Lachman, Silvia Sanza. *Commission* Home & Dramatic 15%; Translation & Foreign 20%. *Overseas associates* Scott Ferris Associates.

SBC Enterprises, Inc.
See **Puddingstone Literary**

Jack Scagnetti Talent & Literary Agency

5118 Vineland Avenue, Suite 102, North Hollywood CA 91601
☎001 818 762 3871
Contact *Jack Scagnetti*

FOUNDED 1974. Works mostly with established/published authors. *Handles* non-fiction, fiction, film and TV scripts. No reading fee for outlines. *Commission* Home & Dramatic 10%; Foreign 15%.

Susan Schulman, A Literary Agency

454 West 44th Street, New York NY 10036
☎001 212 713 1633/4/5
Fax 001 212 581 8830

FOUNDED 1979. *Specialises* in non-fiction of all types but particularly in psychology-based self-help for men, women and families. Other interests include business, the social sciences, biography, language and linguistics. Fiction interests include contemporary fiction, including women's, mysteries, historical and thrillers 'with a cutting edge'. Always looking for 'something original and fresh'. No unsolicited mss. Query first including outline and three sample chapters with IRCs. No reading fee. Represents properties for film and television, and works with agents in appropriate territories for translation rights. *Commission* Home & Dramatic 15%; Translation 20%. *Overseas associates* Plays: **Rosica Colin Ltd** and **The Agency Ltd**, London; Film: **Michelle Kass Associates**, London; Children's books: Marilyn Malin, London, Commercial fiction: **MBA Literary Agents** London.

Shapiro-Lichtman-Stein Talent Agency

8827 Beverly Boulevard, Los Angeles CA 90048
☎001 310 859 8877   Fax 001 310 859 7153

FOUNDED 1969. Works mostly with established/published authors. *Handles* film and TV scripts. Unsolicited mss will not be read. *Commission* Home & Dramatic 10%; Foreign 20%.

The Shepard Agency

Pawling Savings Bank Building, Suite 3, Southeast Plaza, Brewster NY 10509
☎001 914 279 2900/3236
Fax 001 914 279 3239

Contact *Jean Shepard, Lance Shepard*

FOUNDED 1987. *Handles* non-fiction: business, food, self-help and travel; some fiction: adult, children's and young adult and the occasional script. No pornography. *Specialises* in business. Send query letter, table of contents, sample chapters and IRCs for response. No reading fee. *Commission* Home & Dramatic 15%; Translation 20%.

Lee Shore Agency Ltd

440 Friday Road, Pittsburgh PA 15209
☎001 412 821 0440   Fax 001 412 821 6099

Contact *Cynthia Sterling, Tricia Smith, Mark Maier, Jennifer Blose*

FOUNDED 1988. *Handles* non-fiction, including textbooks, and mass-market fiction: horror, romance, mystery, westerns, science fiction. Also some young adult and, more recently, screenplays. *Specialises* in New Age, self-help, how-to and quality fiction. No children's. No unsolicited mss. Send IRCs for guidelines before submitting work. Reading fee charged. CLIENTS include Mel Blount, Francisco Cruz, Dr Laura Essen, Dr Lynn Hawker, Susan Sheppard. *Commission* Home 15%; Dramatic 20%.

Bobbe Siegel Literary Agency

41 West 83rd Street, New York NY 10024
☎001 212 877 4985   Fax 001 212 877 4985

Contact *Bobbe Siegel*

FOUNDED 1975. Works mostly with established/published authors. *Specialises* in literary fiction, detective, suspense, historical, fantasy, biography, how-to, women's interest, fitness, health, beauty, sports, pop psychology. No scripts. No cookbooks, crafts, children's, short stories or humour. First approach with letter including IRCs for response. No reading fee. Critiques given if the writer is taken on for

representation. CLIENTS include Michael Buller, Eileen Curtis, Margaret Mitchell Dukore, Primo Levi, John Nordahl, Curt Smith. *Commission* Home 15%; Dramatic & Foreign 20%. (Foreign/Dramatic split 50/50 with sub-agent.) *Overseas associates* **John Pawsey**, London; others in other countries.

The Evelyn Singer Literary Agency, Inc.

PO Box 594, White Plains NY 10602
☎001 914 949 1147/914 631 5160

Contact *Evelyn Singer*

FOUNDED 1951. Works mostly with established/published authors. *Handles* fiction and non-fiction, both adult and children's. Adult: health, medicine, how-to, diet, biography, celebrity, conservation, political, serious novels, suspense and mystery. Children's: educational non-fiction for all ages and fiction for the middle/teen levels. No picture books unless the author is or has an experienced book illustrator. No formula romance, poetry, sex, occult, textbooks or specialised material unsuitable for trade market. No scripts. No unsolicited mss. First approach with letter giving writing background, credits, publications, including date of publication and publisher. IRCs essential. No phone calls. No reading fee. 'Accepts writers who have earned at least $25,000 from freelance writing.' CLIENTS include John Armistead, Mary Elting, Franklin Folsom, William F. Hallstead, Rose Wyler. *Commission* Home 15%; Dramatic 20%; Foreign 25%. *Overseas associates* **Laurence Pollinger Limited**, London.

Michael Snell Literary Agency

PO Box 1206, Truro MA 02666–1206
☎001 508 349 3718

President *Michael Snell*
Vice President *Patricia Smith*

FOUNDED 1980. Adult non-fiction, especially science, business and women's issues. *Specialises* in business and computer books (professional and reference to popular trade how-to); general how-to and self-help on all topics, from diet and exercise to parenting, health, sex, psychology and personal finance, plus literary and suspense fiction. No unsolicited mss. Send outline and sample chapter with return postage for reply. No reading fee for outlines. Brochure available on how to write a book proposal. Rewriting, developmental editing, collaborating and ghostwriting services available on a fee basis. Send IRCs. *Commission* Home 15%.

Southern Writers
5120 Prytania Street, New Orleans LA 70115
☎001 504 899 5889
President *William Griffin*

FOUNDED 1979. *Handles* fiction and non-fiction of general interest. No scripts, short stories, poetry, autobiography or articles. No unsolicited mss. Approach in writing with query. Reading fee charged to authors unpublished in the field. *Commission* Home 15%; Dramatic & Translation 20%.

Spieler Literary Agency
154 West 57th Street, Room 135,
New York NY 10019
☎001 212 757 4439   Fax 001 212 333 2019
The Spieler Agency/West, 1328 Sixth Street, #3, Berkeley, CA 94710
☎001 510 528 2616   Fax 001 510 528 8117
Contact *Joseph Spieler, Lisa M. Ross, John Thornton, Emily Block (New York); Victoria Shoemaker (Berkeley)*

FOUNDED 1980. *Handles* literary fiction and non-fiction. No how-to or genre romance. *Specialises* in history, science, ecology, social issues and business. No scripts. Approach in writing with IRCs. No reading fee. CLIENTS James Chace, Amy Ehrlich, Paul Hawken, Joe Kane, Walter Laqueur, Catherine MacCoun, Akio Morita, Marc Reisner. *Commission* Home & Dramatic 15%; Translation 20%. *Overseas associates* **Abner Stein, The Marsh Agency**, London.

Philip G. Spitzer Literary Agency
50 Talmage Farm Lane, East Hampton NY 11937
☎001 516 329 3650   Fax 001 516 329 3651
Contact *Philip Spitzer*

FOUNDED 1969. Works mostly with established/published authors. *Specialises* in general non-fiction and fiction – thrillers. No reading fee for outlines. *Commission* Home & Dramatic 15%; Foreign 20%.

Lyle Steele & Co. Ltd Literary Agents
511 East 73rd Street, Suite 6, New York NY 10021
☎001 212 288 2981
President *Lyle Steele*

FOUNDED 1985. *Handles* general non-fiction and category fiction, including mysteries (anxious to see good British mysteries), thrillers, horror and occult. Also North American rights to titles published by major English publishers.

No scripts unless derived from books already being handled. No romance. No unsolicited mss: query with IRCs in first instance. No reading fee. *Commission* 10%. *Overseas associates* worldwide.

Gloria Stern Agency
2929 Buffalo Speedway, Suite 2111,
Houston TX 77098
☎001 713 963 8360   Fax 001 713 963 8460
Contact *Gloria Stern*

FOUNDED 1976. *Specialises* in non-fiction, including biography, history, politics, women's issues, self-help, health, science and education; also adult fiction. No scripts, how-to, poetry, short stories or first fiction from unpublished authors. First approach by letter stating content of book, including one chapter, list of competing books, qualifications as author and IRCs. No reading fee. *Commission* Home 10–15%; Dramatic 10%; Foreign 20% shared; Translation 20% shared. *Overseas associates* **A. M. Heath & Co. Ltd**, London, and worldwide.

Gloria Stern Agency (Hollywood)
12535 Chandler Boulevard, Suite 3, North Hollywood CA 91607
☎001 818 508 6296   Fax 001 818 508 6296
Contact *Gloria Stern*

FOUNDED 1984. *Handles* film scripts, genre (romance, detective, thriller and sci-fi) and mainstream fiction; electronic media. 'No books containing gratuitous violence.' Approach with letter, biography and synopsis. Reading fee charged by the hour plus possible 'distribution' charges. *Commission* Home 15%; Offshore 20%.

Jo Stewart Agency
201 East 66th Street, Suite 18G, New York NY 10021
☎001 212 879 1301
Contact *Jo Stewart*

FOUNDED 1978. *Handles* fiction and non-fiction. No scripts. No unsolicited mss; send query letter first. No reading fee. *Commission* Home 10%; Foreign 20%; Unpublished 15%. *Overseas associates* **John Johnson (Authors' Agent) Ltd**, London.

Gunther Stuhlmann Author's Representative
PO Box 276, Becket MA 01223
☎001 413 623 5170
Contact *Gunther Stuhlmann, Barbara Ward*
FOUNDED 1954. *Handles* literary fiction, biogra-

phy and serious non-fiction. No film/TV scripts unless from established clients. No short stories, detective, romance, adventure, poetry, technical or computers. *Specialises* in 20th-century literature, translations of Japanese and Spanish literature, and modern American writers. Query first with IRCs, including sample chapters and synopsis of project. 'We take on few new clients.' No reading fee. CLIENTS include Joe Bernardini, Julieta Campos, B. H. Friedman, Anaïs Nin, Richard Powers, Otto Rank. *Commission* Home 10%; Foreign 15%; Translation 20%.

H. N. Swanson, Inc.
See **Renaissance**

The Tantleff Office
375 Greenwich Street, Suite 700, New York NY 10013
☎001 212 941 3939   Fax 001 212 941 3948
Contact (scripts) *Jack Tantleff, Jill Bock, Charmaine Ferenczi*

FOUNDED 1986. *Handles* primarily scripts for TV, and represents actors. No unsolicited mss; queries only. No reading fee. CLIENTS include Brian Friel, Marsha Norman, Mark O'Donnell. *Commission* Scripts 10%; Books 15%.

2M Communications Ltd
121 West 27th Street, Suite 601, New York NY 10001
☎001 212 741 1509   Fax 001 212 691 4460
Contact *Madeleine Morel*

FOUNDED 1982. *Handles* non-fiction only: everything from pop psychology and health to cookery books, biographies and pop culture. No scripts. No fiction, children's, computers or science. No unsolicited mss; send letter with sample pages and IRCs. No reading fee. CLIENTS include David Steinman, Janet Wolfe, Donald Woods. *Commission* Home & Dramatic 15%; Translation 20%. *Overseas associates* Thomas Schluck Agency, Germany; Asano Agency, Japan; EAIS, France; Living Literary Agency, Italy; Nueva Agencia Literaria Internacional, Spain.

Susan P. Urstadt, Inc.
PO Box 1676, New Canaan CT 06840
☎001 203 972 8226   Fax 001 203 966 2249
President *Susan P. Urstadt*

FOUNDED 1975. *Specialises* in decorative arts, antiques, gardening, cookery, biography, history, sports, natural history, environment and popular reference. No unsolicited fiction or children's. Query with outline, sample chapter,

author biography and IRCs to cover return postage. *Commission* Home 15%; Dramatic & Foreign 20%.

Van der Leun & Associates
22 Division Street, Easton CT 06612
☎001 203 259 4897
Contact *Patricia Van der Leun*

FOUNDED 1984. *Handles* fiction and non-fiction. No scripts. No science fiction, fantasy or romance. *Specialises* in art and architecture, science, biography and fiction. No unsolicited mss; query first, with proposal and short biography. No reading fee. CLIENTS include David Darling, Robert Fulghum, Marion Winik. *Commission* 15%. *Overseas associates* **Abner Stein**, UK; Michelle Lapautre, France; English Agency, Japan; Carmen Balcells, Spain; Lijnkamp Associates, The Netherlands; Karin Schindler, South America; Susanna Zevi, Italy.

Wallace Literary Agency, Inc.
177 East 70th Street, New York NY 10021
☎001 212 570 9090   Fax 001 212 772 8979
Contact *Lois Wallace, Thomas C. Wallace*

FOUNDED 1988. No unsolicited mss. No faxed queries. *Commission* Rates upon application. *UK representative* **A. M. Heath & Co. Ltd**; *French representative* Michelle Lapautre; *all other European representation* **Andrew Nurnberg Associates**; *Japanese representative* Tuttle-Mori.

The Gerry B. Wallerstein Agency
2315 Powell Avenue, Suite 12, Erie PA 16506
☎001 814 833 5511   Fax 001 814 833 6260
Contact *Gerry B. Wallerstein*

FOUNDED 1984. Adult fiction and non-fiction. No scripts unless by established clients. No children's, textbooks, esoteric or autobiographical (unless celebrity). Broad range of clients, main interest being marketability of material. No unsolicited mss. Send IRCs for information regarding submissions. Reading fee charged for non-established authors. *Commission* Home & Dramatic 15%; Translation 20%.

John A. Ware Literary Agency
392 Central Park West, New York NY 10025
☎001 212 866 4733   Fax 001 212 866 4734
Contact *John Ware*

FOUNDED 1978. *Specialises* in non-fiction: biography, history, current affairs, investigative journalism, science, inside looks at phenomena, medicine and psychology (academic credentials required). Also handles literary fiction, mysteries/thrillers, sport, oral history, Americana and folklore. Unsolicited mss not read. Send query letter first with IRCs to cover return postage. No reading fee. CLIENTS include Caroline Fraser, Jon Krakauer, Jack Womack. *Commission* Home & Dramatic 15%; Foreign 20%.

Waterside Productions, Inc.

2191 San Elijo Avenue, Cardiff by the Sea CA 92007-1839
☎001 619 632 9190   Fax 001 619 632 9295
Contact *William Gladstone*

FOUNDED 1982. *Handles* general non-fiction: computers and technology, psychology, science, business, sports. All types of multimedia. No unsolicited mss; send query letter. No reading fee. *Commission* Home 15%; Dramatic 20%; Translation 25%. *Overseas associates* **Serafina Clarke**, England; Asano Agency, Japan; Ulla Lohren, Sweden; Ruth Liepman, Germany; Vera Le Marie, EAIS, France; Bardon Chinese Media Agency, China; Grandi & Vitali, Italy; DRT, Korea; Mercedes Casanovas, Spain.

Watkins Loomis Agency, Inc.

133 East 35th Street, Suite 1, New York NY 10016
☎001 212 532 0080   Fax 001 212 889 0506
Contact *Nicole Aragi*

FOUNDED 1904. *Handles* fiction and non-fiction. No scripts for film, radio, TV or theatre. No science fiction, fantasy or horror. No reading fee. No unsolicited mss. Approach in writing with enquiry or proposal and s.a.e.. *Commission* Home 15%; UK & Translation 20%. *Overseas associates* **Abner Stein**; **The Marsh Agency**, London.

Wecksler-Incomco

170 West End Avenue, New York NY 10023
☎001 212 787 2239   Fax 001 212 496 7035
Contact *Sally Wecksler, Joann Amparan*

FOUNDED 1971. *Handles* fiction and non-fiction (biographies, performing arts), heavily illustrated books, business and reference. Film and TV rights. No children's books. No unsolicited mss; queries only. No reading fee. *Commission* Home 15%; Translation 20% and British rights 20%.

Cherry Weiner Literary Agency

28 Kipling Way, Manalapan NJ 07726
☎001 908 446 2096   Fax 001 908 792 0506
Contact *Cherry Weiner*

FOUNDED 1977. *Handles* more or less all types of genre fiction: science fiction and fantasy, romance, mystery, westerns. No scripts. No

non-fiction. No unsolicited mss. No submissions except through referral. No reading fee. *Commission* 15%. *Overseas associates* **Abner Stein**, London; Thomas Schluck, Germany; International Editors Inc., Spain.

Wieser & Wieser, Inc.

118 East 25th Street, New York NY 10010
☎001 212 260 0860   Fax 001 212 505 7186
Contact *Olga B. Wieser, George J. Wieser, Jake Elwell*

FOUNDED 1976. Works mostly with established/published authors. *Specialises* in literary and mainstream fiction, serious and popular historical fiction, and general non-fiction: business, finance, aviation, sports, photography, cookbooks, travel and popular medicine. No poetry, children's, science fiction or religious. No unsolicited mss. First approach by letter with IRCs. No reading fee for outlines. *Commission* Home & Dramatic 15%; Foreign 20%.

Ruth Wreschner, Authors' Representative

10 West 74th Street, New York NY 10023
☎001 212 877 2605   Fax 001 212 595 5843
Contact *Ruth Wreschner*

FOUNDED 1981. Works mostly with established/published authors but 'will consider very good first novels, both mainstream and genre, particularly British mystery writers'. *Specialises* in popular medicine, psychology, health, self-help, business. No screenplays or dramatic plays. First approach with query letter and IRCs. For fiction, send a synopsis and first 50 pp; for non-fiction, an outline and two sample chapters. No reading fee. *Commission* Home 15%; Foreign 20%.

Ann Wright Representatives

165 West 46th Street, Suite 1105, New York · NY 10036–2501
☎001 212 764 6770   Fax 001 212 764 5125
Contact *Dan Wright*

FOUNDED 1961. *Specialises* in screenplays for film and TV. Also handles novels, drama and fiction. No academic, scientific or scholarly. Approach by letter; no reply without IRCs. Include outline and credits only. New film and TV writers encouraged. No reading fee. CLIENTS include Ferne Arfin, Theodore Bonnet, Joy Chambers, Tom Dempsey, Jerry D. Hoffman, Michael McKittrick, John Peer Nugent, James O'Hare, Kevin O'Morrison, Brian Reich, William H. Selzer. Signatory to the Writers Guild of America Agreement. *Commission* Home varies according to current trend (10–20%); Dramatic 10% of gross.

Writers House, Inc.

21 West 26th Street, New York NY 10010
☎001 212 685 2400   Fax 001 212 685 1781

Contact *Albert Zuckerman, Amy Berkower, Merrilee Heifetz, Susan Cohen, Susan Ginsburg, Fran Lebowitz, Karen Solem*

FOUNDED 1974. *Handles* all types of fiction, including children's and young adult, plus narrative non-fiction: history, biography, popular science, pop and rock culture. Also represents designers and developers of CD-ROM computer games. *Specialises* in popular fiction, women's novels, thrillers and children's. Represents novelisation rights for film producers such as New Line Cinema. No scripts. No professional or scholarly. For consideration of unsolicited mss, send letter of enquiry, 'explaining why your book is wonderful, briefly what it's about and outlining your writing background'. No reading fee. CLIENTS include Barbara Delinsky, Ken Follett, Eileen Goudge, Stephen Hawking, Michael Lewis, Robin McKinley, Ann Martin, Francine Pascal, Ridley Pearson, Nora Roberts, Cynthia Voigt, F. Paul Wilson. *Commission* Home & Dramatic 15%; Foreign 20%. Albert Zuckerman is author of *Writing the Blockbuster Novel*, published by **Little, Brown & Co.**

Susan Zeckendorf Associates, Inc.

171 West 57th Street, Suite 11B, New York NY 10019
☎001 212 245 2928   Fax 001 212 977 2643

President *Susan Zeckendorf*

FOUNDED 1979. Works with new/unpublished writers. *Specialises* in literary fiction, commercial women's fiction, international espionage, thrillers and mysteries. Non-fiction interests: science, parenting, music and self-help. No category romance, science fiction or scripts. No unsolicited mss. Send query letter describing mss. No reading fee. CLIENTS include Linda Dahl, James N. Frey, Marjorie Jaffe, Laurie Morrow, Una-Mary Parker, Jerry E. Patterson. *Commission* Home & Dramatic 15%; Foreign 20%. *Overseas associates* **Abner Stein**, London; V. K. Rosemarie Buckman, Europe, South America; Tom Mori, Japan, Taiwan. Film & TV representative: Joel Gotler at **Renaissance**.

US Media Contacts in the UK

ABC News Intercontinental Inc.
8 Carburton Street, London W1P 7DT
☎0171 637 9222   Fax 0171 631 5084
**Bureau Chief & Director of News
Coverage, Europe, Middle East &
Africa** *Rex Granum*

Alaska Journal of Commerce
58 Jubilee Place, London SW3 3TQ
☎0171 376 7316   Fax 0171 376 7316
Bureau Chief *Robert Gould*

The Associated Press
12 Norwich Street, London EC4A 1BP
☎0171 353 1515   Fax 0171 353 8118
Chief of Bureau/Managing Director
Myron L. Belkind

The Baltimore Sun
11 Kensington Court Place, London W8 5BJ
☎0171 460 2200   Fax 0171 460 2211
Bureau Chief *Bill Glauber*

Billboard
23 Ridgmount Street, London WC1E 7AH
☎0171 323 6686   Fax 0171 323 2314
International Bureau Chief *Thom Duffy*

Bloomberg Business News
City Gate House, 39—45 Finsbury Square,
London EC2A 1PX
☎0171 256 7500   Fax 0171 374 6138
London Bureau Chief *Paul Sillitoe*

Bridge News
78 Fleet Street, London EC4Y 1HY
☎0171 842 4000   Fax 0171 583 5032
Chief Correspondent (UK) *Timothy Penn*

Business Week
34 Dover Street, London W1X 4BR
☎0171 491 8985   Fax 0171 409 7152
Bureau Manager *Stanley Reed*

Cable News Network Inc.
CNN House, 19—22 Rathbone Place,
London W1P 1DF
☎0171 637 6800   Fax 0171 637 6868
Bureau Chief *Charles Hoff*

CBC Television and Radio
43/51 Great Titchfield Street, London
W1P 8DD
☎0171 412 9200   Fax 0171 631 3095
London Bureau Manager *Sue Phillips*

CBS News
68 Knightsbridge, London SW1X 7LL
☎0171 581 4801   Fax 0171 581 4431
Bureau Chief *Marcy McGinnis*

Chicago Tribune Press Service
169 Piccadilly, London W1V 9DD
☎0171 499 8769   Fax 0171 499 8781
Chief European Correspondent *Ray Moseley*

CNBC
8 Bedford Avenue, London WC1B 3NQ
☎0171 927 6759   Fax 0171 636 2628
Bureau Chief *Karen Nye*

Cox Newspapers
The Atlanta Journal Constitution, 29 Ferry
Street, Isle of Dogs, London E14 3DT
☎0171 537 0765   Fax 0171 537 0766
European Correspondent *Lou Salome*

Dow Jones Telerate-Commodities
& Finance
10 Fleet Place, Limeburner Lane, London
EC4M 7RB
☎0171 832 9522   Fax 0171 832 9894
Chief European Correspondent *James Dyson*

Fairchild Publications of New York
121 Kingsway, London WC2B 6PA
☎0171 831 3607   Fax 0171 831 6485
Bureau Chief *James Fallon*

Forbes Magazine
51 Charles Street, London W1X 7PA
☎0171 495 0120   Fax 0171 495 0170
European Bureau Manager *Howard Banks*

Futures World News
2 Royal Mint Court, Dexter House, London
EC3N 4QN
☎0171 867 8867   Fax 0171 867 1368
Vice President & London Bureau Chief
Barbara Kollmeyer

The Globe and Mail
43—51 Great Titchfield Street, London
W1P 8DD
☎0171 323 0449   Fax 0171 323 0428
European Correspondent *Madelaine Drohan*

International Herald Tribune
63 Long Acre, London WC2E 9JH
☎0171 836 4802   Fax 0171 240 2254
London Correspondent *Erik Ipsen*

Journal of Commerce
Totara Park House, 3rd Floor, 34/36 Gray's
Inn Road, London WC1X 8HR
☎0171 430 2495   Fax 0171 837 2168
Chief European Correspondent *Janet Porter*

Los Angeles Times
150 Brompton Road, London SW3 1HX
☎0171 823 7315   Fax 0171 823 7308
Bureau Chief *William D. Montalbano*

Maclean's Magazine
35 Adam and Eve Mews, London W8 6UG
☎0171 937 0550   Fax 0171 938 3333
London Bureau Chief *Bruce Wallace*

Market News Service Inc.
Wheatsheaf House, 4 Carmelite Street,
London EC4Y 0BN
☎0171 353 4462   Fax 0171 353 9122
Bureau Chief *Jon Hurdle*

McGraw-Hill International
34 Dover Street, London W1X 4BR
☎0171 493 0538   Fax 0171 493 9896
Bureau Chief *David Brezovec*

National Public Radio
Room G-10 East Wing, Bush House, Strand,
London WC2B 4PH
☎0171 257 8086   Fax 0171 379 6486
London Bureau Chief *Michael Goldfarb*

NBC News Worldwide Inc.
8 Bedford Avenue, London WC1B 2NQ
☎0171 637 8655   Fax 0171 636 2628
Bureau Chief *Karen Curry*

The New York Times
66 Buckingham Gate, London SW1E 6AU
☎0171 799 5050   Fax 0171 799 2962
Chief Correspondent *John Darnton*

Newsweek
18 Park Street, London W1Y 4HH
☎0171 629 8361   Fax 0171 408 1403
Bureau Chief *Stryker McGuire*

People Magazine
Brettenham House, Lancaster Place, London
WC2E 7TL
☎0171 499 4080   Fax 0171 322 1125
Special Correspondent *Jerene Jones*

Philadelphia Inquirer
36 Agate Road, London W6 0AH
☎0181 932 8854   Fax 0181 932 8856
Correspondent *Fawn Vrazo*

Reader's Digest Association Ltd
Berkeley Square House, Berkeley Square,
London W1X 6AB
☎0171 629 8144   Fax 0171 408 0748
Editor-in-Chief, British Edition *Russell
Twisk*

Time Magazine
Brettenham House, Lancaster Place, London
WC2E 7TL
☎0171 499 4080   Fax 0171 322 1230
Bureau Chief *Barry Hillenbrand*

United Press International
408 Strand, London WC2R 0NE
☎0171 333 0999   Fax 0171 333 1690
Regional Editor *David Alexander*

USA Today
10 Wardour Street, London W1V 3HG
☎0171 734 4004   Fax 0171 734 6066
Chief European Correspondent *David Lynch*

Voice of America
IPC, 76 Shoe Lane, London EC4A 3JB
☎0171 410 0960   Fax 0171 410 0966
Bureau Chief/Senior Editor *Paul Francuch*

Wall Street Journal
10 Fleet Place, London EC4M 7RB
☎0171 832 9200   Fax 0171 832 9201
London Bureau Chief *Lawrence Ingrassia*

Washington Post
18 Park Street, London W1Y 4HH
☎0171 629 8958   Fax 0171 629 0050
Bureau Chief *Fred Barbash*

Who Weekly
Brettenham House, Lancaster Place, London
WC2E 7TL
☎0171 322 1118   Fax 0171 322 1199
Special Correspondent *Moira Bailey*

Worldwide Television News (WTN)
The Interchange, Oval Road, Camden Lock,
London NW1 7DZ
☎0171 410 5200   Fax 0171 410 8302
President *Robert E.Burke*

Professional Associations and Societies

Alliance of Literary Societies
71 Stepping Stones Road, Coventry
CV5 8JT
☎01203 592231

President *Gabriel Woolf*
Chairman *J. Hunt*
Honorary Secretary *Bill Adams (address above)*

FOUNDED 1974. Acts as a liaison body between member societies and, when necessary, as a pressure group. Deals with enquiries and assists in preserving buildings and places with literary connections. 30–40 societies hold membership. A directory of literary societies is maintained and the ALS produces an annual fanzine, *Chapter One*, which is distributed to affiliated societies, carrying news of personalities, activities and events.

Chapter One details and advertising rates can be obtained from Kenneth Oultram, Editor, Chapter One, Clatterwick Hall, Little Leigh, Northwich, Cheshire CW8 4RJ (☎01606 891303).

Arvon Foundation
Totleigh Barton, Sheepwash, Beaworthy, Devon EX21 5NS
☎01409 231338   Fax 01409 231338

Lumb Bank, Heptonstall, Hebden Bridge, West Yorkshire HX7 6DF
☎01422 843714 Fax 01422 843714

Moniack Mhor, Teavarran, Kiltarlity, Beauly, Inverness-shire IV4 7HT
☎01463 741675

President *Terry Hands*
Chairman *Professor Brian Cox, CBE*
National Director *David Pease*

FOUNDED 1968. Offers people of any age (over 16) and any background the opportunity to live and work with professional writers. Five-day residential courses are held throughout the year at Arvon's three centres, covering poetry, narrative, drama, writing for children, songwriting and the performing arts. A number of bursaries towards the cost of course fees are available for those on low incomes, the unemployed, students and pensioners.

Also runs a biennial poetry competition (see under **Prizes**).

Association for Business Sponsorship of the Arts (ABSA)
Nutmeg House, 60 Gainsford Street, Butlers Wharf, London SE1 2NY
☎0171 378 8143   Fax 0171 407 7527

ABSA is the independent national association that exists to promote and encourage partnerships between the private sector and the arts to their mutual benefit and to that of the community at large. ABSA represents the interests of the business sponsor, in particular those of its business members, and also advises and trains the arts community both individually and corporately on the development of private sector support. A major initiative of ABSA is *Business in the Arts* which encourages business men and women to share their management skills with the arts to their mutual benefit. The *National Heritage Arts Sponsorship Scheme* (commonly known as the 'Pairing Scheme'), is designed to increase the level of sponsorship of the arts.

Association of American Correspondents in London
12 Norwich Street, London EC4A 1BP
☎0171 353 1515   Fax 0171 936 2229

Contact *Sandra Marshall*
Subscription £90 (Organisations)

FOUNDED 1919 to serve the professional interests of its member organisations, promote social cooperation among them, and maintain the ethical standards of the profession. (An extra £30 is charged for each department of an organisation which requires separate listing in the Association's handbook.)

Association of Authors' Agents
c/o Sheil Land Associates Ltd, 43 Doughty Street, London WC1N 2LF
☎0171 405 9351   Fax 0171 831 2127

Secretary *Vivien Green*
Membership £50 p.a.

FOUNDED 1974. Membership voluntary. The AAA maintains a code of practice, provides a forum for discussion, and represents its members in issues affecting the profession.

Association of British Editors

Broadvision, 49 Frederick Road, Edgbaston, Birmingham B15 1HN
☎0121 455 7949   Fax 0121 454 6187

Executive Director/Honorary Secretary
Jock Gallagher
Subscription £50 p.a.

FOUNDED 1985. Independent organisation for the study and enhancement of journalism world-wide. Established to protect and promote the freedom of the Press. Members are expected to 'maintain the dignity and rights of the profession; consider and sustain standards of professional conduct; exchange ideas for the advancement of professional ideals; work for the solution of common problems'. Membership is limited, but open to persons who have immediate charge of editorial or news policies in all media.

Association of British Science Writers (ABSW)

23 Savile Row, London W1X 2NB
☎0171 439 1205   Fax 0171 973 3051

Administrator *Barbara Drillsma*
Membership £25 p.a.; £20 (Associate)

ABSW has played a central role in improving the standards of science journalism in the UK over the last 40 years. The Association seeks to improve standards by means of networking, lectures and organised visits to institutional laboratories and industrial research centres. Puts members in touch with major projects in the field and with experts worldwide. A member of the European Union of Science Journalists' Associations, ABSW is able to offer heavily subsidised places on visits to research centres in most other European countries, and hosts reciprocal visits to Britain by European journalists. Membership open to those who are considered to be *bona fide* science writers/editors, or their film/TV/radio equivalents, who earn a substantial part of their income by promoting public interest in and understanding of science. Runs the administration and judging of the **Glaxo Science Writers' Awards**, for outstanding science journalism in newspapers, journals and broadcasting.

Association of Freelance Journalists

5 Beacon Flats, Kings Haye Road, Wellington, Telford, Shropshire TF1 1RG
Founding President *Martin Scholes*
Subscription £30 p.a.

Offers membership to local correspondents, those making a modest sum writing for the specialist press and those writing for a hobby, with or without an income. Members receive a laminated press card, newsletters, information networking, discounts on services, etc.

Association of Golf Writers

106 Byng Drive, Potters Bar, Hertfordshire EN6 1UJ
☎01707 654112   Fax 01707 654112

Honorary Secretary *Mark Garrod*

FOUNDED 1938. Aims to cooperate with golfing bodies to ensure best possible working conditions.

Association of Illustrators

First Floor, 32–38 Saffron Hill, London EC1N 8FH
☎0171 831 7377   Fax 0171 831 6277

Contact *Stephanie Smith*

FOUNDED 1973 to promote illustration and illustrators' rights, and encourage professional standards. The AOI is a non-profit-making trade association dedicated to its members, to protecting their interests and promoting their work. Talks, seminars, a newsletter, regional groups, legal and portfolio advice as well as a number of related publications such as *Rights, The Illustrator's Guide to Professional Practice*, and *Survive, The Illustrator's Guide to a Professional Career*.

Association of Independent Libraries

Leeds Library, 18 Commercial Street, Leeds, West Yorkshire LS1 6AL
☎01132 453071

Chairman *Geoffrey Forster*

Established to 'further the advancement, conservation and restoration of a little-known but important living portion of our cultural heritage'. Members include the **London Library, Devon & Exeter Institution, Linen Hall Library** and **Plymouth Proprietary Library**.

Association of Learned and Professional Society Publishers

48 Kelsey Lane, Beckenham, Kent BR3 3NE
☎0181 658 0459   Fax 0181 663 3583

Secretary-General *Bernard Donovan*

FOUNDED 1972 to foster the publishing activities of learned societies and academic and professional bodies. Membership is limited to such organisations, those publishing on behalf of member organisations and those closely associated with the work of academic publishers.

Association of Little Presses

86 Lytton Road, Oxford OX4 3NZ
☎01865 718266

Co-ordinator *Chris Jones*
Subscription £12.50 p.a.

FOUNDED 1966 as a loosely knit association of individuals running little presses, who grouped together for mutual self-help and encouragement. First acted as a pressure group to extend the availability of grant aid to small presses and later became more of an information exchange, advice centre and general promoter of small press publishing. Currently represents over 300 publishers and associates throughout Britain. Membership is open to presses and magazines as well as to individuals and institutions.

ALP publishes a twice-yearly magazine, *Poetry and Little Press Information* (PALPI); a *Catalogue of Little Press Books in Print*; information booklets such as *Getting Your Poetry Published* (over 35,000 copies sold since 1973) and *Publishing Yourself: Not Too Difficult After All* which advises those who are thinking of self-publishing, and a regular newsletter. A full list of little presses (some of which, like **Bloodaxe Books**, are now sufficiently established and successful to be considered in the mainstream of the business) is available from ALP.

ALP organises frequent bookfairs. Its main focus, that of supporting members' presses, brings it into contact with organisations worldwide. Over 80% of all new poetry in Britain is published by small presses and magazines but the Association is by no means solely devoted to publishers of poetry; its members produce everything from comics to cookery, novels and naval history.

Association of Scottish Motoring Writers

c/o 85 East King Street, Helensburgh, Argyll & Bute G84 7RG
☎01436 672187   Fax 01436 674118

Contact *Ross Finlay*
Subscription £45 (Full); £25 (Associate)

FOUNDED 1961. Aims to co-ordinate the activities of, and provide shared facilities for, motoring writers resident in Scotland, as well as creating opportunities for them to keep in touch when working outside of Scotland. Membership is by invitation only.

Author-Publisher Network

12 Mercers, Hawkhurst, Kent TN18 4LH
☎01580 753346

Chairman *John Dawes*

Secretary *Daphne Macara*
Subscription £15 (p.a.)

FOUNDED 1993. The association aims to provide an active forum for writers publishing their own work. An information network of ideas and opportunities for self-publishers. Explores the business and technology of writing and publishing. Regular newsletter, seminars and workshops, etc.

Authors North

c/o The Society of Authors, 84 Drayton Gardens, London SW10 9SB
☎0171 373 6642

Secretary *Ray Dunbobbin*

A group within **The Society of Authors** which organises meetings for members living in the North of England.

Authors' Club

40 Dover Street, London W1X 3RB
☎0171 499 8581   Fax 0171 409 0913

Secretary *Mrs Ann Carter*

FOUNDED in 1891 by Sir Walter Besant, the Authors' Club welcomes as members writers, publishers, critics, journalists, academics and anyone involved with literature. Administers the **Authors' Club Best First Novel Award; Sir Banister Fletcher Award; Marsh Biography Award** and the **Marsh Award for Children's Literature in Translation**. Membership fee: apply to secretary.

Authors' Licensing and Collecting Society

74 New Oxford Street, London WC1A 1EF
☎0171 255 2034   Fax 0171 323 0486

Secretary General *Christopher Zielinski*
Subscription £5.88 incl. VAT (free to members of **The Society of Authors** and **The Writers' Guild**); £5 (Residents of EC countries); £7 (Overseas)

A non-profit-making society collecting and distributing payment to writers in areas where they are unable to administer the rights themselves, such as reprography, certain lending rights, private and off-air recording and simultaneous cable retransmission. Open to writers and their heirs.

The Bibliographical Society

c/o The Wellcome Institute Library, 183 Euston Road, London NW1 2BE
☎0171 611 7244   Fax 0171 611 8703

President *R. Myers*

Honorary Secretary D. Pearson
Subscription £28 p.a.

Aims to promote and encourage the study and research of historical, analytical, descriptive and textual bibliography, and the history of printing, publishing, bookselling, bookbinding and collecting; to hold meetings at which papers are read and discussed; to print and publish works concerned with bibliography; to form a bibliographical library. Awards grants and bursaries for bibliographical research. *Publishes* a quarterly magazine called *The Library*.

Book Packagers Association

93A Blenheim Crescent, London W11 2EQ
☎0171 221 9089
Secretary Rosemary Pettit
Subscription £150 p.a.; Associate
  membership £75 p.a.; Overseas
  membership £100 p.a.

Aims to provide members with a forum for the exchange of information, to improve the image of packaging and to represent the interests of members. Activities include meetings, seminars, the provision of standard contracts and a joint stand at London Book Fair.

Book Trust

Book House, 45 East Hill, London
SW18 2QZ
☎0181 870 9055   Fax 0181 874 4790
Chief Executive Brian Perman
Subscription £25 p.a.; £28 (Overseas)

FOUNDED 1925. Book Trust, the independent educational charity promoting books and reading, includes Young Book Trust (formerly Children's Book Foundation). The Trust offers a book information service (free to the public and on subscription to the trade); administers many literary prizes (including the **Booker**); carries out surveys, *publishes* useful reference books and resource materials; houses a children's book reference library, and promotes children's books through activities like Children's Book Week.

Book Trust Scotland

The Scottish Book Centre, 137 Dundee Street, Edinburgh EH11 1BG
☎0131 229 3663   Fax 0131 228 4293
Contact Lindsey Fraser

FOUNDED 1956. Book Trust Scotland works with schools, libraries, writers, artists, publishers, bookshops and individuals to promote the pleasures of reading to people of all ages. It

provides a book information service which draws on the children's reference library (a copy of every children's book published in the previous twelve months), the Scottish children's book collection, a range of press cuttings on Scottish literary themes and a number of smaller collections of Scottish books. Book Trust Scotland administers **The Fidler Award** and the **The Scottish Writer of the Year Prize**; and *publishes* guides to Scottish books and writers, both adult and children's. Book Trust Scotland also produces a range of children's reading posters and Scottish poetry posters.

Booksellers Association of Great Britain & Ireland

Minster House, 272 Vauxhall Bridge Road,
London SW1V 1BA
☎0171 834 5477   Fax 0171 834 8812
Chief Executive Tim Godfray

FOUNDED 1895. The BA helps 3,300 independent, chain and multiple members to sell more books and reduce costs. It represents members' interests to publishers, Government, authors and others in the trade as well as offering marketing assistance, running training courses, conferences, seminars and exhibitions. *Publishes* directories, catalogues, surveys and various other publications connected with the book trade and administers the **Whitbread Book of the Year and Literary Awards**.

BAFTA (British Academy of Film and Television Arts)

195 Piccadilly, London W1V 0LN
☎0171 734 0022   Fax 0171 734 1792
Chief Executive Harry Manley
Subscription £150 p.a.; £75 (Country)

FOUNDED 1947. Membership limited to 'those who have contributed to the industry' over a minimum period of three years. Provides facilities for screening and discussions, encourages research and experimentation, and makes annual awards.

BASCA (British Academy of Songwriters, Composers and Authors)

The Penthouse, 4 Brook Street, London
W1Y 1AA
☎0171 629 0992   Fax 0171 629 0993
Contact Amanda Harcourt
Subscription from £35 + VAT p.a.

FOUNDED 1947. The Academy offers advice and support for songwriters and composers and represents members' interests to the music industry. It also issues a standard contract between publishers and writers and a collaborators' agreement. Members receive the Academy's quarterly magazine and can attend fortnightly legal and financial seminars and creative workshops. The Academy administers Britain's annual awards for composers, the Ivor Novello Awards, now in their 42nd year.

British Amateur Press Association (BAPA)

Flat 36, Priory Park, Botanical Way, St Osyth, Essex CO16 8TE

Secretary/Treasurer L. E. Linford

A non-profit-making, non-sectarian hobby organisation (founded in 1890) to 'promote the fellowship of amateur writers, artists, editors, printers, publishers and other craftsmen/women. To encourage them to edit, print and publish, *as a hobby*, magazines and newsletters, etc' by letterpress and other processes, including photocopiers and computer DTP/word-processors. Not an outlet for placing work commercially, only with other members in their private publications circulated within the association and amongst friends. A fraternity providing contacts between amateur writers, poets, editors, artists, etc. Postal enquiries only, please enclose first-class stamp to the Secretary at the above address.

British American Arts Association

118 Commercial Street, London E1 6NF
☎0171 247 5385   Fax 0171 247 5256

Director *Jennifer Williams*

A non-profit organisation working in the field of arts and education. Conducts research, organises conferences, produces a quarterly newsletter and is part of an international network of arts and education organisations. As well as a specialised arts and education library, BAAA has a more general library holding information on opportunities for artists and performers both in the UK and abroad. It is not a grant-giving organisation.

British Association of Communicators in Business

Bolsover House, 5–6 Clipstone Street, London W1P 7EB
☎0171 436 2545   Fax 0171 436 2545/2565

FOUNDED 1949. The Association aims to be the 'market leader for those involved in corporate media management and practice by providing professional, authoritative, dynamic, supportive and innovative services'.

British Association of Journalists

88 Fleet Street, London EC4Y 1PJ
☎0171 353 3003   Fax 0171 353 2310

General Secretary *Steve Turner*

Subscription National newspaper staff, national broadcasting staff, national news agency staff: £12.50 a month. Other seniors, including magazine journalists, PRs and freelancers who earn the majority of their income from journalism: £7.50 a month. Journalists under 24: £5 a month. Student journalists: Free.

FOUNDED 1992. Aims to protect and promote the industrial and professional interests of journalists.

BAPLA (British Association of Picture Libraries and Agencies)

18 Vine Hill, London EC1R 5DX
☎0171 713 1780   Fax 0171 713 1211

Administrator *Sarah Saunders*

Represents 95 per cent of the British picture library and agency industry offering more than 300 million pictures. The Association offers advice on costs, an annual membership directory, a picture-sourcing database, and produces an internationally admired journal.

British Copyright Council

Copyright House, 29–33 Berners Street, London W1P 4AA
Contact *The Secretary*

Works for the national and international acceptance of copyright and acts as a lobby/watchdog organisation on behalf of creators, publishers and performers on copyright and associated matters. Publications include *Guide to the Law of Copyright and Rights in Performances in the UK*; *Photocopying from Books and Journals*. An umbrella organisation which does not deal with individual enquiries.

The British Council

10 Spring Gardens, London SW1A 2BN
☎0171 930 8466/Press Office: 389 4878
Fax 0171 839 6347

Head of Literature *Jonathan Barker*

The British Council promotes Britain abroad. It provides access to British ideas, talents, expertise and experience in education and training, books and periodicals, the English language, literature and the arts, sciences and technology. An independent, non-political organisation, the British Council works in 109 countries running a mix of offices, libraries, resource centres and English teaching operations.

British Equestrian Writers' Association

Priory House, Station Road, Swavesey, Cambridge CB4 5QJ

☎01954 232084   Fax 01954 231362

Contact *Gillian Newsum*
Subscription £15

FOUNDED 1973. Aims to further the interests of equestrian sport and improve, wherever possible, the working conditions of the equestrian press. Membership is by invitation of the committee. Candidates for membership must be nominated and seconded by full members and receive a majority vote of the committee.

British Film Commission

70 Baker Street, London W1M 1DJ

☎0171 224 5000   Fax 0171 224 1013

Press & Public Relations Manager *Tina McFarling*

FOUNDED 1991 the BFC is funded through the Department of National Heritage. Its remit is to promote the United Kingdom as an international production centre, to encourage the use of British personnel, technical services, facilities and locations, and to provide wide-ranging support to those filming and contemplating filming in the UK.

British Film Institute

21 Stephen Street, London W1P 2LN

☎0171 255 1444   Fax 0171 436 7950

Membership from £11.95–£56.60 p.a. (concessions available)

FOUNDED 1933. Exists to encourage the development of film, television and video in the UK. Its divisions include: National Film and Television Archive; BFI on the South Bank (National Film Theatre, London Film Festival and Museum of the Moving Image); **BFI Production**; **BFI Library and Information Services**; and BFI Research & Education (including Publishing, *Sight and Sound*). It also provides programming support to a regional network of 36 film theatres.

British Guild of Beer Writers

PO Box 900, Hemel Hempstead, Herts HP3 0RJ

☎01442 834900   Fax 01442 834901

Contact *Peter Coulson*
Subscription £40 p.a.

FOUNDED 1988. Aims to improve standards in beer writing and at the same time extend public knowledge of beers and brewing. Publishes a directory of members with details of their publications and their particular areas of interest; this is then circulated to newspapers, magazines, trade press and broadcasting organisations. As part of the plan to improve writing standards and to achieve a higher profile for beer, the Guild offers annual awards, The Gold and Silver Tankard Awards, to writers and broadcasters judged to have made the most valuable contribution towards this end in their work. Meetings are held regularly.

British Guild of Travel Writers

90 Corringway, London W5 3HA

☎0181 998 2223

Chairman *Annette Brown*
Honorary Secretary *John Harrison*
Subscription £50 p.a.

The professional association of travel writers, broadcasters, photographers and editors which aims to serve its members' professional interests by acting as a forum for debate, discussion and 'networking'. It publishes an annual Year Book giving full details of all its members, holds monthly meetings and has a monthly newsletter. Members are required to earn the majority of their income from travel reporting.

British Science Fiction Association

1 Long Row Close, Everdon, Daventry, Northants NN11 3BE

☎01327 361661

Membership Secretary *Paul Billinger*
Subscription £18 p.a. (Reduction for Unwaged)

FOUNDED originally in 1958 by a group of authors, readers, publishers and booksellers interested in science fiction. With a worldwide membership, the Association aims to promote the reading, writing and publishing of science fiction and to encourage SF fans to maintain contact with each other. The Association also offers postal writers' workshops, a magazine chain and an information service.

Publishes Matrix bi-monthly newsletter with comment and opinions, news of conventions, etc. Contributions from members welcomed; *Vector* bi-monthly critical journal – reviews of books and magazines; *Focus* bi-annual magazine with articles, original fiction and letters column. For further information, contact the Membership Secretary at the above address or on e-mail (billingeratenterprise.net).

British Screen Finance
14–17 Wells Mews, London W1P 3FL
☎0171 323 9080   Fax 0171 323 0092
Contact *Simon Perry, Emma Berkofsky*

A private company aided by government grant; shareholders are Rank, Channel 4, Granada and Pathé. Exists to invest in British films specifically intended for cinema release in the UK and worldwide. Divided into two functions: project development (contact *Stephen Cleary*), and production investment (contact *Simon Perry*). British Screen also manages the European Co-production Fund which exists to support feature films co-produced by the UK with other European countries. British Screen develops around 40 projects per year, and has invested in 115 British feature film productions in the last ten years.

British Society of Magazine Editors (BSME)
137 Hale Lane, Edgware, Middlesex
HA8 9QP
☎0181 906 4664   Fax 0181 959 2137
Contact *Gill Branston*

FOUNDED 196. Holds regular lunches and industry forums.

Broadcasting Press Guild
Tiverton, The Ridge, Woking, Surrey
GU22 7EQ
☎01483 764895   Fax 01483 764895
Membership Secretary *Richard Last*
Subscription £15 p.a.

FOUNDED 1973 to promote the professional interests of journalists specialising in writing or broadcasting about the media. Organises monthly lunches addressed by top broadcasting executives, and annual TV and radio awards. Membership by invitation.

Campaign for Press and Broadcasting Freedom
8 Cynthia Street, London N1 9JF
☎0171 278 4430   Fax 0171 837 8868
Subscription £12 p.a. (concessions available); £25 p.a. (Institutions); £20 p.a. (Organisations)

Broadly based pressure group working for more accountable and accessible media in Britain. Advises on right of reply and takes up the issue of the portrayal of minorities. Members receive *Free Press* (bi-monthly), discounts on publications and news of campaign progress.

The Caravan Writers' Guild
Hillside House, Beach Road, Benllech, Anglesey LL74 8SW
☎01248 852248   Fax 01248 852107
Contact *The Secretary*
Subscription £5 joining fee plus £10 p.a.

Guild for writers active in the specialist fields of caravan and camping journalism.

Careers Writers' Association
71 Wimborne Road, Colehill, Wimborne, Dorset BH21 2RP
☎01202 880320
Membership Secretary *Barbara Buffton*

FOUNDED 1979. The association aims to promote high standards of careers writing, improve access to sources of information, provide a network for members to exchange information and experience, hold meetings on topics of relevance and interest to members. Also produces an occasional newsletter and maintains a membership list. Forges links with organisations sharing related interests, and maintains regular contact with national education and training bodies, government agencies and publishers.

Chartered Institute of Journalists
2 Dock Offices, Surrey Quays Road, London SE16 2XU
☎0171 252 1187   Fax 0171 232 2302
General Secretary *Christopher Underwood*
Subscription £150

FOUNDED 1884. The Chartered Institute is concerned with professional journalistic standards and with safeguarding the freedom of the media. It is open to writers, broadcasters and journalists (including self-employed) in all media. Affiliate membership (£100) is available to part-time or occasional practitioners and to overseas journalists who can join the Institute's International Division. Members also belong to the IOJ (Institute of Journalists), an independent trade union which protects, advises and represents them in their employment or freelance work; negotiates on their behalf and provides legal assistance and support. The IOJ (TU) is a certificated trade union which represents members' interests in the workplace, and is also a constituent member of the National Council in the Training of Journalists and the Independent Unions Training Council.

Children's Book Circle

c/o Macmillan Publishers Ltd, 25 Eccleston Place, London SW1W 9NF
☎0171 881 8000   Fax 0171 881 8001
Membership Secretary *Gaby Morgan*

The Children's Book Circle provides a discussion forum for anybody involved with children's books. Monthly meetings are addressed by a panel of invited speakers and topics focus on current and controversial issues. Administers the **Eleanor Farjeon Award**.

Children's Book Foundation

See **Book Trust**

Circle of Wine Writers

44 Oaklands Avenue, Droitwich, Worcestershire WR9 7BT
☎01905 773707   Fax 01905 773707
Vice Chairman *Philippe Boucheron*
Membership £25 p.a.

FOUNDED 1962. Open to all *bona fide* authors, broadcasters, journalists, lecturers and tutors who are engaged in, or earn a significant part of their income from, communicating about wine and spirits. Aims to improve the standard of writing, broadcasting and lecturing about wine; to contribute to the growth of knowledge and interest in wine; to promote wine of quality in the UK and to comment adversely on faulty products or dubious practices which could lead to a fall in consumption; to establish and maintain good relations between the Circle and the wine trade in the best interests of the consumer.

Clé, The Irish Book Publishers Association

The Writers' Centre, 19 Parnell Square, Dublin 1, Republic of Ireland
☎00 353 1 8729090   Fax 00 353 1 8722035
President *Michael Gill*
Administrator *Orla Martin*

FOUNDED 1970 to promote Irish publishing, protect members' interests and train the industry.

Comedy Writers' Association of Great Britain

61 Parry Road, Ashmore Park, Wolverhampton, West Midlands WV11 2PS
☎01902 722729   Fax 01902 722729
Contact *Ken Rock*

FOUNDED 1981 to assist and promote the work of comedy writers. The Association is a self-help group designed to encourage and advise its members to sell their work. It is an international organisation with representatives in Britain, Germany, Cyprus, Sweden, Belgium, Luxembourg, Czechoslovakia, Denmark, Finland and Canada. International seminar with videos of foreign TV comedy programmes, bookshop and business club where members can discuss opportunities. Members often come together to work jointly on a variety of comedy projects for British and overseas productions. *Publishes* regular magazines and monthly market information.

Comhairle nan Leabhraichean/ The Gaelic Books Council

22 Mansfield Street, Glasgow G11 5QP
Chairman *Boyd Robertson*
Director *Ian MacDonald*

FOUNDED 1968. Encourages and promotes Gaelic publishing by offering grants to publishers and writers; providing editorial and word-processing services; retailing Gaelic books; producing a catalogue of all Gaelic books in print, and answering enquiries about them.

Commercial Radio Companies Association

77 Shaftesbury Avenue, London W1V 7AD
☎0171 306 2603   Fax 0171 470 0062
Chief Executive *Paul Brown*
Research Communications Manager *Rachell Fox*

The CRCA is the trade body for the independent radio stations. It represents members' interests to Government, the **Radio Authority**, trade unions, copyright organisations and other bodies.

The Copyright Licensing Agency Ltd

90 Tottenham Court Road, London W1P 0LP
☎0171 436 5931   Fax 0171 436 3986
Chief Executive/Secretary *Peter Shephard*
Office Manager *Kate Gardner*

FOUNDED 1982 by the **Authors' Licensing and Collecting Society (ALCS)** and the **Publishers Licensing Society Ltd (PLS)**, the CLA administers collectively photocopying and other copying rights that it is uneconomic for writers and publishers to administer for themselves. The Agency issues collective and transactional licences, and the fees it collects, after the deduction of its operating costs, are distributed at regular intervals to authors and publishers via their respective societies (i.e. ALCS or PLS). Since 1987 CLA has distributed over £50 million.

Council for British Archaeology

Bowes Morrell House, 111 Walmgate, York YO1 2UA
☎01904 671417   Fax 01904 671384
Information Officer *Mike Heyworth*

FOUNDED 1944 to represent and promote archaeology at all levels. Its aims are to improve the public's awareness in and understanding of Britain's past; to carry out research; to survey, guide and promote the teaching of archaeology at all levels of education; to publish a wide range of academic, educational, general and bibliographical works (see **CBA Publishing**).

Council of Academic and Professional Publishers

See **The Publishers Association**

Crime Writers' Association (CWA)

60 Drayton Road, Kings Heath, Birmingham B14 7LR
Secretary *Judith Cutler*
Membership £40 (Town); £35 (Country)

Full membership is limited to professional crime writers, but publishers, literary agents, booksellers, etc., who specialise in crime are eligible for Associate membership. The Association has regional chapters throughout the country, including Scotland. Meetings are held monthly in central London, with informative talks frequently given by police, scenes of crime officers, lawyers, etc., and a weekend conference is held annually in different parts of the country. Produces a monthly newsletter for members called *Red Herrings* and presents various annual awards.

The Critics' Circle

c/o The Stage (incorporating Television Today), 47 Bermondsey Street, London SE1 3XT
☎0171 403 1818 ext 106 (Catherine Cooper)
Fax 0171 357 9287
President *Allen Robertson*
Honorary General Secretary *Charles Hedges*
Subscription £18 p.a.

Membership by invitation only. Aims to uphold and promote the art of criticism (and the commercial rates of pay thereof) and preserve the interests of its members: professionals involved in criticism of film, drama, music and dance.

Department of National Heritage

2–4 Cockspur Street, London SW1Y 5DH
☎0171 211 6000   Fax 0171 211 6270
Senior Press Officer, Arts *Toby Sargent*

The Department of National Heritage has responsibilities for Government policies relating to the arts, museums and galleries, public libraries, sport, broadcasting, Press standards, film, the built heritage, tourism and the National Lottery. It funds **The Arts Council**, national museums and galleries, **The British Library** (including the new library building at St Pancras), the Public Lending Right and the Royal Commission on Historical Manuscripts. It is responsible within Government for the public library service in England, and for library and information matters generally, where they are not the responsibility of other departments.

Directory Publishers Association

93A Blenheim Crescent, London W11 2EQ
☎0171 221 9089
Contact *Rosemary Pettit*
Subscription £110–£1100 p.a.

FOUNDED 1970 to promote the interests of *bona fide* directory publishers and protect the public from disreputable and fraudulent practices. The objectives of the Association are to maintain a code of professional practice to safeguard public interest; to raise the standard and status of directory publishing throughout the UK; to promote business directories as a medium for advertising; to protect the legal and statutory interests of directory publishers; to foster bonds of common interest among responsible directory publishers and to provide for the exchange of technical, commercial and management information between members. Meetings, seminars, conference, newsletter and representation at fairs.

Drama Association of Wales

The Library, Singleton Road, Splott, Cardiff CF2 2ET
☎01222 452200   Fax 01222 452277
Contact *Gary Thomas*

Runs a large playscript lending library; holds an annual playwriting competition (see under **Prizes**); offers a script-reading service (£10 per script) which usually takes three months from receipt of play to issue of reports. From plays submitted to the reading service, selected scripts are considered for publication of a short run (250–750 copies). Writers receive a percentage of the cover price on sales and a percentage of the performance fees.

East Anglian Writers
47 Christchurch Road, Norwich, Norfolk
NR2 3NE
☎01603 455503   Fax 01603 455503
Chairman *Michael Pollard*

A group of over 80 professional writers living
in Norfolk and Suffolk. Business and social
meetings and informal contacts with regional
publishers and other organisations interested in
professional writing.

Edinburgh Bibliographical Society
Dept of Special Collections, Edinburgh
University Library, George Square, Edinburgh
EH8 9LJ
☎0131 650 3412   Fax 0131 650 6863
Honorary Secretary Dr M. Simpson
Subscription £7; £5 (Students)

FOUNDED 1890. Organises lectures on bibliographical topics and visits to libraries. *Publishes*
a biennial journal called *Transactions*, which is
free to members, and other occasional publications.

Educational Publishers Council
See **The Publishers Association**

Electronic Publishers' Forum
See **The Publishers Association**

The English Association
University of Leicester, University Road,
Leicester LE1 7RH
☎0116 252 3982   Fax 0116 252 2301
Secretary *Helen Lucas*

FOUNDED 1906 to promote understanding and
appreciation of the English language and its literatures. Activities include sponsoring a number of publications and organising lectures and
conferences for teachers, plus annual sixth-
form conferences. Publications include *Year's
Work in Critical and Cultural Theory, English,
Use of English, Primary English, Year's Work in
English Studies, Essays and Studies* and *Year's
Work in English Studies.*

ETmA (Educational Television & Media Association)
37 Monkgate, York YO3 7PB
☎01904 639212   Fax 01904 639212
Administrator *Josie Key*

The ETmA is a 'dynamic association' comprising

a wide variety of users of television and other
electronic media in education. Annual awards
scheme (video competition), and annual conferences. New members always welcome.

Federation of Entertainment Unions
1 Highfield, Twyford, Nr Winchester,
Hampshire SO21 1QR
☎01962 713134   Fax 01962 713288
Secretary *Steve Harris*

Plenary meetings six times annually and meetings
of The Film and Electronic Media Committee
six times annually on alternate months.
Additionally, there are Training & European
Committees. Represents the following unions:
British Actors' Equity Association; Broadcasting
Entertainment Cinematograph and Theatre
Union; Musicians' Union; **National Union of
Journalists**; **The Writers' Guild of Great
Britain**.

The Federation of Worker Writers and Community Publishers (FWWCP)
PO Box 540, Burslem, Stoke on Trent
ST6 6DR
☎01782 822327   Fax 01782 822327
Administrator/Coordinator *Tim Diggles*

The FWWCP is a federation of writing groups
who are committed to writing and publishing
based on working-class experience and creativity. The FWWCP is the membership's collective national voice and has for some time been
given funding by **The Arts Council**.

Founded in 1976, it comprises around 50
member groups, each one with its own identity, reflecting its community and membership.
They represent over 5000 people who regularly (often weekly) meet to offer constructive
criticism, produce books and tapes, perform
and share skills, offering creative and critical
support. There are writers' workshops of long
standing; adult literacy organisations; groups
working mainly in oral and local history;
groups and local networks of writers who
come together to publish, train or perform;
groups with a specific remit to further the aims
of a section of the community such as the
homeless or disabled.

Although diverse in nature, member organisations share the aim to make writing and publishing accessible to people and encourage
them to take an active, cooperative and democratic role in writing, performing and publishing. The main activities include training days

and weekends to learn and share skills, a quarterly magazine, a major annual festival of writing and networking between member organisations.

The FWWCP has published a number of anthologies and is willing to work with other organisations on publishing projects. Membership is only open to groups but individuals will be put in touch with groups which can help them, and become friends of the Federation. Contact the above address for an information leaflet.

Foreign Press Association in London
11 Carlton House Terrace, London SW1Y 5AJ
☎0171 930 0445   Fax 0171 925 0469
Contact *Davina Crole, Catherine Flury*
Membership (not incl. VAT) £100 p.a. (Full); £92.40 (Associate Journalists); £142 (Associate Non-Journalists)

FOUNDED 1888. Non-profit-making service association for foreign correspondents based in London, providing a variety of press-related services.

The Gaelic Books Council
See **Comhairle nan Leabhraichean**

The Garden Writers' Guild
c/o Institute of Horticulture, 14/15 Belgrave Square, London SW1X 8PS
☎0171 245 6943
Contact *Angela Clarke*
Subscription £15; (£10 to Institute of Horticulture members)

FOUNDED 1990. Aims to revise the status and standing of gardening communicators. Administers an annual awards scheme. Operates a mailing service and organises press briefing days.

General Practitioner Writers' Association
West Carnliath, Strathtay, Perth PH9 0PG
☎01887 840380   Fax 01887 840380
Contact *Professor F. M. Hull*
Subscription £30 p.a.; £40 (Joint)

FOUNDED 1986 to promote and improve writing activities within and for general practices. Open to general practitioners, practice managers, nurses, etc. and professional journalists writing on anything pertaining to general practice. Very keen to develop input from interested parties who work mainly outside the profession.

Regular workshops, discussions and a twice-yearly journal, *The GP Writer*.

Guild of Agricultural Journalists
Charmwood, 47 Court Meadow, Rotherfield, East Sussex TN6 3LQ
☎01892 853187
Honorary General Secretary *Don Gomery*
Subscription £30 p.a.

FOUNDED 1944 to promote a high professional standard among journalists who specialise in agriculture, horticulture and allied subjects. Represents members' interests with representative bodies in the industry; provides a forum through meetings and social activities for members to meet eminent people in the industry; maintains contact with associations of agricultural journalists overseas; promotes schemes for the education of members and for the provision of suitable entrants into agricultural journalism.

Guild of Editors
See **The Newspaper Society**

The Guild of Erotic Writers
CTCK PO Box 8431, Deptford, London SE8 4BP
☎0973 767086
Contact *Elizabeth Coldwell, Zak Jane Keir*
Subscription £10 p.a.

FOUNDED 1995. Aims to provide a network for all authors of erotic fiction, both published and unpublished and to promote erotica as a valid form of writing. Members receive quarterly newsletters and a tip sheet on getting work accepted, together with discounts on quarterly conferences and a manuscript-reading service (also available to non-members at 'very competitive rates' – short stories £4.50 for members, £7 non-members).

Guild of Motoring Writers
30 The Cravens, Smallfield, Surrey RH6 9QS
☎01342 843294   Fax 01342 844093
General Secretary *Sharon Scott-Fairweather*

FOUNDED 1944. Represents members' interests and provides a forum for members to exchange information.

The Guild of Regional Film Writers
45 Tides Way, Marchwood, Southampton SO40 4LE
☎01703 872956   Fax 01703 872956
Chairman *Darren Vaughan*

Subscription £40 p.a.

FOUNDED 1987. Aims to encourage, support and promote the work of regional film writers and broadcasters within the film industry. Works closely with distributors, exhibitors and other industry bodies. Members are invited to attend 'Cinema Days' weekends thrice yearly, where new movies are screened and press conferences held. Prospective members should supply three cuttings/tapes for approval.

Humberside Writers' Association (HWA)

'Fairoaks', West Promenade, Driffield,
East Yorkshire YO25 7TZ
☎01377 255542

Chairman *Glynn S. Russell*
Annual membership fee £2

FOUNDED 1987 by local writers, would-be writers and people interested in new writing who gathered together with the backing of their regional arts association to create a platform for local scribblers, published or otherwise. Organises and promotes writing-related events and workshops within the Humberside area. *Publishes* information about events, competitions, workshops, publications and any other news, local or national, about opportunities of interest to members. Regular meetings (last Wednesday of the month) to which writers, publishers and agents are invited; plus day schools, readings, newsletter and library/ resource unit.

Independent Publishers Guild

25 Cambridge Road, Hampton, Middlesex
TW12 2JL
☎0181 979 0250   Fax 0181 979 6393

Secretary *Yvonne Messenger*
Subscription approx. £75 p.a.

FOUNDED 1962. Membership open to independent publishers, packagers and suppliers, i.e. professionals in allied fields. Regular meetings, conferences, seminars, a bulletin and regional groups.

Independent Television Association

See **ITV Network Centre**

Independent Theatre Council

12 The Leathermarket, Weston Street,
London SE1 3ER
☎0171 403 1727/6698 (general/training)
Fax 0171 403 1745

Contact *Charlotte Jones*

The management association and representative body for small/middle-scale theatres (up to 350 seats) and touring theatre companies. Negotiates contracts and has established standard agreements with Equity on behalf of all professionals working in the theatre. In 1991 negotiated with the **Theatre Writers' Union** and **The Writers' Guild** for a contractual agreement covering rights and fee structure for playwrights. Terms and conditions were renegotiated and updated in April 1997. Copies of the minimum terms agreement can be obtained from The Writers' Guild. *Publishes* a booklet, *A Practical Guide for Writers and Companies* (£3.50 plus p&p), which gives guidance both to writers on how to submit scripts to theatres and to theatres on how to deal with them.

Institute of Copywriting

PO Box 1561, Wedmore BS28 4TD
☎01934 713563   Fax 01934 713492

Secretary *Alex Middleton*

FOUNDED 1991 to promote copywriters and copywriting (writing publicity material). Maintains a code of practice. Membership is open to students as well as experienced practitioners. Runs training courses (see entry under **Writers' Courses**). Has a list of approved copywriters. Answers queries relating to copywriting. Contact the Institute for a free booklet.

Institute of Translation and Interpreting

377 City Road, London EC1V 1NA
☎0171 713 7600   Fax 0171 713 7650

Professional association of translators and interpretors. Membership is open to those who satisfy stringent admission criteria and can provide evidence of adequate professional translation or interpreting experience. Offers affiliation and student membership. Benefits include listing in an index which specifies the skills and languages of members. *Publishes* a bi-monthly bulletin and *Directory of Translators & Interpreters*. Member of the International Federation of Translators.

International Association of Puzzle Writers

42 Brigstocke Terrace, Ryde, Isle of Wight
PO33 2PD
☎01983 811688

Contact *Dr Jeremy Sims*

FOUNDED 1966 for writers of brainteasing puzzles, crosswords and word games, and for designers of games in general. Enquiries from publishers seeking material welcome. Aims to provide support and information and to promote the art of puzzle writing and games design to publishers, games manufacturers and the general public. *Publishes* bi-monthly newsletter – contributions welcome. Membership is free but stamps or IRCs are necessary to cover the costs of postage of the newsletter. For further information, send s.a.e. to the above address.

International Cultural Desk
6 Belmont Crescent, Glasgow G12 8ES
☎0141 339 0090   Fax 0141 337 2271
Development Manager *Hilde Bollen*
Information Officer *Anne Robb*

FOUNDED 1994. Aims to assist the Scottish cultural community to operate more effectively in an international context by providing timely and targeted information and advice. The Desk provides and disseminates information on funding sources, international opportunities and cultural policy development in Europe, and also assists with establishing contacts internationally. The Desk is not a funding agency.

   Publishes Communication, a bi-monthly information update about forthcoming international opportunities across the whole range of cultural and artistic activity, and *InFocus*, a new series of specialised guides with an international focus.

Irish Book Publishers Association
See **Clé**

Irish Copyright Licensing Agency Ltd
19 Parnell Square, Dublin 1, Republic of Ireland
☎00 353 1 872 9202   Fax 00 353 1 872 2035
Administrator *Orla O'Sullivan*

FOUNDED 1992 by writers and publishers in Ireland to provide a scheme through which rights holders can give permission, and users of copyright material can obtain permission, to copy.

Irish Writers' Union
19 Parnell Square, Dublin 1 Republic of Ireland
☎00 353 1 872 1302   Fax 00 353 1 872 6282
Secretary *Sam McAughtry*
Subscription £20 p.a.

FOUNDED 1986 to promote the interests and protect the rights of writers in Ireland.

Isle of Man Authors
24 Laurys Avenue, Ramsey, Isle of Man
IM8 2HE
☎01624 815634
Secretary *Mrs Beryl Sandwell*
Subscription £5 p.a.

An association of writers living on the Isle of Man, which has links with **The Society of Authors**.

ITV Network Centre
200 Gray's Inn Road, London WC1X 8HF
☎0171 843 8000   Fax 0171 843 8158

The ITV Network Centre, wholly owned by the ITV companies, independently commissions and schedules the television programmes which are shown across the ITV network. As a successor to the Independent Television Association, it also provides a range of services to the ITV companies where a common approach is required.

IVCA (International Visual Communication Association)
Bolsover House, 5–6 Clipstone Street, London W1P 8LD
☎0171 580 0962   Fax 0171 436 2606
Chief Executive *Wayne Drew*

The IVCA is a professional association representing the interests of the users and suppliers of visual communications. In particular it pursues the interests of producers, commissioners and manufacturers involved in the non-broadcast and independent facilities industries and also business event companies. It represents all sizes of company and freelance individuals, offering information and advice services, publications, a professional network, special interest groups, a magazine and a variety of events including the UK's Film and Video Communications Festival.

The Library Association
7 Ridgmount Street, London WC1E 7AE
☎0171 636 7543   Fax 0171 436 7218
Chief Executive *Ross Shimmon*

The professional body for librarians and information managers, with 26,000 individual and institutional members. **Library Association Publishing** produces 25 new titles each year and has over 200 in print. The *LA Record* is the monthly magazine for members. Further information from Information Services, The Library Association.

The Media Society
56 Roseneath Road, London SW11 6AQ
Contact *Peter Dannheisser*
Subscription £25 p.a.; £10 entry fee
FOUNDED 1973. A registered charity which aims to provide a forum for the exchange of knowledge and opinion between those in public and political life, the professions, industry and education. Meetings (about six a year) usually take the form of luncheons and dinners in London with invited speakers. The society also acts as a 'think tank' and submits evidence and observations to royal commissions, select committees and review bodies.

Medical Journalists' Association
Barley Mow, 185 High Street, Stony Stratford, Milton Keynes MK11 1AP
☎01908 564623
Chairman *John Illman*
Honorary Secretary *Gwen Yates*
Subscription £30 p.a.
FOUNDED 1967. Aims to improve the quality and practice of medical and health journalism and to improve relationships and understanding between medical and health journalists and the health and medical professions. Regular meetings with senior figures in medicine and medico politics; teach-ins on particular subjects to help journalists with background information; weekend symposium for members with people who have newsworthy stories in the field; awards for medical journalists offered by various commercial sponsors, plus MJA's own award financed by members. *Publishes* a detailed directory of members and freelances and two-monthly newsletter.

Medical Writers' Group
The Society of Authors, 84 Drayton Gardens, London SW10 9SB
☎0171 373 6642   Fax 0171 373 5768
Contact *Jacqueline Granger-Taylor*
FOUNDED 1980. A specialist group within **The Society of Authors** offering advice and help to authors of medical books. Administers the **Royal Society of Medicine Prizes**.

National Association of Writers Groups
The Arts Centre, Biddick Lane, Washington, Tyne & Wear NE38 2AB
Contact *The Secretary*
FOUNDED 1995 with the object of furthering the interests of writers' groups throughout the UK. Produces a bi-monthly newsletter, distributed to member groups. Details available from the secretary at the above address.

National Association of Writers in Education
PO Box 1, Sheriff Hutton, York YO6 7YU
☎01653 618429   Fax 01653 618429
Contact *Paul Munden*
Subscription £12 p.a.
FOUNDED 1991. Aims to promote the contribution of living writers to education and to encourage both the practice and the critical appreciation of creative writing. Has over 400 members. Organises national conferences and training courses. *Publishes* a directory of writers who work in schools, colleges and the community (available on the Internet on www.nawe.co.uk) and a magazine, *Writing in Education*, issued free to members three times per year.

National Campaign for the Arts
Francis House, Francis Street, London SW1P 1DE
☎0171 828 4448   Fax 0171 931 9959
Director *Jennifer Edwards*
FOUNDED 1984 to represent the cultural sector in Britain and to make sure that the problems facing the arts are properly put to Government, at local and national level. The NCA is an independent body relying on finance from its members. Involved in all issues which affect the arts: public finance, education, broadcasting and media affairs, the fight against censorship, the rights of artists, the place of the arts on the public agenda and structures for supporting culture. Membership open to all arts organisations (except government agencies) and to individuals. Overseas Associate Membership available.

National Literacy Trust
Swire House, 59 Buckingham Gate, London SW1E 6AS
☎0171 828 2435   Fax 0171 931 9986
Director *Neil McClelland*
Subscription £14 p.a.
FOUNDED 1993. A charitable organisation (Registered Charity No: 1015539) which aims to work with others to enhance literacy standards in the UK, to encourage more reading and writing for pleasure and to seek to raise the profile of literacy in the context of social and technological change. Maintains a database of literacy activities in the UK, undertakes media campaigns, organises seminars and conferences, and *publishes* a quarterly magazine, *Literacy Today*.

National Poetry Foundation
See **Organisations of Interest to Poets**

The National Small Press Centre
See **Organisations of Interest to Poets**

National Union of Journalists
Acorn House, 314 Gray's Inn Road, London
WC1X 8DP
☎0171 278 7916   Fax 0171 837 8143
General Secretary *John Foster*
Subscription £148.50 p.a. (Freelance) or 1%
of annual income if lower; minimum
contribution £57.75

Represents journalists in all sectors of publishing, print and broadcast. Responsible for wages and conditions agreements which apply across the industry. Provides advice and representation for its members, as well as administering unemployment and other benefits.
Publishes various guides and magazines: *Freelance Directory, Fees Guide, The Journalist* and *The Freelance* (see **Magazines**).

Networking for Women in Film, Video and Television
c/o Vera Productions, 30–38 Dock Street,
Leeds, West Yorkshire LS10 1JF
☎0113 242 8646   Fax 0113 245 1238
Contact *Jane Howarth, Al Garthwaite*
Subscription £15 p.a.

FOUNDED 1989. A membership organisation for women working, seeking work, studying or in any way involved in film, video or television. Media studies departments, libraries, careers services are also welcome to join. *Publishes* a quarterly 16–page newsletter with news of activities, upcoming events, reviews, information about production funds, courses, etc. Entries of up to 40 words may be sent for inclusion in the Members' Index circulated throughout the membership to assist geographical/interest-based networking and employment. Contributions to the newsletter are welcome from all members. Advice, help and a campaigning voice for women in media are also on offer.

New Playwrights Trust
Interchange Studios, 15 Dalby Street, London
NW5 3NQ
☎0171 284 2818   Fax 0171 482 5292
Executive Director *Johnathan Meth*
Information & Research Officer
Angela Kelly
Subscription (information available by post)

New Playwrights Trust is the national research and development organisation for writing for all forms of live and recorded performance. *Publishes* a range of information pertinent to writers on all aspects of development and production in the form of pamphlets, and a six-weekly journal which also includes articles and interviews on aesthetic and practical issues. NPT also runs a script-reading service and a link service between writers and producers, organises seminars and conducts research projects. The latter includes research into the use of bilingual techniques in playwriting (*Two Tongues*), documentation of training programmes for writers (*Black Theatre Co-operative*) and an investigation of the relationship between live art and writing *Writing Live*.

New Producers Alliance (NPA)
9 Bourlet Close, London W1P 7PJ
☎0171 580 2480   Fax 0171 580 2484
Contact *Harriet Bass, Victoria Lorkin-Lange*

FOUNDED 1992; current membership of over 1000. Aims to encourage the production of commercial feature films for an international audience and to educate and inform feature film producers, writers and directors. The NPA is an independent networking organisation providing members with access to contacts, information, free legal advice and general help regarding film production. *Publishes* a monthly newsletter and organises meetings, workshops and seminars. The NPA does not produce films so please do not send scripts or treatments.

The New SF Alliance (NSFA)
c/o BBR Magazine, PO Box 625, Sheffield,
South Yorkshire S1 3GY
Contact *Chris Reed*

FOUNDED 1989. Committed to supporting the work of new writers and artists by promoting independent and small press publications worldwide. 'Help with finding the right market for your material by providing a mail-order service which allows you to sample magazines, and various publications including *BBR* magazine and *Scavenger's Newsletter*, which features the latest market news and tips.'

Newspaper Conference
See **The Newspaper Society**

The Newspaper Society
Bloomsbury House, 74–77 Great Russell
Street, London WC1B 3DA
☎0171 636 7014   Fax 0171 631 5119
Director *Dugal Nisbet-Smith*

Young Newspaper Executives' Association *David Brown*

The association of publishers of the regional and local Press, representing 1,400 regional daily and weekly, paid and free, newspaper titles in the UK. The Newspaper Conference is an organisation within the Society for London editors and representatives of regional newspapers. Bloomsbury House is also home to the Guild of Editors and to the Young Newspaper Executives' Association.

Outdoor Writers' Guild

PO Box 520, Bamber Bridge, Preston, Lancashire PR5 8LF
☎01772 696732   Fax 01772 696732
Secretary *Terry Marsh*
Subscription £35 p.a.; Joining fee £20

FOUNDED 1980 to promote, encourage and assist the development of professional standards among those involved in all aspects of outdoor journalism. Membership is not limited to writers but includes other outstanding professional media practitioners in the outdoor world such as broadcasters, photographers, filmmakers, editors, publishers and illustrators. *Publishes* a quarterly journal, *Bootprint*, and an annual *Handbook and Directory* (£25; free to members) as well as guidelines, codes of practice and advice notes. Presents five Awards for Excellence jointly with the Camping and Outdoor Leisure Association (COLA), and its own Award for Photographic Excellence.

PACT (Producers Alliance for Cinema and Television)

45 Mortimer Street, London W1N 7TD
☎0171 331 6000   Fax 0171 331 6700
Chief Executive *John Woodward*
Membership Officer *David Alan Mills*

FOUNDED 1992. PACT is the trade association of the UK independent television and feature film production sector and is a key contact point for foreign producers seeking British co-production, co-finance partners and distributors. Works for producers in the industry at every level and operates a members' regional network throughout the UK with a divisional office in Scotland. Membership services include: a dedicated industrial relations unit; discounted legal advice; a varied calendar of events; business advice; representation at international film and television markets; a comprehensive research programme; various publications: a monthly magazine, an annual members' directory; affiliation with European

and international producers' organisations; extensive information and production advice. Lobbies actively with broadcasters, financiers and governments to ensure that the producer's voice is heard and understood in Britain and Europe on all matters affecting the film and television industry.

PEN

7 Dilke Street, London SW3 4JE
☎0171 352 6303   Fax 0171 351 0220
General Secretary *Gillian Vincent*
Membership £40 (London/Overseas); £35 (members living over 50 miles from London)

English PEN is part of International PEN, a worldwide association of published writers which fights for freedom of expression and speaks out for writers who are imprisoned or harassed for having criticised their governments, or for publishing other unpopular views. FOUNDED in London in 1921, International PEN now consists of 126 centres in 92 countries. PEN originally stood for poets, essayists and novelists, but membership is now also open to published playwrights, editors, translators and journalists. A programme of talks and discussions is supplemented by a twice-yearly mailing and annual congress at one of the centre countries.

The Penman Club

185 Daws Heath Road, Benfleet, Essex SS7 2TF
☎01702 557431
Subscription £15 in the first year; £8.25 thereafter

FOUNDED 1950. Writers' society offering criticism of members' work and general advice. Send s.a.e. for prospectus to the General Secretary.

Performing Right Society

29–33 Berners Street, London W1P 4AA
☎0171 580 5544   Fax 0171 306 4050

Collects and distributes royalties arising from the performance and broadcast of copyright music on behalf of its composer, lyricist and music publisher members and members of affiliated societies worldwide.

Periodical Publishers Association (PPA)

Queens House, 28 Kingsway, London WC2B 6JR
☎0171 404 4166   Fax 0171 404 4167
Contact *Nicholas Mazur*

FOUNDED 1913 to promote and protect the interests of magazine publishers in the UK.

The Personal Managers' Association Ltd

1 Summer Road, East Molesey, Surrey
KT8 9LX
☎0181 398 9796   Fax 0181 398 9796
Co-chairs *Jane Annakin, Marc Berlin,*
   Tim Corrie
Secretary *Angela Adler*
Subscription £250 p.a.

An association of artists' and dramatists' agents
(membership not open to individuals).
Monthly meetings for exchange of information
and discussion. Maintains a code of conduct
and acts as a lobby when necessary. Applicants
screened. A high proportion of play agents are
members of the PMA.

The Picture Research Association (formerly SPREd)

Head Office: 455 Finchley Road, London
NW3 6HN
☎0171 431 9886   Fax 0171 431 9887
General Secretary *Emma Krikler*
Subscription Members: Introductory £30;
   Full £40; Associate £35. Magazine only:
   £25 per year quarterly

FOUNDED 1977 as the Society of Picture
Researchers & Editors. The Picture Research
Association is a professional body for picture
researchers, managers, picture editors and all
those involved in the research, management
and supply of visual material to all forms of the
media. The Association's main aims are to promote the interests and specific skills of its members internationally; to promote and maintain
professional standards; to bring together those
involved in the research and publication of
visual material; to provide a forum for the
exchange of information and to provide guidance to its members. Free advisory service for
members, regular meetings, quarterly magazine,
monthly newsletter and Freelance Register.

Player–Playwrights

9 Hillfield Park, London N10 3QT
☎0181 883 0371
President *Jack Rosenthal*
Contact *Peter Thompson (at the above address)*
Subscription £7.50 p.a., plus £1 per
   attendance

FOUNDED 1948. A society giving opportunity
for writers new to stage, radio and television, as
well as others finding difficulty in achieving
results, to work with writers established in
those media. At weekly meetings (7.45–10.00

p.m., Mondays, St Augustine's Hall, Queen's
Gate, London SW7), members' scripts are read
or performed by actor members and afterwards
assessed and dissected in general discussion.
Newcomers and new acting members are
always welcome.

Poetry Book Society

See **Organisations of Interest to Poets**

Poetry Ireland

See **Organisations of Interest to Poets**

The Poetry Society

See **Organisations of Interest to Poets**

Private Libraries Association

16 Brampton Grove, Kenton, Harrow,
Middlesex HA3 8LG
☎0181 907 6802   Fax 0181 907 6802
Honorary Secretary *Frank Broomhead*
Membership £25 p.a.

FOUNDED 1956. An international society of
book collectors. The Association's objectives
are to promote and encourage the awareness of
the benefits of book ownership, and the study
of books, their production, and ownership; to
publish works concerned with this, particularly
those which are not commercially profitable,
to hold meetings at which papers on cognate
subjects can be read and discussed. Lectures and
exhibitions are open to non-members.

The Professional Authors' and Publishers' Association (PAPA)

292 Kennington Road, London SE11 4LD
☎0171 582 1477   Fax 0171 582 4084
Contact *Tom Deegan, Andy Dempsey*

FOUNDED 1993 to provide self-publishing
authors with an imprint, a book production,
promotion and marketing service, thereby enabling them to avoid exploitation by so-called
'subsidy' or 'partnership' publishers. Authors
using the Association's New Millenium imprint
own the stock of books and receive the greater
proportion of the profits on book sales.

The Publishers Association

1 Kingsway, 3rd Floor, Strand, London
WC2B 6XF
☎0171 580 6321   Fax 0171 636 5375
Chief Executive *Clive Bradley, CBE* (retiring
   end 1997)

The national UK trade association for books,
learned journals, and electronic publications,

with around 300 member companies in the industry. Very much a trade body representing the industry to Government and the European Commission, and providing services to publishers. *Publishes* the *Directory of Publishing* in association with **Cassell**. Also home of the General Books Council (trade books), the Educational Publishers Council (school books), PA's International Division (BDC), the Council of Academic and Professional Publishers, and the Electronic Publishers' Forum.

Publishers Licensing Society Ltd
5 Dryden Street, Covent Garden, London WC2E 9NW
☎0171 829 8486   Fax 0171 829 8488
Manager *Caroline Elmslie*

FOUNDED 1981 to exercise and enforce on behalf of publishers the rights of copyright and other rights of a similar nature; to authorise the granting of licences for the making of reprographic copies; and to receive and distribute to the relevant publisher and copyright proprietors the sums accruing from such licensed use.

Publishers Publicity Circle
48 Crabtree Lane, London SW6 6LW
☎0171 385 3708   Fax 0171 385 3708
Contact *Christina Thomas*

Enables book publicists from both publishing houses and freelance PR agencies to meet and share information regularly. Meetings, held monthly in central London, provide a forum for press journalists, television and radio researchers and producers to meet publicists collectively. A directory of the PPC membership is published each year and distributed to over 2500 media contacts.

The Romantic Novelists' Association
Queens Farm, 17 Queens Street, Tintinhull, Somerset BA22 8PG
☎01935 822808
Contact *Margaret Graham*
Subscription £25 p.a.

Membership is open to published writers of romantic novels, or two or more full-length serials. Associate membership is open to publishers, editors, literary agents, booksellers, librarians and others having a close connection with novel writing and publishing. Meetings are held in London and guest speakers are often invited. *RNA News* is published quarterly and issued free to members. The Association makes

two annual awards. **The Major Award** for the Romantic Novel of the Year, and **The New Writers Award**.

Royal Festival Hall Literature Office
Performing Arts Department, Royal Festival Hall, South Bank Centre, London SE1 8XX
☎0171 921 0907   Fax 0171 928 2049
Head of Literature *Antonia Byatt*

The Royal Festival Hall presents a year-round literature programme covering all aspects of writing. Regular series range from New Voices to Fiction International and there is a biennial Poetry International Festival. Literature events are now programmed in the Voice Box, Purcell Room and Queen Elizabeth Hall. To join the free mailing list, phone 0171 921 0906.

Royal Society of Literature
1 Hyde Park Gardens, London W2 2LT
☎0171 723 5104   Fax 0171 402 0199
President *Lord Jenkins of Hillhead*
Subscription £30 p.a.

FOUNDED 1823. Membership by application to the Secretary. Fellowships are conferred by the Society on the proposal of two Fellows. Membership benefits include a newsletter, lectures, discussion meetings and poetry readings in the Society's rooms. Lecturers have included Patrick Leigh Fermor, Germaine Greer, Seamus Heaney, John Mortimer and Tom Stoppard. Presents the **W. H. Heinemann Prize** and the **Winifred Holtby Memorial Prize**.

Royal Television Society
Holborn Hall, 100 Gray's Inn Road, London WC1X 8AL
☎0171 430 1000   Fax 0171 430 0924
Subscription £55 p.a.

FOUNDED 1927. Covers all disciplines involved in the television industry. Provides a forum for debate and conferences on technical, social and cultural aspects of the medium. Presents various awards including journalism, programmes, technology, design and commercials. *Publishes Television Magazine* eight times a year for members and subscribers.

Science Fiction Foundation
c/o Liverpool University Library, PO Box 123, Liverpool L69 3DA
☎0151 794 2696/2733   Fax 0151 794 2681
The SFF is a national academic body for the fur-

therance of science fiction studies. *Publishes* a thrice-yearly magazine, *Foundation* (see entry under **Magazines**), which features academic articles and reviews of new fiction. It also has a reference library (see entry under **Library Services**), now housed at Liverpool University.

Scottish Daily Newspaper Society

48 Palmerston Place, Edinburgh
EH12 5DE
☎0131 220 4353   Fax 0131 220 4344
Director *Mr J. B. Raeburn*
FOUNDED 1915. Trade association representing publishers of Scottish daily and Sunday newspapers.

Scottish Library Association

Scottish Centre for Information & Library Services, 1 John Street, Hamilton, Strathclyde
ML3 7EU
☎01698 458888   Fax 01698 458899
Director *Robert Craig*
FOUNDED 1908 to bring together everyone engaged in or interested in library work in Scotland. The Association has over 2300 members, covering all aspects of library and information work. Its main aims are the promotion of library services and the qualifications and status of librarians.

Scottish Newspaper Publishers Association

48 Palmerston Place, Edinburgh
EH12 5DE
☎0131 220 4353   Fax 0131 220 4344
Director *Mr J. B. Raeburn*
FOUNDED around 1905. The representative body for the publishers of paid-for weekly and associated free newspapers in Scotland. Represents the interests of the industry to Government, public and other bodies and provides a range of services including industrial relations, education and training, and advertising. It is an active supporter of the Press Complaints Commission.

Scottish Print Employers Federation

48 Palmerston Place, Edinburgh
EH12 5DE
☎0131 220 4353   Fax 0131 220 4344
Director *Mr J. B. Raeburn*
FOUNDED 1910. Employers' organisation and trade association for the Scottish printing industry. Represents the interests of the indus-

try to Government, public and other bodies and provides a range of services including industrial relations. Negotiates a national wages and conditions agreement with the Graphical, Paper and Media Union, as well as education, training and commercial activities. The Federation is a member of Intergraf, the international confederation for employers' associations in the printing industry. In this capacity its views are channelled on the increasing number of matters affecting print businesses emanating from the European Union.

Scottish Publishers Association

Scottish Book Centre, 137 Dundee Street, Edinburgh EH11 1BG
☎0131 228 6866   Fax 0131 228 3220
Director *Lorraine Fannin*
Administrator *Davinder Bedi*
Publicity & Marketing Manager *Susanne Gilmour*
The Association represents nearly 70 Scottish publishers, from multinationals to very small presses, in a number of capacities, but primarily in the cooperative promotion and marketing of their books. The SPA also acts as an information and advice centre for both the trade and general public. *Publishes* seasonal catalogues, membership lists, the annual *Directory of Publishing in Scotland* and regular newsletters. Represents members at international book fairs; provides opportunities for publishers' training; carries out market research; and encourages export initiatives. Also provides administrative back-up for the Scottish Book Marketing Group, organisers of Scottish Book Fortnight and other promotions.

The Society of Authors

84 Drayton Gardens, London SW10 9SB
☎0171 373 6642   Fax 0171 373 5768
General Secretary *Mark Le Fanu*
Subscription £65/70 p.a.
FOUNDED 1884. The Society of Authors is an independent trade union with some 6000 members. It advises on negotiations with publishers, broadcasting organisations, theatre managers and film companies; assists with complaints and takes action for breach of contract, copyright infringement, etc. Together with **The Writers' Guild**, the Society has played a major role in advancing the Minimum Terms Agreement for authors. Among the Society's publications are *The Author* (a quarterly journal) and the *Quick Guides* series to various aspects of writing (all free of charge to members). Other services include vetting of con-

tracts, emergency funds for writers, and various special discounts. There are groups within the Society for scriptwriters, children's writers and illustrators, educational writers, medical writers and translators. Authors under 35, who are not yet earning a significant income from their writing, may apply for membership at a lower subscription of £52. Contact the Society for a free booklet giving further information.

The Society of Authors in Scotland

24 March Hall Crescent, Edinburgh
EH16 5HL
☎0131 667 5230

Secretary *Alanna Knight*

The Scottish branch of **The Society of Authors**, which organises business meetings, social and bookshop events in Scotland.

Society of Civil Service Authors

4 Top Street, Wing, Nr Oakham, Rutland
LE15 8SE

Membership Secretary *Mrs Joan Hykin*
Subscription £12 p.a.

FOUNDED 1935. Aims to encourage authorship by present and past members of the Civil Service and to provide opportunities for social and cultural relationships between civil servants who are authors or who aspire to be authors. Annual competitions, open to members only, are held for short stories, poetry, sonnets, travel articles, humour, etc. Members receive *The Civil Service Author*, a bi-monthly magazine. Occasional meetings in London, one or two weekends outside London.

Society of Freelance Editors and Proofreaders (SFEP)

Mermaid House, 1 Mermaid Court, London
SE1 1HR
☎0171 403 5141

Chair *Kathleen Lyle*
Vice-chair *Mary Fox*
Secretary *Shelagh Brown*
Subscription £35.25 p.a. (Individuals);
£23.50 (Joint); £70 – £176 (Corporate, depending on size of company); plus £10.00 registration fee for new members

FOUNDED 1988 in response to the growing number of freelance editors and their increasing importance to the publishing industry. Aims to promote high editorial standards by disseminating information and through advice and training, and to achieve recognition of the professional status of its members. The Society also supports moves towards recognised standards of training and qualifications, and is currently putting in place accredited and registered membership of SFEP.

Society of Indexers

Mermaid House, 1 Mermaid Court, London
SE1 1HR
☎0171 403 4947   Fax 0171 357 0903

Secretary *Christine Shuttleworth*
Subscription £40 p.a.; £60 (Institutions)

FOUNDED 1957. Publishes *The Indexer* (bi-annual, April and October) and a quarterly newsletter. Issues an annual list of members and *Indexers Available (IA)*, which lists members and their subject expertise. In addition the Society runs an open-learning course entitled *Training in Indexing* and recommends rates of pay (currently £12 per hour).

Society of Picture Researchers & Editors (SPREd)

See **The Picture Research Association**

Society of Sussex Authors

Bookends, Lewes Road, Horsted Keynes, Haywards Heath, West Sussex RH17 7DP
☎01825 790755   Fax 01825 790755

Contact *Michael Legat*
Subscription £8 p.a.

FOUNDED 1968 to promote the interests of its members and of literature, particularly within the Sussex area. Regular meetings and exchange of information; plus social events. Membership restricted to writers who live in Sussex and who have had at least one book commercially published. Meetings are held six times a year in Lewes.

Society of Women Writers and Journalists

110 Whitehall Road, London E4 6DW
☎0181 529 0886

Honorary Secretary *Jean Hawkes*
Subscription £25 (Town); £21 (Country); £15 (Overseas). £10 joining fee

FOUNDED 1894. The first of its kind to be run as an association of women engaged in journalism. Aims to encourage literary achievement, uphold professional standards, and establish social contacts with other writers. Lectures given at monthly lunchtime meetings. Offers advice to members and has regular seminars, etc. *Publishes* a quarterly society journal, *The Woman Journalist*.

Society of Young Publishers
12 Dyott Street, London WC1A 1DF
Subscription £20 p.a.; £15 (Student/
unwaged)

Provides facilities whereby members can increase their knowledge and widen their experience of all aspects of publishing. Open to those in related occupations, with associate membership available for over-35s. *Publishes* a monthly newsletter called *Inprint* and holds meetings on the last Wednesday of each month at **The Publishers Association**.

The South and Mid-Wales Association of Writers (S.A.M.W.A.W)
c/o I.M.C. Consulting Group, Denham House, Lambourne Crescent, Cardiff CF4 5ZW
☎01222 761170   Fax 01222 761304
Contact *Julian Rosser*
Subscription £7 (Single); £12 (Joint)

FOUNDED 1971 to foster the art and craft of writing in all its forms. Provides a common meeting ground for writers, critics, editors, adjudicators from all over the UK and abroad. Organises an annual residential weekend conference and a day seminar in May and October respectively. Holds competitions, two for members only and two which are open to the public, in addition to **The Mathew Pritchard Award for Short Story Writing** .

South Eastern Writers' Association
47 Sunningdale Avenue, Leigh-on-Sea, Essex SS9 1JY
☎01702 77083   Fax 01702 77083
President *Marion Hough*

FOUNDED 1989 to bring together experienced and novice writers, in an informal atmosphere. Non-profit-making, the Association holds a annual residential weekend each spring at Bulphan, Essex. Free workshops and discussion groups included in the overall cost. Previous guest speakers: Simon Brett, Jonathan Gash, George Layton, Maureen Lipman, Terry Pratchett, Jack Rosenthal.

Southwest Scriptwriters
149 St Andrew's Road, Montpelier, Bristol BS6 5EL
☎0117 9445424   Fax 0117 9445413
Secretary *John Colborn*
Subscription £5 p.a.

FOUNDED 1994 to offer encouragement and advice to those writing for stage, screen, radio and TV in the region. The group, which attracts professional writers, enthusiasts and students, meets regularly at the Theatre Royal, Bristol to read aloud and provide critical feedback on members' work, discuss writing technique and exchange market information. Catherine Johnson, writer-in-residence at the Bristol Old Vic, acts as Honorary President and is able to offer information and advice on members' writing.

Sports Writers' Association of Great Britain
c/o English Sports Council Press Office, 16 Upper Woburn Place, London WC1H 0QP
☎0171 273 1555   Fax 0171 383 0273
Secretary *Trevor Bond*
Subscription £23 (incl. VAT) p.a., London; £11.75 (incl. VAT, Regional

FOUNDED 1948 to promote and maintain a high professional standard among journalists who specialise in sport in all its branches and to serve members' interests.

Sussex Playwrights' Club
2 Princes Avenue, Hove, East Sussex BN3 4GD
☎01273 734985
Secretary *Mrs Constance Cox*
Subscription £5 p.a.

FOUNDED 1935. Aims to encourage the writing of plays for stage, radio and TV by giving monthly dramatic readings of members' work by experienced actors, mainly from local drama groups. Gives constructively criticised suggestions as to how work might be improved, and suggests possible marketing. Membership is not confined to writers but to all who are interested in theatre in all its forms, and all members are invited to take part in such discussions. Guests are always welcome at a nominal 50p. Meetings held at New Venture Theatre, Bedford Place, Brighton, East Sussex.

Theatre Writers' Union
c/o GFTU, Central House, Upper Woburn Place, London WC1H 0HY
☎0181 365 3850
Chair *David Edgar*
Administrator *Sheelah Sloane*

Formed in the mid 1970s. Specialises in the concerns of all who write for theatre, of whatever kind. Has national branch network. Actively seeks a membership which represents the diversity of playwriting today. Many members are also active in other media: radio, TV, film and video. Responsible for the very first standard agreements on minimum pay and conditions for playwrights working in British theatre. Any playwright who has written a play is eligible to join. Annual subscription is related to income from playwriting. Members may receive legal and professional advice, copies of standard contracts and regular newsletters. As affiliates to the General Federation of Trade Unions, TWU has access to their legal and education services.

The Translators Association

84 Drayton Gardens, London SW10 9SB
☎0171 373 6642   Fax 0171 373 5768
Secretary *Gordon Fielden*

FOUNDED 1958 as a subsidary group within **The Society of Authors** to deal exclusively with the special problems of literary translators into the English language. Members are entitled to all the benefits and services of the Association, in addition to those of the Society, without extra charge. These include free legal and general advice and assistance on all matters relating to translators' work, including the vetting of contracts and information about improvements in rates of remuneration. Membership is normally confined to translators who have had their work published in volume or serial form or produced in this country for stage, television or radio. Translators of work for industrial firms or government departments are in certain cases admitted to membership if their work, though not on general sale, is published by the organisation commissioning the work. The Association administers several prizes for translators of published work and maintains a database to enable members' details to be supplied to publishers who are seeking a translator for a particular work.

Ver Poets

Haycroft, 61–63 Chiswell Green Lane, St Albans, Hertfordshire AL2 3AL
☎01727 867005
Chairman *Ray Badman*
Editor/Organiser *May Badman*
Membership £10 p.a.; £12.50 or US$25 (Overseas)

FOUNDED 1966 to promote poetry and to help poets. With postal and local members, holds meetings in St Albans; runs a poetry bookstall for members' books and publications from other groups; publishes members' work in magazines and organises poetry competitions,

including the annual **Ver Poets Open** competition. Gives help and advice whenever they are sought and makes information available to members about other poetry groups, events and opportunities for publication.

Voice of the Listener and Viewer

101 Kings Drive, Gravesend, Kent
DA12 5BQ
☎01474 352835

The citizen's voice in broadcasting is an independent, non-profit-making society working to ensure independence and high standards in broadcasting. It is also the only consumer body speaking for listeners and viewers on the whole range of broadcasting issues. VLV is funded by its members and is free from sectarian, commercial and political affiliations. Holds public lectures, seminars and conferences, and has frequent contact with MPs, civil servants, the BBC and independent broadcasters, regulators, academics and other consumer groups. VLV has responded to all parliamentary and public enquiries on broadcasting since 1984 and to all consultation documents issued by the ITC and Radio Authority since 1990. The VLV does not handle complaints.

W.A.T.C.H.

See **Writers and their Copyright Holders**

Welsh Academy

3rd Floor, Mount Stuart House, Mount Stuart Square, Cardiff CF1 6DQ
☎01222 492025   Fax 01222 492930
Director *Kevin Thomas*

FOUNDED 1968. The Welsh Academy is the English Language section of **Yr Academi Gymreig**, the national society of Welsh writers. The Academy exists to promote English literature in Wales. Organises readings, an annual conference (usually held in May) and events such as the **Cardiff Literature Season**. There are three tiers of membership: Fellow (max. 12, an honorary position offered to those who have made an outstanding contribution to the literature of Wales over a number of years); Member (open to all who are deemed to have made a contribution to the literature of Wales whether writers, editors or critics); Associate Member (open to all who are interested in the Academy's work). Publications include: *BWA*, the Academy's newsletter; *The Oxford Companion to the Literature of Wales*; *Writing in Wales*; *The Literature of Wales in Secondary Schools*; *How the Earth Was Formed Quiz And*

Other Poems and Stories by Children; The New Welsh Review; A Bibliography of Anglo-Welsh Literature; Interweave.

Welsh Books Council (Cyngor Llyfrau Cymru)

Castell Brychan, Aberystwyth, Ceredigion SY23 2JB
☎01970 624151   Fax 01970 625385
Director *Gwerfyl Pierce Jones*
Head of Editorial Department *Dewi Morris Jones*

FOUNDED 1961 to stimulate interest in Welsh literature and to support authors. The Council distributes the government grant for Welsh language publications and promotes and fosters all aspects of both Welsh and Welsh interest book production. Its Editorial, Design, Marketing and Children's Books departments and wholesale distribution centre offer central services to publishers in Wales. Writers in Welsh and English are welcome to approach the Editorial Department for advice on how to get their manuscripts published. *Books in Wales/Llais Llyfrau* is a quarterly publication which includes book lists, reviews and articles on various aspects of Welsh writing and publishing (see entry under **Magazines**).

Welsh Union of Writers

4 Teilo Street, Pontcanna, Cardiff CF2 3AQ
☎01222 640041
Secretary *John Harrison*
Subscription £10 p.a.; £5 joining fee

FOUNDED 1982. Independent union. Full membership by application to persons born or working in Wales with at least one publication in a quality journal or other outlet. Associate membership now available for other interested supporters. Lobbies for writing in Wales, represents members in disputes; annual conference and occasional events and publications.

West Country Writers' Association

Malvern View, Garway Hill, Hereford, Hereford & Worcester HR2 8EZ
☎01981 580495
President *Christopher Fry*
Honorary Secretary *Mrs Anne Double*
Subscription £10 p.a.

FOUNDED 1951 in the interest of published authors with an interest in the West Country. Meets to discuss news and views and to listen to talks. Conference and newsletters.

Women in Publishing

c/o The Bookseller, 12 Dyott Street, London WC1A 1DF
Contact *Information Officer*
Membership £20 p.a. (Individuals);
    £15 (Unwaged); £25 (if paid by company)

Aims to promote the status of women working within the publishing industry and related trades, to encourage networking, and to provide training for career and personal development. Meetings held on the second Wednesday of the month at **The Publishers Association** (see entry for address) at 6.30 pm. Monthly newsletter.

Women Writers Network (WWN)

23 Prospect Road, London NW2 2JU
☎0171 794 5861
Membership Secretary *Cathy Smith*
Subscription £30 p.a.; £35 (for non-EEC countries)

FOUNDED 1985. Provides a forum for the exchange of information, support, career and networking opportunities for working women writers. Meetings, seminars, excursions, newsletter and directory. Also has a north west branch; details from the Membership Secretary at the above address.

Writers and their Copyright Holders (W.A.T.C.H.)

The Library, The University of Reading, PO Box 223, Whiteknights, Reading, Berkshire RG6 6AE
☎0118 9318783   Fax 0118 9316636
Contact *Dr David Sutton*

FOUNDED 1994. Provides an on-line database of information about the copyright holders of literary authors. The database is available free of charge on the Internet and the World Wide Web (http:www.lib.utexas.edu/Libs/HRC/WATCH). W.A.T.C.H. is the successor project to the Location Register of English Literary Manuscripts and Letters, and continues to deal with location register enquiries.

Writers in Oxford

41 Kingston Road, Oxford OX2 6RH
☎01865 513844   Fax 01865 510017
Secretary *Maggie Black*
Subscription £15 p.a.

FOUNDED 1992. Open to published authors, playwrights, poets and journalists. Linked to **The Society of Authors** but organised locally. Arranges a programme of meetings, seminars and functions. *Publishes* quarterly newsletter, *The Oxford Writer*.

The Writers' Guild of Great Britain

430 Edgware Road, London W2 1EH
☎0171 723 8074   Fax 0171 706 2413
General Secretary *Alison V. Gray*

Annual subscription 1% of that part of the author's income earned in the areas in which the Guild operates, with a basic subscription of £70 and a maximum of £920

FOUNDED 1959. The Writers' Guild is the writers' trade union, affiliated to the TUC. It represents writers in film, radio, television, theatre and publishing. The Guild has negotiated agreements on which writers' contracts are based with the BBC, Independent Television companies, and **PACT** (the Producers' Alliance for Cinema and Television). Those agreements are regularly renegotiated, both in terms of finance and conditions.

In 1979, together with the **Theatre Writers' Union**, the Guild negotiated the first ever industrial agreement for theatre writers, the TNC Agreement, which covers the Royal National Theatre, the RSC, and the English Stage Company. Further agreements have been negotiated with the Theatre Management Association which covers regional theatre and the **Independent Theatre Council**, the organisation which covers small theatres and the Fringe.

The Guild initiated a campaign over ten years ago which achieved the first ever publishing agreement for writers with the publisher W. H. Allen. Jointly with **The Society of Authors**, that campaign has continued and each year sees new agreements with more publishers. Perhaps the most important breakthrough came with **Penguin** on 20 July 1990. The Guild now also has agreements covering **HarperCollins**, **Random House Group**, **Transworld** and others.

The Guild regularly provides individual help and advice to members on contracts, conditions of work, and matters which affect a member's life as a professional writer. Members are given the opportunity of meeting at craft meetings, which are held on a regular basis throughout the year. Membership is by a points system. One major piece of work (a full-length book, an hour-long television or radio play, a feature film, etc.) entitles the author to full membership; writers who do not qualify for Full Membership may qualify for Associate Membership; they currently pay the basic subscription only of £70. A new type of membership was launched in July 1997 called Candidate Membership. This is open to all those who wish to be involved in writing but have not yet had work published. The subscription fee for this is £35. (Website address: http.www.writers.org.uk/guide)

Yachting Journalists' Association

3 Friars Lane, Maldon, Essex CM9 6AG
☎01621 855943/0468 962936(mobile)
Fax 01621 852212
Honorary Secretary *Peter Cook*
Subscription £30 p.a.

To further the interest of yachting, sail and power, and to provide support and assistance to journalists in the field; current membership is just over 230 with 20 from overseas. A handbook, listing details of members and subscribing PR organisations, press facility recommendations, forthcoming events and other useful information, is published annually in April at a cost to non-members and non-advertisers of £5. Information for inclusion should be submitted by the end of February. The YJA organises the Yachtsman of the Year Awards which are in their 42nd year. Presented annually at the beginning of January, they consist of the Yachtsman of the Year, Young Sailor of the Year and Global Achievement Awards.

Young Newspaper Executives' Association

See **The Newspaper Society**

Yr Academi Gymreig

3rd Floor, Mount Stuart House, Mount Stuart Square, Cardiff CF1 6DQ
☎01222 492064   Fax 01222 492930
Director *Dafydd Rogers*

FOUNDED 1959. National society of Welsh writers. Aims to encourage writing in Welsh. *Publishes Taliesin*, plus books on Welsh literature and an English/Welsh dictionary. Organises readings, conferences and general literary events. Various tiers of membership available.

Words That Offend –
Looking for Libel

The care that writers must take in treading the minefield of libel was illustrated recently by a prominent notice in *The Stage*.

'In Fay Weldon's book *Worst Fears*, one of the main characters is called Jenny Linden. Unfortunately, this character's name is almost identical to that of the actress Jennie Linden. We wish to clarify that the character is in no way connected to Jennie Linden and that any similarities are entirely coincidental. We apologise unreservedly to Jennie Linden for any distress and embarrassment caused by any connection between the character and Jennie Linden.'

Having to apologise for choosing a name at random may seem tough on Miss Weldon but as the law stands, if you are sued for libel your opponent need not prove that you intended to discredit him or even that he has been harmed by whatever you have said. All that is necessary is to indicate that a hurt to reputation has been suffered.

In the search for suitable names for fictional characters, a minimum precaution is to check with the relevant directories.

'If the author has invented a corrupt landlord living in Paddington he should look up the invented name in the London telephone directory and substitute a safe one, if there is someone of that name with a Paddington telephone number,' says Mark Le Fanu of the Society of Authors. 'If one of the characters is a bishop of doubtful sanctity, the author should look in *Crockford's* to make sure that there is no bishop of that name.'

Paul Watkins has cause to regret not checking the list of Old Etonians. His novel *Stand Up Before Your God* based on his schooldays at Eton featured an undesirable called Wilbraham. It was a name plucked from a New York telephone directory. Unfortunately, it happened also to be the name of an Eton contemporary. Neither the author nor the real Wilbraham could remember ever having met. It was an unfortunate misunderstanding which nonetheless ended with Paul Watkins and his publisher Faber paying damages in the region of £15,000.

Where libel has been committed unintentionally or 'innocently' one way out of the trap is an 'offer to make amends'. This escape clause has been available since the 1950s but until last year was rarely taken up because it was hedged by so many technicalities. Now, under the 1996 Defamation Act, the rules have been tightened to allow for a speedy and relatively inexpensive resolution of disputes. If you did not intend to defame and can show that you were not reckless, you can avoid further litigation by offering a published apology, a sum in compensation and a settlement of costs. If the amount to be paid cannot be agreed mutually a judge can make an order.

But there is a downside as Daniel Eilon, a solicitor with Campbell Hooper, points out: 'The offer of amends is not so much a defence as an orderly surrender. If you use it, you cannot plead any of the other recognised defences such as justification, fair comment and privilege.'

Moreover, if you choose to go the hard route with one of the other defences, there is no going back; you no longer have the option to make amends. Lawyers have criticised the 1996 Act for failing to allow for a greater degree of flexibility in settling disputes while welcoming long overdue changes in Britain's archaic and, in many ways, anarchic libel laws. The time limit for starting an action for defamation has been cut from three years to one. (This will curb the use of 'gagging writs' such as those used by the late Robert Maxwell.) There is a new summary procedure under which every defamation claim can come before a judge at an early stage. The judge assesses whether the claim is suitable for summary disposal, or whether it should go for trial, with or without a jury. He has power to award damages up to £10,000. This makes it easier for an ordinary citizen to seek redress against a rich opponent who, otherwise, is liable to keep a trial going as long as possible in the hope that a plaintiff will run out of patience and money.

The broadcaster Derek Jameson was brought to the edge of bankruptcy by an unsuccessful action against the BBC for what he regarded as damaging inferences. When Gillian Taylforth, the *EastEnders* star, lost her case against *The Sun* she faced a legal bill that was said to be around £500,000.

Success, on the other hand, can bring riches. For reasons lost in the deliberations of the jury rooms, awards are invariably out of all proportion to damage suffered. It used to be the rule that compensation for a serious libel should roughly correspond to the price of a good house. Now the guide-line leads to a palace. Speaking up for press colleagues who have found themselves in the High Court, William Rees-Mogg points out that 'if newspaper vans ran amok in London and crashed freely into innocent pedestrians, that would cost their proprietors less than a few defamatory paragraphs'.

For those with the gambling instinct, the chance of jackpot winnings is a powerful draw. It may be a safe general rule, as the Book of Proverbs tells us that 'A good name is rather to be chosen than great riches'. But, in the wonderful world of libel, lawyers are ready to admit that some plaintiffs go for the money. There is the story of a famous critic who was offered a settlement plus an apology or double the money and no apology. He decided he could live without the apology.

There is some hope that the lid has been put on outrageous libel awards now that the Court of Appeal can provide guidelines. Many reformers would go further. They want the responsibility of a jury to be limited to saying if damages should be substantial, moderate, nominal or contemptuous. The judge would then decide on the appropriate figure. A useful compromise would compel juries to explain their calculations. As Lord Donaldson has observed, 'having to give reasons puts a substantial premium on ensuring that the head rules the heart'.

If not money, what is the pull of a libel action? Setting the record straight may be a worthy motive but those who go to court to defend their reputations invariably find that the matter which offends them is publicised yet more heavily and stays longer in the public memory. A sexy case like that featuring Gillian Taylforth produces reams of detailed coverage. It has been argued that while the original story of an unconventional coupling on the A1, as published in *The Sun*, reached 25 per cent of the population, the court proceedings lifted that figure to more than 80 per cent.

Every writer is responsible for his own work. But this should not mean that when he makes mistakes he alone carries the can. Journalists are usually covered by their employers who take on the whole cost of a libel action. Authors, on the other hand, are more exposed to the rigours of legal censorship. A typical publishing contract includes a warranty clause which entitles the publisher to be indemnified by the author against damages and costs if any part of the work turns out to be libellous.

Publishers excuse their weakness of backbone by arguing that only the author is in a position to know whether or not a work is libellous and that the onus should be on the author to check facts before they are published. But why, asks Mark Le Fanu of the Society of Authors, should the risk be borne by the author alone when a publisher deliberately gambles on making money out of a book?

'While it is true that a writer of fiction is much more likely than the publisher to know whether or not a person has been defamed (whether intentionally or unintentionally), the issue is much less clear-cut with non-fiction. Authors are not experts in the arcane mysteries of the 'fair comment' defence to a libel claim. Publishers are well aware that certain sorts of books (eg biographies of the living, business exposés, etc) inevitably carry a libel risk.'

In fairness, it must be said that the indemnity is rarely invoked unless a publisher feels he has been deceived or misled. But, at the very least, the author should insist that his publisher has the manuscript read for libel and that his contract does not specify unlimited liability.

Libel insurance offers some sort of safeguard and a publisher who is insured is clearly preferable to one who is not. But most insurance policies carry severe limitations, not least a ceiling on the payout of damages. Also, reading for libel can be expensive for a book that is in any way controversial. As Richard West discovered when he wrote an investigative volume, 'the lawyer who read it for libel got £1000. The lawyer who wrote in to the publisher to complain on behalf of his client was probably paid about £5000'. Since West himself earned about £500 for his efforts he concluded, not unreasonably, that authorship was a mug's game.

There are many cases where a cost-conscious publisher has played safe by amending a text to a point where it loses its cutting edge and thus its sales appeal. It is not unknown for an entire book to be jettisoned to save on lawyers' bills.

Another limitation on libel insurance is that few policies extend to the US market, where claims and awards can take off like Concorde. There, a thriving libel industry has been made yet more prosperous by enterprising lawyers who assess fees as a percentage of whatever they can persuade juries to award. The consolation for defendants is that while the law of libel in the States is similar to the law here, in practical terms it is more favourable to the authors, in that the reputations of public figures are thought to be in less need of protection. A politician, say, who sues for libel is ridiculed as a bad sport. Whoever puts his head above the parapet, goes the argument, should expect to be shot at. Judges are more understanding of ordinary citizens particularly when there is an inva-sion-of-privacy claim but as a general rule, for libel damages to be awarded in an American court, someone must publish untruths knowing them to be untrue. Even then, there is plenty of leeway.

Peter Marsh, a barrister specialising in defamation, offers these tips for writers about to embark on a controversial project.

'If the subject or subjects of critical comment are still alive, beware; if you are writing a book about real life incidents but have changed names to avoid identification, take extreme care in the choice of names for your characters; remember that damage to a person's reputation can be caused by innuendo. For example, to write of someone that most people thought he was taking advantage of the Inland Revenue may suggest some improper and unethical practice. If a living person is going to be the subject of comment which is expressly or implicitly derogatory, make absolutely sure your facts are correct and can be substantiated. Otherwise, your pub-lisher is going to be propelled into the courtroom naked of a defence.'

In one important respect, authors and publishers suffer more than anyone from the application of the libel laws. At the root of the problem is the ease with which determined plaintiffs can get a book or magazine withdrawn from circu-lation. The process, successfully used by Sir James Goldsmith in his litigation against *Private Eye*, was given a shot in the arm by Robert Maxwell in his tussles with Tom Bower over a biography of which Maxwell did not approve. David Hooper, author of *Public Scandal, Odium and Contempt* points out that the posi-tion of distributors in such situations is extremely perilous: 'They have no means of knowing whether the book is in fact libellous. All they know is that any profit they might have made – and more – will find its way smartly into the hands of their lawyers.' The remedy, says David Hooper, is for anyone seeking to get a book withdrawn to be required to undertake to pay damages if their claims turn out to be without substance.

Is there anything to be said for those who bring libel actions? No better summary of the risks and tribulations for all but the excessively rich appears in Adam Raphael's absorbing indictment, *Grotesque Libels*.

> The problems of a libel action can be stated quite simply. The law is highly technical and the pleadings so complex that even its skilled practitioners often differ on the most basic questions. The costs of the lawyers involved are so high that they make the fees charged by any other profession appear to be a mere bagatelle. The opportunities for obstruction and delay are such that it can take as long as five years to bring a libel action to court. When it eventually does reach the court, the damages left to the whim of a jury are so uncertain that the result is often no sounder than a dodgy fruit machine. A libel action has in fact more in common with a roulette wheel than justice. The net result for both plaintiffs and defendants is that such actions are a nightmare with only the lawyers able to sleep soundly.

No wonder Bernard Levin asserts 'If I were libelled (I have frequently been) and were given the choice of suing or having all my toenails pulled out with red-hot pincers while listening to *Pelléas et Mélisande*, I think it would be a close run thing.'

As for those who are unable to keep out of the courts, the best advice comes from Tom Crone in his book on *Law and the Media*. The libel litigant, he says, must possess two prime qualities – 'a strong nerve and a deep pocket'.

Literary Societies

Most literary societies exist on a shoestring budget; it is a good idea to enclose an A5 s.a.e. with all correspondence needing a reply.

The Abbey Chronicle
See **The Elsie Jeanette Oxenham Appreciation Society**

Margery Allingham Society
3 Corringham Road, Wembley, Middlesex HA9 9PX
☎0181 904 5994   Fax 0181 904 5994
Contact *Mrs Pat Wat*
Subscription £8 p.a.

FOUNDED 1988 to promote interest in and study of the works of Margery Allingham. The London Society *publishes* two newsletters yearly, *The Bottle Street Gazette*. Contributions welcome. Two social events a year. Open membership.

Jane Austen Society
Carton House, Redwood Lane, Medstead, Alton, Hampshire GU34 5PE
☎01705 475855   Fax 01705 788842
Honorary Secretary *Susan McCartan*
Subscription UK: £10 (Annual); £15 (Joint); £30 (Corporate); £150 (Life); Overseas: £12 (Annual); £18 (Joint); £33 (Corporate); £180 (Life)

FOUNDED 1940 to promote interest in and enjoyment of Jane Austen's novels and letters. The society has branches in Bath & Bristol, Midlands, London, Oxford, Kent and Hampshire. Also overseas branches in North America and Australia.

William Barnes Society
75 Prince of Wales Road, Dorchester, Dorset DT1 1PS
☎01305 264405
Contact *Mrs Pamela Holden*
Subscription £6 p.a.

FOUNDED 1983 to provide a forum in which admirers of the Dorset poet could share fellowship and pleasure in his work. William Barnes (1801–86) is best known as the writer of Dorset dialect poetry. His interest in dialect prompted him to become a learned philologist and he published many papers in defence of native English against the incursions of French and Latin. Quarterly meetings and newsletter.

The Baskerville Hounds
6 Bramham Moor, Hill Head, Fareham, Hampshire PO14 3RU
☎01329 667325
Chairman *Philip Weller*
Subscription £6.00 p.a.

FOUNDED 1989. An international Sherlock Holmes society specialising solely in studies of *The Hound of the Baskervilles* and its Dartmoor associations. *Publishes* a quarterly newsletter, an annual journal and specialist monographs. It also organises many social functions, usually on Dartmoor. Open membership.

The Beckford Society
15 Healey Street, London NW1 8SR
☎0171 267 7750   Fax 01985 213195
Secretary *Sidney Blackmore*
Subscription £10 (min.) p.a.

FOUNDED 1995 to promote an interest in the life and works of William Beckford (1760–1840) and his circle. Encourages Beckford studies and scholarship through exhibitions, lectures and publications, including an annual journal, *The Beckford Journal*, and occasional newsletters.

Arnold Bennett Society
106 Scotia Road, Burslem, Stoke on Trent, Staffordshire ST6 4ET
☎01782 816311
Secretary *Mrs Jean Potter*
Subscription £6 (Single); £7 (Family); £5 (Unwaged)

Re-formed in 1954 to promote interest in the life and works of 'Five Towns' author Arnold Bennett and other North Staffordshire writers. Annual dinner and other events. Quarterly newsletter. Open membership.

E. F. Benson Society
The Old Coach House, High Street, Rye, East Sussex TN31 7JF
☎01797 223114   Fax 0171 580 0763
Secretary *Allan Downend*
Subscription £7.50 (UK/Europe); £12.50 (Overseas)

FOUNDED 1985 to promote the life and work

of E. F. Benson and the Benson family. Organises social and literary events, exhibitions and talks. *Publishes* a quarterly newsletter and annual journal, *The Dodo*, postcards and reprints of E. F. Benson articles and short stories. Holds an archive which includes the Seckersen Collection (transcriptions of the Benson collection at the Bodleian Library in Oxford).

E. F. Benson/The Tilling Society
5 Friars Bank, Pett Road, Guestling, East Sussex TN35 4ET
☎01424 812531

Contact *Cynthia Reavell*
Subscription Full starting membership (members receive all back newsletters) £20 (UK); £24 (Overseas); or Annual Membership (members receive only current year's newsletters) £8 (UK); £10 (Overseas).

FOUNDED 1982 for the exchange of news, information and speculation about E. F. Benson and his *Mapp & Lucia* novels. Readings, discussions and twice-yearly newsletter. Acts as a clearing house for every sort of news and activity concerning E. F. Benson.

The Betjeman Society
35 Eaton Court, Boxgrove Avenue, Guildford, Surrey GU1 1XH
☎01483 560882

Honorary Secretary *John Heald*
Subscription £7 (Individual); £9 (Family); £3 (Student); £2 extra each category for overseas members

Aims to promote the study and appreciation of the work and life of Sir John Betjeman. Annual programme includes poetry reading, lectures, discussions, visits to places associated with Betjeman, and various social events. Meetings are held in London and other centres. Regular newsletter and annual journal, *The Betjemanian*.

The Bewick Society
c/o The Dean's Office, Faculty of Arts and Design, University of Northumbria, Squires Building, Sandyford Road, Newcastle upon Tyne NE1 8ST
☎0191 227 3138   Fax 0191 227 4077
Chairman *Kenneth McConkey*
Subscription £7 p.a.

FOUNDED 1988 to promote an interest in the life and work of Thomas Bewick, wood-engraver and naturalist (1753–1828). Organises related events and meetings, and is associated with the Bewick birthplace museum.

Biggles & Co
See **The W. E. Johns Society**

Birmingham Central Literary Association
c/o Birmingham & Midland Institute, Margaret Street, Birmingham B3 3DS
☎0121 236 3591

Contact *The Honorary Secretary*

Holds fortnightly meetings at the Birmingham Midland Institute to discuss the lives and work of authors and poets. Holds an annual dinner to celebrate Shakespeare's birthday.

The George Borrow Society
The Gables, 112 Irchester Road, Rushden, Northants NN10 9XQ
☎01933 312965   Fax 01933 312965
President *Sir Angus Fraser, KCB TD*
Honorary Secretary *Dr James H. Reading*
Honorary Treasurer *Mrs Ena R. J. Reading*
Subscription £8 p.a.

FOUNDED 1991 to promote knowledge of the life and works of George Borrow (1803–81), traveller, linguist and writer. The Society holds biennial conferences (with published proceedings) and informal intermediate gatherings, all at places associated with Borrow. *Publishes* the *George Borrow Bulletin* twice yearly, a newsletter containing scholarly articles, publications relating to Borrow, reports of past events and news of forthcoming events. Member of the **Alliance of Literary Societies** and corporate associate member of the Centre of East Anglian Studies (CEAS) at the University of East Anglia, Norwich (Borrow's home city for many years).

Elinor Brent-Dyer
See **Friends of the Chalet School**

British Fantasy Society
2 Harwood Street, Heaton Norris, Stockport, Cheshire SK4 1JJ
☎0161 476 5368
President *Ramsey Campbell*
Vice-President *Jan Edwards*
Secretary *Robert Parkinson*
Subscription from £17 p.a. (Apply to secretary.)

FOUNDED 1971 for devotees of fantasy, horror and related fields in literature, art and the cinema. *Publishes* a regular newsletter with information and reviews of new books and films, plus related fiction and non-fiction magazines. Annual conference at which the **British Fantasy Awards** are presented.

The Brontë Society

Brontë Parsonage Museum, Haworth,
Keighley, West Yorkshire BD22 8DR
☎01535 642323   Fax 01535 647131

Contact *Membership Secretary*
Subscription £15 p.a. (UK/Europe);
£7.50 (Student); £5 (Junior – to age 14);
£22 (Overseas); Joint subscriptions and life
membership also available

FOUNDED 1893. Aims and activities include the
preservation of manuscripts and other objects
related to or connected with the Brontë family,
and the maintenance and development of the
museum and library at Haworth. The society
holds regular meetings, lectures and exhibitions; and *publishes* information relating to the
family, a bi-annual society journal *Transactions*
and a bi-annual *Gazette*. Freelance contributions for either publication should be sent to
the Publications Secretary at the address above.

The Browning Society

Cherry Tree Cottage, Fyning Lane, Rogate,
Petersfield, Hampshire GU31 5DQ
☎01730 821666

Honorary Secretary *Dr Mairi Calcraft-Rennie*
Subscription £15 p.a.

FOUNDED 1969 to promote an interest in the
lives and poetry of Robert and Elizabeth Barrett
Browning. Meetings are arranged in the London
area, one of which occurs in December at
Westminster Abbey to commemorate Robert
Browning's death.

The John Buchan Society

Limpsfield, 16 Ranfurly Road, Bridge of Weir
PA11 3EL
☎01505 613116

Secretary *Russell Paterson*
Subscription £10 (Full/Overseas);
£4 (Associate); £6 (Junior);
£20 (Corporate); £90 (Life)

To perpetuate the memory of John Buchan and
to promote a wider understanding of his life and
works. Holds regular meetings and social gatherings, *publishes* a journal, and liaises with the John
Buchan Centre at Broughton in the Scottish
borders.

The Charles Bukowski Society

9 Mepham Crescent, Harrow Weald, Harrow,
Middlesex HA3 6QU
☎0181 421 5290   Fax 0181 933 6782

Chairman *Jamie Meakes*
Subscription £10 p.a.

FOUNDED 1997 to promote and encourage
interest in the late American Underground
poet/novelist, Charles Bukowski. *Publishes* a
twice-yearly magazine *Bukowski* which includes
reviews, features and comic strips as well as information on Bukowski events and the society's
own activities. The society has members worldwide. It can also be contacted on the Web at
http://www.jamus.com/buk-society/.

The Burns Federation

The Dick Institute, Elmbank Avenue,
Kilmarnock, Strathclyde KA1 3BU
☎01563 526401   Fax 01563 529661

Honorary Secretary *John Inglis*
Subscription £12 p.a.(Individual);
£25 (Club subscription)

FOUNDED 1885 to encourage interest in the life
and work of Robert Burns and keep alive the
old Scottish Tongue. The Society's interests go
beyond Burns himself in its commitment to the
development of Scottish literature, music and
arts in general. *Publishes* the quarterly *Burns
Chronicle/Burnsian*.

The Byron Society

Byron House, 6 Gertrude Street, London
SW10 0JN
☎0171 352 5112

Honorary Director, Byron Society *Mrs
Elma Dangerfield OBE*
Subscription £18 p.a.

Also: Newstead Abbey Byron Society,
Newstead Abbey, Newstead Abbey Park,
Nottingham NG15 8GE   ☎01623 797392
(Contact: *Mrs Maureen Crisp*)

FOUNDED 1876; revived in 1971. Aims to promote knowledge and discussion of Lord Byron's
life and works, and those of his contemporaries,
through lectures, readings, concerts, performances and international conferences. *Publishes*
annually in April *The Byron Journal*, a scholarly
journal – £5 plus 60p postage.

Randolph Caldecott Society

Clatterwick Hall, Little Leigh, Northwich,
Cheshire CW8 4RJ
☎01606 891303

Honorary Secretary *Kenneth N. Oultram*
Subscription £7–£10 p.a.

FOUNDED 1983 to promote the life and work
of artist/book illustrator Randolph Caldecott.
Meetings held in the spring and autumn in
Caldecott's birthplace, Chester. Guest speakers,
outings, newsletter, exchanges with the society's American counterpart. (Caldecott died
and was buried in St Augustine, Florida.) A

medal in his memory is awarded annually in the US for children's book illustration.

The Carlyle Society, Edinburgh

Dept of English Literature, The University of Edinburgh, David Hume Tower, George Square, Edinburgh EH8 9JX
Fax 0131 650 6898

Contact *The President*
Subscription £2 p.a.; £10 (Life); $20 (US)

FOUNDED 1929 to examine the lives of Thomas Carlyle and his wife Jane, his writings, contemporaries, and influences. Meetings are held about six times a year and occasional papers are published annually. Enquiries should be addressed to the President of the Society at the above address or to the Secretary at 15 Lennox Street, Edinburgh EH4 1QB.

Lewis Carroll Society

Acorns, Dargate, Near Faversham, Kent ME13 9HG
☎01227 751339   Fax 01227 751339
Secretary *Sarah Stanfield*
Subscription Individual: £13 (UK); £15 (Europe); £17 (Outside Europe); £10 (Retired rate); £2 (Additional family members); Institutions: £26 (UK); £28 (Europe); £30 (Outside Europe)

FOUNDED 1969 to bring together people with an interest in Charles Dodgson and promote research into his life and works. *Publishes* quarterly journal *Jabberwocky*, featuring scholarly articles and reviews; plus a newsletter (*Bandersnatch*) which reports on Carrollian events and the Society's activities. Regular meetings held in London with lectures, talks, outings, etc.

Lewis Carroll Society (Daresbury)

Clatterwick Hall, Little Leigh, Northwich, Cheshire CW8 4RJ
☎01606 891303
Honorary Secretary *Kenneth N. Oultram*
Subscription £5 p.a.

FOUNDED 1970. To promote the life and work of Charles Dodgson, author of the world-famous *Alice's Adventures*. Holds regular meetings in the spring and autumn in Carroll's birthplace, Daresbury, in Cheshire. Guest speakers, theatre visits and a newsletter. Appoints annually a 10-year-old 'Alice' who is available for public engagements.

Friends of the Chalet School

4 Rock Terrace, Coleford, Bath, Somerset BA3 5NF
☎01373 812705   Fax 01373 813517
Contact *Ann Mackie-Hunter, Clarissa Cridland*
Subscription £6 p.a.; £5 (Under–18); Outside Europe: details on application

FOUNDED 1989 to promote the works of Elinor Brent-Dyer. The society has members worldwide; *publishes* four newsletters a year and runs a lending library.

The Chesterton Society

11 Lawrence Leys, Bloxham, Near Banbury, Oxfordshire OX15 4NU
☎01295 720869
Honorary Secretary *Robert Hughes*
Subscription £10 p.a.

FOUNDED 1964 to promote the ideas and writings of G. K. Chesterton.

The Children's Books History Society

25 Field Way, Hoddesdon, Hertfordshire EN11 0QN
☎01992 464885   Fax 01992 464885
Membership Secretary *Mrs Pat Garrett*
Subscription £7.50 p.a. (£10 from January 1998)

ESTABLISHED 1969. Aims to promote an appreciation of children's books and to study their history, bibliography and literary content. The Society holds approximately six meetings per year in London and a summer meeting to a collection, or to a location with a children's book connection. Three newsletters issued annually, also an occasional paper. The Society constitutes the British branch of the Friends of the Osborne and Lillian H. Smith Collections in Toronto, Canada, and also liaises with the **Library Association**. In 1990, the Society established its biennial Harvey Darton Award for a book, published in English, which extends our knowledge of some aspect of British children's literature of the past. 1996 winner: Marina Warner *From the Beast to the Blonde*.

The John Clare Society

The Stables, 1A West Street, Helpston, Peterborough PE6 7DU
☎01733 252678
Honorary Secretary *Mrs J. Mary Moyse*
Subscription £9.50 (Individual); £12.50 (Joint); £7.50 (Fully Retired); £9.50 (Joint Retired); £10 (Group/Library);

£3 (Student, Full-time);
£12.50 sterling draft/$25 (Overseas)

FOUNDED 1981 to promote a wider appreciation of the life and works of the poet John Clare (1793–1864). Organises an annual festival in Helpston in July; arranges exhibitions, poetry readings and conferences; and *publishes* an annual society journal and quarterly newsletter.

Wilkie Collins Society

10A Tibberton Square, Islington, London
N1 8SF
Chairman *Andrew Gasson*
Membership Secretary *Louise Marchant (at above address)*
Subscription £8.50 (UK); $12 (US/outside Europe – remittance must be made in UK sterling)

FOUNDED 1980 to provide information on and promote interest in the life and works of Wilkie Collins, one of the first English novelists to deal with the detection of crime. *The Woman in White* appeared in 1860 and *The Moonstone* in 1868. *Publishes* newsletters, a journal and occasional reprints of Collins' work.

The Arthur Conan Doyle Society

PO Box 1360, Ashcroft, British Columbia
Canada V0K 1A0
Joint Organisers *Christopher Roden, Barbara Roden*
Membership Contact *R. Dixon-Smith*,
59 Stonefield, Bar Hill, Cambridge
CB3 8TE
Subscription £15 (UK); £16 (Overseas); Family rates available

FOUNDED 1989 to promote the study and discussion of the life and works of Sir Arthur Conan Doyle. Occasional meetings, functions and visits. *Publishes* an annual journal and twice-yearly news magazine, together with reprints of Conan Doyle's writings.

The Rhys Davies Trust

10 Heol Don, Whitchurch, Cardiff
CF4 2AU
☎01222 529202   Fax 01222 529202
Contact *Meic Stephens*
FOUNDED 1990 to perpetuate the literary reputation of the Welsh prose writer, Rhys Davies (1901–78), and to foster Welsh writing in English. Organises competitions in association with other bodies such as **The Welsh Academy**, puts up plaques on buildings associated with Welsh writers, offers grant-aid for book production, etc.

The Dickens Fellowship

48 Doughty Street, London WC1N 2LF
☎0171 405 2127   Fax 0171 831 5175
Honorary General Secretary *Edward G. Preston*
FOUNDED 1902. Particular aims and objectives are: to bring together lovers of Charles Dickens; to spread the message of Dickens, his love of humanity ('the keynote of all his work'); to remedy social injustice for the poor and oppressed; to assist in the preservation of material and buildings associated with Dickens. Annual conference. *Publishes* journal called *The Dickensian* and organises a full programme of lectures, discussions, visits and conducted walks throughout the year. Branches worldwide.

Early English Text Society

Christ Church, Oxford OX1 1DP
Fax 01865 794199
Executive Secretary *R. F. S. Hamer* (at above address)
Editorial Secretary *Dr H. L. Spencer* (at Exeter College, Oxford OX1 3DP)
Subscription £15 p.a.; $30 (US); $35 (Canada)
FOUNDED 1864. Concerned with the publication of early English texts. Members receive annual publications (one or two a year) or may select titles from the backlist in lieu.

The Eighteen Nineties Society

97D Brixton Road, London SW9 6EE
☎0171 582 4690
Patron *HRH Princess Michael of Kent*
President *Countess of Longford, CBE*
Chairman *Martyn Goff, OBE*
Honorary Secretary *G. Krishnamurti*
Subscription £20 p.a.(UK); $35 (US)
FOUNDED 1963 to bring together admirers of the work of Francis Thompson, the Society widened its scope in 1972 to embrace the artists and literary scene of the entire decade (Impressionism, Realism, Naturalism, Symbolism). Assists members' research into the literature and art of the period; mounts exhibitions; *publishes* an annual journal and a quarterly newsletter, plus biographies of neglected writers and artists of the period under the general title of *Makers of the Nineties*.

The George Eliot Fellowship

71 Stepping Stones Road, Coventry,
Warwickshire CV5 8JT
☎01203 592231
Contact *Mrs Kathleen Adams*

Subscription £8 p.a.; £80 (Life); concessions for pensioners

FOUNDED 1930. Exists to honour George Eliot and promote interest in her life and works. Readings, memorial lecture, birthday luncheon and functions. Issues a quarterly newsletter and an annual journal.

Folly (Fans of Light Literature for the Young)

21 Warwick Road, Pokesdown, Bournemouth, Dorset BH7 6JW

Contact *Mrs Sue Sims*
Subscription £6 p.a. (UK); £7 (Europe); £8.50 (Worldwide)

FOUNDED 1990 to promote interest in a wide variety of children's authors – with a bias towards writers of girls' books and school stories. *Publishes* three magazines a year.

The Franco–Midland Hardware Company

6 Bramham Moor, Hill Head, Fareham, Hampshire PO14 3RU
☎01329 667325

Chairman *Philip Weller*
Subscription £14 p.a.

FOUNDED 1989. 'The world's leading Sherlock Holmes correspondence study group and the most active Holmesian society in Britain.' *Publishes* bi-annual journal and at least six specialist monographs a year. It provides certificated self-study courses and organises monthly functions at Holmes-associated locations. Open membership.

The Gaskell Society

Far Yew Tree House, Over Tabley, Knutsford, Cheshire WA16 0HN
☎01565 634668

Honorary Secretary *Joan Leach*
Subscription £8 p.a.; £12 (Overseas)

FOUNDED 1985 to promote and encourage the study and appreciation of the life and works of Elizabeth Cleghorn Gaskell. Meetings held in Knutsford, Manchester and London; residential study weekends and visits; annual journal and bi-annual newsletter.

The Ghost Story Society

PO Box 1360, Ashcroft, British Columbia Canada V0K 1A0

Joint Organisers *Barbara Roden, Christopher Roden*

Membership Contact *Rosemary Pardoe*, Flat One, 36 Hamilton Street, Hoole, Chester CH2 3JQ

Subscription UK: £13 (Surface mail)/ £14.50 (Airmail); $23 (US); $29.50 (Canada)

FOUNDED 1988. Devoted mainly to supernatural fiction in the literary tradition of M. R. James, Walter de la Mare, Algernon Blackwood, E. F. Benson, A. N. L. Murphy, R. H. Malden, etc. *Publishes* a thrice-yearly journal, *All Hallows*, which includes new fiction in the genre and non-fiction of relevance to the genre.

The Gothic Society

Chatham House, Gosshill Road, Chislehurst, Kent BR7 5NS
☎0181 467 8475   Fax 0181 295 1967

Contact *Jennie Gray*
Subscription £20 p.a.; £23 (Overseas)

FOUNDED 1990 for the amusement of 'those who delight in morbid, macabre and black-hued themes, both ancient and modern Gothick!' *Publishes* high-quality paperbacks on related subjects, and four large-format illustrated magazines yearly together with a quarterly newsletter. Some scope for original and imaginative fiction, but main preference is for history, biography and intelligent but amusing essays on the arts. Members have a definite advantage over writers outside the Society. (Also see **The Gargoyle's Head** under **Small Presses**.)

Rider Haggard Appreciation Society

27 Deneholm, Whitley Bay, Tyne & Wear NE25 9AU
☎0191 252 4516   Fax 0191 252 4516

Contact *Roger Allen*
Subscription £8 p.a. (UK); £10 (Overseas)

FOUNDED 1985 to promote appreciation of the life and works of Sir Henry Rider Haggard, English novelist, 1856–1925. News/books exchange, and meetings every two years.

The Thomas Hardy Society

PO Box 1438, Dorchester, Dorset DT1 1YH
☎01305 251501

Honorary Secretary *Miss Eileen Johnson*
Subscription £12 (Individual); £16 (Corporate); £15 (Individual Overseas); £20 (Corporate Overseas)

FOUNDED 1967 to promote the reading and study of the works and life of Thomas Hardy. Thrice-yearly journal, events and a biennial conference.

The Henty Society

Fox Hall, Kelshall, Royston, Hertfordshire
SG8 9SE
☎01763 287208

Honorary Secretary *Mrs Ann J. King*
Subscription £12 p.a. (UK); £15 (Overseas)

FOUNDED 1977 to study the life and work of George Alfred Henty, and to publish research, bibliographical data and lesser-known works, namely short stories. Organises conferences and social gatherings in the UK and Canada, and *publishes* quarterly bulletins to members. Published in 1996: *G. A. Henty (1832–1902) a Bibliographical Study* by Peter Newbolt.

Sherlock Holmes Society (Northern Musgraves)

Overdale, 69 Greenhead Road, Huddersfield, West Yorkshire HD1 4ER
☎01484 426957   Fax 01484 426957
Contact *David Stuart Davies, Kathryn White*
Subscription £15 p.a. (UK)

FOUNDED 1987 to promote enjoyment and study of Sir Arthur Conan Doyle's Sherlock Holmes through publications and meetings. One of the largest Sherlock Holmes societies in Great Britain. Honorary members include Dame Jean Conan Doyle, Richard Lancelyn Green, Edward Hardwicke and Douglas Wilmer. Past honorary members: Peter Cushing and Jeremy Brett. Open membership. Lectures, presentations and consultation on matters relating to Holmes and Conan Doyle available.

The Sherlock Holmes Society of London

13 Crofton Avenue, Orpington, Kent
BR6 8DU
☎01689 811314

Membership Secretary *R. J. Ellis*
Subscription £9.50 p.a. (Associate); £14 (Full)

FOUNDED 1951 to promote the study of the life and work of Sherlock Holmes and Dr Watson, and their creator, Sir Arthur Conan Doyle. Offers correspondence and liaison with international societies, plus a bi-annual society journal.

Sherlock Holmes

See **The Franco-Midland Hardware Company**

Hopkins Society

Library, Museum & Gallery, Earl Road, Mold, Flintshire CH7 1AP
☎01352 758403   Fax 01352 700236

Contact *Sandra Wynne*
Subscription £5 p.a.

FOUNDED 1990 to celebrate the life and work of Gerard Manley Hopkins; to inform members of any publications, courses or events about the poet. Holds an annual lecture on Hopkins in the spring; produces two newsletters a year; sponsors and organises educational projects based on Hopkins' life and works.

W. W. Jacobs Appreciation Society

3 Roman Road, Southwick, West Sussex
BN42 4TP
☎01273 871017   Fax 01273 871017
Contact *A. R. James*

FOUNDED 1988 to encourage and promote the enjoyment of the works of W. W. Jacobs, and stimulate research into his life and works. *Publishes* a quarterly newsletter free to those who send s.a.e. (9in x 4in). Contributions welcome but no payment made. Preferred lengths 600–1200 words. No subscription charge. Biography, bibliography, directories of plays and films are available for purchase.

Richard Jefferies Society

Eidsvoll, Bedwells Heath, Boars Hill, Oxford
OX1 5JE
☎01865 735678

Honorary Secretary *Lady Phyllis Treitel*
Membership Secretary *Mrs Sheila Povey*
Subscription £7 p.a. (Individual); £8 (Joint);
    Life membership for those over 50

FOUNDED 1950 to promote understanding of the work of Richard Jefferies, nature/country writer, novelist and mystic (1848–87). Produces newsletters, reports and an annual journal; organises talks, discussions and readings. Library and archives. Assists in maintaining museum in Jefferies' birthplace at Coate near Swindon. Membership applications should be sent to *Sheila Povey*, 20 Farleigh Crescent, Swindon, Wiltshire SN3 1JY.

Jerome K. Jerome Society

The Birthplace Museum, Belsize House, Bradford Street, Walsall, West Midlands
WS1 1PN
☎01922 27686   Fax 01922 721065
Honorary Secretary *Tony Gray*
Subscription £5 p.a. (Ordinary);
    £25 (Corporate); £6 (Joint);
    £2.50 (Under 21/Over 65)

FOUNDED 1984 to stimulate interest in Jerome K. Jerome's life and works (1859–1927). One of the Society's principal activities is the support of a small museum in the author's birthplace, Walsall. Meetings, lectures, events and a twice-yearly newsletter *Idle Thoughts*. Annual dinner in Walsall near Jerome's birth date (2nd May).

The W. E. Johns Society
Canna, West Drive, Bracklesham Bay, Chichester, West Sussex PO20 8PF
☎01243 671209

Contact *Jenny Schofield*
Subscription £8 p.a.

Publishes bi-annual magazine, *Biggles Flies Again* and usually holds two meetings (in Hertford and Nottingham) each year.

Johnson Society
Johnson Birthplace Museum, Breadmarket Street, Lichfield, Staffordshire WS13 6LG
☎01543 264972

Secretary *Mrs Norma Hooper*
Subscription £5 p.a.; £7 (Joint)

FOUNDED 1910 to encourage the study of the life, works and times of Samuel Johnson (1709–1784) and his contemporaries. The Society is committed to the preservation of the Johnson Birthplace Museum and Johnson memorials.

Johnson Society of London
255 Baring Road, Grove Park, London SE12 0BQ
☎0181 851 0173

Honorary Secretary *Mrs Z. E. O'Donnell*
Subscription £10 p.a.; £12.50 (Joint)

FOUNDED 1928 to promote the knowledge and appreciation of Dr Samuel Johnson and his works. Regular meetings from October to April in the Vestry Hall of St Edmund the King, Lombard Street in London on the second Saturday of each month, and a commemoration ceremony around the anniversary of Johnson's death, in December, held in Westminster Abbey.

The Just William Society
15 St James' Avenue, Bexhill-on-Sea, East Sussex TN40 2DN
☎01424 216065

Secretary *Michael Vigar*
Treasurer *Phil Woolley*
Subscription £7 p.a. (UK); £10 (Overseas); £5 (Juvenile/Student); £15 (Family)

FOUNDED 1994 to further knowledge of Richmal Crompton's *William* and *Jimmy* books. An annual 'William' meeting is held in April, although this is not currently organised by the Society. The Honorary President of the Society is Richmal Crompton's niece, Richmal Ashbee.

The Keats–Shelley Memorial Association
1 Lewis Road, Radford Semele, Warwickshire CV31 1UB

Contact *Honorary Treasurer* (at 10 Lansdowne Road, Tunbridge Wells, Kent TN1 2NJ. ☎01892 533452 Fax 01892 519142)
Subscription £10 p.a.; £100 (Life)

FOUNDED 1909 to promote appreciation of the works of Keats and Shelley, and their contemporaries. One of the Society's main tasks is the preservation of 26 Piazza di Spagna in Rome as a memorial to the British Romantic poets in Italy, particularly Keats and Shelley. *Publishes* an annual review of Romantic Studies called the *Keats-Shelley Review* and arranges events and lectures for Friends. The review is edited by *Angus Graham-Campbell*, c/o Eton College, Windsor, Berkshire SL4 6DL.

Kent & Sussex Poetry Society
Costens, Carpenters Lane, Hadlow, Kent TN11 0EY
☎01732 851404

Honorary Secretary *Mrs Doriel Hulse* (at the above address)
Subscription £6 p.a.; £3 (non-attending); £2 (per meeting)

FOUNDED 1946 to promote the enjoyment of poetry. Monthly meetings, including readings by major poets, and a monthly workshop. Produces an annual folio of members' work, adjudicated and commented upon by a major poet and runs an open poetry competition (see **Prizes**) bi-annually (next in 1998).

The Kilvert Society
The Old Forge, Kinnersley, Hereford HR3 6QB
☎01544 327426

Secretary *Mr M. Sharp*
Subscription £5 p.a.; £50 (Life)

FOUNDED 1948 to foster an interest in the Diary, the diarist and the countryside he loved. *Publishes* three newsletters each year; during the summer holds three weekends of walks, commemoration services and talks.

The Kipling Society

Tree Cottage, 2 Brownleaf Road, Brighton,
East Sussex BN2 6LBR
☎01273 303719   Fax 01273 303719
Secretary *Mr J. W. Michael Smith*
Subscription £20 p.a.

FOUNDED 1927. The Society's main activities
are: maintaining a specialised library in
London; answering enquiries from the public
(schools, publishers, writers and the media);
arranging a regular programme of lectures,
especially in London and in Sussex, and an
annual luncheon with guest speaker; maintaining a small museum and reference at The
Grange, in Rottingdean near Brighton, issuing
a quarterly journal. This is a literary society for
all who enjoy the prose and verse of Rudyard
Kipling (1865–1936) and are interested in his
life and times. Please contact the Secretary for
further information.

The Kitley Trust

Toadstone Cottage, Edge View, Litton,
Derbyshire SK17 8QU
☎01298 871564

Contact *Rosie Ford*

FOUNDED 1990 by a teacher in Sheffield to
promote the art of creative writing, in memory
of her mother, Jessie Kitley. Activities include:
bi-annual poetry competitions; a 'Get Poetry'
Day (distribution of children's poems in shopping malls); annual sponsorship of a writer for a
school; campaigns; organising conferences for
writers and teachers of writing. Funds are provided by donations and profits (if any) from
competitions.

Charles Lamb Society

1A Royston Road, Richmond, Surrey
TW10 6LT
☎0181 940 3837

General Secretary *Mrs M. R. Huxstep*
Subscription £12 p.a. (Single); £18 (Joint &
    Corporate); US$28 (Overseas Personal);
    US$42 (Overseas Corporate)

FOUNDED 1935 to promote the study of the
life, works and times of English essayist Charles
Lamb (1775–1834). Holds regular monthly
meetings and lectures in London and organises
society events over the summer. *Publishes* a
quarterly bulletin, *The Charles Lamb Bulletin*.
Contributions of Elian interest are welcomed
by the editor *Dr Duncan Wu* at Dept of English
Literature, University of Glasgow, Glasgow
G12 8QQ (E-mail: dwu@arts.gla.ac.uk/
☎0141 332 3836). Membership applications

should be sent to the General Secretary at
1A Royston Road, Richmond TW10 6LT.
The Society's library is housed in the
Guildhall Library, Aldermanbury, London
EC2P 2EJ (☎0171 606 3030). Member of the
Alliance of Literary Societies. Registered
Charity No: 803222.

Lancashire Authors' Association

Heatherslade, 5 Quakerfields, Westhoughton,
Bolton, Lancashire BL5 2BJ
☎01942 791390

General Secretary *Eric Holt*
Subscription £9 p.a.; £12 (Joint);
    £1 (Junior)

FOUNDED 1909 for writers and lovers of
Lancashire literature and history. Aims to foster
and stimulate interest in Lancashire history and
literature as well as in the preservation of the
Lancashire dialect. Meets four times a year
on Saturday at various locations. *Publishes* a
quarterly journal called *The Record* which is
issued free to members and holds eight annual
competitions (open to members only) for both
verse and prose. Comprehensive library with
access for research to members.

The D. H. Lawrence Society

Dept of French, University of Hull,
Cottingham Road, Hull HU6 7RX
Contact *Dr Catherine Greensmith*
Subscription £10; £9 (Concession);
    £11 (Joint); £12 (Europe); £15 (RoW)

FOUNDED 1974 to increase knowledge and the
appreciation of the life and works of D. H.
Lawrence. Monthly meetings, addressed by
guest speakers, are held in the library at
Eastwood (birthplace of DHL). Organises visits
to places of interest in the surrounding countryside, supports the activities of the D. H.
Lawrence Centre at Nottingham University,
has close links with DHL Societies worldwide.
Publishes two newsletters and one journal each
year, free to members.

The Leamington Literary Society

15 Church Hill, Leamington Spa,
Warwickshire CV32 5AZ
☎01926 425733

Honorary Secretary *Mrs Margaret Watkins*
Subscription £6 p.a.

FOUNDED 1912 to promote the study and
appreciation of literature and the arts. Holds
regular meetings every second Tuesday of the
month (except August) at the Regent Hotel,

Leamington Spa, and lectures. The Society has published various books of local interest.

The Wyndham Lewis Society
818 Coltsfoot Road, Ware, Hertfordshire
SG12 7NW
Contact *Mrs Sam Brown*
Subscription £6 p.a. (UK/Europe);
£7.30 p.a. (Institutions); $16–21 (RoW)
(Dollar subs to be sent to Wyndham Lewis
Society, Hugh Anson Cartwright,
229 College Street, Toronto, Ontario
M5T 1R4, Canada. All cheques payable
to The Wyndham Lewis Society)

FOUNDED 1974 to promote recognition of the value of Lewis's works and encourage scholarly research on the man, his painting and his writing. *Publishes* inaccessible Lewis writings; the annual society journal *The Wyndham Lewis Annual* plus two newsletters; and reproduces Lewis's paintings. The journal is chiefly edited by *Paul Edwards*, School of English, Bath College of Higher Education, Newton St. Loe, Bath BA2 9BN.

William Morris Society
Kelmscott House, 26 Upper Mall,
Hammersmith, London W6 9TA
☎0181 741 3735
Contact *David Rodgers*
Subscription £13.50 p.a.

FOUNDED 1953 to promote interest in the life, work and ideas of William Morris (1834–1923), English poet and craftsman.

Violet Needham Society
c/o 19 Ashburnham Place, London SE10 8TZ
☎0181 692 4562
Honorary Secretary *R. H. A. Cheffins*
Subscription £6 p.a. (UK & Europe);
£9 (outside Europe)

FOUNDED 1985 to celebrate the work of children's author Violet Needham and stimulate critical awareness of her work. *Publishes* thrice-yearly *Souvenir*, the Society journal with an accompanying newsletter; organises meetings and excursions to places associated with the author and her books. The journal includes articles about other children's writers of the 1940s and '50s. Contributions welcome.

The Edith Nesbit Society
8 Marlborough Park Avenue, Sidcup, Kent
DA15 9DJ
☎0181 659 5776
Chairman *Nicholas Reed*

Treasurer *Terence Holland*
Subscription £5 p.a.; £7.50 (Joint)

FOUNDED in 1996 to celebrate the life and work of Edith Nesbit (1858–1924), best known as the author of *The Railway Children*. The Society's activities include a regular newsletter, booklets, talks and visits to relevant places.

The Wilfred Owen Association
17 Belmont, Shrewsbury, Shropshire
SY1 1TE
☎01743 235904
Chairman *Helen McPhail*
Subscription Adults £4 (£6 Overseas);
£2 (Senior Citizens/Students/Unemployed);
£10 (Groups/Institutions)

FOUNDED 1989 to commemorate the life and works of Wilfred Owen by promoting readings, visits, talks and performances relating to Owen and his work, and supporting appropriate academic and creative projects. Membership is international with 600 members. *Publishes* a newsletter twice a year. Speakers are available for schools or clubs etc. Special events in 1998 will commemorate the 80th anniversary of Owen's death.

The Elsie Jeanette Oxenham Appreciation Society
32 Tadfield Road, Romsey, Hampshire
SO51 5AJ
☎01794 517149   Fax 01794 517149
Contact *Ms Ruth Allen*
Subscription £6 p.a.

FOUNDED 1989 to promote the works of Elsie J. Oxenham. Publishes a newsletter, *The Abbey Chronicle*, three times a year.

Thomas Paine Society U.K.
43 Wellington Gardens, Selsey, West Sussex
PO20 0RF
☎01243 605730
President *The Rt. Hon. Michael Foot*
Honorary Secretary/Treasurer *Eric Paine*
Subscription (Minimum) £10 p.a. (UK);
£20 (Overseas)

FOUNDED 1963 to promote the life and work of Thomas Paine, and continues to expound his ideals. Meetings, newsletters, lectures and research assistance. Membership badge. The Society has members worldwide and keeps in touch with American and French Thomas Paine associations. *Publishes* magazine, *Bulletin*, twice yearly.

The Polidori Society

Ebenezer House, 31 Ebenezer Street, Langley
Mill, Nottinghamshire NG16 4DA
Founder & President *Franklin Charles Bishop*
Subscription £15 p.a.

FOUNDED 1990 to promote and encourage
appreciation of the life and works of John
William Polidori MD (1795–1821) – novelist,
poet, tragedian, philosopher, diarist, essayist,
traveller and one of the youngest students to
obtain a medical degree (at the age of 19). He
was one-time intimate of the leading figures in
the Romantic movement and travelling companion and private physician to Lord Byron. He
was a pivotal figure in the infamous Villa
Diodati ghost story sessions in which he assisted
Mary Shelley in her creation of the Frankenstein
tale. Polidori introduced into literature the
enduring icon of the vampire portrayed as a
handsome seducer with his seminal work *The
Vampyre – A Tale*, published in 1819. Members
receive exclusive newsletters, unique publications. International membership.

The Beatrix Potter Society

32 Etchingham Park Road, Finchley, London
N3 2DT
☎0181 346 8031

Secretary *Mrs Marian Werner*
Subscription UK: £10 p.a. (Individual);
£15 (Institutional); Overseas: £15 (or
US$25/Can./Aust.$30, Individual);
£22 (US$35/Can./Aust.$47, Institutional)

FOUNDED 1980 to promote the study and
appreciation of the life and works of Beatrix
Potter (1866–1943). Potter was not only the
author of *The Tale of Peter Rabbit* and other
classics of children's literature; she was also a
landscape and natural history artist, diarist,
farmer and conservationist, and was responsible
for the preservation of large areas of the Lake
District through her gifts to the National Trust.
The Society upholds and protects the integrity
of the inimitable and unique work of the lady,
her aims and bequests. Holds regular talks and
meetings in London with visits to places connected with Beatrix Potter. Biennial International Study Conferences are held in the UK
and occasionally in the USA. The Society has
an active publishing programme.

The Powys Society

Keeper's Cottage, Montacute, Somerset
TA15 6XN
☎01935 824077

Honorary Secretary *John Batten*

Subscription £13.50 (UK); £16 (Overseas)

The Society aims to promote public education
and recognition of the writings, thought and
contribution to the arts of the Powys family;
particularly of John Cowper, Theodore and
Llewelyn, but also of the other members of the
family and their close associates. The Society
holds two major collections of Powys published
works, letters, manuscripts and memorabilia.
Publishes the *Powys Society Newsletter* in April,
June and November and *The Powys Journal* in
August. Organises an annual conference as well
as lectures and meetings in Powys places.

The Arthur Ransome Society

Abbot Hall Art Gallery, Kirkland, Kendal,
Cumbria LA9 5AL
☎01539 722464   Fax 01539 722494

Chairman *M. Temple*
Secretary *Dr K. Cochrane*
Contact *Gillian Riding*
Subscription £5 (Junior); £10 (Student);
£15 (Adult); £20 (Family/Overseas);
£40 (Corporate); Concessions for retired
persons

FOUNDED 1990 to celebrate the life and promote the works and ideas of Arthur Ransome,
author of the world-famous *Swallows and
Amazons* titles for children and biographer of
Oscar Wilde. TARS seeks to encourage children and adults to engage in adventurous pursuits, to educate the public about Ransome and
his works, and to sponsor research into his literary works and life.

The Followers of Rupert

31 Whiteley, Windsor, Berkshire SL4 5PJ
☎01753 865562

Membership Secretary *Mrs Shirley Reeves*
Subscription UK: £8; £10 (Joint); Europe,
airmail: £9 (Individual); £11 (Joint);
Worldwide, airmail: £11 (Individual);
£13 (Joint)

FOUNDED in 1983. The Society caters for the
growing interest in the Rupert Bear stories,
past, present and future. *Publishes* the *Nutwood
Newsletter* quarterly which gives up-to-date
news of Rupert and information on Society
activities. A national get-together of members
– the Followers Annual – is held during the
autumn in venues around the country.

The Ruskin Society of London

351 Woodstock Road, Oxford OX2 7NX
☎01865 310987/515962

Honorary Secretary *Miss O. E. Forbes-Madden*

Subscription £10 p.a.

FOUNDED 1986 to promote interest in John Ruskin (1819–1900) and his contemporaries. All aspects of Ruskinia are introduced. Functions are held in London. *Publishes* the annual *Ruskin Gazette*, a journal concerned with Ruskin's influence.

The Dorothy L. Sayers Society

Rose Cottage, Malthouse Lane,
Hurstpierpoint, West Sussex BN6 9JY
☎01273 833444   Fax 01273 835988
Contact *Christopher Dean*
Subscription £10 p.a.

FOUNDED 1976 to promote the study of the life, works and thoughts of Dorothy Sayers; to encourage the performance of her plays and publication of her books and books about her; to preserve original material and provide assistance to researchers. Acts as a forum and information centre, providing material for study purposes which would otherwise be unavailable. Annual seminars and other meetings. Co-founder of the Dorothy L. Sayers Centre in Witham. *Publishes* bi-monthly bulletin and other papers.

The Shaw Society

51 Farmfield Road, Downham, Bromley,
Kent BR1 4NF
☎0181 697 3619   Fax 0181 697 3619
Honorary Secretary *Ms Barbara Smoker*
Subscription £10 p.a. (Individual);
  £14 (Joint)

FOUNDED 1941 to promote interest in the life and works of G. Bernard Shaw. Meetings are held on the last Friday of every month (except July, August and December) at Conway Hall, Red Lion Square, London WC1 (6.30pm for 7pm) at which speakers are invited to talk on some aspect of Shaw's life or works. Monthly playreadings are held on the first Friday of each month (except August). A 'Birthday Tribute' is held at Shaw's Corner, Ayot St Lawrence in Hertfordshire on the weekend nearest to Shaw's birthday (26th July). *Publishes* a quarterly newsletter and a magazine, *The Shavian*, which appears approximately every nine months.

The Robert Southey Society

16 Rhydhir, Longford, Neath Abbey, Neath,
West Glamorgan SA10 7HP
☎01792 814783
Contact *Robert King*
Subscription £10 p.a.

FOUNDED 1990 to promote the work of Robert Southey. *Publishes* an annual newsletter and arranges talks on his life and work. Open membership.

The Friends of Shandy Hall (The Laurence Sterne Trust)

Shandy Hall, Coxwold, York YO6 4AD
☎01347 868465
Honorary Secretary *Mrs J. Monkman*
Subscription £6 (Annual); £60 (Life)

Promotes interest in the works of Laurence Sterne and aims to preserve the house in which they were created (open to the public). *Publishes* annual journal *The Shandean*. An Annual Memorial Lecture is delivered at Shandy Hall each summer.

Robert Louis Stevenson Club

5 Albyn Place, Edinburgh EH2 4NJ
☎0131 225 6665   Fax 0131 220 1015
Contact *Alistair J. R. Ferguson*
Subscription £10 p.a. (Individual);
  £80 (Life)

FOUNDED 1920 to promote the memory of Robert Louis Stevenson and interest in his works.

The R. S. Surtees Society

Manor Farm House, Nunney, Near Frome,
Somerset BA11 4NJ
☎01373 836937   Fax 01373 836574
Contact *Mrs Joan Wright*
Subscription £10

FOUNDED 1979 to republish the works of R. S. Surtees and others.

The Tennyson Society

Central Library, Free School Lane, Lincoln
LN2 1EZ
☎01522 552862   Fax 01522 552858
Honorary Secretary *Miss K. Jefferson*
Subscription £8 p.a. (Individual); £10
  (Family); £15 (Corporate); £125 (Life)

FOUNDED 1960. An international society with membership worldwide. Exists to promote the study and understanding of the life and work of Alfred, Lord Tennyson. The Society is concerned with the work of the Tennyson Research Centre, 'probably the most significant collection of mss, family papers and books in the world'. *Publishes* annually the *Tennyson Research Bulletin*, which contains articles and critical reviews; and organises lectures, visits and seminars. Annual memorial service at Somersby in Lincolnshire.

The Edward Thomas Fellowship

Butlers Cottage, Halswell House, Goathurst, Bridgwater, Somerset TA5 2DH
☎01278 662856

Secretary *Richard Emeny*
Subscription £5 p.a. (Single); £7 p.a. (Joint)

FOUNDED 1980 to perpetuate and promote the memory of Edward Thomas and to encourage an appreciation of his life and work. The Fellowship holds a commemorative birthday walk on the Sunday nearest the poet's birthday, 3 March; issues newsletters and holds various events.

The Trollope Society

9A North Street, Clapham, London
SW4 0HN
☎0171 720 6789   Fax 0171 978 1815

Contacts *John Letts, Phyllis Eden*

FOUNDED 1987 to study and promote Anthony Trollope's works. Linked with the publication of the first complete edition of his novels.

Edgar Wallace Society

Kohlbergsgracht 40, 6462 CD Kerkrade
The Netherlands
☎00 31 455 67 00 50 Fax 00 31 455 67 00 70

Organiser *K. J. Hinz*
Subscription £15 p.a.; £20 (Overseas);
    £10 (Senior Citizens)

FOUNDED 1969 by Edgar's daughter, Penelope, to bring together all who have an interest in Edgar Wallace. Members receive a brief biography of her father by Penelope Wallace, with a complete list of all published book titles. A 24-page quarterly newsletter, *Crimson Circle*, is issued in February, May, August and November.

The Walmsley Society

April Cottage, No 1 Brand Road, Hampden Park, Eastbourne, East Sussex BN22 9PX
☎01323 506447

Honorary Secretary *Fred Lane*
Subscription £8 p.a.; £10 (Family);
    £7 (Students/Senior Citizens)

FOUNDED 1985 to promote interest in the art and writings of Ulric and Leo Walmsley. Two annual meetings, one held in Robin Hood's Bay on the East Yorkshire coast, spiritual home of the author Leo Walmsley. The Society also seeks to foster appreciation of the work of his father Ulric Walmsley. *Publishes* a journal twice-yearly and newsletters, and is involved in other publications which benefit the aims of the Society.

Mary Webb Society

Tansy Cottage, Clunbury, Craven Arms, Shropshire SY7 0HF
Secretary *Margaret Austin*
Subscription £7.50 p.a.

FOUNDED 1972. Attracts members from the UK and overseas who are devotees of the literature of Mary Webb and of the beautiful Shropshire countryside of her novels. *Publishes* annual journal in September, organises summer schools in various locations related to the authoress's life and works. Archives; lectures; tours arranged for individuals and groups.

H. G. Wells Society

49 Beckingthorpe Drive, Bottesford, Nottingham NG13 0DN
Honorary Secretary *J. R. Hammond*
Subscription £12 (UK/EU);
    £18 (Overseas); £20 (Corporate);
    £6 (Concessions)

FOUNDED 1960 to promote an interest in and appreciation of the life, work and thought of Herbert George Wells.

The Charles Williams Society

26 Village Road, London N3 1TL
Contact *Honorary Secretary*

FOUNDED 1975 to promote interest in, and provide a means for, the exchange of views and information on the life and work of Charles Walter Stansby Williams (1886–1945).

The Henry Williamson Society

16 Doran Drive, Redhill, Surrey RH1 6AX
☎01737 763228

Membership Secretary *Mrs Margaret Murphy*
Subscription £8 p.a.; £10 (Family);
    £4 (Students)

FOUNDED 1980 to encourage, by all appropriate means, a wider readership and deeper understanding of the literary heritage left by 20th-century English writer Henry Williamson (1895–1977). *Publishes* annual journal.

The P. G. Wodehouse Society

108 Balmoral Road, Northampton
NN2 6JZ
☎01604 710500

President *Richard Briars*

Contact *Richard Morris*
Subscription £15 p.a. (includes membership of US society)

Relaunched in May 1997 to advance the genius of P. G. Wodehouse – twinned with The Wodehouse Society in the US. Publications include *Wooster Source* and the *By The Way* newsletter. Regular national and international group meetings. Members in most countries throughout the world. Society patrons include Rt. Hon. Tony Blair MP, Sir Edward Cazelet (Wodehouse's grandson) and Stephen Fry.

WW2 HMSO PPBKS Society

3 Roman Road, Southwick, West Sussex
BN42 4TP
☎01273 871017   Fax 01273 871017
Contact *A. R. James*
Subscription £2 p.a.

FOUNDED 1994 to encourage collectors of, and promote research into HM Stationery Office's World War II series of paperbacks, most of which were written by well-known authors, although, in many cases, anonymously. *Publishes* bi-monthly newsletter for those who send s.a.e. (9in x 4in). Contributors welcome; preferred length 600 – 1200 words but no payment made. Bibliography available for purchase (£3); Collectors' Guide (£5).

Yorkshire Dialect Society

51 Stepney Avenue, Scarborough, North Yorkshire YO12 5DW
☎01785 371296
Secretary *Stanley Ellis*
Subscription £8 p.a.

FOUNDED 1897 to promote interest in and preserve a record of the Yorkshire dialect. *Publishes* dialect verse and prose writing. Two journals to members annually. Details of publications are available from the Librarian, YDS, School of English, University of Leeds, Leeds, West Yorkshire LS2 9JT.

Francis Brett Young Society

52 Park Road, Hagley, Near Stourbridge, West Midlands DY9 0QF
☎01562 882973
Honorary Secretary *Mrs Jean Pritchard*
Subscription £5 p.a. (Individuals);
    £7 (Married couples sharing a journal);
    £3 (Students); £5 (Organisations/Overseas);
    £45 (Life)

FOUNDED 1979. Aims to provide a forum for those interested in the life and works of English novelist Francis Brett Young and to collate research on him. Promotes lectures, exhibitions and readings; *publishes* a regular newsletter.

Arts Councils and Regional Arts Boards

The Arts Council of England
14 Great Peter Street, London SW1P 3NQ
☎0171 333 0100   Fax 0171 973 6590
Chairman *Lord Gowrie*
Secretary General *To be appointed*

The 1997/98 government grant dispensed by the Arts Council stands at approximately £186.1 million. From this fund the Arts Council supports arts organisations, artists, performers and others: grants can also be made for particular productions, exhibitions and projects. Grants available to individuals are detailed in the free Arts Council folder: *Development Funds 1997/98*. The total amount set aside for literature in 1997/98 is £1,723,000.

Drama Director *Anna Stapleton* New writing is supported through *Theatre Writing Allocations* (contact the Drama Department for more details).

Literature Director *Gary McKeone* The Literature Department has defined support for writers, education, access to literature including the touring of authors and literary exhibitions, cultural diversity, and an international view of writing including more translation into English among its top priorities. Professor Andrew Motion is chairman of the Literature Advisory Panel. This year the Arts Council will be giving at least 15 grants of £7,000 each to individual writers. Applicants must have at least one published book. Details available from the Literature Department from July 1997.

The Arts Council/
An Chomhairle Ealaion
70 Merrion Square, Dublin 2
☎00 353 1 6611840   Fax 00 353 1 6761302
Literature Officer *Laurence Cassidy*

The Irish Arts Council has programmes under six headings to assist in the area of literature and the book world: a) Writers; b) Literary Organisations; c) Publishers; d) Literary Magazines; e) Participation Programmes; f) Foreign Representation. It also gives a number of annual bursaries (see **Arts Council Literature Bursaries, Ireland**) and organises the **Dublin International Writers' Festival**.

The Arts Council of Northern Ireland
185 Stranmillis Road, Belfast BT9 5DU
☎01232 381591   Fax 01232 661715
Literature Officer *Ciaran Carson*

Funds book production by established publishers, programmes of readings, literary festivals, writers-in-residence schemes and literary magazines and periodicals. Occasional schools programmes and anthologies of children's writing are produced. Annual awards and bursaries for writers are available. Holds information also on various groups associated with local arts, workshops and courses.

Scottish Arts Council
12 Manor Place, Edinburgh EH3 7DD
☎0131 226 6051   Fax 0131 225 9833
Literature Director *Jenny Brown*
Literature Officer *Shonagh Irvine*
Literature Secretary *Catherine Allan*

The Council's work for Scottish-based writers who have a track record of publication includes: bursaries (considered twice yearly); travel and research grants (considered three times yearly); writing fellowships (posts usually advertised) and an international writing fellowship (organised reciprocally with the Canada Council). Also publishes lists of Scottish writers' groups, workshops, circles, awards and literary agents.

The Arts Council of Wales
Museum Place, Cardiff CF1 3NX
☎01222 394711   Fax 01222 221447
Literature Director *Tony Bianchi*
Drama Director *Michael Baker*

Funds literary magazines and book production; *Writers on Tour* and bursary schemes; **Welsh Academy, Welsh Books Council, Hay-on-Wye Literature Festival** and **Tŷ Newydd Writers' Centre** at Cricieth; also children's literature, annual awards. The Council's Drama Board aims to develop theatrical experience among Wales-based writers through a variety of schemes – in particular, by funding writers on year-long attachments.

Arts Council of Wales – North Wales Office

10 Wellfield House, Bangor, Gwynedd
LL57 1ER
☎01248 353248   Fax 01248 351077

Regional Director *Sandra Wynne*
Arts Officer (Literature) *J. Clifford Jones*

The region includes Gwynedd, Clwyd and the Montgomeryshire district of Powys. The Regional Board's role in the field of literature is fourfold: to highlight all aspects of the literary heritage in both English and Welsh; to foster an understanding and appreciation of this tradition; to stimulate others to develop these traditions; to encourage promising new initiatives. Priorities include the *Authors in Residence, Authors on Video* and *Writers on Tour* schemes, and the support of literary circles, Eisteddfodau and community newspapers. Can supply list of names and addresses of regional groups and circles in the region. Contact the Literature Officer.

Arts Council of Wales – South East Wales Office

Victoria Street, Cwmbran, Gwent NP44 3YT
☎01633 875075   Fax 01633 875389

Literature Officer *Bob Mole*

Can supply names and addresses of local groups, workshops and writing courses, and information on local writing schemes, and writers.

Arts Council of Wales – West Wales Office

6 Gardd Llydaw, Jacksons Lane, Carmarthen
SA31 1QD
☎01267 234248   Fax 01267 233084

Regional Executive Officer *Marion Morris*

ACW West Wales covers Carmarthenshire, Ceredigionshire, Pembrokeshire, Neath Port Talbot, City and County of Swansea (formerly the counties of Dyfed and West Glamorgan). It supports a network of writers' groups through the **Arts Council of Wales** *Writers on Tour* scheme and organises an ongoing series of community writing projects. Writers receive additional support through their participation in residencies and other activities in the education and healthcare sectors. In conjunction with the Welsh Language Board, the ACW also supports a network of Welsh language community newspapers. Publishing ventures are referred to other agencies. Supplies a list of names and addresses of over 20 groups in the region, including groups like Carmarthen Writers' Circle.

English Regional Arts Boards

5 City Road, Winchester, Hampshire
SO23 8SD
☎01962 851063   Fax 01962 842033

Chief Executive *Christopher Gordon*
Assistant *Carolyn Nixson*

English Regional Arts Boards is the representative body for the 10 Regional Arts Boards (RABs) in England. Its Winchester secretariat provides project management, services and information for the members, and acts on their behalf in appropriate circumstances. Scotland, Northern Ireland and Wales have their own Arts Councils. The three Welsh Regional Arts Associations are now absorbed into the Welsh Arts Council. RABs are support and development agencies for the arts in the regions. Policies are developed in response to regional demand, and to assist new initiatives in areas of perceived need; they may vary from region to region.

DIRECT GRANTS FOR WRITERS

While most of the RABs designate part of their budget for allocation direct to writers, this is often a minor proportion, which new or aspiring playwrights stand little chance of receiving. Money is more readily available for the professional, though, because of the emphasis on community access to the arts in many of the Boards, this is often allocated to writers' appearances in schools and community settings, theatre workshops, etc, rather than to support the writer at the typewriter. New writing is also encouraged through the funding of small presses and grants to theatre companies for play commissions. Details of schemes available from individual Boards or access to the Regional Arts Pages on can be found at its Website – //www.poptel.org.uk/arts.

Cleveland Arts

Ground Floor, Gurney House, Gurney Street, Middlesbrough, Cleveland TS1 1JL
☎01642 262424   Fax 01642 262429

Contact *Literature Development Officer*

Not one of the Regional Arts Boards, Cleveland Arts is an independent arts development agency working in the county of Cleveland. The company works in partnership with local authorities, public agencies, the business sector, schools, colleges, individuals and organisations to coordinate, promote and develop the arts – crafts, film, video, photography, music, drama, dance, literature, public arts, disability, Black arts, community arts. The Literature Development Officer promotes writing classes, poetry readings and cabarets, issues a free newsletter and assists publishers and writers.

East Midlands Arts

Mountfields House, Epinal Way,
Loughborough, Leicestershire LE11 0QE
☎01509 218292   Fax 01509 262214
Literature Officer *Sue Stewart*
Drama Officer *Helen Flach*

Covers Leicestershire, Nottinghamshire, Derbyshire (excluding the High Peak district) and Northamptonshire. A comprehensive information service for regional writers includes an extensive *Writers' Information Pack*, with details of local groups, workshops, residential writing retreats, publishers and publishing information, regional magazines which offer a market for work, advice on approaching the media, on unions, courses and grants. Also available is a directory of writers, primarily to aid people using the *Artists At Your Service* scheme and to establish *Writers' Attachments*. Writers' bursaries are granted for work on a specific project – all forms of writing are eligible except for local history and biography. Writing for the theatre can come under the aegis of both Literature and Drama. A list of writers' groups is available, plus *Foreword*, the literature newsletter.

Eastern Arts Board

Cherry Hinton Hall, Cambridge CB1 4DW
☎01223 215355   Fax 01223 248075
Literature Officer *Emma Drew*
Drama Officer *Alan Orme*
Cinema & Broadcast Media Officer
  Martin Ayres

Covers Bedfordshire, Cambridgeshire, Essex, Hertfordshire, Norfolk, Suffolk and Lincolnshire. Policy emphasises quality and access. As an arts development agency, emphasis is placed upon work with publishers within the region and on literature in performance. Support is given to projects which develop audiences for literature performances and publishing, including electronic media. It offers a range of bursaries annually for individual published writers. Supplies lists of literary groups, workshops, local writing courses and writers working in the educational sector. Also provides advice on applying for National Lottery funds.

London Arts Board

Elme House, 3rd Floor, 133 Long Acre,
London WC2E 9AF
☎0171 240 1313/Help Line: 0171 240 4578
Fax 0171 240 4580

Principal Literature Officer *John Hampson*
Principal Drama Officer *Sue Timothy*

The London Arts Board is the Regional Arts Board for the Capital, covering the 32 London boroughs and the City of London. Potential applicants for support for literature and other arts projects should contact the Board for information.

North West Arts Board

Manchester House, 22 Bridge Street,
Manchester M3 3AB
☎0161 834 6644   Fax 0161 834 6969
Media Officer – Literature *Bronwel Williams*
Performing Arts Officer – Drama *Jane Dawson*

NWAB covers Cheshire, Greater Manchester, Merseyside, Lancashire and the High Peak district of Derbyshire. Offers financial assistance to a great variety of organisations and individuals through a number of schemes, including Writers' Bursaries, Residencies and Placements and the Live Writing scheme. NWAB publishes a directory of local writers groups, a directory of writers and a range of information sheets covering topics such as performance and publishing. For further details please contact the Literature Department.

Northern Arts Board

9–10 Osborne Terrace, Jesmond, Newcastle upon Tyne NE2 1NZ
☎0191 281 6334   Fax 0191 281 3276
Head of Published and Broadcast Arts
  Janice Campbell

Covers Cumbria, Durham, Northumberland, Teesside and Tyne and Wear, and was the first regional arts association in the country to be set up by local authorities. It supports both organisations and writers and aims to stimulate public interest in artistic events. Offers Writers Awards for published writers to release them from work or other commitments for short periods of time to enable them to concentrate on specific literary projects. It also has a film/TV script development fund operated through the Northern Production Fund. A separate scheme for playwrights is operated by the Northern Playwrights Society. Northern Arts makes drama awards to producers only.

Also funds writers' residencies, and has a fund for publications. Contact list of regional groups and workshops available.

South East Arts

10 Mount Ephraim, Tunbridge Wells, Kent TN4 8AS
☎01892 515210   Fax 01892 549383
Literature Officer *Anne Downes*
Drama Officer *Linda Lewis*

Covers Kent, Surrey, East and West Sussex (excluding the London boroughs). The literature programme aims to raise the profile of contemporary literature across the region, to support new and established writers and encourages creative reading schemes. Priorities include live literature schemes, writers' residencies, and bursaries for writers living in the region. A regular newsletter is available (£3 p.a./£5 to those outside the region).

South West Arts

Bradninch Place, Gandy Street, Exeter, Devon EX4 3LS
☎01392 218188   Fax 01392 413554
Director of Media & Published Arts *David Drake*
Director of Performing Arts *Nick Capaldi*
Media & Published Arts Administrator *Sara Fasey*

Covers the county formerly known as Avon, Cornwall, Devon, Dorset (excluding Bournemouth, Christchurch and Poole), Gloucestershire and Somerset. 'The central theme running through the Board's aims are promoting quality and developing audiences for new work.' The literature policy aims to promote a healthy environment for writers of all kinds and to encourage a high standard of new writing. There is direct investment in small presses, publishers and community groups. Literary festivals, societies and arts centres are encouraged. The theatre department aims to support the development of theatre writing by funding the development of literary management programmes of dramaturgy and seasons of new plays. List of regional groups and workshops available from the Information Service.

Southern Arts

13 St Clement Street, Winchester, Hampshire SO23 9DQ
☎01962 855099   Fax 01962 861186
Literature Officer *Keiren Phelan*
Film, Video & Broadcasting Officer *Jane Gerson*

Theatre Officer *Sheena Wrigley*

Covers Berkshire, Buckinghamshire, Hampshire, the Isle of Wight, Oxfordshire, Wiltshire and South East Dorset. The Literature Department funds fiction and poetry readings, festivals, magazines, bursaries, a literature prize, publications, residencies and a scheme which subsidises writers working in education and the community.

West Midlands Arts

82 Granville Street, Birmingham B1 2LH
☎0121 631 3121   Fax 0121 643 7239
Literature Officer *Adrian Johnson*

There are special criteria across the art forms, so contact the Information Office for details of *New Work & Production* and other schemes as well as for the *Reading (Correspondence Mss Advice) Service*. There are contact lists of writers, storytellers, writing groups etc. WMA supports the regional magazine, *Raw Edge Magazine*: contact PO Box 4867, Birmingham B3 3HD.

Yorkshire & Humberside Arts

21 Bond Street, Dewsbury, West Yorkshire WF13 1AY
☎01924 455555   Fax 01924 466522
Literature Officer *Steve Dearden*
Drama Officer *Shea Connolly*
Administrator *Jill Leahy*

'Libraries, publishing houses, local authorities and the education service all make major contributions to the support of literature. Recognising the resources these agencies command, Yorkshire & Humberside Arts actively seeks ways of working in partnership with them, whilst at the same time retaining its particular responsibility for the living writer and the promotion of activities currently outside the scope of these agencies.' Funding goes to **Yorkshire Art Circus** (community publishing); *Live Writing*, a scheme which subsidises projects involving professional writers and young people at all levels as well as writing and community groups; and awards for local independent publishers. The Board also offers support for literature in performance: it supports the **Ilkley Literature Festival**, The Word Hoard and *the text* magazine. It has a bursary scheme, New Beginnings, for writers; and it holds a list of workshops and writers' groups throughout the region. *Publishes* a writers' directory and a newsletter, *Write Angles*, bi-monthly. Contact the Literature Officer.

Writers' Courses, Circles and Workshops

Courses

Courses are listed under country and county

ENGLAND

Berkshire

University of Reading
Centre for Continuing Education, London Road, Reading, Berkshire RG1 5AQ
☎0118 9318347

Creative writing courses usually include *Life into Fiction; Poetry Workshop; Getting Started; Writers Helping Writers* (with **Southern Arts'** help, the course includes visits from well-known writers); *Writing Fiction*. There is also a support group for teachers of creative writing, a public lecture by a writer and a reading by students of their work. Fees vary depending on the length of course. Concessions available.

Buckinghamshire

Missenden Abbey
Great Missenden, Buckinghamshire HP16 0BD
☎01494 890296   Fax 01494 866737

Residential courses, weekend workshops and a regular writers circle available. The 1997 programme included *Writing Magazine Articles and Getting Them Published; Writing Comedy for Television and Radio; The Art of Travel Writing; A Creative Approach to Non-Fiction Writing; Writing Poetry; Writing for Children.*

National Film & Television School
Beaconsfield Studios, Station Road, Beaconsfield, Buckinghamshire HP9 1LG
☎01494 671234   Fax 01494 674042

Writers' course designed for students who already have experience of writing in other fields. The course is divided into two parts: a self-contained intensive five-week course, concentrating on the fundamentals of screenwriting, and a two-year course for 8–10 students selected from the one-month course: intensive programme of writing and analysis combined with an understanding of the practical stages involved in the making of film and television drama.

Cambridgeshire

National Extension College
18 Brooklands Avenue, Cambridge CB2 2HN
☎01223 316644   Fax 01223 313586

Runs a number of home-study courses on writing. Courses include: *Essential Editing; Creative Writing; Writing for Money; Copywriting; Essential Desktop Publishing; Essential Design.* Contact the NEC for copy of the *Guide to Courses* which includes details of fees.

PMA Training
PMA House, Free Church Passage, St Ives, Cambridgeshire PE17 4AY
☎01480 300653   Fax 01480 496022

One-/two-/three-day editorial, PR, design and publishing courses held in central London. High-powered, intensive courses run by Fleet Street journalists and magazine editors. Courses include: *News Writing; Journalistic Style; Feature Writing; Investigative Reporting; Basic Writing Skills.* Fees range from £150 to £600 plus VAT. Special rates for freelancers.

Cheshire

The College of Technical Authorship – Distance Learning Course
The College of Technical Authorship, PO Box 7, Cheadle, Cheshire SK8 3BT
☎0161 437 4235   Fax 0161 437 4235

Distance learning courses for City & Guilds Tech 536, Part 1, Technical Communication Techniques, and Part 2, Technical Authorship. Individual tuition by correspondence and fax; includes some practical work done at home. Contact: John Crossley, DipDistEd, DipM, MCIM, MISTC, LCGI.

Cleveland

University of Leeds

Adult Education Centre, 37 Harrow Road, Middlesbrough, Cleveland TS5 5NT
☎01642 814987

Creative writing courses held throughout Cleveland, North and West Yorkshire in the autumn, spring and summer terms. Courses are part-time and offered in a range of subjects, at beginners, intermediate and advanced levels and carry undergraduate credit. A range of professional development courses for writers are being developed which carry post-graduate credit. Contact Rebecca O'Rourke for details.

Cumbria

Higham Hall College

Bassenthwaite Lake, Cockermouth, Cumbria CA13 9SH
☎017687 76276   Fax 017687 76013

Residential courses. Summer 1997 programme included *Walking and Writing*, *Short Story Writing*, and *Memoir Writing*. Detailed brochure available.

Derbyshire

Real Writers

PO Box 170, Chesterfield, Derbyshire S40 1FE

Correspondence course with personal tuition from professional writers. In addition to the support and appraisal service, runs an annual short story and poetry competition.

Writers' Summer School, Swanwick

The Hayes, Swanwick, Derbyshire

A week-long summer school of informal talks and discussion groups, forums, panels, quizzes and competitions, and 'a lot of fun'. Open to everyone, from absolute beginners to published authors. Held in August from late Saturday to Friday morning. Cost (1997) £190+, all inclusive. Contact the Secretary, Brenda Courtie at The New Vicarage, Parson's Street, Woodford Halse, Daventry, Northants NN11 3RE (☎01327 261477).

Devon

Dartington College of Arts

Totnes, Devon TQ9 6EJ
☎01803 862224

BA(Hons) course in *Performance Writing*: exploratory approach to writing as it relates to performance. Can be taken as a single honours subject or in combination with *Music, Theatre, Visual Performance* or *Arts Management*. Contact Subject Director, Performance Writing: Caroline Bergvall.

Exeter & Devon Arts Centre

Bradninch Place, Gandy Street, Exeter, Devon EX4 3LS
☎01392 421111   Fax 01392 499929

Holds weekly courses: *Poetry Garage; Poetry Zoo; Creative Writing; Advanced Poetry; Poetry Masterclass* as well as a range of other workshops. There is also a regular programme of poetry and literature events, plus the annual Exeter Poetry Prize. Copies of the Courses & Classes or Events brochures can be obtained free from the Centre.

University of Exeter

Exeter, Devon EX4 4QW
☎01392 264580

BA(Hons) in Drama with a third-year option in *Playwriting*. Contact Professor Peter Thomson.

Dorset

Bournemouth University

School of Media Arts and Communication, Poole House, Talbot Campus, Fern Barrow, Poole, Dorset BH12 5BB
☎01202 595553   Fax 01202 595530

Three-year, full-time BA(Hons) course in *Scriptwriting for Film and Television*. Contact Sue Sykes, Programme Adiminstrator.

Essex

National Council for the Training of Journalists

Latton Bush Centre, Southern Way, Harlow, Essex CM18 7BL
☎01279 430009   Fax 01279 438008

For details of journalism courses, both full-time and via distance learning, please write to the NCTJ enclosing a large s.a.e.. (Internet: http://www.itecharlow.co.uk/nctj and e-mail: NCTJ@itecharlow.co.uk)

Hampshire

Highbury College, Portsmouth

Dovercourt Road, Cosham, Portsmouth, Hampshire PO6 2SA
☎01705 383131   Fax 01705 383131

Courses include: one-year *Pre-entry Magazine Journalism* (mainly post-graduate intake). Run under the auspices of the Periodicals Training Council. One-year *Pre-entry Newspaper Journalism* course, run under the auspices of the National Council for Training of Journalists. One-year Post-Graduate Diploma in *Broadcasting Journalism*, run under the auspices of the Broadcast Journalism Training Council. Contact Mrs Paulette Miller, Faculty Secretary, ☎01705 283287.

King Alfred's College of Higher Education
Winchester, Hampshire SO22 4NR
☎01962 841515   Fax 01962 842280

Three-year course on *Drama, Theatre and Television Studies*, including *Writing for Devised Community Theatre* and *Writing for Television Documentary*. Contact Tim Prentki.

MA course in *Theatre for Development* – one year, full-time course with major project overseas or in the UK. MA course in *Writing for Children* (subject to validation) available on either a one- or two-year basis. Admissions enquiries: Linda Richards (01962 827235); Programme enquiries: Jo Roffey (01962 827375).

University of Southampton
Department of Adult Continuing Education, Southampton SO17 1BJ
☎01703 592833

Creative writing courses and writers' workshops. Courses are held in local/regional centres.

Hertfordshire
West Herts College
Faculty of Visual Communication, Hempstead Road, Watford, Hertfordshire WD1 3EZ
☎01923 257654 (Admissions)

The 24-week postgraduate course in *Writing and Production for the Media* covers two options: *Creative, Business and Technical Writing* and *Radio Writing and Production*. The college also offers a postgraduate diploma in *Publishing* with an option in *Multimedia Publishing*. Contact the Admissions Secretary on the number above.

Humberside
Hull College of Further Education
Queen's Gardens, Hull,
North Humberside HU1 3DG
☎01482 329943   Fax 01482 219079

Offers part-time day/evening writing courses, including *Novel Writing* and *Short Story Writing*, at various centres within the city. Most courses

begin each academic term and last for a period of ten weeks. Publishes an anthology of students' work each year entitled, *Embryo*. Contact Ed Strauss.

Kent
International Forum Ltd
The Oast House, Plaxtol, Sevenoaks,
Kent TN15 0QG
☎01732 810925

Wide range of courses (one-/two-/three-day) on screenwriting and other key creative roles in film and television. Courses run throughout the year and concessions are available for members of certain trade organisations. Also runs Kent Enterprises which offers a range of courses in film and television. Contact: Joan Harrison.

University of Kent at Canterbury
School of Continuing Education, Keynes College, Canterbury, Kent CT2 7NP
☎01227 823662

Creative writing courses. Contact Vicki Inge.

Kent Enterprises
See **International Forum Ltd**

Lancaster
Edge Hill University College
St Helen's Road, Ormskirk,
Lancashire L39 4QP
☎01695 575171

Offers a two-year, part-time MA in *Writing Studies*. Combines advanced-level writers' workshops with closely related courses in critical theory and contemporary writing in English. There is also provision for MPhil- and PhD-level research in writing and poetics. A full range of creative writing courses is available at undergraduate level, in poetry and fiction writing which may be taken as part of a modular BA.

Lancaster University
Department of Creative Writing, Lonsdale College, Bailrigg, Lancaster LA1 4YN
☎01524 594169

Offers practical graduate and undergraduate courses in writing fiction, poetry and scripts. All based on group workshops – students' work-in-progress is circulated and discussed. Visiting writers have included: Carol Ann Duffy, Kazuo Ishiguro, Bernard MacLaverty, David Pownall. Contact Linda Anderson for details.

Leicestershire

Leicester Writing School

Leicester Adult Education College,
Wellington Street, Leicester LE1 6HL
☎0116 2334343   Fax 0116 2334344

Offers a wide range of creative writing and
journalism courses throughout the year with
occasional masterclasses and talks. Manuscript
appraisal by post for short stories and articles.
Novel writing weekend (accommodation
arranged on request) planned for spring 1998.
For details contact Valerie Moore.

London

The Central School of Speech and Drama

Embassy Theatre, Eton Avenue, London
NW3 3HY
☎0171 722 8183   Fax 0171 722 4132

Post-Graduate Diploma in *Advanced Theatre
Practice*. One-year, full-time course aimed at
providing a grounding in principal areas of professional theatre practice – *Writing, Dramaturgy,
Directing, Performance, Puppetry* and *Design*, with
an emphasis on collaboration between the various strands. Entrants to the *Writing* strand are
required to submit two pieces of writing
together with completed application form.
Prospectus available.

The City Literary Institute

Humanities Dept, Stukeley Street, London
WC2B 5LJ
☎0171 430 0542

The Writing School offers a wide range of
courses from *Radio Drama Writing* and *Writing
for Children* to *Autobiographical Writing* and
Writing Short Stories. The Department offers
information and advice during term time.

City University

Northampton Square, London EC1V 0HB
☎0171 477 8268

Creative writing classes include: *Writer's
Workshop; Wordshop* (poetry); *Writer's Craft;
Writing Fiction; Writing Comedy; Playwright's
Workshop; Writing Freelance Articles for Newspapers;
Women Writer's Workshop; Creative Writing*.
Contact: Courses for Adults.

The London Academy of Playwriting

75 Hillfield Park, London N10 3QU
☎0181 444 5228   Fax 0181 444 5228

Two-year, part-time, post-graduate course in
playwriting. Directors: Tony Dinner and Sonja
Lyndon.

London College of Printing & Distributive Trades

Elephant & Castle, London SE1 6SB
☎0171 514 6500

Courses in journalism. Short courses run by
DALI (Developments at the London Institute)
at the Elephant & Castle address above: *Writing
for Magazines; Guide to News Writing; Guide to
Feature Writing; Guide to Effective Business
Writing; Freelance Journalism; Proof Reading; Sub-
editing and Law for Journalists*. Full-time courses
(held at the School of Media Studies, Back
Hill, London EC1R 5EN): BAHons. in
Journalism; HND in *Journalism; Periodical
Journalism for Graduates*. Prospectus and infor-
mation leaflets available.

London School of Journalism

22 Upbrook Mews, London W2 3HG
☎0171 706 3790   Fax 0171 706 3780

Correspondence courses with an individual
and personal approach. Students remain with
the same tutor throughout their course.
Options include: *Short Story Writing; Writing for
Children; Poetry; Freelance Journalism; Improve
Your English; English for Business; Journalism and
Newswriting*. Fees vary but range from £175 for
Enjoying English Literature to £375 for
Journalism and Newswriting. Contact the Student
Administration Office at the above address.

Middlesex University

School of English Cultural and
Communication Studies, White Hart Lane,
London N17 8HR
☎0181 362 5000   Fax 0181 362 6299

Undergraduate courses (full-time, part-time,
associate) for those interested in writing, publishing and the media. Writing & Publishing
Studies Set includes: *Editing* and *Marketing*
(contact Juliet Gardiner); BA(Hons) Writing
Programme includes: *Journalism, Scriptwriting*
and *Narrative* and *Poetry Workshops* (contact
Susanna Gladwin).

Roehampton Institute London

Drama and Theatre Studies Department,
Roehampton Lane, London SW15 5PU
☎0181 392 3230   Fax 0181 392 3289

Three-year BA(Hons) programmes in *Drama
and Theatre Studies* and *Film and Television
Studies* include courses on writing for stage and
screen. Contact Jeremy Ridgman.

Thames Valley University
St Mary's Road, London W5 5RF
☎0181 579 5000

Offers a course in *Scriptwriting for Television, Stage and Radio*. Aims to provide the fundamental principles of the craft of script writing.

University of Westminster
Harrow Campus, Watford Road, Harrow, Middlesex HA1 3TP
☎0171 911 5910

The 1997 Summer School courses included *Scriptwriting for Film and Television* and *Broadcast Journalism*.

Greater Manchester
University of Manchester
Department of American Studies, Arts Building, Oxford Road, Manchester M13 9PL
☎0161 275 3054   Fax 0161 275 3054

Offers a one-year MA in *Novel Writing*. Contact Mrs Alex Sherwood.

University of Salford
Admissions Office, The Crescent, Salford, Greater Manchester M5 4WT
☎0161 295 6026

MA in *Television and Radio Scriptwriting*. Two-year, part-time course taught by professional writers and producers. Also offers a number of Masterclasses with leading figures in the radio and television industry.

Password Training Ltd
23 New Mount Street, Manchester M4 4DE
☎0161 953 4009   Fax 0161 953 4090

In addition to training for established companies, Password also provides training in self-publishing skills for writers who wish to publish their own work. Elements covered are planning, production, design, marketing, costing and distribution. For further details, contact Claire Turner, Training Manager.

The Writers Bureau
Sevendale House, 7 Dale Street, Manchester M1 1JB
☎0161 228 2362   Fax 0161 228 3533

Comprehensive home-study writing course with personal tuition service from professional writers (fee approx. £219); Professional Business Writing Course which covers the writing of letters, memos, reports, minutes etc.

(£199); and a Poetry Course which covers all aspects of writing poetry (£99).

Merseyside
University of Liverpool
Centre for Continuing Education, 19 Abercromby Square, Liverpool L69 3BX
☎0151 794 6900 (24 hrs)   Fax 0151 794 2544

Introduction to Creative Writing; The Short Story and the Novel; Poetry Workshops; Biography and Autobiography; Science Fiction and Fantasy; Women's Writing; Writing for Children; Travel Writing; Introduction to Journalism; The Art and Craft of Songwriting; Scripting for Radio; Scripting for Theatre; Scripting for Comedy; Scripting for Film and Television; Scriptwriting for Women. New courses under consideration for 1998 include *Scripting for Animation*. Most courses are run in the evening over 10 or 20 weeks and you may, if wished, work towards a university qualification in Creative Writing. Weekend and summer residential courses are possible. No pre-entry qualifications required. Fees vary with concessions for the unwaged and those in receipt of benefit. For further information and copy of current prospectus, phone or write to Keith Birch, Head of Creative Arts (address as above).

Writing in Merseyside
Writers' and Artists' Resource Unit, Toxteth Library, Windsor Street, Liverpool L8 1XF
☎0151 708 0143   Fax 0151 709 8142

A mini-directory which lists facilities, resources and opportunities in the Merseyside area. Excellent publication for putting writers in touch with what's available in their area. Everything from workshops and courses to competitions, research and library facilities, plus tips. Comprehensive course information on all areas of writing is provided.

Norfolk
University of East Anglia
School of English & American Studies, Norwich, Norfolk NR4 7TJ
☎01603 593262

UEA has a history of concern with contemporary literary culture. Among its MA programmes is one in *Creative Writing*, Stream 1: Prose Fiction; Stream 2: Poetry; Stream 3: Script and Screenwriting.

Nottinghamshire

Nottingham Trent University

Humanities Faculty Office (Post Graduate Studies), Clifton Lane, Nottingham NG11 8NS
☎01115 941 8418   Fax 0115 948 6632

MA in *Writing*. Workshop-based, it focuses on the development of your own feature-writing, fiction, lifewriting and poetry. Current visiting professors: Michele Roberts and Miranda Seymour. Application forms available from the above address. For more information contact Janice Greenhalgh on 0115 941 8418 ext 6335.

Somerset

Bath College of Higher Education

Newton Park, Bath BA2 9BN
☎01225 425264

Postgraduate Diploma/MA in *Creative Writing*. Includes poetry, fiction, playwriting and scriptwriting. Visiting writers have included Roy Fisher, Marion Lomax, William Stafford and Fay Weldon. Contact Clare Brandram Jones for details.

Institute of Copywriting

PO Box 1561, Wedmore, Somerset BS28 4TD
☎01934 713563

Comprehensive home-study course covering all aspects of copywriting, including advice on becoming a self-employed copywriter. Each student has a personal tutor who is an experienced copywriter and who provides detailed feedback on the student's assignments. Also a two-day residential course.

University of Bristol

Department for Continuing Education, 8–10 Berkeley Square, Bristol BS8 1HH
☎0117 9287172   Fax 0117 9254975

Courses in Bristol and throughout the surrounding counties (Dorset, Gloucestershire, Somerset, Wiltshire). *Women and Writing*, for women who write or would like to begin to write (poetry, fiction, non-fiction, journals); *Certificate in Creative Writing*. Detailed brochure available.

Staffordshire

Keele University

The Centre for Continuing and Professional Education, Keele University, (Freepost ST1666), Newcastle under Lyme, Staffordshire ST5 5BR
☎01782 583436

Weekend courses on literature and creative writing. The 1997 programme included fiction writing and poetry. Also runs study days where major novelists or poets read and discuss their work.

Surrey

Royal Holloway College

University of London, Egham Hill, Egham, Surrey TW20 0EX
☎01784 443922   Fax 01784 431018

Three-year BA course in *Theatre Studies* during which playwriting can be studied as an option in the second and third years. Contact Dan Rebellato or David Wiles.

University of Surrey

Department of Educational Studies, University of Surrey, Guildford, Surrey GU2 5XH
☎01483 300800 ext. 3013   Fax 01483 300803

The programme 'Courses For All' includes a *Creative Writing* course, held at the University, the Guildford Institute and across the county. For details contact Karen Fisher or Dr Brian Crossley FRSA, Creative Writing Consultant.

Writing School

Nationwide House, Hyland Business Centre, 78–86 Garlands Road, Redhill, Surrey RH1 6NT
☎01737 779065

Correspondence course covering writing for articles, short stories, books, plays and scripts, with a strong emphasis on writing to sell. Fee £259 (1997). Contact the Director of Studies for enrolment details.

Suffolk

University College Suffolk

Suffolk College, Ipswich, Suffolk IP4 1LT
☎01473 296656   Fax 01473 230054

Summer School courses; the 1997 programme included *Writing for Radio*. Contact Janet Clement, Summer School Co-ordinator for details.

Sussex

Chichester Institute of Higher Education

Bishop Otter College, College Lane, Chichester, West Sussex PO19 4PE
☎01243 816000   Fax 01243 816080

Postgraduate Certificate/Diploma MA in *Creative Writing*. Contact Ms Jan Ainsley, Head of English Studies for details.

The Earnley Concourse

Earnley, Chichester, West Sussex
PO20 7JL
☎01243 670392   Fax 01243 670832

Offers a range of residential and non–residential courses throughout the year. The 1997 programme included *Writing for Publication; You Can Sell What You Write*. Brochure available.

Scriptwriters Tutorials

Wish Hill, Sandy Lane, Mayfield,
East Sussex TN20 6UE
☎01435 873914   Fax 0171 720 7047

Offers professional *one-to-one* scriptwriting tuition by working writers in film, television, radio or stage. Beginners, intermediate and advanced courses. Script evaluation service and correspondence courses. Tutors based in London, Oxford and the southern counties.

University of Sussex

Centre for Continuing Education, Education Development Building, Falmer, Brighton, East Sussex BN1 9RG
☎01273 678040   Fax 01273 678848

Courses in creative writing on campus and at locations in East and West Sussex. The University also offers a one-year part-time Certificate in *Creative Writing*, a Postgraduate Diploma in *Dramatic Writing*, and a Postgraduate Diploma in *Creative Writing and Personal Development*. Contact Richard Crane or Marco Santucci.

Tyne & Wear

University of Newcastle upon Tyne

Centre for Continuing Education, Newcastle upon Tyne NE1 7RU
☎0191 222 5680

Writing–related courses include: *Writing From the Inside Out; Dramatic Writing for Film, TV and Radio; Writing Workshops*. Contact the Secretary, Adult Education Programme.

Warwickshire

University of Warwick

Open Studies, Continuing Education Department, Coventry, Warwickshire CV4 7AL
☎01203 523831

Creative writing courses held at the university or in regional centres. Subjects have included:

Starting to Write; Creative Writing; Writing for Radio; Screenwriting for Beginners. A one-year certificate in *Creative Writing* is available.

West Midlands

Sandwell College

Smethwick Campus, Crocketts Lane, Smethwick B66 3BU
☎0121 556 6000

Creative writing courses held afternoons/evenings, from September to July. General courses covering short stories, poetry, auto-biography, etc. Also women's writing courses. Contact Roz Goddard.

University of Birmingham

School of Continuing Studies, Edgbaston, Birmingham B15 2TT
☎0121 414 5607   Fax 0121 414 5619

Day and weekend classes, including creative writing, writing playscripts for beginners. Courses are held at locations throughout Birmingham, the West Midlands, Hereford & Worcester and Shropshire. Detailed course brochures are available from the above address. Please specify which course you are interested in.

The University also offers an MA course in *Playwriting Studies*. This was established by David Edgar in 1970. Contact Brian Crow at the Department of Drama and Theatre Arts (☎0121 414 5993).

Wiltshire

Marlborough College

Marlborough, Wiltshire SN8 1PA
☎01672 892388/9   Fax 01672 892476

Summer school with literature and creative writing included in its programme. Caters for residential and day students. Brochure available giving full details and prices.

Yorkshire

The Northern School of Film and Television

Leeds Metropolitan University, 2 Queen Square, Leeds, West Yorkshire LS2 8AF
☎0113 2831900   Fax 0113 2831901

A relatively new film school, the NSFT offers a Postgraduate Diploma/MA course in *Fiction Screenwriting*. One to two years, full-/part-time. Contact Ian Macdonald.

Open College of the Arts
Houndhill, Worsbrough, Barnsley, South
Yorkshire S70 6TU
☎01226 730495   Fax 01226 730838

The OCA correspondence course, *Starting to Write*, offers help and stimulus, without an emphasis on commercial success, from experienced writers/tutors. Subsequent levels available include specialist poetry, fiction and biographical writing courses. Audio-cassette versions of these courses are available.

Sheffield Hallam University
School of Cultural Studies, Sheffield Hallam University, Psalter Lane, Sheffield S11 8UZ
☎0114 2532256   Fax 0114 2532603

Offers MA in *Creative Writing* (one-year, full-time/two-year, part-time course).

University College Bretton Hall
School of English and Communication Media, Faculty of Art, University College Bretton Hall, West Bretton, Wakefield, West Yorkshire WF4 4LG
☎01924 830261   Fax 01924 830521

Offers one-year full-time/two-years part-time MA course in *Creative Writing* designed for competent though not necessarily published writers. Contact Rob Watson for details.

University College, Scarborough
North Riding College, Filey Road, Scarborough, North Yorkshire YO11 3AZ
☎01723 362392   Fax 01723 362392

BA Single Honours and Combined Honours Degree in which *Theatre Studies* contains *Writing for Theatre*. Contact Dr Eric Prince. University College Scarborough also works closely with the Stephen Joseph Theatre and its artistic director Alan Ayckbourn. The theatre sustains a policy for staging new writers. (See entry under **Theatre Producers**.) The College hosts the annual National Student Drama Festival which includes the International Student Playscript Competition (details from Clive Wolfe on 0181 883 4586).

University of Leeds
See under *Cleveland*

University of Sheffield
Division of Adult Continuing Education, 196–198 West Street, Sheffield S1 4ET
☎0114 2227000

Creative writing courses and workshops. Day/evening classes, residential courses.

IRELAND

Queen's University of Belfast
Institute of Continuing Education, Belfast BT7 1NN
☎01232 273323

Courses have included *Creative Writing* and *Journal Writing*.

University of Ulster
Short Course Unit, Belfast BT37 0QB
☎01232 365131

Creative writing course/workshop, usually held in the autumn and spring terms. Concessions available. Contact the Administrative Officer.

SCOTLAND

University of Aberdeen
Centre for Continuing Education, Regent Building, Regent Walk, Aberdeen AB24 3FX
☎01224 272449   Fax 01224 272478

Creative writing evening class held weekly, taught by published author. Participants may join in at any time.

University of Dundee
Centre for Continuing Education, Perth Road, Dundee DD1 4HN
☎01382 344128

Various creative writing courses held at the University and elsewhere in Dundee, Perthshire and Angus. Detailed course brochure available.

Edinburgh University
Centre for Continuing Education, 11 Buccleuch Place, Edinburgh EH8 9LW
☎0131 650 4400   Fax 0131 667 6097

Several writing-orientated courses and summer schools. Beginners welcome. Intensive two-week course in Playwriting is held in July, culminating in a rehearsed reading by professional actors and recorded on video for participants to take away. Free tuition in word-processing and use of computer room. Course brochure available.

University of Glasgow
Department of Adult and Continuing Education, 59 Oakfield Avenue, Glasgow G12 8LW
☎0141 330 4032/4394 (Brochure/Enquiries)

In 1996/7 ran several writers' workshops and courses at all levels; all friendly and informal.

Both daytime and evening meetings. Tutors are all experienced and published writers in various fields.

University of St Andrews

School of English, The University,
St Andrews, Fife KY16 9AL
☎01334 462666   Fax 01334 462655

Offers postgraduate study in *Creative Writing*. Candidates choose two topics from: *Fiction: The Novel; Craft and Technique in Poetry; The Short Story*, and also write their own poetry and/or prose for assessment.

WALES

Tŷ Newydd Writers' Centre

Llanystumdwy, Cricieth, Gwynedd
LL52 0LW
☎01766 522811   Fax 01766 523095

Residential writers' centre set up by the Taliesin Trust with the support of the **Arts Council of Wales** to encourage and promote writing in both English and Welsh. Most courses run from Monday evening to Saturday morning. Each course has two tutors and takes a maximum of 16 participants. The centre offers a wide range of specific courses. Course tutors have included Gillian Clarke, Liz Lochhead, Clare Boylan and Kevin Crossley-Holland. Early booking essential. Fee £265 inclusive. People on low incomes may be eligible for a grant or bursary. Course leaflet available. (Also see **Organisations of Interest to Poets**.)

University of Glamorgan

Treforest, Pontypridd CF37 1DL
☎01443 482551

MA in *Writing* – a two-year part-time Master of Arts degree for writers of fiction and poets. ESTABLISHED 1993. Contact Professor Tony Curtis at the School of Humanities and Social Sciences.

Also, BA in Theatre and Media Drama. Modules include *Scriptwriting: Theatre, Radio, TV and Video*. Contact Steven Blandford.

Circles and Workshops

Directory of Writers' Circles

Oldacre, Horderns Park Road, Chapel-en-le-Frith, High Peak SK23 9SY
☎01298 812305

Comprehensive directory of writers' circles, containing contacts and addresses of more than 600 groups and circles meeting throughout the country. Some overseas entries too. Available from Jill Dick at the above address. £5 post free.

Alston Hall

Alston Lane, Longridge, Preston, Lancashire
PR3 3BP
☎01772 784661   Fax 01772 785835

Holds regular day-long creative writing workshops. Brochure available.

Black Coral Productions Ltd

See under **Film, TV and Video Production Companies**

Chiltern Writers' Group

Marsh Green House, Bassetsbury Lane, High Wycombe HP11 1QY
☎01494 451654

Invites writers, publishers, editors and agents to speak at its monthly meetings at Wendover Public Library. Regular newsletter and competitions. Annual subscription: £10; concessions: £6. Non-members meeting: £2. Contact Diana Atkinson at the above address.

Concordant Poets Folios

87 Brookhouse Road, Farnborough, Hampshire GU14 0BU

Founded through popular demand ten years ago to encourage and assist poets, while studying techniques and possible marketing outlets. Each poem included is discussed and advised upon from several different viewpoints, with poets gaining valuable knowledge while building (via postal method) a circle of friends with mutual interests. Whether beginner, intermediate or advanced, there is a suitable place in one of the eight folios. For details and enrolment form please send s.a.e. to Barbara Horsfall.

The Cotswold Writers' Circle

Dar-es-Salaam, Beeches Park, Hampton Fields, Minchinhampton, Gloucestershire GL6 9BA

The Circle meets fortnightly in Cirencester. Activities include organising and running two competitions, publishing an anthology of Circle work, etc.. Contact *Charles Hooker*, Honorary Treasurer, for details of the Circle's activities.

Croftspun

Drakemyre Croft, Cairnorrie, Methlick, Ellon, Aberdeenshire AB41 7JN
☎01651 806252

Publishes a small booklet entitled *The Cottage Guide to Writers' Postal Workshops*, a directory giving the contact names and addresses of postal folios for writers (£2 post free – cheques payable to Mrs C. M. Gill).

Destructive Writers

56 Crampton Street, London SE17
☎0181 986 2263

DW is a group of people who write; some already have a (relatively) long experience in writing, some have been or are being published, others are just beginning. DW meets twice a month to discuss stories, exchange tips and ideas, useful information etc.

'Sean Dorman' Manuscript Society

Cherry Tree, Crosemere Road, Cockshutt, Ellesmere, Shropshire SY12 0JP
☎01939 270293

FOUNDED 1957. The Society provides mutual help among writers and aspiring writers in England, Wales and Scotland. By means of circulating manuscript parcels, members receive constructive criticism of their own work and read and comment on the work of others. Each 'Circulator' has up to nine participants and members' contributions may be in any medium: short stories, chapters of a novel, poetry, magazine articles etc. Members may join two such circulators if they wish. Each circulator has a technical section and a letters section in which friendly communication between members is encouraged, and all are of a general nature apart from one, specialising in mss for the Christian market. Full details and application forms available on receipt of s.a.e.. Director: Mary Driver. Subscription £6.50 p.a..

Equinoxe Screenwriting Workshops

Association Equinoxe, 85–89 Quai André Citroën, 75711 Paris, France
☎00 33 1 4425 7146   Fax 00 33 1 4425 7142

FOUNDED 1993, with Jeanne Moreau as president, to promote screenwriting and to establish a link between European and American film production. In association with Canal+, Sony Pictures Entertainment and Media Programme of the European Union, Equinoxe supports young writers of all nationalities by creating a screenwriting community capable of appealing to an international audience. For selected professional screenwriters able to speak either English or French fluently. Contact Claire Dubert.

Gay Authors Workshop

BM Box 5700, London WC1N 3XX
☎0181 520 5223

Established 1978 to encourage and support lesbian/gay writers. Regular meetings and a newsletter. Contact Kathryn Byrd. Membership £5; £2 unwaged.

The Garret

9 High Street, Warwick CV34 4AR
☎01926 492904   Fax 01926 403336

The Garret is a bookshop in Warwick which specialises in creative writing and poetry. The Poets', Writers' & Artists' Gallery holds regular events such as readings, workshops and book signings. More information is available, as well as copies of *WriteUp* (creative writing) and *Poetry Lovers'* catalogues from the above address.

Historical Novel Folio

17 Purbeck Heights, Mount Road, Parkstone, Poole, Dorset BH14 0QP
☎01202 741897

An independent postal workshop – single folio dealing with any period before World War II. Send s.a.e. for details. Contact: Doris Myall-Harris.

The International Inkwell

See under **Editorial, Research and Other Services**

Loch Ryan Writers

Loch Ryan Hotel, 119 Sidbury, Worcester WR5 2DH
☎01905 351143   Fax 01905 351143

Weekend residential writing workshops throughout the year. Emphasis on poetry, but also prose and drama. Contact Gwynneth Royce for details and all-inclusive prices.

London Screenwriters' Workshop
The Holborn Centre, Three Cups Yard, Sandland Street, Holborn, London WC1R 4PZ
☎0171 242 2134

Established by writers in 1983 as a forum for contact, information and tuition. LSW helps new and developing writers in the film, TV and video industries. Organises a continuous programme of workshops, events with industry figures, seminars and courses. Free monthly events and magazine newsletter every two months. Contact Paul Gallagher or Anji Loman Field. Membership £25 p.a..

London Writer Circle
15 Lower Park Road, Loughton, Essex IG10 4NB
☎0181 508 6916

FOUNDED 1924. Aims to help and encourage writers of all grades. Monthly evening meetings with well-known speakers on aspects of literature and journalism, and workshops for short story writing, poetry and feature writing. Occasional social events and quarterly magazine. Subscription: £16 (Town); £9 (Country); £6 (Overseas). Contact Margaret Owen, Membership Secretary at the above address.

Nottingham Writers Contact
U.A.E.C. Centre, 16 Shakespeare Street, Nottingham NG1 4GF
☎01159 288913

A group of professional and amateur writers which meets every third Saturday in the month at the U.A.E.C. Centre, 10.00am – 12.30pm. 'If you are visiting the city contact Keith Taylor at the above telephone number.'

NWP (North West Playwrights)
Contact Theatre, Oxford Road, Manchester M15 6JA
☎0161 274 4418   Fax 0161 274 4418

FOUNDED 1982. Award-winning organisation whose aim is to develop and promote new theatre writing. Operates a script-reading service, Commission and Residency Award Scheme, The Lowdown newsletter and the Summer Workshops – an annual showing of six workshopped plays by local writers. Previous participants include Charlotte Keatley, Kevin Fegan, Lavinia Murray and James Stock. Services available only to North West writers.

Scribo
Flat 1, 31 Hamilton Road, Boscombe, Bournemouth, Dorset BH1 4EQ
☎01202 302533

FOUNDED in the early '70s, Scribo circulates folios (published and unpublished work) to its members, who currently number about 40 and rising. The only criteria for joining is that you must be actively engaged in writing novels. Forum folios discuss anything of interest to novelists; problems are shared and information exchanged. Manuscript folios offer friendly criticism and advice. Besides 'general' mss folios there are four specialist folios: crime; aga-saga/saga/romance; Gothic suspense; fantasy/science-fiction. A new folio has been launched for the more literary novelist. Members – mostly graduates, published and unpublished – would welcome a few similarly dedicated serious novelists. 'No pornography.' Contact: K. Sylvester, P. A. Sylvester. No s.a.e., no reply.

University of Southampton Annual Writers' Conference
Dept of Adult Continuing Education, University of Southampton, Southampton, Hampshire SO17 1BJ
☎01703 593469

Having grown over the past 17 years from a creative writing workshop, this event is now the largest writers' conference in the country attracting international authors, playwrights, poets, agents and editors who give workshops, lectures and seminars to help writers harness their creativity and develop technical skills. The 1998 conference will not be held at its usual venue of Southampton University but at King Alfred's College, Sparkford Road, Winchester on the last weekend in June. The Conference also offers a variety of writing competitions. For programme, booking forms and further information, please write to Barbara Large, Conference Organiser at the University of Southampton address above.

Southport Writers' Circle
53 Richmond Road, Birkdale, Southport, Merseyside PR8 4SB
Runs a poetry competition (see **Prizes**). Contact Alison Chisholm.

Speakeasy
14 Langcliffe Drive, Heelands, Milton Keynes MK13 7AL
☎01908 318722

Invites poets and writers to Milton Keynes

most months. Also runs workshops according to demand. Monthly meetings are held where people can read their own work. Contact Anita Packwood.

University of Stirling
Continuing Education, Airthrey Castle,
Stirling FK9 4LA
☎01786 467940

Holds writers' workshop at Airthrey Castle one evening per week for ten weeks. Covers writing short stories, poetry, novels, letters, diaries, drama, newspaper articles, biography and autobiography, etc.

Ways With Words
See under **Festivals**

Workers' Educational Association
National Office: Temple House, 17 Victoria Park Square, London E2 9PB
☎0181 983 1515   Fax 0181 983 4840

FOUNDED in 1903, the WEA is a voluntary body with members drawn from all walks of life. It runs writing courses and workshops throughout the country and all courses are open to everyone. Branches in most towns and many villages, with 13 district offices in England and 1 in Scotland. Contact your district WEA office for courses in your region. All correspondence should be addressed to the District Secretary.

Cheshire, Merseyside & West Lancashire:
7/8 Bluecoat Chambers, School Lane,
Liverpool L1 3BX (☎0151 709 8023)

Eastern: Botolph House, 17 Botolph Lane,
Cambridge CB2 3RE (☎01223 350978)

East Midlands: 16 Shakespeare Street,
Nottingham NG1 4GF (☎01159 475162)

London: 4 Luke Street, London EC2A 4NT
(☎0171 388 7261/387 8966)

Northern: 51 Grainger Street, Newcastle upon Tyne NE1 5JE (☎0191 232 3957)

North Western: 4th Floor, Crawford House, University Precinct Centre, Oxford Road, Manchester M13 9GH (☎0161 273 7652)

South Eastern: 4 Castle Hill, Rochester,
Kent ME1 1QQ (☎01634 842140)

South Western: Martin's Gate Annexe, Bretonside, Plymouth, Devon PL4 0AT
(☎01752 664989)

Thames & Solent: 6 Brewer Street, Oxford OX1 1QN (☎01865 246270)

Western: 40 Morse Road, Redfield, Bristol BS5 9LB (☎01179 351764)

West Mercia: 78–80 Sherlock Street, Birmingham B5 6LT (☎0121 666 6101)

Yorkshire North: 6 Woodhouse Square, Leeds, W. Yorkshire LS3 1AD (☎01132 453304)

Yorkshire South: Chantry Buildings, 6–20 Corporation Street, Rotherham S60 1NG (☎01709 837001)

Scottish Association: Riddle's Court, 322 Lawnmarket, Edinburgh EH1 2PG
(☎0131 226 3456)

The Writers' Workshop
Frieth, Buckinghamshire RG9 6PR
☎01442 871004

The Writers' Workshop at Frieth offers classes in creative writing, plus workshop opportunities. Professional assessments available. Contact Maggie Prince at the above address.

Yorkshire Playwrights
3 Trinity Road, Scarborough, North Yorkshire YO11 2TD

FOUNDED 1989 out of an initiative by Jude Kelly and William Weston of the **West Yorkshire Playhouse**. A group of professional writers of plays for stage, TV and radio whose aims are to encourage the writing and performance of new plays in Yorkshire. Open to any writers living in Yorkshire who are members of the **Theatre Writers Union**, **The Writers' Guild**, or **The Society of Authors**. Contact the Administrator, Ian Watson for an information sheet.

Editorial, Research and Other Services

Lesley & Roy Adkins

Longstone Lodge, Aller, Langport, Somerset
TA10 0QT
☎01458 250075   Fax 01458 250858
Contact *Lesley Adkins, Roy Adkins*

Offers indexing, research, copy-editing, manuscript criticism/advice, contract writing for publishers, rewriting, book reviews and feature writing. *Special interests* archaeology (worldwide), history and heritage. See also **Lesley & Roy Adkins Picture Library**.

Anagram Editorial Service

26 Wherwell Road, Guildford, Surrey
GU2 5JR
☎01483 33497   Fax 01483 306848
Contact *Martyn Bramwell*

Full range of editorial services available from project development through commissioning, editing and proof-reading to production of finished books. Specialises in earth sciences, natural history, environment, general science and technology. Also author of over 30 non-fiction titles for young readers. Clients include UK, German, American and Middle East publishers, United Nations agencies (UNEP, FAO) and international conservation organisations.

Arioma

Gloucester House, High Street, Borth,
Ceredigion SY24 5HZ
☎01970 871296   Fax 01970 871296
Contact *Moira Smith*

FOUNDED 1987. Staffed by ex-London journalists, who work mainly with authors wanting to self-publish. Editing, indexing, ghost writing, cover design, plus initial help with marketing and publicity. Sample chapter and synopsis required. All types of book welcome, but work must be of a 'sufficiently high standard'. Rates on application. Please send s.a.e. with all submissions.

Astron Ltd

77 New Bond Street, London W1Y 9DB
☎0171 495 2230   Fax 0171 495 4472
Managing Director *Colin Ancliffe*

In addition to a long-standing register of permanent job-seekers within publishing, Astron has a freelance register with details of a large number of experienced people available to undertake all types of freelance assignments within the publishing field.

Authors' Research Services

32 Oak Village, London NW5 4QN
☎0171 284 4316
Contact *Richard Wright*

Research and document supply service, particularly to authors, academics and others without easy access to London libraries and sources of information. Also indexing of books and journals. Rates negotiable.

Joanna Billing

1 Holly Farm Mews, Green Lane, Great
Sutton, South Wirral L66 4XX
☎0151 339 9740
Contact *Joanna Billing*

Specialises in writing, copy-editing, proof-reading, researching, desk-top publishing (with laser printer), word-processing and print production for company newsletters and journals, corporate literature, brochures, training documents, confidential reports, publicity materials and public relations. With expertise in technical and scientific, travel, commercial and education fields.

Brooks Krikler Research

455 Finchley Road, London NW3 6HN
☎0171 431 9886   Fax 0171 431 9887
Contact *Emma Krikler*

Provides a full picture-research service to all those involved in publishing and the media. Educational and non-educational books, magazines, advertising, CD-ROM & Multimedia, brochures, video and computer games manufacturers and designers. The service includes finding, editing and providing images, negotiating all reproduction charges inclusive of full copyright clearance. Has special arrangements with photographic libraries worldwide and a variety of photographers can undertake commissioned work. An on-line service is available with all requests.

D. Buckmaster

Wayfarer House, 51 Chatsworth Road,
Torquay, Devon TQ1 3BJ
☎01803 294663

Contact *Mrs D. Buckmaster*

General editing of mss, specialising in traditional themes in religious, metaphysical and esoteric subjects. Also success and inspirational books or articles.

Graham Burn Productions

9–13 Soulbury Road, Linslade, Leighton Buzzard, Bedfordshire LU7 7RL
☎01525 377963/376390   Fax 01525 382498

Offers complete production services to writers wishing to publish their own material, and pre-press and print services to other publishers.

CIRCA Research and Reference Information Ltd

13–17 Sturton Street, Cambridge CB1 2SN
☎01223 568017   Fax 01223 354643

An editorial co-operative
Approx. turnover £500,000

ESTABLISHED 1989. Specialises in researching, writing and editing of reference works on international politics and economics, including *Cassell Dictionary of Modern Britain; Cassell Dictionary of Modern Politics; Dorling Kindersley World Reference Atlas; Keesing's UK Record; People in Power*. All work is fee-based.

Creative Communications

11 Belhaven Terrace, Glasgow G12 0TG
☎0141 334 9577   Fax 0141 334 9577

Contact *Ronnie Scott*

Creative Comunications delivers professional corporate communication services to leading Scottish organisations. It also provides effective writing (including copywriting and script writing), editing and newspaper design, and consults on all aspects of communications. Recent activities include developing copy for World Wide Web and interactive CD-ROM projects.

The Critical Eye

c/o Breese Books Ltd, 164 Kensington Park Road, London W11 2ER

ESTABLISHED 1994. The Critical Eye provides an honest and direct assessment, from a publisher's point of view, of the first 50 pages of manuscripts submitted by writers. This is probably the only critical evaluation service run by an established publisher. The cost of a Critical Eye report and evaluation is currently £95. A detailed information pack is available on request.

E. Glyn Davies

Cartref, 21 Claremont Avenue, Bishopston, Bristol BS7 8JD
☎0117 9756793   Fax 0117 9246248

Contact *E. Glyn Davies*

Editorial services for writers whose first language is not English: rewriting, revision, proofreading, translation into English. Quotations on request.

Deeson Editorial Services

Ewell House, Faversham, Kent ME13 8UP
☎01795 535468   Fax 01795 535469

Contact *Dr Tony Deeson, Dominic Deeson*

ESTABLISHED 1959. A comprehensive research/writing/editing service for books, magazines, newspapers, articles, annual reports, submissions, presentations. Design and production facilities. Specialists in scientific, technical, industrial and business-to-business subjects including company histories.

Flair for Words

5 Delavall Walk, Eastbourne, East Sussex BN23 6ER
☎01323 640646

Directors *Cass and Janie Jackson*

ESTABLISHED 1988. Offers wide range of services to writers, whether beginners or professional, through the Flair Network. Offers assessment, editing and advisory service. Publishes bi-monthly newsletter, handbooks on all aspects of writing, and audio tapes.

F. G. & K. M. Gill

11 Cranmore Close, Aldershot, Hampshire GU11 3BH
☎01252 25881/650339   Fax 01252 25881

Contacts *Fred and Kathie Gill*

ESTABLISHED over 18 years. Proof-reading, copy-editing and indexing services. Fiction and non-fiction (all subjects). Clients include UK, North American and continental publishers. Rates on application.

Indexing Specialists

202 Church Road, Hove, East Sussex BN3 2DJ
☎01273 738299   Fax 01273 323309

Contact *Richard Raper*

ESTABLISHED over 30 years. Indexes in a wide

range of subjects for all manner of books, journals and other publications. Also offers copy-editing and proof-reading services. Quotations available on request.

Ink Inc. Ltd
1 Anglesea Road, Kingston on Thames, Surrey KT1 2EW
☎0181 549 3174   Fax 0181 287 7493
Managing Director *Richard Parkes*
Editorial Head *Barbara Leedham*

Publishing consultants. Clients range from very small dtp operations to large plcs. Advise on every aspect of publishing, including production, design, editorial, marketing, distribution and finance. Also take on editorial, design, production and project management work.

The International Inkwell
Cafe du Livre, Rue de la Mairie, 11170 Montolieu, Aude, France
☎00 33 468248117   Fax 00 33 468248321
London address: 96 Edith Grove, Chelsea, London SW10   (☎01273 748134)
Contact *Lucia Stuart*

Set in the French medieval village of Montolieu, which boasts 14 bookshops to a population of 800, The International Inkwell rents rooms for writers. Open from June to September, groups are welcome for writing courses, reading weeks or forums. For further details contact Lucia Stuart in France between May and September or in London between November and April.

J G Editorial
54 Mount Street, Lincoln LN1 3JG
☎01522 530758   Fax 01522 575679
Contact *Jenni Goss*

ESTABLISHED 1988. Freelance editors with 21 years' experience offering full editorial service to authors and typesetters. Independent critique service for fiction, general non-fiction and academic/business (no poetry) – includes structure and presentation; rewriting/ghosting; word processing/presentation/keying; project management; editorial reports; copy and disk editing (IBM/AppleMac); proofreading. Quotations on request.

J. P. Lethbridge
245 St Margaret's Road, Ward End, Birmingham B8 2DY
☎0121 783 0548
Contact *J. P. Lethbridge*

Experienced historical researcher. Searching through old newspapers and checking birth, marriage and death certificates a speciality. Special interest in crime. Rates negotiable.

The Literary Consultancy
PO Box 12939, London N8 9WA
☎0181 372 3922/374 2812
Fax 0181 372 3922/274 2812
Contact *Rebecca Swift, Hannah Griffiths*

Founded by former publishers to offer an editorial service and advice for aspiring writers. Will provide an appraisal of fiction, poetry and most categories of non-fiction. Charges range from £40 for a short story to £300 for a full mss of 300 pages.

LJC Permission Services
8 Burstow House, Skipton Way, Horley, Surrey RG6 8LP
☎07000 782332   Fax 07000 782331
Contacts *Robert Young, Louisa Clements*

A copyright clearing agency used widely by publishers and authors who wish to reproduce copyright material. The agency undertakes to obtain permission for articles, photographs, artwork and music to be reproduced in another publication or on cassettes. Part of the service includes preparing acknowledgement copy if requested and negotiating the reproduction fee with the copyright holder. Full breakdown of costs on larger projects. Large database of copyright sources. Multimedia permissions also undertaken. Fixed fee per permission.

Duncan McAra
28 Beresford Gardens, Edinburgh EH5 3ES
☎0131 552 1558   Fax 0131 552 1558
Contact *Duncan McAra*

Consultancy on all aspects of general trade publishing: editing, rewriting, copy-editing, proofreading. *Specialises* in art, architecture, archaeology, biography, film, military and travel. Also runs a literary agency (see **UK Agents**).

Deborah Manley
57 Plantation Road, Oxford OX2 6JE
☎01865 310284
Contact *Deborah Manley*

Offers (to publishers) editorial reports, copy-editing, writing, rewriting, research, anthologising, indexing, proof-reading and caption copy. Specialises mainly in children's, reference and travel. NUJ rates.

Minett Media

6 Middle Watch, Swavesey, Cambridge
CB4 5RN
☎01954 230250   Fax 01954 232019

Contact *Dr Steve Minett, Gunnel Minett*

Specialises in the proactive and strategic management of trade press activities. Produces press releases and feature articles for multi-national business-to-business companies, offering a comprehensive editorial service (including site visits anywhere in Europe, writing draft text, securing approval and best effort at publication in the international trade press). Also offers complete-package production of business-to-business, multi-language customer magazines (including translation, design, artwork, repro, printing and distribution) and enquiry database management.

Murder Files

Marienau, Brimley Road, Bovey Tracey,
Devon TQ13 9DH
☎01626 833487   Fax 01626 835797

Contact *Paul Williams*

Crime writer and researcher specialising in UK murders. Can provide information on thousands of well-known and less well-known cases dating from 1400. Copies of press cuttings relating to murder available for cases from 1920 onwards. Research also undertaken for general enquirers, writers, TV, radio, video, etc. Rates on application.

Northern Writers Advisory Services (NWAS)

77 Marford Crescent, Sale, Cheshire
M33 4DN
☎0161 969 1573

Contact *Jill Groves*

Offers publishing services such as copy-editing, proof-reading, word-processing and desktop publishing (with laser printing). Does much of its work with societies (mainly local history), and small presses. NWAS's specialist subject is history of all types, but especially local and family history. Also handles biographies. Rates on application, but 'very reasonable'.

Ormrod Research Services

Weeping Birch, Burwash, East Sussex
TN19 7HG
☎01435 882541   Fax 01435 882541

Contact *Richard Ormrod*

ESTABLISHED 1982. Comprehensive research service: literary, historical, academic, biographical, commercial. Critical reading with report, editing, indexing, proof-reading, ghosting. Verbal quotations available.

Out of Print Book Service

13 Pantbach Road, Birchgrove, Cardiff
CF4 1TU
☎01222 627703

Contact *L. A. Foulkes*

FOUNDED 1971. Covers all subjects including fiction and non-fiction. No charge for search. Send s.a.e for details.

Pages Editorial & Publishing Services

Ballencrieff Cottage, Ballencrieff Toll,
Bathgate, West Lothian EH48 4LD
☎01506 632728   Fax 01506 632728

Contact *Susan Coon*

Contract-publishing service for magazines and newsletters, including journalism, editing, advertising, production and mailing. Also editorial advice, word processing and short-run publishing service for authors and publishers.

Roger Palmer Limited, Media Contracts and Copyright

18 Maddox Street, Mayfair, London
W1R 9PL
☎0171 499 8875   Fax 0171 499 9580

Contact *Roger Palmer, Stephen Aucutt*

ESTABLISHED 1993. Drafts, advises on and negotiates all media contracts (on a regular or *ad hoc* basis) for publishers, literary and merchandising agents, packagers, charities and others. Manages and operates clients' complete contracts functions, undertakes contractual audits, devises contracts systems, advises on copyright and related issues and provides training and seminars. Growing private client list, with special rates for members of **The Society of Authors**. Roger Palmer (Managing Director) was for many years Contracts and Intellectual Property Director of the Hodder & Stoughton Group; Stephen Aucutt (Senior Consultant) was previously Contracts Manager for Reed Children's Books.

Penman Literary Service

185 Daws Heath Road, Benfleet, Essex
SS7 2TF
☎01702 557431

Contact *Mark Sorrell*

ESTABLISHED 1950. Advisory, editorial and typing service for authors. Rewriting, ghosting, proof-reading; critical assessment of mss.

Perfect English

11 Hill Square, Upper Cam, Dursley,
Gloucestershire GL11 5NJ
☎01453 547320　　　　Fax 01453 542439

Contact *James Alexander*

'Meticulous reading and editing to remove errors of spelling, grammar, punctuation, word choice and meaning. Mss returned fully checked and as perfect as possible within the structure and style of the original material.' Rates on application.

Plain Words (Business Writers)

96 Wellmeadow Road, London `
SE6 1HW
☎0181 698 5269/697 3227
Fax 0181 461 5705

Contact *Henry Galgut, Judy Byrne*

Provide industrial and commercial businesses with a copywriting and editing service. Sectors served include oil, petrochemicals, banking, public transport, travel, retail, publishing and catering. Henry Galgut and Judy Byrne have backgrounds in human resource management, consulting, journalism, psychology and psychotherapy.

Reading & Righting (Robert Lambolle Services)

618B Finchley Road, London
NW11 7RR
☎0181 455 4564　　　　Fax 0181 455 4564

Contact *Robert Lambolle*

Reader/literary editor, with agency, publishing and theatre experience. Offers detailed manuscript evaluation, analysis of prospects and next-step guidelines. Fiction, non-fiction, drama and screenplays. Special interests include cinema, the performing arts, popular culture, psychotherapy and current affairs. Also editorial services, creative writing workshops and lectures. Services do not include representing writers in an agent's capacity. Send s.a.e. for detailed leaflet on procedure and terms.

Science and Technology Reference Publishing

2 Pell Hill Cottages, Wadhurst, East Sussex
TN5 6DS
☎01892 783652

Contact *Peter Lafferty*

Specialises in researching, writing and editing of reference works such as dictionaries and encyclopedias in science and technology, including *Hutchinson Dictionary of Science* and *Hutchinson Encyclopedia of Science*. Works for children and general family audiences a particular interest.

Scriptmate

See **Book-in-Hand Ltd** under **Small Presses**

Strand Editorial Services

16 Mitchley View, South Croydon, Surrey
CR2 9HQ
☎0181 657 1247　　　　Fax 0181 657 1247

Contact *Derek Bradley*

All stages of editorial production of house journals, magazines, newsletters, publicity material, etc. Short-term, long-term and emergency projects. Sub-editing, proof-reading, and book reviews (education, training and business). Reasonable rates (negotiable).

Teral Research Services

45 Forest View Road, Moordown,
Bournemouth, Dorset BH9 3BH
☎01202 516834　　　　Fax 01202 516834

Contact *Terry C. Treadwell*

All aspects of research undertaken but specialises in all military, aviation, naval and defence subjects, both past and present. Extensive book and photographic library, including one of the best collections of World War One aviation photographs. Terms by arrangement.

WORDSmith

2 The Island, Thames Ditton, Surrey
KT7 0SH
☎0181 339 0945　　　　Fax 0181 339 0945

Contact *Michael Russell*

Copy-editing, both on paper and on-screen. Specialises in rewriting and abridging, particularly new writer fiction. Also magazine articles and stories, company literature, user guides, copywriting, film-script editing. Everything from 2000 to 200,000 words. Please phone for details.

The Writers Advice Centre for Children's Books

Palace Wharf, Rainville Road, London
W6 9HN
☎0181 874 7347　　　　Fax 0181 874 7347

Contact *Louise Jordan*

Offers editorial and marketing advice to children's writers – both published and unpublished – by Readers who are all currently connected with children's publishing. Plus personal introductions to publishers/agents where appropriate. Also runs courses and a small agenting service.

The Writers' Exchange
14 Yewdale, Clifton Green, Swinton
M27 8GN
☎0161 281 0544

Contact *Mike Wright, The Secretary*

FOUNDED 1978. Full range of copywriting, ghostwriting and editorial services, including appraisal service for amateur writers preparing to submit material to or having had material rejected by, literary agents and/or publishers. Novels, short stories, film, TV, radio, and stage plays. Appraisal fee £5 per 1000 words. Send s.a.e. for details.

Press Cuttings Agencies

The Broadcast Monitoring Company
89½ Worship Street, London EC2A 2BE
☎0171 377 1742   Fax 0171 377 6103

Television, radio, national and European press monitoring agency. Cuttings from national and all major European press available seven days a week, with early morning delivery. Also monitoring of all news and current affairs programmes – national, international and satellite. Retrospective research service and free telephone notification. Sponsorship evaluation from all media sources.

Durrants Press Cuttings Ltd
103 Whitecross Street, London EC1Y 8QT
☎0171 588 3671   Fax 0171 374 8171

Wide coverage of all print media sectors; foreign press in association with agencies abroad; current affairs and news programmes from UK broadcast media. High speed, early morning press cuttings from the national press. Overnight delivery via courier to most areas or first-class mail. Well presented, laser printed, A4 cuttings. Monthly reading fee of £40 plus 80p per cutting.

International Press–Cutting Bureau
224–236 Walworth Road, London SE17 1JE
☎0171 708 2113   \   Fax 0171 701 4489
Contact *Robert Podro*

Covers national, provincial, trade, technical and magazine press. Cuttings are normally sent twice weekly by first-class post and there are no additional service charges or reading fees. Subscriptions for 100 and 250 cuttings are valid for six months. Larger subscriptions expire after one year even if the total number of cuttings

subscribed for has not been reached. 100 cuttings (£146, plus VAT); 250 (£330, plus VAT).

Premium Press Monitoring
Bear Wharf, 27 Bankside, London SE1 9DP
☎0171 203 3500   Fax 0171 203 0101
Contact *Richard Jenkinson*

Offers an overnight national press monitoring service with same day, early morning delivery. Also coverage of regional papers and weekly/ monthly business/trade magazines. Rates on application.

Press Express
3rd Floor, 53–56 Great Sutton Street, London EC1V 0DE
☎0171 689 0123   Fax 0171 689 1412
Contact *Charles Stuart Hunt*

High-speed overnight press cuttings.

Romeike & Curtice
Hale House, 290–296 Green Lanes, London N13 5TP
☎0800 289543   Fax 0181 882 6716
Contact *Richard Silver*

Covers national and international dailies and Sundays, provincial papers, consumer magazines, trade and technical journals, national radio/TV logs and teletext services. Back research and advertising checking services are also available.

We Find It (Press Clippings)
103 South Parade, Belfast BT7 2GN
☎01232 646008   Fax 01232 646008
Contact *Avril Forsythe*

Specialises in Northern Ireland press and magazines, both national and provincial. Rates on application.

Bursaries

Aosdána

An Chomhairle Ealaíon (The Arts Council),
70 Merrion Square, Dublin 2,
Republic of Ireland
☎00 353 1 6611840   Fax 00 353 1 6761302
Literature Officer *Laurence Cassidy*

Aosdána is an affiliation of creative artists engaged in literature, music and the visual arts, and consists of not more than 200 artists who have gained a reputation for achievement and distinction. Membership is by competitive sponsored selection and is open to Irish citizens or residents only. Members are eligible to receive an annuity for a five-year term to assist them in pursuing their art full-time.
Award IR£8000 (annuity).

Arts Council Literature Bursaries, Ireland

An Chomhairle Ealaíon (The Arts Council),
70 Merrion Square, Dublin 2,
Republic of Ireland
☎00 353 1 6611840   Fax 00 353 1 6761302
Literature Officer *Laurence Cassidy*

Bursaries in literature awarded to creative writers of fiction, poetry and drama in Irish and English to enable concentration on, or completion of, specific projects. A limited number of bursaries may be given to non-fiction projects. Open to Irish citizens or residents only. Final entry date 28 March.
Award IR£3000–£8000.

Arts Council Theatre Writing Bursaries

Arts Council of England, 14 Great Peter Street, London SW1P 3NQ
☎0171 333 0100 ext 431   Fax 0171 973 6590
Contact *John Johnston*

Intended to provide experienced playwrights with an opportunity to research and develop a play for the theatre independently of financial pressures and free from the need to write for a particular market. Bursaries are also available for theatre translation projects. Writers must be resident in England. Writers resident in Wales, Scotland or Northern Ireland should approach their own Arts Council. Final entry date 6 January 1998.
Award £3000.

Arts Council Writers' Awards

14 Great Peter Street, London SW1P 3NQ
☎0171 333 0100   Fax 0171 973 6590
Literature Assistant *Valerie Olteanu*

ESTABLISHED 1965. The Arts Council offers 15 bursaries a year. Applications should be accompanied by a c.v., description and sample of work in progress, statement of annual income and three copies of a previously published creative work. Judges will make their choices principally on the grounds of artistic quality, basing that judgment on their reading of work in progress and evidence before them of the writer's past achievement. Past winners include: Donald Atkinson, Olivia Fane, Jonathan Treitel, Subniv Babuta, Jon Silkin, Margaret Wilkinson, Robert Edric, Sue Thomas, Sally Cline, Jocelyn M. Ferguson, Lavinia Greenlaw, Charlotte Cory, David Gale, Nicola Barker, Ruth Padell, Duncan Sprott. Final entry date 30 September.
Award 15 awards of £7000.

The Authors' Contingency Fund

The Society of Authors, 84 Drayton Gardens, London SW10 9SB
☎0171 373 6642   Fax 0171 373 5768

This fund makes modest grants to published authors who find themselves in sudden financial difficulties.

The Authors' Foundation

The Society of Authors, 84 Drayton Gardens, London SW10 9SB
☎0171 373 6642   Fax 0171 373 5768

Annual grants to writers whose publisher's advance is insufficient to cover the costs of research involved. Application by letter to The Authors' Foundation giving details, in confidence, of the advance and royalties, together with the reasons for needing additional funding. Grants are sometimes given even if there is no commitment by a publisher, so long as the work will almost certainly be published. £60,000 was distributed in 1996. Contact the Society of Authors for an information sheet. Final entry date 30 April.

The K. Blundell Trust

The Society of Authors, 84 Drayton Gardens, London SW10 9SB
☎0171 373 6642   Fax 0171 373 5768

Annual grants to writers whose publisher's advance is insufficient to cover the costs of research. Author must be under 40, has to submit copy of his/her previous book and the work must 'contribute to the greater understanding of existing social and economic organisation'. Application by letter. Contact the Society of Authors for an information sheet. Final entry date 30 April. Total of £15,000 available.

Alfred Bradley Bursary Award
c/o Network Radio Drama, BBC North, New Broadcasting House, Oxford Road, Manchester M60 1SJ
☎0161 200 2020
Contact *Melanie Harris*

ESTABLISHED 1992. Biennial award in commemoration of the life and work of the distinguished radio producer Alfred Bradley. Aims to encourage and develop new writing talent in the **BBC North** region. There is a change of focus for each award; the theme for the 1997 award was Verse Drama. Entrants must live or work in the North region. The award is given to help authors to pursue a career in writing for radio. Support and guidance is given from regional BBC radio producers. Previous winners: Lee Hall, Julie Clark.
Award not less than £3000 a year for 2 years.

British Academy Small Personal Research Grants
20–21 Cornwall Terrace, London NW1 4QP
☎0171 487 5966   Fax 0171 224 3807
Contact *Assistant Secretary, Research Grants*

Quarterly award to further original creative research at postdoctoral level in the humanities and social sciences. Entrants must no longer be registered for postgraduate study, and must be resident in the UK. Final entry dates end of September, November, February and April.
Award maximum £5000.

Cholmondeley Awards
The Society of Authors, 84 Drayton Gardens, London SW10 9SB
☎0171 373 6642   Fax 0171 373 5768

FOUNDED 1965 by the late Dowager Marchioness of Cholmondeley. Annual non-competitive awards for the benefit and encouragement of poets of any age, sex or nationality, for which submissions are not required. Presentation date: June. 1997 winners: Alison

Brackenbury, Gillian Clarke, Tony Curtis, Anne Stevenson.
Award (total) £8000, usually shared.

The Economist/Richard Casement Internship
The Economist, 25 St James's Street, London SW1A 1HG
☎0171 839 7000

Contact *Business Affairs Editor (re. Casement Internship)*

For a journalist under 24 to spend three months in the summer writing for *The Economist* about science and technology. Applicants should write a letter of introduction along with an article of approximately 600 words suitable for inclusion in the Science and Technology Section. Competition details normally announced in the magazine late January and 4–5 weeks allowed for application.

Fulbright T. E. B. Clarke Fellowship in Screenwriting
The Fulbright Commission, Fulbright House, 62 Doughty Street, London WC1N 2LS
☎0171 404 6880   Fax 0171 404 6834
Contact *Programme Director*

Award offered to a young (normally, under 35) British film screenwriter to spend nine months in the US developing his/her expertise and experience. The successful candidate will follow postgraduate courses in screenwriting at a US institution, attend real-life story conferences and write a screenplay and some treatments during the award period. At the time of going to press, funding for this award was unconfirmed for 1998/99. Please contact the Fulbright Commission for details.
Award Air travel and grant of £18,000 plus approved tuition fees.

Fulton Fellowship
David Fulton (Publishers) Ltd, Ormond House, 26/27 Boswell Street, London WC1N 3JD
☎0171 405 5606   Fax 0171 831 4840
Contact *David Fulton*

ESTABLISHED 1995. Annual award to support research in special educational needs. Recipients will have the opportunity to publish their work in a form accessible to teachers with the help of the publisher, David Fulton and the Centre of the Study of Special Education at Westminster College, Oxford. 1996 Fellow: Deborah Eyre.

The Tony Godwin Memorial Award

The Tony Godwin Memorial Trust,
c/o Laurence Pollinger Limited, 18 Maddox Street, London W1R 0EU
☎0171 629 9761　　　　Fax 0171 629 9765
Contact *Lesley Hadcroft (at above address)*
Chairman *Iain Brown* (0171 627 4244)

Biennial award established to commemorate the life of Tony Godwin, a prominent publisher in the 1960s/70s. Open to all young people (under 35 years old) who are UK nationals and working, or intending to work, in publishing. The award provides the recipient with the means to spend at least one month as the guest of a publishing house in the US in order to learn about American publishing. The recipient is expected to submit a report upon return to the UK. Final entry date for next award: 31 December, 1997. Previous winners: George Lucas (Hodder), Richard Scrivener (Penguin). *Prize* Bursary of approx. US$5000.

Eric Gregory Trust Fund

The Society of Authors, 84 Drayton Gardens, London SW10 9SB
☎0171 373 6642　　　　Fax 0171 373 5768

Annual competitive awards of varying amounts are made each year for the encouragement of young poets under the age of 30 who can show that they are likely to benefit from an opportunity to give more time to writing. Open only to British-born subjects resident in the UK. Final entry date, 31 October. Presentation date, June. Contact the Society of Authors for further information. 1997 winners: Matthew Clegg, Sarah Corbett, Polly Clark, Tim Kendal, Graham Nelson, Matthew Welton. *Award* (total) £28,000.

The Guardian Research Fellowship

Nuffield College, Oxford OX1 1NF
☎01865 278520　　　　Fax 01865 278676
Contact *Warden's Secretary*

One-year fellowship endowed by the Scott Trust, owner of *The Guardian*, to give someone working in the media the chance to put their experience into a new perspective, publish the outcome and give a *Guardian* lecture. Applications welcomed from journalists and management members, in newspapers, periodicals or broadcasting. Research or study proposals should be directly related to experience of working in the media. Accommodation and meals in college will be provided, and a 'modest' supplementary stipend might be arranged to ensure the Fellow does not lose out from the stay. Advertised annually in November.

Hawthornden Castle Fellowship

Hawthornden Castle, The International Retreat for Writers, Lasswade, Midlothian EH18 1EG
☎0131 440 2180
Administrator *Adam Czerniawski*

ESTABLISHED 1982 to provide a peaceful setting where published writers can work without disturbance. The Retreat houses five writers at a time, who are known as Hawthornden Fellows. Writers from any part of the world may apply for the fellowships. No monetary assistance is given, nor any contribution to travelling expenses, but once arrived at Hawthornden, the writer is the guest of the Retreat. Application on forms provided must be made by the end of September for the following calendar year. Previous winners include: Les Murray, Alasdair Gray, Helen Vendler, Olive Senior, Hilary Spurling.

Francis Head Bequest

The Society of Authors, 84 Drayton Gardens, London SW10 9SB
☎0171 373 6642　　　　Fax 0171 373 5768

Provides grants to published British authors over the age of 35 who need financial help during a period of illness, disablement or temporary financial crisis.

Ralph Lewis Award

University of Sussex Library, Brighton, East Sussex BN1 9QL
☎01273 678158　　　　Fax 01273 678441

ESTABLISHED 1985. Triennial award set up by Ralph Lewis, a Brighton author and art collector who left money to fund awards for promising manuscripts which would not otherwise be published. The award is given in the form of a grant to a UK-based publisher in respect of an agreed three-year programme of publication of literary works by new authors or by established authors using new styles or forms. No direct applications from writers. Previous winners: **Peterloo Poets** (1989–91); **Serpent's Tail** (1992–94); **Stride Publications** (1997–99).

London Arts Board: Publishing New Writing Fund

London Arts Board, Elme House, 133 Long Acre, London WC2E 9AF
☎0171 240 1313　　　　Fax 0171 240 4580

Aims to support and develop small presses and literary magazines in the publishing of new or under-represented fiction and poetry. This fund is only open to groups for whom publishing is a central activity. Contact the Principal Literature Officer for further details and deadline.

Macaulay Fellowship

An Chomhairle Ealaíon (The Arts Council), 70 Merrion Square, Dublin 2, Republic of Ireland
☎00 353 1 6611840   Fax 00 353 1 6761302
Literature Officer *Laurence Cassidy*

To further the liberal education of a young creative artist. Candidates for this triennial award must be under 30 on 30 June, or 35 in exceptional circumstances, and must be Irish citizens or residents. The Fellowship will be made in Literature in 1999.
Award IR£3500.

The John Masefield Memorial Trust

The Society of Authors, 84 Drayton Gardens, London SW10 9SB
☎0171 373 6642   Fax 0171 373 5768

This trust makes occasional grants to professional poets (or their immediate dependants) who are faced with sudden financial problems.

Somerset Maugham Trust Fund

The Society of Authors, 84 Drayton Gardens, London SW10 9SB
☎0171 373 6642   Fax 0171 373 5768

The annual awards arising from this Fund are designed to encourage young writers to travel and to acquaint themselves with other countries. Candidates must be under 35 and their publishers must submit a published literary work in volume form in English. They must be British subjects by birth. Final entry date 31 December. Presentation in June. 1997 winners: Rhidian Brook *The Testimony of Taliesin Jones*; Kate Clanchy *Slattern*; Philip Hensher *Kitchen Venom*; Francis Spufford *I May Be Some Time*.
Award £5000 each.

National Poetry Foundation Grants

27 Mill Road, Fareham, Hampshire PO16 0TH
☎01329 822218
Contact *Johnathon Clifford*

The **National Poetry Foundation** considers applications for grant aid of up to £1000 where other funding is not available and the product will benefit poetry in general. Send details together with s.a.e. to NPF (Grants) at the above address.

The Airey Neave Trust

40 Charles Street, London W1X 7PB
☎0171 495 0554   Fax 0171 491 1118
Contact *Hannah Scott*

INITIATED 1989. Annual research fellowships for up to three years – towards a book or paper – for serious research connected with national and international law, and human freedom. Must be attached to a particular university in Britain. Interested applicants should come forward with ideas, preferably before March in any year.

New London Writers' Awards

London Arts Board, Elme House, 133 Long Acre, London WC2E 9AF
☎0171 240 1313   Fax 0171 240 4580
Contact *John Hampson*

ESTABLISHED 1993/94. Four bursaries, of £3,500 each, are awarded annually to London writers. Application form available from the above address. Final entry date: mid-January 1998. Previous winners include: Pauline Melville, Leena Dhingra, Maura Dooley, Kirsty Gunn, Mick Imlah, Bridget O'Connor.
Awards £3500 each.

Newspaper Press Fund

Dickens House, 35 Wathen Road, Dorking, Surrey RH4 1JY
☎01306 887511   Fax 01306 876104
Director/Secretary *Peter Evans*

Aims to relieve distress among journalists and their dependants. Limited help available to non-member journalists. Continuous and/or occasional financial grants; also retirement homes for eligible beneficiaries. Information and subscription details available from The Secretary.

Northern Arts Literary Fellowship

Northern Arts, 10 Osborne Terrace, Jesmond, Newcastle upon Tyne NE2 1NZ
☎0191 281 6334   Fax 0191 281 3276
Contact *Published & Broadcast Arts Department*

A competitive fellowship tenable at and co-sponsored by the universities of Durham and Newcastle upon Tyne for a period of two academic years.
Award £15,000 p.a.

Northern Arts Writers Awards

Northern Arts, 10 Osborne Terrace, Jesmond, Newcastle upon Tyne NE2 1NZ
☎0191 281 6334   Fax 0191 281 3276
Contact *Published & Broadcast Arts Department*

Awards are offered to established authors

resident in the **Northern Arts** area on the basis of literary merit. Application spring/summer. Also available, one-month residencies at the Tyrone Guthrie Centre, Ireland.

Award Variable.

The PAWS (Public Awareness of Science) Drama Script Fund

The PAWS Office, OMNI Communications, Osborne House, 111 Bartholomew Road, London NW5 2BJ
☎0171 267 2555   Fax 0171 482 2394

Contacts *Barrie Whatley, Andrew Millington*

ESTABLISHED 1994. Annual award aimed at encouraging television scriptwriters to include science and engineering scenarios in their work. Grants (currently £2000) are given to selected writers to develop their script ideas into full treatments; prizes are awarded for the best of these treatments (Grand Prix currently £5000). The PAWS Fund holds meetings enabling writers to meet scientists and engineers and also offers a contacts service to put writers in 'one-to-one' contact with specialists who can help them develop their ideas.

Pearson Television Theatre Writers' Scheme

1 Stephen Street, London W1P 1PJ
☎0181 948 1154

Contact *Jack Andrews*

Awards bursaries to playwrights. Applicants must be sponsored by a theatre which then submits the play for consideration by a panel. Each award allows the playwright a twelve-month attachment. Applications invited via theatres at the end of 1997 and the end of 1998. For up-to-date information, contact Jack Andrews.

The Margaret Rhondda Award

The Society of Authors, 84 Drayton Gardens, London SW10 9SB
☎0171 373 6642   Fax 0171 373 5768

Competitive award given to a woman writer as a grant-in-aid towards the expenses of a research project in journalism. Triennial. Final entry date 31 December 1998 (for 1999 award). Presentation date May. 1996 winner: Laura Spinney.

Award (total) approx. £1000.

The Royal Literary Fund

144 Temple Chambers, Temple Avenue, London EC4Y 0DA
☎0171 353 7150

Secretary *Mrs Fiona Clark*

Grants and pensions are awarded to published authors in financial need, or to their dependants. Examples of author's works are needed for assessment by Committee. Write for further details and application form.

Southern Arts Literature Award

13 St Clement Street, Winchester, Hampshire SO23 9DQ
☎01962 855099   Fax 01962 861186

Contact *Literature Officer*

Offers an annual award of £3,500 to a published writer living in the region to assist a specific project. Awards can be used to cover a period of unpaid leave while writing from home, to finance necessary research and travel, or to purchase equipment. Final entry date: 17 October.

Laurence Stern Fellowship

Department of Journalism, City University, Northampton Square, London EC1V 0HB
☎0171 477 8224   Fax 0171 477 8574

Contact *Bob Jones*

FOUNDED 1980. Awarded to a young journalist experienced enough to work on national stories. It gives them the chance to work on the national desk of the *Washington Post*. Benjamin Bradlee, the *Post*'s Vice-President, selects from a shortlist drawn up in March/April. 1996 winner: Gary Younge. Full details available on the web: http://www.city.ac.uk/journalism

Thames Television Theatre Writers' Scheme

See **Pearson Television Theatre Writers' Scheme**

David Thomas Prize

The Financial Times (W), 1 Southwark Bridge, London SE1 9HL
☎0171 873 3000   Fax 0171 873 3924

Managing Editor *Robin Pauley*

FOUNDED 1991. Annual award in memory of David Thomas, *FT* journalist killed on assignment in Kuwait in April 1991, whose 'life was characterised by original and radical thinking coupled with a search for new subjects and orthodoxies to challenge'. The award will provide an annual study/travel grant to enable the recipient to take a career break to explore a theme in the fields of industrial policy, Third World development or the environment. Entrants may be of any nationality; age limits vary. A given theme, which changes from year to year, is announced in the early autumn. The 1996 theme was: 'Home Truths From Abroad': a policy idea from outside the UK for the next

British Prime Minister. Entrants submit up to 800 words on the theme, together with a brief c.v. and proposal outlining how the award could be used to explore the theme further. Award winners are required to write an essay of 1500–2000 words at the end of the study period, which is considered for publication in the newspaper. Final entry date end December/early January.

Prize £3000 travel grant.

Tom-Gallon Trust

The Society of Authors, 84 Drayton Gardens, London SW10 9SB
☎0171 373 6642   Fax 0171 373 5768

A biennial award is made from the Trust Fund to fiction writers of limited means who have had at least one short story accepted. Authors wishing to enter should send a list of their already published fiction, giving the name of the publisher or periodical in each case and the approximate date of publication; one published short story; a brief statement of their financial position; an undertaking that they intend to devote a substantial amount of time to the writing of fiction as soon as they are financially able to do so; and an s.a.e. for the return of work submitted. Final entry date 20 September 1998. Presentation date June.

Award £1000.

The Betty Trask Awards

The Society of Authors, 84 Drayton Gardens, London SW10 9SB
☎0171 373 6642   Fax 0171 373 5768

These annual awards are for authors who are under 35 and Commonwealth citizens, awarded on the strength of a first novel (published or unpublished) of a traditional or romantic nature. The awards must be used for a period or periods of foreign travel. Final entry date 31 January; presentation June. Contact The Society of Authors for an information sheet. 1997 winners: Alex Garland *The Beach*; Josie Barnard *Poker Face*; Ardashi Vakil *Beach Boy*; Diran Adebayo *Some Kind of Black*; Sanjida O'Connell *Theory of Mind*.

Award (total) £25,000.

The Travelling Scholarships

The Society of Authors, 84 Drayton Gardens, London SW10 9SB
☎0171 373 6642   Fax 0171 373 5768

Annual, non-competitive awards for the benefit of British authors, to enable them to travel abroad. 1997 winners: William Palmer, Jo Shapcott and James Simmons.

Award (total) £6000.

UEA Writing Fellowship

University of East Anglia, University Plain, Norwich, Norfolk NR4 7TJ
☎01603 592734   Fax 01603 593522
Director of Personnel & Registry Services
  J. R. L. Beck

ESTABLISHED 1971. Awarded to a writer of established reputation in any field for a period of six months, January to end June. The duties of the Fellowship are discussed at interview. It is assumed that one activity will be the pursuit of the Fellow's own writing. In addition the Fellow will be expected to (a) offer an undergraduate creative writing course in the School of English and American Studies during the Spring semester, and to read and grade work received; (b) offer 15 less formal sessions of one hour or more made up of readings, workshops, tutorials, and/or visits to seminars; (c) arrange, with help from UEA and **Eastern Arts**, additional visits and readings by other writers from outside the university; (d) make contact with groups around the county, and participate with Eastern Arts in organising off-campus visits for writers from the performance programme. It is hoped that (b), (c) and (d) above will involve students from the University as a whole, as well as participants from the city and the region. An office and some limited secretarial assistance will be provided, and some additional funds will be available to help the Fellow with the activities described. Applications should be lodged with the Director of Personnel & Registry Services in the autumn; candidates should submit at least two examples of recent work. Previous winner: Peter Reading.

Award £5000 plus free flat on campus.

The David T. K. Wong Fellowship

School of English and American Studies, University of East Anglia, Norwich, Norfolk NR4 7TJ
☎01603 592810   Fax 01603 507728

New annual fellowship founded by retired Hong Kong senior civil servant, journalist and businessman, David Wong, to give writers the chance to produce a work of fiction in English set in the Far East. The aim of the Fellowship is 'to promote better understanding of the Far East and excellence in the writing of literature'. Applications will be considered from published and unpublished writers of any age and nationality. An original piece of fiction of no more than 10,000 words must be submitted with an application form, available from the above address, by 31 October.

Award £25,000.

Prizes

'...One thing I am persuaded of: the world of communications has to be fed by travel. Nothing can be done without it. Proust wrote: "The real voyage of discovery consists not in seeking new lands but in seeking with new eyes." This is an ultimate truth, never to be overlooked. But it has surely to be qualified by the likelihood that "new eyes" are very greatly stimulated by new faces, new sights and sounds. To me, travel is the life-blood of literature. We have to find at first hand how other people live and die, what they say, how they smell, how they are made. I recommend travel to young authors.

'And also to authors not so young. So far, you have been too polite to ask me how I intend to use the handsome prize-money that goes with the British Literature Award. I can say right away that I intend it for my travels, starting with a lovely, new, suitable motor car, which I hope will bear me in and out of our famous tunnel with ever more ease and pleasure.'

Dame Muriel Spark, taken from her acceptance speech – British Literature Award, 1997

ABSW/Glaxo Science Writers' Awards

Association of British Science Writers, 23 Savile Row, London W1X 2NB
☎0171 439 1205   Fax 0171 973 3051
ABSW Administrator *Barbara Drillsma*

A series of annual awards for outstanding science journalism in newspapers, journals and broadcasting.

J. R. Ackerley Prize

English Centre of International PEN, 7 Dilke Street, London SW3 4JE
☎0171 352 6303   Fax 0171 351 0220

Commemorating the novelist/autobiographer J. R. Ackerley, this prize is awarded for a literary autobiography, written in English and published in the year preceding the award. Entry restricted to nominations from the Ackerley Trustees only ('please do not submit books'). Previous winners include: Paul Binding *St Martin's Ride*; Germaine Greer *Daddy, We Hardly Knew You*; John Osborne *Almost a Gentleman*; Barry Humphries *More Please*; Blake Morrison *And When Did You Last See Your Father?*; Paul Vaughan *Something in Linoleum*.

Acorn–Rukeyser Chapbook Contest

Mekler & Deahl, Publishers, 237 Prospect Street South, Hamilton, Ontario, Canada L8M 2Z6
☎001 905 312 1779   Fax 001 905 312 8285
Contact *James Deahl, Gilda Mekler*

ESTABLISHED in 1996, this annual award is named after the poets Milton Acorn and Muriel Rukeyser in order to honour their achievements as populist poets. Poets may enter as many as 30 poems for a fee of £5. Final entry date: 31 October. Contact the above address for a copy of the rules.

Prize (Canadian) $100 and publication of the manuscript.

Age Concern Book of the Year
See **The Seebohm Trophy**

Aldeburgh Poetry Festival Prize

Goldings, Goldings Lane, Leiston, Suffolk IP16 4EB
☎01728 830631   Fax 01728 832029
Festival Coordinator *Michael Laskey*

ESTABLISHED 1989 by the Aldeburgh Poetry Trust. Sponsored by the Aldeburgh Bookshop for the best first collection published in Britain or the Republic of Ireland in the preceding twelve months. Open to any first collection of poetry of at least 40 pp. Final entry date 1 October. Previous winners: Donald Atkinson, Susan Wicks, Gwyneth Lewis, Glyn Wright.

Prize £500, plus an invitation to read at the following year's festival.

Alexander Prize

Royal Historical Society, University College London, Gower Street, London WC1E 6BT
☎0171 387 7532   Fax 0171 387 7532
Contact *Literary Director*

Awarded for a historical essay of not more than 8000 words. Competitors may choose their own subject for the essay, but must submit their choice for approval in the first instance to the Literary Director of the Royal Historical Society.
Prize £250.

Allied Domecq Playwright Award

c/o Scope Ketchum Sponsorship, Tower House, 8–14 Southampton Street, London WC2E 7HA
☎0171 379 3234   Fax 0171 465 8241
Contact *Lucy McCrickard, Lucy Cohn*

ESTABLISHED 1995. Biennial award, founded by Allied Domecq and the **Bush Theatre** in London, to encourage new writing talent. Open to writers (over the age of 18) who have not yet had a play produced professionally. Entrants must submit a 1000-word outline plus examples of previously completed work. First winner: Jacinta Stringer.
Prize £5000 to help with development of the outline; if appropriate, the play will be staged at the Bush Theatre.

An Duais don bhFilíocht i nGaeilge

An Chomhairle Ealaíon (The Arts Council), 70 Merrion Square, Dublin 2, Republic of Ireland
☎00 353 1 6611840   Fax 00 353 1 6761302
Literature Officer *Laurence Cassidy*

Triennial award for the best book of Irish poetry. Works must have been published in the Irish language in the preceding three years. Next award in 1998.
Prize £1500.

Hans Christian Andersen Awards

IBBY, Nonnenweg 12, Postfach CH-4003, Basle, Switzerland
☎00 41 61 272 2917   Fax 00 41 61 272 2757
Executive Director *Leena Maissen*

The highest international prizes for children's literature: The Hans Christian Andersen Award for Writing ESTABLISHED 1956; The Hans Christian Andersen Award for Illustration ESTABLISHED 1966. Candidates are nominated by National Sections of IBBY (The International Board on Books for Young People). Biennial prizes are awarded, in even-numbered years, to an author and an illustrator whose body of work has made a lasting contribution to children's literature. Next award 1998. 1996 winners: Award for

Writing: Uri Orlev (Israel); Award for Illustration: Klaus Ensikat (Germany).
Award Gold medals.

Eileen Anderson Central Television Drama Award

Central Broadcasting, Central House, Broad Street, Birmingham B1 2JP
☎0121 634 4232   Fax 0121 634 4137
Head of Regional Affairs *Kevin Johnson*

ESTABLISHED 1987 with money left by the late Dr Eileen Anderson and contributed to by **Central Television**, this is an annual award to encourage new theatre writing in the Midlands. Open to all new plays or an adaptation commissioned or premièred by a building-based theatre company in the Central region. Previous winners include: David Edgar *Pentecost* (premièred at the **Royal Shakespeare Company**'s The Other Place); Sean Street *Honest John* (premièred on Community Tour by the **Royal Theatre Northampton**); Vilma Hollingbery & Michael Napier Brown *Is This the Day?* (premièred at the Royal Theatre Northampton); Lucy Gannon *Wicked Old Nellie* (**Derby Playhouse**); Timberlake Wertenbaker *The Love of the Nightingale* (commissioned by the RSC's The Other Place); Pam Gem's *The Blue Angel* (premièred at the RSC's The Other Place) and Rod Dungate for *Playing By The Rules* (premièred at the **Birmingham Repertory Theatre**).
Prize £1500, plus trophy worth an additional £500 designed each year by a local college of education. A plaque is awarded to the theatre which commissioned the work.

The Aristeion Prize

Commission of the European Communities, Culture Unit, Rue de la Loi 200, B–1049 Brussels, Belgium
☎00 32 22 99 92 40   Fax 00 32 22 99 92 83
Contact *The Culture Unit*

ESTABLISHED 1990 to bring knowledge and appreciation of European literature to a wider public and to celebrate the strength and diversity of the European literary tradition. Member countries of the EC nominate their best works of literature and translation from the last three years. Sponsored by the Commission. 1996 winners: Salman Rushdie *The Moor's Last Sigh* and Christoph Ransmayr *Morbus Kithara* (Joint Literary Prize winners); Thorkild Bjornvig *Udsat På Hjertets Bjerge* by Rainer Maria Rilke (Translation Prize).
Prize 20,000 ecus (about £14,000) for each category.

Rosemary Arthur Award

National Poetry Foundation, 27 Mill Road, Fareham, Hampshire PO16 0TH

Contact *Johnathon Clifford*

ESTABLISHED 1989. Annual award to get poets of merit published in book form. Anyone resident in the UK who has not previously had a book published may submit 40 poems together with s.a.e. and £5 reading fee at any time during the year. The winner is announced in February.

Award Complete funding for a book of the poet's work, plus £100 and an engraved carriage clock.

Arvon Foundation International Poetry Competition

Kilnhurst, Kilnhurst Road, Todmorden, Lancashire OL14 6AX

☎01706 816582   Fax 01706 816359

Contact *David Pease*

ESTABLISHED 1980. Biennial competition (odd years) for poems written in English and not previously broadcast or published. There are no restrictions on the number of lines, themes, age of entrants or nationality. No limit to the number of entries. Entry fee: £3.50 per poem. Previous winners: Paul Farley *Laws of Gravity*; Don Paterson *A Private Bottling*.

Prize (1st) £5000 and £5000 worth of other prizes sponsored by Duncan Lawrie Limited.

The Asher Prize

See **The Royal Society of Medicine Prizes**

Authors' Club First Novel Award

Authors' Club, 40 Dover Street, London W1X 3RB

☎0171 499 8581   Fax 0171 409 0913

Contact *Mrs Ann Carter*

ESTABLISHED 1954. This award is made for the most promising work published in Britain by a British author, and is presented at a dinner held at the Authors' Club. Entries for the award are accepted from publishers and must be full-length – short stories are not eligible. Previous winners: T. J. Armstrong *Walter and the Resurrection of G.*; Nadeem Aslam *Season of the Rainbirds*; David Park *The Healing*; Andrew Cowan *Pig*.

Award £750.

BAAL Book Prize

BAAL Publications Secretary, School of Education, Open University, Milton Keynes MK7 6AA

☎01908 653383   Fax 01908 654111

Contact *David Graddol*

Annual award made by the British Association for Applied Linguistics to an outstanding book in the field of applied linguistics. Final entry at the end of February. Nominations from publishers only. Previous winners: Ruth Lesser and Lesley Milroy *Linguistics and Aphasia*; *Dictionary of British Sign Language*; Susan Berk-Seligson *The Bilingual Courtroom*; Joshua A. Fishman *Reversing Language Shift*.

The Barclays Bank Prize

See **Lakeland Book of the Year Awards**

Verity Bargate Award

The Soho Theatre Company, 21 Dean Street, London W1V 6NE

☎0171 287 5060   Fax 0171 287 5061

Contact *Paul Syrett*

To commemorate the late Verity Bargate, founder and director of the **Soho Theatre Company**. This award is presented bi-annually for a new and unperformed full-length play. Send s.a.e. for details; if submitting scripts, enclose one s.a.e. script-size and one standard-size. The Soho Theatre Company also runs many courses for new writers. Previous winners: Adrian Pagan, Frazer Grace, Lyndon Morgans, Diane Samuels, Judy Upton, Angela Meredith.

Award £1500, plus production by the Soho Theatre Company.

The Herb Barrett Award

Canadian Poetry Association, Hamilton Chapter, 237 Prospect Street South, Hamilton, Ontario, Canada L8M 2Z6

☎001 905 521 9196

Contact *James Deahl*

ESTABLISHED in 1996, this annual award is named in honour of Herb Barrett, founder of the Hamilton Chapter of the Canadian Poetry Association. Poets may enter one or two haiku for a fee of £5. Final entry date: 30 November. Contact the above address for a copy of the rules.

Prize (Canadian) $75, $50 and $25; anthology publication for the winners and all other worthy entries.

The Shaunt Basmajian Chapbook Award

Canadian Poetry Association, PO Box 22571, St George Postal Outlet, Toronto, Ontario, Canada M5S 1V0

☎001 416 944 3985

Contact *Allan Briesmaster*

ESTABLISHED 1996. Annual award named in

honour of poet Shaunt Basmajian, a founder of the Canadian Poetry Association. Up to 24 pages of poetry may be submitted for an entry fee of £5. Open to any type of poetry. Final entry date: 30 November. A copy of the rules is available from the above address.

Prize (Canadian) $100 and publication of the winning manuscript.

H. E. Bates Short Story Competition

Events Team, Directorate of Environment Services, Northampton Borough Council, Cliftonville House, Bedford Road, Northampton NN4 7NR
☎01604 233500   Fax 01604 238796
Contact *Liz Carroll-Wheat*

Named after the late H. E. Bates, one of the masters of the short story form. Entries should preferably be typed, 2000 words maximum on any subject. Any writer resident in Great Britain is eligible and there are categories for children under 11 and under 16.

Prize (1st) £200.

BBC Wildlife Magazine Awards for Nature Writing

BBC Wildlife Magazine, Broadcasting House, Whiteladies Road, Bristol BS8 2LR
☎0117 9738402   Fax 0117 9467075

Annual competition for professional and amateur writers. The competition was suspended in 1997 and at the time of going to press plans for its future resumption were unknown.

BBC Wildlife Magazine Poetry Awards

PO Box 229, Bristol BS99 7JN
☎0117 9738402   Fax 0117 9467075
Contact *Rosamund Kidman Cox*

Annual award for a poem, the subject of which must be the natural world and/or our relationship with it. Entrants may submit one poem only of no more than 50 lines with the entry form which appears in the magazine. Closing date for entries is in April. 1996 winner: Sheila Hamilton.

Prizes Poet of the Year: £500, publication in the magazine, plus reading of the poem on Radio 4's *Poetry Please*; eight runners-up prizes: £75 plus publication in the magazine; four young poets awards.

Samuel Beckett Award

c/o Faber & Faber, 3 Queen Square, London WC1N 3AU
☎0171 465 0045   Fax 0171 465 0034
Contact *Editorial Department*

The rules for this award are currently under review, 'largely as a reflection of prevailing conditions in the theatre and television as they affect new plays'. Nevertheless, a watching brief is being kept on plays that would have been eligible under the existing rules.

David Berry Prize

Royal Historical Society, University College London, Gower Street, London WC1E 6BT
☎0171 387 7532   Fax 0171 387 7532

Annual award for an essay of not more than 10,000 words on Scottish history. Candidates may select any subject from the relevant period, providing it has been submitted to, and approved by, the Council of the Royal Historical Society.

Prize £250.

Besterman Medal

See **The Library Association Besterman Medal**

The BFC Mother Goose Award

Books for Children, 4 Furzeground Way, Stockley Park, Uxbridge, Middlesex UB11 1DP
☎0181 606 3061   Fax 0181 606 3099
Contact *Marisa Summers, Editorial Coordinator*

ESTABLISHED 1979. Annual award for the most exciting newcomer to British children's book illustration. 1997 winner: Clare Jarrett *Catherine and the Lion.*

Prize £1000, plus Golden Egg trophy.

Birdwatch Bird Book of the Year

c/o Birdwatch Magazine, Bow House, 153–159 Bow Road, London E3 2SE
☎0181 983 1855
Contact *Dominic Mitchell*

ESTABLISHED in 1992 to acknowledge excellence in ornithological publishing – an increasingly large market with a high turnover. Annual award. Entries, from publishers, must offer an original and comprehensive treatment of their particular ornithological subject matter and must have a broad appeal to British-based readers. Previous winners: *Terns of Europe and North America* Klaus Malling Olsen and Hans Larsson; *Birds in Europe – Their Conservation Status* Graham Tucker and Melanie Heath; *The Birds of Israel* Hadoram Shirihai.

James Tait Black Memorial Prizes

University of Edinburgh, David Hume Tower, George Square, Edinburgh EH8 9JX
☎0131 650 3619   Fax 0131 650 6898

Contact *Department of English Literature*

ESTABLISHED 1918 in memory of a partner of the publishing firm of **A. & C. Black Ltd**. Two prizes, one for biography and one for fiction. Closing date for submissions: 30 September. Each prize is awarded for a book published in Britain in the previous twelve months. Prize winners are announced in December each year. Previous winners include: Diarmaid MacCulloch *Thomas Cranmer: A Life*; Graham Swift *Last Orders*; Alice Thompson *Justine*; Christopher Priest *The Prestige*; Gitta Sereny *Albert Speer: His Battle with Truth*; Alan Hollinghurst *The Folding Star*, Doris Lessing *Under My Skin*; Caryl Phillips *Crossing the River*; Richard Holmes *Dr Johnson and Mr Savage*.

Prizes £3000 each.

Boardman Tasker Award

14 Pine Lodge, Dairyground Road, Bramhall, Stockport, Cheshire SK7 2HS
☎0161 439 4624

Contact *Dorothy Boardman*

ESTABLISHED 1983, this award is given for a work of fiction, non-fiction or poetry, whose central theme is concerned with the mountain environment and which can be said to have made an outstanding contribution to mountain literature. Authors of any nationality are eligible, but the book must have been published or distributed in the UK for the first time between 1 November 1997 and 31 October 1998. Entries from publishers only. 1996 winner: Audrey Salkeld *A Portrait of Leni Riefenstahl*.

Prize £2000 (at Trustees' discretion).

Booker Prize for Fiction

Book Trust, Book House, 45 East Hill, London SW18 2QZ
☎0181 870 9055   Fax 0181 874 4790

Contact *Sandra Vince*

The leading British literary prize, set up in 1968 by Booker McConnell Ltd, with the intention of rewarding merit, raising the stature of the author in the eyes of the public and increasing the sale of the books. The announcement of the winner has been televised live since 1981, and all books on the shortlist experience a substantial increase in sales. Eligible novels must be written in English by a citizen of Britain, the Commonwealth, the Republic of Ireland or South Africa, and must be published in the UK for the first time between 1 October and 30 September of the year of the prize. Self-published books are no longer accepted. Entries are accepted from UK publishers who may each submit not more than two novels within the appropriate scheduled publication dates. The judges may also ask for certain other eligible novels to be submitted to them. Annual award. Previous winners include: James Kelman *How Late It Was, How Late*; Ben Okri *The Famished Road*; Michael Ondaatje *The English Patient*; Barry Unsworth *Sacred Hunger*; Roddy Doyle *Paddy Clarke Ha, Ha, Ha*; Pat Barker *The Ghost Road*. 1996 winner: Graham Swift *Last Orders*

Prize £20,000.

Author of the Year Award
Booksellers Association of Great Britain and Ireland

272 Vauxhall Bridge Road, London SW1V 1BA
☎0171 834 5477   Fax 0171 834 8812

Contact *Administrator*

Founded as part of BA Annual Conference to involve authors more closely in the event. Authors must be British or Irish. Not an award open to entry but voted on by the membership. Previous winner: Kate Atkinson.

Award £1000 plus trophy.

Border Television Prize
See **Lakeland Book of the Year Awards**

The BP Natural World Book Prize

Book Trust, Book House, 45 East Hill, London SW18 2QZ
☎0181 870 9055   Fax 0181 874 4790

Contact *Sandra Vince*

ESTABLISHED in 1996 as an amalgamation of the Natural World Book Prize (the magazine of the Wildlife Trusts) and the BP Conservation Book Prize. Award for a book on creative conservation of the environment. Entries from UK publishers only. Previous winner: David Quammen *The Song of the Dodo*; Runner-up: Richard Mabey *Flora Britannica*.

Prizes (1st) £5000; Runner-up: £1000.

The Michaél Breathnach Literary Memorial Award

Cló Iar-Chonnachta Teo, Indreabhán, Conamara, Co. Galway, Republic of Ireland
☎00 353 91 593307   Fax 00 353 91 593362

Editor *Nóirín Ní Ghrádaigh*

As part of their 10-year celebration, **Cló Iar-**

Chonnachta have established an annual award for the best Irish-language work in any literary form; novel, drama, poetry collection or short story collection. Open to writers under 30 years of age. Closing date for entries on 1 December annually.

Prize IR£1000.

Bridport Arts Centre
The Bridport Prize
Arts Centre, South Street, Bridport, Dorset DT6 3NR

☎01308 427183   Fax 01308 427183

Contact *Bridport Prize Administrator*

Annual competition for poetry and short story writing. Unpublished work only, written in English. Winning stories are read by leading London literary agent and an anthology of prize-winning entries is published. Also runs a young writers competition with variable prizes. Final entry date 30 June (early April for young writers award). Send s.a.e. for entry forms.

Prizes £2,500, £1000 & £500 in each category, plus supplementary runners-up prizes.

Katharine Briggs Folklore Award
The Folklore Society, University College London, Gower Street, London WC1E 6BT

☎0171 387 5894

Contact *The Convenor*

ESTABLISHED 1982. An annual award in November for the book, published in Britain and Ireland between 1 June and 30 May in the previous calendar year, which has made the most distinguished non-fiction contribution to folklore studies. Intended to encourage serious research in the field which Katharine Briggs did so much to establish. The term folklore studies is interpreted broadly to include all aspects of traditional and popular culture, narrative, belief, custom and folk arts. Previous winners include: Claudia Kinmouth *Irish Country Furniture 1700–1950*.

Prize £50, plus engraved goblet.

British Book Awards
Publishing News, 43 Museum Street, London WC1A 1LY

☎0171 404 0304   Fax 0171 242 0762

ESTABLISHED 1988. Viewed by the book trade as the one to win, 'The Nibbies' are presented annually in February. The 1996 Awards were in the following categories: Children's Book; Distributor; Editor; Publisher Marketing; Bookshop Marketing; Illustrated Book; Author; Book; Innovation in Publishing; Independent Bookseller; Chain Bookseller; Services to Bookselling; Publisher. Each winner receives the prestigious Nibbie and the awards are presented to those who have made the most impact in the book trade during the previous year. Previous winners have included: Alan Bennett, Sebastian Faulks, Jung Chang, Anne Fine, Books etc., and the publisher **Little, Brown**.

For further information contact: Merric Davidson, 12 Priors Heath, Goudhurst, Cranbrook, Kent TN17 2RE (☎/Fax 01580 212041).

British Comparative Literature Association/British Centre for Literary Translation Competition
Dept of Literature, University of Essex, Wivenhoe Park, Colchester, Essex CO4 3SQ

Competition Secretary *Dr Leon Burnett*

ESTABLISHED 1983. Annual competition open to unpublished literary translations from all languages. Maximum submission 25 pages. Special prizes for translations from Swedish (biennial). Final entry date 28 February.

Prizes (1st) £350; (2nd) £150; plus publication for all winning entries in the Association's annual journal *Comparative Criticism* (**Cambridge University Press**). Other entries may receive commendations.

British Fantasy Awards
2 Harwood Street, Heaton Norris, Stockport, Cheshire SK4 1JJ

☎0161 476 5368 (after 6 p.m.)

Secretary *Robert Parkinson*

Awarded by the **British Fantasy Society** by members at its annual conference for Best Novel and Best Short Story categories, among others. Previous winners include: Piers Anthony, Clive Barker, Ken Bulmer, Ramsey Campbell.

British Literature Prize
See **David Cohen British Literature Prize**

British Press Awards
Press Gazette, EMAP Business Communications, 33–39 Bowling Green Lane, London EC1R 0DA

☎0171 505 8000   Fax 0171 505 8220

'The Oscars of British journalism'. Open to all British morning and Sunday newspapers sold nationally and news agencies. March event. Run by the *Press Gazette*.

British Science Fiction (Association) Award

60 Bournemouth Road, Folkestone, Kent CT19 5AZ

☎01303 252939

Award Administrator *Maureen Speller*

ESTABLISHED 1966. The BSFA awards a trophy each year in three categories – novel, short fiction and artwork – published in the preceding year. Previous winners: Iain Banks *Feersum Endjinn*; Paul di Filippo *The Double Felix*.

James Cameron Award

City University, Department of Journalism, Northampton Square, London EC1V 0HB

☎0171 477 8221   Fax 0171 477 8594

Contact *The Administrator*

Annual award for journalism to a reporter of any nationality, working for the British media, whose work is judged to have contributed most during the year to the continuance of the Cameron tradition. Administered by City University Department of Journalism. 1996 winner: Maggie O'Kane, *The Guardian*.

The County of Cardiff International Poetry Competition

The Welsh Academy, 3rd Floor, Mount Stuart House, Mount Stuart Square, Cardiff CF1 6DQ

☎01222 492025   Fax 01222 492930

Contact *Kevin Thomas*

ESTABLISHED 1986. An annual competition for unpublished poems in English of up to 50 lines. Launched in the spring with an autumn closing date.

Prize (total) £5000.

Carey Award

Society of Indexers, Mermaid House, 1 Mermaid Court, London SE1 1HR

☎0171 403 4947   Fax 0171 357 0903

Secretary *Christine Shuttleworth*

A private award made by the Society to a member who has given outstanding services to indexing. The recipient is selected by Council with no recommendations considered from elsewhere.

Carmarthen Writers' Circle Short Story Competition

Lower Carfan, Tavern Spike, Whitland, Pembrokeshire SA34 0NP

☎01994 240441

Contact *Jenny White*

ESTABLISHED 1990. Annual. All stories must be unpublished and not yet accepted for publication. Entries *must* be anonymous and an A4 cover page giving story title, name, address and telephone number must be attached to submissions. Any number may be submitted; entry fee £4 per story. Stories must be typed in double-spacing on one side of A4 paper. Send s.a.e. for details. Also holds an annual open poetry competition. Entry fee of £2 per poem.

Prizes Short Story Competition: (1st) £120; (2nd) £80; (3rd) £60. All prize winners will be put on tape for the Talking Newspaper and considered by Radio 4 for broadcasting. Open Poetry Competition: (1st) £100; (2nd) £70; (3rd) £50; children's prize and local prize for West Wales.

Carnegie Medal

See **The Library Association Carnegie Medal**

Sid Chaplin Short Story Competition

Shildon Town Council, Civic Centre Square, Shildon, Co Durham DL4 1AH

☎01388 772563   Fax 01388 777648

Contact *T. Toward*

FOUNDED 1986. Annual themed short story competition (1996 subject was 'Friendship') open to residents in the Northern Arts area. Maximum 3000 words; £1 entrance fee (Juniors free). All stories must be unpublished and not broadcast and/or performed. Final entry date usually 31st December. *Prizes* (1st) £300; (2nd) £150; (3rd) £75; (Junior) £50.

Children's Book Award

The Federation of Children's Book Groups, The Old Malt House, Aldbourne, Wiltshire SN8 2DW

☎01672 540629   Fax 01672 541280

Coordinator *Marianne Adey*

ESTABLISHED 1980. Awarded annually for best book of fiction suitable for children. Unique in that it is judged by the children themselves. Previous winners include: Dick King-Smith *Harriet's Hare*; Ian Strachan *The Boy in the Bubble*; Mick Inkpen *Threadbear*; Robert Swindells *Room 13*; Elizabeth Laird *Kiss the Dust*; Jaqueline Wilson *The Suitcase Kid* and *Double Act*.

Award A splendid silver and oak sculpture made by Graham Stewart and Tim Stead, plus portfolio of letters, drawings and comments from the children who took part in the judging;

category winners receive silver bowls designed by the same artists and portfolios.

Children's Book Circle Eleanor Farjeon Award
See **Eleanor Farjeon Award**

Arthur C. Clarke Award for Science Fiction
60 Bournemouth Road, Folkestone, Kent CT19 5AZ
☎01303 252939   Fax 01303 252939
Administrator *Paul Kincaid*

ESTABLISHED 1986. The Arthur C. Clarke Award is given yearly to the best science fiction novel with first UK publication in the previous calendar year. Both hardcover and paperback books qualify. Made possible by a generous donation from Arthur C. Clarke, this award is selected by a rotating panel of six judges nominated by the **British Science Fiction Association**, the International Science Policy Foundation and the **Science Fiction Foundation**. Previous winners include: Paul J. McAuley *Fairyland*; Pat Cadigan *Fools*; Jeff Noon *Vurt*; Marge Piercy *Body of Glass*; Pat Cadigan *Synners*; Colin Greenland *Take Back Plenty*.
Award £1000 plus trophy.

The Cló Iar-Chonnachta Literary Award
Cló Iar-Chonnachta Teo, Indreabhán, Conamara, Co. Galway, Republic of Ireland
☎00 353 91 593307   Fax 00 353 91 593362
Editor *Nóirín Ní Ghrádaigh*

As part of their 10-year celebration, **Cló Iar-Chonnachta** have established an annual prize for a newly written and unpublished work in the Irish language. Awarded in 1996 for the best novel, 1997 for the best poetry collection, and 1998 for the best short story collection or drama. Last date of entry for 1997 Poetry Award: 1 December 1996.
Prize IR£5000.

David Cohen British Literature Prize in the English Language
Arts Council of Great Britain, 14 Great Peter Street, London SW1P 3NQ
☎0171 333 0100   Fax 0171 973 6590
Literature Director *Dr Alastair Niven*
Literature Assistant *Karen Woods*

ESTABLISHED 1993. By far the most valuable literature prize in Britain, the British Literature Prize, launched by the **Arts Council**, is awarded biennially. Anyone is eligible to suggest candidates and the award recognises writers who use the English language and who are British citizens, encompassing dramatists as well as novelists, poets and essayists. The prize is for a lifetime's achievement rather than a single play or book and is donated by the David Cohen Family Charitable Trust in association with Coutts Bank. The David Cohen Trust was set up in 1980 by David Cohen, general practitioner son of a property developer. The Trust has helped composers, choreographers, dancers, poets, playwrights and actors. The Council is providing a further £10,000 to enable the winner to commission new work, with the dual aim of encouraging young writers and readers. 1997 winner: Dame Muriel Spark. Previous winners: Harold Pinter, V. S. Naipaul.
Award £30,000, plus £10,000 towards new work.

Collins Biennial Religious Book Award
HarperCollins Publishers, 77-85 Fulham Palace Road, London W6 8JB
☎0181 741 7070   Fax 0181 307 4064
Contact *Jeremy Yates-Round*

Biennial award given for the book which has made the most distinguished contribution to the relevance of Christianity in the modern world, written by a living citizen of the Commonwealth, the Republic of Ireland or South Africa. Previous winners include: John MacQuarrie *Jesus Christ in Modern Thought*. The award scheme is currently on hold – all enquiries to Jeremy Yates-Round.
Award £5000.

The Commonwealth Writers Prize
Book Trust, Book House, 45 East Hill, London SW18 2QZ
☎0181 870 9055   Fax 0181 874 4790
Contact *Sandra Vince*

ESTABLISHED 1987. An annual award to reward and encourage the upsurge of new Commonwealth fiction. Any work of prose or fiction is eligible, i.e. a novel or collection of short stories. No drama or poetry. The work must be written in English by a citizen of the Commonwealth and be first published in the year before its entry for the prize. Entries must be submitted by the publisher to the region of the writer's Commonwealth citizenship. The four regions are: Africa, Eurasia, S. E. Asia and South Pacific, Caribbean and Canada. Previous winners: Louis de Bernières *Captain Corelli's Mandolin* (Best Book); Adib Khan *Seasonal Adjustments* (Best First Book).

Prizes £10,000 for Best Book; £3000 for Best First Book; 8 prizes of £1000 for each best and first best book in four regions.

The Thomas Cook/*Daily Telegraph* Travel Book Award

The Thomas Cook Group, PO Box 227, Thorpe Wood, Peterborough PE3 6PU
☎01733 503566   Fax 01733 503596

Contact *Jennifer Rigby, Publishing*

Annual award given to the author of the book, published (in the English language) in the previous year, which most inspires the reader to want to travel. Submissions by publishers only. Previous winners: Gavin Bell *In Search of Tusitala: Travels in the South Pacific after Robert Louis Stevenson*; William Dalrymple *City of Djinns*; Nik Cohn *The Heart of the World*; Stanley Stewart *Frontiers of Heaven*.

Award £7500.

The Duff Cooper Prize

54 St Maur Road, London SW6 4DP
☎0171 736 3729   Fax 0171 731 7638

Contact *Artemis Cooper*

An annual award for a literary work of biography, history, politics or poetry, published by a recognised publisher (member of **The Publishers Association**) during the previous 12 months. The book must be submitted by the publisher, not the author. Financed by the interest from a trust fund commemorating Duff Cooper, first Viscount Norwich (1890–1954). 1996 winner: Gitta Sereny *Albert Speer*.

Prize £2000.

Rose Mary Crawshay Prize

The British Academy, 20–21 Cornwall Terrace, London NW1 4QP
☎0171 487 5966   Fax 0171 224 3807

Contact *British Academy Secretary*

ESTABLISHED 1888 by Rose Mary Crawshay, this prize is given for a historical or critical work by a woman of any nationality on English literature, with particular preference for a work on Keats, Byron or Shelley. The work must have been published in the preceding three years.

Prizes normally two of approximately £500 each.

Crime Writers' Association (Cartier Diamond Dagger)

60 Drayton Road, Kings Heath, Birmingham B14 7LR

Contact *The Secretary*

An annual award for a lifetime's outstanding contribution to the genre. 1996 winner: Colin Dexter, creator of Inspector Morse.

Crime Writers' Association (John Creasey Memorial Dagger for Best First Crime Novel)

60 Drayton Road, Kings Heath, Birmingham B14 7LR

Contact *The Secretary*

ESTABLISHED 1973 following the death of crime writer John Creasey, founder of the **Crime Writers' Association**. This award, sponsored by **Chivers Press**, is given annually for the best crime novel by an author who has not previously published a full-length work of fiction. Nominations from publishers only. Previous winners include: Laurie King *A Grave Talent*; Doug J. Swanson *Big Town*.

Award Dagger, plus cheque.

Crime Writers' Association (The Macallan Dagger for Non-Fiction)

60 Drayton Road, Kings Heath, Birmingham B14 7LR

Contact *The Secretary*

Annual award for the best non-fiction crime book published during the year. Previous winners include: Antonia Fraser *The Gunpowder Plot*; Martin Beales *Dead Not Buried*; David Canter *Criminal Shadows*; Alexandra Artley *Murder in the Heart*; Charles Nicholl *The Reckoning*; John Bossy *Giordano Bruno and the Embassy Affair*.

Award Dagger, plus cheque (sum varies).

Crime Writers' Association (The Macallan Gold and Silver Daggers for Fiction)

60 Drayton Road, Kings Heath, Birmingham B14 7LR

Contact *The Secretary*

Two annual awards for the best crime fiction published during the year. Nominations for Gold Dagger from publishers only. Previous winners include: Val McDermid *The Mermaids Singing*; Minette Walters *The Scold's Bridle*; Patricia Cornwell *Cruel and Unusual*; Ben Elton *Popcorn* (Gold); Peter Lovesey *The Summons*;

Peter Hoeg *Miss Smilla's Feeling for Snow*; Sarah Dunant *Fatlands*; Peter Lovesey *Bloodhounds* (Silver).
Award Dagger, plus cheque (sum varies).

Crime Writers' Association (The Macallan Short Story Dagger)
60 Drayton Road, Kings Heath, Birmingham B14 7LR
Contact *The Secretary*

ESTABLISHED 1993. An award for a published crime story. Publishers should submit three copies of the story by 30 September. 1996 winner: Ian Rankin *Herbert in Motion*.
Prize Dagger, plus cheque.

The Daily Telegraph Nirex Young Science Writer Awards
Electric Echo, 334A Goswell Road, London EC1V 7LQ
☎0171 713 5525
Contact *Gerry Fallon*

Celebrating its 10th anniversary, the awards are open to anyone aged between 16–28 for a short article (maximum 700 words) on any scientific or science-related subject suitable for publication in *The Daily Telegraph*. Prizes include a trip to the US for the annual meeting of the American Association for the Advancement of Science. Entry details from the above address or on the Internet at http://www. science-writer.co.uk.

Harvey Darton Award
See **The Children's Books History Society** under **Literary Societies**

The Hunter Davies Prize
See **Lakeland Book of the Year Awards**

Isaac & Tamara Deutscher Memorial Prize
Department of International Relations, London School of Economics, Houghton Street, London WC2A 2AE
☎0171 955 7181
Secretary *Dr Justin Rosenberg*

An annual award in recognition of, and as an encouragement to, outstanding research in or about the Marxist tradition. Made to the author of an essay or full-scale work published or in manuscript. Final entry date 1 May.
Award £200.

George Devine Award
17A South Villas, London NW1 9BS
☎0171 267 9793 (evenings)
Contact *Christine Smith*

Annual award for a promising new playwright writing for the stage in memory of George Devine, artistic director of the **Royal Court Theatre**, who died in 1965. The play does not need to have been produced. Send two copies of the script to Christine Smith by March. Information leaflet available.
Prize £5000.

Denis Devlin Memorial Award for Poetry
An Chomhairle Ealaíon (The Arts Council), 70 Merrion Square, Dublin 2, Republic of Ireland
☎00 353 1 6611840   Fax 00 353 1 6761302
Literature Officer *Laurence Cassidy*

Triennial award for the best book of poetry in English by an Irish poet, published in the preceding three years. Next award 1999.
Award £1500.

Dillons First Fiction Award
Dillons UK Ltd., Publicity Dept., Royal House, Prince's Gate, Homer Road, Solihull, West Midlands B91 3QQ
☎0121 703 8000
Contact *Ruth Killick, Tracey Lewis*

ESTABLISHED 1994. Annual award to 'acknowledge and encourage new novel-writing talent'. Open to full-length first novels written in English by a UK or Irish resident. Books must be published in the UK during the calendar year of the award. 1997 winner: Patricia Duncker *Hallucinating Foucault*.
Prize £5000 plus extensive promotion in all Dillons branches.

Dog Watch Open Poetry Competition
267 Hillbury Road, Warlingham, Surrey CR6 9TL
☎01883 622121
Contact *Michaela Edridge*

ESTABLISHED 1993. Dog Watch is a charity that rescues and finds new homes for badly abused dogs. The annual prize is awarded only to authors of unpublished works. Final entry date is 1st November each year and entrants should send s.a.e. for details.
Prize (1st) £50; (2nd) £30; (3rd) £20.

Drama Association of Wales Playwriting Competition

The Library, Singleton Road, Splott, Cardiff CF2 2ET

☎01222 452200   Fax 01222 452277

Contact *Gary Thomas*

Annual competition held to promote the writing of one act plays in English and Welsh of between 20 and 45 minutes' playing time. The theme of the competition is changed each year – the 1997 title was *The Winds of Change*. Application forms from the above address.

Prizes £100; £50; £25, plus special prizes for the most outstanding author under the age of 25, the best play with an all-female cast and the best play in the Welsh language. Winning plays will be considered for publication.

Eccles Prize

Columbia Business School, 810 Uris Hall, New York NY 10027, USA

☎001 212 854 2747   Fax 001 212 854 3050

Contact *Office of Public Affairs*

ESTABLISHED 1986 by Spencer F. Eccles in commemoration of his uncle, George S. Eccles, a 1922 graduate of the Business School. Annual award for excellence in economic writing. One of the US's most prestigious book prizes. Books must have a business theme and be written for a general audience. Previous winners: *The Warburgs* Ron Chernow; *The New Palgrave Dictionary of Money and Finance* ed. Peter Newman, Murray Milgate and John Eatwell; *The Prize* Daniel Yergin.

The T.S. Eliot Prize

The Poetry Book Society, Book House, 45 East Hill, London SW18 2QZ

☎0181 870 8403/
877 1615 (24-hour answerphone/fax)

Contact *Clare Brown, Director*

ESTABLISHED 1993. Annual award named after T. S. Eliot, one of the founders of the Poetry Book Society. Open to books of new poetry published in the UK and Republic of Ireland during the year and over 32 pages in length. At least 75 per cent of the collection must be previously unpublished in book form. Final entry date is in September/October. Previous winners: *First Language* Ciaran Carson; *The Annals of Chile* Paul Muldoon; *My Alexandria* Mark Doty; *Subhuman Redneck Poems* Les Murray.

The Encore Award

The Society of Authors, 84 Drayton Gardens, London SW10 9SB

☎0171 373 6642   Fax 0171 373 5768

ESTABLISHED 1990. Awarded to an author who has had one (and only one) novel previously published. Details from **The Society of Authors**. 1996 winner: A.L. Kennedy *So I Am Glad*.

Prize (total) £7500.

Envoi Poetry Competition

Envoi, 44 Rudyard Road, Biddulph Moor, Stoke on Trent, Staffordshire ST8 7JN

☎01782 517892

Contact *Roger Elkin*

Run by *Envoi* poetry magazine. Competitions are featured regularly, with prizes of £200, plus three annual subscriptions to *Envoi*. Winning poems along with full adjudication report are published. Send s.a.e. to Competition Secretary, 17 Millcroft, Bishops Stortford, Hertfordshire CM23 2BP.

Esquire/Apple/Waterstone's Non-Fiction Award

National Magazine Co Ltd, 72 Broadwick Street, London W1V 2BP

☎0171 439 5000   Fax 0171 439 5067

Editor *Rosie Boycott*

ESTABLISHED 1993 by *Esquire* as a major annual literary award. 1996 winner: Peter Godwin *Mukina*. The award was suspended for 1997 and at the time of going to press its future is uncertain.

European Literary Prize/European Translation Prize

See **The Aristeion Prize**

Geoffrey Faber Memorial Prize

Faber & Faber Ltd, 3 Queen Square, London WC1N 3AU

☎0171 465 0045   Fax 0171 465 0034

ESTABLISHED 1963 as a memorial to the founder and first chairman of **Faber & Faber**, this prize is awarded in alternate years for the volume of verse and the volume of prose fiction published in the UK in the preceding two years, which is judged to be of greatest literary merit. Authors must be under 40 at the time of publication and citizens of the UK, Commonwealth, Republic of Ireland or South Africa. 1996 winner: Kathleen Jamie *The Queen of Sheba*.

Prize £1000.

Eleanor Farjeon Award

c/o Children's Book Circle, Hampshire
County Library, 81 North Walls, Winchester,
Hampshire SO23 8BY
☎01962 846086   Fax 01962 856615
Contact *Anne Marley*

This award, named in memory of the much-loved children's writer, is for distinguished services to children's books either in this country or overseas, and may be given to a librarian, teacher, publisher, bookseller, author, artist, reviewer, television producer, etc. Nominations from members of the **Children's Book Circle**. 1996 winner: *Books for Keeps*.
Award £750.

Fawcett Society Book Prize

New Light on Women's Lives, Fifth Floor, 45
Beech Street, London EC2Y 8AD
☎0171 628 4441   Fax 0171 628 2865
Contact *Charlotte Burt*

Awarded annually to the author of the book which gives us a greater understanding of women's lives, whether it be a book of fiction, non-fiction, biography, etc. All works submitted for the prize are placed in the **Fawcett Library** at London Guildhall University. Previous winners: Stella Tillyard *Aristocrats*; Jung Chang *Wild Swans*; Margaret Forster *Daphne du Maurier*.
Prize £2000.

The Fidler Award

c/o Book Trust Scotland, The Scottish Book
Centre, 137 Dundee Street, Edinburgh
EH11 1BG
☎0131 229 3663   Fax 0131 228 4293

Sponsored by Hodder Children's Books for an unpublished novel for children aged 8–12, to encourage authors new to writing for this age group. Authors should not previously have had a novel published for this age group. The award is administered by **Book Trust Scotland**. Final entry date end October. Previous winners: Theresa Breslin *Simon's Challenge*; Catherine McPhail *Run Zan Run*. 1996 winner: John Smirthwaite *The Falcon's Crest*.
Award £1000, plus publication.

Fish (Publishing) Short Story Prize

Fish Publishing, Durrus, Bantry, Co Cork,
Republic of Ireland
☎00 353 27 61246   Fax 00 353 27 61246
Contact *Clem Cairns, Jula Walton*

ESTABLISHED 1994. Annual award which aims to discover, encourage and publish exciting new literary talent. Stories of 5000 words maximum which have not been published previously may be entered; an entry fee of £8 is charged for the first entry and £5 thereafter. Closing date: mid-November. Honorary Patrons: Roddy Doyle and Dermot Healy. Previous winner: Molly McCloskey *The Stranger*.
Prize £1000; the best 15 stories are published.

Sir Banister Fletcher Award

The Authors' Club, 40 Dover Street, London
W1X 3RB
☎0171 499 8581   Fax 0171 409 0913
Contact *Mrs Ann Carter*

This award was created by Sir Bannister Fletcher, who was president of the **Authors' Club** for many years. The prize is donated by Nelson Hurst & Marsh, insurance brokers, and is presented annually for the best book on architecture or the fine arts published in the preceding year. Submissions: Fletcher Award Committee, RIBA, 66 Portland Place, London W1N 4AD. Previous winners: Richard Weston *Alvar Aalto*; Dr Megan Aldrich *Gothic Revival*; Professor Thomas Markus *Building and Power*; John Onians *Bearers of Meaning: Classical Orders in Antiquity*; Sir Michael Levey *Giambattista Tiepolo: His Life and Art*; John Allan *Berthold Lubetkin – Architecture and The Tradition of Progress*.
Award £750.

The John Florio Prize

The Translators Association, 84 Drayton
Gardens, London SW10 9SB
☎0171 373 6642   Fax 0171 373 5768
Contact *Kate Pool*

Biennial award for the best translation into English of a twentieth-century Italian work, published by a British publisher in the two years preceding the prize. Previous winners include: Emma Rose for *His Mother's House* by Marta Morazzoni.
Prize £1000.

The Forward Prizes for Poetry

Colman Getty PR, Carrington House,
126–130 Regent Street, London W1R 5FE
☎0171 439 1783   Fax 0171 439 1784
Contact *Liz Sich, Margot Weale*

ESTABLISHED 1992. Three awards, sponsored by Forward Publishing, Waterstone's and Tolman Cunard, for the best collection of poetry, the best first collection of poetry, and the best single poem which is not already part of an anthology or collection. All entries must be published in the UK or Eire and submitted by poetry publishers (collections) or newspaper and magazine editors (single poems). Previous winners: Thom Gunn, Simon Armitage, Jackie Kay, Carol Ann Duffy, Don Paterson, Vicki Feaver, Alan Jenkins, Kwame Dawes, Iain Crichton Smith, Sean O'Brien, Jane Duran, Jenny Joseph, John Fuller, Kate Clanchy, Kathleen Jamie.

Prizes £10,000 for best collection; £5000 for best first collection; £1000 for best single poem.

Anne Frankel Prize

The Critics' Circle, c/o The Stage (incorporating Television Today), 47 Bermondsey Street, London SE1 3XT
☎0171 403 1818 ext 106   Fax 0171 357 9287
Contact *Catherine Cooper*

ESTABLISHED 1991. Annual prize for young film critics in memory of the late Anne Frankel, who wrote on film. Set up by her father William Frankel, former editor and now chairman of the *Jewish Chronicle*. Age limit for entrants is 25. Entries should be self-submitted and have been published in a local/national/student newspaper or periodical. Submit three examples of work, sending four copies of each to the above address. Final entry date usually end August.

Prize £500.

The Frogmore Poetry Prize

The Frogmore Press, 42 Morehall Avenue, Folkestone, Kent CT19 4EF
Contact *Jeremy Page*

ESTABLISHED 1987. Awarded annually and sponsored by the Frogmore Foundation. The winning poem, runners-up and short-listed entries are all published in the magazine. Previous winners have been: David Satherley, Caroline Price, Bill Headdon, John Latham, Diane Brown, Tobias Hill, Mario Petrucci.

Prize The winner receives 100 guineas and a life subscription to the biannual literary magazine *The Frogmore Papers*.

David Gemmell Cup

Hastings Writers Group, 39 Emmanuel Road, Hastings, East Sussex TN34 3LB
☎01424 442471
Contact *Mrs R. Bartholomew* (for entry form)

ESTABLISHED 1988. Annual award to encourage writers of short fiction (1500 words) resident in East and West Sussex, Kent, Surrey, London and London boroughs. Final entry date: end August. The competition is organised by Hastings Writers' Group and is presented by its sponsor David Gemmell. Previous winners: Wendy Brewer, Barbara Couvela, Stella Radford, Carol Bostock, Sarah Mills.

Prizes (1st) £250 plus David Gemmell Cup; (2nd) £150; (3rd) £100; (4th) £50; (5th) £30; (6th) £20. Additionally, certificates of commendation issued at the discretion of the judge, David Gemmell.

Glaxo Science Writers' Awards
See **ABSW/Glaxo Science Writers' Awards**

Glenfiddich Awards

27 Fitzroy Square, London W1P 5HH
☎0171 383 3024   Fax 0171 383 4593

A series of awards to writers and broadcasters who have contributed most to the civilised appreciation of food and drink through articles, books, illustration and photography published in the UK. Also covers TV and radio programmes, as well as a Special Award for outstanding work or event. 1997 winners: Food Book of the Year: *Passion for Flavour* Gordon Ramsay; Drink Book of the year: no overall winner, Andrew Jeffords *Evening Standard Wine Guide 1997* was highly commended; Food Writer of the Year: Simon Hopkinson for work in *The Independent Magazine*; Drink Writer of the Year: Roger Protz for work in *The Guardian Weekend*; Magazine Cookery Writer of the Year: Ruth Watson for work in Sainsbury's *The Magazine*; Newspaper Cookery Writer of the Year: Rowley Leigh for work in *The Guardian Weekend*; Restaurant Writer of the Year: Charles Campion for work in *ES Magazine*; Wine Writer of the Year: Andrew Jefford for work in the *Evening Standard*; Regional Writer of the Year: Neil MacLean for work in *The Sunday Times*, Scotland; TV Programme of the Year: *Techno:Food*, BBC Education programme featuring chef Paul Rankin, directed by Mark Holness, produced by series producer Cassie Braban and executive producer Richard Langridge; Radio Programme of the Year: *Farming Today – Spam*, presented by Jeremy Cherfas and produced by Ruth Kiely for BBC Radio 4; Visual Award: Martin Brigdale for photography in *Sauces* by Michel Roux; 1997 Special Award: Joanna Blythman for her investigative food journalism in *The Guardian* and her book *The Food We Eat*; 1997 Glenfiddich Trophy Winner: BBC Education.

Award Overall winner (chosen from the category winners) £3000, plus the Glenfiddich Trophy (which is held for one year); category winners £800 each, plus a case of Glenfiddich

Single Malt Scotch Whisky and an engraved commemorative quaich.

Edgar Graham Book Prize

c/o Department of Development Studies, School of Oriental and African Studies, Thornhaugh Street, Russell Square, London WC1H 0XG

☎0171 436 7295   Fax 0171 323 6605

Contact *The Secretary*

ESTABLISHED 1984. Biennial award in memory of Edgar Graham. Aims to encourage research work in Third World agricultural and industrial development. Open to published works of original scholarship on agricultural and/or industrial development in Asia and/or Africa. No edited volumes. Next award 1998; final entry date 30 September 1997.

Prize £1500.

Kate Greenaway Medal

See **The Library Association Kate Greenaway Medal**

The Guardian Children's Fiction Award

The Guardian, 119 Farringdon Road, London EC1R 3ER

☎0171 278 2332   Fax 0171 837 2114

Children's Book Editor *Joanna Carey*

ESTABLISHED 1967. Annual award for an outstanding work of fiction for children by a British or Commonwealth author, first published in the UK in the preceding year, excluding picture books and previous winners. Final entry date: end December. Previous winners: Melvin Burgess *Junk*; Lesley Howarth *MapHead*; Rachel Anderson *Paper Faces*; Hilary McKay *The Exiles*; William Mayne *Low Tide*; Sylvia Waugh *The Mennyms*. 1996 joint winners: Philip Pullman *Dark Materials I: Northern Lights* and Alison Prince *The Sherwood Hero*.

Award £1500.

The Guardian Fiction Prize

The Guardian, 119 Farringdon Road, London EC1R 3ER

☎0171 278 2332   Fax 0171 837 2114

Contact *Literary Editor*

ESTABLISHED 1965. An annual award for a novel published by a British, Irish or Commonwealth writer, which is chosen by the literary editor in conjunction with the paper's regular reviewers of fiction. Previous winners: James Buchan *Heart's Journey into Winter*; Seamus Deane *Reading in the Dark*; Candia

McWilliam *Debatable Land*; Alasdair Gray *Poor Things*; Alan Judd *The Devil's Own Work*; Pat Barker *The Eye in the Door*.

Prize £3000.

W. H. Heinemann Prize

Royal Society of Literature, 1 Hyde Park Gardens, London W2 2LT

☎0171 723 5104   Fax 0171 402 0199

ESTABLISHED 1945. Works of any kind of literature may be submitted by publishers under this award, which aims to encourage genuine contributions to literature. Books must be written in the English language and have been published in the previous year; translations are not eligible for consideration. Preference tends to be given to publications which are unlikely to command large sales: poetry, biography, criticism, philosophy, history. Final entry date: 31 October. Up to three awards may be given. Previous winners: Tony Harrison *The Shadow of Hiroshima* and *Permanently Bard*; Theo Richmond *Konin*.

Prize £5000.

Felicia Hemans Prize for Lyrical Poetry

University of Liverpool, PO Box 147, Liverpool, Merseyside L69 3BX

☎0151 794 2458   Fax 0151 794 2454

Contact *The Registrar*

ESTABLISHED 1899. Annual award for published or unpublished verse. Open to past or present members and students of the University of Liverpool. One poem per entrant only. Closing date 1 May.

Prize £30.

Heywood Hill Literary Prize

10 Curzon Street, London W1Y 7FJ

☎0171 629 0647

Contact *John Saumarez Smith*

ESTABLISHED 1995 by the Duke of Devonshire to reward a lifetime's contribution to the enjoyment of books. Three judges chosen annually. No applications are necessary for this award. 1996 winner: Penelope Fitzgerald.

Prize £10,000.

David Higham Prize for Fiction

c/o Book Trust, Book House, 45 East Hill, London SW18 2QZ

☎0181 870 9055   Fax 0181 874 4790

Contact *Sandra Vince*

ESTABLISHED 1975. An annual award for a first

novel or book of short stories published in the UK in the year of the award by an author who is a citizen of Britain, the Commonwealth, the Republic of Ireland or South Africa. Previous winners: Vikram Chandra *Red Earth and Pouring Rain*; Fred D'Aguiar *The Longest Memory*; Nicola Barker *Love Your Enemies*; John Loveday *Halo*; Elspeth Barker *O Caledonia*; 1996 winner: Linda Grant *The Cast Iron Shore*.
Award £1000.

William Hill Sports Book of the Year

Greenside House, Station Road, Wood Green, London N22 4TP
☎0181 918 3731   Fax 0181 918 3728
Contact *Graham Sharpe*

ESTABLISHED 1989. Annual award introduced by Graham Sharpe of bookmakers William Hill. Sponsored by William Hill and thus dubbed the 'bookie' prize, it is the first, and only, Sports Book of the Year award. Final entry date September. Previous winners include: John Feinstein *A Good Walk Spoiled*; Simon Kuper *Football Against the Enemy*; Stephen Jones *Endless Winter*; Nick Hornby *Fever Pitch: A Fan's Life*; Colin McRae *Dark Trade*.
Prize (reviewed annually) £10,000 package including £5000 cash, hand-bound copy, free bet and a day at the races. Runners-up prizes.

Hilton House Poet of the Year/ Hilton House Open Competition

Hilton House (Publishers), Hilton House, 39 Long John Hill, Norwich, Norfolk NR1 2JP
☎01603 449845
Contact *Michael K. Moore*

ESTABLISHED 1995. Annual awards to promote interest in poetry and to encourage high standards. Unpublished poems only, of up to 30 lines; no limit to number of entries. Best poems selected will be published in Hilton House anthology series for that year. Final entry dates: 31st March (Poet of the Year); 31st August (Open Competition). Previous winners: Michael Roy, Paul J. Thornber.
Prizes (for both competitions) 1st £200; 2nd £100; 3rd £150.

Calvin & Rose G. Hoffman Prize

King's School, Canterbury, Kent CT1 2ES
☎01227 595501
Contact *The Headmaster*

Annual award for distinguished publication on Christopher Marlowe, established by the late Calvin Hoffman, author of *The Man Who was Shakespeare* (1955) as a memorial to himself and his wife. For unpublished works of at least 5000 words written in English for their scholarly contribution to the study of Christopher Marlowe and his relationship to William Shakespeare. Final entry date 1 September. Previous winners: Prof. Dr Kurt Tetzeli von Rosador, Dr R. Dutton, Prof. R. Danson, Prof. T. Cartelli, Dr. David Pascoe, Dr Lisa Hopkins, Prof. J. Shapiro, Prof. J. Bate, Dr Ruth Lunney.

Winifred Holtby Memorial Prize

Royal Society of Literature, 1 Hyde Park Gardens, London W2 2LT
☎0171 723 5104   Fax 0171 402 0199

ESTABLISHED 1966 by Vera Brittain who gave a sum of money to the RSL to provide an annual prize in honour of Winifred Holtby who died at the age of 37. Administered by the **Royal Society of Literature**. The prize is for the best regional novel of the year written in the English language. The writer must be of British or Irish nationality, or a citizen of the Commonwealth. Translations, unless made by the author himself of his own work, are not eligible for consideration. If in any year it is considered that no regional novel is of sufficient merit the prize money may be awarded to an author, qualified as aforesaid, of a literary work of non-fiction or poetry, concerning a regional subject. Publishers are invited to submit works (three copies of each) published during the current year to the Secretary, labelled 'Winifred Holtby Prize'. Final entry date 31 October. Previous winners: Paul Watkins *Archangel*; Jim Crace *Signals of Distress*; Carl MacDougall *The Lights Below*.
Prize £800.

L. Ron Hubbard's Writers of the Future Contest

PO Box 218, East Grinstead, West Sussex RH19 4GH
Contest Administrator *Andrea Grant-Webb*

ESTABLISHED 1984 by L. Ron Hubbard to encourage new and amateur writers of science fiction, fantasy and horror. Quarterly awards with an annual grand prize. Entrants must submit a short story of up to 10,000 words, or a novelette less than 17,000 words, which must not have been previously published. The contest is open only to those who have been published professionally. Previous winners: R. Gregory, Edwina Mayer, M. W. Keiper,

Arlene C. Harris, Russell William Asplund. Send s.a.e. for entry form.

Prizes (1st) £640, (2nd) £480 and (3rd) £320 each quarter; Annual Grand Prize: £2,500. All winners are awarded a trip to the annual L. Ron Hubbard Achievement Awards which include a series of professional writers' workshops, and are published in the *L. Ron Hubbard Presents Writers of the Future* anthology.

Ilkley Literature Festival Poetry Competition

Manor House Museum, Ilkley, West Yorkshire LS29 9DT
☎01943 601210

Contact *David Porter*

Annual open poetry competition run by the **Ilkley Literature Festival**. Final entry date August each year. entry fee: £2.50 per poem. Previous winners: Anthony Dunn, John Sewell.

Prize (total) £600.

The Richard Imison Memorial Award

The Society of Authors, 84 Drayton Gardens, London SW10 9SB
☎0171 373 6642   Fax 0171 373 5768

Contact *The Secretary, The Broadcasting Committee*

Annual award established 'to perpetuate the memory of Richard Imison, to acknowledge the encouragement he gave to writers working in the medium of radio, and in memory of the support and friendship he invariably offered writers in general, and radio writers in particular'. Administered by the Society of Authors, the purpose is 'to encourage new talent and high standards in writing for radio by selecting the radio drama by a writer new to radio which, in the opinion of the judges, is the best of those submitted. An adaptation for radio of a piece originally written for the stage, television or film will not be eligible. Any radio drama first transmitted in the UK between 1 January and 31 December by a writer or writers new to radio, is eligible, provided the work is an original piece for radio and it is the first dramatic work by the writer(s) that has been broadcast. Submission may be made by any party to the production in the form of two copies of an audio cassette (not-returnable) accompanied by a nomination form. 1996 winner: Lee Hall *I Love U Jimmy Spud*.

Prize £1000.

The Independent/Scholastic Story of the Year

Postal box address changes each year (see below)

ESTABLISHED 1993. Open competition for the best short story for children aged 6–9. One story per entrant (between 1500–2500 words). Details of the competition, including the postal box address, are published in *The Independent* in March/April of each year.

Prize £2000; two runners-up of £500 each. The winning story will be published in the newspaper and in an anthology published by **Scholastic Children's Books**, along with a selection of the best entries.

The International IMPAC Dublin Literary Award

Dublin City Public Libraries, Administrative Headquarters, Cumberland House, Fenian Street, Dublin 2, Republic of Ireland
☎00 353 1 6619000   Fax 00 353 1 6761628

ESTABLISHED 1995. Sponsored by a US-based management consultancy firm, IMPAC, this prize is awarded for a work of fiction written and published in the English language or written in a language other than English and published in English translation. Initial nominations are made through municipal public libraries in world capital cities, each library putting forward three books to the panel of judges in Dublin. 1997 winner: Javier Maras *A Heart So White*.

Prize IR£100,000.

International Reading Association Literacy Award

International Reading Association, 800 Barksdale Road, PO Box 8139, Newark, Delaware 19714-8139, USA
☎001 302 731 1600   Fax 001 302 731 1057

Director of Research *Terry Salinger*

The International Reading Association is a non-profit education organisation devoted to improving reading instruction and promoting literacy worldwide. In addition to the US $10,000 award presented each year on International Literacy Day (September 8), the organisation gives more than 25 awards in recognition of achievement in reading research, writing for children, media coverage of literacy, and literacy instruction.

International Student Playscript Competition

See **University College, Scarborough** under **Writers' Courses, Circles and Workshops**

Irish Times International Fiction Prize

The Irish Times Ltd, 10–16 D'Olier Street, Dublin 2, Republic of Ireland
☎00 353 1 679 2022   Fax 00 353 1 670 9383

Administrator, Book Prizes *Gerard Cavanagh*

FOUNDED 1989. Biennial award to the author of a work of fiction written in the English language and published in Ireland, the UK or the US in the two years of the award. Next award to be announced in October 1997, the short list having been announced in September. Books are nominated by literary critics and editors only. Previous winners: J. M. Coetzee *The Master of Petersburg*; E. Annie Proulx *The Shipping News*; Norman Rush *Mating*; Louis Begley *Wartime Lies*.
Prize IR£7500.

Irish Times Irish Literature Prizes

The Irish Times Ltd, 10–16 D'Olier Street, Dublin 2, Republic of Ireland
☎00 353 1 679 2022   Fax 00 353 1 670 9383

Administrator, Book Prizes *Gerard Cavanagh*

FOUNDED 1989. Biennial prizes awarded in three different categories: fiction (a novel, novella or collection of short stories), non-fiction prose (history, biography, autobiography, criticism, politics, sociological interest, travel, current affairs and belles-lettres), and poetry (collection or a long poem or a sequence of poems, or a revised/updated edition of a previously published selection/collection). The author must have been born in Ireland or be an Irish citizen, but may live in any part of the world. Books are nominated by literary editors and critics, and are then called in from publishers. Previous winners: Paddy Devlin *Straight Left* (non-fiction); Kathleen Ferguson *A Maid's Tale* (fiction); Robert Greacen *Collected Poems* (poetry); Brian Keenan *An Evil Cradling*; John MacKenna *The Fallen and Other Stories*.
Prizes IR£5,000 each category.

Jewish Quarterly Literary Prizes

PO Box 2078, London W1A 1JR
☎0171 629 5004   Fax 0171 629 5110

Contact *Gerald Don*

Formerly the H. H. Wingate Prize. Annual awards (one for fiction and one for non-fiction) for works which best stimulate an interest in and awareness of themes of Jewish interest. Books must have been published in the UK in the year of the award and be written in English by an author resident in Britain, Commonwealth, Israel, Republic of Ireland or South Africa. Previous winners: Amos Oz *Black Box*; Anton Gill *The Journey Back from Hell*; Bernice Rubens *Kingdom Come*; Leo Abse *Wotan My Enemy*; Ronald Harwood *Home*; Alan Isler *The Prince of West End Avenue*; Theo Richmond *Konin: A Quest*.
Prizes Fiction: £4000; Non-fiction: £3000; Poetry: £1000.

Mary Vaughan Jones Award

Cyngor Llyfrau Cymru (Welsh Books Council), Castell Brychan, Aberystwyth, Dyfed SY23 2JB
☎01970 624151   Fax 01970 625385

Contact *The Administrator*

Triennial award for distinguished services in the field of children's literature in Wales over a considerable period of time.
Award Silver trophy.

Kent & Sussex Poetry Society Open Competition

8 Edward Street, Southborough, Tunbridge Wells, Kent TN4 0HP
☎01892 543862

Chairman *Clive R. Eastwood*

After 1996 this open poetry competition will become biennial and, therefore, will not run in 1997. No details available for 1998 at the time of going to press. Queries to the Chairman.

Kent Short Story Competition

Kent Literature Festival, The Metropole Arts Centre, The Leas, Folkestone, Kent CT20 2LS
☎01303 255070

Contact *Ann Fearey*

ESTABLISHED 1992. For a short story of up to 3000 words by anyone over the age of 16. Sponsored by Midland Bank and supported by **South East Arts** and Shepway District Council. Send s.a.e. for entry forms, available from March.
Prizes (1st) £275; (2nd) £150; (3rd) £100.

Kraszna-Krausz Book Awards

122 Fawnbrake Avenue, London SE24 0BZ
☎0171 738 6701   Fax 0171 738 6701

Administrator *Andrea Livingstone*

ESTABLISHED 1985. Annual award to encourage and recognise ourstanding achievements in the publishing and writing of books on the art, practice, history and technology of photography and the moving image (film, television, video and related screen media). Books in any language, published worldwide, are eligible. Entries must be submitted by publishers only. Prizes for books on still photography alternate annually with those for books on the moving image (1997: moving image). Previous winners: Eve Arnold *In Retrospect*; Larry J. Schaaf *Records of the Dawn of Photography*.

Prizes £10,000 in each of the main categories; £1000 special commendations.

Lakeland Book of the Year Awards

Cumbria Tourist Board, Ashleigh, Holly Road, Windermere, Cumbria LA23 2AQ
☎015394 44444   Fax 015394 44041
Contact *Regional Publicity Officer*

Four annual awards set up by Cumbrian author Hunter Davies and the Cumbria Tourist Board. The **Hunter Davies Prize** was established in 1984 and is awarded for the book which best helps visitors or residents enjoy a greater love or understanding of any aspect of life in Cumbria and the Lake District. Three further awards were set up in 1993 with funding from the private sector: **The Tullie House Prize** is for the book which best helps develop a greater appreciation of the built and/or natural environment of Cumbria; **The Barclays Bank Prize** is for the best small book on any aspect of Cumbrian life, its people or culture, and **The Border Television Prize** is for the book which best illustrates the beauty and character of Cumbria. Final entry date mid-March. 1996 winners: Hunter Davies Prize: June Thistlethwaite *Cumbrian Women Remember*; Border Television Prize: Mary E. Burkett and David Sloss *Read's Point of View*; Barclays Bank Prize: Ethel Fisher *Seaton Past and Present*; Tullie House Prize: Susan Denyer and Janet Martin *The National Trust: A Century in the Lake District*.

Prize £100 and certificate.

Lancashire County Library/NWB Children's Book of the Year Award

Lancashire County Library Headquarters, 143 Corporation Street, Preston, Lancashire PR1 2UQ
☎01772 264010   Fax 01772 555919
Assistant County Librarian, Operations and Development *D. G. Lightfoot*

ESTABLISHED 1986. Annual award sponsored by the National Westminster Bank for a work of original fiction suitable for 11–14-year-olds. The winner is chosen by 13–14-year-old secondary school pupils in Lancashire. Books must have been published between 1 September and 31 August in the year of the award and authors must be UK residents. Final entry date 1 September each year. Previous winners: Robert Westall *Gulf*; Brian Jacques *Salamandastron*; Robin Jarvis *The Whitby Witches*; Ian Strachan *The Boy in the Bubble*; Garry Kilworth *The Electric Kid*.

Prize £500 plus engraved glass decanter.

The Library Association Besterman Medal

7 Ridgmount Street, London WC1E 7AE
☎0171 636 7543   Fax 0171 436 7218

ESTABLISHED 1970. Sponsored by Whitaker Bibliographic Services. Awarded annually for an outstanding bibliography or guide to literature first published in the UK during the preceding year. Recommendations for the award are invited from members of **The Library Association**. Among criteria taken into consideration in making the award are: authority of the work and quality of articles or entries; accessibility and arrangement of the information; scope and coverage; quality of indexing; adequacy of references; accuracy of information; physical presentation; and the originality of the work. Previous winners include: Heather Creaton *Bibliography of Printed Works on London History to 1939*; John McIlwaine *Africa: A Guide to Reference Material*; Katherine Pantzer *A Short-title Catalogue of Books Printed in England, Scotland, Ireland and English Books Printed Abroad 1475–1640 Vol 3*.

Award Medal.

The Library Association Carnegie Medal

7 Ridgmount Street, London WC1E 7AE
☎0171 636 7543   Fax 0171 436 7218

ESTABLISHED 1936. Sponsored by Peters Library Service. Presented for an outstanding book for children written in English and first published in the UK during the preceding year. This award is not necessarily restricted to books of an imaginative nature. Previous winners include: Anne Fine *Flour Babies*; Theresa Breslin *Whispers in the Graveyard*.

Award Medal.

The Library Association Kate Greenaway Medal

7 Ridgmount Street, London WC1E 7AE
☎0171 636 7543   Fax 0171 436 7218

ESTABLISHED 1955. Sponsored by Peters Library Service. Presented annually for the most distinguished work in the illustration of children's books first published in the UK during the preceding year. Previous winners include: Alan Lee *Black Ships Before Troy*; Gregory Rogers *Way Home*.

Award Medal.

The Library Association McColvin Medal

7 Ridgmount Street, London WC1E 7AE
☎0171 636 7543   Fax 0171 436 7218

ESTABLISHED 1970. Sponsored by Whitaker Bibliographic Services. Annual award for an outstanding reference book first published in the UK during the preceding year. Books eligible for consideration include: encyclopedias, general and special; dictionaries, general and special; biographical dictionaries; annuals, yearbooks and directories; handbooks and compendia of data; atlases. Recommendations invited from members of **The Library Association**. Previous winners include: Colin Matthew *The Gladstone Diaries*; Ray Desmond *Dictionary of British and Irish Botanists*; Edward Peget-Tomlinson *The Illustrated History of Canal and River Navigation*.

Award Medal.

The Library Association Walford Award

7 Ridgemount Street, London WC1E 7AE
☎0171 636 7543   Fax 0171 436 7218

Awarded to an individual who has made a sustained and continual contribution to British bibliography over a period of years. The nominee need not be resident in the UK. The award is named after Dr A. J. Walford, a bibliograper of international repute. Previous winners include: Prof. Stanley Wells, Prof. J. D. Pearson and Prof. R. C. Alston

Award Cash prize and certificate.

The Library Association Wheatley Medal

7 Ridgmount Street, London WC1E 7AE
☎0171 636 7543   Fax 0171 436 7218

ESTABLISHED 1962. Sponsored by Whitaker Bibliographic Services. Annual award for an outstanding index first published in the UK during the preceding three years. Whole work must have originated in the UK and recommendations for the award are invited from members of **The Library Association**, the **Society of Indexers**, publishers and others. Previous winners include: Elizabeth Moys *British Tax Encyclopedia*; Paul

Nash *The World of Environment 1972–1992*; Richard Raper *The Works of Charles Darwin*.

Award Medal.

Lichfield Prize

c/o Tourist Information Centre, Donegal House, Bore Street, Lichfield, Staffordshire WS13 6NE
☎01543 252109   Fax 01543 417308

Contact *Mrs Alison Bessey* at Lichfield District Council on 01543 414000 ext. 2047

ESTABLISHED 1988. Biennial award initiated by Lichfield District Council to coincide with the Lichfield Festival. Run in conjunction with James Redshaw Booksellers of Lichfield and 1997 Prize co-sponsors, **Hodder & Stoughton** publishers. Awarded for a previously unpublished novel set in the Lichfield district area, and contemporary or historical, but not futuristic. Previous winners include: Valerie Kershaw *Rockabye*; Gary Coyne *The Short Caution*. Next award 1999. Final entry date in April of that year.

Prize £5000, plus possible publication.

Literary Review Grand Poetry Competition

See *Literary Review* under **Magazines**

Lloyds Private Banking Playwright of the Year Award

Tony Ball Associates Plc, 174–178 North Gower Street, London NW1 2NB
☎0171 380 0953   Fax 0171 387 9004

Contact *Stephen Harrison*

LAUNCHED in February 1994. The Award aims to provide support and encouragement for writing talent to flourish and gain greater recognition, as well as to help widen interest in regional and London theatres. Playwrights must be of British or Irish nationality and have written a new play which was first performed in the previous year. Nominations are made by theatre critics from which a shortlist of ten is selected. The winner is announced in February/March. 1996 winner: Peter Whelan *The Herbal Bed*.

Prize £25,000.

London Writers Competition

See **Wandsworth London Writers Competition**

Longman-*History Today* Book of the Year Award

c/o *History Today*, 20 Old Compton Street, London W1V 5PE
☎0171 439 8315

Contact *Gordon Marsden, Marion Soldan*

ESTABLISHED 1993. Annual award set up as joint initiative between the magazine *History Today* and the publisher **Addison Wesley Longman** to mark the past links between the two organisations, to encourage new writers, and to promote a wider public understanding of, and enthusiasm for, the study and publication of history. Submissions are made by publishers only. Previous winners: Orlando Figes *A People's Tragedy: The Russian Revolution 1891–1924*; Paul Binski *Westminster Abbey and the Plantagenets*; Nicholas Timmins *Five Giants: A Biography of the Welfare State*.

Prize £1000.

Lost Poet

PO Box 136, Norwich, Norfolk NR3 3LJ
☎01603 440944   Fax 01603 440940
Contact *Tricia Frances*

Lost Poet runs four literary competitons per year. All profits go to the work of The Light Foundation whose aim is to 'help the population become more aware of personal, planetary and evolutionary issues'. For more details, send s.a.e. to the above address.

Prizes reflect the amount of entries received.

Sir William Lyons Award

The Guild of Motoring Writers,
30 The Cravens, Smallfield, Surrey
RH6 9QS
☎01342 843294   Fax 01342 844093
Contact *Sharon Scott-Fairweather*

An annual competitive award to encourage young people in automotive journalism and to foster interests in motoring and the motor industry. Entrance by two essays and interview with Awards Committee. Applicants must be British, aged 17–23 and resident in UK. Final entry date 1 August. Presentation date December.

Award £1000 plus trophy.

McColvin Medal

See **The Library Association McColvin Medal**

Agnes Mure Mackenzie Award

The Saltire Society, 9 Fountain Close, 22 High Street, Edinburgh EH1 1TF
☎0131 556 1836   Fax 0131 557 1675
Administrator *Kathleen Munro*

ESTABLISHED 1965. Biennial award in memory of the late Dr Agnes Mure Mackenzie for a published work of distinguished Scottish historical research of scholarly importance (including intellectual history and the history of science). Editions of texts are not eligible. The 1998 award is open to books published between 1st January 1997 and 31st December 1998. Nominations are invited and should be sent to the Administrator.

Prize Bound and inscribed copy of the winning publication.

W. J. M. Mackenzie Book Prize

Political Studies Association, Dept of Politics, University of Nottingham, Nottingham NG7 2RD
☎0115 9514797   Fax 0115 9514859
PSA Administrative Secretary *Lynn Corken*

ESTABLISHED 1987. Annual award to best work of political science published in the UK during the previous year. Submissions from publishers only. Final entry date in March. Previous winners: James Mayall *Nationalism and International Society*; Brian Barry *Theories of Justice*; Avi Shlaim *Collusion Across the Jordan*; Colin Crouch *Industrial Relations and European State Tradition*; Iain Hampsher-Monk *A History of Modern Political Thought*; Patrick Dunleavy *Democracy, Bureaucracy and Public Choice*.

Prize £100, plus travel/attendance at three-day annual conference.

McKitterick Prize

Society of Authors, 84 Drayton Gardens, London SW10 9SB
☎0171 373 6642   Fax 0171 373 5768
Contact *Awards Secretary*

Annual award for a full-length work in the English language, first published in the UK or unpublished. Open to writers over 40 who have not had any adult novel published other than the one submitted. Closing date 16 December. 1997 winner: Patricia Duncker *Hallucinating Foucault*.

Prize £4–5000.

Enid McLeod Prize

Franco–British Society, Room 623,
Linen Hall, 162–168 Regent Street, London
W1R 5TB
☎0171 734 0815   Fax 0171 734 0815
Executive Secretary *Mrs Marian Clarke*

ESTABLISHED 1982. Annual award to the author of the work of literature published in the UK which, in the opinion of the judges, has contributed most to Franco-British understanding. Any full-length work written in English by a citizen of the UK, Commonwealth, Republic of Ireland, Pakistan, Bangladesh and South

Africa. No English translation of a book written originally in any other language will be considered. Nominations from publishers for books published between 1 January and 31 December of the year of the prize. Previous winners: Gillian Tindall *Célestiné, Voices from a French Village*; Jonathan Keates *Stendhal*; Sebastian Faulks *Birdsong*; Margaret Crosland *Simone de Beauvoir – The Woman and Her Work*; Frank Giles *The Locust Years*.

Prize Cheque.

Macmillan Prize for a Children's Picture Book

Macmillan Children's Books, 25 Eccleston Place, London SW1W 9NF

☎0171 881 8000   Fax 0171 881 8001

Contact *Marketing Dept., Macmillan Children's Books*

Set up in order to stimulate new work from young illustrators in art schools, and to help them start their professional lives. Fiction or non-fiction. **Macmillan** have the option to publish any of the prize winners.

Prizes (1st) £1000; (2nd) £500; (3rd) £250.

Macmillan Silver PEN Award

The English Centre of International PEN, 7 Dilke Street, London SW3 4JE

☎0171 352 6303   Fax 0171 351 0220

Sponsored by **Macmillan Publishers**. An annual award for a volume of short stories written in English by a British author and published in the UK in the year preceding the prize. Nominations by the PEN Executive Committee only. Previous winners: Jane Gardham *Going into a Dark House*; Nicola Barker *Love Your Enemies*; Clive Collins *Misunderstandings*; John Arden *Cogs Tyrannic*; Pauline Melville *Shape-Shifter*. 1996 winner: Fay Weldon *Wicked Women*.

Prize £500, plus silver pen.

The Mail on Sunday Novel Competition

Postal box address changes each year (see below)

Annual award ESTABLISHED 1983. Judges look for a story/character that springs to life in the 'tantalising opening 50–150 words of a novel'. Details of the competition, including the postal box address, are published in *The Mail on Sunday* each summer. Previous winners: Jill Roe, Judy Astley, Simon Levack, Sarah Cooper, Terry Eccles, Jillian Hart.

Awards (1st) £400 book tokens and a weekend writing course at the **Arvon Foundation**; (2nd) £300 tokens; (3rd) £200 tokens; three runners-up receive £150 tokens each.

The Mail on Sunday/John Llewellyn Rhys Prize

Book Trust, Book House, 45 East Hill, London SW18 2QZ

☎0181 870 9055   Fax 0181 874 4790

Contact *Sandra Vince*

ESTABLISHED 1942. An annual young writer's award for a memorable work of any kind. Entrants must be under the age of 35 at the time of publication; books must have been published in the UK in the year of the award. The author must be a citizen of Britain or the Commonwealth, writing in English. Previous winners: Matthew Kneale *Sweet Thames*; Jason Goodwin *On Foot to the Golden Horn*. 1996 winner: Melanie McGrath *Motel Nirvana*.

Prize £5000 (1st); £500 for shortlisted entries.

Marsh Award for Children's Literature in Translation

Authors' Club, 40 Dover Street, London W1X 3RB

☎0171 499 8581   Fax 0171 409 0913

Contact *Mrs Ann Carter*

ESTABLISHED 1995 and sponsored by the Marsh Christian Trust, the award aims to encourage translation of foreign children's books into English. It is a biennial award (first year: 1996), open to British translators of books for 4–16-year-olds, published in the UK by a British publisher. Any category will be considered with the exception of encyclopedias and reference. No electronic books. First winner: Anthea Bell *A Dog's Life* by Christine Nostlinger.

Prize £750.

Marsh Biography Award

Authors' Club, 40 Dover Street, London W1X 3RB

☎0171 499 8581   Fax 0171 409 0913

Contact *Mrs Ann Carter*

A biennial award for the most significant biography published over a two-year period by a British publisher. Previous winners: Hugh & Mirabel Cecil *Clever Hearts*; Patrick Marnham *The Man Who Wasn't Maigret*; Selina Hastings *Evelyn Waugh*. Next award October 1997.

Award £3500, plus silver trophy presented at a dinner.

Kurt Maschler Award

Book Trust, Book House, 45 East Hill,
London SW18 2QZ
☎0181 870 9055   Fax 0181 874 4790
Contact *Sandra Vince*

ESTABLISHED 1982. Annual award for 'a work
of imagination in the children's field in which
text and illustration are of excellence and so
presented that each enhances, yet balances the
other'. Books published in the current year in
the UK by a British author and/or artist, or by
someone resident for ten years, are eligible.
Previous winners: Kathy Henderson and
Patrick Benson *The Little Boat*; Trish Cooke,
illus. Helen Oxenbury *So Much*; Karen Wallace,
illus. Mike Bostock *Think of an Eel*; Raymond
Briggs *The Man*; Colin McNaughton *Have You
Seen Who's Just Moved in Next Door to Us?*. 1996
winner: Babette Cole *Drop Dead*.
Award £1000 plus bronze Emil trophy.

MCA Book Prize

122 Fawnbrake Avenue, London SE24 0BZ
☎0171 738 6701   Fax 0171 738 6701
Administrator *Andrea Livingstone*

ESTABLISHED 1993. Annual award sponsored
by the Management Consultancies Association
to recognise and reward books that contribute
stimulating, original and progressive ideas on
management. Entries should have been published first in the UK during the calendar year
of the Award and written by British subjects
living in the UK. Submissions by publishers
only. Previous winners: Colin Egan *Creating
Organizational Advantage*; Clive Morton
Becoming World Class; Richard Whittington
What is Strategy and Does it Matter?.
Prizes £5000 for best management book. In
addition, a prize of £2000 for best management book by a writer under 35 may be given.

Meyer-Whitworth Award

Arts Council of England, 14 Great Peter
Street, London SW1P 3NQ
☎0171 333 0100 ext 431   Fax 0171 973 6590
Contact *The Drama Director*

In 1908 the movement for a National Theatre
joined forces with that to create a memorial to
William Shakespeare. The result was the
Shakespeare Memorial National Theatre
Committee, the embodiment of the campaign
for a National Theatre. This award, bearing the
name of but two protagonists in the movement, has been established to commemorate all
those who worked for the SMNT. Endowed
by residual funds of the SMNT, the award is
intended to help further the careers of UK
playwrights who are not yet established, and to
draw contemporary theatre writers to the public's attention. The award is given to the writer
whose play most nearly satisfies the following
criteria: a play which embodies Geoffrey
Whitworth's dictum that 'drama is important
in so far as it reveals the truth about the relationships of human beings with each other and
the world at large'; a play which shows promise
of a developing new talent; a play in which the
writing is of individual quality. Nominations
from professional theatre companies. Plays
must have been written in the English language
and produced professionally in the UK in the
12 months preceding the award.
Award £8000.

MIND Book of the Year/ Allen Lane Award

Granta House, 15–19 Broadway, London
E15 4BQ
☎0181 519 2122 ext. 225 Fax 0181 522 1725

ESTABLISHED 1981. Annual award, in memory
of Sir Allen Lane, for the author of a book
published in the current year (fiction or non-
fiction), which furthers public understanding of
mental health problems. Previous winners:
Sapphire *Push*; Linda Hart *Phone at Nine Just to
Say You're Alive*.
Award £1000.

The Mitchell Prize for Art History/The Eric Mitchell Prize

c/o The Burlington Magazine, 14–16 Duke's
Road, London WC1H 9AD
☎0171 388 8157   Fax 0171 388 1230
Executive Director *Caroline Elam*

ESTABLISHED 1977 by art collector, philan-
thropist and businessman, Jan Mitchell, to draw
attention to exceptional achievements in the history of art. Consists of two prizes: The Mitchell
Prize, given for an outstanding and original contribution to the study and understanding of
visual arts, and The Eric Mitchell Prize, given for the
most outstanding first book in this field. The
prizes are awarded to authors of books in English
that have been published in the previous 12
months (i.e. 1 January – 31 December 1996 for
the 1997 award). Books are submitted by publishers before the end of February. Previous winners: The Mitchell Prize: *Colour and Culture* John
Gage; The Eric Mitchell Prize: *Fra Angelico at
San Marco* William Hood.
Prizes $15,000 (Mitchell Prize); $5000 (Eric
Mitchell Prize)

Scott Moncrieff Prize

The Translators Association, 84 Drayton Gardens, London SW10 9SB
☎0171 373 6642

Contact *Kate Pool*

An annual award for the best translation published by a British publisher during the previous year of a French work, which must have been published within the last 150 years. Previous winners include: David Coward for his translation of *Belle de Seigneur* by Albert Cohen.

Prize £1000.

The Montagu of Beaulieu Trophy

Guild of Motoring Writers, 30 The Cravens, Smallfield, Surrey RH6 9QS
☎01342 843294   Fax 01342 844093

Contact *Sharon Scott-Fairweather*

First presented by Lord Montagu on the occasion of the opening of the National Motor Museum at Beaulieu in 1972. Awarded annually to a member of the **Guild of Motoring Writers** who, in the opinion of the nominated jury, has made the greatest contribution to recording in the English language the history of motoring or motor cycling in a published book or article, film, television or radio script, or research manuscript available to the public.

Prize Trophy.

The Mother Goose Award

See **The BFC Mother Goose Award**

Shiva Naipaul Memorial Prize

The Spectator, 56 Doughty Street, London WC1N 2LL
☎0171 405 1706   Fax 0171 242 0603

Contact *Emma Bagnall*

ESTABLISHED 1985. Annual prize given to an English language writer of any nationality under the age of 35 for an essay of not more than 4000 words describing a culture alien to the writer. Final entry date is in March. Previous winner: Miranda France.

Prize £3000.

NASEN Special Educational Needs Awards

The Educational Publishers Council, The Publishers Association, 19 Bedford Square, London WC1B 3HJ
☎0171 580 6321   Fax 0171 636 5375

ESTABLISHED 1992. Organised by the National Association for Special Education Needs (NASEN) and the **Educational Publishers Council**. Two awards: the *Academic Book Award*, for a book which enhances the knowledge and understanding of those engaged in the education of children with special needs; the *Children's Book Award*, for a book written for children under the age of 16 which does most to put forward a positive image of children with special education needs. Books must have been published in the UK within the two years preceding the award. Previous winners: Paul Greenhalgh *Emotional Growth and Learning* (Academic); David Hill *See ya, Simon* (Children's).

Prize £500.

NCR Book Award for Non-Fiction

NCR, 206 Marylebone Road, London NW1 6LY
☎0171 725 8253   Fax 0171 724 6519

Contact *The Administrator*

ESTABLISHED 1987 (first award made 1988), the NCR Book Award for Non-Fiction is for a book written in English by a living writer from Britain, the Commonwealth or Republic of Ireland, and published in the UK. One of the UK's single most valuable annual book prizes, with a total prize money of £31,000, and the only major prize specifically for non-fiction. Only publishers may submit titles, limited to three per imprint. The award covers all areas of adult non-fiction except academic, guidebooks and practical listings (such as cookery books). Titles must be published in the 12 months between 1 April and 31 March. A shortlist of four books is announced in mid-April and the winning book in early/mid-May. The aim of the award is to stimulate interest in non-fiction writing, reading and publishing in the UK. 1997 winner: Orlando Figes *A People's Tragedy*.

Prizes(1st) £25,000 and computer equipment; three runners-up shortlisted £1500 and computer equipment.

Nobel Prize

The Nobel Foundation, PO Box 5232, 102 45 Stockholm, Sweden
☎00 46 8 663 0920   Fax 00 46 8 660 3847

Contact *Information Section*

Awarded yearly for outstanding achievement in physics, chemistry, physiology or medicine, literature and peace. FOUNDED by Alfred Nobel, a chemist who proved his creative ability by inventing dynamite. In general, individuals cannot nominate someone for a Nobel Prize. The rules vary from prize to prize but the following are eligible to do so for Literature: members of the Swedish Academy and of other academies, institutions and societies similar to it in membership and aims; professors of history of literature or of languages at universities or colleges; Nobel Laureates in Literature; presidents of authors' organisations which are representative of the literary activities of their respective countries. British winners of the literature prize, first granted in 1901, include Rudyard Kipling, John Galsworthy and Winston Churchill. Recent winners: Seamus Heaney; Camilio Jose Cela (Spain); Octavio Paz (Mexico); Nadine Gordimer (South Africa); Derek Walcott (St Lucia); Toni Morrison (USA); Kenzaburo Oe (Japan). Nobel Laureate in Literature 1996: Ms Wislawa Szymborska (Poland).

Prize 1996: SEK7,400,000 (about £700,000), increasing each year to cover inflation.

The Noma Award for Publishing Africa

PO Box 128, Witney, Oxfordshire OX8 5XU
☎01993 775235   Fax 01991 709265
Contact *Mary Jay, Secretary to the Managing Committee*

ESTABLISHED 1979. Annual award, founded by the late Shoici Noma, President of Kodansha Ltd, Tokyo, to encourage the publication of works by African writers and scholars within Africa. The award is for an outstanding book, published in Africa by an African writer, in three categories: scholarly and academic; literature and creative writing; children's books. Entries, by publishers only, by 31 March for a title published in the previous year. Previous winners: Paul Tiyambe Zeleza *A Modern Economic History of Africa – Vol 1: The Nineteenth Century*; Marlene van Niekerk *Triomf.*

Prize US$ 10,000 and presentation plaque.

Northern Short Stories Competition

ARC Publications, Nanholme Mill, Shaw Wood Road, Todmorden, Lancashire OL14 6DA
☎01706 812338   Fax 01706 818948
Contact *Rosemary Jones*

ESTABLISHED 1988. Annual award set up to stimulate the writing and reading of quality short fiction. Open to all living in the area covered by the three Northern regional arts boards (**North West Arts**, **Northern Arts**, **Yorkshire & Humberside Arts**) as well as Derbyshire and Lincolnshire. Final entry date 30 June. Please send s.a.e. for entry forms which are available from March onwards.

Prize Guaranteed same-year publication in anthology, plus small cash prize.

C. B. Oldman Prize

Aberdeen University Library, Queen Mother Library, Meston Walk, Aberdeen AB9 2UE
☎01224 272592   Fax 01224 487048
Contact *Richard Turbet*

ESTABLISHED 1989 by the International Association of Music Libraries, UK Branch. Annual award for best book of music bibliography, librarianship or reference published the year before last (i.e. books published in 1996 considered for the 1998 prize). Previous winners: Andrew Ashbee, Michael Talbot, Donald Clarke, John Parkinson, John Wagstaff, Stanley Sadie, William Waterhouse, Richard Turbet.

Prize £150.

One Voice Monologue Competition

c/o Pro Forma, Box 29, Neath, West Glamorgan SA11 1WL
Contact *Nicola Davies*

ESTABLISHED 1992. An international competition run by playwright Nicola Davies with the support of a team of writers/actors. The competition has been supported by Catrin Collier, Sir Anthony Hopkins, Simon Callow and Miriam Margolyes. Finalists' work is performed at the Finals and published in a glossy illustrated book. The Catrin Collier Random House award enables the winner to spend a day in London with novelist Catrin Collier and an editor from **Random House**. There are two categories: Monologue/Duologue and Story. Please send s.a.e. for entry form. Final entry date October 1998. In 1997, the competition was extended to include a morning of workshops with actors and readers and Q/A sessions with Catrin Collier and editors. Surgeries were also available for entrants to discuss their entries with readers/judges on a one-to-one basis.

Orange Prize for Fiction

Book Trust, 45 East Hill, London SW18 2QZ
☎0181 870 9055   Fax 0181 874 4790
Contact *Sandra Vince*

ESTABLISHED 1996. Annual award founded by a group of senior women in publishing to 'create the opportunity for more women to be rewarded for their work and to be better known by the reading public'. Awarded for a full-length novel written in English by a woman of any nationality, and published in the UK between

1 April and 31 March of the following year. 1996 winner: Helen Dunmore *A Spell of Winter*.

Prize £30,000 and a work of art (a limited edition bronze figurine to be known as 'The Bessie' in acknowledgement of anonymous prize endowment).

The Orwell Prize

The Political Quarterly, 8a Bellevue Terrace, Edinburgh EH7 4DT
☎0131 557 2517   Fax 0131 557 2517
Contact *Bernard Crick*

Jointly ESTABLISHED in 1993 by the George Orwell Memorial Fund and the *Political Quarterly* to encourage and reward writing in the spirit of Orwell's 'What I have most wanted to do ... is to make political writing into an art'. Two categories: book or pamphlet; newspaper and/or articles, features, columns, or sustained reportage on a theme. Submissions by editors or publishers only. Previous winners: Melanie Phillips (journalism); Fergal Keane (book).

Prizes £1000 for each category.

Outposts Poetry Competition

Outposts, 22 Whitewell Road, Frome, Somerset BA11 4EL
☎01373 466653
Contact *Roland John*

Annual competition for an unpublished poem of not more than 40 lines run by **Hippopotamus Press**.

Prize £1000.

OWG/COLA Awards for Excellence

Outdoor Writers' Guild, PO Box 520, Bamber Bridge, Preston, Lancashire PR5 8LF
☎01772 696732   Fax 01772 696732
Contact *Terry Marsh*

ESTABLISHED 1980. Annual award by the **Outdoor Writers' Guild** and the Camping & Outdoor Leisure Association to raise the standard of outdoor writing, journalism and broadcasting. Winning categories include best book, best guidebook, best feature, best technical report. Open to OWG members only. Final entry date March. Previous winners include: Leigh Hatts, Steve Venables, Hazel Constance, Catherine Moore, John and Anne Nuttall, Roland Smith, Terry Marsh, Peter and Leni Gillman, Alastair Macdonald, Richard Gilbert.

Prize (total) £1250.

Catherine Pakenham Award

The Sunday Telegraph, 1 Canada Square, Canary Wharf, London E14 5DT
☎0171 538 6259   Fax 0171 513 2512
Contact *Joanne Henwood*

ESTABLISHED in 1970, the award is designed to ecourage women journalists as they embark on their careers. Open to women aged 18–25 who have had at least one piece of work published. Previous winners: Elizabeth Brooks, Esther Oxford, Polly Toynbee.

Award £1000 and a writing commission with one of the Telegraph publications; three runner-up prizes of £200 each.

Peer Poetry Competition

26(w) Arlington House, Bath Street, Bath BA1 1QN
☎01225 445298
Contact *Competition Editor*

Bi-annual open competition. At least two, preferably more, poems of any type or style required, up to approximately 200 lines or 2000 words, typed in duplicate on two single-sided A4 sheets. Fee £2.50 per side. Winners chosen by the votes of subscribers to *Peer Poetry Magazine* and all successful entrants are published in the magazine. Closing dates: end of April and October. S.a.e. (IRC) essential for replies and return of scripts.

Prizes £120 (1st); £60 (2nd); £30 (3rd).

PEN Awards

See **Macmillan Silver PEN Award; Silver PEN Non-Fiction Award**

Peterloo Poets Open Poetry Competition

2 Kelly Gardens, Calstock, Cornwall PL18 9SA
☎01822 833473
Contact *Lynn Chambers*

ESTABLISHED 1986. Annual competition sponsored by Marks & Spencer for unpublished English language poems of not more than 40 lines. Final entry date 1 March. Previous winners: John Watts, David Craig, Rodney Pybus, Debjani Chatterjee, Donald Atkinson, Romesh Gunesekera, Shafi Ahmed, Anna Crowe, Carol Ann Duffy, Mimi Khalvati, John Lyons, M. R. Peacocke, Carol Shergold, David Simon, Maureen Wilkinson, Chris Woods.

Prize £4000 (1st).

Poetry Business Competition

The Studio, Byram Arcade, Westgate,
Huddersfield, West Yorkshire HD1 1ND
☎01484 434840   Fax 01484 426566

Contact *The Competition Administrator*

ESTABLISHED 1986. Annual award which aims
to discover and publish new writers. Entrants
should submit a manuscript of poems. Entry
fee £15. Winners will have their work published by the **Poetry Business** under the
Smith/Doorstop imprint. Final entry date end
of October. Previous winners include: Pauline
Stainer, Michael Laskey, Mimi Khalvati, David
Morley, Julia Casterton, Liz Cashdan, Moniza
Alvi, Selima Hill. Send s.a.e. for full details.

Prize Publication of full collection; runners-
up have pamphlets; 20 complimentary copies.

Poetry Life Poetry Competition

Poetry Life, 14 Pennington Oval, Lymington,
Hampshire SO41 8BQ

Contact *Adrian Bishop*

ESTABLISHED 1993. Open competition for
original poems in any style which have not
been published in a book. Maximum length of
80 lines. Entry fee of £3 per poem. Send s.a.e.
for details.

Prize £500 (1st); £100 (2nd); £50 each (3rd
& 4th).

The Poetry Society's National Poetry Competition

The Poetry Society, 22 Betterton Street,
London WC2H 9BU
☎0171 240 4810   Fax 0171 240 4818

Contact *Competition Organiser*

One of Britian's major open poetry competitions. Closing date 31 October. Poems on any
theme, up to 40 lines. For rules and entry form
send s.a.e. to the Competition Organiser at the
above address.

Prizes (1st) £5000; (2nd) £1000; (3rd)
£500; 10 commendations of £50 plus a Mont
Blanc pen.

Poetry Update Poem of the Month Competition

3 Fulham Broadway, London SW6 1AA

A monthly competition for poems of any style
and length. No limit to the number of entries
but they must be original work and previously
unpublished. Entry fee of £3 per poem.
Closing date is the last day of every month.

Prize £100. Winning poem will be published in *Poetry Update* on the Internet.

Peter Pook Humorous Novel Competition

See **Emissary Publishing** under **UK Publishers**

The Portico Prize

The Portico Library, 57 Mosley Street,
Manchester M2 3HY
☎0161 236 6785

Contact *Miss Emma Marigliano*

ESTABLISHED 1985. Administered by the
Portico Library in Manchester. Biennial award
(odd-numbered years) for a published work of
fiction or non-fiction set wholly or mainly in
the North-West/Cumbria. Previous winners
include: John Stalker *Stalker*; Alan Hankinson
Coleridge Walks the Fells; Jenny Uglow *Elizabeth
Gaskell: A Habit of Stories*.

Prize £2500.

The Dennis Potter Television Play of the Year Award

Room C210, BBC, Centre House, 56 Wood
Lane, London, W12 7SB
☎0181 576 8536

ESTABLISHED 1994 in memory of the late television playwright to 'bring out courageous and
imaginative voices'. Annual award for writers
who have not had single plays produced on
television. Nominees are put forward by independent and BBC producers. 1996 winner:
John Milarky *Lah a Note to Follow Soh*.

Prize Commission worth £10,000.

Premio Langhe Ceretto – Sei Per La Cultura Del Cibo

Biblioteca Civica 'G. Ferrero', Via Paruzza 1,
12051 Alba, Italy
☎00 39 173 290092   Fax 00 39 173 362075

Contact *Gianfranco Maggi*

ESTABLISHED 1991. Annual award, founded by
the wine company F. Illi Ceretto, for published
works dealing with historical, scientific, dieto-
logical, gastronomical or sociological aspects of
food and wine. Previous winners: E. Gowers,
A. Kanafani-Zahar, J. Bottero.

The Premio Valle Inclán

The Translators Association, 84 Drayton
Gardens, London SW10 9SB
☎0171 383 6642   Fax 0171 373 5768

Contact *Kate Pool*

ESTABLISHED 1996. An annual award for the
best translation published by a British publisher

during the previous year of a work written in the Spanish language.

Prize £1,000.

The Mathew Prichard Award for Short Story Writing

95 Celyn Avenue, Lakeside, Cardiff CF2 6EL
Competition Secretary *Mrs Betty Persen*
Organiser *Philip Beynon*

ESTABLISHED 1996 to provide sponsorship and promote Wales and its writers. Competition open to all writers in English; the final entry date is 1 March each year.

Prizes (1st) £1000; (2 runners-up) £250 each.

Pulitzer Prizes

The Pulitzer Prize Board, 702 Journalism, Columbia University, New York NY 10027, USA
☎001 212 854 3841/2

Awards for journalism in US newspapers, and for published literature, drama and music by American nationals. Deadline 1 February (journalism); 1 March (music); 1 March (drama); 1 July for books published between 1 Jan–30 June, and 1 Nov for books published between 1 July–31 Dec (literature). 1996 winners included: Richard Ford *Independence Day*. Previous winners: Carol Shields *The Stone Diaries*; E. Annie Proulx *The Shipping News*; David Levering Lewis *W. E. B. DuBois*; David Remnick *Lenin's Tomb: The Last Days of the Soviet Empire*.

Puppy Lifeline Short Story and Poetry Competition

Farplace, Sidehead, Westgate, Co Durham DL13 1LE
☎01388 517397   Fax 01388 517397
Contact *Jan Edwards, National Fundraising Officer*

ESTABLISHED 1997 to help raise funds for Puppy Lifeline's rescue and rehoming work. Annual competition for writers and poets. Closing date for entries is 31 July each year. Submissions can be any length up to 5000 words; entry fee of £3 per short story and £2 per poem, payable to Puppy Lifeline. Send s.a.e. for details.

Prizes £100 (story); £60 (poem) plus runners-up prizes.

Real Writers Short Story Competition

PO Box 170, Chesterfield, Derbyshire S40 1FE
ESTABLISHED 1994. Short story competition with two categories: 5000 and 1200 words

maximum. Entry fees: £4 for each 1200-word entry and £3 for each story up to 5000 words. Entry forms giving further details of competition rules available from the above address.

Prizes £200 for each category.

Trevor Reese Memorial Prize

Institute of Commonwealth Studies, University of London, 28 Russell Square, London WC1B 5DS
☎0171 580 5876   Fax 0171 255 2160
Contact *Seminar and Conference Secretary*

ESTABLISHED 1979 with the proceeds of contributions to a memorial fund to Dr Trevor Reese, Reader in Commonwealth Studies at the Institute and a distinguished scholar of imperial history (d.1976). Biennial award (next award 1998) for a scholarly work, usually by a single author, in the field of Imperial and Commonwealth History published in the preceding two years. Final entry date March 1998. All correspondence relating to the prize should be marked *Trevor Reese Memorial Prize*. Previous winner: Professor D. K. Fieldhouse *Merchant Capital and Economic Decolonization: the United Africa Company 1929–1989*.

Prize £1000.

Regional Press Awards

Press Gazette, EMAP Business Communications, 33–39 Bowling Green Lane, London EC1R 0DA
☎0171 505 8000   Fax 0171 505 8220

Comprehensive range of journalist and newspaper awards for the regional press. Five newspapers of the year, by circulation and frequency, and a full list of journalism categories. Open to all regional journalists, whether freelance or staff. June event. Run by the *Press Gazette* .

Renault UK Journalist of the Year Award

Guild of Motoring Writers, 30 The Cravens, Smallfield, Surrey RH6 9QS
☎01342 843294   Fax 01342 844093
Contact *Sharon Scott-Fairweather*

Originally the Pierre Dreyfus Award and ESTABLISHED 1977. Awarded annually by Renault UK Ltd in honour of Pierre Dreyfus, president director general of Renault 1955–75, to the member of the **Guild of Motoring Writers** who is judged to have made the most outstanding journalistic effort during the year.

Prizes (1st) £1500, plus trophy.

The Rhône-Poulenc Prizes for Science Books

COPUS, c/o The Royal Society, 6 Carlton House Terrace, London SW1Y 5AG
☎0171 839 5561 ext. 2580 Fax 0171 451 2693

Contact *Imelda Topping*

ESTABLISHED 1987 by COPUS (Committee on the Public Understanding of Science) with the Science Museum. Sponsored by Rhône-Poulenc. Annual awards for popular non-fiction science and technology books judged to contribute most to the public understanding of science. Books must be published during the previous calendar year in their first English edition in the UK. The prizes, totalling £20,000, are divided between two categories: the Rhône-Poulenc Prize awarded for a book for general readership, and the Junior Prize for books written primarily for young people. Final entry date January. 1996 winners: Arno Karlen *Plague's Progress*; Chris Maynard *The World of Weather* (Junior Prize).

Prizes Rhône-Poulenc Prize £10,000; Junior Prize £10,000.

Rhyme International Prize

c/o Orbis Magazine, 199 The Long Shoot, Nuneaton, Warwickshire CV11 6JQ
☎01203 327440   Fax 01203 327440

Contact *Mike Shields*

ESTABLISHED 1982. Annual competition aimed at promoting rhyming poetry. Minimum entry fee £5 (£2.50 per poem). Entries may fall into two categories: rhymed poems of less than 50 lines; or formal: sonnet, villanelle, etc. Final entry date end September.

Prize (1996 total) £1500.

John Llewellyn Rhys Prize

See **The Mail on Sunday/John Llewellyn Rhys Prize**

Rogers Prize

Academic Trust Funds, Room 234, University of London, Senate House, London WC1E 7HU
☎0171 636 8000 ext. 3147

Contact *The Secretary of the Academic Trust Funds*

Annual award for an essay or dissertation on alternately a medical or surgical subject, which is named and appointed by the University of London – in 1997 for 'An Essay for the Advance in Surgery'. Essays and dissertations must be in English and shall be typewritten or printed and submitted by 30 June.

Prize £250.

Romantic Novelists' Association Major Award

3 Arnesby Lane, Peatling Magna, Leicester LE8 5UN
☎0116 2478330   Fax 0116 2478330

Organiser *Jean Chapman*

ESTABLISHED 1960. Annual award for the best romantic novel of the year, open to non-members as well as members of the **Romantic Novelists' Association**. Novels must be published between specified dates which vary year to year. Authors must be based in the UK. 1997 winner: Susan Gee *The Hours of the Night*. Previous winners include: Rosamunde Pilcher *Coming Home*; Susan Kay *Phantom*; Reay Tannahill *Passing Glory*; Elizabeth Buchan *Consider the Lily*; Charlotte Bingham *A Change of Heart*. Contact the Organiser for entry form.

Award £5000.

Romantic Novelists' Association New Writers Award

RNA, Queen's Farm, 17 Queen Street, Tintinhull, Somerset BA22 8PG

Contact for enquiries *Margaret Graham*

ESTABLISHED 1962, the award is for unpublished writers in the field of the romantic novel. Entrants are required to join the Association as probationary members. Mss entered for this award must be specifically written for it.

Rooney Prize for Irish Literature

Rooney Prize, Strathin, Templecarrig, Delgany, Co. Wicklow, Republic of Ireland
☎00 353 1 287 4769   Fax 00 353 1 287 2595

Contact *Jim Sherwin, Barbara Norman*

ESTABLISHED 1976. Annual award to encourage young Irish writing to develop and continue. Authors must be Irish, under 40 and published. A non-competitive award with no application procedure.

Prize IR£5000.

Royal Economic Society Prize

c/o University of York, York YO1 5DD
☎01904 433764   Fax 01904 433575/9

Contact *Prof. Mike Wickens*

Annual award for the best article published in *The Economic Journal*. Open to members of the Royal Economic Society only. Next award 1998. Final entry date December 1997. Previous winners: Drs O. P. Attanasio & Guglielmo Weber; Prof. M. H. Pesaran; Prof. J. Pemberton.

Prize £3000.

Royal Society of Literature Awards

See **Winifred Holtby Memorial Prize** and **W. H. Heinemann Prize**

The Royal Society of Medicine Prizes

The Society of Authors, 84 Drayton Gardens, London SW10 9SB
☎0171 373 6642   Fax 0171 373 5768
Contact *Jacqueline Granger-Taylor*

Annual award in five categories: textbook, illustrated textbook, atlas, electronic format and first textbook, published in the UK in the year preceding the awards. Previous winners: S. G. Hillier, H.C. Kitchener and J. P. Neilson *Essentials of Reproductive Medicine*; Christopher D. M. Fletcher *Diagnostic Histopathology of Tumors*; Jatin O. Shah *Head and Neck Surgery, 2nd edition*. **The Asher Prize** for a first textbook: Charles Fox and Anthony Pickering *Diabetes in the Real World*.

Prizes £1000 (each category).

The RTZ David Watt Memorial Prize

RTZ Corporation Plc, 6 St James's Square, London SW1Y 4LD
☎0171 930 2399   Fax 0171 930 3249

INITIATED in 1987 to commemorate the life and work of David Watt. Annual award, open to writers currently engaged in writing for newspapers and journals, in the English language, on international and political affairs. The winners are judged as having made 'outstanding contributions towards the greater understanding and promotion of national and international political issues'. Entries must have been published during the year preceding the award. Final entry date 31 March. The 1996 winner was Máire Nic Suibhne for her article 'A paler shade of orange?', published in the *The Guardian Weekend*. Previous winners include: Martin Wolf for 'If you go down to the woods today', published in the *Financial Times*; David Rose for 'Silent Revolution', published in the *Observer*; Martin Woollacott of *The Guardian* for 'Grail or bitter cup?'.

Prize £5000.

Runciman Award

Anglo-Hellenic League, Flat 4, 68 Elm Park Gardens, London SW10 9PB
☎0171 352 2676   Fax 0171 351 5657
Contact *Arthur Foss*

ESTABLISHED 1985. Annual award, founded by the Anglo-Hellenic League and funded by the Onassis Foundation, to promote Anglo-Greek understanding and friendship. Named after Sir Steven Runciman, former chairman of the Anglo-Hellenic League.

Prizes are offered for works in three historical categories: Greece from earliest times to the foundation of Constantinople, capital of the Roman Empire at Byzantium, in 324; Byzantium and post-Byzantium from 324 until 1821; the modern Hellenic world from 1821 to the present.

Awards may be given for a work of fiction, drama or non-fiction; concerned academically or non-academically with the history of any period; biography or autobiography, the arts, archaeology; a guide book or a translation from the Greek of any period.

Final entry date in February; awards presented in May. Previous winners include: *The Empire of Manuel I Komnenos 1143–1180* Paul Magdalino; *Crete: the Battle and the Resistance* Antony Beevor; *A Concise History of Greece* Richard Clogg; *An Introduction to Modern Greek Literature* Roderick Beaton; *The Diffusion of Classical Art in Antiquity* Sir John Boardman.

Awards up to £9000.

The SAGA Prize

Book Trust, Book House, 45 East Hill, London SW18 2QZ
☎0181 870 9055   Fax 0181 874 4790
Contact *Sandra Vince*

ESTABLISHED 1995. Annual award for the best unpublished novel by a black writer born in Great Britain or the Republic of Ireland and having a black African ancestor. Established by Marsha Hunt and sponsored by The SAGA Group. Mss must be unpublished and of no more than 80,000 words. Entry fee of £15 per mss. Final entry date is in June. 1996 winner: Joanna Traynor *Sister Josephine*.

*Prize £3000 plus publication by **Virago Press**.*

Sagittarius Prize

Society of Authors, 84 Drayton Gardens, London SW10 9SB
☎0171 373 6642   Fax 0171 373 5768

ESTABLISHED 1990. For first published novel by an author over the age of 60. Final entry date mid-December. 1997 winner: Barbara Hardy *London Lovers*.

Prize £2000.

The Salaman Prize for Non-Fiction

42 Irwin Avenue, Heworth Green, York
YO3 7TU
☎01904 422464

Contact *A. Mitchell*

ESTABLISHED 1994. Annual award for the best published work of non-fiction by writers living in, born in, or writing about the North of England. Named after Redcliffe Salaman, author of *The History & Social Influence of the Potato*, the prize is awarded in association with the York and District Writers Circle. £4 administration fee for each entry; further details and entry forms from the above address. Final entry date is in May. Previous winners: *Horse Omnibus* Roy Shadwell; *Charlotte Brontë and Her 'Dearest Nell'* Barbara Whitehead; *George Hudson – The Rise and Fall of the Railway King* Brian Bailey.

Prize £150, £50 book tokens, donated by Blackwell's Bookshop, trophy and certificate.

The Saltire Literary Awards

Saltire Society, 9 Fountain Close, 22 High Street, Edinburgh EH1 1TF
☎0131 556 1836   Fax 0131 557 1675

Administrator *Kathleen Munro*

ESTABLISHED 1982. Annual awards, one for Book of the Year, the other for Best First Book by an author publishing for the first time. Open to any author of Scottish descent or living in Scotland, or to anyone who has written a book which deals with either the work and life of a Scot or with a Scottish problem, event or situation. Nominations are invited from editors of leading newspapers, magazines and periodicals. Previous winners: Scottish Book of the Year: *The Kiln* William McIlvanney; Best First Book: *Slattern* Kate Clanchy.

Cash prize.

Sandburg-Livesay Anthology Contest

Mekler & Deahl, Publishers, 237 Prospect Street South, Hamilton, Ontario, Canada L8M 2Z6
☎001 905 312 1779   Fax 001 905 312 8285

Contact *James Deahl, Gilda Mekler*

FOUNDED 1996. Annual award named after the poets Carl Sandburg and Dorothy Livesay to honour their achievement as populist poets. Up to ten poems may be entered for a fee of £5. A copy of the rules is available from the above address. Final entry date 31 October.

Prizes US$100 for the best poem in the anthology.

Schlegel-Tieck Prize

The Translators Association, 84 Drayton Gardens, London SW10 9SB
☎0171 373 6642   Fax 0171 373 5768

Contact *Kate Pool*

An annual award for the best translation of a German 20th-century work of literary merit and interest published by a British publisher during the preceding year. Previous winners include: David McLintock for his translations of *Caesar* by Christian Meier and *Extinction* by Thomas Bernhardt.

Prize £2200.

Scottish Arts Council Book Awards

Scottish Arts Council, 12 Manor Place, Edinburgh EH3 7DD
☎0131 226 6051   Fax 0131 225 9833

Literature Officer *Shonagh Irvine*

A number of awards are given biannually to authors of published books in recognition of high standards in new writing from new and established writers. Authors should be Scottish, resident in Scotland or have published books of Scottish interest. Applications from publishers only.

Award £1000 each.

Scottish Book of the Year

See **The Saltire Literary Awards**

The Scottish Writer of the Year Prize

c/o Book Trust Scotland, The Scottish Book Centre, 137 Dundee Street, Edinburgh EH11 1BG
☎0131 229 3663   Fax 0131 228 4293

Contact *Kathryn Ross*

ESTABLISHED 1987. Sponsored by United Biscuits (Holdings) plc for the best substantial work of an imaginative nature, including TV and radio scripts and writing for children (for 8–16 years), first published, performed, filmed or transmitted between 1st August and 31st July. Writers born in Scotland, or who have Scottish parents, or who have been resident in Scotland for a considerable period, or who take Scotland as their inspiration are all eligible. Submissions accepted in English, Scots or Gaelic. Recent winners: Janice Galloway, William Boyd and Alan Spence.

Prize £10,000, plus £1,000 to each of the other four shortlisted writers.

SCSE Book Prizes

Department of Education Studies, University of Reading, Bulmershe Court, Reading, Berkshire RG6 1HY
☎01189 318861   Fax 01189 318863
Contact *Professor P. Croll*
Annual awards given by the Standing Conference on Studies in Education for the best book on education published during the preceding year and for the best book by a new author. Nomination by members of the Standing Conference and publishers.
Prizes £1000 and £500.

The Seebohm Trophy – Age Concern Book of the Year

1268 London Road, London SW16 4ER
☎0181 679 8000
Contact *Michael Addison, Jane Marsh*
ESTABLISHED 1995. Annual award in memory of the late Lord Seebohm, former President of Age Concern England. Awarded to the author and publisher of a non-fiction title published in the previous calendar year which, in the opinion of the judges, is most successful in promoting the well-being and understanding of older people. Final entry by the end of March for presentation in October. 1996 winner: *Connecting Gender and Ageing: A Sociological Approach* eds. Sara Arber and Jay Ginn.
Prize £1000 (author); Trophy (publisher), for one year.

Bernard Shaw Translation Prize

The Translators Association, 84 Drayton Gardens, London SW10 9SB
☎0171 373 6642   Fax 0171 373 5768
Contact *Kate Pool*
ESTABLISHED 1990. Triennial award funded by the Anglo-Swedish Literary Foundation for the best translation of a Swedish work published in the UK in the three years preceding the closing date. Next entry date 31 December 1999. Winners include: David McDuff for *A Valley in the Midst of Violence* by Gösta Ågren.
Prize £1000.

Signal Poetry for Children Award

Thimble Press, Lockwood, Station Road, South Woodchester, Stroud, Gloucestershire GL5 5EQ
☎01453 873716/872208   Fax 01453 878599
Contact *Nancy Chambers*
This award is given annually for particular excellence in one of the following areas: single-poet collections published for children; poetry anthologies published for children; the body of work of a contemporary poet; critical or educational activity promoting poetry for children. All books for children published in Britain are eligible regardless of the original country of publication. Unpublished work is not eligible. Previous winners include: Philip Gross *The All-Nite Café*; Helen Dunmore *Secrets*.
Award £100 plus certificate designed by Michael Harvey.

André Simon Memorial Fund Book Awards

5 Sion Hill Place, Bath BA1 5SJ
☎01225 336305   Fax 01225 421862
Contact *Tessa Hayward*
ESTABLISHED 1978. Three awards given annually for the best book on drink, best on food and special commendation in either. Previous winners: Rick Stein *Taste of the Sea* (food); Anthony Hanson *Burgundy* and Remington Norman *Rhone Renaissance* (drink book joint winners); Robert Neil *The French, the English and the Oyster* (special award).
Awards £2000 (best books); £1000 (special commendation); £200 to shortlisted books.

Smarties Book Prize

Book Trust, Book House, 45 East Hill, London SW18 2QZ
☎0181 870 9055   Fax 0181 874 4790
Contact *Sandra Vince*
ESTABLISHED 1985 to encourage high standards and stimulate interest in books for children, this prize is given for a children's book (fiction), written in English by a citizen of the UK or an author resident in the UK, and published in the UK in the year ending 31 October. There are three age-group categories: 5 and under, 6–8 and 9–11. Previous winners include: *Oops!* Colin McNaughton (5 and under); *Butterfly Lion* Michael Morpurgo (6–8); *The Firework-maker's Daughter* Philip Pullman (9–11).
Prizes in each category: £2,500 (gold); £1000 (silver); £500 (bronze).

W. H. Smith Literary Award

W. H. Smith Ltd., Audrey House, Ely Place, London EC1N 6SN
☎0171 404 4242 Fax 0171 404 4242 ext. 5653
Contact *Tricia Ryan*
FOUNDED 1959. Annual prize awarded to a UK, Republic of Ireland or Commonwealth citizen for the most oustanding contribution to English

literature, published in English in the UK in the preceding year. Writers cannot submit work themselves. Previous winners include: Alice Munro *Open Secrets*; Vikram Seth *A Suitable Boy*; Michèle Robert *Daughters of the House*; Thomas Pakenham *The Scramble for Africa*; Derek Walcott *Omeros*; 1996 winner: Simon Schama *Landscape and Memory*. Four previous winners have gone on to win the Nobel Prize for Literature – Derek Walcott, Nadine Gordimer, Patrick White and Seamus Heaney.

Prize £10,000.

W. H. Smith's Thumping Good Read Award

W. H. Smith Ltd., Greenbridge Road, Swindon, Wiltshire SN3 3LD
☎01793 562128   Fax 01793 562590
Contact *Catherine Hickson*

ESTABLISHED 1992 to promote new writers of popular fiction. Books must have appeared on W. H. Smith's bestseller list for the first time and must have been published in the 12 months preceding the award. Submissions, made by publishers, are judged by a panel of customers to be the most un-put-down-able from a shortlist of six. Final entry date February each year. Previous winners: Robert Harris *Fatherland*; Thomas Eidson *St Agnes' Stand*; Andrew Klavan *True Crime*. 1997 winner: David Baldacci *Absolute Power*.

Award £5000.

W. H. Smith's Young Writers' Competition

Dept. GWC, PO Box 985, Swindon SN38 7XU
☎01793 451300

Annual awards for poems or prose by anyone in the UK aged 16 or under. There are four age groups. Over 60 individual winners have their work included in a paperback every year.

Prize (total) over £7000.

Sony Radio Awards

ZAFER Productions, 47–48 Chagford Street, London NW1 6EB
☎0171 723 0106
Contact *Francesca Watt, Alan Zafer*

ESTABLISHED 1981 by the **Society of Authors**. Sponsored by Sony. Annual awards to recognise excellence in radio broadcasting. Entries must have been broadcast in the UK between 1 January and 31 December in the year preceding the award. The categories for

the awards are reviewed each year. 1996 Awards included: The Society of Authors' Award for Best Radio Writer.

Southern Arts Literature Prize

Southern Arts, 13 St Clement Street, Winchester, Hampshire SO23 9DQ
☎01962 855099   Fax 01962 861186
Contact *Literature Officer*

ESTABLISHED 1991, this prize is awarded annually to an author living in the **Southern Arts** region for the most promising work of prose or poetry published during the year. The 1997 prize will be awarded for poetry. Previous winner: Jon Stallworthy *Louis MacNeice* (biography). Final entry date 30 June.

Prize £1000, plus a craft commission to the value of £600.

Southport Writers' Circle Poetry Competition

53 Richmond Road, Birkdale, Southport, Merseyside PR8 4SB
Contact *Mrs Alison Chisholm*

For previously unpublished work which has not been entered in any other current competition. Entry fee £1.50 first poem, plus £1 for each subsequent entry. Open category (any subject any form) and humorous category; maximum 40 lines. Closing date end April. Poems must be entered under a pseudonym, accompanied by a sealed envelope marked with the pseudonym and title of poem, containing s.a.e.. Entries must be typed on A4 paper and be accompanied by the appropriate fee payable to Southport Writers' Circle. No application form is required. Envelopes should be marked 'Poetry Competition'. Postal enquiries only. No calls.

Prizes (1st) £100; (2nd) £50; (3rd) £25 in each category.

Ian St James Awards

c/o The New Writers' Club, PO Box 60, Cranbrook, Kent TN17 2ZR
☎01580 212626   Fax 01580 212041

ESTABLISHED 1989. Administered by the New Writers' Club. Presented annually to approximately 10 writers of short stories. These awards are 'an opportunity for talented and as yet unpublished writers to achieve recognition'. Ian St James is a successful novelist who hopes to attract both literary and commercial fiction from aspiring writers. Winning entries are published in a paperback anthology. The Ian St James Awards are open to international writers who have not had a novel or novella previously published. Final entry date 30 April each year. Previous top prize winners: Kate Atkinson *Karmic Mothers*; Joshua Davidson *The Saviour*; Anna McGrail *The Welfare of the Patient*. Entry forms available from around October from above address.

Award Top prize: £2000 plus runners-up cash prizes. Shortlisted stories are published throughout the year in *The New Writer* magazine.

Stand Magazine Poetry Competition

Stand Magazine, 179 Wingrove Road, Newcastle upon Tyne NE4 9DA
☎0191 273 3280

Contact *The Administrator*

Biennial award for poems written in English and not yet published, broadcast or under consideration elsewhere. Next award 1998. Final entry date 30 June 1998. Send s.a.e. for entry form.
Prize (total) £2500.

Stand Magazine Short Story Competition

Stand Magazine, 179 Wingrove Road, Newcastle upon Tyne NE4 9DA
☎0191 273 3280

Contact *The Administrator*

Biennial award for short stories written in English and not yet published, broadcast or under consideration elsewhere. Next award 1999. Closing date 30 June 1999. Send s.a.e. for entry form.
Prize (total) £2500.

Staple First Editions Project 1997–98

Tor Cottage, 81 Cavendish Road, Matlock, Derbyshire DE4 3HD
☎01629 582764

Contact *Donald Measham*

Biennial open competition for single-author collections (poetry, prose) run by *Staple* magazine. Final entry date 1 February 1998. Publication of winning poetry monograph, July 1998; of fiction collection, March 1999.
Prize half shares of £500, complimentary copies, publication, promotion and distribution to subscribers and to the book trade.

Steinbeck Award

William Heinemann Ltd, Michelin House, 81 Fulham Road, London SW3 6RB
☎0171 581 9393   Fax 0171 225 9095

Contact *The Awards Secretary*

ESTABLISHED 1994. Bi-annual award, sponsored by **William Heinemann** to support a young writer (under 40) for a new full-length work of fiction, first published in the UK, and written in the spirit of the works of John Steinbeck. Final closing date end of February 1998. Entries are submitted by publishers and not authors. Information sheet available. Previous winner: John Gregory Brown *Decorations in a Ruined Cemetery*.
Prizes £10,000, of which £5000 is donated to a charity chosen by the winner.

The Stern Silver PEN Non-Fiction Award

English Centre of International PEN, 7 Dilke Street, London SW3 4JE
☎0171 352 6303   Fax 0171 351 0220

ESTABLISHED 1986 and sponsored, from 1997, by the family of James Stern in memory of their father. An annual award, the winner being nominated by the PEN Executive Committee, for an outstanding work of non-fiction written in English and published in England in the year preceding the prize. Previous winners: Alan Bullock *Hitler and Stalin*; Brian Keenan *An Evil Cradling*; John Hale *The Civilization of Europe in the Renaissance*; Eric Hobsbawm *Age of Extremes*; Neal Ascherson *Black Sea*.
Prize £1000, plus silver pen.

Sunday Times Award for Small Publishers

Independent Publishers Guild, 25 Cambridge Road, Hampton, Middlesex TW12 2JL
☎0181 979 0250   Fax 0181 979 6393

Contact *Yvonne Messenger*

ESTABLISHED 1988, the first winner was **Fourth Estate**. Open to any publisher producing between five and forty titles a year, which must primarily be original titles, not reprints. Entrants are invited to submit their catalogues for the last twelve months, together with two representative titles. Previous winners: **Nick Hern Books**; **Tarquin Publications**. 1996 winner: **Ellipsis London**.

Sunday Times Special Award for Excellence in Writing

The Sunday Times, 1 Pennington Street, London E1 9XW
☎0171 782 5774   Fax 0171 782 5798

Contact *The Literary Editor*

ESTABLISHED 1987. Annual award to fiction and non-fiction writers. The panel consists of

Sunday Times journalists, publishers and other figures from the book world. Previous winners: Anthony Burgess, Seamus Heaney, Stephen Hawking, Ruth Rendell, Muriel Spark, William Trevor, Martin Amis, Ted Hughes and Harold Pinter. No applications; prize at the discretion of the Literary Editor.

Sunday Times Young Writer of the Year Award

The Society of Authors, 84 Drayton Gardens, London SW10 9SB
☎0171 373 6642   Fax 0171 373 5768
Contact *Awards Secretary*

ESTABLISHED 1991. Annual award given on the strength of the promise shown by a full-length published work of fiction, non-fiction, poetry or drama. Entrants must be British citizens, resident in Britain and under the age of 35 at the closing date of 31 December. The work must be by one author, in the English language, and published in Britain during the 12 months prior to the closing date. Full details available from the above address. Previous winners: Katherine Pierpoint *Truffle Beds*; Andrew Cowan *Pig*; William Dalrymple *City of Djinns*; Simon Armitage *Xanadu and Kid*.
Prize £5000.

The Talkies

9–10 Barnard Mews, London SW11 1QU
☎0171 582 0536   Fax 0171 582 4917
Contact *Peter Dean, Sean King, Sam Warren*

Annual award ESTABLISHED in 1995 by *Talking Business* magazine to recognise the best in spoken word publishing, production, design and retailing. There are 19 awards with the 'Talkie of the Year' being picked from the winners of all the categories. Contact *Talking Business* for entry form. Final entry date late July. Previous Talkie of the Year winners: *Alan Bennett Diaries*; *This Sceptred Isle*.
Prizes Framed certificate for all winners, plus logo award for Best Reader and Talkie of the Year.

Reginald Taylor and Lord Fletcher Essay Prize

Journal of the British Archaeological Association, Institute of Archaelogy, 36 Beaumont Street, Oxford OX1 2PG
Contact *Dr Martin Henig*

A biennial prize, in memory of the late E. Reginald Taylor and of Lord Fletcher, for the best unpublished essay, not exceeding 7500 words, on a subject of archaeological, art history or antiquarian interest within the period from the Roman era to AD 1830. The essay should show *original* research on its chosen subject, and the author will be invited to read the essay before the Association. The prize is now included in the British Archaeological Awards scheme and the presentation will be made along with the other awards in November 1998. The essay may be published in the journal of the Association if approved by the Editorial Committee. Closing date for entries is 1 June 1998. All enquiries by post please. No phone calls. Send s.a.e. for details.
Prize £300 and a medal.

The Teixeira Gomes Prize

The Translators Association, 84 Drayton Gardens, London SW10 9SB
☎0171 373 6642   Fax 0171 373 5768
Contact *Kate Pool*

ESTABLISHED 1989. Triennial award funded by the Calouste Gulbenkian Foundation and the Portuguese Book Institute for the best translation of a work by a Portuguese national published in the UK in the three years preceding the closing date, or unpublished. Previous winners: Giovanni Pontiero *The Gospel According to Jesus Christ* by Jose Saramago. Final entry date is 31 December 1997 for 1998 award.

David Thomas Prize

See entry under **Bursaries, Fellowships and Grants**

Anne Tibble Poetry Competition

Events Team, Directorate of Environment Services, Northampton Borough Council, Cliftonville House, Bedford Road, Northampton NN4 7NR
☎01604 233500   Fax 01604 238796

Entries should preferably be typed, 20 lines maximum, any subject. Writers must be resident in the UK; categories for children under 11 and under 16.
Prize £200 (1st).

The Times Educational Supplement Books and Resources Awards

Times Educational Supplement, Admiral House, 66–68 East Smithfield, London E1 9XY
☎0171 782 3000   Fax 0171 782 3200
Contact *Literary Editor*

ESTABLISHED 1973. Annual awards made for the

best books used in schools, and for innovative mixed media resources (first awarded in 1996). The books must have been published in Britain. Previous winners: Junior Information Book Award: *Children Just Like Me* Barnabas and Anabel Kindersley; Senior Information Book Award: Joint winners *Young Citizen's Passport* Citizenship Foundation; *Keeping Clean: A Very Peculiar History* Daisy Kerr. Primary Schoolbook Award: *Discovery: Dinosaurs* Dougal Dixon; Secondary Schoolbook Award: *GCSE Biology* D. G. Mackean.

The Tir Na N-Og Award
Cyngor Llyfrau Cymru (Welsh Books Council), Castell Brychan, Aberystwyth, Dyfed SY23 2JB
☎01970 624151   Fax 01970 625385

An annual award given to the best original book published for children in the year prior to the announcement. There are three categories: Best Welsh Fiction; Best Welsh Non-fiction; Best English Book with an authentic Welsh background.
Awards £1000 (each category).

Marten Toonder Award
An Chomhairle Ealaíon (The Arts Council), 70 Merrion Square, Dublin 2, Republic of Ireland
☎00 353 1 6611840   Fax 00 353 1 6761302
Literature Officer *Laurence Cassidy*

A triennial award for creative writing. Next award will be offered in Literature in 1998. Given to an established writer in recognition of achievement. Open to Irish citizens or residents only.
Award IR£4500.

The Betty Trask Prize
See entry under **Bursaries, Fellowships and Grants**

The Trewithen Poetry Prize
Treskewes Cottage, Trewithen Moor, Stithians, Truro, Cornwall TR3 7DU
Contact *Competition Secretary*

ESTABLISHED 1995 in order to promote poetry with a rural theme. Entry forms available from the above (enclose s.a.e.). Closing date: 31 October. Entry fee of £2.50 for first poem, £1.50 for subsequent entries. Previous winners include: Elizabeth Rapp, David Smart, Sylvia Oldroyd, Ann Drysdale.
Prizes (total) £400 plus publication in *The Trewithen Chapbook*.

The Tullie House Prize
See **Lakeland Book of the Year Awards**

UNESCO/PEN Short Story Competition
English Centre of International PEN, 7 Dilke Street, London SW3 4JE
☎0171 352 6303

ESTABLISHED 1993. Biennial award, funded by UNESCO and administered by the English Centre of PEN. It is intended to reward the efforts of those who write in English despite the fact that it is not their mother tongue (the Irish, Scots and Welsh are not eligible). Entries in the form of short stories not exceeding 1500 words should be submitted to the writer's home country PEN centre. The top three entries are then forwarded to the English PEN centre for final judging. Final entry date end December of year preceding award. First awarded March 1993. Previous winner: Kiruvin Boon *The Dream*.
Prizes (1st) $3000; (2nd) $2000; (3rd) $500.

Unicorn Arts Theatre National Young Playwrights' Competition
Unicorn Theatre for Children, Arts Theatre, Great Newport Street, London WC2H 7JB
☎0171 379 3280   Fax 0171 836 5366
Contact *Ruth Burgess*

Annual awards to young playwrights aged 6–16 for plays on a theme decided by the theatre. Three age groups: 6–8; 9–12; 13–16. The plays are judged by a committee of writers. The winners take part in workshops on the plays with members of the Unicorn Theatre professional company, with rehearsed readings on stage the following spring. Final entry date end December.

T. E. Utley Memorial Award
111 Sugden Road, London SW11 5ED
☎0171 228 3900
Contact *The Secretary*

Annual award ESTABLISHED 1988 in memory of the political journalist T. E. Utley. In 1996, two awards were given for unpublished essays by aspiring journalists who were still at school or university.
Prizes £2500 (under 25); £1500 (under 18).

Ver Poets Open Competition
Haycroft, 61–63 Chiswell Green Lane, St Albans, Hertfordshire AL2 3AL
☎01727 867005
Contact *May Badman*

Various competitions are organised by **Ver Poets**, the main one being the annual Open for unpublished poems of no more than 30 lines written in English. Entry fee £2 per poem. Entries must be made under a pseudonym, with name and address on form or separate sheet. *Vision On*, the anthology of winning and selected poems, and the adjudicators' report are normally available from mid-June. Final entry date 30 April. Back numbers of the anthology are available for £2, post-free.

Prizes (1st) £500; (2nd) £300; two runners-up £100.

Vogue Talent Contest

Vogue, Vogue House, Hanover Square, London W1R 0AD
☎0171 499 9080   Fax 0171 408 0559
Contact *Frances Bentley*

ESTABLISHED 1951. Annual award for young writers and journalists (under 25 on 1 January in the year of the contest). Final entry date mid-April. Entrants must write three pieces of journalism on given subjects.

Prizes £1000, plus a month's paid work experience with *Vogue*; (2nd) £500.

The Vondel Translation Prize

The Translators Association, 84 Drayton Gardens, London SW10 9SB
☎0171 373 6642   Fax 0171 373 5768
Contact *Kate Pool*

ESTABLISHED 1995. Triennial award funded by the Foundation for the Production and Translation of Dutch Literature and the Ministry of the Flemish Community for the best translation of a Dutch or Flemish work published in the UK or the USA. Next entry date 31 December 1998.

Prize £1000.

Wadsworth Prize for Business History

Business Archives Council, The Clove Building, 4 Maguire Street, London SE1 2NQ
☎0171 407 6110
Chairman *Mrs Lenore Symons*

ESTABLISHED 1978. Annual award for the best book published on British business history. Previous winners: Dr T. R. Gourvish and Dr R. Wilson *The British Brewing Industry: A History*; Dr Geoffrey Tweedale *Steel City*.

Prize £500.

Arts Council of Wales Book of the Year Awards

Arts Council of Wales, Museum Place, Cardiff CF1 3NX
☎01222 394711   Fax 01222 221447
Contact *Tony Bianchi*

Annual non-competitive prizes awarded for works of exceptional literary merit written by Welsh authors (by birth or residence), published in Welsh or English during the previous calendar year. There is one major prize in English, the Book of the Year Award, and one major prize in Welsh, Gwobr Llyfr y Flwyddyn. Shortlists of three titles in each language are announced in April; winners announced in May.

Prizes £3000 (each); £1000 to each of four runners-up.

Walford Award

See **The Library Association Walford Award**

Wandsworth London Writers Competition

Room 224, Town Hall, Wandsworth High Street, London SW18 2PU
☎0181 871 7037   Fax 0181 871 7630
Contact *Arts Office*

An annual competition, open to all writers of 16 and over who live, work or study in the Greater London Area. There are two categories, all for previously unpublished work, in poetry and short story.

Prizes £1000 for each class, divided between the top three in each category; plus two runners-up in each class.

The Harri Webb Prize

10 Heol Don, Whitchurch, Cardiff CF4 2AU
☎01222 529202
Contact *Meic Stephens*

ESTABLISHED 1995. Annual competition to commemorate the Welsh poet, Harri Webb, for a single poem in any of the categories in which he wrote: ballad, satire, song, polemic. The poems are chosen by three adjudicators; no submissions. 1996 winner: Alun Rees.

Prize £100.

Wellington Town Council Award

The Civic Buildings, Town Bank, Wellington, Telford, Shropshire TF1 1LX
☎01952 222935   Fax 01952 222936
Contacts *Martin Scholes, Derrick Drew*

ESTABLISHED 1995. Annual short story competition to promote the ancient town of Wellington. Open to all for a minimum fee of £2.50; prizes are sponsored so all entry fee monies go to charity. 1996 winners: Ann Palmer (Best Shropshire Entry); Jenny Amphlett (Best Story for Children).

Prizes Trophies and money.

Wheatley Medal
See **The Library Association Wheatley Medal**

Whitbread Book of the Year and Literary Awards
Minster House, 272 Vauxhall Bridge Road, London SW1V 1BA
☎0171 834 5477   Fax 0171 834 8812
Contact *Gillian Cronin*

ESTABLISHED 1971. Publishers are invited to submit books for this annual competition designed for writers who have been resident in Great Britain or the Republic of Ireland for three years or more. The awards are made in two stages. First, nominations are selected in four categories: novel, first novel, biography and poetry. One of these is then voted by the panel of judges as Whitbread Book of the Year. 1996 winners: Beryl Bainbridge *Every Man for Himself* (novel); John Lanchester *The Debt to Pleasure* (first novel); Diarmaid MacCulloch *Thomas Cranmer: A Life* (biography); Seamus Heaney *The Spirit Level* (poetry and Book of the Year). For the first time, in 1996, the Children's Award was separated out into the Whitbread Children's Book of the Year Award, the winner being Anne Fine for *The Tulip Touch*.

Awards £21,000 (Book of the Year); £8000 (Children's Book of the Year); £2000 (all nominees).

Whitfield Prize
Royal Historical Society, University College London, Gower Street, London WC1E 6BT
☎0171 387 7532   Fax 0171 387 7532
Contact *Literary Director*

ESTABLISHED 1977. An annual award for the best new work within a field of British history, published in the UK in the preceding calendar year. The book must be the author's first (solely written) history book and be an original and scholarly work of historical research. Final entry date end December.

Prize £1000.

John Whiting Award
Arts Council of England, 14 Great Peter Street, London SW1P 3NQ
☎0171 333 0100 ext 431   Fax 0171 973 6590
Contact *The Drama Director*

FOUNDED 1965. Annual award to commemorate the life and work of the playwright John Whiting (*The Devils, A Penny for a Song*). Any writer who has received during the previous two calendar years an award through the **Arts Council's Theatre Writing Schemes** or who has had a première production by a theatre company in receipt of annual subsidy is eligible to apply. Awarded to the writer whose play most nearly satisfies the following criteria: a play in which the writing is of special quality; a play of relevance and importance to contemporary life; a play of potential value to the British theatre. Closing date for entries: 6 January 1998.

Prize £6000.

Alfred and Mary Wilkins Memorial Poetry Competition
Birmingham & Midland Institute, 9 Margaret Street, Birmingham B3 3BS
☎0121 236 3591
Administrator *Mr P. A. Fisher*

An annual competition for an unpublished poem not exceeding 40 lines, written in English by an author over the age of 15 and living, working or studying in the UK. The poem should not have been entered for any other poetry competition. Six prizes awarded in all.

Prizes (total) £400.

Griffith John Williams Memorial Prize
3rd Floor, Mount Stuart House, Mount Stuart Square, Cardiff CF1 6DQ
☎01222 492064   Fax 01222 492930
Contact *Dafydd Rogers*

FOUNDED 1965. Biennial award in honour of the first president of the **Welsh Academy.** It aims to promote writing in Welsh. Entries must be the first published work of authors or poets writing in Welsh. Work must have been published in the two-year period preceding the award.

Award £400.

Raymond Williams Community Publishing Prize
Literature Dept, Arts Council of England, 14 Great Peter Street, London SW1P 3NQ
☎0171 333 0100   Fax 0171 973 6590
Contact *Karen Woods*

ESTABLISHED 1990. Award for published work which exemplifies the values of ordinary people and their lives – as often embodied in Raymond Williams' own work. Submissions may be in the form of poetry, fiction, biography, auto-biography, drama or even local history, pro-viding they are literary in quality and intent. They are likely to be produced by small community or cooperative presses, but other forms of publication will be considered. Final entry date end April. Winner announced in July. 1996 winner: *Voices of Ferrier, an Oral History of a Council Estate* published by the Greenwich Community College Press.

Prizes (1st) £3000; runner-up £2000. Prizes are divided between publisher and author.

H. H. Wingate Prize
See **Jewish Quarterly Literary Prize**

Wolfson History Awards
Wolfson Foundation, 18–22 Haymarket, London SW1Y 4DQ
☎0171 930 1057   Fax 0171 930 1036
Contact *The Director*
ESTABLISHED 1972. An award made annually to authors of published historical works, with the object of encouraging historians to communicate with general readers as well as with their pro-fessional colleagues. Previous winners include: H. G. C. Matthew *Gladstone: 1875–1898*; Fiona MacCarthy *William Morris*; John G. C. Rohl *The Kaiser and His Court: Wilhelm II and the Government of Germany*; Lord Skidelsky *John Maynard Keynes: The Economist as Saviour 1920–1937*.

Award (total) £25,000.

Woolwich Young Radio Playwrights' Competition
Independent Radio Drama Productions Ltd, PO Box 518, Manningtree, Essex CO11 1XD
Contact *Marja Giejgo*
ESTABLISHED 1990 and sponsored by the Woolwich Building Society, with writer and broadcaster Melvyn Bragg as patron. This is a national scheme which aims to discover and professionally produce radio drama writing talent among young people aged 25 and under. The competition involves national and regional script writing competitions with vari-ous workshop programmes at independent and BBC local radio stations. Send s.a.e. for further details. Writers selected for production receive a **Writers' Guild** approved contract.

The Writers Bureau Poetry and Short Story Competition
The Writers Bureau, Sevendale House, 7 Dale Street, Manchester M1 1JB
☎0161 228 2362
Competition Secretary *Angela Cox*
ESTABLISHED 1994. Annual award. Poems should be no longer than 40 lines and short stories no more than 2000 words. £3.50 entry fee.

Prizes in each category: (1st) £300; (2nd) £200; (3rd) £100.

The Writers' Guild Awards
430 Edgware Road, London W2 1EH
☎0171 723 8074   Fax 0171 706 2413
Originally ESTABLISHED 1961 and relaunched in 1991. Five categories of awards: radio (orig-inal drama, comedy/light entertainment, dramatisations, children's); theatre (West End, fringe, regional, children's); books (non-fic-tion, fiction, children's); film (best screenplay); television (original play/film, original drama series, original drama serial, dramatisation/adaptation, situation comedy, light entertain-ment, children's). There are also awards for: Non-English Language, New Writer of the Year (won by Diran Adebayo in 1996), Lifetime Achievement (won by Wole Soyinka in 1996) and The Writers' Guild Award which is given to an individual or institution in recog-nition of their outstanding contribution towards the developing and fostering of new writing in any field represented by the Guild (won by the **Arvon Foundation** in 1996). The various short-lists are prepared by a differ-ent jury in each category and presented to the full Guild membership for its final vote.

Xenos Short Story Competition
Xenos magazine, 29 Prebend Street, Bedford MK40 1QN
☎01234 349067
Annual short story competition open to all. Each year has a specific theme; send s.a.e. or IRC for details and entry form. No entries accepted with-out official entry form. Closing date 30 June.

Prizes Three cash prizes of £50 plus publi-cation in *Xenos*; three runners-up receive an annual subscription to the magazine plus publi-cation.

Yorkshire Open Poetry Competition
See **Ilkley Literature Festival Poetry Competition**

Yorkshire Post Art and Music Awards

Yorkshire Post, PO Box 168, Wellington Street, Leeds, West Yorkshire LS1 1RF
☎0113 2432701

Contact *Margaret Brown*

Two annual awards made to the authors whose work has contributed most to the understanding and appreciation of art and music. Books should have been published in the preceding year in the UK. Previous winners: Charles Hemming *British Landscape Painters: A History and Gazetteer;* David Cairns *Berlioz: The Making of An Artist.*
   Award £1000 each.

Yorkshire Post Best First Work Awards

Yorkshire Post, PO Box 168, Wellington Street, Leeds, West Yorkshire LS1 1RF
☎0113 2432701

Contact *Margaret Brown*

An annual award for a work by a new author published during the preceding year. Previous winners include: Harriet O'Brien *Forgotten Land.*
   Prize £1000.

Yorkshire Post Book of the Year Award

Yorkshire Post, PO Box 168, Wellington Street, Leeds, West Yorkshire LS1 1RF
☎0113 2432701

Contact *Margaret Brown*

An annual award for the book (either fiction or non-fiction) which, in the opinion of the judges, is the best work published in the preceding year. 1997 winner: John Ehrman *The Younger Pitt, Vol. III: The Consuming Struggle.*
   Prize £1200.

Young Science Writer Awards
See **The Daily Telegraph Nirex Young Science Writer Awards**

Holding on to PLR

There was a great fuss last year when a cost conscious minister at the Department of National Heritage came up with a ruse for saving the Government £127,000 on Public Lending Right. How his nerve ends must have tingled with excitement as he worked out the figures on his pocket calculator. The PLR Fund for 1996/97 had been held at £5 million but with fewer books going out of the libraries this meant an increase of the rate per loan from 2p to 2.07p. Not so, said the minister. How much more economical it would be to keep the 2p rate while reducing the total grant proportionately.

That he did not get away with it says more for the effective lobbying by writers' organisations than the innate decency of politicians. Having claimed that it was intending to use any money clawed back from PLR 'to fund projects connected with books and reading', the Department of National Heritage decided that the best way of doing this was to leave things as they were. The result was a modest extra payout to over 20,000 authors and pocket money cheques to another 100 authors who otherwise would not have received anything at all.

PLR has been with us since 1984 when 6000 authors were signed up. Today, there are over 25,000 authors on the PLR register which continues to expand by about 2000 names a year. A quarter of those registered do not qualify for payments and the majority come in at less than £100. On the other hand, at the last count, 98 authors received cheques of £6000, the highest maximum level (Catherine Cookson, Danielle Steel, Dick Francis and Ruth Rendell lead the top earners) and 1800 authors made in excess of £500.

The curiosity is that you can never be sure which category you fall into until you test your popularity on the library shelves. For example, there are children's writers who earn modest royalties but clean up on PLR because they write books which are borrowed frequently and read quickly. Many of the authors of adult fiction who receive the maximum payment do not appear in the bestseller lists. Their chief source of income is their hardback sales to libraries.

To qualify for PLR, an author must be resident in the United Kingdom or Germany (the latter as part of a reciprocal deal). For a book to be eligible it must be printed, bound and put on sale with an ISBN. It must not be mistaken for a newspaper or periodical, or be a musical score. Crown copyright is excluded, also books where authorship is attributed to a company or association. But – and this is where mistakes often occur – the author does not have to own copyright to be eligible for PLR. Anyone who has disclaimed copyright as part of a flat fee commission, for instance, will still have a claim if his name is on the title page.

Under PLR, the sole writer of a book may not be its sole author. Others named on the title page or elsewhere in the book, such as illustrators, translators, compilers, editors and revisers, may have a claim to authorship. Where there are joint authors – two writers, say, or a writer and illustrator – they can strike their own bargain on how their entitlement is to be split. But translators may apply, without reference to other authors, for a 30 per cent fixed share (to be divided equally between joint translators). Similarly, an editor or compiler may register a 20 per cent share provided he has written 10 per cent of the book or at least ten pages of text. Joint editors or compilers must divide the 20 per cent share equally.

Authors and books can be registered for PLR only when application is made during the author's lifetime. However, once an author is registered, the PLR on his books continues for the period of copyright. If he wishes, an author can assign PLR to other people and bequeath it by will. If a co-author is dead or untraceable, the remaining co-author can still register for a share of PLR so long as he provides supporting evidence as to why he alone is making application.

A note on German PLR. Some authors wonder why their payments are so small. The answer is that under the German system there is a 10 per cent deduction for administration, a further 10 per cent for a 'social fund', which is set aside for making *ex gratia* payments to authors who are in need, and yet another 45 per cent for 'social security'. After the 65 per cent deductions, the remaining amount is divided between the authors (who take 70 per cent) and the publishers (who take 30 per cent). Furthermore, under German law, the translator is entitled to 50 per cent of the author's share, and if there are editors involved, they are also entitled to a percentage of the fee.

There are various ideas for extending PLR. Much thought, for example, has gone into the question of rewarding authors of reference books which are consulted on library premises but rarely taken out on loan. Complex sampling procedures have been rejected as too expensive and time consuming. Instead, payment is likely to be based on the average number of loans of a book in the lending stock. Also, there is a good argument for extending PLR to all authors living in the European Union. This might persuade other European countries to follow Germany's example with reciprocity payments to UK authors. But given the limits on public spending, the DNH is stalling on any extension of PLR that demands extra funding.

One overdue change that would not cost a bean is the raising of the minimum payment level from £1 to £10 or possibly £20. But redistribution which favours the better off does not go down well with the writers' associations who have argued successfully for a £5 minimum payment.

PLR application forms and details can be obtained from: The Registrar, PLR Office, Bayheath House, Prince Regent Street, Stockton on Tees, Cleveland TS18 1DF (☎01642 604699)

Library Services

Aberdeen Central Library
Rosemount Viaduct, Aberdeen AB25 1GW
☎01224 634622   Fax 01224 641985

Open 9.00 am to 8.00 pm Monday to Friday
(Reference & Local Studies 9.00 am to 9.00 pm); 9.00 am to 5.00 pm Saturday. Branch library opening times vary.

Open access

General reference and loans. Books, pamphlets, periodicals and newspapers; videos, CDs, records and cassettes; arts equipment lending service; recording studio; DTP and WP for public access; photographs of the Aberdeen area; census records, maps; on-line database, patents and standards. The library offers special services to housebound readers.

Armitt Library
Ambleside, Cumbria LA22 9BL
☎015394 33949

Open 10.00 am to 12.30 pm and 1.30 pm to 4.00 pm Monday, Tuesday, Wednesday, Friday.

Access By arrangement (phone or write)

A small but unique reference library of rare books, manuscripts, pictures, antiquarian prints and museum items, mainly about the Lake District. It includes early guidebooks and topographical works, books and papers relating to Wordsworth, Ruskin, H. Martineau and others; fine art including work by W. Green, J. B. Pyne, John Harden, K. Schwitters, and Victorian photographs by Herbert Bell; also a major collection of Beatrix Potter's scientific watercolour drawings and microscope studies. Museum and Exhibition open from spring 1998, five days per week from 10.00 am to 5.00 pm.

The Athenaeum, Liverpool
Church Alley, Liverpool L1 3DD
☎0151 709 7770   Fax 0151 709 0418

Open 9.00 am to 4.00 pm Monday to Friday

Access To club members; researchers by application only

General collection, with books dating from the 15th century, now concentrated mainly on local history with a long run of Liverpool directories and guides. *Special collections* Liverpool playbills; William Roscoe; Blanco White; Robert Gladstone; 18th-century plays; 19th-century economic pamphlets; the Norris books; Bibles; Yorkshire and other genealogy. Some original drawings, portraits, topographical material and local maps.

Bank of England Library and Information Services
Threadneedle Street, London EC2R 8AH
☎0171 601 4715   Fax 0171 601 4356

Open 9.30 am to 5.30 pm Monday to Friday

Access For research workers by prior arrangement only, when material is not readily available elsewhere

50,000 volumes of books and periodicals. 3000 periodicals taken. UK and overseas coverage of banking, finance and economics. *Special collections* Central bank reports; UK 17th–19th-century economic tracts; Government reports in the field of banking.

Barbican Library
Barbican Centre, London EC2Y 8DS
☎0171 638 0569

Open 9.30 am to 5.30 pm Monday, Wednesday, Thursday, Friday; 9.30 am to 7.30 pm Tuesday; 9.30 am to 12.30 pm Saturday

Open access

Situated on Level 2 of the Barbican Centre, this is the Corporation of London's largest lending library. Limited study facilities are available. In addition to a large general lending department, the library seeks to reflect the Centre's emphasis on the arts and includes strong collections, including videos, on painting, sculpture, theatre, cinema and ballet, as well as a large music library with books, scores, cassettes and CDs (sound recording loans available at a small charge). Also houses the City's main children's library and has special collections on finance, natural resources, conservation, socialism and the history of London. Service available for housebound readers.

Barnsley Public Library
Central Library, Shambles Street, Barnsley, South Yorkshire S70 2JF
☎01226 773930   Fax 01226 773955

Open 9.30 am to 8.00 pm Monday and Wednesday; 9.30 am to 6.00 pm Tuesday,

Thursday, Friday; 9.30 am to 5.00 pm
Saturday; Archive Collection: 9.30 am to
1.00 pm and 2.00 pm to 6.00 pm (closed all
day Thursday and Saturday afternoon)

Open access
General library, lending and reference.
Archive collection of family history and local
firms; local studies: coalmining, local authors,
Yorkshire and Barnsley; European Business
Information Unit; music library (books, CDs,
records, tapes); large junior library. (Specialist
departments are closed on certain weekday
evenings and Saturday afternoons.)

BBC Written Archives Centre
Peppard Road, Caversham Park, Reading,
Berkshire RG4 8TZ
☎0118 9469280/1/2   Fax 0118 9461145

Contact *Jacqueline Kavanagh*
Open 9.30 am to 5.30 pm Monday to Friday

Access For reference, by appointment only on
Wednesday to Friday.
Holds the written records of the BBC,
including internal papers from 1922 to 1974
and published material to date. Charges for
certain services.

Bedford Central Library
Harpur Street, Bedford MK40 1PG
☎01234 350931   Fax 01234 342163

Open 9.30 am to 7.00 pm Monday and
Wednesday; 9.30 am to 5.30 pm Tuesday,
Thursday, Friday; 9.30 am to 4.00 pm
Saturday

Open Access
Reference and lending library with a wide
range of stock, including books, music (CD-
ROMs and cassettes), audio books and videos,
information services, children's library, local
history library, Internet facilities, gallery and
coffee bar.

Belfast Public Libraries:
Central Library
Royal Avenue, Belfast BT1 1EA
☎01232 243233   Fax 01232 332819

Open 9.30 am to 8.00 pm Monday and
Thursday; 9.30 am to 5.30 pm Tuesday,
Wednesday, Friday; 9.30 am to 1.00 pm
Saturday

Open access To lending libraries; reference
libraries by application only
Over 2 million volumes for lending and reference. *Special collections* United Nations/Unesco

depository; complete British Patent Collection;
Northern Ireland Newspaper Library; British
and Irish government publications. The Central
Library offers the following reference departments: Humanities and General Reference; Irish
and Local Studies; Business and Law; Science
and Technology; Fine Arts, Language and
Literature; Music and Recorded Sound. The
lending library, supported by twenty branch
libraries and two mobile libraries, offers special
services to hospitals, prisons and housebound
readers.

BFI Library and Information Services
21 Stephen Street, London W1P 2LN
☎0171 255 1444   Fax 0171 436 2338

Open 10.30 am to 5.30 pm Monday and
Friday; 10.30 am to 8.00 pm Tuesday and
Thursday; 1.00 pm to 8.00 pm Wednesday;
Telephone Enquiry Service operates from
10.00 am to 5.00 pm

Access For reference only; annual and limited
day membership available
The world's largest collection of information
on film and television including periodicals,
cuttings, scripts, related documentation, personal papers. Information available through
SIFT (Summary of Information on Film and
Television).

Birmingham and Midland Institute
9 Margaret Street, Birmingham B3 3BS
☎0121 236 3591   Fax 0121 212 4577

Administrator & General Secretary *Philip Fisher*

Access For research, to students (loans
restricted to members)
ESTABLISHED 1855. Later merged with the
Birmingham Library (now renamed the
Priestley Library), which was founded in 1779.
The Priestley Library specialises in the humanities, with approximately 100,000 volumes in
stock. Founder member of the **Association of
Independent Libraries**. Meeting-place of
many affiliated societies including many
devoted to poetry and literature.

Birmingham Library Services
Central Library, Chamberlain Square,
Birmingham B3 3HQ
☎0121 235 2615   Fax 0121 233 4458

Open 9.00 am to 8.00 pm Monday to Friday;
9.00 am to 5.00 pm Saturday
Over a million volumes. *Research collections*

include the Shakespeare Library; War Poetry Collection; Parker Collection of Children's Books and Games; Johnson Collection; Milton Collection; Cervantes Collections; Early and Fine Printing Collection (including the William Ridler Collection of Fine Printing); Joseph Priestley Collection; Loudon Collection; Railway Collection; Wingate Bett Transport Ticket Collection; Labour, Trade Union and Co-operative Collections. Photographic Archives: Sir John Benjamin Stone; Francis Bedford; Francis Frith; Warwickshire Photographic Survey; Boulton and Watt Archive; Charles Parker Archive; Birmingham Repertory Theatre Archive and Sir Barry Jackson Library; Local Studies (Birmingham); Patents Collection; Song Sheets Collection; Oberammergau Festival Collection.

Bradford Central Library
Princes Way, Bradford, West Yorkshire BD1 1NN
☎01274 753600   Fax 01274 395108
Open 9.00 am to 7.30 pm Monday to Friday; 9.00 am to 5.00 pm Saturday

Open access
Wide range of books and media loan services. Comprehensive reference and information services, including major local history collections and specialised business information service. Bradford Libraries runs its own publishing programme, and has a number of creative writing projects – *In Your Own Write* (for local writers), *The Writeplace* (DTP facility for writers), *Poem of the Month*, and an annual programme of performance events.

Brighton Central Library
Church Street, Brighton, East Sussex BN1 1UE
☎01273 691195   Fax 01273 625234
Open 10.00 am to 7.00 pm Monday to Friday (closed Wednesday); 10.00 am to 4.00 pm Saturday
Reference Library ☎01273 601197 Fax 01273 695882

Access Limited stock on open access; all material for reference use only
FOUNDED 1869, the library has a large stock covering most subjects. Specialisations include art and antiques, history of Brighton and Sussex, family history, local illustrations, HMSO, business and large bequests of antiquarian books and ecclesiastical history.

Bristol Central Library
College Green, Bristol BS1 5TL
☎0117 9276121   Fax 0117 9221081
Open 10.00 am to 7.30 pm Monday to Thursday; 9.30 am to 7.30 pm Friday; 9.30 am to 5.00 pm Saturday
Open Access
Lending, reference, art, music, commerce and local studies are particularly strong.

British Architectural Library
Royal Institute of British Architects, 66 Portland Place, London W1N 4AD
☎0171 580 5533   Fax 0171 631 1802
Members' Information Line (Premium rate): 0891 234 444; Public Information Line (Premium rate): 0891 234 400
Open 1.30 pm to 5.00 pm Monday; 10.00 am to 8.00 pm Tuesday; 10.00 am to 5.00 pm Wednesday, Thursday, Friday; 10.00 am to 1.30 pm Saturday
Access Free to RIBA members; non-members must buy a day ticket (£10/£5 concessions but on Tuesday between 5–8.00 pm and Saturday £5/£2.50); annual membership (£96/£48 concessions); loans available to RIBA and library members only
Collection of books, drawings, manuscripts, photographs and periodicals, 400 of which are indexed. All aspects of architecture, current and historical. Material both technical and aesthetic, covering related fields including: interior design, landscape architecture, topography, the construction industry and applied arts. Brochure available; queries by telephone, letter or in person. Charge for research £40 per hour (min. charge £10).

The British Library Business Information Service (BIS)
25 Southampton Buildings, London WC2A 1AW
☎0171 412 7454/7977 (Free)/0171 412 7457 (Priced Enquiry Service)   Fax 0171 412 7453
Open 9.30 am to 9.00 pm Monday to Friday; 10.00 am to 1.00 pm Saturday; Free Enquiry Service 9.00 am to 5.00 pm Monday to Friday; Priced Enquiry Service 9.00 am to 5.00 pm Monday to Friday
Open access
BIS holds the most comprehensive collection of business information literature in the UK. This includes market research reports and journals, directories, company annual reports,

trade and business journals, house journals, trade literature and CD-ROM services.

British Library Department of Manuscripts

Great Russell Street, London WC1B 3DG
☎0171 412 7513   Fax 0171 412 7745

Open 10.00 am to 4.45 pm Monday to Saturday; enquiries and applications up to 4.30 pm (closed 3–15 November, 1997)

Access Reading facilities only, by British Library reader's pass and supplementary mss pass, for which a written letter of recommendation is required

Two useful publications, *Index of Manuscripts in the British Library*, Cambridge 1984–6, 10 vols, and *The British Library: Guide to the Catalogues and Indexes of the Department of Manuscripts* by M. A. E. Nickson, help to guide the researcher through this vast collection of manuscripts dating from Ancient Greece to the present day. Approximately 300,000 mss, charters, papyri and seals are housed here.

British Library Map Library

Great Russell Street, London WC1B 3DG
☎0171 412 7700   Fax 0171 412 7780

Open 10.00 am to 4.30 pm Monday to Saturday

Access By British Library reader's pass or Map Library day pass

A collection of two million maps, charts and globes with particular reference to the history of British cartography. Maps for all parts of the world in wide range of scales and dates, including the most comprehensive collection of Ordnance Survey maps and plans. *Special collections* King George III Topographical Collection and Maritime Collection, and the Crace Collection of maps and plans of London.

British Library Music Library

Great Russell Street, London WC1B 3DG
☎0171 412 7752   Fax 0171 412 7751

Open 9.30 am to 4.45 pm Monday to Friday; on Saturday material is made available 10.00 am to 4.45 pm in the Manuscripts students' room

Access By British Library reader's pass
Special collections The Royal Music Library (containing almost all Handel's surviving autograph scores) and the Paul Hirsch Music Library. Also a large collection (about one and a quarter million items) of printed music, both British and foreign.

British Library National Sound Archive

29 Exhibition Road, London SW7 2AS
☎0171 412 7440   Fax 0171 412 7441

Open 10.00 am to 5.00 pm Monday to Friday (Thursday till 9.00 pm)

Listening service (by appointment) 10.00 am to 5.00 pm Monday to Friday

Northern Listening Service

British Library Document Supply Centre, Boston Spa, West Yorkshire: 9.15 am to 4.30 pm Monday to Friday

Open access
An archive of over 1,000,000 discs and more than 125,000 tape recordings, including all types of music, oral history, drama, wildlife, selected BBC broadcasts and BBC Sound Archive material. Produces a thrice-yearly newsletter, *Playback*.

British Library Newspaper Library

Colindale Avenue, London NW9 5HE
☎0171 412 7353   Fax 0171 412 7379

Open 10.00 am to 4.45 pm Monday to Saturday (last newspaper issue 4.15 pm)

Access By British Library reader's pass or Newspaper Library pass (available from and valid only for Colindale)

English provincial, Scottish, Welsh, Irish and Commonwealth foreign newspapers from c.1700 are housed here. London newspapers from 1801 and many weekly periodicals are also in stock as well as selected newspapers from overseas. (London newspapers pre-dating 1801 are housed in Great Russell Street.) Readers are advised to check availability of material in advance.

British Library Oriental and India Office Collections

Orbit House, 197 Blackfriars Road, London SE1 8NG
☎0171 412 7873   Fax 0171 412 7641

Open 9.30 am to 5.45 pm Monday to Friday; 9.30 am to 12.45 pm Saturday

Open access By British Library reader's pass or day pass (identification required)

A comprehensive collection of printed volumes and manuscripts in the languages of North Africa, the Near and Middle East and all of Asia, plus official records of the East India Company and British government in India until 1947. Also prints, drawings and paintings by British artists of India.

British Library Reading Room

Great Russell Street, London WC1B 3DG
☎0171 412 7676 (Reading Room/
Bibliographical holdings enquiries)
Fax 0171 412 755

☎0171 412 7677 (Admissions)

The British Library Reading Room leaves the
Great Russell Street address on October 29th
1997 and reopens at the new St Pancras building on November 24th: 96 Euston Road,
London NW1 2DB (☎/fax numbers un-
changed). Opening hours unconfirmed at the
time of going to press but unlikely to differ
greatly from current times. However, it is recommended that a telephone enquiry be made
in advance of a visit to the new Library.

Open 9.00 am to 5.00 pm Monday, Friday,
Saturday; 9.00 am to 9.00 pm Tuesday,
Wednesday, Thursday (closed week
following the last complete week in
October). The Admissions Office is open
9.00 am to 4.30 pm Monday, Friday,
Saturday; 10.00 am to 6.00 pm Tuesday,
Wednesday, Thursday.

Access By British Library reader's pass

Large and comprehensive stock of books and
periodicals relating to the humanities and social
sciences for reference and research which cannot easily be done elsewhere. Leaflet *Applying
for a Reader's Pass* available for guidance. The
permanent exhibition on the history of printing and binding will move to the new Library.
Telephone for details.

British Library Science Reference and Information Service

25 Southampton Buildings, London
WC2A 1AW
☎0171 412 7494/7496 (General Enquiries)
Fax 0171 412 7495

Also at: 9 Kean Street, London WC2B 4AT
(Life sciences enquiries)
☎0171 412 7288   Fax 0171 412 7217

And: Chancery House Reading Room,
Chancery Lane, London WC2A 1AW
☎0171 412 7901   Fax 0171 412 7912

Open Southampton Buildings: 9.30 am to
9.00 pm Monday to Friday; 10.00 am to
1.00 pm Saturday. Kean Street and
Chancery House Reading Room: 9.30 am
to 5.30 pm Monday to Friday.

General enquiries tel as above; British and EPO
Patent enquiries: 0171 412 7919; Foreign
Patent enquiries: 0171 412 7902; Business
enquiries: 0171 412 7454/7977.

Open access

The national library for modern science,
technology, medicine, business, patents, trade
marks and designs, it is the most comprehensive
reference collection in Western Europe of such
literature from the whole world. The primary
purpose is to make this information readily
accessible, so no prior arrangement or reader's
ticket is necessary. The library has enquiry and
referral services and priced services (especially in
business information, the environment, and
industrial property); online database search;
photocopying service; runs courses and seminars; and publishes a wide range of publications
from newsletters to definitive bibliographies.

PRICED RESEARCH SERVICE CONTACT DETAILS:
Business Information Service
☎0171 412 7457   Fax 0171 412 7453
Environmental Information Service
☎0171 412 7955   Fax 0171 412 7954
Health Care Information Service
☎0171 412 7477   Fax 0171 412 7954
Social Policy Information Service
☎0171 412 7536   Fax 0171 412 7761
STM search (science, technology and medicine):
☎0171 412 7477   Fax 0171 412 7954

British Library Social Policy Information Service

Great Russell Street, London WC1B 3DG
☎0171 412 7536   Fax 0171 412 7761

Open 9.30 am to 4.45 pm (last admissions
4.30pm) Monday to Friday

Access By British Library reader's pass

Provides an information service on social
policy, public administration, and current and
international affairs, and access to current and
historical official publications from all countries
and intergovernmental bodies, including
House of Commons sessional papers, UK legislation, UK electoral registers, up-to-date reference books on official publications and on the
social sciences, a major collection of statistics
and a browsing collection of recent social science books and periodicals.

British Psychological Society Library

c/o Psychology Library, University of
London, Senate House, Malet Street, London
WC1E 7HU
☎0171 636 8000 ext. 5060
Fax 0171 436 1494

Open Term-time: 9.00 am to 9.00 pm
Monday to Thursday; 9.30 am to 6.30 pm

Friday; 9.00 am to 5.30 pm Saturday (holidays: 9.00 am to 6.00 pm Monday to Friday; 9.30 am to 5.30 pm Saturday)

Access Members only; Non-members £6.50 day ticket

Reference library, containing the British Psychological Society collection of periodicals – over 140 current titles housed alongside the University of London's collection of books and journals. Largely for academic research. General queries referred to **Swiss Cottage Library** which has a very good psychology collection.

Bromley Central Library

London Borough of Bromley - Leisure & Community Services, High Street, Bromley, Kent BR1 1EX

☎0181 460 9955   Fax 0181 313 9975

Open 9.30 am to 6.00 pm Monday, Wednesday, Friday; 9.30 am to 8.00 pm Tuesday and Thursday; 9.30 am to 5.00 pm Saturday

Open Access

A large selection of fiction and non-fiction books for loan, both adult and children's. Also videos, CDs, cassettes, language courses, open learning packs for hire. Other facilities include a business information service, CD-ROM, Ramesis, local studies library, 'Upfront' teenage section, large reference library with photocopying, fax, microfiche and film facilities and specialist 'Healthpoint' and 'Careerpoint' sections. Specialist collections include: H. G. Wells, Walter de la Mare, Crystal Palace, The Harlow Bequest, and the history and geography of Asia, America, Australasia and the Polar regions.

CAA Library and Information Centre

Aviation House, Gatwick Airport, West Sussex RH6 0YR

☎01293 573725   Fax 01293 573181

Open 9.30 pm to 4.30 pm Monday to Friday

Open Access

Books, periodicals and reports on air transport, air traffic control, electronics, radar and computing.

Cambridge Central Library (Reference Library & Information Service)

7 Lion Yard, Cambridge CB2 3QD

☎01223 365252   Fax 01223 362786

Open 9.30 am to 7.00 pm Monday, Wednesday, Thursday; 9.30 am to 5.00 pm

Tuesday and Friday; 12 noon to 7.00 pm Wednesday; 9.30 am to 5.00 pm Saturday

Access Open

Large stock of books, periodicals, newspapers, maps, plus comprehensive collection of directories and annuals covering UK, Europe and the world. Microfilm and fiche reading and printing services. On-line access to news and business databases. News databases on CD-ROM; Internet access. Monochrome and colour photocopiers.

Camomile Street Library

12–20 Camomile Street, London EC3A 7EX

☎0171 247 8895   Fax 0171 377 2972

Open 9.30 am to 5.30 pm Monday to Friday

Open access

The new City of London lending library, replacing the Bishopsgate Library. Wide range of fiction and non-fiction books and language courses on cassette, foreign fiction, paperbacks, maps and guides for travel at home and abroad, children's books, a selection of large print, and collections of music CDs and of videos.

Cardiff Central Library

Frederick Street, St David's Link, Cardiff CF1 4DT

☎01222 382116   Fax 01222 238642

Open 9.00 am to 6.00 pm Monday, Tuesday, Friday; 9.00 am to 8.00 pm Wednesday and Thursday; 9.00 am to 5.30 pm Saturday

General lending library with the following departments: leisure, music, children's, local studies, information, science and humanities.

Carmarthen Public Library

St Peter's Street, Carmarthen SA31 1LN

☎01267 224833   Fax 01267 221839

Open 9.30 am to 7.00 pm Monday, Tuesday, Wednesday Friday; 9.30 am to 5.00 pm Thursday and Saturday

Open access

Comprehensive range of fiction, non-fiction, children's books and reference works in English and in Welsh. Large local history library – newspapers/census returns on microfilm. Large Print books, books on tape, CDs, cassettes, and videos available for loan.

Catholic Central Library

47 Francis Street, London SW1P 1QR

☎0171 834 6128

Open 10.00 am to 5.00 pm Monday to Friday; 10.00 am to 1.30 pm Saturday

Open access For reference (non-members must sign in; loans restricted to members)

Contains books, many not readily available elsewhere, on theology, religions worldwide, scripture and the history of churches of all denominations.

The Centre for the Study of Cartoons and Caricature
See entry under **Picture Libraries**

City Business Library
1 Brewers Hall Garden, London EC2V 5BX
☎0171 638 8215   Fax 0171 332 1847
☎0171 480 7638 (recorded information)
Open 9.30 am to 5.00 pm Monday to Friday
Open access Local authority public reference library run by the Corporation of London.

Books, pamphlets, periodicals and newspapers of current business interest, mostly financial. Aims to satisfy the day-to-day information needs of the City's business community, and in so doing has become one of the leading public resource centres in Britain in its field. Strong collection of directories for both the UK and overseas, plus companies information, market research sources, management, law, banking, insurance, statistics and investment.

City of London Libraries
See **Barbican Library; Camomile Street Library; City Business Library; Guildhall**

Commonwealth Institute
Kensington High Street, London W8 6NQ
☎0171 603 4535   Fax 0171 602 7374
Open 11.00 am to 4.00 pm Tuesday to Friday; 1.00 pm to 4.45 pm Saturday
Access For reference (Loan service available to 'Friends' of the CI)

Special collection Books and periodicals on Commonwealth countries. Also a collection of directories and reference books on the Commonwealth and information on arts, geography, history and literature, cultural organisations and bibliography. The Commonwealth Literature Library includes fiction, poems, drama and critical writings.

Commonwealth Secretariat Library
Marlborough House, Pall Mall, London SW1Y 5HX
☎0171 747 6164   Fax 0171 747 6168
Open 9.15 am to 5.00 pm Monday to Friday

Access For reference only, by appointment

Extensive reference source concerned with economy, development, trade, production and industry of Commonwealth countries; also human resources including women, youth, health, management and education.

Coventry Central Library
Smithford Way, Coventry, Warwickshire CV1 1FY
☎01203 832314   Fax 01203 832440
Open 9.00 am to 8.00 pm Monday, Tuesday, Thursday, Friday; 9.30 am to 8.00 pm Wednesday; 9.00 am to 4.30 pm Saturday
Open access

Located in the middle of the city's main shopping centre. Approximately 120,000 items (books, records, cassettes and CDs) for loan; plus reference collection of business information and local history. *Special collections* Cycling and motor industries; George Eliot; Angela Brazil; Tom Mann Collection (trade union and labour studies); local newspapers on microfilm from 1740 onwards. Over 500 periodicals taken. CCTV available for people with visual handicap. 'Peoplelink' community information database available.

Derby Central Library
Wardwick, Derby DE1 1HS
☎01332 255389   Fax 01332 369570
Open 9.30 am to 7.00 pm Monday, Tuesday, Thursday, Friday; 9.30 am to 1.00 pm Wednesday and Saturday

LOCAL STUDIES LIBRARY
25B Irongate, Derby DE1 3GL
Open 9.30 am to 7.00 pm Monday and Tuesday; 9.30 am to 5.00 pm Wednesday, Thursday, Friday; 9.30 am to 1.00 pm Saturday
Open access

General library for lending, information and Children's Services. The Central Library also houses specialist private libraries: Derbyshire Archaeological Society; Derby Philatelic Society. The Local Studies Library houses the largest multimedia collection of resources in existence relating to Derby and Derbyshire. The collection includes mss deeds, family papers, business records including the Derby Canal Company, Derby Board of Guardians and the Derby China Factory.

Devon & Exeter Institution Library

7 Cathedral Close, Exeter, Devon EX1 1EZ
☎01392 251017

Open 9.00 am to 5.00 pm Monday to Friday

Access Members only

FOUNDED 1813. Contains over 36,000 volumes, including long runs of 19th-century journals, theology, history, topography, early science, biography and literature. A large and growing collection of books, journals, newspapers, prints and maps relating to the South-West.

Doncaster Libraries and Information Services

Central Library, Waterdale, Doncaster, South Yorkshire DN1 3JE
☎01302 734305　　　　Fax 01302 369749

Open 9.30 am to 6.00 pm Monday to Friday; 9.30 am to 4.00 pm Saturday

Open Access
Books, cassettes, CDs, videos, picture loans. Reading aids unit for people with visual handicap; activities for children during school holidays, including visits by authors, etc. Occasional funding available to support literature activities.

Dorchester Library (part of Dorset County Library)

Colliton Park, Dorchester, Dorset DT1 1XJ
☎01305 224440/224448　　Fax 01305 266120

Open 10.00 am to 7.00 pm Monday; 9.30 am to 7.00 pm Tuesday, Wednesday, Friday; 9.30 am to 5.00 pm Thursday; 9.00 am to 1.00 pm Saturday

Open Access
General lending and reference library, including Local Studies Collection, special collections on Thomas Hardy, The Powys Family, William Barnes and T. E. Lawrence. Periodicals, children's library, playsets.

Dundee District Libraries

Central Library, The Wellgate, Dundee DD1 1DB
☎01382 434318　　　　Fax 01382 434642

Open Lending Departments: 9.30 am to 7.00 pm Monday, Tuesday, Thursday, Friday; 10.00 am to 7.00 pm Wednesday; 9.30 am to 5.00 pm Saturday. General Reference Department: 9.30 am to 9.00 pm Monday, Tuesday, Thursday, Friday; 10.00 am to 7.00 pm Wednesday; 9.30 am to 5.00 pm Saturday. Local History Department: 9.30 am to 5.00 pm Monday, Tuesday, Friday, Saturday; 10.00 am to

7.00 pm Wednesday; 9.30 am to 7.00 pm Thursday.

Access Reference services available to all; lending services to those who live, work or study within Dundee City

Adult lending, reference and children's services. Art, music, audio and video lending services. Schools service (Agency). Housebound and mobile services. *Special collections*: The Wighton Collection of National Music; The Wilson Photographic Collection; The Lamb Collection.

English Nature

Northminster House, Peterborough, Cambridgeshire PE1 1UA
☎01733 455000　　　　Fax 01733 68834

Open 9.00 am to 5.00 pm Monday to Thursday; 9.00 am to 4.30 pm Friday;

Access To *bona fide* students only. Telephone for appointment

Information on nature conservation, nature reserves, SSSIs, planning, legislation, etc.

Equal Opportunities Commission Library

Overseas House, Quay Street, Manchester M3 3HN
☎0161 833 9244　　　　Fax 0161 835 1657

Open 10.00 am to 4.00 pm Monday to Friday

Access For reference

Books and pamphlets on equal opportunities and gender issues. Non-sexist children's books and Equal Opportunities Commission publications. Also an information service with periodicals and press cuttings.

Essex County Council Libraries

County Library Headquarters, Goldlay Gardens, Chelmsford, Essex CM2 0EW
☎01245 284981　　　　Fax 01245 492780

Essex County Council Libraries has 90 static libraries throughout Essex as well as 15 mobile libraries and four special-needs mobiles. Services to the public include books, newspapers, periodicals, CDs, cassettes, videos, pictures and CD-ROM as well as postal cassettes for the blind and subtitled videos. Specialist subjects and collections are listed below at the relevant library.

Chelmsford Library

PO Box 882, Market Road, Chelmsford, Essex CM1 1LH
☎01245 492758 Fax 01245 492536

Open: 9.00 am to 7.00 pm Monday to Friday; 9.00 am to 5.00 pm Saturday

Science and technology, business information, social sciences and medical.

Colchester Library
Trinity Square, Colchester, Essex CO1 1JB
☎01206 562243 Fax 01206 562413
Open: 9.00 am to 7.30 pm Monday, Tuesday, Wednesday, Friday; 9.00 am to 5.00 pm Thursday and Saturday

Local studies, music scores and education. Harsnett collection (early theological works 16th/17th-century); Castle collection (18th-century subscription library); Cunnington, Margaret Lazell and Taylor collections.

Grays Library
Orsett Road, Grays, Essex RM17 5DX
☎01375 383611 Fax 01375 370806
Open: 9.00 am to 7.30 pm Monday, Tuesday, Thursday, Friday; 9.00 am to 5.00 pm Wednesday and Saturday

Picture loans. County periodicals collection.

Harlow Library
The High, Harlow, Essex CM20 1HA
☎01279 413772 Fax 01279 424612
Open: 9.00 am to 7.30 pm Monday, Tuesday, Thursday, Friday; 9.00 am to 5.00 pm Wednesday and Saturday

Fiction, language and literature. Sir John Newson Memorial collection; Maurice Hughes Memorial collection.

Loughton Library
Traps Hill, Loughton, Essex IG10 1HD
☎0181 502 0181 Fax 0181 508 5041
Open: 9.00 am to 7.30 pm Monday, Tuesday, Wednesday, Friday; 9.00 am to 5.00 pm Saturday (closed Thursday)

Jazz archive.

Saffron Walden Library
2 King Street, Saffron Walden, Essex CB10 1ES
☎01799 523178 Fax 01799 513642
Open: 9.00 am to 7.00 pm Monday, Tuesday, Thursday, Friday; 9.00 am to 5.00 pm Saturday (closed Wednesday)

VICTORIAN STUDIES.

Southend Library
Victoria Avenue, Southend-on-Sea, Essex SS2 6EX
☎01702 612621 Fax 01702 469241
Open: 9.00 am to 7.00 pm Monday to Friday; 9.00 to 5.00 pm Saturday

Art, history and travel. Turner collection.

Witham Library
18 Newland Street, Witham, Essex CM8 2AQ
☎01376 519625 Fax 01376 501913
Open: 9.00 am to 7.00 pm Monday, Tuesday, Thursday, Friday; 9.00 am to 5.00 pm Saturday (closed Wednesday)

Drama. Dorothy L. Sayers collection.

The Fawcett Library
London Guildhall University, Calcutta House, Old Castle Street, London E1 7NT
☎0171 320 1189 Fax 0171 320 1188
Contact *Reference Librarian*
Open University term-time: 10.15 am to 8.30 pm Monday; 9.00 am to 8.30 pm Wednesday; 9.00 am to 5.00 pm Thursday and Friday. During University vacation: 9.00 am to 5.00 pm Monday, Wednesday to Friday

Open access Members of staff and students at London Guildhall University and to *bona fide* researchers employed in higher education institutions funded by the (UK) Funding Councils and DENI. Otherwise, full membership including borrowing rights £30 or £7 for full-time students and the unwaged. Day fee (reference only) £3 or £1.50 for students and the unwaged. Bring a student ID card or similar to claim concessionary rate and two passport-type photographs if intending to join as an annual member

The Fawcett Library, national research library for women's history, is the UK's oldest and most comprehensive research library on all aspects of women in society, with both historical and contemporary coverage. The Library includes materials on feminism, work, education, health, the family, law, arts, sciences, technology, language, sexuality, fashion and the home. The main emphasis is on Britain but many other countries are represented, especially the Commonwealth and the Third World. Established in 1926 as the library of the London Society of Women's Service (formerly Suffrage), a non-militant organisation led by Millicent Fawcett. In 1953 the Society was renamed after her and the library became the Fawcett Library.

Collections include: women's suffrage, work, education; women and the church, the law, sport, art, music; abortion, prostitution. Mostly British materials but some American and Commonwealth works. Books, journals, pamphlets, archives, photographs, posters, postcards, audiovisual materials, artefacts, scrapbooks, albums and press cuttings dating mainly from the 19th century although some materials date from the 17th century.

Foreign and Commonwealth Office Library

King Charles Street, London SW1A 2AH
☎0171 270 3925   Fax 0171 270 3270

Access By appointment only

An extensive stock of books, pamphlets and other reference material on all aspects of historical, socio-economic and political subjects relating to countries covered by the Foreign and Commonwealth Office. Particularly strong on colonial history, early travel works, and photograph collections, mainly of Commonwealth countries and former colonies, c. 1850s– 1960s.

Forestry Commission Library

Forest Research Station, Alice Holt Lodge, Wrecclesham, Farnham, Surrey GU10 4LH
☎01420 22255   Fax 01420 23653

Open 9.00 am to 5.00 pm Monday to Thursday; 9.00 am to 4.30 pm Friday

Access By appointment for personal visits

Approximately 10,000 books on forestry and arboriculture, plus 500 current journals. CD-ROMS include TREECD (1939 onwards). Offers a Research Advisory Service for advice and enquiries on forestry (☎01402 23000) with a charge for consultations and diagnosis of tree problems exceeding 10 minutes.

French Institute Library

17 Queensberry Place, London SW7 2DT
☎0171 838 2144   Fax 0171 838 2145

Head Librarian *Odile Grandet*
Deputy Head Librarian *Pascale Mukerjee*
Open 12.00 pm to 7.00 pm Tuesday to Friday; 12 noon to 6.00 pm Saturday

Open access For reference and consultation (loans restricted to members)

A collection of over 40,000 volumes mainly centred on French cultural interests with special emphasis on language, literature and history. Books in French and English. Collection of 1000 videos; 250 periodicals; 1000 CDs (French music); 50 CD-ROMs; Children's library (8000 books); also a special collection about 'France Libre'. Inter-library loans; quick information service; Internet access. Group visit on request.

John Frost Newspapers

8 Monks Avenue, Barnet, Hertfordshire EN5 1DB
☎0181 440 3159   Fax 0181 440 3159

Contact *John Frost, Andrew Frost*

A collection of 60,000 original newspapers (1630 to the present day) and 100,000 press cuttings available, on loan, for research and rostrum work (TV and audiovisual documentaries/presentations). Historic events, politics, sports, royalty, crime, wars, personalities etc., plus many in-depth files.

Gloucestershire County Library Arts & Museums Service

Quayside House, Shire Hall, Gloucester GL1 2HY
☎01452 425020   Fax 01452 425042

Open access

The service includes 39 local libraries – call the number above for opening hours; and seven mobile libraries telephone 01452 425039 for timetable/route enquiries

Goethe-Institut Library

50 Princes Gate, Exhibition Road, London SW7 2PH
☎0171 411 3452   Fax 0171 584 3180

Librarian *Regine Friederici*
Open 11.00 am to 8.00 pm Monday to Thursday; 10.00 am to 1.00 pm Saturday

Library specialising in German literature and books/audiovisual material on German culture and history: 27,000 books (4,800 of them in English), 134 periodicals, 14 newspapers, 2,600 audiovisual media (including 800 videos), selected press clippings on German affairs from the German and UK press, information service, photocopier, video facility for six viewers. Also German language teaching material for teachers and students of German.

Greater London Record Office

See **London Metropolitan Archives**

Guildford Institute of University of Surrey Library

Ward Street, Guildford, Surrey GU1 4LH
☎01483 562142

Librarian *Mrs Anne Milton-Worssell, BA, ALA*
Open 10.00 am to 3.00 pm Tuesday to Friday (under review and occasionally closed at lunchtime)

Open access To members only but open to enquirers for research purposes

FOUNDED 1834. Some 10,000 volumes of which 7500 were printed before the First World War. The remaining stock consists of recently published works of fiction, biography and travel. Newspapers and periodicals also available. *Special collections* include an almost complete run of the *Illustrated London News* from 1843-1906, a collection of Victorian scrapbooks, and about 400 photos and other pictures relating to the Institute's history and the town of Guildford.

Guildhall Library

Aldermanbury, London EC2P 2EJ
☎See below   Fax 0171 600 3384

Access For reference (but much of the material is kept in storage areas and is supplied to readers on request; proof of identity is required for consultation of certain categories of stock)

Part of the Corporation of London libraries. Seeks to provide a basic general reference service but its major strength, acknowledged worldwide, is in its historical collections. The library is divided into three sections, each with its own catalogues and enquiry desks. These are: Printed Books; Manuscripts; the Print Room.

PRINTED BOOKS
Open 9.30 am to 5 pm Monday to Saturday
☎0171 332 1868/1870

Strong on all aspects of London history, with wide holdings of English history, topography and genealogy, including local directories, poll books and parish register transcripts. Also good collections of English statutes, law reports, parliamentary debates and journals, and House of Commons papers. Home of several important collections deposited by London institutions: the Marine collection of the Corporation of Lloyd's, the Stock Exchange's historical files of reports and prospectuses, the Clockmakers' Company library and museum, the Gardeners' Company, Fletchers' Company, the Institute of Masters of Wine, International Wine and Food Society and Gresham College.

MANUSCRIPTS
Open 9.30 am to 4.45 pm Monday to Saturday (no requests for records after 4.30 pm)
☎0171 332 1863

The official repository for historical records relating to the City of London (except those of the Corporation of London itself, which are housed at the Corporation Records Office). Records date from the 11th century to the present day. They include archives of most of the City's parishes, wards and livery companies, and of many individuals, families, estates, schools, societies and other institutions, notably the Diocese of London and St Paul's Cathedral, as well as the largest collection of business archives in any public repository in the UK. Although mainly of City interest, holdings include material for the London area as a whole and beyond.

PRINT ROOM
Open 9.30 am to 5.00 pm Monday to Friday
☎0171 332 1839

An unrivalled collection of prints and drawings relating to London and the adjacent counties. The emphasis is on topography, but there are strong collections of portraits and satirical prints. The map collection includes maps of the capital from the mid-16th century to the present day and various classes of Ordnance Survey maps. Other material includes photographs, theatre bills and programmes, trade cards, book plates and playing cards as well as a sizeable collection of Old Master prints.

Guille–Alles Library

Market Street, St Peter Port, Guernsey, Channel Islands GY1 1HB
☎01481 720392   Fax 01481 712425

Open 9.00 am to 5.00 pm Monday, Tuesday, Thursday, Friday, Saturday; 9.00 am to 8.00 pm Wednesday

Open Access For residents; payment of returnable deposit by visitors
Lending, reference and information services.

Health Information Library (Westminster)

Marylebone Library, Marylebone Road, London NW1 5PS
☎0171 641 1039   Fax 0171 641 1044

Open 9.30 am to 8.00 pm Monday, Tuesday, Thursday, Friday; 10.00 am to 8.00 pm Wednesday; 9.30 am to 5.00 pm Saturday; 1.30 pm to 5.00 pm Sunday

Open access
Located in Westminster's Marylebone public library. Books, pamphlets and periodicals covering all aspects of medicine and the health services.

Hereford and Worcester County Libraries

Libraries and Arts Department, County Hall, Spetchley Road, Worcester WR5 2NP
☎01905 766240   Fax 01905 766244

Open Opening hours vary in branches across the county; all full-time libraries open at least one evening a week until 7.00 pm or 8.00 pm, and on Saturday until 1 pm

Access For reference to anyone; loans to members only (membership criteria: resident, educated, working, or an elector in the county or neighbouring authorities; temporary membership to other visitors. Proof of identity and address required)

Reference and lending libraries. Non-fiction and fiction for all age groups, including large print, sound recordings (CD, cassette, vinyl), videos, maps, local history, CD-ROMs for reference at main libraries. *Special collections* Carpets and Textiles; Needles & Needlemaking; Stuart Period; Cidermaking; Beekeeping; Housman and John Masefield.

University of Hertfordshire Library
College Lane, Hatfield, Hertfordshire
AL10 9AD
☎01707 284677   Fax 01707 284670

Open Term-time: 8.30 am to 10.00 pm Monday to Friday; 11.00 pm to 6.00 pm Saturday, Sunday; Holidays: 9.00 am to 5.00 pm Monday to Friday

Access For reference; loans available to members of HERTIS.

280,000 volumes and 2000 journals in science technology and social science, including law, across all five of the university's campuses. There are four other site libraries: at the Business School at Hertford, at the Watford campus near Radlett (education and humanities), at the Art & Design building in Hatfield and at the Law School in St Albans. Desk research, postal interlibrary loans and consultancy undertaken by HERTIS Information and Research Unit which is based at Hatfield and has capacity for up to 300 subscribing companies and organisations.

HERTIS
See **University of Hertfordshire Library**

Highgate Literary and Scientific Institution Library
11 South Grove, London N6 6BS
☎0181 340 3343

Open 10.00 am to 5.00 pm Tuesday to Friday; 10.00 am to 4.00 pm Saturday (closed Monday)
Annual membership £33 single; £51 household
40,000 volumes of general fiction and non-fiction, with a children's section and extensive archives. *Special collections* on local history, London, and local poets Samuel Taylor Coleridge and John Betjeman.

Highland Libraries, The Highland Council, Cultural and Leisure Services
Library Support, 31A Harbour Road, Inverness IV1 1UA
☎01463 235713   Fax 01463 236986

Open Library opening hours vary to suit local needs. Contact Administration and support services for details (8.00 am to 6.00 pm Monday to Friday)

Open access
Comprehensive range of lending and reference stock: books, pamphlets, periodicals, newspapers, compact discs, audio and video cassettes, maps, census records, genealogical records, photographs, educational materials, etc. Highland Libraries provides the public library service throughout the Highlands with a network of 41 static and 12 mobile libraries.

Holborn Library
32–38 Theobalds Road, London
WC1X 8PA
☎0171 413 6345/6

Open 10.00 am to 7.00 pm Monday and Thursday; 10.00 am to 6.00 pm Tuesday and Friday; 10.00 am to 5.00 pm Saturday (closed all day Wednesday)

Open access
London Borough of Camden public library, specialising in law. Also includes the London Borough of Camden Local Studies and Archive Centre.

Sherlock Holmes Collection (Westminster)
Marylebone Library, Marylebone Road, London NW1 5PS
☎0171 641 1206   Fax 0171 641 1019

Open 9.30 am to 5.00 pm Monday, Tuesday, Thursday, Friday; 10.00 am to 5.00 pm Wednesday (closed Saturday)

Telephone for Access By appointment only
Located in Westminster's Marylebone Library. An extensive collection of material from all over the world, covering Sherlock Holmes and Sir Arthur Conan Doyle. Books, pamphlets, journals, newspaper cuttings and photos, much of which is otherwise unavailable in this country. Some background material.

Imperial College Library
See **Science Museum Library**

Imperial War Museum

Department of Printed Books, Lambeth Road, London SE1 6HZ

☎0171 416 5000   Fax 0171 416 5374

Open 10.00 am to 5.00 pm Monday to Saturday (restricted service Saturday; closed on Bank Holiday Saturdays and last two full weeks of November for annual stock check)

Access For reference (but at least 24 hours' notice must be given for intended visits)

A large collection of material on 20th-century life with detailed coverage of the two world wars and other conflicts. Books, pamphlets and periodicals, including many produced for short periods in unlikely wartime settings; also maps, biographies and privately printed memoirs, and foreign language material. Additional research material available in the following departments: Art, Documents, Exhibits and Firearms, Film, Sound Records, Photographs. Active publishing programme based on reprints of rare books held in library. Catalogue available.

Instituto Cervantes

22 Manchester Square, London W1M 5AP

☎0171 935 1518   Fax 0171 935 6167

Open 9.30 am to 6.30 pm Monday to Thursday; 9.30 am to 5.00 pm Friday (closed Saturday)

Open access For reference and lending

Spanish literature, history, art, philosophy. The library houses a collection of books, periodicals, videos, slides, tapes, CDs, cassettes, films and CD-ROMs specialising entirely in Spain and Latin America.

Italian Institute Library

39 Belgrave Square, London SW1X 8NX

☎0171 235 1461   Fax 0171 235 4618

Open 10.00 am to 1.00 pm and 2.00 pm to 5.00 pm Monday to Friday

Open access For reference

A collection of over 26,000 volumes relating to all aspects of Italian culture. Texts are mostly in Italian, with some in English.

Jersey Library

Halkett Place, St Helier, Jersey JE2 4WH

☎01534 59991 (Lending)/59992 (Reference)
Fax 01534 69444

Open 9.30 am to 5.30 pm Monday, Wednesday, Thursday, Friday; 9.30 am to 7.30 pm Tuesday; 9.30 am to 4.00 pm Saturday

Open access

Books, periodicals, newspapers, CDs, cassettes, CD-ROMs, videos, microfilm, specialised local studies collection.

Kent County Central Library

Kent County Council Arts & Libraries, Springfield, Maidstone, Kent ME14 2LH

☎01622 696511   Fax 01622 753338

Open 10.00 am to 6.00 pm Monday, Tuesday, Wednesday, Friday; 10.00 am to 7.00 pm Thursday; 9.00 am to 4.00 pm Saturday

Open access

50,000 volumes available on the floor of the library plus 250,000 volumes of non-fiction, mostly academic, available on request to staff. English literature, poetry, classical literature, drama (including playsets), music (including music sets). Strong, too, in sociology, art and history. Loans to all who live or work in Kent; those who do not may consult stock for reference or arrange loans via their own local library service.

Lansdowne Library

Meyrick Road, Bournemouth, Dorset BH1 3DJ

☎01202 556603   Fax 01202 291781

Open 10.00 am to 7.00 pm Monday; 9.30 am to 7.00 pm Tuesday, Thursday, Friday; 9.30 am to 5.00 pm Wednesday; 9.00 am to 1.00 pm Saturday

Open access

General lending and reference library, County Music Library, collection of Government publications. Children's section, periodicals.

The Law Society

50 Chancery Lane, London WC2A 1SX

☎0171 320 5810/5811/5884
Fax 0171 242 1309

Head of Press Office *David McNeill*
Press Relations Manager *Catherine Slaytor*
Open 8.30 am to 5.30 pm with out-of-hours answerphone and mobile phone back-up

Access Library restricted to solicitors/members but press office available to all journalists for advice, information and assistance.

Provides all information about solicitors, the legal profession in general, law reform issues etc.

Leeds Central Library

Calverley Street, Leeds, West Yorkshire
LS1 3AB
☎0113 2478274   Fax 0113 2478268

Open 9.00 am to 8.00 pm Monday and
Wednesday; 9.00 am to 5.30 pm Tuesday
and Friday; 9.30 am to 5.30 pm Thursday;
10.00 am to 5.00 pm Saturday

Open Access to lending libraries; Reference
material on request
Lending Library covering all subjects.
Music Library contains scores, books and
audio.
Information for Business Library holds
company information, market research, statistics, directories, journals and computer-based
information.
Art Library (in Art Gallery) has a major
collection of material on fine and applied arts.
Local & Family History Library contains
an extensive collection on Leeds and Yorkshire, including maps, books, pamphlets, local
newspapers, illustrations and playbills. Census
returns for the whole of Yorkshire also available. International Genealogical Index and
parish registers.
Reference Library with over 270,000 volumes, including extensive files of newspapers
and periodicals plus all government publications since 1960. *Special collections* include
military history, Judaic, early gardening books,
and mountaineering.
Leeds City Libraries has an extensive network of 65 branch and mobile libraries.

Leeds Library

18 Commercial Street, Leeds, West Yorkshire
LS1 6AL
☎0113 2453071

Open 9.00 am to 5.00 pm Monday to Friday

Access To members; research use upon application to the librarian
FOUNDED 1768. Contains over 120,000
books and periodicals from the 15th century
to the present day. *Special collections* include
Reformation pamphlets, Civil War tracts, Victorian and Edwardian children's books and
fiction, European language material, spiritualism and psychical research, plus local material.

Lincoln Central Library

Free School Lane, Lincoln LN2 1EZ
☎01522 549160 (Reference)/510800(Lending)
Fax 01522 535882

Open 9.30 am to 7.00 pm Monday to Friday;
9.30 am to 4.00 pm Saturday

Linen Hall Library

17 Donegall Square North, Belfast BT1 5GD
☎01232 321707   Fax 01232 438586
Librarian *John Gray*
Open 9.30 am to 5.30 pm Monday, Tuesday,
Wednesday, Friday; 9.30 am to 8.30 pm
Thursday (5.30 pm in July and August);
9.30 am to 4.00 pm Saturday

Open access For reference (loans restricted to
members)
FOUNDED 1788. Contains about 200,000
books. Major Irish and local studies collections,
including the Northern Ireland Political
Collection relating to the current troubles (c.
90,000 items).

Literary & Philosophical Society of Newcastle upon Tyne

23 Westgate Road, Newcastle upon Tyne
NE1 1SE
☎0191 232 0192

Librarian *Pat Southern*
Open 9.30 am to 7.00 pm Monday,
Wednesday, Thursday, Friday; 9.30 am to
8.00 pm Tuesday; 9.30 am to 1.00 pm
Saturday

Access Members; research facilities for *bona
fide* scholars on application to the Librarian
200-year-old library of 140,000 volumes,
periodicals (including 130 current titles), classical
music on vinyl recordings and CD, plus a collection of scores. A programme of lectures and
recitals provided. Recent publications include:
*History of the Literary and Philosophical Society of
Newcastle upon Tyne, Vol. 2 (1896–1989)* Charles
Parish; *Bicentenary Lectures 1993* ed. John
Philipson.

Liverpool City Libraries

William Brown Street, Liverpool LE3 8EW
☎0151 225 5429   Fax 0151 207 1342

Open 9.00 am to 7.30 pm Monday to
Thursday; 9.00 am to 5.00 pm Friday;
10.00 am to 4.00 pm Saturday

Open access

**Arts and Recreation, Social Sciences,
Rare and Antiquarian Department**
Reference library with a total stock in excess of
120,000 volumes and 24,000 maps, plus book
plates, prints and autographed letters. *Special
collections* Walter Crane and Edward Lear illustrations, Kolmscott Press, Audubon.

**Business Information, Commerce and
Technology** Reference library with extensive

stock dealing with all aspects of science, commerce and technology, including British and European standards and patents and trade directories.

Music Library Extensive stock relating to all aspects of music. Includes 128,000 volumes and music scores, 18,500 records, and over 3000 cassettes and CDs. *Special collections* Carl Rosa Opera Company Collection and Earl of Sefton's early printed piano music.

Record Office and Local History Department Printed and audiovisual material relating to Liverpool, Merseyside, Lancashire and Cheshire, together with archive material mainly on Liverpool. Some restrictions on access, with 30-year rule applying to archives.

London College of Printing & Distributive Trades: Department of Learning Resources

Elephant and Castle, London SE1 6SB
☎0171 514 6500   Fax 0171 514 6597

Access By arrangement

The Department of Learning Resources operates from the three sites of the college at: Elephant & Castle; Davies Street (W1); Back Hill (Clerkenwell). Books, periodicals, slides, CD-ROM, videos and computer software on all aspects of the art of the book, printing, management, film/photography, graphic arts, plus retailing. *Special collections* Private Press books and the history and development of printing and books.

The London Library

14 St James's Square, London SW1Y 4LG
☎0171 930 7705/6   Fax 0171 930 0436

Librarian *Mr A. S. Bell*

Open 9.30 am to 5.30 pm Monday to Saturday (Thursday till 7.30 pm)

Access Members only (£120 p.a. 1997 price)

With over a million books and 8300 members, The London Library 'is the most distinguished private library in the world; probably the largest, certainly the best loved'. Founded in 1841, it is a registered charity and wholly independent of public funding. Its permanent collection embraces most European languages as well as English. Its subject range is predominantly within the humanities, with emphasis on literature, history, fine and applied art, architecture, bibliography, philosophy, religion, and topography and travel. Some 6000–7000 titles are added yearly. Most of the stock is on open shelves to which members have free access. Members may take out up to 10 volumes; 15 if

they live more than 20 miles from the Library. The comfortable Reading Room has an annexe for users of personal computers. There are photocopiers and CD-ROM workstations, and the Library also offers a postal loans service.

Prospective members are required to submit a refereed application form in advance of admission, but there is at present no waiting list for membership. The London Library Trust may make grants to those who are unable to afford the full annual fee; details on application.

London Metropolitan Archives

40 Northampton Road, London EC1R 0HB
☎0171 332 3822   Fax 0171 833 9136

Open 9.30 am to 4.45 pm Monday to Friday

Access For reference only

Formerly, the Greater London Record Office Library. Covers all aspects of the life and development of London, specialising in the history and organisation of local government in general, and London in particular. Books on London history and topography, covering many subjects. Also London directories dating back to 1677, plus other source material including Acts of Parliament, Hansard reports, statistical returns, atlases, yearbooks and many complete sets of newspapers and magazines.

Lord Louis Library

Orchard Street, Newport, Isle of Wight PO30 1LL
☎01983 527655/823800 (Reference Library)
Fax 01983 825972

Open 9.30 am to 5.30 pm Monday to Friday (Saturday till 5.00 pm)

Open access

General adult and junior fiction and non-fiction collections; local history collection and periodicals. Also the county's main reference library.

Manchester Central Library

St Peters Square, Manchester M2 5PD
☎0161 234 1900   Fax 0161 234 1963

Open 10.00 am to 8.00 pm Monday to Thursday; 10.00 am to 5.00 pm Friday and Saturday; Commercial and European Units: 10.00 am to 6.00 pm Monday to Thursday; 10.00 am to 5.00 pm Friday and Saturday

Open access

One of the country's leading reference libraries with extensive collections covering all subjects. Subject departments include: Commercial, European, Technical, Social Sciences,

Arts, Music, Local Studies, Chinese, General Readers, Language & Literature. Large lending stock and VIP (visually impaired) service available.

Marylebone Library (Westminster)
See **Health Information Library; Sherlock Holmes Collection**

Ministry of Agriculture, Fisheries and Food
Whitehall Place Library, 3 Whitehall Place, London SW1A 2HH
☎0171 270 8000/8421   Fax 0171 270 8419
MAFF Helpline 0645 335577 (local call rate) – general contact point which can provide information on the work of MAFF, either directly or by referring callers to appropriate contacts. Available 9.00 am to 5.00 pm Monday to Friday (excluding Bank Holidays)

Open 9.30 am to 5.00 pm Monday to Friday

Access For reference (but at least 24 hours notice must be given for intended visits)
Large stock of volumes on temperate agriculture.

The Mitchell Library
North Street, Glasgow G3 7DN
☎0141 287 2999   Fax 0141 287 2815
Contact *Mrs F. MacPherson*
Open 9.00 am to 8.00 pm Monday to Thursday; 9.00 am to 5.00 pm Friday and Saturday
Open access
Europe's largest public reference library with stock of over 1,200,000 volumes. It subscribes to 46 newspapers and more than 2,000 periodicals. There are collections in microform, records, tapes and videos, as well as CD-ROM, illustrations, photographs, postcards etc.
The library is divided into a number of subject departments including the arts department which contains a number of special collections, eg the Robert Burns Collection (5000 vols), the Scottish Poetry Collection (12,000 items) and the Scottish Drama Collection (1,650 items).

National Library of Scotland
George IV Bridge, Edinburgh EH1 1EW
☎0131 226 4531/459 4531
Fax 0131 220 6662
Open Main Reading Room: 9.30 am to 8.30 pm Monday, Tuesday, Thursday,

Friday; 10.00 am to 8.30 pm Wednesday; 9.30 am to 1.00 pm Saturday. Map Library: 9.30 am to 5.00 pm Monday, Tuesday, Thursday, Friday; 10.00 am to 5.00 pm Wednesday; 9.30 am to 1.00 pm Saturday. Scottish Science Library: 9.30 am to 5.00 pm Monday, Tuesday, Thursday, Friday; 10.00 am to 8.30 pm Wednesday.

Access To reading rooms and Map Library, for research not easily done elsewhere, by reader's ticket
Collection of over 6 million volumes. The library receives all British and Irish publications. Large stock of newspapers and periodicals. Many special collections, including early Scottish books, theology, polar studies, baking, phrenology and liturgies. Also large collections of maps, music and manuscripts including personal archives of notable Scottish persons.

National Library of Wales
Aberystwyth, Ceredigion SY23 3BU
☎01970 623816   Fax 01970 615709
Open 9.30 am to 6.00 pm Monday to Friday; 9.30 am to 5.00 pm Saturday (closed Bank Holidays and first week of October)
Access To reading rooms and map room by reader's ticket, available on application
Collection of over 4 million books and including large collections of periodicals, maps, manuscripts and audiovisual material. Particular emphasis on humanities in printed foreign material, and on Wales and other Celtic areas in all collections.

National Meteorological Library and Archive
London Road, Bracknell, Berkshire RG12 2SZ
☎01344 854843   Fax 01344 854840
Open Library & Archive: 8.30 am to 4.30 pm Monday to Friday; Archive closed between 1.00 pm and 2.00 pm
Access By Visitor's Pass available from the reception desk; advance notice of a planned visit is appreciated
The major repository of most of the important literature on the subjects of meteorology, climatology and related sciences. The Library houses a collection of books, journals, articles and scientific papers, plus published climatological data from many parts of the world. The Technical Archive (The Scott Building, Sterling Centre, Eastern Road, Bracknell, Berks RG12 2PW) holds the document collec-

tion of meteorological data and charts from England, Wales and British overseas bases, including ships' weather logs. Records from Scotland are stored in Edinburgh and those from Northern Ireland in Belfast.

The Natural History Museum Library

Cromwell Road, London SW7 5BD
☎0171 938 9191   Fax 0171 938 9290
Open 10.00 am to 4.30 pm Monday to Friday
Access To *bona fide* researchers, by reader's ticket on presentation of identification (telephone first to make an appointment)

The library is in five sections: general; botany; zoology; entomology; earth sciences. The sub-department of ornithology is housed at Zoological Museum, Akeman Street, Tring, Herts HP23 6AP (☎01442 834181). Resources available include books, journals, maps, manuscripts, drawings and photographs covering all aspects of natural history, including palaeontology and mineralogy, from the 14th century to the present day. Also archives and historical collection on the museum itself.

Newcastle upon Tyne City Library

Princess Square, Newcastle upon Tyne NE99 1DX
☎0191 261 0691   Fax 0191 261 1435

Open 9.30 am to 8.00 pm Monday and
Thursday; 9.30 am to 5.00 pm Tuesday, Wednesday, Friday; 9.00 am to 5.00 pm Saturday

Open access
Extensive local studies collection, including newspapers, illustrations and genealogy. Also business, science, humanities and arts, educational guidance unit, open learning resource centre, marketing advice centre, patents advice centre.

Norfolk Library & Information Service

Norfolk and Norwich Central Library, Central Lending Service, 71 Ber Street, Norwich, Norfolk NR1 3AD
☎01603 215215

Central Reference & Information Service and Norfolk Studies
Gildengate House, Upper Green Lane, Norwich, Norfolk NR3 1AX
☎01603 215222   Fax 01603 215258
Open Lending Library, Reference and Information Service and Norfolk Studies:

10.00 am to 8.00 pm Monday to Friday; 9.00 am to 5.00 pm Saturday

Open access
Reference and lending library with wide range of stock for loan, including books, recorded music, music scores, plays and videos. (The collections were severely damaged by fire in August 1994 and are in the process of being rebuilt.) Houses the 2nd Air Division Memorial Library and has a strong Local Studies Library. Extensive range of reference stock including business information. On-line database and CD-ROM services. Public fax and colour photocopying. Information brokerage provides in-depth research services.

Northamptonshire Libraries & Information Service

Library HQ, PO Box 259, 27 Guildhall Road, Northampton NN1 1BA
☎01604 20262   Fax 01604 26789
Since 1991, the Libraries and Information Service have run two to three programmes of literary events for adults each year. Programmes so far have included visiting authors, poetry readings, workshops and other events and activities. The programmes are supported by regular touring fiction displays, writers' advice sessions and dedicated notice boards in libraries across the county.

Northumberland Central Library

The Willows, Morpeth, Northumberland NE61 1TA
☎01670 512385   Fax 01670 519985
Open 10.00 am to 8.00 pm Monday, Tuesday, Wednesday, Friday; 9.30 am to 12.30 pm Saturday (closed Thursday)

Open access
Books, periodicals, newspapers, cassettes, CDs, video, microcomputers, CD-ROM, Internet access, prints, microforms, vocal scores, playsets, community resource equipment. *Special collections* **Northern Poetry Library**: 13,000 volumes of modern poetry (see entry: **Organisations of Interest to Poets**); cinema: comprehensive collection of about 5000 volumes covering all aspects of the cinema; family history.

Nottingham Central Library

Angel Row, Nottingham NG1 6HP
☎0115 9412121   Fax 0115 9504207
Open 9.30 am to 7.00 pm Monday to Friday; 9.00 am to 1.00 pm Saturday

Open access

General public lending library: business information, the arts, local studies, religion, literature. Videos, periodicals, spoken word, recorded music, search service – textual information on CD-ROM on public access machines. *Special collection* on D. H. Lawrence. Extensive back-up reserve stocks. Drama and music sets for loan to groups.

Nottingham Subscription Library Ltd

Bromley House, Angel Row, Nottingham NG1 6HL
☎0115 9473134

Librarian *Julia Wilson*

Open 9.30 am to 5.00 pm Monday to Friday; also first Saturday of each month from 10.00 am to 12.30 pm for members only

FOUNDED 1816. Collection of 30,000 books including local history, topography, biography, travel and fiction.

Office for National Statistics

1 Drummond Gate, London SW1V 2QQ
☎0171 533 6262   Fax 0171 533 6261

Open 9.30 am to 4.30 pm Monday to Friday

Access By appointment only

All published Census data from 1801 onwards for the UK. Population and health statistics from 1837 onwards. Some foreign censuses and statistics (incomplete; most are out-housed and require one week's notice for retrieval). International statistics (WHO, UN, etc). Government Social Survey reports, 1941 onwards. Small stock of books on demography, vital registration, epidemology, survey methodology, census taking.

Orkney Library

Laing Street, Kirkwall, Orkney KW15 1NW
☎01856 873166   Fax 01856 875260

Open 9.00 am to 8.00 pm Monday to Friday; 9.00 am to 5.00 pm Saturday. Archives: 9.00 am to 1.00 pm and 2.00 pm to 4.45 pm Monday to Friday

Open access

Local studies collection. Archive includes sound and photographic departments.

Oxford Central Library

Westgate, Oxford OX1 1DJ
☎01865 815549   Fax 01865 721694

Open 9.15 am to 7.00 pm Monday, Tuesday, Thursday, Friday (Wednesday and Saturday till 5.00 pm); Centre for Oxfordshire Studies closed on Mondays; Special arrangements over Bank Holidays

General lending and reference library including the Centre for Oxfordshire Studies. Also has audio visual materials, children's library, music library, periodicals, and Business Information Point.

PA News Library

292 Vauxhall Bridge Road, London SW1V 1AE
☎0171 963 7012   Fax 0171 963 7065

Open 8.00 am to 8.00 pm Monday to Friday; 8.00 am to 6.00 pm Saturday; 9.00 am to 5.00 pm Sunday

Open Access

PA News, the 24-hour national news and information group, offers public access to its press cutting archive. Covering a wide range of subjects, the library includes over 14 million cuttings dating back to 1928. Personal callers welcome or research undertaken by in-house staff.

Penzance Library

Morrab House, Morrab Gardens, Penzance, Cornwall TR18 4DQ
☎01736 64474

Librarian *L. Lowdon*

Open 10.00 am to 4.00 pm Tuesday to Friday; 10.00 am to 1.00 pm Saturday

Access Non-members may use the library for a small daily fee, but may not borrow books

An independent subscription lending library of over 60,000 volumes covering virtually all subjects except modern science and technology, with large collections on history, literature and religion. There is a comprehensive Cornish collection of books, newspapers and manuscripts including the Borlase letters; a West Cornwall photographic archive; many runs of 18th- and 19th-century periodicals; a collection of over 2000 books published before 1800.

Plymouth Central Library

Drake Circus, Plymouth, Devon PL4 8AL
Fax 01752 385905

Open Access

LENDING DEPARTMENTS:
Lending ☎01752 385912
Children's Department ☎01752 385916
Music & Drama Department ☎01752 385914

Open 9.30 am to 7.00 pm Monday, Friday;

9.30 am to 5.30 pm Tuesday, Wednesday, Thursday; 9.30 am to 4.00 pm Saturday

The Lending departments offer books on all subjects; language courses on cassette and foreign language books; the Holcenberg Jewish Collection; books on music and musicians, drama and theatre; music parts and sets of music parts; play sets; videos; song index; cassettes and CDs.

REFERENCE DEPARTMENTS:
Reference ☎01752 385907/8
Business Information ☎01752 385906
Local Studies & Natural History Department ☎01752 985909

Open 9.00 am to 7.00 pm Monday to Friday; 9.00 am to 4.00 pm Saturday

The Reference departments include an extensive collection of Ordnance Survey maps and town guides; community and census information; marketing and statistical information; Patents and British Standards; books on every aspect of Plymouth; naval history; Mormon Index on microfilm; Baring Gould manuscript of 'Folk Songs of the West'.

Plymouth Proprietary Library

Alton Terrace, 111 North Hill, Plymouth, Devon PL4 8JY
☎01752 660515

Librarian *Camilla M. Blackman*

Open Monday to Saturday from 9.30 am (closing time varies)

Access To members; visitors by appointment only

FOUNDED 1810. The library contains approximately 17,000 volumes of mainly 20th-century work. Member of the Association of Independent Libraries.

The Poetry Library

See entry under **Organisations of Interest to Poets**

Polish Library

238–246 King Street, London W6 0RF
☎0181 741 0474   Fax 0181 746 3798

Open 10.00 am to 8.00 pm Monday and Wednesday; 10.00 am to 5.00 pm Friday; 10.00 am to 1.00 pm Saturday (library closed Tuesday and Thursday)

Access For reference to all interested in Polish affairs; limited loans to members and *bona fide* scholars only through inter-library loans

Books, pamphlets, periodicals, maps, music, photographs on all aspects of Polish history and culture. *Special collections* Emigré publications; Joseph Conrad and related works; Polish underground publications; bookplates.

Poole Central Library

Dolphin Centre, Poole, Dorset BH15 1QE
☎01202 673910   Fax 01202 670253

Open 10.00 am to 7.00 pm Monday; 9.30 am to 7.00 pm Tuesday to Friday; 9.00 am to 1.00 pm Saturday

Open access

General lending and reference library, including Healthpoint health information centre, HATRICS business information centre, children's library, periodicals.

Press Association Library

See **PA News Library**

Harry Price Library of Magical Literature

University of London Library, Senate House, Malet Street, London WC1E 7HU
☎0171 636 8000 ext 5031 Fax 0171 436 1494

Open 9.30 am to 5.15 pm Monday to Friday; 9.30 am to 1.00 pm, 2.00 pm to 5.15 pm Saturday (by prior appointment only); Monday evenings in term time (by prior appointment only)

Restricted access For reference only, restricted to members of the University and *bona fide* researchers (apply in writing); items must be requested from, and consulted in, the Special Collections Reading Room

Over 14,000 volumes and pamphlets on psychic phenomena and pseudo-phenomena; books relating to spiritualism and its history, to hypnotism, telepathy, astrology, conjuring and quackery.

Public Record Office

Ruskin Avenue, Kew, Richmond, Surrey TW9 4DU
☎0181 876 3444   Fax 0181 878 8905

Also at: The Family Record Centre, 1 Myddleton Street, London EC1 1UW

Open 9.30 am to 5.00 pm Monday, Wednesday, Friday; 10.00 am to 7.00 pm Tuesday; 9.30 am to 7.00 pm Thursday; 9.30 am to 5.00 pm Saturday

Access For reference, by reader's ticket, available free of charge on production of proof of identity (UK citizens: banker's card or driving licence; non-UK: passport or national identity card. Telephone for further information)

Over 168 kilometres of shelving house the national repository of records of central Government in the UK and law courts of England and Wales, which extend in time from the 11th–20th century. Medieval records and the records of the State Paper Office from the early 16th–late 18th century, plus the records of the Privy Council Office and the Lord Chamberlain's and Lord Steward's departments. Modern government department records, together with those of the Copyright Office dating mostly from the late 18th century. Under the Public Records Act, records are normally only open to inspection when they are 30 years old.

Reading Central Library

Abbey Square, Reading, Berkshire
RG1 3BQ
☎0118 9509245　　　　Fax 0118 9589039

Open 9.30 am to 5.00 pm Monday and Wednesday; 9.30 am to 7.00 pm Tuesday, Thursday, Friday; 9.30 am to 4.00 pm Saturday

Open access

Lending library; county reference library; county local studies library, bringing together every aspect of the local environment and human activity in Berkshire; county business library; county music and drama library. Special collections: Mary Russell Mitford; local illustrations.

Public meeting room available.

Religious Society of Friends Library

Friends House, 173 Euston Road, London
NW1 2BJ
☎0171 387 3601　　　　Fax 0171 388 1977

Quaker history, thought and activities from the 17th century onwards. Supporting collections on peace, anti-slavery and other subjects in which Quakers have maintained long-standing interest. Also archives and manuscripts relating to the Society of Friends. Closed until early 1998 due to Friends House building work. Send s.a.e. for leaflet on closure, Quaker libraries and microfilm publications.

Richmond Central Reference Library

Old Town Hall, Whittaker Avenue, Richmond, Surrey TW9 1TP
☎0181 940 5529　　　　Fax 0181 940 6899

Open 10.00 am to 6.00 pm Monday, Thursday, Friday (Tuesday till 1.00 pm;

Wednesday till 8.00 pm and Saturday till 5.00 pm)

Open access

General reference library serving the needs of local residents and organisations.

Royal Geographical Society Library (with the Institute of British Geographers)

1 Kensington Gore, London SW7 2AR
☎0171 591 3040　　　　Fax 0171 591 3001

Open 10.00 am to 5.00 pm Monday to Friday

Access to the library and reading rooms restricted to use by Fellows and members

Books and periodicals on geography, topography, cartography, voyages and travels. The Map Room, open since 1854 to the general public for reference purposes only, houses map and chart sheets, atlases and RGS-sponsored expedition reports. Photographs on travel and exploration are housed in the picture library, for which an appointment is necessary. (See entry under **Picture Libraries**.)

Royal Society Library

6 Carlton House Terrace, London
SW1Y 5AG
☎0171 839 5561　　　　Fax 0171 930 2170

Open 10.00 am to 5.00 pm Monday to Friday

Access For research only, to *bona fide* researchers on application to the Head of Fellowship and Information Services.

History of science, scientists' biographies, science policy reports, and publications of international scientific unions and national academies from all over the world.

RSA (Royal Society for the Encouragement of Arts, Manufactures & Commerce)

8 John Adam Street, London WC2N 6EZ
☎0171 930 5115　　　　Fax 0171 839 5805

Archivist *Susan Bennett*

Open 10.00 am to 1.00 pm Monday, Tuesday, Wednesday, Thursday and 2.00pm to 5.00 pm Wednesdays only; 10.00 am to 1.00 pm Friday

Access to Fellows of RSA; by application and appointment to non-Fellows (£6.00 for a yearly ticket)

Archives of the Society since 1754. A collection of approximately 5000 volumes; international exhibition material.

Royal Society of Medicine Library
1 Wimpole Street, London W1M 8AE
☎0171 290 2940   Fax 0171 290 2939

Open 9.00 am to 8.30 pm Monday to Friday;
   10.00 am to 5.00 pm Saturday

Access For reference only, on introduction by
Fellow of the Society (temporary membership
may also be granted)
   Books and periodicals on general medicine,
biochemistry and biomedical science. Extensive historical material.

Royal Statistical Society Library
University College London, Gower Street,
London WC1E 6BT
☎0171 387 7050 ext. 2628
Fax 0171 380 7727/7373

Contact *D Chatarji*

Access RSS fellows registered with University
College London Library
   Statistics (theory and methodology), mathematical statistics, applied statistics, econometrics.

Science Fiction Foundation Research Library
Liverpool University Library, PO Box 123,
Liverpool L69 3DA
☎0151 794 2696/2733   Fax 0151 794 2681

Access For research, by appointment only
   (telephone first)
   This is the largest collection outside the US
of science fiction and related material – including autobiographies and critical works. *Special
collection* Runs of 'pulp' magazines dating back
to the 1920s. Foreign-language material
(including a large Russian collection), and the
papers of the Flat Earth Society. The collection
also features a growing range of archive and
manuscript material, including the Eric Frank
Russell archive.

Science Museum Library
Imperial College Road, off Exhibition Road,
London SW7 5NH
☎0171 938 8234   Fax 0171 938 9714

Open 9.30 am to 9.00 pm Monday to Friday
   (closes 5.30 pm outside academic terms);
   9.30 am to 5.30 pm Saturday

Open access Reference only; no loans
   National reference library for the history and
public understanding of science and technology, with a large collection of source material.
Operates jointly with Imperial College Central
Library.

Scottish Poetry Library
See entry under **Organisations of Interest
to Poets**

Sheffield Libraries and Information Services
Central Library, Surrey Street, Sheffield
S1 1XZ
☎0114 2734711   Fax 0114 2735009
Sheffield Archives
52 Shoreham Street, Sheffield S1 4SP
☎0114 2734756   Fax 0114 2735066

Open 9.30 am to 5.30 pm Monday to
   Thursday; 9.00 am to 1.00 pm and 2.00 pm
   to 4.30 pm Saturday (documents should be
   ordered by 5.00 pm Thursday for Saturday)

Access By reader's pass
   Holds documents relating to Sheffield and
South Yorkshire, dating from the 12th century
to the present day, including records of the
City Council, churches, businesses, landed
estates, families and individuals, institutions and
societies.

Arts and Social Sciences Reference Service
☎0114 2734747/8

Open 10.00 am to 8.00 pm Monday; 9.30 am
   to 5.30 pm Tuesday and Friday; 9.30 am to
   8.00 pm Wednesday; 9.30 am to 4.30 pm
   Saturday (closed Thursday)

Access For reference only
   A comprehensive collection of books, periodicals and newspapers covering all aspects of
arts (excluding music) and social sciences.

Music and Video Service
☎0114 2734733

Open as for Arts and Social Services above

Access For reference (loans to ticket holders
only)
   An extensive range of books, records, CDs,
cassettes, scores, etc. related to music. Also a
video cassette loan service.

Local Studies Service
☎0114 2734753

Open as for Arts & Social Sciences above
   (except Wednesday 9.30 am to 5.30 pm)

Access For reference (advance notice advisable)
   Extensive material covering all aspects of
Sheffield and its population, including maps,
photos and taped oral histories.

Business, Science and Technology Reference Services
☎0114 2734736–8

Open as for Arts & Social Sciences above

Access For reference only

Extensive coverage of science and technology as well as commerce and commercial law. British patents and British and European standards with emphasis on metals. Hosts the World Metal Index. The business section holds a large stock of business and trade directories, plus overseas telephone directories and reference works with business emphasis.

Sheffield Information Service
☎0114 2734760/1

Open 10.00 am to 5.30 pm Monday; 9.30 am to 5.30 pm Tuesday, Wednesday, Friday; 9.30 am to 4.30 pm Saturday (closed Thursday)

Full local information service covering all aspects of the Sheffield community and a generalist advice service on a sessional basis.

Shetland Library
Lower Hillhead, Lerwick, Shetland
ZE1 0EL
☎01595 693868   Fax 01595 694430

Open 10.00 am to 7.00 pm Monday, Wednesday, Friday; 10.00 am to 5.00 pm Tuesday, Thursday, Saturday

General lending and reference library; extensive local interest collection including complete set of *The Shetland Times*, *The Shetland News* and other local newspapers on microfilm and many old and rare books; audio collection including *Linguaphone* courses and talking books/newspapers. Junior room for children. Disabled access and Housebound Readers Service (delivery to reader's home). Mobile library services to rural areas. Open Learning Service. Same day photocopying service. Publishing programme of books in dialect, history, literature.

Shoe Lane Library
Hill House, Little New Street, London
EC4A 3JR
☎0171 583 7178

Open 9.30 am to 5.30 pm Monday, Wednesday, Thursday, Friday; 9.30 am to 6.30 pm Tuesday

Open access

Corporation of London general lending library, with a comprehensive stock of 48,000 volumes, most of which are on display. Some specialisation in graphics, advertising and illustrated works.

Shrewsbury Library
Castlegates, Shrewsbury, Shropshire SY1 2AS
☎01743 255300   Fax 01743 255309

Open 9.30 am to 5.00 pm Monday and Wednesday; 9.30 am to 1.00 pm Thursday; 9.30 am to 7.30 pm Tuesday and Friday; 9.30 am to 4.00 pm Saturday

Open access

The largest public lending library in Shropshire. Books, cassettes, CDs, talking books, videos, language courses. Public Internet access. Strong music, literature and art book collection. Reference and local studies provision in adjacent buildings.

Spanish Institute Library
See **Instituto Cervantes**

St Bride Printing Library
Bride Lane, London EC4Y 8EE
☎0171 353 4660   Fax 0171 583 7073

Open 9.30 am to 5.30 pm Monday to Friday

Open access

Corporation of London public reference library. Appointments advisable for consultation of special collections. Every aspect of printing and related matters: publishing and bookselling, newspapers and magazines, graphic design, calligraphy and type, papermaking and bookbinding. One of the world's largest specialist collections in its field, with over 40,000 volumes, over 2000 periodicals (200 current titles), and extensive collection of drawings, manuscripts, prospectuses, patents and materials for printing and typefounding. Noted for its comprehensive holdings of historical and early technical literature.

Suffolk County Council Libraries & Heritage
St Andrew House, County Hall, St Helens Street, Ipswich, Suffolk IP4 1LJ
☎01473 583000   Fax 01473 584549

Open Details on application to St Andrew House above. Major libraries open six days a week

Access A single user registration card gives access to the lending service of 41 libraries across the county

Full range of lending and reference services. *Special collections* include Suffolk Archives and Local History Collection; Benjamin Britten

Collection; Edward Fitzgerald Collection; Seckford Collection and Racing Collection (Newmarket). The Suffolk Infolink service gives details of local groups and societies and is available in libraries throughout the county.

Sunderland City Library and Arts Centre

28–30 Fawcett Street, Sunderland, Tyne & Wear SR1 1RE
☎0191 514 1235   Fax 0191 514 8444
Open 9.30 am to 7.30 pm Monday and Wednesday; 9.30 am to 5.00 pm Tuesday, Thursday, Friday; 9.30 am to 4.00 pm Saturday

The city's main lending and reference library. Local studies and children's sections, plus sound and vision department (CDs, cassettes, videos, talking books). The City of Sunderland maintains a further 19 branch libraries. Special services available to housebound readers, hospitals and schools, plus two mobile libraries.

Swansea Central Reference Library

Alexandra Road, Swansea SA1 5DX
☎01792 655521   Fax 01792 645751
Open 9.00 am to 7.00 pm Monday, Tuesday, Wednesday, Friday; 9.00 am to 5.00 pm Thursday and Saturday. The library has a lending service but hours tend to be shorter – check in advance (☎01792 654065).

Access For reference only (Local Studies closed access: items must be requested on forms provided)
    General reference material (approx. 50,000 volumes); also British standards, statutes, company information, maps, etc. Local studies: comprehensive collections on Wales; Swansea & Gower; Dylan Thomas. Local maps, periodicals, illustrations, local newspapers from 1804. B&w and colour photocopying facilities and microfilm/microfiche copying facility.

Swiss Cottage Library

88 Avenue Road, London NW3 3HA
☎0171 413 6533/4
Open 10.00 am to 7.00 pm Monday and Thursday; 10.00 am to 6.00 pm Tuesday and Friday; 10.00 am to 5.00 pm Saturday (closed all day Wednesday)

Open access
    Over 300,000 volumes in the lending and reference libraries and 300 periodicals (200 current titles). Home of the London Borough of Camden's Information and Reference Services.

Theatre Museum Library & Archive

1e Tavistock Street, London WC2E 7PA
☎0171 836 7891   Fax 0171 836 5148
Open 10.30 am to 4.30 pm Tuesday to Friday
Access By appointment only
    The Theatre Museum was founded as a separate department of the Victoria & Albert Museum in 1974 and moved to its own building in Covent Garden in 1987. The museum (open Tuesday to Sunday 11.00 am to 7.00 pm) houses permanent displays, temporary exhibitions, a studio theatre, and organises a programme of special events, performances, lectures and guided visits. The library houses the UK's largest performing arts research collections, including books, photographs, designs, engravings, programmes, press cuttings, etc. All the performing arts are covered but strengths are in the areas of theatre history, ballet, circus and stage design. The Theatre Museum has acquired much of the British Theatre Association's library and is providing reference access to its collections of play texts and critical works.

Truro Library

Union Place, Pydar Street, Truro, Cornwall TR1 1EP
☎01872 79205 (Lending)/72702 (Reference)
Open 9.30 am to 5.00 pm Monday to Thursday; 9.30 am to 7.00 pm Friday; 9.30 am to 1.00 pm Saturday

Books, cassettes, CDs and videos for loan through branch or mobile networks. Reference, local studies, music and drama. *Special collections* on the visual arts and maritime studies. Opening hours vary at branch libraries throughout the county.

United Nations Office and Information Centre

Millbank Tower (21st Floor), 21–24 Millbank, London SW1P 4QH
☎0171 630 1981   Fax 0171 976 6478
Open Information Centre: 9.30 am to 1.00 pm and 2.00 pm to 5.30 pm Monday to Friday. Reference Library: 2.00 pm to 5.00 pm Monday; 10.00 am to 1.00 pm and 2.00 pm to 5.00 pm Tuesday, Wednesday, Thursday; 10.00 am to 1.00 pm Friday

Open access To Information Centre only; Reference Library by appointment only
    A full stock of official publications and documentation from the United Nations.

Western Isles Libraries

Public Library, Keith Street, Stornoway, Isle of Lewis HS1 2QG
☎01851 703064   Fax 01851 705657

Open 10.00 am to 5.00 pm Monday to Thursday; 10.00 am to 7.00 pm Friday; 10.00 am to 1.00 pm Saturday

Open access
General public library stock, plus local history and Gaelic collections including maps, printed music and cassettes; census records and Council minutes; music collection (cassettes). Branch libraries on the isles of Barra, Benbecula, Harris and Lewis.

City of Westminster Archives Centre

10 St Ann's Street, London SW1P 2XR
☎0171 641 2180/5180   Fax 0171 641 2179

Open 9.30 am to 7.00 pm Monday to Friday; 9.30 am to 5.00 pm Saturday

Access For reference
Comprehensive coverage of the history of Westminster and selective coverage of general London history. 22,000 books, together with a large stock of maps, prints, photographs, and theatre programmes.

Westminster Music Library

Victoria Library, 160 Buckingham Palace Road, London SW1W 9UD
☎0171 798 2192   Fax 0171 798 2181

Open 1.00 pm to 7.00 pm Monday to Friday; 10 am to 5.00 pm Saturday

Open access
Located at Victoria Library, this is the largest public music library in the South of England, with extensive coverage of all aspects of music, including books, periodicals and printed scores. No recorded material, notated only. Lending library includes a small collection of CDs, cassettes and videos.

Westminster Reference Library

35 St Martin's Street, London WC2H 7HP
☎0171 641 4636 (General Media & Performing Arts)   Fax 0171 641 4640

Business and Official Publications
☎0171 641 4634

Information for Business Service
☎0171 641 4603 (fee-based service)

Open 10.00 am to 7.00 pm Monday to Friday; 10.00 am to 5.00 pm Saturday

Access For reference only

A general reference library with emphasis on the following: Art & Design (see separate entry); Performing Arts – theatre, cinema, radio, television and dance; Official Publications – major collection of HMSO publications from 1947, plus parliamentary papers dating back to 1906, and a ten-year file of key statistical publications from OECD, UN, Unesco, etc.; Maps – an excellent map and town plan collection for Britain, plus international material; Business – UK directories, trade directories, company and market data; Periodicals – long files of many titles. One working day's notice is required for some monographs and most older periodicals. Official EU Depository Library – carries all official EU material.

Westminster Reference Library (Art & Design Department)

2nd Floor, Westminster Reference Library, St Martin's Street, London WC2H 7HP
☎0171 641 4638   Fax 0171 641 4640

Open 10.00 am to 7.00 pm Monday to Friday; 10.00 am to 5.00 pm Saturday

Access For reference only (stacks are closed to the public)
Located on the second floor of the City of Westminster's main reference library. An excellent reference source for fine and applied arts, including antiques, architecture, ceramics, coins, costume, crafts, design, furniture, garden history, interior decoration, painting, sculpture, textiles. Complete runs of major English Language periodicals such as *Studio*; exhibition catalogues; guidebooks to historic houses, castles, gardens and churches. Some older books and most periodicals earlier than 1980 are in storage and at least one day's notice is required before they can be obtained.

The Wiener Library

4 Devonshire Street, London W1N 2BH
☎0171 636 7247   Fax 0171 436 6428

Open 10.00 am to 5.30 pm Monday to Friday

Access By letter of introduction (readers needing to use the Library for any length of time should become members)
Private library – one of the leading research centres on European history since the First World War, with special reference to the era of totalitarianism and to Jewish affairs. Founded by Dr Alfred Wiener in Amsterdam in 1933, it holds material that is not available elsewhere. Books, periodicals, press archives, documents, pamphlets, leaflets and brochures. Much of the material can be consulted on microfilm.

Vaughan Williams Memorial Library

English Folk Dance and Song Society, Cecil Sharp House, 2 Regent's Park Road, London NW1 7AY
☎0171 284 0523 Fax 0171 284 0523
Open 9.30 am to 5.30 pm Monday to Friday

Access For reference to the general public, on payment of a daily fee; members may borrow books and use the library free of charge

A multi-media collection: books, periodicals, manuscripts, tapes, records, CDs, films, videos. Mostly British folk culture and how this has developed around the world. Some foreign language material, and some books in English about foreign cultures. Also, the history of the English Folk Dance and Song Society.

Dr Williams's Library

14 Gordon Square, London WC1H 0AG
☎0171 387 3727 Fax 0171 388 1142
Open 10.00 am to 5.00 pm Monday, Wednesday, Friday; 10.00 am to 6.30 pm Tuesday and Thursday
Annual subscription £10; ministers of religion and certain students £5

Open access To reading room (loans restricted to subscribers)

Primarily a library of theology, religion and ecclesiastical history. Also philosophy, history (English and Byzantine). Particularly important for the study of English Nonconformity.

Wolverhampton Central Library

Snow Hill, Wolverhampton WV1 3AX
☎01902 312025 Fax 01902 714579
Open 10.00 am to 7.00 pm Monday to Thursday; 10.00 am to 5.00 pm Friday and Saturday

Archives & Local Studies Collection

42–50 Snow Hill, Wolverhampton WV2 4AB
☎01902 717703
Open 10.00 am to 5.00 pm Monday, Tuesday, Friday, Saturday (limited archive production between 12.00 pm and 2.00 pm; archives must be booked in advance on Saturdays); 10.00 am to 7.00 pm Wednesday (closed Thursday)

General lending and reference libraries, plus children's library. Also audiovisual library holding cassettes, CDs, videos and music scores.

York Central Library

Museum Street, York YO1 2DS
☎01904 655631 Fax 01904 611025
Lending Library
Open 9.30 am to 8.00 pm Monday, Tuesday, Friday; 9.30 am to 1.00 pm Wednesday; 9.30 am to 5.30 pm Thursday; 9.30 am to 4.00 pm Saturday

General lending library including videos, CDs, music cassettes, audio books and children's storytapes.

Reference Library
Open 9.00 am to 8.00 pm Monday, Tuesday, Wednesday, Friday; 9.00 am to 5.30 pm Thursday; 9.00 am to 1.00 pm Saturday

General reference library; organisations database; local studies library for York and surrounding area; business information service; microfilm/fiche readers for national and local newspapers; census returns and family history resource; general reference collection. Maintains strong links with other local history resource centres, namely the Borthwick Institute, York City Archive and York Minster Library. CD-ROM facility.

Young Book Trust Children's Reference Library

Book House, 45 East Hill, London SW18 2QZ
☎0181 870 9055 Fax 0181 874 4790
Open 9.00 am to 5.00 pm Monday to Friday

Access For reference only

A comprehensive collection of children's literature, related books and periodicals. Aims to hold all children's titles published within the last two years. An information service covers all aspects of children's literature, including profiles of authors and illustrators. Reading room facilities.

Zoological Society Library

Regent's Park, London NW1 4RY
☎0171 449 6293 Fax 0171 586 5743
Open 9.30 am to 5.30 pm Monday to Friday

Access To members and staff; non-members by application and on payment of fee

160,000 volumes on zoology including 5000 journals (1300 current) and a wide range of books on animals and particular habitats. Slide collection available and many historic zoological prints.

Picture Libraries

A–Z Botanical Collection Ltd
82–84 Clerkenwell Road, London
EC1M 5RJ
☎0171 336 7942   Fax 0171 336 7942
Contact *Robin McGeever*
150,000 transparencies, specialising in plants and related subjects.

Acme
See **Popperfoto**

Action Plus
54–58 Tanner Street, London SE1 3PH
☎0171 403 1558   Fax 0171 403 1526
Specialist sports and action library with a vast comprehensive collection of small-format colour and b&w images covering all aspects of over 120 professional and amateur sports from around the world. As well as personalities, events, venues etc, also covers themes such as success, celebration, dejection, teamwork, effort and exhaustion. Offers same-day despatch of pictures or alternatively, clients with Macintosh and modem or ISDN links can receive digital images direct.

Lesley & Roy Adkins Picture Library
Longstone Lodge, Aller, Langport, Somerset
TA10 0QT
☎01458 250075   Fax 01458 250858
Colour coverage of archaeology, heritage and related subjects (UK and Europe), prehistoric, Roman, medieval and recent sites and monuments, landscapes and countryside, housing, art and architecture, towns, villages and religious monuments. Prompt service. No service charge if pictures are used. Catalogue and rates available.

The Advertising Archive Limited
45 Lyndale Avenue, London NW2 2QB
☎0171 435 6540   Fax 0171 794 6584
Contact *Suzanne or Larry Viner*
With half a million images, the largest collection of British and American press ads and magazine cover illustrations in Europe. Material from 1870 to the present day. Visitors by appointment. Research undertaken; rapid service, competitive rates. Exclusive UK agents

for *Saturday Evening Post* cover illustrations including artwork of Norman Rockwell and Josef Leyendecker.

AFP (Agence France Presse)
See **Popperfoto**

AKG London Ltd, Arts and History Picture Library
10 Plato Place, 72–74 St Dionis Road, London SW6 4TU
☎0171 610 6103   Fax 0171 610 6125
Contact *Julia Engelhardt*
Collection of 125,000 images with computerised access to nine million more kept in the Berlin AKG Library. *Specialises* in art, archaeology, history, topography, music, personalities and film.

Bryan & Cherry Alexander Photography
Higher Cottage, Manston, Sturminster Newton, Dorset DT10 1EZ
☎01258 473006   Fax 01258 473333
Contact *Cherry Alexander*
Artic and Antartic specialists; indigenous peoples, wildlife and science in polar regions; Norway and Iceland.

Allsport (UK) Ltd
3 Greenlea Park, Prince George's Road, London SW19 2JD
☎0181 685 1010   Fax 0181 648 5240
Contact *Lee Martin*
A large specialist library with 6 million colour transparencies, covering 140 different sports and top sports personalities. Represented in 27 countries worldwide. Large studio and digital wiring facilities through Macintosh picture desk. Online digital archive access available via ISDN and Internet.

Alvey & Towers
9 Rosebank Road, Countesthorpe, Leicestershire LE8 5YA
☎0116 2779184   Fax 0116 2779184
Contact *Emma Rowen*
Collection of approximately 20,000 transparencies, mainly of the modern railway

industry and all related supporting industries. In addition, also covers architecture, gardens, industry, people, scenics, transport and travel.

Andalucia Slide Library
Apto 499, Estepona, Malaga 29 680, Spain
☎00 34 527 93647   Fax 00 34 527 93647
Contact *Chris Chaplow*

Specialist library covering all aspects of Spain and Spanish life and culture. Cities, white villages, landscapes, festivals, art, gastronomy, leisure, tourism. Commissions undertaken.

Andes Press Agency
26 Padbury Court, London E2 7EH
☎0171 613 5417   Fax 0171 739 3159
Contact *Val Baker, Carlos Reyes*

80,000 colour transparencies and 300,000 b&w, specialising in social documentary, world religions, Latin America and Britain.

Heather Angel/Biofotos
Highways, 6 Vicarage Hill, Farnham, Surrey GU9 8HJ
☎01252 716700   Fax 01252 727464
Contacts *Lindsay Bamford, Valerie West*

Constantly expanding worldwide natural history, wildlife and landscapes: polar regions, tropical rainforest flora and fauna, all species of plants and animals in natural habitats from Africa, Asia (notably China and Malaysia), Australasia, South America and USA, urban wildlife, pollution, biodiversity, global warming. Catalogue available. Commissions undertaken. Complete picture/text packages a speciality.

Animal Photography
4 Marylebone Mews, New Cavendish Street, London W1M 7LF
☎0171 935 0503   Fax 0171 487 3038

Colour and b&w coverage of horses, dogs, cats, zoos, the Galapagos Islands, East Africa. Commissions undertaken.

Aquarius Picture Library
PO Box 5, Hastings, East Sussex TN34 1HR
☎01424 721196   Fax 01424 717704
Contact *David Corkill*

Over one million images specialising in cinema past and present, television, pop music, ballet, opera, theatre, etc. The library includes various American showbiz collections. Film stills date back to the beginning of the century. Interested in film stills, the older the better. Current material is supplied by own suppliers.

Aquila Photographics
PO Box 1, Studley, Warwickshire B80 7JG
☎0152785 2357   Fax 0152785 7507

Natural history library specialising in birds, British and European wildlife, North America, Africa and Australia, environmental subjects, farming, habitats and related subjects, domestic animals and pets.

Arcaid
The Factory, 2 Acre Road, Kingston upon Thames, Surrey KT2 6EF
☎0181 546 4352   Fax 0181 541 5230

The built environment, historic and contemporary architecture and interior design by leading architectural photographers. Covers international and British subjects, single images and series, with background information. Visitors welcome by appointment. Commissions undertaken.

Architectural Association Photo Library
34–36 Bedford Square, London WC1B 3ES
☎0171 887 4078/4086   Fax 0171 414 0782
Contact *Valerie Bennett, Vanessa Norwood*

200,000 35 mm transparencies on architecture, historical and contemporary. Archive of large-format b&w negatives from the 1920s and 1930s.

Ardea London Ltd
35 Brodrick Road, London SW17 7DX
☎0181 672 2067   Fax 0181 672 8787

Wildlife, natural history, conservation and environmental topics in colour and b&w. Animals, birds, plants and fish in their natural habitat worldwide.

Art Directors & Tripp Photo Library
57 Burdon Lane, Cheam, Surrey SM2 7BY
☎0181 642 3593/661 7104
Fax 0181 395 7230
Contact *Helene Rogers, Bob Turner*

Enlarged newly-merged library with over 750,000 images. Extensive coverage of all countries, lifestyles, religion, peoples, etc.. Backgrounds a speciality. Two new catalogues available free to professionals.

Artbank Illustration Library
8 Woodcroft Avenue, London NW7 2AG
☎0181 906 2288   Fax 0181 906 2289

Illustration and art library holding thousands of

images by many renowned contemporary illustrators. Large-format transparencies. Catalogue available on faxed request. Represents a diverse group of UK and American illustrators for commissioned work. Portfolios available for viewing.

Aspect Picture Library Ltd
40 Rostrevor Road, London SW6 5AD
☎0171 736 1998/731 7362
Fax 0171 731 7362

Colour and b&w worldwide coverage of countries, events, industry and travel, with large files on art, namely paintings, space, China and the Middle East.

Audio Visual Services
Imperial College School of Medicine at St Mary's, London W2 1PG
☎0171 725 1739   Fax 0171 724 7349
Contact B. Tallon

Colour and b&w, mostly 35 mm colour. Clinical medicine, contemporary and historical, including HIV-AIDS material and history of penicillin. Commissions undertaken.

Australia Pictures
28 Sheen Common Drive, Richmond TW10 5BN
☎0181 898 0150/876 3637
Fax 0181 898 0150/876 3637
Contact John Miles

Collection of 4000 transparencies covering all aspects of Australia: Aboriginal people, paintings, Ayers Rock, Kakadu, Tasmania, underwater, reefs, Arnhem Land, Sydney. Also Africa, Middle East and Asia.

Autosport Photographic
38–42 Hampton Road, Teddington, Middlesex TW11 0JE
☎0181 943 5918   Fax 0181 943 5922
Contact Tim Wright

Collection of one million images of Formula 1, touring and club cars. Now incorporates Classic & Sportscar.

Aviation Images – Mark Wagner
42B Queens Road, London SW19 8LR
☎0181 944 5225   Fax 0181 944 5335
Contact Mark Wagner

250,000+ aviation images, civil and military, technical and generic. Mark Wagner is the photographer for *Flight International* magazine. Member of **BAPLA** and RAeS.

Aviation Photographs International
15 Downs View Road, Swindon, Wiltshire SN3 1NS
☎01793 497179   Fax 01793 434030

The 250,000 colour photos comprise a comprehensive coverage of army, naval and airforce hardware ranging from early pistols to the latest ships. Extensive coverage of military and civil aviation includes modern together with many air-to-air views of vintage/warbird types. Commissions undertaken for additional photography and research.

Aviation Picture Library
35 Kingsley Avenue, London W13 0EQ
☎0181 566 7712   Fax 0181 566 7714
Contact Austin John Brown, Chris Savill

Specialists in the aviation field but also a general library which includes travel, architecture, transport, landscapes and skyscapes. *Special collections*: aircraft and all aspects of the aviation industry; aerial obliques of Europe, USA, Caribbean and West Africa; architectural and town planning. Commissions undertaken on the ground and in the air.

Axel Poignant Archive
115 Bedford Court Mansions, Bedford Avenue, London WC1B 3AG
☎0171 636 2555   Fax 0171 636 2555
Contact Roslyn Poignant

Anthropological and ethnographic subjects, especially Australia and the South Pacific. Also Scandinavia (early history and mythology), Sicily and England.

Barnaby's Picture Library
Barnaby House, 19 Rathbone Street, London W1P 1AF
☎0171 636 6128   Fax 0171 637 4317
Contact Mary Buckland

Colour and b&w coverage of a wide range of subjects: nature, transport, industry and historical, including a collection on Hitler. Commissions undertaken.

Barnardos Photographic and Film Archive
Tanners Lane, Barkingside, Ilford, Essex IG6 1QG
☎0181 550 8822   Fax 0181 550 0429
Contact John Kirkham

Specialises in social history (1874 to present day), child care, education, war years, emigration/migration. Half a million prints, slides, negatives. Images are mainly b&w, colour since late 1940s/early 50s. Archive of 200 films dating back to 1905. Visitors by appointment Mon–Fri 9.30 am to 4.30 pm.

Colin Baxter Photography Limited

Woodlands Industrial Estate, Grantown-on-Spey PH26 3NA
☎01479 873999   Fax 01479 873888
Contact *Colin B. Kirkwood*

Over 50,000 images specialising in Scotland. Also the Lake District, Yorkshire, the Cotswolds, France, Iceland and a special collection on Charles Rennie Mackintosh's work. *Publishes* books, calendars, postcards and greetings cards on landscape, cityscape and natural history containing images which are primarily, but not exclusively, Colin Baxter's. Also publishers of the *Worldlife Library* of natural history books.

BBC Natural History Unit Picture Library

Broadcasting House, Whiteladies Road, Bristol BS8 2LR
☎0117 9746720   Fax 0117 9238166
Contacts *Helen Gilks, Victoria Keble Williams*

A collection of 80,000 transparencies of wildlife of the world. Other subjects covered include plants, landscapes, environmental issues and photos relating to the making of the Natural History Unit's films. Wildlife sound recordings and film footage also available.

The Photographic Library Beamish, The North of England Open Air Museum

Beamish, The North of England Open Air Museum, Beamish, County Durham DH9 0RG
☎01207 231811   Fax 01207 290933
Assistant Keeper, Resource Collections
  Jim Lawson

Comprehensive collection; images relate to the North East of England and cover agricultural, industrial, topography, advertising and shop scenes, people at work and play. Also on laser disk for rapid searching. Visitors by appointment weekdays.

Francis Bedford

See **Birmingham Library Services** under **Library Services**

Ivan J. Belcher Colour Picture Library

57 Gibson Close, Abingdon, Oxfordshire OX14 1XS
☎01235 521524   Fax 01235 521524

Extensive colour picture library specialising in top-quality medium-format transparencies depicting the British scene. Particular emphasis on tourist, holiday and heritage locations, including famous cities, towns, picturesque harbours, rivers, canals, castles, cottages, rural scenes and traditions photographed throughout the seasons. Mainly of recent origin, and constantly updated.

Andrew Besley PhotoLibrary

2 Reawla Lane, Reawla, Near Hayle, Cornwall TR27 5HQ
☎01736 850086   Fax 01736 850086
Contact *Andrew Besley*

Specialist library of 20,000 images of West Country faces, places and moods.

BFI Stills, Posters and Designs

British Film Institute, 21 Stephen Street, London W1P 2LN
☎0171 255 1444   Fax 0171 323 9260

Holds images from more than 60,000 films and TV programmes on 6 million b&w prints and over 500,000 colour transparencies. A further 20,000 files hold portraits of film and TV personalities and cover related general subjects such as studios, equipment, awards. Also holds original posters and set and costume designs. Visitors welcome by appointment only (from 10.00 am to 6.00 pm).

Birmingham Repertory Theatre Archive and Sir Barry Jackson Library

See **Birmingham Library Services** under **Library Services**

Blackwoods Picture Library

See **Geoslides Photography**

Anthony Blake Photo Library

54 Hill Rise, Richmond, Surrey TW10 6UB
☎0181 940 7583   Fax 0181 948 1224

'Europe's premier source' of food and wine related images. From the farm and the vineyard to the plate and the bottle. Cooking and kitchens, top chefs and restaurants, country trades and markets, worldwide travel. Extensive new Italian section. Many recipes available to accompany   transparencies.   Commissions accepted. Free brochure available.

Boats & Boating Features (Keith Pritchard)

9 High Street, Southwell, Portland, Dorset DT5 2EH

☎01305 861006   Fax 01305 861006

Contact *Keith Pritchard*

Around 20,000 colour transparencies of small craft, historic and modern boats up to 100ft, boating events, people and places in Britain and overseas.

Chris Bonington Picture Library

Badger Hill, Nether Row, Hesket Newmarket, Wigton, Cumbria CA7 8LA

☎016974 78286   Fax 016974 78238

Contact *Frances Daltrey*

Based on the personal collection of climber and author Chris Bonington and his extensive travels and mountaineering achievements; also work by Doug Scott and other climbers, including the Peter Boardman and Joe Tasker Collections. Full coverage of the world's mountains, from British hills to Everest, depicting expedition planning and management stages, the approach march showing inhabitants of the area, flora and fauna, local architecture and climbing action shots on some of the world's highest mountains.

Boulton and Watt Archive

See **Birmingham Library Services** under **Library Services**

The Bridgeman Art Library

17–19 Garway Road, London W2 4PH

☎0171 727 4065   Fax 0171 792 8509

Sales & Marketing Manager *Sarah Pooley*

Fine art photo archive acting as an agent to more than 650 museums, galleries and picture owners around the world. Large-format colour transparencies of paintings, sculptures, prints, manuscripts, antiquities and the decorative arts. The Library is currently expanding at the rate of 500 new images each week. Collections represented by the library include the British Library, the National Galleries of Scotland, the National Library of Australia, and the National Gallery of South Africa. Catalogues of stock are available in printed form and on CD-ROM. Please call for a free brochure or visit our web siste on the Internet. The site address is www.bridgeman.co.uk.

British Library Reproductions

British Library, Great Russell Street, London WC1B 3DG

☎0171 412 7638   Fax 0171 412 7771

New address from November 1997: 96 Euston Road, St Pancras, London NW1 2DB

Twelve million books and approximately five million other items available for photography, microfilming or photocopying by Library staff. Specialist subjects include illuminated manuscripts, stamps, music, maps, botanical and zoological illustration, portraits of historical figures, history of India and South East Asia. All copies should be ordered as far in advance as possible. However, for photographs for commercial reproduction a picture library service is now available which enables orders to be processed more quickly.

Brooklands Museum Picture Library

Brooklands Museum, The Clubhouse, Brooklands Road, Weybridge, Surrey KT13 0QN

☎01932 857381   Fax 01932 855465

Contact *John Pulford, Curator of Collections; Julian Temple, Curator of Aviation*

About 40,000 b&w and colour prints and slides. Subjects include: Brooklands Motor Racing 1907–1939; British aviation and aerospace 1908–present day – particularly BAC, Hawker, Sopwith and Vickers aircraft built at Brooklands.

Hamish Brown Scottish Photographic

26 Kirkcaldy Road, Burntisland, Fife KY3 9HQ

☎01592 873546

Contact *Hamish M. Brown*

Colour and b&w coverage of most topics and areas of Scotland (sites, historic, buildings, landscape, mountains), also travel and mountains abroad, Ireland and Morocco. Commissions undertaken.

Bubbles Photolibrary

23A Benwell Road, London N7 7BL

☎0171 609 4547   Fax 0171 607 1410

Pregnancy, babies, children, teenagers, general lifestyle, health, old age, medical, still lives of food.

Caledonian Newspapers Picture Library

195 Albion Street, Glasgow G1 1QP
☎0141 552 6255   Fax 0141 553 2642

Over 6 million images: b&w and colour photographs from *c.*1900 from the *Herald* (Glasgow) and *Evening Times*. Current affairs, Scotland, Glasgow, Clydeside shipbuilding and engineering, personalities, World Wars I and II, sport.

Camera Press

21 Queen Elizabeth Street, London SE1 2PD
☎0171 378 1300   Fax 0171 278 5126

High-quality photofeatures and up-to-date coverage of international events, celebrities, royals, fashion and beauty, and general stock.

Camera Ways Ltd Picture Library

Court View, Stonebridge Green Road,
Egerton, Ashford, Kent TN27 9AN
☎01233 756454   Fax 01233 756242

Contacts *Derek, Caryl, Jonathan, Steve*

Founded by award-winning film-maker and photographer, Derek Budd, the library specialises in rural activities and natural history. It contains 35mm and 6x4.5mm, colour and b&w images as well as 16mm film and video footage on Beta SP. Coverage includes: wildlife habitats, flora and fauna of Britain and Europe, traditional country crafts and people, village scenes, landscapes, gardens, coastal and aquatic life, dinosaurs, aerial surveys, storm damage and M.O.D. reserves. A creative service is available from their Technical Artist & Wildlife Illustrator; commissions undertaken in all aspects of commercial multi-media photography, 16mm film, broadcast and corporate video production. 35mm digital film scanning and transmission, image manipulation and page-making facilities also available with 'Adobe' software.

Capital Pictures

54a Clerkenwell Road, London EC1M 5PS
☎0171 253 1122   Fax 0171 253 1414

Contact *Phil Loftus*

350,000 images. *Specialises* in famous people from the worlds of showbusiness, rock and pop, television, politics, royalty and film stills.

The Casement Collection

Erin Lodge, Jigs Lane South, Warfield,
Berkshire RG42 3DR
☎01344 302067   Fax 01344 303158

Colour and b&w travel library, particularly strong on North America and the Gulf. Not just beaches and palm trees. Based on Jack Casement's collection, with additions by other photographers. Digitised images available.

J. Allan Cash Ltd

74 South Ealing Road, London W5 4QB
☎0181 840 4141   Fax 0181 566 2568

Colour and b&w coverage of travel, natural history, people, space, sport, industry, agriculture and many other subjects. New material regularly contributed by 300 plus photographers.

Central Press Collection

See **The Hulton Getty Picture Collection**

The Centre for the Study of Cartoons and Caricature

The Templeman Library, University of Kent at Canterbury, Canterbury, Kent CT2 7NU
☎01227 823127   Fax 01227 823127

Contacts *Robert Edwards, Jane Newton*

A national research archive of over 85,000 20th century cartoons and caricatures, supported by a library of books, papers, journals, catalogues and assorted ephemera. A computer database provides for quick and easy catalogued access. A source for exhibitions and displays as well as a picture library service. *Specialises* in historical, political and social cartoons – British and international.

CEPHAS Picture Library

Hurst House, 157 Walton Road, East Molesey, Surrey KT8 0DX
☎0181 979 8647   Fax 0181 224 8095

The wine industry and vineyards of the world is the subject on which Cephas has made its reputation. 70,000 images, mainly original 6x7s, make this the most comprehensive and up-to-date archive in Britain. Almost all wine-producing countries and all aspects of the industry are covered in depth. Spirits, beer and cider also included. A major food and drink collection now also exists, through preparation and cooking, to eating and drinking. Call for free 114-page catalogue.

Christel Clear Marine Photography

Roselea, Church Lane, Awbridge, Near Romsey, Hampshire SO51 0HN
☎01794 341081   Fax 01794 340890

Contact *Nigel Dowden, Christel Dowden*

Over 60,000 images on 35mm and 645 transparency: yachting and boating from Grand Prix sailing to small dinghies, cruising locations and harbours. Recent additions include angling, fly fishing and travel. Visitors by appointment.

Christian Aid Photo Section
PO Box 100, London SE1 7RT
☎0171 523 2235   Fax 0171 620 0719

Pictures are mainly from Africa, Asia and Latin America, relating to small-scale, community-based programmes. Mostly development themes: agriculture, health, education, urban and rural life.

Christie's Images
1 Langley Lane, London SW8 1TH
☎0171 582 1282   Fax 0171 582 5632
Contact *Edward Schneider*

The UK's largest fine art photo library. 150,000 images of fine and decorative art. An extensive list of subjects is covered through paintings, drawings and prints of all periods as well as silver, ceramics, jewellery, sculpture, textiles and many other decorative and collectable items. Staff will search files and database to locate specific requests or supply a selection for consideration.

The Cinema Museum
The Old Fire Station, 46 Renfrew Road, London SE11 4NA
☎0171 820 9991   Fax 0171 793 0849

Colour and b&w coverage (including stills) of the motion picture industry throughout its history, including the Ronald Grant Archive. Smaller collections on theatre, variety, television and popular music.

John Cleare/Mountain Camera
Hill Cottage, Fonthill Gifford, Salisbury, Wiltshire SP3 6QW
☎01747 820320   Fax 01747 820320

Colour and b&w coverage of mountains and wild places, climbing, trekking, expeditions, wilderness travel, landscapes and people from all continents. Geographical features, the Himalaya and the British countryside, both landscapes and country walking, are specialities. Commissions and consultancy work undertaken in all these fields. Researchers welcome by appointment.

The Clifton Archive
Suite 314, 28 Old Brompton Road, South Kensington, London SW7 3DL
Fax 0171 581 4851

Also at: Apartado 297, Los Cristianos, 38650 Arona, Tenerife, Canary Isles
Contact *Alan Clifton*

Established in 1956 by photographer Alan Clifton. A collection of 300,000 b&w 35mm negatives and 200,000 colour 35mm transparencies which includes a large travel section and over 500 personalities.

Close-Up Picture Library
14 Burnham Wood, Fareham, Hampshire PO16 7UD
☎01329 239053
Director *David Stent*

Specialises in the close-up angle of all aspects of life: people, places, animal and bird-life and the environment in general. Also a wide range of pictures covering travel in Europe and the Orient, multicultural, ethnic and educational issues. Photographers with quality material always welcome: no minimum initial submission; 50% commission on 35mm.

Stephanie Colasanti
38 Hillside Court, 409 Finchley Road, London NW3 6HQ
☎0171 435 3695   Fax 0171 435 9995

Colour coverage of Europe, Africa, Asia, United Arab Emirates, the Caribbean, USA, Australia, New Zealand, the Pacific Islands and South America: people, animals, towns, agriculture, landscapes, carnivals, markets, archaeology, religion and ancient civilisations. Travel assignments undertaken. Medium-format transparencies (2″ square).

Michael Cole Camerawork
The Coach House, 27 The Avenue, Beckenham, Kent BR3 2DP
☎0181 658 6120   Fax 0181 658 6120
Contact *Michael Cole, Derrick Bentley*

Probably the largest and most comprehensive collection of tennis pictures in the world; incorporating the library of Le Roye Productions, a company which covered Wimbledon from 1945–70, and MCC coverage of all major tennis events, worldwide, since 1970. Also small travel picture library: English countryside, Venice, Moscow, USA, etc. 200,000 35mm colour slides, 3,600 2-inch and 6x7cm colour transparencies, 270,000 b&w negatives and a vast quantity of b&w movie film.

Collections
13 Woodberry Crescent, London N10 1PJ
☎0181 883 0083   Fax 0181 883 9215
Contact *Laura Boswell, Brian Shuel*

250,000 colour and b&w images making a collection of collections about the British Isles. 'Our "area" collections aim to cover Great Britain, Ireland and the many smaller islands eventually – and we are doing well so far.' Subjects include two of Britain's major collections on pregnancy, birth, childhood and education by Anthea Sieveking and Sandra Lousada, the customs of Britain by Brian Shuel, landscapes by Fay Godwin, large collections of castles, waterways, railways, bridges and London, and a large variety of smaller specialities. Also building an unusual collection on the emergency services. Visitors welcome by appointment.

COMSTOCK Photolibrary

28 Chelsea Wharf, 15 Lots Road, London SW10 0QQ

☎0171 351 4448   Fax 0171 352 8414

Contact *Helena Kovac*

Extensive coverage of business, people, industry, science, futuristic, world travel, landscapes, medical and natural history. Also desktop photography and CD-ROM. Free catalogue on request. Provides access to over four million images.

Concannon Golf History Library

11 Cheyne Gardens, Westcliff, Bournemouth, Dorset BH4 8AF

☎01202 765773   Fax 01202 765773

Contact *Rosemary Anstey*

Private collection of historic golfing images 1750–1950. Players, courses, Ryder Cup, Open Championship, golf architecture, memorabilia, US golf. Specialist advice. Commissions undertaken.

Corbis UK Ltd

12 Regents Wharf, All Saints Street, London N1 7RL

☎0171 843 4444   Fax 0171 278 1408

Contacts *Helen Menzies, Anna Calvert*

Access to a digital archive of over half a million images, plus one of the world's largest picture sources, Bettmann. With over 17 million images, the archive is home to scores of individual collections including two of the most important news libraries: UPI (1907–90) and Reuters (1985 to the present day, from the original negatives). Specialist subjects include news events, sports, cinema, war, social history, entertainment, people, geography, and early coverage of the Wild West, native Americans and the American Civil War. Other major components provide comprehensive coverage of world history from woodcuts and engravings to early photographs. A 6000-image directory has been published and a free catalogue is available.

Sylvia Cordaiy Photo Library

72 East Ham Road, Littlehampton, West Sussex BN17 7BQ

☎01903 715297   Fax 01903 715297

Over 130 countries on file from the obscure to main stock images – Africa, North, Central and South America, Asia, Atlantic, Indian and Pacific Ocean islands, Australasia, Europe, polar regions. Covers travel, architecture, ancient civilisations, people worldwide, environment, wildlife, natural history, Antarctica, domestic pets, livestock, veterinary treatment, equestrian, ornithology, flowers. UK files cover cities, towns villages, coastal and rural scenes, London Transport, railways, shipping and aircraft (military and civilian). Aerial photography. Backgrounds and abstracts. Also the Paul Kaye B/W archive.

Country Life Picture Library

King's Reach Tower, Stamford Street, London SE1 9LS

☎0171 261 6337   Fax 0171 261 6216

Contact *Camilla Costello*

Over 150,000 b&w negatives dating back to 1897, and 15,000 colour transparencies. Country houses, stately homes, churches and town houses in Britain and abroad, interiors of architectural interest (ceilings, fireplaces, furniture, paintings, sculpture), and exteriors showing many landscaped gardens. Visitors by appointment. Open Tuesday to Friday.

County Visuals

The Design Studio, Professional Services Dept, Kent County Council, Springfield, Maidstone, Kent ME14 2LT

☎01622 696209   Fax 01622 686170

Contact *Tony Hemsted*

A small but comprehensive library of colour transparencies specialising in the wide spectrum of attractions, activities, developments and general countryside scenes across the county of Kent.

Philip Craven Worldwide Photo-Library

Surrey Studios, 21 Nork Way, Nork, Banstead, Surrey SM7 1PB

☎01737 373737   Fax 01737 373737

Contact *Philip Craven*

Extensive coverage of British scenes, cities, villages, English countryside, gardens, historic buildings and wildlife. Worldwide travel and wildlife subjects on medium- and large-format transparencies.

CTC Picture Library

CTC Publicity, Longfield, Midhurst Road, Fernhurst, Haslemere, Surrey GU27 3HA

☎01428 655007   Fax 01428 641071

Contact *Neil Crighton*

One of the biggest specialist libraries in the UK with 250,000 slides covering world and UK agriculture, horticulture, and environmental subjects. Also a small section on travel.

Sue Cunningham Photographic

56 Chatham Road, Kingston upon Thames, Surrey KT1 3AA

☎0181 541 3024   Fax 0181 541 5388

Extensive coverage of many geographical areas: South America (especially Brazil), Eastern Europe from the Baltic to the Balkans, Zambia, Gambia, Western Europe including the UK. Colour and b&w. Member of **BAPLA**.

James Davis Travel Photography

65 Brighton Road, Shoreham, West Sussex BN43 6RE

☎01273 452252   Fax 01273 440116

Travel collection: people, places, emotive scenes and tourism. Constantly updated by James Davis and a team of photographers, both at home and abroad. Same-day service available.

Douglas Dickins Photo Library

2 Wessex Gardens, Golders Green, London NW11 9RT

☎0181 455 6221

Worldwide colour and b&w coverage, specialising in Asia, particularly India, Indonesia and Japan. Meeting educational requirements on landscape, archaeology, history, religions, customs, people and folklore.

C M Dixon

The Orchard, Marley Lane, Kingston, Canterbury, Kent CT4 6HJ

☎01227 830075   Fax 01227 831135

Colour coverage of ancient civilisations, archaeology and art, ethnology, mythology, world religion, museum objects, geography, geology, meteorology, landscapes, people and places from many countries including most of Europe, former USSR, Ethiopia, Iceland, Jordan, Morocco, Sri Lanka, Tunisia, Turkey, Egypt, Uzbekistan.

Dominic Photography

4B Moore Park Road, London SW6 2JT

☎0171 381 0007   Fax 0171 381 0008

Contact *Zoë Dominic, Catherine Ashmore*

Colour and b&w coverage of the entertainment world from 1957 onwards: dance, opera, theatre, ballet, musicals and personalities.

Philip Dunn Picture Library

Jasmine Cottage, Marston, Church Eaton, Staffordshire ST20 0AS

☎01785 840674/0860 523599

Fax 01785 840674

Contact *Philip Dunn*

Constantly expanding collection of some 50,000 b&w/colour images of travel, people, activities and places in Britain and overseas. Commissions undertaken.

Patrick Eagar Photography

5 Ennerdale Road, Kew Gardens, Surrey TW9 3PG

☎0181 940 9269   Fax 0181 332 1229

Colour and b&w coverage of cricket from 1965. Test matches, overseas tours and all aspects of the sport. Also a constantly expanding wine library (colour) of vineyards, grapes, cellars and winemakers of France, Italy, Germany, Lebanon, Australia, New Zealand, South Africa (and England). Digital photograph transmission by modem.

Ecoscene

The Oasts, Headley Lane, Passfield, Liphook, Hampshire GU30 7RX

☎01428 751056   Fax 01428 751057

Contact *Sally Morgan*

Expanding colour library of over 80,000 transparencies specialising in all aspects of the environment: pollution, conservation, recycling, restoration, natural history, habitats, education, landscapes, industry and agriculture. All parts of the globe are covered with specialist collections covering Antarctica, Australia, North America. Sally Morgan, who runs the library, is a professional ecologist and expert source of information on all environmental topics. Photographic and writing commissions undertaken.

Edifice

14 Doughty Street, London WC1N 2PL

☎0171 405 9395   Fax 0171 267 3632

Contact *Philippa Lewis, Gillian Darley*

Colour coverage of architecture, buildings of all possible descriptions, gardens, urban and rural landscape. *Specialises* in details of ornament, period style and material. British Isles, USA, Africa, Europe and Japan all covered. Detailed list available, visits by appointment.

English Heritage Photographic Library

23 Savile Row, London W1X 1AB

☎0171 973 3338   Fax 0171 973 3330

Contact *Celia Sterne*

Images of English castles, abbeys, houses, gardens, Roman remains, ancient monuments, battlefields, industrial and post-war buildings, interiors, paintings, artifacts, architectural details, conservation, archaeology.

EPA (European Pressphoto Agency)

See **Popperfoto**

Mary Evans Picture Library

59 Tranquil Vale, Blackheath, London SE3 0BS

☎0181 318 0034   Fax 0181 852 7211

Collection of historical illustrations documenting social, political, cultural, technical, geographical and biographical themes from ancient times to the recent past (up to mid-20th century). Photographs, prints and ephemera backed by large book and magazine collection. Many special collections including Sigmund Freud, the **Fawcett Library** (women's rights), the Meledin Collection (20th-century Russian history) and individual photographers such as Roger Mayne. Brochure sent on request. Compiled the *Picture Researcher's Handbook*, published by **Routledge**.

Express Newspapers Syndication

Ludgate House, 245 Blackfriars Road, London SE1 9UX

☎0171 922 7902/3/4/5/6 Fax 0171 922 7871

Syndication Manager *Jamie Maskey*

One and a half million images updated daily, with strong collections on personalities, royalty, showbiz, sport, fashion, nostalgia and events. Electronic transmission available.

Eye Ubiquitous

65 Brighton Road, Shoreham, East Sussex BN43 6RE

☎01273 440113   Fax 01273 440116

Contact *Paul Seheult*

General stock specialising in social documentary worldwide, including the work of Tim Page, and now incorporating the **James Davis Travel Library** (see entry).

Chris Fairclough Colour Library

Whinfields, Cranleigh Road, Ewhurst, Surrey GU6 7RN

☎01483 277992   Fax 01483 267984

Contact *Jane Eaton*

General colour library with special collections on religion, education, travel, children, people and places.

Falklands Pictorial

Vision House, 16 Broadfield Road, Heeley, Sheffield, South Yorkshire S8 0XJ

☎0114 2589299   Fax 0114 2550113

Colour and b&w photographs showing all aspects of Falklands life from 1880 to the present day.

Famous Pictures and Features

Studio 4, Limehouse Cut, 46 Morris Road, London E14 6NQ

☎0171 537 7055   Fax 0171 537 7056

Pictures and features agency with a growing library of colour transparencies dating back to 1985. Portrait, party and concert shots of rock and pop stars plus international entertainers, film and TV celebrities. The library is supplied by a team of photographers from the UK and around the world, keeping it up-to-date on a daily basis.

Farmers Weekly Picture Library

Quadrant House, The Quadrant, Sutton, Surrey SM2 5AS

☎0181 652 4914   Fax 0181 652 4005

Library Manager *Barry Dixon*

Britain's largest agricultural picture library holds more than 200,000 transparencies covering all aspects of farming, country life and the environment. The collection is continually updated.

ffotograff

10 Kyveilog Street, Pontcanna, Cardiff CF1 9JA

☎01222 236879   Fax 01222 229326

Contact *Patricia Aithie*

Library and agency specialising in travel, exploration, the arts, architecture, traditional culture, archaeology and landscape. Based in Wales but specialising in the Middle and Far East; Yemen and Wales are unusually strong aspects of the library. Churches and cathedrals of Britain and Crusader castles. Abstract paintings and detailed photographic textures suitable for book covers. Digital transfer by ISDN and modem available.

Financial Times Pictures

1 Southwark Bridge, London SE1 9HL
☎0171 873 3671   Fax 0171 873 4606

Photographs from around the world ranging from personalities in business, politics and the arts, people at work and other human interests and activities. 'FT Graphics are outstanding in their ability to make complex issues comprehensible.' Delivery via Modem, ISDN, E-mail or Newscom.

Fine Art Photographic Library Ltd

2A Milner Street, London SW3 2PU
☎0171 589 3127   Fax 0171 584 1944

Contact *Linda Hammerbeck*

Over 20,000 large-format transparencies, with a specialist collection of 19th-century paintings.

Fogden Natural History Photos

Mid Cambushinnie Cottage, Kinbuck, Dunblane, Perthshire FK15 9JU
☎01786 822069   Fax 01786 822069

Contact *Susan Fogden*

Natural history collection, with special reference to rain forests and deserts. Emphasis on quality rather than quantity; growing collection of around 10,000 images.

Food Features

Hardwicke Court, Waverley Lane, Farnham, Surrey GU9 8ES
☎01252 781433   Fax 01252 784091

Contacts *Steve Moss, Alex Barker*

Specialised high-quality food and drink photography, features and tested recipes. Clients' specific requirements can be incorporated into regular shooting schedules.

Ron & Christine Foord Colour Picture Library

155B City Way, Rochester, Kent ME1 2BE
☎01634 847348   Fax 01634 847348

Specialist library with over 1000 species of British and European wild flowers, plus garden flowers, trees, indoor plants, pests and diseases, mosses, lichen, cacti and the majority of larger British insects.

The Football Archive

14–15 Perseverance Works, 38 Kingsland Road, London E2 8DD
☎0171 613 1400   Fax 0171 613 1800

Contacts *Peter Robinson*

FOUNDED in 1995 as a specialist football library.

Based on the work of FIFA's former director of photography, Peter Robinson, the library consists of over 100,000 colour and b&w images dating from the 1960s to the present day.

Forest Life Picture Library

231 Corstorphine Road, Edinburgh EH12 7AT
☎0131 334 0303   Fax 0131 314 6285

Contact *Douglas Green, Neill Campbell*

The official image bank of the Forestry Commission, the library provides a single source for all aspects of forest and woodland management. The comprehensive subject list includes tree species, scenic landscapes, employment, wildlife, flora and fauna, conservation, sport and leisure.

Werner Forman Archive Ltd

36 Camden Square, London NW1 9XA
☎0171 267 1034   Fax 0171 267 6026

Colour and b&w coverage of ancient civilisations, the Near and Far East and primitive societies around the world. A number of rare collections. Subject lists available.

Formula One Pictures

Suite 8, King Harold Court, Sun Street, Waltham Abbey, Essex EN9 1ER
☎01992 787800   Fax 01992 714366

Contacts *John Townsend, Clive Rose*

500,000 35mm colour slides, b&w and colour negatives of all aspects of Formula One grand prix racing including driver profiles and portraits.

Robert Forsythe Picture Library

16 Lime Grove, Prudhoe, Northumberland NE42 6PR
☎01661 834511

Contact *Robert Forsythe, Fiona Forsythe*

25,000 transparencies of industrial and transport heritage; plus a unique collection of 50,000 items of related publicity ephemera from 1945. Image finding service available. Robert Forsythe is a transport/industrial heritage historian and consultant. Nationwide coverage, particularly strong on Northern Britain. A bibliography of published material is available.

Fortean Picture Library

Henblas, Mwrog Street, Ruthin LL15 1LG
☎01824 707278   Fax 01824 705324

Contact *Janet Bord*

30,000 colour and 45,000 b&w images: mysteries and strange phenomena worldwide, including ghosts, UFOs, witchcraft and monsters; also antiquities, folklore and mythology. Subject list available.

The Fotomas Index

12 Pickhurst Rise, West Wickham, Kent BR4 0AL
☎0181 776 2772   Fax 0181 776 2772
Contact *John Freeman*

General historical collection, mostly pre-1900. Subjects include London, topography, art, satirical, social and political history.

Fox Photos

See **The Hulton Getty Picture Collection**

The Francis Frith Collection

The Old Rectory, Bimport, Shaftesbury, Dorset SP7 8AT
☎01747 855669   Fax 01747 855065
Contact *John Buck*

330,00 b&w photographs of British topography from 1860 to 1969 depicting 7000 British towns and villages.

John Frost Newspapers

See under **Library Services**

Galaxy Picture Library

1 Milverton Drive, Ickenham, Uxbridge, Middlesex UB10 8PP
☎01895 637463   Fax 01895 623277
Contact *Robin Scagell*

Specialises in astronomy, space, telescopes, observatories, the sky, clouds and sunsets. Composites of foregrounds, stars, moon and planets prepared to commission. Editorial service available.

Garden and Wildlife Matters Photo Library

'Marlham', Henley's Down, Battle, East Sussex TN33 9BN
☎01424 830566   Fax 01424 830224
Contact *Dr John Feltwell*

Collection of 80,000 6x4 and 35mm images. General gardening techniques and design; cottage gardens and USA designer gardens. 5000 species of garden plants. Flowers, wild and house plants, trees and crops. Environmental, ecological and conservation pictures, including sea, air, noise and freshwater pollution; Eastern Europe, Mediterranean. Recycling in all its forms, agriculture, forestry, horticulture and oblique aerial habitat shots from Europe, USA and SE Asian rainforests.

The Garden Picture Library

Unit 12, Ransome's Dock, 35 Parkgate Road, London SW11 4NP
☎0171 228 4332   Fax 0171 924 3267
Contact *Sally Wood*

'Our inspirational images of gardens, plants and gardening offer plenty of scope for writers looking for original ideas to write about.' Special collections include al fresco food, floral graphics and the still life photography of Linda Burgess. From individual stock photos to complete features, photographers submit material from the UK, Europe, USA and Australia on 35mm and medium formats. In-house picture research can be undertaken on request. Visitors to the library are welcome by appointment and copies of promotional literature are available on request.

Leslie Garland Picture Library

69 Fern Avenue, Jesmond, Newcastle upon Tyne, Tyne & Wear NE2 2QU
☎0191 281 3442   Fax 0191 281 3442
Contact *Leslie Garland, ABIPP, ARPS*

Most subjects in the geographic area of North Yorkshire, Cleveland, Cumbria, Durham, Tyne & Wear, Northumberland, Borders and Dumfries and Galloway – major cities, towns, sights and scenes, heritage, etc. Norway – cities, sights and scenes, hydro-electric power. Applied science and engineering – bridges, cranes, ship building, chemical plants, field studies, geography and geology, physics and chemistry experiments, etc., and a range of still-life studies of miscellaneous subjects – household objects, cats eyes, hydraulic rams, galvanised steel, crash barriers, etc. Most on medium format. Brochure available. Commissions undertaken.

Ed Geldard Picture Collection

7 Ellergreen House, Nr Burnside, Kendal, Cumbria LA9 5SD
☎01539 728609
Contact *Ed Geldard*

Approximately 10,000 colour transparencies and b&w negs, all by Ed Geldard, specialising in mountain landscapes: particularly, the mountain regions of the Lake District; and the Yorkshire limestone areas, from valley to summit. Commissions undertaken.   Books published: *Wainwright's Tour of the Lake District* and *Wainwright in the Limestone Dales*.

Genesis Space Photo Library

Greenbanks, Robins Hill, Raleigh, Bideford,
Devon EX39 3PA
☎01237 471960   Fax 01237 472060

Contact *Tim Furniss*

Contemporary and historical colour and b&w
spaceflight collection including rockets, space-
craft, spacemen, Earth, moon and planets.
Stock list available on request.

Geo Aerial Photography

4 Christian Fields, London SW16 3JZ
☎0181 764 6292/0115 9819418
Fax 0181 764 6292/0115 9815474/9819418

Contact *Kelly White*

Established 1990 and now a growing collection
of aerial oblique photographs from the UK, Asia,
Africa and Scandinavia – landscapes, buildings,
industrial sites etc. Commissions undertaken.

GeoScience Features

6 Orchard Drive, Wye, Kent TN25 5AU
☎01233 812707   Fax 01233 812707

Fully computerised and comprehensive library
containing the world's principal source of vol-
canic phenomena. Extensive collections, providing scientific detail with technical quality, of
rocks, minerals, fossils, microsections of botanical and animal tissues, animals, biology, birds,
botany, chemistry, earth science, ecology,
environment, geology, geography, habitats,
landscapes, macro/microbiology, peoples, sky,
weather, wildlife and zoology. Over 300,000
original colour transparencies in medium- and
35mm-format. Subject lists and CD-ROM
catalogue available on application. Incorporates
the RIDA photolibrary.

Geoslides Photography

4 Christian Fields, London SW16 3JZ
☎0181 764 6292
Fax 0181 764 6292/0115 9819418

Contact *John Douglas*

Established in 1968. Landscape and human
interest subjects from the Arctic, Antarctica,
Scandinavia, UK, Africa (south of Sahara),
Middle East, Asia (south and southeast); also
Australia, via Blackwoods Picture Library. Also
specialist collections of images from British
India (the Raj) and Boer War.

Martin and Dorothy Grace

40 Clipstone Avenue, Mapperley, Nottingham
NG3 5JZ
☎0115 9208248   Fax 0115 9626802

Colour coverage of Britain's natural history,

specialising in trees, shrubs and wild flowers.
Also ferns, birds and butterflies, habitats, landscapes, ecology. Subject lists available. Member
of **BAPLA**.

Ronald Grant Archive

See **The Cinema Museum**

Greater London Photograph Library

London Metropolitan Archives,
40 Northampton Road, London EC1R 0HB
☎0171 332 3822   Fax 0171 833 9136

Contact *The Senior Librarian*

Approximately 500,000 images of London,
mostly topographical and architectural. Subjects
include education, local authority housing,
transport, the Thames, parks, churches, hospitals, war damage, pubs, theatres and cinemas.
Also major redevelopments like the South Bank,
The City, Covent Garden and Docklands.

Sally and Richard Greenhill

357A Liverpool Road, London N1 1NL
☎0171 607 8549   Fax 0171 607 7151

Colour and b&w photos of a social documentary nature: child development, pregnancy and
birth, education and urban scenes in London
and Northern England. Also Modern China
1971–95, Hong Kong, USA, longhouse life in
Sarawak, and other material from around the
world.

V. K. Guy Ltd

Silver Birches, Troutbeck, Windermere,
Cumbria LA23 1PN
☎015394 33519   Fax 015394 32971

Contact *Vic Guy, Pauline Guy, Mike Guy,
    Paul Guy, Nicola Guy*

British landscapes and architectural heritage.
20,000 5x4in transparencies, suitable for
tourism brochures, calendars, etc. Colour catalogue available.

Angela Hampton 'Family Life Pictures'

Holmleigh, Victoria Road, Freshwater Bay,
Isle of Wight PO40 9PX
☎01983 754140   Fax 01983 754140

Contact *Angela Hampton*

Over 50,000 transparencies on all aspects of contemporary lifestyle, including pregnancy, childbirth, babies, children, parenting, behaviour,
education, medical, holidays, pets, family life,
relationships, teenagers, women and men's

health, over-50's retirement. Also comprehensive stock on domestic and farm animal life. Isle of Wight travel pictures in 35mm. Commissions undertaken. Offers fully illustrated text packages on most subjects and welcomes ideas for collaboration from journalists with proven, successful background.

Tom Hanley
61 Stephendale Road, London SW6 2LT
☎0171 731 3525   Fax 0171 731 3525

Colour and b&w coverage of London, England, Europe, Canada, India, the Philippines, Brazil, China, Japan, Korea, Taiwan, the Seychelles, Cayman Islands, USA. Also pop artists of the 60s, First World War trenches, removal of London Bridge to America, and much more. Current preoccupation with Greece, Turkey, Spain and Egypt, ancient and modern.

Robert Harding Picture Library
58–59 Great Marlborough Street, London W1V 1DD
☎0171 287 5414   Fax 0171 631 1070

Over two million colour images covering a wide range of subjects – travel, people, architecture, scenics, sport, lifestyle, food, industry and agriculture. Syndication of many titles from IPC Magazines, BBC Magazines and Burda Group.

Harpur Garden Library
44 Roxwell Road, Chelmsford, Essex CM1 2NB
☎01245 257527   Fax 01245 344101
Contact *Jerry Harpur, Marcus Harpur, Susan Rowley*

Jerry Harpur's personal collection of gardens in Britain, France, Australia, South Africa, the US, Morocco and Japan (35mm and 6x7, colour). Inspired partly by contemporary designers and horticulturalists but also includes historic gardens: formal gardens, front and back gardens, plant associations, gardens in all four seasons, garden containers, fences, hedges, herbs, hillsides, seaside, lawns, paths, paving, rock, arbours, scented, fruit and vegetables, ornaments, water and integrated gardens.

Jim Henderson AMPA Photographer
Crooktree, Kincardine O'Neil, Aboyne, Aberdeenshire AB34 4JD
☎01339 882149   Fax 01339 882149
Contact *Jim Henderson, AMPA*

Scenic and general activity coverage of the North-East Scotland-Grampian region and Highlands for tourist, holiday and activity illustration. Specialist collection of over 100 Aurora Borealis displays from 1989–1996 in Grampian. Large collection of recent images of Egypt: Cairo through to Abu-Simbel. Commissions undertaken.

Heritage and Natural History Photographic Library
37 Plainwood Close, Summersdale, Chichester, West Sussex PO19 4YB
☎01243 533822
Contact *Dr John B. Free*

Specialises in insects (particularly bees and beekeeping), tropical and temperate agriculture and crops, archaeology and history worldwide.

John Heseltine Picture Library
Hill House, Tetbury Hill, Avening, Gloucestershire GL8 8LT
☎01453 835792   Fax 01453 835858
Contact *John Heseltine*

Over 100,000 colour transparencies of landscapes, architecture, food and travel with particular emphasis on Italy and the UK.

Christopher Hill Photographic Library
17 Clarence Street, Belfast BT2 8DY
☎01232 245038   Fax 01232 231942
Contact *Janet Smyth*

A comprehensive collection of landscapes of Northern Ireland, from Belfast to the Giant's Causeway, updated daily. Images of farming, food and industry. 'We will endeavour to supply images overnight.'

Hobbs Golf Collection
5 Winston Way, New Ridley, Stocksfield, Northumberland NE43 7RF
☎01661 842933   Fax 01661 842933
Contact *Michael Hobbs*

Specialist golf collection: players, courses, art, memorabilia and historical topics (1300–present). 40,000+ images – mainly 35mm colour transparencies and b&w prints. Commissions undertaken.

David Hoffman Photo Library
21 Norman Grove, London E3 5EG
☎0181 981 5041/0468 402932
Fax 0181 980 2041
Contact *David Hoffman*

Commissioned photography and stock library with a strong emphasis on social issues built up from 35mm journalistic and documentary work dating from the late 1970s. Files on drugs and drug use, policing, disorder, riots, major strikes, youth protest, homelessness, housing, environmental demonstrations and events, waste disposal, alternative energy, industry and pollution. Wide range of images especially from UK and Europe but also USA, Venezuela and Thailand. General files on topical issues and current affairs plus specialist files from leisure cycling to local authority services.

Holt Studios International Ltd
The Courtyard, 24 High Street, Hungerford, Berkshire RG17 0NF
☎01488 683523   Fax 01488 683511
Commercial Director *Andy Morant*

Specialist photo library covering world agriculture and horticulture both from a pictorial and a technical point of view. Commissions undertaken worldwide.

The Bill Hopkins Collection
See **The Special Photographers Library**

Kit Houghton Photography
Radlet Cottage, Spaxton, Bridgwater, Somerset TA5 1DE
☎01278 671362   Fax 01278 671739
Contact *Kit Houghton, Debbie Cook*

Specialist equestrian library of over 150,000 transparencies on all aspects of the horse world, with images ranging from the romantic to the practical, and many competition pictures including all Olympic Games from 1984. On-line facility available for transmission of pictures.

Houses and Interiors
82–84 Clerkenwell Road, London EC1M 5RJ
☎0171 336 7942   Fax 0171 336 7943

40,000 images of houses and gardens. Large format and 35mm. Specialises in reselling of illustrated articles and features for magazines. Member of **BAPLA**.

Chris Howes/Wild Places Photography
51 Timbers Square, Roath, Cardiff CF2 3SH
☎01222 486557   Fax 01222 486557
Contact *Chris Howes, Judith Calford*

Expanding collection of over 50,000 colour transparencies and b&w prints covering travel, topography and natural history worldwide, plus action sports such as climbing. *Specialist areas* include caves, caving and mines (with historical coverage using engravings and early photographs), wildlife, landscapes and the environment, including pollution and conservation. Europe (including Britain), USA, Africa and Australia are all well represented within the collection. Commissions undertaken.

The Hulton Getty Picture Collection
Unique House, 21–31 Woodfield Road, London W9 2BA
☎0171 266 2660   Fax 0171 266 2658

The Hulton Getty Picture Collection, the largest picture resource in Europe, holds over 15 million images from ancient history through the early years of photography up to present day. News events, sport, royalty, war, social history, people and places – photos, lithographs, etchings, engravings, woodcuts. A unique source of visual and reference material which includes the Keystone, Three Lions, Fox Photos and Central Press collections. Manages Mirror Syndication International. Also publishes material on CD-ROM (both Windows and Macintosh). Catalogue available.

Jacqui Hurst
66 Richford Street, Hammersmith, London W6 7HP
☎0181 743 2315/0860 563484
Fax 0181 743 2315
Contact *Jacqui Hurst*

A specialist library of traditional and contemporary designers and crafts, regional food producers and markets. The photos form illustrated essays of how something is made and finish with a still life of the completed object. The collection always being extended and a list is available on request. Commissions undertaken.

The Hutchison Library
118B Holland Park Avenue, London W11 4UA
☎0171 229 2743   Fax 0171 792 0259

Worldwide contemporary images from the straight-forward to the esoteric and quirky. With over half a million documentary colour photographs on file and more than 200 photographers continually adding new work, this is an ever-growing resource covering people, places, customs and faiths, agriculture, industry and transport. *Special collections* include the environment and climate, family life (including pregnancy and birth), ethnic minorities worldwide (including Disappearing World archive), conventional and alternative medicine, and music around the world. Search service available.

Illustrated London News Picture Library

20 Upper Ground, London SE1 9PF
☎0171 805 5585   Fax 0171 805 5905

Engravings, photographs and illustrations from 1842 to the present day, taken from magazines published by Illustrated Newspapers: *Illustrated London News; Graphic; Sphere; Tatler; Sketch; Illustrated Sporting and Dramatic News; Illustrated War News 1914–18; Bystander; Britannia & Eve*. Social history, London, Industrial Revolution, wars, travel. Brochure available. Visitors by appointment.

The Image Bank

17 Conway Street, London W1P 6EE
☎0171 312 0300   Fax 0171 391 9111
4 Jordan Street, Manchester M15 4PY
☎0161 236 9226   Fax 0161 236 8723.
14 Alva Street, Edinburgh EH2 4QG
☎0131 225 1770   Fax 0131 225 1660.
Contact, London *Paul Walker*
Contact, Manchester *Rowan Young*
Contact, Edinburgh *Roddy McRae*

Stock photography, illustration and film footage. Over 20 million constantly updated images from 450 photographers and 337 illustrators. Free catalogue available. Creative advertising, editorial and corporate commissions undertaken. For magazines, partworks and books, contact the publishing department. Visitors welcome.

Images Colour Library

15/17 High Court Lane, The Calls, Leeds, West Yorkshire LS2 7EU
☎0113 2433389   Fax 0113 2425605
12–14 Argyll Street, London W1V 1AB
☎0171 734 7344   Fax 0171 287 3933

A general contemporary library specialising in top-quality advertising, editorial and travel photography. Catalogues available. Visitors welcome. See also **Landscape Only**.

Images of Africa Photobank

11 The Windings, Lichfield, Staffordshire WS13 7EX
☎01543 262898   Fax 01543 417154
Contact *Jacquie Shipton*
Owner *David Keith Jones, ABIPP, FRPS*

Over 135,000 images covering 14 African countries: Botswana, Egypt, Ethiopia, Kenya, Malawi, Namibia, Rwanda, South Africa, Swaziland, Tanzania, Uganda, Zaire, Zambia and Zimbabwe. 'Probably the best collection of photographs of Kenya in Europe.' Wide range of topics covered. Particularly strong on African wildlife with over 80 species of mammals including many sequences showing action and behaviour. Popular animals like lions and elephants are covered in encyclopedic detail. More than 100 species of birds and many reptiles are included. Other strengths include National Parks & Reserves, natural beauty, tourism facilities, traditional and modern people. Most work is by David Keith Jones, ABIPP, FRPS; several other photographers are represented. Colour brochure available.

Imperial War Museum Photograph Archive

Lambeth Road, London SE1 6HZ
☎0171 416 5333   Fax 0171 416 5379

A national archive of photographs of war in this century. Mostly the two world wars but also other conflicts involving Britain and the Commonwealth. Mostly b&w. Visitors welcome to the Museum's All Saints Annexe, Austral Street, five minutes walk from main building. Appointments preferred.

The Interior Archive Ltd

7 Chelsea Studios, 410 Fulham Road, London SW6 1EB
☎0171 370 0595   Fax 0171 385 5403
Contact *Karen Howes*

Several thousand images of interiors, architecture, design and gardens.

International Photobank

Loscombe Barn Farmhouse, West Knighton, Dorchester, Dorset DT2 8LS
☎01305 854145   Fax 01305 853065

Over 300,000 transparencies, mostly medium-format. Colour coverage of travel subjects: places, people, folklore, events. Assignments undertaken for guide books and brochure photography.

The Isle of Wight Photo Library

The Old Rectory, Calbourne, Isle of Wight PO30 4JE
☎01983 531575   Fax 01983 531253
Contact *The Librarian*

Stock material represents all that is best on the Isle of Wight – landscapes, seascapes, architecture, gardens, boats.

Robbie Jack Photography

45 Church Road, Hanwell, London W7 3BD
☎0181 567 9616   Fax 0181 567 9616

Contact *Robbie Jack*

Built up over the last 14 years, the library contains over 250,000 colour transparencies of the performing arts – theatre, dance, opera and music. Includes West End shows, the RSC and Royal National Theatre productions, English National Opera and Royal Opera. The dance section contains images of the Royal Ballet, English National Ballet, the Rambert Dance Company, plus many foreign companies. Also holds the largest selection of colour material from the Edinburgh International Festival. Researchers are welcome to visit by appointment.

Jayawardene Travel Photo Library

7A Napier Road, Wembley, Middlesex
HA0 4UA
☎0181 902 3588   Fax 0181 902 7114

Contacts *Marion Jayawardene, Rohith Jayawardene*

100,000 colour transparencies, specialising in worldwide travel and travel-related subjects. Most topics featured have been covered in depth, with more than 500 different images per destination. Regularly updated, all are originals and shot in 35mm- and medium-format. Commissions undertaken. New photographers welcome (please telephone first) – minimum initial submission: 100 transparencies per destination.

Trevor Jones Thoroughbred Photography

The Hornbeams, 2 The Street, Worlington, Suffolk IP28 8RU
☎01638 713944   Fax 01638 713945

Contact *Trevor Jones, Gill Jones*

Extensive library of high-quality colour transparencies depicting all aspects of thoroughbred horse racing dating from 1987. Major group races, English classics, studs, stallions, mares and foals, early morning scenes, personalities, jockeys, trainers and prominent owners. Also international work: USA Breeders Cup, Arc de Triomphe, French Classics, Irish Derby, Dubai racing scene, Japan Cup and Hokkaido stud farms; and more unusual scenes such as racing on the sands at low tide, Ireland, and on the frozen lake at St Moritz. Visitors by appointment.

Katz Pictures

13/15 Vine Hill, London EC1R 5DX
☎0171 814 9898   Fax 0171 814 9899

Contact *Alyson Whalley*

Contains an extensive collection of colour and b&w material covering a multitude of subjects from around the world – business, environment, industry, lifestyles, politics plus celebrity portraits from the entertainment world. Also Hollywood portraits and film stills dating back to the twenties. Represents *Life* and *Time* magazines for syndication in the UK and can offer a complete selection of material spanning over 50 years.

The Keystone Collection

See **The Hulton Getty Picture Collection**

David King Collection

90 St Pauls Road, London N1 2QP
☎0171 226 0149   Fax 0171 354 8264

Contact *David King*

250,000 b&w original and copy photographs and colour transparencies of historical and present-day images. Russian history and the Soviet Union from 1900 to the fall of Khrushchev; the lives of Lenin, Trotsky and Stalin; the Tzars, Russo-Japanese War, 1917 Revolution, World War I, Red Army, Great Patriotic War etc. Special collections on China, Eastern Europe, the Weimar Republic, American labour struggles, Spanish Civil War. Open to qualified researchers by appointment, Monday to Friday, 10 – 6. Staff will undertake research; negotiable fee for long projects. David King's latest photographic book, *The Commissar Vanishes*, documents the falsification of photographs and art in Stalin's Russia.

The Kobal Collection

4th Floor, 184 Drummond Street, London
NW1 3HP
☎0171 383 0011   Fax 0171 383 0044

Colour and b&w coverage of Hollywood films: portraits, stills, publicity shots, posters, ephemera. Visitors by appointment.

Kodak Motoring Picture Library

National Motor Museum, Beaulieu, Hampshire SO42 7ZN
☎01590 612345   Fax 01590 612655

Contact *Simon Priestley, Jonathan Day*

A quarter of a million b&w images, plus 50,000 colour transparencies covering all forms of motoring history from the 1880s to the present day. Commissions undertaken. Own studio.

Kos Picture Source Ltd

7 Spice Court, Ivory Square, Plantation
Wharf, London SW11 3UE
☎0171 801 0044   Fax 0171 801 0055

Worldwide marine subjects from yachting to
seascapes. Constantly updated, covering all
aspects of water-based subjects.

Landscape Only

12–14 Argyll Street, London W1V 1AB
☎0171 734 7344   Fax 0171 287 3933

Premier landscape collection, featuring the
work of top photographers Charlie Waite,
Nick Meers, Joe Cornish and many others.
Colour brochure available.

Frank Lane Picture Agency Ltd

Pages Green House, Wetheringsett,
Stowmarket, Suffolk IP14 5QA
☎01728 860789   Fax 01728 860222

Colour and b&w coverage of natural history
and weather. Represents Silvestris Fotoservice,
Germany, and works closely with Eric and
David Hosking, plus 200 freelance photographers.

André Laubier Picture Library

4 St James Park, Bath, Avon BA1 2SS
☎01225 420688   Fax 01225 420688

An extensive library of photographs from 1935
to the present day in 35mm- and medium-format. Main subjects are: archaeology and architecture; art and artists (wood carving, sculptures, contemporary glass); botany; historical
buildings, sites and events; landscapes; nature;
leisure sports; events; experimental artwork
and photography; people; and travel. Substantial stock of many other subjects including:
birds, buildings and cities, folklore, food and
drink, gardens, transport. Special collection:
Images d'Europe (Austria, Britain, France,
Greece, Italy, Spain, Turkey and former
Yugoslavia). Private collection: World War II
to D-Day. List available on request. Photo
assignments, artwork, design, and line drawings
undertaken. Correspondence welcome in
English, French or German.

The Erich Lessing Archive of Fine Art & Culture

c/o AKG London Ltd, Arts and History
Picture Library, 10 Plato Place, 72–74 St
Dionis Road, London SW6 4TU
☎0171 610 6103   Fax 0171 610 6125

Computerised archive of large-format transparencies depicting the contents of many of the
world's finest art galleries as well as ancient
archaeological and biblical sites. Over 70,000
pictures can be viewed on microfiche. Represented by AKG London Ltd.

Life File Ltd

76 Streathbourne Road, London SW17 8QY
☎0181 767 8832   Fax 0181 672 8879

Contact *Simon Taylor*

300,000 images of people and places, lifestyles,
industry, environmental issues, natural history
and customs, from Afghanistan to Zimbabwe.
Stocks most of the major tourist destinations
throughout the world, including the UK.

Lindley Library, Royal Horticultural Society

80 Vincent Square, London SW1P 2PE
☎0171 821 3050   Fax 0171 630 6060

Contact *Jennifer Vine*

18,0000 original drawings and approx. 8000
books with hand-coloured plates of botanical
illustrations. Appointment is absolutely essential; all photography is done by own photographer.

Link Picture Library

33 Greyhound Road, London W6 8NH
☎0171 381 2261/2433   Fax 0171 385 6244

Contacts *Orde Eliason*

40,000 images of South Africa, India and Israel.
A more general collection of colour transparencies from 100 countries worldwide,
including an archive on musicians. Link
Picture Library has an international network
and can source material not in its file from
Japan, USA, Holland, Scandinavia, Germany
and South Africa. Original photographic commissions undertaken.

London Aerial Photo Library

PO Box 25, Ashwellthorpe, Norwich,
Norfolk NR16 1HL
☎01508 488320   Fax 01508 488282

Contact *Sandy Stockwell*

60,000 colour negatives of aerial photographs
covering most of Britain, with particular
emphasis on London and surrounding counties. No search fee. Photocopies of library
prints are supplied free of charge to enquirers.
Welcomes enquiries in respect of either general
subjects or specific sites and buildings.

London Transport Museum Photographic Library

39 Wellington Street, London WC2E 7BB
☎0171 379 6344   Fax 0171 497 3527
Contacts *Hugh Robertson, Simon Murphy*

Around 100,000 b&w images from the 1860s and 10,000 colour images from c.1975. *Specialist collections* poster archive, underground construction, corporate design and architecture, street scenes, London Transport during the war. Collection available for viewing by appointment on Monday, Wednesday and Friday. No loans system but prints and transparences can be purchased.

The Ludvigsen Library Limited

73 Collier Street, London N1 9BE
☎0171 837 1700   Fax 0171 837 1776
Contact *Neil King, Paul Parker*

Approximately 250,000 images (both b&w and many colour transparencies) of automobiles and motorsport, from 1920s through 1970s. Glass plate negatives from the early 1900s; Formula One, Le Mans, motor car shows, vintage, antique and classic cars from all countries. Includes the Dalton-Watson Collection and noted photographers such as Max le Grand and Rodolfo Mailander. Extensive information research facilities for writers and publishers.

Lupe Cunha Photos

19 Ashfields Parade, London N14 5EH
☎0181 882 6441   Fax 0181 882 6303
Children, health, pregnancy and general women's interest. Also special collection on Brazil. Commissions undertaken.

MacQuitty International Photographic Collection

7 Elm Lodge, River Gardens, Stevenage Road, London SW6 6NZ
☎0171 385 6031/384 1781
Fax 0171 384 1781
Contact *Dr Miranda MacQuitty*

Colour and b&w collection on aspects of life in over 70 countries: dancing, music, religion, death, archaeology, buildings, transport, food, drink, nature. Visitors by appointment.

Magnum Photos Ltd

Moreland Buildings, 2nd Floor, 5 Old Street, London EC1V 9HL
☎0171 490 1771   Fax 0171 608 0020
Head of Library *Heather Vickers*

FOUNDED 1947 by Cartier Bresson, George Rodger, Robert Capa and David 'Chim' Seymour. Represents over 50 of the world's leading photo-journalists. Coverage of all major world events from the Spanish Civil War to present day. Also a large collection of personalities.

The Raymond Mander & Joe Mitchenson Theatre Collection

The Mansion, Beckenham Place Park, Beckenham, Kent BR3 2BP
☎0181 658 7725   Fax 0181 663 0313
Contact *Richard Mangan*

Enormous collection covering all aspects of the theatre: plays, actors, dramatists, music hall, theatres, singers, composers, etc. Visitors welcome by appointment.

Terry Marsh Picture Library

27 Camwood, Clayton Green, Bamber Bridge, Preston, Lancashire PR5 8LA
☎01772 321243   Fax 01772 321243
Contact *Terry Marsh*

Mainly 35 mm colour coverage of landscapes and countryside features generally throughout the UK and France, in particular Cumbria, North Yorkshire, Lancashire, southern Scotland, Isle of Skye, Wales, Cornwall, French Alps, French Pyrenees and Provence. Commissions undertaken.

S & O Mathews Photography

The Old Rectory, Calbourne, Isle of Wight PO30 4JE
☎01983 531247   Fax 01983 531253
Library of colour transparencies of landscapes, gardens and flowers.

MC Picture Library

119 Wardour Street, London W1V 3TD
☎0171 565 6108   Fax 0171 494 1839
Contact *Steven Lai*

Leisure-related subjects including cookery, gardening, DIY, crafts and needlecrafts, antiques and collectibles. Unique collection of sex-related material – both photography and illustration. The majority of transparencies are medium format. Clients are welcome to visit by appointment. Complimentary colour brochure available upon request.

Institution of Mechanical Engineers

1 Birdcage Walk, London SW1H 9JJ
☎0171 973 1289   Fax 0171 222 4557
Contact *Corporate Communications*

800 contemporary images on mechanical engineering can be borrowed free of charge.

Medimage
32 Brooklyn Road, Coventry CV1 4JT
☎01203 668652   Fax 01203 668562
Contact *Anthony King, Catherine King*

10,000 medium format colour transparencies of Mediterranean countries covering a wide range of subjects – agriculture, archaeology, architecture, arts, crafts, education, festivals, flora, geography, history, industry, landscapes, markets, recreation, seascapes, sports and transport. The collection is added to on a regular basis and photographic commissions are undertaken. No search fees. Pictures by other photographers are not accepted.

Meledin Collection
See **Mary Evans Picture Library**

Lee Miller Archives
Burgh Hill House, Chiddingly, Near Lewes, East Sussex BN8 6JF
☎01825 872691   Fax 01825 872733
The work of Lee Miller (1907–77). As a photo-journalist she covered the war in Europe from early in 1944 to VE Day with further reporting from the Balkans. Collection includes photographic portraits of prominent Surrealist artists: Ernst, Eluard, Miró, Picasso, Penrose, Carrington, Tanning, and others. Surrealist and contemporary art, poets and writers, fashion, the Middle East, Egypt, the Balkans in the 1930s, London during the Blitz, war in Europe and the liberation of Dachau and Buchenwald.

Mirror Syndication International
20th Floor, 1 Canada Square, Canary Wharf, London E14 5PA
☎0171 266 1133   Fax 0171 266 2563
Managing Director *Frank Walker*

Major photo library specialising in current affairs, personalities, royalty, sport, pop and glamour, plus extensive British and world travel pictures. Major motion picture archive up to 1965. Agents for Mirror Group Newspapers. Syndicator of photos and text for news/features.

Monitor Syndication
17 Old Street, London EC1V 9HL
☎0171 253 7071   Fax 0171 250 0966
Colour and b&w coverage of leading international personalities. Politics, entertainment, royals, judicial, commerce, religion, trade

unions, well-known buildings. Syndication to international, national and local media.

Moroccan Scapes
Seend Park, Seend, Wiltshire SN12 6NZ
☎01380 828533   Fax 01380 828630
Contact *Chris Lawrence*

Specialist collection of Moroccan material: scenery, towns, people, markets and places, plus the Atlas Mountains. Over 16,000 images.

Mountain Camera
See **John Cleare**

Moving Image Communications Ltd
The Basement, 2–4 Dean Street, London W1V 5RN
☎0171 437 5688   Fax 0171 437 5649
Contact *Michael Maloney*

11,000 hours of quality archive and contemporary images; computer catalogued for immediate access. Collections include: Britain 1925–96, The Cuban Archive, Medical Technology, 1950's Classic Travelogues, Subaqua Films, Space Exploration, Vintage Slapstick, British Airways 1984–96, Seascapes and Landscapes, TVAM Interviews/Funnies 1983–92. In addition, Moving Image provides an external research and copyright clearance service. In-house researchers can locate images using long-established contacts with footage sources worldwide.

Museum of Antiquities Picture Library
University and Society of Antiquaries of Newcastle upon Tyne, Newcastle upon Tyne NE1 7RU
☎0191 222 7846   Fax 0191 222 8561
Contact *Lindsay Allason-Jones*

25,000 images, mostly b&w, of special collections including: Hadrian's Wall Archive (b&ws taken over the last 100 years); Gertrude Bell Archive (during her travels in the Near East, 1900–26); and aerial photographs of archaeological sites in the North of England. Visitors welcome by appointment.

Museum of London Picture Library
London Wall, London EC2Y 5HN
☎0171 600 3699 ext. 254 Fax 0171 600 1058
Contact *Gavin Morgan, Stewart Drew*

Comprehensive coverage of the history and

archaeology of London represented in paintings, photographs and historic artefacts. Special files include Roman and medieval archaeology, costume, suffragettes and Port of London.

National Galleries of Scotland Picture Library

National Galleries of Scotland, Belford Road, Edinburgh EH4 3DR
☎0131 556 8921, ext 319 Fax 0131 315 2963
Contacts *Deborah Hunter, Helen Nicoll*

Over 30,000 b&w and several thousand images in colour of works of art from the Renaissance to present day. Specialist subjects cover fine art (painting, sculpture, drawing), portraits, Scottish, historical, still life, photography and landscape. Colour leaflet, scale of charges and application forms available on request.

National Maritime Museum Picture Library

Greenwich, London SE10 9NF
☎0181 312 6631   Fax 0181 312 6632
Manager *Chris Gray*

Over 3 million maritime-related images and artefacts, including oil paintings from the 16th century to present day, prints and drawings, historic photographs, plans of ships built in the UK since the beginning of the 18th Century, models, rare maps and charts, instruments, etc. Over 50,000 items within the collection are now photographed and with the Historic Photographs Collection form the basis of the picture library's stock.

National Medical Slide Bank

Wellcome Centre Medical Photo Library, 210 Euston Road, London NW1 2BE
☎0171 611 8746   Fax 0171 611 8577
Contact *Julie Dorrington*

Specialist section of the **Wellcome Centre Medical Photographic Library**, it comprises 16,000 slides covering clinical and general medicine with associated pathology and medical imaging. 12,000 images on videodisc.

National Meteorological Library and Archive

See under **Library Services**

National Monuments Record

National Monuments Record Centre, Kemble Drive, Swindon, Wiltshire SN2 2GZ
☎01793 414600   Fax 01793 414606
The National Monuments Record is the first stop for photographs and information on England's heritage. Over 7 million photographs, documents and drawings are held. English architecture from the first days of photography to the present, air photographs covering every inch of England from the first days of flying to the present, and archaeological sites. The record is the public archive of the Royal Commission on the Historical Monumenets of England, which surveys buildings and archaeological sites. The London office specialises in the architecture of the capital city – for more information phone 0171 208 8200.

National Portrait Gallery Picture Library

St Martin's Place, London WC2H 0HE
☎0171 306 0055 exts. 259/260/261
Fax 0171 306 0092/0056
Contact *Shruti Patel*

Over 700,000 images - portraits of famous British men and women dating from medieval times to the present day. Various formats/media.

National Railway Museum Picture Library

Leeman Road, York YO2 4XJ
☎01904 621261   Fax 01904 611112
1.5 million images, mainly b&w, covering every aspect of railways from 1866 to the present day. Visitors by appointment.

The National Trust Photographic Library

36 Queen Anne's Gate, London SW1H 9AS
☎0171 222 9251   Fax 0171 222 5097
Contact *Gayle Mault*

Collection of mixed-format transparencies covering landscape and coastline throughout England, Wales and Northern Ireland; also architecture, interiors, gardens, paintings and conservation. Brochure available on request. Profits from the picture library are reinvested in continuing the work of the Trust.

Natural History Museum Picture Library

Cromwell Road, London SW7 5BD
☎0171 938 9122/9035   Fax 0171 938 9169
Contact *Martin Pulsford, Lodvina Mascarenhas*

12,000 large-format transparencies on natural history and related subjects: extinct animals, dinosaurs, fossils, anthropology, minerals, gemstones, fauna and flora. No wildlife pictures but many images of historic natural history art. Commissions of museum specimens undertaken.

Natural History Photographic Agency
See **NHPA**

Natural Science Photos
33 Woodland Drive, Watford, Hertfordshire WD1 3BY
☎01923 245265   Fax 01923 246067
Colour coverage of natural history subjects worldwide. The work of some 150 photographers, it includes angling, animals, birds, reptiles, amphibia, fish, insects and other invertebrates, habitats, plants, fungi, geography, weather, scenics, horticulture, agriculture, farm animals and registered dog breeds. Researched by experienced scientists Peter and Sondra Ward. Visits by appointment. Commissions undertaken.

Nature Photographers Ltd
West Wit, New Road, Little London, Tadley, Hampshire RG26 5EU
☎01256 850661   Fax 01256 851157
Contact *Dr Paul Sterry*

Over 150,000 images on worldwide natural history and environmental subjects. The library is run by a trained biologist and experienced author on his subject.

Peter Newark's Pictures
3 Barton Buildings, Queen Square, Bath BA1 2JR
☎01225 334213   Fax 01225 334213
Over 1 million images covering world history from ancient times to the present day. Incorporates two special collections: American history in general with strong Wild West collection; and the military collection: military/ naval personalities and events. Subject list available. Visitors welcome by appointment.

NHPA (Natural History Photographic Agency)
Little Tye, 57 High Street, Ardingly, West Sussex RH17 6TB
☎01444 892514   Fax 01444 892168
Library Manager *Tim Harris*

Extensive coverage on all aspects of natural history – animals, plants, landscapes, environmental issues. 120 photographers worldwide provide a steady input of high-quality transparencies. Specialist files include the unique high-speed photography of Stephen Dalton, extensive coverage of African and American wildlife, also rainforests, marine life and the polar regions. UK agents for the ANT collection of Australasian material. Loans are generally made direct to publishers; individual writers must request material via their publisher.

The Northern Picture Library
Greenheys Business Centre, 10 Pencroft Way, Manchester M15 6JJ
☎0161 226 2007   Fax 0161 226 2022
Wide selection of subjects from the UK and abroad. Mostly colour, some b&w. Industry, business, sport, farming, scenic, personalities, jazz musicians (and some classical), space, and many more. Special collection on the North West of England. Commissions undertaken.

NRSC – Air Photo Group
Arthur Street, Barwell, Leicestershire LE9 8GZ
☎01455 849227   Fax 01455 841785
Leading supplier of colour aerial photography in the UK. Commissions undertaken.

Observer Colour Library
PO Box 33, Edenbridge, Kent TN8 5PB
☎01342 850313   Fax 01342 850244
Half a million pictures from the *Observer* magazine, from 1962 to end 1992.

Odhams Periodicals Library
See **Popperfoto**

Only Horses Picture Agency
27 Greenway Gardens, Greenford, Middlesex UB6 9TU
☎0181 578 9047   Fax 0181 575 7244
Colour and b&w coverage of all aspects of the horse. Foaling, retirement, racing, show jumping, eventing, veterinary, polo, breeds, personalities.

Open University Photo Library
Room 163 A Block, Walton Hall, Milton Keynes MK7 6AA
☎01908 658408   Fax 01908 653744
Contact *Debbie Nicholls-Brien*

Education, industry and social welfare collection. 5000 b&w images dating from the early 1970s.

Oxford Picture Library
1 North Hinksey Village, Oxford OX2 0NA
☎01865 723404   Fax 01865 725294
Contact *Annabel Webb, Chris Andrews, Angus Palmer*

Specialist collection on Oxford: the city, university and colleges, events, people, spires and shires; also the Cotswolds, architecture and landscape from Stratford-upon-Avon to Bath; the Chilterns and Henley on Thames, with aerial views of all of the above; plus Channel Islands, especially Guernsey and Sark. General collection includes wildlife, trees, plants, clouds, sun, sky, water and teddy bears. Commissions undertaken.

Oxford Scientific Films Photo Library

Long Hanborough, Witney, Oxfordshire
OX8 8LL
☎01993 881881   Fax 01993 882808

Senior Account Manager *Suzanne Aitzetmuller*
Account Managers *Alex Harper, Dee Williams*

Collection of 300,000 colour transparencies of wildlife and natural science images supplied by over 300 photographers worldwide, providing comprehensive coverage of behaviour, life histories, close-ups, high speed and some special effects, as well as scenic environmental shots. Macro and micro photography. UK agents for Animals Animals and Photo Researchers, USA, Okapia, Germany and Dinodia, India. Now also incorporating the Survival Anglia Photo Library. Research by experienced and specialist researchers for specific and creative briefs. Visits welcome, by appointment.

PA News Photo Library

PA News Centre, 292 Vauxhall Bridge Road, London SW1V 1AE
☎0171 963 7038/7039   Fax 0171 963 7066

PA News, the 24-hour national news and information group, offers public access to its photographic archives. Photographs, dating from 1890 to the present day, cover everything from news and sport to entertainment and royalty, with around 50 new pictures added daily. Personal callers welcome (9.00am to 5.30pm weekdays; 9.00am to 5.00pm Saturday) or research undertaken by in-house staff.

Hugh Palmer

Knapp House, Shenington, Near Banbury, Oxfordshire OX15 6NE
☎01295 670433   Fax 01295 670709

Extensive coverage of gardens from Britain and Europe, as well as rural landscapes and architecture. Medium-format transparencies from numerous specialist commissions for books and magazines.

Panos Pictures

1 Chapel Court, Borough High Street, London SE1 1HH
☎0171 234 0010   Fax 0171 357 0094

Documentary colour and b&w library specialising in Third World and Eastern Europe, with emphasis on environment and development issues. Leaflet available. All profits from this library go to the Panos Institute to further its work in international sustainable development.

Papilio Natural History & Travel Library

44 Palestine Grove, Merton, London SW19 2QN
☎0181 687 2202   Fax 0181 687 2202

Contact *Robert Pickett, Justine Bowler*

100,000 colour transparencies of natural history, including birds, animals, insects, flowers, plants, fungi and landscapes; plus travel worldwide including people, places and cultures. Commissions undertaken. Full company information pack available. Visits by appointment only. Member of **BAPLA**.

Charles Parker Archive

See **Birmingham Library Services** under **Library Services**

David Paterson Photo-Library

88 Cavendish Road, London SW12 0DF
☎0181 673 2414   Fax 0181 675 9197

Travel, landscapes, nature from the UK, Europe, North Africa, the Himalayas, Japan, Scotland and the USA.

Ann & Bury Peerless Picture Library

St David's, 22 King's Avenue, Minnis Bay, Birchington-on-Sea, Kent CT7 9QL
☎01843 841428   Fax 01843 848321

Contact *Ann or Bury Peerless*

Specialist collection on world religions: Hinduism, Buddhism, Jainism, Christianity, Islam, Sikhism. Geographical areas covered: India, Pakistan, Bangladesh, Sri Lanka, Cambodia, Thailand, Russia, Republic of China, Spain, Poland. 10,000 35mm colour transparencies.

Performing Arts Library

52 Agate Road, London W6 0AH
☎0181 748 2002   Fax 0181 563 0538

Colour and b&w pictures of all aspects of the performing arts, including classical music, opera, theatre, ballet and contemporary dance, musicals, concert halls, opera houses and festivals.

Photo Flora
46 Jacoby Place, Priory Road, Edgbaston,
Birmingham B5 7UN
☎0121 471 3300   Fax 0121 471 3300

Specialist in British and European wild plants, with colour coverage of most British and many European species (rare and common) and habitats; also travel in India, Nepal, Egypt, China, Thailand and Tibet.

Photo Library International Ltd
PO Box 75, Leeds, West Yorkshire LS7 3NZ
☎0113 2623005   Fax 0113 2625366

Contemporary colour coverage of most subjects, including industry.

Photo Press Defence
Sherwell House, 54 Staddiscombe Road,
Plymouth, Devon PL9 9NB
☎01752 401800   Fax 01752 402800
Contact *David Reynolds, Jessica Kelly*

Leading source of military photography covering all areas of the UK Armed Forces, supported by a research agency of facts and figures. More than 100,000 images. Campaigns in Aden, the Falklands, Ulster, the Gulf and Yugoslavia covered. Specialist collections include the Royal Marine Commandos and Parachute Regiment training. Visitors welcome by appointment.

Photo Resources
The Orchard, Marley Lane, Kingston,
Canterbury, Kent CT4 6JH
☎01227 830075   Fax 01227 831135

Colour and b&w coverage of archaeology, art, ancient art, ethnology, mythology, world religion, museum objects.

Photofusion
17A Electric Lane, London SW9 8LA
☎0171 738 5774   Fax 0171 738 5509
Contact *Liz Somerville*

Colour and b&w coverage of contemporary social issues including babies and children, disablement, education, the elderly, environment, family, health, housing, homelessness, people general and work. Brochure available.

The Photographers' Library
81A Endell Street, London WC2H 9AJ
☎0171 836 5591   Fax 0171 379 4650

Covers people, lifestyles, commerce, holiday people, travel destinations, industry, landscapes, health. Brochure available.

Photomax
118–122 Magdalen Road, Oxford
OX4 1RQ
☎01865 241825   Fax 01865 794511
Contact *Max Gibbs, Barry Allday*

All aspects of the aquarium hobby are covered: aquarium fish, tropical freshwater, tropical marine, coldwater, marine invertebrates (tropical); aquarium plants; water lilies. Expanding. Commissions undertaken.

Photos Horticultural
169 Valley Road, Ipswich, Suffolk
IP1 4PJ
☎01473 257329   Fax 01473 233974

Colour coverage of all aspects of gardening in Britain and abroad, including extensive files on plants in cultivation and growing wild.

PictureBank Photo Library Ltd
Parman House, 30–36 Fife Road, Kingston
upon Thames, Surrey KT1 1SY
☎0181 547 2344   Fax 0181 974 5652

250,000 colour transparencies covering people (girls, couples, families, children), travel and scenic (UK and world), moods (sunsets, seascapes, deserts, etc.), industry and technology, environments and general. Commissions undertaken. Visitors welcome. Member of **BAPLA**. New material on medium/large format welcome.

Pictures Colour Library
4th Floor, The Italian Building,
41 Dockhead, London SE1 2BS
☎0171 252 3300   Fax 0171 252 3345

Location, lifestyle, food, still life, sport, animals, industry and business. Visitors welcome.

Pitkin Guides Ltd
Healey House, Dene Road, Andover,
Hampshire SP10 2AA
☎01264 334303   Fax 01264 334110
Contact *Sarah Pickering*

Colour transparencies of English cathedrals; plus a large collection of b&w prints. Also London and a few other cities. No visitors.

H. G. Ponting
See **Popperfoto**

Popperfoto
The Old Mill, Overstone Farm, Overstone,
Northampton NN6 0AB
☎01604 670670   Fax 01604 670635

Home to over 13 million images, covering 150
years of photographic history. Renowned for
its archival material, a world-famous sports
library and stock photography. Popperfoto's
credit line includes Reuters, Bob Thomas
Sports Photography, UPI, AFP & EPA, Acme,
INP, Planet, Paul Popper, Exclusive News
Agency, Victory Archive, Odhams Periodicals
Library, Illustrated, Harris Picture Agency, and
H. G. Ponting which holds the Scott
1910–1912 Antarctic expedition. Colour from
1940, b&w from 1870 to the present. Major
subjects covered worldwide include events,
personalities, wars, royalty, sport, politics,
transport, crime, history and social conditions.
Material available on the same day to clients
throughout the world. Mac-desk available.
Researchers welcome by appointment. Free
catalogue available.

PPL Photo Agency Ltd
68 East Ham Road, Littlehampton, West
Sussex BN17 7BE
☎01903 730614   Fax 01903 730618
Contacts *Barry Pickthall, Jon Nash*

2 million pictures of sailing and boating, watersports, travel, water and coastal scenes. British
Steel Multimedia Library – all aspects of steel
and steel making. Construction, science and
technology, transport, mining and industry.

Premaphotos Wildlife
Amberstone, 1 Kirland Road, Bodmin,
Cornwall PL30 5JQ
☎01208 78258   Fax 01208 72302
Contact *Jean Preston-Mafham, Library Manager*

Natural history worldwide. Subjects include
flowering and non-flowering plants, fungi, slime
moulds, fruits and seeds, galls, leaf mines,
seashore life, mammals, birds, reptiles, amphibians, insects, spiders, habitats, scenery and culti-
vated cacti. Commissions undertaken. Visitors
welcome. 'Make sure your name is on our mailing list to receive regular, colourful mailers.'

Professional Sport
8 Apollo Studios, Charlton Kings Mews,
London NW5 2SA
☎0171 482 2311   Fax 0171 482 2441

Colour and b&w coverage of tennis, soccer,
athletics, golf, cricket, boxing, winter sports

and many minor sports. Major international
events including the Olympic Games, World
Cup soccer and all Grand Slam tennis events.
Also news and feature material supplied worldwide. Computerised library with in-house processing and studio facilities; Macintosh photo
transmission services available for editorial and
advertising.

PWA International Ltd
City Gate House, 399–425 Eastern Avenue,
Gants Hill, Ilford, Essex IG2 6LR
☎0181 518 2057   Fax 0181 518 2241
Contact *Terry Allen*

Over 250,000 images of beauty, cookery and
craft plus a comprehensive library of story illustrations comprising work by some of the UK's
best-known illustrators.

Railfotos
Millbrook House Ltd., Calthorpe House,
30 Hagley Road, Edgbaston, Birmingham
B16 8QY
☎0121 454 1308
Fax 0121 454 4224 quote Millbrook House

One of the largest specialist libraries dealing
comprehensively with railway subjects worldwide. Colour and b&w dating from the turn of
the century to present day. Up-to-date material
on UK, South America and Far East (except
Japan), especially China. Visitors by appointment.

Redferns Music Picture Library
7 Bramley Road, London W10 6SZ
☎0171 792 9914   Fax 0171 792 0921

Music picture library covering every aspect of
popular music from 1920's jazz to present day.
Over 12,000 artists on file plus other subjects
including musical instruments, recording studios, crowd scenes, festivals, etc. Brochure
available.

Reed International Books Picture Library
Michelin House, 81 Fulham Road, London
SW3 6RB
☎0171 225 9212   Fax 0171 225 9053
Contact *Sally Claxton*

400,000 images of cookery and gardening.

Remote Source
See **Royal Geographical Society Picture Library**

Retna Pictures Ltd

1 Fitzroy Mews, Cleveland Street, London
W1P 5DQ
☎0171 209 0200   Fax 0171 383 7151

Colour and b&w coverage of international
rock and pop performers, actors, actresses,
entertainers and celebrities. Also a general stock
library covering a wide range of subjects,
including travel, people, sport and leisure, flora
and fauna, and the environment.

Retrograph Archive Ltd

164 Kensington Park Road, London
W11 2ER
☎0171 727 9378/9426   Fax 0171 229 3395

Contact *Jilliana Ranicar-Breese*

'Number One for nostalgia!' A vast archive of
commercial and decorative art (1860–1960).
Worldwide labels and packaging for food,
wine, chocolate, soap, perfume, cigars and cigarettes; fine art and commercial art journals,
fashion and lifestyle magazines, posters,
Victorian greeting cards, scraps, Christmas
cards, Edwardian postcards, wallpaper and gift-
wrap sample books, music sheets, folios of decorative design and ornament – Art Nouveau
and Deco; hotel, airline and shipping labels;
memorabilia, tourism, leisure, food and drink,
transport and entertainment. Lasers for book
dummies, packaging, mock-ups, film/TV
action props. Colour brochure on request.
Medium format. Picture research service.
Design consultancy service. Victorian-style
montages conceived, designed and styled
(RetroMontages).

Rex Features Ltd

18 Vine Hill, London EC1R 5DX
☎0171 278 7294/3362   Fax 0171 696 0974

Established in the 1950s. Colour and b&w
coverage of news, politics, personalities, show
business, glamour, humour, art, medicine, science, landscapes, royalty, etc.

Royal Air Force Museum

Grahame Park Way, Hendon, London NW9
5LL
☎0181 205 2266   Fax 0181 200 1751

Contact *Christine Gregory*

About a quarter of a million images, mostly
b&w, with around 1500 colour in all formats,
on the history of aviation. Particularly strong
on the activities of the Royal Air Force from
the 1870s to 1970s. Researchers are requested
to enquire in writing only.

The Royal Collection

Windsor Castle, Windsor, Berks SL4 1NJ
☎01753 868286   Fax 01753 620046

Contact *Gwyneth Campling, Nicole Tetzner*

Photographic material of items in the Royal
Collection, particularly oil paintings, drawings
and watercolours, works of art, and interiors
and exteriors of royal residences. 35,000 colour
transparencies plus 25,000 b&w negatives.

Royal Geographical Society Picture Library

1 Kensington Gore, London SW7 2AR
☎0171 591 3060   Fax 0171 591 3061

Contact *Joanna Scadden, Daisy Jellicoe*

A strong source of geographical and historical
images, both archival and modern, showing the
world through the eyes of photographers and
explorers from the 1830s to the present day. The
Remote Source Collection provides up-to-date
transparencies from around the world, highlighting aspects of cultural activity, environmental
phenomena, anthropology, architectural design,
travel, mountaineering and exploration. Offers a
professional and comprehensive service for both
commercial and academic use.

Royal Opera House Archives

Royal Opera House, Covent Garden, London
WC2E 9DD
☎0171 240 1200   Fax 0171 212 9489

Contact *Francesca Franchi*

Information and illustrations covering the his-
tory of the three Covent Garden Theatres,
1732 to the present, including the three Royal
Opera House Companies – Birmingham
Royal Ballet, The Royal Ballet and The Royal
Opera. Visitors welcome by appointment.

The Royal Photographic Society

The Octagon, Milsom Street, Bath BA1 1DN
☎01225 462841   Fax 01225 448688

Contact *Debbie Ireland*

History of photography, with an emphasis on
pictorial photography as an art rather than a
documentary record. Photographic processes
and cameras, landscape, portraiture, architecture, India, Victorian and Edwardian life.

RSPB Images

21-22 Great Sutton Street, London EC1V 0DN
☎0171 608 7325   Fax 0171 608 0770

Contact *Zoe Beech*

Colour and b&w images of birds, butterflies,

moths, mammals, reptiles and their habitats. Also colour images of all RSPB reserves. Growing selection of various habitats. Total number of slides now 52,000, available digitally or in any desired format.

RSPCA Photolibrary
RSPCA Trading Limited, Causeway, Horsham, West Sussex RH12 1HG
☎01403 223150   Fax 01403 241048
Photolibrary Manager *Tim Sambrook*

Over 25,000 colour transparencies and over 5000 b&w/colour prints. A comprehensive collection of natural history pictures representing the work of over 100 photographers. Has a unique photographic record of the work of the RSPCA including animal hospitals, veterinary treatment, wildlife rehabilitation work, cruelty to animals, animal welfare education, RSPCA inspectors at work, and other animal welfare issues such as environmental problems and cruel sports.

Russia and Republics Photolibrary
Conifers House, Cheapside Lane, Denham, Uxbridge, Middlesex UB9 5AE
☎01895 834814/0956 304384 (mobile)
Fax 01895 834028

Images of Russia and the Republics: cities, museums, cathedrals, markets, landmarks, landscapes, resorts, traditional costumes and dances, craftsmen at work.

Salamander Picture Library
129–137 York Way, London N7 9LG
☎0171 267 4447   Fax 0171 267 5112
Contact *Terry Forshaw*

Approximately 250,000 images, colour and b&w, of American history, collectibles, cookery, crafts, military, natural history, space and transport.

Peter Sanders Photography
24 Meades Lane, Chesham, Buckinghamshire HP5 1ND
☎01494 773674   Fax 01494 773674
Contact *Peter Sanders, Hafsa Garwatuk*

The world of Islam in all its aspects from religion and industry to culture and arts. Areas included are Saudi Arabia, Africa, Asia, Europe and USA. Now expanding to all religions.

Science & Society Picture Library
Science Museum, Exhibition Road, London SW7 2DD
☎0171 938 9750   Fax 0171 938 9751
Contact *Angela Murphy, Venita Paul*

25,000 reference prints and 100,000 colour transparencies, incorporating many from collections at the Science Museum, the National Railway Museum and the National Museum of Film, Photography and Television. Collections illustrate the history of: science, industry, technology, medicine, transport and the media. Plus three archives documenting British society in the twentieth century.

The Scottish Highland Photo Library
Croft Roy, Crammond Brae, Tain, Ross-shire IV19 1JG
☎01862 892298   Fax 01862 892298
Contact *Hugh Webster*

120,000 colour transparencies of the Scottish Highlands and Islands. Not just a travel library; images cover industry, agriculture, fisheries and many other subjects of the Highlands and Islands. Submissions from photographers welcome. Commissions undertaken.

Seaco Picture Library
Sea Containers House, 20 Upper Ground, London SE1 9PF
☎0171 805 5831   Fax 0171 805 5926
Contact *Maureen Elliott*

Approx. 250,000 images of containerisation, shipping, fast ferries, manufacturing, fruit farming, ports, hotels and leisure.

Mick Sharp Photography
Eithinog, Waun, Penisarwaun, Caernarfon, Gwynedd LL55 3PW
☎01286 872425   Fax 01286 872425
Contacts *Mick Sharp, Jean Williamson*

Colour transparencies (6x4.5cm and 35mm) and black & white prints (5"x4" and 6x4.5cm negatives) of subjects connected with archaeology, ancient monuments, buildings, churches, countryside, environment, history, landscape, past cultures and topography from Britain and abroad. Photographs by Mick Sharp and Jean Williamson, plus access to other specialist collections on related subjects. Commissions undertaken.

Phil Sheldon Golf Picture Library
40 Manor Road, Barnet, Hertfordshire EN5 2JQ
☎0181 440 1986   Fax 0181 440 9348

An expanding collection of over 300,000 quality images of the 'world of golf'. In-depth worldwide tournament coverage including every Major championship & Ryder Cup since 1976. Instruction, portraits, trophies and over 300 golf courses from around the world. Also the Dale Concannon collection covering the period 1870 to 1940 and the classic 1960s collection by photographer Sidney Harris.

Skishoot–Offshoot

Hall Place, Upper Woodcott, Whitchurch, Hampshire RG28 7PY
☎01635 255527   Fax 01635 255528
Contact *Felice Eyston, Peter Hardy*

Predominantly skiing and snowboarding, but also a travel library specialising in France. Commissions undertaken.

The Skyscan Photolibrary

Oak House, Toddington, Cheltenham, Gloucestershire GL54 5BY
☎01242 621357   Fax 01242 621343
The Skyscan Photolibrary is based on a unique collection of low-level aerial views of Britain taken from remotely controlled cameras suspended beneath a tethered barrage balloon. From castles to cottages, landscapes to landfills, this bird's eye view takes a new look at Britain. Recently expanded to include collections of striking images from photographers across the aviation spectrum; ballooning, paragliding and other aerial sports; aircraft, both military and civil air, air to air, RAF life; international air to ground images – in fact, 'anything aerial!' Commissions undertaken.

SOA Photo Library

87 York Street, London W1H 1DU
☎0171 258 0202   Fax 0171 258 01881
Contact *Brigitte Bott, Lorna Allen*

75,000 colour slides, 10,000 b&w photos covering *Stern* productions, celebrities, sports, travel & geographic, advertising, social subjects. Representatives of Photonica, Voller Ernst, Interfoto and many freelance photographers. Catalogues available.

Solo Syndication Ltd

49–53 Kensington High Street, London W8 5ED
☎0171 376 2166   Fax 0171 938 3165
Syndication Manager *Trevor York*
Photo Sales *Danny Howell, Nick York*
Online transmissions *Geoff Malyon* (☎0171 937 3866)
Three million images from the archives of the *Daily Mail, Mail on Sunday, Evening Standard* and *Evening News* together with current pictures

from *Woman, Woman's Own, Woman's Weekly* and *Woman's Realm*. Also photo portfolios from Australia, South Africa and 1000 colour travel slides of Spain from **Visions of Andalucia**. Main library encompassing celebrities, royalty, political figures, crime, sports, beauty, cuisine, health, fashion and general. Hard prints or Mac-to-mac delivery. 24-hour service.

Sotheby's Picture Library

34–35 New Bond Street, London W1A 2AA
☎0171 408 5383   Fax 0171 408 5062
Contact *Joanna Ling*
The library mainly consists of several thousand selected transparencies of pictures sold at Sotheby's. Images from the 15th to the 20th century. Oils, drawings, watercolours and prints. 'Happy to do searches or, alternatively, visitors are welcome by appointment.'

South American Pictures

48 Station Road, Woodbridge, Suffolk IP12 4AT
☎01394 383963/383279   Fax 01394 380176
Contact *Marion Morrison*
Colour and b&w images of South/Central America, Cuba, Mexico and New Mexico (USA), including archaeology and the Amazon. Frequently updated. There is an archival section, with pictures and documents from most countries.

The Special Photographers Library

21 Kensington Park Road, London W11 2EU
☎0171 221 3489   Fax 0171 792 9112
Contacts *Chris Kewbank*
Represents over 100 contemporary fine art photographers who are unusual in style, technique or subject matter. Also has exclusive access to the Bill Hopkins Collection – an archive of thousands of vintage pictures dating back to the early 20th century.

Spectrum Colour Library

41–42 Berners Street, London W1P 3AA
☎0171 637 1587   Fax 0171 637 3681
A large collection including travel, sport, people, pets, scenery, industry, British and European cities, etc. All pictures are also available in digital format. Visitors welcome by appointment.

Frank Spooner Pictures Ltd

Unit B7, Hatton Square, 16–16A Baldwin's Gardens, London EC1N 7US
☎0171 405 9943   Fax 0171 831 2483
Subjects include current affairs, show business,

fashion, politics, travel, adventure, sport, personalities, films, animals and the Middle East. Represented in more than 30 countries and handles UK distribution of Harry Benson, and Gamma Presse Images and Roger-Viollet of Paris. Commissions undertaken.

The Still Moving Picture Co.
67A Logie Green Road, Edinburgh EH7 4HF
☎0131 557 9697   Fax 0131 557 9699
Contact *John Hutchinson, Sue Hall*
250,000 colour, b&w and 16mm film coverage of Scotland and sport. The largest photo and film library in Scotland, holding the Scottish Tourist Board library among its files. Scottish agents for **Allsport (UK) Ltd**.

Still Pictures' Whole Earth Photolibrary
199 Shooters Hill Road, Blackheath, London SE3 8UL
☎0181 858 8307   Fax 0181 858 2049
Contacts *Theresa de Salis, Mark Edwards*
FOUNDED 1970, the library is a leading source of pictures illustrating the human impact on the environment, Third World development issues, industrial ecology, wildlife, endangered species and habitats. 250,000 colour medium-format transparencies, 100,000 b&w prints. Over 300 leading photographers from around the world supply the library with stock pictures.

Stockfile
5 High Street, Sunningdale, Berkshire SL5 0LX
☎01344 872249   Fax 01344 872263
Contact *Jill Behr, Steven Behr*
Specialist cycling- and skiing-based collection covering most aspects of these activities, with emphasis on mountain biking. Expanding adventure sports section.

Sir Benjamin Stone
See **Birmingham Library Services** under **Library Services**

Survival Anglia Photo Library
See **Oxford Scientific Films**

Tate Gallery Picture Library
Tate Gallery Publishing Ltd, Millbank, London SW1P 4RG
☎0171 887 8867   Fax 0171 887 8900
Contact *Carlotta Gelmetti*
Approximately 8000 images of British art from

the 16th century; international 20th century painting and sculpture. Colour transparencies of more than half the works in the main collection of the Gallery are available for hire. For a fee, orders can be taken for other works to be photographed, depending on their condition or location. B&w prints of nearly all the works in the collection can be purchased. Colour slides and prints can be made on request providing a colour transparency exists. Not open for private research and applications should be made by telephone or fax.

Telegraph Colour Library
The Innovation Centre, 225 Marsh Wall, London E14 9FX
☎0171 987 1212   Fax 0171 538 3309
Contact *Norma Lilley*
Leading stock photography agency covering a wide subject range: business, sport, people, industry, animals, medical, nature, space, travel and graphics. Free catalogue available. Same-day service to UK clients.

3rd Millennium Music Ltd
22 Avon, Hockley, Tamworth, Staffordshire B77 5QA
☎01827 286086   Fax 01827 286086
Managing Director *Neil Williams*
Archive specialising in classical music ephemera, particularly portraits of composers, musicians, conductors and opera singers comprising of old and sometimes very rare photographs, postcards, prints, cigarette cards, stamps, First Day Covers, concert programmes, Victorian newspapers, etc. Also modern photos of composer references such as museums, statues, busts, paintings, monuments, memorials and graves. Other subjects covered include ballet and dance, musical instruments, concert halls, opera houses, bandstands, 'music in art', manuscripts, church organs, opera scenes, music-cartoons, ethnic music, jazz, military bands, orchestras and other music groups.

Bob Thomas Sports Photography
See **Popperfoto**

Three Lions Collection
See **The Hulton Getty Picture Collection**

Patrick Thurston Photolibrary
10 Willis Road, Cambridge CB1 2AQ
☎01223 352547   Fax 01223 366274
Colour photography of Britain: scenery, people,

museums, churches, coastline. Also various countries abroad. Commissions undertaken.

Rick Tomlinson Marine Photo Library

18 Hamble Yacht Services, Port Hamble, Hamble, Southampton, Hampshire SO31 4NN

☎01703 458450   Fax 01703 458350

Contacts *Rick Tomlinson, Julie Birchall*

ESTABLISHED 1985. *Specialises* in marine subjects. 60,000 35mm transparencies of yachting, racing, cruising, Whitbread Round the World Race, tall ships, RNLI Lifeboats, Antarctica, wildlife and locations.

Topham Picturepoint

PO Box 33, Edenbridge, Kent TN8 5PB

☎01342 850313   Fax 01342 850244

Contact *Alan Smith*

Eight million contemporary and historical images, ideal for advertisers, publishers and the travel trade. Delivery on line.

B. M. Totterdell Photography

Constable Cottage, Burlings Lane, Knockholt, Kent TN14 7PE

☎01959 532001   Fax 01959 532001

Contact *Barbara Totterdell*

Specialist volleyball library covering all aspects of the sport.

Tessa Traeger Library

7 Rossetti Studios, 72 Flood Street, London SW3 5TF

☎0171 352 3641   Fax 0171 352 4846

Food, gardens, travel and artists.

Travel Ink Photo and Feature Library

The Old Coach House, 14 High Street, Goring on Thames, Nr Reading, Berkshire RG8 9AR

☎01491 873011   Fax 01491 875558

Contact *Abbie Enock*

Around 80,000 colour images covering about 130 countries (including the UK). Close links with other specialist libraries mean most topics can be accessed. Subjects include travel, tourism, lifestyles, business, industry, transport, children, religion, history, activities. Specialist collections on Hong Kong (including construction of the Tsing Ma bridge), Greece, North Wales, Germany, the Cotswolds and France.

Peter Trenchard's Image Store Ltd

The Studio, West Hill, St Helier, Jersey, Channel Islands JE2 3HB

☎01534 869933   Fax 01534 889191

Contact *Peter Trenchard, FBIPP, AMPA*

Slide library of the Channel Islands - mainly tourist and financial-related. Commissions undertaken.

Tropix Photographic Library

156 Meols Parade, Meols, Wirral, Merseyside L47 6AN

☎0151 632 1698   Fax 0151 632 1698

Contact *Veronica Birley*

Leading specialists on the developing world in all its aspects. Environmental topics widely covered. Assignment photography undertaken at home and overseas. New collections welcome, especially parts of Africa and Latin America, and environmental; please write with details enclosing four first-class stamps. All submissions (35 mm+ colour transparencies only) must be accompanied by detailed accurate captions, prepared according to Tropix specifications.

True North Picture Source

5 Brunswick Street, Hebden Bridge, West Yorkshire HX7 6AJ

☎01422 845532   Fax 01422 845532

Contact *John Morrison*

30,000 transparencies on 35 mm and 6x4.5 cm format on the life and landscape of the north of England, photographed by John Morrison.

Ulster Museum

Botanic Gardens, Belfast BT9 5AB

☎01232 383000 ext 3113   Fax 01232 383103

Contact *Mrs Pat McLean*

Affectionately known as the 'treasure house of Ulster', the Ulster Museum is a national museum for Northern Ireland. Specialist subjects: art – fine and decorative, late 17th–20th century, particularly Irish art, archaeology, ethnography, treasures from the Armada shipwrecks, geology, botany, zoology, local history and industrial archaeology. Commissions welcome for objects not already photographed.

Universal Pictorial Press & Agency Ltd

29–31 Saffron Hill, London EC1N 8FH

☎0171 421 6000   Fax 0171 421 6006

News Editor *Peter Dare*

Photo archive dates back to 1944 and contains approximately four million pictures. Colour and b&w coverage of news, royalty, politics, sport, arts, and many other subjects. Commissions undertaken for press and public relations. Fully interactive digital photo archive in addition to bulletin board accessible via ISDN or modem. Full digital scanning, retouching and transmission facilities.

UPI
See **Popperfoto**

V & A Picture Library
Victoria and Albert Museum, South Kensington, London SW7 2RL
☎0171 938 8352/8354/8452
Fax 0171 938 8353

45,000 colour and half a million b&w photos of decorative and applied arts, including ceramics, ivories, furniture, costumes, textiles, stage, musical instruments, toys, Indian, Far Eastern, Islamic objects, sculpture, painting and prints, from medieval to present day.

Valley Green
Barn Ley, Valley Lane, Buxhall, Stowmarket, Suffolk IP14 3EB
☎01449 736090   Fax 01449 736090
Contact *Joseph Barrere*

Approximately 9–10,000 transparencies of plants, with a comprehensive coverage of hardy perennials. Also photographs, watercolours and line drawings available. Artistic and photographic commissions undertaken.

Venice Picture Library
2a Milner Street, London SW3 2PU
☎0171 589 3127   Fax 0171 584 1944

25,000 35mm images of Venice, its buildings, people, animals and atmosphere. Member of **BAPLA**.

Victory Archive
See **Popperfoto**

The Vintage Magazine Company Ltd
203–213 Mare Street, London E8 3QE
☎0181 533 7588   Fax 0181 533 7283

A large collection of movie stills and posters, photographs, illustrations and advertisements covering music, glamour, social history, theatre posters, ephemera, postcards.

The Charles Walker Collection
12–14 Argyll Street, London W1V 1AB
☎0171 734 7344   Fax 0171 287 3933

One of the foremost collections in the world on subjects popularly listed as 'Mystery, myth and magic'. The collection includes astrology, occultism, witchcraft and many other related areas. Catalogue available.

John Walmsley Photo Library
April Cottage, Warners Lane, Albury Heath, Guildford, Surrey GU5 9DE
☎01483 203846   Fax 01483 203846

Specialist library of learning/training/working subjects. Comprehensive coverage of learning environments such as playgroups, schools, colleges, universities. Images reflect a multi-racial Britain. Plus a section on complementary medicine with over 30 therapies from acupuncture and yoga to more unusual tones like moxibustion and metamorphic technique. Commissions undertaken. Subject list available on request.

Warwickshire Photographic Survey
See **Birmingham Library Services** under **Library Services**

Waterways Photo Library
39 Manor Court Road, Hanwell, London W7 3EJ
☎0181 840 1659   Fax 0181 567 0605

A specialist photo library on all aspects of Britain's inland waterways. Top-quality 35mm-and medium-format colour transparencies, plus a large collection of b&w. Rivers and canals, bridges, locks, aqueducts, tunnels and waterside buildings. Town and countryside scenes, canal art, waterway holidays, boating, fishing, windmills, watermills, watersports and wildlife.

Philip Way Photography
426–432 Essex Road, London N1 3PJ
☎0171 704 0494   Fax 0171 226 0435
Contact *Philip Way*

Over 1000 images of St Paul's Cathedral – historical exteriors, interiors and events (1982– 1997).

Wellcome Centre Medical Photographic Library
210 Euston Road, London NW1 2BE
☎0171 611 8348   Fax 0171 611 8577
Contact *Catherine Draycott, Heather Ercilla, Michele Minto, Julie Dorrington*

Approximately 160,000 images on the history of medicine and human culture worldwide, including modern clinical medicine. Incorporates the **National Medical Slide Bank**.

Eric Whitehead Photography

PO Box 33, Kendal, Cumbria LA9 4SU
☎015394 48894   Fax 015394 48294

Incorporates the Cumbria Picture Library. The agency covers local news events, PR and commercial material, also leading library of snooker images.

Derek G. Widdicombe-Worldwide Photographic Library

Oldfield, High Street, Clayton West, Huddersfield, West Yorkshire HD8 9NS
☎01484 862638   Fax 01484 862638
Contact *Derek G. Widdicombe*

Around 150,000 images (mostly the work of Derek Widdicombe) in colour and b&w. Landscapes, seascapes, human interest, architecture, moods and seasons, buildings and natural features in Britain and abroad.

Wilderness Photographic Library

Mill Barn, Broad Raine, Sedbergh, Cumbria LA10 5ED
☎015396 20196   Fax 015396 21293
Contact *John Noble*
Striking colour images from around the world, from polar wastes to the Himalayas and Amazon jungle. Subjects: mountains, the Arctic, deserts, icebergs, wildlife, rainforests, glaciers, geysers, exploration, caves, rivers, eco-tourism, people and cultures, canyons, seascapes, marine life, weather, geology, volcanoes, mountaineering, skiing, conservation, adventure sports, national parks.

David Williams Picture Library

50 Burlington Avenue, Glasgow G12 0LH
☎0141 339 7823   Fax 0141 337 3031
Colour coverage of Scotland and Iceland. Smaller collections of the Faroes, France and Western USA. Landscapes, historical sites, buildings, geology and physical geography. Medium format and 35 mm. Catalogue available. Commissions undertaken.

Vaughan Williams Memorial Library

English Folk Dance and Song Society, Cecil Sharp House, 2 Regent's Park Road, London NW1 7AY
☎0171 284 0523   Fax 0171 284 0523
Mainly b&w coverage of traditional/folk music, dance and customs worldwide, focusing on Britain and other English-speaking nations. Photographs date from the late 19th century to the 1970s.

Windrush Photos, Wildlife and Countryside Picture Agency

99 Noah's Ark, Kemsing, Sevenoaks, Kent TN15 6PD
☎01732 763486   Fax 01732 763285
Contact *David Tipling*
Specialists in birds (worldwide) and British wildlife. A large collection of black and white images covering British wildlife and angling, and shooting scenes dating back to the 1930s. High quality photographic and features commissions are regularly undertaken for publications in the UK and overseas. The agency acts as ornithological consultants for all aspects of the media.

The Wingfield Sporting Art Library

Old Chancellor House, Hyde Park Gate, London SW7 5DQ
☎0171 581 2964   Fax 0171 581 2964
Contact *Mary Ann Wingfield*
Sporting works of art, both historical and contemporary, covering 50 different sports. Commissions undertaken.

Woodfall Wild Images

14 Bull Lane, Denbigh, Denbighshire LL16 3SN
☎01745 815903   Fax 01745 814581
Contacts *David Woodfall, Martin Barlow*
Environmental, conservation, landscape and wildlife photographic library. A constantly-expanding collection of images reflecting a wide range of subjects, 'from mammals to marine, insects to industry, rivers to rainforest, and pollution to people changing our world, for the better and for the worse'.

World Pictures

85a Great Portland Street, London W1N 5RA
☎0171 437 2121/436 0440
Fax 0171 439 1307
Contacts *David Brenes, Carlo Irek*
600,000 colour transparencies of travel and emotive material.

WWF UK Photolibrary

Panda House, Weyside Park, Catteshall Lane, Godalming, Surrey GU7 1XR
☎01483 426444   Fax 01483 426409
Contact *Amanda Freestone*

Specialist library covering natural history, endangered species, conservation, environment, forests, habitats, habitat destruction, and pollution in the UK and abroad. 10,000 colour slides (35mm).

Yemen Pictures

28 Sheen Common Drive, Richmond TW10 5BN
☎0181 898 0150/876 3637
Fax 0181 898 0150

Large collection (4000 transparencies) covering all aspects of Yemen – culture, people, architecture, dance, qat, music. Also Africa, Australia, Middle East, and Asia.

York Archaeological Trust Picture Library

Cromwell House, 13 Ogleforth, York YO1 2JG
☎01904 663000   Fax 01904 640029

Specialist library of rediscovered artifacts, historic buildings and excavations, presented by the creators of the highly acclaimed Jorvik Viking Centre. The main emphasis is on the Roman, Anglo-Saxon and Viking periods.

The John Robert Young Collection

61 De Montfort Road, Lewes, East Sussex BN7 1SS
☎01273 475216   Fax 01273 475216
Contact *Jennifer Barrett*

50,000 transparencies and monochrome prints on travel, religion and military subjects.

Balancing the Books –
Tax and the Writer

'No man in this country is under the smallest obligation, moral or other, to arrange his affairs as to enable the Inland Revenue to put the largest possible shovel in his stores.

'The Inland Revenue is not slow, and quite rightly, to take every advantage which is open to it . . . for the purpose of depleting the taxpayer's pockets. And the taxpayer is, in like manner, entitled to be astute to prevent as far as he honestly can the depletion of his means by the Inland Revenue.'
Lord Clyde, *Ayrshire Pullman v Inland Revenue Commissioners, 1929.*

Income Tax

What is a professional writer for tax purposes?
Writers are professionals while they are writing regularly with the intention of making a profit; or while they are gathering material, researching or otherwise preparing a publication.

A professional freelance writer is taxed under Case II of Schedule D of the *Income and Corporation Taxes Act 1988*. The taxable income is the amount received, either directly or by an agent, on his behalf, less expenses wholly and exclusively laid out for the purposes of the profession. If expenses exceed income, the loss can either be carried forward and set against future income from writing or set against other income which is subject to tax in the same year. If tax has been paid on that other income, a repayment can be obtained, or the sum can be offset against other tax liabilities. Special loss relief can apply in the opening year of the profession. Losses made in the first four years can be set against income of up to five earlier years.

Where a writer receives very occasional payments for isolated articles, it may not be possible to establish that these are profits arising from carrying on a continuing profession. In such circumstances these 'isolated transactions' may be assessed under Case VI of Schedule D of the *Income and Corporation Taxes Act 1988*. Again, expenses may be deducted in arriving at the taxable income, but, if expenses exceed income, the loss can only be set against the profits from future isolated transactions, or other income assessable under Case VI.

Expenses
A writer can normally claim the following expenses:

(a) Secretarial, typing, proofreading, research. Where payment for these are made to the author's wife or husband, they should be recorded and entered in the spouse's tax return as earned income which is subject to the usual personal allowances. If payments reach taxable levels, PAYE should be operated.

(b) Telephone, telegrams, postage, stationery, printing, maintenance, insurance, dictation tapes, batteries, any equipment or office requisites used for the profession.

(c) Periodicals, books (including presentation copies and reference books) and other publications necessary for the profession, but amounts received from the sale of books should be deducted. Some inspectors of tax allow only capital allowances on books (see (l) below).

(d) Hotels, fares, car running expenses (including repairs, petrol, oil, garaging, parking, cleaning, insurance, licence, road fund tax, depreciation), hire of cars or taxis in connection with:
   (i) business discussions with agents, publishers, co-authors, collaborators, researchers, illustrators, etc.
   (ii) travel at home and abroad to collect background material.

(e) Publishing and advertising expenses, including costs of proof corrections, indexing, photographs, etc.

(f) Subscriptions to societies and associations, press cutting agencies, libraries, etc., incurred wholly for the purpose of the profession.

(g) Premiums to pension schemes such as the *Society of Authors Retirement Benefits Scheme*. Depending on age, up to 40% of net earned income can be paid into a personal pension plan.

(h) Rent, council tax and water rates, etc., the proportion being determined by the ratio which the number of rooms are used exclusively for the profession bears to the total number of rooms in the residence. But see note on *Capital Gains Tax* below.

(i) Lighting, heating and cleaning. A carefully estimated figure of the business use of these costs can be claimed as a proportion of the total.

(j) Agents' commission. Accountancy charges and legal charges incurred wholly in the course of the profession including cost of defending libel actions, damages in so far as they are not covered by insurance and libel insurance premiums. However, where in a libel case, damages are awarded to punish the author for having acted maliciously the action becomes quasi-criminal and costs and damages may not be allowed.

(k) TV and video rental (which may be apportioned for private use), and cinema or theatre tickets, if wholly for the purpose of the profession, e.g. playwriting.

(l) Capital allowances for equipment, e.g. car, TV, radio, hi-fi sets, tape and video recorders, dictaphones, typewriters, desks, bookshelves, filing cabinets, photographic equipment. Allowances vary in the Finance Acts depending upon political and economic views prevailing. At present they are set at 25%. On motor cars the allowance is 25% in the first year and

25% of the reduced balance in each successive year limited to £2000 each year. In the case of motor cars bought after 11 March 1992 the limit is £3000 each year. The total allowances in the case of all assets must not exceed the difference between cost and eventual sale price. Allowances will be reduced to exclude personal (non-professional) use where necessary.

(m) Lease rent. The cost of lease rent of equipment is allowable; also on cars, subject to restrictions for private use and for expensive cars.

(n) Tax relief is available for three-year (minimum) covenants to charities. With effect from 1 October 1990 individuals can obtain tax relief on one-off charitable gifts subject to certain generous limits.

NB It is always advisable to keep detailed records. Diary entries of appointments, notes of fares and receipted bills are much more convincing to the Inland Revenue than round figure estimates.

It has recently been announced that there is a fundamental change in the method of assessment of income of the self-employed to the 'current year' basis. This will operate for most existing businesses with effect from 1996/7 but anyone who is just starting to write for profit should take professional advice as regards the date to choose for their accounting year end.

Capital Gains Tax

The exemption from Capital Gains Tax which applies to an individual's main residence does not apply to any part of that residence which is used exclusively for business purposes. The effect of this is that the appropriate proportion of any increase in value of the residence since 31 March 1982 can be taxed, when the residence is sold, subject to a deduction for the increase in the retail price index (indexation), at the maximum rate of 40% (at present).

Writers who own their houses should bear this in mind before claiming expenses for the use of a room for writing purposes. Arguments in favour of making such claims are that they afford some relief now, while Capital Gains Tax in its present form may not stay for ever. Also, where a new house is bought in place of an old one, the gain made on the sale of the first study may be set off against the cost of the study in the new house, thus postponing the tax payment until the final sale. For this relief to apply, each house must have a study, and the author must continue his profession throughout. On death there is an exemption of the total Capital Gains of the estate. Some relief from tax will be given on Council Tax.

NB Writers can claim that their use is non-exclusive and restrict their claim to the cost of extra lighting, heating and cleaning to avoid Capital Gains Tax liability.

Can a writer average out his income over a number of years for tax purposes?

Under Section 534 of the *Income and Corporation Taxes Act 1988,* a writer may in certain circumstances spread over two or three fiscal years lump sum payments, whenever received, and royalties received during two years from the date of first publication or performance of work. Points to note are:

(a)   The relief can only be claimed if the writer has been engaged in preparing and collecting material and writing the book for more than twelve months.

(b)   If the period of preparing and writing the work exceeds twelve months but does not exceed twenty-four months, one-half of the advances and/or royalties will be regarded as income from the year preceding that of receipt. If the period of preparing and writing exceeds twenty-four months, one-third of the amount received would be regarded as income from each of the two years preceding that of receipt.

(c)   For a writer on a very large income, who otherwise fulfils the conditions required, a claim under these sections could result in a tax saving. If his income is not large he should consider the implication, in the various fiscal years concerned, of possible loss of benefit from personal and other allowances and changes in the standard rate of income tax.

It is also possible to average out income within the terms of publishers' contracts, but professional advice should be taken before signature. Where a husband and wife collaborate as writers, advice should be taken as to whether a formal partnership agreement should be made or whether the publishing agreement should be in joint names.

Is a lump sum paid for an outright sale of the copyright or part of the copyright exempt from tax?
No. All the money received from the marketing of literary work, by whatever means, is taxable. Some writers, in spite of clear judicial decisions to the contrary, still seem to think that an outright sale of, for instance, the film rights in a book is not subject to tax.

Remaindering
To avoid remaindering authors can usually purchase copies of their own books from the publishers. Monies received from sales are subject to income tax but the cost of books sold should be deducted because tax is only payable on the proft made.

Is there any relief where old copyrights are sold?
Section 535 of the *Income and Corporation Taxes Act 1988* gives relief where not less than ten years after the first publication of the work the author of a literary, dramatic, musical or artistic work assigns the copyright therein wholly or partially, or grants any interest in the copyright by licence, and:

(a)   the consideration for the assignment or grant consists wholly or partially of a lump sum payment, the whole amount of which would, but for this section, be included in computing the amount of his/her profits or gains for a single year of assessment, and

(b) the copyright or interest is not assigned or granted for a period of less than two years.

In such cases, the amount received may be spread forward in equal yearly instalments for a maximum of six years, or, where the copyright or interest is assigned or granted for a period of less than six years, for the number of whole years in that period. A 'lump sum payment' is defined to include a non-returnable advance on account of royalties.

It should be noted that a claim may not be made under this section in respect of a payment if a prior claim has been made under Section 534 of the *Income and Corporation Taxes Act 1988* (see section on spreading lump sum payments over two or three years) or vice versa.

Are royalties payable on publication of a book abroad subject to both foreign tax as well as UK tax?

Where there is a Double Taxation Agreement between the country concerned and the UK, then on the completion of certain formalities no tax is deductible at source by the foreign payer, but such income is taxable in the UK in the ordinary way. When there is no Double Taxation agreement, credit will be given against UK tax for overseas tax paid. A complete list of countries with which the UK has conventions for the avoidance of double taxation may be obtained from the Inspector of Foreign Dividends, Lynwood Road, Thames Ditton, Surrey KT7 0DP, or the local tax office.

Residence Abroad

Writers residing abroad will, of course, be subject to the tax laws ruling in their country of residence, and as a general rule royalty income paid from the United Kingdom can be exempted from deduction of UK tax at source, providing the author is carrying on his profession abroad. A writer who is intending to go and live abroad should make early application for future royalties to be paid without deduction of tax to HM Inspector of Taxes, Foreign Division, Prudential Building, 72 Maid Marian, Nottingham NG1 6AS. In certain circumstances writers resident in the Irish Republic are exempt from Irish Income Tax on their authorship earnings.

Are grants or prizes taxable?

The law is uncertain. Some Arts Council grants are now deemed to be taxable, whereas most prizes and awards are not, though it depends on the conditions in each case. When submitting a statement of income and expenses, such items should be excluded, but reference made to them in a covering letter to the Inspector of Taxes.

What if I disagree with a tax assessment?

Income Tax law requires the Inspector of Taxes to make an assessment each year calculating the amount of income tax payable on the 'profits' of the profession. Even though accounts may have already been submitted the assessment can quite possibly be estimated and overstated.

The taxpayer has the right of appeal within 30 days of receipt of the assessment and can request that the tax payable should be reduced to the correct liability which he must estimate as accurately as possible. However, if he underestimates the amount, interest can become payable on the amount by which he underpays when the correct liability is known.

What is the item 'Class 4 N.I.C.' which appears on my tax assessment?

All taxpayers who are self-employed pay an additional national insurance contribution if their earned income exceeds a figure which is varied each year. This contribution is described as Class 4 and is calculated in the tax assessment. It is additional to the self-employed Class 2 (stamp) contribution but confers no additional benefits and is a form of levy. It applies to men aged under 65 and women under 60. Tax relief is given on half the Class 4 contributions.

Value Added Tax

Value Added Tax (VAT) is a tax currently levied at 17.5% on:

(a) the total value of taxable goods and services supplied to consumers,
(b) the importation of goods into the UK,
(c) certain services from abroad if a taxable person receives them in the UK for the purpose of their business.

Who is Taxable?

A writer resident in the UK whose turnover from writing and any other business, craft or art on a self-employed basis is greater than £47,000 annually, before deducting agent's commission, must register with HM Customs & Excise as a taxable person. A business is required to register:

– at the end of any month if the value of taxable supplies in the past 12 months has exceeded the annual threshold; or

– if there are reasonable grounds for believing that the value of taxable supplies in the next 12 months will exceed the annual threshold.

Penalties will be claimed in the case of late registration. A writer whose turnover is below these limits is exempt from the requirements to register for VAT, but may apply for voluntary registration, and this will be allowed at the discretion of HM Customs & Excise.

A taxable person collects VAT on outputs (turnover) and deducts VAT paid on inputs (taxable expenses) and where VAT collected exceeds VAT paid, must remit the difference to HM Customs & Excise. In the event that input exceeds output, the difference will be repaid by HM Customs & Excise.

Outputs (Turnover)

A writer's outputs are taxable services supplied to publishers, broadcasting organisations, theatre managements, film companies, educational institutions, etc. A taxable writer must invoice, i.e. collect from, all the persons (either individuals or organisations) in the UK for whom supplies have been made, for fees, royalties or other considerations plus VAT. An unregistered writer cannot and must not invoice for VAT. A taxable writer is not obliged to collect VAT on royalties or other fees paid by publishers or others overseas. In practice, agents usually collect VAT for the registered author.

Taxable at the standard rate	*Taxable at the zero or special rate*	*Exempt*
Rent of certain commercial premises	Books (zero)	Rent of non-commercial premises
Advertisements in newspapers, magazines, journals and periodicals	Periodicals (zero)	Council Tax
	Coach, rail, and air travel (zero)	Postage
Agent's commission (unless it relates to monies from overseas, when it is zero-rated)	From 1.4.94 electricity (8%)	Services supplied by unregistered persons
Accountant's fees	Gas (8%)	Subscriptions to the Society of Authors, PEN, NUJ, etc.
Solicitor's fees *re* business matters	Other fuel (8%)	Wages and salaries
Agency services (typing, copying, etc.)		Insurance
Word processors, typewriters and stationery		Taxicab fares
Artists' materials		
Photographic equipment		
Tape recorders and tapes		
Hotel accommodation		*Outside the scope of VAT*
Motor-car expenses		PLR (Public Lending Right)
Telephone		Profit shares
Theatres and concerts		Investment income

NB This list is not exhaustive.

Remit to Customs

The taxable writer adds up the VAT which has been paid on taxable inputs, deducts it from the VAT received and remits the balance to Customs. Business with HM Customs is conducted through the local VAT Offices of HM Customs which are listed in local telephone directories, except for tax returns which are sent direct to the Customs and Excise VAT Central Unit, Alexander House, 21 Victoria Avenue, Southend on Sea, Essex SS99 IAA.

Accounting

A taxable writer is obliged to account to HM Customs & Excise at quarterly intervals. Returns must be completed and sent to VAT Central Unit by the dates shown on the return. Penalties can be charged if the returns are late.

It is possible to account for the VAT liability under the Cash Accounting Scheme (Note 731), whereby the author accounts for the output tax when the invoice is paid or royalties, etc., are received. The same applies to the input tax, but as most purchases are probably on a 'cash basis', this will not make a considerable difference to the author's input tax. This scheme is only applicable to those with a taxable turnover of less than £350,000 and, therefore, is available to the majority of authors. The advantage of this scheme is that the author does not have to account for VAT before receiving payment, thereby relieving the author of a cash flow problem.

It is also possible to pay VAT by nine estimated direct debits, with a final balance at the end of the year (see leaflet 732).

Registration

A writer will be given a VAT registration number which must be quoted on all VAT correspondence. It is the responsibility of those registered to inform those to whom they make supplies of their registration number. The taxable turnover limit which determines whether a person who is registered for VAT may apply for cancellation of registration is £45,000.

Voluntary Registration

A writer whose turnover is below the limits may apply to register. If the writer is paying a relatively large amount of VAT on taxable inputs – agent's commissions, accountant's fees, equipment, materials, or agency services, etc. – it may make a significant improvement in the net income to be able to offset the VAT on these inputs. An author who pays relatively little VAT may find it easier, and no more expensive, to remain unregistered.

Fees and Royalties

A taxable writer must notify those to whom he makes supplies of the Tax Registration Number at the first opportunity. One method of accounting for and paying VAT on fees and royalties is the use of multiple stationery for 'self-billing', one copy of the royalty statement being used by the author as the VAT invoice. A second method is for the recipient of taxable outputs to pay fees, including authors' royalties, without VAT. The taxable author then renders a tax invoice for the VAT element and a second payment, of the VAT element, will be made. This scheme is cumbersome but will involve only taxable authors. Fees and royalties from abroad will count as payments for exported services and will accordingly be zero-rated.

Agents and Accountants

A writer is responsible to HM Customs for making VAT returns and payments. Neither an agent nor an accountant nor a solicitor can remove the responsibility, although they can be helpful in preparing and keeping VAT returns and accounts. Their professional fees or commission will, except in rare cases where the adviser or agent is himself unregistered, be taxable at the standard rate and will represent some of a writer's taxable inputs.

Income Tax – Schedule D

An unregistered writer can claim some of the VAT paid on taxable inputs as a business expense allowable against income tax. However, certain taxable inputs fall into categories which cannot be claimed under the income tax regulations. A taxable writer, who has already offset VAT on inputs, cannot charge it as a business expense for the purposes of income tax.

Certain Services From Abroad

A taxable author who resides in the United Kingdom and who receives certain services from abroad must account for VAT on those services at the appropriate tax rate on the sum paid for them. Examples of the type of services concerned include: services of lawyers, accountants, consultants, provisions of information and copyright permissions.

Inheritance Tax

Inheritance Tax was introduced in 1984 to replace Capital Transfer Tax, which had in turn replaced Estate Duty, the first of the death taxes of recent times. Paradoxically, Inheritance Tax has reintroduced a number of principles present under the old Estate Duty.

The general principle now is that all legacies on death are chargeable to tax (currently 40%), except for legacies between spouses which are exempt, as are the first £200,000 of legacies to others. Gifts made more than seven years before death are exempt, but those made within this period are taxed on a sliding scale. No tax is payable at the time of making the gift.

In addition, each individual may currently make gifts of up to £3000 in any year and these will be considered to be exempt. A further exemption covers any number of annual gifts not exceeding £250 to any one person.

If the £3000 is not utilised in one year it, or the unused balance, can be given in the following year (but no later), plus that year's exemptions. Gifts out of income, which means those which do not reduce one's capital or one's living standards, are also exempt if they are part of one's normal expenditure.

At death all assets are valued: they will include any property, investments, life policies, furniture and personal possessions, bank balances and, in the case of authors, the value of their copyrights. All, with the sole exception of copyrights, are capable (as assets) of accurate valuation, and, if necessary, can be turned into cash. The valuation of copyright is, of course, complicated, and frequently gives rise to difficulty. Except where they are bequeathed to the owner's husband or wife, very real problems can be left behind by the author.

Experience has shown that a figure based on two to three years' past royalties may be proposed by the Inland Revenue in their valuation of copyright. However, it all depends. If a book is running out of print or if, as in the case of educational books, it may need revision at the next reprint, these factors must be taken into account. In many cases the fact that the author is no longer alive and able to make personal appearances, or provide publicity, or write further works, will result in lower or slower sales. Obviously this is an area in which help can be given by the publishers, and in particular one needs to know what their future intentions are, what stocks of the books remain, and what likelihood there will be of reprinting.

There is a further relief available to authors who have established that they have been carrying on a business, normally assessable under Case II of Schedule D, for at least two years prior to death. It has been possible to establish that copyrights are treated as business property and in these circumstances, 'business property relief' is available. This relief at present is at 100% on business assets including copyrights, so that the tax saving can be quite substantial. The Inland Revenue may wish to be assured that the business is continuing and consideration should therefore be given to the appointment, in the author's will, of a literary executor who should be a qualified business person or, in certain circumstances, the formation of a partnership between the author and his or her spouse, or other relative, to ensure that it is established that the business is continuing after the author's death.

If the author has sufficient income, consideration should be given to building up a fund to cover future liabilities. One of a number of ways would be to take out a whole life assurance policy which is assigned to the children, or other beneficiaries, the premiums on which are within the annual exemption of £3000. The capital sum payable on the death of the assured is exempt from inheritance tax.

Anyone wondering how best to order his affairs for tax purposes, should consult an accountant with specialised knowledge in this field. Experience shows that a good accountant is well worth his fee which, incidentally, so far as it relates to matters other than personal tax work, is an allowable expense.

The information contained in this section is adapted from **The Society of Authors** *Quick Guides to Taxation* (Nos 4 and 7), with the kind help of A. P. Kernon, FCA, who will be pleased to answer questions on tax problems. Please write to A. P. Kernon, c/o *The Writer's Handbook*. 34 Ufton Road, London N1 5BX.

Stop Press

UK Publishers

Context Limited
Grand Union House, 20 Kentish Town Road,
London NW1 9NR
☎0171 267 8989   Fax 0171 267 1133
FOUNDED 1986. Electronic publisher of UK
and European legal and official information on
CD-ROM and online. TITLE *Justis* cartoons
CD-ROM, developed jointly with **The
Centre for the Study of Cartoons and
Caricature** at the University of Kent (see
entry under **Library Services**), contains over
18,000 political cartoons published in Brtish
newspapers from 1912–90. No unsolicited
mailshots; enquiries only.

Fitzwarren Publishing
PO Box 6887, London N19 3SG
☎0171 686 4129   Fax 0171 686 4129
Contact *Emma Prinsley*
Publishes two or three books a year, mainly layman's handbooks on legal matters. All six
books published so far have followed a rigid
128-page format. Written approaches and synopses from prospective authors welcome.
Authors, although not necessarily legally qualified, are expected to know their subject as well
as a lawyer would.
Royalties paid twice a year.

Small Presses

Ferry Publications
PO Box 9, Narberth, Pembrokeshire
SA68 0PE
☎01834 891460   Fax 01834 891463
Managing Editor *Miles Cowsill*
FOUNDED 1987 to publish ferry and shipping
books. 3–4 titles a year. TITLES *Only Britanny
Ferries*; *P&O The Fleet*; *Ferries of Portsmouth*.
Unsolicited mss, synopses and ideas welcome.
Royalties paid.

Magazines

The First Word Bulletin
Calle Domingo Fernandez 5, Box 500,
28036 Madrid, Spain
☎00 34 1 359 6418   Fax 00 34 1 320 8961
Owner *The First Word Bulletin Associates*
Publisher/Editor *G. W. Amick*
Circulation 5000
FOUNDED 1995. QUARTERLY international
magazine, printed in Madrid and distributed to
the English-speaking community worldwide.
Welcomes articles on self-improvement, both
mental and physical, also environmental problems and cures. Human interest, alternative
medicine, fiction and non-fiction, nature stories,
young adult and senior citizen retirement articles. 400 words maximum. Approach in writing
with s.a.e. and IRCs. *Payment* £30.

Company Index

The following codes have been used to classify the index entries:

A	UK Publishers	L	Film, TV and Video Production
A1	Irish Publishers		Companies
AB	Writer's Courses, Circles and Workshops	M	Theatre Producers
AA	European Publishers	N	US Publishers
AU	Audio Books	O	US Agents
B	Poetry Presses	P	US Media Contacts in the UK
C	Poetry Magazines	Q	Professional Associations
D	Organisations of Interest to Poets	R	Arts Councils and Regional Arts
E	UK Packagers		Boards
EE	Book Clubs	S	Bursaries, Fellowships and Grants
F	UK Agents	T	Prizes
G	National Newspapers	U	Libraries
H	Regional Newspapers	V	Picture Libraries
HH	News Agencies	W	Small Presses
I	Magazines	X	Festivals
J	National and Regional Television	Y	Editorial, Research and other Services
J1	European Television Companies	YY	Press Cuttings Agencies
K	National and Regional Radio	Z	Literary Societies

Subject Index

Sterling Publishing Co. Inc. 441
Time-Life Inc. 442

Gardening & Horticulture: Small Presses
New Arcadian Press 160
Sawd Books 165
Silent Books Ltd 165

Gay/Lesbian: Agents (UK)
Morris (Jay) & Co., Authors' Agents 196

Gay/Lesbian: Magazines
Attitude 252
Gay Times 276
Pink Paper, The 297

Gay/Lesbian: Publishers (European)
Rowohlt Taschenbuch Verlag GmbH 410

Gay/Lesbian: Publishers (UK)
Absolute Press 1
Gay Men's Press (GMP Publishers Ltd), The 34
Onlywomen Press Ltd 61
Scarlet Press 73

Gay/Lesbian: Publishers (US)
Bantam Doubleday Dell Publishing Group Inc. 424
Temple University Press 441

Gay/Lesbian: Theatre Producers
Gay Sweatshop 382

Gay/Lesbian: Writers Courses
Gay Authors Workshop 524

Genealogy: Libraries
Guildhall Library 591
Leeds Central Library 594
Newcastle upon Tyne City Library 597
Northumberland Central Library 597
York Central Library 605

Genealogy: Magazines
Family Tree Magazine 272

Genealogy: Publishers (Irish)
Flyleaf Press 95

Genealogy: Publishers (UK)
Countryside Books 22
Manchester University Press 54
Phillimore & Co. Ltd 64

Geography: Libraries
Royal Geographical Society Library 600

Geography: Picture Libraries
Cleare (John)/Mountain Camera 612
Corbis UK Ltd 613
Dixon (C M) 614
Evans (Mary) Picture Library 615
Garland (Leslie) Picture Library 617
GeoScience Features 618
Medimage 625
Natural Science Photos 627
Royal Geographical Society Picture Library 631
SOA Photo Library 633
Williams (David) Picture Library 637

Geography: Publishers (European)
Bra Böcker (Bokförlaget) AB 416
Istituto Geografico de Agostini SpA 412

Orell Füssli Verlag 417
Presses Universitaires de France (PUF) 409
Societa Editrice Internazionale – SEI 412
Ullstein (Verlag) GmbH 411

Geography: Publishers (UK)
Chapman (Paul) Publishing Ltd 19
Dalesman Publishing Co. Ltd 23
Darf Publishers Ltd 23
Freeman (W. H.) 32
Fulton (David) (Publishers) Ltd 33
HarperCollins Publishers Ltd 38
Liverpool University Press 51
Routledge 72
Ward Lock Educational Co. Ltd 84

Geography: Publishers (US)
Lerner Publications Co. 432

Geology: Picture Libraries
Dixon (C M) 614
Garland (Leslie) Picture Library 617
GeoScience Features 618
Medimage 625
Ulster Museum 635
Wilderness Photographic Library 637
Williams (David) Picture Library 637

Geology: Publishers (European)
Bra Böcker (Bokförlaget) AB 416
Istituto Geografico de Agostini SpA 412
Orell Füssli Verlag 417
Presses Universitaires de France (PUF) 409
Societa Editrice Internazionale – SEI 412
Ullstein (Verlag) GmbH 411

Geology: Publishers (UK)
Dalesman Publishing Co. Ltd 23
Freeman (W. H.) 32
National Museums of Scotland (NMS Publishing) 58
Scottish Academic Press 74

Geology: Small Presses
Geological Society Publishing House 155

Germany: Agents (UK)
Howarth (Tanja) Literary Agency 192

Germany: Libraries
Goethe-Institut Library 590

Germany: Picture Libraries
King (David) Collection 622
Travel Ink Photo & Feature Library 635

Germany: Prizes
Schlegel-Tieck Prize 569

Golf: Magazines
Amateur Golf 249
Golf Monthly 276
Golf Weekly 276
Golf World 276
Scottish Golfer 304
Today's Golfer 312

Golf: Picture Libraries
Concannon Golf History Library 613
Hobbs Golf Collection 619
Professional Sport 630
Sheldon (Phil) Golf Picture Library 632

Golf: Professional Associations
Association of Golf Writers 469

Golf: Small Presses
Grant Books 155

Government: Film, TV and Video Production Companies
Central Office of Information Film & Video 352

Government: Libraries
Bank of England Library and Information Services 581
Belfast Public Libraries: Central Library 582
British Library Social Policy Information Service 585
Guildhall Library 591
London Metropolitan Archives 595
Office for National Statistics 598
Public Record Office 599
Westminster Reference Library 604

Government: Publishers (UK)
Business Education Publishers Ltd 14
Hobsons Publishing 42
Reed (William) Directories 69
Stationery Office Publishing 78

Government: Publishers (US)
ABC-Clio, Inc. 421
New England (University Press of) 435

Greece: Picture Libraries
Hanley (Tom) 619
Travel Ink Photo & Feature Library 635

Greece: Prizes
Runciman Award 568

Greece: Publishers (UK)
Boulevard Books & The Babel Guides 11

Guidebooks: Publishers (Audio)
WALKfree Productions Ltd 106

Guidebooks: Publishers (Irish)
Collins Press, The 95
Gill & Macmillan 96

Guidebooks: Publishers (UK)
AA Publishing 1
Allan (Ian) Ltd 2
B & W Publishing 6
Cicerone Press 20
Constable & Co. Ltd 21
Cook (Thomas) Publishing 22
Dalesman Publishing Co. Ltd 23
Donald (John) Publishers Ltd 25
HarperCollins Publishers Ltd 38
Haynes Publishing 40
Impact Books Ltd 45
Little, Brown & Co. (UK) 51
Michelin Tyre plc 56
Prion Books Ltd 66
Quiller Press 67
Random House UK Ltd 67
Reardon Publishing 69
Robson Books Ltd 71
SB Publications 73
Settle Press 75
Telegraph Books 80
West One (Trade) Publishing Ltd 85

736 SUBJECT INDEX

King Alfred's College, Winchester
International Forum of ...
University of ...
Liverpool, Edge Hill College of ...

THE MACMILLAN GOOD ENGLISH HANDBOOK

Compiled by
Godfrey Howard

This completely new handbook is written and designed for writers to flip open whenever there's any hesitation over grammar or usage – and find *at a glance* a clearcut and authoritative answer.

For the first time – and about time! – here is an indispensable guide to English that sweeps away the cobwebs and frees the language from the arthritic grip of linguisitic Colonel Blimps.

The Macmillan Good English Handbook uses a consensus of over a hundred writers to offer a reliable balance between traditional grammar and what is truly out of touch with the language on the brink of the new millennium.

£9.99 Hardback 384pp